Allegra

THE LAW OF
PUBLIC COMMUNICATION

Second Edition

**THE LONGMAN SERIES
IN PUBLIC COMMUNICATION**

THE
LAW OF
P U B L I C
COMMUNICATION

Second Edition

KENT R. MIDDLETON
UNIVERSITY OF GEORGIA

BILL F. CHAMBERLIN
UNIVERSITY OF FLORIDA

Longman
New York & London

The Law of Public Communication, second edition

Longman, 95 Church Street, White Plains, N.Y. 10601

Associated companies:
Longman Group Ltd., London
Longman Cheshire Pty., Melbourne
Longman Paul Pty., Auckland
Copp Clark Pitman, Toronto

Executive editor: Gordon T. R. Anderson
Development editor: Elsa van Bergen
Production editor: Halley Gatenby and The Book Studio, Inc.
Text design adaptation: Betty L. Sokol
Cover design: David Levy
Text art: J & R Services, Inc.
Production supervisor: Anne P. Armeny

Library of Congress Cataloging-in-Publication Data

Middleton, Kent.
    The law of public communication / Kent R. Middleton, Bill F.
Chamberlin.—2nd ed.
        p.   cm.—(The Longman series in public communication)
    Includes bibliographical references
    ISBN 0–8013–0449–0
    1. Freedom of the press—United States.   2. Press law—United
States.   3. Freedom of speech—United States.   I. Chamberlin, Bill
F., 1944– . II. Title. III. Series.
    KF4774.M53   1991
    342.73′0853—dc20
    [347.302853]   90–42987
                                                                  CIP

2 3 4 5 6 7 8 9 10-DO-9594939291

For Margaret, Hillary, and Arthur,
and for Jeanne, Evelyn Thayer,
and the memory of Charles H. Chamberlin

CONTENTS

PREFACE

The second edition of *The Law of Public Communication* reflects changes in the law and, like the first edition, reflects the diverse interests of students enrolled in schools and departments of journalism and mass communication. The text treats traditional journalism law comprehensively but also includes the law affecting new technologies, public relations, and advertising. The second edition includes U.S. Supreme Court decisions affecting libel, the student press, emotional distress, flag burning, computer privacy, and the speech rights of corporations since the first edition was published in 1988. It also includes revised sections on the fairness doctrine, indecency, cable television, and dial-a-porn.

Professors who have adopted *The Law of Public Communication* often have expressed appreciation for our recognition not only that communication law has moved beyond journalism and broadcasting, but that the majority of students in journalism schools are planning careers outside of newspapers and over-the-air broadcasting stations. Students of advertising and public relations frequently comprise 50–60 percent of the student body in schools of journalism and mass communication. In addition, the distinction between print and broadcasting students is blurring as the technologies of publishing and broadcasting merge into telecommunications.

To reflect these changes in the law and student enrollment, *The Law of Public Communication* covers not only journalism law but also the law of commercial and electronic communication. The libel chapter, for example, discusses how both news media and non media businesses can defend themselves in defamation suits. The privacy chapter deals not only with photos in news publications, but also in telecommunications and in public relations and advertising contexts. Likewise, the sections on the federal Freedom of Information Act discuss both journalists' access to government records and the extensive use of the FOI Act by competing businesses.

The book also includes extended treatment of the electronic media and sections on corporate and public relations law. Chapter 12, "The Electronic Media," outlines the regulatory framework for new communication technologies increasingly available to public communicators. Chapter 6, "Corporate Speech," includes sections on the emerging definition of corporate speech rights in referenda and elections and discusses communication law affecting lobbyists, foreign agents, management, unions, and corporations whose stock is publicly traded. Chapter 5, "Intellectual Property," includes sections on commercial performance rights and trademarks.

The second edition of *The Law of Public Communication* reflects U.S. Supreme Court decisions through June 1990 as well as other major changes in media law during the previous three years. The section on student press law in Chapter 2, "The First Amendment," has been substantially enlarged. Also added to Chapter 2 is treatment of the Supreme Court's flag-burning cases. A section on negligence has been added to Chapter 4, "Privacy." In Chapter 12, the sections on the fairness doctrine, indecency, cable, and new technologies have been substantially reworked to reflect the significant changes in those areas during the last few years.

We are pleased that Longman is committed to publishing yearly updates to *The Law of Public Communication* so that neither professors nor students need use textbooks that are two or three years out of date, an eternity in communication law. Longman and the authors are committed to publishing either a new edition of the text or a comprehensive update, coordinated with the text, each January. The updates are packaged with the latest edition of the textbook so that instructors do not have to order the updates separately. However, instructors can also ask local bookstores to order separate updates for the number of used textbooks the bookstores buy back.

The Law of Public Communication is a practical book for students planning careers in communication. The text explains the law as it applies to the daily work of writers, editors, speakers, artists, and photographers. The innumerable statutes and cases are presented in a cohesive narrative that is understandable, even to students studying law for the first time. While students have generally praised *The Law of Public Communication* for its readability, we have tried even harder in the second edition than in the first to make the complexities of communication law understandable to undergraduates who are new to the law. Frequent summaries help students retain major points. Added to this edition are several graphic illustrations.

Communication law is a liberal arts course. It is therefore important that students learn not only the practical rules but also the principles, theory, and methods of analysis of such a dynamic and challenging subject. Students need to understand how the law evolves so that they can keep abreast of inevitable shifts after they graduate. We try to discuss cases in sufficient detail—often with quotations—for students to learn to identify legal issues, court holdings, and judicial rationale while gaining professional guidance. We also discuss theories of the press and the legal tools and tests used by the courts in First Amendment analysis. The text is extensively, but unobtrusively, footnoted to document the scholarship on which statements are based and to suggest further reading for the student or professor.

The Law of Public Communication focuses on the law as it affects communicators, not as it regulates the business aspects of communication companies. In most places, the book discusses regulation of communication content—what people can say or publish. Therefore, we devote little space to broadcast-license renewal procedures but quite a bit of space to political broadcasting. Taxes on the media are important in this book only if they restrict what might be said or published. We leave discussion of newsroom safety standards and labor contracts to business law and management courses.

We would like to thank the many people who have helped and encouraged us. We want to express our appreciation to the professors and students who submitted comments and suggestions, all of which were helpful and many of which were incorporated into the text. We welcome reactions to the second edition.

We pay special tribute to the late Gordon T. R. (Tren) Anderson, executive editor of college publishing at Longman. Tren was a superb editor and project director and a valued friend.

Among the many communication professors who contributed by commenting on the first edition and drafts of the second edition are Jeremy Cohen, Stanford University; David Eshelman, Central Missouri State; Robert L. Hughes, Virginia Commonwealth University; Ivan Preston, University of Wisconsin; Herbert Strentz, Drake University; Robert Trager, University of Colorado; and Ruth Walden, University of North Carolina. We would like to acknowledge the special contribution of time and effort given by F. Leslie Smith at the University of Florida.

We would also like to thank attorneys Norman Davis, of Steel, Hector & Davis, Miami; Mark Goodman, executive director, of the Student Press Law Center; and Samuel Terilli, of the *Miami Herald*.

We also thank Sally Askew, associate research librarian; José Rodriguez, retired assistant professor; Erwin Surrency, professor and director, and the staff of the Law Library at the University of Georgia; and Arthur R. Donnelly, associate librarian and associate director, and Rosalie M. Sanderson, assistant librarian, and the staff of the Legal Information Center, College of Law, and Dolores C. Jenkins, associate university librarian, at the University of Florida. Help from Georgia graduate students Linda MacColl, Timothy McCollum, and Laura Sweep is also gratefully acknowledged; as is the assistance of Sigman Splichal, Linda Perry, and Matthew Bunker, doctoral students at the University of Florida; and Barbara Walker, assistant to the director of the Brechner Center for Freedom of Information, University of Florida.

We also thank Jeanne Chamberlin for her direct and indirect contributions to the book.

Kent R. Middleton
Bill F. Chamberlin

1

PUBLIC COMMUNICATION AND THE LAW

Many have called *Westmoreland v. CBS* the libel trial of the century. It certainly has the credentials. The top U.S. military officer in Vietnam, General William C. Westmoreland, sued one of the three major television networks for $120 million. The two sides to the dispute spent several million dollars in legal expenses, the most for any libel trial in history. The suit spawned several legal sideshows—court battles over the location of the trial, the protection of confidential sources, and the presence of cameras in the courtroom. The trial itself questioned Vietnam War tactics and the integrity of one of the most powerful news organizations in the world.

Westmoreland sued CBS after the network aired a 1982 documentary called "The Uncounted Enemy: A Vietnam Deception." The program claimed that Westmoreland had led a conspiracy to underestimate enemy strength in Vietnam. The network contended that "the highest levels of American military intelligence" had deliberately misled President Johnson, the Congress, the Joint Chiefs of Staff, and the American public in order to convince them the country was winning a war it was actually losing. However, Westmoreland argued that because of shoddy journalism CBS presented only one side of the story. Westmoreland said that CBS misrepresented an argument within the military over how the enemy ought to be counted.

Neither Westmoreland nor CBS "won" the libel suit after 18 weeks of trial. In 1985, the lawyers for both sides agreed to settle out of court before the case reached the jury. CBS did not have to pay monetary damages to Westmoreland, but the network's reputation was severely battered.[1]

Although the Westmoreland case was not decided in court, the law of libel dictated the outcome. Libel law required Westmoreland to prove more than that he had been defamed by CBS. Libel law required that Westmoreland, as a public official, also prove that CBS had knowingly broadcast falsehoods or had recklessly disregarded the truth during the preparation of the story. Westmoreland may not have been able to prove falsehood or recklessness because CBS produced witnesses who endorsed its version of the truth.

Libel law and other law that affect public communication are the subjects of this book. The book will also discuss confidential news sources and cameras in the courtroom as well as privacy, copyright, pornography, and access to government-held information. The book focuses on the law affecting the content of public communication, including printed publications, electronic media, public relations, and advertising.

This chapter will examine legal concepts and procedures important to an understanding of the law of communication. It will talk about the purpose and organization of law. It will also describe court procedures, explain how students can find legal materials, and discuss how communicators can work with lawyers.

THE SOURCES OF LAW

Law can be defined in many ways, but for our purposes it is the system of rules that governs society. Law serves many functions in our society. It regulates the behavior

---

[1]*See generally* R. Adler, *Reckless Disregard* (1986); D. Kowet, *A Matter of Honor* (1984); R. Smolla, *Suing the Press* 198–237 (1986); Lewis, "Annals of Law: The Sullivan Case," *The New Yorker,* Nov. 5, 1984, at 84–95.

of citizens and corporations, restricting, for example, what advertisers can say about their products. It provides a vehicle to settle disputes, as in the Westmoreland libel case. And law limits the government's power to interfere with individual rights, such as the right to speak and publish.

The law in the United States comes primarily from six sources: constitutions, statutes, administrative rules and regulations, executive actions, the **common law,*** and the law of **equity.**

Constitutional Law

Constitutions are the supreme source of law in the United States and are the most direct reflection of the kind of government desired by the people of the country. Constitutions of both the federal and state governments supersede all other declarations of public policy. The Constitution of the federal government and those of the 50 state governments establish the framework for governing. They outline the structure of government and define governmental authority and responsibilities.

Frequently, a constitution limits the powers of government, as in the case of the Bill of Rights, the first 10 amendments to the U.S. Constitution. The Bill of Rights, printed in the appendix of this book, protects the rights and liberties of U.S. citizens against infringement by government. The First Amendment, particularly the prohibition against laws abridging freedom of speech and the press, provides the foundation for communication law.

The federal constitution is the ultimate law of the land. Any federal law, state law, or state constitution that conflicts with the U.S. Constitution cannot be enforced; the U.S. Constitution prevails. Similarly, a state constitution prevails in conflicts with the **statutory** or common law in the same state.

The U.S. Supreme Court, the nation's highest judicial authority, has the last word on the meaning of the federal constitution. Each state's supreme court is the interpreter of that state's constitution. Only the U.S. Supreme Court can resolve conflicts between the state and federal constitutions. The courts make constitutional law when they decide a case or controversy by interpreting a constitution. In 1980, the U.S. Supreme Court said the First Amendment required that the public and press ordinarily be permitted to attend trials.[2] Constitutional law can be understood only by reading the opinions of the courts.

Constitutions are hard to amend and therefore are changed infrequently. Amendments to the U.S. Constitution can only be proposed by two-thirds of the members of both houses of Congress or by a convention called by two-thirds of the state legislatures. Amendments must be ratified by three-fourths of the state legislatures or by state constitutional conventions in three-fourths of the states.

Statutory Law

A major source of law in the United States is the collection of statutes and ordinances written by legislative bodies—the U.S. Congress, the 50 state legislatures, county

---

*Definitions for the terms printed in boldface can be found in the Glossary beginning on page 633.
[2]Richmond Newspapers v. Virginia, 448 U.S. 555, 6 Media L. Rep. 1833 (1980).

commissions, city councils, and countless other lawmaking bodies. Statutes set forth enforceable rules to govern social behavior. Areas of communication law controlled by statutes include advertising, copyright, electronic media, obscenity, and access to government-held information.

Almost all of this country's criminal law, including a prohibition against the mailing of pornography, is statutory. Statutes not only prohibit antisocial acts, but also frequently provide for the oversight of acceptable behavior. For example, a primary purpose of the federal Communications Act of 1934 is to administer the use of the broadcast spectrum in the public interest.

The process of adopting statutes allows lawmakers to study carefully a complicated issue—such as how to regulate the use of the electromagnetic spectrum—and write a law accordingly. The process permits anyone or any group to make suggestions through letters, personal contacts, and hearings. In practice, well-organized special interests, such as broadcasters and cable television system operators, frequently have enough influence to thwart proposals contrary to their interests.

The adoption of a statute does not conclude the lawmaking process. Executive branch officials interpret statutes in order to administer them in the daily operation of government. Judges add meaning when either the statutes themselves or their application are challenged in court. Judges explain the statutes as they apply to specific problems and conflicts, as occurred when the U.S. Supreme Court was asked in 1983 to interpret the 1976 Copyright Act. The Court ruled that a provision in the act limiting the copying of copyrighted materials does not bar homeowners from taping television programs on home VCRs.[3] In 1989, the Court said a provision in the federal Freedom of Information Act allows the FBI to refuse to disclose individual criminal records in a computer data base. The Court said that giving the records to a reporter would constitute an "unwarranted" invasion of privacy, one of the stated exceptions to the disclosure requirements in the act.[4]

The courts can invalidate municipal or county laws that conflict with state or federal law. The courts can strike down state statutes that conflict with federal laws or the state or federal constitutions. In 1974, the U.S. Supreme Court declared unconstitutional a Florida statute that required newspapers to print a reply to published attacks on political candidates. The Supreme Court ruled that a statute requiring a response violates First Amendment protection for freedom of the press.[5]

State and federal laws may conflict when the states try to regulate matters **preempted** by the federal government. For example, under the Constitution, Congress can regulate aspects of the economy to the exclusion of the states. In 1984, the U.S. Supreme Court nullified an Oklahoma statute banning the advertising of wine on cable television. The Oklahoma law conflicted with the 1976 Copyright Act and regulations adopted by the Federal Communications Commission (FCC). The federal laws prohibit the editing of national and regional television programming carried by cable systems. The Supreme Court said federal law preempts state television regulation.[6]

---

[3]Sony Corp. v. Universal City Studios, 464 U.S. 417, 7 Media L. Rep. 2065 (1984).
[4]Department of Justice v. Reporters Comm. for Freedom of the Press, 109 S. Ct. 1468, 16 Media L. Rep. 1545, (1989).
[5]Miami Herald Publishing Co. v. Tornillo, 418 U.S. 241, 1 Media L. Rep. 1898 (1974).
[6]Capital Cities Cable, Inc. v. Crisp, 467 U.S. 691, 10 Media L. Rep. 1873 (1984).

Administrative Law

Administrative law, the rules and decisions made by administrative agencies, has mushroomed in the last few decades and now dominates several areas of communication law. Administrative agencies are created by legislative bodies to supervise specialized activities that require more attention than a legislature can provide. Agencies such as the Federal Communications Commission adopt rules and **adjudicate** disputes as authorized by statute.

Congress established the FCC in the 1934 Communications Act to regulate telephone, telegraph, and radio communications. Other agencies that oversee communications include the Federal Trade Commission (FTC), which regulates advertising; the Securities and Exchange Commission (SEC), which controls the communication of corporations registered to sell securities; the Federal Election Commission (FEC), which regulates political campaign contributions and expenditures; the National Labor Relations Board (NLRB), which regulates communication between labor and management; and the Copyright Royalty Tribunal (CRT), which distributes user fees to copyright holders.

Administrative agencies develop detailed regulatory plans and procedures, monitor industry practices, and discourage and penalize undesirable behavior. For example, the FCC has declared that broadcasters must provide programming on issues important to their communities. In the 1960s and 1970s, the FCC regularly required broadcast licensees to fill out programming reports. In a few cases, the FCC decided that a broadcaster's local programming was not sufficiently serving the public interest and refused to renew the station's license.

Congress has provided administrative agencies with two kinds of legal authority. The agencies can establish enforceable rules and regulations through an administrative procedure known as **rule making.** Administrative agencies can adopt legally enforceable rules as long as they follow procedures established by law. Rule making will be explained in the chapters on advertising and electronic media of this book. The administrative agencies also can resolve complaints initiated by business competitors, the public, or the agency itself. Each side in the dispute has a chance to be heard. Federal agency regulations and decisions can be challenged in federal courts.

Executive Actions

The president, and other governmental executive officers, can also make law. The president can exercise power in a number of ways, including appointments, executive orders, proclamations, and executive agreements with foreign countries. Much of the presidential authority derives from article II of the U.S. Constitution, including the declaration that the president shall "take Care that the Laws be faithfully executed."[7] The Supreme Court has allowed the chief executive broad discretion under the clause. In addition, Congress often grants the president the authority to administer the statutes it passes.

Perhaps the president's greatest influence on communication law comes from the power to nominate judges to the federal courts, including the U.S. Supreme

---

[7]See also U.S. Const. art. II, sec. 2 (appointment power).

Court. The political and judicial philosophies of the judges, and particularly their interpretation of the First Amendment, influence the legal climate for communicators. The president also nominates the members of several administrative agencies, including the Federal Communications Commission, the Federal Trade Commission, and the Securities and Exchange Commission. Orders from the top officer in the executive branch of government seldom directly affect the law of public communication. The presidential orders establishing procedures for classifying documents important to the national security constitute a major exception.

Common Law

The most important source of law during the early development of the country was the common law, often called judge-made law. The common law is the continually growing accumulation of rulings made by the courts in individual disputes, as opposed to the body of general rules adopted by legislatures. Judicial decisions, for example, have created a law of privacy that provides individuals with limited protection against media disclosure of highly personal information.

Common law in the United States grew out of the English common law. For centuries, judges in England, under the authority of the king, decided controversies on the basis of tradition and custom. These rulings became **precedents** for future decisions that, together, became the law of the land. When the English colonized America, they brought English common law principles with them.

Common law is primarily state law. Each state has its own judicial traditions. Long ago the U.S. Supreme Court ruled that there is no federal common law.

The common law recognizes the importance of stability and predictability in the law. When editors are considering articles for publication, they need to know, for example, which stories may violate rights of privacy. In the common law, editors can know which stories present risks by understanding the decisions made by the courts in previous privacy cases. The common law is based on the judicial policy of **stare decisis,** which roughly means ''let past decisions stand.'' In the common law, a judge decides a case by applying the law established by other judges in earlier, similar cases. The reliance on precedent not only provides continuity, but also restricts judicial abuse of discretion.

While the common law promotes stability, it also allows for flexibility. The common law can adjust to fit changing circumstances because each judge can interpret and modify the law. Judges have five options when considering a case. They can (1) apply a precedent directly, (2) modify a precedent to fit the present circumstances, (3) establish a new precedent by distinguishing the new case from the previous judicial tradition, (4) overrule a previous precedent as no longer appropriate, or (5) ignore precedent. In most cases, precedent is followed, or adjusted to meet the facts at hand. Judges only rarely directly overrule previous precedents. Ignoring precedents greatly increases the risks of an opinion being overturned by a higher court.

The common law recognizes the superiority of both constitutional law and statutory law. The common law is relied upon only when a statute or constitutional provision is not applicable. The task of lawmaking in a representative form of government is assigned to the legislatures. Sometimes legislatures incorporate portions of the common law into a statute, a process called ''codification.'' In 1976,

Congress rewrote the federal copyright statute to reflect judicially created exceptions to copyright infringement.

Sometimes, people confuse the common law with constitutional law. Both are embodied, at least in part, in judicial opinions based on precedent. However, constitutional law is based on judicial interpretation of a constitution, while common law is based on custom and practice.

Common law is not written down in one book. It can be understood only by reading recorded court decisions that may be in hundreds of different volumes. While the 1976 copyright statute is located in one volume of the United States Code, the common law of privacy can be found only by looking in numerous volumes of state and federal judicial opinions.

Law of Equity

The sixth source of law, equity, is historically related to the common law. Although *equity* is a legal term, it means what it sounds like. The law of equity allows courts to take action that is fair or just.

The law of equity developed because English common law only allowed individuals to collect monetary compensation awards after an injury had occurred. Under the law of equity, a **litigant** could petition the king to "do right for the love of God and by way of charity."[8] The law of equity allowed for preventive action and for remedial action other than monetary compensation.

Unlike England, the United States and most individual states have never had separate courts of equity. Equity developed in the same courts that decided common-law cases, but juries are never used in equity suits. In addition, although judges sitting in equity must consider precedent, they have substantial discretion to order a remedy they believe fair and appropriate.

Equity is significant in communication law primarily because of the preventive possibilities it provides. A judge could use it, for example, to halt the publication of a story he or she believed would severely endanger national security. Punishment after publication would not protect national security.

SUMMARY

Law in the United States comes from constitutions, statutes, administrative agencies, executive orders, common law, and equity. Constitutions outline the structure of government and define governmental authority and responsibilities. In the United States, the First Amendment to the federal constitution protects the right to free speech and to a free press. Statutes are enforceable rules written by legislative bodies to govern social behavior. Administrative agencies make law as they adopt rules and adjudicate disputes, as authorized by statute. Executive orders are issued by the top officer in the executive branch of government. The common law is a collec-

---

[8]H. Abraham, *The Judicial Process* 14 (1986).

tion of judicial decisions based on custom and tradition. Equity provides alternatives to the legal remedies available through the common law.

THE COURTS

Although all three branches of government in the United States help make law, an understanding of the judiciary is particularly important to a student of the law of public communication.

There are 52 court systems in the country: the federal system, a system for each state, and another in the District of Columbia. The structures of the 52 systems are generally similar, but the state systems operate independent of the federal system under the authority of the individual state constitutions and state laws.

Most court systems consist of three layers (see Figure 1.1). On the bottom layer are the trial courts, where the facts of each case are evaluated in light of the applicable law. The middle layer for both the federal system and many states is an intermediate **appellate court.** Finally, all court systems maintain a court of ultimate appeal, usually called a supreme court. The federal court system is the most important for the law of public communication.

The Federal System

The U.S. Constitution mandates only one federal court, the U.S. Supreme Court, but provides for "such inferior courts as the Congress may from time to time ordain and establish."[9]

The Constitution also spells out the **jurisdiction,** or areas of responsibility, of the federal courts. Arguably, the most important federal jurisdiction for communication law is the resolution of disputes involving the Constitution, laws, and treaties of the United States. The federal courts must decide any controversy over the meaning of the First Amendment, including the constitutionality of statutes that ban the burning of the American flag. The federal courts must also resolve any conflict in the interpretation of federal statutory law, such as the 1934 Communications Act. The federal courts must also hear controversies involving the United States, such as when the federal government seeks a court order to obtain the name of a confidential news source. The federal courts must also hear controversies between citizens or corporations of different states. Frequently, for example, the two parties in a libel suit, the person suing and the publisher or broadcaster being sued, live in different states. Matters not specifically assigned to the federal courts by the Constitution must be tried in the state courts.

Congress created the federal judicial system in 1791 with the adoption of the Federal Judiciary Act. The federal system includes 94 trial courts, the U.S. district courts; 13 intermediate appellate courts, the judicial circuits of the U.S. Courts of

---

[9]U.S. Const. art. III, sec. 1.

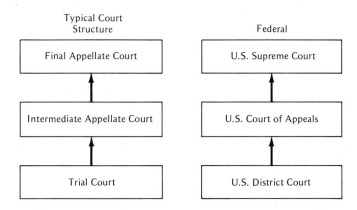

Figure 1.1. Comparative examples of federal and state court structures.

Appeals; and the highest appellate court, the U.S. Supreme Court. Courts with special jurisdiction, such as the U.S. Tax Court, are not generally important to the law of public communication.

Trial Courts Almost all court cases begin in the trial courts, also called courts of **original jurisdiction.** Trial courts examine the facts, or evidence, in a case and then apply the appropriate law. Only trial courts employ juries.

There is at least one federal district court in every state. Many states have more than one, and many districts have more than one judge. In 1987, there were 575 district court judgeships. The Westmoreland libel trial took place in New York City before a judge in the U.S. District Court for the Southern District of the state of New York.

Intermediate Appellate Courts Every person who loses in a trial court has the right to at least one appeal. In the federal system, that appeal is made to an intermediate appellate court. Appellate courts do not hold new trials or reevaluate the facts of cases. Rather, their responsibility is to ensure that trial courts use the proper procedures and apply the law correctly.

Appellate court judges decide cases primarily on the basis of lower court records and the lawyers' written arguments, called *briefs.* The judges also hear a short oral argument by attorneys for both sides. If an appellate court discovers a trial court made an error, a case may be **remanded,** or sent back, to a lower court for a new trial. Cases can be remanded for other reasons as well.

An appeal of a federal district court decision will ordinarily be considered in one of the 13 circuits of the U.S. Courts of Appeals (see Figure 1.2). The jurisdictions of 12 of these courts are defined geographically. The thirteenth, the U.S. Court of Appeals for the Federal Circuit, handles only specialized appeals.

An individual appeals court may include as many as 28 judges, but most cases are heard by a panel of three. Particularly important cases will be heard ***en banc,*** that is, by all the judges of the court. For example, in 1984, the U.S. Court of Appeals for

Figure 1.2.   The thirteen circuits of the U.S. Courts of Appeals.

the District of Columbia Circuit decided *en banc* that a newspaper column written by Rowland Evans and Robert Novak was not libelous. The appeals court, overturning a decision by a three-judge panel of the same court, said the column contained constitutionally protected opinion.[10]

The decisions of the U.S. Courts of Appeals are binding precedents for the federal district courts under their jurisdiction. Opinions of the Courts of Appeals may be persuasive authority but are not binding on state courts in the same jurisdiction deciding similar issues. Although federal appeals court decisions are not binding outside their jurisdiction, they are frequently influential.

Three circuits of the U.S. Courts of Appeals are particularly important to communication law. The Second Circuit, which hears appeals from federal courts in New York, decides a large number of media cases since New York City is the center of commercial telecommunications and the headquarters for many magazines, book publishers, advertising and public relations agencies, and several major newspapers. The Court of Appeals for the D.C. Circuit hears most of the appeals of decisions made by the Federal Communications Commission and the Federal Trade Commission. The Ninth Circuit, with jurisdiction for the West Coast, frequently decides film, television, and copyright cases.

---

[10]Ollman v. Evans & Novak, 750 F.2d 970, 11 Media L. Rep. 1433 (1984), *cert. denied,* 471 U.S. 1127, 11 Media L. Rep. 2015 (1985).

The U.S. Supreme Court   Although the U.S. Supreme Court can exercise both original and appellate jurisdiction, it is primarily an appellate court. The Constitution specifically limits the occasions when the Supreme Court can be the first court to consider a legal controversy, and the Court has done so only about 150 times in the history of the country.[11] However, because the Court has the last word in the interpretation of federal law, the Court's appellate duties make it one of the most powerful institutions in the world. Appellate cases reach the Court from all other federal courts, federal regulatory agencies, and state supreme courts.

The nine Supreme Court justices, like all federal judges, are appointed by the president and confirmed by the Senate. In this century, the Senate has refused to confirm only five Supreme Court nominees, including the controversial conservative Robert Bork. Bork would have replaced Justice Lewis F. Powell, Jr., who retired from the Court in 1987. Justices are appointed for life, or as long as they choose to remain on the Court. They can be removed only by an impeachment conviction.[12]

When Judge Bork was rejected by the Senate, President Ronald Reagan nominated Anthony M. Kennedy, who had been a judge on the U.S. Court of Appeals for the Ninth Circuit. Once confirmed in 1988, Justice Kennedy became part of a five-person conservative majority in many cases before the Court. Other conservative justices are Chief Justice William H. Rehnquist and Justices Antonin Scalia, Byron R. White, and Sandra Day O'Connor.[13] Those justices who are considered "conservative" and those who are "liberal" do not always vote as blocs. Both Kennedy and Scalia joined the more liberal justices on the Court in key 1989 cases protecting First Amendment values. For example, Kennedy and Scalia joined Justices William J. Brennan, Jr., Thurgood Marshall, Harry A. Blackmun, and John Paul Stevens in striking down a Florida law that prohibited newspapers from printing the names of rape victims.[14] Kennedy and Scalia also voted with Brennan, Marshall, and Blackmun to hold that flag burning is protected by the First Amendment.[15] Justice Brennan retired in 1990 and was replaced by David H. Souter.

The Court accepts only 150 to 200 cases a year from the more than 4,300 appeals it receives.[16] In 1988, Congress passed legislation giving the Supreme Court nearly total discretion in selecting the cases it will hear.[17] Until then, the Court was required to hear several kinds of appeals accounting for 20 percent of its caseload. Now, even more than before, most cases reach the court by a writ of ***certiorari,*** a Latin term indicating the Court is willing to review a case.

The process of submitting a case to the Supreme Court for review begins when an attorney files a written argument, called a petition for *certiorari,* asking the Court to review a decision by a federal court or state supreme court. Four Supreme Court jus-

---

[11]H. Abraham, *The Judiciary* 178–79 (1986).

[12]U.S. Const. art. III, sec. 1; *see* S. Mermin, *Law and the Legal System* 327 (1982).

[13]*See, e.g.,* Savage, "Justice Consistently Conservative; Kennedy's Record Sours Liberals' Victory on Bork," *Los Angeles Times,* June 11, 1989, at 1; Kamen, "Divisive Issues at Center Stage as Court Term Ends," *Washington Post,* July 5, 1989, at 1.

[14]Florida Star v. B.J.F., 109 S. Ct. 2603, 16 Media L. Rep. 1801 (1989).

[15]Texas v. Johnson, 109 S. Ct. 2533 (1989).

[16]*E.g.,* "Supreme Court Is Expected to Gain Wide Freedom in Selecting Cases," *New York Times,* June 9, 1988, at 25.

[17]Review of Cases by the Supreme Court, Pub. L. No. 100–352, 102 Stat. 662 (1988).

tices must vote "yes" for the Court to grant a writ of *certiorari* and put the case onto its calendar. The justices try to choose cases involving significant legal issues or containing lower court error. They also may grant *certiorari* when federal appellate courts have decided the same issue differently.

The Court rejects more than 95 percent of the petitions for *certiorari,* usually with no explanation. When a petition for *certiorari* is denied, the lower court decision stands. A refusal by the Supreme Court to accept a case is not an affirmation of the lower court's opinion.

If the Supreme Court accepts a case, the review process is much the same as it is for other appellate courts. The attorneys file briefs arguing their position. The briefs generally present the facts of the case, the issues involved, a review of the actions of the lower courts, and legal arguments. The Supreme Court justices review the written arguments and then listen to what is usually a half hour of oral argument from each attorney. The justices often interrupt attorneys to ask questions or challenge the arguments being presented. The time limit is precise. An attorney arguing before the Court is expected to stop in the middle of a sentence if the light in front of the lectern signals that time has expired.

Following oral arguments, the justices meet in chambers to discuss the case. No one else is permitted to be present. Once the justices have voted, a justice voting with the majority will be designated to write the Court's opinion. If the chief justice is part of the majority, he decides who will write the opinion of the Court. If the chief justice votes in the minority, the most senior justice on the majority decides who will write the Court's opinion.

The choice of author for each opinion can be significant. Because the individual justices have different political philosophies, different views of the role of the Court, and different interpretations of law, they not only vote differently but also explain Court decisions in different ways. Conservative justices, such as Chief Justice Rehnquist and Justice Scalia, are inclined to interpret the Constitution narrowly and restrict the role of the Court, an approach called *strict constructionism.* Conservative justices are more likely to defer to the decisions of government officials. Conservative justices are also more inclined to protect property rights and less likely to protect civil rights than more liberal justices. Liberal justices, such as Justice Marshall, are more concerned about protecting individual rights and less concerned about property rights. Liberal justices are usually more willing to read the Constitution expansively.

When the chief justice and the most senior justice differ markedly in political philosophy—the situation for more than 20 years—the chief justice may want to write the Court's opinion, or control who does, whenever possible. Liberals Hugo Black, William O. Douglas, and Brennan were most senior when conservative Warren E. Burger served as chief justice. Brennan was the most senior justice when Rehnquist became chief justice in 1986.

After a justice drafts an opinion that is expected to be the opinion of the Court, the draft is circulated to the other justices for editing and comment. Drafts of dissenting opinions may be shared as well. The justices may bargain over, and compromise on, the language in the drafts. Votes may shift. The justices reviewing the drafts have several options. They can agree to support the proposed opinion of the Court. They can agree with the proposed opinion of the Court but write a concurring opinion, adding their own thoughts. They can agree with the Court's decision but disagree with the points made in the Court's opinion and write their own. Finally, justices may dissent, writing a dissenting opinion or joining one written by another justice. During the review process, the draft proposed as the opinion of the Court may gain or lose support.

In close votes, both the concurring and dissenting opinions can be particularly important. A majority of the justices deciding a case, usually five, must agree to any point of law for the Court's opinion to become binding precedent. Therefore, in a 5–4 decision, all five justices in the majority must agree to one opinion in order for it to have precedential value. If one of the five writes a concurring opinion questioning any language in the majority opinion, the precedential value of the case will be weakened. Lower courts may have a harder time determining the majority's intentions if the Supreme Court is strongly divided and thus may be less likely to follow the majority opinion.

Lower courts have had difficulty interpreting the Supreme Court's 1972 *Branzburg v. Hayes* decision. In *Branzburg,* a 5–4 majority said that the First Amendment did not ordinarily protect journalists who refuse to reveal confidential sources to grand juries. However, Justice Lewis F. Powell, Jr., though he voted with the majority, wrote a concurring opinion suggesting that he would provide more First Amendment protection for journalists who conceal their sources than the majority opinion implied. Powell's opinion led many lower courts to believe that Powell might join the four dissenting justices instead of the rest of the majority if confidential news source cases involving different circumstances came before the court.[18]

Sometimes none of the draft opinions presented to the Court attract the five votes necessary for a majority. In such a situation, the draft with the most support becomes the plurality opinion of the Court, as occurred in *Richmond Newspapers v. Virginia.* Although the justices in *Richmond Newspapers* voted 7–1 that the First Amendment required that trials be open to the public, no more than three justices agreed to any one opinion explaining why courtrooms could not be closed during trials.[19]

Chief Justice Burger wrote the opinion for the Court even though only Justices White and Stevens joined him. Justice Brennan was among the seven justices who decided that the press and the public have a right to attend criminal trials. However, Brennan, instead of joining Burger's opinion, wrote a concurring opinion to explain his reasons for the decision. Justice Marshall signed on to Brennan's opinion rather than Burger's. Two other justices, the late Potter Stewart and Blackmun, also concurred in the judgment of the Court, but wrote separate opinions expressing their reasons. Rehnquist dissented; Powell did not participate in the case.

On another occasion, in what is known as the Pentagon Papers case, each of the nine justices wrote his own opinion. Although the Court voted 6–3 that the *New York Times* and the *Washington Post* could report a secret Defense Department study, the only opinion issued on behalf of the Court was an unsigned, three-paragraph *per curiam* opinion. A *per curiam* opinion is "by the court" as a whole rather than an opinion attributed to any one justice. The Court's opinion said only that the govern-

---

[18]408 U.S. 655 (1972).
[19]448 U.S. 555, 6 Media L. Rep. 1833 (1980).

ment had not sufficiently justified barring news stories based on the Defense Department study.[20] The justices could not agree on the reasons a **prior restraint** was unjustified. When the Supreme Court is so divided that a majority cannot agree on major legal issues, the high court offers little guidance to lower courts facing similar circumstances.

Technically, the Supreme Court's decisions apply only to the case being decided. The Supreme Court's opinions do not establish statutelike law. However, lower courts assume the Supreme Court will decide similar cases in similar ways so they adjudicate conflicts before them accordingly. Otherwise lower court judges risk being overturned.

The Supreme Court, in its role as interpreter of the U.S. Constitution, has assumed the power to consider the constitutionality of all legislation. This means that the Supreme Court can declare that any act of Congress violates the Constitution and is therefore invalid. The Court has declared that at least part of a federal statute was unconstitutional only about 135 times in the history of the country. The Court has also declared about 970 state laws and state constitutional provisions to be at least in part unconstitutional.[21]

The Court's review of the constitutionality of statutes is important to communication law. The Supreme Court has frequently expanded freedom of expression by invalidating state and federal statutes found to conflict with the First Amendment. Ordinarily, in most areas of law, the Court presumes a statute to be constitutional unless demonstrated otherwise. But in cases involving "fundamental" civil liberties such as free expression, the Court often presumes a limitation on those liberties to be unconstitutional unless the government can establish a "compelling" or "overriding" interest. The Court's protection of First Amendment values is discussed more thoroughly in Chapter 2.

However, regardless of the Supreme Court holding in a case, neither it nor any other court can enforce its own decisions. Enforcement becomes the job of the executive branch. When the Supreme Court rules against the executive branch, it relies upon tradition and its own prestige to achieve compliance. In 1974, public respect for the Court forced President Nixon to obey an order to release secret White House tapes to a special prosecutor investigating the Watergate scandal.[22]

The State Systems

Most state court systems are organized much like the federal courts. Each state has trial courts, similar to the federal district courts, which handle nearly any kind of civil or criminal case. These courts, often called county courts, are ordinarily the first state courts to consider individual libel or privacy cases. These trial courts also handle appeals for a number of subordinate trial courts responsible for minor civil matters, traffic violations, and criminal misdemeanors.

State court systems provide either one or two levels of appellate courts. In some states, appeals go directly from the county courts to what is usually called the state

---

[20]New York Times Co. v. United States, 713 U.S. 403, 1 Media L. Rep. 1031 (1971).
[21]H. Abraham, *The Judiciary* 293 (1986).
[22]United States v. Nixon, 418 U.S. 683 (1974).

supreme court. But many states have intermediate appellate courts to moderate the work load of the supreme court. State courts of appeals, like the federal circuit courts, often use small panels of judges. State appellate court decisions are binding both on lower state courts and federal courts in the same jurisdiction.

The decisions of state supreme courts, usually made up of seven to nine justices, constitute the law of the state and are binding on all of the state's courts. Each state supreme court is the final arbiter of its own state constitution unless a federal constitutional question is involved. A losing **party** in a state supreme court case may have recourse before the U.S. Supreme Court only if a substantial federal question is involved.

Most state court judges are elected, usually in nonpartisan elections.

SUMMARY

There are 52 court systems: one for the federal government, one for the District of Columbia, and one for each state. Most court cases originate in the trial courts, where the facts of each case are applied to the law. Appeals courts ensure that the trial courts use the proper procedures and apply the law correctly. The federal court system consists of federal district courts, the 13 circuits of the U.S. Courts of Appeals, and the U.S. Supreme Court.

THE LITIGATION PROCESS: CIVIL AND CRIMINAL

In criminal law, the government punishes individuals who commit illegal acts such as murder, arson, and theft. Civil law resolves disputes between two private parties. The dispute can be over a dog bite or a news story. Most communication cases are usually brought in civil court rather than criminal court.

A crime is an antisocial act as defined by law, usually a statute adopted by a state legislature. State criminal statutes forbid behavior such as murder and rape and specify punishment, usually a jail sentence or a fine or both. Criminal law is enforced by government law enforcement officers. Once suspects are arrested, they are prosecuted by government attorneys. Even the names of cases, such as *State of Ohio v. Sheppard,* suggest the government involvement in criminal law. One example of criminal law discussed in this book is obscenity law. Both the federal and state governments prosecute individuals who distribute obscene publications.

Understanding criminal law is important to journalists because many report news of the criminal courts. Several issues discussed in this book—access to courtrooms, prejudicial pretrial publicity, and cameras in the courtroom—relate directly to criminal court proceedings.

In contrast to criminal law, civil law concerns claims by individuals or organizations that they have been wronged by another. A person may sue a neighbor for medical costs after being bitten by the neighbor's dog. Or a man may sue a newspaper for inaccurately reporting that he is an adulterer. A legal wrong committed by one person against another is often called a **tort.** Civil law provides the opportunity for a "peaceful'' resolution when one person accuses another of committing a tort. If the person suing wins, he or she often recovers monetary **damages.** If the person being sued wins, frequently no money changes hands except to pay the fees of the lawyers. In civil law, there are no fines or jail terms.

Civil law, including libel and privacy, is a significant part of the law of public communication. Civil suits are more likely to be based on common law than statutory law. In media law, in particular, the government is not ordinarily involved except to provide neutral facilities—the judge, the jury, and the courthouse—to help settle the dispute. However, a civil suit can be based on a statute, and a person or group can sue the government.

A Civil Suit

A civil case begins when the person suing, called the **plaintiff,** files a legal complaint against the person being sued, the **defendant.**

In April 1976, Dr. Ronald Hutchinson, then the research director at a Michigan state mental hospital, filed a civil complaint against Senator William Proxmire of Wisconsin in the U.S. District Court for the Western District of Wisconsin. Hutchinson complained that Proxmire had libeled him by giving a "Golden Fleece" award to his research on monkeys. Proxmire had said, a year earlier, that the American public was being "fleeced" by the nearly half million dollars spent for Hutchinson's research by the National Science Foundation, the National Aeronautics and Space Administration, and the Office of Naval Research. The agencies were examining the problems faced by humans confined in close quarters for long periods of time, as in space or in underwater exploration. Proxmire said, however, that the federal government ought to get out of the "monkey business." He said the "transparent worthlessness" of Hutchinson's research was taking a bite out of the American taxpayer. Hutchinson's civil complaint said Proxmire had humiliated him and held him up to public scorn, damaged his professional and academic standing, and damaged his ability to attract research grants.[23]

Once a complaint has been filed at the courthouse, a defendant, in this case Senator Proxmire, is served with a summons, a notice to appear in court. The penalty for not appearing could be loss of the case or a citation for contempt of court. Defendants often respond to complaints by denying the accusations. Senator Proxmire "answered" the complaint, in part, by filing a motion for **summary judgment,** a common tactic in communication cases. A judge can grant a summary judgment to either a defendant or a plaintiff if the judge believes that the two sides in a case agree on the facts of the dispute, and that one should win as a matter of law. Summary judgments can defeat a suit in its early stages, saving attorney fees and avoiding the often unpredictable outcome of a jury decision. Summary judgments are discussed more thoroughly in Chapter 3.

Hutchinson's complaint, Proxmire's answer, and a reply by Hutchinson are called the *pleadings,* documents stating the nature of a case. Sometimes the two sides in a dispute file a series of documents in an attempt to narrow the issues. Frequently,

---

[23]Hutchinson v. Proxmire, 443 U.S. 111, 5 Media L. Rep. 1279 (1979).

the two sides will ask a judge for a pretrial conference in another attempt to narrow the issues or even to settle the case.

Meanwhile, the parties, sometimes called litigants, begin what is called **discovery.** Discovery is the information-gathering process. During discovery—which, in major cases, can take several years—each side tries to gather information on its behalf and find out as much as possible about the evidence available to the other party. The lawyers often prepare interrogatories, written questions that must be answered under oath by people who might have relevant information. Then lawyers frequently take depositions, that is, ask questions in person that also must be answered under oath.

During discovery, lawyers may request that the judge issue a **subpoena** requiring a journalist, or someone else, to testify or bring documents or other evidence to court. A subpoena must be served to the person named in it. Failure to comply with a subpoena can result in contempt of court. Journalists frequently fight subpoenas on the grounds that revealing sources or evidence will limit their future news-gathering ability, a subject discussed in Chapter 10.

In the Hutchinson case, the judge granted time for discovery after receiving Senator Proxmire's motion for summary judgment. The two parties exchanged interrogatories and subsequently the answers. Hutchinson requested a trial by jury. He also asked to amend his complaint, a motion that was granted over the objection of Senator Proxmire. In the amended complaint, Hutchinson said the "Golden Fleece" announcement not only libeled him, but also infringed on his rights of privacy and peace and tranquility. Both Hutchinson, the plaintiff, and Proxmire, the defendant, filed the results of depositions in November 1976. Shortly thereafter, Hutchinson filed a brief, along with five volumes of exhibits, arguing against Proxmire's motion for summary judgment. Senator Proxmire filed a reply brief with exhibits.

In April 1977, about a year after Hutchinson's complaint was filed, the district court judge granted Senator Proxmire's motion for summary judgment.[24] If the summary judgment had not been granted, the case would have gone to trial.

A jury trial is required if the two parties disagree on the facts of a case and one of the parties insists on a jury. In a jury trial, both sides present their cases and then the judge explains the relevant law to the jurors. The jury is asked to apply the law to the facts, and it may set monetary damages as part of the verdict. If a judge believes the jury verdict is contrary to law, or that the damages are excessive, he or she can overturn the jury's decision. This occurred early in the 1980s when a judge decided that a jury verdict in favor of Mobil Oil president William Tavoulareas, and against the *Washington Post,* was contrary to libel law.[25]

Once a judgment has been recorded in a case, either party can appeal. The person who appeals is known as the **petitioner;** the person fighting the appeal is called the **respondent.** The petitioner in one appeal may be the respondent in another appeal. In Hutchinson's suit, Hutchinson became a petitioner when he appealed the grant of summary judgment to the U.S. Court of Appeals for the Seventh Circuit, where it was upheld. Hutchinson's petition of *certiorari* to the U.S. Supreme Court was ac-

---

[24]431 F. Supp. 1311, 2 Media L. Rep. 1769 (W.D. Wis. 1977).
[25]Tavoulareas v. Washington Post Co., 567 F. Supp. 651, 9 Media L. Rep. 1553 (D.D.C. 1983), *aff'd,* 817 F.2d 762 (D.C. 1987) *(en banc).*

cepted. Proxmire was the respondent both before the Seventh Circuit and the Supreme Court. The Supreme Court reversed the decision of the Seventh Circuit, and Hutchinson and Proxmire eventually settled out of court. Hutchinson received $10,000 in damages and an apology from Senator Proxmire. The Supreme Court opinion, *Hutchinson v. Proxmire,* is discussed in Chapter 3.

A Criminal Case

The key steps in a criminal prosecution are substantially the same in most states. The procedures may be labeled differently or occur in different sequence.

A criminal action begins with a law enforcement investigation. The government's case against an individual begins with the arrest, or apprehension, of the person suspected of committing a crime. The case of Dr. Sam Sheppard, important to communication law, began with his arrest in July 1954. Sheppard, a Cleveland, Ohio, osteopath, was arrested on a charge of murdering his wife, Marilyn. The one-month investigation prior to the arrest established that Mrs. Sheppard had been killed with a blunt instrument, that Dr. Sheppard was in the house at the time, that there was no money missing from the home, and that no readable fingerprints could be found.[26] The investigation included an inquest ordered by the coroner to determine if a murder had been committed. Extensive, sensational publicity, discussed in Chapter 9, began immediately.

After an arrest, the person accused of a crime appears before a magistrate for a preliminary hearing. At the hearing, the person is advised of the nature of the crime and reminded of his or her right to counsel and the right to remain silent. The primary purpose of a preliminary hearing is to determine if there is sufficient evidence, or **probable cause,** to justify further detention or a trial. Sheppard appeared before a magistrate, was informed of the charge, and was bound over to the grand jury.

If the magistrate decides that there is probable cause, he or she will set the bail; that is, announce the amount of money that must be posted before the accused can be released from jail. The bail is intended to ensure that the accused appears in court. Sheppard was denied bail.

The next step, depending on the state, could be the filing by the prosecutor of a criminal information, a document formally accusing the person of a crime. Or, the prosecutor may take the evidence to a grand jury to seek an **indictment,** the formal accusation by a grand jury. Only about half of the states have grand juries, and their role in the criminal justice system varies. On August 17, 1954, a grand jury in Ohio indicted Sheppard for first-degree murder.[27]

An arraignment usually follows the formal accusation. The arraignment is the official, formal reading of the indictment or information to the accused. The accused is asked to plead guilty or not guilty.

If the defendant pleads not guilty, the focus turns to pretrial preparation and negotiation. Both the prosecution and defense engage in discovery, the pretrial fact-

---

[26]State v. Sheppard, 128 N.E.2d 471, 484, 485, 494 (1955).

[27]State v. Sheppard, 128 N.E.2d 471 (1955); Sheppard v. Maxwell, 384 U.S. 333, 1 Media L. Rep. 1220 (1966); Ohio Rev. Code Ann. sec. 2937.02 (1984).

finding. Both sides may submit a variety of motions to the judge. The defense may move for an adjustment or dismissal of the charges. Or, as in Sam Sheppard's case, a defense attorney may ask that a trial be relocated or delayed because of extensive pretrial publicity. The judge in the Sheppard trial denied both motions.

During the pretrial maneuvers, the prosecution and defense may agree to resolve the case through a *plea bargain*. In plea bargaining, a trial is avoided due to the defendant's willingness to plead guilty to reduced charges, a process that resolves cases 15 times more frequently than jury verdicts.[28] Plea bargains not only save time and money, but also avoid the uncertainty inherent in a trial court decision.

A trial can take place before a judge or a jury. Criminal defendants can waive their right to a jury trial. After the jury announces the verdict of guilty or not guilty, a judge pronounces the sentence. A jury in the Common Pleas Court of Cuyahoga County, Ohio, decided that Sam Sheppard "purposely and maliciously" killed his wife, the requirement for second-degree murder in Ohio. The judge sentenced Sheppard to life in prison, the mandatory penalty in Ohio for the crime of second-degree murder.

Sheppard appealed to the Court of Appeals of Ohio for Cuyahoga County, an intermediate appellate court, in 1955. He argued that there were nearly 40 errors in the conduct of the trial, including the denial of motions to move the trial and to postpone the trial. He also argued that the jury had been improperly selected and prejudicial evidence was improperly allowed during the trial. The three-judge panel decided that Sheppard "has been afforded a fair trial by an impartial jury and . . . substantial justice has been done."[29] Sheppard also lost a 1956 appeal in the Ohio Supreme Court. The U.S. Supreme Court denied *certiorari* the same year.[30] Nine years later the U.S. Supreme Court agreed to consider Sheppard's contention that he was denied a fair trial because of sensational media coverage. That story is told in Chapter 9.

SUMMARY

Criminal law prohibits antisocial behavior as defined by statute. Violations are punishable by jail sentence and/or fine. Criminal law is enforced by the government. A criminal action begins with an investigation and an arrest. A preliminary hearing is held to determine if there is sufficient evidence to justify a trial. Then either a prosecutor or a grand jury formally accuses a person of a crime. After the accused responds to the charge during an arraignment, both the prosecution and the defense engage in pretrial fact-finding, known as discovery.

Civil law involves disputes between two private parties. A plaintiff sues a defendant for damages. After the plaintiff files a civil complaint and the defendant responds, the two parties engage in discovery.

Both civil and criminal cases can be dismissed or otherwise resolved before trial.

---

[28]H. Abraham, *The Judicial Process* 140 (1986).
[29]State v. Sheppard, 128 N.E.2d at 504.
[30]State v. Sheppard, 128 N.E.2d 471 (Ohio Ct. App. 1955), *aff'd,* 135 N.E.2d 340 (Ohio 1956), *cert. denied,* 352 U.S. 910 (1956).

FINDING THE LAW

A professional communicator does not need to be a lawyer to find and read the law. Most law libraries have friendly and knowledgeable librarians ready to help. The next few pages should provide enough background to enable students to know what to ask for. Although a nonlawyer can find the law with very little assistance, reading and understanding the law takes time and practice.

Court Documents

The book you are reading is footnoted. The citations provide the information necessary to find a court case, and they are a lot easier to understand than they may appear.

Footnote 23 referred to *Hutchinson v. Proxmire,* 443 U.S. 111, 5 Media L. Rep. 1279 (1979). The first name in the citation, Hutchinson, refers to the person initiating the legal action, whether filing a complaint or an appeal. The second name, Proxmire, refers to the object of the action. The rest of the citation tells where the legal document can be found. The abbreviation between the numbers refers to the court reporter where the case is found. The "U.S." in the example stands for *United States Reports,* the official legal reporter for the U.S. Supreme Court. The number in front of the "U.S." refers to the volume in which the case can be found. The number after the "U.S." refers to the page on which the case begins. Therefore, *Hutchinson v. Proxmire* can be found in volume 443 of *United States Reports,* beginning on page 111.

The second abbreviation in the *Hutchinson* citation, "Media L. Rep.," stands for *Media Law Reporter,* a second publication in which the case can be found. In *Media Law Reporter,* the case *Hutchinson v. Proxmire* begins on page 1279 of volume 5. *Media Law Reporter* is a specialized commercial reporting system for media law cases available in many law libraries and some journalism libraries. Court opinions are available much sooner in *Media Law Reporter* than they are in *United States Reports.*

The final number in the citation for *Hutchinson v. Proxmire* is the year the opinion was issued. The case was decided in 1979.

Any government or academic law library should have the *United States Reports.* However, the same legal opinions that are published in *United States Reports* are also reported commercially in reporting systems such as West Publishing Company's *Supreme Court Reporter.* The West Publishing Company version of *Hutchinson v. Proxmire* can be found at 99 S. Ct. 2675 (1979). The Lawyers Co-operative Publishing Company publishes what is called *United States Supreme Court Reports: The Lawyer's Edition. Hutchinson v. Proxmire,* therefore, can also be found at 61 L. Ed.2d 411 (1979). Both commercial systems reporting Supreme Court opinions publish the decisions more quickly than the government. The commercial reporters are reliable and just as useful for most purposes as the official reporters. Both commercial companies also publish numerous other legal reference services.

Only the West Publishing Company prints the opinions of the 13 circuits of the U.S. Courts of Appeals. The federal appeals court opinion in the *Hutchinson* case can be found at *Hutchinson v. Proxmire,* 579 F.2d 1027 (7th Cir. 1978). The "F" stands for *Federal Reporter.* The "2d" means that volume 579 is in the second series of volumes of the *Federal Reporter.* If the citation had been 579 F. 1017, the case would have been found in the first series. The first series of the *Federal Reporter* was issued from 1880 to 1924 and stopped with volume 300. In the *Federal Reporter* citation for *Hutchinson,* there is an abbreviation within the parentheses next to the date. The "7th Cir." stands for the Seventh Circuit of the U.S. Courts of Appeals, the court that heard the case. When the court issuing a decision is not readily apparent by the discussion in the text of this book, it is usually named next to the date.

The most comprehensive collection of federal district court decisions is found in the *Federal Supplement.* The summary judgment issued by the federal district court judge in *Hutchinson v. Proxmire* can be found at 432 F. Supp. 1311 (W.D. Wis. 1977). The abbreviations within the parentheses indicate which court heard the case, in this instance, the U.S. District Court for the Western District of the state of Wisconsin. Not even the *Federal Supplement* publishes all the opinions issued by the federal district courts.

This book will frequently refer to state court cases. Although most state trial court opinions are not published, the appellate opinions are—sometimes in both the official state reports and the West version. Both citations, *State v. Sheppard,* 100 Ohio App. 345 (1955), and *State v. Sheppard,* 128 N.E.2d 471 (1955), refer to the same opinion of the Ohio Court of Appeals. In the opinion, the court denied the first appeal by Sam Sheppard after he was convicted of murdering his wife. The first citation is to the official Ohio reports; the second to the West Publishing Company version.

West publishes state cases in seven "regional" reporters. "NE" stands for the Northeastern region, "SE" for the Southeastern region, "P" for the Pacific, and so forth (see Figure 1.3). Again, the "2d" refers to the second series, in this case of the Northeastern reporter. The state of Ohio has separate reporters for the intermediate appellate courts and for the Ohio Supreme Court. West uses the same reporting system for both. The Ohio Supreme Court opinion in the Sheppard case can be found at 165 Ohio St. 293 (1956) and 135 N.E.2d 340 (1956).

Most of the case opinions cited above are available in yet another source, computerized data bases found in most law libraries. The two commercial data bases specializing in legal materials are *Lexis* and *Westlaw,* which provide court opinions more quickly than the print services and provide extraordinary capabilities for searching for specific subjects. *Lexis* and *Westlaw* are often not available to undergraduates. However, they are sometimes used in the footnotes in this book because they were the only places a few court opinions could be found at the time of publication.

The legal citations in this book and elsewhere not only reveal where to find a court case, but they also often provide a case history. Citations therefore will include a short description of the action taken by courts and administrative agencies. For example, the abbreviation *aff'd* indicates an appellate court affirmed a lower court action. *Rev'd* stands for reversed. *Cert. denied* means that the U.S. Supreme Court rejected the petition for *certiorari.* **Sub. nom.** means that a different name is being used for the same case.

In a citation a few pages back, footnote 30 tells the reader that a decision in the case *State v. Sheppard* by the Court of Appeals of Ohio was affirmed by the Ohio Supreme Court. The name of the state, standing alone with the date, indicates that

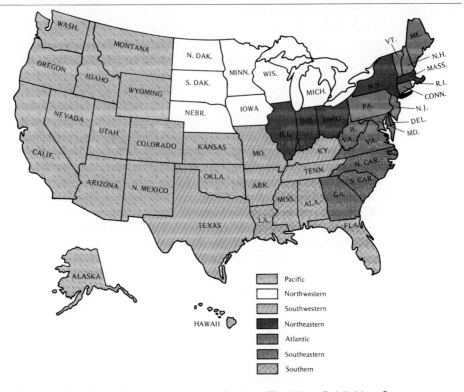

Figure 1.3. West's Regional Reporter System. The West Publishing Company arranges state court cases into a series of regional reporters.

the decision was made by the state's supreme court. Footnote 30 indicates the United States Supreme Court refused to take the case. There was no change in the case name as the dispute traveled through the court system.

Once a court opinion is found in a law library, the next task is to figure out what it means. One aid often available is a collection of small paragraphs just under the name of the case. These *headnotes* summarize major legal points addressed in the opinion. In addition to the headnotes, many reporting systems provide a syllabus for the case. The syllabus summarizes the principal facts of the case and the decision of the court. Neither the headnotes nor the syllabus are "official" because they are not written by the courts.

Following the headnotes, the syllabus, and a list of attorneys involved in the case, the reporting system will usually indicate who wrote the opinion of the court. In many reporting systems, the votes of the other judges or justices are recorded only if they dissented or wrote a concurring opinion. If a judge's name is not mentioned, it can be assumed that he or she voted for the court opinion. In the Supreme Court case *Hutchinson v. Proxmire,* Chief Justice Burger wrote the majority opinion. Justice Stewart joined the majority opinion, except that he disagreed with one footnote. Justice Brennan wrote a dissenting opinion. Since there is no note indicating that a justice did not participate in deciding the case, all nine voted in the case. Therefore, a reader can conclude that the Court decided all the issues in *Hutchinson,* except for the footnote objected to by Stewart, by an 8–1 vote.

A student reading a court opinion should first look for the issue, or issues, that the court is addressing. Sometimes a court opinion will say, "The issue before the court is . . . " At other times the issue may be hidden in the language of an opinion. Sometimes a court opinion will not clearly address any one issue. In some cases, the justices disagree on the major issue being addressed. Still, understanding the issue helps a reader determine what is important in an opinion.

Knowing the issue, or the *question,* as it is often called, helps locate the resolution, or *holding,* of the case. When a reader knows the legal question a court is posing, the court's answer should be easier to find. One of the questions in *Hutchinson v. Proxmire* was whether Hutchinson, a research scientist receiving federal funds for his work, was a "**public figure**" as defined by the Court. The holding for that issue was "no," Hutchinson was not a public figure. The holding of a case should lead to the point of law, a brief statement of the meaning of the opinion. The libel chapter discusses that the Court ruled in *Hutchinson v. Proxmire* that research scientists receiving government funding are not automatically public figures in libel suits.

Many times, in addition to identifying the issue and the holding, it is important to try to find the major reasons, or the rationale, for a court's decision. A court may support its rulings by referring to such evidence as previous court decisions, its interpretation of a statute, the legislative documents leading up to the passage of a statute, a court's understanding of history, or its understanding of "good" public policy. When the Supreme Court ruled in *Hutchinson v. Proxmire* that Hutchinson was not a public figure, it relied on language in previous Supreme Court opinions discussing the definition of *public figure.*

As mentioned earlier in the chapter, some court decisions cannot be fully understood without reading concurring and dissenting opinions. The lone Brennan dissent in *Hutchinson* was not a major factor in the disposition of the case. But remember: When all nine justices participate in a case, five must agree on any point of law for it to be considered legal precedent.

The level and function of a court rendering an opinion are other factors to be kept in mind when reading court opinions. The importance of a court opinion varies with the level of the court. An opinion by a federal district court judge does not have the same impact on the law as an opinion by the U.S. Supreme Court. Opinions by trial courts, such as a federal district court, have the least influence on other courts. Decisions in a trial court are more apt to be dependent on the facts of an individual case than at other levels of the court system. The decisions are often made by juries rather than judges, who are legal professionals. Trial courts are responsible for the smallest geographical jurisdictions and trial court opinions are the least likely to be *reported,* or published. Opinions by intermediate appellate courts carry more precedential value. Judges rather than juries are examining cases in light of the law as a whole. Appellate courts review the decisions of several trial courts and all appellate court opinions are reported. Of course, supreme court decisions carry the most weight.

Legislative Documents

Court opinions are not the only place law is found. There are several important legal documents generated by the legislative system.

The most important documents produced by the legislative process, the statutes, are compiled by the federal government and each state government. Statutes passed by Congress are published in chronological order for each session of Congress in *United States Statutes at Large.* The citation for the 1934 Communications Act, as originally adopted, is 48 Stat. 1064 (1934). The 1934 Communications Act can be found on page 1064 of volume 48 of *United States Statutes at Large.* The Communications Act and other federal statutes can also be found in the *United States Code,* a compilation of active federal law. The code is arranged by 50 topics, or "titles," and is published about every six years. The 1934 Communications Act, as amended, can be found in title 47 of the *United States Code.* The citation for the section requiring that broadcasters provide equal opportunities for political candidates is 47 U.S.C. sec. 315.

Both West Publishing Company and the Lawyers Co-operative Publishing Company publish annotated versions of the statutes that provide references to historical changes in the laws, notes about court decisions interpreting the statutes, and a list of pertinent publications discussing the law. West prints the *U.S. Code Annotated,* and the Lawyers Co-op prints the *U.S. Code Service.* Citations to the equal opportunities section of the 1934 Communications Act are 47 U.S.C.A. sec. 315 and 47 U.S.C.S. sec. 315, respectively. Both services provide a "popular name index" so that statutes can be found if only the commonly used, rather than legal, name is known. The Trademark Act of 1946, for example, can be found by looking under "Lanham Act," the commonly used name. The *U.S. Code Service* also provides references to law review articles.

Proposed legislation, committee reports, hearings, and floor debates for the U.S. Congress are readily available on most major university campuses. Libraries that serve as one of 1,300 federal document depositories keep a copy of every bill submitted to each house of Congress. The depositories receive most of the documents printed by the U.S. Government Printing Office, including the transcripts of congressional hearings, committee reports on legislation, and other committee staff studies. The committee reports—which document the background, history, purpose, and explanations of bills passed by the committees—are available in a West publication, *United States Code Congressional and Administrative News.* The *Congressional Record* is the published version of what is said on the floor of the U.S. House and Senate. It is not what was actually said, but an amended version. The floor debates, committee hearings, and committee reports constitute what is called the *legislative history* of a bill. In contrast to the extensive legislative history available for congressional action, information about state legislative activity is sometimes scarce.

Commerce Clearing House publishes the *Congressional Index* (CI), an excellent place to find the status of bills introduced into Congress, including information about hearings and committee votes. The *Congressional Quarterly Weekly Report* provides regular updates on the progress of legislation and reports on votes in both houses. A good index for congressional materials is the *Congressional Information Service Index.* The *Monthly Catalog of United States Government Publications* indexes most documents published by the government.

Administrative Documents

The rules and regulations of the administrative agencies are printed in the *Federal Register,* published daily by the government. The *Federal Register,* abbreviated *FR* in textual matter and Fed. Reg. in citations, also publishes proposed rules, federal legal notices, documents ordered published by Congress, and presidential proclamations and executive orders. The Congressional Information Service provides an effective index to the *Federal Register.*

A compilation of administrative regulations can be found in the *Code of Federal Regulations,* or *CFR.* The *CFR*, a commercial service updated annually, is to administrative law what the *United States Code* is to statutory law. The regulations of the administrative agencies are organized into 50 "titles" parallel to the titles of the *United States Code.* Regulations adopted by the Federal Communications Commission to enforce the 1934 Communications Act can be found in title 47 of the *CFR.* The rules affecting the right of persons attacked during controversial broadcasts to reply on the air are spelled out as 47 C.F.R. section 73.1920 (1989).

Each of the federal administrative agencies publishes official reports containing agency decisions. The FCC used to call its official reports the *Federal Communications Commission Reports,* abbreviated F.C.C. in a citation. Since 1986, the FCC has instead published the *FCC Record* (FCC Rcd.). The FTC publishes *Federal Trade Commission Decisions* (F.T.C.). Other publications important to communication law include *Decisions and Orders of the National Labor Relations Board* (N.L.R.B.), *Securities and Exchange Commission Decisions and Reports* (S.E.C.), and *Copyright Decisions* (Copy. Dec.), published by the Copyright Royalty Tribunal.

In addition, numerous commercial services provide excellent research resources for scholars studying administrative agencies. For the study of telecommunications, the best service is *Pike & Fischer Radio Regulations,* a privately published loose-leaf service updated regularly. Another specialized publication is the *Commerce Clearing House Copyright Law Report.*

Other Resources

There also are general resource materials that can be helpful in finding and understanding the law. The two major legal encyclopedias are *American Jurisprudence 2d* (cited as Am. Jur. 2d) and *Corpus Juris Secundum* (C.J.S.). Although the titles are formidable, both can provide extensive subject indexes that lead to short legal summaries and pertinent legal citations.

A good way to find all the cases related to a particular topic is to use one of the many legal digests. West Publishing Company, in particular, provides digests for the Supreme Court, for all federal courts, for individual states, and for groups of states. The digests contain brief case summaries.

One way to begin a search is through computerized indexes such as *Lexis* and *Westlaw,* mentioned earlier. Another way is to examine extensively footnoted law review articles. The two major indexes to law reviews are *Current Law Index* and *Index to Legal Periodicals.*

An easy-to-understand guide to legal research is *The Legal Research Manual; A Game Plan for Legal Research and Analysis,* by Christopher and Jill Wren. It is available in paperback from A-R Editions, Inc., Madison, Wisconsin.

An indispensable tool for legal writing is *A Uniform System of Citation,* recognized as the authority in legal style. The publication, popularly known as the "Harvard Blue Book," is in its fourteenth edition. Not only is the Blue Book a handy guide for legal citations, but it also can be used as a guide to the kinds of publications available. The Blue Book is indeed blue and is published by the Harvard Law Review Association.

Anyone doing legal research should also be acquainted with *Black's Law Dictionary,* the most widely used dictionary for legal terminology.

Updating

Law is constantly changing. Frequently, the bound volumes of statutes, regulations, and court opinions become outdated soon after they reach the shelves. To keep up with new developments, legal researchers rely extensively on "advance sheets," "pocket parts," and *Shepard's Citations.*

Advance sheets are early paperback versions of opinions or other legal research materials that eventually will be available in hardbound books. Pocket parts are paperback supplements to statutes, codes, and regulations usually found in a back "pocket" of a bound volume. Anyone using legal research materials should be sure to check for advance sheets or pocket parts in order to ensure the law has not been changed.

Shepard's Citations allows anyone studying the law to be certain that a specific court opinion or administrative agency ruling is still valid law. *Shepard's* tells a legal researcher when an opinion such as *Hutchinson v. Proxmire* has been mentioned in subsequent court decisions. *Shepard's* can be used to determine if a court opinion has been overturned or to see how the law has developed since the opinion being "shepardized" was decided.

SUMMARY

Most legal citations contain, in order, the name of the legal action, the volume of the legal reporting service containing information about the action, the abbreviation for the legal reporting service, the first page of the information cited, and the year of the action. The citation may also include the name of the court issuing the opinion.

The official reporter for the U.S. Supreme Court is the *United States Reports.* The opinions of the U.S. Courts of Appeals can be found in the *Federal Reporter.* Federal district court opinions are printed in the *Federal Supplement.* State appellate court opinions are often printed by the state and by West Publishing Company in regional reports. Students examining a case should look for the issue, the holding, and the court's rationale.

Statutes are first printed in the *United States Statutes at Large* and then are compiled in the *United States Code.* Administrative rules and regulations are first printed in the *Federal Register* and then compiled in the *Code of Federal Regulations.*

WORKING WITH LAWYERS

Many communicators will not conduct their own legal research as often as they will call a lawyer. Because public communication often raises questions of law, professional communicators frequently need lawyers. Communicators should not fear or avoid lawyers; rather, communicators should use lawyers intelligently.

Most communicators will not have direct access to a lawyer in their first job. Newspapers, for example, generally prefer that legal questions be taken to a supervisor. In newsrooms, city editors and managing editors ordinarily can answer relatively simple legal questions and usually decide when a lawyer needs to be consulted. Some major daily newspapers and large advertising and public relations firms hire staff lawyers, known as in-house attorneys. Others engage a law firm they can call as needed. Even the smallest communications organization should have someone to call when legal questions arise.

Lawyers, whose fees often range from $100 to $250 an hour, should be used only when necessary. When possible, lawyers should be used to prevent a legal conflict rather than to resolve one. Therefore, a lawyer should be consulted in the following cases:

- When a communicator is served with, or receives, a subpoena, a summons, or an arrest warrant. Communicators need the advice of a lawyer before responding to a legal document.
- When there is a concern that a story being considered for publication could lead to a libel or privacy suit. Attorneys can help assess the risks of stories, such as major investigative stories.
- When a news medium is asked to print retractions or corrections. Some seemingly innocent and well-intentioned efforts to correct errors can increase rather than decrease the risk of a suit if a lawyer is not consulted.
- When a communicator is approached by a lawyer hired by someone else. A layperson should not respond to the legal moves of an adversary.
- When a communicator is considering an action that may be illegal. Reporters sometimes consider trespassing, breaking and entering, or obtaining stolen documents in pursuit of a story. Sometimes it is obvious when an act is illegal; often it is not. Reporters need to understand the legal consequences of their actions. A lawyer may be able to help.

Lawyers can do more than help communications professionals make legal decisions. They can also help communicators do their jobs. For example, lawyers can help obtain access to closed records or meetings by explaining to reporters and officials the rights of the public and press. Lawyers can also help public relations specialists complete forms required by the Securities and Exchange Commission, the Federal Communications Commission, and other administrative agencies.

When communicators work with lawyers, they should remember that lawyers, like other professionals, are trained to do some tasks and not others. Lawyers can help resolve a legal conflict, but they cannot eliminate the sloppy writing or editing that may have caused a suit in the first place. Attorneys can explain the probable risks and consequences of a story or an ad. They can discuss the factors that ought to be considered in deciding how to avoid **liability.** An attorney should know the questions an opposing attorney will ask about a story and what kind of arguments are likely to be made in a libel trial.

Lawyers are not usually qualified to tell a communicator what to write or how to edit. Some lawyers are insensitive to the problems, values, and commitments of journalists. Some attorneys regularly advise cutting stories to avoid trouble. They routinely suggest eliminating the defamatory portions of stories without regard to the public importance of the information. The job of a lawyer, according to James Goodale, a prominent media attorney, should be "to figure out how to get the story published," not trimmed or killed.[31] The lawyer should explain legal risks; the communicator should make the editorial decisions after weighing those risks.

Public communicators may sometimes need a personal attorney. An employer might refuse to represent an employee in court, especially if the employee acts contrary to instructions or without consulting a supervisor. In the early 1970s, the *New York Times* refused to defend one of its reporters, Earl Caldwell, when he refused to testify before a grand jury. The *Times* wanted Caldwell to respond to a grand jury subpoena by entering the grand jury room, even if he refused to answer questions. However, Caldwell refused even to enter the grand jury room, which is closed to the public and the press. Caldwell believed that once he went behind closed doors his sources would no longer trust his promises to keep what he knew confidential. When Caldwell was found in contempt of court for refusing to testify, the *Times* did not provide him with a company attorney. Caldwell's case was considered by the Supreme Court in *Branzburg v. Hayes,* a case mentioned earlier in this chapter and discussed in Chapter 10.

An attorney needs to know all of the facts that pertain to a legal issue. Communicators should hold nothing back. If confessions to lawyers about careless reporting or writing are embarrassing, they are even more so if first revealed by an opposing lawyer in front of a jury. Attorneys need to know the worst in order to present the best case.

SUMMARY

Legal advice can be an expensive but necessary part of modern communication. Lawyers should be called when a communicator must respond to an official document or someone else's attorney. Lawyers should be consulted when a communicator is considering an act that may be illegal. Lawyers should review stories that could lead to libel or privacy suits. Lawyers can explain the risks of publishing a story, but they should not be allowed to act as editors.

---

[31]Rambo, "Litigious Age Gives Rise to Media Law," *presstime,* Nov. 1981, at 7.

LIMITATIONS OF LAW

This book focuses on the law. Professional communicators need to know the law in order to do their job effectively and without unnecessary risk. However, the law does not resolve all questions that may arise in public communication.

For one thing, the law does not necessarily protect every action that a professional communicator believes to be in the public interest. Libel law does not always protect a newspaper that wants to report an allegation of government corruption. In addition, reporters who refuse to reveal the names of sources for a story about government corruption could go to jail. At times, communicators have to decide whether a story is worth a jail sentence or a libel suit. They have to consider whether the public benefit of a story outweighs the risk of jail or a suit. The fact that a journalist may not be protected by law is not the only factor to be considered.

Conversely, the law may allow behavior contrary to personal or professional ethics. Ethics is the consideration of moral rights and wrongs. Ethics involves honesty, fairness, and motivation. It also involves respect for the emotional well-being, dignity, and physical safety of other human beings. The law, as reflected in statutes and court decisions, does not always parallel personal and professional codes of conduct. The First Amendment frequently permits expression, such as the publication of the name of rape victims, that many journalists consider unethical. Ethical questions are raised by the publication of highly personal information, the publication of pretrial information about criminal defendants, and the refusal of journalists to reveal their news sources, all of which are at least sometimes permitted by law. Communicators base decisions on whether behavior is morally "right" or "wrong" as well as its legality. However, a discussion of ethics is left for another book and another class. The purpose of this book is to help professional communicators understand the law that affects their performance. The law, however, is not meant to be an end unto itself.

2

THE FIRST AMENDMENT

In no other country do people enjoy the freedom of expression exercised by Americans. The legal foundation of American freedom to speak and publish is the First Amendment. "Congress shall make no law," the First Amendment says, "respecting an establishment of religion, or prohibiting the free exercise thereof; or abridging the freedom of speech, or of the press; or the right of the people peaceably to assemble, and to petition the government for a redress of grievances." This categorical language, embedded in the supreme law of the land, gives Americans a broad right to speak and publish on matters of conscience and consequence without fear of reprisal by the government.

Despite the categorical prohibition against government interference, the freedom to speak and publish is not absolute. Sometimes the government may bar dissemination of expression that threatens national security or public safety. More frequently expression will be punished *after* dissemination because it defames someone or invades a citizen's privacy.

Communication law, the subject of this book, is the system by which society determines the exceptions to freedom of expression. Exceptions to freedom of expression depend on what is said, who is speaking, and the harm that speech or writing may cause. Whether speech may be prohibited or punished also depends on the standards of judgment employed by the courts and the theory underpinning the law.

THEORY OF FREEDOM OF EXPRESSION

Freedom of expression is highly valued and protected by the Constitution because it is thought to serve essential values. Free speech is valued because it advances important social goals, such as the discovery of truth, the continuance of self-government, and the promotion of change with stability. Freedom of expression is also valued because it helps the individual find fulfillment.

Considerable effort has been invested in trying to create a "theory" of freedom of expression to explain in each case when freedom of expression should be protected and why. Some First Amendment theorists emphasize one value over others,[1] while others agree with Professor Kent Greenawalt that "[t]there is no single correct way of presenting the justifications . . . for a principle of freedom of speech."[2] The late law professor Harry Kalven thought it fruitless to try to construct a theory of freedom of expression because each case in which speech may be halted or punished involves too many conflicting values and complex facts to be explained by an overarching theory. It is better, Kalven said, to "think small,"[3] deciding each court case as it arises without attempting to reconcile every decision with every other in a consistent structure. Whether or not Kalven is right, no comprehensive First Amendment theory has been developed. But underlying individual court decisions are values that are generally agreed to be served by freedom of expression.

Attainment of Truth

The argument that freedom of expression helps the search for truth assumes that rational decisions emerge from consideration of all facts and arguments. An individual who seeks knowledge and truth, says Professor Thomas I. Emerson, carries on a continuous Socratic dialogue. A citizen, Emerson says,

> must hear all sides of the question, especially as presented by those who feel strongly and argue militantly for a different view. He must consider all alternatives, test his judgment by exposing it to opposition, make full use of different minds to sift the true from the false. Conversely, suppression of information, discussion, or the clash of opinion prevents one from reaching the most rational judgment, blocks the generation of new ideas, and tends to perpetuate error.[4]

The argument that freedom of expression speeds the search for truth is frequently summarized in the metaphor of the marketplace of ideas. The best test of

---

[1]*See* Baker, "Commercial Speech: A Problem in the Theory of Freedom," 62 *Iowa L. Rev.* 1 (1976); Meiklejohn, "The First Amendment Is an Absolute," 1961 *Sup. Ct. Rev.* 245.

[2]"Free Speech Justifications," 89 *Colum. L. Rev.* 119, 127 (1989).

[3]*See* Karst, "The First Amendment and Harry Kalven: An Appreciative Comment on the Advantages of Thinking Small," 13 *U.C.L.A. L. Rev.* 1 (1965).

[4]T. Emerson, *Toward a General Theory of the First Amendment* 7 (1963).

truth, according to the late Supreme Court Justice Oliver Wendell Holmes, is the power of a thought "to get itself accepted in the competition of the market."[5] Just as shoppers in the commercial marketplace seek the best products, participants in the marketplace of ideas seek the most original, truthful, or useful information. Like shoppers in a commercial market, consumers in the marketplace of ideas must be wary that they do not get inferior goods. In theory, good ideas, like good products, will prevail in a free market.

The marketplace-of-ideas metaphor can be traced to the bad marital relations of John Milton, the English poet and essayist. In 1644, Milton published an essay titled *Areopagitica,* which was Milton's response to criticism he had received earlier for publishing without government license a tract urging that English divorce laws be liberalized so that he could extricate himself from an unpleasant union. In *Areopagitica,* Milton argued that Parliament should allow unlicensed printing.

Milton said that licensing is a bad idea because it deprives citizens of knowledge and ideas that could inprove their lives. Furthermore, Milton argued, censorship is impractical; the censor's pencil does not prevent the circulation of influential ideas. In addition, Milton said that most people are not fit to be censors. Those with the intelligence to be discerning censors would not want such a boring and repulsive task. Besides, Milton concluded, it is good for a citizen's intellect to distinguish good ideas from bad. In his most famous passage, Milton said that the free competition of ideas leads to truth:

> And though all the winds of doctrine were let loose to play upon the earth, so Truth be in the field, we do injuriously, by licensing and prohibiting, to misdoubt her strength. Let her and Falsehood grapple; who ever knew Truth put to the worse, in a free and open encounter?[6]

Despite his laissez faire argument, Milton did not believe that all expression should be permitted. As a Puritan, he was not ready to allow free discussion of Catholicism or atheism.

Nineteenth-century philosopher John Stuart Mill thought it "idle sentimentality" to argue, as Milton did, that truth always prevails in combat with falsehood. "History teems," Mill wrote, "with instances of truth put down by persecution." Yet, Mill valued free speech fully as much as Milton, not because truth would always prevail but because truth has no chance to prevail without freedom of expression.

It robs the human race, Mill said, to silence the opinion of even one person. If a correct opinion is suppressed, he said, people are "deprived of the opportunity of exchanging error for truth." If the opinion is wrong, people "lose, what is almost as great a benefit, the clearer perception and livelier impression of truth, produced by its collision with error."[7]

Not all students of freedom of expression embrace the metaphor of the marketplace of ideas. One commentator, following Mill, questions whether citizens are sufficiently rational to choose truth over falsehood.[8] Critics also question whether the

---

[5]Abrams v. United States, 250 U.S. 616 (1919).
[6]*Areopagitica,* in *32 Great Books of the Western World* 409 (1952).
[7]J.S. Mill, *On Liberty* 24 (Gateway 1955).
[8]Baker, "Scope of the First Amendment Freedom of Speech," 25 *U.C.L.A. L. Rev.* 964 (1978).

consolidation of the media, particularly large urban newspapers, has not restricted the marketplace of ideas from what it was in the days of small, independent newspapers. In 1947, The Commission on Freedom of the Press, a panel of scholars and intellectuals, warned that concentration of media ownership threatened to create a private censorship as restrictive as government censorship.[9]

In the 1960s and 1970s, Dean Jerome Barron of the National Law Center, George Washington University, argued that the marketplace of ideas meant little to minorities, dissidents, and fringe groups who could not gain access for their ideas in the monopoly daily newspapers in most American cities. Barron argued that a right of citizen access to American newspapers should be created through advertising columns. Barron said anyone should be able to buy space in a newspaper to express ideas in an editorial advertisement and that newspapers should be required to print replies from public officials who are libeled.[10] However, the First Amendment forbids requiring newspapers to publish advertisements or replies.

The argument that concentration of media ownership restricts the marketplace of ideas does not go unchallenged. Ownership of big-city newspapers may become increasingly concentrated, but most publishers feel obligated to publish a wide range of views. Furthermore, the number of channels of communication continues to grow. Serious newspapers thrive in the suburbs around big cities, challenging the monopoly of metropolitan dailies for advertisers, readers, and news scoops. Meanwhile, cable television erodes the dominance of the television networks with more channels and specialized programming. In addition, dozens of radio stations can be heard in major cities. The marketplace of ideas is a commercial marketplace that does not present every viewpoint, particularly not extreme views, but the marketplace of ideas is not an empty metaphor.

Governance

Besides aiding the search for truth, freedom of expression also contributes to democratic governance. "The root purpose of the First Amendment," Professor Emerson says, "is to assure an effective system of freedom of expression in a democratic society."[11]

Alexander Meiklejohn, an influential philosopher and academic leader, was the best-known proponent of the theory that freedom of expression is to be valued primarily for its contribution to governance. For Meiklejohn, the discovery of truth was valuable, but the role of freedom of expression in democratic governance was much more so. "No one can deny," Meiklejohn wrote, "that the winning of the truth is important for the purposes of self-government." But, Meiklejohn said, truth

> is not our deepest need. Far more essential, if men are to be their own rulers, is the demand that whatever truth may become available shall be placed at the disposal of all the citizens of the community. The First Amendment is not, primarily, a device

---

[9]Commission on Freedom of the Press, *A Free and Responsible Press* (1947).

[10]J. Barron, *Freedom of the Press for Whom?* 6 (1973). *See also* Barron, "Access to the Press—a New First Amendment Right," 80 *Harv. L. Rev.* 1641 (1967).

[11]T. Emerson, *System of Freedom of Expression* 17 (1970).

for the winning of new truth, though that is very important. It is a device for the sharing of whatever truth has been won. Its purpose is to give to every voting member of the body politic the fullest possible participation in the understanding of those problems with which the citizens of a self-governing society must deal.[12]

Meiklejohn said the primary purpose of the First Amendment is that citizens understand "the issues which bear upon our common life." Therefore, he said, "no idea, no opinion, no doubt, no belief, no counterbelief, no relevant information," may be kept from the people. "Under the compact upon which the Constitution rests, it is agreed that men shall not be governed by others, that they shall govern themselves."

Meiklejohn said speech that contributes to "the business of government" should be absolutely protected from government intervention. Meiklejohn's primary hope was that freedom of expression would protect discussion, beliefs, and associations necessary for responsible voting because, to Meiklejohn, voting was the key act of self-governance. Voting, he said, is "the official expression of a self-governing man's judgment on issues of public policy."

In response to criticism that his focus on political expression was too narrow, Meiklejohn expanded his definition of political speech. He said that governance in a democracy requires absolute First Amendment protection for communications about education, philosophy, science, literature, the arts, and public issues. From discussion of philosophy, science, and the arts, the voter derives the knowledge, intelligence, and sensitivity to human values necessary for "sane and objective judgment" in the voting booth, Meiklejohn said.[13] Meiklejohn's elastic definition of political speech made it difficult for him to limit the range of expression meriting "absolute" protection.

Check on Government Power

A variation on the writings that emphasize the value of political speech is Professor Vincent Blasi's argument that freedom of expression is to be valued as a check on abuses of governmental authority. Blasi sees the media as an institutional counterweight to government. To Blasi, freedom of expression, particularly as exercised by larger media, is a countervailing power to federal, state, and local governments in which corruption seems to increase with their budgets. Abuse of government, Blasi says, "is an especially serious evil—more serious than the abuse of private power, even by institutions such as large corporations which can affect the lives of millions of people."[14] Blasi, then, sees a role for the institutional media as the proverbial "watch dog," checking government conduct during periods of wrongdoing.

The First Amendment, Blasi argues, is most valuable during such "pathological" periods as Watergate, when the government may be most tempted to suppress

---

[12]A. Meiklejohn, *Free Speech and Its Relation to Self-Government* 88–89 (1948). *See also* Bork, "Neutral Principles and Some First Amendment Problems," 47 *Indiana L. J.* 1 (1971).

[13]"The First Amendment Is an Absolute," 1961 *Sup. Ct. Rev.* 245, 256–57. For criticism, *see* Chafee, "Book Review," 62 *Harv. L. Rev.* 891 (1949); L. Tribe, *American Constitutional Law* 577 (1978).

[14]Blasi, "The Checking Value in First Amendment Theory," 1977 *Am. B. Found. Res. J.,* 521, 538.

free expression.[15] Blasi does not deny that freedom of expression serves other values, such as promoting self-governance and enhancing individual dignity. But Blasi is more interested in power relationships. To him, the press can expose political corruption if it scrutinizes government operations in a system that recognizes the First Amendment checking function of the press.

Change with Stability

A fourth social purpose of freedom of expression, one also related to governance, is the contribution of free speech to orderly change. As Professor Emerson wrote,

> suppression of expression conceals the real problems confronting a society and diverts public attention from the critical issues. It is likely to result in neglect of the grievances which are the actual basis of the unrest, and thus prevent their correction. For it both hides the extent of opposition and hardens the position of all sides, thus making a rational compromise difficult or impossible. Further, suppression drives opposition underground, leaving those suppressed either apathetic or desperate. It thus saps the vitality of the society or makes resort to force more likely.[16]

Freedom of expression, therefore, can be thought of as a "safety valve." Where there is freedom of expression, dissidents have a chance to work their ideas into the social fabric without resorting to a violent underground cell. Ideas that society deems worthless can be rejected with little threat to the stability of society. Where there is freedom of expression, consensus can develop to support orderly change. Free expression promotes both flexibility and stability. Tradition and change coexist. As Emerson says, where there is freedom of expression, society is better able to maintain "the precarious balance between healthy cleavage and necessary consensus."

Fulfillment

Freedom of expression is valued not only because of the social values it promotes, but also because speaking freely enriches the life of the speaker or publisher. Freedom of expression, Professor Emerson says, is justified as a right of the individual "purely in his capacity as an individual. It derives from the widely accepted premise of Western thought that the proper end of man is the realization of his character and potentialities as a human being."[17] Freedom of expression is a fundamental good, says Professor Laurence Tribe, "an end in itself, an expression of the sort of society we wish to become and the sort of persons we wish to be."[18]

The notion that freedom of expression is necessary to protect the integrity of the individual reflects the influence of natural law in American jurisprudence. Natural law, popular in the seventeenth and eighteenth centuries, posited that people are

---

[15]Blasi, "The Pathological Perspective and the First Amendment," 85 *Colum. L. Rev.* 449 (1985). *See also* Abrams, "The Press *Is* Different: Reflections on Justice Stewart and the Autonomous Press," 7 *Hofstra L. Rev.* 563 (1979).

[16]T. Emerson, *Toward a General Theory of the First Amendment* 12 (1963).

[17]*Id.* at 4–5.

[18]L. Tribe, *American Constitutional Law* 785 (2d ed. 1988).

born, as English philosopher John Locke said, with fundamental rights of life, liberty and property, rights which the government has a contract with its citizens to protect.[19] The influence of natural law can be seen in the American Declaration of Independence and in the guarantees of liberty and equality in the Bill of Rights. The Bill of Rights protects the integrity of the individual not only from government suppression of free speech, but also from unreasonable searches and forced confessions.

Of course, self-fulfillment does not have to be directed inward. Exercising one's right to speak may also serve the social and political values of free speech. One might say with philosopher Wolfgang Freidmann that the individual's rights of liberty and equality find their highest fulfillment when a citizen participates in what Lincoln called "Government of the People."[20]

Some writers find the concept of "natural rights" too vague and sentimental for making principled decisions in free speech cases.[21] Does the fundamental right of self-expression include the right to shout obscenities? Burn a draft card? Shoot an adversary? It is hard to answer these questions when freedom of expression is justified on the grounds of an unprovable natural right to fulfillment. Nevertheless, the American legal system, more than any other, has been molded by the principles of natural law.[22]

SUMMARY

While First Amendment theorists emphasize different values, the discussion usually centers on the relative importance of social and individual values. Freedom of expression is said to be justified because it leads toward truth, promotes self-governance, checks government abuses, and advances orderly change. Freedom of expression is also valued as fundamental to human fulfillment.

SCOPE OF THE FIRST AMENDMENT: WHO IS PROTECTED

Whether people have a right to speak in specific circumstances depends in part on who they are. The average adult has greater First Amendment rights than students, prisoners, and some government employees. Publishers enjoy fuller freedoms of expression than broadcasters and nonmedia corporations.

Adults

Adults exercising their right of free expression may serve social goals and fulfill themselves at the same time. Adults enjoy First Amendment rights to speak and publish,

---

[19]J. Locke, *Of Civil Government* (1955). *See also* J.-J. Rousseau, *The Social Contract* (1960).
[20]W. Friedmann, *Legal Theory* 419–20 (5th ed. 1967).
[21]*E.g.,* Schauer, "The Role of the People in First Amendment Theory," 74 *Calif. L. Rev.* 761 (1986).
[22]W. Friedmann, *Legal Theory* 136–37 (5th ed. 1967).

join associations, and receive information. Adults also enjoy freedom from being compelled to speak.

Speaking and Publishing The right to speak and publish is basic to freedom of expression. The First Amendment specifically protects the rights of speech and the press. Any citizen with sufficient resources may publish and distribute a newspaper, pamphlet, or book. Any adult also enjoys the right to converse on a public sidewalk or expound on a political or religious theme at a public meeting or a speaker's corner. Some argue the government has an affirmative obligation to encourage speech in public parks, sidewalks, airports, bus terminals, and other "public forums."[23]

Freedom of expression includes the individual's right to participate in symbolic forms of expression such as marching, demonstrating, contributing money to a political campaign, and burning the American flag. Symbolic expression, which is speech melded with conduct, is not permitted in all places and at all times, but is nevertheless protected by the First Amendment along with more "pure" speech and publishing.

Associating Besides the right to speak and publish, a citizen has a First Amendment right to associate with others. Alexis de Tocqueville noted that the "most natural privilege of man, next to the right of acting for himself, is that of combining his exertions with those of his fellow creatures and of acting in common with them."[24] The right of association is found in the First Amendment rights of assembly, speech, and petition. By joining a religious, political, or ideological group, individuals strengthen their individual right to speak. Thus, associations are protected from government interference not only because of the inalienable right of individuals to band together, but also because associations advance political and social issues.

Citizens have a constitutional right to band together to advocate political change,[25] undertake litigation,[26] or worship their god.[27] Associations enjoying these rights include the conservative John Birch Society and the more liberal National Association for the Advancement of Colored People. The right of association guarantees these ideological groups the rights enjoyed by individuals to speak, publish, pamphleteer, lobby, and march.

Receiving Information The First Amendment does not protect just the right to talk, write, and associate; it protects the interchange of ideas. Speaking and publishing mean little if one cannot also hear or acquire information. The right to speak and publish therefore implies an audience to hear, to read, and to respond.

The Supreme Court has recognized a constitutional right to receive information.[28] Laborers, for example, have a right to hear what a labor organizer has to say.[29]

---

[23]Emerson, "The Affirmative Side of the First Amendment," 15 *Ga. L. Rev.* 795 (1981).

[24]P. Bradley, ed. *Democracy in America* 196 (1945). *See* Raggi, "An Independent Right to 'Freedom of Association,' " 12 *Harv. C.R.–C.L. L. Rev.* 1 (1977).

[25]Cousins v. Wigoda, 419 U.S. 477 (1975).

[26]NAACP v. Button, 371 U.S. 415 (1963).

[27]Serbian Eastern Orthodox Diocese v. Milivojevich, 426 U.S. 696 (1976).

[28]Martin v. Struthers, 319 U.S. 141 (1943).

[29]Thomas v. Collins, 323 U.S. 516 (1945).

Consumers have a right to receive some forms of commercial advertising[30] and corporate communication.[31] Regulations on broadcasting, too, are supposed to promote the rights of listeners and viewers to receive information.[32]

The constitutional right of a citizen to receive information is not as strong as the right to speak and publish. The right to receive derives from, and is subsidiary to, the right to speak and publish.[33] The right to receive, therefore, is difficult to assert. The Supreme Court has recognized the right of the press and public to have access to many court proceedings,[34] but the Court has recognized no constitutional right of access for the press and public to prisons,[35] or to foreign countries declared off limits by the State Department.[36] Likewise, public access to government records and meetings depends on state and federal statutes opening the documents and proceedings, not on a First Amendment right of access.[37]

Likewise, Americans have been denied access to foreign speakers. The U.S. government has frequently denied Americans access to foreign speakers by refusing to issue entry visas, often under authority of the recently repealed McCarran-Walter Immigration Act of 1952. Under this McCarthy-era legislation, the attorney general could deny entry to Communists or others whose admission might be ''prejudicial to the public interest.'' The McCarran-Walter Act was used many times to deny entry to foreigners because of their political beliefs. Among those denied visas were Ernest Mandel, a distinguished Belgian journalist and Marxist scholar, who had been invited to speak at Stanford University.[38] Also excluded were the Italian novelist and chemist Primo Levi and Mexican novelist and Nobel Laureate Carlos Fuentes. In 1984, the Immigration and Naturalization Service estimated that it blocked 8,000 people from 98 countries because of their beliefs or political affiliations.[39] In 1990, Congress passed legislation barring the government from denying short-term visas to foreigners because of their political beliefs.[40]

Soliciting Funds   Individuals and ideological groups also have a First Amendment right to contribute money and to solicit funds to further their cause. **Political action committees** associated with corporations and unions can raise and contribute money to support political candidates as part of their right of association. The Supreme Court has also said that charitable appeals are protected by the First Amendment because they ''involve a variety of speech interests—communication of information, the dissemination and propagation of views and ideas, and the advocacy of causes.''[41]

---

[30]Virginia State Bd. of Pharmacy v. Virginia Citizens Consumer Council, Inc., 425 U.S. 748, 1 Media L. Rep. 1930 (1976).

[31]First Nat'l Bank of Boston v. Bellotti, 435 U.S. 765, 3 Media L. Rep. 2105 (1978).

[32]Red Lion Broadcasting Co. v. FCC, 395 U.S. 367, 1 Media L. Rep. 2053 (1969). *See generally* Lee, ''The Supreme Court and the Right to Receive Expression,'' 1987 *Sup. Ct. Rev.* 303.

[33]R. Dworkin, *Taking Rights Seriously* 93 (1977).

[34]Richmond Newspapers, Inc. v. Virginia, 448 U.S. 555, 6 Media L. Rep. 1833 (1980).

[35]Houchins v. KQED, 438 U.S. 1, 3 Media L. Rep. 2521 (1978).

[36]Zemel v. Rusk, 381 U.S. 1, 1 Media L. Rep. 2299 (1965).

[37]*See* Federal Freedom of Information Act, 5 U.S.C.A. sec. 552a (1977).

[38]Kleindienst v. Mandel, 408 U.S. 753 (1972).

[39]''Congress Drops Barrier to Aliens Based on Beliefs,'' *New York Times,* Feb. 2, 1990, at 1, 4.

[40]*Id.*

[41]Village of Schaumburg v. Citizens for a Better Environment, 444 U.S. 620, 632 (1980).

The solicitation of funds, the Court said, is "characteristically intertwined with informative and perhaps persuasive speech seeking support for particular causes or for particular views on economic, political, or social issues."

The First Amendment right to solicit barred an Illinois town from requiring newspaper representatives soliciting subscriptions to have a permit.[42] An Illinois court ruled that a suburban ordinance requiring a commercial solicitor to have a permit did not apply to a newspaper seeking subscriptions in a door-to-door campaign. The Court said a newspaper subscription solicitation, like a political, charitable, or religious solicitation, is protected by the First Amendment.

The First Amendment right to solicit funds, however, does not bar the government from stopping begging, according to a federal appeals court. The U.S. Court of Appeals for the Second Circuit ruled that the New York Metropolitan Transportation Authority did not violate the First Amendment when it prohibited panhandlers from the subways. Most individuals who beg are simply collecting money, the court said. They do not convey any social or political message meriting First Amendment protection, the court said. However, Judge Meskill, in dissent, said beggars, like representatives of a charity, often explain the purpose of their solicitation and "perhaps engage in a discussion regarding social issues," such as the nature of poverty.[43]

Compelling Speech   The freedom of expression belonging to individuals and associations includes freedom from compelled speech. "The right to speak and the right to refrain from speaking are complementary components of the broader concept of 'individual freedom of mind,'" the Supreme Court has said.[44] Therefore, the government cannot compel schoolchildren to salute the flag if their families' religious beliefs forbid it.[45] Nor can the government, consistent with the First Amendment, compel a citizen to affirm a belief in God,[46] associate with a political party in order to get a job,[47] or adhere to an ideology.[48]

In *Wooley v. Maynard,* the Supreme Court said that the government of New Hampshire could not require a Jehovah's Witness to display "Live Free or Die" on his automobile license plate. The Court said the New Hampshire statute requiring the phrase on the plates unconstitutionally required citizens to use their private property as a "mobile billboard" for a state's ideological message. George and Maxine Maynard, both Jehovah's Witnesses, found the slogan repugnant on moral, religious, and political grounds. According to their beliefs, it is immoral to value freedom above life or to give up one's life for the state.[49]

The Supreme Court has also ruled that a public utility is protected from having to carry messages from a consumer group in the company's billing envelopes. A company, like an individual, has a right to avoid associations it opposes.[50]

---

[42]Chicago Tribune v. Downers Grove, 508 N.E.2d 439, 14 Media L. Rep. 1273 (Ill. App. 1987).
[43]Young v. New York City Transit Auth., 903 F.2d 146 (2d Cir. 1990).
[44]Wooley v. Maynard, 430 U.S. 705 (1977).
[45]West Virginia State Bd. of Educ. v. Barnette, 319 U.S. 624 (1943).
[46]Torcaso v. Watkins, 367 U.S. 488 (1961).
[47]Elrod v. Burns, 427 U.S. 347 (1976)
[48]Wooley v. Maynard, 430 U.S. 705 (1977).
[49]*Id.*
[50]Pacific Gas & Elec. Co. v. Public Utilities Comm. of California, 475 U.S. 1 (1986).

Freedom from compelled speech is of particular importance to ideological associations. The government is not supposed to withhold privileges or benefits from an association or compel disclosure of a group's membership.[51] Because of the right of association, minor political parties may be exempted from laws requiring disclosure of political contributions and expenditures if disclosure might subject the parties to threats, harassment, or reprisals.[52] The Supreme Court ruled that a newspaper could not publish the names of contributors to a counterculture church because disclosure might embarrass contributors and weaken the ability of the church to collect contributions.[53]

However, the First Amendment does permit the government to require a number of disclosures by individuals and groups. Later chapters will discuss constitutionally acceptable compulsory disclosure by advertisers, corporations, lobbyists, contributors to political campaigns, and by journalists ordered to testify before grand juries and courts.

High School Students

First Amendment rights are not the exclusive property of adults. Speaking and publishing by young people is also constitutionally protected. High school students, however, have weaker rights than college students.

High school students, like adults, are persons with fundamental rights, the Supreme Court said in 1969 in *Tinker v. Des Moines Independent School District.*[54] Students' First Amendment rights, therefore, "do not stop at the schoolhouse gate," the Court said. Students in the American system of state-operated schools should not be viewed, the Court said, as "closed-circuit recipients of only that which the State chooses to communicate."

In the *Tinker* case, the Court ruled 7–2 that the First Amendment prohibited the school system in Des Moines from barring students who wished to wear black arm bands to protest the war in Vietnam. In a majority opinion written by Justice Fortas, the Court said that the arm bands were a form of symbolic expression akin to "pure speech" protected by the First Amendment. It is especially appropriate that freedom of expression be protected in the school system, the Court said, because,

> The classroom is peculiarly the "marketplace of ideas." The Nation's future depends upon leaders trained through wide exposure to that robust exchange of ideas which discovers truth "out of a multitude of tongues, [rather] than through any kind of authoritative selection."[55]

State-operated schools, Fortas said, may not be "enclaves of totalitarianism."

Although its decision in *Tinker* was very expansive, the Court did not say that high school students' rights of free expression are absolute. The Court said student

---

[51]L. Tribe, *American Constitutional Law* 1010–1022 (2d ed. 1988).
[52]Buckley v. Valeo, 424 U.S. 1 (1976) (per curiam).
[53]Seattle Times v. Rhinehart, 467 U.S. 20, 10 Media L. Rep. 1705 (1984).
[54]393 U.S. 503 (1969).
[55]*Id.* at 512, *quoting* Keyishian v. Board of Regents, 385 U.S. 589, 603 (1967).

speech can be curbed if it "materially disrupts classwork or involves substantial disorder or invasion of the rights of others." The Court saw no evidence that the black arm bands would interfere with the school's work or collide with the rights of other students. Until the mid 1980s, courts following *Tinker* generally ruled that high school administrators could censor student speech only if it presented a genuine possibility of disruption, was libelous, was obscene, or promoted illegal activity.

While high schoool students enjoy First Amendment rights, it has always been recognized, as the Supreme Court noted in *Tinker,* that restrictions may be applied "in light of the special circumstances of the school environment." High schools, besides being places of intellectual inquiry and debate, are places where community values are inculcated in the young. With this educational function in mind, the Supreme Court has sharply limited the First Amendment rights of high school students.

In 1988, the Court upheld the censorship of two articles from the student newspaper, *Spectrum,* at Hazelwood East High School near St. Louis. In *Hazelwood School District v. Kuhlmeier,* the Court ruled 5–3 that school authorities could impose any reasonable regulation on school-sponsored speech. The Court upheld the deletions by Hazelwood principal Robert Reynolds of an article about teen pregnancies and one about divorce. The newspaper was produced in Journalism II, a class taught for credit.

Students at Hazelwood East argued the articles were constitutionally protected because they were not disruptive under the Court's test in *Tinker.* But the Supreme Court refused to apply the *Tinker* disruption standard because the stories in *Spectrum* were school-sponsored expression. The Court said the disruption standard is appropriate for students' "personal expression," such as black arm bands, but is not necessary when expression is sponsored by the school and serves the school's educational mission as *Spectrum* did. The Court said educators "do not offend the First Amendment by exercising editorial control over the style and content of student speech in school-sponsored expressive activities so long as their actions are reasonably related to legitimate pedagogical concerns."

Legitimate Pedagogical Concerns   The Court first concluded in *Hazelwood* that *Spectrum* was not a "public forum." A public forum is government-owned property on which free discussion is protected. Streets and parks are traditional public forums because they have always been open for "assembly, communicating thoughts between citizens, and discussing public questions."[56] Government property, such as a university meeting room, may also be a public forum if it is dedicated to public debate through a policy of opening the property indiscriminately to campus or community speakers.[57] The government may not stop speech in a public forum absent a compelling interest.

Students at Hazelwood East argued that *Spectrum* was a public forum because the school had adopted policies guaranteeing publication of "diverse viewpoints." Students also noted that *Spectrum* was more than just a classroom exercise; every three weeks, 4,500 copies were distributed widely on campus and in the community.

---

[56]*See* Perry Educ. Assoc. v. Perry Local Educators' Assoc., 460 U.S. 37, 45 (1983).
[57]*See* Widmar v. Vincent, 454 U.S. 263 (1981).

Writing for the Court, Justice White said *Spectrum* was not like streets and parks or like a university meeting room that has been dedicated to public debate. *Spectrum,* White said, had never been dedicated "by policy or by practice" to use by the public. Rather, *Spectrum* was more like an army base, which is government property that is not dedicated to free expression, but is retained for its nonspeech purposes.[58] Even if civilian speakers or entertainers are invited onto an army base, the government has not dedicated the property as a public forum.

To Justice White, *Spectrum* could be regulated because it was school-sponsored expression. White said *Spectrum* was a "laboratory" paper because it was published in Journalism II, a class for which students received credit and grades. *Spectrum* was a "regular classroom activity" in which the journalism teacher selected the editors, scheduled publication, decided the number of pages, assigned story ideas, edited, and sought approval from the principal before publication.

The Court said educators may regulate school-sponsored expression "to assure that participants learn whatever lessons the activity is designed to teach." Journalism II was designed to teach students journalistic skills and "the legal, moral, and ethical restrictions imposed upon journalists within the school community."

The Court also said educators could govern school-sponsored expression to assure that "readers or listeners are not exposed to material that may be inappropriate for their level of maturity." It was therefore reasonable for Reynolds, the Hazelwood East principal, to delete the article about teen pregnancy, in part, because he thought references to sexual activity and birth control were "inappropriate" for 14-year-old freshmen at the school and for even more sensitive younger siblings at home.

Finally, the Court said it was reasonable for school administrators, as publishers and producers of school-sponsored expression, to assure that views of a student are not erroneously attributed to the school. A school may, the Court said, "disassociate itself " from speech that might be disruptive, inconsistent with "the shared values of a civilized social order," or which is not neutral in a political controversy. The Court said, for example, a school might not want to be associated with student expression that is "ungrammatical, poorly written, inadequately researched, biased or prejudiced, vulgar or profane, or unsuitable for immature audiences."

Thus, it was reasonable, in the Court's view, for the Hazelwood principal to censor the story about teen pregnancy because publication might invade the privacy of one of the few pregnant students at the school. Reynolds could also delete the divorce story because he felt parents referred to in the piece had been unfairly denied a chance to respond. One named student complained in the story that her father "was always out of town on business or out late playing cards with the guys."

Justice Brennan, in a very sharp dissent harkening back to the Court's decision involving black arm bands in *Tinker,* argued that the wide powers of censorship granted to school administrators by the Court majority threatened to create "enclaves of totalitarianism" in the public schools. Brennan, who was joined in dissent by Justices Marshall and Blackmun, said the First Amendment does not permit a school to bar student communication simply because it may be at odds with a school's

---

[58]*See* Greer v. Spock, 424 U.S. 828 (1976).

pedagogical message. Administrators' desire to avoid discomfort and unpleasantness does not justify official suppression of student speech, Brennan said.

To Brennan, *Spectrum* was a public forum dedicated to vigorous public debate. Brennan wanted the Court to employ the constitutional test enunciated in *Tinker* barring student expression only if it disrupts educational processes. Brennan saw no threat of disruption in the articles about pregnancy and divorce.

The dissenters also argued it was unconstitutional to bar student publications on such vague criteria as whether the subject of an article was "inappropriate" or too sensitive. These amorphous criteria leave unlimited discretion to school administrators, the dissenters said.

Limits of School-Sponsored Speech   Yet to be determined following *Hazelwood* is the breadth of expression that may be censored because it is school-sponsored. Clearly, expression deriving from a class is school-sponsored, the Court said, because it is part of the curriculum. But the Supreme Court suggested in *Hazelwood* that school-sponsored expression included most student speech at school. Educators, the court said, "have authority over any school-sponsored publications, theatrical productions, and other expressive activities that students, parents, and members of the public might reasonably perceive to bear the imprimatur of the school." All of these activities, the Court said, "may fairly be characterized as part of the school curriculum," even if they do not occur in traditional classrooms. They are part of the curriculum, the Court said, as long as they are "supervised by faculty members and designed to impart particular knowledge or skills to student participants and audiences."

Speech that "bears the imprimatur" of the school, and is therefore not "personal expression" like the arm bands in *Tinker,* includes expression at assemblies that students must attend. Two years before *Hazelwood,* the Supreme Court held in *Bethel School District v. Fraser,*[59] that a Washington state school could suspend Matthew N. Fraser for a lewd speech nominating a student government candidate. In his nominating speech, Fraser said his candidate was firm, "firm in his pants, he's firm in his shirt, his character is firm. . . . "

A school does not violate the First Amendment, the Court said, if it determines that vulgar and lewd speech should be punished, particularly when younger students are present. It was appropriate, the Court said, for the school to teach pupils that vulgar speech and lewd conduct are "wholly inconsistent with the 'fundamental values' of public school education."

While the Supreme Court says that administrators may regulate most student expression in high schools, lower courts have ruled since *Hazelwood* that schools may not necessarily regulate student expression just because the school system pays for a publication or advises student editors. A federal district court in New York said a trial should be held to determine whether *The Crow's Nest,* a noncredit extracurricular publication funded by a New York City high school, "bore the imprimatur" of the school or was a public forum. *The Crow's Nest* was paid for by the school and advised by a teacher, but the paper was not produced in a class. *The Crow's Nest* was

---

[59]478 U.S. 675 (1986).

also different from *Spectrum* because the paper included a disclaimer in its masthead saying that the paper did not express the views of the Board of Education, the school administration, or its faculty adviser. The court denied summary judgment to the school in a suit by an adviser who was fired for allowing a student to publish an article opposing a federal holiday for Martin Luther King, Jr.[60]

Another court, in a case that was later settled, ruled that a trial should determine whether a school-funded magazine at a high school in Ridgefield, Connecticut, was a public forum or a school-sponsored publication furthering the school's educational mission.[61] Although the publication, *Lodestar,* was funded by the school, its history suggested to the court the publication was not just a school activity. In the settlement, the magazine and school agreed that the school could withdraw funding if *Lodestar* wished to publish material the school thought contrary to its educational mission. Students, however, would still be allowed to distribute *Lodestar* on campus, presumably as expression akin to black arm bands that is personal to the student.[62]

In a third case, the U.S. Court of Appeals for the Ninth Circuit said that even a publication produced in a classroom might be a public forum if school policy or practices dedicate the publication to public debate. In a case involving a high school newspaper in Clark County, Nevada, the Ninth Circuit also said that administrative regulations on student expression should not discriminate against would-be speakers, barring speech the administration disagrees with and permitting speech it supports.

However, the Ninth Circuit upheld the power of the Nevada school system to bar advertisements by Planned Parenthood in a high school newspaper produced in a journalism class. Although the Ninth Circuit said that even a classroom publication could be dedicated as a public forum, the court said the Clark County school system had not created a public forum in its high school newspaper by policy or practice. Like the Supreme Court in *Hazelwood,* the Ninth Circuit said that the school policy "invests principals with broad authority and discretion to control the content of advertisements" appearing in school publications. The court, therefore, said a principal could bar advertisements for family planning in high school newspapers if the school system did not wish to be associated with "any position other than neutrality" on the subject of teenage family planning.[63]

The court also concluded that the school system did not discriminate by barring advertisements by Planned Parenthood but allowing other advertisements. Within a principal's discretion, the court said, is the authority to dissociate the school from "potentially sensitive subjects" such as birth control and abortions. The regulations barring Planned Parenthood's advertisements had a valid educational purpose that was not discriminatory, the court said.

While high school administrators enjoy broad authority to censor expression that is associated with the school, courts generally rule that administrators must permit campus distribution of "underground" and "alternative" publications that are produced off-campus and are therefore not school-sponsored. While a school system may punish even this personal student expression if it is disruptive, libelous, or pro-

[60]Romano v. Harrington, 725 F. Supp. 687 (E.D.N.Y. 1989).

[61]Lodestar v. Board of Educ., Civ. No. B-88-257 (D. Conn. 1989).

[62]"Lodestar Suit Ends in Out-of-court Settlement," *Student Press Law Center Rep.,* Winter 1989–90, at 16.

[63]Planned Parenthood of S. Nevada, Inc. v. Clark County School Dist., 887 F.2d 935 (9th Cir. 1989).

poses illegal activities, the U.S. Court of Appeals for the Ninth Circuit ruled that a school system may not review all nonschool-sponsored student publications before they are distributed on campus.[64] As a later section will discuss, the Ninth Circuit ruling is consistent with a long line of cases holding that government review of a publication before distribution is unconstitutional.

The *Hazelwood* decision, of course, does not require administrators to censor school-sponsored expression. The decision says only that censorship of expression bearing the imprimatur of the school does not violate the First Amendment if reasonable regulations serve the school's educational purpose. In fact, several states, including California, Massachusetts, and Iowa, limit school officials' powers of censorship far more than *Hazelwood* permits. In 1988, Iowa adopted a law guaranteeing public school students freedom of expression except when speech is obscene, libelous, slanderous, or will incite students to break the law, or cause substantial disruption of the school.[65] To protect schools from liability for student speech, the Iowa law, like one in Massachusetts,[66] says student expression is not to be deemed an expression of school policy, nor is the school system liable if it fails to censor. Similar legislation has been introduced in other states.

University Students

The *Kuhlmeier* decision, which affects students' expression in high schools, does not diminish the greater First Amendment freedoms usually enjoyed by students at state colleges and universities. Indeed, since *Kuhlmeier,* the U.S. Court of Appeals for the First Circuit has said in *dicta* that the *Hazelwood* decision does not permit the same censorship of the college press that it permits of the high school press.[67] The First Circuit's statement is consistent with a 1972 ruling in which the Supreme Court said that First Amendment protections apply with the same force on college campuses as in the community at large.[68] A year later, the Court ruled in *Papish v. Board of Curators*[69] that state university officials lack the authority to ban offensive student expression.

In *Papish,* a divided Supreme Court held that the University of Missouri could not put Barbara Papish, a 32-year-old journalism graduate student, on probation for distributing the *Free Press Underground,* an off-campus paper. One issue of the paper contained a political cartoon depicting a club-wielding policeman raping the Statue of Liberty. Inside the paper was an article headlined "Motherfucker Acquitted." The article concerned the acquittal of a New York youth for assault and battery. The university said the publication was "indecent conduct or speech," the distribution of which violated the bylaws of the University's Board of Curators.

Overturning the U.S. Court of Appeals for the Eighth Circuit, the U.S. Supreme Court ruled 6–3 that the "mere dissemination of ideas—no matter how offensive to

---

[64]Burch v. Barker, 861 F.2d 1149 (9th Cir. 1988).
[65]"Iowa Rattles *Hazelwood,*" *Student Press Law Center Rep.* Fall 1989, at 4.
[66]M.G.L.A. c. 71, sec. 82 (1982).
[67]Student Government Ass'n v. Board of Trustees, 868 F.2d 473 (1st Cir. 1989).
[68]Healy v. James, 408 U.S. 169, 180 (1972).
[69]410 U.S. 667 (1973).

good taste—on a state university campus may not be shut off in the name alone of 'conventions of decency.'" Contrary to the Court's high school decision in *Kuhlmeier*, the Court in *Papish* said that college students cannot be held to a higher standard of expressive conduct on a state university campus than off. The First Amendment, the Court said in *Papish,* "leaves no room for the creation of a dual standard in the academic community with respect to the content of speech."

Although *Papish* involved an off-campus paper, a federal court in Michigan ruled recently that the First Amendment bars university administrators from prohibiting tasteless and offensive speech in campus media as well. The Michigan court struck down as unconstitutional the University of Michigan policy that barred verbal or physical behavior that "stigmatizes or victimizes" individuals because of their race, ethnicity, religion, sex, sexual orientation, or age. The university policy was similar to regulations passed at several universities, including Stanford and Duke, to halt racial jokes and slurs against women, blacks, and gays in campus media.

However, the federal court ruled the University of Michigan regulation unconstitutional, declaring that Michigan policy was too vague because people would not know what the prohibited "stigmatizing" language is. The court said the policy was also too broad because it prohibited not only speech that might be disruptive or obscene, but also distasteful speech that is nevertheless protected by the First Amendment.[70] Other universities have withdrawn similar regulations.

Government Employees

The right to speak and publish does not belong only to private citizens. The government and its employees also share the right, although with limitations. Government officials have a right, sometimes a legislated duty, to communicate with the public through press conferences, press releases, state of the union addresses, and public reports.[71] Furthermore, government employees, like other citizens, may speak as private persons on public issues and vote for the political candidate of their choice.

The Supreme Court has ruled that a government employee may not be fired for making hostile remarks about the president. In *Rankin v. McPherson,* the Court ruled 5–4 that Ardith McPherson could not be fired from her clerical job in the Harris County, Texas, constable's office for saying, after hearing of the attempt to assassinate President Reagan, "If they go for him again, I hope they get him."[72]

McPherson said she "didn't mean anything" by the statement, which was part of a conversation about how the Reagan administration had cut Medicaid and food stamps. A fellow employee who overheard the remark reported it to a superior who fired McPherson.

The Supreme Court balanced a government employer's interest in promoting office efficiency against an employee's right as a citizen to comment upon matters of public concern. The majority, in an opinion written by Justice Marshall, said that McPherson's remark dealt with a matter of public concern because it was made dur-

---

[70]Doe v. University of Michigan, 721 F. Supp. 852 (E.D. Mich. 1989).
[71]Emerson, "The Affirmative Side of the First Amendment," 15 *Ga. L. Rev.* 795 (1981).
[72]483 U.S. 378 (1987).

ing a conversation about the president's policies just after an attempt on his life. Both the administration's policies and an assassination attempt are matters of public concern.

The Court said a threat to kill the president would not be protected by the First Amendment. However, Ardith McPherson's comment was ruled to be a caustic and unpleasantly sharp verbal attack on a public official that was within the robust debate protected by the First Amendment. Furthermore, the majority found no evidence that McPherson's comment interfered with the efficient functioning of the constable's office.

While the law permits public employees to state political views, a federal statute prohibits lower- and middle-level government employees from managing or actively working on political campaigns. This prohibition is to ensure that high-level government officials do not bias government agencies by coercing their employees to work in election campaigns.[73] In 1990, however, President Bush vetoed legislation that would have allowed federal workers to participate in many partisan political activities from which they were banned by federal law.[74]

The First Amendment does not forbid the government from censoring its own publications. However, government agencies that publish news and information may have their own free-press policies. Department of Defense policy, for example, states that armed forces publications should provide "a free flow of news and information . . . without censorship or news management." When the General Accounting Office found censorship of *Stars and Stripes,* the armed forces newspaper, it recommended that the autonomy of editors be guaranteed by appointing civilian editors with fixed terms of three to five years.[75] The GAO found censorship of articles on politically sensitive subjects, including articles critical of the Department of Defense.

Prisoners

Prisoners enjoy lesser rights to speak, publish, and receive information than adults who are not incarcerated. The U.S. Supreme Court has ruled that prison officials may enact reasonable restrictions on communication to ensure safe, secure penal institutions.[76] Wardens may censor prisoner mail to nonprisoners to protect the security and order of a prison and to promote rehabilitation.[77] To protect security, prisons may also bar prisoners from receiving books that are not mailed directly from publishers, book clubs, or book stores.[78] Prisoners may also be denied access to a periodical a warden might find "detrimental to the security, good order, or discipline of the institution or if it might facilitate criminal activity."[79]

---

[73]5 U.S.C.A. sec.7324 (1980). United States Civil Service Comm. v. National Ass'n of Letter Carriers, 413 U.S. 548 (1973).

[74]"Senate Upholds Veto on U.S. Workers' Politicking," *New York Times,* June 22, 1990, at 13.

[75]Garneau, "Stars & Stripes & Censorship," *Editor & Publisher,* Dec. 17, 1988, at 10.

[76]Turner v. Safley, 482 U.S. 78 (1987).

[77]Procunier v. Martinez, 416 U.S. 396, 413 (1974).

[78]Bell v. Wolfish, 441 U.S. 520 (1979).

[79]Thornburgh v. Abbott, 109 S. Ct. 1874 (1989).

Corporations

Corporations, as well as individuals and ideological associations, possess First Amendment rights to speak and publish. The corporate press has First Amendment rights similar to those of individuals, but nonmedia corporations, such as banks and insurance companies, have lesser rights.

The "Press"   The "press" is the only business specifically protected by the First Amendment; indeed, it is the only business singled out for special protection in the Constitution. The modern corporate press, therefore, has the same "right" to publish as the individual. The modern corporate press, like its forebears in individual print shops, serves the social purposes of the First Amendment by providing the political ideas and commentary necessary for a democratic government.

The press protected by the First Amendment is not limited to newspapers. "The press in its historic connotation," Chief Justice Hughes wrote several decades ago, "comprehends every sort of publication which affords a vehicle of information and opinion."[80] Publications protected from government interference by the press clause of the First Amendment include pamphlets, books, magazines, and newsletters.

The print media enjoy the fullest protection. The government can seldom bar the press from publishing,[81] nor can it require the press to publish news stories, advertisements,[82] apologies, retractions,[83] or other items.

Corporate broadcasters also enjoy First Amendment rights. But over-the-air broadcasters are subject to more government restrictions because they operate on a limited electromagnetic band that is owned by the public. Broadcasters are therefore licensed by the government and are obligated—unlike publishers—to operate in the "public interest."[84] Among regulations imposed on broadcasters that are not imposed on publishers is a requirement that broadcasters provide access to political candidates. The First Amendment rights of cable system owners and the operators of new communications technologies are evolving in legislatures and the courts.[85]

Publishers and broadcasters must abide by normal business laws requiring them to pay taxes, honor advertising contracts, avoid antitrust violations, and discourage discrimination.[86] Publishers and broadcasters may also be sued for libel, invasion of privacy, and other damage they cause.

Nonmedia Corporations   Some people argue that nonmedia corporations, such as gas companies and banks, should not have First Amendment rights. Nonmedia corporations, it is argued, are large, impersonal entities, created through government charters, whose speech would not serve the First Amendment interests of personal

---

[80]Lovell v. Griffin, 303 U.S. 444 (1938).

[81]*See generally* New York Times Co. v. United States, 402 U.S. 713 (1971).

[82]*E.g.,* Person v. New York Post Corp., 427 F. Supp. 1297, 2 Media L. Rep. 1666 (E.D.N.Y.), *aff'd,* 573 F.2d 1294, 3 Media L. Rep. 1784 (2d Cir. 1977).

[83]Miami Herald Publishing Co. v. Tornillo, 418 U.S. 241, 1 Media L. Rep. 1898 (1974).

[84]Red Lion Broadcasting Co. v. FCC, 395 U.S. 367, 1 Media L. Rep. 2053 (1969).

[85]*See, e.g.,* City of Los Angeles v. Preferred Communications, Inc., 476 U.S. 488, 12 Media L. Rep. 2244 (1986).

[86]*E.g.,* Home Placement Service, Inc. v. Providence Journal Co., 682 F.2d 274 (1st Cir. 1982), *cert. denied,* 460 U.S. 1028 (1983).

fulfillment. A nonmedia corporation, it is argued, has no personality, dignity, or self-worth to be protected by a constitutional right to publish. Furthermore, it is feared that corporate resources used in politics will undermine democracy. Yet, nonmedia corporations, like the media, may want to make social and political statements. Furthermore, citizens may want to hear corporate political as well as commercial statements.

Recognizing the value of corporate political and commercial statements and the interest of citizens in receiving these messages, the Supreme Court has granted limited First Amendment rights to nonmedia corporations.[87] But corporate speech is subject to many restrictions that would not be tolerated on media corporations. For example, nonmedia corporations are prohibited from supporting a candidate in an election with corporate funds.[88] The danger of corporate money corrupting an election is considered too great to permit corporate participation. Corporate commercial speech is also regulated.

SUMMARY

First Amendment freedoms are enjoyed to a greater or lesser degree by adults, students, government employees, prisoners, and corporations. The First Amendment freedoms of adults and ideological associations include freedom to speak, publish, join with others, receive information, solicit funds, and refuse to speak. High school students may distribute nondisruptive personal communication on campus, but high school administrators may impose reasonable regulations on school-sponsored expression to advance the educational mission. University students enjoy the same rights as adults off campus.

Government employees may speak and vote as private citizens, but middle-level employees are barred from participating in political campaigns. Prisoners must adhere to regulations adopted to ensure the safety and security of the prison. First Amendment protections of the print media equal those of adults. Broadcasters are subject to more control because of the limited public spectrum on which they operate. Nonmedia corporations enjoy limited First Amendment status because they are legal creations controlling concentrated wealth.

SCOPE OF THE FIRST AMENDMENT: THE HIERARCHY OF PROTECTED EXPRESSION

Just as different speakers enjoy different rights to speak and publish, so are different kinds of expression treated differently. Even though the First Amendment categorically bars Congress from abridging freedom of expression, political and social ex-

[87]First Nat'l Bank of Boston v. Bellotti, 435 U.S. 765, 3 Media L. Rep. 2105 (1978).
[88]Austin v. Michigan Chamber of Commerce, 110 S. Ct. 1391 (1990).

pression enjoys maximum protection. Commercial and nonobscene sexual expression is less protected, and obscenity, false advertising, and "fighting words" are excluded from constitutional consideration.

Political and Social Expression

The most valued and most protected speech—the expression that arguably contributes most to individual fulfillment as well as to democratic governance—is expression dealing with political, social, religious, and cultural issues. Following the teachings of Alexander Meiklejohn, some jurists and commentators place a higher value on political speech than on other social and cultural commentary. However, it is virtually impossible to distinguish between political and social expression. Even Meiklejohn included in his definition of political speech expression about education, philosophy, science, literature, the arts, and public issues.[89] The inseparability of political, religious, and educational expression is illustrated in the continuing public confrontations over the teaching of evolution in American public schools. Citizens' statements about evolution reflect their scientific and religious training and affect their votes on school bond issues and political candidates.

Unable or unwilling to distinguish between political and social expression, the courts protect both at the highest constitutional level. Seldom does the First Amendment allow government to prohibit, require, or alter discussion about elections, referenda, labor, race, health, agriculture, religion, education, and other political and social issues.

Political and cultural expression may take many forms. It is protected in almost any written form, such as news stories, magazine articles, editorial advertisements, posters, and poetry. Political and cultural expression is also protected when delivered verbally in speeches, lectures, films, and broadcasts. Political and social expression may also be communicated in symbolic form, such as black arm bands,[90] political campaign contributions,[91] marches, slogans, and symbols.[92] One court ruled that a rugby match between the United States and South Africa was protected by the First Amendment and could not be canceled by the governor of New York because of the "singularly dramatic racial issue involved."[93]

In one of the Supreme Court's most controversial recent decisions, the justices ruled 5–4 that burning the American flag is protected political expression. In *Texas v. Johnson*,[94] the Court overturned the conviction of Gregory Lee Johnson for burning the flag in violation of a Texas statute. The Court ruled that the Texas statute, which prohibited intentional desecration of the flag so as to "seriously offend" others, unconstitutionally punished Johnson for expression of political opinion.

Johnson burned the flag during the 1984 Republican National Convention in

[89]"The First Amendment Is an Absolute," 1961 *Sup. Ct. Rev.* 245, 256–57.
[90]Tinker v. Des Moines Indep. School Dist., 393 U.S. 503 (1969).
[91]Buckley v. Valeo, 424 U.S. 1 (1976).
[92]Spence v. Washington, 418 U.S. 405 (1974).
[93]Selfridge v. Carey, 522 F. Supp. 693, 7 Media L. Rep. 2042 (N.D.N.Y. 1981).
[94]109 S. Ct. 2533 (1989).

Dallas to protest policies of the Reagan administration. Johnson set the flag on fire after dousing it with kerosene in front of City Hall. While the flag burned, protestors chanted, "America, the red, white, and blue, we spit on you." Several witnesses testified that they had been seriously offended, but no one was injured or threatened with injury.

The Supreme Court rejected Texas' argument that the statute simply protected the flag as a national symbol, much as federal law protects the Lincoln Memorial from grafitti artists. Writing for the majority, Justice Brennan said the statute unconstitutionally barred political speech. Brennan noted that the United States has a long history of protecting expression that is critical, defiant, and contemptuous of the flag and other national symbols. Respect for the flag and national unity should be fostered, Brennan said, through persuasion and example, not through punishment of flag burners. Brennan also noted there was no evidence that Johnson's incendiary act threatened to start a riot.

In a dissenting opinion, Chief Justice Rehnquist said he considered the public burning of the American flag to be "no essential part of any exposition of ideas." The Chief Justice, who was joined in dissent by Justices White and O'Connor, said burning a flag is like an "inarticulate grunt or roar" that might easily be regulated by the government because it is not speech. Rehnquist also said Johnson's flag burning had a tendency to incite a breach of the peace.

Shortly after the Court's decision was handed down, Congress adopted the Flag Protection Act of 1989, which made it illegal to knowingly mutilate, deface, defile, burn, or trample on an American flag.[95] Violators could be imprisoned for up to a year and fined up to $100,000. Congress tried to avoid unconstitutional content regulations in the statute by omitting the requirement of the Texas statute that conduct be "offensive" to be illegal. Congress attempted only to protect the "physical integrity" of the flag as a symbol of the nation.

However, the Supreme Court, in a 5–4 decision relying on *Johnson,* ruled that the federal statute was, like the Texas statute, an unconstitutional restraint on political speech. In a decision written by Justice Brennan, the Court ruled that the federal statute's protection of the integrity of the flag as a symbol of national ideals was unconstitutional because the law would punish political treatment of the flag that violated those ideals.[96]

Congress' unconstitutional attempt to bar communication with the statute can be seen, the Court said, in the legislature's criminalization of conduct by anyone who knowingly "mutilates," "defaces" or "physically defiles" the flag. Each of these terms, the Court said, "unmistakably connotes disrespectful treatment of the flag and suggests a focus on those acts likely to damage the flag's symbolic value."

Although all forms of political and social expression are protected by the First Amendment, speech may be prohibited or punished if it incites a riot or other illegal action. Furthermore, the time, place, and manner of the more symbolic and physical forms of political and social expression may be regulated.

---

[95] 18 U.S.C.A. §700 (Supp. 1990).
[96] United States v. Eichman, 58 U.S.L.W. 4744 (1990).

Commercial and Sexual Expression

Less protected in the First Amendment hierarchy than political and social expression are commercial advertising and nonobscene sexual expression. Commercial advertising, the Supreme Court says, may be more heavily regulated than political and cultural expression because advertising is hardier and more easily verified. Advertising is hardy, and therefore will not be curtailed by regulation, because it is motivated by economic gain, the Court says.[97] Advertising is more easily verifiable than political speech because advertisers are in a position to substantiate their commercial claims, often with scientific tests. Because of the hardiness and verifiability of commercial speech, the Supreme Court says there is less reason to tolerate inaccurate or misleading commercial speech than there is to tolerate false political speech. Therefore, it is constitutional for the government to ban, alter, or require commercial statements even though the government usually may not ban, alter, or require political statements.

Nonobscene sexual expression is also less protected by the constitution than political and social commentary. Nonobscene sexual films, plays, and magazines may be examined for obscenity before distribution, whereas political and other more highly valued expression cannot.[98] Furthermore, the display of nonobscene sexual plays, movies, and printed materials can be restricted to certain zones within a city without violating the First Amendment.[99]

"Indecent" language—what one can think of as four-letter words—also enjoys less constitutional protection than other speech, at least when indecency is broadcast so that children might hear it. Vulgar words are fully protected in print aimed at adults, but can be barred in broadcasts because of the intrusiveness of broadcasts into homes where children may be listening.[100]

Obscenity, False Advertising, and Fighting Words

A few narrow categories of content at the bottom of the First Amendment hierarchy are excluded from constitutional protection. The excluded categories of expression are remnants of a "two-tier" theory of freedom of speech in which only one tier is protected.[101] Advertising was once among the categories of speech excluded from constitutional protection by definition, but commercial expression that is not false or misleading now enjoys some constitutional protection from government regulation. However, obscenity, false commercial advertising, and "fighting words" are excluded by definition. These categories of content are not thought to contribute to self-fulfillment or the robust debate that the First Amendment is supposed to encourage.

---

[97]Virginia State Bd. of Pharmacy v. Virginia Citizens Consumer Council, Inc., 425 U.S. 748, 1 Media L. Rep. 1930 (1976).

[98]Freedman v. Maryland, 380 U.S. 51, 1 Media L. Rep. 1126 (1980).

[99]City of Renton v. Playtime Theatres, Inc., 475 U.S. 41 (1986), 12 Media L. Rep. 1721 (1986).

[100]See Farber, "Content Regulation and the First Amendment," 68 Geo. L. J. 727 (1980); Redish, "The Content Distinction in First Amendment Analysis," 34 Stan. L. Rev. 113 (1981).

[101]See Kalven, "Metaphysics of the Law of Obscenity," Sup. Ct. Rev. 1 (1960).

The exclusion of obscenity from constitutional protection will be discussed in the chapter on obscenity. The chapters on advertising and corporate speech will define the false and misleading commercial speech that, like obscenity, is considered unworthy of First Amendment protection.

Fighting words were declared to be outside of constitutional protection by the Supreme Court in 1942. In *Chaplinsky v. New Hampshire,* the Supreme Court defined fighting words as epithets "likely to provoke the average person to retaliation, and thereby cause a breach of the peace." Chaplinsky was convicted for calling a marshal in Rochester, New Hampshire, a "goddamned racketeer and a damned Fascist." Although the marshal did not strike Chaplinsky, the court said that "goddamned racketeer" and "damned Fascist" were epithets likely to provoke the average person to physical retaliation. Chaplinsky, therefore, had no First Amendment right to make his provocative statements.

Fighting words are excluded from constitutional protection because, "by their very utterance," they "inflict injury or tend to incite an immediate breach of the peace." Fighting words are so offensive that "men of common intelligence would understand" that they are "likely to cause an average addressee to fight," the Court said. Fighting words, like the lewd and obscene, are "no essential part of any exposition of ideas, and are of such slight social value as a step to truth that any benefit that may be derived from them is clearly outweighed by the social interest in order and morality.[102]

To be considered fighting words, an offensive expression must "have a direct tendency to cause acts of violence by the person to whom, individually, the remark is addressed."[103] Fighting words are delivered one-on-one. The fighting words doctrine does not apply in cases where groups of people are provoked or agitated. A man walking in a California courthouse with "Fuck the Draft" on the back of his jacket did not issue fighting words, the Supreme Court said, because the offensive epithet "was not directed at some particular person."[104] The vulgar phrase was a constitutionally protected political comment on the unpopular war the country was waging at the time in Vietnam.

SUMMARY

Despite the categorical language of the First Amendment prohibiting abridgments of free expression, the Supreme Court has structured a hierarchy of protected expression. Political and social commentary sits at the top of the hierarchy, enjoying the most protection under the First Amendment. Lower down and less protected are commercial and nonobscene sexual expression. Excluded from First Amendment consideration are obscenity, false advertising, and fighting words.

---

[102]Chaplinsky v. New Hampshire, 315 U.S. 568 (1942).
[103]Gooding v. Wilson, 405 U.S. 518 (1972).
[104]Cohen v. California, 403 U.S. 15, 20 (1971).

THE PROCESS OF REGULATION

Deciding First Amendment cases is usually a matter of weighing conflicting values, such as freedom of expression versus an individual's right to a good reputation. Whether freedom of expression or conflicting values prevail depends upon who makes the decision and the procedures and standards the decision-maker employs. This section discusses the processes and assumptions courts rely on to ensure that maximum freedom of expression is preserved even as it may be restricted. Among the courts' operational assumptions are the importance of judicial review, a bias against **content regulations,** and an unwillingness to defer to restrictions imposed by legislatures and lower courts. Among the courts' analytical and procedural tools are an ability to scrutinize regulations for **overbreadth** and **vagueness** and a reliance on "**First Amendment due process.**"

Judicial Review and the Fourteenth Amendment

Under the Constitution, federal judges have a duty to uphold the rights protected by the Bill of Rights. The federal courts, therefore, are the final interpreters of freedom of expression. Judges have broad authority to review the constitutionality of restrictions imposed on expression by legislatures, lower courts, and administrative agencies.

It is proper that federal judges rather than legislators or executive branch administrators be the guardians of free expression. Federal judges, appointed for life, can take the long view, free of political pressures. The late Professor Alexander Bickel pointed out that judges have "the leisure, the training, and the insulation to follow the ways of the scholar in pursuing the ends of government."[105] Only a judicial determination in First Amendment cases, the Supreme Court has said, "ensures the necessary sensitivity to freedom of expression."[106]

The authority of federal courts to review the constitutionality of state laws restricting speech derives from the **Fourteenth Amendment.** The Fourteenth Amendment was intended to prohibit the states from violating citizens' rights protected by the Bill of Rights in the federal Constitution. The Fourteenth Amendment prohibits any state from enforcing a law that would (1) abridge the privileges or immunities of citizens of the United States, (2) deprive any person of life, liberty, or property, without due process of law, or (3) deny any person equal protection of the laws. (See appendix.)

The Fourteenth Amendment, adopted in 1868, was meant by its author, Representative John Bingham of Ohio, to end the "dual citizenship" under which Americans had lived from the time the Constitution was ratified through the Civil War.[107] Originally, the Bill of Rights barred only the federal government from interfering with a citizen's rights. Only Congress, not state governments, was barred from passing legislation violating the First Amendment, the Fourth Amendment, and other

---

[105]A. Bickel, *The Least Dangerous Branch* 25–26 (1962).
[106]Freedman v. Maryland, 380 U.S.51, 1 Media L. Rep. 1126 (1965).
[107]I. Brant, *The Bill of Rights* 325 (1965).

amendments guaranteeing a citizen's rights. Before the Civil War, Americans had a dual citizenship, one state, one federal. A state legislature could limit speech, schooling, voting, or other rights in ways that the federal government could not.[108] The Fourteenth Amendment was supposed to give blacks full citizenship after the war and guarantee to citizens of every state the same rights they enjoyed as American citizens.

However, it was not until the late nineteenth century that the Supreme Court began to rule that the Bill of Rights applied to the states through the Fourteenth Amendment. In 1925, in the case of *Gitlow v. New York,* the Court said it "assumed" that First Amendment rights protected from abridgment by Congress are "among the fundamental personal rights and 'liberties' protected by the due process clause of the Fourteenth Amendment from impairment by the states."[109] However, the Court upheld the conviction of Benjamin Gitlow for distributing revolutionary literature in violation of a state criminal anarchy statute.

The Supreme Court first struck down a state statute violating the press clause of the First Amendment in *Near v. Minnesota* in 1931. The Minnesota statute declared unconstitutional in *Near* permitted prepublication restraints on "malicious, scandalous, and defamatory" publications. In declaring the prior restraints unconstitutional, Chief Justice Charles Evans Hughes said,

> It is no longer open to doubt that the liberty of the press, and of speech, is within the liberty safeguarded by the due process clause of the Fourteenth Amendment from invasion by state action. It was found impossible to conclude that this essential personal liberty of the citizen was left unprotected by the general guaranty of fundamental rights of person and property.[110]

Since *Near v. Minnesota,* almost all of the clauses of the Bill of Rights have been applied to the states in a process frequently called **incorporation.** Case by case, the Supreme Court incorporated the various clauses of the Bill of Rights into the Fourteenth Amendment. Therefore, an ordinance permitting a county sheriff to refuse arbitrarily a parade permit denies citizens their First Amendment rights as surely as if the U.S. Attorney General denied the permit. Similarly, an unreasonable search by a county sheriff violates the Fourth Amendment just as if the illegal search were conducted by an F.B.I. agent.

Bias against Content Regulations

One of the courts' operating assumptions when deciding freedom of expression cases is that the government should not regulate the content of what is said. Government may sometimes regulate when and where speech is made, but generally may not control what is published or spoken. Ordinarily, the Supreme Court has said, the constitutional guarantee of freedom of expression means that "government has no power to restrict expression because of its message, its ideas, its subject matter, or its con-

---

[108]*See* Barron v. Baltimore, 7 Peters 243 (1833).
[109]Gitlow v. New York, 268 U.S. 652, 666 (1925).
[110]Near v. Minnesota, 283 U.S. 697, 707, 1 Media L. Rep. 1001, 1003 (1931).

tent.''[111] Content regulations are viewed skeptically by the courts because it is through the content of messages that citizens exercise their right to fulfill themselves and it is the content of expression that contributes ideas to democratic debate.

The courts are less skeptical of noncontent or "time, place, and manner" regulations. Time, place, and manner regulations do not restrict what is said but control when or where expression occurs. For example, the courts would say it is a constitutional time, place, or manner restriction to ban civil rights marches in residential neighborhoods at 3 A.M., when householders are sleeping. The restriction is aimed at the time and place of the expression, not the political content of the march. A city could schedule the march at a less disruptive time and location.

Deference to Legislatures and Lower Courts

When reviewing legislation or court decisions that restrict freedom of expression, the Supreme Court is less deferential to statutes and judicial rulings than when less fundamental rights are at stake. The Supreme Court assumes that legislation is constitutional if it determines zoning, highway construction, seatbelt requirements, and other matters that do not affect fundamental rights, such as freedom of speech. The Supreme Court generally does not second-guess the will of the majority as expressed through legislatures in decisions affecting taxes, business regulations, and other commercial matters that do not involve civil or personal rights. As long as such legislation has a "rational basis," the courts will accept it as constitutional.[112] The government need show no "compelling" need for its regulation.

However, when the Supreme Court judges the constitutionality of restrictions on fundamental rights such as free speech, it abandons its assumption that legislative enactments are constitutional. "Deference to a legislative finding cannot limit judicial inquiry when First Amendment rights are at stake," the Supreme Court has said.[113] When the government wishes to restrict freedom of expression, the Supreme Court requires the government to show that its regulation is not just "reasonable," but is justified by a compelling need to curb speech.

The Supreme Court also views very cautiously content restrictions imposed by lower courts. In cases not involving fundamental rights, the Supreme Court is likely to accept the facts of a case as presented by a lower court. Only if a decision is "clearly erroneous" will the higher court overturn a lower court decision.[114] However, in freedom-of-expression cases, the Supreme Court said appellate courts have an obligation to "make an independent examination of the whole record" of lower court decisions to ensure "that the judgment does not constitute a forbidden intrusion on the field of free expression."[115] In legal jargon, this is the power of de novo review. This more comprehensive review of lower court decisions is necessitated by the fundamental rights at stake in freedom-of-expression cases.

---

[111]Police Dep't v. Mosley, 408 U.S. 92 (1972).
[112]United States v. Carolene Prods. Co., 304 U.S. 144, 152 (1938).
[113]Landmark Communications, Inc. v. Virginia, 435 U.S. 829; 3 Media L. Rep. 2153 (1978).
[114]Inwood Laboratories, Inc. v. Ives Laboratories, Inc., 456 U.S. 844 (1982).
[115]Bose Corp. v. Consumers Union of United States, Inc., 466 U.S. 485, 10 Media L. Rep. 1625 (1984).

Overbreadth and Vagueness

When the courts review the constitutionality of state or federal restraints on the content of expression, they carefully examine restrictive legislation to ensure that it does not encroach on protected freedoms. Particularly when political speech is at issue, the Supreme Court requires strict scrutiny of restrictive legislation to ensure that the government has demonstrated a "sufficiently important interest" to justify an infringement on free expression and to ensure that the government has employed the "least drastic means" to accomplish its ends. The Supreme Court does not require such strict scrutiny when reviewing restrictions on less valued expression, such as commercial advertising, or when judging the constitutionality of newsrack ordinances and other regulations that determine when and where expression may take place, but do not regulate its content.

When scrutinizing laws that limit the content of expression, the Supreme Court examines legislation for overbreadth and vagueness. Statutes and ordinances that are too broad or vague may be declared unconstitutional because they extend government restrictions too far into areas of protected expression. The statutes are declared unconstitutional because they are not "narrowly tailored" to restrict only offensive expression, but no more. An unconstitutionally vague law is one that is written so unclearly that persons "of common intelligence must necessarily guess at its meaning and differ as to its application."[116] A vague law is unconstitutional because it inhibits speech by making speakers unnecessarily cautious.[117]

In an early flag desecration case, the Supreme Court ruled that a criminal statute was unconstitutionally vague because it prohibited anyone from publicly treating a United States flag "contemptuously." A man named Goguen was convicted under the statute for wearing a small flag on the seat of his pants.[118] The Court said the statute was unconstitutionally vague because what is "contemptuous to one man may be a work of art to another."

Under a vague law prohibiting contemptuous treatment of the flag, the Supreme Court said a police officer might arrest a war protester who disrespectfully used a flag to protect himself from the rain but not arrest a member of the American Legion who regretfully used a flag for the same purpose. A statute that leaves authorities such broad discretion to curb expression is unconstitutionally vague.

In another vagueness case, a federal judge ruled that the University of Michigan policy banning speech or action that "stigmatizes or victimizes" an individual was also vague.[119] The policy was designed to halt racial jokes and slurs against women and gays on campus. Both "stigmatize" and "victimize" are general terms that elude precise definition, the court said. A university lawyer admitted to the judge that he could not distinguish between speech that is merely offensive, and therefore protected, and speech that stigmatizes or victimizes, and therefore would not be protected. A policy that does not define the line between protected and unprotected speech is unconstitutionally vague.

---

[116]Connally v. General Constr. Co., 269 U.S. 385, 391 (1926).
[117]*See* Amsterdam, "The Void for Vagueness Doctrine," 109 *U. Pa. L. Rev.* 67 (1960).
[118]Smith v. Goguen, 415 U.S. 566, 573 (1974).
[119]Doe v. University of Michigan, 721 F. Supp. 852 (E.D. Mich. 1989).

An overbroad law, unlike a vague one, may be quite clear about what it prohibits, but it prohibits too much. In *Houston v. Hill,* the Supreme Court struck down a Houston Municipal Code that made it unlawful for any person to "oppose, molest, abuse or interrupt any policeman in the execution of his duty."[120] Raymond Hill was charged with violating the law after he shouted at a policeman to pick on someone his own size.

Although Hill was acquitted, the Supreme Court agreed with him that the ordinance was unconstitutionally overbroad. The Houston ordinance, Justice Brennan wrote for the Court,

> is not limited to fighting words nor even to obscene or opprobrious language, but prohibits speech that "in any manner . . . interrupt[s]" an officer. The Constitution does not allow such speech to be made a crime. The freedom of individuals verbally to oppose or challenge police action without thereby risking arrest is one of the principal characteristics by which we distinguish a free nation from a police state.

The University of Michigan harassment policy was also overbroad because it interfered with academic freedom. The federal district court noted that a Michigan graduate student had been charged with harassing students because he openly stated his belief that homosexuality is a disease. Although the student was not punished following a hearing on the charges, the court said the harassment policy was overbroad because it subjected constitutionally protected academic opinions to possible punishment.

First Amendment Due Process

If the government wishes to ban an obscene movie, close a courtroom, or otherwise restrict expression, the First Amendment requires that careful procedures be followed. Procedures that are sometimes called *First Amendment due process* require that the judge be the final arbiter of what is protected expression. A judge makes a determination after a hearing in which the government bears the burden of proving why expression should be stopped.[121]

First Amendment due process requires the government to prove that speech is unprotected rather than requiring the media to prove the expression is protected. The government bears the burden of proof so that the media will not become defensive and censor themselves. Citizens who know they must prove their conduct is lawful, the Supreme Court has said, will "steer far wider of the unlawful zone than if the State must bear these burdens."[122] Thus, the government must prove a film is obscene and therefore should not be shown; it is unconstitutional for the courts to assume that a film is obscene and then require a theater owner to prove that it is not.[123] Similarly, the government must bear the burden of proving why a publication might be so dan-

---

[120]482 U.S. 451 (1987).
[121]*See* Monaghan, "First Amendment 'Due Process,' " 83 *Harv. L. Rev.* 518 (1970).
[122]Speiser v. Randall, 357 U.S. 513, 526 (1958).
[123]Freedman v. Maryland, 380 U.S. 51, 1 Media L. Rep. 1126 (1965).

gerous to the national interest that publication should not be allowed,[124] or why closing a courtroom is necessary for a fair trial.[125]

When the government proposes a prior restraint on expression, due process usually requires that the government post notice of a hearing at which media attorneys can challenge the proposed restriction.[126] At the hearing, attorneys for the media argue that the government cannot demonstrate a compelling need for the restriction it proposes. In obscenity cases, due process requires that a censorship board hold a hearing at which attorneys for theater owners can argue against government charges that a work is obscene.[127]

If an administrative board bans speech, due process also requires that the would-be speaker or theater owner be allowed a rapid appeal to a federal court. Only a judge can make the final determination whether expression can be banned. A rapid judicial appeal, or expedited review, is sometimes required in statutes. The Flag Protection Act of 1989, which barred mutilation of the American flag, said that an appeal of any federal district court decision interpreting the constitutionality of the statute would be taken directly to the Supreme Court. Furthermore, the statute provided that the Supreme Court expedite the appeal "to the greatest extent possible."[128]

SUMMARY

The Supreme Court, the final arbiter of what expression is protected by the First Amendment, has the power under the Fourteenth Amendment to declare state laws violative of the First Amendment. In reviewing the constitutionality of restrictions on expression, the courts operate with a bias against regulations that limit the content of expression, as opposed to regulations on the time, place, and manner of speech. Because of the important values at stake in freedom-of-expression cases, the appellate courts do not assume that either legislation or lower court decisions restricting speech are constitutional. Furthermore, courts carefully scrutinize restrictive legislation for overbreadth and vagueness to ensure minimum curbs on freedom of expression. When considering banning or limiting expression, the courts also ensure First Amendment due process by placing the burden of justifying restrictions on the government and providing for adversary hearings at which the media may challenge restrictions.

TESTS

Whether expression is protected in specific cases depends on the test, or constitutional standard, a court employs. Courts use different tests to reconcile society's interests in

---

[124]New York Times v. United States, 403 U.S. 713, 1 Media L. Rep. 1031 (1971).
[125]Richmond Newspapers, Inc. v. Virginia, 448 U.S. 555, 6 Media L. Rep. 1833 (1980).
[126]See L. Tribe, *American Constitutional Law* 1059–60 (2d ed. 1988).
[127]Freedman v. Maryland, 380 U.S. 51, 1 Media L. Rep. 1126 (1968).
[128]Pub. L. 101–131, sec. 3, 103 Stat. 777 (1989).

freedom of expression with conflicting social interests, such as national security, individual reputation, orderly streets, and honest commercial markets. The test a court employs determines the point at which freedom of expression may have to defer to other social interests. The result reached when a test is applied in a particular case will depend on the values at stake, whether an individual or corporation is talking, and the status of expression in the First Amendment hierarchy.

At the turn of the century, courts employed a **bad-tendency test,** whereby speech might be prohibited or punished if it had a tendency to cause a riot or some other social harm. More recently, courts have tested the constitutionality of some restrictions by whether the speech presents a "clear and present danger" to society. Another test, frequently employed by the Burger–Rehnquist Court, is a *balancing test,* by which the Court weighs interests in free speech against conflicting social interests. Some previous members of the Court have also urged First Amendment **absolutism,** or protection of all speech.

Bad-Tendency Test

The bad-tendency test, accepted by a majority of the Supreme Court in the early twentieth century, provides virtually no First Amendment protection for speech. Under the bad-tendency test, expression may be halted or punished if it has the vaguest "tendency" to cause a substantial evil. The bad-tendency test, now abandoned, is unconstitutionally vague because it gives a speaker no warning which speech is protected and which speech is not.[129] The most innocuous threat may have a tendency—though extremely remote—to cause a disturbance.

The Supreme Court cited the bad-tendency test in *Gitlow v. New York* when it said the state could punish those who abuse freedom of expression by words that, among other things, are "inimical to the public welfare" or "tend . . . to corrupt public morals."[130] Under the now-discredited bad-tendency test, virtually any social or public interest could justify suppression of expression. The bad-tendency test cuts off expression long before it may pose any danger to society. The mere intent to cause harm could be grounds for punishing speech, even if harm to society is unlikely.

Clear-and-Present-Danger Test

A second test, and one that would appear to provide more certain protections to free speech, is the **clear-and-present-danger test.** Justice Oliver Wendell Holmes first stated the clear-and-present-danger standard in *Schenck v. United States.*[131] Expression should be punished, Holmes said, only when words "are used in such circumstances and are of such a nature as to create a clear and present danger that they will bring about the substantive evils that Congress has a right to prevent."

The clear-and-present-danger test, if applied literally, should leave a judge much less room than a bad-tendency test to punish speech. If the clear-and-present-danger

---

[129]T. Emerson, *Toward a General Theory of the First Amendment* 50–51 (1963); Z. Chafee, *Free Speech in the United States* 42–51 (1969).

[130]268 U.S. 652, 667 (1925).

[131]249 U.S. 47 (1919).

test were applied literally, judges would not punish speech because of some vague tendency of danger or because of a criminal intent that poses no immediate danger. The clear-and-present-danger test would appear to be a much more rigorous and objective standard than the bad-tendency test, allowing free expression up to the point where there is concrete evidence that speech poses a serious, immediate danger that the state may rightly halt.

The clear-and-present-danger test, however, has often been applied loosely to halt or punish speech that presents no imminent danger. In fact, a conviction for rather innocuous expression was upheld in the case in which Justice Holmes set forth the clear-and-present-danger test. In *Schenck,* two Socialists, Charles Schenck and Elizabeth Baer, were sent to jail for expression that appeared to present no immediate danger. The Supreme Court upheld their convictions for conspiring to violate the Espionage Act of 1917 by distributing one-page circulars arguing against the draft. The Espionage Act, as strengthened in 1918, made it a crime to willfully cause or attempt to cause insubordination or disloyalty in military forces or to obstruct recruiting.[132] Convictions could result in fines of up to $10,000 and prison terms of up to 20 years.

Schenck's anti-draft circular, in "impassioned language," intimated "that conscription was despotism in its worst form and a monstrous wrong against humanity in the interest of Wall Street's chosen few." People were duty-bound to oppose the draft, the circular said. Schenck's flier apparently convinced no one to avoid the draft, although it was established at the trial that at least a few conscripts received one.

How could Holmes conclude that Schenck's ineffective flier presented a clear and present danger to the United States war effort? Perhaps the answer is, as Professor Jeremy Cohen argues, that Holmes did not view Schenck's flier as speech.[133] Cohen argues that Holmes viewed Schenck's planning and distribution of the antiwar circular as illegal acts punishable under the espionage statute, not as speech. Holmes compared the circulars, which he noted were being distributed in wartime, to falsely shouting "fire" in a theater, an illegal act that the Justice said raised no issues of freedom of expression.

While distribution of Schenck's insignificant flier may have appeared to Holmes to be illegal action, Holmes viewed similar expression a short time later to be speech that should be protected because it did not present a clear and present danger. In this later case, however, *Abrams v. United States,* Holmes was in the minority.

In *Abrams,* the Court upheld the espionage conviction of four immigrants whose fliers criticized the dispatch of American troops to Russia.[134] In his dissent, Holmes treated the fliers, which were not widely circulated, as expression worthy of First Amendment protection. In a now-famous phrase, Holmes said that even opinions we "loathe and believe to be fraught with death" should not be suppressed "unless they so imminently threaten immediate interference with the lawful and pressing purposes

---

[132]Espionage Act of 15 June 1917, 40 Stat. 217.

[133]*Congress Shall Make No Law: Oliver Wendell Holmes, the First Amendment, and Judicial Decision Making* (1989).

[134]Abrams v. United States, 250 U.S. 616 (1919) (dissenting opinion).

of the law that an immediate check is required to save the country.'' Holmes thought Abrams' fliers presented no imminent danger.

Several times after *Schenck* and *Abrams,* the Supreme Court purported to apply a clear-and-present-danger test but upheld convictions for expression that presented no imminent threat. During the McCarthy era in the 1950s, a Supreme Court plurality upheld the conviction of nearly a dozen members of the Communist Party for "conspiring" to advocate the forcible overthrow of the government.[135] While applying a version of the clear-and-present-danger test in *Dennis v. United States,* the plurality admitted that the defendant and his comrades posed no immediate danger of violence. Nevertheless, the Court upheld their conviction, saying the government need not wait to stop speech "until the catalyst is added" if "the ingredients of the reaction are present." It was enough, the Court said, that Dennis and his friends established a "highly organized conspiracy, with rigidly disciplined members subject to call when the leaders . . . felt the time had come for action."

The Court's version of the clear-and-present-danger test in *Dennis* amounted to little more than a one-time balancing of free speech interests and general security considerations during a politically charged era. Whether or not one agrees with the Court's results, the justices in the plurality did not rigorously scrutinize the speech of Dennis and his cohorts to determine whether it presented an immediate danger.

By 1957, the Court began to examine the facts of cases more carefully to determine if speech in fact presented an imminent danger. In *Yates v. United States,* the Court, applying the clear-and-present-danger test more literally, ruled that a conspiracy to advocate the overthrow of the government was too far removed from immediate danger to be punished. The Court said a clear and present danger could be found only if there were advocacy of direct illegal action.[136]

In 1969, the Court employed a variation of the clear-and-present-danger test that is still active precedent. In the 1969 case, *Brandenburg v. Ohio,*[137] the Court overturned the conviction of Ku Klux Klan members for racist provocations. The Court struck down an Ohio Criminal Syndicalism statute under which a Ku Klux Klan leader had been convicted for advocating . . . unlawful methods of industrial or political reform. Brandenburg was fined $1,000 and sentenced to 1–10 years in prison for telling Klansmen at a televised meeting:

> We're not a revengent [sic] organization, but if our President, our Congress, our Supreme Court, continues to suppress the white, Caucasian race, it's possible that there might have to be some revengence [sic] taken.

Brandenburg then told of plans to march on Congress "four hundred thousand strong" on the Fourth of July.

The Supreme Court did not decide whether Brandenburg's hateful comments were protected expression, but the Court did overturn his conviction because the statute permitted convictions for "mere advocacy" of illegal action at some distant time.

---

[135]Dennis v. United States, 341 U.S. 494 (1951).

[136]354 U.S. 298 (1957).

[137]395 U.S. 444 (1969) (per curiam). *See* Linde, " 'Clear and Present Danger' Re-examined: Dissonance in the Brandenburg Concerto," 22 *Stan. L. Rev.* 1163, 1166 (1970).

To be constitutional, the Court said, an advocacy statute can only punish speech that "is directed to inciting or producing imminent lawless action and is likely to incite or produce such actions."

Four years later, the Court again employed its incitement variation of the clear-and-present-danger test to overturn the conviction of a street protester. In *Hess v. Indiana,* the Court overturned the conviction of a demonstrator who was arrested during an antiwar demonstration on a college campus for shouting, "We'll take the fucking street later."[138]

After an objective evaluation of the facts, the Court concluded that Hess's statement, at best, "could be taken as counsel for present moderation." At worst, the statement "amounted to nothing more than advocacy of illegal action at some indefinite future time." To sustain a conviction, the Court said, it was necessary to show that the words "were intended to produce, and likely to produce, imminent disorder."

Balancing Test

Another test for determining when free-speech interests must defer to other social interests is balancing. In a sense, all tests of speech protection, including the clear-and-present-danger test, require a balancing of values.[139] But when courts deliberately employ a balancing test, they consciously weigh speech interests against conflicting social and personal interests. Chief Justice Vinson explained balancing in 1950 when he said it is the duty of the courts to determine which of two conflicting interests demands the greater protection in particular circumstances.[140]

Courts engage in what is called *ad hoc balancing* when judges treat each case separately, placing speech considerations on one side of the scales and conflicting values on the other side. In ad hoc balancing, there are no definitions or single standards for guidance. Ad hoc balancing should provide more flexibility to a judge than a literally applied clear-and-present-danger standard because the judge engaged in balancing can assign different weights to different facts as they appear and reappear in each case. But what is gained in flexibility is lost in predictability. In fact, ad hoc balancing risks making First Amendment protections indefinable; judges balancing speech interests against other personal and social interests may rule for either side in any case.[141] Ad hoc balancing creates opportunities for biased judgments because judges may impose their own values where there are no objective standards.

To put more uniformity and predictability into balancing, courts engage in what is sometimes called **definitional balancing.** In definitional balancing, courts define the outer limit of free speech before the balancing test is applied in individual cases. Thus, definitional balancing reduces the vagueness of ad hoc balancing by providing defined standards that can be applied in similar cases.

For example, in libel cases involving the media and a public official, the media's

---

[138]414 U.S. 105 (1973). *See also* Healy v. James, 408 U.S. 169 (1972).

[139]P. Freund, *The Supreme Court of the United States* 42–44 (1961).

[140]Am. Communications Ass'n v. Douds, 339 U.S. 382 (1950).

[141]M. Nimmer, *Nimmer on Freedom of Speech* sec. 2.02 at 2-10–2-11 (1984).

freedom of expression is balanced against the official's right to a good reputation. However, the media bring a defined advantage to the scales in individual cases. This is because the Supreme Court has ruled that the media's freedom of expression includes protection to publish false, defamatory statements about public officials, provided the statements are not published with what is called *actual malice.*

Because the Supreme Court has ruled that public officials must prove the media published defamatory statements with malice, officials know before they file a libel suit that the courts will not engage in **ad hoc balancing** of the officials' interest in reputation against the media's First Amendment rights. The media's constitutional freedom to make false but nonmalicious statements is defined beforehand.[142] Thus, the media have a decided advantage—one mandated by the First Amendment—when an official's reputation is balanced against the media's freedom of expression.

Absolutism

Even more protective of expression than the clear-and-present-danger test is **absolutism.** First Amendment absolutists argue that all speech—at least all political speech— is protected by the categorical language of the First Amendment, language that tells Congress it can pass "no law" abridging free expression. To the late Justice Hugo Black, an absolutist, the categorical language of the First Amendment should be read literally. " 'No law,' " Black said, "means 'no law.' " Justice Black said the federal government is "without any power whatever under the Constitution to put any type of burden on speech and expression of ideas of any kind."[143] Professor Alexander Meiklejohn argued that political speech should be protected absolutely.[144]

Justice Black's absolutism has never enjoyed the support of even a significant minority of the Supreme Court. Other justices, with the exception of Justice William O. Douglas, found Black's absolutism unrealistic. The Court's majority has concluded that there are times when freedom of expression must give way to other personal and social values such as national security or public tranquillity.

Even Justice Black conceded it was reasonable to abridge constitutionally protected demonstrations by limiting when and where they might be held. Justice Black wrote the Court's opinion in a case holding that students might be arrested for conducting a nonviolent civil rights demonstration that interfered with the functioning of a jail.[145] Absolutists presumably would also concede that the government may abridge perjury and fraudulent speech.

Although absolutism has not prevailed as First Amendment doctrine, the First Amendment does protect two kinds of speech absolutely. One is speech critical of the government. Newspapers and broadcasters can say whatever they want about a city, state, or other government. It is not possible to libel the government, although it is possible to libel individuals within the government.[146] Another absolute protection is

---

[142]New York Times v. Sullivan, 376 U.S. 254, 1 Media L. Rep. 1527 (1964); M. Nimmer, *Nimmer on Freedom of Speech* sec. 2.03 at 2-15–2-17 (1984).

[143]Ginzburg v. United States, 383 U.S. 463, 476, 1 Media L. Rep. 1409, 1414 (1966) (dissenting opinion).

[144]"The First Amendment Is an Absolute," 1961 *Sup. Ct. Rev.* 245.

[145]Adderley v. Florida, 385 U.S. 39 (1966).

[146]*E.g.,* Philadelphia v. Washington Post, 482 F. Supp. 897, 5 Media L. Rep. 2221 (E.D.Pa. 1979).

afforded broadcasters fulfilling *equal time* requirements mandated by federal communications law. Because broadcast stations are required to provide equal access opportunities to political candidates, the broadcasters are absolutely protected from libel suits resulting from those broadcasts.[147]

SUMMARY

Courts apply tests in individual cases to determine whether freedom of expression or conflicting social and personal values will prevail. Whether expression is protected depends not only on the value of the content in question but also on the constitutional test a court chooses. The discredited bad-tendency test permitted suppression of almost any expression that presented a vague danger to social or personal interests. A clear-and-present-danger test, if applied literally, provides more protection for freedom of expression by prohibiting speech only when there is objective evidence of an imminent danger. Absolutists would protect almost all speech by definition, but the absolutist test has never won support of a majority on the Supreme Court. Most often, the courts employ a balancing test. *Ad hoc* balancing gives judges great flexibility but makes First Amendment protections unpredictable. Definitional balancing brings more uniform standards to First Amendment adjudication.

PRIOR RESTRAINTS AND POSTPUBLICATION PUNISHMENT

Another assumption in the law of public communication is the unconstitutionality of restraints before publication. William Blackstone, the English jurist, wrote more than 200 years ago that liberty of the press

> consists in laying no *previous* restraints upon publications, and not in freedom from censure for criminal matter when published. Every freeman has an undoubted right to lay what sentiments he pleases before the public: to forbid this is to destroy the freedom of the press: but if he publishes what is improper, mischievous, or illegal, he must take the consequences of his own temerity.[148]

The founders, who were familiar with Blackstone, saw elimination of prior restraints as a primary goal when they adopted the First Amendment.[149] The primacy of no restraints before publication has also been noted by the modern Supreme Court. "Prior restraints on speech and publication," the Supreme Court has said, "are the most serious and the least tolerable infringement on First Amendment rights."[150]

Although not all scholars would agree,[151] prior restraints are thought to be more

---

[147]Farmers Educ. and Coop. Union of Am. v. WDAY, Inc., 360 U.S. 525 (1959).

[148]Blackstone, 4 *Commentaries on the Laws of England* 151–52 (Gifford 1820) (emphasis in the original).

[149]L. Levy, *Emergence of a Free Press* (1985).

[150]Nebraska Press Ass'n v. Stuart, 427 U.S. 539 (1976).

[151]*See* M. Redish, *Freedom of Expression: A Critical Analysis,* 127–71 (1984).

inhibiting to free expression than subsequent punishment. For the publisher, prior restraints are a direct curb on publication whereas the possibility of prosecution after publication is a more remote threat.

Prior restraints also bring a wider range of expression under government scrutiny than postpublication prosecution. Under a system of prior restraints, all public expression may be censored by a central authority. In contrast, the government is limited in the number of publications it has the resources and evidence to prosecute after the fact.[152]

Prior restraints are also thought to be more damaging than subsequent punishment because prior restraints deny the public access to valuable facts and ideas. In a regime of subsequent punishment, the public may reject published ideas as silly, dangerous, or unworkable. But where prior restraints are permitted, the public has no opportunity to judge the worth of suppressed ideas or to offer criticism that might strengthen weak proposals. Perhaps most important, citizens subject to extensive prior restraints may be intimidated to write or speak at all.

The Supreme Court established the presumption that prior restraints are unconstitutional in the 1931 case of *Near v. Minnesota.*[153] In *Near,* the Court struck down a state nuisance statute that permitted an injunction to halt "malicious, scandalous, or defamatory" publications. Under the statute, publishers could avoid an injunction if they could prove that a publication was true and made with good motives for justifiable ends. Publishers who printed in defiance of an injunction could be held in contempt of court.

The constitutionality of the statute was tested by Jay M. Near, an anti-Semitic publisher from Duluth whose *Saturday Press* accused Minneapolis police chief Frank Brunskill of failure to pursue a "Jewish gangster" who allegedly controlled gambling, bootlegging, and racketeering in the city. Near's publication asserted that "[p]ractically every vendor of vile hooch, every owner of a moonshine still, every snake-faced gangster and embryonic yegg in the Twin Cities is a JEW." The trial court declared the paper a nuisance and issued an injunction to bar Near from publishing more defamatory and scandalous matter. The Minnesota Supreme Court upheld the trial court, but the U.S. Supreme Court, in a 5–4 decision, reversed.

Chief Justice Charles Evans Hughes, citing Blackstone and Madison, wrote that the main purpose of the guarantee of freedom of expression is to prevent previous restraints upon publication. Hughes said the prohibition on prior restraints is even more important in the twentieth century than it was in the eighteenth because the opportunities for the press to expose official corruption have multiplied as the government has become more complex.

Hughes said the Minnesota statute imposed unconstitutional prior restraints because it permitted courts to enjoin publication of expression critical of public officials. It is the essence of censorship, Hughes said, to suppress a newspaper, under threat of being held in contempt, for publishing charges of official dereliction. Defamed officials may sue a newspaper after publication for libel, the Court said, but it is unconstitutional to bar all publication because statements might be libelous.

---

[152]T. Emerson, *The System of Freedom of Expression* 506 (1970).
[153]283 U.S. 697 (1931).

The Court also rejected imposing prior restraints because a publication might be "scandalous." Charges of government misconduct may indeed cause public scandal, the Court said, but "a more serious public evil would be caused by authority to prevent publication."

The Court also found unacceptable the statutory requirement that publishers trying to avoid **injunctions** prove their good motives, justifiable ends, and the truth of their publications. Under such vague standards, a legislature or court would have complete discretion to determine what are "justifiable ends" and to "restrain publication accordingly," Hughes said.

Chief Justice Hughes did not say that the constitutional prohibition on prior restraints is absolute. In dicta—statements not essential to the ruling in the case—the Court suggested that prior restraints might be permissible in wartime, to bar expression obstructing military recruiting or announcing the number and location of troops or the sailing dates of troop transports. Hughes also suggested a prior restraint might be acceptable on obscenity and on speech that incited acts of civil violence or the violent overthrow of the government. "The constitutional guaranty of free speech," Hughes said, does not "protect a man from an injunction against uttering words that may have all the effect of force."

Prior restraints may take many forms. They may appear as an injunction as was issued in the *Near* case, as licensing, in contracts or other agreements, and in discriminatory taxes.

Injunctions

Courts quite willingly issue injunctions to halt obscenity, false advertising, and fraud. As Professor Laurence Tribe suggests, prior restraints are justified in such cases because the courts may determine as easily before publication as after whether a statement is obscene, false, or fraudulent.[154] Furthermore, delaying dissemination of such expression is less damaging to freedom of expression than delaying political speech because of the lesser value of commercial and sexual expression.

However, prior restraints are not as easily obtained on political speech and other expression in which the harm may be difficult to determine ahead of time and in which the harm caused by a restraint may be severe. *New York Times v. United States* is a dramatic case demonstrating the Supreme Court's unwillingness to grant prior restraints on political speech when the government cannot make a clear showing that publication will cause a severe harm.[155]

In *New York Times v. United States,* frequently referred to as the *Pentagon Papers* case, the Supreme Court refused to bar publication of a series of stories in the *New York Times* and other newspapers based on a secret Pentagon study of the Vietnam War. The Pentagon Papers, a 47-volume, classified history of American involvement in Vietnam, was commissioned by Defense Secretary Robert McNamara before he left office in 1968. The papers documented how Republican and Democratic administrations had misled the American people about the nation's objectives

---

[154]L. Tribe, *American Constitutional Law* 1048 (2d ed. 1988).
[155]403 U.S. 713, 1 Media L. Rep. 1031 (1971). *See* S. Ungar, *The Papers & The Papers* (1975).

in Southeast Asia. One of the minor authors of the Pentagon Papers, Daniel Ellsberg, acting without authorization, provided the classified documents to the *Times* and later to the *Washington Post.*

After publication began in the *Times* on Sunday, June 13, 1971, the administration of President Nixon asked the Justice Department to seek an injunction on the grounds that continued publication would cause irreparable danger to the national interest. The government argued that publication would prolong the war in Vietnam and disrupt the administration's diplomacy. The country learned later that the Nixon administration feared that publication of the Pentagon Papers might frighten the Chinese from secret negotiations to open diplomatic relations with the United States. The administration feared the Chinese would be wary of conducting confidential discussions with the U.S. if the confidential details of the Pentagon Papers were being exposed on the front page of the *New York Times.*

In New York, the U.S. Court of Appeals for the Second Circuit enjoined publication of the papers in the *Times,* but the Court of Appeals for the District of Columbia Circuit refused to stop publication in the *Post.* The Supreme Court temporarily stopped publication in the *Post* and granted expedited review of both cases.

The Supreme Court ruled, 6–3, that the First Amendment did not permit an injunction. A brief, unsigned opinion for the court, a *per curiam* opinion, freed the papers to publish because the government, the Court said, had not met its "heavy burden" of proof to overcome the presumption that prior restraints are unconstitutional. While the newspapers were pleased to resume publication, the Court's opinion provided little guidance about when injunctions violate the First Amendment. The terse majority opinion did not define the government's heavy burden or explain why the government had not met the burden in the *Pentagon Papers* case.

The Court's "real" opinion is found in nine separate opinions written by the six concurring and three dissenting justices. On the majority side, justices Black and Douglas asserted their absolutism, arguing they could not imagine a situation in which the government could meet its "heavy burden" to justify a prior restraint. On the contrary, Justice Black said, the newspapers should be "commended" for revealing the government's involvement in Vietnam.

Justice Brennan, citing *Near v. Minnesota,* said prior restraints might be justified in wartime if the government presented clear evidence that publication presented an imminent danger. However, Congress had not declared war in Vietnam, and Brennan saw no evidence that publication of the Pentagon Papers presented an immediate danger to the national security.

Justices Stewart, White, and Marshall said a prior restraint might be justified if Congressional legislation had authorized one in such a case. But Congress had earlier rejected the opportunity to provide for injunctions against publication of national security information. Justice Stewart, in an opinion joined by Justice White, suggested the Court might issue an injunction even without Congressional authorization if the government proved publication would "surely result in direct, immediate, and irreparable damage" to the nation. In any case, the government had not met that burden, Stewart said, although he was convinced that publication of the Pentagon Papers would cause some harm.

The three dissenters, Chief Justice Burger and Justices Harlan and Blackmun, thought the *Pentagon Papers* cases should not be decided with such speed. To Chief

Justice Burger, the cases were decided with "unseemly haste," which Burger said precluded reasonable, deliberate judicial treatment. The dissenters wanted the courts in New York and Washington to proceed with the cases so that a more complete record could be established.

Chief Justice Burger suggested the *Times's* demand for an immediate end to prior restraint was hypocritical after the *Times* spent three months editing the stolen papers before beginning publication. The chief justice was also disappointed that the newspaper did not return the stolen papers as, in his view, any responsible citizen would return lost property to its owner.

The press trumpeted the Court's decision in the *Pentagon Papers* case allowing publication to proceed, but the victory was not without cost, according to Professor Alexander Bickel, who represented the *New York Times* before the Supreme Court. While the press beat the government's first attempt to enjoin publication of national security information, Bickel saw a danger in the reservations and limits the justices included in their opinions. The *Pentagon Papers* decision revealed that a majority of the Supreme Court might be willing to impose an injunction on political speech in the future. The press was also put on notice that it might be prosecuted after publication under existing or yet-to-be-written criminal statutes. Thus, Bickel thought the press might have been freer before the *Pentagon Papers* victory—a victory that defined and limited First Amendment freedoms. "Those freedoms which are neither challenged nor defined are the most secure," Bickel said.[156]

The government's power to halt national security publications was tested again in 1979, when a federal court in Wisconsin stopped publication of an article about the hydrogen bomb. The article, which described in general terms how easy it might be to build a bomb, was to appear in the small-circulation magazine *The Progressive.* Most of the information for the article came from public sources. Using Justice Stewart's suggested test from the *Pentagon Papers* case, District Judge Robert E. Warren ruled that the article, "The H-Bomb Secret: How We Got It; Why We're Telling It," presented an "immediate, direct, irreparable harm to the interests of the United States."[157]

Even though the article was based in large measure on public information, the court found an imminent danger in publication of "concepts that are not found in the public realm, concepts that are vital to the operation of the bomb." The court said the article could allow a medium-size nation to move faster in developing a hydrogen weapon than it otherwise might and thus irreparably harm the security of the United States. Publication also violated provisions of the Atomic Energy Act prohibiting disclosure of "restricted data," including information about the design and manufacture of atomic weapons.

The media did not learn if an appeals court would uphold the prior restraint on *The Progressive* because the government dropped its suit after information similar to that in the *The Progressive* article was published elsewhere.

---

[156]A. Bickel, *The Morality of Consent* 60 (1975).

[157]United States v. The Progressive, Inc., 467 F. Supp. 990 (W.D.Wis. 1979), *dismissed,* 610 F.2d 819, 5 Media L. Rep. 2441 (7th Cir. 1979).

Prepublication Agreements

Besides injunctions, prior restraints may also take the form of a government contract or restrictive prepublication agreement. Although government employees have a right to speak as private citizens, their speech may be restricted in a number of ways that private citizens' speech may not be. Government employees with access to confidential information are prohibited from releasing data that would jeopardize national security, reveal business secrets, or invade privacy.

Federal employees throughout the Executive Branch sign so-called "standard" nondisclosure forms prohibiting disclosure of "classified" and, on some forms, "classifiable" information. Employees who divulge information in violation of the agreements may lose their security clearances or their jobs.

The term "classifiable" was challenged as unconstitutionally vague and broad because it might permit punishing an employee for disclosing information that only speculation suggests might be classified at some future time. However, a federal court ruled that the term "classifiable" was constitutional as used on the forms as long as it was defined to include only unclassified information that an employee should know meets the standards for classification and is in the process of being classified.[158]

CIA employees must sign an employment contract that subjects them to lifetime censorship. Former CIA intelligence officer Frank Snepp paid a heavy price for publishing a book in violation of his agreement with the CIA. Snepp, a former intelligence officer in Vietnam, published a book critical of the American evacuation of Vietnam. Snepp violated his contract with the CIA by publishing before submitting the manuscript to the CIA as his preemployment secrecy agreement required. Although the CIA conceded Snepp's book, *Decent Interval,* contained no classified material, the agency brought a suit for breach of contract. Upholding the CIA's contractual claims, the Supreme Court rejected Snepp's argument that prepublication review of unclassified material was an unconstitutional prior restraint.[159]

Even Snepp's publication of unclassified material relating to intelligence activities might be detrimental to national interests, the Court said. Snepp's publication, the Court said, might inadvertently reveal classified information and perhaps inhibit sources from confiding in the CIA because the agency could not keep a secret.

In a footnote, the Court suggested that the CIA's censorship powers did not depend exclusively on the prepublication contract. Even in the absence of an agreement, the Court said, "the CIA could have acted to protect substantial government interests by imposing reasonable restrictions on employee activity that in other contexts might be protected by the First Amendment." To punish Snepp, the Supreme Court imposed a "constructive trust" on all of his earnings from the book, as well as earnings on movies and talks resulting from his work as an intelligence officer in Vietnam. Earnings go into the trust and revert to the government.

In 1990, a federal appeals court denied Snepp's attempt to modify his prior-censorship agreement with the government. Snepp argued that the agreement should be modified to allow him to publish a manuscript even if it is not approved by the CIA, unless the CIA sought an injunction to stop him. Snepp sought to shift the bur-

---

[158]National Fed'n of Fed. Employees v. United States, 695 F. Supp. 1196 (D.C.D.C. 1988).
[159]Snepp v. United States, 444 U.S. 507, 5 Media L. Rep. 2409 (1980).

den of acquiring an injunction to the government after a slow review of a Snepp manuscript by the CIA's Prepublication Review Board scuttled a proposed television miniseries about Snepp's experiences in Vietnam.

However, the U.S. Court of Appeals for the Fourth Circuit upheld the existing agreement that requires Snepp to wait for CIA approval before publishing a manuscript and to bear the burden of challenging a CIA denial Snepp considers too broad or slow. The court found no reason to impose the burden of obtaining judicial review upon the CIA because of "the sensitivity of the area and confidentiality of the relationship in which the information was obtained.[160]

The Supreme Court's enforcement of the secrecy agreement in the Snepp case, despite the lack of classified information in Snepp's book, goes considerably further than two earlier lower court cases that permitted prior restraints of classified information under preemployment secrecy agreements. In *United States v. Marchetti*, the U.S. Court of Appeals for the Fourth Circuit ruled that the CIA could censor classified national defense information learned by an agent while employed by the agency. But the court in *Marchetti*, unlike the court in *Snepp*, ruled that the First Amendment precludes restraints on publication of unclassified information that has already been disclosed. Victor Marchetti, a former agent, published a book with several blank spaces where the agency had deleted what it said was classified material.[161]

Prepublication agreements between authors and state institutions may also bar publication. A Massachusetts court barred public viewing of a documentary about an institution for the criminally insane because the producer failed to get permission from patients as he had earlier agreed to.[162] In New York, a court enjoined publication of a book by a psychiatric analyst who was said to have violated an implied agreement not to publicize a patient's treatment.[163]

Licensing

Licensing as a form of prior restraint was well-known to the framers of the Constitution. In 1643, the English Parliament passed a law forbidding publication of any book, pamphlet, or paper without registration with the Stationers' Company, a group of 97 London stationers who were given a monopoly by the Crown on all printing. Milton wrote *Areopagitica,* his famous pamphlet championing a free press, in opposition to this act.

Under the Printing Act of 1662, London stationers controlled the printing, importing, and selling of all publications. Nothing could be printed, imported, or sold that was "heretical, seditious, schismatical, or offensive" to the Church of England. It was also an offense to print anything offensive to any officer of government, to a

---

[160]U.S. v. Snepp, 17 Media L. Rep. 1579 (4th Cir. 1990), *quoting* United States v. Marchetti, 466 F.2d 1309 (4th Cir.), *cert. denied,* 409 U.S. 1063 (1972).

[161]466 F.2d 1309 (4th Cir.), *cert. denied,* 409 U.S. 1063, 1 Media L. Rep. 1051 (1972). *See also* Alfred A. Knopf, Inc. v. Colby, 509 F.2d 1362 (4th Cir.), *cert. denied,* 421 U.S. 992 (1975).

[162]Commonwealth v. Wiseman, 249 N.E.2d 610 (Mass. 1969).

[163]Doe v. Roe, 400 N.Y.S.2d 668 Sup. Ct. (1977).

corporation, or to any private person.[164] By the 1690s, economically powerful commercial printers forced an end to English licensing, but licensing continued in the colonies into the next century.

The modern Supreme Court finds an unconstitutional licensing when officials are left too much discretion in administering otherwise constitutional regulations. Local governments may require permits for some forms of communications, including parades and commercial solicitation, but too much discretion in the hands of the permit issuer is considered an unconstitutional form of licensing.

In a series of cases in the 1930s and 1940s, the Supreme Court struck down overbroad and vague religious solicitation ordinances. In one of these cases, *Lovell v. Griffin,* a unanimous Court declared unconstitutional a Griffin, Georgia, ordinance that banned any pamphleteering or leafletting without prior written permission from the city manager.[165]

Alma Lovell, a Jehovah's Witness, was convicted under the law for leafletting without first getting permission. In her appeal, Lovell argued the ordinance violated the First Amendment.

Writing for the Court, Chief Justice Hughes said that the ordinance was overbroad because it barred distribution of all literature without a permit. The ordinance was not limited to specific problems such as litter or libel. Hughes said the law left unchecked discretion in the city manager to control printed communication in the town. Such a licensing system, the Court said, was unconstitutional.

More recently, the Supreme Court struck down a Lakewood, Ohio, ordinance that required publishers to obtain a permit from the mayor before placing newsracks on public sidewalks. The ordinance also required newspaper companies to return each year to renew their permits. In a challenge brought by the Plain Dealer Publishing Co., the Supreme Court ruled that the ordinance violated the First Amendment.[166]

A licensing statute "placing unbridled discretion in the hands of a government official or agency," Justice Brennan wrote for the Court, "constitutes a prior restraint and may result in censorship." The licensor's unfettered discretion intimidates parties into censoring their own speech, even if the discretion is never abused, Brennan said. A newspaper that depends on the mayor's approval each year may feel compelled to support the mayor's policies, the Court said.

Not all licensing is unconstitutional. Later chapters will discuss permissible licensing of broadcast stations, investment advisers, and lawyers.

Discriminatory Taxation

After licensing ended in England, the government taxed publications and advertisements as an alternative means of control. A discriminatory tax, or a "tax on knowledge" as it was called in colonial times, is not a prior restraint on a specific story. A tax on the press is a prior restraint because it curtails the ability of publishers to disseminate information and, consequently, of citizens to receive it. Taxation by the En-

---

[164]F. Siebert, *Freedom of the Press in England, 1476–1776,* at 239–41 (1952).
[165]Lovell v. Griffin, 303 U.S. 444 (1938).
[166]City of Lakewood v. Plain Dealer Publishing Co., 486 U.S. 750 (1988).

glish Crown made publications less profitable, thus making them vulnerable to control through government subsidies and bribery.[167] Taxes on the press did not end in England until 1855. The notorious Stamp Acts under which colonial publications were taxed helped precipitate the American Revolution.

The First Amendment does not exempt publishers and broadcasters from the laws regulating all businesses. The media must abide by tax, safety, antitrust, labor, and other laws that regulate businesses. However, the First Amendment may be used to strike down business regulations that are based on content or that place a disproportionate burden on the media.

The Supreme Court has consistently ruled that discriminatory taxes on the media are unconstitutional. In 1936, the Court struck down a tax on large newspapers in Louisiana because it was not a general business tax. The law imposed a license tax of 2 percent on the gross receipts of the thirteen newspapers in the state that had a circulation of more than 20,000 copies. Publishers subject to the tax were required to file sworn financial reports every three months under penalty of a fine of up to $500 and imprisonment up to six months.

The tax was adopted to diminish criticism of Governor Huey Long by the large papers in the state. Notable among the more critical papers was the *New Orleans Times-Picayune*. Governor Long did not see the tax as a tax on knowledge, but rather as a tax on lying because, in his view, the big papers in the state lied about him.

To Justice Sutherland, who delivered the opinion of the Supreme Court, the tax was an unconstitutional restraint on the press because it limited advertising revenue and restricted circulation. The tax therefore violated the First and Fourteenth Amendments. The Court said that owners of newspapers are not immune from any of "the ordinary forms of taxation for support of the government," but they cannot be subjected to taxes "single in kind" that place a restraint on the press. Such a tax is unconstitutional, Justice Sutherland said, because "it is seen to be a deliberate and calculated device in the guise of a tax to limit the circulation of information to which the public is entitled."[168]

More recently the court struck down a Minnesota tax on ink and paper that applied only to larger users of the two products. Although there was no indication that the Minnesota legislature was trying to mute the state's large papers as the Louisiana legislature had, the tax was still ruled to be unconstitutional. Justice O'Connor, in her opinion for the Court, was willing to permit a special tax on newspapers if the state could meet its heavy constitutional burden to justify such a tax. But Minnesota had no interest of compelling importance to justify a special tax on large newspapers. The threat of a burdensome tax placed only on newspapers, O'Connor said, "can operate as effectively as a censor" to check critical comment of the government by the press.[169]

Similarly, the Supreme Court ruled in 1987 that an Arkansas sales tax that was applied to general circulation magazines but not to religious, professional, trade, or sports journals was unconstitutionally discriminatory. Because the tax treated some

---

[167]F. Siebert, *Freedom of the Press in England 1476–1776,* at 305–22 (1952).

[168]Grosjean v. American Press Co., 297 U.S. 233 (1936).

[169]Minneapolis Star & Tribune Co. v. Minnesota Commissioner of Revenue, 460 U.S. 575, 9 Media L. Rep. 1369 (1983).

magazines less favorably than others, it suffered from the same type of discrimination identified in the Minnesota case, the Court said.[170]

Courts in California[171] and Colorado[172] have upheld general business taxes that do not discriminate against publications, but several attempts to extend general taxes to advertising have failed. Bills to tax advertising were voted down in 1989 in Massachusetts and Colorado. Earlier, the Florida legislature repealed the state's five percent sales tax on services, including advertising. The tax, which had been in effect for five months, was opposed by the Association of National Advertisers. Advertisers filed suits charging the tax violated the First Amendment, but the Florida Supreme Court ruled otherwise in an advisory opinion. The state lost millions of dollars when businesses refused to advertise and groups canceled conventions in Florida.

Punishment after Publication

Punishment after publication, rather than prior restraint, is the preferred method of curbing expression, if it is to be limited at all. Most of this book will discuss the circumstances under which the media may be punished in civil or criminal court for dissemination of dangerous, false, defamatory, invasive, obscene, or otherwise damaging communication.

Of considerable legal and practical interest to the media is whether they can be punished for disseminating legally acquired government information that is not supposed to be released. The Supreme Court has not ruled definitively on the circumstances in which the media might be punished for publishing secret, confidential, and private information that is deliberately leaked from government files or inadvertently given to the media.

The Supreme Court has said that the media might be punished for publishing private or confidential information from government files if punishment would serve an important government purpose. But the Court has ruled that privacy interests did not outweigh freedom of the press in a case in which law enforcement officers mistakenly gave the name of a rape victim to a reporter.[173] Similarly, the Court ruled that government interests in confidentiality did not outweigh press rights when officials revealed the name of a juvenile offender whose identity was supposed to remain confidential.[174]

The Supreme Court has also never determined when, if ever, the media may be punished for disseminating leaked national security information. However, the Court did refuse to review an appeals court decision upholding the conviction of a government employee who leaked classified photos to the press. In *United States v. Morison,* the Supreme Court refused to review the conviction for espionage of a civilian

---

[170]Arkansas Writers' Project, Inc. v. Ragland, 481 U.S. 221, 14 Media L. Rep. 1313 (1987). *See also* Texas Monthly, Inc. v. Bullock, 108 S. Ct. 2842 (1989).

[171]Times Mirror Co. v. City of Los Angeles, 192 Cal. App.3d 170, 237 Cal. Rptr. 346, 14 Media L. Rep. 1289, *appeal dismissed,* 108 S. Ct. 743 (1988). *But see* Redwood Empire Publishing Co. v. California State Board of Equalization, 16 Media L. Rep. 1257 (Cal. Ct. App. 1989).

[172]Catholic Archdiocese of Denver v. Denver, 741 P.2d 333, 14 Media L. Rep. 1964 (Colo. 1987).

[173]Florida Star v. B.J.F., 109 S. Ct. 2603 (1989).

[174]Smith v. Daily Mail, 443 U.S. 97 (1979). *See also* Landmark Communications v. Virginia, 435 U.S. 829 (1978) (confidential investigation of a judge).

Navy analyst who passed a "secret" satellite photo of a Soviet aircraft carrier to *Jane's Defense Weekly,* a prominent British defense magazine.[175] Samuel Loring Morison, who worked at the Naval Intelligence Support Center at Suitland, Maryland, received a two-year sentence for selling the picture and a typed summary of a secret report about an explosion at a Soviet naval base.

The government charged Morison with violating the Espionage Act of 1917 by intentionally giving information pertinent to the national defense to "a person not entitled to receive it." Morison was also charged with violating a federal theft statute and an employment agreement not to disclose classified information.

The U.S. Court of Appeals for the Fourth Circuit said it could find no evidence in congressional reports or court opinions to support Morison's contention that the Espionage Act applies only to "classic spying" for another government and not to documents leaked to the press. In addition, the Fourth Circuit rejected Morison's contention that the prohibition in the Espionage Act on disclosing "national defense" information is unconstitutionally vague and overbroad.

The court said Morison could not claim that he did not know he was violating the statute because he was an experienced intelligence officer who had been taught the regulations protecting the security of national defense information. The court also said that the term "national defense" in the Espionage Act, as defined by the trial court, applied to no more materials than necessary to protect the government's interest in national security, and therefore was not unconstitutionally overbroad. The Fourth Circuit also upheld Morison's conviction for theft of property and violation of his employment agreement with the military not to reveal classified information.

Critics of the *Morison* decision argue that the ruling will inhibit government employees from releasing even unclassified national defense information out of fear of prosecution, either for espionage and theft or for violation of a preemployment agreement. *New York Times* columnist Anthony Lewis suggested that the logic of the *Morison* decision might mean that a Defense Department employee could be prosecuted for espionage for revealing to the press a White House plan to sell arms to Iran in exchange for hostages. Another possibility is that the press would also be charged with espionage for publishing national defense information that might be read by "a person not entitled to receive it."

SUMMARY

Although prior restraints on content are presumed to be unconstitutional, they are permitted on a number of types of expression. Injunctions may be imposed on false advertising, publications that would violate a copyright, and obscenity. Injunctions might also be imposed on political speech in national security cases, but only if the government meets an undefined "heavy" evidentiary burden.

The courts have upheld preemployment contracts in which government employees agree to a review of all writings before publication. Licensing that leaves unbridled discretion to government officials is also an unconstitutional prior restraint.

---

[175]U.S. v. Morison, 844 F.2d 1057, 15 Media L. Rep. 1369, *cert. denied,* 109 S. Ct. 259 (1988).

Courts accept general business taxes on the media, but discriminatory taxes based on the content of what is published are an unconstitutional prior restraint.

Postpublication punishments are permitted for some libelous, false, fraudulent, and invasive communications. The Supreme Court has also said that the media may be liable for publication of confidential and secret government information. However, the Court has never held the media liable for such a publication.

NONCONTENT REGULATIONS: TIME, PLACE, AND MANNER

While the courts discourage regulations aimed at the content of speech, they are more tolerant of "noncontent" regulations that incidentally restrict speech but are designed to accomplish other goals. These noncontent, or content-neutral, regulations are constitutional, even if they incidentally impinge on speech, provided the regulations serve a substantial government interest. For example, noncontent regulations that incidentally limit free speech have been upheld if their main purpose was to facilitate the military draft, maintain the smooth flow of traffic, ensure uncluttered sidewalks, and preserve the ambience of public parks. To be constitutional, noncontent regulations must not only be content neutral and serve a significant government interest, but must also be drawn narrowly so as to impinge as little as possible on protected expression.

A leading example of a constitutionally acceptable regulation that incidentally affects, but is not aimed at, expression is the military draft law prohibiting American men from destroying or mutilating their draft cards. The Supreme Court upheld the constitutionality of this prohibition as it was applied to a draft card burner in *United States v. O'Brien*.[176] David O'Brien burned his draft card on the steps of the courthouse in Boston to oppose the war in Vietnam and the selective service system.

The Supreme Court did not evaluate the political expression embodied in O'Brien's incendiary act. Instead, the Court focused on the purposes of the Universal Military Training and Service Act under which O'Brien was prosecuted. The Court ruled that O'Brien could be punished without violation of the First Amendment because the draft law furthers a substantial government interest unrelated to the suppression of free expression. The draft law was adopted, the Court said, not to regulate speech, but to allow armies to be raised more quickly and efficiently by requiring eligible men to carry classification certificates. O'Brien was convicted, not for his protest against the war, the Court said, but because he frustrated the government's interest in an efficient system of military mobilization. The Court was also satisfied that the law was written so that it impinged on constitutionally protected speech as little as possible.

The content neutrality of the military draft law can be contrasted with the Texas flag burning statute that the Supreme Court said was unconstitutional in *Texas v. Johnson*.[177] The Texas statute was an unconstitutional content regulation because it

---

[176]391 U.S. 367 (1968).
[177]109 S. Ct. 2533 (1989).

only punished those whose disrespectful treatment of the flag "offended" patriotic bystanders. The military draft law, on the other hand, had no such speech-related purpose.

While noncontent or content-neutral regulations may result in the punishment of expression as in *O'Brien,* more often noncontent regulations "channel" expression into certain times and places. These so-called **"time, place, and manner" regulations** are constitutional if they are not designed to suppress expression but are aimed at furthering nonspeech interests such as health, safety, and a pleasing environment. To be constitutional, these time, place, and manner restrictions must also be narrowly tailored, and leave ample alternative channels for communication of information. Time, place, and manner regulations have been developed for a number of public forums, including streets and sidewalks, parks, and fairs.

Public Streets and Sidewalks

It is well established that the government may regulate the hours and frequency of marches and demonstrations on public streets and sidewalks. The right to demonstrate does not include the right to keep householders awake at 3 A.M. The government may also prohibit public speakers from harassing pedestrians and from littering. But in a series of cases in the 1930s and 1940s, the Supreme Court ruled that ordinances restricting public meetings, pamphleteering, leafleting, and solicitation on public property were unconstitutional content regulations if they invested too much discretion in authorities.[178]

In 1988, a divided Supreme Court ruled that a District of Columbia Code provision barring signs near foreign embassies was also an unconstitutional content regulation. In *Boos v. Barry,* a five-person majority declared unconstitutional a provision prohibiting signs within 500 feet of an embassy if the signs were designed to bring a foreign government "into public odium."[179] The District of Columbia said the ordinance was necessary if the city was to fulfill its obligations under international law to shield diplomats from speech that "offends their dignity." Michael Boos challenged the law when he was prevented from displaying a sign stating "RELEASE SAKHAROV" in front of the Soviet Embassy. Another plaintiff in the case wanted to display a sign reading "STOP THE KILLING" in front of the Nicaraguan Embassy.

In the opinion for the Court, Justice O'Connor said the provision barring the signs was an unconstitutional content-based restriction because it made the ability of demonstrators to display political signs in a public forum depend "entirely upon whether their picket signs are critical of the foreign government." Signs supporting a foreign government were permitted under the law, but unfavorable signs were not. Furthermore, the Court said the "dignity" of diplomats, protected under international law, was not a sufficiently compelling government interest to justify barring free expression. The plurality also found a "dignity" standard too subjective to apply

---

[178]*E.g.,* Lovell v. Griffin, 303 U.S. 444 (1938). *See also* Schneider v. New Jersey, 308 U.S. 147 (1939); Jones v. Opelika, 316 U.S. 584 (1942).
[179]108 S. Ct. 1005 (1988).

in cases involving free speech. The Court also said the statute barring signs was not sufficiently narrow.

The court did uphold another provision in the Washington code limiting groups of people near foreign embassies. The Court held constitutional a provision permitting officials to disperse crowds near an embassy if the officials "reasonably believe that a threat to the security or peace of the embassy is present."

In *Frisby v. Schultz,* the Supreme Court upheld a city picketing ordinance that was aimed at protecting the privacy of homes, not at restricting demonstrators' content. In *Frisby,* the Court upheld a Brookfield, Wisconsin, ban on picketing "before or about the residence or dwelling" of anyone in Brookfield, a suburb of Milwaukee.[180] The ordinance was adopted to stop opponents of abortion from picketing the home of Dr. Benjamin Victoria, a physician who performed abortions. The pickets, sometimes numbering more than 40, were peaceful, but they shouted slogans, sometimes trespassed, and told neighborhood children the doctor was a "baby killer."

The majority of the Court said the city could constitutionally ban picketing directed to a particular residence because such expression could invade the privacy of a "captive audience" within the home by forcing occupants to hear speech. "One important aspect of residential privacy," Justice O'Connor said in her opinion for the Court, "is protection of the unwilling listener."

Applying the Court's usual analysis in cases of time, place, and manner restrictions on speech in public forums, the Court said the ordinance was content neutral because it did not halt a specific message. The ordinance was also sufficiently narrow, as Justice O'Connor interpreted it, because it only barred picketing in front of a particular residence. The Court also noted that picketers were free to march and hand out leaflets elsewhere in the community. "General marching through residential neighborhoods, or even walking a route in front of an entire block of houses, is not prohibited by the ordinance," she said.

While time and manner restrictions may be imposed on picketers in front of private homes, the Supreme Court struck down an Illinois statute that aimed at the content of a demonstrator's protest. The Court declared unconstitutional a statute that permitted picketing in front of residences only if the picketing involved a labor issue. The Court said the law was an unconstitutional content regulation because it discriminated against citizens who wanted to picket the mayor's house on issues other than labor, such as the mayor's busing policies. The Court said that the discriminatory content regulation was not necessary to preserve the significant state interest in the privacy of the mayor's residence.[181]

Parks

The Supreme Court has ruled that maintaining attractive federal parks in the nation's capital is a sufficient government interest to outweigh the symbolic expression of sleep. The Supreme Court ruled the National Park Service could constitutionally prevent citizens from protesting President Reagan's policies toward the homeless by

---

[180]108 S. Ct. 2495 (1988).
[181]Carey v. Brown, 447 U.S. 455 (1980).

sleeping in Lafayette Park in Washington, D.C. Sleep may be symbolic speech, but the Supreme Court said the Park Service could prohibit camping in the park to ensure that the parks remained intact and attractive.

The Court said the park rule against sleep was not promulgated to stifle dissent. Thus, citizens protesting Reagan's policies could pitch tents in the federal park, but could not dramatize their "homelessness" by sleeping there.[182] The Court said a prohibition less restrictive than a ban on camping in federal parks might encourage so many people to sleep in parks as a form of symbolic expression that the Park Service would have a "difficult problem."

The Supreme Court has also upheld regulations on the volume of rock music in a public park. In *Ward v. Rock Against Racism,* the Court upheld New York City regulations requiring groups performing in Central Park to use a sound system provided and operated by the city. The city adopted the regulations after area residents complained of too much noise at some events and audiences complained of too little amplification at others. Rock Against Racism, an antiracist rock group, charged that the regulations violated rights of expression. In a 6–3 decision, the Supreme Court ruled that the regulations were content neutral and narrowly tailored to provide adequate amplification without disturbing surrounding neighborhoods.[183]

In *Rock Against Racism,* the Supreme Court said a time, place, and manner regulation is constitutional even if it is not the narrowest possible. Until 1989, regulations, to be constitutional, had to be the "least restrictive" or "least intrusive" into protected expression. However, in *Rock Against Racism,* the Court ruled that regulations might be constitutional if they were narrow, but not necessarily the narrowest possible.

Newsracks

In another time, place, and manner decision, the Supreme Court ruled that an ordinance barring newsracks in residential areas was an unconstitutional content regulation. In *City of Lakewood v. Plain Dealer Publishing Co.,*[184] the Court struck down an Ohio ordinance requiring a permit from the mayor before a newspaper publisher could place newsracks on public sidewalks. The Court ruled the Lakewood ordinance was unconstitutional on its face because it gave too much discretion to a public official to determine whether expression may be distributed. Even though the ordinance required the mayor to state reasons for denying a permit, the Court ruled, 4–3, that the ordinance was unconstitutional because it vested "unbridled discretion" in a government official.

Justice White, dissenting with Justices Stevens and O'Connor, argued that the ordinance should not be struck down as invalid on its face because newspapers have no First Amendment right to place newsracks on sidewalks in the first place. The government cannot bar distribution of a newspaper, the dissenters said, but the government does not have to provide public sidewalks for newsracks if it does not want

---

[182]Clark v. Community for Creative Non-Violence, 468 U.S. 288 (1984).
[183]Ward v. Rock Against Racism, 109 S. Ct. 2746 (1989).
[184]108 S. Ct. 2138 (1988).

to. There are many alternatives to newsracks by which publishers may distribute their papers, the dissenters said.

A Swarthmore, Pennsylvania, ordinance limiting placement of newspaper boxes was ruled to be unconstitutionally broad. The Swarthmore ordinance prohibited newspaper boxes on public sidewalks except in the central business district during daylight hours, and then only if the boxes were set up by merchants, not publishers.

A federal court said the city had a legitimate interest in limiting the size, appearance, advertising, and placement of newspaper boxes on streets and sidewalks to permit unobstructed passage of pedestrians on a sidewalk that is not overly commercial. However, the court said a municipality cannot prevent crowding and over-commercialization of the sidewalks by prohibiting publishers from placing newspaper boxes on the sidewalk. The court said the overbroad ordinance violated publishers' First Amendment right to distribute their newspapers and citizens' rights to receive them.[185]

In other newsrack decisions, a federal court in Rhode Island ruled that a Newport ordinance barring newsracks from all public rights of way was unconstitutional.[186] The New York Court of Appeals ruled that a public official does not have the discretion to refuse newsrack space to a free newspaper,[187] and a federal court in New York said the government may not prohibit a newspaper from installing newsracks at some turnpike stops but not at others.[188]

State Fairs

The Supreme Court has also upheld time, place, and manner regulations at a state fair. In *Heffron v. International Society for Krishna Consciousness,* the Court upheld a Minnesota statute that limited the sales, exhibition, and distribution of materials to fixed locations on the state fair grounds. The Supreme Court said that the restriction, which was challenged by the Krishnas, was constitutional because it was not based on the content or subject matter of the materials distributed. All religious, political, or ideological groups seeking a permit to distribute literature in fixed booths had an equal chance under a first-come-first-served basis. No government official had control over what content was distributed.[189]

The Supreme Court said Minnesota's interest in maintaining the orderly movement of the crowd at the state fair outweighed the Krishnas' First Amendment interest in unrestricted access to the fairgoers for the purpose of distributing religious literature and soliciting donations. The flow of the crowd and the demands of safety are more pressing at a fair than they might be on the streets, the Court noted. Furthermore, disorder might result if the Krishnas were allowed to intercept all fair patrons.

The Krishnas also argued unsuccessfully that Minnesota could ensure the safety and mobility of citizens at the state fair with regulations that were less restrictive than limiting solicitation to fixed booths on the fair grounds. The Supreme Court agreed

---

[185]Philadelphia Newspapers, Inc. v. Borough of Swarthmore, 381 F. Supp. 228 (E.D.Pa. 1974).
[186]Providence Journal v. Newport, 665 F. Supp. 107, 14 Med. L. Rep. 1545 (D.R.I. 1987).
[187]New York City v. American School Publications, 69 N.Y.2d 676, 514 Media L. Rep. 1153 (N.Y. 1987).
[188]Gannett v. White, 14 Media L. Rep. 2037 (N.D.N.Y. 1987).
[189]452 U.S. 640, 7 Media L. Rep. 1489 (1981).

with Minnesota that the state might have more of a problem than it could manage if Krishnas and other groups that wanted to solicit fairgoers were not restricted to fixed booths.

Finally, the Supreme Court noted that the Krishnas had adequate alternative channels for disseminating their message. Even though the Krishnas could not freely circulate within the fair grounds to distribute literature and solicit donations, they could mingle with the crowd to discuss their beliefs with anyone who would listen. In addition, the Krishnas could sell and distribute literature outside the fair grounds.

SUMMARY

Regulations that are not directed at restricting expression, but which incidentally impinge on free speech, are constitutional if they are content neutral, serve a substantial government interest, are narrowly written, and leave alternative channels of communication.

The Supreme Court has ruled that the government interest in efficient military mobilization justifies a prohibition on the burning of draft cards even though political expression is incidentally infringed. The Court has also ruled that officials may not ban citizens' use of public streets and parks but may limit expression to preserve public order, the integrity of parks, and the privacy of private residences. The courts have also ruled that placement of newsracks may be limited to allow the smooth flow of pedestrians in a pleasing environment, but that officials may not have absolute power to bar newsracks. The Supreme Court has ruled that solicitation at state fairs may be limited to fixed booths.

3

LIBEL

Shakespeare recognized the importance of individual reputation in 1604:

> Who steals my purse steals trash; tis something, nothing;
> Twas mine; tis his, and has been slave to thousands;
> But he that filches from me my good name
> Robs me of that which not enriches him,
> And makes me poor indeed.[1]

Three and a half centuries later a member of the U.S. Supreme Court said protection of reputation is the foundation of liberty. In 1966, the late Potter Stewart said the "rights and values of private personality transcend more than personal interests." He said society's willingness to protect individual reputation from "unjustified invasion and wrongful hurt" reflects the social value of the "dignity and worth of every human being—a concept at the root of any decent system of ordered liberty."[2]

Stewart pointed to libel law, "as imperfect as it is," as the only legal means to vindicate or redress a reputation that has been falsely tarnished. In the United States, people can sue for printed or spoken words that tend "to diminish the esteem, respect, good will or confidence" others have in them or form language that incites "adverse, derogatory or unpleasant feelings or opinions" about them.[3] People who believe they have been libeled can sue to recover monetary compensation.

However, the same law that allows individuals to sue when their reputations have been damaged creates considerable problems for professional communicators. The Libel Defense Resource Center, an organization that monitors developments in libel law, reported that the average award in media libel cases between 1987 and 1988 was $432,000. In 1988, the U.S. Supreme Court let stand a $3.5 million libel verdict for the broadcast of a commentary that accused the Brown & Williamson Tobacco Corporation of marketing cigarettes to children.[4] A few years earlier, the *Alton* (Illinois) *Telegraph* lost a $9.2 million jury verdict, and, while appealing, settled out of court for $1.4 million rather than risk bankruptcy.[5]

Even the libel cases won by the media are a major financial burden. One libel insurance agent estimated that the average cost for the media to defend a libel case through trial is $150,000.[6] The *Alton Telegraph* spent $600,000, abut a third of which was paid by insurance.[7] The cost of libel insurance itself skyrocketed in the mid-1980s, climbing 200 percent for many papers in one year alone.[8]

More than one local paper has significantly reduced the reporting of government wrongdoing out of the fear of libel suits. After the *Alton Telegraph*'s costly legal battle, the paper's editor would not pursue a lead about possible official misconduct.

---

[1] *Othello,* Act III.

[2] Rosenblatt v. Baer, 383 U.S. 75, 92, 1 Media L. Rep. 1558, 1564 (1966) (concurring opinion).

[3] *Prosser and Keeton on Torts* sec. 111, at 773 (5th ed. 1984).

[4] Brown & Williamson Tobacco Corp. v. Jacobson, 827 F.2d 1119, 14 Media L. Rep. 1497 (1987), *cert. denied,* 485 U.S. 993 (1988).

[5] Curley, "How Libel Suit Sapped the Crusading Spirit of a Small Newspaper," *Wall Street Journal,* Sept. 29, 1983, at 1.

[6] Genovese, "Libel Update," *presstime,* April 1986, at 37.

[7] Gannett Center for Media Studies, *The Cost of Libel: Economic and Policy Implications* 5 (1986).

[8] Newsom, "Insurance," *presstime,* April 1986, at 9.

"Let someone else stick their neck out this time," he said. Then he asked, "Wouldn't you be gun-shy if you nearly lost your livelihood and your home?"[9] One publisher of four weekly newspapers in Pennsylvania said he stopped publishing investigative stories after being sued 11 times in seven years. "I finally had to make a choice," he said. "I decided to abandon my obligation to the First Amendment and run my newspapers as a business."[10]

In one sense, libel appeared to be less of a problem for the media in the last years of the 1980s than in the first part of the decade. Media executives, libel insurance companies, lawyers representing the media, and the Society of Professional Journalists (SPJ) reported substantial drops in the number of libel suits filed against the media.[11] However, at least one attorney for a major newspaper chain said the decline in libel litigation has not reached the smaller newspapers.[12] In addition, media companies were still losing 60 percent of the libel cases at the trial level.[13]

The costs of libel for media companies, combined with the tension between personal reputation on the one hand and robust public debate on the other, make defamation one of the most important issues in mass media law. It also is one of the most complicated. Libel law is complex in part because it developed primarily as state law, and therefore exists in 50 versions. In addition, during the last 25 years the U.S. Supreme Court has applied the First Amendment to libel. Finally, many aspects of libel law are not logical. In the words of a prominent legal scholar, the late Dean William Prosser: "It must be confessed at the beginning that there is a great deal of the law of defamation which makes no sense."[14]

This chapter will explain the general principles of libel that apply in most jurisdictions. The chapter begins with a discussion of libel terminology and the legal burden borne by a person suing for libel. Defenses to a libel suit are then discussed. Finally, the chapter reviews libel damage awards, postpublication measures that may deter libel suits, and libel reform proposals.

LIBEL TERMINOLOGY

Defamation is expression that tends to damage a person's standing in the community. Defamation can take the form of either libel or slander. Most defamation cases are taken to civil rather than to criminal court.

Libel and Slander

Written or printed defamation is libel. Traditionally, oral defamation is slander. The distinction between libel and slander is important because a person successfully suing

---

[9]Curley, "How Libel Suit Sapped the Crusading Spirit of a Small Newspaper," *Wall Street Journal,* Sept. 29, 1983, at 1.

[10]Zucchino, "Publish *and* Perish," *Wash. J. Rev.,* July 1985, at 28.

[11]*E.g.,* Society of Professional Journalists, *Media Litigation '88* (Nov. 4, 1988); Wong, "In Wake of Westmoreland, Sharon Cases, Libel Suits against the Media Decline," *Wall Street Journal,* Oct. 17, 1988, at B8.

[12]"Libel Suits Wane, Press Study Finds," *New York Times,* Dec. 3, 1988, at 12.

[13]"Report Says Media Faring Better in Libel Suits," *Broadcasting,* Sept. 11, 1989, at 133.

[14]*Prosser on Torts* sec. 111, at 737 (4th ed. 1971).

for libel will probably win a larger damage award than someone suing for slander. In addition, someone suing for libel usually does not have as much to prove as someone suing for slander. In slander suits, plaintiffs must show the defamation caused them a financial loss. Only rarely do plaintiffs suing for libel have to prove actual monetary loss.

Historically, plaintiffs could win libel suits more easily than slander suits in part because written defamation was believed to cause more harm to a person's reputation. The printed word was more enduring than speech and could be circulated more widely. In addition, the writing of defamation was considered to be evidence of greater deliberation and intent to damage someone's reputation.[15]

However, the distinction between libel and slander is blurred in broadcasting. The *Restatement (Second) of Torts,* an influential summary of tort law, argues that defamation by the printed or broadcast word should be treated the same. The *Restatement* notes that radio and television reach large audiences. In fact, a story on a network evening newscast reaches more homes than any single newspaper or magazine. In addition, the *Restatement* contends, broadcasting can damage a reputation just as easily as print because, as a mass medium, it has the same credibility and prestige.[16]

Yet, in some states, defamation on the broadcast media is still considered slander.[17] In other states, broadcast defamation is considered libel only if it is read from a prepared script.[18]

Criminal Libel and Civil Libel

The differences between criminal and civil libel parallel the differences between criminal and civil law in general.

Most early libel law was criminal law. Governments adopted criminal libel statutes to prevent breaches of the peace. Libel of public officials, disrespect for the dead, and aspersions upon the chastity of women were punishable because they could lead to violence. Criminal libel was based on the concept that an individual should use the criminal justice system rather than a pistol to avenge a sullied reputation. The government prosecuted the case, as it would any crime. The defendant, if found guilty, could be fined or jailed.

However, in the twentieth century, virtually all libel cases are civil suits. Individuals who believe they are defamed sue for monetary damages. The development of civil libel has given Americans an alternative to putting people in jail for something they say. The move away from criminal libel has come in spite of a 1952 Supreme Court opinion, *Beauharnais v. Illinois,* now largely discredited.[19] By a narrow 5–4 margin, the Court upheld an Illinois statute that made it a crime to libel any race, color, creed, or religion. The law had been used to prosecute a man for distributing racist literature. The U.S. Supreme Court said that libelous remarks directed at ethnic and racial groups were not protected by the First Amendment.

---

[15]Rice v. Simmons, 2 Del. (2 Harr.) 417, 422 (1838). *See Restatement (Second) of Torts* sec. 568(3) (1977).

[16]*Restatement (Second) of Torts* sec. 568A and 568A comment a (1977).

[17]*Id.; e.g.,* Cal. Civ. Code secs. 46, 48.5 (West 1989).

[18]*E.g.,* Christy v. Staufer Publications, Inc., 437 S.W.2d 814 (Tex. Civ. App. 1969); R. Smolla, *Law of Defamation* sec. 1.04[4], at 1-10 (1989).

[19]343 U.S. 250 (1952).

While *Beauharnais* has never been overturned, most observers believe the decision has been eclipsed by more recent developments. First, under current libel law, ethnic and racial slurs directed at large groups are not considered defamatory. A specific individual must be identified for a libelous statement to be actionable and, frequently, no individuals are named in attacks on groups such as blacks and Hispanics. In addition, in 1966, the Supreme Court said a state's common law that punished speech tending to breach the peace was too vague to be constitutional. In *Ashton v. Kentucky,* the Court unanimously overturned the conviction of Steve Ashton under Kentucky criminal libel law allowing the state to punish conduct "calculated to create disturbances of the peace." Ashton had been fined $3,000 and sentenced to six months in prison for printing a pamphlet during a bitter labor dispute in Hazard, Kentucky. The pamphlet attacked the chief of police, the sheriff, and the co-owner of the *Hazard Herald* for their failure to support striking miners. For example, the pamphlet said Sheriff Charles Combs had bought off a jury after "intentionally blinding a boy with tear-gas" and beating him while his hands were cuffed. The pamphlet also said Combs was indicted for murder in another incident: "Yet he is still the law in this county and has support of the rich man because he will fight the pickets and the strike." Ashton's conviction was affirmed by the Kentucky Court of Appeals, but reversed by the U.S. Supreme Court.

Justice William O. Douglas, writing for eight of the justices, said Kentucky's common law crime of libel based on a breach of the peace was too imprecise to withstand constitutional scrutiny. Vague laws give officials too much discretion in determining which speech is permissible, Douglas asserted. Under the Kentucky crime for breach of peace, Douglas said that speakers could not know when their speech was "calculated to create disturbances of the peace" under the law. The Kentucky crime of libel, he added, was determined not so much by the nature of what a person wrote but by the boiling point of those who read it. "This kind of criminal libel 'makes a man a criminal simply because his neighbors have no self-control and cannot refrain from violence,'" Douglas continued, quoting First Amendment scholar Zechariah Chafee.[20] Douglas pointed out that the Supreme Court had previously said that a function of free speech was "to invite dispute." Douglas, quoting the Court in *Terminiello v. Chicago,* said that free speech may best serve its purpose

> when it induces a condition of unrest, creates dissatisfaction with conditions as they are, or even stirs people to anger.[21]

Douglas said that, in order to adequately protect freedom of speech, prosecutions under general and ill-defined laws designed to regulate breach of the peace could not be tolerated.

The Supreme Court also limited the ability of states to prosecute for criminal libel in *Garrison v. Louisiana.* Two years before *Ashton,* the Court said criticism about public officials could not be prosecuted as criminal libel unless the statements were made with the knowledge they were false or with reckless disregard for the truth.

---

[20]Ashton v. Kentucky, 384 U.S. 195, 200 (1966), *quoting* Z. Chafee, *Free Speech in the United States* 151 (1954).
[21]384 U.S. at 199–200, *quoting* 337 U.S. 1, 4 (1949).

The Court reversed the conviction of New Orleans prosecutor Jim Garrison, who had accused eight judges of being lazy, inefficient, and sympathetic to "racketeer influences."[22]

Despite cases such as *Ashton* and *Garrison,* some states still maintain the authority to prosecute criminal libel cases, either under state statute or common law precedent. However, the constitutionality of criminal libel laws is suspect and prosecutions are extremely rare. In fact, in the last 30 years, few prosecutions against the media, if any, have been successful. The focus of libel law today is on civil libel, the topic of the rest of the chapter.

THE PLAINTIFF

A person who files a libel complaint becomes the plaintiff in a libel suit. Any individual, business, nonprofit corporation, or unincorporated association can legally sue. A government institution cannot.

Living Individuals

Any living individual can sue for libel. Everyone has a *personal* right to sue to protect his or her reputation. However, because reputation is personal to each individual, no person can sue for damage to the reputation of another.

Therefore, under the common law, the right to sue for damage to reputation dies with each individual. No friend or relative can sue on behalf of a dead person whose reputation may be defiled.[23] While people can leave houses, cars, copyright in books, and other *property* rights to heirs, they cannot do the same with *personal* rights such as the right to reputation. Descendants of George Washington, Al Capone, Lyndon B. Johnson, and Dr. Martin Luther King, Jr., cannot sue newspapers, books, or broadcasts for defaming their ancestors.

However, some states, such as New Jersey, have adopted statutes that allow a dead person's relatives to pursue a libel suit filed by the individual prior to death. In 1983, a federal court said New Jersey law allowed the family of Kenneth N. MacDonald to continue a suit he filed against *Life* magazine before he died in 1982. MacDonald, once vice-chairman of the New Jersey Casino Control Commission, sued for a 1981 article linking him to the FBI's Abscam investigation of official corruption and mob influence.[24]

Organizations

Businesses or corporations can sue only if the defamation is said to damage the corporation itself rather than individual officers. A business can sue for stories about

---

[22]Garrison v. Louisiana, 379 U.S. 64, 1 Media L. Rep. 1549 (1964).
[23]*Restatement (Second) of Torts* sec. 560 (1977).
[24]MacDonald v. Time, Inc., 554 F. Supp. 1053 (D.N.J. 1983).

business practices, such as financial mismanagement or attempts to deceive the public through advertising.

Nonprofit corporations, such as churches and charitable organizations, can sue for language damaging their ability to obtain donations.[25] Unincorporated associations, including labor unions, can sue for language that would tend to damage their ability to attract members, conduct business, or obtain financial support.[26]

Government

Units of government cannot sue for criticism of government conduct. Governments cannot sue on their own behalf, on behalf of employees, or on behalf of the public they serve no matter how false or unreasonable the criticism. Appellate courts have consistently held that governments cannot be defamed.[27] The U.S. Supreme Court has declared that libel suits by government institutions are unconstitutional.[28] The right to criticize government has been held to be too important to the process of self-government to decide otherwise.

The U.S. Supreme Court, in *New York Times v. Sullivan,* implicitly endorsed language used by the Illinois Supreme Court in 1923.[29] The Illinois court, when rejecting a libel suit by the City of Chicago, said that ''no court of last resort in this country has ever held, or even suggested, that prosecutions for libel on government have any place in the American system of jurisprudence.'' Chicago had sued the *Chicago Tribune* for printing that it was ''broke,'' its ''credit was shot to pieces,'' and bankruptcy for the city was ''just around the corner.'' Chicago said the articles damaged its credit in the bond market and accounted for a substantial financial loss to the city. The Illinois Supreme Court said that even if the *Tribune*'s stories resulted in an increase in taxes, it was better that irresponsible individuals or newspapers not be punished than for all citizens to be ''in jeopardy of imprisonment or economic subjection'' for criticizing ''an inefficient or corrupt government.''[30]

The fact that government cannot be libeled should not lead communicators to be careless about what they say about government. Government employees can sue as individuals for language that damages their reputations if they have been named or otherwise identified in defamatory stories.

SUMMARY

Defamation is expression that can damage a person's reputation. Printed defamation and most broadcast defamation are considered to be libel. Slander is spoken

---

[25]*Restatement (Second) of Torts* secs. 561, 562, and 562 comment a (1977).

[26]*Id.* at secs. 562 and 562 comment a.

[27]*E.g.,* Johnson City v. Cowles Communications, Inc., 477 S.W.2d 750 (Tenn. 1972); Louisiana v. Time, Inc., 249 So.2d 328 (La. 1971). *See also* Philadelphia v. Washington Post Co., 482 F. Supp. 897 (E.D. Pa. 1979).

[28]*See* Rosenblatt v. Baer, 383 U.S. 75, 1 Media L. Rep. 1558 (1966); New York Times Co. v. Sullivan, 376 U.S. 254, 1 Media L. Rep. 1527 (1964).

[29]New York Times Co. v. Sullivan, 376 U.S. at 291–92, 1 Media L. Rep. at 1542.

[30]City of Chicago v. Tribune Co., 139 N.E. 86, 91 (1923).

defamation. Although most early libel law was criminal law aimed at preventing breaches of the peace, civil libel law—where one person or organization sues another for monetary damages—is now dominant.

Individuals and organizations, including businesses, can sue for libel. However, governments cannot sue.

THE PLAINTIFF'S BURDEN OF PROOF

A plaintiff, in order to win a libel suit, must establish certain claims to the satisfaction of a jury. This obligation is called the plaintiff's **burden of proof.** In order to sue successfully for libel, a plaintiff must prove

1. defamation, that there was defamatory language;
2. identification, that the defamation was about the plaintiff;
3. publication, that the defamation was disseminated; and
4. **fault**, that the defamation was published as a result of negligence or recklessness.

A plaintiff must prove all four points; proving only that the language was defamatory, for example, is not sufficient.

Almost all plaintiffs must also prove that a defamatory statement was false. However, falsity is usually related to fault. Falsity usually occurs because a communicator is careless or reckless, and therefore falsity will be discussed in the fault section of the chapter.

In addition, in order to receive monetary damages in a libel action, most plaintiffs must also prove that a defamation caused personal harm, such as a loss to reputation, emotional distress, or the loss of business revenues, a subject discussed toward the end of the chapter.

Even if libel plaintiffs meet their burden of proof, they may not win their libel suits. The courts recognize that certain kinds of defamatory publications benefit society, and therefore ought to be protected. However, public communicators can avoid the risk of losing many libel suits by preparing stories with a plaintiff's burden of proof in mind. If a published story contains defamatory language, does it identify anyone? If it does, could a defendant establish recklessness or negligence in court? Could the subject of a story prove harm to reputation, emotional well-being, or financial condition?

Defamation

The *Restatement (Second) of Torts* declares that defamatory communications tend to expose a person "to hatred, ridicule or contempt." Defamation may reflect unfavorably on someone's morality or integrity or discredit a person in his or her occupation. Also, defamation is language that restricts a person's social contacts by suggesting or asserting that he or she has a mental illness or a particular undesirable and contagious disease.[31]

A story or advertisement can be defamatory only if a significant segment of the average and reasonable people in the community believe it can damage an individual's reputation. Language cannot simply appear defamatory to a very small group of people or a minority with views quite different from those of the general population. In court, a judge usually determines whether a printed or broadcast message is capable of a defamatory meaning. A jury determines whether that message, in its everyday meaning, defamed the person suing.[32]

Even when juries decide that language is defamatory, plaintiffs may not win their libel suits. In fact, public communicators regularly use defamatory language when they report crime news, for example. To write that a person is accused of embezzlement is defamatory because it may damage his or her reputation. However, the person accused of embezzling cannot win a libel suit unless the report is false because of a journalist's carelessness or recklessness. A libel plaintiff must establish that a communicator published defamatory language, but that is only one of the four burdens of proof that must be satisfied to win a libel case.

Defamatory Content   The words and phrases most often involved in libel suits are those stating or suggesting criminal activity, serious moral failings, or incompetence in business or professional life. More than 80 percent of 400 libel cases studied by Stanford law professor Marc A. Franklin fell into one of these categories.[33] Words also can be defamatory if they imply that a person is unpatriotic, mentally incompetent, an alcoholic, or infected by a loathsome disease. Both businesses and business products can be libeled.

Crime   Stories about crime make up a significant proportion of the news, and the assertion that someone committed, or is accused of committing, a crime is defamatory on its face. If a newspaper or broadcast station falsely reports that someone is suspected or convicted of rape, drug use, or drunken driving, that person may be able to win a libel suit. A court ruled that the *Washington Post* printed libel when it erroneously reported that Michael Donaldson pleaded guilty to a charge of murder.[34] Similarly, a court said an Indiana couple used defamatory language when they told a real estate agent that Marshall Agnew was a thief.[35]

Imprecision in crime reporting can result in a successful libel suit. A New York court said Mrs. Hazel Robart was defamed when she was falsely reported to have been charged with driving an uninsured motor vehicle. She had instead been issued a ticket, but was never charged, for failing to carry state insurance identification.[36] In a

---

[31]*Restatement (Second) of Torts* sec. 559 (1977).

[32]*Id.* at secs. 559 comment e, 563 comment c, and 614.

[33]Franklin, "Winners and Losers and Why: A Study of Defamation Litigation," in 1980 *Am. B. Found. Res. J.* 455, 481–82.

[34]Donaldson v. Washington Post Co., 3 Media L. Rep. 1436 (D.C. Super. Ct. 1977).

[35]Agnew v. Hiatt, 10 Media L. Rep. 2389 (Ind. Ct. App. 1984).

[36]Robart v. Post-Standard, 425 N.Y.S.2d 891, 6 Media L. Rep. 1058 (N.Y. App. Div. 1980), *aff'd,* 52 N.Y.2d 843, 6 Media L. Rep. 2375 (N.Y. 1981).

similar vein, a reporter should not write that a man who has just shot a neighbor has committed murder. A prosecutor or jury may decide the man acted in self-defense or otherwise lacked the criminal intent required for a charge of murder.

Occupation　Allegations of incompetence, unethical practices, or criminal activity related to work accounted for more than three-quarters of the libel cases studied by Professor Franklin. Nearly 40 percent of the plaintiffs in the study worked in manufacturing or general business. Government employees, including law enforcement personnel and teachers, were the plaintiffs nearly 30 percent of the time. Professionals were the plaintiffs 14 percent of the time. Elected public officials or candidates for office were the plaintiffs 6 percent of the time.[37]

Libel law protects businessmen, professionals, laborers, and government employees from false charges that they lack the intelligence, ability, or credentials to do their jobs. Statements that a doctor has only a mail-order medical degree or that a president of a savings and loan association is "incapable" of administration are defamatory.[38]

Remarks that professionals do not perform the services promised or that they violate professional ethics could damage their reputations. A Kentucky appeals court said that an article in the *Louisville Times,* "An Elderly Woman's Story of the Living Hell of Drugs," defamed Dr. Charles E. Pearce. The story recounted the tale of 76-year-old Hattie Rose Ludwig, who said she became addicted to drugs while under Dr. Pearce's care. The court said the story left the impression that Pearce injected Ludwig with drugs for no valid medical purpose but only to take her money. The court said the "natural and probable effect of this story on the mind of the average lay reader" would be to hold Dr. Pearce up to hatred, contempt, or disgrace. The court ruled that Dr. Pearce should have the chance to prove in a trial that the story was false.[39]

Charges of corruption can also be defamatory. An Illinois appeals court ruled that the *Wall Street Journal* could be sued for an article that accused business executive Robert Crinkley of payoffs to foreign governments. The *Journal* reported that Crinkley, president of the radiographics division of G.D. Searle and Company, resigned after disclosures that he made payments to foreign governments in order to obtain business. The court said that although such payments were not illegal at the time, the false allegations did impugn Crinkley's integrity.[40]

Of course, not every story that generates a complaint is libelous. A federal appeals court said that criticism of a criminal law class at Stanford University in *Newsweek* was not defamatory. *Newsweek* said that Professor Stanley Kaplan's criminal law course was "recognized as the easiest five credits" at Stanford. The article reported that some students listened to the lectures over the radio while they sunned themselves by the pool, the professor required only a midterm and a final, the grades "exactly mirror the curve" for grades at Stanford, and two students took the final exam in top hats and three-piece suits while drinking champagne. The U.S. Court of

---

[37]Franklin, "Winners and Losers and Why: A Study of Defamation Litigation," in 1980 *Am. B. Found. Res. J.* 455, 477–78, 482.

[38]Newton v. Family Fed. S & L, 616 P.2d 1213 (Or. Ct. App. 1980).

[39]Pearce v. Courier-Journal & Louisville Times Co., 683 S.W.2d 633, 11 Media L. Rep. 1498 (Ky. Ct. App. 1985).

[40]Crinkley v. Dow Jones & Co., 456 N.E.2d 138, 9 Media L. Rep. 2248 (Ill. App. Ct. 1983).

Appeals for the Ninth Circuit said the story said nothing directly about the teacher's ability or integrity, and maybe nothing derogatory about the course. The court said that any implication that the class was worthless because it was easy was "strained."[41]

Business   Businesses can only sue for damage to the corporate reputation and not for damage to any individual's reputation. Businesses may sue for stories that claim they provide poor service, lack integrity, or have committed a crime. Businesses also might sue for language that asserts that they cheat their customers, are financially insolvent, or are intentionally selling harmful or ineffective products.

Writers need to be particularly careful when they are tempted to use such words as *fraud, cheated, ripped-off,* and *gypped.* Charges that a business is deceptive could cause the loss of customers. A federal court said that a reporter's assertion that a retail meat company deceptively advertised the price and quality of its beef could be defamatory. Donna Deaner, a reporter for WTAE-TV in Pittsburgh, broadcast that a Steaks Unlimited sales agent said the beef at a sale was "lovely, fully dressed and trimmed" and a "fantastic bargain." But Deaner said the beef came from "old tough animals" and was tenderized "with a variety of chemicals to make it palatable." She also said the meat was not much cheaper than what could be purchased in supermarkets. Although the U.S. Court of Appeals for the Third Circuit said the report could be defamatory, it ruled that Steaks Unlimited could not meet other elements of its burden of proof.[42]

The reputation of a business can also be damaged by allegations that it is financially unstable or insolvent. Greenmoss Builders, a construction company, won $350,000 when a credit-reporting agency falsely said the company had filed for bankruptcy. A 17-year-old employee of the credit agency had inadvertently attributed the bankruptcy petition of a former Greenmoss employee to the company itself.[43]

A business also may be able to win a libel suit if a publication or broadcast contends that it manufactures or promotes products that could damage the public health or safety. The Brown & Williamson Tobacco Corporation won $3.5 million in damages after a Chicago television commentator falsely accused the company of trying to sell Viceroy cigarettes to children. Walter Jacobson of WBBM-TV said Viceroy's strategy was to convince young people that smoking cigarettes was an "illicit pleasure" such as drinking alcoholic beverages, smoking pot, and engaging in sexual activities. Jacobson said Viceroy wanted to "present the cigarette as an initiation into the adult world" and a "declaration of independence." Jacobson's commentary said Viceroy lied when it contended it was not trying to sell cigarettes to children. However, Brown & Williamson proved the accusation false—the company had rejected the "illicit pleasure" strategy aimed at children and fired the ad agency that proposed it.[44]

At least a few states limit libel suits related to business and occupation through what is called the single instance rule. Courts in New York and Florida have held that

---

[41]Kaplan v. Newsweek, 776 F.2d 1053, 12 Media L. Rep. 1277 (9th Cir. 1985).

[42]Steaks Unlimited, Inc. v. Deaner, 623 F.2d 264, 6 Media L. Rep. 1129 (3d Cir. 1980).

[43]Dun & Bradstreet, Inc. v. Greenmoss Builders, Inc., 472 U.S. 749, 11 Media L. Rep. 2417 (1985).

[44]Brown & Williamson Tobacco Corp. v. Walter Jacobson, 644 F. Supp. 1240, 13 Media L. Rep. 1263 (1986), *aff'd in part,* 827 F.2d 1119, 14 Media L. Rep. 1497 (1987), *cert. denied,* 485 U.S. 993 (1988).

"language charging a professional person with ignorance or error on a single occasion" is not defamatory without proof of specific monetary loss. The courts have suggested that readers and viewers know that everyone makes mistakes at some time, and therefore a report of a single error will not damage a professional's reputation.

In New York and Florida, it is only defamatory to accuse a professional of "general" incompetence, ignorance, or lack of skill. A journalist may be able to report falsely that a professional once made an error as long as the story does not imply the incident is typical. Thus, a New York court said former district attorney Nat Hentel could not claim his reputation was damaged by criticism of his handling of one murder case. A book, *The Alice Crimmins Case,* suggested that Hentel's political aspirations dictated his interest in the prosecution of a mother accused of murdering her children. Author Ken Gross said Hentel was out for "a quick kill," worried that he would be "dismissed at the polls as an impotent prosecutor" if he allowed the Crimmins case to "dribble away." The court said the criticism fell under the single instance rule.[45]

Product Disparagement or Trade Libel   Business libel should be distinguished from product disparagement, also called trade libel. Product disparagement defames the quality or usefulness of a commercial product rather than the company that produced it. Stories suggesting that a brand of scissors cannot cut, a manufacturer's basketball does not bounce, or a prescription drug causes cancer are examples of trade libel. The comments criticize the products without contending the companies are trying to cheat their customers. The purpose of trade libel is to compensate for the loss of sales rather than for damage to reputation.

Plaintiffs have a hard time winning product disparagement suits. They must not only meet the burden of proof required of all libel plaintiffs, but must also comply with two additional requirements. First, a trade libel plaintiff must prove financial damage to the business. Bob Diefenderfer could not do that after a Sheridan, Wyoming, radio station suggested that merchandise he was trying to sell after a fire was not

> worth the paper cartons it was packed in. . . . Radios had picked up moisture, dishes and glassware, subject to terrific heat, were brittle, turquoise Indian stones in jewelry were permanently discolored. . . . The Navajo rugs were scorched and the colors ran together. The record stock was wet and useless, since they would warp.[46]

A trial judge ruled the merchandise on sale at Bob's War Surplus Store was worth more than the paper cartons. However, the judge said Diefenderfer had not proven his store had lost money because of the broadcast. Diefenderfer's claims of damage were "uncertain, conjectural and speculative," said the court. The Wyoming Supreme Court affirmed the lower court decision.

In addition to loss of business, a plaintiff in a trade libel case must establish that defamation was published with **malice,** either intent to do harm, knowledge of falsity,

---

[45]Hentel v. Alfred A. Knopf, Inc., 8 Media L. Rep. 1908 (N.Y. Sup. Ct. 1982). *See Restatement (Second) of Torts* sec. 573 comment d (1977).
[46]Diefenderfer v. Totman, 280 P.2d 284, 285 (Wyo. 1955).

or reckless disregard for the truth.[47] The malice requirement prevented the Bose Corporation from winning damages for a false statement printed in *Consumer Reports* about the Bose 901 speaker system. The magazine said that sound from the speakers, rather than running back and forth "along the wall," wandered "about the room." A violin appeared to be "10 feet wide and a piano stretched from wall to wall." A district court judge was persuaded that the publication caused an eight-month decline in the sales growth of the speaker system. He decided that Bose should be compensated $115,000. However, a federal appeals court overturned the ruling, deciding that Bose had not adequately established that *Consumer Reports* knew the publication was false. That ruling was upheld by the U.S. Supreme Court.[48]

A single story can be both business defamation and trade libel. Anyone disparaging a product can, at the same time, imply that the manufacturer was dishonest, fraudulent, or incompetent. Such was the ruling of a New York state appeals court when the manufacturers of a sleep aid called Snooze sued NBC and Jack Paar for a televised comment that the product was full of habit-forming drugs, led to weight loss, and would make a person feel like "a run-down hound dog." The court said the broadcast not only defamed the product but also implied fraud and deceit on the part of the company that would put such an "unwholesome and dangerous" product on the market.[49]

Personal Character, Habits, and Obligations   Although a majority of recent libel suits have involved criticism of people for their work, Professor Marc Franklin's study demonstrated that many suits are still filed for attacks on personal character traits or life-style. An important ingredient of every reputation is what friends and acquaintances think about a person's behavior and beliefs. An individual's reputation can be damaged by stories that imply the person exhibits bad character, vicious motives, or antisocial behavior.

More specifically, a story that suggests that someone is dishonest, cruel, or does not live up to social obligations can be defamatory. A federal district court said that a broadcast news segment that could be interpreted to portray Amrit Lal as a slum landlord was capable of a defamatory meaning. The court said WCAU-TV in Philadelphia may have defamed Lal when it reported an allegation by students that he would not make necessary repairs on his property. The tenants complained of leaky roofs, faulty wiring, and "other eyesores." The court said the broadcast could be interpreted as accusing Lal of being an "unscrupulous" person who "preys upon the economically disadvantaged."[50] The court said the report could deter people from associating or dealing with Lal, an issue that needed to be determined at trial. Other courts have said that people were libeled when they were accused of being hypocrites, liars, cowards, cheats, or unwilling to pay their bills.[51]

---

[47]*E.g., Restatement (Second) of Torts* secs. 623A comment d, 626, 633, 634 (1977); R. Smolla, *The Law of Defamation* sec. 11.02[2] [e], at 11–33 (1989).

[48]Bose Corp. v. Consumers Union of United States, Inc., 508 F. Supp. 1249, 7 Media L. Rep. 1069, *enforced,* 529 F. Supp. 357, 7 Media L. Rep. 2481 (D. Mass. 1981), *rev'd,* 692 F.2d 189, 8 Media L. Rep. 2391 (1st Cir. 1982), *aff'd,* 466 U.S. 485, 10 Media L. Rep. 1625 (1984).

[49]Harwood Pharmacal Co. v. NBC, 174 N.E.2d 602 (N.Y. 1961).

[50]Lal v. CBS, 551 F. Supp. 356, 9 Media L. Rep. 1113 (E.D. Pa. 1982), *aff'd,* 726 F.2d 97, 10 Media L. Rep. 1276 (1984).

[51]*Restatement (Second) of Torts* sec. 569(g) (1977); *Prosser and Keeton on Torts* sec. 111, at 775 (5th ed. 1984).

Assertions that either a husband or wife has not fulfilled marital or familial obligations also may be libelous. A court said a woman defamed her ex-husband when she said "he abandoned me, made no provisions for my support, treated me with complete indifference and did not display any affection or regard for me."[52] In many jurisdictions it is defamatory to say that a man or woman is divorced or that a couple is having marriage problems.[53]

Assertions that a person's sexual conduct deviates from generally accepted norms are usually defamatory. A jury awarded a Virginia woman $25,000 in 1985 after the *Charlottesville* (Virginia) *Daily Progress* falsely said she was pregnant and unmarried.[54] A story that asserts that a man has made improper advances toward a woman ordinarily will be considered to have damaged his reputation.[55] Juries are also likely to decide that stories falsely reporting that a woman has been raped are defamatory. Many people still consider rape victims to be social outcasts.

A claim that a person is a homosexual is also defamatory. So is language that suggests a person performs sexual favors for a living. A jury awarded author and television personality Pat Montandon $251,000 in damages after deciding that *TV Guide* had falsely implied she had been a prostitute. When Montandon had consented to appear on "The Pat Michaels Show," the program's producer submitted an item to *TV Guide* that read:

> From Party Girl to Call Girl? How far can the "party-girl" go until she becomes a "call-girl" is discussed wth T-V personality Pat Montandon, author, "How to Be a Party Girl" and a masked-anonymous prostitute!

The version appearing in the magazine had been substantially edited:

> From Party Girl to Call Girl. Scheduled guest: TV Personality Pat Montandon and author of "How to Be a Party Girl."

Besides changing the introductory question to an assertion, *TV Guide* made it appear that Montandon was the only person to discuss the featured topic. Court testimony indicated that the average reader would conclude from the *TV Guide* item that Montandon had progressed from a woman who liked parties to a prostitute. An appeals court affirmed the jury's verdict.[56]

Also libelous are assertions that someone is crazy, insane, an idiot, or mentally ill.[57] Former presidential candidate and senator Barry Goldwater won $75,000 after a 1964 issue of *Fact* magazine said he was paranoid, sadistic, anti-Semitic, and uncertain about his masculinity. The publication, printed to alert the public to the "dangers" of a Goldwater presidency, contained numerous distortions and fabrications.

---

[52]Brown v. DuFrey, 134 N.E.2d 469 (Ct. App. N.Y. 1956).

[53]*E.g.,* Brewer v. Memphis Publishing Co., 626 F.2d 1238, 6 Media L. Rep. 2025 (5th Cir. 1980), *cert. denied,* 452 U.S. 962 (1981).

[54]*E.g.,* Gazette v. Harris, 325 S.E.2d 713, 11 Media L. Rep. 1609 (Va. 1985).

[55]*E.g.,* Brewer v. Memphis Publishing Co., 626 F.2d at 1244, 6 Media L. Rep. at 2029; *Prosser and Keeton on Torts* sec. 111, at 775 (5th ed. 1984); *Restatement (Second) of Torts* sec. 569(f) (1977).

[56]Montandon v. Triangle Publications, Inc., 45 Cal. App.3d 938, *cert. denied,* 423 U.S. 893 (1975).

[57]*Restatement (Second) of Torts* sec. 559(c) (1977).

A federal appeals court affirmed a jury's decision that the accusations of insanity and mental instability were false and defamatory.[58]

Allegations that a person is suffering from a nervous breakdown or is going to a psychiatrist do not necessarily imply severe mental illness or abnormality; yet they still can be damaging to a person's career. Usually, the jury will decide whether the imputation has lowered a person's esteem in the eyes of others.

Although alcoholism is legally an illness, the accusation that someone is an alcoholic is still considered to be damaging to a person's reputation. An individual who is falsely reported to be an alcoholic, a drunkard, arrested for drunk driving, or a member of Alcoholics Anonymous may be able to successfully sue for libel.[59] To say that someone had a drink is not defamatory under most circumstances, but a report of raucous activity because of drinking can be. Actress Carol Burnett won $200,000 when the *National Enquirer* inaccurately reported she was obnoxious after drinking too much at the Rive Gauche, an expensive restaurant in Washington, D.C.[60]

A story can be libelous if it has the tendency to inhibit personal contact. Persons reported to have a particularly undesirable and contagious disease may be shunned.[61] Therefore, people can successfully sue for inaccurate reports that they have a sexually transmitted disease such as AIDS, genital herpes, or syphilis. A false report that a person has contracted infectious hepatitis could also lead to a successful libel suit. However, to say that someone has a cold or the flu would not be defamatory, even though both are contagious. Colds and the flu do not carry the social stigma attached to AIDS; neither are they ordinarily as damaging to the health as either AIDS or hepatitis. People do not avoid social contact with individuals who have colds in the same way they shun known carriers of the AIDS-related or hepatitis viruses. Neither have courts generally held that false reports of cancer are defamatory even though some people argue that cancer victims are shunned. Cancer is not believed to be contagious and is not considered to be damaging to esteem or reputation.[62]

In fact, many statements that embarrass, annoy, or hurt someone's feelings do not necessarily damage reputation. Ordinarily, a story that falsely asserts a woman is 52 years old rather than 32 does not defame her even though it might embarrass her and make her angry. Neither is it libelous to claim that someone has no sense of humor or is angry. Age and a lack of humor usually have little to do with bad character. Similarly, people described as poor can probably not sue successfully unless a story implies the poverty is the result of character flaws such as laziness or incompetence. Ordinarily the assertion that someone is poor does not suggest he or she is immoral, insane, or a criminal.[63]

In addition, relatives, partners, or subordinates of someone named in a defamatory story cannot ordinarily win suits by claiming they were libeled. Since damage to reputation is an individual matter, defamation of one person does not "rub off" onto

---

[58]Goldwater v. Ginzburg, 414 F.2d 324 (1969).

[59]*Prosser and Keeton on Torts* sec. 111, at 775 (5th ed. 1984).

[60]Burnett v. National Enquirer, 144 Cal. App.3rd 991, 9 Media L. Rep. 1921 (Cal. Ct. App. 1983), *appeal dismissed,* 465 U.S. 1014 (1984).

[61]*Restatement (Second) of Torts* sec. 559(c) (1977).

[62]Chuy v. Philadelphia Eagles Football Club, 595 F.2d 1265, 4 Media L. Rep. 2537 (3rd Cir. 1979).

[63]*See* R. Sack, *Libel, Slander, and Related Problems* 45–46 (1980).

another, regardless of the relationship between the two.[64] One court said that Senate staff members close to Wisconsin senator Joseph McCarthy could not claim they had been defamed by a film disparaging the late senator.[65] Friends, relatives, or associates of a person libeled can successfully sue for damage to their own reputations only if they can convince a court they are inextricably linked to the defamation in a story.

Politics, Religion, and Race   People can lose face if a story questions their patriotism or accuses them of being aligned with a political group that pursues goals contrary to national policy. It can be defamatory to assert falsely that someone is a traitor or a spy, believes in anarchy, or wants to overthrow the government by force. In 1975, a former Arizona state attorney general was awarded $485,000 after an editorial in the *Arizona Republic* said he had Communist sympathies.[66]

A story falsely reporting that an individual is a member of a discredited organization—such as the Nazi party—is defamatory.[67] It is also libelous to suggest that a person has been kicked out of a religious order or that a religious organization is not what it purports to be.[68] Both statements imply an insincerity of faith unacceptable to many people.

However, courts have held that the use of derogatory nationalistic and racial terms may not damage reputation. To call someone a spic, chink, polack, nigger, or cracker may be degrading and offensive but probably not libelous. An individual might be able to win a libel suit only if there were proof of harm to reputation. But ordinarily terms such as chink or nigger do not reflect on the individual character or beliefs of the persons subject to the verbal abuse.

Humor and Ridicule   Humor is dangerous because what is funny to some is not to others. A publication that generates laughs at someone's expense, or makes a person the butt of a joke, is not necessarily libelous. However, humor can become libelous if it subjects people to ridicule by suggesting they do not deserve respect. A major difficulty for writers is that even the courts disagree on where the line between harmless humor and ridicule should be drawn.

To illustrate, courts have generally ruled that false obituaries planted in newspapers are bad jokes but do not damage the reputation of the living.[69] A New York court even ruled that it was not defamatory to assert that the corpse of someone who was very much alive was lying in state at the address of a saloon. Even had readers known the address was that of a bar, the judge said, the obituary did not expose the plaintiff to public hatred, shame, odium, ridicule, aversion, or disgrace. The judge said, at worst, the publication "might cause some amusement to plaintiff's friends."[70] How-

---

[64]*Restatement (Second) of Torts* sec. 564 and comment e (1977).

[65]Cohn v. NBC, 414 N.Y.S.2d 906, 4 Media L. Rep. 2533 (N.Y. App. Div. 1979), *aff'd*, 430 N.Y.S.2d 265, 6 Media L. Rep. 1398 (N.Y. 1980).

[66]Phoenix Newspapers, Inc. v. Church, 537 P.2d 1345 (Ariz. 1975), *appeal dismissed*, 425 U.S. 908 (1976), *reh'g denied*, 425 U.S. 985 (1976).

[67]Holy Spirit Ass'n v. Sequoia Elsevier Publishing Co., 4 Media L. Rep. 1744 (N.Y. Sup. Ct. 1978).

[68]*See* Church of Scientology v. Minnesota State Medical Ass'n Found., 264 N.W.2d 152, 3 Media L. Rep. 2177 (Minn. 1978).

[69]*E.g.,* Cohen v. New York Times Co., 138 N.Y.S. 206 (1912).

[70]Cardiff v. Brooklyn Eagle, Inc., 75 N.Y.S.2d 222 (Kings Co. 1947).

ever, another court concluded that a paper mill employee was libeled when a newspaper column implied he was preoccupied with saving money when he died. George Powers was awarded $50 when a writer said he was "a classic example of typical Yankee thrift"—he was building his own casket and would soon be digging his own grave. Powers said neither assertion was true. The court said the story made him appear foolish, weird, and unnatural and was therefore defamatory.[71]

Forms of Libel   Libel suits are most often filed because of the words printed or broadcast in news stories, editorials, and letters to editors. Defamatory words also appear in headlines and advertisements. Although individual words often carry a defamatory meaning, sometimes words are defamatory only in combination or because of circumstances not known to a reasonably prudent writer or editor. Libel also can occur in the use of photographs, cartoons, caricatures, and video.

Words   Some words are defamatory on their face, that is libelous per se. Courts have held that some words can, by themselves, if used inaccurately, damage a person's reputation. Words that are libelous *per se* have clear, unambiguous, and commonly agreed to meanings. Among the many "red flag" words that are defamatory on their face are *unethical, adulterer, thief, drunkard,* and *cheat.*

However, many words and phrases can have more than one meaning. Some states have adopted what is called the *innocent construction rule,* which provides that if language is capable of a nondefamatory meaning, it should be construed that way. The Illinois Supreme Court has said courts should find words and implications nonactionable if, "given their natural and obvious meaning," they can reasonably be interpreted "innocently."[72] Applying the innocent construction rule, an Illinois appellate court said that a school board member's suggestion that a high school superintendent could lose certification and be criminally penalized was not defamatory. School board member Charles Garrison, after initiating a state investigation into the administration of Zion-Benton High School, said

> Whatever legal ramifications result from that investigation—which could range from the superintendent losing his certification to criminal penalties—is up to the state's attorney.

Garrison also said the public would "demand changes" when the investigation was complete. Zion-Benton superintendent, Gene Cartwright, said Garrison's remark put his job into jeopardy because readers would believe he was a criminal. However, the Illinois court said Cartwright was not defamed because, under the innocent construction rule, Garrison's comment could reasonably be interpreted to mean he was leaving to the state's attorney whether Cartwright had done anything "legally wrong" or whether "legal ramifications" would result from the investigation. The court said Garrison's comments did not imply that Cartwright was unfit to be a school administrator.[73]

---

[71]Powers v. Durgin-Snow Publishing Co., 144 A.2d 294 (Me. 1958).
[72]*E.g.,* Chapski v. Copley Press, 442 N.E.2d 195, 198, 8 Media L. Rep. 2403, 2406 (Ill. 1982).
[73]Cartwright v. Garrison, 447 N.E.2d 446, 9 Media L. Rep. 1819 (Ill. App. Ct. 1983).

The meaning of words must be considered in context.[74] A plaintiff cannot successfully contend that an isolated word or sentence is defamatory when the thrust of the article or book in which it appears is a neutral or favorable impression of the person. Therefore, a New York court said a survivor of a terrorist attack was not defamed by a book that falsely portrayed him fleeing the scene alone without warning companions. The book, *The Blood of Israel,* told the story of the terrorist attack on Israeli athletes during the 1972 Olympic Games. The survivor, Shaul Ladany, said the book implied he was a coward because it inaccurately described his leaving the scene of the attack alone. In fact, Ladany had left his apartment with several teammates.

However, a federal district court said the book as a whole was not defamatory. Although the book falsely portrayed Ladany leaving the building without warning his teammates, it gave the impression that Ladany thought he was alone in the apartment before he fled. In addition, the court said, the book implied that escape "was the only prudent course." Although individual passages in the book might have been defamatory, the court said, the thrust of the entire book was not.[75]

Words also have to be considered in their social context. Whether language is considered defamatory may change with the time and place. For example, in most areas of the country, the Ku Klux Klan is held in contempt for its racism and violence. A false accusation that a person is a member of the Klan would often be considered damaging to reputation. However, in some communities, the Klan's commitment to white superiority is shared by many—many who may be members of a jury. A jury may decide that Klan membership is not contemptuous and that a person falsely labeled as a Klan member has not been defamed.[76]

In 1976, a federal judge ruled that assertions that a U.S. citizen worked for the CIA could be defamatory. Ordinarily, a statement that a person works for the government is not considered damaging to his or her reputation. More specifically, an allegation that a person worked for the CIA would not have exposed the individual to hatred, contempt, or ridicule for most of the post–World War II era. However, an assertion that a citizen was a CIA employee during the 1960s and 1970s could have been defamatory because many people believed that the CIA was engaged in illegal activity and did not always function in the best interest of the country.[77]

Innuendo and Circumstance   People can be libeled not only by words that are defamatory on their face but also by implication or innuendo. Sometimes a defamatory meaning can be implied rather than stated outright. In an example mentioned above, *TV Guide* did not say directly that author Pat Montandon had been a call girl. Rather, a reader could have inferred she had been a prostitute from the fact that Montandon was listed as the only guest on a program titled "From Party Girl to Call Girl."

Similarly, writers may imply that a person is involved in criminal activity by using a nickname such as "Jake the Mugger," or by saying that Jake spent the night

---

[74]*Restatement (Second) of Torts* sec. 563 comment d (1977).
[75]Ladany v. William Morrow & Co., 465 F. Supp. 870, 4 Media L. Rep. 2153 (S.D.N.Y. 1978).
[76]*See Restatement (Second) of Torts* sec. 559(e) (1977).
[77]*See* Oliver v. The Village Voice, Inc., 417 F. Supp. 235 (S.D.N.Y. 1976).

in jail or refused to take a lie detector test.[78] An Illinois court said bribery was implied by the comment that a municipal garbage contract was awarded after "two hundred forty pieces of silver changed hands—thirty for each alderman."[79]

In some states, libel by innuendo is called libel *per quod*.[80] However, libel *per quod* more frequently means libel that is not apparent in the words themselves. Libel *per quod* is often distinguished from libel *per se,* when words by themselves can hurt a reputation. In libel *per quod,* the words are defamatory only because of facts not known by reasonably prudent reporters and editors. For example, a birth notice naming the parents of a baby is not usually libelous, even if the names are wrong. However, a man falsely identified as the father might successfully sue if he is a bachelor and the mother has a reputation for promiscuity, information that an editor in a large city might not know. With the addition of information not available to newspaper personnel, what appears to be a harmless birth announcement can turn into an item that could damage a person's reputation.[81]

In Washington State, Phillip and Donna Pitts won $2,000 in damages when the *Spokane Chronicle* falsely reported that Phillip Pitts was granted a divorce in 1961. Pitts had been granted a divorce in 1960 and married Donna shortly afterward. The paper had mistakenly reported a 1961 modification of the divorce decree. The Washington Supreme Court agreed that the error made it appear to readers who knew about the 1960 divorce that the marriage of Phillip and Donna Pitts was illegal and that he was a bigamist.[82]

The distinction between libel *per se* and libel *per quod* is only significant in states that add to the plaintiff's burden of proof when the libel is not apparent by the words alone. In some states, in the case of libel *per quod,* the person suing must prove in court the truth of the facts that make the otherwise innocent story defamatory. Further, some states also require that a plaintiff claiming libel *per quod* prove a specific dollar loss and ill will on the part of the publication, in addition to elements of proof ordinarily required of a libel plaintiff.[83]

Headlines   Courts are split over whether a headline alone can result in a successful libel suit. In many jurisdictions, a suit will not be successful if a defamatory headline is clarified in the story. In those states, the headline and article must be read as a whole. The Hawaii Supreme Court rejected Councilman William Fernandes's contention that a headline in the *Hawaiian Advertiser* was libelous because it implied he exercised improper influence on behalf of his brother. The court said that, although the headline said "Brother Helps in Kauai Zoning Request," the article explained that Fernandes's efforts had been approved by the Kauai County Board of Ethics.[84]

However, the *Restatement (Second) of Torts* asserts that readers often miss im-

---

[78]*E.g.,* Molnar v. Star-Ledger, 471 A.2d 1209, 10 Media L. Rep. 1823 (N.J. Super. Ct. App. Div. 1984); *Restatement (Second) of Torts* sec. 569 comment d and 571 comment c (1977).

[79]Catalano v. Pechous, 419 N.E.2d 350, 6 Media L. Rep. 2511 (Ill. 1980), *cert. denied,* 451 U.S. 911 (1981).

[80]*See, e.g.,* Bruck v. Cincotta, 371 N.E.2d 874 (1978).

[81]*See Prosser and Keeton on Torts* sec. 111, at 776 (5th ed. 1984); Karrigan v. Valentine, 339 P.2d 52 (Kan. 1959).

[82]Pitts v. Spokane Chronicle Co., 388 P.2d 976 (1964).

[83]*See* R. Sack, *Libel, Slander, and Related Problems* 94-111 (1980); R. Smolla, *Law of Defamation* sec. 7.06, at 7-11 (1989).

[84]Fernandes v. Tenbruggencate, 649 P.2d 1144, 8 Media L. Rep. 2577 (1982).

portant parts of a story because they see only the headlines or read the article itself "hastily or imperfectly."[85] For those reasons, some courts hold that a headline by itself may be considered libelous even if the article provides clarification. The *New Orleans Times-Picayune* paid $10,000 in damages for the headline "Bid Specs Reported 'Rigged.'" The article below the headline correctly reported that a consultant concluded that bid specifications for a school for the deaf appeared to favor specific manufacturers. A Louisiana appellate court said preferential treatment may or may not be illegal or improper but that the word *rigged* in the headline itself was defamatory because it denoted "fraudulent, illegal and improper" activity.[86]

Advertisements　Advertisements can also be defamatory. Although ads that claim one business is better than another are often not libelous, an ad that claims the competitor provides poor service may be. For example, an advertisement that asserts one camera shop develops film faster and produces color prints that resist fading longer than another is not defamatory. However, in 1962, the Pennsylvania Supreme Court said the Cosgrove Studio and Camera Shop may have been defamed when a competitor implied that Cosgrove misled consumers, ruined film, and produced poor prints in the "small city" of Hazelton. Cosgrove had advertised that the store would give customers a free roll of film for every roll brought in for processing. Competitor Cal R. Pane responded the following day with an ad that, without referring directly to Cosgrove, advised readers to "Use Common Sense—You Get Nothing for Nothing." Pane's ad told consumers that he would not inflate the price of film processing in order to give customers free film, implying that Cosgrove had raised prices to compensate for the "free" film. Still referring to Cosgrove, according to the court, Pane's ad also said he would not print blurred negatives, would not ruin film by speeding up the developing process, and would not use inferior chemicals and paper. The court said the ad, if false, libeled Cosgrove. The court said the ad suggested Cosgrove lacked integrity and provided poor service, conduct incompatible with what a customer expected of a business.[87]

Photographs, Cartoons, and Layout　Photographs can also be the basis of a successful libel suit if they do not accurately reflect what the photographer saw, either because the lens created an optical illusion or because the picture was altered.[88] More often, however, defamation occurs because of the combination of a picture and a nearby headline, story, or cutline.

　　The Supreme Judicial Court of Massachusetts said a Boston lawyer was entitled to a jury trial because the juxtaposition of a headline and a picture was capable of being defamatory. Mitchell Mabardi testified before a congressional committee in 1962 that he had refused to participate in the fraudulent purchase of land for highways. A *Boston Herald-Traveler* story reporting a full day of testimony before the committee referred to Mabardi's comments but did not use his name. However,

---

[85]*Restatement (Second) of Torts* sec. 563 comment d (1977).
[86]Forrest v. Lynch, 347 So.2d 1255, 3 Media L. Rep. 1187 (La. Ct. App. 1977).
[87]Cosgrove Studio & Camera Shop, Inc. v. Pane, 182 A.2d 751 (1962).
　　[88]*See* R. Sack, *Libel, Slander, and Related Problems* 64 (1980); R. Smolla, *Law of Defamation* sec. 4.07[2] [a], at 7-26 (1989).

Mabardi's picture and name, without further explanation, appeared immediately below the headline "Settlement Upped $2,000: $400 Kickback Told." The headline applied to a state official discussed in the hearings and also pictured. The official had recently been convicted for taking a kickback in exchange for artificially raising the price the government paid for land. The Massachusetts court said that because Mabardi's role in the committee hearings had not been explained in the story, a large number of readers could have inferred he was involved in the scandal referred to in the headline and discussed in the story.[89]

Illustrating stories with inappropriate pictures can also be libelous. The use of file photos to illustrate stories with defamatory implications can be risky. Public communicators also take risks when they accept photographs and identifying information from other sources. For example, a jury decided that a South Dakota trucking firm was defamed when a picture of one of its sales posters was used inappropriately in *Fleet Owner,* a trucking industry magazine. *Fleet Owner* editors used a picture of a sign announcing an equipment auction by Drotzmann's, Inc., to illustrate a story about trucking companies going out of business. The editors of *Fleet Owner* had selected the Drotzmann's sales poster from a batch of auction posters given to the magazine to illustrate problems in the industry. The article and picture combined to create the false impression that Drotzmann's was going out of business. A jury awarded the firm $245,000 in damages before an appellate court ordered a new trial on other grounds.[90]

Many political cartoons carry a defamatory message. Many will be protected by the courts as opinion, discussed later in the chapter. However, a Missouri appeals court ruled that a cartoon defamed a psychic by portraying her as callous and unfeeling toward her clients and implying that she had no professional skill. The court said the drawing depicted Patricia Buller as a "bizarrely dressed figure, seated in bed, and surrounded by an incomprehensible array of charts and diagrams." The psychic in the drawing had just provided a "reading" that was "obviously meaningless" to the client. The client is "confused, even dismayed." However, the psychic does nothing to dispel the confusion but instead asks for money and summons the next client. The court ruled that the drawing, although representing the cartoonist's opinion, depicted Buller falsely as a greedy charlatan and was defamatory *per se.*[91]

SUMMARY

Libel plaintiffs must establish that a publication or broadcast holds them up to hatred, ridicule, or contempt. Most defamation involves assertions that individuals committed a crime or are incompetent or unethical in their occupation. Both businesses and products can be defamed. Also defamatory are suggestions of deviant sexual habits, irresponsible or unethical behavior, mental deficiencies, loathsome diseases, and a lack of patriotism. Defamation can occur because of photographs, cutlines, and headlines as well as stories.

---

[89]Mabardi v. Boston Herald-Traveler Corp., 198 N.E.2d 304 (Mass. 1964).
[90]Drotzmann's, Inc. v. McGraw-Hill, Inc., 500 F.2d 830 (8th Cir. 1974).
[91]Buller v. Pulitzer Publishing, 684 S.W.2d 473, 11 Media L. Rep. 1289 (Mo. Ct. App. 1984).

Judges determine whether words are capable of defamatory meaning, and jurors determine if the person suing was actually defamed. Isolated words taken out of context cannot be defamatory. However, a person can be libeled by the implication of words or by words that take on a defamatory meaning because of facts not known by a writer or editor.

Identification

Libel plaintiffs, in addition to establishing that an expression is defamatory, must also prove that the defamatory language is about them individually. Persons who are part of a large group that is libeled are usually unable to sue because they cannot show the defamation is about them individually.

Identifying Individuals The identification requirement means that plaintiffs must prove the defamatory language is "of or concerning" them. They must be able to show that at least one reader or viewer could identify them as the object of defamatory remarks. A person can be identified by name, nickname, signature, caricature, description, picture, or set of circumstances.[92]

Many libel suits involve the inadvertent naming of the wrong person. A careless police reporter can erroneously copy the name "Adams" instead of "Adamson" from police records. Or a reporter may use the wrong middle initial or address. In 1974, the *Springfield* (Massachusetts) *Union* lost a $60,000 suit for reporting that Anthony Liquori of Agawam, Massachusetts, pleaded guilty to conspiring to break into two businesses. A reporter for the paper obtained Anthony Liquori's name from the court record. Because the court record did not include Liquori's address, the reporter looked up the name of Anthony Liquori in the Agawam phone book. There was only one, so he used it without confirming its accuracy. Unfortunately for the paper, the address identified the wrong person. The Anthony Liquori who had pleaded guilty was then living in Springfield, not Agawam, and the Anthony Liquori listed in the phone book successfully sued for libel.[93]

The Liquori case demonstrates that checking identification in one place is not always enough. It also demonstrates the importance of a thorough identification. Media lawyers recommend identifying story subjects three ways if possible: full name, including a middle initial; address; and occupation. Listing ages also can help identify people with certainty. In 1980, the now-defunct *Washington Star* won a libel suit because it printed a complete identification. The paper, relying on a police officer at the scene, said the person who shot Dr. Michael J. Halberstam was Jerry Summerlin, 22, of the 5500 block of Dana Place, N.W., Washington, D.C. Jerry Gene Summerlin of 8809 Plymouth Street in Silver Spring, Maryland, sued, claiming he had been wrongfully identified as the man who killed Halberstam. But a federal district court judge said the *Star*'s story had provided enough information to ensure that someone with the same name as the murder suspect would not be unfairly stigma-

---

[92]*See Restatement (Second) of Torts* sec. 564 (1977); *Prosser and Keeton on Torts* sec. 111, at 783 (5th ed. 1984).
[93]Liquori v. Republican Co., 396 N.E.2d 726, 5 Media L. Rep. 2180 (Mass. App. Ct. 1979).

tized. Jerry Gene Summerlin was not 22 and did not live on Dana Place. Further, Jerry Gene Summerlin had not been hospitalized with internal injuries as the man arrested for Halberstam's murder had been. Halberstam had hit his assailant with his car as he was driving himself to the hospital.[94]

The courts have ruled that readers or viewers can identify a person by the facts in a story even if the person is not named. The *Kentucky Post,* for example, printed at least two articles about a fight in 1974 between two boys, Donnie Cholmondelay, 12, and Jeff Girdler, 11. A single blow to Jeff's head had sent him into a coma and he died a year later. The *Post* printed one story that said that Jeff's head had been hit repeatedly. Another said that Jeff's head had been pounded repeatedly against the pavement and that he had been savagely beaten into insensibility. Although Donnie's name was never used, he won a libel judgment for the inaccurate stories portraying him as brutal. The court said Donnie's friends and acquaintances familiar with the incident were certain to recognize who had fought with Jeff.[95]

Similarly, readers may identify people they know in works of fiction if authors do not adequately disguise their characters. The real people who may be the basis of unflattering or defamatory portrayals in the book might sue. Whether an author intended to portray a real person is irrelevant.[96] A person identified through name, occupation, physical characteristics, or personality traits may be able to sue successfully if the character portrayal would damage reputation. In 1980, a federal appeals court said that Melanie Geisler should have the chance to prove in court that a reasonable reader would believe she was the central character in a book, *Match Set,* by Orlando Petrocelli. The leading character, also named Melanie Geisler, was a transsexual who participated in a scheme to fix tennis tournaments and who was lured into graphically portrayed sexual conduct. Author Petrocelli depicted the fictional Melanie Geisler as young, attractive, and honey-blonde, ''her body . . . firm and compact, though heavier than she would like,'' a description that fit the *real* Melanie Geisler. Both the real Melanie Geisler and the author, Petrocelli, once worked at the same small publishing firm. The real Melanie Geisler said Petrocelli's book defamed her because she was an ''upstanding individual'' and the mother of two children. The U.S. Court of Appeals for the Second Circuit reversed a lower court ruling that Geisler's suit ought to be dismissed because her complaint had not contained enough evidence that she had been legally identified in *Match Set.* Although the Second Circuit said Geisler's complaint was adequate to justify a trial, it said that in order to win she would have to show additional circumstances existed that would cause reasonable readers to confuse the real and the fictional Melanie Geisler. The court suggested that the real Melanie Geisler would have to show that her friends corresponded to those in the book, that she was an athletic prodigy like the fictional character, or that friends who read *Match Set* believed she was the person portrayed.[97]

Group Libel   Since defamation is a matter of personal reputation, large groups of people—such as union members, doctors, Republicans, or Polish Americans—can-

---

[94]Summerlin v. Washington Star, 7 Media L. Rep. 2460 (D.C.D.C. 1981).
[95]E.W. Scripps Co. v. Cholmondelay, 569 S.W.2d 700, 3 Media L. Rep. 2462 (Ky. Ct. App. 1978).
[96]*See* R. Sack, *Libel, Slander, and Related Problems* 121–22 (1980).
[97]Geisler v. Petrocelli, 616 F.2d 636, 6 Media L. Rep. 1023 (1980).

not usually sue successfully for libel. In addition, when a defamatory remark is made about a large group of people, individual members of the group also have difficulty suing successfully because individuals are frequently not identifiable. Individuals can successfully sue for a defamatory comment made about a group only if they can show the language was "of and concerning" them personally.[98]

The courts consistently rule that people belonging to groups of more than 100 members cannot ordinarily claim that defamatory comments about the group as a whole apply to them individually. Individual members of such large groups cannot successfully sue for such allegations as "all doctors are quacks" or "most politicians are corrupt." One of more than 5,000 Kentucky Fried Chicken outlets could not convince the Kentucky Supreme Court it was defamed when Colonel Harland Sanders, the chain's original owner, criticized the food produced by his successors. The Bowling Green, Kentucky, outlet sued Sanders for telling the *Louisville Courier-Journal* that the gravy being served by the chain was a combination of "wallpaper paste" and "sludge." Sanders said the crispy recipe was "nothing in the world but a damn fried doughball stuck on some chicken." The court said it was obvious that Sanders had no particular restaurant in mind. The court said that nothing in the article identified the Bowling Green restaurant from the more than 5,000 Kentucky Fried Chicken outlets around the world. A reference to all did not identify one.[99]

Similarly, several Butte, Montana, businessmen whose buildings had burned down were not allowed to sue *Time* magazine for a comment that could have applied to at least 200 people. *Time,* while describing Butte's depressed economy in 1975, said that "arson has become common as people who are unable to sell their devalued buildings burn them for the insurance." About a third of 160 fires in downtown Butte between 1965 and 1975 had been attributed to arson. Several men who jointly owned two buildings said the *Time* article falsely suggested they burned the structures to collect insurance money. The Montana Supreme Court said, however, that too many people owned buildings that had burned in Butte for a reasonable reader to believe that *Time*'s comment was directed at the plaintiffs.[100]

If a story is about a group of fewer than 100 members, a court may say that defamatory comments about the group apply to each group member. For example, the Oklahoma Supreme Court said an assertion that University of Oklahoma football players used illegal drugs libeled every member of the team. A 1958 article in *True* magazine said that "members" of the 60-man team used an amphetamine nasal spray, thereby increasing their aggressiveness and competitive spirit. The article did not name any team members or say how many players received the "spray jobs." However, one member of the team, fullback Dennit Morris, was awarded $75,000 in libel damages by a jury. The Oklahoma Supreme Court affirmed the verdict, explaining that the magazine's accusation exposed every player to hatred and contempt.[101]

In contrast, courts usually rule that defamatory comments about *one* or a *few*

---

[98]*Restatement (Second) of Torts* sec. 564A (1977); *Prosser and Keeton on Torts* sec. 111, at 784 (5th ed. 1984).

[99]Kentucky Fried Chicken, Inc. v. Sanders, 563 S.W.2d 8, 3 Media L. Rep. 2054 (1978).

[100]Granger v. Time, Inc., 568 P.2d 535, 3 Media L. Rep. 1021 (1977).

[101]Fawcett Publications, Inc. v. Morris, 377 P.2d 42 (Okla.), *appeal dismissed, cert. denied,* 376 U.S. 513 (1962), *reh'g denied,* 377 U.S. 925 (1964). *See also* Brady v. Ottaway Newspapers, 445 N.Y.S.2d 786, 8 Media L. Rep. 1671 (N.Y. App. Div. 1981).

unidentified members of a group of 15 to 100 members do not identify any of the individuals in the group. A federal appeals court said that a story about the activities of one unidentified policeman did not libel any of 21 officers in the Bellingham, Massachusetts, police department. A column in the *Woonsocket Call and Evening Reporter* closed with the question: "Is it true that a Bellingham cop locked himself and a female companion in the back of a cruiser in a town sandpit and had to radio for help?" The U.S. Court of Appeals for the First Circuit said that "by no stretch of the imagination" could the question in the newspaper be considered a blanket slur, applying to each of the 21 officers. The court added that to allow every member of a group to sue in such a circumstance "would chill communication to the marrow."[102]

The First Circuit said, however, that a defamatory statement aimed at a substantial portion of a small group would present a different question. Other courts have agreed that statements encompassing *most* of a group could be seen as a *blanket slur* defaming everyone. In one case, all 25 salesmen in the menswear section of the Neiman-Marcus department store in Dallas were allowed to sue when a book, *U.S.A. Confidential,* asserted that "most of the sales staff" were "fairies."[103]

The smaller the group the more likely it is that every individual in it might be able to sue regardless of qualifying language. Courts often decide that defamatory language aimed at groups of fewer than 15 may be "of or concerning" each of the individuals in the group. A 1977 column in the *Detroit News* accused the leadership of Teamster Local 299, a group of seven people, of illegal activity. Writer Dan Girard discussed "thieves who run the Teamster Union," "thugs who run Local 299," and "union hoods." A Michigan appellate court said the president and secretary/treasurer of the local could sue for libel because the reference was to a group of seven "whose identities are readily ascertainable from the content of the article."[104]

SUMMARY

A libel plaintiff must demonstrate that defamatory language refers to him or her. Many suits result from inaccurate identification. People who can show they can be recognized as characters in defamatory works of fiction may be able to successfully sue for libel.

Communicators should be careful that libelous language about a group will not be considered to identify any single individual. Defamatory language about groups larger than 100 people is reasonably safe. However, individuals may be able to sue successfully for defamatory language pertaining to all members of groups of fewer than 100. For groups of fewer than 100, restrictive phrases such as "a few of" or "a couple of" can sometimes ensure that individuals in the group cannot claim to be

---

[102]Arcand v. Evening Call, 567 F.2d 1163, 3 Media L. Rep. 1748 (1977). *See also Restatement (Second) of Torts* sec. 564A comment c (1977); *Prosser and Keeton on Torts* sec. 111, at 784 (5th ed. 1984).

[103]Neiman-Marcus Co. v. Lait, 13 **F.R.D.** 311 (S.D. N.Y. 1952).

[104]Lins v. Evening News, 342 N.W.2d 573, 578, 9 Media L. Rep. 2380, 2383–84 (Mich. App. 1983).

identified. If a story is about a group with fewer than 15 members, any reference to the group may be considered "of and concerning" anyone in the group.

Publication

Libel plaintiffs, in addition to proving that defamatory language identifies them, must prove that the libel reaches someone other than themselves. The *publication* of defamation, in the legal sense, requires at least three persons—the person uttering or publishing the defamation, the person being defamed, and a person hearing or seeing the defamation.

Newspapers and magazines *publish* when they circulate one copy of one issue. Radio and television stations *publish* when they air a broadcast. A libel plaintiff is not required to prove that subscribers or viewers heard or read a defamatory "publication." Courts assume publications and broadcast signals reach an audience.[105]

Libel can be *published* not only through newspapers and broadcast stations but also in press releases, interoffice memos, conversations, interviews, and business letters. In 1969, Joseph Melosi and William Lhotka, reporters for the *Alton* (Illinois) *Telegraph,* mentioned in a memo to a U.S. Justice Department investigator that they suspected a local builder, James C. Green, was connected to organized crime. The memo was passed to federal bank regulators, who forced a savings and loan association to cut off credit to Green. Even though nothing was published in the paper, Green sued, claiming that he lost his business as a result of the memo. Green won a jury verdict and eventually agreed to a settlement of $1.4 million with the paper.[106]

Reporters can effectively *publish* defamation by asking questions during interviews. Theodor Schuchat, a free-lance writer, was ordered to pay $1,500 in damages after he falsely stated in interviews that insurance executive Leonard Davis was a convicted felon. Davis had been tried for perjury but not convicted. Schuchat said he made the remark as part of a technique of "throwing a lot of things out" during interviews in an attempt to "to get a response." A federal appeals court refused to protect Schuchat's comments even though they were made in private conversations rather than printed in the paper.[107]

Communicators are also usually liable for repeating, therefore *republishing,* defamatory remarks. Plaintiffs are not restricted to suing the first person to utter or write a libelous comment; they can also sue anyone responsible for disseminating it. A citizen who accuses a doctor of medical malpractice can be sued for libel; but so can the reporter who uses the accusation in a news story, the editors who review the copy, and the publisher of the newspaper that prints it. The writer of a letter to the editor can be sued for libel, but so can the editor who prepares it for the editorial page and

---

[105]*See Restatement (Second) of Torts* sec. 559 comment e (1977); Hornby v. Hunter, 385 S.W.2d 473 (Tex. Civ. App. 1964).

[106]*See* footnote 5 in this chapter and Green v. Alton Telegraph, 438 N.E.2d 203, 8 Media L. Rep. 1345 (Ill. App. 1982).

[107]Davis v. Schuchat, 510 F.2d 731 (D.C. Cir. 1975).

the newspaper that publishes it.[108] A newspaper or broadcast station also can be sued for defamation in an ad regardless of who wrote the copy. Therefore, newspapers and broadcast stations take risks when copying defamatory ads or stories from other media.[109] This is true even if the second publication properly attributes the story or indicates "it is only publishing a rumor."[110]

SUMMARY

Publication, one element of the burden of proof for libel plaintiffs, means that defamation is communicated to a third party. Anyone participating in the process of publishing defamation can be liable. A republication of a libel is a new libel.

Fault

A libel plaintiff proving defamation, identification, and publication also must prove that a medium erred in the preparation of a story, or published with *fault*. The U.S. Supreme Court has said that the First Amendment bars plaintiffs from collecting damages for loss of reputation unless they can show that defendants published or broadcast with fault, usually negligence or recklessness. The Court, by providing constitutional protection for defamatory language, revolutionized libel law. Fault is the central issue in nearly 90 percent of libel suits filed against the media, according to one study.[111]

The degree of fault that must be proved depends on who is suing and the subject of the libel. Public officials or public figures have the heavy burden of establishing that defamation was published with knowing falsity or reckless disregard for the truth. The burden of proof for anyone else depends on state law. Most states require that private persons show only media negligence, which is much easier to prove than recklessness. The Supreme Court requires all persons involved in a matter of public concern to prove the falsity of any defamation.

Before the 1964 Supreme Court case *New York Times v. Sullivan,* libel law was common law. Prior to *Times v. Sullivan,* libel law in most states was governed by the rule of **strict liability.** That is, libel plaintiffs could win suits by proving only that someone had published defamatory language that identified them. The defamation was presumed to be false and presumed to have damaged the person's reputation, regardless of how hard a journalist may have tried to be accurate. A defendant in a libel suit could win only by overriding the presumption of falsity through the establishment of a legally recognized defense, such as proof of truth.

---

[108]*See, e.g., Prosser and Keeton on Torts* sec. 113, at 799 (5th ed. 1984); Weaver v. Pryor Jeffersonian, 569 P.2d 967, 3 Media L. Rep. 1425 (Okla. 1977).

[109]An exception, the protection that permits the publication of wire copy, is explained in the negligence section of this chapter.

[110]*Restatement (Second) of Torts* sec. 578 comment a and comment b (1977); *Prosser and Keeton on Torts* sec. 113, at 799 (5th ed. 1984).

[111]Soloski, "The Study and the Libel Plaintiff: Who Sues for Libel?" and Bezanson, "Libel Law and Realities of Litigation: Setting the Record Straight," 71 *Iowa L. Rev.* 215, 218, 229–31 (1985).

However, in *New York Times v. Sullivan,* the U.S. Supreme Court began the process of constitutionalizing libel. The Court said in *Times v. Sullivan* that requiring a defendant in a libel case to prove truth did not adequately protect a robust debate about the conduct of public officials. The Court said falsity was ''inevitable'' in free debate and ''must be protected if the freedoms of expression are to have the breathing space' that they 'need . . . to survive.' ''[112] The Court said the First Amendment right to freely debate the performance of public officials was a fundamental principle of American government. Punishment for the criticism of government officials, inherited from the British in the form of seditious libel, was discredited in the early days of the Republic, according to the Court.

Seditious Libel in the United States   During the formative years of the United States, the country substantially relied on English common law. In England, during the seventeenth and eighteenth centuries, any criticism of government officials—always proclaimed by the officials to be false, scandalous, and malicious—was called seditious libel. The government justified the punishment of seditious libel by arguing that criticism of public officials could provoke violent retaliation by the official or trigger public unrest. Truth was not a defense. In fact, officials believed truth was more damaging than falsehood because true statements were more likely to provoke a violent response. Moreover, in English common law, the members of the public sitting on the jury could only decide whether the accused printed or said the words as charged. The judge decided whether the expression was seditious. A person convicted of seditious libel could be fined, imprisoned, pilloried, and whipped.[113]

In one famous case in the American colonies, a jury rebelled against the common law of seditious libel. The jury found the now-legendary printer John Peter Zenger, publisher of the *New-York Weekly Journal,* not guilty of seditious libel in 1734 even though he had printed criticism of New York governor William Cosby. Cosby's high-handed land deals and manipulation of the courts had made him unpopular. Zenger's lawyer, Andrew Hamilton, conceded that Zenger had published the remarks critical of Cosby, theoretically settling the only issue the jury could legally decide. However, the jury, apparently swayed by Hamilton's arguments for a citizen's right to truthfully criticize public officials, returned a verdict of not guilty.

The Zenger verdict, as welcome as it was to advocates of unfettered political expression, did not change the law. In 1791, at the time the Bill of Rights was adopted, truth was still not a defense and juries were still limited to determining whether the publication had occurred as charged. Both the federal common law and state statutes permitted jail terms and fines for seditious libel.[114]

In addition, just seven years after the adoption of the First Amendment forbidding government abridgment of the freedom of the press, Congress passed laws intended to punish criticism of the Federalists, then in power. The Federalists were afraid that the Republicans would destroy the young American republic by fostering the radical French ideas that had led to the bloody French Revolution. The Federal-

---

[112]New York Times Co. v. Sullivan, 376 U .S. at 271–72, 1 Media L. Rep. at 1534, *quoting* NAACP v. Button, 371 U.S. 415, 433 (1963).
[113]L. Levy, *Emergence of a Free Press* 9 (1985).
[114]*Id.* at 173–219.

ists hoped to stop Republican rhetoric with the adoption of the Alien and Sedition Acts of 1798. The Alien Act allowed the president to deport anyone not born in the United States who was "dangerous to the peace" or suspected of "secret machinations against the government." The Sedition Act prohibited any conspiracy to oppose the government and "any false, scandalous and malicious writing" against the government or government officials. Violators could be punished by fines of up to $5,000 and jail terms for as long as five years.[115]

Although the Sedition Act permitted the defense of truth and gave juries the power to determine whether publications printed sedition, these reforms meant little. According to historian James Morton Smith, the juries were dominated by Federalists. In addition, the judges required the accused to prove the truth "to the marrow"—documenting every word of every statement. Critical opinions that could not be proven true were judged false.

The Federalists prosecuted more than a dozen persons under the Sedition Act, including newspaper editors and writers in Boston, Philadelphia, and Richmond. Congressman Matthew Lyon was fined $1,000 and sentenced to four months in jail after he wrote for the *Vermont Journal* that President Adams was continually grasping for power and possessed "an unbounded thirst for ridiculous pomp, foolish adulation, and selfish avarice."[116] Although the Supreme Court never ruled on the constitutionality of the Alien and Sedition Acts, individual Supreme Court justices sat on courts that prosecuted government critics.

The Republicans argued that the Alien and Sedition Acts violated the First Amendment, but historian Leonard Levy contends the statutes reflected the conventional understanding of the term *freedom of the press* at the time. Levy argues that most politicians in the late eighteenth century believed in freedom of expression as it was defined by famed English legal commentator William Blackstone. Blackstone said liberty of the press only meant freedom from prior restraint on publication and not freedom from punishment for publishing words that were "improper, mischievous, or illegal."[117]

The Republicans, led by Thomas Jefferson, defeated the Federalists in the election of 1800, and the Alien and Sedition Acts were not renewed. Levy argues that prosecutions under the acts helped sensitize Americans to the dangers of punishing criticism of government and government officials. Liberal theorists of the period argued fiercely that freedom of expression was hollow unless false criticism of government was tolerated, and their message seems to have been heard.[118] In 1812, the Supreme Court eliminated the federal common law of seditious libel.[119] In 1836, Senator John C. Calhoun said in a Senate report that *no one* doubted that the Sedition Act was invalid. Indeed, a few years later Congress repaid fines levied under the Sedi-

---

[115]*See generally* J. M. Smith, *Freedom's Fetters* 3–21, 438–42 (1956).

[116]*Id.* at 226, 235, 421–22.

[117]W. Blackstone, *Commentaries on the Laws of England,* London, 1765–69, book 4, 151–52. *See generally* L. Levy, *Emergence of a Free Press* (1985). *But see, e.g.,* J. Smith, *Printers and Press Freedom; The Ideology of Early American Journalism* (1988) (early Americans generally had a libertarian understanding of press freedom incompatible with the idea of seditious libel).

[118]Levy, "Liberty and the First Amendment: 1790–1800," 68 *Am. Hist. Rev.* 29 (1962).

[119]United States v. Hudson & Goodwin, 7 Cranch 32 (1812).

tion Act on the grounds that the act was unconstitutional.[120] State prosecutions for seditious libel became less and less frequent.[121] The courts declared that government could not be libeled, a point already noted in this chapter. Finally, in 1964, in *New York Times v. Sullivan,* the U.S. Supreme Court declared that the Sedition Act of 1798 had been unconstitutional.

Constitutional Protection for Libel about Public Officials

In *New York Times v. Sullivan,* the Supreme Court said the First Amendment protects criticism of government officials even if the remarks are false and defamatory. The Court said public officials cannot successfully sue for libel unless they establish that defamation has been published with knowing falsity or reckless disregard for the truth. This burden of proof for public officials has come to be known as *New York Times* **actual malice.** The new constitutional protection for criticism of public officials announced in *New York Times v. Sullivan* superseded, in part, the libel laws of the 50 states.

Protecting a Robust Debate

The case that provided the media with constitutional protection for the criticism of public officials was a product of the civil rights struggle in the South in the early 1960s. A Montgomery, Alabama, police official sued the *New York Times* for a March 19, 1960, advertisement purchased by a committee of civil rights activists including the well-respected A. Philip Randolph. The full-page ad, titled "Heed Their Rising Voices," said that "thousands of Southern Negro students are engaged in widespread non-violent demonstrations" affirming "the right to live in human dignity." The efforts were being met, the ad continued, "by an unprecedented wave of terror." The ad purported to document the "wave of terror" and sought support for the civil rights movement in the South and its major leader, Dr. Martin Luther King, Jr.[122]

The ad contained several false statements. Nine student leaders were not expelled for singing at the state capital as stated in the ad. They were expelled for demanding service at a Montgomery courthouse lunch counter. The dining hall had not been padlocked, and there was no attempt "to starve" students into "submission," as the ad had claimed. The only students barred were those without the required tickets. The police, although deployed in large numbers, had not "ringed" the Alabama State College campus. King had been arrested four times instead of seven, as the ad had declared. There was conflicting evidence about whether King had been assaulted. The *New York Times* ad staff could have checked the accuracy of the ad against the *Times*'s news stories of the same events but had not.

The Montgomery commissioner in charge of police, L. B. Sullivan, demanded that the *Times* publish a retraction. The paper refused and asked Sullivan why he believed the ad referred to him. Sullivan did not respond but joined three other Montgomery officials and Alabama Governor John Patterson in suing the *Times* for $3 million. At the trial, Sullivan argued that although he was not named in the ad, the charges of police abuse defamed him because he supervised the police department.

[120]*See* New York Times Co. v. Sullivan, 376 U.S. at 276, 1 Media L. Rep. at 1536.
[121]*See* J. M. Smith, *Freedom's Fetters* 432 n.32 (1956).
[122]376 U.S. at 256–58, 1 Media L. Rep. at 1528–30.

The Alabama judge trying the case, relying on the rule of strict liability, instructed the jury that the ad was libelous on its face and that damage to reputation need not be proved. The judge told the jury that it only had to decide that the statements were published in the *Times* and were "of and concerning" Sullivan. The jury awarded Sullivan $500,000, the largest libel judgment in Alabama history at that time.[123] The judgment was upheld by the Supreme Court of Alabama. However, the U.S. Supreme Court voted unanimously to reverse the Alabama court.

Justice William J. Brennan, Jr., writing for the Supreme Court, said that Alabama's libel law was unconstitutional because it did not adequately safeguard freedom of speech and press as required by the First and the Fourteenth Amendments. Brennan said that at issue was

> a profound national commitment to the principle that debate on public issues should be uninhibited, robust, and wide-open, and that it may well include vehement, caustic and sometimes unpleasantly sharp attacks on government and public officials.[124]

Brennan said that a civil libel suit brought by a public official such as Sullivan created the same kind of dangers to First Amendment freedoms as a seditious libel prosecution initiated by a government. He said, "the court of history" had found that the Sedition Act of 1798, which had authorized punishment for criticism of government and public officials, was inconsistent with the First Amendment. He argued that the fear of large damage awards under civil libel laws such as the one in Alabama created greater "hazards to protected freedoms" than the criminal penalties of seditious libel laws. Brennan said First Amendment freedoms could not survive if a "pall of fear and timidity" was imposed upon those who otherwise offer public criticism.[125]

Brennan added that a privilege to criticize official conduct was "appropriately analogous" to protection accorded a public official sued for libel by a private citizen. Public officials are granted some immunity from libel suits so that they are not inhibited from "fearless, vigorous, and effective administration." The same kind of consideration should support "the privilege for the citizen-critic," Brennan argued. "It is as much his duty to criticize as it is the official's duty to administer."

Brennan rejected Sullivan's argument that constitutional guarantees did not protect the *Times* because the defamation had occurred in an advertisement. Sullivan had cited the Supreme Court's 1942 decision *Valentine v. Chrestensen,* in which the Court denied constitutional protection to a handbill it had called "purely commercial advertising."[126] In *Times v. Sullivan,* however, Brennan argued that the ad in the *Times* was not purely commercial speech. The ad "communicated information, expressed opinion, recited grievances and sought financial support" on behalf of a cause "of the highest public concern." Brennan said the fact that the *Times* was paid for the ad was as immaterial as the fact that books and newspapers are sold. He added:

---

[123]Lewis, "Annals of Law: The Sullivan Case," *The New Yorker,* Nov. 5, 1984, at 52, 55.
[124]376 U.S. at 270, 1 Media L. Rep. at 1533–34.
[125]*Id.* at 278, 1 Media L. Rep. at 1537.
[126]*See* 316 U.S. 52 (1942).

Any other conclusion would discourage newspapers from carrying "editorial advertisements" of this type, and so might shut off an important outlet for the promulgation of information and ideas by persons who do not themselves have access to publishing facilities.[127]

Brennan also rejected the argument that the falsity of some of the statements in the *Times* ad destroyed any legal protection the paper might have had. He said constitutional protection did not depend on the "truth, popularity, or social utility" of the ideas and beliefs expressed. The national commitment to the free expression of political beliefs presumed exaggeration and error. Indeed, truth for one person could be error for another, Brennan said.

Brennan said that if critics of public officials could be penalized for honest mistakes, they would tend to avoid controversy:

> A rule compelling the critic of official conduct to guarantee the truth of all of his factual assertions—and to do so on pain of libel judgments virtually unlimited in amount—leads to a comparable "self-censorship."[128]

Brennan said potential critics of government may be "chilled" from even speaking the truth for fear of the expense and uncertainty of a libel trial.

Because a requirement that defendants prove the truth of their remarks "dampens the vigor and limits the variety of public debate," the Supreme Court established a new constitutional rule to provide better protection for the criticism of public officials. No longer would courts, such as those in Alabama, be able to presume the falsity of defamation and require the defendant to prove the truth of the remarks to successfully defend a libel suit. Instead, Brennan said, public officials could recover damages for defamation relating to their official conduct only if they could prove the statement was made with "actual malice." To prove *New York Times* actual malice an official would have to establish that a defendant published the statement either (1) knowing it was false, or (2) exercising reckless disregard for the truth.

In *Times v. Sullivan,* the Court said the ad in the *Times* had not been published with actual malice. Brennan said a statement by a *Times* employee that he thought the advertisement was "substantially correct" was reasonable. The Court was satisfied with the *Times'*s reliance on the good reputation of those listed as sponsors of the ad, particularly the chair of the "committee" submitting the ad, well-known civil rights advocate A. Philip Randolph. The Court said the fact that stories contradicting the ad existed in the *Times'*s own files did not mean that employees responsible for the ad knew it was false.[129] The *Times'*s failure to check the ad against the news stories might be evidence of negligence, but it did not demonstrate recklessness, the Court said. Neither was the *Times'*s failure to retract the errors in the ad evidence of actual malice. The *Times* had asked Sullivan why he believed the ad referred to him, but he did not reply.

Although the Supreme Court ruled the *New York Times* should not be held liable

---

[127]376 U.S. at 266, 1 Media L. Rep. at 1532.
[128]*Id.* at 279, 1 Media L. Rep. at 1537.
[129]*Id.* at 260–61, 285–88, 1 Media L. Rep. at 1529–30, 1540–41.

for the civil rights ad, the *Sullivan* opinion left many unanswered questions about the new constitutional protection for libel. For example, who would be considered a public official? What kind of conduct constituted *New York Times* actual malice? Would anyone besides public officials have to prove *New York Times* actual malice?

Defining Public Officials The *Sullivan* Court said that public officials would have to prove actual malice in order to collect damages for defamation relating to their official conduct, but the Court did not define *public official* or *official conduct*. The Court said only that Sullivan was a public official because he was an elected city commissioner, and the allegations in the ad related to his conduct as the commissioner in charge of the police department.[130]

In the nearly three decades since *Sullivan,* courts have substantially agreed that anyone elected to a public office would be a "public official" required to prove *New York Times* actual malice. Among those fitting the category are U.S. senators, federal and state legislators, mayors, town council members, school board members, and elected judges.[131]

In addition, the courts have said that nonelected government employees responsible for public policy are *public officials.* The Supreme Court, shortly after *Times v. Sullivan,* declared that a former supervisor of a county-owned ski resort was a public official. In *Rosenblatt v. Baer,* the Court said the decision in *Times v. Sullivan* was motivated by "a strong interest in debate" about public issues and the people in position to significantly influence the resolution of those issues. Therefore, the term *public official* applied to government employees "who have, or appear to the public to have, substantial responsibility for or control over the conduct of governmental affairs."[132]

Lower courts interpreting the Supreme Court's language have looked for persons directly responsible for formulating public policy, supervising public funds, or maintaining the public health and welfare. Other important criteria are the amount of direct contact with the public and the degree to which an official can make decisions in the name of the government. Lower courts have designated as public officials a school superintendent, a town tax assessor, an administrator of a county motor pool, a county medical examiner, a director of financial aid at a state college, the director of an antipoverty agency, and various military officers. Among those not considered to be public officials because of their lack of control over public policy are paid consultants, police informants, and the director of a university print shop.[133] The courts' criteria indicate that the head of a city public works department would be considered a public official because of his or her responsibility for public policy, public safety, and public funds. An auditor could be. An auditor is usually not responsible for public policy, but plays a key role in the government's use of public funds. A receptionist or a janitor in the same department probably would not be. They exercise little, if any, control over public policy and do not, in their government jobs, play an important role in the debate of public issues.

---

[130]*Id*. at 283 n. 23, 1 Media L. Rep. at 1539 n. 23.
[131]B. Sanford, *Libel and Privacy* para. 7.2.3.1, at 208–210 (1987 Supp.).
[132]Rosenblatt v. Baer, 383 U.S. 75, 85, 1 Media L. Rep. 1558, 1561–62 (1966).
[133]*See* B. Sanford, *Libel and Privacy* para. 7.2.2.2, at 205–207 (1987 Supp.).

Law enforcement personnel, regardless of rank, are ordinarily considered public officials. The courts have said that a police chief, a deputy sheriff, and a federal drug enforcement agent were public officials. Frequently, policemen without rank, "the cops on the beat," are categorized as public officials, too. The courts are conscious of the frequent contact patrolmen have with the public, their authority, and their ability to exercise force. That force "can result in significant deprivation of constitutional rights and personal freedoms, not to mention bodily injury and financial loss."[134]

Public officials are required to prove *New York Times* actual malice only for defamatory statements about their official conduct and not for statements about their private lives. However, the Supreme Court has interpreted official conduct broadly. In *Garrison v. Louisiana,* the Court said that an assertion that judges were lazy, "vacation-minded," and sympathetic to criminals was a comment about their official conduct. The Court unanimously reversed the Louisiana Supreme Court's determination in a criminal libel case that Jim Garrison, the district attorney for New Orleans Parish, had attacked the judges' personal integrity rather than their official conduct. Justice Brennan, writing for the U.S. Supreme Court, said the *New York Times* rule protected any discussion "which might touch on an official's fitness for office." He said few personal attributes were more germane "than dishonesty, malfeasance, or improper motivation."[135]

A few years later the Court said that any accusation that a public official had committed a crime was related to the person's fitness for office. The Court ruled that Leonard Damron, the mayor of Crystal River, Florida, had to prove *New York Times* actual malice in order to win a suit he filed against the Ocala Star-Banner Company. The *Star-Banner* had falsely reported that Damron had been charged with perjury.[136] The courts also have routinely held that discussions of the official conduct of former public officials is protected under the *Times v. Sullivan* rule.[137]

SUMMARY

The U.S. Supreme Court, in *New York Times v. Sullivan,* said for the first time that the First Amendment provides protection for the publication of false statements damaging reputation. The Court said that public officials suing the media for statements about their official conduct must prove defamation was published with knowing falsehood or reckless disregard for the truth. The Court said that such a heavy burden of proof on public officials was necessary to protect a robust debate on important public issues. *Times v. Sullivan* eliminated state common law libel that held that officials could win libel suits by showing only that the media had disseminated defamatory information about them.

The Supreme Court's commitment to the robust criticism of public officials

---

[134]Gray v. Udevitz, 656 F.2d 588, 591, 7 Media L. Rep. 1872, 1875 (10th Cir. 1981).

[135]Garrison v. Louisiana, 379 U.S. 64, 77, 1 Media L. Rep. 1548, 1553 (1964).

[136]Ocala Star-Banner Co. v. Damron, 401 U.S. 295, 1 Media L. Rep. 1624 (1971), relying upon language in Monitor Patriot v. Roy, 401 U.S. 265, 277, 1 Media L. Rep. 1619, 1624 (1971).

[137]*E.g.,* Gray v. Udevitz, 656 F.2d 588, 7 Media L. Rep. 1872 (10th Cir. 1981).

underscored the Court's rejection of seditious libel. The meaning of the First Amendment, as interpreted by the Court in the twentieth century, is not limited to a ban on prior restraints. The Court has also said that, after the Alien and Sedition Acts of 1798, the country cannot tolerate the punishment of even false criticism of public officials without a showing of *New York Times* actual malice.

Courts after *Times v. Sullivan* have defined public officials to include anyone elected to public office as well as government employees responsible for policy making or for public funds, health, or safety.

Defining Public Figures   In 1967, only three years after the landmark *New York Times v. Sullivan* case, the U.S. Supreme Court said public figures, as well as public officials, must prove *New York Times* actual malice. But it took the Court another seven years to settle on the definition of *public figure* used today.

In 1967, in *Curtis Publishing Co. v. Butts* and *Associated Press v. Walker,* a majority of the Court agreed that Wally Butts and retired Army general Edwin Walker were public figures. Butts was nationally known as athletic director and former football coach of the University of Georgia; Walker had publicly argued against federal enforcement of school integration in the South. Seven justices said public figures were persons who engaged in activities that commanded public interest and who could counter defamatory remarks through their access to the media. At least four justices agreed that Butts may have been a public figure by his "position alone." The same four said that Walker had purposefully thrust himself into the "vortex" of an important public controversy.[138]

In 1971, the *Rosenbloom v. Metromedia,* a plurality of only three justices said that the constitutional protection of *Times v. Sullivan* extended to anyone involved in a matter of public concern, regardless of whether they were famous or unknown. Justices Brennan, Burger, and Blackmun said that George Rosenbloom, arrested in a Philadelphia police campaign against pornography, had to prove *New York Times* actual malice. Rosenbloom had sued Philadelphia radio station WIP, claiming that the station had stated in its news stories as fact that he distributed obscene books and magazines. Later, a judge ruled that the publications confiscated by police were not legally obscene.[139] A divided Supreme Court said the burden of proof that applied to public officials and public figures also applied to private persons involved in an event of public interest.

However, in 1974, the Court rejected the *Rosenbloom* standard. In *Gertz v. Welch,* the Court said that ordinarily only public officials and people who become involved in matters of public interest by their own choosing would have to prove *New York Times* actual malice. The Court refined the public figure criteria it had applied in *Butts* and *Walker.*

Criteria for Public Figures   In *Gertz v. Welch,* the Supreme Court said that public figures are either persons of widespread fame or notoriety or people who have in-

---

[138]388 U.S. 130, 1 Media L. Rep. 1568 (1967).
[139]403 U.S. 29, 1 Media L. Rep. 1597 (1971).

jected themselves into the debate about a controversial public issue for the purpose of affecting the outcome.

The Supreme Court said that Elmer Gertz, a prominent Chicago civil rights attorney, was not a public figure. Gertz had been hired by the parents of a boy killed by a Chicago policeman, Richard Nuccio. Although Nuccio had been convicted of second-degree murder, the parents filed a civil suit for damages. Gertz had nothing to do with the murder trial, but *American Opinion,* a publication reflecting the views of the John Birch Society, portrayed him as the architect of a "frame-up" of Nuccio. The magazine pictured Gertz as part of a nationwide conspiracy to discredit local law enforcement agencies and replace them with a national police force that would support a Communist dictatorship. Gertz was inaccurately called a Leninist, a Communist-fronter, and an official of the Marxist League for Industrial Democracy. *American Opinion* also said that Gertz had been an officer of the National Lawyers Guild, which it described as a Communist organization. The magazine falsely reported that the police had a file on Gertz that took "a big Irish cop to lift."[140]

Both the trial court and the appeals court ruled that Gertz must prove *New York Times* actual malice because the issue of police effectiveness is a matter of public interest. The Supreme Court reversed those decisions 5–4. Justice Lewis F. Powell, Jr., writing the Court's opinion, said tension necessarily exists "between the need for a vigorous and uninhibited press" and the legitimate interest in protecting reputation. Powell said the Court, in order to ensure that the freedoms of speech and press have adequate breathing space, had extended the constitutional protection for libel announced in *New York Times v. Sullivan* to defamatory falsehoods about public figures, those persons who had played major roles in the resolution of public issues. However, Powell said, when private persons are defamed during discussions of public issues, they should receive more protection of their reputations.

Powell said that public figures, like public officials, are different from private individuals because (1) they invite attention and comment and (2) they ordinarily have access to "channels of effective communication" so that they can counteract false statements about them. Powell said that public figures, like public officials, seek their status by playing an influential role in the affairs of society. They voluntarily expose themselves to an increased risk of public scrutiny and defamatory falsehoods. In addition, Powell said, public persons, because of their access to media, can minimize damage to their reputations. They can "contradict the lie or correct the error." A private person, on the other hand, relinquishes

> no part of his interest in the protection of his own good name, and consequently he
> has a more compelling call on the courts for redress of injury inflicted by defamatory
> falsehood.[141]

Powell said private persons are also more vulnerable to injury. Private persons normally have few opportunities to counter false statements and therefore need greater protection from the law.

---

[140]Gertz v. Robert Welch, Inc., 418 U.S. 323, 325, 1 Media L. Rep. 1633, 1634 (1974).
[141]*Id.* at 345, 1 Media L. Rep. at 1642.

Powell identified two principal kinds of public figures, since labeled (1) "all-purpose" and (2) "limited," or "vortex," public figures. All-purpose public figures "occupy positions of such pervasive power and influence that they are deemed public figures for all purposes." Powell said that "more commonly, those classed as public figures have thrust themselves to the forefront of particular public controversies in order to influence the resolution of the issues involved."[142] Powell implied that individuals who voluntarily inject themselves into a public controversy would have to prove *New York Times* actual malice only for defamatory falsehoods related to that controversy, thus the labels of "limited" and "vortex" public figures.

Powell said that Gertz was neither an all-purpose nor vortex public figure. Although Gertz had published several books and articles on legal subjects and had served as an official in several civic and professional associations, none of the jurors at the libel trial said they had heard of him. Powell said that participation in community and professional affairs should not make a person a public personality "for all aspects of his life" unless there is "clear evidence of general fame or notoriety in the community, and pervasive involvement in the affairs of society."[143]

If Gertz did not have widespread fame and notoriety, neither had he "thrust himself into the vortex" of the public issue raised by *American Opinion* or "engage[d] the public's attention in an attempt to influence" the outcome of that issue. The Court said Gertz's participation in the controversy surrounding Nuccio was limited to representing a private client. He had never discussed either the criminal or the civil litigation with the press. The Court implied that a person did not become a public figure simply by representing a client in a controversial case.

The Supreme Court, after determining that Gertz was a private person who did not have to show actual malice, sent the case back to the trial court. In 1983, more than 14 years after Gertz sued, he was awarded damages, interest on the damages, and court fees—a total of $482,000.[144]

The *Gertz* case, like *Times v. Sullivan,* raised a host of new questions. Justice Powell used several terms—*fame, notoriety, pervasive power, influence, voluntarily thrust,* and *public controversies*—that he did not define. Shortly after *Gertz,* one federal court judge said the Supreme Court's definitions made the process of trying to determine who was, and who was not, a public figure "much like trying to nail a jellyfish to the wall."[145] To be sure, lower courts have struggled with the Supreme Court's definitions.

All-Purpose Public Figures   One of Powell's two categories of public figures in *Gertz* included people with special prominence in society—those who exercise general power or influence and those who occupy a position of continuing news value. Such *all-purpose* public figures have achieved widespread fame or notoriety and must prove *New York Times* actual malice in any defamation suit they file. They must

---

[142]*Id.*

[143]*Id.* at 352, 1 Media L. Rep. at 1643–44.

[144]Lewis, "Annals of Law: The Sullivan Case," *The New Yorker,* Nov. 5, 1984, at 52, 79.

[145]Rosanova v. Playboy Enterprises, Inc., 411 F. Supp. 440, 443 (1976), *aff'd,* 580 F.2d 859, 4 Media L. Rep. 1550 (5th Cir. 1978).

prove knowing falsehood or reckless disregard for the truth for stories about their private lives as well as their public activities.

One federal appeals court said that the all-purpose public figure

> is a well-known "celebrity," his name a "household word." The public recognizes him and follows his words and deeds, either because it regards his ideas, conduct, or judgment as worthy of its attention or because he actively pursues that consideration.[146]

Courts have had limited opportunities to categorize nationally known persons as all-purpose public figures. A federal appeals court said a famous entertainer, Johnny Carson, was an all-purpose public figure.[147] Other federal courts put a prominent political writer, William F. Buckley, Jr.,[148] and a publicly owned insurance company with assets of a billion dollars into the all-purpose public figure category.[149] Actress Carol Burnett was presumed to be a public figure without explanation in her suit against the *National Enquirer*.[150] Presumably, former presidents Richard Nixon, Gerald Ford, Jimmy Carter, and Ronald Reagan would be all-purpose public figures for defamation related to their activities after they left office. Actress and activist Jane Fonda also probably has sufficient fame and notoriety that she would be considered an all-purpose public figure.

The U.S. Supreme Court said that Mary Alice Firestone was not an all-purpose public figure even though she was a prominent member of Palm Beach society and former wife of Firestone tire heir Russell Firestone. Mrs. Firestone sued *Time* magazine after a "Milestones" item incorrectly reported that Russell Firestone had won a divorce on the grounds "of extreme cruelty and adultery." Although cruelty and adultery were issues in the divorce trial, the trial court did not say they were the reasons the divorce was granted.

The Supreme Court categorized Mrs. Firestone as a private person for the purpose of her suit even though she was "prominent among the 400' of Palm Beach Society" and an "active" member of the "sporting set." She subscribed to a clipping service to keep track of the times she was mentioned in the newspapers. Her marital difficulties were "well known" and her suit for divorce became a "veritable *cause célèbre* in social circles across the country."[151] However, the Supreme Court said that Mrs. Firestone "did not assume any role of especial prominence in the affairs of society, other than perhaps Palm Beach society."[152]

Although the courts have recognized only a few all-purpose public figures at the national level, judges also have declared that people with fame or notoriety at local and regional levels are public figures. When the Supreme Court decided that Elmer Gertz was not a public figure, Justice Powell focused his evaluation on Gertz's lack

[146]Waldbaum v. Fairchild Publications, Inc., 627 F.2d 1287, 1294, 5 Media L. Rep. 2629, 2633 (D.C. Cir.), *cert. denied,* 449 U.S. 898 (1980).
[147]Carson v. Allied News Co., 529 F.2d 206, 5 Media L. Rep. 2646 (7th Cir. 1976).
[148]Buckley v. Littell, 539 F.2d 882, 1 Media L. Rep. 1762 (2d Cir. 1976), *cert. denied,* 429 U.S. 1062 (1977).
[149]Reliance Insurance Co. v. Barron's, 442 F. Supp. 1341, 3 Media L. Rep. 1033 (S.D.N.Y. 1977).
[150]Burnett v. National Enquirer, Inc., 144 Cal. App.3d 991, 9 Media L. Rep. 1921 (Cal. Ct. App. 1983).
[151]Firestone v. Time, Inc., 271 So.2d 745, 751 (1972).
[152]Time, Inc. v. Firestone, 424 U.S. 448, 453, 1 Media L. Rep. 1665, 1667 (1976).

of fame and notoriety *in the community* rather than a lack of fame nationwide.[153] Conversely, the Kansas Supreme Court said that Myron Steere's activities in Franklin County, Kansas, gave him sufficient fame and notoriety to be an all-purpose public figure. Steere, who had practiced law in the area for 32 years, sued the Associated Press for saying in 1975 that he was being censured by the State Board of Law Examiners for his defense of a woman accused of murdering her husband. Steere was a former county attorney and had once served as a special counsel to the county commissioners during a controversial construction project. The court said he "was a prominent participant in numerous social activities" and served as an officer and representative for many professional, fraternal, and social activities.[154]

Generalizations about all-purpose public figures are risky. There are few cases, and courts hesitate to say that individual plaintiffs have to prove *New York Times* actual malice for every libel suit they file.

Limited, or Vortex, Public Figures   Justice Powell's second category of public figures in *Gertz* included people who have injected themselves into a debate about a public controversy for the purpose of affecting the outcome. Such people are *limited* public figures because they have to prove *New York Times* actual malice only for defamation directly connected to their voluntary activity. For libel suits affecting any other part of their lives, they are private persons. The Supreme Court said Elmer Gertz was a private person because he had not actively thrust himself into any issue related to the prosecution of the policeman Richard Nuccio. Gertz had not tried to influence public opinion as part of a Communist plot to discredit the police.

In cases after *Gertz,* the Supreme Court has made it clear that persons will be classified as limited, or vortex, public figures only if

1. the alleged defamation involves a public controversy,
2. the person suing for libel has voluntarily participated in the discussion of that controversy, and
3. the person suing for libel has tried to affect the outcome of the controversy.

All three criteria must be met before a person will be considered a limited public figure, although court discussions of the last two are frequently merged. In addition, lower courts sometimes consider other factors discussed by the Supreme Court in *Gertz,* including access to media for the purpose of rebutting a defamatory remark.

In the case of the first criterion for a limited public figure, that the defamation must involve a public controversy, the Court has not explained what it means by *public controversy.* The Court has only indicated that public controversy should be understood narrowly. In *Time v. Firestone,* the Court said the term did not refer to all controversies that attracted the public's interest. When the Court declared that Mrs. Firestone was not a public figure, it asserted that a divorce proceeding was

---

[153]Gertz v. Robert Welch, Inc., 418 U.S. at 352, 1 Media L. Rep. at 1644.
[154]Steere v. Cupp, 602 P.2d 1267, 5 Media L. Rep. 2046 (1979).

not the sort of "public controversy" referred to in *Gertz,* even though the marital difficulties of extremely wealthy individuals may be of interest to some portion of the reading public.[155]

A better definition of *public controversy* has been used by the U.S. Court of Appeals for the D.C. Circuit. In *Waldbaum v. Fairchild Publications,* the D.C. Circuit said that a public controversy had to be a "real dispute" over a specific issue affecting a segment of the general public. The D.C. Circuit said the outcome of a *public controversy* has "foreseeable and substantial ramifications" for those not directly participating in the debate. News coverage is an indication of a *public controversy,* but newsworthiness itself is not a sufficient criterion, the court said.[156]

The D.C. Circuit said Eric Waldbaum, in his suit against a trade publication called *Supermarket News,* was a public figure because he injected himself into controversy as the president of an innovative consumer cooperative. Greenbelt Consumer Services, the second of its kind in the country, owned retail supermarkets, furniture and gift outlets, and service stations. Waldbaum sued *Supermarket News* for a five-sentence item that announced his ouster as Greenbelt president. The article said that the co-op had been "losing money" and "retrenching" with Waldbaum in charge.

The D.C. Circuit said Waldbaum was a limited public figure because he set policies and standards in the supermarket industry. The court said Waldbaum thrust himself into public controversies over unit pricing and open dating in supermarkets by battling traditional industry practices. He also invited the public and press to meetings about topics ranging from "supermarket practices to energy legislation and fuel allocation."[157] The court said Waldbaum's activities generated considerable comment from trade journals and newspapers such as the *Washington Post.* His policies were debated within the supermarket industry and by retailers and consumers in the Washington, D.C., area.

Public controversies identified by the courts, in addition to supermarket business practices, include the value of protein supplements in the human diet[158] and alleged recruiting violations in a college basketball program.[159] A court said the infamous rape trial of the black youths known nationally as the "Scottsboro Boys" focused on the controversy of fair justice for blacks in the court system.[160] The courts have also considered controversial a campaign to recall city council members,[161] the firing of an administrator of a large public hospital,[162] and the solicitation of funds by a cancer research foundation that did not meet the standards of the Better Business Bureau.[163]

Issues that have not been considered public controversies by the courts include a

---

[155]424 U.S. at 454, 1 Media L. Rep. at 1667.

[156]627 F.2d at 1292, 5 Media L. Rep. at 2635–36.

[157]*Id.* at 1290, 5 Media L. Rep. at 2630. *See also id.* at 1298–1300, 5 Media L. Rep. at 2637–38.

[158]Hoffman v. Washington Post Co., 433 F. Supp. 600, 3 Media L. Rep. 1143 (D.D.C. 1977).

[159]Barry v. Time, Inc., 584 F. Supp. 1110, 10 Media L. Rep. 1809 (N.D. Cal. 1984).

[160]Street v. NBC, 645 F.2d 1227, 7 Media L. Rep. 1001 (6th Cir.), *cert. granted,* 454 U.S. 815, *cert. dismissed,* 454 U.S. 1095 (1981).

[161]Weingarten v. Block, 102 Cal. App.2d 129, 5 Media L. Rep. 2585, *cert. denied,* 449 U.S. 899 (1980).

[162]Gadd v. News-Press Publishing, 10 Media L. Rep. 2362 (Fla. Cir. Ct. 1984).

[163]National Found. for Cancer Research v. Council of Better Business Bureaus, 705 F.2d 98, 9 Media L. Rep. 1915 (4th Cir.), *cert. denied,* 464 U.S. 830 (1983).

fight among company stockholders that would have no impact on the general public[164] and the demonstration of an air-powered automobile. A court said the car may be of some interest to the public but had not been part of a dispute.[165]

Once the courts determine that a story is about a public controversy, they must determine the nature and purpose of a person's participation in that controversy. Five years after *Gertz,* the Supreme Court said that limited public figures must thrust themselves into controversies with the intent of affecting the outcomes. Public figures must initiate their own participation in the debate over a public controversy. It is not enough for someone to become involuntarily involved in a controversy or to do something controversial, such as using government funds for questionable research or committing a crime. Public figures must also make an effort to affect the resolution of the controversy.

In *Hutchinson v. Proxmire,* a suit discussed in Chapter 1, the Supreme Court said the fact that a research scientist received substantial federal funds did not make him a public figure. Neither did the scientist's publication of research findings in professional journals. The scientist, Dr. Ronald Hutchinson, sued Senator William Proxmire for criticizing the half-million dollars spent by three government agencies on Hutchinson's study of monkeys. Proxmire gave one of his Golden Fleece awards for wasteful government spending to the National Science Foundation, the Office of Naval Research, and the National Aeronautics and Space Administration for sponsoring Hutchinson's research. Hutchinson was trying to help federal agencies resolve problems faced by humans confined in close quarters in space and under the ocean. He was looking for visible ways to determine aggressive tendencies in animals, such as the clenching of jaws. Senator Proxmire ridiculed the research on the U.S. Senate floor, in a newsletter to constituents, and in comments made on a nationally televised talk show. Proxmire said that Hutchinson "has made a fortune from his monkeys and in the process made a monkey out of the American taxpayer." Hutchinson contended the comments had damaged both his reputation among his professional colleagues and his ability to obtain research grants.

The Supreme Court, in an opinion written by Chief Justice Burger, said that simply being the recipient of public money does not make a person a public figure. If such were the case, Burger said, "everyone who received or benefited from the myriad public grants for research could be classified as a public figure—a conclusion that our previous opinions have rejected." Burger said that Hutchinson had not thrust himself or his views into a public controversy for the purpose of influencing others. He had become involved in a controversy created by Senator Proxmire. Burger said that Hutchinson had never assumed a role of prominence in the broad question of how public money should be spent: "Neither his applications for federal grants nor his publications in professional journals can be said to have invited that degree of public attention and comment . . . essential to meet the public figure level."[166] In addition, Burger noted that Hutchinson had not enjoyed the regular access to the media necessary for a public figure. He was only offered access after Proxmire directed attention to him.

---

[164]Denny v. Mertz, 318 N.W.2d 141, 8 Media L. Rep. 1369 (Wis. 1982).
[165]Re v. Gannett, 480 A.2d 662, 10 Media L. Rep. 2267 (Del. Super. Ct. 1984).
[166]443 U.S. 111, 135, 5 Media L. Rep. 1279, 1290 (1979).

If receiving public funding does not make a person a public figure, neither does involvement in a criminal proceeding. In *Wolston v. Reader's Digest,* the Court said that a man who refused to testify before a federal grand jury investigating Soviet spy activities was not a public figure, even though he received substantial media attention. Ilya Wolston, said to be a Russian spy in a book published by *Reader's Digest,* had been cited for contempt of court in 1958 for his failure to testify. Wolston sued both *Reader's Digest* and John Barron, the author of the book published in 1974, *KGB, The Secret Work of Soviet Agents.* Wolston said he had never been a Soviet spy nor had he been convicted of espionage.

The Court said Wolston had not thrust himself into the forefront of the controversy over Soviet espionage in the United States. Justice William Rehnquist, writing for six of the justices, said that Wolston was "dragged unwillingly" into the spotlight. Wolston never discussed the espionage investigation with the press, Rehnquist said, and limited his involvement to what was necessary to defend himself in court. Rehnquist said the fact that Wolston decided not to appear before the grand jury, knowing that his action might attract publicity, did not make him a public figure.[167]

Neither had Wolston, according to Rehnquist, tried to influence public opinion. He did not "in any way seek to arouse public sentiment in his favor and against the investigation."

Rehnquist acknowledged that Wolston's activities were newsworthy but said that media attention alone did not determine who would be classified as a public figure: "A private individual is not automatically transformed into a public figure just by becoming involved in or associated with a matter that attracts public attention." Rehnquist said criminals did not automatically become public figures on matters related to their convictions.[168]

The combination of *Hutchinson* and *Wolston* severely limited the possibility that private persons could involuntarily become public figures. In the Supreme Court's 1974 *Gertz* opinion, Justice Powell said that someone could become a public figure through no purposeful action on his or her part but that such instances "must be exceedingly rare."[169] Indeed, the number of occasions in recent years that lower courts have determined that a plaintiff was an involuntary public figure have been "exceedingly rare." Although there have been a few exceptions, lower courts generally do not recognize involuntary public figures, and some commentators question the concept's survival.[170]

Instead, the courts almost always find that people who do not seek public attention or controversy are not public figures, even though they may be controversial themselves. For example, a California court said that a high school teacher who became the focus of a book-banning controversy did not attain public figure status. The court said there was no evidence that Virginia Franklin intentionally triggered a controversy when she told students to read a book of underground writings of the 1960s.

---

[167]443 U.S. 157, 167, 5 Media L. Rep. 1273, 1277 (1979).

[168]*Id.* at 167–68, 5 Media L. Rep. at 1278.

[169]Gertz v. Robert Welch, Inc., 418 U.S. at 345, 1 Media L. Rep. at 1642.

[170]*E.g.,* R. Smolla, *Law of Defamation* para. 2–14[1][a], at 2–43 (1989); McCrory, Bernius, Jones, & Grygiel, "Constitutional Privilege in Libel Law" in J. Goodale, ed., 1 *Communications Law 1989* at 577–79. *But see, e.g.,* Dameron v. Washington Magazine, Inc., 779 F.2d 736, 12 Media L. Rep. 1508 (D.C. Cir. 1985).

The court said Franklin did not initiate media contact. She only participated in the controversy to the extent required by her job.[171] Similarly, a federal appeals court said a political campaign aide for successful senatorial candidate Orrin Hatch had not become a public figure. A Hatch opponent suggested that the aide, W. Andrew Lawrence, had once been a "bag man" for former vice president Spiro Agnew. Lawrence sued, contending that *bag man* implied illegal activity. The court said Lawrence had not thrust himself into prominence in his role as a campaign aide. He specialized in administration and made no speeches or media appearances.[172]

Business people do not ordinarily become public figures simply because their business practices or products are criticized, even if they respond to the charges.[173] Neither will they usually be considered to have injected themselves into controversial public issues solely by standard advertising and public relations practices.[174] However, businesses or business people who initiate aggressive advertising or public relations campaigns related to controversial issues may become public figures. A federal appeals court categorized Greenbelt co-op executive Eric Waldbaum as a public figure because he promoted precedent-breaking business policies vigorously. Waldbaum knew how to use the news media and held press conferences to discuss Greenbelt's policies and operations. He used a monthly newspaper, *Co-op Consumer,* for an aggressive consumer education campaign. In the words of the trial judge, Waldbaum was "an activist, projecting his own image and that of the cooperative."[175]

Courts regularly conclude that political candidates are public figures if they sue for defamatory comments made about their candidacies. The Supreme Court has said that criticism about political candidates must be accorded as much constitutional protection as criticism about officeholders. In *Monitor Patriot v. Roy,* a losing candidate for a New Hampshire seat in the U.S. Senate sued after being called a former small-time bootlegger in a syndicated political column. The Court said that the candidate, Alphonse Roy, had to prove *New York Times* actual malice. Justice Potter Stewart, writing for the majority, said the principal activity of a political candidate is to put before the voters "every conceivable aspect of his public and private life that he thinks may lead the electorate to gain a good impression of him."[176] The Court said that a candidate's integrity or qualities as a father or husband may become matters of public concern.

The courts usually decide that people who voluntarily try to change the minds of others about public issues are limited public figures. Among persons the courts have determined to be public figures for trying to affect the outcome of public controversies were an outspoken foe of fluoridating water[177] and a person circulating a petition and purchasing advertising to oppose county land acquisition.[178] Also designated a

---

[171]Franklin v. Lodge 1108, 97 Cal. App.3d 915, 5 Media L. Rep. 1977 (Cal. Ct. App. 1979).

[172]Lawrence v. Moss, 639 F.2d 635, 6 Media L. Rep. 2377 (10th Cir. 1981), *cert. denied,* 451 U.S. 1031 (1981).

[173]*E.g.,* General Products v. Meredith Corp., 526 F. Supp. 546, 7 Media L. Rep. 2257 (E.D. Va. 1981).

[174]*E.g., see* Vegod Corp. v. ABC, 603 P.2d 14, 18, 5 Media L. Rep. 2043, 2045 (1980). *But see* Steaks Unlimited, Inc. v. Deaner, 468 F. Supp. 779, 4 Media L. Rep. 2569 (W.D. Pa. 1979), *aff'd,* 623 F.2d 264, 6 Media L. Rep. 1129 (3rd Cir. 1980).

[175]Waldbaum v. Fairchild Publications, Inc., 627 F.2d at 1300, 5 Media L. Rep. at 2637.

[176]*See* Monitor Patriot Co. v. Roy, 401 U.S. 265, 274, 1 Media L. Rep. 1619, 1623 (1971).

[177]Yiamouyiannis v. Consumers Union, 619 F.2d 932, 6 Media L. Rep. 1065 (2d Cir. 1980).

[178]Cloyd v. Press, 629 S.W.2d 24, 8 Media L. Rep. 1589 (Tenn. App. 1981).

limited public figure was Liberty Lobby, a self-avowed citizens' lobby. Liberty Lobby claims to promote "patriotism, nationalism, lawfulness, protection of the national interests of the United States and the economic interests of its citizens."[179]

Other Limited Public Figures   In addition, some courts confer limited public figure status on entertainers and athletes who are not pervasively involved in public issues. Although entertainers and athletes often have fame and notoriety, courts are reluctant to impose the all-purpose public figure status on persons who have not become involved in political activities. At the same time, the courts believe that because entertainers and athletes have sought public attention during their careers, they ought to have to prove *New York Times* actual malice for the limited purpose of defamation about their public performances. For example, the U.S. Court of Appeals for the Fifth Circuit said Anita Brewer was a public figure even though the court was not sure she was an all-purpose public figure and even though she had not injected herself into a public controversy.

Anita Wood Brewer, along with her husband, sued the *Memphis Commercial Appeal* for falsely reporting that they were divorced and that she had a "reunion" with former boyfriend Elvis Presley. Mrs. Brewer was known as an entertainer in her own right as well as for her earlier relationship with Presley. The court did not say that she would have to prove *New York Times* actual malice for every libelous story about her. It only said she was a public figure in the suit over the *Commercial Appeal*'s story because it focused on her romance with Presley, a relationship that had advanced her career. The Fifth Circuit said Mrs. Brewer had entered a profession that required public appearances and invited press attention. Therefore she fit the *Gertz* criteria of voluntarily risking public exposure and having access to the press for the purpose of rebuttal.[180] Other plaintiffs treated similarly include a football player,[181] a prominent writer for *Sports Illustrated*,[182] a person promoting newly acquired radio stations,[183] and a seminude dancer.[184]

Time Lapse   The Supreme Court has not said whether a public figure can become a private person over time. In the absence of Supreme Court direction, several lower courts have said that public figures do not lose their public figure status with a lapse of time, at least when the libel concerns the same issues that led to the public attention in the first place.

For example, a federal appeals court said that Victoria Price Street, who accused the nine black "Scottsboro Boys" of raping her in 1931, was a public figure 50 years later. Street sued NBC for a network docudrama that portrayed her as a woman trying to send innocent boys to the electric chair. The U.S. Court of Appeals for the Sixth Circuit said that Street had been a public figure in the 1930s because of her

---

[179]Liberty Lobby, Inc. v. Anderson, 562 F. Supp. 201, 9 Media L. Rep. 1524 (D.D.C. 1983). *See* Liberty Lobby, Inc. v. Anderson, 9 Media L. Rep. 1526 (D.D.C. 1983).

[180]Brewer v. Memphis Publishing Co., 626 F.2d at 1253–55, 6 Media L. Rep. at 2038–41.

[181]*E.g.,* Chuy v. Philadelphia Eagles Football Club, 595 F.2d 1265, 4 Media L. Rep. 2537 (3d Cir. 1979) (*en banc*).

[182]Maule v. NYM Corp., 429 N.E.2d 416, 7 Media L. Rep. 2092 (N.Y. 1981).

[183]Howard v. Buffalo Evening News, 453 N.Y.S.2d 516, 8 Media L. Rep. 2592 (N.Y. App. Div. 1982).

[184]Griffin v. Kentucky Post, 10 Media L. Rep. 1159 (Ky. Cir. Ct. 1983).

prominent role in the issue, her access to the media, and her effort to aggressively promote her version of the case outside of the courtroom. She was still a public figure nearly 50 years later because "once a person becomes a public figure in connection with a particular controversy, that person remains a public figure for purposes of later commentary or treatment of *that controversy*" (emphasis in original).

The Sixth Circuit said that the rationale for giving the media constitutional protection for reporting about public figures did not change with time. For one thing, past public figures do not lose access to the media for the purpose of discussing their role in a controversy. In addition, the Sixth Circuit said, fading memories and disappearing sources create problems of accuracy and verifiability that need to be considered in order to protect a vigorous public debate. At the same time, the court said, the passage of time "does not automatically diminish the significance of events or the public's need for information." The Sixth Circuit said the case of the Scottsboro boys, "the most famous rape case of the twentieth century," focused the nation's attention on the treatment of blacks by the courts. The court said that as long as fair justice for blacks is an issue, the case of the Scottsboro boys would remain "a living controversy."[185]

SUMMARY

The Supreme Court said in *Gertz v. Welch* that public figures are either persons of widespread fame or notoriety or people who inject themselves into the debate about a controversial public issue for the purpose of affecting the outcome. Public figures are people who voluntarily subject themselves to public exposure and who have ready access to the media themselves. The Supreme Court said that persons of widespread fame and notoriety are public figures for all purposes either because of their prominence or because of the influence they exercise in society. Limited public figures are persons who voluntarily thrust themselves into a public controversy with the intent of having an impact on the way that controversy is resolved. Limited public figures must prove *New York Times* actual malice only for media discussion of that issue.

New York Times *Actual Malice*   Once a court decides that a person is a public official, a public figure, or a private person, the focus of the libel case turns to the quality of the research, writing, and editing of the libelous story or advertisement. All libel plaintiffs must prove *fault,* meaning negligence or recklessness, to win their suit. Public officials and public figures must establish *New York Times* actual malice, defined as knowledge of falsity or reckless disregard for the truth. Proof of *New York Times* actual malice requires an examination of the "state of mind" of writers and editors.

Reckless Disregard for the Truth   Public officials and public figures most often try to prove *New York Times* actual malice by providing evidence that journalists

---

[185]Street v. NBC, 645 F.2d at 1235, 7 Media L. Rep. at 1007–1008 (6th Cir.), *cert. granted,* 454 U.S. 815, *cert. dismissed,* 454 U.S. 1095 (1981).

demonstrated a reckless disregard for the truth. The Supreme Court has said that plaintiffs can establish reckless disregard only if they can prove that defamatory statements were made with a "high degree of awareness of their probable falsity."[186] In *St. Amant v. Thompson,* the Court said a candidate for sheriff did not exercise reckless disregard because he believed the truth of false statements he made in a televised speech. Phil A. St. Amant charged that his opponent in Baton Rouge, Louisiana, a deputy sheriff named Herman Thompson, illegally accepted money from E.G. Albin, the president of a Teamsters union local. St. Amant based his charges on an affidavit from a union member who opposed Albin in an internal union struggle. St. Amant did not consider that his accusations might be defamatory and made no effort to verify his information. Thompson sued, and the state supreme court upheld a jury verdict for Thompson.

The Louisiana Supreme Court said that St. Amant had recklessly disregarded whether the statements about Thompson were true. The U.S. Supreme Court disagreed 8–1. Justice Byron White, writing for the Court, said reckless conduct was not measured by whether a reasonably prudent person would have published or investigated before publishing. Rather, White said, "There must be sufficient evidence to permit the conclusion that the defendant in fact entertained serious doubts as to the truth of his publication."[187]

However, White emphasized that the Court's decision does not automatically protect journalists who argue that they believe the statements they publish are true. A journalist cannot successfully contend a story is written in good faith if there are "obvious reasons" to doubt the credibility of a source or the accuracy of the source's information, White said. Neither can remarks be "based wholly on an unverified anonymous telephone call." White said courts still may find *New York Times* actual malice if defamatory remarks are fabricated or "so inherently improbable that only a reckless man would have put them into circulation."[188]

The inquiry into whether a journalist entertained "serious doubts" about the truth or falsity of a story requires the courts to try to reconstruct the publishing process. The courts ask whether a journalist adequately investigated a story given the time available. The courts consider whether the reporter chose reliable sources, ignored warnings that the story was wrong, or disregarded inconsistencies. Other factors that could contribute to a finding of *New York Times* actual malice include a mistake in interpretation, a use of the wrong terms, and a biased selection of facts. Proof of motives such as ill will or hatred could be considered. So could an intent to print sensational stories in order to attract readers. The failure to print a retraction could also be a factor. Ordinarily, one of these items alone would not be sufficient evidence of *New York Times* actual malice—however, a combination of them could be.

The Supreme Court has said that a journalist adhering to standard newsgathering procedures will not be found to be reckless.[189] Carelessness alone should not

---

[186]Garrison v. Louisiana, 379 U.S. at 74, 1 Media L. Rep. at 1552.

[187]390 U.S. 727, 731, 1 Media L. Rep. 1586, 1588 (1968).

[188]*Id.* at 732, 1 Media L. Rep. at 1588.

[189]*See* Greenbelt Coop. Publishing Co. v. Bresler, 398 U.S. 6, 12–13, 1 Media L. Rep. 1589, 1592 (1970).

lead to a decision that a story was published with *New York Times* actual malice.[190] Rather, a publication must have used reporting techniques considered unacceptable and unreasonable by responsible journalists.

In 1989, the Supreme Court unanimously upheld a $200,000 libel award when it agreed with lower court decisions that the staff of the *Hamilton* (Ohio) *Journal News* had published stories during an election campaign with reckless disregard for the truth.[191] The Supreme Court said the *Journal News* published with actual malice because the paper's staff intentionally avoided the truth in its preparation of a story about a losing judicial candidate, Daniel Connaughton.

Connaughton had sued the *Journal News* for reporting on the front page a week before the election that he had used "dirty tricks" in his campaign for a municipal judgeship. The *Journal News* reported that local resident Alice Thompson said that she and her sister had been offered jobs and a Florida vacation "in appreciation" for their help in discrediting Connaughton's opponent, incumbent Municipal Judge James Dolan. Thompson's sister, Patsy Stephens, said a key Dolan aide accepted cash from her in exchange for "disposing" of minor criminal charges against her former husband, relatives, and friends. Patsy Stephens first revealed those charges to Connaughton in a tape-recorded interview. Connaughton subsequently filed a written criminal complaint and the aide was eventually convicted.

In *Harte-Hanks Communications v. Connaughton,* the Court held that staff members of the *Journal News* had not only failed to investigate adequately the story alleging that Connaughton had used underhanded tactics to discredit his election opponent, but the staff also had purposefully avoided the truth. The Court ruled that the staff made a "deliberate decision not to acquire knowledge" that would have revealed the probable falsity of Thompson's charges that she and her sister had been offered jobs and a Florida vacation. The Court found that it was "utterly bewildering" that the paper's staff did not interview Thompson's sister, Patsy Stephens, the person in the best position to corroborate or contradict Thompson's story. The Court also noted that the staff did not listen to the tapes of Connaughton's principal interview with Stephens, tapes that cast doubt on Thompson's claims.

Although a failure to investigate a story adequately does not by itself constitute reckless disregard for the truth, the Court said, the failure to interview Patsy Stephens and listen to the Stephens–Connaughton tape may have been motivated by a fear that Stephens and the tapes would have contradicted the story the paper had already planned to run. The Court said the *Journal News* staff should have suspected Thompson's allegations. Thompson had a criminal record, had been treated for mental instability, and had told the *Journal News* that she opposed Connaughton's candidacy. In addition, not only had Connaughton directly denied Thompson's charges, but her story was contradicted by the six other witnesses to the Stephens–Connaughton conversation. Further, a Thompson allegation that Connaughton only planned to use his taped interview with Stephens to secretly blackmail incumbent Judge Dolan into resigning had proven to be false. The *News Journal* staff knew that

---

[190]*See, e.g.,* Pauling v. Globe-Democrat Publishing Co., 362 F.2d 188 (8th Cir. 1966), *cert. denied,* 388 U.S. 909 (1967) and Glover v. Herald Co., 549 S.W.2d 858, 2 Media L. Rep. 1846 (Mo.), *cert. denied,* 434 U.S. 965 (1977).

[191]Harte-Hanks Communications, Inc. v. Connaughton, 109 S. Ct. 2678, 16 Media L. Rep. 1881 (1989).

Connaughton had openly turned over the information he had to the county prosecutor. Finally, the Court said a *Journal News* editorial published before the paper had completed its interviews for the story provided additional evidence that the paper's staff was not interested in the truth. The editorial, said the Court, appeared to prejudge the outcome of the paper's investigation by predicting that information about the integrity of the candidates for the judgeship might surface in the last days of the campaign.

The Court said the *News Journal* staff had published with reckless disregard for the truth because it intentionally avoided an adequate investigation of Alice Thompson's charges against Daniel Connaughton. The paper should have questioned Thompson's reliability, particularly when her story was challenged by seven sources. The paper also had evidence that directly contradicted one aspect of Thompson's allegations. Yet, the paper failed to interview a key source or listen to a crucial tape recording. In fact, the editorial suggested the paper had made up its mind to print Thompson's story before the staff had finished its inquiry.

The Supreme Court, in finding the *News Journal* had published with *New York Times* actual malice, did not rely on evidence that the paper printed the Connaughton story to support an editorial policy or to boost circulation. The U.S. Court of Appeals for the Sixth Circuit had emphasized in its decision that the *Journal News* had published the Connaughton story because it opposed Connaughton's candidacy and wanted a competitive advantage over a "bitter rival," the *Cincinnati Enquirer.* However, the Supreme Court said that a newspaper's collective state of mind, including commercial and political motives, could be one issue—but not the only one—in deciding whether a paper acted with actual malice.

In addition to *Connaughton* and *St. Amant,* two earlier Supreme Court cases provide good illustrations of the factors the Supreme Court considers when determining whether journalists have acted with reckless disregard for the truth. In one of the two cases, a plurality of the Court said in 1967 that a magazine staff, in reporting an alleged plot to fix a football game, exhibited an extreme departure from standard journalism practices. In *Curtis Publishing Co. v. Butts,* three of the justices explicitly said the magazine acted with reckless disregard for the truth, a point agreed to in the Supreme Court's opinion in *Connaughton* 20 years later.[192]

In *Curtis v. Butts,* University of Georgia athletic director Wally Butts sued the *Saturday Evening Post* for a story that said Butts had conspired to fix a 1962 Georgia–Alabama football game. Although, the Supreme Court said, Butts was well known and well respected as a former college coach, the *Post* charged that Butts revealed his school's significant football secrets to Alabama football coach Bear Bryant just before a game between the two schools. The *Post* obtained the information for the article, "The Story of a College Football Fix," from George Burnett, an Atlanta insurance salesman who had no reporting experience and who had been on probation for bad-check charges. Burnett claimed that he was accidentally connected to a telephone conversation in which he overheard Butts tell Bryant about Georgia's strategy for the Alabama game.

---

[192]*Id.* at 2698, 16 Media L. Rep. at 1897. *See also id.* at 2683, 16 Media L. Rep. at 1885 (explanation of relationship between the *Butts* standard of extreme departure from ordinary reporting practices and *New York Times* actual malice).

Although *Saturday Evening Post* editors said they recognized the need for a thorough investigation of Burnett's charges, the Supreme Court said the editors did not do even elementary checking during the editing process. The Court said the *Post* did not check the notes Burnett claimed he made during the phone call. Editors did not check the story with an individual who was supposed to have been with Burnett when he overheard the Butts–Bryant call. No one at the magazine attempted to find out if Alabama had adjusted its game plan. No one looked at Georgia–Alabama game films to see if Burnett's allegations that the game was fixed were accurate. No one even checked the story with a football expert before publication. Indeed, said the Court, experts who testified at the libel trial said Burnett's notes did not contain information useful to an opposing team that could not have been gathered by watching readily available films of Georgia's previous games. In addition, *Post* staff members did not initiate any inquiries after Butts and his daughter told them before publication that the story was false. The Supreme Court upheld a jury verdict of $460,000 for Butts.

In contrast, in *Associated Press v. Walker,* a majority of the Court said that the AP did not act with actual malice in its reporting of a riot on the University of Mississippi campus. The AP reported in September 1962, that a retired army officer, Major General Edwin Walker, encouraged the use of violence and personally led a charge against federal marshals during a racial dispute at the university. In fact, Walker spoke to students at the university while federal marshals were enforcing a court order to enroll the university's first black student, James Meredith. However, Walker said he advocated peaceful protest, a plea that was rejected by the crowd. Walker denied taking part in the charge against federal marshals. The AP story was filed by a young stringer who, said the Court, witnessed the events and had given "every indication of being trustworthy and competent." Walker was awarded $500,000 in a Texas court but the Supreme Court reversed the decision. In *AP v. Walker,* decided on the same day as *Curtis v. Butts,* the Supreme Court found that the AP did not report the story with reckless disregard for the truth.

Justice John Harlan's opinion for the Court distinguished *Walker* from *Butts,* using several criteria:

- Deadline pressure. The story about violence at the University of Mississippi was a news story needing immediate dissemination. The magazine piece about the football game was not hot news.
- Sources used. The information in the AP story came from an apparently reliable witness with some journalism background. Burnett's criminal background should have raised doubts.
- Standard journalistic practices. There was no evidence of improper or incompetent story preparation by employees of the AP. However, *Post* editors did not investigate the Butts story even after he told them it was false.
- Believability of story. There was no obvious reason AP editors should have doubted the Walker story. Walker was known to have talked to students at the University of Mississippi the day of the violence. The dispatches from the stringer, with a minor exception, were consistent. In addition, conduct attributed to Walker in the AP dispatch was considered believable given prior statements Walker had made about the need to defy federal court orders in

segregation disputes. In contrast, *Post* personnel should have asked football experts whether Burnett's charges that the Alabama–Georgia game was fixed were believable. *Post* editors should have asked whether Burnett's story made sense in light of Butts's standing among his peers. In addition, the *Post* staff should have asked whether the films of the Georgia–Alabama game supported Burnett's contentions.

- Motivation. The *Post,* in serious financial trouble, had announced a new editorial policy of "sophisticated muckraking" designed to "provoke people, make them mad."[193]

Harlan's opinion should not be taken as a prescription for *New York Times* actual malice. The Supreme Court has refused to establish "one infallible definition" of reckless disregard for the truth.[194] However, *Butts, Walker, Connaughton,* and *St. Amant* illustrate some of the factors the courts consider when trying to determine whether a journalist had or should have had serious doubts about the truth of a defamatory statement.

Knowing Falsehood Although public officials and public figures who have to prove *New York Times* actual malice usually try to establish reckless disregard for the truth, a few provide evidence that journalists published with knowledge that a defamatory story was false. Public officials and public figures can win libel suits by demonstrating that libelous stories were fabricated. In *Cantrell v. Forest City Publishing,* a case discussed in Chapter 4, the U.S. Supreme Court said that a reporter acted with *New York Times* actual malice when he fabricated an interview with a West Virginia widow.[195] In *Goldwater v. Ginzburg,* the U.S. Court of Appeals for the Second Circuit said that *Fact* magazine knowingly published defamatory falsehoods about 1964 presidential candidate Barry Goldwater. In *Goldwater,* the court said *Fact* editor Ralph Ginzburg and managing editor Warren Boroson decided shortly after the Republican nominating convention to warn the public about a Goldwater presidency in a "Goldwater issue." The court said that Ginzburg and Boroson decided to attack Goldwater's character "on preconceived psychiatric or psychological grounds of their own fabrication."[196] Before Boroson had begun his research, the court said, he wrote that the Goldwater profile would say that the candidate had "deep-seated doubts about his masculinity." Ginzburg wrote in one of the magazine's articles that Goldwater had had two nervous breakdowns although Ginzburg knew the charge had been denied by Goldwater and by Goldwater's physician. Ginzburg also asserted that Goldwater suffered a serious mental disease without discussing his conclusions with experts in psychiatry. A second article was based on a mail questionnaire to psychiatrists. However, Ginzburg edited and altered some of the letters he received so that they were misleading and inaccurate as printed. The Second Circuit, noting that Ginzburg had created numerous false statements to support his predetermined views, af-

---

[193]388 U.S. 130, 1 Media L. Rep. 1568 (1967).
[194]St. Amant v. Thompson, 390 U.S. at 730, 1 Media L. Rep. at 1588.
[195]419 U.S. 245, 1 Media L. Rep. 1815 (1974).
[196]Goldwater v. Ginzburg, 414 F.2d 324, 329, 1 Media L. Rep. 1737, 1739 (1969).

firmed a jury verdict that the *Fact* articles were published with *New York Times* actual malice.

In 1981, actress Carol Burnett proved that the *National Enquirer* had knowingly printed a false story when it said she made a fool of herself in an expensive Washington, D.C., restaurant. The four-sentence item in the *Enquirer* said that "a boisterous" Carol Burnett argued with Henry Kissinger. Burnett supposedly "traipsed around the place offering everyone a bite of her dessert" and "really raised eyebrows when she accidentally knocked a glass of wine over one diner and started giggling instead of apologizing."

The trial court established that the basis of the story came from a free-lance tipster who emphasized that Burnett was not drunk. One *Enquirer* writer expressed doubts that the tipster could be trusted. Another could verify only that Burnett shared her dessert and "carried on a good-natured conversation with Kissinger." No one told *Enquirer* columnist Brian Walker, the author of the story, that Burnett and Kissinger had an argument. The description of "boisterous" and the wine-spilling story were only unverified hearsay. The trial judge suggested that Walker added "embellishment . . . to spice up' the item." The judge said Walker at least had serious doubts about the truth of the publication and there was "a high degree of probability" that he fabricated part of the story.[197]

However, even if a writer admits making a false statement, the remark may not have been made with knowing falsehood. In *Bose Corporation v. Consumers Union,* the U.S. Supreme Court decided that *Consumer Reports* had not acted with knowledge of falsity when it used the wrong prepositional phrase in a review of speaker systems. The Court said that a Consumers Union engineer wrote that sound from the Bose 901 speaker moved "around the room" although what he heard, he said in testimony, was sound that moved back and forth "across the wall." Lower court judges said that statements suggesting "such grotesque qualities" in sound such as instruments wandering around the room "could have no effect other than to harm the reputation of the product."[198] However, Justice John Paul Stevens, who wrote the Supreme Court's opinion in *Bose,* said that the fact that a mistake was made did not establish that the engineer, Arnold Seligson, realized he was publishing a falsehood at the time of the publication. Stevens said Seligson's error was "the sort of inaccuracy that is commonplace in the forum of robust debate to which the *New York Times* rule applies."[199]

The Supreme Court also has said that a plaintiff may not be able to prove knowledge of falsity even if the truth was readily available to a public communicator at the time of publication. In *New York Times v. Sullivan,* Justice Brennan said the fact that the paper's own files contradicted an ad it printed did not establish that *Times* personnel knew the story was false. The Court could find no evidence that *Times* employees responsible for the ad knew it contained errors.[200]

---

[197]Burnett v. National Enquirer, Inc., 7 Media L. Rep. 1321 (Cal. Super. Ct. 1981), *aff'd on other grounds,* 144 Cal. App.3d 991, 9 Media L. Rep. 1921 (Cal. Ct. App. 1983).
[198]Bose Corp. v. Consumers Union of United States, Inc., 508 F. Supp. at 1268, 7 Media L. Rep. at 1070.
[199]466 U.S. at 513, 10 Media L. Rep. at 1638.
[200]367 U.S. at 286, 1 Media L. Rep. at 1540.

Inquiry into a Journalist's Mind   The proof necessary for *New York Times* actual malice, evidence of knowing falsehood or reckless disregard of the truth, seemingly requires courts to know what journalists were thinking during the preparation of a story. The necessity to prove knowing falsehood or a "high degree of awareness of their probable falsity," as mentioned in *St. Amant v. Thompson,* at least encourages plaintiffs' lawyers to examine the thought processes, or "the state of mind," of journalists. During the pretrial discovery phase of libel litigation, writers and editors are frequently required to discuss their evaluation of the information they collected and the sources they interviewed. Writers are asked if they believed what their sources told them. Editors are asked if they doubted the truth of the story, and, if so, if they asked reporters to provide more documentation. Both writers and editors are asked why they published what they did and why some information never reached their readers, listeners, or viewers.

Many journalists argue that detailed examinations of news decisions interfere with editorial processes and therefore violate the First Amendment. They contend that writers and editors are reluctant to express doubts about a story in the newsroom knowing that those doubts could be used against them in court. Journalists claim that juries cannot understand decisions made under deadline pressure not to pursue tips that might lead to a more complete story.

Nevertheless, in 1979, in *Herbert v. Lando,* the U.S. Supreme Court said that journalists could be required to testify about thought processes and editorial conversations during the publication process. *Herbert v. Lando* began with a 1973 "Sixty Minutes" broadcast that examined allegations of a cover-up of atrocities committed by U.S. troops in Vietnam. The program questioned the widely discussed accusations made by Colonel Anthony Herbert, a retired Army officer. Herbert sued, claiming that the program falsely and maliciously portrayed him as a liar. Herbert said "Sixty Minutes" falsely suggested he made up the war-crimes charges to explain why he was relieved of his command.

Herbert conceded in a federal district court that he was a public figure. Herbert's attorneys asked questions for more than a year about the preparation of the story, trying to prove *New York Times* actual malice. The questioning of Barry Lando, the producer of the Herbert segment of "Sixty Minutes," resulted in nearly 3,000 pages of testimony. Yet Lando refused to answer questions about his evaluation of the information gathered for the story on the grounds that the First Amendment protected against an inquiry "into the state of mind" of editors. The district court judge rejected the First Amendment argument and ruled that an examination of Lando's state of mind was appropriate under the federal rules of discovery. The judge allowed Lando to appeal the ruling before the case was tried.

An appeals court reversed the trial court judge, but the Supreme Court, in a 6–3 vote, held that the First Amendment did not bar inquiry into the editorial process. Justice Byron White, who wrote the Court's opinion, said that using "state-of-mind" evidence was not a recent development but was instead deeply rooted in the common law of libel. White argued that the Court, in constitutionalizing libel law, had not intended that the First Amendment prevent a plaintiff from obtaining evidence needed to prove *New York Times* actual malice. Indeed, he said, the *Times* rule "made it essential" that public officials and public figures "focus on the conduct and state of mind" of defendants. If public officials and public figures were prevented from asking about the thoughts, opinions, and conclusions of journalists, White said, the balance between the protection of reputation and the protection for the First Amendment guarantees of freedom of speech and press would be unacceptably skewed in favor of the press.

White rejected the argument that investigations into the "state of mind" would have "an intolerable chilling effect" on editorial decision making. White contended that the media had a self-interest in taking any necessary precautions, including a "frank interchange of fact and opinion," to avoid publishing a story that was the result of a knowing falsehood or reckless error. White said he did not believe that discussions between reporters and editors were "so subject to distortion and . . . misunderstanding" that they should be immune from courtroom examination. However, he said, investigations into the editorial process should only be permitted when someone suing for libel had to prove *New York Times* actual malice. Inquiry into the "state of mind" should not be permitted "merely to satisfy curiosity."[201]

The Supreme Court returned the *Herbert v. Lando* case to the federal district court judge for trial. The trial judge eventually granted summary judgment to CBS for most of Herbert's complaint on grounds he could not prove *New York Times* actual malice. In 1986, a federal appeals court ordered the case dismissed.[202]

While Herbert lost his suit, the impact of the Supreme Court's decision remains. Many observers contend that *Herbert v. Lando* has contributed to the extraordinarily long and expensive pretrial fact-finding that is common to libel litigation. However, Justice White, in his majority opinion, said the only way to avoid extensive discovery was to eliminate libel law.

SUMMARY

Public officials and public figures are required to prove *New York Times* actual malice, knowing falsehood or reckless disregard of the truth, in order to win libel suits. The Supreme Court has said plaintiffs must demonstrate that journalists had serious doubts about the truth of a defamatory story before publication. In order to determine whether journalists exercised reckless disregard, courts examine the amount of time available to journalists for story preparation and whether standard news-gathering techniques were used. Courts also consider the believability of the story, the depth and breadth of the investigation, the credibility of sources, and motives for publication. Plaintiffs can also establish *New York Times* actual malice if they can prove a journalist fabricated a story or otherwise knowingly printed false defamation. The Supreme Court has ruled that public communicators can be required to testify to what they knew and were thinking during the writing, editing, and production phases of defamatory stories.

Fault for Private Persons   The 1974 Supreme Court case *Gertz v. Welch* not only provided the current definition for public figures but also eliminated the doctrine of

---

[201]441 U.S. 153, 4 Media L. Rep. 2575 (1979).
[202]781 F.2d 298 (2d Cir.), *cert. denied,* 476 U.S. 1182 (1986).

strict liability in libel law. Before 1974, libel plaintiffs who were not public officials or public figures had to prove only that they had been defamed in order to win their suits. They did not have to prove a newspaper or broadcast station was also careless or reckless. Since *Gertz v. Welch,* every person suing the media for libel must prove some form of fault. In most states, private persons must prove negligence, the lack of ordinary care. In addition, in 1986, the Supreme Court said that private persons involved in matters of public concern must prove any defamation to be false before they can win a libel suit.

Eliminating Strict Liability In *Gertz v. Welch,* the Court tried to balance the interest in protecting the erroneous statements "inevitable" in a debate on public issues and the interest in protecting individual reputations from defamatory falsehoods. Justice Powell, writing for the majority, said that private persons suing for defamation should not have to meet the same heavy burden of proof imposed on public officials and public figures. On the other hand, Powell said, publishers or editors should not be automatically liable for damages for printing defamatory language, a concept known as strict liability. Under strict liability, publishers are liable for the publication of any false defamation, even if they take "every reasonable precaution" to ensure accuracy. Powell said a rule of strict liability for private persons would threaten the vigorous public debate the Court wanted to protect in *Times v. Sullivan.*[203]

In an effort to accommodate the interests of private reputation and public debate, the Court said each state could determine its own burden of proof for private individuals as long as editors exercising reasonable care would not be held liable. Twenty-nine states[204] as well as the District of Columbia and Puerto Rico have chosen negligence as the burden of proof for private persons. Four states require private persons involved in matters of public interest to prove *New York Times* actual malice, adopting the rule recommended by three Supreme Court justices in *Rosenbloom v. Metromedia.*[205] New York State requires private persons to prove "gross irresponsibility,"[206] a standard more rigorous than negligence but less demanding than actual malice. Several states have recognized the *Gertz* requirement of fault for private persons but have not adopted a specific burden of proof.[207]

Negligence Negligence, the fault requirement most states have adopted for private persons suing for libel, is a standard of liability used widely in tort law. Negligence means a failure to act as a reasonable person would in similar circumstances. In libel law, the issue is whether a writer exercised reasonable care in determining whether a story was true or false.[208]

---

[203]418 U.S. at 345–48, 1 Media L. Rep. at 1642–43.

[204]The states are Alabama, Arizona, Arkansas, California, Delaware, Florida, Georgia, Hawaii, Illinois, Iowa, Kansas, Kentucky, Maryland, Massachusetts, Michigan, Minnesota, Mississippi, New Mexico, Ohio, Oklahoma, Oregon, Pennsylvania, South Carolina, Tennessee, Texas, Utah, Virginia, Washington, and Wisconsin. *See generally* McCrory, Bernius, Jones, & Grygiel, "Constitutional Privilege in Libel Law," in J. Goodale, ed., 1 *Communications Law 1989* at 589–94; H. Kaufman, ed., *Libel Defense Resource Center 50–State Survey 1989.*

[205]Alaska, Colorado, Indiana, and New Jersey.

[206]*See* Chapadeau v. Utica Observer-Dispatch, Inc., 341 N.E.2d 569, 1 Media L. Rep. 1693 (N.Y. 1975).

[207]Connecticut, Louisiana, Montana, New Hampshire, North Carolina, and Wyoming.

[208] *See Restatement (Second) of Torts* sec. 580B comment g (1977).

Negligence, as well as reckless disregard for the truth, is the failure to check a story's facts adequately before publication. A *New York Times* columnist and First Amendment scholar, Anthony Lewis, has said the failure to check a story's facts is negligence if a story is believable. The failure to check, Lewis said, is *New York Times* actual malice if a story appears hard to believe or the reporter knew the story was probably false.[209]

States apply the term *negligence* in one of two ways. Many states define negligence as a failure to do what "a reasonably prudent person" would do.[210] Other states define negligence by a professional standard: a failure to be as careful as an ordinarily prudent person in the same occupation.[211] In the first case, journalists are compared to reasonable people generally. Such a standard does not take into consideration the daily occupational hazards of journalism, such as deadline pressures or sources unwilling to talk. In the case of the professional standard, the performance of journalists is compared to the reasonable actions of their peers in similar situations. Witnesses can testify to the kinds of behavior considered acceptable within the profession.

No court has provided a definitive list of journalism practices considered to be negligent. The Supreme Court suggested in *New York Times v. Sullivan* that the *Times*'s advertising staff may have been negligent when it failed to check the paper's news columns to verify the accuracy of an advertisement calling for support for civil rights activities in the South.[212] One academic study reports that juries are likely to decide a journalist was negligent if they find

1. a failure to contact the person who is being defamed (unless there was a thorough investigation otherwise),
2. a failure to verify information through proper sources, or
3. a discrepancy between the reporter and the only source(s) relied upon.[213]

Negligence often occurs because of reliance on the wrong sources or inadequate fact-checking. Negligence can also arise through errors in note-taking, the misuse of professional or technical jargon, and typographical errors. A single breakdown in generally accepted reporting practices may constitute negligence.

A South Carolina reporter made several mistakes that constituted negligence when he erroneously reported that James Jones pleaded guilty to pirating stereo tapes in violation of copyright laws. Jones had been arrested and arraigned in 1975, along with his father, an uncle named Jack Jones, and two others. Two months later the father and uncle pleaded guilty, but the charges against James Jones were dismissed. The reporter said he published what he had been told by a U.S. attorney, but the attorney said he read the reporter the names of those who pleaded guilty directly from the record, a record that did not include the name of James Jones.

---

[209]Lewis, "Annals of Law: The Sullivan Case," *The New Yorker,* Nov. 5, 1984, at 52, 73.

[210]Memphis Publishing Co. v. Nichols, 569 S.W.2d 412, 418, 4 Media L. Rep. 1573, 1578 (Tenn. 1978). For lists of states adopting each standard, *see, e.g.,* McCrory, Bernius, Jones, & Grygiel, "Constitutional Privilege in Libel Law," in J. Goodale, ed., 1 *Communications Law 1989* at 597–603.

[211]Martin v. Griffin Television, Inc., 549 P.2d 85 (Okla. 1976).

[212]New York Times Co. v. Sullivan, 376 U.S. at 287–88, 1 Media L. Rep. at 1541.

[213]W. W. Hopkins, "Negligence Ten Years after *Gertz v. Welch,*" *Journ. Monographs,* August 1985, at 93.

The South Carolina Supreme Court said a jury understandably decided that the reporter violated acceptable reporting standards because he did not check court records himself or contact the Joneses, whom he knew. The court said the six days between the guilty pleas and the published story gave the reporter plenty of time to check his information. The state supreme court reinstated a jury verdict of $35,000, which had been set aside by the trial judge.[214]

A court found a Springfield, Massachusetts, reporter to be negligent when he relied only on a phone book for the address of Anthony Liquori, a man who pleaded guilty to conspiring to break into a business. The reporter obtained Liquori's name from the court record, which did not list an address. Instead of tracking down the address through official records, the reporter looked up Anthony Liquori in the phone book. The reporter assumed the person listed in the phone book was the same man in the court record. However, the Liquori who pleaded guilty did not live in the community, and the reporter attributed the guilty plea to the wrong individual.[215]

Another Massachusetts newspaper was found negligent when an editor failed to check a suspicious report about an "excellent citizen." An inexperienced reporter, who had trouble hearing court testimony, wrote that John J. Stone was charged with illegal possession of drugs. The editor, who had known Stone for 20 years, was surprised by the story but failed to inquire. Indeed, Stone's son, Jeffrey, was the person charged with possessing illegal drugs.[216] Also negligent was a reporter in Kentucky whose stories reporting that one boy "savagely beat" another were contradicted in court by two of his sources. Both the police chief and the mother of one of the boys said the reporter inaccurately reported their interviews.[217]

On the other hand, a reporter is not apt to be found negligent if a story is based on several sources or if a source verifies the reporter's version of events. A Florida appeals court said a reporter was not negligent in falsely printing that Hersh and Ogenia Karp faced deportation after being charged with illegally entering the country. Although no such charges were filed, the reporter had relied on an officer of the Immigration and Naturalization Service who had provided accurate information before. Fortunately for the journalist, the official testified that the published article was an accurate account of what he told the reporter. The court noted that the reporter had tried to reach the Karps for their version of the events.[218]

Courts have held that the publication of defamatory wire service stories without checking is ordinarily not negligent. In one case, the Massachusetts Supreme Judicial Court affirmed a summary judgment for four newspapers that were sued for publishing wire service stories about a criminal investigation involving Kenneth A. Appleby of West Springfield. Appleby had filed 94 libel suits against newspapers and broadcast stations in the region, contending they published false defamatory stories about an investigation culminating in his conviction for rape, kidnapping, and assault and battery. Appleby said he was damaged by false statements about his homosexuality, the torture and murder of young homosexual men, and his interest in the Nazi party.

[214]Jones v. Sun Publishing Co., 191 S.E.2d 12, 8 Media L. Rep. 1388, *cert. denied,* 459 U.S. 944 (1982).
[215]Liquori v. Republican Co., 396 N.E.2d 726, 5 Media L. Rep. 2180 (Mass. App. Ct. 1979).
[216]Stone v. Essex County Newspapers, 330 N.E.2d 161 (Mass. 1975).
[217]Scripps v. Cholmondelay, 569 S.W.2d 702, 3 Media L. Rep. 2462 (Ky. Ct. App. 1977).
[218]Karp v. Miami Herald Publishing Co., 359 So.2d 580, 3 Media L. Rep. 2581 (Fla. D. Ct. App. 1978).

The Massachusetts supreme court, in affirming the judgment of the trial court, said that "reasonable reliance" on stories obtained from "a reputable wire service" was not negligence, even in the case of the *Holyoke Transcript-Telegram,* located about 10 miles from West Springfield. The court noted that both the Associated Press and United Press International had excellent reputations for accuracy. The court said independent corroboration by individual newspapers and broadcast stations would be impractical and therefore impose a heavy burden on the media's ability to report national and world news.[219]

The Massachusetts court did not, however, indicate that newspapers and broadcast stations could always rely on wire service copy without checking it. The court noted that none of the Appleby stories were "so inherently improbable or inconsistent" that the newspapers should have had some reason to doubt their accuracy. Nor, said the court, was there evidence that the newspapers knew, or should have known, information about Appleby that raised doubts about the truth of the wire service stories. If a newspaper or broadcast station has a reason to doubt a wire service story, the Massachusetts court said, publication without verification could become the basis of a negligence suit that could go to trial.

The requirement that libel plaintiffs prove at least negligence also provides broadcast stations with protection from defamatory statements made by members of the public participating in call-in shows and other live broadcasts. Some states protected broadcast stations exercising reasonable care even before *Gertz.* A few states either provide broadcasters with absolute immunity for live third-party statements or require private-person plaintiffs to prove *New York Times* actual malice when libelous statements are made during controversial programs.[220]

Still, the courts have not provided clear guidelines for the kinds of precautions broadcasters should take to avoid liability during call-in shows. For example, courts disagree whether the failure to use a tape-delay system during live broadcasts is reckless disregard for the truth. The Montana Supreme Court said that the failure to use a taping device that allows a talk-show host a few seconds to censor calls is not reckless. In *Adams v. Frontier Broadcasting,* Bob Adams sued radio station KFBC after an anonymous caller said on a talk show that Adams had been discharged as state insurance commissioner because he was dishonest. The Montana Supreme Court said that use of a tape-delay system could restrict a robust public debate.[221] However, in Louisiana, a state appeals court said the direct broadcast of anonymous defamatory remarks without any attempt to verify them constituted reckless disregard.[222] If the lack of a tape delay is deemed reckless, it also will be considered negligent.

In general, most courts expect only a good-faith effort on the part of public communicators to block a live defamatory remark or to determine the accuracy of a news story. Courts do not usually demand an unreasonably exhaustive investigation before a defamatory story is published or broadcast. A journalist who contacts the persons

---

[219]Appleby v. Daily Hampshire Gazette, 478 N.E.2d 721, 11 Media L. Rep. 2372 (1985).

[220]*See generally, e.g.,* Hughes, "Radio Libel Laws: Relics That May Have Answer for Reform Needed Today," 63 *Journ. Q.* 288 (Summer 1986).

[221]Adams v. Frontier Broadcasting, 555 P.2d 556, 2 Media L. Rep. 1166 (1976).

[222]Snowden v. Pearl River Broadcasting Corp., 251 So.2d 405 (La. App. 1971).

most directly affected by a story and checks story information carefully with sources known to be reliable will not ordinarily be found negligent, even if a story is false.

Falsity   In 1986, the Supreme Court declared that private persons involved in matters of public interest not only had to prove a medium was at fault but also had to prove falsity. Until then, the Court had not specifically eliminated the common law doctrine of presumed falsity in the case of private persons even though it had eliminated the common law doctrine of strict liability. At least a few state courts had continued to hold that private-person plaintiffs could win libel suits without proving a defamatory statement was false. In those states, libel defendants may have had to prove the truth of their publications in order to win libel cases.

In *Philadelphia Newspapers v. Hepps,* the Supreme Court said the private persons suing, rather than the defendants, would be held responsible for proving their version of cases.[223] In *Hepps,* a corporation that franchised a chain of Thrifty stores sued the *Philadelphia Inquirer* for linking the chain to organized crime. The *Inquirer* had said the Thrifty chain, which sold beer, soft drinks, and snacks, used its criminal connections to obtain favorable rulings from the state liquor control board. Pennsylvania law, consistent with *Gertz,* required the corporation, General Programming, to prove negligence in order to win its suit. However, Pennsylvania common law did not require General Programming or other plaintiffs to prove the defamatory language to be false. Rather, the defendants had the burden of proving truth in order to avoid losing the suit.

The Supreme Court said, in a 5–4 decision, that the Constitution required General Programming to prove the falsity of defamatory remarks, as well as negligence, in order to win its suit. Justice Sandra Day O'Connor, who wrote the majority opinion, said the Court's libel opinions had shown that the First Amendment protects speech about public figures and matters of public concern. She noted that public officials and public figures already must prove falsity as part of *New York Times* actual malice. She said that, to ensure that truthful speech was not deterred, the Constitution requires that private persons involved in matters of public interest must also establish falsehood when suing for libel. O'Connor said the question of who has the burden of proof in private-person cases only becomes important when the evidence is ambiguous—when truth or falsity cannot be proven in court. O'Connor said that, as a practical matter, requiring private persons to prove falsity will not significantly add to their burden of proof. She said that a plaintiff's proof of fault, usually negligence, will generally include evidence of falsity as well.

The Court limited its ruling in *Hepps.* The opinion does not apply to all private persons, only to those involved in matters of public interest. Private persons not involved in matters of public concern still must prove negligence, but not necessarily falsity. In addition, Justice O'Connor said her opinion applies only to defamation in the mass media. Private persons defamed in a speech or an unpublished memo might not have to prove falsity.

---

[223]475 U.S. 767, 12 Media L. Rep. 1977 (1986).

SUMMARY

In *Gertz v. Welch,* the U.S. Supreme Court said that persons who do not qualify as public officials or public figures must show fault in order to win their libel suits. Most states have said that private persons must prove negligence, or a lack of reasonable care on the part of journalists. Negligence often involves the failure to check information adequately or to use the most appropriate sources. In 1986, the Supreme Court ruled that private persons involved in matters of public concern must also prove that defamation is false.

Summary Judgment

In order for a plaintiff to win a libel suit, he or she must prove defamation, identification, publication, and fault. If a judge can be satisfied before trial that the plaintiff cannot prove his or her case, the judge may award the defendant a summary judgment. Summary judgments are decisions by judges that conclude cases before trial.

A judge can agree to a defendant's motion for summary judgment if there is no "genuine" dispute over the "material" facts of a case that need to be decided by a jury, and the media defendant should win as a matter of law. Judges cannot resolve factual disputes, such as whether the defendant published defamatory language or whether the plaintiff is a public figure, before a trial. But, if both parties in the case agree on the facts, judges can determine whether, on the basis of those facts, the law would allow the plaintiff to win. If the plaintiff cannot possibly win as a matter of law, there is no reason to hold a trial. If, for example, before a trial, a public-figure plaintiff cannot present sufficient evidence to prove that a newspaper exercised reckless disregard for the truth, a judge can rule that the case should be disposed of through a summary judgment.

Media defendants like summary judgments because they keep cases from juries, where the media have lost as many as 40 percent of the time in 1987 and 1988.[224] Summary judgments also save lawyers' fees since cases do not last as long as they otherwise would.

Summary judgments have been particularly useful in cases involving public figures who must prove *New York Times* actual malice. In 1986, the Supreme Court said that libel plaintiffs must provide the same kind of evidence to defeat a motion of summary judgment that would be necessary to win at trial. In order to defeat a defense motion for summary judgment, libel plaintiffs must prove *New York Times* actual malice with clear and convincing evidence. In *Anderson v. Liberty Lobby,* the founder of a self-described citizens lobby, Willis Carto, sued columnist Jack Anderson for accusing him of being an "American Hitler." In responding to the suit, Anderson contended that Carto was a public figure who could not prove knowing falsehood or reckless disregard for the truth. Anderson documented the time his organization spent on the story and listed the sources used for the story. The trial court awarded Anderson a summary judgment on the grounds that Anderson's thorough

---

[224]"Report Says Media Faring Better in Libel Suits," *Broadcasting,* Sept. 11, 1989, at 133.

investigation precluded a finding of *New York Times* actual malice. A federal appeals court partially reversed the trial court, contending Carto should not have been required to provide the same evidence to defeat a summary judgment as he would have to in order to win at trial. However, the Supreme Court **vacated** the ruling of the appeals court, remanding the case to the lower courts. The Supreme Court said the appeals court had not required a sufficiently rigorous burden of proof to defeat Anderson's motion for summary judgment.[225]

SUMMARY

Summary judgments dismissing libel cases can be issued by judges finding that plaintiffs could not meet their burden of proof at trial.

DEFENSES

While plaintiffs try to establish their burden of proof in libel cases, defendants not only try to counter those arguments but also try to convince the court that they have a legal defense for publishing defamatory language. Before the Supreme Court developed the constitutional protection for defamatory falsehoods, communicators had to rely on protection from libel suits provided by the states through the common law and state statutes. The states recognized several legal defenses that allowed the publication of defamatory information that would benefit society.

The constitutionalizing of libel law has not eliminated the need for common law and statutory defenses. The three most important defenses in the post–*Times v. Sullivan* era protect statements that are provably true, stories based on official records and proceedings, and opinion. The other defenses are statutes of limitations, the absolute privilege of government officials, a narrowly defined absolute privilege for broadcasters, consent, neutral reportage, self-defense, and a qualified privilege for internal communications. Any one of the defenses can defeat the recovery of damages by a plaintiff.

Statutes of Limitations

A state's statute of limitations, the only defense that requires no effort on the part of a communicator, is a sure way to defeat a libel suit. For almost all criminal or civil action, prosecutors and plaintiffs must begin the legal proceeding within a specified amount of time, usually one or two years for libel suits. When the specified time period is up, a legal action cannot be initiated. Statutes of limitations allow the courts to concentrate on new legal claims and put a limit on the length of time a person is responsible for any single act.[226]

---

[225]477 U.S. 242, 12 Media L. Rep. 2297 (1986).
[226]For a list of state statutes of limitations, see B. Sanford, *Libel and Privacy* App. C, at 701–704 (1987 Supp.).

In most jurisdictions, the statute of limitations is governed by the *single-publication rule*—that is, the clock begins running on the date of original publication. Individual sales or displays of the same edition of a newspaper, book, or magazine after the original publication do not restart the clock.[227] However, a new edition of a publication or a new newscast, even on the same day as the first, may allow a person to sue a second time for what could be the same libel.[228]

A few states cling to the old common law rule that a libel is published every time the article is displayed, sold, or circulated to a third party.[229] In these jurisdictions, the media are in constant jeopardy because a plaintiff can sue 10 years after the first publication date.

How is the date of original publication decided? Most states use the date that the libelous publication is released for sale. For magazines, for example, the release date is not the date on the cover. It is the date the magazine is generally available to its readers. Hence, attorney Michael J. Morrissey sued the publishers of the book *Spooks: The Haunting of America—The Private Use of Secret Agents* too late. Morrissey sued on December 1, 1980, within a year of the December 19, 1979, official publication date of the paperback edition. However, a federal appeals court said the one-year clock for the statute of limitations began on November 20, 1979, the time the paperback version "was generally available for sale in bookstores throughout the United States."[230]

SUMMARY

Statutes of limitations can be used to defend libel suits. Persons wishing to sue for libel must generally file the suit within a year or two of the publication of the alleged defamatory remark.

Truth

In most states, a libel defendant who can prove the truth of a defamatory statement in court will win a libel case. In a few states, evidence that a true statement was printed with ill will might defeat the defense.

Although proof of truth will almost always defeat a libel suit, the defense of truth is less important than it was before 1964. The reason is that the Supreme Court, in *New York Times v. Sullivan* and the cases that followed, has shifted the burden of proof in libel litigation. Before 1964, any defamatory communication was assumed to be false. The libel defendant had the responsibility to prove the statement to be true.

---

[227]*E.g., Prosser and Keeton on Torts* sec. 113, at 800 (5th ed. 1984); *Restatement (Second) of Torts* sec. 577A (3) and comment on subsection (3) (1977).

[228]*Restatement (Second) of Torts* sec. 577 comment d (1977); *e.g.,* Cox Enterprises, Inc. v. Gilreath, 235 S.E.2d 633, 3 Media L. Rep. 1031 (1977).

[229]*See Prosser and Keeton on Torts* sec. 113, at 800 (5th ed. 1984); B. Sanford, *Libel and Privacy* para. 13.2.4, at 511 (1987 Supp.).

[230]Morrissey v. William Morrow & Co., 739 F.2d 962, 10 Media L. Rep. 2305 (4th Cir. 1984), *cert. denied,* 469 U.S. 1216 (1985).

Since 1964, public officials and public figures have had to prove falsity as a part of establishing knowing falsehood or reckless disregard for the truth. If a public person cannot demonstrate that a remark is false, the libel defendant wins, without being required to prove truth. In 1986, in *Philadelphia Newspapers v. Hepps,* the Supreme Court said that private persons suing for stories about public issues also must bear the burden of establishing falsity. Still, the defense of truth is important because a communicator who can prove the truth of a statement will almost always win a libel suit.

Proving truth in court can be difficult, however. The truth of a statement must be proven by using witnesses, exhibits, and statements made under oath. In discussions of public issues, the truth of a matter is often elusive. Sometimes the truth may never be known, as is demonstrated by the case *Wilson v. Scripps-Howard Broadcasting Co.* In *Wilson,* television station WMC-TV in Memphis, Tennessee, reported that Shelby Wilson's cattle were starving. The station said many of Wilson's herd had died because he did not have the money to feed them. Wilson argued that his cattle had died because of the weather and sued for libel.

During the trial, both Wilson and WMC-TV called several credible witnesses to support their versions of the truth. Wilson's witnesses were himself, his wife, his banker, his ranch foreman, a ranch hand, a business associate, a neighboring rancher, and an expert in animal husbandry. They argued that Wilson was not in financial difficulty, and his cattle were sufficiently nourished. WMC-TV countered with testimony from four neighboring farmers, a former ranch hand for Wilson, a cattle buyer, two newspaper reporters, and a veterinarian. The defendant's witnesses contended that many of Wilson's cattle had died of starvation because he did not have the money to feed them adequately. The jury could not decide whether the statements in the broadcast were true. It decided the case in favor of Wilson only because the judge mistakenly told jurors that WMC-TV had the burden to prove the truth of its broadcast. The judge said that if the station could not prove its story was correct, Wilson should win. A federal appeals court reversed the decision, saying that Wilson had the burden to prove the story was false. The appeals court said that since the jury could not determine with certainty the truth or falsity of the statement, the defendant, the broadcast station, should win.[231]

Sometimes the evidence necessary to prove the truth of a publication or broadcast is not available. If a secretary confidentially tells a reporter that an office executive is taking bribes, the secretary may refuse to testify in court for fear of losing a job. Or, even if the secretary is willing to testify, he or she might lack the credibility to be a good witness. The secretary may have reported the executive to authorities only after being refused a promotion. Even reporters who witness events for themselves cannot be certain that their versions of the truth will be accepted by juries. Other witnesses might effectively contradict what has been reported.

The determination of truth rests on the overall impression, or "gist," of a statement. A story must be substantially true but need not be true in every detail. Minor errors will not destroy the defense of truth. Hence, the Connecticut Supreme Court upheld a summary judgment in favor of a Stamford newspaper, *The Advocate,* for a

---

[231]642 F.2d 371, 7 Media L. Rep. 1169 (6th Cir.), *cert. granted,* 454 U.S. 962, *cert. dismissed,* 454 U.S. 1130 (1981); B. Sanford, *Libel and Privacy* para. 6.3.3, at 171 (1987 Supp.).

story linking state senator William E. Strada, Jr., to reputed crime figures. The story was true except for an inaccurate statement that the FBI had investigated a Strada trip with stops in Las Vegas and New Orleans. In fact, the FBI had investigated a Strada trip to Reno. The court said the impact of the story on the reader would have been no different if the details of the trip had been accurate. The story was "substantially" true.[232]

Sometimes, however, a story can leave a false defamatory impression even if every individual statement is accurate. In *Memphis Publishing Co. v. Nichols,* the *Memphis Press–Scimitar* was held liable because it left critical facts out of a 1971 article about a shooting.[233] The *Press–Scimitar* truthfully reported that a Mrs. Newton shot Ruth Nichols when she found Mrs. Nichols and Mr. Newton together in the Nichols home. But the paper did not report that Mr.Nichols and two neighbors were in the Nichols home at the same time. The court said the omission left the false impression that Mr. Newton and Mrs. Nichols were committing adultery. The Tennessee Supreme Court said that literal truth of statements in a story does not protect an article that conveys a defamatory meaning.

In addition, accurate reports of false statements do not qualify for the defense of truth. Therefore, the *Baton Rouge* (Louisiana) *State Times* was not protected when it said that a junior-senior high school had been poorly designed. The story, based on information from an insurance company report, said that plans did not provide for either adequate drainage or access to water lines. A Louisiana appeals court said that the defense of truth required more than evidence that the story accurately reflected the insurance report. The *State Times* had to prove that what the report said was true by showing that the building was poorly designed.[234]

In a few states, it still may be possible for a plaintiff to defeat the defense of truth with evidence of **common law malice.**[235] Long before Justice Brennan used the term *actual malice* in *New York Times v. Sullivan* to stand for knowing falsehood or reckless disregard for the truth, common law malice could defeat libel defenses protecting the publication of truth, opinion, and the reporting of official proceedings. When courts look for common law malice, unlike *New York Times* actual malice, they are *only* considering the motivation for a defamation publication. Unlike *New York Times* actual malice, the common law relies on the dictionary meaning of the word *malice.* Common law malice refers to improper motives, including ill will, spite, hatred, hostility, or deliberate intent to harm.

In some jurisdictions, plaintiffs must still demonstrate ill will or hatred to win suits for trade libel and libel *per quod.* However, common law malice is largely an artifact of the past. Motive has been substantially discredited as a criterion for punishing speech as defamation has received First Amendment protection beginning with *New York Times v. Sullivan.*[236] Motive is too hard to determine and too imprecise a

[232]Strada v. Connecticut Newspapers, Inc., 477 A.2d 1005, 10 Media L. Rep. 2165 (1984). *See also Restatement (Second) of Torts* sec. 581A comment f (1977).

[233]569 S.W.2d 412, 420, 4 Media L. Rep. 1573, 1579 (1978).

[234]Miller, Smith & Champagne v. Capital City Press, 142 So.2d 462 (La. Ct. App. 1962). *See also Restatement (Second) of Torts* sec. 581A comment e (1977).

[235]*See generally* H. Kaufman, *Libel Defense Resource Center 50-State Survey 1989.*

[236]*E.g., Restatement (Second) of Torts* sec. 581A comment a (1977); Franklin and Bussel, "The Plaintiff's Burden in Defamation: Awareness and Falsity," 25 *Wm. & Mary L. Rev.* 851 (1984).

standard to distinguish protected speech from unprotected speech. Many states have stopped using common law malice or have substituted the constitutional test of *New York Times* actual malice.

SUMMARY

In most jurisdictions, a defamatory statement that can be proven to be true will be protected. The statement must substantially reflect the proven truth. Minor errors will not defeat the truth defense. Although, in the past, defendants were required to prove truth to win libel suits, the Supreme Court has declared that the burden of proof is now on most plaintiffs to prove falsity.

Absolute Privileges

Some false and defamatory statements are completely protected by law. Absolute privileges protect a defamatory message regardless of its accuracy or the motives of the speaker. Three absolute privileges are important to professional communicators. The spoken and written words of public officials acting in their official capacity are privileged. An absolute privilege also exists any time a person who is defamed consents to the defamatory publication. In addition, broadcasters have been granted an absolute privilege to air the false defamatory speech of political candidates.

Privilege for Government Officials   Government officials acting in their official capacity have absolute privilege from libel litigation. The courts have decided that open and uninhibited communication in government must be protected at the risk of damaging individual reputations; public officials must be able to do their jobs without "the constant dread of retaliation."[237] Therefore, the official statements of executive branch officers and the remarks of legislators during official proceedings are privileged. Also privileged are all of the comments made during judicial proceedings—including those by judges, lawyers, and witnesses.[238]

U.S. senators and representatives are protected from libel suits by the Constitution, which declares that they "shall not be questioned in any other place" for "speech or debate in either house" of Congress.[239] However, the Supreme Court has said the constitutional protection applies only to comments within the walls of the two chambers. In *Hutchinson v. Proxmire,* the Court said that Senator William Proxmire's libelous criticism of Dr. Ronald Hutchinson's research on monkeys was privileged on the floor of the Senate.[240] Proxmire was not privileged when he made the same comments in press releases, in his constituent newsletter, and in a nationally televised talk show. The Court said that nothing in the history or language of the Constitution suggested that the absolute privilege extended beyond the chambers of

[237]Gregoire v. Biddle, 177 F.2d 579, 581 (2d Cir. 1949).
[238]*See* B. Sanford, *Libel and Privacy* para. 10.4, at 393–413 (1987 Supp.).
[239]U.S. Const. art. I, sec. 6.
[240]443 U.S. at 123–30, 5 Media L. Rep. at 1285–89.

Congress. The clause protected only matters that were an "integral part of the deliberative and communicative processes" of U.S. senators and representatives, including comments made in committee reports and during congressional committee meetings. Communication with constituents and promotional activities are not privileged.

States have enacted privileges for state legislators similar to those granted to members of Congress by the U.S. Constitution. Many states also provide either an absolute or a qualified privilege for subordinate legislators such as city council members. A qualified privilege protects speech only on certain conditions that vary from state to state. A qualified privilege can be defeated by such "abuses" as inaccuracies, common law malice, or a failure of the speech to fulfill a governmental purpose.[241]

Federal executive branch officials with policy-making authority have a broader absolute privilege than members of Congress, in large part because of a 1959 Supreme Court ruling in *Barr v. Matteo*. William G. Barr, an acting director of the U.S. Office of Rent Stabilization, issued a press release condemning two agency officials, John J. Madigan and Linda Matteo. Barr said Madigan and Matteo violated the spirit of a federal law when they permitted employees to receive cash for accumulated leave time. He said the two would be suspended. Madigan and Matteo sued Barr for libel and won in trial court. Barr appealed, and the U.S. Supreme Court said that an absolute privilege protected comments within an official's line of duty. Defamation was protected even if the speech or document was not required by the job.[242] *Barr* has been applied to official letters and statements before grievance boards.

States also have adopted an absolute privilege for governors and cabinet-level officers. Most states provide a qualified privilege to lower-echelon officers of state and local government.[243]

Consent   A settled area of law prohibits people who agree to an activity that harms them from collecting compensation. In libel, this means that people who initiate or authorize publications that damage their own reputations cannot successfully sue.[244]

Explicit consent to defamatory publication is rare. Few people authorize the publication of a remark that may damage their reputation. However, in addition to explicit consent, the courts have, on rare occasions, recognized an implied consent. Consent can be inferred when the person suing for libel encouraged or participated in the defamatory publication, knowing what was about to be printed. The Tennessee Supreme Court said that the Reverend Robert L. Langford consented to a defamatory publication when he agreed to talk to the Vanderbilt student newspaper, *Hustler,* about his suit for libel and privacy against the campus humor magazine. Langford, a Methodist minister, was suing *Chase,* the humor magazine, for falsely implying that his wife was sexually promiscuous and his 1-year-old daughter wanted to be.

---

[241]B. Sanford, *Libel and Privacy* para. 10.4.4, at 407–10 (1987 Supp.); R. Smolla, *Law of Defamation* secs. 8.04[2] and [3], 8.07[2], at 8-15, 8-16, 8-19 (1989).

[242]360 U.S. 564 (1959).

[243]*E.g., Restatement (Second) of Torts* sec. 598A (1977); R. Smolla, *Law of Defamation* secs. 8.05[2] [a] and [3] [b], 8.07[2], at 8-17, 8-18, 8-19 (1989).

[244]*See Prosser and Keeton on Torts* sec. 114, at 822 (5th ed. 1984); B. Sanford, *Libel and Privacy* para. 10.4.6, at 411–13 (1987 Supp.).

Langford told the newspaper reporters that he wanted publicity about his suit against *Chase.* Langford encouraged the students to see his lawyers for details of the suit. Subsequently, *Hustler* published that Langford was suing *Chase. Hustler* reproduced the page in *Chase* that triggered the suit and described the charges in Langford's words. Langford sued the paper as well as the magazine, but the Tennessee court said *Hustler's* presentation of the dispute was privileged because Langford had either invited it or consented to it.[245]

Professional communicators should not rely on the fact that a person about to be defamed in a story is willing to talk to them for publication as the only protection against a libel suit. Court decisions do not adequately explain when the consent defense will be recognized. However, the defense may be available to communicators if people knowingly react for publication to the fact that a newspaper or broadcast station is about to carry a story that defames them.

Privilege for Broadcasts by Political Candidates

Broadcast stations have been granted an absolute privilege to air libel during political broadcasts. In 1959, the Supreme Court said that broadcasters would not be held accountable for defamatory remarks made by political candidates during time provided under the equal opportunities provision, section 315, of the 1934 Communications Act. Until the Supreme Court's decision, section 315 presented a catch-22 for broadcasters.

Section 315 requires that broadcasters who provide airtime to political candidates must provide equal opportunities for opponents. The law also prohibits broadcasters from censoring the candidates' comments in order to foster a "full and unrestricted discussion of political issues by legally qualified candidates."[246] However, although section 315 prohibits broadcast stations from censoring candidates, it does not protect broadcasters from libel suits based on candidates' comments. In other words, the 1934 Communications Act, standing by itself, requires broadcasters to carry programming that would make them vulnerable to libel suits.

In 1959, in *Farmers Educational and Cooperative Union of America v. WDAY,* the Supreme Court ruled that broadcasters are immune from liability for defamation by political candidates. The Court acted after WDAY-TV of Fargo, North Dakota, was sued for comments made by W. C. Townley, a colorful independent candidate for the U.S. Senate. Townley, who was granted time under section 315, said that Communists controlled the North Dakota Farmers Union. Although WDAY-TV personnel had warned Townley beforehand that his comment was libelous, the station was sued by the Farmers Union for $100,000. The U.S. Supreme Court, in a 5–4 vote, upheld lower court rulings in favor of WDAY-TV.

The Court said that Congress, in adopting the Communications Act, intended that broadcast stations have no control over the presentations by political candidates. Otherwise, a station might censor all remarks, even those "faintly objectionable . . . out of an excess of caution." The Court said that if it allowed Farmers Union to sue WDAY, there could be two possible results. Licensees could refuse to permit any candidates to use their facilities, contrary to the intent of section 315 to stimulate vigor-

---

[245]Langford v. Vanderbilt University, 318 S.W.2d 568 (Tenn. 1958).
[246]*See* Farmers Educ. and Coop. Union of America v. WDAY, Inc., 360 U.S. 525, 529 (1959).

ous political discussion. Or, the Court said, broadcasters would be liable for defamation because they did what was required of them by law, a result the Court considered "unconscionable."

SUMMARY

Defamatory statements made by public officials in their official capacity are absolutely privileged and cannot be the basis of a successful libel suit. In addition, persons who have consented to the publication of defamation about themselves cannot successfully sue for libel. Broadcasters are also protected from liability when providing time to political candidates under the equal opportunities rule of the 1934 Communications Act.

Qualified Privileges

Unlike absolute privileges, qualified privileges require at least accuracy and an absence of ill will by writers and editors. The most significant qualified privilege for journalists is the privilege to publish defamatory information from government proceedings. Other privileges important to professional communicators are those that protect the use of defamation in self-defense, the use of defamatory language to discuss matters of mutual interest, and news reports of defamatory comments made by unofficial sources.

Reporter's Privilege A qualified privilege protects the reporting of defamatory comments made in official proceedings as long as the stories are fair and accurate. In many states, the stories also have to be attributed and printed without ill will. The reporter's privilege has been justified by the public's need to be informed about the actions of government. Since most citizens cannot observe government directly, those watching for them need to be able to report without fear of being sued. Some states limit the privilege to the press.[247]

The reporter's qualified privilege, the most important common law defense in the post-*Times v. Sullivan* era, is one of the few protections for the publication of false defamatory statements made by news sources. The defense not only defeats libel claims, but also frustrates the filing of many suits.

The privilege usually protects only the reports of *official* proceedings, including legislative, executive, and judicial activities at all levels of government. The privilege covers reports of government actions and records as well as reports of meetings and hearings. In order for the privilege to apply, proceedings must have a legal basis and must deal with a matter of public concern. Usually, meetings must be open to the public, and documents must be available to the public.[248]

---

[247] *See* Medico v. Time, Inc., 643 F.2d 134, 137–38 n.9, 6 Media L. Rep. 2529, 2531 n.9 (3d Cir. 1981).
[248] *Restatement (Second) of Torts* sec. 611 and sec. 611 comment d (1977).

Official Proceedings: Legislative Branch   The reporter's qualified privilege protects news reports of official proceedings of governmental bodies authorized to enact or repeal statutes. The privilege applies to the activities of the U.S. Congress, state legislatures, county commissions, city councils, community school boards, and university boards of trustees.[249] Organizations such as the local Parent-Teacher Association do not qualify since the PTA cannot pass legislation that can be enforced by legal sanctions.

The privilege applies to fair and accurate stories on official meetings, hearings, and reports of legislative bodies and their committees. The privilege protects reports of the comments of anyone recognized to speak during official meetings. Reporters need not worry about the truth of the remarks made in official proceedings or reports. Hence, the Barton County, Missouri, *Democrat* was privileged when it reported that a man attending a city council meeting accused Gregg Shafer, a local policeman, of "knocking up" the man's 16-year-old daughter. The comments came during a discussion of who should run the police department. A Missouri appeals court said the *Democrat* was not responsible for investigating the truth or falsity of the accusation. Otherwise, the court said, a newspaper would be unable to fully report derogatory statements made at public meetings of official bodies.[250]

Journalists will probably be protected by the privilege as long as a quorum is present, minutes are being taken, and the legislative body appears to be conducting official business. The *Passaic* (New Jersey) *Daily News* was privileged when it reported a defamatory comment made during a special meeting of the Clifton City Council. The council had met to consider fiscal issues. However, during the meeting, City Manager John L. Fitzgerald was asked why he did not promote Chester R. Swede and Raymond DeLucca to the rank of police sergeant. Fitzgerald, who admitted to having a few drinks before the meeting, said Swede and DeLucca had been "insubordinate" and "should have been fired." A few months later, with Fitzgerald retired, the council voted to exonerate Swede and DeLucca of any charges. When the patrolmen sued the *Daily News* for printing Fitzgerald's charges, the New Jersey court said the council meeting had been privileged. The court said that although the meeting took place in a conference room rather than the regular meeting room, the council conducted official business and minutes were taken. The meeting was not only official but also public, since the press was allowed to attend.[251]

However, a reporter may not be privileged to report defamatory comments made in the halls outside a council meeting or state legislative session. The remarks will not be considered to be part of a legislative proceeding, even if they are made by a council member or a state legislator.

The reporter's privilege applies to reports of defamatory statements in petitions or complaints made to an official body as long as those documents have been officially received. Petitions to recall a public official may not be protected until the documents are accepted by the appropriate government office. In addition, meetings and discussions by citizens' groups prior to the submission of petitions may not be protected.

---

[249]*Restatement (Second) of Torts* sec. 611 comment d (1977).
[250]Shafer v. Lamar Publishing Co., 621 S.W.2d 709, 7 Media L. Rep. 2049 (Mo. Ct. App. 1981).
[251]Swede v. Passaic Daily News, 153 A.2d 36 (1959).

Official Proceedings: Executive Branch   The reach of the privilege to report executive branch activities is far from clear. Official actions, publications, and proclamations are clearly protected. Stories about informal communication within the executive branch or by executive officers are not protected. However, the courts have not provided guidelines for determining when actions and documents become official and which executive branch employees fall within the boundaries of the privilege.

Stories based on official reports are privileged. Therefore, the *New York Times* was protected when it reported the results of an investigation by New York City's Department of Consumer Affairs into the sales practices of air-conditioner repair shops.[252] Likewise, the *Tampa Tribune* was privileged when it reported that the Stable Lounge was identified as a "trouble spot" in information provided by the county sheriff.[253] Stories based on government investigations in progress or on investigatory documents not available to the public have not generally been privileged. There are recent exceptions, however.[254]

Generally speaking, accurate stories about officials acting and speaking in their official capacity will be protected. Most legal authorities argue the reporter's privilege is triggered when official conduct is clothed by an official's absolute privilege.[255] The higher ranking the official, the more likely the protection will apply. Articles based on official press conferences often will be privileged.[256] The privilege applied when California attorney general Evelle J. Younger released, at a press conference, a report by the state's Organized Crime Control Commission. The document contained the names of 92 people suspected of having connections to organized crime. When Gerald Hay Kilgore, identified as a bookie in the report, sued several media organizations, the California Supreme Court said the reports of the press conference were privileged. The court said California law provided a privilege for fair and accurate reports of a public meeting legally convened by a public official for a lawful purpose.[257]

However, in many jurisdictions, informal remarks made by public officials apart from an official report or proceeding are not protected. For example, the privilege did not protect a story repeating the accusations of Anthony Mitchell, a prosecuting attorney in Camden County, New Jersey. Mitchell asserted in an argument with a local police chief that Les Rogers, a prominent Camden politician, had ordered the police to "fix" criminal cases. The argument took place both in a courtroom and in a judge's chambers, but court had been adjourned. The New Jersey Supreme Court said Mitchell's comments were not made during official court proceedings and they did not constitute an official statement of the county prosecutor's office.[258]

---

[252]Freeze Right Refrigeration & Air Conditioning Services, Inc. v. City of New York, 475 N.Y.S.2d 383, 10 Media L. Rep. 2032 (N.Y. App. Div. 1984).

[253]Hatjioannou v. Tribune Co., 8 Media L. Rep. 2637 (Fla. Cir. Ct. 1982). *See also Restatement (Second) of Torts* sec. 611 comment d (1977).

[254]*E.g.,* Medico v. Time, Inc., 643 F.2d 134, 6 Media L. Rep. 2529 (3d Cir. 1981).

[255]*See Prosser and Keeton on Torts* sec. 114, at 793 (5th ed. 1984); *Restatement (Second) of Torts* sec. 612 comment c (1977).

[256]*See* R. Sack, *Libel, Slander, and Related Problems* 321 (1980); R. Smolla, *Law of Defamation* sec. 8.10[2] [d], at 8-36 (1989).

[257]Kilgore v. Younger, 640 P.2d 793, 8 Media L. Rep. 1886 (Cal. 1982).

[258]Rogers v. Courier Post Co., 66 A.2d 869 (N.J. 1949).

Stories about quasi-judicial proceedings in the executive branch are usually protected. In 1985, the *Louisville Times* was protected for most of a story reporting that Dr. Charles E. Pearce was being investigated for prescribing excessive or needless drugs. The article was primarily based on proceedings before the Kentucky Board of Medical Licensure.[259] Stories about public hearings will be privileged if the hearings are supervised by an official with the power to investigate complaints.[260]

Arrest reports are privileged but usually only after a suspect has been officially booked.[261] The suspect usually must be officially charged with a crime, and the name of the suspect must be entered on a police blotter. The blotter itself—the list of the suspect's name, address, age, and charge—is privileged in those states where it is an official public record. Journalists need to be particularly careful when reporting arrests. People can be picked up by police without being arrested. Police can pick up people for questioning, "invite" them to the police station, or simply remove them from the street. In addition, the police sometimes tell reporters that someone who has been arrested will be charged with a crime and then, for one reason or another, charges are never filed.

The informal disclosure by a law enforcement officer that an arrest has been made is not privileged in every state. Reporters may not be privileged when they rely on the word of an officer at the scene of a crime, obtain information from an officer over the phone, or take the information from a police "hot line." For example, an appeals court said the District of Columbia hot line that provided crime reports for the media was not privileged. The *Washington Evening Star* relied on the hot line to say that John Phillips was charged with homicide after shooting his wife during an argument. The police later classified the shooting as an accident. The Court of Appeals for the District of Columbia affirmed a lower court ruling that the hot line consisted of unofficial police statements rather than a privileged official police report. The appeals court allowed a jury award of $1 in nominal damages to Phillips to stand.[262]

Informal police reports may not only lack privilege but may not be verifiable. The media often have no protection for defamatory statements if the police officer on the scene, or the desk officer over the telephone, later denies a reporter's version of a conversation.

If journalists have to be careful about where they obtain information, they also have to be careful not to add information unavailable from official records. If journalists add to the reports of privileged proceedings and comments or information from other sources, the supplementary materials may not be protected. Although the *Louisville Times* was privileged when it reported from official proceedings that the drug prescriptions written by Dr. Charles E. Pearce were being investigated, other information in the same story was not privileged. The *Times* was not protected for a paragraph reporting that 79-year-old Hattie Rose Ludwig contended she became a

[259]Pearce v. Courier-Journal & Louisville Times Co., 683 S.W.2d 622, 11 Media L. Rep. 1498 (Ky. Ct. App. 1985).

[260]*Restatement (Second) of Torts* sec. 611 comment d (1977).

[261]*See Prosser and Keeton on Torts* sec. 115, at 836–37 (5th ed. 1984); *Restatement (Second) of Torts* sec. 611 comment h (1977).

[262]Phillips v. Evening Star Newspaper Co., 424 A.2d 78, 6 Media L. Rep. 2191 (D.C. 1980), *cert. denied,* 451 U.S. 989 (1981), *aff'd* 2 Media L. Rep. 2201 (D.C. Super. Ct. 1977).

drug addict while a patient of Dr. Pearce. Although Ludwig's allegation had only been used to illustrate the charges under investigation in an official proceeding, it arose during an interview that was not privileged. When Dr. Pearce sued the paper for libel, a Kentucky appeals court affirmed a summary judgment for the newspaper in the case of the information taken from official proceedings. However, the court allowed Pearce to sue for the information obtained from Hattie Rose Ludwig.[263]

In addition, contrary to a frequently repeated myth, the word *alleged* in crime stories does not always protect the media from libel suits. Some reporters write that "police alleged that Joe Crook robbed the Dodge City Bank" when they cannot accurately, or with certainty, say "police have charged Joe Crook with robbing the Dodge City Bank." Ordinarily, reporters use the word *alleged* when the police say Joe Crook robbed the bank but there is no official charge and journalists have no evidence to support the allegation. Some journalists believe that use of the word *alleged* protects them from liability when they cannot rely on the reporter's privilege to report the contents of official documents.[264] The use of *alleged* may tell readers that a reporter is unsure of a charge, but it does not protect a reporter from a successful libel suit if information gathered from unprivileged sources is false.

Official Proceedings: Judicial Branch   The privilege to cover judicial proceedings is particularly important since practically every issue taken to court is potentially defamatory. The reporter's privilege pertains to anything said during the official judicial process by all legitimate participants, including judges, witnesses, jurors, litigants, and attorneys. In some jurisdictions, reports of uninvited outbursts from observers might not be privileged.

The privilege applies to fair and accurate reports of all judicial proceedings, no matter how minor the court. The privilege covers the report of indictments, warrants signed by a judge, trials, judicial orders, verdicts, and judgments entered at the court clerk's office. Reports of depositions—sworn statements made by witnesses under oath—are also privileged. So is the coverage of pretrial proceedings, such as hearings.

However, in many states, the privilege applies only once the judicial process begins. Often, a judge has to take action in a case, if only to set a court date or to meet with the parties in chambers, before the privilege applies to documents in the case. News stories about the instigation of a civil lawsuit, for example, may not be privileged even though a complaint is filed with the court clerk.[265] The privilege to report court proceedings often does not begin with the filing of a complaint because courts want to frustrate people who might be inclined to file a frivolous suit in order to obtain news coverage protected by libel law.

Therefore, before a civil suit becomes a part of the judicial process, journalists may be liable for reporting remarks made in a civil complaint that later cannot be proven true. When a man named Emerson sued Wallace Sanford for "alienation of

---

[263]Pearce v. Courier-Journal & Louisville Times Co., 683 S.W.2d 633, 11 Media L. Rep. 1498 (Ky. Ct. App. 1985). *See Restatement (Second) of Torts* sec. 611 comment f (1977).

[264]*See also Webster's New World Dictionary of American English* (3rd college ed. 1988).

[265]*See Prosser and Keeton on Torts* sec. 115, at 837 (5th ed. 1984); *Restatement (Second) of Torts* sec. 611 commente (1977).

affections," a 1941 report in the *Boston Herald-Traveler* based on the civil complaint was not privileged. Emerson said Sanford induced Emerson's wife to leave him after Sanford met her in secret. At trial, Emerson produced no evidence to back up his charges, and Sanford sued the newspaper. The Supreme Judicial Court of Massachusetts upheld a lower court's decision to award Sanford $2,000. The court said Emerson's official complaint was a public record in the sense that it was available for general public inspection. However, the court refused to declare that the information in public records could be published without regard to its truth or falsity. The court said that Massachusetts did not provide a privilege for repeating defamatory charges in complaints not yet acted upon by a judge. To be safe, the court added, a newspaper need "only" wait to report court proceedings "rather than to search the files of cases not yet brought before the court." The court did not consider evidence presented during the trial to be relevant to a suit based on the *Herald-Traveler's* story about the complaint.[266] However, some states do provide a privilege for the reporting of civil complaints.

Ordinarily, the privilege to cover the judicial process extends only to proceedings that are public. Closed court sessions for juvenile cases and for the testimony of victims in sexual assault cases are often not privileged. Similarly, in most states, stories relying on documents or records officially withheld from the public are not privileged.[267] This often includes papers filed in juvenile and divorce cases.

Although journalists need to know the state law governing reporter's privilege, they are not expected to make technical determinations of what constitutes an official legal proceeding. If a proceeding appears to be legal, and if the people in attendance act as if it is legal, then an accurate report of the proceeding should be protected even if false, defamatory statements are made. Reporters are not expected to know, for example, when a judge takes an action beyond the court's authority.[268]

Unofficial Proceedings In some states, reporters are privileged to report unofficial but open meetings held to discuss matters of public concern.[269] The privilege may apply to public meetings of union members, church members, political parties, and medical and bar associations. The privilege could be used to report a Chamber of Commerce "forum" or a meeting to discuss the removal of public officials. The U.S. Court of Appeals for the Ninth Circuit ruled that the *Moscow Idahonian* was privileged when it reported defamatory comments made at an unofficial public meeting of citizens at Moscow High School. Some at the meeting argued that a grand jury ought to investigate the legal maneuvers that followed a fight between a University of Idaho student and a lawyer named Murray Estes. One speaker implied that Judge John K. Borg acted unethically when he dismissed a charge brought against Estes for assault with a deadly weapon. Borg sued for libel, using Estes as his attorney. After a trial court ruled that the story in the *Idahonian* was accurate, the Ninth Circuit said the press performed "its most valuable function" when it truthfully reported proceed-

---

[266]Sanford v. Boston Herald-Traveler Corp., 61 N.E.2d 5 (1945).

[267]*See Prosser and Keeton on Torts* sec. 115, at 837 (5th ed. 1984).

[268]*See* Lee v. Brooklyn Union Publishing Co., 103 N.E. 155 (1913); *Restatement (Second) of Torts* sec. 611 comment g (1977).

[269]*See Restatement (Second) of Torts* sec. 611 comment i (1977).

ings related to the administration of law. The court said the public in a representative government must be informed.[270]

Reports of private gatherings such as the annual meetings of corporations, are not generally privileged. Such meetings usually are not concerned with public problems but with private interests, such as those of stockholders. However, in some states, a report of a meeting of a private organization may be privileged if the meeting pertains to matters of public interest and is open to the public.[271]

Conditions of Privilege: Accuracy and Fairness   Any story and headline based on an official proceeding must accurately reflect what was said. Relatively minor errors will not defeat the privilege, but a substantial error or distortion can. *Time* magazine could not claim a privilege when it erroneously reported the reason Russell Firestone was granted a divorce from his wife Mary Alice, a case discussed earlier in the chapter.[272]

A story must not only be accurate to be privileged, but it must also provide a balanced presentation of the proceeding. A story cannot report only the arguments on one side of a debate or only the arguments for the prosecution. This was noted by the U.S. Court of Appeals for the Sixth Circuit when Victoria Price Street, the white woman who accused nine black ''Scottsboro Boys'' of raping her in 1931, sued NBC. The network, in defending its docudrama about the case, claimed a privilege to report a judicial proceeding. The court said, however, that the movie was not an accurate account of the trial. Witnesses who corroborated the story of the former Victoria Price were not shown. Portions of the show depicting Price as a perjurer and a promiscuous woman were emphasized. The flashbacks used presented only one side. The privilege was not allowed.[273]

Of course, journalists can report the events in court for a day even if only the prosecution is presenting its case. However, reporters will be expected to report the case when the defense is presenting its side.[274]

Conditions of Privilege: Attribution and Common Law Malice   In most cases, the reader, viewer, or listener must be told that a story is a report of an official proceeding in order for the story to be privileged. This means that both the story and the headline must include an attribution. The old *Washington Daily News* once printed a story that asserted that William F. and Josephine P. Hughes were charged with making bogus money and passing the bills on an air tour of the country. There was no attribution. The paper told the court it obtained the information from an announcement made by the U.S. Secretary of the Treasury. The U.S. Court of Appeals for the District of Columbia said, however, that a statement made by a newspaper on its own authority was not privileged. The fact that the official announcement and the story were similar was not sufficient to qualify for the privilege.[275]

---

[270]Borg v. Boas, 231 F.2d 781 (1956).

[271]*See Prosser and Keeton on Torts* sec. 115, at 836 (5th ed. 1984); *Restatement (Second) of Torts* sec. 611 comment i (1977).

[272]Time, Inc. v. Firestone, 424 U.S. at 457–58, 1 Media L. Rep. at 1668. *See* 424 U.S. 448 (1976).

[273]Street v. NBC, 645 F.2d at 1223, 7 Media L. Rep. at 1005.

[274]*Restatement (Second) of Torts* sec. 611 comment f (1977).

[275]Hughes v. Washington Daily News Co., 193 F.2d 922 (1952).

A few courts have ruled that journalists could not rely on the reporter's privilege if they did not base their stories on official documents. In Louisiana, a court ruled the privilege did not apply when a *Baton Rouge State Times* reporter obtained false defamatory information from another newspaper, the *Morning Advocate.* The *Morning Advocate* said that Ronald E. Melon had been arrested on three drug-related charges, including possessing methamphetamines for the purpose of distributing them. The reporters for the *Morning Advocate* based their story on a press release from the East Baton Rouge Parish sheriff's office that named Melon among four persons arrested on a series of charges. Ronald Melon had not been arrested for the possession of methamphetamines with the intent to distribute, and he sued both newspapers.

A Louisiana appeals court granted a privilege to the *Morning Advocate* for a "reasonable interpretation" of the press release. The court said the press release could have been interpreted to mean that all four men had been arrested for all the crimes or that each of the four had been arrested for at least one of the crimes. However, the court said it could not grant a privilege to the reporter for the *State Times,* who did not see the official document in the first place but relied on the report of the other paper.[276]

The reporter's privilege can also be defeated by a showing of ill will or other improper purpose. The *Restatement (Second) of Torts* says ill will or improper purpose can no longer defeat the privilege, but the precedent remains in many states.[277]

Neutral Reportage   Historically, the media have not been privileged to report newsworthy but defamatory charges made outside an official proceeding. However, a few courts have adopted a legal defense that protects reporters who accurately repeat defamatory charges made about public figures. A doctrine called *neutral reportage* allows the media to report newsworthy statements by reliable sources even if the reporter doubts the accuracy of the remarks. The few courts that have adopted neutral reportage say the protection is important to the public debate of controversial issues encouraged by the First Amendment.

Legal recognition of neutral reportage arose out of the controversy over the use of the pesticide DDT. Three scientists sued the *New York Times* for reporting that they had been accused of being "paid liars" as "scientist-spokesmen" for the pesticide industry. *Times* reporter John Devlin obtained from officials of the National Audubon Society the names of industry scientists the organization accused of misleading the public about the impact of DDT on bird life. The organization's 1971 Christmas Bird Count said that certain scientists were being paid to say that DDT did not kill birds. The society said the scientists were misusing the bird-count data to say that bird life in North America was thriving in spite of the use of pesticides. The scientists' claims, the society said, were "false and misleading, a distortion of the facts for the most self-serving reasons." Devlin included the names of the scientists in the story even though both of those he reached denied the charges.

A federal jury awarded $20,000 to each of the scientists, but the U.S. Court of

---

[276]Melon v. Capital City Press, 407 So.2d 85, 8 Media L. Rep. 1165 (La. Ct. App. 1981).
[277]*See Restatement (Second) of Torts* sec. 611 (1977); *Prosser and Keeton on Torts* sec. 115, at 838 (5th ed. 1984).

Appeals for the Second Circuit reversed the judgment. The court said the First Amendment protected the "accurate and disinterested reporting" of charges made by a "responsible, prominent organization" such as the National Audubon Society, even though a reporter believes the charges to be false. The court said that the fact that the accusations were made was newsworthy. The press should not have to suppress newsworthy statements because it seriously doubted their truth. The court said the public interest in being informed about "sensitive issues" required that the press be able to report defamatory charges without having to assume responsibility for them.[278]

So far courts have adopted the privilege of neutral reportage for only limited situations. Usually, the charges must be

1. newsworthy and related to a public controversy,
2. made by a responsible person or organization,
3. about a public official or public figure,
4. accurately reported alongside opposing views, and
5. reported impartially.

Neutral reportage has thus far been adopted in only a handful of jurisdictions. It has been accepted by the U.S. Court of Appeals for the Eighth Circuit, several federal district courts, and state appellate courts in Ohio, Vermont, and Florida. Reaction by courts in Illinois and New York is mixed. The privilege has been rejected by the state supreme courts in Kentucky and South Dakota and an appeals court in Michigan.[279] Courts that have rejected neutral reportage have been hesitant to allow the media to print statements known to be or suspected of being false. The courts have been unwilling to provide protection beyond *New York Times* actual malice for stories about public figures and public officials.

Self-Interest or Self-Defense   The concept of self-defense, like consent, discussed earlier, runs through most areas of the law. People can use reasonable means to defend their self-interest, whether against assault, unfair business practices, or libel. In libel law, self-defense means that individuals or businesses are protected when publishing libelous language to combat attacks on their own reputations.[280]

Courts have held that publishers and broadcast stations can use the self-defense privilege not only to reply on their own behalf but also on behalf of others. The Virginia Supreme Court of Appeals said that a trial court did not adequately consider self-defense when adjudicating a dispute between the *Princess Anne Free Press* and the *Virginia Beach Sun-News*. The trial court awarded $30,000 to J. Willcox Dunn, editor of the *Free Press,* who was called a "deliberate liar" and a "fugitive from truth" in the *Sun-News,* a competing publication. However, the comments in the

---

[278]Edwards v. National Audubon Soc'y, Inc., 556 F.2d 113, 2 Media L. Rep. 1849, *cert. denied sub nom.* Edwards v. New York Times Co., 434 U.S. 1002 (1977).

[279]*See* McCrory, Bernius, Jones, & Grygiel, "Constitutional Privilege in Libel Law" in J. Goodale, ed., 1 *Communications Law 1989* at 641–50.

[280]*Restatement (Second) of Torts* sec. 594 comment k (1977); *Prosser and Keeton on Torts* sec. 115, at 825 (5th ed. 1984).

Sun-News were printed in response to a campaign by Dunn against what he called the "Kellam machine." Dunn concentrated his attacks on Floyd Kellam, a county judge, and Sidney Kellam, a business and political leader who owned part of the *Sun-News*. Dunn charged that the majority of officeholders in Princess Anne County and Virginia Beach were part of the Kellam machine and associated with criminals. Indeed, Dunn said, the *Sun-News* was part of the machine. The Virginia appellate court sent the libel suit back to the trial court to consider whether the *Sun-News* had published in defense of itself and others attacked by Dunn.[281]

Businesses, besides using the self-defense privilege to reply to a defamatory attack, also can use it to protect a lawful self-interest. For example, a business would have a libel defense if it told potential customers that a competitor was using trade secrets stolen from the business's facilities.[282] Although self-interest is a qualified privilege applicable only under certain conditions, it provides more protection than would ordinarily be available for accusing a business of stealing trade secrets, which is obviously defamatory language. The defense will not protect defamation used for no other reason than to woo customers away from a competitor. In libel law, as well as in law generally, an argument of self-defense will not protect the acts of an aggressor.[283]

Neither will writers be protected if they go beyond what is reasonably necessary to defend themselves or others. The self-defense privilege can be used as a right to reply as long as the level of invective does not exceed that of the attack. A famous example of an inappropriate reply is a 1949 syndicated column by Westbrook Pegler. Pegler was accused by Quentin Reynolds of causing the death of the writer Heywood Broun by calling Broun a liar. Reynolds, in the *New York Herald-Tribune Book Review,* said that Broun brooded over the attack and could not rest or sleep although he had been sick. Reynolds accused Pegler of "moral homicide." In reply, Pegler accused Reynolds and "his wench" of public nudity. He also said Reynolds proposed marriage to Broun's widow on the way to her husband's grave. In addition, Pegler accused Reynolds of being a "war profiteer" and a coward. A federal appeals court said that Pegler's column exceeded the bounds of the self-defense privilege. Pegler's column was not related to Reynolds's charges but was "a wholly separate personal attack upon Reynolds."[284]

Comments made in self-defense can only be disseminated as broadly as necessary to protect the reputation at stake. Further distribution can defeat the privilege. Self-defense also can be defeated by a showing of improper motive or *New York Times* actual malice.[285]

Privileges for Messages of Mutual Interest Two related privileges protect communications among persons with common interests. In the first, members of an organi-

---

[281]Haycox v. Dunn, 104 S.E.2d 800 (1958).

[282]*See* Converters Equip. Corp. v. Condes Corp., 258 N.W.2d 712 (Wis. 1977).

[283]*Restatement (Second) of Torts* sec. 594 comments f, g, and h (1977); R. Sack, *Libel, Slander, and Related Problems* 302 (1980). *See* Mid-America Food Serv. v. ARA Servs. Inc., 578 F.2d 691 (8th Cir. 1978).

[284]Reynolds v. Pegler, 223 F.2d 429 (2d Cir. 1955).

[285]*Prosser and Keeton on Torts* sec. 115, at 825 (5th ed. 1984); *Restatement (Second) of Torts* sec. 594 comment a and comment on clause (b) (1977).

zation are privileged in their discussions of mutual affairs. The privilege protects communications between business partners and corporation employees that defame third parties. It protects, for example, the conversations in newsrooms about potentially defamatory stories. The privilege also applies to defamation among members of religious or professional societies, fraternities, labor unions, and educational organizations.

A second privilege protects a defamatory message that affects the welfare of the receiver, particularly if the information has been requested. This privilege usually protects credit agency reports, letters of reference to prospective employers, and comments of employees to employers about fellow employees and customers. The Illinois Supreme Court said a defamatory comment made by an officer of Hayes Freight Lines about a former employee was privileged. The officer, David Ratner, was filling out a verification of employment for Seymour Zeinfield, who was seeking a mortgage from Park Forest Homes. Ratner said Zeinfield left the company owing it ''a substantial amount of money,'' and he found it difficult to vouch for him. Zeinfield sued, but the Illinois court said Ratner only responded in good faith to an inquiry that affected the well-being of Park Forest Homes.[286]

Neither of the privileges for messages of common interest can be relied upon if the information involved is communicated to anyone not sharing the same interests. Therefore, neither privilege would apply to an employer's statements to the media about the firing of an employee. The privileges can also be defeated with ill will or *New York Times* actual malice.[287]

SUMMARY

The reporter's qualified privilege to report official proceedings is the most important of the common law defenses. Reporters will be protected from libel suits as long as they report official proceedings and records fairly and accurately, with proper attribution, and without ill will. The privilege does not protect the reporting of an official's informal comments outside of an official meeting.

A few courts have declared that reporters should be protected when accurately reporting false defamatory statements made outside of official proceedings. The defense of neutral reportage, as the privilege is called, usually applies only when the defamatory remarks are made about public officials or public figures by responsible people or organizations. The charges usually must be newsworthy, related to a public controversy, and reported impartially, including a reaction from the person defamed.

The courts protect libelous remarks communicated only among members of a group with a strong common interest. The courts also protect defamatory information provided to individuals or organizations for their well-being. Businesses can publish defamation to protect their interests. An individual or mass medium cannot be

---

[286]Zeinfield v. Hayes Freight Lines, Inc., 243 N.E.2d 217 (Ill. 1968).
[287]*Prosser and Keeton on Torts* sec. 115, at 828–30 (5th ed. 1984).

successfully sued for libel if the defamatory remarks were made in reply to libelous remarks first uttered by the plaintiff.

Protection for Opinion

The chapter so far has concentrated on defamatory assertions of fact that can be proven either true or false. The common law protects factual statements harmful to reputation that are provably true, such as an assertion that former Cincinnati baseball All-Star Pete Rose filed false income tax returns. The First Amendment even protects assertions of fact that are false and defamatory if the statements were published without negligence or reckless disregard for the truth. Therefore, the Associated Press won a libel suit brought by Major General Edwin Walker even though the AP falsely said Major General Walker led a mob attacking federal marshals at the University of Mississippi.

However, statements of opinion that may damage reputation but cannot be proven true or false present different problems for the courts. Statements of "pure" opinion are, by definition, expressions of belief or judgment rather than assertions of fact. Courts have long recognized that protection for opinion from successful libel suits is important because the punishment of opinion involves the punishment of ideas. Courts have not wanted to restrict, for example, the criticism of literature, public officials, and business practices when the commentary depends more on judgment than on factual allegations. Yet the courts do not want to shield from liability fact-laden expressions, such as "the mayor is corrupt," which could hide a false accusation of criminal behavior.

In addition, courts ordinarily do not permit libel judgments for exaggerated speech that is intended to convey opinion rather than factual information. Most courts would rule the word *stupid* is not actionable when used figuratively, as in "You stupid idiot. You locked us out of the house." The word *stupid* is actionable only when a speaker means to describe a person with a low level of intelligence, which can be proven true or false. However, determining when such words as *stupid, liar, blackmailer,* and *traitor* are used figuratively and when they are used descriptively is a difficult task for the courts.

Communicators expressing an opinion can receive qualified protection from libel suits under both constitutional law and the common law.

Constitutional Protection   The U.S. Supreme Court has said the First Amendment protects statements of opinion in two ways. First, the Constitution exempts from liability opinion in the form of exaggerated language that cannot reasonably be interpreted by a reader or viewer as a statement of fact. Second, the Court has said opinion is protected by the constitutional rule, announced in *Philadelphia Newspapers v. Hepps,* that a plaintiff must prove falsity to win a libel suit. The Supreme Court has said that the Constitution does not protect opinion that implies a provably false defamatory assertion.

Figurative Language and Rhetorical Hyperbole   The Supreme Court has said that the First Amendment protects picturesque and exaggerated speech that cannot "reasonably [be] interpreted as stating actual facts."[288] The Court has said that whether figurative or exaggerated statements convey opinion or assertions of fact often depends on the context of remarks. Words such as *blackmail* and *traitor* that may have a specific factual meaning in some circumstances may be protected as "loose, figurative" language or "rhetorical hyperbole" in others, the Court said.

To determine whether a statement is an expression of opinion or a factual assertion may require an examination of the language in the context of the complete article. A word or statement with a commonly understood meaning might be intentionally exaggerated or used metaphorically to make a point. In *Greenbelt Publishing v. Bresler,* for example, the Court said the word *blackmail* did not defame real estate developer Charles Bresler when it was used to describe his offer to the city of Greenbelt, Maryland.

Bresler sued the *Greenbelt News Review* for libel after the newspaper reported citizen comments made at a city council hearing. Several speakers said Bresler was blackmailing the city because he refused to sell a piece of land until the city helped him obtain favorable zoning for another. Justice Potter Stewart, writing for the Supreme Court, said it was "simply impossible to believe" that a reader of the *News Review* would have interpreted *blackmail* to mean that Bresler was being charged with a crime. To the contrary, Stewart said,

> even the most careless reader must have perceived that the word was no more than rhetorical hyperbole, a vigorous epithet used by those who considered Bresler's negotiating position extremely unreasonable.[289]

The Court said that not only was the newspaper's story a fair and accurate report of an official proceeding, but that the use of *blackmail* was a constitutionally protected expression of opinion.

In contrast, the Supreme Court decided in 1990 that the use of the word *lied* in a newspaper column was a factual assertion rather than protected opinion. In *Milkovich v. Lorain Journal Co.,* the Court decided 7–2 that a sports column in the Willoughby, Ohio, *News-Herald* strongly implied that a high school wrestling coach lied under oath. In *Milkovich,* sports columnist J. Theodore Diadiun criticized a court decision lifting penalties imposed on a high school wrestling team by the Ohio High School Athletic Association. The athletic association had placed the Maple Heights High School wrestling team on probation after seven persons were injured in a brawl at a Maple Heights wrestling match. Maple Heights wrestling coach Michael Milkovich testified that he was not responsible for the brawl before both an athletic association hearing and an Ohio trial court reviewing the association's decision. Diadiun said in his column that Milkovich inspired fans to attack opponents from Mentor High School. In addition, Diadiun said, anyone attending the meet "knows in his heart" that Milkovich "lied at the hearing after . . . having given his solemn oath to tell the truth." Diadiun also said that Maple Heights students learned a lesson: "If you get in a jam, lie your way out."[290]

---

[288]Milkovich v. Lorain Journal Co., 17 Media L. Rep. at 2018, *quoting* Hustler Magazine, Inc. v. Falwell, 485 U.S. at 50, 14 Media L. Rep. at 2283 (1988).

[289]Greenbelt Coop. Publishing Ass'n v. Bresler, 398 U.S. at 14, 1 Media L. Rep. at 1593 (1970).

[290]Milkovich v. Lorain Journal Co., 17 Media L. Rep. 2009 (1990).

Although the News Journal Co. argued that Diadiun's comments were constitutionally protected opinion, the Supreme Court disagreed. The Court in *Milkovich* emphasized the importance of protecting "imaginative expression" and "rhetorical hyperbole" that could not be understood by the reasonable reader to be statements of fact, and that "has traditionally added much to the discourse of our Nation." However, seven of the nine Court justices believed that Diadiun's use of the word *lied* was not "loose, figurative or hyperbolic language" but an accusation that Milkovich had committed the crime of perjury. The Court said little to explain how it arrived at its conclusion or how other courts should decide similar cases. It only quoted another court's impression that "the clear impact in some nine sentences [of the Diadiun column] and a caption is that [Milkovich] 'lied at the hearing.' "[291] The U.S. Supreme Court said an examination of the article as a whole did not negate that impression. The Supreme Court reversed an opinion of the Ohio Court of Appeals, and remanded the case for trial.

To determine whether expression is a statement of opinion or an assertion of fact, courts not only examine a word or phrase in the context of the rest of an article but also often consider the setting of the remarks. One court said that "some types of writing or speech by custom or convention signal to readers or listeners that what is being read or heard is likely to be opinion, not fact."[292] Although the Supreme Court in *Milkovich* did not pay serious attention to the location of Diadiun's comments in a sports column, other courts have often said that reasonable readers expect to see strongly stated opinions, rather than precise statements of fact, in editorials, columns, and reviews of art, movies, and restaurants.

Courts also frequently note the nation's tradition of "sharp and biting writing" on political and social issues.[293] In a case endorsed in *Milkovich,* the Supreme Court recognized that "exaggerated rhetoric was commonplace in labor disputes." In *National Association of Letter Carriers v. Austin,* the Court said the word *traitor* did not convey a defamatory meaning when applied to a "scab," an employee who crossed a picket line to work. A letter carriers union newspaper printed a list of the names of 15 "scabs" just below an "explanation." In an essay often attributed to Jack London, a "scab" is said to be "a traitor to his God, his country, his family and his class." However, the Supreme Court said that the word *traitor* was used in a "loose, figurative sense" rather than to mean that the workers had committed treason.[294]

In *Greenbelt v. Bresler,* where the Supreme Court said that the word *blackmail* had not been used in its literal sense, the Court noted that debates about controversial issues at city council meetings are usually heated. The Court said the preservation of "free political discussion," so that people could participate in government decision making, "is a fundamental principle of our constitutional system."[295]

Writers should be aware that the use of epithets, insults, hyperbole, and name-

---

[291]17 Media L. Rep. at 2019, *quoting* Scott v. News-Herald, 496 N.E.2d 699, 707, 13 Media L. Rep. 1241, 1246 (1986).

[292]Ollman v. Evans and Novak, 750 F.2d at 983, 11 Media L. Rep. at 1444.

[293]*E.g., id.,* at 983–84, 11 Media L. Rep. at 1446.

[294]418 U.S. at 264, 268 (1975).

[295]Greenbelt Coop. Publishing Ass'n v. Bresler, 398 U.S. at 11–12, 1 Media L. Rep. at 1592, *quoting* Stromberg v. California, 283 U.S. 359, 369 (1931).

calling can be risky. Although courts often protect extreme language on the grounds that epithets and insults do not have meanings that can be supported by facts, a court may decide that in context the extreme language connotes an accusation subject to proof of truth. Writers cannot be certain in advance whether a court will decide that words such as *traitor, hypocrite,* or *liar* in context are assertions of fact as decided in *Milkovich* or exaggerated rhetoric in the sense that the word *blackmail* was used in the Greenbelt, Maryland, city council meeting. In addition, *Milkovich* demonstrates that expression is not automatically protected because it appears in an editorial, column, or movie or restaurant review.

Expression Not Provably False   The Supreme Court has not only said that the First Amendment protects figurative speech and rhetorical hyperbole, but in its 1990 *Milkovich* decision the Court also ruled that the First Amendment protects any expression about matters of public concern that cannot be proven false. The Court said that the constitutional requirement that plaintiffs must prove defamatory comments false, explained in *Philadelphia Newspapers v. Hepps,* ensures protection for opinion that does not contain a provably false connotation.

Therefore, the Court suggested the *Hepps* requirement protected "pure" opinion since statements of opinion cannot be proven true or false. For example, the Court said in *Milkovich,* no one could prove false the statement that "Mayor Jones shows his abysmal ignorance by accepting the teachings of Marx and Lenin," and therefore the statement would be constitutionally protected.

However, the courts have only been willing to protect expression as opinion as long as the opinion is not subject to proof of truth. The courts have said that if a statement is subject to verification, it conveys factual information that ought to be tested for accuracy rather than opinion that ought to be protected.[296] In *Milkovich,* the Court said, the suggestion in Theodore Diadiun's sports column that the wrestling coach, Michael Milkovich, lied under oath was a factual statement capable of verification. Diadiun's comment could not be constitutionally protected as opinion because it was not a subjective assertion but a comment that could be proven true or false. A court could determine whether Milkovich committed perjury by examining transcripts from the hearing and trial testimony and interviewing witnesses.

In *Milkovich,* the Supreme Court suggested that editorials, columns, and other expressions of opinion should not be constitutionally protected if they are based on information that is either incorrect or incomplete. Therefore, to say that a person is "a despicable human being" is a statement of opinion but one that would not be protected if it is based on false assertions that the person is sexist, racist, miserly, and physically abusive of family members. Neither will writers be protected, said the Court in *Milkovich,* if their interpretation of accurate information is erroneous and defamatory.

Because the courts, after the *Milkovich* decision, will often protect constitutional opinion only when a plaintiff cannot demonstrate the falsity of a remark, writers of columns and editorials can protect themselves by basing their opinions on facts

---

[296]*See* Ollman v. Evans & Novak, 750 F.2d at 981, 11 Media L. Rep. at 1442.

that can be substantiated. In 1983, a *Time* magazine inference that lawyer Jerome Lewis was one of the "shadier practitioners" of law was protected because *Time* reporters had established that Lewis had been found guilty of malpractice and fraud.[297] The *Wilmington* (Delaware) *News-Journal* was protected when it said that former County Director Melvin A. Slawik had abused his office even though the paper did not explain why. Slawik had previously pleaded guilty to a charge of obstruction of justice.[298] However, published opinions should not be based on "gut reactions," or rumors or other information that may be false.

If the Supreme Court is not willing to protect opinion that can be proven to be false, neither is it willing to protect opinion that contains provably false connotations. The Court said expressions of opinion should not be constitutionally protected if they imply the existence of information that can be proven to be wrong. The Court said it did not want to protect the statement "John Jones is a liar" as opinion because the comment implies knowledge of facts that could lead a listener to believe that Jones has lied. The Court believed that the truth or falsity of the accusation that Jones lied should be tested in court.

Even before *Milkovich,* courts sometimes decided that vague accusations using words such as *bastard, hypocrite, corrupt,* and *liar* were not used figuratively or as rhetorical hyperbole but instead implied the existence of unstated defamatory facts. A New York appeals court said in *Rinaldi v. Holt, Rinehart & Winston, Inc.* that the word *corrupt* would mean to the average reader that an official had committed illegal and unethical actions, an accusation susceptible to proof in court.[299] In *Rinaldi,* and under the rule in *Milkovich* and *Hepps,* an accusation that an official was *corrupt* would be constitutionally protected expression only if the official could not prove that he or she was innocent of wrongdoing.

The Supreme Court, in *Milkovich,* also did not want to protect false assertions of fact couched as opinions. Therefore, the Supreme Court would not protect the statement, "In my opinion John Jones is a liar," only because it was prefaced with the words, "in my opinion." Quoting a case opinion of the U.S. Court of Appeals for the Second Circuit, the Supreme Court said "it would be destructive of the law of libel if a writer could escape liability . . . simply by using, explicitly or implicitly, the words 'I think.' "[300]

The Supreme Court, in *Milkovich,* not only required that protected opinion be free of provably false assertions and connotations, but also that the opinions be about a matter of public concern. The requirement in *Hepps* that plaintiffs must prove falsity was limited to matters of public concern.

The Supreme Court did not define "matters of public concern" in *Milkovich,* however; nor has it explained the term previously. In *Hepps,* the state licensing of a chain of stores that sold liquor was a matter of public concern. However, in *Dun &*

---

[297]Lewis v. Time, Inc., 710 F.2d 549, 9 Media L. Rep. 1985 (9th Cir. 1983). *See Restatement (Second) of Torts* sec. 566 comment c (1977).

[298]Slawik v. News-Journal Co., 428 A.2d 15, 17, 7 Media L. Rep. 1112, 1113 (Del. 1981).

[299]366 N.E.2d 1299, 2 Media L. Rep. 2169 (N.Y.), *cert. denied,* 434 U.S. 969 (1977).

[300]17 Media L. Rep. at 2017, *quoting* Cianci v. New Times Publishing Co., 639 F.2d 54, 64, 6 Media L. Rep. 1625, 1632 (1980).

Bradstreet v. Greenmoss Builders, a case discussed later in the chapter, a defamatory private credit report sent to five subscribers was not a matter of public concern.

Protected Opinion in the Lower Courts   During much of the 1970s and 1980s, many lower courts ruled that defamatory opinions were completely protected from successful libel suits by the Constitution.[301] The lower courts relied substantially on **dicta** in the 1974 Supreme Court decision *Gertz v. Welch.* In *Gertz,* the Court said that

> Under the First Amendment there is no such thing as a false idea. However perni-
> cious an opinion may seem, we depend for its correction not on the conscience of
> judges and juries but on the competition of other ideas.[302]

In *Milkovich,* the Court rejected the interpretation that it had intended in *Gertz* to provide absolute constitutional protection for opinion. In *Milkovich,* the Court said that the constitutional protection for opinion provided by such cases as *Hepps* and *Greenbelt* made it unnecessary to create a wholesale exemption from liability for "anything that might be labeled 'opinion.'" The Court said that existing constitutional doctrine provided adequate "breathing space" for freedom of expression without the need to create an artificial category of protected speech.

Because the lower courts had based many of their opinions in the 1970s and 1980s on *Gertz,* lawyers and legal scholars expect changes in the lower court treatment of opinion after *Milkovich.* However, many of the points made in *Milkovich* had already been adopted in the lower courts. Almost all lower courts faced with opinion cases have already said that statements are constitutionally protected only if the language used, taken in context, cannot be verified. Many courts have also declared that assertions of fact will not be protected even if couched in terms of opinion. Some courts have also held that protected opinion could not connote a false defamatory implication. Yet, immediately after *Milkovich*, it was unclear how the lower courts would integrate their previous decisions, *Milkovich,* and the common law protection of fair comment and criticism.

Defense of Fair Comment   The fact that the Supreme Court declared in *Milkovich* that there is no absolute constitutional protection for opinion *per se* concerned at least some media lawyers. Immediately after *Milkovich,* some lawyers said the precedents of *Hepps, Greenbelt,* and *Letter Carriers* might not protect some expressions of opinion as effectively as lower court interpretations of the Constitution had in the past. The lawyers said more suits involving opinion would likely go to trial rather than be resolved in pretrial stages, and trial judgments over issues of truth or falsity were often hard to predict. Those lawyers suggested that writers may need to look to the common law, to some degree neglected in recent years, in addition to the Constitution for protection of opinion.

Long before any court had declared that opinion was constitutionally protected,

---

[301]Trager and Chamberlin, "The Dangerous Exception to Protection for Opinion," 11 *Comm. & L.,* 1, 51 (Dec. 1989).

[302]418 U.S. at 339–40, 1 Media L. Rep. at 1640.

the common law defense of fair comment provided a qualified privilege for criticism of public officials, persons involved in public issues, consumer goods, cultural activities, and other matters of public interest. The most important difference between constitutional protection and common law protection for opinion is that the media have an increased burden of proof for the common law defense. While the constitutional protection imposes a burden on plaintiffs to prove falsity, the common law requires that journalists ensure a factual basis for an opinion. The common law also specifies that communicators establish that an opinion is their own opinion, is about a matter of public interest, is fair, and is printed without ill will. However, communicators who meet the common law requirements of fair comment should find legal protection for opinion even in a changing legal environment.[303]

Subject of Public Interest   To be protected by the common law privilege of fair comment, criticism must relate to matters of widespread public interest. Fair comment applies to criticism of anyone who presents his or her services or goods to the public. It applies to any person or institution fulfilling a public function, appealing for public support, participating in a public activity, inviting the public's judgment, or participating in a public controversy. It does not apply to statements about private life.

Among the persons and organizations falling under the fair comment rules are:

- those participating in events relating to the nation's economic and social welfare, such as strikes and demonstrations;
- public institutions, such as schools, hospitals, charities, and churches, and the employees who staff them, such as teachers, doctors, nurses, and ministers;
- hotels and restaurants;
- writers, artists, entertainers, and athletes;
- mass media and their employees;
- scientists; and
- manufacturers of products available to the public as well as the products themselves.[304]

The courts have not discussed how the common law requirement that an opinion be about a subject of public interest compares to the constitutional requirement that an opinion be about a matter of public concern.

Opinion Based on Fact   To be protected under the defense of fair comment and criticism, statements must be expressions of opinion rather than assertions of fact. Courts have historically had some difficulty distinguishing opinion from fact, but generally have considered the same kinds of criteria mentioned by the Supreme Court

---

[303] *See Restatement of Torts* sec. 606 (1938); *Restatement (Second) of Torts* sec. 566 comment a (1977); R. Smolla, *Law of Defamation* secs. [4] [a] and [4] [b], at 6-8 to 6-10 (1989); Sack, "Common Law Libel and the Press: A Primer" in J. Goodale, ed., 1 *Communications Law 1989* at 365.

[304] *See* R. Sack, *Libel, Slander, and Related Problems* 169–72 (1980).

in *Milkovich.* Courts usually consider statements to be opinion and thus eligible for protection if, in context, the comments are not susceptible to being proved true or false.

For an expression of opinion to be protected by the common law, the Supreme Court noted in *Milkovich,* the opinion cannot state or imply a false statement of fact. Indeed, the common law predicates protection on the grounds that an opinion is supported by a fact stated in the article or widely known in the community. The common law does not generally require that the basis for an opinion be fully proven or documented; rather, writers are supposed to provide readers, viewers, and listeners with a basis for evaluating a published or broadcast opinion.

Although, before *Milkovich,* a court ruled that *Time* magazine was protected by the First Amendment when it called Jerome Lewis one of the "shadier practitioners" of law, *Time* also could have relied on the common law. The magazine not only printed its opinion, but also told readers that Lewis had been convicted of malpractice and fraud.[305] Similarly, in many jurisdictions, the *Wilmington News-Journal* could have relied on the common law as well as the Constitution to defend its statement that former County Director Melvin A. Slawik abused his office. Although the *News-Journal* had not published the fact that Slawik had pleaded guilty to a charge of obstruction of justice, that fact was widely known in the community.[306]

However, courts will not allow a defendant protection under the common law if facts supporting an opinion are not published or widely known. In fact, some courts insist the basis of the opinion must be discussed or referred to in the same article, editorial, or column. Therefore, the *Baltimore Morning Sun* lost a suit filed after it said in an editorial that Edgar Gordon Kirby was "infamous" and suggested Kirby harbored a questionable motive when he called the city police commissioner incompetent. Kirby said the *Sun* implied he was corrupt. The *Sun* said its opinion was sufficiently supported by the fact that Kirby had been dismissed from the police force for planting false evidence at the scene of a police raid and refusing to take a lie-detector test during the investigation that followed. Although Kirby's dismissal from the force was not mentioned in the editorial, the *Sun* contended the pertinent facts were readily available to the public. But a Maryland appeals court disagreed, contending the facts supporting an opinion must be clearly stated in the publication, or at least referred to in a "recognizable" way in the same publication. The court said "nothing in the editorial" explained to the reader why Kirby was believed to be infamous or "a man with a motive." The appeals court upheld a trial court verdict in favor of Kirby.[307]

Critic's Own Opinion   The common law requires that opinion, to be protected, must be held by the person communicating it. Fair comment does not protect newspapers, for example, when they publish someone else's opinion in letters to the editor or in news columns. Fair comment did not protect *Look* magazine when it reported remarks critical of San Francisco Giant baseball star Orlando Cepeda. A federal appeals court said the magazine could not rely on the defense when it published an as-

---

[305]Lewis v. Time, Inc., 710 F.2d 549, 9 Media L. Rep. 1985 (9th Cir. 1983). *See Restatement (Second) of Torts* sec. 566 comment c (1977).
[306]Slawik v. News-Journal Co., 428 A.2d 15, 7 Media L. Rep. 1112 (Del. 1981).
[307]A. S. Abell Co. v. Kirby, 176 A.2d 340 (1962).

sertion by Giant team executives that Cepeda was "temperamental, uncooperative and underproductive."[308] Presumably, the Giant executives themselves could have successfully used the defense if they had been sued. In contrast, the constitutional protection appears to apply to opinions printed or broadcast in the media without regard to whose opinions they are.[309]

Fairness and Ill Will   Under the common law defense of fair comment and criticism, some courts have held that criticism had to be "fair" or "reasonable" in order to be protected. Some courts say *fair* only means an opinion must be based on fact, as already discussed.[310] Courts have been divided over whether vehement or vituperative language might be unfair.

The common law privilege can be defeated by a showing of an intent to harm. Thus far, there is general agreement that the constitutional privilege is not subject to such a test.[311]

SUMMARY

Between 1974 and 1990, several courts followed the dicta of *Gertz v. Welch* to assert that opinion is constitutionally protected. In 1990, in *Milkovich v. Lorain Journal Co.,* the U.S. Supreme Court said the First Amendment does not provide a separate protection for opinion but that expressions of opinion would often be protected by existing precedent.

In the cases of *Greenbelt Cooperative Publishing Association v. Bresler* and *National Association of Letter Carriers v. Austin,* the Supreme Court established that whether comments were to be considered assertions of fact or expressions of opinion must be determined in context. Courts should examine such factors as the nature of an article and the circumstances of the expression in order to determine whether comments were "loose, figurative" language or rhetorical hyperbole that should not be taken as factual assertions, and therefore receive constitutional protection as opinion.

In *Milkovich,* the Supreme Court said that opinion is also protected by the constitutional requirement, announced in *Philadelphia Newspapers v. Hepps,* that plaintiffs have to prove statements about matters of public concern to be false in order to win libel suits. Therefore, statements that are not provably false, including "pure" opinions, would be protected. However, said the Court, an opinion that implies a false factual connotation will not be protected. Neither will statements be protected simply because they are prefaced with "I think" or "in my opinion."

---

[308]Cepeda v. Cowles Magazines & Broadcasting, Inc., 328 F.2d 869, 871, 873 (9th Cir. 1964).

[309]*See* Mishovsky v. Oklahoma Publishing, 642 P. 2d 587, 7 Media L. Rep. 2607, *cert. denied,* 459 U.S. 923, 8 Media L. Rep. 2302 (1982); *Restatement (Second) of Torts* sec. 566 comment c (1977).

[310]*See* R. Sack, *Libel, Slander, and Related Problems* 163–76 (1980); Note, "Fact and Opinion after *Gertz v. Robert Welch, Inc.*: The Evolution of a Privilege," 34 *Rutgers L. Rev.* 81, 87–89, 104 (1981).

[311]*See* Note, "Fact and Opinion after *Gertz v. Robert Welch, Inc.*: The Evolution of a Privilege," 34 *Rutgers L. Rev.* 81, 102; R. Sack, *Libel, Slander, and Related Problems* 179–80 (1980).

Writers uncertain about how the Supreme Court's *Milkovich* opinion will be interpreted by the lower courts can look to the common law requirements for additional protection for opinion. The common law defense of fair comment and criticism can protect an opinion from a successful libel suit if the opinion has a basis in fact. In addition, under fair comment, writers must also be able to establish that a statement is a personal opinion, is about a matter of public interest, is fair, and was published without an intent to harm.

DAMAGE, INJURY, OR HARM

Libel plaintiffs, in order to win their suits, must first satisfy their burden of proof and then defeat any defense offered by the media. However, in order to win any money in their suits, most plaintiffs must also prove they were damaged. Demonstration of harm to reputation, emotional well-being, or financial status must usually be established in order for a plaintiff to win monetary damages.

The nature of damages has been substantially altered by the constitutionalizing of libel in *New York Times v. Sullivan* and *Gertz v. Welch.* For example, since *Gertz,* the only plaintiffs who can win substantial monetary damages without proving harm or injury are those who can prove the defamation was published with knowing falsehood or reckless disregard for the truth. Even so, juries have substantial latitude in determining the amount of damage awards. Appeals courts can alter jury damage awards only if they find the awards to be ''excessive.''

Among the most important categories of libel damages are presumed damages, compensatory damages, and **punitive damages.** However, terms such as *presumed damages* can have different meanings in different states.

Presumed Damages

Before *Times v. Sullivan* and *Gertz,* winning libel plaintiffs won damages on the presumption that a person who was defamed was damaged. This practice meant that plaintiffs could recover damages without providing evidence of a damaged reputation. Plaintiffs had only to establish that defamatory language about them was published.

In *Times v. Sullivan,* the Supreme Court said that presumed damages could not be awarded to public officials who do not prove *New York Times* actual malice. In *Gertz,* the Court seemed to extend the same rule to all libel plaintiffs. However, a few years later, in *Dun & Bradstreet v. Greenmoss Builders,* the Court ruled that private persons suing for defamation that does not relate to matters of public concern do not have to prove *New York Times* actual malice to collect punitive damages. *Dun & Bradstreet* is discussed further in the next section.

In *Gertz,* the Supreme Court said the government has an interest in compensating private individuals only when damage to reputation can be demonstrated. Justice Powell, writing the majority opinion, said the ''largely uncontrolled discretion of juries to award damages where there is no loss'' of reputation increases the likelihood of dampening the "exercise of First Amendment freedoms." In addition, presumed damages invite "juries to punish unpopular opinion rather than to compensate individuals for injury."[312]

Nevertheless, in 1987, a federal district court permitted a jury to award entertainer Wayne Newton $50,000 in presumed damages for an NBC report linking him to organized crime. Newton was eligible to receive presumed damages, since, as a public figure, he had to prove *New York Times* actual malice to win his suit against NBC. The jury believed that NBC gave viewers the impression that Newton asked an organized crime figure, Guido Penosi, to help him raise money to buy a Las Vegas hotel. NBC implied that Penosi obtained a hidden interest in the casino, a violation of state law. The jury originally awarded Newton $5 million in presumed damages, but the trial court judge said the award "shocks the conscience" because NBC had not tarnished "Newton's outstanding reputation."[313] In 1990, a federal appeals court reversed the trial court's decision that NBC had acted with actual malice.

Compensatory Damages

Compensatory damages are intended to be monetary compensation for the harm to reputation caused by a libelous remark. In deciding compensatory damage awards, juries consider the degree of fault involved, the number of people who may have read or heard the defamation, the seriousness of the defamatory charge, the degree of the injury suffered, and the character and reputation of the litigants. Two of the most important forms of compensatory damages are **actual damages** and **special damages.**

Actual Damages   In *Gertz,* the Supreme Court said plaintiffs who cannot prove *New York Times* actual malice can collect only for actual damages. One way, but not the only way, to show actual injury is to prove a monetary loss, such as the financial loss a restaurant might suffer after a libelous review. However, libel can cause harm to individuals in many ways other than hurting their pocketbooks. Defamatory falsehoods can impair reputation and standing in the community and cause humiliation, mental anguish, and suffering. The Court said that all damage awards for actual injury must be supported by "competent evidence."

Entertainer Wayne Newton was originally awarded $225,000 in actual damages for physical and mental suffering in his suit against NBC. The trial court judge said there was "ample evidence" that Newton was "very upset" over NBC's broadcasts, and was treated for an ulcer because of the "stress and psychic trauma" created by the broadcasts.[314]

Elmer Gertz, the Chicago lawyer called a Communist by a John Birch Society publication, won $100,000 in actual damages. A federal appeals court said that Gertz had demonstrated actual injury, in part, by testifying to his own mental distress, anxiety, and embarrassment. Several attorneys testified that a lawyer who had been called a Communist would suffer significant damage to his professional reputation.

---

[312]418 U.S. at 349–50, 1 Media L. Rep. at 1643–44.
[313]Newton v. NBC, 677 F. Supp. 1066, 14 Media L. Rep. 1914 (1987), rev'd, 18 Media L. Rep. 1001 (9th Cir. 1990).
[314]*Id.*

Another witness said he had heard the defamation printed in *American Opinion* repeated.[315]

In another case, a court awarded $50,000 in actual damages to a Virginia couple, E. Grey and Carolyn Lewis, falsely accused of physically abusing their son. Two articles and an editorial in the *Alexandria Port Packet* "horrified," "mortified," and "humiliated" Mrs. Lewis. She was "scared to death" she was going to be put into prison. She isolated herself for six months, lost sleep, and suffered stomach pains because of her "public humiliation." The Lewises also became afraid to discipline their 5-year-old daughter for fear that someone would hear about it.[316]

The Supreme Court's requirement that injury to reputation be shown rather than presumed has had little practical effect on the size of damage awards. The Court has provided no guidelines for what kind of proof of injury is acceptable, and proof of damage to reputation is necessarily speculative without demonstrated monetary loss. Personal humiliation and mental anguish, in particular, do not carry price tags.

However, courts have said that some plaintiffs cannot prove their reputation has been damaged even if they are defamed. A plaintiff's reputation may be "so hopelessly bad or so unassailable that no words can affect it harmfully."[317] Plaintiffs who are "libel proof" are relatively rare, but in 1985 the Massachusetts Supreme Judicial Court ruled that the reputation of a man convicted of several serious crimes could not be damaged further. Anthony Jackson was serving a life sentence for murder. He also had been convicted for armed assault, unlawfully carrying a firearm, kidnapping, rape, and unarmed robbery. He was under indictment for four additional murders. The court said that even if the *Boston Globe* defamed Jackson by falsely accusing him of car theft, he already had such a poor reputation that additional damage was impossible.[318] If a jury is convinced that even a plaintiff with a good reputation has not been seriously damaged by a defamatory remark, the jury may award only nominal damages—something as little as $1.

Special Damages   Special damages, unlike actual damages, *require* proof of out-of-pocket loss, such as financial harm to a business. Monetary loss is the only kind of injury sufficient to justify special damages. Evidence of special damages, sometimes called specific damages, is required before plaintiffs can win trade libel suits. Some states also require plaintiffs to prove special damages when suing for slander or libel *per quod,* libel based on circumstances not apparent to the reasonably prudent editor.[319] Plaintiffs often have a hard time proving that their loss of business was due to a defamatory article.

Punitive Damages

The big-money awards in libel usually come from punitive damages. Punitive damages are intended to punish a publication for defamation rather than compensate the

---

[315]Gertz v. Robert Welch Inc., 680 F.2d 527, 8 Media L. Rep. 1769 (7th Cir. 1982).

[316]Gazette, Inc. v. Harris, 325 S.E.2d 713, 11 Media L. Rep. 1609 (Va. 1985).

[317]*Restatement (Second) of Torts* sec. 559 comment d (1977).

[318]Jackson v. Longcope, 476 N.E.2d 617, 11 Media L. Rep. 2282 (1985).

[319]*See, e.g.,* R. Sack, *Libel, Slander, and Related Problems* 345–46 (1980); R. Smolla, *Law of Defamation* sec. 9.07, at 9-16 (1989).

plaintiff for injury to reputation. Justice Powell said in *Gertz* that punitive damages are "private fines" levied by juries "to punish reprehensible conduct and to deter its future occurrence." Justice Powell, as well as many commentators, have said that punitive damages are irrelevant to the social interest of libel law, that of vindicating reputation.

Elmer Gertz won $300,000 in punitive damages in addition to his $100,000 in compensatory damages. Wayne Newton won $5 million in punitive damages in a trial his suit against NBC before the verdict was overturned on appeal. He had also won to the $50,000 he received in presumed damages and $225,000 in actual damages.

Mind-boggling jury awards of more than $1 million, known as "megaverdicts," are often reduced by judges. A jury awarded Carol Burnett $1.3 million in punitive damages, a figure eventually cut to $150,000 by a California appellate court. She also won $50,000 in compensatory damages.[320]

Many commentators and the Supreme Court itself have been concerned that large punitive damage awards lead to self-censorship by the media.[321] The Supreme Court has said that all plaintiffs, except for private plaintiffs involved in private issues, can only win punitive damages by proving *New York Times* actual malice. Some states, including Washington, Oregon, and Massachusetts, do not permit punitive damages.[322] Others, before allowing punitive damage awards, require evidence of intent to harm reputation or refusal to run a retraction in addition to proof of *New York Times* actual malice.[323]

In 1989, the Supreme Court, in a case unrelated to libel law, upheld in general the ability of plaintiffs in civil suits to sue for punitive damages.[324] In the same year, the Court also denied review of a newspaper's appeal of a $2.2 million libel judgment, all but $200,000 for punitive damages. The Court rejected a petition for *certiorari* by the *Pittsburgh Post-Gazette,* which had argued that punitive damage awards violated not only the First and Fourteenth Amendments, but also the Eighth Amendment's prohibition against excessive fines.[325]

Different Damage Standards for Private Issues

In 1985, more than a decade after *Gertz*, the Supreme Court said the *Gertz* limitations on presumed and punitive damages did not apply to all libel suits. In *Dun & Bradstreet v. Greenmoss Builders,* the Court ruled that when a false defamatory statement about a private person is not a "matter of public concern," a plaintiff could collect presumed and punitive damages without having to prove *New York Times* actual malice. A divided Court did not define "matters of public concern," but the decision may affect only nonmedia communication and specialized business publications.

---

[320]Burnett v. National Enquirer, Inc., 7 Media L. Rep. 1321 (Cal. Super. Ct. 1981), *aff'd on other grounds*, 144 Cal. App.3d 991, 9 Media L. Rep. 1921 (Cal. Ct. App. 1983).

[321]*See* Gertz v. Robert Welch, Inc., 418 U.S. at 349, 1 Media L. Rep. at 1644 and, *e.g.,* Lewis, "Annals of Law: The Sullivan Case," *The New Yorker,* Nov. 5, 1984, at 55, 82.

[322]*E.g.,* Stone v. Essex County Newspaper, 330 N.E.2d 161 (Mass. 1975); Taskett v. King Broadcasting Co., 546 P.2d 81, 1 Media L. Rep. 1716 (Wash. 1976).

[323]*See* R. Sack, *Libel, Slander, and Related Problems* 352–53 (1980).

[324]Browning-Ferris Industries, Inc. v. Kelco Disposal Inc., 109 S. Ct. 2909 (1989).

[325]*See* Disalle v. P.B. Publishing Co., 557 A.2d 724, 15 Media L. Rep. 1873 (Pa. 1988), *cert. denied,* 109 S. Ct. 3216 (1989).

In *Dun & Bradstreet,* the Supreme Court said that Greenmoss Builders, a contractor, did not have to prove *Times* rule actual malice after being falsely defamed in a credit report. Dun & Bradstreet, a credit-reporting agency, had told five subscribers that Greenmoss Builders had filed for bankruptcy. Dun & Bradstreet had inadvertently attributed the bankruptcy petition of a former Greenmoss employee to Greenmoss itself. A jury awarded Greenmoss Builders $50,000 in presumed damages and $300,000 in punitive damages without finding *New York Times* actual malice. The Supreme Court upheld the damages.

Justice Powell, writing the Court opinion, said the credit report did not require the same protection from defamation suits that was necessary to protect the debate of public issues. Powell said that since the credit report was solely of interest to Dun & Bradstreet and the business audience, there was no threat to a meaningful dialogue of ideas about government. In addition, he said, the regulation of credit reports would be unlikely to stifle speech because of the substantial commercial demand for them. However, Powell did not indicate what other kinds of speech might be considered private and therefore beyond the *Gertz* protection. He said the protection depended on the "content, form and context" of the speech.[326]

SUMMARY

The U.S. Supreme Court has said that public officials, public figures, and private persons involved in matters of public concern can collect only presumed and punitive damages if they prove *New York Times* actual malice. Presumed damages do not require proof of harm. Punitive damages are intended to punish a publication for false defamatory remarks. Public officials, public figures, and private persons involved in matters of public concern who do not prove *New York Times* actual malice must show actual injury in order to be eligible for damages. Actual injury can mean proof of damage to reputation or mental anguish as well as actual monetary loss. Special damages are awarded only after proof of monetary loss.

PREVENTING LIBEL SUITS

Legal defenses may help protect a publication once a suit has been filed. However, a carefully considered media response to the first sign of dissatisfaction by a person named in a story may keep a publication or broadcast station out of court altogether. The effective handling of complaints and the willingness to publish a retraction can prevent many people who believe they have been defamed from filing libel suits. In addition, retractions can reduce damage awards at trials in some states.

---

[326]472 U.S. 749, 11 Media L. Rep. 2417 (1985).

Handling Complaints

A study published by three scholars, then at the University of Iowa, has suggested that old-fashioned courtesy may do more to prevent libel suits than previously realized.

Professors Randall Bezanson, Gilbert Cranberg, and John Soloski said libel plaintiffs typically do not sue immediately after reading what they believe to be an inaccurate story about themselves in the newspaper. The Iowa study found that about half of the 160 libel plaintiffs studied said they contacted the media to ask for an explanation before contacting a lawyer or filing a complaint. The plaintiffs usually sued only after they decided they were treated rudely by the press. In some cases, media personnel cursed the person for complaining. Sometimes, staff members told the person complaining that the newspaper does not make mistakes. At other times complaints were passed around the newsroom without a satisfactory resolution.

The professors participating in the Iowa study noted that journalists' reluctance to correct errors stems in part from their conditioning to resist publishing a story about everyone's pet project. As one editor, Arnold Carson of the *Des Moines Register,* said, journalists "have to say no every day"—to the couple who wants a picture published of their daughter winning the county midteen beauty contest, to the business with a new promotion, and to the local politician attending a ribbon-cutting. Carson said the same tough mindset carries over

> to a place where it shouldn't—dealing with people after the fact, in connection with news stories in which they've been harmed or think they've been harmed or been wronged . . . a place where we ought to have a good deal more compassion and understanding and take a good deal more time in hearing people out.[327]

The Iowa project stressed the need to reduce the media's defensiveness in handling complaints. People agitated by news coverage want to believe they have at least been heard. The scholars said that editors should teach reporters that the press can have a major impact on individual reputations and that courteous responses to complaints are a newsroom priority. The professors also suggested the media develop systematic procedures for handling complaints.

Retractions

Journalists also can sometimes avoid a libel suit by printing a retraction. Some people who believe they have been defamed decide not to sue if a newspaper or broadcast station admits to the falsity of a defamatory publication.

A retraction can be a part of a written settlement, signed by both parties, that prohibits the person complaining from suing. In addition, more than 30 states have retraction statutes that provide legal protection to the media willing to retract false defamatory publications. The retraction statutes vary widely. Some prohibit the recovery of punitive damages if a newspaper or broadcast station retracts a defamatory

---

[327]Cranberg, "Fanning the Fire: The Media's Role in Libel Litigation," 71 *Iowa L. Rev.* 221, 222 (Oct. 1985).

falsehood. Others restrict the plaintiff to recovering special damages through proof of out-of-pocket loss if a retraction is published.[328]

In many states, the request for a retraction by a reader or viewer must be made within a certain time following publication. Often, a statute requires that the media be given an opportunity to retract before a suit is filed.

Ordinarily, in order to reduce damages, retractions must be full and fair, free of damaging innuendoes. Retractions need to be an honest effort to repair any damage done. They often need to be published within a limited amount of time and given the same emphasis and prominence as the defamatory statement. A California court said a retraction by the *San Francisco Examiner* did not meet the statutory requirement that a retraction must be given the same prominence as the defamation. A Sunday edition of the paper erroneously identified the suspect in a shooting as Willie Lee Beasley instead of Willie Ray Beasley. The paper published a retraction on Wednesday, three days later. But the court was not satisfied because Wednesday circulation was 150,000 compared to 450,000 on Sunday. The court also said the retraction was not published "in as conspicuous a manner" as the libel.[329]

Even if a retraction does not reduce damages by law, a jury may award lower damages if a retraction is published. However, courts have said that a failure to retract by itself is not evidence of *New York Times* actual malice or negligence.[330]

Most experts recommend that the media retract a defamatory statement only after consulting a lawyer. A lawyer can ensure that a retraction does not exacerbate a complaint. A retraction that repeats a libel may provoke a suit instead of keeping a publication or broadcast station out of court. In addition, a retraction written without legal assistance might not meet state statutory requirements.

SUMMARY

Libel suits may be avoided if initial informal complaints are handled courteously by publications and broadcast stations. Sometimes damages can be avoided by printing retractions, particularly if they meet the requirements of state retraction statutes.

IDEAS FOR REFORM

Despite retraction opportunities, libel suits became an increasing problem for the media in the mid-1980s. Media companies were losing more than two-thirds of the libel suits tried before a jury. Juries frequently awarded defendants more than a million dollars in damages. The costs of libel insurance skyrocketed.

---

[328] *See generally Prosser and Keeton on Torts* sec. 116, at 845–47 (5th ed. 1984); R. Sack, *Libel, Slander, and Related Problems* 372–83 (1980) (including discussions of retractions under the common law). *But see* Boswell v. Phoenix Newspapers, 730 P.2d 186, 13 Media L. Rep. 1785 (Ariz. 1986) (retraction statute violates state constitution).

[329] Beasley v. Hearst Corp., 11 Media L. Rep. 2067 (Cal. Super. Ct. 1985).

[330] *See* New York Times Co. v. Sullivan, 376 U.S. at 286, 1 Media L. Rep. at 1540; Walters v. Sanford Herald, 228 S.E.2d 766, 2 Media L. Rep. 1959 (N.C. Ct. App. 1977).

Libel plaintiffs were not pleased either. Trials seldom vindicated their reputations because the focus was on the constitutional protections of the press rather than the truth or falsity of a defamatory story. In addition, although plaintiffs frequently won at the trial level, they seldom won on appeal.

As a result of a general dissatisfaction with libel law, several reforms were proposed in the late 1980s. The proposal receiving the most attention was a model statute developed by the Washington Annenberg Program, a branch of Northwestern University. In 1988, an Annenberg study group representing both the media and media critics drafted a model law that would direct the focus of libel disputes to the truth or falsity of a story, instead of the issue of *New York Times* actual malice. Annenberg's model statute would also eliminate most large monetary damage awards.

Annenberg's proposed Libel Reform Act recommends a low-cost dispute-settlement procedure. In the initial stage of the process, a person claiming to be libeled first seeks a retraction or a chance to reply. If either a retraction or reply is granted, the aggrieved person cannot sue for damages. However, if a media organization does not offer a retraction or an opportunity to reply, the person offended can sue. Under the Annenberg plan, the issue to be resolved is the truth of the publication rather than whether the publication was published with negligence or reckless disregard for the truth. The constitutional protections of negligence and recklessness would not be factors in the case.

In addition, either side in the dispute can require that a trial be limited to the question of the truth of the report instead of an award of monetary damages. The Annenberg proposal provides for vindicating reputation by seeking to discover the truth rather than by compensating a damaged reputation with a monetary judgment, as in the case of current libel law. The losing side in a suit under the Annenberg plan would be required to pay the winner only attorneys' fees. If both sides of a dispute want to try a case for damages, the Annenberg proposal eliminates the chance of recovering punitive damages.

Media representatives criticize the Annenberg proposal for abandoning constitutional protections such as *New York Times* actual malice, even in return for protection against monetary damages. Media representatives also fear that state legislators enacting the Annenberg proposal into law would drop aspects more favorable to the media.[331] Media critics protest the Annenberg plan's effective elimination of damage awards. Defense lawyer John Walsh, who represented former Mobil Oil President William Tavoulareas in his libel suit against the *Washington Post,* said the plan would provide no means of recovery for "businesses wiped out overnight" by false stories.[332]

Bills similar to the Annenberg proposal have failed in California, Connecticut, Iowa, and Illinois.

The Annenberg model statute was but one of many reform proposals. The University of Iowa project suggested arbitration rather than litigation for libel disputes, but could not find people willing to participate in experimental projects. In another effort, a judge tried an innovative approach to jury instructions when former Israeli

---

[331]Mauro, "The Annenberg Libel Plan," *Wash. Journ. Rev.,* April 1989, at 7.
[332]*Id.*

Defense Minister Ariel Sharon sued *Time* magazine. Instead of asking a jury whether *Time* acted with *New York Times* actual malice, Judge Abraham Sofaer first asked the jury if *Time*'s story was defamatory. When the jury replied that Sharon had been defamed, Sofaer asked if the story was false. The jury responded by deciding *Time*'s story was false, and the jury's declaration that *Time* had printed a false defamatory story about Sharon received widespread media play. However, Judge Sofaer finally asked the jury if the *Time* story was published with reckless disregard for the truth. The jury said that although the story was false and defamatory it was not printed with reckless disregard for the truth. *Time* technically won the suit because, although the story was ruled to be false and defamatory, Sharon had not met all of the elements of his burden of proof. Both sides claimed victory, however: Sharon's reputation had been vindicated and *Time* did not have to pay monetary damages. Since the Sharon case, some judges have adopted Sofaer's approach to jury instructions as a way to clarify the issues in a libel trial.[333]

In spite of the several innovative proposals for changing libel law, the chances of significant reform in the near future seem unlikely. Media executives fear that changes in the system will infringe on First Amendment values. Perhaps more important, the libel threat for the press diminished significantly toward the end of the 1980s. The media began to win more jury decisions, several of the megaverdicts were reduced on appeal, and the number of libel suits dropped dramatically. The changing climate does not mean that libel is no longer a significant issue for media professionals. It only means the momentum for reform was waning in the early 1990s.

SUMMARY

The combination of frequent losses in libel trials and multimillion dollar verdicts in the mid-1980s led to several proposals for changes in libel law. However, a major reduction in the number of libel suits toward the end of the decade sharply decreased media interest in major changes in libel law, and the prospects for significant reform looked slim in 1990.

---

[333]*E.g.,* "A General Loses His Case; The Jury Finds No 'Malice,' but Chastises *Time,*" *Time,* Feb. 4, 1985, at 64; "Time Cleared of Libeling Sharon but Jurors Criticize Its Reporting," *New York Times*, Jan. 25, 1985, at A1.

4

PRIVACY

mission from the children's parents to publish the picture and to name the children in the story. The paper was not able to claim it was publishing information from a public record because names of retarded school children were withheld from the public under a Mississippi statute.

In another case from a conservative jurisdiction, a newspaper was ruled to have invaded privacy for publishing a picture taken at a county fair. The Alabama Supreme Court upheld a $4,000 jury award to Flora Bell Graham, a 44-year-old housewife, for a picture that was taken when air jets blew her dress over her head as she emerged from the Fun House at the fair. The picture, published in the *Daily Times Democrat* in Cullman County, revealed Graham's legs and panties. A reader could identify Graham because her children were also in the picture.

Generally, pictures taken at public events are newsworthy and therefore preclude a successful privacy suit. But the Alabama court said the *Times Democrat* photo of Graham's legs was offensive to modesty and decency because it revealed private information in which the public had no legitimate interest. It would be "illogical, wrong, and unjust," the court said, to hold that one involuntarily "enmeshed in an embarrassing pose" forfeits her right of privacy because she happens to be part of a public scene.[14]

Public Domain   While citizens may consider information about their marital, financial, and medical affairs to be private, the law may not consider such information private if the public is already aware of it. The media are generally free to disseminate information that appears in public records or is revealed through a person's public activities. Although cases to be discussed later will show that a plaintiff does not always lose a claim to privacy in information available to the public, it is generally true, as the *Restatement (Second) of Torts* concludes: "There is no liability when the defendant merely gives further publicity to information about the plaintiff that is already public."[15]

Private information may pass into the public domain on official records. The Iowa Supreme Court ruled that Robin Howard could not sue for invasion of privacy when a newspaper published that she had been sterilized involuntarily while a patient at a government home. The fact of her sterilization, the court said, was a public, as opposed to a private, fact because it was part of a public record forwarded to the governor's office in a file of complaints against the home. "Because the documents were public," the court said, "the information which they contained was in the public domain," and Howard could not sue for invasion of privacy.[16]

Private information may also become public through a person's public speaking and activities. Oliver Sipple, a decorated Vietnam veteran who saved President Gerald Ford from being shot, lost a privacy suit because his private life was ruled to be part of the public domain. Sipple, who was well-known as a leader in the San Francisco gay community, saved Ford's life during a 1975 visit to the city by deflecting the hand of Sarah Jane Moore as she aimed a gun at the president. Sipple unsuccessfully

[14]Daily Times Democrat v. Graham, 162 So.2d 474 (Ala. 1964).

[15]*Restatement (Second) of Torts* sec. 652 D comment b (1977).

[16]Howard v. Des Moines Register, 283 N.W.2d 289 (Iowa 1979), *cert. denied,* 445 U.S. 904 (1980).

sued several newspapers for their publication of the fact that he was homosexual. Sipple said the publication of information about his sexual life caused him embarrassment with his family and friends in the Middle West.[17]

A California appellate court ruled that Sipple's sexual orientation was not a private matter. Sipple, through his activism in the gay community, made no secret of his sexual orientation. His homosexuality was in the public domain, the court said.

People who participate in public affairs do not abandon all claims to privacy in their intimate affairs. The California Court of Appeals ruled that the sex-change operation of Toni Diaz, the first female president of the student body at the College of Alameda, was private. Unlike Oliver Sipple, who participated publicly in gay organizations, Diaz tried to conceal her sexual identity after the operation by legally changing her identification records, including her driver's license, Social Security forms, and high school records.[18]

The court ruled Diaz could bring a privacy suit against the *Oakland Tribune* for the paper's revelation of her earlier sexual identity. The court said that her sexuality was a private matter that was neither newsworthy nor part of a public record.

SUMMARY

The private-facts tort is the publication of information that "(a) would be highly offensive to a reasonable person and (b) is not of legitimate concern to the public." Courts have found revelation of details about illnesses, hospitalization, retardation, or intimate parts of the body to be highly offensive invasions of privacy. Information that has passed into the public domain by appearing in public records or as part of public activities is generally not "private."

Defenses

While the media lose a few private-facts cases, particularly those in which medical details are revealed, more often the media successfully argue that dissemination of their stories and pictures are protected by the First Amendment, are newsworthy, or are published with consent.

First Amendment   Journalists often argue the First Amendment should protect them whenever they publish truthful information, particularly truthful information from official sources. Although the Supreme Court has refused to recognize complete protection for publication of truthful information, it has ruled that the First Amendment protects publication of most truthful information that is lawfully acquired from official records or court proceedings.

In *Cox Broadcasting Corp. v. Cohn,* the Supreme Court established nearly complete First Amendment protection for the media to report information from official

---

[17]Sipple v. Chronicle Publishing Co., 201 Cal. Rptr. 665, 10 Media L. Rep. 1690 (Ct. App. 1984).
[18]Diaz v. Oakland Tribune, 188 Cal. Rptr. 762, 9 Media L. Rep. at 1121 (Cal. App. 1983).

records available in open court.[19] In *Cox,* the Supreme Court ruled 8–1 that a Georgia father could not bring a privacy suit against a television station for reporting the name of his daughter in violation of a Georgia statute. The statute made publication or broadcast of the name of a rape victim a misdemeanor.

The case arose from the 1971 murder and rape of a 17-year-old girl. Six youths were indicted for murder and rape, but the murder charges were later dropped. Despite substantial press coverage of the crime, the victim's name was never publicized, perhaps because of the statute. Eight months after the murder, the six youths appeared in court to enter pleas to indictments for rape. During a recess in the proceedings, a reporter for Atlanta station WSB-TV learned the name of the rape victim by reading the indictments provided by the court clerk. Later that day, the station named the victim in a report on the court proceedings. The victim's father brought a civil suit claiming that his privacy was invaded by WSB's broadcast of his daughter's name.

The Georgia Supreme Court ruled that the father's privacy suit should go to trial, but the U.S. Supreme Court reversed. The Supreme Court said the First Amendment did not permit a privacy suit against the media for disseminating private information contained in public records that are part of an open-court proceeding. "The commission of crime, prosecutions resulting from it, and judicial proceedings arising from the prosecutions," Justice White wrote for the majority, "are without question events of legitimate concern to the public and consequently fall within the responsibility of the press to report the operations of Government." By their very nature, the Court said, public records "are of interest to those concerned with the operation of government, and a public benefit is performed by the reporting of the true contents of the records by the media." The Court did say that a state might declare records containing very sensitive private information not be made public. But the press cannot be liable in a private suit for publishing information from official records introduced in court.

In 1989, the Court extended First Amendment protection to publication of private information acquired by the press from a county sheriff. In *Florida Star v. B.J.F.,* the Court reversed a judgment against a weekly Jacksonville newspaper for publishing the full name of B.J.F., a rape victim, in violation of a state statute.[20] The statute barred an "instrument of mass communication" from printing, publishing, or broadcasting the name of the victim of a sexual offense.

A reporter-trainee for the weekly *Florida Star* acquired the name from a press release prepared by the Duval County sheriff's department and published it in violation of the paper's own policy not to publish names of rape victims. A sign at the sheriff's department warned that names of rape victims were not matters of public record.

In her privacy suit, B.J.F. claimed that publication of her name caused her emotional distress. She testified that her mother received threatening phone calls and that she had been compelled to move to a new residence, change her phone number, and begin mental health counseling. A jury awarded B.J.F. $75,000 in compensatory damages and $25,000 in punitive damages for the paper's violation of the statute. A

[19]420 U.S. 469, 1 Media L. Rep. 1819 (1975).
[20]109 S. Ct. 2603 (1989).

Florida appeals court affirmed the jury award, and the Florida Supreme Court refused review. The U.S. Supreme Court reversed.

The Court did not rule that the First Amendment protects publication of all information from public records. The *Star* argued that the press release from which the paper acquired B.J.F.'s name was a public record similar to court records from which the name of the rape victim was acquired in *Cox Broadcasting v. Cohn.* But in *B.J.F.,* the Supreme Court limited its *Cox* ruling to information acquired in open court. In a majority decision written by Justice Marshall, the Court said that the First Amendment interest in reporting of law enforcement records is less than the First Amendment interest in reporting open court proceedings, where the press has traditionally had a role ensuring the fairness of trials.

The Court also refused in *B.J.F.,* as it refused in *Cox,* to rule that the First Amendment protects publication of all truthful information. Justice Marshall said the sensitive and significant interests presented in clashes between the First Amendment and privacy rights should be balanced in each case. Relying on an earlier decision in *Smith v. Daily Mail Publishing Co.,* the Court said the government may constitutionally punish a newspaper for publishing lawfully obtained, truthful information about a matter of public significance only if the government can show that punishment will "further a state interest of the highest order."

Applying the *Daily Mail* balancing test to the *B.J.F.* case, the Court determined that the weekly newspaper had lawfully obtained truthful information about a matter of public significance. The commission and investigation of violent crime, such as rape, is a subject of "paramount public import," the Court said.

The reporter's acquisition of the name from a sheriff's department press release was certainly lawful. If the government wishes to keep information confidential, the Court said, it should establish stronger safeguards on disclosure, not punish the press. Citizens hurt by dissemination of information released by the government should seek restitution from the government, not the media, the Court said. Indeed, the Duval sheriff's department had earlier settled a civil suit with B.J.F. for $2,500.

Continuing his balancing analysis, Justice Marshall said that punishing the *Star* would not further the significant state interests in protecting rape victims' privacy and safety and encouraging them to report rapes without fear of exposure or reprisal. The Florida statute cannot be assumed to protect the privacy of a rape victim, the Court said, because it punishes publication of a victim's name in an "instrument of mass communication," but allows dissemination by other means, such as by gossips or the victim herself. "When a State attempts the extraordinary measure of punishing truthful publication in the name of privacy, it must demonstrate its commitment to advancing this interest by applying its prohibition evenhandedly, to the smalltime disseminator as well as the media giant," the Court said.

The Court also objected because the Florida statute made the press liable whether or not the name was already public, regardless of whether publication was offensive to anyone, and without consideration of the publisher's motives. Such automatic liability, without case-by-case weighing of competing values, motives, and damages is unconstitutional where important First Amendment interests are at stake, the Court said.

Justice White, in a dissenting opinion joined by Chief Justice Rehnquist and Justice O'Connor, argued that the majority opinion would "obliterate" liability for publication of private facts. "If the First Amendment prohibits wholly private persons (such as B.J.F.) from recovering for the publication of the fact that she was raped, I doubt that there remain any 'private facts' which persons may assume will not be" disseminated by the media, Justice White said. The dissenters found no public interest in publishing the names, addresses, and phone numbers of crime victims.

After *B.J.F.* was decided, the Court vacated and remanded a Pennsylvania Supreme Court decision upholding a fine against the *Easton* (Pennsylvania) *Express* for publication of part of a wiretap transcript. Publication of the transcript, which was included in a file of pretrial discovery materials deposited in a court clerk's office, violated a state statute prohibiting disclosure of confidential information.[21] The Pennsylvania court upheld a $1,000 fine and $17,000 in lawyers' fees against the newspaper for disclosing the wiretap information. The transcript recounted a taped conversation with an illegal gambling suspect.

In vacating the lower court decision, the U.S. Supreme Court told the Pennsylvania Court to reconsider whether punishment of the newspaper for publishing lawfully acquired truthful information served a state interest of the highest order. The newspaper argued that the state has a far less compelling interest in protecting the confidentiality of evidence against a criminal suspect than it did in protecting the privacy of a rape victim in *B.J.F.*

In a case decided before *B.J.F.*, a California appeals court ruled that the safety of a witness and the state's interest in conducting a criminal investigation might outweigh a newspaper's First Amendment interest in publishing the name of the witness. In a case that was later settled out of court, the California Court of Appeals denied summary judgment to the *Los Angeles Times* in a privacy suit over publication of the name of a woman who could identify a murder suspect still at large.[22] The woman, called Jane Doe in court papers, saw the murderer of her roommate as he fled her apartment. Doe sued the Times-Mirror Co., publisher of the *Los Angeles Times,* for invasion of privacy, claiming the identification made her a target of the murderer.

The Times-Mirror Co. argued that summary judgment should be granted because the First Amendment protects publication of newsworthy public information gained from public sources. In disputed testimony, the *Times* said a summer intern obtained Jane Doe's real name over the phone from an official at the coroner's office. The paper also said the name was in the public domain because police interviewed Doe at a public restaurant and Doe told friends of finding her roommate's body.

The California Appeals Court denied summary judgment, concluding that the First Amendment provides no absolute protection from liability for printing the name of a witness who can identify a murder suspect still at large. "The individual's safety and the state's interest in conducting a criminal investigation may take precedence over the public's right to know the name of the individual," the court said.

The court said Doe's talk with friends about the incident did not necessarily place her identity in the public domain. "Talking to selected individuals does not

---

[21]Easton Publishing Co. v. Boettger, 110 S. Ct. 225 (1989), *vacating,* Boettger v. Loverro, 555 A.2d 1234, 16 Media L. Rep. 1467 (Pa. 1989). *See also* Cape Publications, Inc. v. Hitchner, 16 Media L. Rep. 2337 (Fla. 1989).

[22]Times-Mirror Co. v. San Diego Superior Court, 744 Cal. Rptr. 556, 15 Media L. Rep. 1129 (Cal. Ct. App. 1988).

render private information public," the court said. Furthermore, the court said, even if names appear on a public record, "the press can [not] print names in connection with sensitive information with impunity." Before a trial could be held, the case was settled for an undisclosed sum after the U.S. Supreme Court refused review.[23]

A few lower courts have recognized broader First Amendment protections for the media in private-facts cases than the Supreme Court has. The U.S. Court of Appeals for the Fourth Circuit ruled that the First Amendment protects publication of information about a figure only tangentially related to a subject of public interest. In *Campbell v. Seabury Press,* the court affirmed summary judgment for Seabury Press in a privacy suit brought by Carlyne Campbell, former wife of Joseph Campbell, who was the brother of a religious and civil rights leader. The book, an autobiography of the civil rights leader, discussed the influence of Joseph Campbell on his younger brother. Carlyne Campbell said her privacy was invaded when the book mentioned her home life and marriage to Joseph Campbell. Carlyne Campbell conceded references to her were true and that the book about her brother-in-law was newsworthy, but she said her marriage was of no public interest.

The court, however, said the First Amendment mandates a privilege to publish or broadcast facts about public figures and other matters of public interest. The court said Seabury's references to Carlyne Campbell were privileged because she had a logical connection to the newsworthy relationship between the civil rights leader, who wrote the book, and Carlyne Campbell's husband. "Likewise," the court said, "accounts of his brother's marriage as they impacted on the author have the requisite logical nexus to fall within the ambit of constitutional protection."[24]

Newsworthiness   While the Supreme Court cautiously extends First Amendment protections to publication of private information from official records, the common law has long provided a broad newsworthiness defense for the media in private-facts cases. Not surprisingly, newsworthiness is most likely to outweigh privacy interests when the media report on public records, public proceedings, and the public activities of police, firefighters, and other officials. But the newsworthiness defense is also successful in cases involving information that is of no particular public importance, but is strange, unusual, or simply interesting.

Public Occurrences   The newsworthiness defense extends beyond official records to public occurrences, both official and unofficial. A Kansas City court ruled against a youth who filed a privacy suit because he was shown on television being frisked just after he was mistakenly arrested. The court said criminal complaints, subsequent police action, and the arrest of suspects are matters of proper public concern. The court recognized that the youth was "undoubtedly embarrassed" by the publicity given to his arrest. Nevertheless, the court concluded, the media were not liable for invasion of privacy at a newsworthy event because the picture showing him being searched "merely depicted a normal incident to such an arrest."[25]

---

[23] "Witness, *Times* Settle Privacy Suit," *News Media Update,* April 15, 1989, at 2.

[24] Campbell v. Seabury Press, 614 F.2d 395, 5 Media L. Rep. 2612 (5th Cir. 1980). *See also* Gilbert v. Medical Economics, 665 F.2d 305, 7 Media L. Rep. 2372 (10th Cir. 1981).

[25] Williams v. KCMO Broadcasting Division—Meredith Corp., 472 S.W.2d 1 (Kans. City Ct. Appl.1971). *See also* Jacova v. Southern Radio & Television Co., 83 So.2d 34 (Fla. 1955).

In a much-discussed case, Hilda Bridges lost a privacy suit against a Florida newspaper over publication of a dramatic nude photograph. The photo in *Cocoa Today* showed Bridges running partially nude across a parking lot on the arm of a policeman. Bridges was rushed from her former apartment after her estranged husband fatally shot himself. He had earlier forced Bridges to disrobe and threatened to kill her. Police surrounded the apartment when they learned that Bridges was a hostage. The media arrived shortly thereafter. Police stormed the apartment at the sound of gunfire.

Although Bridges was holding a towel over her front as she fled the apartment, her hips were exposed in the published picture. The jury awarded Bridges $10,000 in her privacy suit against *Cocoa Today,* but an appellate judge ruled for the newspaper because the picture was of a newsworthy event in a public place. Bridges's public exposure in an event involving a suicide, threatened murder, and police was of public interest, the court said, just as crime, arrests, police raids, accidents, and fires are of public interest. The newspaper, in its defense, pointed out that tan lines on Bridges's hips showed she revealed more of herself on the beach than *Cocoa Today* revealed in the newspaper. The paper also pointed out that it had not published several more revealing pictures.[26]

Oliver Sipple, the homosexual who saved President Ford's life, lost his privacy suit not only because his sexual orientation was in the public domain, but also because the court ruled his sexuality was newsworthy. Sipple agreed that saving the president's life was a newsworthy act, but he argued that his sexual life was not newsworthy because it had no relation to saving the president. However, the court said Sipple's sexuality was newsworthy because his courageous act cast the often-stereotyped homosexuals in a positive light. There was also a newsworthy question whether President Ford was delaying public expression of gratitude to Sipple because of Sipple's homosexuality.[27]

The ethics of publishing Sipple's sexual identity was complicated. While Sipple said he was embarrassed, other members of the gay community, seeking positive publicity about gays, had urged the media to tell the public of Sipple's homosexuality. In ruling against Sipple in his privacy suit, the court said the publication was not intended to embarrass him. The court said publication was an attempt to "dispel the false public opinion that gays were timid, weak and unheroic figures."

The Strange and Unusual   "Newsworthiness" is an elastic term. Not only does it include information in official records and public events, but also revelation of people's oddities, foibles, skills, talents, style of living, and natural gifts. "News" has been said to include "all events and items of information that are out of the ordinary humdrum routine, and which have 'that indefinable quality of interest which attracts public attention.' "[28] People may be newsworthy, as we saw in the Carlyne Campbell case discussed earlier, even if they have only a tangential relationship to other news-

---

[26]Cape Publishing v. Bridges, 423 So.2d 426, 8 Media L. Rep. 2535 (Fla. App. 1982), *cert. denied,* 464 U.S. 893 (1983). *See also* Taylor v. K.T.V.B., 525 P.2d 984 (Idaho 1976).

[27]Sipple v. Chronicle Publishing Co., 201 Cal. Rptr. 665, 10 Media L. Rep. 1690 (Ct. App. 1984).

[28]Prosser, "Privacy," 48 *Calif. L. Rev.* 383, 412, *quoting* Sweenek v. Pathé News, 16 F. Supp. 746, 747 (E.D.N.Y. 1936).

worthy people and events. So broad is the range of newsworthy information recognized by the courts that former Chicago law professor Harry Kalven wondered if the revelation of private facts would remain a tort.[29]

The public activities of well-known athletes, performers, and other celebrities are newsworthy, but so are the unusual talents, abilities, and quirks of less well-known people. A California court ruled in favor of *Sports Illustrated* in a privacy suit over a story it published about Michael S. Virgil, once one of the greatest surfers on the California coast. Virgil sued after *Sports Illustrated* told readers that he ate insects, dived off stairs to impress women, put out cigarettes in his mouth, and deliberately hurt himself to collect unemployment insurance so he could spend time surfing. The court said the magazine's revelations were not sufficiently embarrassing to outweigh their newsworthiness. The court said the publication was not morbid or sensational and was related to a "legitimate journalistic attempt" to explain Virgil's daring surfing style.[30]

Unusual intellectual talents made William James Sidis a newsworthy public figure as a teenager. Though only a youth, Sidis's intellectual ability was so developed that he gave lectures to the math department at Harvard. Because of the newsworthiness of his outstanding talents, Sidis lost a privacy suit many years later when the *New Yorker* wrote a story about the sad and unfulfilling development of Sidis's life.[31]

Curiosities and oddities are also newsworthy. Newsworthiness encompasses the sad, the macabre, the hair-raising, and the tasteless. Courts have found newsworthiness in the family of a man kicked to death by a youth gang,[32] in pictures of auto accident victims,[33] and in the picture of the juvenile victim of a street accident.[34] When 12-year-old Troyce Brindel Meetze delivered a baby, the birth was newsworthy, the South Carolina Supreme Court said, because it was an unusual biological occurrence "which would naturally excite public interest."[35] The birth also became part of the public record.

Newsworthiness over Time   Generally speaking, once people are newsworthy, they remain newsworthy. William James Sidis, the brilliant teenage mathematician retained his newsworthiness nearly 30 years later when his undistinguished life was nearing a lonely end. In 1937, the *New Yorker* published a "Where Are They Now?" piece on Sidis, a child prodigy in 1910. The article described the life of a man who had become a reclusive clerk spending his time collecting streetcar transfers and living in a simple room in a shabby Boston neighborhood.[36]

As a child prodigy, the court said, Sidis inspired both admiration and curiosity. Nearly three decades later, the question of whether Sidis fulfilled his early promise

---

[29]Kalven, "Privacy in Tort Law—Were Warren and Brandeis Wrong?" 31 *Law & Contemporary Problems* 326, 336 (1966).

[30]Virgil v. Sports Illustrated, Inc., 424 F. Supp. 1286 (S.D. Cal. 1976).

[31]Sidis v. F–R Publishing Corp., 113 F.2d 806, 1 Media L. Rep. 1775 (2d Cir.), *cert. denied,* 311 U.S. 711 (1940).

[32]Jenkins v. Dell Publishing Co., 251 F.2d 447 (3d Cir. 1958).

[33]Kelley v. Post Publishing Co., 98 N.E.2d 286 (Mass. 1951).

[34]Leverton v. Curtis Publishing Co., 192 F.2d 974 (3d Cir. 1951).

[35]Meetze v. Associated Press, 95 S.E.2d 606 (S.C. 1956).

[36]Sidis v. F–R Publishing Corp., 113 F.2d 806, 1 Media L. Rep. 1775 (2d Cir. 1940). *See also* Cohen v. Marx, 211 P.2d 320 (Cal. Ct. App. 1949).

remained a matter of public concern. "The article in the *New Yorker* sketched the life of an unusual personality, and it possessed considerable popular news interest," the court said. The court continued:

> Regrettably or not, the misfortunes and frailties of neighbors and "public figures" are subjects of considerable interest and discussion to the rest of the population. And when such are the mores of the community, it would be unwise for a court to bar their expression in the newspapers, books, and magazines of the day.

Information in public records will usually remain newsworthy, particularly if the records relate to the subject of a later newsworthy story. The Oklahoma Supreme Court ruled that publication of 20-year-old FBI allegations, including two mistaken charges, did not invade privacy because they came from a public record.[37] Even where records have been expunged or erased newsworthiness is likely to remain. A federal court in Illinois ruled a corporate officer had no privacy claim where a credit reporting company accurately published the officer's criminal record even though the record was more than two years old and had been expunged.[38]

Information from old public records may retain its newsworthiness even if the information is used in stories of little newsworthiness. The Louisiana Supreme Court ruled a weekly newspaper, the *Iberville South,* did not invade Carlysle Roshto's privacy when it republished a 25-year-old story about Roshto's conviction for cattle theft. Publication of Roshto's criminal record had no relation to any current public issue; the item appeared in the paper's "Page from Our Past" feature, which was made up of randomly chosen stories from earlier issues. Roshto sued for invasion of privacy because he had worked hard after his release from prison, had been pardoned, and had hidden his conviction from the people in the community. The court suggested that the paper was insensitive to publish Roshto's story but ruled the paper would not be punished for publishing truthful, accurate, and nonmalicious information.[39]

A few courts in California have expressed sympathy for rehabilitated criminals who bring privacy claims over media stories revealing their past. But these cases do little to undermine the general rule that publishing information from public records, even old records, does not invade a person's privacy. In *Briscoe v. Reader's Digest Association, Inc.,* the Supreme Court of California held that Marvin Briscoe could sue for invasion of privacy over a truthful report that he had participated in an unsuccessful hijacking attempt 11 years earlier. The court said Briscoe could pursue his privacy suit because a jury could find that his criminal past was no longer newsworthy after more than a decade of living within the law.[40] Nevertheless, a federal district court dismissed Briscoe's privacy claim on the grounds that reports of his court records were public information, that he was newsworthy, and that publication had not been made with malice.[41]

---

[37]McCormack v. Oklahoma Publishing Co., 613 P.2d 737 (Okla. 1980).

[38]Anonymous v. Dun & Bradstreet, 3 Media L. Rep. 2376 (N.D. Ill. 1978).

[39]Roshto v. Hebert, 439 So.2d 428, 9 Media L. Rep. 2417 (La. 1983). *See also* Shifflet v. Thomson Newspapers, 8 Media L. Rep. 1199 (Ohio 1982).

[40]93 Cal. Rptr. 866 (Cal. 1971).

[41]Briscoe v. Reader's Digest Ass'n Inc., 1 Media L. Rep. 1852 (C.D. Cal. 1972).

Consent   Besides asserting a First Amendment or newsworthiness defense, defendants in private-facts cases may also argue the plaintiff consented to publication. Consent may be explicit or implied. One who is involved in a newsworthy public event, whether voluntarily or involuntarily, will usually be held to have given an implied consent to be photographed and written about. Similarly, people who talk to a reporter give implied consent for use of their names because they should anticipate publication. However, there may be no implied consent if people interviewed do not understand who they are talking to or that their interview might be published or broadcast.[42]

The more private the facts, the stronger the need for a journalist or public relations practitioner to obtain explicit written consent to publish a name or picture. Journalists and public relations practitioners should be particularly careful to obtain consent when intending to publish information about medical and psychological conditions and private facts about children. Minors may not give consent.

The South Carolina Supreme Court ruled a young father did not consent to have his name published when he talked with a reporter because the father did not understand the nature of the story. The court ruled that Craig Hawkins, the teenage father of an illegitimate child, never gave consent to Multimedia to use his name in a story about teen pregnancies. Although the reporter identified herself to Craig and to his mother during brief telephone conversations, the reporter did not ask Craig's permission to use his name in the story. Craig understood the newspaper was doing a "survey" on teenage pregnancy, not a story in which individual minors would be identified. The court ruled Craig gave no implied consent because he never understood enough about how his name might be used to make an informed choice. Whether publication of Craig's name was newsworthy should be left to a jury, the court said. Craig obtained a verdict against Multimedia for $1,500 actual and $25,000 punitive damages.[43]

It may be difficult to know who has authority to give consent to disseminate private information at institutions housing the sick, the retarded, and the young. Releases obtained by television journalist Bill Moyers permitting CBS to film mental patients at Creedmoor State Hospital in New York were invalid because they were not signed by the proper authority. The hospital's Consent for Patient Interview form required that a patient's consent be witnessed by a physician who had determined a patient was capable of giving consent. The court said that permission forms secured by Moyers were invalid because they were signed by a psychologist, not by a medical doctor.[44]

Consent to publish private information should be broad enough to cover the uses intended by the media. For example, a book publisher with permission to publish the picture of a woman bathing should not pass the picture to a newspaper for publication to a much broader audience.[45] Consent to have one's picture published in news columns does not include consent to have the picture used in a commercial context.

---

[42]Prahl v. Brosamle, 295 N.W.2d 768 (Wis. App. 1980).

[43]Hawkins v. Multimedia, Inc., 344 S.E.2d 145, 12 Media L. Rep. 1878 (S.C. 1986), *cert. denied,* 479 U.S. 1012 (1986).

[44]Delan v. CBS, 445 N.Y.S.2d 898, 7 Media L. Rep. 2453 (Sup. Ct. 1981), *modified,* 458 N.Y.S.2d 608, 9 Media L. Rep. 1130 (A.D. 1983).

[45]McCabe v. Village Voice, 550 F. Supp. 525, 8 Media L. Rep. 2583 (E.D. Pa. 1982).

Where proper consent is lacking, a presentation containing intimate private information may be enjoined. The Massachusetts Supreme Court barred filmmaker Frederick Wiseman from showing to the general public his documentary of the Massachusetts Correctional Institution at Bridgewater. Wiseman was blocked, in part, because the filmmaker failed to get written releases from all inmates. The documentary, *Titicut Follies,* showed deplorable conditions in the institution. Because consent was lacking, the court said Wiseman could show his documentary only to doctors, lawyers, social workers, and others with a professional interest in the institution.[46]

SUMMARY

Defendants in private-facts cases may claim a First Amendment privilege, newsworthiness, or consent. The Supreme Court has ruled that publication of private information contained in court records is constitutionally protected. So is lawfully acquired information in official government records, unless a plaintiff can demonstrate that punishment would advance a state interest of the highest order.

Newsworthy names and pictures also may be disseminated. Newsworthiness is a broad defense, including information gathered in public places and information about public figures and interesting events. One can also disseminate private information if given implied or explicit consent. The media should be most careful to get written consent when acquiring information about mental and physical illness and minors.

INTRUSION AND TRESPASS

The Fourth Amendment to the Constitution prohibits government agents from making unreasonable searches and seizures. The Fourth Amendment protects citizens from unjustified government searches of their homes and offices and unwarranted seizures of their papers and possessions. Law enforcement officers must get a search warrant from the judiciary before searching private property and seizing private materials. The search warrant is issued after law enforcement officers have convinced a judge there is probable cause to believe that a search of a specific place will reveal evidence related to a specific crime.

The Fourth Amendment does not protect citizens only from unreasonable physical searches by government agents. It also protects citizens from unwarranted government snooping with electronic devices. In a case in which FBI agents bugged a public telephone booth without a warrant, the Supreme Court ruled that a citizen's Fourth Amendment rights had been violated. The Fourth Amendment protects people, not places, from government intrusion, the Court said.[47]

While the Fourth Amendment protects citizens from unreasonable government intrusions, tort law protects citizens from intrusions by private citizens, including re-

---

[46]Commonwealth v. Wiseman, 249 N.E.2d 610 (Mass. 1969).
[47]Katz v. United States, 389 U.S. 347 (1967).

porters. In the common law of privacy, intrusion is a highly intrusive physical, electronic, or mechanical invasion of another's solitude or seclusion.[48] Intrusion includes the secretly recorded conversation, the overly aggressive surveillance, the long-distance photograph made with a telephoto lens. Intrusion is part of privacy law because an intrusion violates citizens' rights to be left alone and to control information about themselves.

Intrusion is a tort of information gathering, not a tort of publishing or broadcasting. Journalists gathering information with a secret camera or tape recorder may be liable for intrusion regardless of what they learn or whether they publish it. "Where there is intrusion," a federal circuit judge said,

> the intruder should generally be liable whatever the content of what he learns. An eavesdropper to the marital bedroom may hear marital intimacies, or he may hear statements of fact or opinion of legitimate interest to the public; for purposes of liability that should make no difference.[49]

Whether an act intrudes upon the privacy of another depends on whether that person has a reasonable expectation of privacy. Is the person in a place where he or she can reasonably assume that secret photographs will not be taken or secret recordings made? One may have an expectation of privacy in some public places, such as an enclosed phone booth, but generally the more public the surroundings, the less the expectation of privacy.

Intrusion into Public and Quasi-Public Places

"What a person knowingly exposes to the public . . . is not a subject of Fourth Amendment protection," the Supreme Court has said.[50] Therefore, government agents do not need a search warrant to watch a mooonshiner in an open field,[51] view marijuana plants from a helicopter in a backyard greenhouse,[52] or listen to one side of an easily overheard telephone conversation in a public place.[53] In tort law, too, a private person has little expectation of privacy in public places.

Permitted Surveillance   Common law decisions generally hold that people in public and quasi-public places must assume they might be photographed or recorded, particularly if they are officials carrying out their public duties. Media personnel therefore can photograph, film, and record what they easily see or hear in public places, provided they do not harass, trespass, or use electronic and photo devices to enhance hearing and vision. A California statute reflects the law generally when it says tape recording at public meetings is not an intrusion where "the parties to the

---

[48]*Restatement (Second) Torts* sec. 652B (1977).
[49]Pearson v. Dodd, 410 F.2d 701, 705, 1 Media L. Rep. 1809, 1812 (D.C. Cir. 1969).
[50]Katz v. United States, 389 U.S. 347, 351 (1967).
[51]Hester v. United States, 265 U.S. 57 (1924).
[52]Florida v. Riley, 109 S. Ct. 693 (1989).
[53]United States v. Llanes, 398 F.2d 880 (2d Cir. 1968); United States v. McLeod, 493 F.2d 1186 (7th Cir. 1974).

communication may reasonably expect that the communication may be overheard or recorded."[54]

It is not an intrusion for a TV crew to record police publicly frisking a suspect[55] or to take a picture of private property from a public sidewalk. John W. Bisbee lost an intrusion suit over a picture taken from a sidewalk of his Ocean Township estate. Bisbee had no suit for intrusion, a New Jersey court said, because the picture "merely represented a view which is available to any bystander."[56]

Courts are divided over whether a restaurant is a private place in which a diner may expect to be free from unwanted photographers and interviewers. The Iowa Supreme Court ruled that a restaurant might be a sufficiently secluded place that a patron could sue the media for unwanted filming of a diner. The Iowa court ruled Theresa Stessman had a cause of action against the American Black Hawk Broadcasting Company for filming her despite her objection as she dined in a public restaurant.[57] In allowing the suit to proceed, the court said filming a person in a private dining room "might conceivably be a highly offensive intrusion upon that person's seclusion."

However, a federal court in Maine ruled that a *National Enquirer* reporter did not intrude when she persistently sought to interview and photograph a Henry Dempsey at a restaurant as well as outside his home.[58] The court said it is not intrusive to attempt to take a photograph in a restaurant open to the public, or to attempt interviews without passing the threshold of the home. The reporter's attempts to interview may have been "annoying," the court said, but they were not "highly offensive" and therefore did not constitute intrusion.

Journalists may record and photograph what they can easily see or overhear in the public sections of jails. Radio reporter Carl Connerton did not intrude on attorney Marvin Holman when he recorded Holman hollering and banging from an Arkansas jail cell after he was charged with drunk driving. The recording was not intrusive even though one of Holman's associates told Connerton not to record. "The boisterous complaints which were recorded were not made with the expectation of privacy or confidentiality," the federal court said.[59]

Whether it is an intrusion to photograph an inmate in his cell without permission is not clear. On the one hand, an inmate is housed in a quasi-public institution and has almost no right of privacy. Because prisoners have little privacy to protect, at least one court ruled a prisoner could not sue over a surreptitious picture taken while he was asleep.[60] On the other hand, jail inmates are not completely without civil rights. Inmates are protected, for example, by the Fourth Amendment from having to undress in front of guards of the opposite sex.[61] One court ruled that a prisoner could

---

[54]Cal. Penal Code Sec. 632(c) (West 1986). *See also* Ill. Ann. Stat. ch. 38, sec. 14-3(c) (Smith-Hurd Supp. 1989).

[55]Prahl v. Brosamle, 295 N.W.2d 768, 774 (Wis. Ct. App. 1980).

[56]Bisbee v. Conover, 9 Media L. Rep. 1298, 1299 (N.J. Super. App. Div. 1982). *See also* Mark v. King Broadcasting Co., 618 P.2d 512 (1980); Neff v. Time, Inc., 406 F. Supp. 858 (W.D. Pa. 1976).

[57]Stessman v. American Black Hawk Broadcasting Co., 416 N.W.2d 685, 14 Media L. Rep. 2073 (1987).

[58]Dempsey v. National Enquirer, Inc. 702 F. Supp. 927, 16 Media L. Rep. 1396 (D. Maine 1988).

[59]Holman v. Central Arkansas Broadcasting Co., Inc., 610 F.2d 542, 5 Media L. Rep. 2217 (8th Cir. 1979).

[60]Jenkins v. Winchester Star, 8 Media L. Rep. 1403 (W.D. Va. 1981). *See also* Rifkin v. Esquire, 8 Media L. Rep. 1384 (C.D. Cal. 1982).

[61]Lee v. Downs, 641 F.2d 1117 (4th Cir. 1981).

pursue a civil rights suit against a warden who permitted a camera crew to film the prisoner.[62] Even though no intrusion suit was brought against the film crew, a warden may be reluctant to permit press photographers and camera crews into a prison if inmates can then bring suits charging a violation of their civil rights.

Harassment, Assault, and Overzealous Shadowing

Not all news-gathering practices in public places are permitted. A famous case involving Jacqueline Onassis illustrates how aggressive journalism can cross over to illegal harassment. Although the case of *Galella v. Onassis* is not an intrusion case, it illustrates where overzealous reporting becomes intrusive.[63]

Photographer Ron Galella, in his pursuit of photos and information about Mrs. Onassis, guided children into glass doors, bumped the parents of the Kennedy children's schoolmates, blocked passages, temporarily blinded people with his flashbulbs, spied with telephoto lenses, trailed Mrs. Onassis hour after hour, chased her in his car, and snooped in her packages while she was shopping. He also impersonated family employees, spooked John Junior's horse, and circled Mrs. Onassis in a motorboat while she was swimming.

When Onassis sued over this list of intrusive activities, Galella complained that Onassis was camera-shy and uncooperative. However, the court ruled that Galella was liable for assault, battery, harassment, and infliction of emotional distress. "The essence of the privacy interest," the federal district court said,

> includes a general "right to be left alone," and to define one's circle of intimacy; to shield intimate and personal characteristics and activities from public gaze; to have moments of freedom from the unremitted assault of the world and unfettered will of others in order to achieve some measure of tranquillity for contemplation or other purposes, without which life loses its sweetness.[64]

A federal district court enjoined Galella from taking pictures of Onassis from closer than 150 feet. A federal appeals court affirmed most of the lower court ruling but reduced to 25 feet the distance that Galella must remain from Onassis. After several violations, Galella was held in contempt of court and ordered to pay Onassis $10,000.[65]

Overzealous surveillance or shadowing that falls short of harassment or assault may nevertheless be intrusive. The New York Court of Appeals, the state's highest court, ruled that Ralph Nader could bring a suit against General Motors for hiring people to follow him so closely that they could see the denomination of the bills Nader withdrew from a bank. The court said that "mere observation" in a public place does not amount to an invasion of privacy, but that surveillance "may be so 'overzealous' as to render it actionable." The fact that Nader was in the lobby of a public building "did not give anyone the right to try to discover the amount of money he was withdrawing."[66]

---

[62]Smith v. Fairman, 98 F.R.D. 445 (C.D. Ill. 1982).

[63]353 F. Supp. 196 (S.D.N.Y. 1972), *aff'd,* 487 F.2d 986, 1 Media L. Rep. 2425 (2d Cir. 1973).

[64]353 F. Supp. at 232.

[65]Galella v. Onassis, 533 F. Supp. 1076 (S.D.N.Y. 1982).

[66]Nader v. General Motors Corp., 307 N.Y.S.2d 647 (N.Y. 1970).

However, aggressive news gathering, including "ambush interviews," may not be intrusive. One federal court ruled an "aggressive and possibly abrasive" interview is not an intrusion in a public or semipublic place as long as it does not amount to "unabated hounding." In *Machleder v. Diaz,* a reporter entered the property of a hazardous waste company without permission and asked questions of the president. There was no intrusion because the executive's willingness to talk constituted consent to the interview.[67] Another court ruled that aggressive phoning—ten unwanted calls over several months—to obtain comments on newsworthy events is not intrusive, but constitutes "routine newsgathering activities."[68]

SUMMARY

Intrusion is the physical or technological violation of another's privacy. Generally, the media can record or take pictures of what is easily seen or heard in public and quasi-public places. However, the media are not permitted to engage in harassment, assault, or overzealous surveillance, even in a public place.

Intrusion into Private Places

Perhaps of more concern to citizens and the media than intrusion into public places is intrusion into private places. Even the most well-known public figures have a right to private retreats where they are free to talk, joke, and perhaps be irresponsible without being accountable to the outside world. A person has a justifiable expectation in a private place to be free from the telephoto lens,[69] the hidden microphone, and the trespasser crouching below his or her window. The law has long held that it is illegal to peep, snoop, or eavesdrop on people in private places. Peering in someone's window or pressing one's ear to the door may be trespass, intrusion, or both.[70] It is also an invasion of privacy to open someone's mail[71] or to tap someone's telephone.

Third-Party Tape-recording   Only law enforcement officers operating under a valid search warrant may legally bug a room or tap a telephone. Bugging, wiretapping, and eavesdropping are prohibited by the Constitution, by federal and state statutes, and by common law.[72] Bugging, wiretapping, and eavesdropping are a form of *third-party* monitoring conducted without the knowledge of parties to a conversation. Not only is it against the law for a third party to intercept telephone conversations transmitted over wires, it is also illegal to intercept wireless telephone conversations, electronic mail, and satellite transmissions of video teleconferences and

---

[67]Machleder v. Diaz, 538 F. Supp. 1364 (S.D.N.Y. 1982).

[68]Lee v. The Columbian, 16 Media L. Rep. (Wash. Sup. Ct. 1989).

[69]Souder v. Pendleton Detectives, Inc., 88 So.2d 716 (La. Ct. App. 1956).

[70]A. Westin, *Privacy and Freedom* 333–34 (1967); Souder v. Pendleton Detectives, Inc., 88 So.2d 716 (La. Ct. App. 1956).

[71]Vernars v. Young, 539 F.2d 966 (3d Cir. 1976).

[72]Omnibus Crime Control and Safe Streets Act of 1968, 18 U.S.C. sec. 2511 (1976); Katz v. United States, 389 U.S. 347 (1967).

data.[73] Third-party monitoring is a particularly offensive intrusion because, as Justice Douglas observed in a bugging case involving law enforcement officers, it "intrudes upon the privacy of those not even suspected of crime and intercepts the most intimate of conversations."[74] Regardless of what the third party might see or hear, it is an intrusion to place a secret camera or bug in a bedroom, in an office, or on a telephone line.[75]

Participant Monitoring   The law is more tolerant of participants who record their own conversations than of third parties who record the conversations of others. *Participant monitoring* occurs when at least one party to a conversation is aware of a secret recorder or transmitter. Some people contend that secret participant tape-recording is unethical and unnecessary, but lawyers, businessmen, public relations practitioners, and journalists sometimes secretly record telephone conversations to establish an accurate record without inhibiting candor. Unannounced recording protects journalists against false charges that a source was misquoted. Investigative reporters, like police informants, will sometimes carry a secret tape recorder or transmitter to document drug deals and other wrongdoing. It is estimated that half of the household telephone answering machines sold in the United States permit secret taping of conversations.[76]

  Federal Law   Federal law and the law in about 40 states permits one party to a conversation to record or transmit a conversation without telling the other party. In these jurisdictions, participant tape-recording is considered no more intrusive than orally retelling a conversation to a third party. Citizens are generally free to recount conversations, even private conversations, to friends, neighbors, colleagues, or journalists. Doctors, lawyers, and ministers are prohibited by law from divulging confidential conversations with their clients, but other citizens are not.[77]

    Although federal law permits participant recording, section 2511 of the Federal Wiretap Statute forbids a participant from secretly recording a conversation for the purpose of committing a crime or a tort.[78] Civil penalties for violation of the act can result in a fine of $10,000.[79] It is a crime or a tort for a participant in a conversation to make a recording with the intent to blackmail or threaten someone with the recording.[80] It may also violate the federal statute to interview under a false identity.[81] However, Congress intended that the federal statute not be invoked against journalists simply because their surreptitious recordings may result in news stories that "embarrass" someone.[82]

---

[73]Electronic Communications Privacy Act of 1986, Pub. L. 99-508, 100 Stat. 1848 (1986).

[74]Berger v. New York, 388 U.S. 41, 64–65 (1967) (concurring opinion).

[75]Hamberger v. Eastman, 206 A.2d 239 (N.H. 1964). *See* McDaniel v. Atlanta Coca-Cola Bottling Co., 2 S.E.2d 810 (Ga. App. 1939).

[76]Bradsher, "That Private Phone Conversation May Be on Tape," *New York Times,* Dec. 17, 1989, at 1.

[77]*See generally* Middleton, "Journalists and Tape Recorders: Does Participant Monitoring Invade Privacy," 2 *Comm/Ent L. J.* 287 (1979–80).

[78]18 U.S.C.A. sec. 2511 (2)(d) (Supp. 1989); Katz v. United States, 389 U.S. 347 (1967).

[79]18 U.S.C.A. sec. 2520 (c) (2) (B) (Supp. 1989). *See* United States v. Turk, 526 F.2d 654 (5th Cir. 1976).

[80]United States v. Phillips, 540 F.2d 319, 325 (8th Cir.), *cert. denied,* 429 U.S. 1000 (1976).

[81]W.C.H. of Waverly v. Meredith, 13 Media L. Rep. 1648 (W.D. Mo. 1986).

[82]Boddie v. American Broadcasting Cos., 694 F. Supp. 1304, 16 Media L. Rep. 1100 (N.D. Ohio 1989).

Contrary to the federal wiretap statute, the Federal Communications Commission requires telephone companies to prohibit telephone subscribers from recording conversations unless all parties to the conversation are told of the recording in advance either with an announcement or a beep tone. However, the telephone regulations do not require a warning before recording calls to an emergency number or calls recorded under court order.[83] A person making an illegal call has little or no expectation of privacy.

More important, the telephone company regulations prohibiting participant recording are seldom enforced. Highly competitive phone companies have little incentive to seek out violators, and the penalty—removal of a subscriber's phone—is only a slight deterrent. It is easy to obtain another number. Furthermore, telephone company regulations mandated by the FCC may be preempted by provisions of the Federal Wiretap Statute that permit participant recording.

An FCC rule that is enforced requires broadcasters to notify callers immediately if a telephone conversation is being recorded for broadcast.[84] But broadcasters, like anyone else, need provide no notice of a secret participant telephone recording not intended for broadcast, if participant recording is legal under state law. Furthermore, the FCC rule requiring notice of telephone conversations taped for broadcast does not require notice of face-to-face conversations intended for broadcast.

State Prohibitions   Statutes in about 10 states prohibit participant tape-recording.[85] At least one state court has upheld the constitutionality of the prohibition on participant monitoring. In a case involving a reporter's unannounced telephone recordings, the Florida Supreme Court rejected reporters' arguments that secret tape-recording was needed to corroborate a journalist's story. The court said that secret recording is not an "indispensable" tool of news gathering and that the First Amendment does not include a right to corroborate news stories with secret recordings.[86]

Illinois law prohibits tape-recording a conversation unless all parties to the conversation give consent, but the statute was held not to bar secret videotaping without sound of a policeman's official conduct in a massage parlor. The Illinois appeals court ruled that undercover police officer Arlyn Cassidy had no privacy claim when a television station filmed him from behind a two-way mirror as he investigated activities at a massage parlor. After watching a model change her lingerie several times, Officer Cassidy made several suggestive remarks and physical advances. He arrested the model for solicitation after the model established "sufficient" physical contact. At that moment, a television crew rushed out of the adjoining room shouting, "Channel 7 News."[87] The television crew was watching the proceedings with the consent of the model.

---

[83]Use of Recording Devices in Connection with Telephone Service, 86 F.C.C.2d 313 (1981), *reconsideration granted in part,* 48 Fed. Reg. 51,773 (1983).

[84]*In re* Amendment of Section 1206: Broadcast of Telephone Conversations, 65 P&F Rad. Reg.2d 444 (1988).

[85]California, Florida, Illinois, Maryland, Massachusetts, Montana, New Hampshire, Oregon, Pennsylvania, and Washington.

[86]Shevin v. Sunbeam Television Corp., 351 So.2d 723 (Fla. 1977), *appeal dismissed,* 435 U.S. 920, *reh'g denied,* 435 U.S. 1018 (1978).

[87]Cassidy v. ABC, 377 N.E.2d 126 (Ill. App. 1978).

Cassidy charged that the unannounced filming violated the Illinois statute prohibiting secret sound-recording and intruded into his privacy. The Illinois appeals court ruled that the statute prohibiting participant monitoring was not violated because the television camera recorded no sound. The camera, therefore, was not an "eavesdropping device" under the statute.

The Illinois court of appeals also ruled that Cassidy had little expectation of privacy. Cassidy was a public official acting in an official capacity. "In our opinion," the court said, "the very status of the policeman as a public official is tantamount to an implied consent to informing the general public by all legitimate means regarding his activities in discharge of his public duties."[88] There was no allegation, the court noted, that the broadcast crew had attempted to impede police work. Furthermore, Cassidy's expectation of privacy was less than it might have been because he suspected he might be under surveillance. When he entered the modeling room, he noticed "camera lights" and asked the model if they were on TV. She replied, "Sure, we're making movies." Under the circumstances, Cassidy had no expectation of privacy, the court said.

Secret Recording as a Tort   Regardless of federal and state statutes, secret recording by a participant to a conversation may be an intrusion, particularly if subterfuge is used to bring electronic eavesdropping equipment into a private place. Secret recording in an office or other business location where a person's expectation of privacy is less than in a home may not be an intrusion, but the law is not clear.

In one well-known case from California, a federal court ruled secret transmitting and photographing by two journalists in a private home was an intrusion. In *Dietemann v. Time, Inc.,* the U.S. Court of Appeals for the Ninth Circuit ruled that A. A. Dietemann, a quack doctor, could collect damages from Time for invasion of his privacy by two *Life* magazine employees who secretly used a voice transmitter and camera in the doctor's den. The journalists gained entrance to Dietemann's house by giving false names. One *Life* staffer secretly photographed the doctor as he waved a wand over bottles of body tissue and rubbed what he said was the cancerous breast of the other journalist. Meanwhile a transmitter in the journalist's purse transmitted the conversation to a tape recorder in a nearby police car.[89]

The federal appeals court affirmed a lower court ruling awarding $1,000 to Dietemann for the journalists' electronic intrusion into a private place. Dietemann's den, the Ninth Circuit said, "was a sphere from which he could reasonably expect to exclude eavesdropping newsmen." When a person invites another into a private place, the court said,

> he does not and should not be required to take the risk that what is heard and seen will be transmitted by photograph or recording, or in our modern world, in full living color and hi-fi to the public. . . . A different rule could have a most pernicious effect upon the dignity of man and it would surely lead to guarded conversations and conduct where candor is most valued, *e.g.,* in the case of doctors and lawyers.[90]

---

[88]60 *Id.* at 132.
[89]Dietemann v. Time, Inc., 449 F.2d 245, 1 Media L. Rep. 2417 (1971).
[90]*Id.* at 249.

The court rejected *Life*'s claim that concealed electronic instruments are essential to investigative reporting and that their use is protected by the First Amendment. "We agree," the court said, "that newsgathering is an integral part of news dissemination. We strongly disagree, however, that the hidden mechanical contrivances are 'indispensable tools' of newsgathering."

In a passage that has been cited frequently, the court wrote,

> The First Amendment has never been construed to accord newsmen immunity from torts or crimes committed during the course of newsgathering. The First Amendment is not a license to trespass, to steal, or to intrude by electronic means into the precincts of another's home or office.[91]

In a case of surreptitious tape-recording in a lawyer's office, the Kentucky Supreme Court came to a different conclusion than that of the Ninth Circuit in the *Dietemann* case. The Kentucky court upheld a lower court's dismissal of an intrusion claim by an attorney who was secretly recorded by a client, Kristie Frazier. Frazier, an indicted drug dealer, carried a hidden tape recorder to a meeting with attorney Tim McCall at the suggestion of two *Louisville Courier Journal* reporters. Frazier was to get taped corroboration for her claims that McCall had offered to arrange with a judge to keep Frazier out of jail for a fee of $10,000. But during the secretly taped conversation, attorney McCall denied being able to fix Frazier's case with the judge.[92]

In ruling that Frazier's surreptitious recording did not intrude into McCall's privacy, the Kentucky trial court said the *McCall* case was not like the *Dietemann* case, where intrusion was found. The Kentucky court noted that Kristie Frazier did not give a false identity to gain entry to McCall's office as the *Life* employees did at Dr. Dietemann's. Frazier was not an intruder because Tim McCall knew whom he was talking to.

The Kentucky trial court also said McCall had less expectation of privacy than Dietemann did, because McCall suspected that Frazier might be secretly recording their conversation. At one point, McCall asked Frazier if she was carrying a recorder and continued the conversation when she said no. The Kentucky court said McCall should have asked Frazier to leave when he suspected she had a recorder. "By continuing the conversation, McCall consented to her presence," the court said.

SUMMARY

Bugging and wiretapping are prohibited. But secret recording by one party to a conversation is permitted by federal statute and statutes in 40 states. However, participant monitoring may violate federal law if done to commit a crime or a tort. Unannounced telephone recordings also violate seldom-enforced telephone regulations. Unannounced participant telephone recordings also violate FCC regulations if the recordings are intended for broadcast. In contrast, participant monitoring violates

---

[91]*Id.*

[92]McCall v. Courier Journal & Louisville Times Co., 6 Media L. Rep. 1112 (Ky. Ct. App. 1980), *rev'd*, 623 S.W.2d 882 (Ky. 1981), *cert. denied*, 456 U.S. 975 (1982).

statutes in ten states and may be a tort, particularly if conducted in very private settings under false pretenses. Surreptitious recording may not be an intrusion in business settings where expectations of privacy are lower, particularly if no deceit is used to gain entry.

Trespass

Closely related to intrusion and often claimed simultaneously with intrusion is trespass. While intrusion does not require a physical invasion of someone's property, trespass does. Trespass is entering private property or inviting someone to go onto private property without consent of the owner or "possessor" of the property.[93] Merely going onto private property or posted public property without permission may be a trespass, whether or not the trespasser uses intrusive tape recorders, secret cameras, and other technological devices. The violation lies in the trespass, not in what is learned or published as a result of the trespass. Property owners need not prove their property was damaged, but punitive damages usually will be awarded only if the trespass is willful or malicious.[94]

It is not a trespass to enter private property with the consent of the owner or possessor of the property. Usually the possessor of private property is the owner, but a person who rents also "possesses" property. A tenant may grant or deny access to an apartment or rental house, regardless of the wishes of the property owner.[95] For brief periods during emergencies, fire and police officials may also control access to private property, but even during an emergency, the owner of property can deny access to the media.[96]

Once journalists enter private property to ask questions, they gain an implied consent to remain if the property owner agrees to talk.[97] However, journalists may become trespassers if they refuse to leave when asked. They may also be trespassers if they misrepresent the purpose of the interview[98] or fail to identify themselves as reporters.[99] When journalists misrepresent themselves or their purpose, courts may rule that property owners do not consent to the journalists' presence when the owners agree to talk.

Journalists are likely to be ruled trespassers if their news gathering disrupts the normal activities on private property open to the public. A New York court awarded $1,200 in compensatory damages to Le Mistral, a fashionable Manhattan restaurant, for trespass by a Channel 2 news crew that burst into the establishment during lunchtime in July 1972. The Channel 2 reporter wanted to question management about the

---

[93]*Restatement (Second) of Torts* sec. 158 at 277 (1965).

[94]Le Mistral, Inc. v. Columbia Broadcasting Sys., 402 N.Y.S.2d 815, 3 Media L. Rep. 1913 (App. Div. 1978); Belluomo v. KAKE TV & Radio, Inc., 596 P.2d 832 (Kan. Ct. App. 1979).

[95]Lal v. CBS, 551 F. Supp. 356, 9 Media L. Rep. 1112 (E.D. Pa. 1982), *aff'd,* 726 F.2d 97, 10 Media L. Rep. 1276 (3d Cir. 1984).

[96]Prahl v. Brosamle, 295 N.W.2d 768, 773 (Wis. Ct. App. 1980); Anderson v WROC-TV, 441 N.Y.S.2d 220, 7 Media L. Rep. 1787 (Sup. Ct. 1981).

[97]Machleder v. Diaz, 538 F. Supp. 1364 (S.D.N.Y. 1982).

[98]Belluomo v. KAKE TV & Radio, Inc., 596 P.2d 832 (Kan. Ct. App. 1979).

[99]Prahl v. Brosamle, 295 N.W.2d 768 (Wis. Ct. App. 1980).

restaurant's inclusion on a list of establishments violating the city health code. Consternation followed when the bright TV lights were turned into the dining room. Before management could remove the news crew, patrons waiting to be seated left the restaurant. Diners left without paying. Some customers hid behind napkins and tablecloths and others dived under tables.[100]

In upholding Le Mistral's trespass claim, a New York appeals court said it was not necessary for the television crew to disrupt the business in order to gather information. The station could have called ahead to make an appointment with the manager and perhaps interview him about the health code matters in his office. The appeals court directed a new trial on the issue of punitive damages, which require a showing of malice in New York.

Accompanying Officials   Consent to enter property can be explicit or can be implied under a theory of *custom and usage.* Store owners give implied consent under the doctrine of custom and usage when they open their doors to the public. Under the doctrine, a customer does not need explicit permission to enter a privately owned store to make a purchase. Custom creates a privilege for peaceful entry. Likewise, a property owner gives implied consent to a traveler to come onto private property to ask directions, a salesman to make a pitch, or a journalist to ask questions. As long as these outsiders heed no-trespassing signs and honor requests to leave, their peaceful entry onto private property is permitted by the doctrine of custom and usage.[101]

The Florida Supreme Court extended the custom-and-usage doctrine to allow journalists to accompany officials onto private property at the scene of a calamity. In *Florida Publishing Co. v. Fletcher,* the Florida court said it was not a trespass for a *Florida Times-Union* photographer to accompany fire officials into the burned-out house of Kleena Ann Fletcher after a fire that killed Mrs. Fletcher's 17-year-old daughter, Cindy.[102] Mrs. Fletcher, who was out of town at the time of the fire, learned of her daughter's death by reading a news account in the *Times-Union.* Accompanying the article was a picture of a "Silhouette of Death" taken by a *Times-Union* photographer in Cindy's bedroom. A silhouette of Cindy's body was formed on the floor where the fire burned around her after she was overcome. Authorities requested that the *Times-Union* photographer take the picture when the fire marshal's camera ran out of film. The picture, besides being published in the paper, became part of the official record.

Mrs. Fletcher said the custom-and-usage doctrine should not apply to journalists accompanying officials because, unlike a householder who expects salesmen to visit occasionally, Mrs. Fletcher was not aware of the journalistic custom of accompanying officials. Therefore, Mrs. Fletcher argued, she did not give the implied consent that the doctrine of custom and usage assumes. Furthermore, Mrs. Fletcher said, she would not have given consent to the journalist had she been home at the time of the fire.

The Florida Supreme Court disregarded Mrs. Fletcher's argument, ruling that

---

[100]Le Mistral, Inc. v. Columbia Broadcasting Sys., 402 N.Y.S.2d 815, 3 Media L. Rep. 1913 (App.Div. 1978).

[101]*See* Fletcher v. Florida Publishing Co., 319 So.2d 100, 109 (Fla. Ct. App. 1975); 75 *Am. Juris. 2d* (Trespass) sec. 41 (1974).

[102]Florida Publishing Co. v. Fletcher, 340 So.2d 914 (Fla. 1976), *cert. denied,* 431 U.S. 930 (1977).

the doctrine of custom and usage does apply when reporters accompany officials onto private property at the scene of a calamity. Important in the Florida court's decision to grant summary judgment for the *Times-Union* on the trespass count was the fact that law enforcement officials and the media sent several affidavits swearing how common it is for journalists to accompany officials onto private property at disaster scenes. The Florida court also noted that officials invited the press onto Mrs. Fletcher's property and that the photographer served a quasi-official function when he took a photo of the silhouette for authorities' files.

Other courts have not been willing to extend the doctrine of custom and usage to allow journalists to accompany officials onto private property, at least when the occupants of the property are present. A New York court ruled that WROC-TV employees trespassed when they accompanied Ronald Storm of the Humane Society of Rochester and Monroe County on an investigation. Storm, who had a search warrant, was investigating a complaint that animals were being mistreated at the home of Joy E. Brenon.[103] Brenon objected when the TV crew accompanied Storm into the house and shot footage.

The New York court said the authority of officials to enter private property to perform their duty "does not extend by invitation, absent an emergency, to every and any other member of the public, including members of the news media." The court said the Florida Supreme Court's ruling in the *Fletcher* case expanding the custom-and-usage doctrine to journalists accompanying officials is a "self-created custom and practice" that gives the media greater right to go onto private property than an official who needs a warrant. A state official such as Ronald Storm may go onto private property with a search warrant, the court said, but the officer's authority to go onto private property does not extend to people he may invite to accompany him, including journalists.[104]

The state of trespass law creates uncertainty for journalists. On the one hand journalists serve legitimate public interests covering fires, shootings, storms, and other newsworthy events on private property. On the other hand, they have no assurance that they will not be sued for trespass if they enter private property, even if accompanying officials. The journalists' dilemma will remain as long as they have no First Amendment defense to trespass charges. Because of the First Amendment interests reporters serve, some argue that journalists should not be held liable for trespass unless it can be shown that the journalists knew they were trespassing and that they caused identifiable damage to people or private property.[105]

Receiving Stolen Information What are journalists' liabilities if they receive stolen information from someone who may have trespassed to get it? In the major case on this question, national columnist Drew Pearson was not held liable for obtaining pri-

---

[103]Anderson v. WROC-TV, 441 N.Y.S.2d 220, 7 Media L. Rep. 1987 (Sup. Ct. 1981).

[104]*See also* Miller v. National Broadcasting Company, 232 Cal. Rptr. 668 (Cal. App. 1987); Green Valley School, Inc. v. Cowles Florida Broadcasting, Inc., 327 So.2d 810 (Fla. App. 1976); Prahl v. Brosamle, 295 N.W.2d 768 (Wis. App. 1980); and Middleton, "Journalists, Trespass, and Officials: Closing the Door on *Florida Publishing Co. v. Fletcher*," *Pepperdine L. Rev.* 259 (1989).

[105]Allen v. Combined Communications, 7 Media L. Rep. 2417 (Colo. Dist. Ct. 1981). *See* Watkins, "Private Property vs. Reporter Rights—A Problem in Newsgathering," 54 *Journ. Q.* 690 (1977).

vate information about Senator Thomas Dodd, information Pearson knew was stolen by the senator's staff. Pearson was not liable for intrusion or trespass because Pearson himself had not trespassed and had not encouraged what may have been a trespass by Pearson's staff.[106]

In addition, the federal appeals court rejected Senator Dodd's assertion that Pearson should be held liable for "conversion" of the senator's property. Conversion is the unauthorized exercise of ownership rights over someone else's property, usually denying the owner use of his or her own property.[107] The court of appeals ruled that there was no conversion because Dodd was not deprived of the use of his files. Pearson received photocopies of originals that had been immediately returned to their proper place in the senator's office.

Furthermore, the court did not consider the letters from constituents, office records, and other routine business of a senator to be "property" because it had no economic value. The court said information in a senator's files was not like a literary creation, scientific invention, or secret business plan whose economic value depends on its being confidential.

While *Pearson v. Dodd* is the major case on theft of stolen property, people in the media should not feel secure that stolen documents can be published with impunity as long as media personnel themselves do not trespass, steal, or encourage theft. Chief Justice Burger, in his dissent in the *Pentagon Papers* case, said the *New York Times* should have been held liable under a theory of stolen property for publishing the stolen government history of the Vietnam War.[108] Since the 1971 Pentagon Papers case, some of the liberals who prevailed against the chief justice in 1971 have been replaced with justices more in tune with the views of Burger and other conservative justices. Furthermore, receiving stolen property could violate a state statute prohibiting the receipt of such goods.[109]

SUMMARY

Trespass, the physical entry onto private property, is closely related to the intrusion tort. A journalist, like any citizen, can be held liable for trespass. The Florida Supreme Court says journalists may accompany authorities onto private property at a disaster scene, but other jurisdictions have not applied the Florida court's reasoning to cases where the owner is present to object. A journalist may avoid liability for trespass or intrusion for obtaining stolen documents, but the Supreme Court has not ruled on this point.

---

[106]Pearson v. Dodd, 410 F.2d 701, 1 Media L. Rep. 1809 (D.C. Cir.), *cert. denied,* 395 U.S. 947 (1969). *See also* Bilney v. Evening Star, 406 A.2d 652, 5 Media L. Rep. 1931 (Md. Ct. App. 1979).

[107]89 *Corpus Juris Secundum,* Trover and Conversion, sec. 1 at 531 (1955). *See* Dennis, "Purloined Information as Property: A New First Amendment Challenge," 50 *Journ. Q.*. 456 (1973).

[108]New York Times v. United States, 403 U.S. 713, 1 Media L. Rep. 1039 (1971).

[109]People v. Kunkin, 100 Cal. Rptr. 845, *rev'd,* 107 Cal. Rptr. 184 (1973).

FALSE LIGHT

A third privacy tort is called false light. It is illustrated by the case of John W. Gill, whose picture was snapped as he sat with his arm around his wife, Sheila, at the counter of their ice cream concession at the Farmers' Market in Los Angeles. As Gill leaned forward, touching his cheek to his wife's, the famous photographer Henri Cartier-Bresson took a photograph without the Gills' knowledge or consent. The photograph was published a short time later in the *Ladies Home Journal* to illustrate a story about love. Under the Gills' picture appeared the caption, "Publicized as glamorous, desirable, 'love at first sight' is a bad risk." The accompanying story said that love at first sight, the kind the Gills were portrayed as representing, is the "wrong" kind because it is founded upon "100% sex attraction."[110]

The Gills sued the publisher of the *Journal* for invasion of privacy. Their complaint was not that their affectionate moment was captured and publicized, but that their picture, with the caption and article, portrayed them falsely. The California Supreme Court ruled the Gills had a cause of action for invasion of privacy. "It is not unreasonable," said the court, to believe that the portrayal of the couple's relationship as based solely on sex "would be seriously humiliating and disturbing."

The *Restatement (Second) of Torts* defines the false-light tort as the dissemination of highly offensive false publicity about someone with knowledge of, or reckless disregard for, the falsity.[111] The interest protected by the law "is the interest of the individual in not being made to appear before the public in an objectionable false light or false position, or in other words, otherwise than he is."[112]

The false-light tort provokes disagreement over its relation to libel and other privacy torts, over what constitutes a "highly offensive" publication, and over how much the First Amendment should protect the media from plaintiffs, like the Gills, who assert difficult-to-prove injuries of mental anguish and emotional distress. "False light invasion of privacy has caused enough theoretical and practical problems," one commentator concludes, "to make a compelling case for a stricter standard of birth control in the evolution of the common law."[113]

As the Gill case illustrates, the false-light tort has much in common with libel. Indeed, the Gills claimed in their privacy suit that the picture, caption, and story would hurt their reputation for industry, decency, and morality. Dean William Prosser contended the interest protected by the false-light tort, like the interest protected by libel law, "is clearly that of reputation with the same overtones of mental distress as in defamation."[114] Not surprisingly, false-light claims are often filed concurrently with defamation suits.

In both libel and false-light litigation, a plaintiff claims to be the victim of falsehoods. Defenses are also similar. False-light defendants, like libel defendants, may claim that the plaintiff is not identified by the publication, that the publication is true, and that the publication is a privileged report of official proceedings. Furthermore,

---

[110]Gill v. Curtis Publishing Co., 239 P.2d 630 (Cal. 1952).
[111]*See Restatement (Second) of Torts* sec. 632E (1977).
[112]*Id.,* comment b.
[113]Zimmerman, "False Light Invasion of Privacy: The Light that Failed," 64 *N.Y.U. L. Rev.* 364, 366 (1989).
[114]Prosser, "Privacy," 48 *Calif. L. Rev.* 383, 400 (1960).

because false-light privacy, like libel, has been "constitutionalized," false-light defendants may also claim that the offending publication is opinion protected by the First Amendment and that the plaintiff must prove fault, usually actual malice.

While false light shares similarities with libel, the false-light plaintiff does not sue for lost reputation, but, like someone suing over publication of embarrassing facts, is seeking recompense, as the Gills were, for the psychic harms of mental distress and humiliation. The late law professor Melville Nimmer thought the false-light tort was a natural derivative of the private-facts tort. Comparing false light and embarrassing facts, Nimmer said an individual has the same privacy interest in "maintaining a haven from society's searching eye" whether true or false information is being revealed.[115] "The injury to the plaintiff's peace of mind which results from the public disclosure of private facts may be just as real where that which is disclosed is not true."

Another similarity between the false-light tort and the embarrassing-facts tort is the requirement that a plaintiff in both cases prove the offending material is widely disseminated. Libel plaintiffs must prove that a defamatory remark is "published" to at least one other person besides the plaintiff; a single business letter may constitute publication in a libel case. But a false-light plaintiff, like an embarrassing-facts plaintiff, must prove that the false information is widely disseminated. False-light privacy is a tort of publicity.

Reflecting the uncertain parentage, purpose, and effectiveness of the false-light tort, several states have refused to recognize it, either finding little relationship between false light and privacy or seeing the tort adequately covered by the law of libel.[116] Courts in Massachusetts and New York have not decided whether to recognize the false-light tort.

Highly Offensive Publications

While there is substantial inconsistency in judicial rulings in false-light cases, the highly offensive publications that result in false-light suits may be seen to belong to two broad categories: distortion and fictionalization.

Distortion   Distortion, the most common false-light claim against the media, results from the false impression created when a broadcaster or publisher omits information or uses it out of context. In a case of selective editing, a federal district court in Pennsylvania refused to set aside a jury award of $1 to Clare Randall Uhl, who sued CBS over a documentary that falsely suggested Uhl was an unsportsmanlike hunter.

In the documentary titled "The Guns of Autumn," CBS opened a sequence with wild geese walking in a clearing next to a field. Next, the viewer saw Uhl and other hunters, their guns aimed nearly parallel to the ground, firing from behind nearby cornstalks. Finally, Uhl was shown picking up a goose lying on the ground. Uhl said the editing erroneously portrayed him shooting birds on the ground instead of in flight. A federal district court agreed with the jury finding that falsely suggesting that

---

[115]Nimmer, "The Right to Speak from *Times* to *Time:* First Amendment Theory Applied to Libel and Misapplied to Privacy," 56 *Calif. L. Rev.* 935, 958 (1968).

[116]States that have not chosen to recognize the false-light tort include Minnesota, Missouri, North Carolina, Ohio.

a hunter shoots birds on the ground is highly offensive to the average person, at least in areas of the country, like western Pennsylvania, where wild geese "darken the noonday sky."[117]

The context in which information is used can also be distorting, particularly when one is portrayed in an offensive sexual milieu. The U.S. Court of Appeals for the Fifth Circuit ruled that Mrs. Ed Braun was portrayed falsely when her picture was published in Larry Flynt's *Chic* magazine, a publication devoted to sex. The picture Flynt published showed Braun in a bathing suit feeding a diving pig named Ralph at a family amusement park in Texas where Braun worked. *Chic* acquired the picture of Braun from the park management by misrepresenting the nature of the magazine. Although *Chic* did not alter Braun's picture, Braun objected to publication next to stories and pictures about enlarging men's breasts, preparing a Chinese concoction from animals' sexual organs, and demonstrating navel jewelry on nude models.[118] Braun said she was terrified, embarrassed, and humiliated when she learned of the publication.

The court ruled that a jury could have reasonably found that *Chic* cast Braun in a false light by the unauthorized publication of her picture in a magazine "devoted exclusively to sexual exploitation and to disparagement of women." The court said that it could consider the "overall impression" of the magazine in determining that the publication cast Braun in a false light. The court agreed that publication of the photo might erroneously imply that Braun consented to publication of her picture or that she approved of the opinions expressed in *Chic*. A jury might reasonably conclude, the court said, that either misrepresentation was highly offensive.

Offensive distortions may also be created in more newsworthy contexts. A West Virginia appeals court ruled that Sue Crump, a miner, may have been falsely portrayed as a harassment victim. A photo of Crump illustrated a newspaper article, "Women Enter 'Man's' World," that described one woman miner being stripped, greased, and sent from a mine. Another female miner was reported to have been dangled from a 200-foot water tower. Crump had not been harassed, but the court said she might have been put in a false light because many people asked her after the article appeared if she had been victimized at the mine.[119]

File photos and television footage of street scenes used to illustrate stories may cast a person in a false light if offensive characteristics are wrongly ascribed to individuals shown. A federal court allowed Linda K. Duncan to pursue a suit against a Washington, D.C., television station for falsely suggesting she had herpes. The suit arose from footage WJLA shot of pedestrians, including Duncan, in the capital. Duncan had no false-light claim for the 6 o'clock news broadcast that showed her walking down K Street with other pedestrians. It was not an invasion of privacy for the station to show a close-up of Duncan while the reporter made general statements about herpes. These statements did not suggest Duncan had the disease.

The false-light claim arose from an edited version of the report shown on the 11 o'clock news. As the camera focused on Duncan in the late-night newscast, the reporter said, "For the 20 million Americans who have herpes, it's not a cure." In

---

[117]Uhl v. CBS, 476 F. Supp. 1134 (W.D. Pa. 1979).

[118]Braun v. Flynt, 726 F.2d 245, 10 Media L. Rep. 1497 (5th Cir. 1984). *But see* Faucheux v. Magazine Management, 5 Media L. Rep. 1697 (E.D. La. 1979).

[119]Crump v. Beckley Newspapers, 320 S.E.2d 70, 10 Media L. Rep. 2225 (W. Va. 1983).

refusing summary judgment for WJLA, the court said the juxtaposition of the close-up of Duncan and the commentary about 20 million Americans with herpes supported an inference that Duncan had herpes. A jury could decide whether the false inference was sufficiently offensive for Duncan to prevail in a false-light suit.[120]

In contrast, the New York Court of Appeals ruled that Clarence Arrington had no false-light suit against the *New York Times* because characteristics of blacks that Arrington found offensive in an article were not attributed to him. Arrington's picture ran on the cover of the *New York Times Magazine* to illustrate a story about middle-class blacks. Arrington's picture was snapped without his knowledge as he walked down a Manhattan street in a dark business suit. The article portrayed middle-class blacks as "materialistic, status-conscious and frivolous individuals without any sense of moral obligation to those of their race who are economically less fortunate." Arrington said the cover photo falsely cast him as one of the insensitive, callous blacks discussed in the article.[121]

However, the New York Court of Appeals, while not ruling whether New York recognizes the false-light tort, said the article did not portray Arrington as holding the ideas or opinions of insensitive blacks. Furthermore, the court said the picture and article about the upward mobility of minorities, a newsworthy social issue, were not sufficiently offensive to allow Arrington to sue.

Fictionalization   A second category of false light is fictionalization. Fictionalizing, a very elusive tort, is the addition of fictional dialogue or characters to what are otherwise essentially factual works. Fictionalization ranges from the relatively limited embellishment of news stories to the much more elaborate addition of dialogue, characters, scenes, mannerisms, beliefs, and thoughts in fictionalized books, short stories, and "docudramas."

An example of embellishment of the news is a story in the *Cleveland Plain Dealer* about Margaret Cantrell and her family five months after the Silver Bridge crashed into the Ohio River killing Cantrell's husband, Melvin. *Plain Dealer* reporter Joseph Eszterhas wrote the story after a visit to the Cantrell home in Point Pleasant, West Virginia. Without seeing or interviewing Cantrell, who was not at home when Eszterhas visited, the reporter wrote, "Margaret Cantrell will talk neither about what happened nor about how they are doing. She wears the same mask of non-expression she wore at the funeral."[122]

Margaret Cantrell sued for invasion of privacy, arguing that she was cast in a false light through Eszterhas's deliberate falsifications that implied she was interviewed. She also charged that the article exaggerated the family's poverty. Cantrell said the article made the family objects of pity and ridicule and caused her and her son mental distress, shame, and humiliation.

Agreeing with Cantrell, a majority of the Supreme Court ruled that Eszterhas placed Margaret Cantrell in a false light with malice through his "significant misrep-

---

[120]Duncan v. WJLA-TV, Inc., 106 F.R.D. 4, 10 Media L. Rep. 1395 (D.D.C. 1984).

[121]Arrington v. New York Times, 5 Media L. Rep. 2581 (Sup. Ct. 1980), *aff'd,* 433 N.Y.S.2d 164, 6 Media L. Rep. 2354 (App. Div. 1980), *aff'd in part,* 449 N.Y.S.2d 941, 8 Media L. Rep. 1351 (N.Y. 1982), *cert. denied,* 103 S. Ct. 787 (1983).

[122]Cantrell v. Forest City Publishing Co., 419 U.S. 245, 1 Media L. Rep. 1815 (1974).

resentations,'' primarily the false implication that the reporter interviewed Cantrell during his visit and that he observed her wearing ''the same mask of non-expression'' that he had seen at Melvin Cantrell's funeral.

Fictionalizing that portrays a plaintiff falsely need not be negative or disparaging to be highly offensive. Baseball player Warren Spahn successfully sued over a fictionalized biography that exaggerated the more laudatory aspects of his life. The author of the biography, which was intended for children, greatly romanticized several aspects of Spahn's life, including his relationship with his father and his military service. Exaggerating Spahn's wartime combat, the author said Spahn ''raced into the teeth of the enemy barrage.'' The portrayal was positive—exaggeratedly and embarrassingly so—but did not hurt Spahn's reputation. Indeed, the publication may have enlarged his reputation. But if so, the enhanced reputation came at the expense of truth. The portrayal was highly offensive to Spahn because it represented the ballplayer as something he was not.[123]

Another Supreme Court case, *Time, Inc. v. Hill,* illustrates a positive treatment that casts a false light. The Hill family was portrayed falsely in a 1955 *Life* magazine article titled ''True Crime Inspires Tense Play.'' In the article, *Life* reported on a broadway play that depicted the ''ordeal'' of the Hill family when three convicts held the Hills hostage in their home for 19 hours during a weekend in 1952. *Life* said the play was a ''heart-stopping account of how a family rose to heroism in a crisis.'' *Life* photographed scenes from the play that were said to be reenacted at the house where the Hills were ''besieged.'' One picture over the caption, ''brutish convict,'' showed the son being ''roughed up.'' Another picture, captioned ''daring daughter,'' showed the daughter biting the hand of a convict.[124]

Although the weekend in 1952 was most unpleasant for the Hill family, the convicts did not mistreat the family during their captivity as the *Life* article claimed. In fact, the three convicts treated the Hills courteously and released them unharmed. The Hills neither displayed the heroics nor endured the intimidation portrayed in the article. After their captivity, the family moved from Pennsylvania to Connecticut, but the fictionalized article in *Life* renewed memories that the Hill family was trying to forget. The lower courts upheld the false-light claim, but the Supreme Court reversed on other grounds. The Supreme Court in *Time, Inc. v. Hill* recognized the false-light tort but ruled that plaintiffs, even private plaintiffs like the Hills, must, like public figure libel plaintiffs, prove *New York Times* actual malice if they are involved in a newsworthy issue. The fault requirement in false-light cases will be discussed shortly.

Minor Falsification   Minor falsehoods that offend only hypersensitive individuals are not sufficiently offensive to support a false-light suit. A federal court ruled that a false statement that parents ''instituted a suit'' against a psychiatrist for the death of their daughter ''but later abandoned'' it was too insignificant an error to support a false-light suit. The story should have said that the parents consulted an attorney about bringing a suit, but had not begun legal action.[125]

---

[123]Spahn v. Julian Messner, Inc., 274 N.Y.S.2d 877, *aff'd,*286 N.Y.S.2d 832 (N.Y. 1967).
[124]Time, Inc. v. Hill, 385 U.S. 374, 1 Media L. Rep. 1791 (1967).
[125]Rinsley v. Brandt, 700 F.2d 1304 (10th Cir. 1983).

A federal district court ruled that a photo and story that falsely suggested a couple resold American consumer goods in Latin America was also not sufficiently offensive to permit a false-light suit. The photo appeared in *Forbes* magazine illustrating a story about Latin American tourists who boost the Miami economy by buying consumer goods in Florida and reselling them at high profits at home. In the photo, Maxwell Fogel, a Philadelphia dentist, and his wife, Anna, were shown standing at an airport counter in Miami next to several boxes. The photo accompanied an article about the benefit to the Miami economy of sales to Latin Americans who ship their purchases home, sometimes reselling them at four times the purchase price. The caption under the Fogels' picture said: "The Load: Some Latins buy so much in Miami they've been known to rent an extra hotel room just to store their purchases."[126]

The Fogels, who said they were photographed while waiting to acquire ticket information, charged in their false-light and libel suit that the photograph created the false impression that they were buying merchandise for resale in Latin America and were masquerading as citizens of another country. A federal judge granted summary judgment for the magazine on both libel and false-light claims. The judge said the Fogels' appearance in the photo did not imply that the couple participated in the Latin American trade. Furthermore, the judge said neither the Fogels' reputation nor privacy would be violated if the photo and story did imply they bought goods in the U.S. for resale elsewhere.

Clearly unbelievable falsification will also not support a false-light suit. The U.S. Court of Appeals for the Tenth Circuit ruled that a beauty queen had no libel or false-light suit against *Penthouse* magazine because the story that offended her was so obviously unbelievable. The story told of a fictional Miss Wyoming's memories of making men levitate during sex.[127] The court said the story was neither libelous nor an invasion of the privacy of a real Miss Wyoming who sued. The court said the story "described something physically impossible in an impossible setting." The reader would realize, the court said, that the offensive sections of the story were "pure fantasy and nothing else."

SUMMARY

The false-light tort is the knowing dissemination of highly offensive false publicity. A person may be placed in a false light through highly offensive distortion resulting from omissions and from the use of pictures and broadcast footage out of context. Plaintiffs may also be cast in a false light through embellishment of news and fictionalization in books, short stories, docudramas, and other media. One is not necessarily cast in a false light by minor or fanciful fictionalization or by creative embellishment.

---

[126]Fogel v. Forbes, Inc., 500 F. Supp. 1081 (E.D. Pa. 1981).
[127]Pring v. Penthouse International, Ltd., 695 F.2d 438 (10th Cir. 1982), *cert. denied,* 462 U.S. 1132 (1983).

Fault

The media are protected in false-light suits by the First Amendment fault requirement imported by the Supreme Court from the law of libel. In *Time, Inc. v. Hill,* decided three years after *New York Times v. Sullivan,* the Court ruled that false-light plaintiffs involved in issues of public interest may not successfully sue for false light without proving that publication was made with *New York Times* actual malice.

As in *Sullivan,* the *Hill* Court said that the press would be saddled with too great a burden if it had to verify "to a certainty" the accuracy of the facts in news articles. The Court said that sanctions against either innocent or negligent misstatement in stories of public interest could discourage the press from exercising its First Amendment guarantees. Thus, the Hills had to prove malice even though they were private persons involuntarily drawn into an issue of public interest.

Malice in false-light cases, like malice in libel, is comprised of a combination of reckless or knowing practices, such as fabrication of quotes, reliance on unreliable sources, and failure to heed warnings. Eszterhas published with malice in the *Cantrell* case because he misrepresented that he had interviewed Mrs. Cantrell. Similarly, the author of the unauthorized biography of Warren Spahn published with malice because he not only invented dialogue, created imaginary incidents, and attributed thoughts and feelings to Spahn, but also, like Eszterhas, failed to interview the subject of the work. The author of the Spahn biography also failed to interview any members of Spahn's family or any baseball player who knew him.[128]

A federal court also found malice in the case of Larry Flynt's *Chic* magazine and its publication of Mrs. Braun's photo. The magazine "acted with entire disregard for the falsity of their portrayal of Mrs. Braun," the court said. Not only was her picture published in an offensive sexual context, but the editor misrepresented the nature of the magazine to acquire permission to publish the picture.[129]

Since *Cantrell,* some courts, citing *Gertz v. Welch,* have argued that private false-light plaintiffs, like private libel plaintiffs, should have a lesser burden of proof than actual malice. These courts, which see the false-light tort as paralleling libel, focus on the status of the plaintiffs—whether they are private persons or public figures—rather than on public interest in the subject. These courts see a natural symmetry in requiring private plaintiffs in both libel and false light to shoulder a similar burden of proof.

Other courts require private and public false-light plaintiffs to prove reckless disregard as public figures, but not private persons, must in libel. Courts requiring all false-light plaintiffs to prove malice focus on protecting publication of newsworthy issues. They argue that the First Amendment imposes a heavier burden on private false-light plaintiffs than on private libel plaintiffs because the false-light plaintiff's claims of mental suffering and shame are less demonstrable than the reputational harm asserted by private libel plaintiffs. The press would be exposed to excessive lia-

---

[128]Spahn v. Julian Messner, Inc., 274 N.Y.S.2d 877, *aff'd,* 286 N.Y.S.2d 832 (N.Y. 1967).
[129]Braun v. Flynt, 726 F.2d 245, 10 Media L. Rep. 1497 (5th Cir. 1984). *But see* Faucheux v. Magazine Management, 5 Media L. Rep. 1697 (E.D. La. 1979).

bility to private false-light plaintiffs, it is argued, if the plaintiff were not required to prove malice.

The fault requirement poses a particularly dicey problem when real people recognize themselves as "fictional" characters in novels and docudramas. Fiction writers usually write from their own experience, but they disguise the real people on whom their work is based by transforming them, making composite characters, and using other literary devices. However, real people may be identified in works that purport to be pure fiction or fictionalizations of real events. Plaintiffs identified in either work might sue for libel or false-light privacy.

The identification problem is illustrated in a libel case in which author Gwen Davis Mitchell did not adequately disguise a psychologist who conducted nude encounter groups in her popular novel *Touching,* which was a fictionalized account of the author's experiences in a California nude therapy group called the Nude Marathon. The encounter group was conducted by Dr. Paul Bindrim.

Mitchell thought she had transformed her experiences in the Nude Marathon sufficiently that she created a work of fiction in which Dr. Bindrim could not be identified. The leader of the therapy group in the novel was a Dr. Simon Herford, a crude, vulgar psychiatrist who used four-letter words frequently with his patients. Dr. Herford was "a fat Santa Claus type" with "long white hair, white sideburns, a cherubic rosy face and rosy forearms." The real Dr. Bindrim was a clean-shaven, trim psychologist—not a psychiatrist—who did not use profanity with his patients.[130]

Despite the differences between Herford and Bindrim in speech, physical appearance, and professional credentials, a few witnesses said they recognized Dr. Bindrim in the character of Dr. Herford by the pattern of Herford's conduct in situations similar to actual occurrences in the Nude Marathon. Thus, fabricated dialogue that Mitchell thought would increase the distance between her fictional doctor and the real one was ruled to have libeled Bindrim by making him out to be crude and unprofessional. Bindrim won $75,000 in damages from Doubleday and Mitchell.

The Bindrim case is a warning that once real people convince a jury they are identified in a fictional work, the author's attempts at disguise become evidence of falsification and, in the *Bindrim* case, defamation. Attempts to disguise real people may also be evidence of malice because malice is knowing falsehood. As the court said in *Bindrim,* "Mitchell's reckless disregard for the truth was apparent from her knowledge of the truth of what transpired at the encounter, and the literary portrayals of that encounter."

SUMMARY

All false-light plaintiffs must meet a fault requirement. Courts divide over whether private plaintiffs must prove actual malice or some lesser fault.

---

[130]Bindrim v. Mitchell, 155 Cal. Rptr. 29, 5 Media L. Rep. 1113 (Cal. Ct. App. 1979), *cert. denied,* 444 U.S. 984 (1979).

COMMERCIALIZATION

The fourth branch of privacy law is appropriation. The *Restatement (Second) of Torts* says that a person is liable for invasion of privacy if he or she "appropriates to his own use or benefit the name or likeness of another."[131] An appropriation is usually the unauthorized commercial use of another's name or picture in an advertisement, poster, public relations promotion, or other commercial context.

The injury suffered by an appropriation plaintiff may take two forms. A plaintiff whose identity is used for commercial purposes may suffer shame and humiliation similar to that suffered by a private-facts plaintiff or may suffer loss of a commercial property. Celebrities, in particular, lose the "publicity" value in endorsements and other commercial opportunities when their identities are appropriated without their consent.

Appropriation and Unauthorized Publicity

Appropriation was the first branch of privacy law to develop following publication of Brandeis and Warren's 1890 article in the *Harvard Law Review*. Although Brandeis and Warren did not discuss commercial appropriation, the appropriation tort, as it developed at the turn of the century, is consistent with Brandeis and Warren's concern that people be able to control what is said about them. To publish peoples' names or pictures in commercial contexts without their permission is in a sense to deny them the right to be left alone. Pirating one's identity for commercial gain may cause the same mental distress as the revelation of personal information that concerned Brandeis and Warren.

The law of appropriation originated in New York, where a disproportionate number of appropriation cases are still filed because of the concentration of publishing, broadcasting, public relations, and advertising there. Under the New York Civil Rights Statute, adopted in 1903, it is a tort and a misdemeanor to use a person's name, portrait, or picture without consent for "advertising purposes or for the purposes of trade."[132]

The appropriation sections of the New York Civil Rights Statute were adopted in response to a case in 1902 in which the New York Court of Appeals, the state's highest court, refused to recognize a right of privacy. In *Roberson v. Rochester Folding Box Co.,* the Court of Appeals ruled that Abigail Roberson of Albany had no legal claim to assert when the Franklin Mills Company used the young girl's picture, without her permission, in advertisements for the company's flour.[133] Franklin Mills's advertisements, which referred to Roberson as "The Flour of the Family," were circulated in stores, warehouses, saloons, and other public places. Roberson said she had been "greatly humiliated by the scoffs and jeers of persons who recognized her face and picture."

---

[131]*Restatement (Second) of Torts* sec. 652C (1977).
[132]*Civil Rights Law* (McKinney) secs. 50–51 (1976).
[133]63 N.E. 442 (N.Y. 1902).

When the Roberson family sued for invasion of privacy, the New York court ruled in a 4–3 decision there was no law of privacy. While not unsympathetic to the Roberson claim, the court was unwilling to recognize a legal remedy for such a purely mental injury as invasion of privacy. The court feared it could not contain the privacy tort if the new category of legal wrong were recognized. If the commercial publication of unauthorized photos may be barred, the court said, what is to prevent the courts from halting the publication of unauthorized photos in news columns? If the unauthorized publication of a person's likeness can be barred, then why not publication of a description or commentary about a person's looks? Furthermore, the court wondered how it could adequately distinguish between public figures, who abandon much of their right of privacy, and private persons, who do not. Not the least of the court's fears was a deluge of litigation by plaintiffs with ill-defined claims of mental suffering. This imagined barrage of lawsuits would place too great a burden on the press to defend itself, the court said.

After a storm of public disapproval over the court's refusal to recognize a right of privacy, the New York legislature passed a privacy statute prohibiting the unauthorized commercial use of a person's name, portrait, or picture. About the same time, the Georgia Supreme Court became the first state supreme court to recognize commercial appropriation as a violation of a right of privacy.[134] Upon learning of the Georgia decision, Louis Brandeis wrote he was glad that the right to privacy was finding judicial recognition.[135]

Since the turn of the century, many courts have compensated private citizens like Abigail Roberson for the shame, humiliation, and mental distress suffered when their privacy is invaded through the unauthorized commercial exploitation of their identities. Celebrities and public figures, too, have sued successfully for invasion of privacy when their names, pictures, acts, and talents have been commercially appropriated without permission. But some courts have balked at compensating baseball stars, movie actors, singers, and other celebrities for loss of privacy when their identities are commercially appropriated. These courts argue that celebrities who make their living from public performances should not be compensated for invasion of privacy when their identities are appropriated because celebrities do not suffer the psychic damage of most privacy plaintiffs. Celebrities, who make their living from public exposure, do not suffer the shame and humiliation that a private appropriation plaintiff may suffer. Celebrities, rather, suffer a commercial loss, a loss of their publicity rights.

The right of publicity, recognized in more than 20 states, is the right of celebrities and public figures to exploit the significant commercial value in their names, pictures, styles, voices, and other distinctive features and talents. Unlike a right of privacy, the right of publicity is a property right that can be marketed and, in some jurisdictions, willed to one's heirs. "[I]nfringement of the right of publicity looks to an injury to the pocketbook," one commentator notes, while "an invasion of appropriation privacy looks to an injury to the psyche."[136] Unauthorized appropriation of celebrities'

---

[134]Pavesich v. New England Life Ins. Co., 50 S.E. 68 (Ga. 1905).

[135]M. Urofsky & D. Levy, eds., I *Letters of Louis D. Brandeis* 306 (1971).

[136]McCarthy, "Public Personas and Private Property: The Commercialization of Human Identity," 79 *Trademark Rep.* 681, 687 (1989).

identities does not necessarily cause mental distress, but may diminish their publicity value, particularly if the appropriation is extensive or tasteless.

Unlike a privacy right, a property interest does not necessarily die with the owner.[137] In legal jargon, the right of publicity may be "descendible." About ten states recognize the right of people to will the publicity value in their name or identity to their estate or heirs. At least six states—California, Florida, Nebraska, Oklahoma, Utah, and Virginia—have adopted statutes providing for descendibility.[138]

States recognizing the inheritability of publicity rights tend to emphasize the right of each person to enjoy and pass to one's heirs the fruits of one's industry. In California, a publicity statute prohibits for 50 years after death the commercial use of the name, voice, signature, photograph, or likeness of any "deceased personality" without prior consent of the person or his agent. A deceased personality is anyone who has commercial value in his or her identity at the time of death. However, it is not a violation of the California law or other state statutes recognizing the descendibility of publicity rights, to use the identity of a dead person in news, public affairs, sports stories, political campaigns, or in a book, magazine, musical work, film, or television program.

Some states do not recognize a right for people to will publicity rights to their heirs, whether or not the celebrities exploit the rights commercially during their lifetime.[139] Instead of emphasizing the right of individuals to pass the product of their work to their descendants, these states tend to emphasize the personal nature of the right of publicity and the difficulties in treating such rights as independent of the people who made them valuable. In these states, rights of publicity die with the person.

Unauthorized appropriation and violation of publicity rights can take many forms, including the unauthorized use of a person's name or identity in advertising and trade purposes.

Advertisements   The vast majority of appropriation and publicity cases involve the unauthorized use of a person's name or identity in an advertisement to attract attention to a product or service. In a typical case, businessman Donald Manville was allowed to collect minimal damages for invasion of privacy when his picture ran without his permission in newspaper advertisements for Norge self-service laundries. Manville had posed for a picture in front of a laundry with the understanding that the photo would be used in a news story, not as it was published in an advertisement in which he endorsed Norge laundries as good investments.[140]

Actress Pola Negri won an appropriation suit against a company that used her picture from the film *Bella Donna* to advertise an antihistamine called Polaramine Repetabs.[141] The drug company that ran the ads argued that Negri had no appropria-

---

[137]*Prosser and Keeton on Torts* 778 (5th ed., 1984).

[138]Cal. Civ. Code secs. 990, 3344 (West Supp. 1989); Fla. Stat. Ann. sec. 540.08 (Harrison 1987); Rev. Stat. Neb. secs. 20-202, 20-208 (1987); Okla. Stat. Ann., tit. 21, sec. 839.2 (West 1983); Utah Code Ann. sec. 76-9-406 (1978); Va. Code sec. 8.01-40 (1984).

[139]*E.g.,* R.I. Gen. Laws sec. 9-1-28 (1985); W. Va. Code sec. 47-2-7 (1986); *see generally,* Felcher & Rubin, "The Descendibility of the Right of Publicity: Is There Commercial Life after Death?" 89 *Yale L. J.* 1125 (1980).

[140]Manville v. Borg-Warner Corp., 418 F.2d 434 (10th Cir. 1969).

[141]Negri v. Schering Corp., 333 F. Supp. 101 (S.D.N.Y. 1971).

tion claim because she was not identifiable in the 40-year-old picture. The actress's looks had changed considerably in four decades. Yet, a federal court in New York ruled that the picture from her film was a recognizable likeness of Negri.

In an unusual case, a New York court ruled that Susan Cohen could pursue an appropriation case even though only a few people could recognize her picture, which was used without permission in an advertisement for a skin treatment. The court ruled that Cohen could go to trial even though only close friends and relatives could identify her as the nude woman in a magazine advertisement for Au Natural, a remedy to aid people with "fatty lumps and bumps that won't go away." Neither Cohen's face, nor the face of her daughter, Samantha, were visible in the ad because their picture was shot from behind. The picture in the ad was taken without Cohen's knowledge at Woodstock, N.Y., as mother and daughter walked nude through shallow water. Nevertheless, Cohen's husband and friends recognized her because of her slender neck, two dimples on her back, her indented elbows, and flowing hair.[142]

Identification resulting in commercial appropriation can also be made through nicknames and slogans. The S.C. Johnson & Son Co. violated football player Elroy Hirsch's right of publicity by using his nickname, Crazylegs, as the name of a women's shaving gel.[143] Johnny Carson's right of publicity was violated by the manufacturer of portable toilets. The manufacturing company never used Carson's full name or picture but appropriated his identity by using the phrase "Here's Johnny," the same phrase used to introduce Carson on his nightly television program. The company also appropriated Carson's personality by calling its portable toilet "The World's Foremost Commodian."[144]

A celebrity might also successfully sue if he or she is identified through a "look-alike." Jacqueline Onassis obtained an injunction to stop magazine fashion advertisements in which Barbara Reynolds, an Onassis look-alike, was shown at a "legendary" private wedding—"no tears, no rice, no in-laws, no smarmy toasts, for once no Mendelssohn." Reynolds appeared in the Christian Dior ad with actress Ruth Gordon and television personality Gene Shalit. A *Newsweek* magazine story characterized the actors in the much-discussed ads as "idle, rich, suggestively decadent, and aggressively chic."[145]

In ruling for Onassis in her appropriation suit, the court said that imitators can simulate the voice or hairstyle of the famous in noncommercial settings, but that "no one is free to trade on another's name or appearance and claim immunity because what he is using is similar to but not identical with the original." Reynolds "may capitalize on the striking resemblance of facial features at parties, TV appearances, and dramatic works," the court said, but she may not use her face in commercial advertisements that are deceptive or would promote confusion.

In a "sound-alike" case, a California jury awarded Bette Midler $400,000 for an automobile advertisement in which a singer imitated Midler's voice. The U.S. Court of Appeals for the Ninth Circuit had held that a jury should determine whether the

[142]Cohen v. Herbal Concepts, 10 Media L. Rep. 1561 (N.Y. App. Div. 1984).

[143]Hirsch v. S.C. Johnson & Son, Inc., 280 N.W.2d 129 (Wis. 1979).

[144]Carson v. Here's Johnny Portable Toilets, Inc., 698 F.2d 831, 9 Media L. Rep. 1153 (6th Cir. 1983).

[145]Onassis v. Christian Dior-New York, Inc., 472 N.Y.S.2d 254, 10 Media L. Rep. 1859 (Sup. Ct. Spec. Term 1984).

Ford Motor Company and the advertising agency, Young & Rubicam, Inc., appropriated Midler's identity by broadcasting an ad with a singer who was hired to sing "Do You Want to Dance" because she sounded like Midler.[146] Several people testified that they thought Midler was singing in the commercials.

The Ninth Circuit said it is a tort in California for advertisers to deliberately imitate the distinctive voice of a widely known professional singer to sell a product. Young & Rubicam had acquired permission to use the song, but not to imitate Midler's voice. The Ford Motor Company was dropped from the suit.

Trade Purposes   Appropriations do not always occur in advertisements for commercial products. It is also possible to appropriate peoples' identities or violate their right of publicity through the unauthorized use of their names or likenesses in public relations promotions, posters, and other commercial purposes that do not advertise a product. The New York privacy statute bars the unauthorized commercial use of someone's name not only in advertising but also for "purposes of trade."

The model Christy Brinkley sued successfully under the trade section of the New York law to stop unauthorized use of her picture on posters sold in stores. The posters did not advertise any products but traded on Brinkley's good looks and popularity without her consent.[147] In another trade case, a man was allowed to bring an appropriation suit when his picture was used without permission in a Minox camera manual. The manual served an educational purpose, but also was ruled to be an appropriation of the man's identity for commercial purposes.[148]

In the case of a broadcast station promotion, the Supreme Court of Utah ruled that KTFX-TV in Salt Lake County violated a state statute prohibiting the commercial use of a person's identity when the station broadcast a listener's name and phone number. The station broadcast Jean W. Jeppson's name and phone number during a dialing-for-dollars game designed to increase station viewership. The station called Jeppson in March, 1977, and asked if her television was on:

"No," Jeppson said on the air.

"Oh, that is unfortunate," the TV announcer said, "because you could have won $50."

"Well now," said Jeppson, "I'll tell you. I'd rather have peace in my home than all that garbage on television, even for $50."

Later that afternoon, Jeppson received several rude, abusive, and threatening calls from viewers who did not share her distaste for commercial television. Jeppson sued the station for invasion of privacy because of the emotional distress she said the calls caused her. The Utah court ruled that use of Jeppson's name and phone number in a campaign to increase viewers violated the state statute prohibiting the use of someone's identity for advertising.[149]

In another promotional, the Shaklee Corporation appropriated the identity of the author Heloise Bowles in a motivational campaign for the company's distributors. Heloise was the author of books and a syndicated newspaper column of house-

---

[146]Midler v. Ford Motor Co., 849 F.2d 460, 15 Media L. Rep. 1620 (9th Cir. 1988).
[147]Brinkley v. Casablancas, 438 N.Y.S.2d 1004, 6 Media L. Rep. 1983 (App. Div. 1981).
[148]Selsman v. Universal Photo Books, Inc., 238 N.Y.S.2d 686 (App. Div. 1963).
[149]Jeppson v. United Television, Inc., 580 P.2d 1087, 3 Media L. Rep. 2513 (Utah 1978).

hold hints. Shaklee, which makes and sells household cleansers, food supplements, and cosmetics, appropriated Heloise's identity by making it appear that Heloise endorsed Shaklee's products.[150]

Shaklee bought 100,000 copies of *All Around the House,* one of several of Heloise Bowles's writings containing hints on how to make household chores easier. Distributing the books to the company's 240,000 distributors was not an appropriation of Heloise's name. However, a federal district court said Shaklee advertisements sent to the distributors did appropriate Heloise's name. The ads said, "Welcome to a new Shaklee Woman, Heloise," a woman who "will soon be helping you to open doors and make more sales with Shaklee." Shaklee also altered the back cover of the book to say, "Heloise and Shaklee all around the house just naturally make your day easier." The court said Shaklee's unauthorized association of Heloise's name with the company's products amounted to an unauthorized endorsement for which the court awarded $75,000 in damages.

The court rejected Shaklee's argument that there was no appropriation because the promotional advertisements and book were sent only to company distributors, not to the general consumer. The court noted that the ads went to 240,000 distributors who, besides being employees, were themselves consumers of Shaklee products. More than half a million consumers saw the Heloise advertisements if one counts, as the court did, the spouses and friends who read the company materials sent to distributors.

Identifying a person in a corporate documentary that builds good will but does not advertise a product has been ruled not to be a misappropriation. The U.S. Court of Appeals for the Fifth Circuit ruled that Anheuser Busch Companies did not appropriate Roy Benavidez's identity by depicting him as a hero in a documentary about valiant Hispanic soldiers. Benavidez appeared in an 80-second segment of the 13-minute film titled *Heroes.* The documentary recounted the exploits of Hispanic Congressional Medal of Honor recipients.

The Corporate Relations Department of Anheuser Busch Companies supervised and paid for the film, which was developed at the request of the National Association of Latino Elected and Appointed Officials from information supplied by the Department of Defense. The film was made available to schools, government agencies, veterans' organizations, and Hispanic organizations. It may also have been shown at Anheuser Busch hospitality centers where the company distributes free beer.[151]

Benavidez conceded that the film was "merely an inoffensive documentary" that did not advertise or promote Anheuser-Busch products. The only reference to Anheuser Busch was a credit at the end. But Benavidez said Anheuser Busch capitalized on his good name and reputation by showing the film at the company's hospitality centers. The appeals court, however, affirming a federal district court, said there was insufficient commercial benefit to Anheuser Busch to support a misappropriation claim even if the film were shown at the centers. No beer was sold at the centers, no orders were taken or solicited, and no one was forced to watch the film. Undoubtedly Anheuser Busch "may enjoy increased good will in the Hispanic community as

---

[150]National Bank of Commerce v. Shaklee Corp., 503 F. Supp. 533 (W.D. Tex. 1980).
[151]Benavidez v. Anheuser Busch Inc., 873 F.2d 102, 16 Media L. Rep. 1733 (5th Cir. 1989).

a result of the production and showing of *Heroes,*" the court said. "This incidental benefit, however, does not rise to the level of commercial benefit sufficient to support a claim for misappropriation."

Appropriation may also occur if an entertainer imitates too closely another's act or performance. Bob Russen's "The Big El Show," a memorial tribute to the late Elvis Presley, was enjoined pending a trial on the question whether the show, which imitated Elvis concerts, violated the right of publicity Elvis left to his estate when he died. The court issued the injunction because Elvis's estate showed evidence of being able to win at trial.

The court said the show, which closely imitated Elvis's stage performances, served "primarily to commercially exploit" Presley's likeness. Had the show been primarily parody, satire, or criticism of Presley's performances, it would have been protected entertainment under the First Amendment. But, the court said, "entertainment that is merely a copy or imitation, even if skillfully and accurately carried out, does not really have its own creative component and does not have a significant value as pure entertainment."[152]

Under New York law, extensive fictionalization of a person's identity may constitute an unauthorized commercial use for "purposes of trade." Baseball player Warren Spahn brought a successful appropriation suit, as well as false-light suit, over an unauthorized, largely fictionalized biography that portrayed him falsely as a war hero and model family man.[153] The author reported and fabricated incidents and dialogue without the benefit of interviews with Spahn's family, friends, or professional colleagues. The court ruled that such fictionalizing constituted commercialization of Spahn's name under the New York law. The court said an unauthorized, factual biography would be a protected newsworthy publication, but extensive fictionalizing made the Spahn biography a commercial appropriation.

Although extensive fictionalizing may be considered an appropriation, it is not an appropriation to make an *incidental* reference to a real person in a book, film, play, musical, or other work, whether fact or fiction. For example, a reference in the movie *Country Girl* to "Stillman's Gym"—a place to find "a punch-drunk fighter"—was ruled to be only an incidental reference.[154] The filmmaker had not appropriated the name of the gym for commercial purposes.

Shaul Ladany, a member of the Israeli Olympic team that was attacked at the 1972 games in Munich, was only mentioned incidentally in a book about the attack, *The Blood of Israel.* Even though Ladany was mentioned on 13 pages of the book by French journalist Serge Groussard, sometimes in considerable detail, the court said Ladany's treatment was incidental to a large, newsworthy book containing more than 100 characters.[155] The court said Ladany's treatment was no more a trade purpose than mentioning a person in a scene in a novel.

---

[152]Estate of Presley v. Russen, 513 F. Supp. 1339, 1359 (D.N.J. 1981).

[153]Spahn v. Julian Messner, Inc., 286 N.Y.S.2d 832 (N.Y. 1967), *appeal dismissed,* 393 U.S. 1046 (1969). *See* Garner v. Triangle Publications, 97 F. Supp. 546 (S.D.N.Y. 1951).

[154]Stillman v. Paramount Pictures Corp., 153 N.Y.S.2d 190 (App. Div. 1956), *aff'd* 184 N.Y.S.2d 856 (N.Y. 1959).

[155]Ladany v. William Morrow & Co., 465 F. Supp. 870 (S.D.N.Y. 1978). *See also* Damron v. Doubleday, Doran & Co., 231 N.Y.S. 444 (Sup. Ct. 1928), *aff'd,* 234 N.Y.S. 773 (App. Div. 1928). (Single mention of name in a novel as "local color" is not an appropriation.)

SUMMARY

Appropriation is the unauthorized commercialization of another. Appropriation may or may not be accompanied by the mental stresses associated with invasions of privacy. A violation of one's right of publicity, however, is the taking of the marketable, sometimes inheritable, property interest celebrities own in their looks, voices, and talents. Appropriation and violation of publicity rights may occur in unauthorized advertisements, promotions, and performances.

Defenses

There are two important defenses in commercialization suits: newsworthiness and consent.

Newsworthiness Newsworthiness is a broad defense. Publication or broadcast of names and pictures in news reports of political, social, and entertainment events are usually not considered to be commercial appropriation. The fact that the media are commercial enterprises motivated by profit and supported by advertising does not diminish the newsworthiness of the items they publish and broadcast. "It is the content of an article or picture, not the media's motive to increase circulation, which determines whether an item is newsworthy," the New York Court of Appeals has said.[156]

Courts sometimes discuss newsworthiness in terms of a First Amendment privilege. In a case of political speech, the Utah Supreme Court ruled that the First Amendment protected a politician from a publicity suit when he published constituents' pictures in campaign literature. Postal workers who posed with Senator Orrin Hatch said the picture reproduced in reelection literature constituted an implicit endorsement of the senator, which they did not intend and which violated their publicity rights. But the Utah court ruled that the campaign literature was newsworthy information protected by the First Amendment. Because of the First Amendment privilege, the court said persons who pose with or inadvertently appear with public officials or candidates may not claim their identity has been appropriated if the picture is taken in a public or semipublic place.[157]

Even without constitutional protection, Senator Hatch would have defeated the postal workers' publicity claim because the court ruled the senator appropriated nothing of value from them. A political endorsement by an unknown member of the general public has no "intrinsic value," the court said. In addition, the court said the workers had no appropriation claim because use of their names and likenesses was "incidental to the purpose of showing Senator Hatch in the company of workers. Other workers' pictures would have sufficed as well."

---

[156]Stephano v. News Group Publications, Inc., 474 N.E.2d 580 (1984).
[157]Cox v. Hatch, 761 P.2d 556, 16 Media L. Rep. 1366 (Utah 1988).

The New York Supreme Court ruled that a political poster was also constitutionally protected newsworthy expression. In *Paulsen v. Personality Posters, Inc.,*[158] the court said that a poster of presidential candidate and comedian Pat Paulsen was protected by the First Amendment even though it was being sold for profit. Unlike the poster of Christy Brinkley which merely capitalized on the model's good looks, the Paulsen poster provided political comment on a mock presidential campaign in which Paulsen was participating. The poster showed Paulsen holding an unlit candle in one hand and cradling a rubber tire in his other arm. A "FOR PRESIDENT" sash was draped across his chest as if he were a contestant in a beauty pageant.

The court said the poster was constitutionally protected political commentary even though Paulsen was "only kidding" about his candidacy for president. "When a well-known entertainer enters the presidential ring, tongue in cheek or otherwise, it is clearly newsworthy and of public interest," the court said. "A poster which portrays plaintiff in that role, and reflects the spirit in which he approaches said role, is a form of public interest presentation to which protection must be extended." The protected status of the poster was not altered, the court said, because the poster might be merely entertaining to some.

In a case that more clearly involves entertainment news, a federal court in New York ruled that the First Amendment protected a magazine that published a photo of actress Ann-Margret partially nude. Ann-Margret brought a publicity and appropriation suit against *High Society Magazine* for publishing the photograph taken from a film. Ruling against the actress, the court said that coverage of the actress's topless appearance in a movie was protected by the First Amendment. Newsworthy matters protected by the First Amendment, the court said, include items "of entertainment and amusement." Ann-Margret's movie appearance would be of great interest to many people, the court said.[159]

Events may be newsworthy even if they are commercially sponsored. The newsworthiness of an Elvis Presley press conference allowed producers of a "talking magazine" to reproduce and distribute large segments of the conference even though the event was staged as a commercial promotion by Presley's record company.[160] The recorded segments of the conference appeared in *Current Audio Magazine,* a magazine that included written and photographic material supplemented with a stereo record that included interviews and commentary. RCA Corp., which sponsored the press conference, said the extensive coverage of the conference, including the voice recording, violated the company's exclusive contract with Presley. But the court said a press conference of a popular singing star is newsworthy. "To hold, as [RCA] urges, that one who has freely and willingly participated in a press conference has some property right which supersedes the right of its free dissemination . . . would constitute an impermissible restraint upon the free dissemination of thoughts, ideas, newsworthy events, and matters of public interest," the court said.

The picture on the cover of a book or magazine is newsworthy if the subject is a newsworthy event or is reasonably related to a newsworthy subject inside the publica-

---

[158]299 N.Y.S.2d 501 (Sup. Ct. 1968).
[159]Ann-Margret v. High Society Magazine, Inc., 498 F. Supp. 401 (S.D.N.Y. 1980).
[160]Current Audio, Inc. v. RCA Corp., 337 N.Y.S.2d 949 (Sup. Ct. 1972).

tion. *New York Magazine* won an appropriation suit brought by Duncan Murray after the magazine published a cover photo of Murray at the city's St. Patrick's Day parade. In a picture taken by a free-lance photographer, Murray was dressed in the "striking attire" of an Irish hat, a green bow tie, and a green pin. The New York Court of Appeals said the picture was newsworthy because Murray participated in "an event of public interest to many New Yorkers." Furthermore, the picture was related to a newsworthy article on Irish immigrants in the magazine.[161]

If a cover picture is not related to newsworthy content inside a publication, the use may be considered an appropriation. A black teen received $1,500 under the New York appropriation statute for the unauthorized use of her picture on the cover of a book about getting into college. The picture was used, not because the teen was a subject of the book, but to promote sales to minorities. The publisher was unaware that the free-lancer who took the picture had no written consent to use the picture for a commercial purpose.[162]

Incidental Advertising   Courts have consistently ruled it is not an appropriation for publishers and broadcasters to use previously published or broadcast news in advertisements promoting the media's own publications and programs. In one well-known case, *Holiday* magazine successfully defended itself against an appropriation suit brought when the magazine advertised itself with previously published pictures of actress Shirley Booth.

Holiday had photographed Ms. Booth wearing a fashionable hat and immersed in water up to her neck at a resort in the West Indies.[163] After the picture was published in a newsworthy travel story, *Holiday* used the picture again in an advertisement for the magazine. Booth sued for appropriation under the New York Civil Rights Statute. In ruling for *Holiday*, New York Appellate Judge Charles Breitel said:

> . . . so long as the reproduction was used to illustrate the quality and content of the periodical in which it originally appeared, the statute was not violated, albeit the reproduction appeared . . . for purposes of advertising the periodical.

Such commercial uses are not an appropriation because they do not imply that the person pictured endorses the publication. The use of the person is said to be only "incidental" to the media advertisement.

Broadcast footage that has never been aired may also be used to advertise programs. The Oregon Supreme Court ruled that a station did not appropriate the identity of an accident victim when it used tape of the woman receiving emergency medical care in an advertisement for the station's special report on emergency medical services. The tape of the victim, which she said caused her mental anguish, was not broadcast either in the special or in a regular news program. Nevertheless, the court ruled the ad did not invade the victim's privacy. Her appearance in a commer-

---

[161]Murray v. New York Magazine, 318 N.Y.S.2d 474 (N.Y. 1971).

[162]Spellman v. Simon & Schuster, 3 Media L. Rep. 2406 (N.Y. 1978).

[163]Booth v. Curtis Publishing Co., 223 N.Y.S.2d 737, 744 (App. Div.), *aff'd,* 182 N.E.2d 812 (N.Y. 1962). *See also* Namath v. Sports Illustrated, 363 N.Y.S.2d 276, (N.Y. Co.), *aff'd,* 371 N.Y.S.2d 10 (App. Div. 1975), *aff'd,* 352 N.E.2d 584 (N.Y. 1976).

cial context, if any, was at most only incidental to the broadcaster's goals of promoting the special report, the court said.[164]

The Whole Act In the only publicity case on which the Supreme Court has ruled, the high court held that the First Amendment does not protect the media if they reproduce a performer's complete act. In *Zacchini v. Scripps-Howard,* the Supreme Court ruled that the First Amendment did not bar a human cannonball from pursuing a publicity suit against a television station that broadcast his entire act during a news program.[165]

WEWS-TV in Cleveland broadcast Zacchini's act on the news even though Zacchini asked the news team not to. WEWS's coverage consisted of a 15-second news clip of Zacchini from the time he blasted from the cannon until he landed safely in a net. The segment did not show Zacchini inspecting the cannon and net as drumrolls built tension. In the newscast, the station's free-lance reporter said the film did not do justice to Zacchini's exciting act and that viewers should see it at the fair.

Zacchini sued for $25,000, saying that WEWS-TV had appropriated his professional property without consent. He did not seek to stop publicity about his act, but to be paid for it. The Supreme Court of Ohio ruled that the news broadcast was protected by the First Amendment because it was of legitimate public interest. But the U.S. Supreme Court held that the First Amendment did not provide a privilege to broadcast someone's whole act. The Court did not consider the drumrolls and Zacchini's inspections before blast off to be part of the act.

WEWS argued that the station's broadcast of Zacchini's flight was a constitutionally protected report of a newsworthy event. But Justice White, writing for the five-person majority, did not focus on the newsworthiness of WEWS's report. Instead, he concentrated on Zacchini's act as a "professional property" that the station appropriated in its entirety. White said Zacchini might have had no case if WEWS had simply reported that Zacchini was performing at the fair. The station might have even shown a picture of Zacchini. But broadcasting the entire act violated Zacchini's publicity interest in his act. Broadcasting his entire act, the Court said, posed "a substantial threat to the economic value of that performance" because viewers of the broadcast might not pay to see Zacchini in person.

In dissent, Justice Powell, joined by Justices Brennan and Marshall, argued that the broadcast segment about Zacchini's act was a constitutionally protected report of a newsworthy event. The dissenters rejected the majority's focus on whether the whole act was taken. A better analysis than viewing the performance simply as an economic property, they said, was to focus on what use the station made of the footage. Because the film was part of a regular news program, the dissenters said the station should be protected by the First Amendment from either a right of publicity or appropriation suit. An exception to a First Amendment privilege would arise, they said, if the station's newscast was a subterfuge for "private or commercial exploitation."

Although the media lost the *Zacchini* case, the Court's decision does not greatly inhibit reporting. The case is limited by its unusual facts, facts that would seldom be

---

[164]Anderson v. Fisher Broadcasting Co., 712 P.2d 803, 12 Media L. Rep. 1604 (Or. 1986).
[165]Zacchini v. Scripps-Howard Broadcasting Co., 433 U.S. 562 (1977).

duplicated. Rarely would reporters risk violating a right of publicity by reporting "all" of an act or performance. Football games, ice pageants, and plays are too long for the evening news and admission of the media is usually controlled by the promoter.

SUMMARY

Newsworthiness is a broad defense allowing the use of information of public interest in commercial contexts. Courts have recognized a First Amendment privilege for newsworthy information used in campaign literature, commercial political posters, and entertainment news. Newsworthiness has also been recognized in reports of commercially staged press conferences. Newsworthy names and photos may also be used in incidental advertising for a publication or broadcast program. The Supreme Court has ruled that reporting all of a performer's act on the evening news is not privileged by the First Amendment.

Consent Besides newsworthiness, the other major defense in commercialization cases is consent. A broadcaster or publisher generally need not acquire consent to present people in newsworthy reports because newsworthy uses of a person's identity are not considered commercial appropriations. However, advertisers and public relations practitioners normally should acquire written consent from participants in commercial ads and promotions. As with any contract, consent agreements should be written, should state the parties to the agreement, state the scope and duration of the terms, and provide for consideration. Consideration is the payment for the use of the name or picture.

A name or picture should not be used commercially after consent has expired. Actor Charles Welch was awarded $1,000 compensatory damages and $15,000 punitive damages because the Mr. Christmas company used Welch's broadcast commercials after the contract for use had run out. The contract gave Mr. Christmas the right to run the ads only in 1973 and 1974, but the company also ran them in 1975.[166]

Altering or falsifying materials may also violate a consent agreement. Maryland Manger, the author of a prizewinning letter on "Why I am Glad I Chose Electrolysis as a Career," won an appropriation suit against the Kree Institute of Electrolysis because the institute changed her letter to make it look as though Manger endorsed the institute's electrolysis machine.[167]

Manger was the winner of a contest conducted by Kree, an institute that taught electrolysis and sold the Radiomatic electrolysis machine that permanently removed superfluous hair. Manger, who used a different machine, signed a consent form permitting Kree to publish her winning letter and picture in Kree's magazine. A jury ruled that Kree appropriated Manger's identity in violation of the consent agreement when the institute's publication referred to her as a "Kree operator" and changed her

---

[166]Welch v. Mr. Christmas, Inc, 447 N.Y.S.2d 252 (App. Div.), *aff'd*, 57 N.Y.2d 971, 8 Media L. Rep. 2366 (1982).
[167]Manger v. Kree Institute of Electrolysis, Inc., 233 F.2d 5 (2d Cir. 1956).

letter so that she endorsed the Radiomatic, an electrolysis machine she did not use. The U.S. Court of Appeals for the Second Circuit said Kree's editing was substantial enough to violate the consent agreement Manger had signed.

Releases must be signed by mentally competent adults. Parents must sign for minors. Actress Brooke Shields learned that agreements signed by parents on behalf of minors are usually binding. When Shields turned 17, she tried to enjoin publication of nude photos taken of her in a bathtub when she was 10. Shield's mother had signed a contract granting photographer Gary Gross unlimited rights to take and use the innocent photos of Brooke in return for $450. Shields, who as a teen made provocative advertisements for Calvin Klein clothes, said the nonpornographic bathtub photos embarrassed her simply because "they are not me now." But the court ruled that a parent's consent is binding for a minor. "A parent who wishes to limit the publicity and exposure of her child," the court said, "need only limit the use authorized in the consent."[168]

An oral or implied agreement is not satisfactory under the New York Civil Rights Law and may not be binding in other jurisdictions. Betty Frank Lomax, a radio announcer and interviewer, was allowed to sue in New York for appropriation because her employer made her appear at sales meetings and hand out autographed pictures to promote the station. Lomax had reluctantly agreed to participate in these commercial activities to keep her job but was still allowed to sue because her employer had not acquired written consent to use her identity commercially.[169]

Often consent may take the form of a broad model release form. The broadest model releases give the advertiser unrestricted rights to take, copyright, alter, sell, and publish a model's or actor's photograph. Unrestricted-use contracts give great flexibility to advertisers and the media, but a model who signs such an open-ended contract may later regret the broad terms. A highly paid professional model, Mary Jane Russell, signed a release granting unrestricted use of her picture to photographer Richard Avedon. Avedon took several pictures of Russell for use in advertisements for Marboro Books. Russell had no objection to Marboro's use of her picture showing her in bed, next to her "husband's" bed, reading an educational book. The caption said, "For People Who Take Their Reading Seriously."

Russell, however, objected when the picture was sold to Springs Mills, Inc., a manufacturer of bed sheets, and used in commercial ways Russell considered objectionable. Russell's photo was retouched in Springs Mills's ads so that she appeared to be reading a pornographic book. Springs Mills also added captions suggesting a "lost weekend" and other risqué activities. Russell said the bed sheet ad contradicted her modeling image as an intelligent, well-bred young wife in socially approved situations.

A New York court said the unrestricted consent form Russell signed barred an appropriation suit for Marboro's sale or Springs Mills's purchase of the original photograph. However, the court said unrestricted consent did not block a suit for libel. The court said Springs Mills might have so altered the emphasis, background, and

---

[168]Shields v. Gross, 451 N.Y.S.2d 419, 8 Media L. Rep. 1928 (App. Div. 1982), *aff'd as modified,* 58 N.Y.2d 338, 9 Media L. Rep. 1466 (1983). A federal court also refused an injunction in Shields v. Gross, 563 F. Supp. 1253, 9 Media L. Rep. 1879 (S.D.N.Y. 1983).
[169]Lomax v. New Broadcasting Co., 238 N.Y.S.2d 781 (App. Div. 1963).

context of Russell's picture as to make it an essentially different—and perhaps libelous—picture.[170]

SUMMARY

The media should have written consent to use one's name or picture for commercial purposes. Oral consent may be unsatisfactory. Consent agreements, signed by competent adults, should state the parties to the agreement, the scope and duration of the terms, and provide for consideration. A name or picture should not be used commercially after consent has expired.

EMOTIONAL DISTRESS AND OTHER TORTS

As the libel and privacy chapters illustrate, plaintiffs suing the media for libel and invasion of privacy often claim anxiety, humiliation, and other emotional distress. Sometimes, however, plaintiffs claim emotional distress as a separate tort, independent of defamation, invasion of privacy, or other wrong.

Courts have been reluctant to recognize liability for the intangible harms of emotional distress just as they have been reluctant to recognize liability for the mental suffering of the plaintiff whose privacy has been invaded. The law does not easily award damages where, as in emotional distress and privacy cases, it may be difficult to prove that a defendant acted wrongly or that a plaintiff claiming mental suffering is really hurt. Minor insults and threats are an unfortunate fact of life. "It would be absurd," a legal text notes, "for the law to seek to secure universal peace of mind."[171] Law may be an especially inappropriate remedy when the source of mental discomfort is a publisher or broadcaster with a First Amendment mandate to promote robust debate that may be disquieting.

Nevertheless, courts do recognize two emotional distress torts: intentional and negligent infliction of emotional distress. Plaintiffs also claim negligence by the media causes physical and financial harm.

Intentional Infliction of Emotional Distress

A plaintiff can sue for intentional infliction of emotional distress when another's conduct is "so outrageous in character, and so extreme in degree, as to go beyond all possible bounds of decency, and to be regarded as atrocious, and utterly intolerable in a civilized community."[172] Conduct is sufficiently shocking to support an emotional distress suit when, for example, a person delivers a rat to a customer who or-

---

[170]Russell v. Marboro Books, Inc., 183 N.Y.S.2d 8 (Sup. Ct. 1955).

[171]*Prosser and Keeton on the Law of Torts* 56 (5th ed. 1984).

[172]*Restatement (Second) of Torts,* sec. 46, comment d (1965). *See* Drechsel, "Negligent Infliction of Emotional Distress: New Tort Problem for the Mass Media," 12 *Pepperdine L. Rev.* 889 (1985).

dered bread,[173] spreads a false rumor that someone's son hanged himself,[174] or harasses a debtor with repeated abusive threats of lawsuits and ruined credit.[175] The victim suffers rather ill-defined, subjective mental anguish and emotional upset. The victim may also suffer tangible damages such as ulcers and lost wages.

The media have seldom been sued for intentional infliction of emotional distress, but some public figures have tried to sue the media for emotional distress when they cannot successfully sue for libel or invasion of privacy. Public figures have viewed intentional infliction of emotional distress as an attractive alternative to libel and false-light privacy suits because the fault requirements of libel and privacy law did not apply in cases of intentional infliction. However, in a recent decision pitting *Hustler* magazine against the Rev. Jerry Falwell, the U.S. Supreme Court ruled that public figures may not successfully sue the media for intentional infliction without meeting the requirements of a libel suit, including the malice requirement imposed by the First Amendment.

In *Hustler Magazine, Inc. v. Falwell,* the Supreme Court ruled that public figures may not collect damages for emotional distress inflicted by a cartoon or carica-ture unless the publication contains false statements that are published with malice as defined in *New York Times v. Sullivan.* The Court's decision, in the case of a crude parody portraying Falwell as an incestuous drunkard, means that public figures will seldom be able to sue successfully for even the most biting satire or criticism unless it is defamatory and published with malice.[176]

Falwell charged that *Hustler* magazine engaged in outrageous conduct by pub-lishing an advertisement satirizing an advertisement for Campari Liqueur. In the real Campari advertisement, celebrities talk about their "first time," that is, their first encounter with Campari Liqueur. But in the parody, Falwell's "first time" is a sexual encounter with his mother in an outhouse in Lynchburg, Virginia. Falwell's mother is portrayed as a drunken and immoral woman, and Falwell appears as a hypocrite and habitual drunkard. At the bottom of the page is a disclaimer stating, "ad parody—not to be taken seriously." (See Parody, Figure 4.1.)

Falwell sued for libel, invasion of privacy, and intentional infliction of emo-tional distress. The U.S. Court of Appeals for the Fourth Circuit ruled that the par-ody did not invade privacy under Virginia law because it was not used for trade purposes. There was no libel, the court said, because no reasonable person would believe that the statements about Falwell in the parody were factual. However, the Fourth Circuit did rule the outrageous language of the parody caused Falwell emo-tional distress. The Supreme Court, in a unanimous decision written by Chief Justice Rehnquist, reversed.

Chief Justice Rehnquist agreed with Falwell that the *Hustler* advertisement was "doubtless gross and repugnant in the eyes of most." But the Court said the ad was constitutionally protected because it contained ideas and opinions about a public fig-ure. The Chief Justice noted that the heart of the First Amendment is protection of the free flow of ideas and opinions on matters of public interest and concern. Even

---

[173]Great Atlantic and Pacific Tea Co. v. Roch, 153 A. 22 (Md. 1931).
[174]Bielitski V. Obadiak, 61 Dom. L. Rep. 494 (1921).
[175]*Prosser and Keeton on the Law of Torts* 61 (5th ed. 1984).
[176]Hustler Magazine, Inc. v. Falwell, 108 S. Ct. 876, 14 Media L. Rep. 2281 (1988).

Figure 4.1.   Reproduced with permission of L.F.P. Inc., and Larry Flynt.

false defamatory statements about public officials and figures are protected if they are not published with "knowing falsehood or reckless disregard for the truth."

The caricature of Falwell in *Hustler* was constitutionally protected because it too contained ideas and opinions about a public figure. The ad did not contain "actual facts" about Falwell "or actual events in which [he] participated." The advertisement contained statements about Falwell that were so outrageous that they could not be true, and no one thought they were. The very outrageousness of the parody placed it in the realm of ideas and opinion.

The Court said the *Hustler* cartoon was a tasteless version of political cartoons that have flayed public figures through American history. Justice Rehnquist compared the advertising parody to political cartoons of Thomas Nast castigating the Tweed Ring in New York and cartoons of George Washington portrayed as an ass. Cartoons may be offensive, but they contain constitutionally protected ideas and opinion.

Falwell argued that he should collect damages, not because the parody was false, but because it was so offensively outrageous. But the Court said an "outrageousness" standard of liability is unconstitutional because it is too subjective and would punish the publisher's motives.

Rehnquist said public debate might suffer no harm if courts could punish outrageous cartoons, but the Chief Justice said he doubted there is any principled way to make a distinction between outrageous and reasonable cartoons. " 'Outrageousness' in the area of political and social discourse," he said,

> has an inherent subjectiveness about it which would allow a jury to impose liability on the basis of the jurors' tastes or views, or perhaps on the basis of their dislike of a particular expression. An "outrageousness" standard thus runs afoul of our longstanding refusal to allow damages to be awarded because the speech in question may have an adverse emotional impact on the audience.[177]

The Court also said that holding Larry Flynt, publisher of *Hustler,* liable for outrageous political opinions would unconstitutionally punish him for bad motives. In debate about public affairs, the First Amendment protects many things "done with motives that are less than admirable," the Court said. Indeed, the Court noted, a political cartoon is often "intentionally injurious"; the purpose of a political cartoon is to be "a weapon of attack, of scorn and ridicule and satire." In a word, the cartoonist's motive is to be outrageous.

SUMMARY

The media are seldom sued successfully for intentional infliction of emotional distress. Attempts by public figures to employ intentional infliction suits as substitutes for libel and privacy suits were stalled when the Supreme Court ruled in the *Falwell* case that the First Amendment bars public figures from successfully suing the media for outrageous satire or parodies unless the publications contain false statements and are published with malice.

---

[177]*Id. at 882, 14 Media L. Rep. at 2285. See generally* Smolla, "Emotional Distress and the First Amendment: An Analysis of *Hustler v. Falwell,"* 20 *Ariz. St. L. J.* 369 (1988).

Negligent Infliction of Emotional Distress

Emotional distress may be inflicted negligently as well as intentionally. The negligent defendant acts less egregiously than the defendant who intentionally inflicts emotional distress. People act negligently if they breach a duty of care owed to the plaintiff and that breach of duty is the likely cause of injury to the plaintiff.[178] Plaintiffs sue the media—usually unsuccessfully—for negligence that the plaintiffs say results in emotional distress, physical harm, or financial losses.

Sometimes plaintiffs lose emotional distress suits against the media because the negligent publication causes insignificant harm. Marcy Decker lost her suit for negligent infliction of emotional distress against *The Princeton Packet* because the injury she suffered from premature publication of an obituary was too insignificant to sustain a suit. The New Jersey Supreme Court ruled that the "annoyance, embarrassment, and irritation" Decker may have felt when she read her obituary in the *Packet* was too insubstantial to permit a suit.[179] The New Jersey Supreme Court affirmed a lower court that said, "While we appreciate the shock plaintiff may have felt in reading of her death, it was necessarily quickly dissipated by her certain knowledge the announcement was premature."[180]

More often, the media win negligence suits because they owe no duty of care to their audiences and imposing a duty on the media might inhibit a free press. A duty of care arises from the relationship between two parties. Licensed doctors owe a duty of care to their patients and furniture movers are contractually obligated to transport goods unharmed. But the relationship of the media to their mass audience is usually too remote for the media to owe a duty of care.

The *Village Voice* won a negligent infliction suit because the newspaper owed no duty of care to the plaintiff, Margaret Tatta. Tatta complained that she received very alarming, sexually explicit telephone calls after the *Voice* negligently published an advertisement that mistakenly carried her phone number. The ad, published under the heading of adult entertainment, read: "Your fantasies, beautifully role-played, privately, daily 11 A.M. to 10 P.M., 475-3371." The telephone number, which belonged to Tatta, was apparently a misprint.[181]

The New York Supreme Court dismissed Tatta's emotional distress suit because the paper lacked a relationship with its readers that imposed liability for its negligent publications. There was no contract between the *Voice* and Tatta that might establish a duty of care. Nor was there a state-imposed duty of care as there is between a doctor and patient or a lawyer and client. Furthermore, Margaret Tatta had not been hurt by relying on anything the *Voice* printed. She was injured, if at all, not by the newspaper, but by readers of the paper who called her as a result of the paper's unintended error.

Not only was the relationship between Tatta and the *Village Voice* too distant for the paper to be liable, the social cost of holding a newspaper liable to the public for unintentional errors would be too great, the court said. A federal judge made this same point when he said:

---

[178]*Prosser and Keeton on the Law of Torts* 164–65 (5th ed. 1984).
[179]Decker v. Princeton Packet, Inc., 561 A.2d 1122, 16 Media L. Rep. 2194 (N.J. 1989).
[180]Decker v. Princeton Packet, Inc., 541 A.2d 292, 15 Media L. Rep. 1775 (N.J. Sup. Ct. 1988).
[181]Tatta v. News Group Publications, Inc., 12 Media L. Rep. 2318 (N.Y. Sup. Ct. 1986).

the chilling effect of imposing a high duty of care on those in the business of news dissemination and making that duty run to a wide range of readers or TV viewers would have a chilling effect which is unacceptable under our constitution.[182]

While the media generally owe no duty to the public for negligent publications or broadcasts, courts have occasionally ruled that the media may be liable for publishing the name of a sexual assault victim and others who may be harassed or assaulted if their name is disseminated. While the rationale of these cases is not fully developed, the harm from publication is apparently grave enough that the media may have a duty to foresee the damage that publication will cause. A New York appellate court refused summary judgment for the American Broadcasting Company on a negligent infliction claim by two rape victims whose identities were revealed over the air. The women agreed to be interviewed on camera for a series on condition that they not be identified. However, the faces and voices of the women were identifiable in a televised promotion and in two parts of a broadcast series. One identification occurred after the women complained of distress caused by comments from people who recognized them in an early broadcast. One victim had never told her family about the rape.[183]

Perhaps a more compelling case for media liability for negligent infliction of emotional distress arises when revelation of a person's name subjects her to harassment or physical harm by an assailant who is known to be at large. The Missouri Supreme Court ruled that Sandra Hyde could bring an emotional distress suit against the City of Columbia and a Columbia newspaper over a story about her successful escape from an abductor who was still at large. After the story appeared, Hyde was followed and telephoned with threatening calls. In one call, a man said, "I'm glad you're not dead yet, I have plans for you before you die."[184]

In denying the newspaper's request to dismiss the case, the Missouri court said the newspaper could reasonably foresee from the assailant's past conduct, reported character, and tendency toward violence that the publication of Hyde's name and address would create a temptation for the abductor to harm her. Publication of her name created the conditions that subjected Hyde to emotional distress by the unknown assailant. Hyde settled before trial for $6,000 from the city.[185]

SUMMARY

In cases of negligent infliction of emotional distress, courts have ruled that the media owe no duty of care to the general readership. However, courts have ruled that the media may be liable for negligently disseminating the name of a rape or abduction victim, particularly if the assailant is still at large.

---

[182]Tumminello v. Bergen Evening Record, Inc., 454 F. Supp. 1156 (D.N.J. 1978).
[183]Doe v. ABC, 543 N.Y.S.2d 455, 16 Media L. Rep. 1958 (A.D. 1989).
[184]Hyde v. City of Columbia, 637 S.W.2d 251 (Mo. App. 1982), *cert. denied,* 459 U.S. 1226 (1983).
[185]*News Media & Law,* Sept.–Oct. 1983, at 41.

Physical Harm

The media are sued not only for negligence leading to emotional distress, but also for negligent publications and broadcasts that are said to lead to suicides, rapes, murders, and other physical harm. These cases are often called ''copycat'' cases because someone in the audience imitates a violent act that has been seen or heard in the media. The media generally win these cases because their broadcast or publication fails to ''incite'' harmful conduct. Cases involving physical harm resulting from a broadcast or publication can be divided into two categories, those in which someone in the audience is harmed and those in which someone in the audience harms someone else.

Harm to the Audience In violence cases, the media usually prevail because courts create a First Amendment privilege, not because of a lack of duty to the audience. Only if the media ''incite'' harmful acts are they liable. For example, in *Herceg v. Hustler,* the U.S. Court of Appeals for the Fifth Circuit ruled the First Amendment protected the magazine from a negligence suit over the death of a young reader. The court said the First Amendment protected *Hustler Magazine* from liability for the death of Troy D., 14, who died while engaging in a masturbatory practice he read about in *Hustler.* The appeals court reversed a jury award to Troy's mother, Diane Herceg, of $69,000 in actual damages and $100,000 in punitive damages, for the death of her son while attempting ''autoerotic asphyxia,'' a practice he had read about in the August 1981 edition of the magazine.

Hustler published a detailed article about autoerotic asphyxia, which entails masturbation while ''hanging'' oneself. By cutting off the blood supply to the brain at the moment of orgasm, one is supposed to increase sexual pleasure. *Hustler* warned its readers not to attempt autoerotic asphyxia because it is dangerous. The article began with accounts of people who died trying it.[186] Nevertheless, Troy D. tried autoerotic asphyxia after reading the article. Troy's nude body was found hanging by the neck in the boy's closet the next morning. A jury decided that the article incited Troy's fatal act. The Fifth Circuit reversed the lower court.

The appeals court first determined that the article on autoerotic asphyxia was constitutionally protected speech because it was not obscene or otherwise outside of First Amendment consideration. The court then ruled that *Hustler* should not be held liable because the article did not ''incite'' the boy's death. The incitement test, which courts have employed in several media cases involving physical harm, is drawn from *Brandenburg v. Ohio,* a case discussed in Chapter 2. In *Brandenburg,* the Supreme Court ruled that provocative speech might be punished if it were ''directed to inciting or producing imminent lawless action.'' The incitement test has most often been used in cases where speech might incite a riot or other public disturbance, not in cases of a solitary individual, such as Troy D., copying a dangerous practice written about in a magazine.

Nevertheless, the Fifth Circuit ruled that *Hustler* was not liable for Troy's death because the publication did not incite the fatal act. The Fifth Circuit did not evaluate the magazine's duty to readers or the danger of publishing an article about autoerotic

---

[186]Herceg v. Hustler Magazine, Inc., 814 F.2d 1017, 13 Media L. Rep. 2345 (5th Cir. 1987).

asphyxia. Relying on a First Amendment privilege, the court said that even if the article described in glowing terms the pleasures of autoerotic asphyxia, "no fair reading of it can make its content advocacy, let alone incitement to engage in the practice." Noting that the incitement test is usually invoked in cases involving speech arousing unrest in a crowd, the Fifth Circuit questioned whether a magazine purchased for solitary reading could ever incite a reader to imminent lawless action.

A California appeals court ruled that a popular song did not incite a despondent young man's suicide. The court ruled that the First Amendment barred the parents of 19-year-old John McCollum from suing CBS Records and singer Ozzy Osbourne for the suicide of their son. The McCollums claimed that Osbourne and CBS negligently disseminated music and album covers demonstrating a preoccupation with despair and recommending suicide as desirable. In one recording, Osbourne is alleged to have sung:

> Ah know people
> You really know where its at
> You got it
> Why try, why try
>
> Get the gun and try it
> Shoot, shoot, shoot[187]

The California appeals court affirmed dismissal of the case because the song did not incite imminent lawless action. There is no incitement, the court said, in art that evokes "a mood of depression as it figuratively depicts the darker side of human nature."

Moving beyond the First Amendment considerations, the court said that CBS could not be held liable for negligence because the company owed no duty to the McCollums. CBS and Osbourne could not reasonably have foreseen that suicide would result from listening to Osbourne's music, the court said. The music and lyrics had been recorded years before McCollum killed himself and there was no "dynamic interaction" between the singer and his audience, no "importuning" of particular listeners. Perhaps most important, the court said, "it is simply not acceptable to a free and democratic society to impose a duty upon performing artists to limit and restrict their creativity in order to avoid the dissemination of ideas in artistic speech which may adversely affect emotionally troubled individuals."

In a variation of the Osbourne case, two families sued the heavy metal band Judas Priest for allegedly including subliminal messages in their songs that drove two young men to commit suicide. The families contended that the rock group's album "Stained Class" contained the subliminal messages "Let's be dead" and "Do it," which incited two young men to form a suicide pact. The plaintiffs said the messages were masked by being played backward. The plaintiffs also argued that Judas Priest and CBS Records were liable for manufacturing and marketing a faulty product.[188]

A Nevada District Court judge had earlier ruled that subliminal messages are not protected by the First Amendment, but the judge had not determined whether such

---

[187]McCollum v. CBS, 249 Cal. Rptr. 187, 15 Media L. Rep. 2001 (Cal. App. 1988).
[188]Rohter, "Rock Band Is Sued in Suicides of 2 Men," *New York Times,* July 17, 1990, at B1, B8.

messages appeared in the Judas Priest album, and, if so, whether they had any relationship to the double suicide.[189]

Harm by the Audience   The First Amendment not only bars suits against the media when someone in the audience is harmed, but also when someone in the audience harms someone else. NBC won a negligence suit over the network's broadcast of *Born Innocent,* a drama in which a girl is raped with a "plumber's helper" on the bathroom floor of a state-run home. A few days after the broadcast, four youths who had seen *Born Innocent* raped a girl with a bottle on a California beach. The girl, Olivia N., argued NBC should have foreseen that the film, broadcast without a warning that it was violent, was likely to be imitated.[190]

A California appeals court was unwilling to hold NBC liable because the program did not encourage or incite the rape. As in other negligence cases, the court said the cost to the media of liability would be too high. "Realistically," the court said, "television networks would become significantly more inhibited in the selection of controversial materials if liability were to be imposed on a simple negligence theory."

The media have also won negligence suits over advertising as well as news and entertainment programs that lead a member of the audience to commit violence against another. In one dramatic case, the U.S. Court of Appeals for the Fifth Circuit ruled that *Soldier of Fortune* magazine was not liable for publishing an advertisement that led to an assassination. The appeals court overturned a $9.4 million judgment against *Soldier of Fortune* for negligently publishing an advertisement that resulted in a contract killing.[191]

The *Soldier of Fortune* case arose from a suit by the mother and son of a Sandra Black, who was assassinated by a man named John Wayne Hearn. Black's husband hired Hearn to kill his wife after Hearn answered an ad Black had placed in *Soldier of Fortune* magazine. The ad said: "EX-MARINES.—'67-'69 Nam vets . . . weapons specialist—jungle warfare, pilot, . . . high risk assignments U.S. or overseas."

Black's mother and son convinced a jury that *Soldier of Fortune* was negligent because the magazine should have known that a person placing an advertisement with terms such as "high risk assignments" was soliciting illegal activity. "High risk assignments," the relatives said, is a term commonly used to advertise contract killing. Several other ads in the magazine had also been linked to violent crimes. The jurors awarded Black's son and mother actual damages of more than $1.9 million and punitive damages of $7.5 million.

Overturning the lower court, the Fifth Circuit did not engage in a First Amendment "incitement" analysis, perhaps because the *Soldier of Fortune* advertisement was commercial speech that enjoys less constitutional protection than news and entertainment. But the Fifth Circuit did rule that a magazine could not be expected to foresee that publication of an ad containing such terms as "high risk assignments" would lead to a murder. The Fifth Circuit agreed that the magazine owed a duty of reasonable care to protect the public from serious crimes. But the appeals court said the magazine had not violated that duty. Given the ambiguous nature of Hearn's ad

---

[189]Vance v. Judas Priest, 16 Media L. Rep. 2241 (Nev. D.C. 1989).

[190]Olivia N. v. NBC, 178 Cal. Rptr. 888, 7 Media L. Rep. 2359 (Cal. App. 1981).

[191]Eimann v. Soldier of Fortune, 880 F.2d 830, 16 Media L. Rep. 2148 (5th Cir. 1989). *But see* Norwood v. Soldier of Fortune Magazine, 651 F. Supp. 1397, 13 Media L. Rep. 2025 (1987).

and the pervasiveness of advertising in American society, the court said one could not expect a publisher to foresee that the advertisement for high risk assignments would lead to murder.

While the court recognized that Hearn's ad presented a risk of serious harm, the court concluded that, on balance, a publisher could not be asked to screen and refuse to publish all ambiguous ads. The ad was ambiguous because it did not directly recruit illegal assignments. Indeed, an advertisement for "high risk assignments" could have sought, as Hearn claimed, bodyguards instead of assassins. Furthermore, the link between other ads in the magazine and crime did not mean that Hearn was seeking criminal employment when he responded to the ad. Even had the publisher of *Solider of Fortune* checked Black's background before running the advertisement, he would have found no criminal record. Thus, there was no reason for *Soldier of Fortune* to know that Black's advertisement for Vietnam vets was seeking someone to commit a criminal act.

While the media generally owe no duty to their broad audiences to withhold stories or advertisements that might result in physical harm, at least one court has ruled that the media may be liable for negligently encouraging the audience to engage in reckless conduct that causes physical injury. The California Supreme Court ruled that the First Amendment did not bar a negligence action against a radio station whose on-air promotion stimulated reckless conduct among teen-age drivers that resulted in the death of a motorist.

The case resulted from a station's public relations promotion in which a popular disk jockey drove from place to place in southern California. Meanwhile, the station encouraged its teen-age audience to hurry to the disk jockey's next stop to claim a prize. One youthful listener, following the disk jockey at high speeds on the California freeways, forced another car to overturn, killing the driver.

In *Weirum v. RKO General, Inc.,* the California Supreme Court ruled the station was liable because it was "foreseeable that defendant's youthful listeners, finding the prize had eluded them at one location, would race to arrive first at the next site and in their haste would disregard the demands of highway safety." The teens were not imitating a media presentation as youths had in the *Born Innocent* rape case; nor was the audience in *Weirum* warned to be careful. In *Weirum,* the station's broadcast promotion stimulated the audience—teen-age listeners—to irresponsible, dangerous conduct that resulted in a death.[192]

The court said the station should have foreseen that its promotion created an unreasonable risk to other motorists by encouraging reckless conduct by the youthful contestants. Giving short attention to the station's First Amendment claims, the court said, "The First Amendment does not sanction the infliction of physical injury merely because achieved by word, rather than act."

The court's consideration of the First Amendment may have been brief because the dangerous broadcasts were a commercial promotion. In the autoerotic asphyxia case discussed earlier, the U.S. Court of Appeals for the Fifth Circuit said *Hustler* magazine merited stronger First Amendment protections than the radio broadcast in *Weirum* because the broadcast "was merely a promotional device to encourage listeners to continue listening to the radio station." But perhaps of more importance in

---

[192]123 Cal. Rptr. 468, 539 P.2d 36 (Cal. 1975).

distinguishing *Weirum* from other cases is the radio station's direct encouragement of an immature audience to engage in dangerous conduct.

SUMMARY

Courts have generally held that the First Amendment incitement test protects the media from negligence suits filed when a program or article results in harm to someone in the audience or when someone in the audience harms another person. However, a California court ruled that the media may be liable for injuries caused when a commercial promotion encourages the audience to engage in conduct that leads to physical harm.

Economic Harm

Negligence suits have been brought against the media not only for mental distress and physical injury, but also for economic injury. Courts generally rule in cases of financial harm, as they do in mental distress cases, that the media owe no duty to investors and other readers or viewers who are hurt economically by the negligent dissemination of false financial information.

In *Gutter v. Dow Jones, Inc.,* the Supreme Court of Ohio ruled that the owner of the *Wall Street Journal* was not liable to a reader for an error in corporate bond listings that mistakenly indicated the bond's interest. Phil Gutter, an investor, bought the bond, believing the interest was different than it was. When the value of the bonds declined shortly after Gutter's purchase, the investor lost nearly $1,700. Gutter sued Dow Jones, publisher of the *Journal,* for negligently misrepresenting the bonds, knowing that investors would rely on the listings. The Ohio Supreme Court dismissed the case.[193]

The court said that the newspaper owed no duty to Gutter because he was a general newspaper reader, not the member of some limited group to which a paper might owe a duty. Like other courts, the Ohio court said holding a newspaper liable to the whole public imposes too great a burden on freedom of expression. Furthermore, the court said it was not justifiable for Gutter to rely on the mistaken news account to buy the bonds without first checking the status of the bonds with a broker. In sum, the public policy and constitutional concerns "tilt decidedly in favor of the press," the court said, when a newspaper makes a negligent error in a news story that results in economic harm. Similar results have been reached when unintentional errors have appeared on a ticker tape,[194] in commercial loose-leaf summaries of finances of corporations,[195] and in advertisements for investment opportunities.[196]

While publishers of mass circulation financial information may owe no duty of care to their broad audiences, publishers of commissioned financial reports may owe

---

[193]Gutter v. Dow Jones, Inc., 490 N.E.2d 898, 12 Media L. Rep. 1999 (1986).
[194]Jaillet v. Cashman, 194 N.Y.S. 947 (A.D. 1922), *aff'd,* 139 N.E. 714 (N.Y. 1923).
[195]First Equity Corp. v. Standard & Poor's Corp., 869 F.2d 175, 16 Media L. Rep. 1282 (2d Cir. 1989).
[196]Pittman v. Dow Jones, 662 F. Supp. 921, 14 Med. L. Rep. 1284, 1285 (E.D. La. 1987), *aff'd,* 14 Media L. Rep. 2384 (5th Cir. 1987). *See generally* 58 *American Jurisprudence* 2d *Newspapers, Periodicals & Press Assns.* sec. 22 (1971).

a duty of accuracy to their clients and to their clients' competitors, at least if the reports are commercial speech. The South Carolina Supreme Court ruled that a public relations consulting firm, Booz-Allen & Hamilton, owed a duty of care to the South Carolina State Ports Authority for negligently preparing an economic report that the ports authority said caused it financial harm. The ports authority claimed that the $75,000 report contained false economic information about the depth and convenience of the port at Charleston. The authority said the errors hurt the state in its competition for world shipping trade with the port at Savannah, Georgia.[197]

The report was commissioned by the Georgia Ports Authority to evaluate the commercial advantages of the Savannah and Charleston ports. The report, which was highly favorable to Savannah, was distributed by the Georgia authority to several foreign customers and potential customers. The South Carolina State Ports Authority, along with Charleston harbor pilots and union workers, claimed the report hurt them financially by reducing the shipping business in Charleston.

The South Carolina Supreme Court ruled that Booz-Allen had no responsibility to harbor pilots and dock workers if false statements in the report reduced shipping in the Charleston port. "The relationship, if any, flowing between a consultant and someone distantly affected by his work is far too attenuated to rise to the level of a duty flowing between them," the Court said.

However, Booz-Allen was ruled to have a duty to the South Carolina State Ports Authority, a direct competitor of the Georgia Ports Authority that hired the consulting firm. Booz-Allen, the court said, owed a duty to the South Carolina Ports Authority to exercise due care to accurately report factual commercial data concerning the Charleston port, if the agency knew or should have known that the Georgia Ports Authority intended to use the report as a marketing device. In other words, a consulting firm such as Booz-Allen should foresee how a client's competitor, such as the South Carolina State Ports Authority, could be injured by mistakes in a commercial report.

The constitutionality of the South Carolina court's holding that an economic consulting firm owes a duty of accuracy to a client's competitor was upheld by the U.S. District Court for the District of Columbia.[198] The federal court ruled that the Booz-Allen report was commercial speech that was not entitled to as much First Amendment protection as political speech. The First Amendment permits holding a defendant liable for negligent preparation of commercial speech, the court said.

SUMMARY

As in cases of negligent infliction of emotional distress, the media are generally not liable to mass audiences for errors that result in financial loss. However, publishers of economic and financial reports may have a duty of accuracy to their clients and clients' competitors.

---

[197]South Carolina State Ports Authority v. Booz-Allen & Hamilton, Inc., 346 S.E.2d 324 (S.C. 1986).
[198]South Carolina State Ports Authority v. Booz-Allen & Hamilton, Inc., 676 F. Supp. 346, 14 Med. L. Rep. 2132 (D.C.D.C. 1987).

5

INTELLECTUAL PROPERTY

If privacy law protects the person, the law of intellectual property protects the imaginative creations of that person. Copyright law allows authors, songwriters, photographers, painters, and other creative people to control the commercial copying and use of their intellectual property. The law of unfair competition, which includes trademark law, permits companies to control the commercial use of their names, slogans, and other creative identification symbols.

Intellectual property, unlike privacy, was recognized in the Constitution when it was adopted in 1789. Article 1, Section 8, of the Constitution gives Congress the power "to promote the Progress of Science and useful Arts, by securing for limited Times to Authors and Inventors the exclusive Right to their respective Writings and Discoveries." Section 8 encourages intellectual creativity of benefit to the whole society by granting creative people exclusive commercial control over their intellectual expression for a fixed period. Intellectual property is not protected as a fundamental right by the Bill of Rights, but protection for intellectual property derives in part—as does protection for fundamental rights—from natural law. In natural law, citizens are entitled to the products of their intellectual as well as physical labor.[1]

Article I, Section 8, recognizes two kinds of intellectual property: inventions and writings. Inventions are protected under patent law. Patent law gives inventors 17 years in which to enjoy exclusive commercial exploitation of the machines, processes, manufactured products, and designs they create. Inventors obtain patents from the U.S. Office of Patent and Trademark for novel inventions that are not obvious and that add to the sum of useful knowledge.[2] Writings are protected by the federal copyright statute, the primary subject of this chapter. Trademarks and other creative symbols that are not writings are protected by a federal trademark statute and by common law.

COPYRIGHT

The British government originated copyright shortly after Gutenberg invented the printing press as a way to control what was published. In 1556, the British Crown

---

[1]*See* A. Latman, *The Copyright Law: Howell's Copyright Law Revised and the 1976 Act* (5th ed. 1979).
[2]35 U.S.C.A. sec. 100 *et seq.* (1984).

granted the Stationers' Company a monopoly on printing, primarily to check the spread of the Protestant Reformation. By requiring that all published works be registered with the Stationers' Company, the government made it easier to block dissemination of heretical writings.

In time, the government's interest in controlling heresy was outweighed by publishers' interests in exploiting publications commercially. The government gradually relinquished its copyright control to publishers and authors. The first statute to recognize the rights of authors was the Statute of Anne of 1710. The Statute of Anne granted authors the exclusive right to publish new works for a renewable 14-year term. Works had to be registered at Stationers' Hall, not so that the government could easily identify the heretical, but so that the copyright holders could prove their claims of originality when they thought others were copying their work.

The first federal copyright act in the United States was adopted on May 31, 1790,[3] shortly after the Constitution authorized Congress to enact a copyright law. The first copyright act protected an author of any "book, map or chart" for a renewable 14-year term. Protection for prints was added in 1802,[4] musical compositions in 1831,[5] photographs in 1865,[6] and paintings in 1870.[7]

The federal copyright statute has been revised twice in this century, once in 1909 and again in 1976, largely because of technological advances. The 1909 act was continually strained by the development of the motion picture, phonograph, radio, television, computer, tape recorder, photocopy machine, satellite, cable, and other communication technologies of what has now become known as the information age.[8]

Congress adopted the 1976 copyright act after 20 years of study. The Copyright Revision Act of 1976 made several changes that make it easier for authors to control when and how their work is used by others. The 1976 revision, which went into effect in 1978, also made copyright law more uniform by preempting state copyright law. However, even since 1976, technological advances have forced Congress and the courts to make changes in copyright law affecting cable television, satellite transmissions, home recording of television programs, and copyright in computer chips and rental movies.

Copyrightable Works

Copyright, which the Constitution says protects "writings," protects much more expression than words on a printed page. The copyright statute says that copyright subsists in "original works of authorship fixed in any tangible medium of expression . . . from which they can be perceived, reproduced, or otherwise communicated." Copyrightable works of authorship include literary, musical, dramatic, pictorial, graphic,

---

[3] 1 Stat. 124 (1790).
[4] 2 Stat. 171 (1802).
[5] 4 Stat. 436 (1831).
[6] 13 Stat. 540 (1865).
[7] 16 Stat. 212 (1870).
[8] *See* D. Bell, *The Coming of Post-Industrial Society* (1973); National Commission on New Technological Uses of Copyrighted Works, *Final Report* 3 (1979).

and sculptural works. Literary works include books, newspapers, magazines, corporate house organs, newsletters, and annual reports.[9]

To be original, a work does not have to be unique, novel, or even good. Rather, the work must be created independently with a modicum of intellectual effort.[10] The Copyright Office in Washington will not deny copyright because a work may be obscene[11] or fraudulent.[12] Nor is the office concerned whether a work is of high quality.

But a copyrightable work must be original and fixed in a tangible medium. The work is *fixed* in a tangible medium of expression as soon as it is created or recorded. A short story is fixed as it emerges from a typewriter, a photo when the shutter clicks. A tape of a football game becomes a fixed work of authorship as a camera crew and director select shots, broadcast, and simultaneously record the game.

Copyright protects expression, but not the idea of creating the expression or the facts contained in the expression. A writer can copyright a story about abortion but not the idea of writing the story or the facts within it. Others can write a similar story using the same facts, providing the new authors do their own research and use their own language, style, and sequencing. The historical fact that Hitler died is not copyrightable, but a particular version of the story of his death is.[13]

Photographers may copyright the unique combination of lighting, contrast, mood, and other elements that comprise a picture. Photographers may not copyright the idea of taking a picture or the individual elements of the picture. Rather the copyright holder copyrights the entirety of the composition. Anyone is free to take the same photograph from the same place and copyright the resulting picture with a unique expression of tone and feeling. However, others are not free to copy the original picture.[14]

Editing techniques and frequently used devices in television productions may be copyrighted. A federal court in Minnesota ruled that one advertiser may have infringed the copyright of another by employing the same actress and using similar editing techniques in an advertisement.[15] The court found substantial similarity between two advertisements, both of which were brief, rapidly paced spots employing Deborah Shelton of the television series "Dallas." While the use of Deborah Shelton could not be copyrighted, the combination of artistic choices—including the choice of actors and actresses, the composition of each frame, pace of editing, camera angle, hairstyle, jewelry, decor, and makeup—could be.

A federal court in New York ruled that the original selection, organization, and presentation of frequently used devices in a television show are also copyrightable. The district court said a trial should determine whether the producers of the television game show "Bamboozle" infringed the copyright in the similar show "To Tell the

---

[9]*See* M. Simon, *Public Relations Law* 146 (1969).

[10]Bleistein v. Donaldson Lithographing Co., 188 U.S. 239 (1903).

[11]*See* Clancy v. Jartech, 666 F.2d 403 (9th Cir. 1982), *cert. denied,* 459 U.S. 826 (1982); Mitchell Brothers v. Cinema Adult Theater, 604 F.2d 852 (5th Cir. 1979), *cert. denied,* 445 U.S. 917 (1980).

[12]Belcher v. Tarbox, 486 F.2d 1087 (9th Cir. 1973).

[13]A.A. Hoehling v. Universal City Studios, Inc., 618 F.2d 972 (2d Cir. 1980). *See also* Suid v. Newsweek Magazine, 503 F. Supp. 146 (D.C.D.C. 1980).

[14]Bleistein v. Donaldson Lithographing Co., 188 U.S. 239 (1903).

[15]C. Blore & Don Richman, Inc. v. 20/20 Advertising Inc., 674 F. Supp. 671 (D. Minn. 1987).

Truth,"[16] Both shows involved celebrities guessing which one of several panelists' stories was true. The court noted that none of the elements of the game shows could be copyrighted individually, not the idea of a show in which people lie nor the use of contestants to guess who is lying. Neither could the use of celebrity guests, the system of asking questions, or the employment of a master of ceremonies be copyrighted. But, the court said, the combination of these often-used devices can be protected. It is the "original selection, organization, and presentation" of these stock devices that is copyrightable.

Copyright can be placed not only on individual stories, photos, and programs, but also on *compilations* and *derivative works*. A compilation is a work formed by the collecting and assembling of preexisting materials or data that are "selected, co-ordinated, or arranged in such a way" as to create an original work. A compilation may be the assembly of discrete facts that, individually, would not be copyrightable. A telephone book, a dictionary of trivia, data bases, and Dow Jones's stock lists are copyrightable compilations even though the individual items in them are not copyrightable.[17]

Compilations include *collective works*, such as magazines, newspapers, anthologies, and corporate reports. Collective works may have several different copyrighted works within them. The publisher of a magazine or anthology must have permission of the individual copyright holders to compile the new collective work.

A derivative work is a transformation or adaptation of an existing work. Derivative works include translations, movie versions of plays and novels, and dolls based on cartoon characters. Derivative works are created when copyright owners or licensees recast, transform, or adapt a work.[18]

One cannot copyright procedures, processes, systems, methods of operation, concepts, principles, or discoveries,[19] many of which can be protected by patent law. Copyright also does not protect useful items such as tables and chairs, or formats, layouts, or typefaces, which are considered too unoriginal to merit copyright protection.

A format is the general plan or organization of a work, the shape and size of a publication, the length of a broadcast, or the number of minutes of music to be included at a certain time each week in a television show. The layout is the plan or arrangement of elements on the page. One cannot copyright the decision to print six columns on a page instead of eight, to leave two inches of white space at the bottom of every page, to center all headlines over their stories, or to publish pictures on every other page.

After lengthy consideration, the federal Copyright Office decided that formats and layouts should not be protected because the number of ways that stories, pictures, and type can be placed on a page is too limited to allow one person or company exclusive control. The Copyright Office feared that injunctions might be issued to

---

[16]Barris/Fraser Enterprises v. Goodson-Todman Enterprises Ltd., 35 *Pat., Trademark & Copyright J.* (BNA) 280 (Feb. 11, 1988).

[17]Eckes v. Card Prices Update, 736 F.2d 859 (2d Cir. 1984); Dow Jones & Co. v. Board of Trade of the City of Chicago, 546 F. Supp. 113 (S.D.N.Y. 1982).

[18]17 U.S.C.A. sec. 101 (1977).

[19]17 U.S.C.A. sec. 102(b) (1977).

halt publication of constitutionally protected literary works because of copyright questions over relatively unimportant layout and format issues.[20] For similar reasons, typefaces are not copyrightable.

Notice, Registration, and Deposit   Copyright lasts for the life of the author plus 50 years. The benefit of copyright, therefore, can be willed to one's survivors for 50 years after the death of the copyright holder. Works already copyrighted in 1978 retain their copyright for up to 75 years. If a company is the copyright holder, copyright runs for 100 years from the date of creation or 75 years from the date of publication, whichever is shorter. Under the copyright statute of 1909, copyright lasted a maximum of two 28-year terms.

Copyright for the encoded messages in semiconductor chips lasts for only 10 years. Computer chips are treated as a special case because of the exceptionally rapid changes in microchip technology.[21]

Notice   To protect copyright, authors should place copyright notice on their work, register it, and deposit copies with the Copyright Office in Washington, D.C. Copyright notice is the sign attached to a work warning would-be copiers that they need permission to reproduce that work. Copyright notice signifies that authors have not abandoned their work to the public domain. Notice has three elements: (1) the letter C in a circle (©), the word *copyright,* or the abbreviation *copr.*; (2) the year of first publication; and (3) the name of the copyright owner. A copyright notice may look like this: © 1990 Thomas R. Jones.

A copyright notice should be placed where it will be easily seen. A copyright notice will normally be placed on, or just after, the title page of a book, on the title page or the masthead of a magazine, on the front page or masthead of a newspaper, or near the title of a film. If notice on the front of a photograph or painting would damage the work, notice can be put on the back. Notice should be placed on a computer program so that it appears on the user's terminal at sign-on.

While it is recommended that notice be placed on copyrighted works, an author's work does not pass into the public domain if notice is omitted. United States membership in the Berne Convention for the Protection of Literary and Artistic Works[22] protects American authors' works in member countries whether or not their works display a notice of copyright. Infringers of authors' works in the member countries may be enjoined or held liable for damages for violating the copyright of works containing no notice.

American publishers and producers of films, records, and tapes hope that American membership in the Berne Convention, the strongest international copyright agreement, will dissuade other countries from pirating American works. American membership in the Berne Convention became effective in March, 1989. Unauthorized copying of American productions, particularly in the Middle and Far East, is estimated to cost copyright holders $1.3 billion annually.[23]

---

[20]46 Fed. Reg. 30651–30653 (June 10, 1981).

[21]Semiconductor Chip Protection Act of 1984, Pub. L. 98-620, 17 U.S.C.A. secs. 901–914 (Supp. 1989).

[22]Berne Convention Implementation Act of 1988, Pub. L. 100-568, 102 Stat. 2854 (Oct. 31, 1988).

[23]"Two Worst Copyright Pirates Are China and Saudi Arabia, Report Says," 37 *Pat., Copyright & Trademark J.* (BNA) 673 (April 27, 1989). The report was published by the International Intellectual Property Alliance.

While notice is not required, placing notice on copyrighted works is advisable. Notice deters would-be infringers by warning them that copyright is claimed. Furthermore, an infringer is barred from claiming "innocent" infringement of works bearing copyright notice. An author may not collect damages from an innocent infringer who does not know a work is copyrighted. Copyright notice is also necessary for free-lancers' bulk registration of a year's work.

Copyright notice on a newspaper, periodical, anthology, or other collective work covers all contributions to the work except for advertisements inserted on behalf of outside businesses or organizations.[24] For example, a general copyright notice on the *New York Times* covers all staff and free-lance stories and pictures, even though free-lance writers and photographers may retain copyright ownership in their work. But the general *Times* copyright notice does not cover advertisements except ads for the *Times* itself. Advertisers who want to protect themselves from innocent infringement of work published in newspapers and magazines must attach a separate copyright notice to each ad.

Individual contributors to collective works may attach separate copyright notice to their contributions if they and the publisher agree. Separate copyright notice on a story or picture can serve as the credit line. Free-lance writers and other contributors to collective works will want a separate notice on their contributions if they wish to take advantage of the efficiency and low cost of bulk registration of their work.

Registration and Deposit   In the days of the English Star Chamber, the British Crown required deposit of all works in London so that the government could more easily check for heresy and sedition. Now, however, registration is not a tool of suppression. Registration is a way of protecting authors' rights in their work. The person who first registers a work has a strong legal claim to copyright ownership in the event of a dispute. First registration is *prima facie* evidence of copyright ownership.

An author registers a work with the Register of Copyrights in Washington, D.C., by submitting the proper form and a registration fee of $10. Registration should be made within three months of publication. Usually an author "deposits" one copy of an unpublished work or two copies of a published work at the same time. To save time and money, newspaper publishers can deposit copies of their work on microfilm.[25] Free-lance writers and photographers can register up to a year's worth of work in a group for one $10 fee.[26]

The 1976 copyright revision permits authors to register unpublished works. Under the 1909 statute, it was difficult to establish ownership of unpublished work because unpublished materials could not be registered. Authors could sue under state common law if someone copied their unpublished manuscript or pictures, but it was often difficult to establish the original authorship. Authors would mail a copy of the unpublished work to themselves and leave the envelope unopened so that they might establish by the postmark that they were the first authors if a copyright dispute arose. But defendants in copyright suits challenged the validity of the postmarks and the

---

[24]17 U.S.C.A. sec. 404(a) (1977).
[25]Copyright Office, Press Release, Sept. 4, 1979.
[26]17 U.S.C.A. secs. 407–408 (1977); 37 C.F.R. sec. 202.3(b) (5) (Supp. 1989).

integrity of the package seals. Now, authors of unpublished works may establish authorship by registering their works in Washington.

Copyright protection does not depend on registration any more than it depends on notice. A work is protected when it is fixed in a tangible medium, whether or not it is registered. But the law includes strong incentives for authors to register their work. An author may not sue for infringement until a work is registered. The copyright owners who register their work within 90 days of publication may sue an infringer for damage to the value of their copyright—such as lost sales—, for profits the infringer illegally gained, and for attorney's fees. Copyright owners may also ask a court to stop further infringement.

The owner of a properly registered copyright may also sue for "statutory" damages. These are awards of up to $100,000 that copyright owners may claim without proving that infringement damaged them financially,[27] a proof that is often difficult. Statutory damages are awarded to owners of registered copyrights simply because the copyright is infringed. However, owners of works that are infringed while unregistered may not sue for statutory damages or attorney's fees.[28]

Copyright Ownership

Copyright belongs to the "author" of a work. But the legal author is not necessarily the creator of a work. When a work is "made for hire," copyright belongs to the party who hires an employee or commissions a free-lancer to create a work. The federal government cannot copyright works.

Works Made for Hire A work made for hire is either (1) "a work prepared by an employee within the scope of his or her employment" or (2) "a work specially ordered or commissioned" for a collective work, such as a magazine, if a work-for-hire agreement is signed.[29] Works created by employees within the scope of their employment include stories, pictures and other items created by staff reporters, artists, publicists, photographers, and copywriters while on the job. This work belongs to the publisher, broadcaster, public relations firm, or advertising agency which employs the creator.[30] Works for hire belong to the employer on the theory that the company that assigns the task, risks the resources to carry it out, and directs the work should also own the copyright. Employers, as copyright owners, may allow employees to publish or display their work elsewhere, but employers do not have to.

Even an article written in off-hours may be a work for hire if the article is the direct result of one's employment. A federal court in Indiana ruled that Miles Laboratories owned the copyright in a scientific article written outside the office by one of the company's employees because the article was a direct result of the employee's work at Miles. The court said the article was within the scope of the employee's work at Miles because the company initiated and supported the research that led to the

---

[27]17 U.S.C.A. sec. 504(c) (Supp. 1989). *See generally* D. Johnston, *Copyright Handbook* (2d ed. 1982).

[28]U.S.C.A. sec. 412 (1977).

[29]17 U.S.C.A. sec. 101. (1977).

[30]*See, e.g.,* United States Ozone Co. v. United States Ozone Company of America, 62 F.2d 881 (7th Cir. 1933) (Company owns copyright in pamphlet written by employee during working hours).

article. The company also had a policy requiring employees to submit articles relating to work.[31]

In recent years, some courts have ruled that free-lance writers and artists were employees when they created work on commission. These courts said that free-lancers were employees creating works within the "scope of their employment" even though they received no regular salary, medical insurance, or other fringe benefits common for employees. Companies commissioning free-lance work could claim copyright in works for hire merely because they paid for, supervised, or retained the right to supervise the work.[32]

However, in 1989, the U.S. Supreme Court ruled that independent writers and artists are not "employees" creating works for hire unless several evidences of the usual employer–employee relationship are present. In *Community for Creative Non-Violence v. Reid,*[33] the Supreme Court said that independent contractors are not employees unless they meet several criteria of employment such as being supervised, being provided a place to work, receiving fringe benefits, and having a long-term, salaried relationship with an employer. The Court ruled that James Earl Reid, a sculptor working on commission, was not an employee because he was a skilled professional who supplied his own tools, worked in his own studio, received no regular salary or benefits, and had only a short-term business relationship with the organization that commissioned his sculpture. After *Reid,* free-lance photographers and writers should seldom be considered employees.[34]

Even if free-lance writers and artists working on commission will seldom be "employees," they may create a "work for hire" if a work is "specially ordered or commissioned" for a collective work, such as a magazine or newspaper, and both parties sign a work-for-hire agreement. Before the copyright law was revised in 1976, free-lance writers and artists surrendered all rights in commissioned works when they endorsed the check for their work. Under the revised law, free-lancers do not create a work for hire unless both parties "expressly agree" in a written contract that "the work shall be considered a work made for hire."[35] Now, unless there is a written contract with work-for-hire language, free-lance photographers and writers who sell a work to a publisher give permission for only one-time publication. All other rights remain with the free-lancer.

Free-lance writers and artists may encounter media companies that demand copyright ownership in commissioned works by insisting that a work-for-hire agreement be signed. Whether a free-lancer signs a work-for-hire contract will depend on the strength of his or her bargaining position, whether either party needs complete copyright control, and who has conceived of, directed, and paid for the work.[36]

---

[31]Marshall v. Miles Laboratories, Inc., 647 F. Supp. 1326 (N.D. Ind. 1986).

[32]*E.g.,* Aldon Accessories, Ltd. v. Spiegel, Inc., 738 F.2d 548, 553 (2d Cir. 1984); Arthur Retlaw & Associates, Inc. v. Travenol Laboratories, Inc., 582 F. Supp. 1010 (N.D. Ill. 1984); Town of Clarkstown v. Reeder, 566 F. Supp. 137, 141 (S.D.N.Y. 1983).

[33]109 S. Ct. 2166 (1989).

[34]*See* Middleton, "Agency Law & Works for Hire: Are Freelancers Employees?" 11 *Newspaper Research J.* 90 (1990).

[35]17 U.S.C.A. sec. 101. (1977).

[36]*See* Middleton, "Copyright and the Journalist: New Powers for the Free-Lancer," 56 *J.Q.* 38 (1979).

Government and Copyright The copyright statute prohibits federal employees from copyrighting work created as part of their official duties.[37] However, government employees may copyright speeches and writings composed on their own time. The U.S. Court of Appeals for the District of Columbia Circuit ruled that Admiral Hyman Rickover could copyright speeches written during his off-duty hours. The court said Rickover owned the copyright because the speeches were not "statements called for by his official duties."[38]

Works commissioned by the federal government from outside organizations may be copyrighted by the firms performing the work if the government deems it in the public interest for the company to own copyright. Public television station WQED in Pittsburgh was permitted to copyright a bicentennial series called "Equal Justice Under Law," a series that had been commissioned by the Judicial Conference to increase public understanding of the courts.[39]

SUMMARY

Copyright encourages creativity by granting authors exclusive rights in original works of authorship for a limited period. Copyrightable works include literary, pictorial, and graphic creations, compilations, and derivative works. Copyright does not depend on notice or registration, although both are recommended either for protection from innocent infringement or for eligibility to sue for statutory damages. Works created on the job are works made for hire and are owned by the employer. Newspaper and magazine publishers commission a work for hire from free-lance writers and photographers only if a contract specifies that it is a work for hire. The federal government may not copyright the work of its employees.

Rights

The Copyright Act grants a "bundle" of rights to copyright owners. These rights include the power to authorize derivative works, to distribute copies of a work, to perform and display a work publicly, and to copy works. This bundle of rights gives authors great flexibility in controlling the commercial use of their work.

Derivative Works A derivative work is a transformation or adaptation of an existing work.[40] The author of a novel or other work may create a derivative work or authorize others to create any number of derivative works, such as sequels, films, plays, and cartoons derived from the original. Separate copyright in each derivative work is important because only the copyright owner can sue for infringement. Film producers want their own copyright in a motion picture based on a novel so they can

[37]17 U.S.C. secs. 101, 105.

[38]Public Affairs Associates v. Rickover, 284 F.2d 262 (D.C. Cir. 1960), *vacated for insufficient record,* 369 U.S. 111 (1962).

[39]Schnapper v. Foley, 667 F.2d 102 (D.C. Cir. 1981).

[40]17 U.S.C.A. sec. 101 (1977).

sue if a film is infringed. Similarly, book publishers want their own copyrights so they can protect their commercial interest in a book. Because copyright is *divisible,* authors can authorize separate copyrights on any number of derivative works while retaining copyright in the underlying work.

Divisibility of copyright is much like the power of a landowner to grant water rights to one person, oil rights to another, a right of way for a road to a third, while retaining ownership in the underlying land.[41] Thus, the author of a novel can permit the publisher of the book to own a copyright in the book. The producer of a film based on the novel can have a separate copyright for the film. Meanwhile, the author of the novel retains the right to authorize the creation of comic strip characters, T-shirts, and other works derived from the novel.

Distribution   The right to distribute includes the power to publish, sell, loan, or rent a copyrighted work. The right of copyright owners to distribute their works includes the right to pick the time when a work will be distributed, if at all. The right of copyright owners to pick the time of publication or distribution was reiterated by the Supreme Court in a case in which the *Nation* magazine pirated excerpts from President Ford's memoirs.

In *Harper & Row, Publishers, Inc. v. Nation Enterprises,* the Supreme Court ruled that the *Nation* violated the copyright held by Harper & Row by publishing several stolen excerpts of Ford's memoirs that were to be published in *Time* magazine. *Time* had an exclusive contract with Harper & Row to publish excerpts from the memoirs before the hardbound book was distributed. The Supreme Court said, "Publication of an author's expression before he has authorized its dissemination seriously infringes the author's right to decide when and whether it will be made public."[42]

A contract permitting distribution of a work in one medium does not extend to new technologies. The U.S. Court of Appeals for the Ninth Circuit ruled that Paramount Pictures Corporation infringed the copyright on the song "Merry-Go-Round" by copying and distributing videotapes of the film *Medium Cool* in which the song appeared.[43] Under a license agreed to in 1969, Paramount had the right to distribute the film with the song in movie theaters and to exhibit it on television. However, the 1969 license did not give Paramount the right to make and sell videocassettes of the movie, the court said. In the contract, the copyright owner retained all rights except for performance of the song when the film was shown in theaters and on television.

Paramount argued that selling the videocassettes was no different than exhibiting the film on television as the original contract allowed. But the court ruled that the copyright holder in 1969 could not have considered videocassettes to be like television broadcasts because videocassettes were not then invented or envisioned. "We would frustrate the purpose of the [Copyright] Act," the court said, "were we to construe this license—with its limiting language—as granting a right in a medium that had not

---

[41]*See* W. Strong, *The Copyright Book* 36 (2d ed. 1984).
[42]471 U.S. 539, 11 Media L. Rep 1969 (1985).
[43]Cohen v. Paramount Pictures Corp., 7 U.S.P.Q.2d 1570 (9th Cir. 1988).

been introduced to the domestic market at the time the parties entered into the agreement.''

While distribution rights include the right to sell a copy of a work, distribution rights do not include control over—and therefore royalties from—resale of a copy. The author's control and receipt of royalties stop with the ''first sale'' of each copy of a book or videocassette. The author may receive a royalty on the first sale, but not subsequent resales or rentals for private use. Thus, a library may loan or resell copies of books it owns without consulting or paying the copyright owner. Similarly a videocassette store may resell or rent cassettes to private individuals without paying additional royalties. However, special legislation bars stores from renting records without a royalty agreement.[44]

Performance and Display   Copyright owners have a right not only to authorize derivative works and distribute their work but also to display and perform their work publicly. Artists, composers, playwrights, and film producers who own a copyright can either bar public performance or demand royalties for public performance or display of their work. A public performance can be live, projected from film or tape, or broadcast to an audience.

Composers and lyricists cannot monitor all the broadcast stations, concert halls, jazz clubs, and movie sound tracks where their work might be publicly performed. Nor would songwriters and composers have the time to negotiate a royalty agreement for each performance of their work. Rather than try to police every public performance, composers and writers let music clearinghouses grant performance rights and collect the royalties for public performances of their work.

Two clearinghouses, the American Society of Composers, Authors and Publishers (ASCAP) and Broadcast Music, Inc. (BMI), control more than 90 percent of the copyrighted music played on the air. Performers obtain licenses to perform works listed with the clearinghouses; the clearinghouses then receive a percentage of the proceeds from the performances and distribute it to member copyright holders according to a formula.

Over-the-Air Broadcasting   What constitutes a public performance of a song or other work varies with different technologies. Broadcast of a copyrighted work over the air is a public performance. Royalties on over-the-air broadcasts of copyrighted work are paid by the broadcaster. Citizens who listen to or view over-the-air broadcasts do not pay royalties because they are passive receivers of a broadcasting service intended for the public. As long as citizens pick up over-the-air broadcasts for their own personal enjoyment, not for commercial use, they need pay no royalties.

However, when over-the-air broadcasts are *retransmitted* to a large number of people for commercial purposes, the retransmissions become public performances for which royalties should be paid. The Gap chain of stores infringed copyright when it piped copyrighted radio music into 420 clothing stores with an average size of 3,500 square feet. These large establishments, the courts have said, should subscribe to a musical background service.[45] Similarly, it is an infringing ''performance'' of copy-

---

[44]Record Rental Amendment of 1984, Pub. L. 98-450, 17 U.S.C.A. 109(a) (Supp. 1989).
[45]Solar Music v. Gap Stores, 516 F. Supp. 923 (1981), *aff'd,* 688 F.2d 84 (2d Cir.1981); Broadcast Music, Inc. v. United States Shoe Corp., 678 F.2d 816 (9th Cir. 1982).

righted material if a business sends radio signals into hotel dining rooms, public meeting rooms, theaters, ballrooms, and other rooms where people outside the normal circle of family would meet.

Over-the-air broadcasts may be used in very limited commercial contexts without becoming a public performance on which royalties must be paid. Hotels and apartment houses can pipe local broadcast signals to private guest rooms and apartments if no separate fee is charged.[46] The owner of a small bar or restaurant can play a single radio or television "of a kind commonly used in private homes" for the enjoyment of a few customers without it becoming a public performance.[47] In these limited cases, the over-the-air broadcast is not being retransmitted to a broader public for commercial purposes.

Cable and Satellites   Cable and satellite transmissions, unlike over-the-air broadcasts, are not intended for the general public. Cable programming, which is usually imported to the cable system from a satellite, is intended to be distributed only to those who subscribe or pay a fee. Because cable and satellite transmissions are not intended for public use, it is an illegal public performance to hook into a cable system or intercept scrambled satellite transmissions to a cable system. It is also illegal to intercept the microwave transmissions of pay TV, subscription TV, or other services that are intended for select paying audiences.[48]

A federal court in Texas ruled that the Echo Motor Hotel violated the Federal Communications Act by picking up ESPN, HBO, and other commercial signals on a satellite dish for viewing on guests' television sets. The motel's commercial use of the broadcasts, the court noted, caused the local cable company, which previously had wired the Echo Motel, to lose the motel as a customer.[49] ESPN, HBO, and other copyright owners were thus losing royalties the cable system would have paid if the motel were connected.

It is also illegal for small businesses to show satellite transmissions of network programs that have been blacked out in an area. These transmissions used by network stations for over-the-air broadcast are not intended for public consumption. These satellite transmissions often do not include advertisements and may contain sections not intended for public viewing. Several bars in the St. Louis area were restrained from showing St. Louis Cardinal football games that had been blacked out in the area because Busch Stadium in St. Louis had not sold out 72 hours before game time. Unlike radio or over-the-air TV programs shown in a neighborhood bar, the satellite signals could not be picked up on a household receiver and were not transmitted "for the use of the general public."[50]

Private individuals are also prohibited from connecting to a cable system without paying or from intercepting and unscrambling satellite transmissions of cable or

---

[46]17 U.S.C.A. sec. 111(a) (1) (1977), *overturning,* Buck v. Jewell-LaSalle Realty Co., 283 U.S. 191 (1931).

[47]17 U.S.C.A. sec. 106 (1977).

[48]*See* Movie Systems, Inc. v. Heller, 710 F.2d 492 (8th Cir. 1983); National Subscription Television v. S&H TV, 644 F.2d 820 (9th Cir. 1981).

[49]Entertainment and Sports Programming Network, Inc. v. Edinburg Community Hotel, 623 F. Supp. 647 (S.D. Tex. 1985).

[50]National Football League v. McBee and Bruno's, 792 F.2d 726, 12 Media L. Rep. 2265 (8th Cir. 1986).

over-the-air broadcasts. However, it is legal for dish owners to intercept unscrambled satellite broadcasts if there is no local company that provides them. In addition, rural residents not served by over-the-air or cable systems can arrange to receive satellite transmissions of network and superstation programming for a few cents each month per channel.[51]

Operators of cable systems do not have to pay royalties to transmit local over-the-air TV broadcasts and network programs, broadcasts that are intended for public viewing. Local broadcasters usually welcome having their signal carried in sharp focus on nearby cable systems.[52] But cable operators do pay for nonnetwork distant signals such as independent stations WGN in Chicago, WTBS in Atlanta, and various religious and country stations. Cable operators pay royalties under a *compulsory license* that guarantees the operators the right to use the distant signals provided the operators pay a royalty agreed upon by the cable and motion picture industries and the Copyright Royalty Tribunal. The Copyright Royalty Tribunal was created by the Copyright Revision Act of 1976 to collect and distribute royalties from compulsory licenses.

Under their compulsory licenses, cable systems pay royalties into a general copyright fund that is distributed by the Copyright Royalty Tribunal. The fees are based on the gross receipts of the cable system. Every five years the Copyright Royalty Tribunal must adjust the rates cable operators pay to use copyrighted programs.

Microwave system operators and other common carriers that bring independent broadcast signals across country to cable systems do not pay copyright royalties as long as they do not edit the signal they transmit.[53] These "passive" carriers pay no fees because they do not perform the work publicly. The cable systems that receive the transmissions perform them. Because microwave system operators pay no royalties, cable systems receive transmissions at lower cost and are able to offer a wider spectrum of programming to subscribers.

Copying One of the most important rights of copyright ownership is the exclusive right to control copying of a work. The right to copy is essential to the copyright owner of a book, newspaper, phonograph record, sheet music, and motion picture. By prohibiting unauthorized copying, the copyright law protects the commercial incentive for authors to be creative. Technology has undermined the ability of copyright owners to protect their intellectual property from illicit copying. Photocopying machines and video and sound recorders make it easy for individuals and businesses to make unauthorized copies of copyrighted works. The president of the Motion Picture Association of America described the marketing of a doublecassette recorder that copies videotapes as a "brazen call to thievery."[54]

Whatever the technological challenges, the copyright statute does not give the copyright holder an absolute right to control copying. Exceptions are made for public

---

[51]Satellite Home Viewer Act of 1988, Pub. L. 100-667 (Nov. 16, 1988).

[52]Hubbard Broadcasting Inc. v. South Satellite Systems, Inc., 777 F.2d 393 (8th Cir. 1985).

[53]Eastern Microwave v. Doubleday Sports, 691 F.2d 125 (2d Cir. 1982), *cert. denied,* 459 U.S. 1226 (1983); WGN Continental Broadcasting Co. v. United Video, Inc., 693 F.2d 622, 8 Media L. Rep. 2170 (7th Cir. 1982).

[54]Valenti, "A Film Ripoff by the Japanese," *New York Times,* Feb. 6, 1985.

libraries and public broadcasting stations. Furthermore, the fair-use doctrine permits limited copying of copyrighted works for public comment and criticism.

Public libraries have a privilege to photocopy an article to fill individual requests by noncommercial users. In a decision upheld by an evenly divided U.S. Supreme Court, the federal Court of Claims ruled that government libraries run by the National Institutes of Health and the National Library of Medicine could make numerous copies of articles from a single scientific journal to fill requests for single copies from library patrons. In *Williams & Wilkins Co. v. U.S.,* the Court of Claims said that finding copyright infringement in such copying would hamper medical research. The court also thought there was insufficient evidence that the multiple copies hurt the journal publishers financially. Furthermore, the court noted that Congress had not prohibited the photocopying. On review, the Supreme Court split 4–4, thus upholding the lower court decision.[55]

While the *Williams* decision permits nonprofit libraries to make copies for noncommercial use, it does not authorize corporate libraries, research centers, and public relations offices to reproduce copyrighted scientific and technical articles to further corporate commercial goals. Commercial and corporate libraries are supposed to pay royalties for copies of copyrighted articles, a subject discussed in the section on fair use.

An exception to the prohibition on unauthorized copying is also granted to the Library of Congress so that it can tape newscasts and spot coverage of news events off the air for the American Television and Radio Archives.[56] The Library of Congress can make these tapes available to researchers and scholars and also deposit them in nonprofit libraries that can make them available for research. Nonprofit public libraries can also tape off-the-air news programs and distribute them in limited numbers to scholars and researchers.[57]

Moral Rights   Countries belonging, as the United States does, to the Berne Convention for the Protection of Literary and Artistic Works are required to protect the "moral rights" of artists and writers in their work. Moral rights include the right to be known as the author of one's work, to prevent deforming changes, to prevent others from using a work in a way that reflects poorly on the author, and to withdraw a published work from distribution if it no longer represents an author's views.[58] A related right permits artists to profit from resales of their work.

Although the Berne Convention recognizes moral rights, the United States agreed to join the convention in 1988 only after American publishers and art dealers were satisfied that signing the accord would not add new moral rights requirements to United States copyright law.[59] American publishers and art dealers were prepared to oppose joining the Berne Convention if membership would limit their editing powers, bar them from altering works, and give artists a percentage of profits from sales after

---

[55]Williams & Wilkins Co. v. United States, 487 F.2d 1345 (Ct. Cl. 1973), *aff'd,* 420 U.S. 376 (1975).

[56]2 U.S.C.A. sec. 170 (1985).

[57]17 U.S.C.A. sec. 108(f) (3) (1977).

[58]H. Henn, *Copyright Law: A Practitioner's Guide* 176 (1988).

[59]"House Unanimously Passes Berne Implementation Legislation," 36 *Pat., Copyright & Trademark J.* (BNA) 25 (May 12, 1988).

the first sale of a copy. The U.S. was able to join the Berne Convention without adding moral rights because signatories to the convention may recognize moral rights in their own way, including through the law of defamation, privacy, and unfair competition, laws which are already well-developed in the U.S.

While the federal copyright law does not contain moral rights provisions, a few states have adopted moral rights laws to protect artists. The New York Arts and Cultural Affairs Law prohibits display or reproduction of noncommercial artwork and photography in an altered, defaced, or mutilated form, if the artist's reputation could be damaged.[60] The law also guarantees artists the right to have their names appear on their work or to have their names removed if a work has been altered in such a way that an artist's reputation might suffer from association with the work. A similar statute in California also provides that artists may receive 5 percent of the proceeds from the sale of their work after the first sale.[61]

Support for broader protection of moral rights appears to be increasing. In 1989, the Copyright Office recommended that Congress "seriously consider a unified system of moral rights."[62] The Copyright Office followed the urgings of film directors, screenwriters, and actors who object to colorization of black-and-white films, editing of films for television schedules, and "panning" to adapt wide-screen films to smaller video screens.

While Congress has not prevented colorization, it did create a National Film Registry of distinguished motion pictures that must be labeled if they are altered. Congress created a 13-member National Film Preservation Board that selects up to 25 "culturally, historically, or aesthetically significant" films each year for inclusion on the registry.[63] Selected films must be at least ten years old. Under terms of the act, registered black-and-white films must be labeled if they are colorized or otherwise altered. Among the first 25 "culturally, historically or aesthetically significant" films named to the registry in 1989 are *Citizen Kane, Casablanca, Gone With the Wind,* and *Snow White and the Seven Dwarfs.*[64]

SUMMARY

Copyright owners control a bundle of rights. These are the rights to distribute their work, create derivative works, and perform, display, and copy their work. At least two states have also enacted limited moral rights allowing copyright owners in artworks to guarantee the integrity of their work after it is sold, to have their name attached to their work and, in California, to receive part of the proceeds from later sales of the work.

The right of copyright owners to perform their works does not prohibit homeowners and small businesses from playing standard radio and television sets for fam-

---

[60]Arts & Cultural Affairs Law, sec. 14.03 (McKinney Supp. 1990).

[61]California Civil Code, secs. 986–987 (West Supp. 1989). *See* W. Strong, *The Copyright Book* 99–100 (2d ed. 1984).

[62]"Film Alteration Report Recommends Consideration of Moral Rights System," 37 *Pat., Copyright & Trademark J.* (BNA) 498 (March 16, 1989).

[63]National Film Preservation Act, Pub. L. 100-446, 2 U.S.C. 178 (1988).

[64]Molotsky, "Cinematic Treasures Picked for Posterity," *New York Times,* Sept. 20, 1989, at 15.

ily, friends, and a few customers, but it is an illegal performance for businesses to set up commercial sound systems to retransmit over-the-air broadcasts.

Unauthorized home or business use of commercial satellite broadcasts and cable programs is generally illegal because such programs are not intended for the general public and cannot be picked up with a single home receiving set.

Infringement

Plaintiffs in copyright cases must prove that they own copyright in an original work and that the defendants copied it. Even if plaintiffs can prove that their work is original and that they own the copyright, they often have difficulty proving that the work has been copied. Typically, a plaintiff has no witnesses to testify to the copying. Lacking direct evidence, copyright owners can nevertheless prove copying if they can establish that a defendant had access to the copyrighted work and that the original and the copy are substantially similar.

Access Copyright protects any original literary or artistic expression, even if, by coincidence, it closely resembles someone else's work. It becomes important, therefore, in copyright suits whether the alleged infringers had access to the copyrighted original. If they had no access to the plaintiff's work, they could not have copied it. A plaintiff, therefore, must prove that a defendant had a reasonable opportunity to see or copy the plaintiff's work.

It is easy to prove access to a widely disseminated work. Miller Brewing Company had no difficulty proving that Carling O'Keefe Breweries had access to Miller Lite advertisements that were broadcast over the air and on cable.[65] Similarly, Universal City Studios, producer of the movie *Jaws,* easily established that Film Ventures International, producer of the movie *Great White,* had easy access to *Jaws.* Both the movie *Jaws* and the book on which it was based had been seen or read by millions.[66]

However, failure to prove access helped defeat author Sonya Jason's infringement suit against the writers and producers of the film *Coming Home.* Jason claimed that Nancy Dowd, a screenwriter for the film, may have received one of the few hundred copies of Jason's book that circulated in southern California where Dowd and the star of the film, Jane Fonda, lived. However, a federal judge ruled that Jason had established only a "bare possibility" that Dowd and others connected with the film had seen one of the relatively few copies of her book circulating in southern California.[67] A bare possibility was insufficient evidence to establish access.

Substantial Similarity Besides proving access, a copyright plaintiff must prove that the works are substantially similar. It is easy to prove substantial similarity in those rare cases in which the pirate copies verbatim much of the original work. There was no question of substantial similarity in *Quinto v. Legal Times of Washington, Inc.* because it was easily demonstrated that a Washington legal publication reprinted 92

---

[65]Miller Brewing Co. v. Carling O'Keefe Breweries, 452 F. Supp. 429 (W.D.N.Y. 1978).

[66]Universal City Studios, Inc. v. Film Ventures Int'l, Inc., 543 F. Supp. 1134 (C.D. Calif. 1982).

[67]Jason v. Fonda, 526 F. Supp. 774 (1981).

percent of a copyrighted work verbatim.[68] Some works are so "strikingly similar" to the original, perhaps because of unusual plot twists or the repetition of errors, that the similarities can be explained only by copying, not by coincidence. In cases of striking similarity, courts may not require evidence that the defendant had access to the original.

More often, however, copying will not be as obvious. One copyright authority said determining "substantial similarity" between two works is "one of the most difficult questions in copyright law."[69] Substantial similarity is somewhere between literal reproduction and no similarity. "[T]he test for infringement of copyright is of necessity vague," Judge Learned Hand observed.[70]

Courts determining substantial similarity often examine whether the underlying ideas and the manner of expression are similar in the two works.[71] The films *Jaws* and *Great White* shared several similarities. Each starred sharks that threatened coastal towns on the Atlantic seaboard. The manner of expression was also the same in the two films. The films also shared similar major characters, sequences of events, and development and interplay of characters. Each film included teen-age victims of the shark, a crusty English sea captain, and a shark expert. Each had an explosive ending. Finding the two films substantially similar, the court said, "In light of the great similarity of expression, it would seem fair to conclude that the creators of *Great White* wished to be as closely connected with the plaintiff's motion picture *Jaws* as possible."[72]

In contrast, a federal appeals court ruled that ABC's "The Greatest American Hero" was not substantially similar to Warner Brothers' *Superman* movies. The idea of each was similar—a character with superhuman powers battles evil—but a federal court said Warner Brothers could not "claim a protected interest in the theme of a man dressed in a cape and tights who has the power to fly, resist bullets, crash through walls and break handcuffs with his bare hands."[73]

But while the ideas were similar, the characters were very different. Unlike Superman, ABC's hero, Ralph Hinckley, was slight, informally dressed, and weak-chinned, "the antithesis of the Superman character image." Unlike Superman, the flying Hinckley crashed into buildings and penetrated walls only with great difficulty. Although he was impervious to bullets, Hinckley, unlike Superman, feared being shot.

SUMMARY

Authors who think their copyright has been infringed must prove that the work in question is original to them, that the infringer had access to the copyrighted work, and that the copy is substantially similar to the original. In determining substantial

---

[68]506 F. Supp. 554 (D.D.C. 1981).

[69]M. Nimmer and D. Nimmer, 3 *Nimmer on Copyright,* sec. 13.03[A] (1989).

[70]Peter Pan Fabrics, Inc. v. Martin Weiner Corp., 274 F.2d 487, 489 (2d Cir. 1960).

[71]Sid and Marty Kroft Television Productions v. McDonald's Corp., 562 F.2d 1157 (9th Cir. 1977).

[72]Universal City Studios, Inc. v. Film Ventures Int'l, Inc., 543 F. Supp. 1134 (C.D. Calif. 1982).

[73]Warner Brothers Inc. v. American Broadcasting Companies, 523 F. Supp. 611, 615-16 (S.D.N.Y. 1981).

similarity, courts examine whether the works have the same idea and manner of expression.

Fair Use

Although a substantial similarity between a copy and a copyrighted work is evidence of infringement, a substantial similarity between a copy and an original is permitted if the copying is a "fair use."[74] The fair-use doctrine is the law's attempt to reconcile society's interest in encouraging creativity with its conflicting interest in ensuring that knowledge of creative achievement is widely disseminated and discussed. For a journalist or critic to discuss copyrighted work, it is usually necessary to copy at least small portions of it. Therefore, the copyright law permits fair use of copyrighted work, that is, limited copying for educational and critical purposes.

Fair use, one expert declared, is "a privilege in others than the owner of a copyright to use the copyrighted material in a reasonable manner without his consent, notwithstanding the monopoly granted to the owner" by the copyright.[75] The fair-use doctrine developed in the common law and was embodied in section 107 of the Copyright Revision Act.[76] Section 107 permits limited copying of copyrighted work, usually only for "productive" purposes such as news reporting, criticism, and comment. For copying to be a fair use, the copier should be "engaged in creating a work of authorship whereby he adds his own original contribution to that which is copied."[77]

The factors to be considered when a court is determining if copying is a fair use are

1. the purpose and character of the use, including whether such use is of a commercial nature or is for nonprofit educational purposes;
2. the nature of the copyrighted work;
3. the amount and substantiality of the portion used in relation to the copyrighted work as a whole; and
4. the effect of the use upon the potential market for, or value of, the copyrighted work.

Most important in fair-use decisions is the commercial damage copying might cause to a copyrighted work.

Purpose and Character of the Use   Section 107 does not define the uses of copyrighted material that are "fair," but the preamble to section 107 says that fair use is likely to be found when the purpose is "criticism, comment, news reporting, teaching

---

[74]M. Nimmer and D. Nimmer, 3 *Nimmer on Copyright* sec. 13.05, at 13-64–65 (1989).

[75]Rosemont Enterprises, Inc. v. Random House, Inc., 366 F.2d 303, 306 (2d Cir. 1966), *cert. denied,* 385 U.S. 1009 (1967), *quoting,* Ball, *The Law of Copyright and Literary Property* 260 (1944).

[76]H. Rep. No. 94-1476, 94th Cong., 2d Sess. 66, *reprinted in,* 1976 *U.S. Code Cong. & Admin. News* 5659, 5680.

[77]3 *Nimmer on Copyright,* sec. 13.05[A], at 13-69 (1989).

(including multiple copies for classroom use), scholarship or research.'' At the time the copyright law was adopted, the Senate suggested fair use would include

> quotation of excerpts in a review or criticism for purposes of illustration or comment; quotation of short passages in a scholarly or technical work, for illustration or clarification of the author's observations; use in a parody of some of the content of the work parodied; summary of an address or article, with brief quotations, in a news report . . . reproduction by a teacher or student of a small part of a work to illustrate a lesson; reproduction of a work in legislative or judicial proceedings or reports; incidental and fortuitous reproduction, in a newsreel or broadcast, of a work located in the scene of an event being reported.[78]

News and Comment   The law tries to encourage the dissemination of knowledge. It therefore permits reporters and scholars to quote brief excerpts from copyrighted works without paying royalties. Scholars may quote short passages of a written work or reproduce small sections of a painting for the purpose of discussion and criticism. Journalists may quote briefly from copyrighted works in news stories.

When the Senate suggested that *incidental and fortuitous reproduction* of a copyrighted work is a fair use, it meant that copyrighted material may be used if it appears as background to events being reported. A federal district court in New York City found such incidental copying when WABC, Channel 7, broadcast footage of a high school band playing a copyrighted song, ''Dove sta Zaza,'' in a parade in Little Italy. The court said the station's brief use of the copyrighted song was fair use because the use was incidental to a news event.[79] Similarly, broadcast footage or publication of a photograph of a copyrighted painting would be fortuitous and therefore a fair use if the painting were the backdrop for a news interview.

Satire and Parody   Another purpose permitted by ⳑne fair-use doctrine is satire and parody. Even if there is substantial similarity between an original and a parody or satire, the defense of fair use may prevail if the purpose of the parody is to comment upon the original, not supplant the market for it. ''Parody in its proper role,'' a federal court has said, ''creates something new by drawing from the old; but when it has the effect of refashioning or destroying the old, it is not protected.''[80] Parody becomes copyright violation when the copying ''goes beyond what is necessary merely to allude to or 'conjure up' the object of the parody.''

A three-hour, three-act play, *Scarlett Fever,* which purported to be a parody of the film *Gone With the Wind,* was not considered to be a fair use because the play followed the script of the film too closely. Although names were changed so that Scarlett O'Hara in the film became Shady Charlotte O'Mara in the parody and Rhett Butler became Brett Studler, the play moved in sequence through the major episodes

---

[78]Sen. Jud. Comm. Rep. 93-983, *A Report to Accompany S. 1361,* Copyright Law Revision, 93rd Cong., 2d Sess. 115 (1974).

[79]Italian Book Corp. v. ABC, 458 F. Supp. 65 (S.D.N.Y. 1978).

[80]D.C. Comics, Inc. v. Unlimited Monkey Business, Inc., 598 F. Supp. 110, 119 (N.D.Ga. 1984).

of *Gone With the Wind.* The play also utilized backdrops depicting scenes reminiscent of the major settings in the film, such as the plantation house at Tara, called Tiarra in the parody.[81]

The court said the play, taken in its entirety, was "not the sort of original critical comment meant to be protected by the fair use defense, but rather is predominantly a derivative or adaptive use of the copyrighted film and novel." The producers of the play drew on the copyrighted work far more extensively than is permissible to "conjure up" the subjects or characters parodied, the court said.

A federal appeals court ruled copyright was not infringed when a parody itself was copied in its entirety as comment and criticism. The U.S. Court of Appeals for the Ninth Circuit ruled it was fair for the Rev. Jerry Falwell to reproduce a copyrighted *Hustler* magazine parody ridiculing Falwell. Falwell reproduced the parody to criticize pornography and *Hustler* publisher Larry Flynt.

The parody that Falwell reproduced was the same Campari Liqueur parody for which the Supreme Court denied Falwell compensation for emotional distress. (See Chapter 4.) However, the Ninth Circuit said Falwell's Moral Majority and the "Old Time Gospel Hour" did not violate *Hustler*'s copyright when they copied the parody and sent it to thousands of listeners to raise money for a campaign against Flynt and pornography.[82]

The Ninth Circuit noted that Falwell's copying of the entire parody in a fundraising campaign would normally not be a fair use. But the court ruled that the public interest in allowing Falwell to defend himself against a personal attack rebuts the presumption of unfairness. To make an understandable response, Falwell needed to reproduce the whole parody, the court said. The court also observed that Falwell did not attempt to sell the parody or to present it as his own. Nor did the court think republication would damage *Hustler*'s commercial market.

Teaching and Noncommercial Research Teaching and noncommercial research are also purposes for which limited copying is permitted under the fair-use doctrine. Although Congress did not determine what photocopying is permissible for nonprofit classroom and scholarly research, guidelines for such photocopying were agreed upon by representatives of the Authors League of America, the Association of American Publishers, and the Ad Hoc Committee of Educational Institutions and Organizations on Copyright Law Revision. These guidelines were included in the House report accompanying the copyright act and have been cited by many courts.[83]

The guidelines allow a teacher or researcher to make a single copy of a chapter in a book, or a single article from a periodical or newspaper. The guidelines also permit a teacher to make multiple copies for a class provided that the copies are brief and maximum teaching effectiveness does not allow time to obtain permission from the copyright owner.

---

[81]Metro-Goldwyn-Mayer, Inc. v. Showcase Atlanta Cooperative Productions, Inc., 479 F. Supp. 351, 5 Media L. Rep. 2092 (N.D.Ga. 1979).

[82]Hustler v. Moral Majority, 796 F.2d 1148, 13 Media L. Rep. 1151 (9th Cir. 1986).

[83]H.R. Rep. No. 94-1476, 94th Cong., 2d Sess., Copyright Law Revision, to accompany S.22 at 68–70.

Personal Entertainment It is usually not a fair use to copy a work, particularly a whole work, for one's own pleasure or entertainment. Such copying is not a fair use because it has no productive purpose. Photocopying a book, for example, simply to avoid the cost of purchasing it, violates copyright, even if the copier intends only to read the book without further lending or copying.

However, in *Sony Corporation of America v. Universal City Studios, Inc.,* the U.S. Supreme Court ruled that it is a fair use for homeowners to record complete copyrighted television shows off the air for their personal, noncommercial use. The case is known as the Betamax decision after Sony's home recorder, the Betamax. The film producers who brought the suit argued that Sony was a "contributory infringer" because the company advertised and sold the machines that made the home recordings. But the Supreme Court ruled that home recording is a fair use and that Sony was not a contributory infringer.[84]

Instead of requiring that living room copiers pursue some productive purpose for their TV recordings, the Supreme Court was satisfied that home copiers do not have a commercial purpose. "If the Betamax were used to make copies for a commercial or profit-making purpose, such use would presumptively be unfair," the Court said. But most people record television shows so that they can watch them at a later time. In the jargon of the broadcast industry, this practice is known as *time-shifting.* Time-shifting, the court noted, is "a noncommercial, nonprofit activity."

Justice Blackmun, in his dissent in the Betamax case, argued that permitting the recording of complete copyrighted programs for no productive use "risks eroding the very basis of copyright law, by depriving authors of control over their works and consequently of their incentive to create." Blackmun and three other justices who joined him in dissent argued that noncommercial home recording of complete copyrighted programs by millions of individuals nationwide presented a significant potential harm to the market of the copyrighted work. Blackmun said copying of whole works for nonproductive purposes should not be considered a fair use even if the purpose of the recording is personal entertainment.

Advertising Copying copyrighted materials for commercial purposes is unlikely to be a fair use. Thus, courts are apt to find copyright infringement if copyrighted material is used in commercial advertising without comment or criticism. For example, a federal court found a copyright infringement when the Vogue School of Fashion Modeling reproduced the copyrighted covers of *Vogue* magazine in the school's promotional campaign. The Vogue School had no relation to the magazine.[85]

In a case involving *Consumer Reports,* a federal court ruled that an advertiser may infringe the consumer magazine's copyright by accurately quoting a favorable product evaluation. The court said a trial should be held to determine whether The New Regina Corporation and its advertising agency violated *Consumer Reports'* copyright and trademark by quoting the magazine's positive rating of the vacuum cleaner. New Regina quoted *Consumer Reports'* high rating for its vacuum cleaner in a television advertisement.[86]

---

[84]464 U.S. 417 (1984).
[85]Condé Nast Publications, Inc. v. Vogue School of Fashion Modeling, Inc., 105 F. Supp. 325 (S.D.N.Y. 1952).
[86]Consumers Union of United States, Inc. v. The New Regina Corp., 664 F. Supp. 753 (S.D.N.Y. 1987).

The federal district court, in its four-part analysis of fair use, said the vacuum cleaner advertisements appropriated the most significant portion of *Consumer Reports'* product research and used it for a commercial purpose. Harm to a copyright is presumed, the court noted, where copyrighted expression is used for commercial purposes.

Most important to the court, however, was the effect the advertisement might have on *Consumer Reports'* potential market. Consumers Union claimed that the public would lose confidence in the organization's neutrality if manufacturers could associate Consumers Union with advertised products by routinely publishing its evaluations. Circulation of *Consumer Reports* would decline as public confidence waned, Consumers Union argued.

Similarly, a federal court ruled the Amana Refrigeration Company infringed a copyright when it quoted favorable magazine articles in 200,000 promotional brochures. Not only did Amana reprint favorable product evaluations from copyrighted articles in *Consumer Reports,* the company also ignored less favorable articles, thus making the brochures misleading.[87]

While reprinting copyrighted material in commercial advertisements may constitute an infringement, reprinting copyrighted materials in comparative advertisements is fair use. The U.S. Court of Appeals for the Fifth Circuit ruled it was a fair use for the *Miami Herald* to copy the copyrighted covers of *TV Guide* in ads for the newspaper's competing television listings booklet. The court recognized that the *Miami Herald* copied the *TV Guide* covers for commercial purposes. But the court said that reproducing copyrighted material in a comparative advertisement is a productive fair use because the ad comments upon, criticizes, and presents information about competing products. The Fifth Circuit also noted that comparing competing products in advertisements furthers the public interest by helping consumers make more rational decisions.[88]

The *Miami Herald* case would have been different, the court noted, had the *Herald* copied *TV Guide*'s listings—the essence of a television booklet—instead of merely its descriptive cover. The court also said the case would have been different if the *Herald* had misrepresented *TV Guide.*

Scooping a News Competitor   The Supreme Court has ruled that a news organization that steals and publishes a competitor's news may infringe copyright. In *Harper & Row, Publishers, Inc. v. Nation Enterprises, Inc.,* the Supreme Court held that the political magazine the *Nation* violated Harper & Row's copyright when the *Nation* printed 300 to 400 words from President Ford's not-yet-published memoirs, *A Time to Heal.*[89] After the *Nation* published its article, *Time* canceled an agreement with Harper & Row to publish excerpts from the book just before the hardbound edition went on sale. The *Nation*'s purpose, to "scoop" *Time,* was not considered to be a fair use.

The Court did not question that the passages the *Nation* published were news-

---

[87]Amana Refrigeration, Inc. v. Consumers Union of United States, Inc., 431 F. Supp. 324, 326–27 (N.D. Iowa 1977).

[88]Triangle Publications, Inc. v. Knight-Ridder Newspapers, Inc., 626 F.2d 1171, 6 Media L. Rep. 1734 (1980).

[89]471 U.S. 539, 11 Media L. Rep. 1969 (1985).

worthy. The quoted passages explained Ford's pardon of President Nixon. Nevertheless, the Court said the passages infringed copyright because the *Nation*'s purpose was not simply to report news, but to beat Harper & Row and *Time* to the marketplace. "The *Nation*'s use," wrote Justice Sandra Day O'Connor for the majority, "had not merely the incidental effect but the *intended purpose* of supplanting the copyright holder's commercially valuable right of first publication." The *Nation,* in the Court's opinion, was less interested in reporting news than in creating a news event of its own. Furthermore, the character of the use was hardly fair, the Court said, where the *Nation* acted in bad faith by knowingly exploiting a stolen manuscript.

Corporate Copying   Corporate copying for commercial purposes is not a fair use. Corporations have been known to buy one subscription to a scientific or technical journal and then make several copies of articles for different departments within the organization. Such extensive copying has led to a number of protests by copyright owners. In 1985, 600 publishers filed a class action suit against Texaco for large-scale unauthorized photocopying from copyrighted scientific and technical journals for which the company allegedly made only "token" payments. The suit has been pursued by the Association for Copyright Enforcement, an organization formed and funded by the 14,000 members of the Copyright Clearance Center who publish some 110,000 publications.[90]

The Copyright Clearance Center in Salem, Massachusetts, is an organization created by publishers and authors to collect and distribute royalties. Companies or individuals who wish to photocopy articles from scientific and technical journals registered with the Copyright Clearance Center are supposed to pay royalties to the center for distribution to the copyright owner. The CCC pays authors according to individual transaction licenses specifying the charge per copy on the article. The charge per copy is often listed on the front page of copyrighted articles.

About 50 companies, including A.T.& T., the Amoco Corporation, and Dow Chemical Company, sign year-long licenses with the Copyright Clearance Center. Each company's annual fee, which may exceed $100,000, is calculated from the amount of copying at the company over a two-month period. In 1988, the Copyright Clearance Center distributed $1 million in royalties to 400 publishers, a fraction of the royalties publishers of scientific and technical publications think they should receive.[91]

Commercial copying of broadcast programs, like commercial copying of printed articles, is not a fair use. The U.S. Court of Appeals for the Eleventh Circuit ruled that a commercial broadcast "clipping service" infringed the copyrighted newscasts the service copied off the air. WXIA-TV in Atlanta obtained an injunction against Carol Duncan's TV News Clips, a company that taped the evening news and sold segments to individuals and institutions that wanted a record of televised coverage of their activities.

---

[90]Reid, "Texaco Photocopy Suit Moves Toward Trials," *Publishers Weekly,* June 30, 1989, at 22; McDowell, "Royalties from Photocopying Grow," *New York Times,* June 13, 1988, at sec. IV, p. 9.
    [91]*Id.*

The Eleventh Circuit said Duncan's "unabashedly commercial" purpose heavily influenced the court's decision to rule that the recording and sale of broadcast news segments was not a fair use.[92] The court distinguished TV News Clips from a newspaper clipping service, which buys the newspapers it clips and sends to customers. TV News Clips was buying nothing. In fact, the court said that TV News Clips could impair WXIA's market for news clips if the station chose to sell them.

Nature of the Copyrighted Work   Besides considering the purpose and character of copying, courts ruling on fair use also consider the nature of the work: its length, the effort involved in creating it, and its availability. Some works, because of their nature, have less copyright protection than others. Works such as data bases, lists, and stock tables, which require much effort but not much originality, receive less copyright protection than works such as novels and plays that embody more originality.[93] News reports are less protected than movies and novels because the news contains facts that are used in comment and criticism of public events.

Some works are of such a nature that copying even a small amount may be an infringement. A few words from a brief poem, for example, might be an infringement. Copying a small excerpt from a commercial newsletter may also be an infringement, particularly if the copying is for a commercial purpose. Commercial newsletters typically have only a few pages, a modest circulation, and a hefty subscription price. Publishers of newsletters of this nature cannot afford to let much be copied by others for free. Copying even a few lines might significantly damage the market value of the newsletter.[94]

The courts are very protective of unpublished manuscripts and letters. In the case in which the *Nation* magazine published excerpts from Gerald Ford's memoirs, the Supreme Court said the unpublished nature of the memoirs was a "key, though not necessarily determinative, factor" tending to negate a defense of fair use. In the *Nation* case, the Court was concerned that the copyright owner lose its right of first publication.[95]

Unpublished letters are also protected from extensive unauthorized copying. Copyright in letters belongs to the person who writes them. The U.S. Court of Appeals for the Second Circuit enjoined Ian Hamilton and Random House from publishing a biography of the reclusive author J.D. Salinger because the biography contained extensive excerpts and close paraphrases from several of Salinger's unpublished letters. Many of the letters were available for public viewing, if not copying, in various libraries. However, the court said the fact that the letters were unpublished was a critical element in finding that the copying was not a fair use.[96]

---

[92]Pacific and Southern Co. v. Duncan, 744 F.2d 1490, 1496, 11 Media L. Rep. 1135, 1138 (11th Cir. 1984). *See also* Robertson v. Batten, Barton, Durstine & Osborne, 146 F. Supp. 795 (S.D.Cal. 1956).

[93]New York Times Co. v. Roxbury Data Interface, Inc., 434 F. Supp. 217 (1977).

[94]Wainwright Securities, Inc. v. Wall Street Transcript Corp., 558 F.2d 91, 2 Media L. Rep. 2153 (2d Cir. 1977), *cert. denied* 434 U.S. 1014 (1978).

[95]Harper & Row, Publishers, Inc. v. Nation Enterprises, Inc., 471 U.S. 539 (1985).

[96]Salinger v. Random House, Inc., 811 F.2d 90, 13 Media L. Rep. 954 (2d Cir. 1987). *See also,* New Era Publications Int'l, ApS v. Henry Holt and Co., 695 F. Supp. 1493 (S.D.N.Y. 1988), *aff'd,* 873 F.2d 576 (2d Cir. 1989), *cert. denied,* 110 S. Ct. 1168 (1990).

Journalists and historians object that authors and their heirs may bar extensive quoting from public, but unpublished, letters. Historian Arthur Schlesinger, Jr., suggests that copyright should not be permitted to deny responsible scholars use of quotations that help establish historical points. Scholars should be able to publish widely from unpublished materials in libraries, court records, and public repositories.[97]

Amount and Substantiality of the Portion Used   The greater the amount of work copied, the weaker the fair-use defense. But determining substantiality is more than a question of the quantity copied; it is also a question of the quality.

Quantity   It is generally not a fair use to copy all or most of a copyrighted work, regardless of the purpose. For example, the *Legal Times of Washington* violated the copyright of Dave Quinto when it published 92 percent of an article Quinto wrote for the *Harvard Law Record*.[98] The Betamax case, therefore, is unusual because the Supreme Court ruled it was a fair use for homeowners to record entire copyrighted television programs off the air for personal entertainment. In this atypical case, the court reasoned that home copying by individuals for noncommercial purposes would not damage the commercial market for the copyright holder.

As a general rule, a critic or reporter should not quote more than two or three paragraphs of a book or journal at one time. Nor should a person copy more than a stanza of a poem or a single chart or graph from a technical treatise, even if the copying is for the purpose of criticism or comment.[99] It is not a defense in a copyright violation case simply to acknowledge the source of a copied work if much of the work is copied.

In the *Salinger* case, discussed previously, the Second Circuit Court of Appeals ruled that Ian Hamilton's biography used substantial portions of Salinger's unpublished letters. Hamilton quoted or closely paraphrased at least one-third of 17 letters and at least 10 percent of 42 letters. The paraphrased material frequently exceeded 10 lines from a single letter. The letters were quoted or paraphrased on at least 40 percent of the book's 192 pages.[100]

Quality   Even if the amount of material copied is small, copying may be an infringement if the "quality" of material taken is high. In *Harper & Row v. the Nation*, the Supreme Court said that the 300 to 400 words quoted by the *Nation* from President Ford's memoirs were an insubstantial portion of Ford's book, but were substantial qualitatively because they were "the heart of the book." The *Nation* took "the most interesting and moving parts" of the manuscript, the Court said. The quoted passages qualitatively embodied Ford's distinctive expression.

---

[97]Schlesinger, "The Judges of History Rule," *Wall St. J.,* Oct. 26, 1989, at 16.
[98]Quinto v. Legal Times of Washington, Inc., 506 F. Supp. 554, 7 Media L. Rep. 1057 (D.C.D.C. 1981).
[99]W. Strong, *The Copyright Book* 137 (3d ed. 1990).
[100]Salinger v. Random House, Inc., 811 F.2d 90, 13 Media L. Rep. 1954 (2d Cir. 1987).

The Supreme Court said the *Nation*'s copying was similar to CBS's infringement of Charlie Chaplin films when the network copied brief but important segments. CBS used no clips longer than four minutes from Chaplin films in a broadcast running more than an hour. But a federal court found an infringement because the network took the highest-quality scenes.[101]

In the *Salinger* case, too, the Second Circuit said Ian Hamilton's use of Salinger's letters was significant from a qualitative as well as quantitative standpoint. The court said the copied passages perhaps did not constitute the "heart of the book" as they did in the *Nation* case. But the court said the quoted and paraphrased passages from Salinger's letters were an important ingredient in Hamilton's biography. "To a large extent," the court said, the quoted passages "make the book worth reading." The biography copies "virtually all of the most interesting passages of the letters, including several highly expressive insights about writing and literary criticism."[102]

Effect upon the Plaintiff's Potential Market   The effect of copying on the plaintiff's commercial market is the single most important factor for determining fair use.[103] This last criterion is a question of the effect of copying not only on the present market but also on the potential market. Critical to a determination of the commercial effect of copying is whether the copy has the same function as the original and therefore competes with, or supplants, the original in the marketplace.

In *Wainwright Securities Inc. v. Wall Street Transcript Corp.,* the U.S. Court of Appeals for the Second Circuit ruled that summaries of commercial reports were a copyright violation because they made it unnecessary to purchase the original.[104] The *Wall Street Transcript,* a financial newspaper, printed 250- to 300-word abstracts of research reports published by Wainwright Securities. Each year, Wainwright wrote 275 in-depth analyses of corporations, evaluating their financial characteristics, their ability to take advantage of changes in their industry, growth prospects, and profit expectations. The *Wall Street Transcript* summarized Wainwright Securities' reports very effectively—so effectively that the *Transcript* advertised that it was not necessary to buy the reports.

In ruling that the *Wall Street Transcript*'s summaries violated Wainwright's copyright, the Second Circuit said that the *Transcript* was not making its own analysis and was not commenting on or criticizing Wainwright's work. Nor was the *Transcript* taking only brief quotes or seeking the opinions of others on the work. Instead, the *Transcript* "appropriated almost verbatim the most creative and original aspects of the reports, the financial analyses and predictions, which represent a substantial investment of time, money and labor." By summarizing the reports, the *Transcript* lowered the commercial value of Wainwright's reports. The *Transcript*'s summaries were, in effect, serving the same function as Wainwright's reports, the court said.

In *Harper & Row v. The Nation,* the Supreme Court ruled that the 300 to 400

---

[101]Roy Export Company v. Columbia Broadcasting System, Inc., 672 F.2d 1095, 8 Media L. Rep. 1637 (2d Cir. 1982), *cert. denied,* 459 U.S. 826 (1982).

[102]Salinger v. Random House, Inc., 811 F. 2d 90, 13 Media L. Rep. 1954 (2d Cir. 1987).

[103]Harper and Row, Publishers, Inc. v. Nation Enterprises, 471 U.S. 539, 11 Media L. Rep. 2469 (1985); Triangle Publications, Inc. v. Knight-Ridder Newspapers, Inc., 626 F. 2d 1171, 6 Media L. Rep. 1739 (5th Cir. 1980).

[104]558 F.2d 91, 2 Media L. Rep. 2153 (2d Cir. 1977), *cert. denied,* 434 U.S. 1014 (1978).

words quoted in the *Nation* from President Ford's memoirs had a potential and actual effect on the market for the Ford book.[105] Most immediately, Harper and Row lost $12,500 as a result of the *Nation*'s publication because *Time* magazine canceled a contract to serialize parts of the memoirs. The *Nation,* by printing sections of the book licensed to *Time,* took the part of the market *Time* would have had. More important, the Court said, the *Nation*'s publication of unreleased manuscript "poses substantial potential for damage to the marketability of first serialization rights in general."

In the *Salinger* case, the Second Circuit Court of Appeals protected Salinger's potential market for his letters even though the author disavowed any intention to publish his letters during his lifetime. Nevertheless, the court said copyright protected Salinger's opportunity to sell his letters for publication should he change his mind. Salinger's literary agent estimated the letters might be worth more than $500,000.[106]

In the Betamax case, the majority and the dissenters disagreed sharply over whether home recording of copyrighted television shows jeopardizes the commercial market for TV production studios. The majority of the Court ruled, as the federal district court had, that the potential harm to the market for studio productions was speculative. The Court demanded that a "meaningful likelihood of future harm" be shown where, as in Betamax, the copiers use their tapes for noncommercial purposes. The Court was not satisfied that such a meaningful likelihood of future harm was demonstrated. On the contrary, the Court said, producers, broadcasters, and advertisers might benefit from home recording because time-shifting allows more people to view a broadcast.[107]

Justice Blackmun, joined by Justices Marshall, Powell, and Rehnquist, dissented in the Betamax case, in large measure because they thought home recording of complete over-the-air broadcasts did present a potential risk to the market for the copyrighted works. Blackmun saw a potential danger to the producers' market for televised reruns, rental exhibitions, and re-releases in theaters if millions of homeowners individually record whole programs and build tape libraries. Potential damage to copyright holders' market was sufficient, the dissenters argued, that homeowners should have to pay a royalty for copying whole programs off the air for a nonproductive use.

The Public Interest   Even though copying or displaying copyrighted work may interfere with a copyright owner's market, some courts have suggested that the public's interest in receiving information may justify copying even though copying might not be a fair use. The clearest statement of the public-interest rationale appeared in *Rosemont Enterprises, Inc. v. Random House, Inc.*[108] Rosemont Enterprises, a company connected to the financier Howard Hughes, owned the copyright to three *Look* magazine articles about Hughes that appeared in 1954. A 1966 biography of Hughes contained 27 percent of the first *Look* article. In all, some 14 percent of all the *Look*

[105]471 U.S. 539 (1985), 11 Media L. Rep. 2469.
[106]Salinger v. Random House, Inc., 811 F. 2d 90, 13 Media L. Rep. 1954 (2d Cir. 1987).
[107]464 U.S. 417 (1984).
[108]366 F.2d 303 (2d Cir. 1966), *cert. denied,* 385 U.S. 1009 (1967).

articles was copied in the biography. Rosemont sought an injunction against publication of the biography, which Rosemont said violated its copyright.

Without specifically mentioning the First Amendment, the U.S. Court of Appeals for the Second Circuit ruled that enjoining publication of the biography would deprive the public of an opportunity to become acquainted with the life of a person of extraordinary talents. " 'Everyone will agree,' " the court said, " 'that at some point the public interest in obtaining information becomes dominant over the individual's desire for privacy.' Thus, in balancing the equities at this time in our opinion the public interest should prevail over the possible damage to the copyright owner." The court said that a narration of Hughes's "initiative, ingenuity, determination and tireless work . . . ought to be available to a reading public."

The public interest also figured in the calculations of a federal court in a case involving the assassination of John F. Kennedy. Author Thomas Thompson published a book in which he questioned the conclusion of the official Warren Commission investigation that Lee Harvey Oswald acted alone when he killed the president. In the book, Thompson printed charcoal sketches of copyrighted photographs of the assassination taken by Abraham Zapruder, a Dallas dress manufacturer who happened to be taking home movies of the presidential motorcade when Kennedy was shot. In *Time, Inc. v. Bernard Geis Associates,* a federal district court ruled that Thompson's charcoal sketches did not violate Zapruder's copyright because there was "a public interest in having the fullest information available on the murder of President Kennedy."[109]

The *Geis Associates* decision, however, did not depend on the public-interest rationale. Beyond the hint that the public had a First Amendment interest in the sketches, the court relied on the fair-use doctrine. The court noted that Thompson did research in support of an original theory on the assassination, a theory that was explained more clearly with the sketches. Furthermore, people did not buy Thompson's book for the pictures, but for his theory about the assassination. Thompson's book about the assassination was not a commercial substitute for *Life* magazine's copyrighted pictures from which the sketches were made.

The public-interest rationale is founded in the notion that some ideas of public importance cannot be conveyed without appropriating the copyrighted expression in which those ideas appear. In the *Geis* case, Thompson arguably could not present his theory of the assassination as fully as the public interest deserves without the sketches of the copyrighted pictures. The late copyright authority Melville Nimmer argued that public discussion of important public events such as the Kennedy assassination and the My Lai massacre cannot be complete unless news photographs of the events are available to the public. Nimmer said that democratic dialogue requires public access to the expression in some copyrighted news photographs. To Nimmer, it was not sufficient that the public have access to the facts or ideas about an important news event. The public must also have access to copies of the photo itself.[110]

However, the public-interest rationale, as the Supreme Court has noted in the Ford memoirs case, is at odds with the scheme of copyright protection.[111] The public

---

[109]293 F. Supp. 130, 146 (S.D.N.Y. 1968).

[110]*Nimmer on Freedom of Speech* (Student Edition) sec. 2.05[C] (1989).

[111]Harper and Row, Publishers, Inc. v. Nation Enterprises, 471 U.S. 539, 11 Media L. Rep. 2469 (1985).

may have the greatest interest in a photo or story that requires the most work, imagination, and risk to create. Thus, the public interest may be greatest in those properties that are the most valuable to their author, properties that copyright is supposed to protect. The Supreme Court was unwilling to diminish copyright protection in the Ford memoirs even though the *Nation* magazine argued the "substantial public import of the subject matter."

SUMMARY

The fair-use doctrine attempts to balance the competing social interests of encouraging creativity by granting a copyright and permitting comment and criticism of creative works. In determining fair use, courts consider the purpose of the copying, the nature of the work, the substantiality of the copying, and the effect of the copying on the market. A related, but different, consideration is the public interest in receiving copyrighted information.

Courts are least likely to find a fair use when works are copied for a commercial purpose and the copyright owner's commercial market is damaged. Nevertheless, copying may be a fair use, even in commercial advertising, if the copying furthers comment and criticism. Copying the whole of any copyrighted work is usually an infringement, but not in the case of copyrighted television programs copied for personal use in the home.

UNFAIR COMPETITION

Copyright protects the property value in the expression of information and ideas. However, copyright does not protect the property value in signs, titles, names, and slogans that businesses use to differentiate themselves. These commercial symbols are considered too "trivial" for protection under copyright law. However, the considerable commercial value of these symbols and the effort and money companies invest creating them can be protected from theft and misleading uses by the law of unfair competition.

Unfair competition, like *reasonableness* and *negligence,* is a vague term that purposely leaves wide discretion to judges. Competition is unfair at that indefinite point where market competition begins to confuse or mislead the consumer. The law of unfair competition protects businesses and advertisers from false statements by competitors. But the law's principal purpose is to protect consumers from being confused or misled. The law of unfair competition is concerned with the morality of commercial promotions.[112]

In early common law, unfair competition was often equated with "passing off." A company passes off or "palms off" when it offers a product as someone else's by using similar labeling, packaging, or advertising. Unfair competition now has a

---

[112]J. McCarthy, *Trademarks and Unfair Competition,* sec. 1.1 (2d ed. 1984).

broader consumer orientation, encompassing several commercial practices that confuse the consumer. Prohibited forms of unfair competition include misappropriating the work of others, using similar titles in a misleading way, stealing trade secrets, and advertising falsely. False advertising is discussed in the chapter on advertising. Theft of trade secrets is treated in the chapter about access to government records. Misappropriation and trademark infringement are discussed here.

Misappropriation

Misappropriation is the unauthorized taking of the benefit of someone else's investment of time, effort, and money. Misappropriation is often referred to as "piracy." The Supreme Court established misappropriation as a separate tort in 1918 in a case in which the Court ruled that the International News Service misappropriated the news from the Associated Press. INS employees misappropriated AP news by taking fresh dispatches from the AP office bulletin boards and early editions of newspapers and putting the dispatches on the INS wire, sometimes after rewriting them, sometimes not.[113]

The misappropriation recognized by the Supreme Court in the 1918 case was the taking by INS of AP's expenditure of time and effort in gathering and assembling facts. The Supreme Court noted that facts in a news report cannot be copyrighted. Nor can the effort and money expended to gather news be copyrighted. Furthermore, AP placed no copyright notice on its news reports. Nevertheless, INS was liable for misappropriation. Misappropriation, the Court said, "is taking material that has been acquired . . . as the result of organization and the expenditure of labor, skill, and money, and which is salable."

A news organization, the Court said, may use a story by another news agency as a tip from which a new story can be developed through independent effort and expense. But the "bodily appropriation of a statement of fact or a news article, with or without rewriting, but without independent investigation or other expense," is misappropriation.

Radio stations that broadcast verbatim newspaper reports without permission of the publisher also misappropriate the time and effort invested by the newspaper staff in researching, writing, and publishing its reports.[114] It is probably a misappropriation, too, to take data from computerized scientific, business, or financial data bases. As yet, the facts in a data base cannot be copyrighted, but the time and effort invested to assemble the facts can be protected against misappropriation.

Trademarks

Another form of unfair competition is misuse of another's trademark so as to confuse the public. A trademark is the word, name, or symbol used by a company to identify itself as the source of goods. The amended Lanham Trademark Act of 1946

---

[113]International News Service v. Associated Press, 248 U.S. 215 (1918).
[114]*See* Veatch v. Wagner, 116 F. Supp. 904 (1953); Pottstown Daily News Publishing Co. v. Pottstown Broadcasting, 192 A.2d 657 (Pa. 1963).

defines a trademark as "any word, name, symbol, or device" used by a manufacturer or merchant "to identify and distinguish his goods . . . from those manufactured or sold by others and to indicate the source of the goods."[115] Familiar trademarks include "M&M's," "Burger King," "Scrabble," "TV Guide," "Xerox," "Styrofoam," "Kleenex," and "Stetson." Slogans such as "Where There's Life There's Bud" can also be trademarks. American Express owns a trademark in "Going Places," the title of a house organ published for employees.[116] Trademarks associate a product with a specific source, whether or not the consumer can actually name the company that distributes M&M chocolate candies or Budweiser beer.

Closely related to trademarks are service marks. A service mark is a symbol used in sales or advertising to identify services as opposed to products. "Revolv-A-Count" is a service mark used in the sale or advertising of a credit service run by a home furnishings company.[117] "Home of the Whopper" is a service mark identifying Burger King's restaurant services and distinguishing them from others. "Elvis" and "Elvis in Concert" are service marks identifying entertainment services that Elvis Presley provided while alive and Presley's estate owns rights to now.[118] A broadcaster's call sign, such as "WXBQ," may also be registered as a service mark identifying the source of news, entertainment, and advertising services. Titles, character names, and other distinctive features of radio and television programs may also be service marks.

Trademarks and service marks have value as intellectual property because they represent a portion of the good will of a company. Trademarks and service marks are signals to consumers of the uniform quality of goods and services. Trademarks reduce the time and effort customers expend to buy desired products. Because of the commercial value of trademarks, a company can acquire exclusive use of a distinctive trademark.[119]

Registration Trademark rights are created, not through registration, but through adoption and use on goods in trade. Unlike copyright and patents, trademark does not depend on originality, invention, or discovery, although a company's trademark may indeed embody imagination. Owners of trademarks are given exclusive use of their marks because of their marks' distinctiveness. The distinctiveness depends on the success of the mark in causing the public to associate a product or service with the company that provides it.

Trademarks and service marks are protected under common law but registration with the federal government under the Lanham Trademark Act provides recorded notice worldwide of a company's claim to ownership in a trademark or service mark. Trademark registration applications include a drawing of the mark and payment of a fee. A registered mark is denoted with a circled R (®) and the phrase *Registered in the U.S. Patent and Trademark Office* or the abbreviated version *Reg. U.S. Pat. & Tm.*

---

[115]15 U.S.C.A. sec. 1127 (Supp. 1989).

[116]American Express Co. v. Darcon Travel Corp., 215 *U.S. Pat. Q.* 529 (Trademark Trial and Appeal Board 1982).

[117]*In re* John Breumer Co., 136 *U.S. Pat. Q.* 94 (1963).

[118]Estate of Presley v. Russen, 513 F. Supp. 1339 (D.N.J. 1981).

[119]J. McCarthy, *Trademarks and Unfair Competition* sec. 2.1 (2d ed. 1984).

Off. If a trademark registration is pending, companies sometimes print *Trademark Pending* or *TM.*

The Patent and Trademark Office in Washington may issue provisional approval before a mark is used in commerce if the company filing for registration demonstrates a "bona fide intention" to use the mark in commerce within six months. Once the mark is used, the Patent and Trademark Office can issue a registration certificate.[120] Registration must be renewed every 10 years and can be renewed each decade for as long as the mark is used.[121]

Inherently Distinctive Marks   To be registered, a mark must either be inherently distinctive or it must be a descriptive mark that has acquired a "secondary meaning." Words such as "reader," "best," or "nationwide" cannot normally be registered as trademarks because they merely describe the function, use, size, or quality of goods. Names such as "Tasty" candy, "Oyster House" restaurant, and "Ivy League" clothes cannot be registered as trademarks because, as merely descriptive terms, they are in the public domain.

A mark is inherently distinctive, or a *strong* mark, if it is fanciful, arbitrary, or suggestive.[122] A mark is fanciful if it is coined specifically for the purpose of being a trademark. "Kodak" photographic equipment, "Ovaltine" drink mix, and "Clorox" bleach are coined terms that have no meaning other than to identify the source of certain products.

A mark is also inherently distinctive if it is arbitrary. An arbitrary mark consists of common words or symbols whose usual meaning has no relation to the product or service to which the words are attached. The "Stork Club" restaurant is an arbitrary trademark because storks have nothing to do with a restaurant. "Old Crow" whiskey, the "Nova" television series, the "Flash" music group, and "Apple" computers are all arbitrary marks. These are strong marks, immediately identifying the source of specific products or services.

Suggestive marks, a third type of inherently distinctive or strong mark, are distinctive because they suggest what a product does without describing it. "Brilliant" furniture polish suggests the quality of the product. The polish in the bottle is not brilliant, but the mark suggests one's furniture will be. The same word, *brilliant,* could not be a trademark for a diamond because *brilliant* would merely describe a gem. "Vanish" toilet bowl cleaner and "Coppertone" suntan oil are other suggestive trademarks that do not merely describe a product.

Federal appeals courts disagree whether the "LA" on the label of low-alcohol beers is descriptive or suggestive. The U.S. Court of Appeals for the Eighth Circuit ruled that "LA" is a distinctive mark that suggests, but is not the descriptive initials for, light-alcohol, low-alcohol, or less-alcohol beer. Ruling that the Anheuser-Busch Company owns the LA trademark, the Eighth Circuit enjoined the Stroh Brewery Company from using the term "Schaefer LA." The court said initials are not descriptive unless they have become synonymous with specific descriptive words. "LA,"

---

[120]15 U.S.C.A. sec. 1051 (Supp. 1989).
[121]*Id.* at sec. 1058.
[122]J. McCarthy, *Trademarks and Unfair Competition,* secs. 11:1–11:4.

however, was not associated in the public mind with a specific descriptive term such as "light alcohol," the court said. The court based its ruling, in part, on a consumer survey in which only 24.4 percent of the people polled thought "LA" was a descriptive term, and three-quarters of those surveyed supported Anheuser-Busch's contention that "LA" suggested Anheuser-Busch's LA beer.[123]

Nevertheless, the U.S. Court of Appeals for the Seventh Circuit ruled that "LA" is descriptive and therefore is not protected under the Lanham Trademark Act.[124] In a ruling against Anheuser-Busch, the court agreed that G. Heileman Brewing Company and other brewers could use the "LA" designation on their light beers. The Seventh Circuit said the "L" and the "A" are merely initials that describe the low alcohol content of the beer. Furthermore, the court saw no danger of confusion among consumers if several companies used the "LA" designation. Confusion would not occur, the court said, because beer companies also put their names on their labels.

Secondary Meaning   Although marks cannot be registered if they merely describe goods or services, descriptive marks can be registered if they acquire a _secondary meaning_. A secondary meaning is the drawing power or the commercial magnetism that develops over time in a title or in a corporate, business, or professional name. A secondary meaning is the mental association in a buyer's mind between a mark or symbol and the source of a product, even though the mark is not inherently distinctive.[125] A mark acquires a secondary meaning when the name and the business become one in the public mind.

Vogue is a word of common usage, but it has acquired a secondary meaning, at least when the term appears on a magazine. Over time, _Vogue_, as the name of a magazine, has acquired an association between the magazine and the clothing and accessories "worn by the American woman of discriminating and fashionable tastes."[126]

Look is not an inherently distinctive word, either, but it, too, acquired a secondary meaning as the title of _Look_ magazine. On the magazine, _Look_ identified Cowles Magazines and Broadcasting, Inc. as the source of a family picture magazine. The secondary meaning was established by long publication, heavy advertising, and the sale of millions of copies. _Look_ was a trademark that could not be used by others even though the title was not copyrightable and even though the word _Look_ is not a strong, arbitrary, or suggestive mark.[127] Other marks that began as weak descriptive names but developed secondary meanings include American Airlines, Kentucky Fried Chicken, and Payless drugstores.

A secondary meaning in one context does not prevent another company from using the same descriptive word in another setting. _Look_'s secondary meaning in connection with Cowles' picture magazine did not prevent the Elysium Company from publishing a magazine titled _Nude Look. Nude Look,_ a California court ruled, would not create confusion with _Look_ because Elysium's _Nude Look_ was printed with dif-

---

[123]Anheuser-Busch, Inc. v. The Stroh Brewery Co., 750 F.2d 631 (8th Cir. 1984).

[124]G. Heileman Brewing Co. v. Anheuser-Busch, Inc., 873 F.2d 985 (7th Cir. 1989).

[125]J. MacCarthy, _Trademarks and Unfair Competition,_ 2d ed., at sec. 15:2 (1984).

[126]Condé Nast Publication, Inc. v. Vogue School of Fashion Modeling, Inc., 105 F. Supp. 325, 331 (S.D.N.Y. 1952).

[127]Cowles Magazines and Broadcasting, Inc. v. Elysium, Inc., 63 Cal. Rptr. 507 (Cal. Ct. App. 1967).

ferent typography, in a magazine about a different subject, and with a different format, price, and frequency of publication.[128]

Infringement   The purpose of trademark policies is to protect consumers from being misled about the source of goods or services in the market. When one company infringes the trademark of another, it confuses the consumer. In deciding whether a trademark has been infringed, courts consider such things as the strength of the marks, the similarity in appearance of the products, the meaning of the marks, the kinds of goods in question, and the intention of the defendant in using the mark. A plaintiff in a trademark case may sue to have the infringing use enjoined and to collect illegal profits, damages, attorneys' fees, and court costs.

A federal court in New Jersey found sufficient likelihood of confusion to constitute infringement when Bob Russen used trademarks belonging to Elvis Presley's estate in promotions for Russen's "The Big El Show," an entertainment program imitating the dead singer's performances. Promotion for "The Big El Show" included use of "Elvis Presley," "TCB," and the "Elvis Pose," all words and symbols registered to Presley's estate. TCB with a lightning bolt is a trademark Presley placed on letterheads, jackets, and the tails of airplanes to identify his entertainment services. The Elvis Pose is an image of Elvis in a jump suit holding a microphone and singing.[129]

The federal court said that "Elvis Presley," the "Elvis Pose," and "TCB" are strong marks distinguishing entertainment services provided first by Presley and then by his estate. Russen was using marks essentially identical to Presley's. Furthermore, the services Russen offered were very similar to Presley's. "The Big El Show" was a careful imitation of Presley's performances, and Russen's intent was to capitalize on Elvis's popularity.

In finding a likelihood of confusion, the court did not suggest that people who bought tickets for "The Big El Show" would think Elvis was alive. But, the court said, the ordinary ticket buyer would likely believe incorrectly that "The Big El Show" was "related to, associated with, or sponsored by" Elvis Presley's estate.

A parody of *Cliff's Notes,* the famous college study guides to the great books, did not infringe the *Cliff's Notes* trademark, the federal appeals court in New York ruled.[130] The parody, *Spy Notes,* published by the editors of *Spy* magazine, purported, tongue-in-cheek, to summarize *Slaves of New York* and other hip urban novels. The U.S. Court of Appeals for the Second Circuit ruled that consumers would not be confused because *Spy Notes* used red, blue, and white on the cover, colors very different from *Cliff's Notes*'s distinctive yellow cover. In addition, *Spy Notes,* which condensed trendy novels instead of great books, contained the word "satire" five times on the front cover and sold for twice the price of *Cliff's Notes.* Whatever minimal likelihood of confusion *Spy Notes* presented, it was insufficient to justify an injunction against a constitutionally protected parody, the court said.

---

[128]*Id.*

[129]Estate of Presley v. Russen, 513 F. Supp. 1339 (D.N.J. 1981).

[130]Cliff's Notes, Inc. v. Bantam Doubleday Dell Publishing Group, Inc., 886 F.2d 490, 16 Media L. Rep. 2289 (2d Cir. 1989).

Dilution   Even if use of a trademark would not deceive or confuse the public, a use might be prohibited if it would tarnish or dilute the value of a mark. About half the states have antidilution statutes. In 1988, Congress amended the trademark law to protect the aura and uniqueness of famous trademarks from dilution. The amendment, section 43 (c) of the trademark law, protects famous trademarks, such as "Kodak" and "Buick," from unauthorized and diluting use on products such as pianos and aspirin.[131]

The dilution theory has frequently been successful in preserving the value of a trademark that has been used in an unwholesome or degrading context. A federal district court in New York enjoined a company from selling posters reading "enjoy cocaine" because the posters, printed in a script and color identical to that used by the Coca-Cola Company, could damage Coca-Cola's reputation. The poster company said the posters were only a satirical spoof, but the court said the unwholesome association of Coca-Cola with an illegal drug could dilute the value of the Coca-Cola trademark. The court did not suggest that consumers would confuse Coca-Cola and cocaine but said consumers might be offended in their mistaken belief that the Coca-Cola Company treated a dangerous drug in a humorous way.[132]

Abandonment   Unlike copyright and patents, which are protected for limited times, a trademark lasts as long as it is used in commerce. Trademarks are lost when they are abandoned. A company can deliberately abandon its trademark by ceasing to use it or by willingly giving it up. More likely, a mark will be lost because companies do not guard against use of the mark as a generic term. Words such as *aspirin, cellophane,* and *linoleum* were trademarks at one time but gradually passed into the public domain because people used the terms to signify generic pain relievers, food wrappings, and synthetic floor coverings. *Escalator, shredded wheat,* and *thermos* were also once trademarks but lost their association with a particular manufacturer and passed into the public domain.

Companies place great value in their trademarks and go to great lengths to keep them from passing into the public domain. A company lawyer may call a journalist who uses a trademark as a generic term. Trademark owners frequently remind the media in advertisements to use trademarks as proper adjectives, not as nouns or verbs. (See the Kimberly-Clark advertisement, Figure 5.1.)

A writer may refer to a "photocopying machine" or a "Xerox photocopying machine," but one should not refer to "the xerox" or write that a person "xeroxed" a copy. *Xerox* and other trademarks are proper adjectives that should appear capitalized or in distinctive type with a lower-case generic noun such as "photocopying machine." One wears a "Stetson" hat or perhaps a "Stetson," but not a "stetson." One plays "Scrabble crossword game," or "Scrabble," but not "scrabble." Journalists who do not want to infringe a trademark or provide free advertising avoid trademarks altogether by describing students "wearing western hats who photocopy their class assignments before playing a crossword game."

---

[131]Trademark Law Revision Act of 1988, Pub. L. 100-446, 2 U.S.C. 178. *See* Sen. Rep. No. 100-515, 100th Cong., 2d Sess. 7, *reprinted in,* 1988 *U.S. Code Cong. & Admin. News* 5577, 5583–84.

[132]Coca-Cola Co. v. Gemini Rising, Inc., 346 F. Supp. 1183 (E.D.N.Y. 1972).

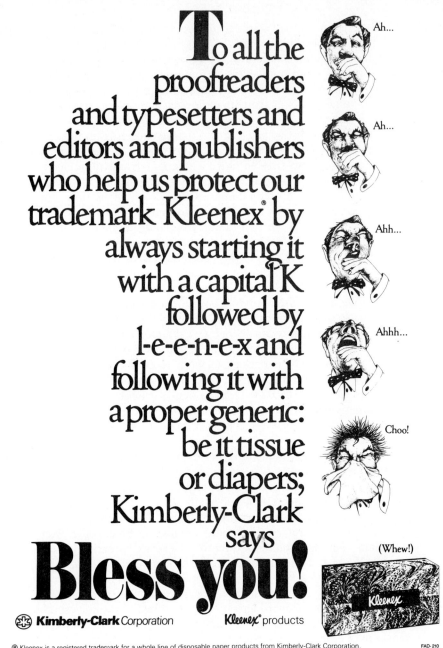

Figure 5.1.   Used with permission of Kimberly-Clark.

276

SUMMARY

The law of unfair competition protects intellectual property not protected by copyright. Under the common law of misappropriation, a person can sue for damages if someone steals uncopyrightable facts or appropriates the time and expense invested in gathering information. Trademark law protects trademarks and service marks, including slogans and titles, from misleading use by others. Both strong marks and descriptive marks that have acquired a secondary meaning can be protected from infringement. Owners of trademarks insist that their marks be capitalized and used as proper adjectives so that the marks do not lose their property value by acquiring a generic meaning.

6

CORPORATE SPEECH

A corporation, Chief Justice John Marshall observed in 1819, is a "mere creature of law" and therefore possesses "only those properties which the charter of creation confers upon it."[1] Because corporations are artificial creations of the state, they do not have the full range of rights of individuals. Unlike an individual, a corporation can be required to testify against itself[2] and has no right of privacy.[3]

For most of American history, nonmedia corporations have possessed no First Amendment rights either. Corporate political speech was restricted out of a fear that a corporation's vast resources might dominate debate and corrupt electoral processes. It was also feared that corporate political speech would violate the rights of shareholders and customers. In the same vein, Justice White and others have argued that speech by impersonal, state-chartered corporations deserves limited First Amendment status at most because it does not further the First Amendment values of "self-expression, self-realization and self-fulfillment."[4] Thus, until recently government regulation of corporate expression in elections, referenda, lobbying, labor-management relations, and securities transactions raised few First Amendment issues. Corporate speech was denied First Amendment protection because it was considered to be part of the economic marketplace, not part of the marketplace of ideas.

Yet nonmedia corporations contribute political and social commentary as well as commercial information to public communication. The Mobil Corporation, for example, frequently prints editorial advertisements in the *New York Times.* The Pacific Gas & Electric Company's monthly newsletter of consumer advice and information circulates to 3 million customers. The *DuPont News,* a 12-page tabloid newspaper, circulates news of the chemical company to nearly 150,000 employees and pensioners,

---

[1]Dartmouth College v. Woodward, 4 Wheat. 518, 636 (1819).
[2]Andresen v. Maryland, 427 U.S. 463 (1976); Wilson v. United States, 221 U.S. 361 (1911).
[3]California Bankers Assn. v. Shultz, 416 U.S. 21 (1974); United States v. Morton Salt Co., 338 U.S. 632 (1950).
[4]First Nat'l Bank of Boston v. Bellotti, 435 U.S. 765, 804–805, 3 Media L. Rep. 2105, 2121 (1978) (dissenting opinion).

several times more people than subscribe to the average daily newspaper. Other corporations contribute to public communication through advertisements, corporate reports, and video productions.[5]

In recent years, the Supreme Court has recognized that profit-making corporations have First Amendment interests in speaking and that consumers have First Amendment interests in hearing what companies have to say. In 1978, the Court ruled that a company could buy advertisements to oppose a personal income tax on the ballot in Massachusetts. A law prohibiting such corporate advertising was declared to violate the First Amendment. A short time later, the Supreme Court ruled that a New York utility could not be barred from telling customers about the advantages of nuclear power. The Court has also ruled that the First Amendment permits profit-making companies to give money to groups for the purchase of advertising in political referenda. Nonprofit "ideological" corporations, such as civil rights and pro-life groups, the Court has said, have an even greater right to speak. Free-speech questions also now arise in corporate lobbying, labor relations, and securities transactions.

The Supreme Court's decisions are not the first recognition that corporations have rights of citizenship. For many years corporations have been held to be "persons" entitled to equal protection and due process of the laws guaranteed by the Fourteenth Amendment.[6] Like individuals, corporations are also protected by the Fifth Amendment against being charged twice for the same crime.[7] Yet it is a relatively recent development for the Court to extend corporate rights of personhood to freedom of expression.

The first section of this chapter examines the expanding corporate rights to speak on referenda and social issues. The second section examines the continuing legal restraints on corporate speech in political elections. The following sections will discuss lobbying, labor-management communication, and corporate speech in connection with securities trading. The First Amendment rights of commercial advertisers is the subject of the next chapter.

REFERENDA AND PUBLIC ISSUES

The First Amendment rights of corporations are most clearly developed in cases involving referenda and public issues. In a referendum, a citizen votes on such propositions as whether to impose an income tax, require deposits on bottles, institute rent control, or build a nuclear power plant. Referenda were initiated early in the century to neutralize the power of well-financed lobbying groups in the legislatures. The reform was supposed to give a citizen a direct voice in governmental policy and discourage legislators from acting only in response to powerful, narrow interests.[8] To keep

---

[5]See Parker, "Corporate Annual Reporting: A Mass Communication Perspective," 12 *Accounting and Bus. Res.* 279 (Autumn 1982).

[6]Santa Clara County v. Southern Pacific R.R. Co., 118 U.S. 394, 396 (1886) (equal protection); Smyth v. Ames, 169 U.S. 466, 522 (1898) (due process).

[7]United States v. Martin Linen Supply Co., 430 U.S. 564 (1977).

[8]See Forrester, "The New Constitutional Right to Buy Elections," 69 *Am. Bar Assoc. J.* 1078 (1983); Easley, "Buying Back the First Amendment: Regulation of Disproportionate Corporate Spending in Ballot Issue Campaigns," 17 *Ga. L. Rev.* 675, 683 (1983).

commercial corporations from dominating debate, several states, including Massachusetts, passed statutes prohibiting corporate participation in referenda.

The Massachusetts law said corporations could not buy ads supporting or opposing a referendum issue unless the ballot measure related directly to the business of the corporation. The First National Bank of Boston challenged the law because the bank wanted to buy newspaper advertisements opposing a personal income tax. The attorney general of Massachusetts, Francis X. Bellotti, said First National's ads would violate the statute because the personal income tax proposal did not relate directly to the bank's business. First National then sued Bellotti, arguing that the state law infringed the company's First Amendment rights.

In ruling for the bank in *First National Bank of Boston v. Bellotti,*[9] and for other corporations in later cases, the Supreme Court has created an almost unlimited First Amendment freedom for nonmedia corporations to spend from their treasuries to support referenda questions and other social issues.

Referenda

Central to the Court's ruling in *Bellotti* was the political nature of First National's proposed advertisement. The Court said that First National's advertisement was constitutionally protected because it was political speech. Expression about a tax referendum is speech "at the heart of the First Amendment's protection," the Court said. Discussion about a referendum issue is "indispensable to decision-making in a democracy," one of the fundamental goals served by the First Amendment.

In making its ruling, the Court did not say that corporations have the same broad First Amendment rights as a newspaper or individual. Indeed, the Court skirted the question of how broad a corporation's right to speak might be. Instead, the Court said the constitutional question was "whether the corporate identity of the speaker deprives this proposed speech of what otherwise would be its clear entitlement to protection." The court said no.

The Court ruled that political speech retains its constitutional status regardless of its corporate source. Thus, First National's referendum advertisements would be constitutionally protected whether or not the referendum related directly to the bank's business. Therefore, the Massachusetts statute was unconstitutional because it permitted corporate referendum advertisements only if they related directly to a company's business.

In declaring the statute unconstitutional, the Court said that government limits on expression in referenda could lead to other unconstitutional regulations. "If a legislature may direct business corporations to 'stick to business,' " the Court said,

> it also may limit other corporations—religious, charitable, or civic—to their respective "business" when addressing the public. Such power in government to channel the expression of views is unacceptable under the First Amendment.[10]

While the Court refused to define the corporate right to speak, it did base its ruling on citizens' rights to receive corporate information. Corporate speech on a ref-

---

[9]435 U.S. 765, 3 Media L. Rep. 2105 (1978).
[10]435 U.S. at 785, 3 Media L. Rep. at 2112–13 (1978).

erendum is constitutionally protected, the Court said, "not so much because it pertains to the seller's business as because it furthers the societal interest in the 'free flow of commercial information'" to the public.

In explaining the First Amendment right to receive information, the Court drew on *Virginia State Board of Pharmacy v. Virginia Citizens Consumer Council,* a case decided two years before *Bellotti.* In *Virginia Pharmacy,* the Court ruled that citizens have a First Amendment right to receive price information about prescription drugs. The Court struck down a Virginia statute that barred pharmacists from advertising the prices of prescription drugs. Citizens need price information, the Court said, to make thoughtful consumer choices that in the aggregate affect political issues such as the allocation of resources. Similarly, in *Bellotti,* the Court said citizens have a right to receive corporate information about a tax referendum.

The Court did not rule in *Bellotti* that all corporate political speech is constitutionally protected. The government might regulate corporate expression, the Court said, if the government demonstrated a compelling interest, such as the need to preserve the integrity of the electoral process from corporate domination. However, the Court rejected Massachusetts's claim that the statute limiting corporate advertising in a referendum was necessary to ensure citizens' faith in the electoral process. There was no evidence, the Court said, that "the relative voice of corporations has been overwhelming or even significant in influencing referenda in Massachusetts, or that there has been any threat to the confidence of the citizenry in government."

To be sure, the Court said, corporate advertising may influence the outcome of a referendum. But, the Court said, "the fact that advocacy may persuade the electorate is hardly a reason to suppress it." Furthermore, the Court said people in a democracy bear the responsibility to judge which speech they choose to believe, whether that of the powerful or the weak.

The Court also rejected the Massachusetts government's contention that the statute barring corporate speech in referenda was necessary to protect shareholders from association with ideas they might oppose. The Court said the Massachusetts legislature did not intend to protect shareholders when it adopted the statute limiting corporate advertising in referenda. If the intention of the legislature was to protect shareholders, the Court said, the lawmakers would also have prohibited corporate lobbying and advertising on issues other than referenda. Yet, the legislature did not protect shareholders from being associated with political views expressed by corporate lobbyists or political advertising beyond referenda.

Furthermore, the Court concluded that the Massachusetts legislation could not have been intended to protect shareholders when it limited corporate advertising in a referendum. This is because the Massachusetts statute prohibited corporate advertisements in a referendum even if all shareholders voted to buy the advertisements. Shareholders who object to the corporate political positions adopted by management should vote in new company directors, the Court said.

Justice White, who dissented in *Bellotti,* argued that nonmedia corporations enjoy no First Amendment right to speak or publish about matters unrelated to their businesses. White thought the Massachusetts statute prohibiting corporate spending in referenda should prevail because speech by an impersonal corporation, chartered by the government, does not serve the First Amendment value of self-fulfillment. The ideas expressed by a company "are not a product of individual choice," Justice White said.

Likewise, Justice Rehnquist, who also dissented in *Bellotti,* argued that the government's power to create a for-profit corporation encompasses the power to regulate it, including regulation of the corporation's speech. The corporation, as a creature of the state, possesses no right to speak or publish, in Rehnquist's view.

Other Matters of Public Concern

While *Bellotti* is a referendum case, the Court viewed First National Bank's proposed advertisement as more than expression about a referendum. To the Court, a referendum is just one of many social and political issues about which corporations might speak. "The freedom of speech and of the press guaranteed by the Constitution," the Court said in *Bellotti,* "embraces at the least the liberty to discuss publicly and truthfully all matters of public concern without previous restraint or fear of subsequent punishment."[11]

The Court's broad vision of constitutionally protected corporate speech was reinforced a few years later when the Court said in *dicta* that a corporate newsletter "receives the full protection of the First Amendment" when it, like a small newspaper, contains "matters of public concern," including energy-saving tips, stories about wildlife conservation, billing information, and recipes.[12]

Besides recognizing First Amendment protection for corporate expression about referenda and matters of public concern, the Court has also ruled that the First Amendment protects corporations which hire professionals to gather signatures on referendum petitions. In *Meyer v. Grant,*[13] the Court held that corporations—or anyone else—may hire professionals to acquire signatures to place a proposal on the ballot. The Court's ruling, which affirmed a lower court decision, struck down a Colorado law that made it a felony to pay persons to circulate petitions.

Under Colorado law, as under the law in many states, proponents of a new law or constitutional amendment may have their proposal placed on the ballot in a general election if they obtain a prescribed number of signatures on an "initiative petition." However, to preserve the integrity of the referendum process, the Colorado legislature prohibited payment for gathering signatures. The statute was challenged by truckers seeking deregulation of their industry. The truckers wanted to pay professional solicitors to gather signatures so that Colorado voters might choose to remove motor carriers from the jurisdiction of the Colorado Public Utilities Commission.

The circulation of a petition, Justice Stevens wrote for the Court, involves "interactive communication concerning political change that is appropriately described as 'core political speech.'" Whether the trucking industry should be deregulated in Colorado is a matter of societal concern that the industry has a right to discuss publicly, the Court said. Furthermore, the Court said "circulation of an initiative petition of necessity involves both the expression of a desire for political change and a discussion of the merits of the proposed change." Colorado's prohibition of paid circulators, Stevens wrote, "restricts access to the most effective, fundamental, and

---

[11]435 U.S. at 776, 3 Media L. Rep. at 2109, *quoting,* Thornhill v. Alabama, 310 U.S. 88, 101–102 (1940).
[12]Pacific Gas and Electric Co. v. Public Utilities Comm'n of California, 475 U.S. 1 (1986).
[13]108 S. Ct. 1886 (1988).

perhaps economical avenue of political discourse, direct one-on-one communication.''

Utilities and the Right to Refuse to Speak

Two years after the Supreme Court ruled in *Bellotti* that corporate political speech is protected, it extended First Amendment protection to speech by a monopoly utility. In *Consolidated Edison Company of New York, Inc. v. Public Service Commission of New York,*[14] the Court upheld the right of Consolidated Edison, a New York utility, to tell its customers that the benefits of nuclear power outweigh the risks. Consolidated Edison advocated nuclear power in brochures enclosed with monthly bills sent to the company's customers. The state Public Service Commission had barred the monopoly utility from enclosing controversial messages in its bills.

Citing *Bellotti,* the Supreme Court said that First Amendment protections would not be denied to the utility simply because a corporation was the source of expression. As a general matter, the Court said, ''the First Amendment means that the government has no power to restrict expression because of its message, its ideas, its subject matter or its content.''[15]

The right of citizens to receive information figured prominently in the Court's reasoning in *Consolidated Edison* as it did in *Bellotti.* In *Consolidated Edison,* the Court said that a monopoly utility could insert controversial messages about nuclear power because customers have a right of access to ''discussion, debate and the dissemination of information and ideas.'' Customers who do not appreciate Consolidated Edison's views on nuclear power can throw the inserts away, the Court said.

Utilities and other corporations not only may express themselves on public issues, they are also protected from having to disseminate messages they oppose. In *Pacific Gas & Electric Co. v. Public Utilities Commission of California,* the Supreme Court ruled a California utility could not be forced to include a newsletter from a consumer group in the company's billing envelopes.[16] In *Pacific Gas & Electric,* the Court overturned a Public Utilities Commission regulation requiring the utility to include materials from a consumer group that often challenged PG&E in rate-making proceedings. The commission had ruled that a monopoly utility must carry the messages of its critic.

The consumer group, Toward Utility Rate Normalization (TURN), tried to raise money through PG&E's billing envelopes. Four times a year, the Public Utilities Commission required PG&E to include TURN's consumer messages in the ''extra space'' of the utility's billing envelopes. The ''extra space'' was space that could be filled without additional postage after the company's bills and legal notices were inserted. During the four months when TURN's messages were carried, Pacific Gas & Electric could not include its own newsletter, *Progress,* unless the utility paid extra postage.

In a 5–3 decision, the Supreme Court ruled it was unconstitutional for the Public Utilities Commission to force Pacific Gas and Electric to carry political views with which the utility disagreed. In an opinion written by Justice Powell and joined by

---

[14]447 U.S. 530, 6 Media L. Rep. 1518 (1980).
[15]447 U.S. at 537, 6 Media L. Rep. at 1522, *quoting,* Police Dept. v. Mosley, 408 U.S. 92, 95 (1972).
[16]475 U.S. 1 (1986).

three other justices, the Court equated the rights of a corporate utility with the rights of a newspaper publisher. The Court said forcing a utility to carry unwanted consumer messages was unconstitutional, just as the Court had earlier ruled it was unconstitutional to force a newspaper to publish a reply by people the paper attacked editorially. (The newspaper case will be discussed in a later chapter.)

Requiring either a utility or a newspaper to carry unwanted messages inhibits their right to speak, the Court said. Speakers may be reluctant to speak if they know their expression may entail an obligation to carry a response. A government-imposed right of access to a newspaper or a corporate billing envelope therefore inescapably dampens freedom of expression and limits the variety of public debate, the Court said.

In addition, the Court said the California Public Utilities Commission order was unconstitutional because it forced PG&E to associate with expression with which the corporation disagreed. Forcing PG&E to carry TURN's messages, the Court said, might either make the utility appear to agree with TURN by remaining silent or force PG&E to respond. Compelling either an uncomfortable silence or a forced response violates the First Amendment, the Court said.

In dissent, Justice Rehnquist argued that PG&E was not forced to associate with views it opposed because the utilities commission required TURN to publish a disclaimer saying PG&E did not necessarily agree with the consumer group's messages. Justice Stevens, in his dissent, argued that requiring a utility to carry consumer messages is little different from the common requirements that corporations disseminate legal notices, alter advertising to make it accurate, print messages on their loan forms, or publish dissident stockholders' proposals.

Indeed, corporations may, consistent with the Constitution, be compelled to disclose much information about the accuracy and sponsorship of their advertisements, the plans of their management, and other business matters. Later sections of this chapter will discuss several of the constitutionally acceptable corporate disclosure requirements. But because of *Pacific Gas & Electric,* the corporate right of association protects corporations from having to disseminate political views with which they disagree.

SUMMARY

The Supreme Court, in a series of decisions, has created a First Amendment right for corporations, including utilities, to speak on matters of public importance. Included among corporate rights are freedom from compelled dissemination of someone else's messages and the right to pay circulators of referendum petitions.

Corporate First Amendment protections are based primarily on the political content of the expression and the right of citizens to receive information. A corporation can use its own means of transmitting messages, such as billing envelopes and newsletters, or it can buy advertising in another medium as the First National Bank of Boston did.

Corporate speech may be halted if the government demonstrates a compelling interest, such as an imminent threat to democratic processes. So far, corporate expenditures have not presented such a threat in the Supreme Court's view.

ELECTIONS

If the First Amendment permits corporations to buy advertising to support referenda and other political and social issues, it might seem likely that corporations could also buy advertising to support political candidates. After all, the Supreme Court has said, freedom of expression "has its fullest and most urgent application precisely to the conduct of campaigns for political office."[17]

The majority in *First National Bank of Boston v. Bellotti,* however, said a profit-making corporation's right to speak on issues of general public interest "implies no comparable right in the quite different context of participation in a political campaign for election to public office."[18] This is one of several times the Court has expressed agreement with federal election law that prohibits profit-making corporations and unions from spending money from their treasuries to support federal candidates. The rationale for these restrictions is to restrict "the influence of political war chests funneled through the corporate form"[19] and to "eliminate the effect of aggregated wealth on federal elections."[20] Law in some states also prohibits corporations and unions from using treasury money to support candidates for state office.

Federal Election Campaign Act

The Federal Election Campaign Act of 1971 prohibits a corporation or union from using money from its treasury "to make a contribution or expenditure in connection with any election to any political office."[21] While *Bellotti* holds that a corporation may buy advertising on referenda or social issues that might be associated with a candidate, corporations may not draw funds from their treasuries either to make contributions to a candidate or to make expenditures on his or her behalf. Contributions are gifts of money or services given directly to a candidate or a candidate's campaign committee. Expenditures are monies spent on advertising advocating the election or defeat of a named candidate. Expenditures made independently of a candidate are not coordinated with a candidate or a campaign. Expenditures that are not independent of a candidate are considered to be contributions.

The Federal Election Campaign Act was passed during the Nixon administration, but the origins of the legislation go back to the turn of the century. One of the first electoral reforms, enacted during the period of Teddy Roosevelt's "trustbusting," was the Tillman Act of 1907, which prohibited corporations from making financial contributions to federal candidates.[22] The Federal Corrupt Practices Act, passed in 1925, extended the Tillman Act prohibitions on corporate contributions to include "anything of value."[23] Twenty-two years later, the Taft-Hartley Act of 1947 barred unions as well as corporations from making either contributions to a candi-

---

[17]Monitor Patriot Co. v. Roy, 401 U.S. 265, 272, 1 Media L. Rep. 1619, 1622 (1971).
[18]435 U.S. at 765, 3 Media L. Rep. at 2102 (1978).
[19]FEC v. Nat'l Conservative Political Action Comm., 470 U.S. 480, 501 (1985).
[20]Pipefitters Local Union v. United States, 407 U.S. 385, 416 (1972).
[21]2 U.S.C.A. sec. 441(a) (1985).
[22]34 Stat. 864 (1907).
[23]43 Stat. 1070 (1925).

date in a federal election or from making expenditures "expressly advocating the election or defeat of a clearly identified candidate."[24]

During debate on the Taft-Hartley Act, Senator Taft said he included the prohibition on corporate and union expenditures to plug a loophole in the earlier law, which only prohibited contributions. "If 'contribution' does not mean expenditure,'" Taft said, "then a candidate for office could have his corporation friends publish an advertisement for him in the newspapers every day for a month before election."[25]

The purpose of the Federal Election Campaign Act and earlier election reform laws is to prevent the corruption that might result if massive corporate capital enters the electoral processes. Corporate contributions to candidates, it is feared, may lead to favored treatment for a contributing corporation if a candidate is elected to office. On the other hand, it is feared that corporate expenditures may lead to corporate dominance of the electoral marketplace of ideas. The corporate expenditure restrictions are meant to ensure that competition among actors in the political arena is truly competition among ideas. In two important decisions, the Supreme Court has ruled that nonprofit ideological corporations are not subject to expenditure limitations imposed by the election laws, but that profit-making business corporations are.

Nonprofit Ideological Corporations   The Supreme Court ruled in *Federal Election Commission v. Massachusetts Citizens for Life, Inc.*[26] that the election law did not bar an anti-abortion group from distributing more than 50,000 copies of a "Special Election Edition" of its newsletter urging the public to vote for named pro-life candidates. The Court acknowledged that Massachusetts Citizens' $10,000 expenditure on the newsletter constituted a corporate expenditure under the federal election law because the publication advocated the election of named candidates. Nevertheless, the Court said the expenditures on political speech by a nonprofit ideological corporation are protected by the First Amendment when the expenditures are not coordinated with a candidate.

In an opinion written by Justice Brennan, the Court said ideological groups such as Massachusetts Citizens for Life may spend money on behalf of candidates because ideological organizations do not threaten the integrity of an election as large, profit-making corporations do. Formed to disseminate political ideas rather than to amass capital, an ideological group is not the "traditional corporation" of immense wealth that concerned Congress when it passed the election law. Therefore, the Court said, the government does not have the same compelling interest to bar election expenditures by ideological corporations as it does to bar expenditures by profit-making business corporations.

Brennan also said the political expenditures by Massachusetts Citizens for Life did not violate the associational rights of members. Individuals who contribute to Massachusetts Citizens for Life are aware of the organization's opposition to abortion, Brennan said. In fact, he said, members "contribute precisely because they sup-

---

[24]Ch. 120, sec. 304, 61 Stat. 159 [current version at 2 U.S.C.A. sec. 441b(a) (1985)].
[25]93 Cong. Rec. 6439, *quoted in,* United States v. United Auto Workers, 352 U.S. 567, 583 (1957).
[26]479 U.S. 238 (1986).

port those purposes.'' The organizations' expenditures, therefore, reflect the political beliefs of its contributors. Citizens for Life, the Court said, is more like a voluntary political association than a business firm and should not lose its right to endorse candidates solely because it is incorporated.

The Court said other corporations might also be exempted from the spending prohibitions of the election law if they were formed to promote political ideas, not to engage in business. Exempted corporations, the Court said, would have no shareholders, would not be established by a business corporation or labor union, and would not accept contributions from either.

Chief Justice Rehnquist, dissenting in *Massachusetts Citizens,* argued that the Court should not ''second guess'' the legislature by making distinctions between nonprofit ideological corporations and profit-making business corporations when the federal election law does not. Congress wanted to bar election expenditures by all corporations, Rehnquist said in his dissent, in which he was joined by three other justices.

Business Corporations   While nonprofit ideological corporations are exempt from federal election expenditure prohibitions, the Court said in *Massachusetts Citizens* that business corporations would not be exempt if they were established by a business, had shareholders, and accepted business contributions. In *Austin v. Michigan Chamber of Commerce,* the Supreme Court ruled that a business corporation could be barred from making expenditures on behalf of political candidates.[27]

In *Michigan Chamber of Commerce,* the Court upheld the constitutionality of a state election law that, like federal law, prohibits corporate expenditures in an election. In *Michigan Chamber of Commerce,* the Court upheld a section of the Michigan Campaign Finance Act prohibiting business corporations from using corporate treasury funds for independent expenditures to support or oppose a candidate in elections for state office. In a 6–3 decision, the Court ruled that the Michigan Chamber of Commerce, a nonprofit corporation funded by the annual dues of member corporations, could be barred from supporting a candidate for state representative.

The Michigan Chamber of Commerce argued that it, like *Massachusetts Citizens for Life,* was exempt from the state prohibition on the use of corporate funds in elections because the Chamber was a nonprofit organization that presented little risk of corrupting elections. However, the Supreme Court, in an opinion written by Justice Marshall, ruled that the Chamber of Commerce was more like a for-profit business than like a nonprofit ideological organization. The Chamber was not created to promote political ideas. Rather, the Chamber had several nonpolitical purposes, including training and promoting the interests of members, three-quarters of which were for-profit corporations.

Like Massachusetts Citizens for Life, the Michigan Chamber of Commerce had no shareholders, but the Court said the Chamber's corporate members were more like shareholders of a business corporation than members of an ideological organization. Members of the Chamber, unlike supporters of ideological groups, belong for non-

---

[27]110 S. Ct. 1391 (1990).

ideological purposes, including financial gain. The money the Chamber spends on behalf of candidates, unlike the money spent by an ideological group, does not reflect the political views of individual contributors. Furthermore, shareholders, unlike contributors to an ideological group, have a financial incentive to remain members even if they disagree with the organization's policy. By contrast, members of an ideological organization, who contribute to advance political goals, have every reason to resign if they disagree with the organization's political positions.

Another factor distinguishing a business corporation such as the Michigan Chamber of Commerce from an ideological group such as Massachusetts Citizens for Life is the influence of business corporations. Massachusetts Citizens for Life was not established by a business and had a policy of not accepting contributions from businesses. Therefore, Massachusetts Citizens for Life could not serve as a conduit for corporate spending that might threaten the political marketplace. However, the Michigan Chamber of Commerce was heavily influenced by business corporations. If Michigan law did not bar expenditures by the Chamber in an election, then corporations might circumvent the expenditure prohibitions by funneling money through the Chamber's general treasury, the Court said.

The Court in *Michigan Chamber of Commerce* noted that the Chamber, by trying to spend money on behalf of political candidates, wished to engage in constitutionally protected expression. The Court therefore required the State of Michigan to demonstrate a compelling reason for curbing expression protected by the First Amendment. The government's compelling interest is to "avoid corruption or the appearance of corruption" in the political arena by reducing the threat that huge corporate treasuries will be used unfairly to influence elections.

It is unfair, the Court said, for large accumulations of wealth, amassed with the help of state laws, to influence elections when the aggregated funds do not reflect public support for a corporation's political ideas. Because members do not contribute to the Michigan Chamber of Commerce to advance an ideological position, political expenditures by the Chamber do not reflect, as expenditures by an ideological organization do, the political views of contributors.

Further justifying prohibitions on corporate expenditures, the Court said, is the fact that companies may amass their huge "political war chests" with the aid of state laws. State business laws granting corporations limited legal and financial liability, perpetual life, and favorable tax treatment, should not be permitted to allow corporations to dominate the political marketplace, the Court said. The limit on independent corporate expenditures is warranted by "the unique state-conferred corporate structure that facilitates the amassing" of money, the Court said.

In his opinion for the Court, Justice Marshall said the Michigan statute was sufficiently narrowly tailored to be constitutional. The statute only prohibited corporations from spending money from their treasuries; it did not bar corporations from operating political committees that collect and spend money contributed from corporate employees, money that therefore reflects the employees' political views, not a corporation's economic interests.

In strong dissents in *Michigan Chamber of Commerce,* Justice Kennedy, joined by Justices O'Connor and Scalia, said the Court's ruling was "the most severe restriction on political speech ever sanctioned by this Court." Kennedy said the Court's hostility to the "corporate form" and its assertion that corporate wealth is evil is too imprecise a reason to justify a ban on independent corporate campaign expenditures.

In another dissent, Justice Scalia said, the fact that corporations amass large treasuries is "not sufficient justification for the suppression of political speech." If corporations may be barred because they have large amounts of money, then wealthy individuals should also be barred, he said.

Prohibited Contributions and Expenditures

Corporate—and union—contributions prohibited by the federal election law include gifts of money, advertising, securities, discounts, membership lists, use of facilities, broadcast time, and services to candidates and their campaigns.[28] Thus, an advertising firm that gives free or reduced-price services to a candidate makes an illegal contribution. Services provided at normal prices are not a contribution. An agency makes an illegal contribution if it takes a loss to benefit a candidate.

It is also an illegal contribution for a corporation or union to allow the free use of its facilities for more than an "occasional, isolated, or incidental" amount of time to produce election materials.[29] The Federal Election Commission, which administers the federal election law, has ruled that use of facilities to promote a candidate should not exceed more than one hour a week and must not interfere with an employee's normal work.[30] In addition, it is considered an illegal contribution for a company to pay for employees' leaves of absence so that they can become active candidates.[31]

A broadcaster who gives free time or news tapes to one candidate but not to his or her opponent also makes an illegal campaign contribution.[32] Similarly, a corporate public affairs department makes an illegal contribution if it gives taped interviews of candidates to broadcasters. The Federal Election Commission ruled the Atlantic Richfield Company made an illegal contribution when its public affairs department gave taped interviews with the major presidential candidates to 145 commercial and cable broadcast stations. Although the tapes did not favor the Republicans or Democrats, the Federal Election Commission said Atlantic Richfield's tapes were "something of value" given on behalf of the candidates by a nonmedia company. The distribution might not have been considered a contribution if the tapes had been obtained from a civic or other nonprofit, nonpartisan group, the FEC said.[33]

It is not an illegal contribution if a publisher includes earlier published editorial material in ads soliciting subscribers. A federal district court ruled that the publisher of *The Pink Sheet of the Left,* a bi-weekly newsletter, did not make an illegal contribution when he solicited subscriptions with mailings that were strongly critical of Senator Edward Kennedy while the senator was a candidate for the Democratic

---

[28]11 C.F.R. 100.7(a) and 100.8(a) (1989); A.O. 1981–33, Fed. Election Camp. Fin. Guide (CCH), para. 5618 (Sept. 21, 1981); A.O. 1978–45, Fed. Election Camp. Fin. Guide (CCH), para. 5337 (Aug. 28, 1978).

[29]11 C.F.R. sec. 114.9(a) (1989).

[30]11 C.F.R. sec. 114.9(a); A.O. 1980–51, Fed. Election Camp. Fin. Guide (CCH), para. 5536 (Sept. 3, 1980).

[31]A.O. 1976–70, Fed. Election Camp. Fin. Guide (CCH) para. 5217 (Sept. 2, 1976).

[32]A.O. 1978–60, Fed. Election Camp. Fin. Guide (CCH), para. 5350 (Sept. 1, 1978).

[33]A.O. 1980–90, Fed. Election Camp. Fin. Guide (CCH), para. 5538 (Sept. 9, 1980). *See also* A.O. 1979–70, Fed. Election Camp. Fin. Guide (CCH), para. 5448 (Jan. 11, 1980).

presidential nomination. The materials critical of Kennedy had been published earlier in *The Pink Sheet.* "[N]ewsletters and other publications," the Court said, "solicit subscriptions, and in their advertising doing so, they publicize content and editorial positions."[34]

Permitted Election Communications

The prohibition on corporate and union campaign expenditures and contributions does not prohibit corporations and unions from participating in election campaigns. Corporations and wealthy individuals can skirt the election laws by spending money on issues, organizations, and get-out-the-vote drives that benefit a candidate indirectly but do not directly advocate his or her election. Corporations and unions may also form and support political action committees that can spend unlimited amounts on behalf of a candidate. Finally, corporations and unions may promote candidates within their corporate or union "family."

Issues, Organizations, and Voter Registration Consistent with the Supreme Court's First Amendment ruling in *First National Bank of Boston v. Bellotti,* corporations may buy advertising to discuss issues associated with a candidate, provided that corporate and union treasury funds are not used to urge the election or defeat of a named candidate. The U.S. District Court of the District of Columbia ruled that the National Organization for Women could send membership solicitation letters critical of Republicans without violating the ban on corporate election expenditures because the letters discussed public issues. The letters, sent to the public during the election campaigns in 1984, urged political action to counter Republican policies. Some politicians named in the letters were running for reelection.[35]

The district court said the letters discussing public issues naturally invoked the names of politicians, but did not violate the election laws because they did not "expressly advocate" the election or defeat of the named candidates. The letters' call for political action could have invited demonstrations, lobbying, letter writing, and other forms of political advocacy besides voting against Republican candidates, the court said.

Besides spending money to discuss issues that might benefit a candidate, corporations and wealthy individuals can contribute large amounts to organizations and programs of interest to candidates. Under a 1979 amendment to the Federal Election Campaign Act, added to promote state "party-building activities," unions and corporations can contribute directly from their dues or treasuries to state parties for minor election activities such as purchasing pins and bumper stickers and supporting nonpartisan get-out-the-vote drives. However, if state law permits, corporations and wealthy individuals can also contribute unlimited amounts to state parties for any purpose. Twenty-eight states permit corporate contributions and 41 permit union

---

[34]Federal Election Comm'n v. Phillips Pub., Inc., 517 F. Supp. 1308 (D.C.D.C. 1981). *See also* Fed. Election Comm'n v. Machinists Non-Partisan Political League, 655 F.2d 380 (D.C. Cir. 1981), *cert. denied,* 454 U.S. 897 (1981).

[35]Federal Election Comm'n v. National Org. for Women, 2 Fed. Election Camp. Fin. Guide (CCH) para. 9274 (May 11, 1989).

contributions, none of which has to be reported at the federal level. During the 1988 elections, Republican and Democratic political parties in Florida received $4.7 million. Parties in Illinois took in $4.4 million, and in Texas, $3.3 million.[36]

In 1980, national parties began raising and distributing state funds, a role for the national parties that violates the intent of the 1979 amendment to the federal election law. Using this "soft money," as it is called, for television advertising to aid candidates for governor or state legislator and for get-out-the-vote drives, both parties can free other contributions for federal campaigns to which corporations and unions cannot legally contribute. Sometimes, too, money raised in one state can be transferred to states where corporate and union contributions to state parties are illegal. Soft money is also used to broadcast from states where soft-money expenditures are permitted into states where they are not.[37]

The propriety of soft money was raised by the contributions of Lincoln Savings and Loan, a failed California S&L, to three voter registration groups backed by Senator Alan Cranston of California. Although these contributions of $850,000 and other contributions were legal, a Congressional investigation was planned to see whether indirect contributions by Lincoln Savings and its head, Charles H. Keating, Jr., influenced Cranston and other legislators to protect the failing S&L from federal regulators.[38] An investigation was also planned to see if Cranston's get-out-the-vote campaigns were truly nonpartisan.

Political Action Committees   Federal election law also permits corporations and unions to form and support political action committees and participate in trade associations that can raise and spend large amounts of campaign money. A PAC has been described as the

> political arm organized by a corporation, labor union, trade association, professional, agrarian, ideological or issue group to support candidates for elective office. PACs raise funds for their activities by seeking voluntary contributions which are pooled together into larger, more meaningful amounts and then contributed to favored candidates or political party committees.[39]

Several media corporations, including 20th Century-Fox Film Co., the Magazine Publishers Association, and the American Advertising Federation have their own political action committees.

PACs are the most visible and controversial outgrowth of the campaign finance reform of the 1970s. During the 1987–88 election cycle, PACs raised nearly $385 million and spent $364 million.[40] "The massive involvement of PACs in federal elections is distorting the entire election process," according to former Senator Barry Goldwater.[41] However, others say PACs are a sound way to collect voluntary contributions

---

[36]Berke, "Tracing Evasion of Campaign Financing Laws," *New York Times,* Dec. 6, 1989, at 17.
[37]*See generally* E. Drew, *Politics and Money: The New Road to Corruption* (1983).
[38]Berke, "How Cash Is Given to Politicians' Interests," *New York Times,* Dec. 10, 1089, at E4.
[39]Alexander, "The PAC Phenomenon," in E. Zuckerman, *Almanac of Federal PACs: 1990,* at ix.
[40]*Id.*
[41]"Senate to Vote on Limiting PAC Contributions," *Cong. Q.,* Nov. 23, 1985, at 2445.

for candidates without corrupting the election process.[42] In any case, PACs do not monopolize political expression in elections. PACs account for only 24 percent of the funds raised by Senate candidates, and 40 percent of the funds raised by House candidates.[43] Furthermore, PACs do not uniformly back conservatives or liberals, but support different, and often opposed, parties, issues, and candidates.

Sponsorship of PACs Corporations and unions can provide sponsorship critical to the success of PACs. A sponsoring company or union can pay for all costs of establishing and operating the *separate segregated fund,* as corporate- or union-sponsored PACs are known legally. The sponsoring corporation, union, trade association, or cooperative can pay the salaries, overhead, and costs of soliciting contributions. Corporate and union officers also can control company PACs and direct their contributions to candidates.[44]

PACs can also be unsponsored or independent of corporations and unions. Independent PACs are established by independent organizations, partnerships, or unincorporated associations such as the California Medical Association. Probably the best known and one of the largest unsponsored PACs is the National Conservative PAC (NCPAC). Unlike sponsored PACs, which can receive unlimited funds for overhead and administrative expenses, unsponsored PACs must pay for overhead and administrative expenses out of money solicited. However, independent PACs can solicit money from a wider range of contributors than sponsored PACs can.

Solicitation of Funds Union and corporate PACs can solicit voluntary contributions from management, stockholders, and their families; union PACs can solicit funds from members and their families. Corporations that have no stock, such as a cooperative or nonprofit organization, are restricted to soliciting contributions from members of the organization.[45] Individuals can contribute up to $5,000 to a PAC during an election and up to $25,000 to all PACs and candidates in an election.

PACs are not supposed to solicit funds beyond their management or union class. Administrative PACs should solicit funds from administrators and shareholders, not from all employees. Union PACs are not supposed to solicit funds from management. Neither management nor union PACs may solicit funds from the general public. If a corporation's or union's solicitation of campaign funds extends beyond its respective shareholders or members to more than an ''incidental'' number of the general public, the organization may be subject to a fine for making an illegal expenditure.[46] The Supreme Court ruled that the National Right to Work Committee, an organization opposing unions, violated the campaign financing laws when it solicited PAC funds from members of the general public who had contributed money to the

---

[42]*E.g.,* ''PACs—Consider the Alternatives,'' *New York Times,* April 28, 1983, at 29; ''PACs—The Voice of Real People,'' *New York Times,* Dec. 2, 1982 at 29. (Advertisements by Mobil Oil Corporation.)

[43]Alexander, ''The PAC Phenomenon,'' in E. Zuckerman, *Almanac of Federal PACs: 1990,* at xi.

[44]2 U.S.C.A. sec. 441b (1985); 11 C.F.R. secs. 114.5(b) and (d) (1989); Pipefitters Local Union No. 562 v. United States, 407 U.S. 385 (1972).

[45]*See* Bread Political Action Comm. v. Fed. Election Comm'n 635 F.2d 621 (7th Cir. 1980), *rev. on other grounds,* 455 U.S. 577 (1982).

[46]The outer limit of nonmembers who can be solicited with members appears to be 15 percent. *See* A.O. 1979-50, Fed. Election Camp. Fin. Guide (CCH), para. 5434 (Oct. 19, 1979).

committee prior to the solicitation but were not members.[47] The Supreme Court ruled that the organization could solicit PAC money only from people who, like stockholders or union members, have "some relatively enduring and independently significant financial or organizational attachment" to the corporation.

A corporate newsletter distributed beyond executive and administrative personnel to all employees may report formation of an executive and administrative PAC but may not solicit contributions from all employees. The FEC ruled that DuPont did not illegally solicit funds from all employees when it announced formation of a PAC for executives and administrators in the *DuPont News,* a 12-page tabloid newspaper that circulates to virtually all 149,000 DuPont employees and pensioners. The articles were not an illegal solicitation beyond executives and administrators because the articles only announced the establishment of the DuPont Good Government Fund. The articles provided "factual, historical or statistical information about the fund and the legal requirements that apply to its activities."[48] The articles did not ask a broad range of employees beyond the administrative family to contribute.

Contributions   PACs contributed $160 million to federal candidates in the 1987–88 election cycle.[49] PAC contributions in 1987–88 were well over twice as large as the $60 million PACs contributed to federal candidates in the 1979–80 elections. Incumbents in 1987–88 received 74 percent of all PAC contributions. Democrats received 62 percent.

PACs can contribute only $5,000 to each candidate in an election, but they can contribute to as many candidates as they want. They can also contribute $15,000 per year to national political parties and up to $5,000 per year to other committees. Furthermore, and most important, PACs and committees can make unlimited "independent expenditures" on advertising and other expenses that benefit a campaign.

Individuals may contribute only $2,000 to each candidate, but may spend unlimited amounts independent of a candidate. The 1971 federal election law, however, limited both contributions and independent expenditures by PACs and individuals. But the Supreme Court in *Buckley v. Valeo* struck down the expenditure limits while upholding the constitutionality of limits on contributions by both PACs and individuals.[50]

The Court in *Buckley* accepted the legislative purpose of contribution limits, which is to discourage political favoritism for large contributors. The Court said bribery laws are insufficient to curb corruption. Wealthy individuals and committees may exact a *quid pro quo* from a politician through contributions as well as bribes. Limits on contributions by PACs and individuals are constitutional, the Court said, because they impose only a "marginal restriction upon the contributor's ability to engage in free communication." Contributions are not direct speech, the Court said, but rather are "indirect or symbolic speech." The Court has also called campaign contributions "speech by proxy."[51] Contributions serve as a general expression of support for can-

---

[47]Federal Election Comm'n v. Nat'l Right to Work Comm., 459 U.S.   ).
[48]A.O. 1983–38, Fed. Election Camp. Fin. Guide, para. 5741, (Dec. 16, 1983).
[49]Fed. Election Comm'n, Press Release, April 9, 1989.
[50]424 U.S. 1 (1976).
[51]California Medical Ass'n v. Fed. Election Comm'n, 453 U.S. 182 (1981).

didates and their views, but do not communicate the underlying basis for the support, the Court said. Limiting contributions, therefore, involves little "direct restraint" on a person's political communication.[52]

Furthermore, the Court in *Buckley* rejected the argument that limitations on contributions violate the right of association of contributing groups. Limits on contributions, the Court said, do not undermine "to any material degree the potential for robust and effective discussion of candidates and campaign issues by individual citizens, associations, the institutional press, candidates, and political parties." Even though individuals and groups cannot make unlimited contributions to candidates, they may exercise First Amendment rights of speech and association by making direct purchases of media advertisements independently in a campaign.

Expenditures   While the Court said in *Buckley* that individual and PAC contributions may be limited without violating the First Amendment, the Court said independent expenditures supporting a candidate, but not coordinated with a campaign, may not be restricted. Thus, PACs and individuals may buy as much television and newspaper advertising on behalf of a candidate as they want, provided their expenditures are not directed by the campaign.

Unlike limits on contributions, curbs on expenditures "impose direct and substantial restraints" on political speech, the Court said. "A restriction on the amount of money a person or group can spend on political communication during a campaign," the Court said, "necessarily reduced the quantity of expression by restricting the number of issues discussed, the depth of their exploration, and the size of the audience reached."[53]

Not only would expenditure limits on PACs and individuals curtail free debate, the Court said, but the limits would not deter corruption. A prohibition on expenditures that expressly advocate the election or defeat of a candidate would still permit individuals and groups to spend unlimited amounts to support candidates without expressly advocating their election or defeat, the Court said.

The Court also rejected the argument that expenditure ceilings are needed to equalize the relative power of rich and poor in an election. In a far-reaching endorsement of the role of money in the marketplace of ideas, the Court said,

> the concept that government may restrict the speech of some elements of our society in order to enhance the relative voice of others is wholly foreign to the First Amendment. . . . The First Amendment's protection against governmental abridgment of free expression cannot properly be made to depend on a person's financial ability to engage in public discussion.[54]

To critics of the election laws, Justice White among them, the Court is naive to distinguish between independent expenditures and contributions to a candidate. "The candidate," Justice White said, "cannot help but know of the extensive efforts

---

[52]Buckley v. Valeo, 424 U.S. 1, 21 (1976).
[53]424 U.S. 1, 21 (1976).
[54]*Id.* at 48–49.

'independently' undertaken on his behalf."[55] Journalist Elizabeth Drew also concluded that pollsters, journalists, consultants, and campaign workers are so interconnected that truly independent campaign expenditures are rare.[56]

Partisan Communications Not only may profit-making corporations use their funds to support election issues, organizations, get-out-the-vote campaigns, and PACs, they may also engage in partisan communication, advocating the election of specific candidates, provided the communications are directed only to the corporate or union "family." A corporation may use corporate funds to urge management, shareholders, and their families to vote for a specific candidate, and unions may use union funds to urge their executive and administrative personnel members, and their families to support specific candidates.[57] Partisan messages by corporations and unions may include extremely opinionated, even vitriolic messages, urging election or defeat of specific candidates, provided they are delivered only to the respective "families" of the corporation or union.

Partisan communications, paid for from corporate or union treasuries, become illegal contributions if they are offered beyond the restricted class of eligible recipients.[58] However, the law permits a corporation or union to invite press coverage of endorsements, candidates' speeches, or other partisan communications to the corporate or union "family."

Disclosure When Congress tried to curb election corruption, it did not want to limit political speech significantly. Indeed, significant limits on speech would be unconstitutional, as the Supreme Court said in *Buckley*. Thus, Congress decided that corruption could be reduced and speech preserved if contributions were limited and contributors and candidates had to reveal sources and uses of campaign funds.

The Federal Election Campaign Act requires each political committee and candidate to register with the Federal Election Commission and to keep detailed records of both contributions and expenditures made "for the purpose of . . . influencing" the nomination or election of a person to federal office.[59] The records must include the name and address of everyone making a contribution of more than $50, along with the date and amount of the contribution.

Federal law also requires disclosure of the source of funding of advertising that "expressly advocates the election or defeat of a clearly identified candidate, or that solicits any contribution, through any broadcasting station, newspaper, magazine, outdoor advertising facility, poster, yard sign, direct mailing or any other form of general public political advertising."[60] The identity of the sponsor must be presented clearly and conspicuously, telling who paid for the ad and whether it was authorized by the candidate. However, the disclosure requirements do not apply to small items

---

[55]Fed. Election Comm'n v. Nat'l Conservative Political Action Comm., 470 U.S. 480 (1985).
[56]E. Drew, *Politics and Money: The New Road to Corruption* 135–45 (1983).
[57]2 U.S.C.A. 441(b) (2) (A) (1985); 11 C.F.R. sec. 114.3(a) (1989).
[58]11 C.F.R. sec.114.3(c) (1) (4) (1989).
[59]2 U.S.C.A. secs. 431(9) (A) (i), 432(e) (1) and (f) (1) (1985).
[60]11 C.F.R. sec. 110.11(a) (1) (1988).

such as bumper stickers, pins, and buttons where it would be inconvenient to print the name of the sponsor.[61]

Each committee and each candidate must also file periodic reports containing the name of each person who has contributed or received more than $200 in a calendar year plus the amount and date of the contributions. Reports filed with the Federal Election Commission must be made available for public inspection and copying. A person who fails to comply with the requirements on making, receiving, or reporting contributions or expenditures aggregating $2,000 or more in one year may be imprisoned for up to a year and fined up to $25,000.[62]

The constitutionality of the election disclosure requirements was upheld in *Buckley v. Valeo*. The court noted that disclosure requirements, unlike limitations on contributions and expenditures, impose no ceiling on campaign-related activities. The disclosure requirements are justified, the Court said, because they tell a voter to whom a candidate may be responsive when in office. Furthermore, the disclosure requirements deter corruption by exposing large contributions and expenditures and providing the records essential for monitoring contributions. The Court concluded that disclosure regulations "appear to be the least restrictive means of curbing the evils of campaign ignorance and corruption."

The Court admitted that disclosure requirements may limit the right of association by deterring some contributions. But the Court said the minor infringement on the right of association was justified by the importance of disclosure to the political process. Nevertheless, the Supreme Court said that minor political parties would not have to disclose contributions and expenditures if there was "a reasonable probability" that compelled disclosure of a party's contributors would subject the party to threats or harassment from government or private individuals.

The Supreme Court forbade the State of Ohio from requiring the Socialist Workers Party to reveal the names of contributors. The Court said in *Brown v. Socialist Workers '74 Campaign Committee* there was a sufficient history of government and private harassment of the party to allow the party to withhold names of contributors and names of recipients of party funds.[63] Similarly, the U.S. Court of Appeals for the Second Circuit ruled that the Communist Party was exempt from record keeping and disclosure requirements because there was undisputed evidence of a reasonable probability that disclosure would subject contributors to threats, harassment, or reprisals.[64]

SUMMARY

Campaign finance laws prohibit corporate and union contributions to candidates and independent expenditures on behalf of candidates in federal elections. The Supreme Court has ruled that a ban on expenditures by business corporations is con-

---

[61] 11 C.F.R. sec. 110.11(a) (2) (1988).
[62] 2 U.S.C.A. sec. 437g (d) (1) (A) (1985).
[63] 459 U.S. 87 (1982).
[64] Fed. Election Comm'n v. Hall-Tyner Election Campaign Comm., 678 F.2d 416 (2d Cir. 1982).

stitutional to prevent corruption or potential corruption of the election process. Restrictions on expenditures by ideological organizations, however, are not permitted. Gifts of "anything of value" are prohibited, including free advertising, airtime, and tapes. However, corporations and individuals can skirt the election law restrictions by spending money on issues and organizations, including state parties, that are associated with a candidate.

Corporations and unions can also participate in elections by forming and soliciting funds for political action committees. Contributions to PACs and the amount that PACs may contribute to candidates are limited by the election law, which was upheld by the Supreme Court in *Buckley v. Valeo*. However, PACs and individuals may spend unlimited amounts independently of a candidate. The Court has also upheld the constitutionality of laws requiring disclosure of campaign contributions and expenditures.

LOBBYING: THE RIGHT TO PETITION

Lobbying is part of everyone's First Amendment right to speak and to petition the government for redress of grievances. This right is not denied because the petitioner is a corporation or union whose motives may be no more lofty than to seek legislation to damage a competitor.[65] Six thousand registered lobbyists reported spending $8.6 million to influence Congress during the first quarter of 1983.[66]

Lobbying the government may be carried out through direct contacts with legislators or through indirect public relations campaigns, sometimes called *grass roots lobbying*. Either form is protected by the First Amendment. However, Congress is concerned that corporate power not corrupt the legislative process any more than corporate power be allowed to corrupt the election process. Because of a perceived threat of corruption in the legislative process, Congress passed the Federal Regulation of Lobbying Act of 1946. The lobbying act, like election law, does not prohibit corporate political activity, but requires disclosure of that activity.[67]

Summarizing the purpose of the lobbying act, the Supreme Court said:

> Present-day legislative complexities are such that individual members of Congress cannot be expected to explore the myriad pressures to which they are regularly subjected. Yet full realization of the American ideal of government by elected representatives depends to no small extent on their ability to properly evaluate such pressures. Otherwise the voice of the people may all too easily be drowned out by the voice of special interest groups seeking favored treatment while masquerading as proponents of the public weal.[68]

---

[65]R.R. Presidents Conference v. Noerr Motor Freight, Inc., 365 U.S. 127 (1961).
[66]Dart, "Lobbyists Moving into Era of Hi-tech Influence," *Atlanta Journal-Constitution,* Nov. 20, 1983, at 1D.
[67]2 U.S.C.A. sec. 261 *et seq.* (1985).
[68]United States v. Harriss, 347 U.S. 612, 625 (1954).

Federal Regulation of Lobbying Act

The lobbying act requires registration by any person who is paid, or who raises money, for the purpose of influencing legislation, either directly through contact with legislators or their staff or indirectly through public relations campaigns. However, the Supreme Court ruled in *United States v. Harriss* that lobbyists and contributions must be disclosed only if the principal purpose is to influence legislation directly.[69] Direct influence includes in-person conversations, telephone calls, and letters to legislators.

Excluded from registration requirements are contributions and persons whose lobbying is indirect or who have only an "incidental" purpose of influencing legislation. Indirect lobbying includes attempts to sway legislators by swaying public opinion.

The Supreme Court ruled that a House Committee on Lobbying Activities could not compel Edward A. Rumely to reveal information about his indirect lobbying. The house committee wanted Rumely to tell who was buying his political books in bulk and distributing them to thousands of citizens. Rumely's organization, the Committee for Constitutional Government, was circulating hundreds of thousands of copies of *The Road Ahead,* a book attempting to stop "the march into socialism and the destruction of our form of government." The book condemned most of the social legislation passed by the Roosevelt and Truman administrations. Occasionally the book recommended the repeal of specific legislation, such as laws granting emergency powers to the president.

Mailing the books in an attempt to influence community sentiment was not a direct representation to congressmen that constituted lobbying under the lobbying act, the Supreme Court said.[70] It was indirect or grass roots lobbying that the Court said need not be reported under the lobbying statute. In a concurring opinion, Justice Douglas argued that requiring disclosure of book purchasers would be "the beginning of surveillance of the press," a violation of the First Amendment.

Corporations usually do not have to register because lobbying is normally not a substantial part of a corporation's business. Also excluded from the registration and disclosure requirements are public officials acting in an official capacity, a "newspaper or other regularly published periodical" that publishes news and editorials in the ordinary course of business, and persons who testify on legislation before a congressional committee. Congress did not want to impair its ability to gather information necessary to legislate. Nor did Congress want to infringe on a citizen's right to petition by requiring citizens who testify to register as lobbyists. In any case, people who testify publicly usually disclose their affiliations and political interests during their testimony. The exemption on registering for people who testify extends to corporate public relations staff who help prepare the witness by gathering information and writing statements.[71]

Nonprofit organizations, such as labor unions and trade associations, often must register because their principal purpose may be to influence legislation.[72] Regis-

---

[69] 347 U.S. 612 (1953).
[70] United States v. Rumely, 345 U.S. 41 (1953).
[71] United States v. Slaughter, 89 F. Supp. 876 (D.C.D.C. 1950).
[72] J. Jacobs, ed., *Federal Lobbying* 4–5 (1989).

tered lobbyists are supposed to report contributions of $500 or more they have received, along with the identity of the contributor, and all expenditures of $10 or more, the identity of the recipient, and the purpose of the expenditure. Lobbyists are also supposed to tell what legislation they have tried to influence and what articles or editorials they have caused to be published. Violation of the lobbying act can result in a fine of up to $5,000 or imprisonment for up to 12 months. Upon conviction, a person is also prohibited from lobbying or appearing before a Congressional committee for three years.[73] However, the act is seldom invoked.

Foreign Agents

Lobbyists who work for foreign "principals" are also supposed to disclose their activities. Just before World War II, Congress was disturbed to learn of well-organized, pro-German and Communist groups distributing large quantities of "anti-democratic material" in the United States. To mitigate the efforts of these new "subverters of democracy, and foreign-policy propagandists," Congress passed the Foreign Agents Registration Act of 1938.[74]

The Foreign Agents Registration Act, like the domestic lobbying act, relies on disclosure of agents' activities, not on suppression of their speech. Under the Foreign Agents Registration Act, agents must report their affiliations, the way they carry out their activities, how they receive and spend money, and how they disseminate information, including "propaganda" they disseminate to influence public opinion. In *Communist Party v. Subversive Activities Control Board,* the Supreme Court said Congress could require registration or disclosure where "secrecy or the concealment of associations has been regarded as a threat to public safety and to the effective, free functioning of our national institutions."[75] Foreign agents are prohibited from spending money to influence an American political election.

Foreign "agents" who are supposed to register include any person or organization that acts as an agent or representative of a foreign principal or "at the order, request, or under the direction or control" of a foreign principal. Foreign principals include governments, political parties, and businesses and organizations. The foreign principal may be a friend or enemy of the United States.[76]

A foreign agent also includes anyone in the United States who acts "as a public relations counsel, publicity agent, information-service employee or political consultant" for a foreign principal. If a law firm representing a foreign government hires an American public relations firm, the public relations firm becomes an agent subject to registration under the act because the firm is "indirectly supervised, directed, controlled, financed, or subsidized" by a foreign principal.

In 1989, four Democratic senators, three of whom had been opposed by a Washington group representing Japanese car dealers, charged that the automotive group was paid by foreigners and should register as a foreign agent. If the automotive group

---

[73]2 U.S.C.A. secs. 267 and 269.
[74]22 U.S.C.A. sec. 611 *et seq.* (1979).
[75]367 U.S. 1, 97 (1961).
[76]22 U.S.C.A. sec. 611 (c) (1) (1979).

were receiving money from foreign automakers, it would be illegal for the dealer organization to spend money to influence an election.[77]

A major exception in the law frees from registration requirements representatives of foreign principals who engage in private, nonpolitical commercial activities. Thus, agents representing foreign businesses do not have to register if the foreign business does not directly promote the foreign policy of a foreign government.[78]

Propaganda   Foreign agents are required to label the "political propaganda" they distribute and file copies of the propaganda with the U.S. Justice Department. Political propaganda is any communication designed to influence the American public about the political interests or policies of a foreign government or to influence the foreign policy of the United States. Disclosures by foreign agents are public records.

When foreign agents distribute a propaganda film, they are supposed to name each station, organization, or theater using it and the dates the film is shown. The U.S. Supreme Court has ruled that the act's requirement that propaganda be labeled does not violate the First Amendment. In its ruling, the Court rejected arguments by California state senator Barry Keene, who argued that the political propaganda label inhibited him from showing three Canadian films about nuclear weapons and pollution because the label was pejorative. Keene said his constituents would be less supportive if they knew he was disseminating films the government had labeled "political propaganda."[79]

The Canadian films were clearly political propaganda as defined in the Foreign Agents Registration Act because they could affect American policy toward Canada. The National Film Board of Canada, which distributed the films in the U.S. from its office in New York, is a registered agent of the Canadian government.

The Court's five-person majority ruled that requiring the propaganda label did not violate Keene's First Amendment rights because the label erects no physical restraint on the showing of the films. Indeed, the Court said the required label could serve First Amendment purposes by increasing debate if a film exhibitor discussed the label when the films were shown.

Furthermore, the Court said the term *propaganda* has a neutral as well as a negative meaning. Congress, the Court said, intended a neutral definition by which *propaganda* means *doctrines, ideas, arguments,* and *facts.* In any case, the Court found no evidence that the label undermined the integrity of the films.

An important hindrance to compliance with the Foreign Agents Act is the stigma of registering under an act passed to cope with "threats to the national security posed by subversives." Typical foreign agents of the 1980s do not represent a fascist foreign power. It has therefore been recommended that the words *agent* and *propaganda* in the act be changed to *representative* and *promotional material,* respectively, to help remove the stigma attached to registration.[80]

---

[77]"Senators Charge Auto Group Is Working as Foreign Agent," *New York Times,* March 19, 1989, at 15.
[78]J. Jacobs, ed., *Federal Lobbying* 22–23 (1989).
[79]Meese v. Keene, 481 U.S. 465 (1987).
[80]The Foreign Agents Registration Act, prepared for the Senate Committee on Foreign Relations, 95th Cong., 1st Sess. 14 (Comm. Print 1977).

that the setting is not coercive. It is considered coercive for an employer to discourage unionization to a small group of employees in the management wing of the building or other places of management authority. Surveillance of employees, such as photographing them talking to union organizers, may also be considered an unlawful threat. In addition, an election may be set aside if management distributes false documents in an election campaign or plants threatening editorials in local newspapers. However, it is unlikely a newspaper's own antiunion editorials would result in a union election being set aside.[87]

Section 7 of the Taft-Hartley Act prohibits the employer from changing "any term or condition of employment" to discourage union membership.[88] Firing or demoting employees because they support a union is an illegal change in the "condition of employment." The U.S. Court of Appeals for the District of Columbia Circuit ruled it was an unfair labor practice for the *Passaic* (New Jersey) *Herald-News* to abruptly stop publishing the weekly column of a journalist who supported a union drive. Management ceased publishing Mitchell Stoddard's column two days after editorial employees voted for the union. It would not have been an unfair practice for the paper to halt Stoddard's long-running column for reasons not related to union activities. However, it was ruled to be unfair to stop it as punishment two days after the union was approved.[89]

The appeals court said Stoddard's case was like *Associated Press v. National Labor Relations Board,*[90] a case in which the U.S. Supreme Court ruled that the wire service could not fire an employee because of his union activity. In the AP case, the Supreme Court rejected AP's argument that the First Amendment prohibited the NLRB from interfering with the AP's decision to fire the employee. Similarly, the NLRB was not prohibited by the First Amendment from barring the *Herald-News* from punishing Stoddard for his support of the union.

While the First Amendment rights of the *Herald-News* management did not include the right to halt a column as punishment for union support, the appeals court ruled that the *Herald-News* did not necessarily have to renew publication of Stoddard's column. The court said the First Amendment prevented the NLRB from requiring the newspaper to publish anything, including Stoddard's column. Therefore, the court remanded the case to the NLRB to pick a remedy other than reinstatement of Stoddard's column. Stoddard settled with the newspaper for a "substantial sum."

Collective Bargaining

Section 8(d) of the Taft-Hartley Act requires companies and unions "to meet at reasonable times and confer in good faith with respect to wages, hours, and other terms and conditions of employment." This means that both parties are supposed to enter

[87]Land o' Frost, 252 N.L.R.B. 1 (1980); Han-Dee Pak, Inc., 232 N.L.R.B. 454 (1977); Midland Nat'l Life Ins. Co., 263 N.L.R.B. 127 (1982); Shopping Kart Food Market, Inc., 228 N.L.R.B. 1311 (1977).

[88]29 U.S.C.A. sec. 158(a) (3) (1973).

[89]Passaic Daily News v. NLRB, 736 F.2d 1543, 10 Media L. Rep. 1905 (D.C. Cir. 1984).

[90]301 U.S. 103 (1937). *See also* "Ex-columnist Wins Settlement Suit against N.J. Daily," *Editor & Publisher,* May 2, 1987, at 144.

contract negotiations with open minds and with a willingness to reach an agreement. If management is unwilling to meet or is unreasonably firm in its offers, labor may file an unfair labor practice charge with the NLRB. Employers fail to bargain in good faith if they take an unyielding attitude on major issues, circumvent the union by dealing directly with employees, or engage in take-it-or-leave-it bargaining, sometimes called *Boulwarism.* Boulwarism takes its name from Lemuel R. Boulware, for many years personnel director at General Electric. Boulware was known for intransigence at the bargaining table coupled with intensive company communications to employees.[91]

A company bargaining in good faith may not bypass the union in an attempt to undermine it, but a company may communicate directly to employees during negotiations to inform them of the status of bargaining.[92] The U.S. Court of Appeals for the Second Circuit upheld an NLRB ruling that General Electric engaged in an unfair labor practice when it took an inflexible position directly to union members, bypassing the International Union of Electrical, Radio and Machine Workers (IUE).[93]

The NLRB hearing examiner, looking at the *totality of conduct,* concluded that General Electric engaged in unfair practices not only by its intransigence, but also because it skirted the union through a broad publicity campaign directed to company employees. By ignoring the union, the company showed it had no intent to bargain in good faith.

A union or company can, if it wants to, appeal directly to the public. During one round of labor negotiations, the United Automobile Workers bought television ads to tell the American public it was struggling with the auto companies to keep American jobs at home.[94]

Strikes

Unions may picket, demonstrate, distribute handbills, buy editorial advertisements, and engage in other forms of expression after a union is formed. Labor and management also may exercise economic power: unions can strike; management can lock strikers out of a plant. The right to strike, though, is established by labor law. It is not a First Amendment right based on the right of speech and association.

The right to picket includes the right to go on private property, although the Supreme Court ruled that this right is not required by the First Amendment.[95] Picketing on private property is governed by the Labor Management Relations Act. The NLRB said it is not sufficient for management to permit picketing only on the edges of a private shopping center where picketing may be ineffective and dangerous. The NLRB said it is reasonable for picketers to demonstrate in front of a store in the middle of a shopping center where strikers may encounter employees and customers of a store at which workers are on strike.[96]

---

[91]*See* H. Northrup, *Boulwarism* (1964).
[92]Safeway Trails Inc., 233 N.L.R.B. 1078 (1977).
[93]NLRB v. General Electric Co., 418 F.2d 736 (2d Cir. 1969).
[94]"Auto Workers Union Airs TV Commercials," *New York Times,* Aug. 28, 1984, at A16.
[95]Hudgens v. NLRB, 424 U.S. 507 (1976).
[96]*Id.;* Scott Hudgens, 230 N.L.R.B. 414 (1977).

Strikers and picketers may also urge the public not to patronize a business. The Supreme Court has ruled that federal labor law permits a union to distribute handbills urging the public not to patronize a shopping mall. In *DeBartolo Corp. v. Florida Gulf Coast Building and Construction Trades Council,*[97] the Court ruled 6–2 that peaceful handbilling is not illegally coercive even if the purpose of the handbills is to pressure merchants to oppose construction by nonunion workers. The Court noted that the union engaged in no violence, picketing, or patrolling that might be coercive. The union was only trying to persuade customers not to shop in the mall. Handbills, unlike coercive picketing, the Court said, depend entirely for their effectiveness on the persuasive force of the ideas they convey.

Because the Court decided the case by interpreting the labor statute, the Court issued no First Amendment ruling. But the Court noted that a union handbill revealing a labor dispute and urging shoppers to buy elsewhere is political speech protected by the First Amendment.

SUMMARY

Corporations and unions have rights of free expression during the organization of a union, collective bargaining, and strikes. However, corporate and union expression is not protected if it is coercive.

SECURITIES TRANSACTIONS

Corporations not only have the right to speak; they may also be required to speak or publish. A number of laws require banks, insurance companies, and other businesses to disclose to the public the details of their financial offerings and the financial strength of their institutions.

Probably the most far-reaching corporate disclosure laws are the securities acts passed during the Roosevelt administration. The securities acts were passed in the 1930s to eliminate abuses that contributed to the stock market crash of 1929. Under the laws, corporations whose stock is publicly traded must disclose financial information to the government, shareholders, and the public when they register and trade securities.

For public relations practitioners, federal and state disclosure requirements mean jobs writing periodic reports and press releases, preparing for annual stockholders' meetings, and advising corporate executives about their disclosure responsibilities. For business journalists, corporate filings with the Securities and Exchange Commission have been said to comprise "the single most intensive research tool" for learning about the operations of American companies.[98] The fundamental purpose of the federal statutes, the Supreme Court said, "was to substitute a philos-

---

[97]108 S. Ct. 1392 (1988).
[98]D. Kirsch, *Financial and Economic Journalism* 241 (1978).

ophy of full disclosure for the philosophy of *caveat emptor* and thus to achieve a high standard of business ethics in the securities industry."[99]

One of the most important securities reforms passed during the New Deal was the Securities Act of 1933. The Securities Act regulates the initial offering and sale of securities.[100] A year later Congress enacted the Securities Exchange Act of 1934, which regulates the trading of securities on stock exchanges after they have been offered.[101] Other measures enacted during the Roosevelt administration to protect investors include the Investment Advisors Act of 1940, which regulates some financial publications.[102]

The securities acts are administered by the Securities and Exchange Commission, created in 1934. The SEC is an independent, bipartisan, quasi-judicial agency like the Federal Trade Commission. The SEC has five members, not more than three of whom can belong to the same political party. They are appointed by the president for five-year staggered terms.

Corporations whose shares are bought and sold on the stock exchanges are mandated by the securities statutes periodically to disclose financial information to the investing public. Even if disclosure is not mandated by statute, a corporation has a duty to disclose information without which investors would be defrauded.

Mandated Disclosure

The Securities Act of 1933 and the Exchange Act of 1934 mandate corporate disclosure to the SEC in connection with the registration and trading of securities.

Registering Securities   The 1933 Securities Act was passed to provide investors the information they need to make intelligent decisions when purchasing new stock offerings. To achieve this goal, Section 5(c) of the Securities Act prohibits a company from "going public" by offering its stock for sale before it has filed a registration statement with the SEC containing extensive financial information about the company.[103] A company whose shares are already traded on an exchange must file registration statements if a new stock offering is made. After a company files a registration statement with the SEC, there is a waiting period during which a company cannot advertise or offer to sell the securities the company hopes investors eventually will buy.

The brief waiting period allows investors "to become acquainted with the information contained in the registration statement and to arrive at an unhurried decision concerning the merits of the securities." After the brief waiting period, a company may advertise the shares for sale.

While a company is waiting to offer shares of stock to the public, it may issue press releases, advertise its products, and continue its other usual communications.

---

[99]SEC v. Capital Gains Research Bureau, Inc., 375 U.S. 180, 186 (1963).

[100]48 Stat. 74, 15 U.S.C.A. sec. 77a *et seq.* (1981).

[101]48 Stat. 881, 15 U.S.C.A. sec. 77b *et seq.* (1981).

[102]54 Stat. 847, 15 U.S.C.A. sec. 80b-1 *et seq.* (1981). *See also* Public Utility Holding Company Act of 1935, 49 Stat. 803, 15 U.S.C.A. sec. 80a-1 *et seq.;* Trust Indenture Act of 1939, 53 Stat. 1149, 15 U.S.C.A. sec. 77 *et seq.*, and Investment Company Act of 1940, 54 Stat. 789, 15 U.S.C.A. sec. 80a-1 *et seq.*

[103]Securities and Exchange Commission v. Arvida Corp., 169 F. Supp. 211 (S.D.N.Y. 1958).

However, the company may not seek purchasers of its new shares of stock until the SEC declares its registration "effective."

In a famous case, the Arvida Corporation violated Section 5(c) of the Securities Act by inviting investors to purchase Arvida stock before a registration statement had been completed.[104] Arvida was formed by the industrialist Arthur Vining Davis when he transferred much of his extensive Florida real estate holdings to the corporation. Davis planned to raise additional capital through an offering of stock to the public. When the financing proposal reached final form, but before registration was filed with the SEC, a press release was issued on the letterhead of Loeb, Rhoades & Co., a New York brokerage.

The Loeb, Rhoades press release said Arvida would have assets of more than $100 million. The release also said that Davis would transfer to Arvida more than 100,000 acres near the Florida "Gold Coast" for development. To help ensure wide dissemination of the press release in the most prestigious papers, the public relations counsel for Loeb, Rhoades invited reporters from the *New York Times,* the *New York Herald-Tribune,* and the *Wall Street Journal* to its offices in time to meet the papers' deadlines. A company official told the reporters that the stock would sell for about $10 a share but declined to answer questions about debt on the property, capitalization of Arvida, the company's balance sheet, or control of the corporation. The substance of the press release appeared in the three New York newspapers and numerous other news media throughout the country.

The SEC charged the release violated Section 5 because it, along with earlier publicity, was calculated "to set in motion the processes of distribution" before registration "by arousing and stimulating investor and dealer interest in Arvida securities."[105] To the SEC, the "arresting references" in the press release to assets in excess of $100 million and to over 100,000 acres on the Florida Gold Coast were part of an illegal selling effort. Indeed, an SEC survey found that within two business days the publicity had resulted in investor interest worth at least $500,000.

The SEC rejected Loeb, Rhoades's contention that the release and publicity about Arvida were legal because they were legitimate news. Section 5(c), the SEC said, "is equally applicable" whether or not "astute public relations activities" make an illegal stock offering appear to have news value. Indeed, the SEC reasoned, "the danger to investors from publicity amounting to a selling effort may be greater in cases where an issue has 'news value' since it may be easier to whip up a speculative frenzy' . . . by incomplete or misleading publicity" and thus aid distribution of an unsound security at inflated prices. This, the SEC concluded, "is precisely the evil which the Securities Act seeks to prevent."[106] The SEC did not want to dam up the normal flow of information, but, the SEC said, the company and its underwriters cannot be part of a publicity campaign that constitutes an offer to sell or solicitation of an offer to buy before registration of a security.

When Arvida's final prospectus was made public, the SEC found support for its decision to enforce the congressionally mandated disclosure system. While the press

---

[104]*Id.* at 213–14.
[105]*In re* Carl M. Loeb, Rhoades & Co., 38 S.E.C. 843, 851 (1959).
[106]*Id.* at 852–53.

release had stressed the great acreage owned by Arvida, the final prospectus describing the stock revealed that the bulk of the land was not usable in its present condition and was located in areas remote from existing development. The final prospectus also revealed significant debt, indicating that the bulk of the money raised through the stock offering might be used to retire the debt rather than to develop the land. The fuller truth disclosed in the final prospectus proved to the SEC's satisfaction the superiority of the mandated disclosure system over investment decisions "brought about by press releases."

The *Arvida* case raised no First Amendment issues, but the SEC noted that Section 5(c) of the 1933 Act "in no way restricts the freedom of news media to seek out and publish financial news." The 5(c) prohibition does not violate the First Amendment rights of underwriters because they are in the business of distributing securities, not news, the SEC said. The restrictions of Section 5(c) do not apply to reporters, who presumably "have no securities to sell."

Trading Securities   While the Securities Act of 1933 is concerned primarily with financial disclosure before a security is first offered for sale, the Securities Exchange Act of 1934 is principally concerned with the trading of securities from one purchaser to another after distribution on the nation's stock exchanges. Under Section 13 of the 1934 Act, large publicly traded corporations are required to file annual, quarterly, and other reports with the SEC about the company's operations.[107] Other sections of the act regulate the solicitation of proxies and tender offers.[108] Proxy statements announce annual and special shareholder meetings. Tender offers are offers to buy shares of another company.

Annual and Quarterly Reports   Annual reports, which must be sent to shareholders and filed for public inspection with the SEC, are one of the most effective mediums through which information is disseminated to the investment community. Corporate reports contain information about management, market information, net sales, earnings, dividends, and other information about the financial condition of the company. The annual report also contains the Management Discussion and Analysis that describes in detail the capital resources, results of company operations, and projected future performance. If a projection turns out to be wrong, a businessperson may be protected from a fraud suit if the projection (1) was prepared with a reasonable basis and (2) was disclosed in good faith.[109]

Much of the information in an annual report is updated in required quarterly reports. Between quarterly reports, publicly traded corporations are mandated to report only a few significant developments to the SEC on form 8-K, or the Interim Report. Companies are required to report changes in control of the company, the buying or selling of significant assets, filing for bankruptcy or receivership, changes in the company's certified public accountants, and the resignation of directors. The law does not require disclosure between quarterly reports of changes in earnings and

---

[107]48 Stat. 881, sec. 13, 15 U.S.C.A. sec. 78 (1981); 17 C.F.R. sec. 240.13a-1, 13a-10, 13a-11 (1985).
[108]48 Stat. 881, sec. 14 *as amended,* 15 U.S.C.A. sec. 78 (1981); 17 C.F.R. sec. 240.14a-1 *et seq.* (1989).
[109]SEC Release No. 33-6084 [1979 Transfer Binder], Fed. Sec. L. Rep.(CCH) para. 82,117.

dividends, a significant new product or discovery, a lawsuit against the company, or other developments that might be of significance to investors.

In any case, information that must be disclosed in the interim report may not be useful by the time the investor receives it. A company has 15 days from the time of the major development to file form 8-K with the SEC.[110] The SEC says a corporation may, "at its option," report other important occurrences, but the law does not require the company to do so unless disclosure is necessary to avoid fraud.

The stock exchanges require the timely disclosure of a much broader range of information than must be disclosed under securities law.[111] But the exchanges do not have the SEC's enforcement powers and are reluctant to use the powers they have.[112] The exchanges may halt trading or "delist" a corporation that violates the disclosure guidelines. But exchanges competing to get corporate listings are reluctant to employ such severe penalties. Even though the enforcement powers of the exchanges are weak, corporations frequently find it serves their interests to disseminate more information about current developments than the law requires.

Proxies and Annual Meetings   Besides reporting regularly in quarterly and annual reports, publicly traded companies must tell shareholders in proxy statements when and where the shareholder meetings will be held and what business will be conducted.[113] Shareholders who will not attend can vote by proxy on various proposals, including management changes and proposals submitted by shareholders. When shareholders vote by proxy, they give their proxy holder, often a committee designated by management, the authority to vote their shares as they instruct on their proxy statement. Through "proxy fights," dissident directors or minority stockholders may "solicit" shareholders to vote their proxies against management. Through proxy fights, dissident shareholders can sometimes vote management out of office, thus gaining control of a company without buying a majority of shares.[114] Under securities law, neither corporations nor dissident stockholders may issue false or misleading statements to shareholders in an effort to sway their votes.

False or misleading proxy solicitations may be halted whether they are targeted directly at shareholders or are communicated more indirectly through speeches, press releases, and television scripts of more general public interest. The U.S. Court of Appeals for the Second Circuit ruled that even a newspaper advertisement placed by a citizens group might be halted if it contained false statements published in an attempt to influence shareholders in a proxy fight.[115]

The case involved a newspaper advertisement purchased by a citizens group opposed to the Long Island Lighting Company, known as LILCO. The ad accused LILCO of mismanagement and of attempting to saddle ratepayers with needless costs of constructing the controversial Shoreham Nuclear Power Plant. The ad urged that LILCO, a private company, be managed by a public authority. The ad was purchased

---

[110]*See* Form 8-K, 42 Fed. Reg. 4429 (1977).
[111]*E.g., American Stock Exchange Disclosure Policies* secs. 401 and 403 (1983).
[112]*See* Dayan, "Correcting Errors in the Press," 5 *Rev. Sec. Reg.* 941, 944 (1972).
[113]48 Stat. 881, sec. 14, *as amended,* 15 U.S.C.A. sec. 78 (1981), 17 C.F.R. sec. 240.14a-1 *et seq.* (1989).
[114]*See* Lewin, "Proxy Battles Proliferating," *New York Times,* April 19, 1983 at 2.
[115]Long Island Lighting Co. v. Barbash, 779 F.2d 793 (2d Cir. 1985).

by a citizens group associated with dissident stockholders who hoped to oust LILCO management in a proxy fight.

LILCO tried to halt the advertisement, claiming it contained false statements attempting to sway LILCO shareholders to vote against management. But a federal district court ruled that the newspaper ad purchased by a citizens group was constitutionally protected expression. The proxy solicitation rules are not applicable "to an advertisement purchased in connection with a serious public debate having important political implications," the court said.[116] However, the U.S. Court of Appeals for the Second Circuit reversed the lower court. The appeals court avoided the First Amendment issue, noting that "[t]he SEC's authority to regulate proxy solicitations has traditionally extended into matters of public interest." The appeals court remanded the case, asking the lower court to determine whether the ad in a general circulation newspaper solicited shareholders' votes.

Tender Offers   Corporate takeovers may be attempted through proxy fights at a company's annual meeting. More often, however, one company makes an offer to stockholders of another to tender their shares for a certain price, usually well above the current market price of a stock. Congress requires that takeover bidders disclose information about themselves to shareholders of the target company. The securities law requires that anyone who rapidly acquires more than five percent of another company file with the SEC, the target company, and the exchange where the target's stock is traded a statement describing the buyer's "background and identity," the source and amount of funds to be used in buying shares, the extent of the buyer's holdings in the target corporation, and the buyer's plans for the target corporation's business or corporate structure.[117]

SUMMARY

The securities laws require stock companies to disclose financial information before shares are offered and while they are being traded. Mandated disclosure includes prospectuses before a stock is offered for sale and periodic reports after trading begins. While companies must disclose a few significant events if they occur between annual reports, corporations may withhold much information if it is not done to conceal fraud. Rules regulating communications to shareholders have been held to extend to political advertisements that might affect shareholders' votes.

Fraud

Corporations that knowingly make false or misleading statements in their annual reports, proxy statements, and other communications mandated by the securities acts

---

[116]Long Island Lighting Co. v. Barbash, 625 F. Supp. 221 (E.D.N.Y. 1985).
[117]17 U.S.C.A. sec. 78m(d) (1981). *See also* Piper v. Chris-Craft Industries, Inc., 430 U.S. 1, 26–37 (1977).

commit fraud. It is also fraudulent for corporate executives to knowingly make false statements in voluntary speeches and press releases if the statements would affect the price of the company's stock.

Most fraud litigation is brought under section 10(b) of the 1934 Act and Rule 10b-5 of the Code of Federal Regulations. Section 10(b) makes it unlawful for a corporation or its agent to be manipulative or deceptive in connection with the purchase or sale of securities. Under Rule 10b-5, it is manipulative or deceptive for a company to make a deliberately misleading material statement. It is also fraudulent for a company to fail to clarify a statement that is necessary to avoid misleading investors. Investors may sue to enjoin deception and to recover money lost because of reliance on deceptive statements.

Materially Deceptive Facts   In order for a statement to be fraudulent, it must involve a material fact. Material facts are facts important to the decision of a reasonable investor to buy, sell, or hold a security. A fact is material in a proxy statement, the Supreme Court said, "if there is a substantial likelihood that a reasonable shareholder would consider it important in deciding how to vote." To be material, it is not necessary that a fact would necessarily change an investor's decision to buy or sell. A fact is material if it would be significant to reasonable shareholders in the "total mix" of their information.[118] Material facts include a sharp change in company earnings, the imminence of a very profitable transaction, and information about a possible merger or bankruptcy.[119]

The U.S. Supreme Court ruled that information about corporate mergers may become material before discussions result in an agreement between negotiating corporations to merge. Once merger discussions become material, companies cannot falsely deny negotiations without committing fraud. In *Basic, Inc. v. Levinson,*[120] the Court applied a probability/magnitude test. The Court said merger negotiations become material either when they are so advanced as to make a merger very probable or at an earlier point in the discussions if the magnitude of the merger would dramatically alter the company.

Misstatements   Materially deceptive facts can be positive misstatements or omissions. It was a material misstatement for the director of the Livingston Oil Company to overstate the corporation's income during a speech to securities analysts. The speech was later distributed to shareholders to encourage more sales of stock.[121] It was also materially misleading for the Baldwin-United Corporation, the troubled piano manufacturer and financial conglomerate, to issue optimistic letters to shareholders and to respond to a negative article in *Forbes* magazine with a document saying, "Baldwin is in its strongest financial position ever."[122] These statements were

---

[118]TSC Industries, Inc. v. Northway, Inc., 426 U.S. 438, 449 (1976).
[119]Dirks v. SEC, 463 U.S. 646 (1983); Northern Trust Co. v. Essaness Theatres Corp., 103 F. Supp. 954 (N.D. Ill. 1952); *In re* Ward La France Truck Corp., 13 S.E.C. 373 (1943).
[120]108 S. Ct. 978 (1988).
[121]Sprayregen v. Livingston Oil Co., 295 F. Supp. 1376 (S.D.N.Y. 1968).
[122]Stoller v. Baldwin-United Corp., 41 Bankruptcy 884 (S.D.Ohio 1985).

misleading because they were not true and the executives making the statements knew they were not true.

Public relations firms cannot avoid liability for fraud if they blindly pass along misleading investment information for their corporate clients. In 1972, a federal judge in Illinois told a corporate financial relations firm it could rely on corporate clients' representations only if the PR firm also made a "reasonable investigation" to satisfy itself that the statements were true.[123] In 1984, the SEC reiterated the financial public relations firm's responsibility not to disseminate corporate information it knows or has reason to know is false.[124]

Omissions More common than misstatements of material facts are deceptive half-truths or omissions. The Electric Autolite Company misled shareholders when it disclosed a proposed merger but failed to tell them in proxy statements that the Autolite board of directors, which recommended a merger with the Mergenthaler Linotype Company, was already under the control of Mergenthaler.[125]

In April 1964, the Texas Gulf Sulphur Company issued a materially deceptive press release when the company dampened rumors of a major copper discovery. In its press release, TGS said press reports of the company's substantial copper discovery in Timmins, Ontario, were exaggerated. The release said public estimates about the size and grade of ore were "without factual basis and have evidently originated by speculation of people not connected with TGS."[126] On the basis of this negative release, several investors sold shares in the company, only to learn from a Texas Gulf Sulphur press release 12 days later that the company had made a 10-million-ton ore strike, one of the largest in history.

In court, Texas Gulf Sulphur said it would have been premature and possibly misleading for the company in its first release to speculate on the size and grade of ore at the mining site. The company had not yet had the ore samples analyzed chemically. But a federal appeals court ruled that the known richness of the ore samples even before chemical analysis was material and did not justify a press release as negative as the company first issued. As evidence that the ore samples were material to investors' decisions even before the samples were chemically analyzed, the court noted that several Texas Gulf Sulphur executives bought additional shares of the company before the ore strike was announced.

The U.S. Court of Appeals for the Second Circuit said the TGS press release misleadingly suggested there was no basis for investor optimism when there was. The court did not require a company to issue a press release to quell rumors, but the Second Circuit said that material facts should be complete and accurate once a company issues a public statement. Instead of saying speculation about a major ore find was without factual basis, Texas Gulf Sulphur should have said nothing, should have told how promising the ore samples were by visual inspection, or should have said the situation was in flux.

How much to reveal, if anything, during searches for raw materials, merger ne-

---

[123]SEC v. Pig 'N' Whistle Corp. [1971–72 Transfer Binder], Fed. Sec. L. Rep. (CCH) para. 93,384 (N.D. Ill. 1972).
[124]Howard Bronson & Co., SEC Release, July 12, 1984, in 16 Sec. Reg. & L. Rep. (BNA) 1207 (July 20, 1984).
[125]Mills v. Electric Autolite Co., 403 F.2d 429, 434 (7th Cir. 1968).
[126]SEC v. Texas Gulf Sulphur Co., 401 F.2d 833, 845 (1968).

gotiations, land acquisitions, and other delicate periods may be a difficult corporate decision. Silence may be difficult to maintain when a company would like to be forthcoming and securities analysts and the media are clamoring for information. Nevertheless, silence may sometimes be the best policy to keep negotiations on track and to avoid charges of fraud for partial revelations.

Sometimes statements may be misleading because of the format of presentation. The American-Hawaiian Steamship Co. was held to have issued a deceptive proxy statement because the company obscured the truth by scattering material facts through a lengthy document.[127] Use of unnecessarily technical terminology also may be misleading. However, the SEC encourages some businesses, including oil companies, to use technical terms familiar to experienced investors where precision is necessary to avoid deception.

Sometimes a company's use of obfuscating technical terms may be misleading. But a company's use of a technical term is not deceptive simply because investors may not be familiar with it. The Sable Company was ruled not to be deceptive when it issued a press release announcing the company was filing a new "investigational" application with the Food and Drug Administration to develop soft contact lenses. Investigational applications are filed when significant product development is necessary before marketing. The company did not say in its release that it usually takes several years before the government approves an investigational product for the market. Investors unfamiliar with the lengthy approval process for investigational applications were disappointed that the company's technology would not lead to higher earnings and stock prices for several years. One investor sued Sable for issuing misleading information. However, a federal district court said that an investor could not use his ignorance to hold Sable liable for a misleading statement. "Where the public can make the evaluation as to how beneficial a certain corporate action will be to the earning picture of that corporation, the omission of information about the decision-making process of a government agency is not a violation of rule 10b-5," the court said. Indeed, the court said the company probably would have misled investors if it had tried to announce a time at which the FDA would approve the lenses for marketing.[128]

Failure to Disclose Payment for Publicity   Another fraud prohibited by securities law is failure of publishers and public relations practitioners to disclose payments for corporate publicity. Such failure can violate Rule 10b-5 or section 17(b) of the Securities Act. Section 17(b) makes it illegal to "publish, give publicity to, or circulate any notice, circular, advertisement, newspaper, article, letter, investment service, or communication about a security without revealing payments received."[129] The purpose of the section is to halt articles in newspapers or periodicals that appear to be unbiased opinion about a company but which in fact are purchased.[130]

Stock Market Magazine was charged with fraud for failing to reveal advertising

---

[127]Gould v. American-Hawaiian Steamship Co., 535 F.2d 761, 774 (3d. Cir. 1976).

[128]Zucker v. Sable, 425 F. Supp. 658 (S.D.N.Y. 1976).

[129]15 U.S.C.A. sec. 77q(b) (1981).

[130]Committee on Interstate and Foreign Commerce. H.R. Rep. No. 85, 73d Cong., 1st Sess. 24 (1933), *cited in,* United States v. Amick, 439 F.2d 351, 365, n.18, *cert. denied,* 404 U.S. 823 (1971).

and reprints sold to companies in return for features in the publication.[131] The U.S. Court of Appeals for the District of Columbia sent the case to a federal district court for a determination whether the magazine, which offers financial news to some 12,000 subscribers, was publishing the articles in exchange for corporate purchases of advertising and reprints. If so, the magazine could be required to disclose these payments. The magazine contended there was no *quid pro quo* that needed to be revealed under the securities laws.

The Court of Appeals told the district court that the fraud investigation into advertising and reprint sales could not constitutionally include inquiry into the origin of articles published in *Stock Market Magazine.* The Securities and Exchange Commission had argued that the magazine should be required to reveal not only that it sold advertising and reprints, but also that featured companies sometimes wrote the articles, paid public relations firms to write them, or paid editors of the *Stock Market Magazine* to write them. The SEC charged that the free articles, which *Stock Market Magazine* published "substantially" as received, also constituted payment that must be disclosed under securities law.

But the appeals court said the First Amendment prohibits inquiry into who pays a writer or how much of an outside article is published. Such inquiry, the court said, would impermissibly interfere with editorial judgments about constitutionally protected content. The First Amendment protects the publisher's right to determine who writes and edits published material, the court said. Content is protected if the writer is paid by a publisher, a public relations firm, or a featured company. A magazine might be required to disclose that it received payments or sold advertising and reprints as a condition for publishing an article, but the First Amendment bars requiring a magazine to disclose who wrote which parts of a business article, the court said.

Public relations practitioners are also supposed to disclose payment from companies they promote. The SEC warned public relations firms in 1984 that they violate the Securities Act if they do not reveal payment for preparation and dissemination of material designed to make a new stock offering look like an attractive investment.[132]

In Connection with a Purchase or Sale Under rule 10b-5, not only must fraudulent statements be material, they must be "in connection with the purchase or sale of any security." The in-connection-with test is met if a corporation issues a materially false or misleading statement on which other investors rely for their purchases or sales. But reliance by investors may be presumed when a company makes materially false or misleading statements. In the *Texas Gulf Sulphur* case, the Second Circuit Court of Appeals said the in-connection-with test was met when Texas Gulf Sulphur issued a misleading statement "reasonably calculated to influence the investing public."[133]

Courts have ruled the in-connection-with test is also met when materially false statements are made in corporate annual reports,[134] product promotions,[135] speeches

---

[131]SEC v. Wall St. Publishing Inst., 851 F.2d 365 (D.C. Cir. 1988), *cert. denied,* 109 S. Ct. 1342 (1989).

[132]Howard Bronson & Co., SEC Release, July 12, 1984, in 16 Sec. Reg. & L. Rep. (BNA) 1207 (July 20, 1984). *See also* SEC v. Pig 'N' Whistle Corp. [1971–1972 Transfer Binder], Fed. Sec. L. Rep.(CCH) para. 93,384 (N.D. Ill. 1972).

[133]Securities and Exchange Commission v. Texas Gulf Sulphur Co., 401 F.2d 833, 862 (1968).

[134]Heit v. Weitzen, 402 F.2d 909 (2d Cir. 1968).

[135]SEC v. Electrogen Indus., Inc. [1967–69 Decisions], Fed. Sec. L. Rep. (CCH) para. 92,156 (E.D.N.Y. 1968).

by corporate directors to securities analysts,[136] and advertisements.[137] In each case, investors may rely on the statements when buying or selling securities. The SEC has also warned companies that statements made during rate-filing hearings, labor negotiations, and in other public circumstances must be factual because they, too, can be heard and relied upon by investors.[138]

The in-connection-with requirement is also met if a corporation engages in insider trading. Corporations engage in insider trading when they or their executives buy or sell stock based on material information that is not yet public. Insider trading is ruled to be fraud because it is unfair.

Duty to Correct Statements Attributed to the Company   A publicly traded corporation has an affirmative duty to correct a published material misstatement if the error originates with the corporation or its agent. In *Green v. Jonhop,*[139] a federal court said a corporation had an obligation to correct falsely optimistic earnings projections made by an underwriter who marketed the company's securities. Corporate silence in the face of falsely optimistic earnings projections, the court said, could fraudulently encourage investors to rely on the underwriter's statements.

A corporation will also have a responsibility to correct misstatements if the company approves or helps draft reports by stock analysts or public relations firms containing material misinformation. The U.S. Court of Appeals for the Second Circuit noted that prepublication review by a corporation of outside analysts' reports of the company is "a risky activity, fraught with danger" because corporate officials, by their participation, make "an implied representation that the information they have reviewed is true or at least in accordance with the company's views."[140]

A corporation may also have a duty to correct its own statements if changing conditions transform accurate statements into misleading statements. A U.S. district court suggested the A.H. Robins Company had a duty to update statements in its stockholder annual reports that the company's Dalkon Shield contraceptive was safer and more effective than other similar devices on the market. A study published after Robins's first reports indicated that the contraceptive was not as safe or effective as Robins first indicated.[141] A court also ruled that the Shattuck Denn Mining Corporation had an obligation to tell investors that a previously announced merger deal had fallen through. Without the update, investors could buy Shattuck's stock with the mistaken belief that the merger would increase profits.[142]

A corporation generally has no duty to respond to market gossip and rumors not attributable to the company.[143] In the *Texas Gulf Sulphur* case, the court said the

---

[136]Sprayregen v. Livingston Oil Co., 295 F. Supp. 1376 (S.D.N.Y. 1968).

[137]*See* Feuerstein, "The Corporation's Obligations of Disclosure under the Federal Securities Laws When It Is Not Trading Its Stock," 15 *N. Y. L. Forum* 385, 393 (1969).

[138]SEC Release No. 34-20560, 49 Fed. Reg. 2468 (Jan. 20, 1984); 17 C.F.R. sec. 241.20560 (1989).

[139]358 F. Supp. 413 (D.Ore. 1973).

[140]Elkind v. Liggett & Myers, Inc., 635 F.2d 156, 163 (2d Cir. 1980).

[141]Ross v. A.H. Robins Co, Inc., 465 F. Supp. 904 (S.D.N.Y. 1979), *rev'd.*, 607 F.2d 545 (2d Cir. 1979), *cert. denied,* 446 U.S. 946, *reh'g denied,* 448 U.S. 911, *on remand,* 100 F.R.D. 5 (1982).

[142]SEC v. Shattuck Denn Mining Corp., 297 F. Supp. 470 (S.D.N.Y. 1968). *See also* Financial Industrial Fund, Inc. v. McDonnell Douglas Corp., 474 F.2d 514 (10th Cir.) (*per curiam*) (*en banc*), *cert. denied,* 414 U.S. 874 (1973).

[143]*See* Sheffey, "Securities Law Responsibilities of Issuers to Respond to Rumors and Other Publicity: Reexamination of a Continuing Problem," 57 *Notre Dame Law.* 755 (1982).

company did not have to respond to speculation about the company's ore discovery because the speculation did not originate with the company. Texas Gulf Sulphur statements were fraudulent because the company responded to rumors in a less than complete statement on its own initiative.

Similarly, a corporation has no duty to respond to an inaccurate interpretive article that is not attributable to the company. The U.S. Court of Appeals for the Second Circuit ruled that the International Controls Corporation had no duty to respond to Dan Dorfman's report in the *Wall Street Journal* about ICC's plan to buy the Electronic Specialty Co. The speculation about the plan turned out to be true, but the price per share Dorfman quoted was considerably higher than ICC was offering. ICC had no duty to respond because the company was not the source of the speculation.[144]

Even if an inaccurate news article is attributed to a company, a corporation probably has no duty to correct the article if information the company provided was accurate. In *Zucker v. Sable,* a federal district court said it would be unreasonable to require a company "to examine every financial publication to ascertain whether the reports of its admittedly accurate press release have been misinterpreted so as to mislead members of the public."[145] In *Zucker,* the newspapers had published misleading stories about the Sable company by omitting the word *investigational,* which had been included in Sable's press release. Sable had filed an investigational application with the Food and Drug Administration for development of plastic lenses. The word *investigational* was a critical omission in the news reports because investigational applications, which indicate time-consuming product research is not complete, can take many years for FDA approval.

Duty to Disclose Insider Trading   Besides a duty to correct its own false or misleading statements, a corporation and its "insiders" also have a duty to disclose material information when they plan to base purchases or sales of company stock on nonpublic information. This duty to disclose to avoid fraud arises from executives' financial responsibility to shareholders and the markets. Publishers of personal investment advisories and some financial journalists may also have a duty to disclose nonpublic information they intend to profit from.

Insiders   The law assumes, although not all legal scholars agree, that it is unfair for insiders to buy and sell a company's stock for their own benefit if they base their decision upon nonpublic material facts. Rule 10b-5 imposes a duty on insiders in this situation either to disclose the information or refrain from trading.[146]

A variation of illegal insider trading is tipping. Tipping is the practice of passing nonpublic material information to friends or brokers so that they can trade. The "tipper" may be liable for fraud along with the "tippee." The *Texas Gulf Sulphur* case is a well-known example of insider trading and tipping. In *Texas Gulf Sulphur,* the federal appeals court found that executives of the mining company violated insider trad-

---

[144]Electronic Specialty Co. v. International Controls Corp., 409 F.2d 937, 949 (2d Cir. 1969). *See also* Greenfield v. Heublein, Inc., 742 F.2d 751 (3d Cir. 1984).

[145]426 F. Supp. 658, 663 (1976). *See also* Mills v. Sarjem Corp., 133 F. Supp. 753 (D.N.J. 1955).

[146]*See* SEC v. Texas Gulf Sulphur Co., 401 F.2d 833 (2d Cir. 1968), *cert. denied sub nom.* Coates v. SEC, 394 U.S. 976 (1969). *But see* H. Manne, *Insider Trading and the Stock Market (1966).*

ing prohibitions by buying stock in the company and also by tipping friends when the insiders learned ahead of the public of the very promising copper ore samples taken at a site in Timmins, Ontario. In ruling that the insiders' stock purchases were illegal, the court said the investing public should have the same access to material corporate information as a corporate insider. Under legislation passed since *TGS* was decided, inside traders may have to repay three times their illegal profits.

Securities statutes do not define *insider* and congressional attempts to define it have failed. But the Supreme Court, agreeing with the SEC, has defined an insider as one who, by virtue of his or her position with the issuer of stock, has access to non-public corporate information that is supposed to be used only for corporate purposes, not for personal benefit.[147] This definition covers corporate officers, directors, controlling stockholders, and corporate public relations executives.

These officers have a duty to disclose material information before trading because of the fiduciary nature of their position. Fiduciaries are people who have a position of trust that prohibits them from acting only in their own self-interest. In the corporate context, the executive is entrusted by the shareholder to manage the shareholder's assets and therefore is supposed to act in the shareholder's interest. To avoid a conflict of interest, an executive must disclose material nonpublic corporate information before selling or buying company stock.[148]

Certain outsiders may acquire the duties of insiders if they "have entered into a special confidential relationship in the conduct of the business of the enterprise and are given access to information solely for corporate purposes."[149] These temporary (or quasi-) insiders include accountants, lawyers, and public relations counsel who have access to nonpublic material information that is intended only for corporate use. These quasi-insiders, like permanent insiders, are supposed to make true and accurate statements about material aspects of a company and are supposed to abstain from trading if they have not disclosed the material information on which trades might be based.

In an effort to curb the increasing number of Wall Street scandals, Congress passed legislation in 1988 that increased penalties, extended liability, and encouraged revelation of insider trading. Under the Insider Trading and Securities Fraud Enforcement Act of 1988, not only are illegal traders and tippers liable, but also those brokers, investment advisers, and other supervisors who fail to take appropriate steps to prevent illegal trading.[150] The act also increases criminal penalties and allows the Securities and Exchange Commission to pay persons who provide information concerning insider trading.

Investment Advisers Several hundred financial newsletters are published in the United States. Until 1985, virtually any financial newsletter from which subscribers

---

[147]Dirks v. SEC, 463 U.S. 646, 653 (1983), *citing,* Chiarella v. United States, 445 U.S. 222, 227 (1980), and *In re* Cady, Roberts & Co., 40 S.E.C. 907 (1961).

[148]*See* Frankel, "Fiduciary Law," 71 *Calif. L. Rev.* 795 (1983).

[149]Dirks v. SEC, 463 U.S. at 655, n.14. *See also* Elkind v. Liggett & Myers, Inc., 635 F.2d 156 (2d Cir. 1980); SEC v. Texas Gulf Sulphur Co., 401 F.2d 833 (2d Cir. 1968); R. Jennings and H. Marsh, *Securities Regulation* 914, n.11 (5th ed. 1982).

[150]Pub. L. 100-704, 102 Stat. 4677 (Nov. 19, 1988). *See also* H. Rpt., No. 100-910, 100th Cong., 2d Sess., *reprinted in,* 1988 *U.S. Code Cong. & Admin. News* 6043.

received investment advice had to be registered with the SEC under the Investment Advisers Act of 1940. Registered investment advisers have a fiduciary duty similar to corporate insiders to reveal conflicts of interest to their clients. Investment advisers who violate their duty to their clients, often by "scalping," can be sued for fraud by the government under provisions of the Investment Advisers Act or by private investors under Rule 10b-5. A publisher who scalps manipulates the market by buying stock, touting it in his publication, and then selling it when the price of the stock rises.[151]

An investment adviser is defined in the Investment Advisers Act as a person who, for pay, advises others "either directly or through publications or writings," on the advisability of buying or selling securities or who "issues analyses or reports on securities."[152] Exempted from the SEC's registration requirements are the publishers of any "bona fide newspaper, news magazine or business or financial publication of general and regular circulation."

Before the Supreme Court's decision in *Lowe v. SEC*,[153] general circulation newspapers were exempted from registration under the Investment Advisers Act because they conduct "customary newspaper activities." However, publications such as the *Lowe Stock Advisory* did have to register because they offer advice to their paying subscribers on when to buy and sell securities. However, the Supreme Court narrowed the definition of an investment adviser in *Lowe* by ruling that Christopher L. Lowe's financial newsletter was not an investment advisory as defined by the act. Lowe, therefore, did not have to register with the SEC.

Lowe's newsletter contained general commentary about the securities markets, reviews of investment strategies, and specific recommendations for buying, selling, or holding stocks. The newsletter also advertised a "telephone hotline" over which subscribers could call to get current information. Lowe's subscriber list fluctuated between 3,000 and 19,000.

The Supreme Court did not decide the First Amendment question of whether the SEC could enjoin publication of an unregistered financial newsletter. Instead, the majority ruled the SEC had no jurisdiction over Lowe's publication because it was a bona fide newspaper exempted from the act. To come to this conclusion, the court made a distinction between *personal* investment advisories that must register with the SEC and *impersonal* financial publications that do not have to register because they are bona fide newspapers.

A financial publication must register with the SEC as a personal investment advisory, the Court said, if it offers "individualized advice attuned to any specific portfolio or any client's particular needs." Only where investment advisers offer personal advice to specific clients does the Court see advisers as having "the kind of fiduciary, person-to-person relationships . . . characteristic of investment adviser-client relationships." Personalized advisers must register because they present a greater potential for fraud than impersonal advisers. In-person advice increases the chances of a client being intimidated, confused, or misled by a skillful talker, the Court said.

---

[151]SEC v. Capital Gains Research Bureau, Inc., 375 U.S. 180 (1963).
[152]SEC v. Wall Street Transcript Corp., 422 F.2d 1371 (2d Cir.), *cert. denied,* 398 U.S. 958 (1970).
[153]469 U.S. 815 (1985).

Lowe's newsletter was not a personal investment advisory, the Court said, because it offered completely disinterested advice to the general public on a regular schedule. Lowe's publications were impersonal advisers exempt from the Investment Advisers Act because they were "published by those engaged solely in the publishing business and are not personal communications masquerading in the clothing of newspapers, news magazines, or financial publications." The Court in *Lowe* suggested, but did not hold, that Lowe's telephone hotline might be subject to the Investment Advisors Act, even though his newsletter was not, because the hotline might be considered "personalized advice" about buying and selling securities.

Financial Journalists and Market Insiders   There is another level of information processors who have access to corporate information but who do not have the fiduciary duties of a corporate insider or investment adviser. People in this group include financial journalists, publishers of impersonal financial newsletters, printers, bank employees, public relations practitioners, and employees of financial brokerage houses. These information handlers are sometimes called *market insiders* because they have access to information about mergers, tender offers, and other sensitive financial intelligence, but they do not have the fiduciary relationship of insiders to companies issuing stock or of investment advisers to their clients.[154]

Although market insiders have no fiduciary duty to market traders, courts have ruled that employees of investment banking firms, financial printers, newspaper publishers, and other processors of market information violate Rule 10b-5 if they misappropriate information about mergers, acquisitions, and other confidential information for their own gain. Under a theory of misappropriation, market insiders have been ruled to violate section 10(b) by taking information about mergers, acquisitions, and other confidential transactions belonging to their employers and using it to tip and trade for their own enrichment.[155] Misappropriation of an employer's property has also been ruled to be fraud under mail and wire statutes that prohibit the use of these interstate channels for illegal schemes.

The U.S. Supreme Court upheld the fraud conviction of R. Foster Winans, a *Wall Street Journal* reporter, who passed financial information to a stockbroker, Peter Brant, who was able to act on the information before it was published in the *Journal's* "Heard on the Street" column. The column contained public information about companies' financial prospects. Such is the influence of the *Wall Street Journal* that the price of a company's stock might fluctuate temporarily because of a favorable or unfavorable mention in the "Heard on the Street" column. Winans's tips resulted in a net profit of $690,000 for Brant and his clients. Winans and his roommate, who was also involved in the scheme, made about $31,000.[156]

The Second Circuit Court of Appeals ruled that Winans violated section 10(b) by misappropriating information belonging to his employer in violation of a conflict-of-interest policy forbidding staff members from trading on information before it was

---

[154]*See* Note, "Drawing the Line on Insiders and Outsiders for Rule 10b-5: *Chiarella v. United States,"* 4 *Harv. J. L. & Pub. Pol.* 203, 207 (1981).

[155]SEC v. Materia, 745 F.2d 197 (2d Cir. 1984), *cert. denied,* 471 U.S. 1053 (1985). *See also* United States v. Newman, 664 F.2d 12, (2d Cir. 1981), *aff'd. after remand,* 722 F.2d 729 (2d Cir.), *cert. denied,* 464 U.S. 863 (1983).

[156]Carpenter v. U.S., 484 U.S. 19, 14 Media L. Rep. 1853 (1987).

published. Like most newspapers, the *Wall Street Journal* claims ownership in all information gathered by its staff.[157]

Although Winans was not a corporate insider and was not trading on insider information, he was not exempt from the fraud provisions of the securities law. The Second Circuit said the securities laws are not aimed "solely at the eradication of fraudulent trading by corporate insiders." The fraud provisions also reach trading activity, such as trading on the basis of improperly obtained information, which the court said is "fundamentally unfair."

The court said Winans's duty to the *Journal* not to violate the paper's conflict-of-interest policy created another duty under section 10(b) not to trade or tip on the basis of misappropriated information. Winans's misuse of the *Journal's* information before publication defrauded the newspaper, the court said, by sullying its reputation for ethical journalism.

The Second Circuit said that holding a journalist liable under a fraud statute did not violate the First Amendment because no government restrictions were placed on publication of the "Heard on the Street" column. The securities law only required that journalists, like other citizens, not engage in fraudulent transactions.

The Supreme Court, in a 4–4 ruling, affirmed Winans's conviction for securities fraud. None of the justices discussed the reason for his or her vote in an opinion. Only eight justices participated in the case because retired Justice Powell had not been replaced. The 4–4 split means that the appeals court decision is precedent only in the Second Circuit. All eight justices also upheld Winans's conviction for wire and mail fraud for his misappropriation of confidential information belonging to the *Journal*.

SUMMARY

Publicly traded corporations are subject to fraud suits under Section 10(b) of the Exchange Act of 1934 if they deliberately make a misleading statement of a material fact or fail to disclose material information when they have a duty to do so. Materially deceptive statements include misstatements and omissions that would affect an investor's decision to buy, sell, or hold a security. In addition, a corporation may have a duty to disclose material information if misleading information circulating in the media originated with the corporation. Corporate insiders and publishers of personal investment advisers also have a duty to disclose material information before using it as a basis for buying or selling securities. Financial journalists and market insiders have also been ruled to have a duty not to trade on market information acquired from their employer.

Adequate Disclosure

The duty to disclose corporate information includes a requirement that disclosure be timely and broad. When a corporation makes a disclosure, whether it is mandated by

---

[157]United States v. Carpenter, 791 F.2d 1024 (2d Cir. 1986).

statute or is made to avoid fraud, the disclosure must be prompt and adequately distributed so that shareholders and other investors will have time to digest the information before insiders buy and sell.

Breadth of Disclosure   Information must be disseminated, the SEC has said, "in a manner calculated to reach the securities marketplace in general through recognized channels of distribution, and public investors must be afforded a reasonable waiting period to react to the information."[158] The procedures to be followed for sufficient dissemination of material information will depend on the market for the corporation's securities. If the corporation has a national market, information should be directed to the national financial press, the major financial communities, and to other areas where the corporation knows there will be interest in its securities. Regional companies can select regional newspapers, magazines, and wire services.

"At a minimum," say the American Stock Exchange Disclosure Policies,

> any public disclosure of material information should be made by an announcement released simultaneously to (a) the national business and financial news-wire services (the Dow Jones News Service and Reuters Economic Services), (b) the national news-wire services (Associated Press and United Press International), (c) The New York Times and the Wall Street Journal, and (d) Moody's Investors Service and Standard & Poor's Corporation. Distribution over private teletype networks can be achieved through the PR Newswire and Business Wire. Dissemination might also be made on an "immediate release" basis to newspapers and broadcast media in areas where the company has plants, offices or to trade publications.

If a company encounters difficulty getting coverage in prominent media, it may need to buy advertisements and send letters to stockholders.

The SEC has said that release of material information over a private wire service to a limited number of institutional subscribers is not adequate dissemination.[159] In *SEC v. Texas Gulf Sulphur Co.,* the U.S. Court of Appeals for the Second Circuit said it was not sufficient for a New York Stock Exchange corporation to publish news of a large mineral discovery only in a Canadian newspaper of limited circulation.[160] In the same case, the Second Circuit said that issuing a news release "is merely the first step in the process of dissemination required for compliance with the regulatory objective of providing all investors with an equal opportunity to make informed investment judgments." The company must also ensure that corporate information is adequately distributed.

Timeliness   While disclosure is supposed to be broad, it is also supposed to be prompt. But the SEC, the courts, and the exchanges permit a company to withhold material information temporarily if the decision to withhold is a good-faith business judgment. Disclosure may be delayed where it would prejudice the ability of a company to pursue corporate objectives or where facts are in a state of flux. The objec-

---

[158]*In re* Fabergé, Inc., 45 S.E.C. 249, 255 (1973). *See also* American Stock Exchange Disclosure Policies, sec. 402.
[159]Fabergé, 45 S.E.C. at 255.
[160]401 F.2d 833, 856 (2d Cir. 1968) *(en banc), cert. denied,* 394 U.S. 976 (1969).

tives of a corporation might be jeopardized, for example, if negotiations for land were disclosed before acquisition was complete. In the *Texas Gulf Sulphur* case, officers of the company were guilty of fraud for misleading the public while insiders bought stock, but the appeals court said it was not wrong for the company to withhold disclosure of the promising drilling results until adjoining land could be acquired.[161] Disclosure of information might also be delayed to allow acquisition of another company[162] or liquidation of a portion of a company's business.[163]

Where circumstances are in a state of flux, corporations may exercise their business judgment to withhold information until the situation has stabilized. In a rapidly changing situation, a series of press releases could cause undesirable fluctuations in the price of a corporation's stock. In such circumstances, it is better to wait until the situation has calmed.

The U.S. Court of Appeals for the Tenth Circuit Court ruled that a corporation can wait to release information until it is "available and ripe for publication."[164] The court said the McDonnell Douglas Corporation did not mislead shareholders when it waited several days for results of an internal evaluation of reduced earnings in the company's aircraft division before issuing a special report. "To be ripe," the court said, information "must be verified sufficiently to permit the officers and directors to have full confidence" in its accuracy. The hazards from an erroneous statement are "obvious," the court said, but it is "equally obvious that an undue delay not in good faith, in revealing facts, can be deceptive, misleading, or a device to defraud." McDonnell Douglas, the court concluded, investigated the expected shortfall as soon as it became known and wasted no time evaluating the information and preparing a release.

SUMMARY

When corporations disclose information, it should be disseminated broadly in a timely fashion. But disclosure may be delayed until information is complete and accurate.

---

[161]401 F.2d at 850, n.12.

[162]Matarese v. Aero Chatillon Corp. [1971–1972 Transfer Binder], Fed. Sec. L. Rep. (CCH) para. 93,322 at 91,731–32 (S.D.N.Y.1971).

[163]Segal v. Coburn Corp. [1973 Transfer Binder] Fed. Sec. L. Rep. (CCH) para. 94,002 (E.D.N.Y. 1973).

[164]Financial Industrial Fund, Inc. v. McDonnell Douglas Corp., 474 F.2d 514, 519 (10th Cir. 1973).

7

ADVERTISING

Until the late nineteenth century, advertisements were primarily announcements. Artisans and merchants in the 1700s and 1800s told their patrons about the arrival of goods through small notices that looked much like today's classified ads. The truth of advertisements was of secondary importance because consumers could examine products and shun merchants who sold inferior merchandise.[1]

With the growth of mass production, advertising became more sophisticated. By the beginning of the twentieth century, manufacturers were using national advertising to convince consumers in distant markets to buy mass-produced, undifferentiated products. Some advertising was dishonest. Patent medicine manufacturers were notorious for their exaggerated promises. Some patent medicine makers bragged that, with the right advertising, they could sell dishwater.

But as mass marketing developed, truth in advertising took on new importance to reputable companies. Procter & Gamble, Burpee Seeds, Quaker Oats, and other producers of brand-name products wanted consumers to have faith in the truth of national advertisements.[2] Endorsing the "rotten apple theory," reputable national advertisers feared that false advertising by one company damaged the credibility of all.

Manufacturers' concern for truth in advertising led to the formation of regulatory organizations within the business community. Truth in advertising was a major theme at the 1911 convention of the Associated Advertising Clubs of America. In 1912, the National Vigilance Committee—later the Better Business Bureau—was created. By the 1930s, a movement within the industry to clean up advertising had resulted in several codes discouraging false and misleading advertising.[3]

---

[1] D. Pope, *The Making of Modern Advertising* 4–5 (1983).
[2] *Id.* at 184–226.
[3] *See* S. Dunn, A. Barban, D. Krugman, & L. Reid, *Advertising: Its Role in Modern Marketing* 24–25 (1990).

Legal regulations also developed. Most states adopted a law similar to one proposed in 1911 by the trade magazine *Printers' Ink*. The *Printers' Ink* statutes, which still form the basis for much state regulation, made it a misdemeanor to disseminate misleading advertising. On the national level, the Federal Trade Commission Act of 1914 established federal authority to outlaw deceptive acts and practices, including false advertising. Later the Food and Drug Administration was established to oversee labeling of food, drugs, cosmetics, and medical devices, and to regulate the advertising of prescription drugs. The Bureau of Alcohol, Tobacco and Firearms, a division of the Treasury Department, oversees advertising and promotion of alcoholic beverages.

State and federal regulation of advertising evolved without raising questions of freedom of expression. Until recently, advertising was outside First Amendment consideration. In 1942, the Supreme Court ruled, in a brief, almost casual, opinion, that the government could regulate advertising without concern for infringing freedom of expression because commercial speech, like fighting words and obscenity, was not protected by the Constitution. However, by 1990, the Supreme Court had long since abandoned its 1942 ruling and established limited First Amendment protections for commercial advertising, thus creating constitutional questions when the government regulates the $130 billion advertising industry.

FIRST AMENDMENT AND ADVERTISING

The case in which the Supreme Court ruled that advertising was outside of First Amendment protection involved the distribution of commercial handbills. In *Valentine v. Chrestensen,* the Court ruled that F. J. Chrestensen had no First Amendment right to distribute handbills advertising tours of a former Navy submarine that Chrestensen moored at a state-owned pier in the East River in New York City.[4] Chrestensen distributed handbills to pedestrians in lower Manhattan advertising 25-cent tours of his $2 million "fighting monster." The handbills promised visitors a glimpse of the kitchen, torpedo compartment, and the crew's sleeping quarters on the S-49 submarine. Children could take the tour for 15 cents.

City officials, however, told Chrestensen to stop distributing his handbills because he was violating the New York City Sanitary Code, which prohibited the distribution of "commercial and business advertising." Chrestensen then added a message to the back of his fliers protesting the restrictions imposed on him under the sanitation code. With a "political" message on one side of his submarine handbills, Chrestensen sought an injunction barring police from interfering with distribution of his constitutionally protected expression.

The U.S. Supreme Court, in a four-page decision in 1942, ruled that New York officials could stop distribution of Chrestensen's fliers without violating the First Amendment. The Court said the fliers were "purely commercial" advertising that fell outside constitutional protection. The Court dismissed the political message appended to the fliers as a ruse not to be taken seriously. The decision in *Valentine v.*

---

[4]316 U.S. 52, 1 Media L. Rep. 1907 (1942).

Chrestensen began the "commercial speech doctrine," which was to deny constitutional protection to commercial advertising until the mid-1970s.

The Court's dismissal in *Valentine* of constitutional consideration for advertising was curt. The Court felt no need to present a detailed rationale for its opinion. However, the Court has long since reconsidered its off-hand denial in *Valentine* of First Amendment status for commercial speech. In a series of cases beginning in the 1970s, the Court has employed the First Amendment to strike down state prohibitions on advertising of drug prices, lawyers' services, abortion referral services, and other products and services. Constitutional protections on commercial speech are weaker than those on political expression, but the Court has long since abandoned its holding that commercial advertising is unprotected by the First Amendment.

Emergence of Constitutional Protections

The Supreme Court took a small first step toward constitutional protection for commercial advertising in its 1964 libel decision in *New York Times v. Sullivan.* Police Commissioner Sullivan, citing *Valentine v. Chrestensen,* argued that criticism of Southern law enforcement officers should have no constitutional status because the criticism was part of a paid advertisement. Another commercial element of the advertisement, according to Sullivan, was its solicitation of funds to support the civil rights movement. The Supreme Court, however, ruled that political expression would not be denied First Amendment protection simply because it appeared in a paid advertisement. Indeed, the Court said it was "immaterial" whether the editorial advertisement was purchased because it "communicated information, expressed opinion, recited grievances, protected claimed abuses, and sought financial support on behalf of a movement whose existence and objectives are matters of the highest public interest and concern."[5]

Protecting "Purely Commercial" Messages While *New York Times v. Sullivan* established that paid political speech enjoys constitutional protection, the case did not create constitutional protection for "purely commercial advertising" such as Chrestensen's original handbills. However, in the 1973 case of *Pittsburgh Press Co. v. Pittsburgh Commission on Human Relations,* the Supreme Court suggested it might be willing to grant constitutional status to "an ordinary commercial proposal."[6]

The *Pittsburgh Press* set *Male* and *Female* column heads over the newspaper's help-wanted ads. These headings, the Court said, promoted sex discrimination in job hiring because success in many of the jobs advertised did not depend on whether the applicant was male or female. The Court, therefore, said the First Amendment permitted the Commission on Human Relations to bar the *Pittsburgh Press* from using separate *Male* and *Female* column heads. However, the Court suggested that government regulations might be prohibited if the column heads promoted legal, nondiscriminatory hiring.

---

[5]376 U.S. 254, 266, 1 Media L. Rep. 1527, 1532 (1964).
[6]413 U.S. 376, 389, 1 Media L. Rep. 1908, 1915 (1973).

A short time later the Court made good on its suggestion that a commercial advertisement for a legal product or service might be constitutionally protected from government interference. In *Bigelow v. Virginia,* the Court struck down a state statute that barred publication of ads for an abortion referral service. Jeffrey C. Bigelow had violated the Virginia statute in 1971 by publishing an ad in the *Virginia Weekly* for the Women's Pavilion, an abortion referral service in New York. The *Virginia Weekly* circulated widely on the campus of the University of Virginia. Abortions at that time were legal in New York but not in Virginia.[7]

In *Bigelow,* the Court did not overturn *Valentine v. Chrestensen* but did seriously undermine it. The Court said in *Bigelow* that the *Chrestensen* decision had not held that "advertising is unprotected *per se*." The *Chrestensen* case did not determine whether commercial advertising is constitutionally protected, the Court said. The Court in *Bigelow* also noted how several justices and commentators had questioned the correctness of the four-page *Chrestensen* decision of 33 years before. Justice Douglas, for example, had second thoughts about *Chrestensen* in 1959 when he dismissed the ruling as "casual, almost offhand."[8]

The *Bigelow* decision did not decisively end the commercial speech doctrine because the abortion referral ad in *Bigelow* was not purely commercial speech. Unlike the original submarine flier in *Chrestensen* and the help-wanted headings in *Pittsburgh Press,* the ad for the abortion referral service in *Bigelow* contained factual material similar to the political content of editorials or news columns. For example, the ad declared, "Abortions are now legal in New York."

Furthermore, abortion itself is not a *purely commercial* transaction. In 1973, the Supreme Court ruled that a woman's constitutional right of privacy includes the right to an abortion.[9] While the right of women to have an abortion is under attack, the constitutional status of abortion gave Jeffrey Bigelow's advertisement for abortion referral services an added First Amendment weight.

A purely commercial advertisement was first protected in *Virginia State Board of Pharmacy v. Virginia Citizens Consumer Council,*[10] a case in which the Supreme Court, as in *Bigelow,* struck down a Virginia statute. In *Virginia Pharmacy,* the Court declared unconstitutional a law prohibiting licensed pharmacists from advertising the prices of prescription drugs. The pharmacists' ads were purely commercial because they did "no more than propose a commercial transaction," the Court said.

The Virginia State Board of Pharmacy argued the prohibition on price advertisements for prescription drugs did not violate the First Amendment because purely commercial speech had not been protected by the First Amendment since *Valentine v. Chrestensen.* The board also argued that aggressive price competition among pharmacists would harm consumers because pharmacists would have less time to compound and dispense drugs. The pressures of advertising, the board said, would either force conscientious pharmacists to diminish their painstaking professional services or go out of business. Furthermore, the Board of Pharmacy argued that competitive

---

[7]421 U.S. 809, 1 Media L. Rep. 1919 (1975).
[8]Cammarano v. United States, 358 U.S. 498, 514 (1959) (concurring opinion).
[9]Roe v. Wade, 412 U.S. 113 (1973).
[10]425 U.S. 748, 1 Media L. Rep. 1930 (1976).

advertising would not necessarily result in the lower drug prices anticipated by the Virginia Citizens Consumer Council.

The Consumer Council, representing a number of prescription drug users, particularly the elderly and infirm, argued that the Virginia statute was a violation of consumers' First Amendment right to receive information necessary to their good health. The Consumer Council also argued that prohibitions on advertising forced consumers to spend more time and money to find the best drugs at the cheapest prices.

In *Virginia Pharmacy,* the Supreme Court recognized a constitutional protection for purely commercial speech motivated by a desire for profit. Justice Harry Blackmun wrote that the price advertising of prescription drugs is protected by the First Amendment even though a

> pharmacist does not wish to editorialize on any subject, cultural, philosophical, or political. He does not wish to report any particularly newsworthy fact, or to make generalized observations even about commercial matters. The "idea" he wishes to communicate is simply this: "I will sell you the X prescription drug at the Y price."[11]

Although price advertising for drugs is "purely commercial," the Court said commercial advertising, like editorial comment, contributes to democratic decision-making served by the First Amendment. In a statement merging the commercial marketplace and the marketplace of ideas, the Court said,

> Advertising, however tasteless and excessive it sometimes may seem, is nonetheless dissemination of information as to who is producing and selling what product, for what reason, and at what price. So long as we preserve a predominantly free enterprise economy, the allocation of our resources in large measure will be made through numerous private economic decisions. It is a matter of public interest that those decisions in the aggregate be intelligent and well informed. To this end, the free flow of commercial information is indispensable.[12]

The Court's First Amendment protection for commercial advertising depended very little on the right of pharmacists to speak or publish. After all, the professional association representing pharmacists opposed lifting the ban on advertising. Of more importance to the Court than a right to speak was the consumer's constitutional interest in receiving information about drug prices. The right to receive would be honored, Justice Blackmun said, because the individual consumer's interest "in the free flow of commercial information may be as keen, if not keener by far, than his interest in the day's most urgent political debate." The Court rejected as "paternalistic" the State Board of Pharmacy's claim that allowing pharmacists to advertise prices of prescription drugs would undermine their professionalism and thereby hurt consumers.

In a very sharp dissent, Justice Rehnquist feared that the "logical consequences" of the *Virginia Pharmacy* decision would be to elevate "commercial intercourse between a seller hawking his wares and a buyer seeking to strike a bargain to the same

---

[11]425 U.S. at 760, 1 Media L. Rep. at 1934.
[12]*Id.* at 765, 1 Media L. Rep. at 1936.

plane as has been previously reserved for the free marketplace of ideas." Rehnquist
did not agree with the majority's assertion that commercial advertising should be protected by the First Amendment because purchasing decisions based on advertising
contribute to public decision-making in a democracy. To Justice Rehnquist, the First
Amendment protects public decision-making on political, social, and other public issues. It does not protect "the decision of a particular individual as to whether to purchase one or another kind of shampoo." Thus, Justice Rehnquist thought the Court's
decision in *Virginia Pharmacy* devalued the First Amendment.[13]

Distinguishing Political and Commercial Speech   Although the majority of justices in *Virginia Pharmacy* appeared to equate commercial advertising with political
speech, in fact the court did not accord commercial speech the same constitutional
status as political expression. Commercial speech came under the constitutional um-
brella in *Virginia Pharmacy* as a second-class form of expression. Starting in *Virginia
Pharmacy* and continuing through other commercial speech decisions, the Court has
permitted many regulations on commercial speech that would not be tolerated on
political speech.

A major difference in the protection of political and commercial speech can be
seen in the Court's tolerance for falsehood in each. While considerable falsehood is
permitted in the political arena because the social price of removing it is too high, the
Court said in *Virginia Pharmacy* that the government may constitutionally ban commercial promotions that are "false or misleading in any way" or that promote products or services that are illegal. The Court also said that prior restraints, which are
presumed to be unconstitutional in the political arena, may be invoked to halt misleading commercial speech. Furthermore, while political expression may not be compelled, the Court said that commercial advertisers might be required to disseminate
warnings, disclaimers, and other messages to ensure that commercial speech is not
misleading. Since *Virginia Pharmacy* was decided, the Supreme Court has even ruled
that truthful advertising may be prohibited.[14]

The constitutional protections for commercial speech are weaker than for political speech, the Supreme Court said, because of "common sense" differences between commercial and political speech. First, the Court said that commercial speech
is hardier than other kinds of expression because of the business person's need to
advertise in a market economy. Advertisers will not be as intimidated by government
regulations as political speakers might be, the Court said, because of the unrelenting
economic pressure on businesses to advertise. In other words, commercial advertising
may be regulated more than political speech because advertising can more easily withstand regulation.

The other "common sense" difference between commercial and political speech
is that commercial speech is more easily verified. Advertisers, the Court said, know
their products well and often make factual statements that can be proven objectively,
perhaps by scientific test. Political statements, in contrast, are often assertions of fact
or opinion that cannot be proved and should not have to be. But because advertisers

---

[13]*Id.* at 781–90, 1 Media L. Rep. at 1942–46.
[14]Posadas de Puerto Rico Assoc. v. Tourism Co. Puerto Rico, 478 U.S. 328, 13 Media L. Rep. 1033 (1986).

may easily verify their statements, the Court said there is less reason to tolerate false and misleading statements in commercial ads than in political debate.

Since *Virginia Pharmacy* was decided, the Supreme Court has issued a number of decisions extending constitutional protection to commercial speech. In 1977, the Court ruled that attorneys have a constitutional right to advertise the prices of routine services, such as a simple will or uncontested divorce.[15] The Court has also extended constitutional protection to illustrations and pictures in attorneys' ads,[16] "For Sale" and "Sold" signs on private houses,[17] advertisements for contraceptives,[18] and promotions for electrical power by a utility.[19] However, the Supreme Court has also ruled that the First Amendment does not protect ads for casinos[20] or sales promotions for Tupperware in college dormitories.[21] The Court's commercial speed decisions have been criticized for being inconsistent and therefore providing little guidance for advertisers wishing to know whether government restrictions are constitutional.

The Court determines the constitutionality of regulations on commercial speech by applying a four-part test set fourth in *Central Hudson Gas & Electric Corp. v. Public Service Commission,*[22] in which the Court upheld the right of a utility to promote the use of electricity.

Four-Part Test

Under the four-part test promulgated in *Central Hudson,* a court must determine first whether commercial expression is eligible for First Amendment protection. Second, a court examines whether the government asserts a substantial interest in regulating the expression. If the speech is eligible and the government asserts a substantial interest, a court next considers whether the regulation directly advances the governmental interest asserted. If so, the court in the fourth step decides whether the regulation is sufficiently narrow to serve the governmental interest but not inhibit protected expression unnecessarily.

Commercial Speech Eligible for Constitutional Consideration   Speech passes the first part of the *Central Hudson* test and is eligible for constitutional protection if it is accurate commercial speech that advertises a legal product or service. False and misleading advertising and advertising for illegal products and services are not eligible for constitutional consideration. The first task of a court, therefore, is to determine whether the expression at issue is eligible commercial speech.

Defining Commercial Speech   An advertisement is commercial speech, the Court said in *Virginia Pharmacy,* if its content does "no more than propose a commercial

---

[15]Bates v. State Bar of Arizona, 433 U.S. 350, 2 Media L. Rep. 2097 (1977).

[16]Zauderer v. Office of Disciplinary Counsel, 471 U.S. 626 (1985).

[17]Linmark Assocs., Inc. v. Township of Willingboro, 431 U.S. 85 (1977).

[18]Bolger v. Youngs Drug Prod. Corp., 463 U.S. 60 (1983); Carey v. Population Services Int'l, 431 U.S. 678, 2 Media L. Rep. 1935 (1977).

[19]Central Hudson Gas & Elec. Corp. v. Public Serv. Comm'n, 447 U.S. 557, 6 Media L. Rep. 1497 (1980).

[20]Posadas de Puerto Rico Assocs. v. Tourism Co. Puerto Rico, 478 U.S. 328, 13 Media L. Rep. 1033 (1986).

[21]Board of Trustees v. Fox, 109 S. Ct. 3028 (1989).

[22]447 U.S. 557, 6 Media L. Rep. 1497 (1980).

transaction."[23] Commercial speech, the Court said, is expression "related solely to the economic interests of the speaker and its audience." Similarly, Justice Brennan once referred to "pure advertising" as "an offer to buy or sell goods and services or encouraging such buying and selling."[24] These definitions adequately describe ads that expressly offer a product or service for sale, particularly at a specific price. Price advertising for prescription drugs, the Supreme Court said in *Virginia Pharmacy,* was a purely commercial proposal. Similarly, a lawyer's offer to write a will at a predetermined price, a homeowner's offer to sell a house, and a salesperson's attempt to sell Tupperware in a university dormitory are purely commercial speech because they do no more than "propose a commercial transaction."

The Supreme Court has also said that commercial speech does not become fully protected political speech merely because it is associated with a political issue. In *Central Hudson,* the Court said that an electric utility's bill inserts promoting the efficient use of electricity were commercial speech even though the inserts were in response to a state-approved energy conservation program. Likewise, in *Bolger v. Youngs Drug Products Corporation,*[25] the Court ruled that leaflets distributed by a condom manufacturer were commercial speech even though they contained information about preventing venereal disease meriting full constitutional protection. Just as F. J. Chrestensen's commercial flier for submarine tours was not transformed into protected political speech because of a political protest appended to the back, the leaflets distributed by a condom manufacturer were not transformed into fully protected political speech simply because they "link[ed] a product to a current public debate." The Court said in *Bolger* that a condom manufacturer's "direct comments" on public issues such as venereal disease would merit full constitutional protection, but not statements "made in the context of commercial transactions." The Court said it feared advertisers would try to immunize false or misleading product information from government regulation if commercial messages were considered to be political when the two were blended. The post office was trying to bar the pamphlets in *Bolger* under a mail statute.

The informational pamphlets at issue in *Bolger* did not propose that readers buy Youngs' condoms. One pamphlet discussed use of condoms generally as a method of preventing the spread of venereal disease. At the end, the pamphlet identified Youngs as the distributor of the flier. Another VD pamphlet described various Trojan-brand condoms manufactured by Youngs without offering them for sale. Nevertheless, the Court ruled the pamphlets were commercial speech because they (1) were conceded to be paid advertisements, (2) made reference to a specific product, and (3) were economically motivated. Not all of these three criteria must be met for an advertisement proposing no commercial transaction to be considered commercial speech. Corporate image ads, for example, might be considered commercial speech even though they mention no products, the Court said.

Relying on *Bolger,* the Federal Trade Commission ruled that a cigarette company's editorial advertisement criticizing a study of smoking and heart disease

---

[23]425 U.S. at 762, 1 Media L. Rep. at 1935.
[24]Dun & Bradstreet v. Greenmoss Builders, 472 U.S. 749, 11 Media L. Rep. 2417 (1985) (dissenting opinion).
[25]463 U.S. 60 (1983).

may also be commercial speech.[26] In a 4–1 decision, the five-member Federal Trade Commission asked an administrative law judge within the FTC to reconsider his earlier contrary ruling. The law judge had ruled that an R. J. Reynolds ad was fully protected political speech, even though the ad misrepresented a Harvard study linking smoking and heart disease.

But the full FTC said the company's advertisement may be commercial speech because it referred to a specific product—cigarettes—and discussed an important attribute of the product—scientists' charges of a link between smoking and heart disease. Before the administrative law judge could reconsider the case, however, R. J. Reynolds agreed not to misrepresent studies linking smoking and health. No determination was made whether the company's editorial advertisement was commercial speech.[27] (See advertisement, Figure 7.1.)

A public relations consultant's economic report has also been ruled to be commercial speech. A federal district court ruled that a $75,000 economic report prepared to help the port at Savannah, Georgia, compete with the port at Charleston, South Carolina, was commercial speech because the report was prepared for a client "embarking on a marketing campaign."[28] In a suit over the accuracy of the report, the federal district court said the report's author, Booz-Allen & Hamilton, could "verify the accuracy of its factual representations" as the Supreme Court said in *Virginia Pharmacy* that commercial advertisers could.

Legal Products and Services   Once a court has determined that commercial speech is at issue, it asks whether the expression promotes a legal product or service. Under the first part of the *Central Hudson* analysis, commercial expression entitled to constitutional protection must promote only products and services that are themselves legal. Ads for prescription drugs, houses, and lawyers' services are eligible for constitutional consideration because they promote lawful products and activities. Similarly, ads promoting electricity and condoms also meet the first part of the test. However, ads for explosives, obscene materials, criminal activities, and discriminatory job opportunities are outside constitutional consideration because they promote illegal products or services.

The Supreme Court has also ruled that slogans, symbols, and advertising that promote the illegal use of legal products are beyond constitutional protection. In *Village of Hoffman Estates v. Flipside, Hoffman Estates,* the Court ruled that logos and slogans on cigarette papers, water pipes, "roach clips," and other drug paraphernalia were outside First Amendment protection because the paraphernalia were marketed for illegal purposes. Although cigarette papers and water pipes have legal uses, the Court said advertising and commercial symbols on and near products could be prohibited if they propose the illegal use of drugs.[29]

In *Hoffman Estates,* drug paraphernalia were displayed next to books and magazines titled *High Times, Marijuana Grower's Guide, Children's Garden of Grass,*

---

[26]R. J. Reynolds Tobacco Co., 3 *Trade Reg. Rep.* (CCH) para. 22,522 (June 2, 1988).

[27]*In re* R. J. Reynolds Tobacco Co., Federal Trade Commission, Doc. No. 9206, May 22, 1989.

[28]South Carolina State Ports Auth. v. Booz-Allen & Hamilton, Inc., 676 F. Supp. 346, 14 Media L. Rep. 2132 (D.C.D.C. 1987).

[29]455 U.S. 489 (1982). *See also* Camille Corp. v. Phares, 705 F.2d 223 (7th Cir. 1983).

Of cigarettes and science.

This is the way science is supposed to work.

A scientist observes a certain set of facts. To explain these facts, the scientist comes up with a theory.

Then, to check the validity of the theory, the scientist performs an experiment. If the experiment yields positive results, and is duplicated by other scientists, then the theory is supported. If the experiment produces negative results, the theory is re-examined, modified or discarded.

But, to a scientist, both positive and negative results should be important. Because both produce valuable learning.

Now let's talk about cigarettes.

You probably know about research that links smoking to certain diseases. Coronary heart disease is one of them.

Much of this evidence consists of studies that show a statistical association between smoking and the disease.

But statistics themselves cannot explain *why* smoking and heart disease are associated. Thus, scientists have developed a theory: that heart disease is *caused* by smoking. Then they performed various experiments to check this theory.

We would like to tell you about one of the most important of these experiments.

A little-known study

It was called the Multiple Risk Factor Intervention Trial (MR FIT).

In the words of the *Wall Street Journal,* it was "one of the largest medical experiments ever attempted." Funded by the Federal government, it cost $115,000,000 and took 10 years, ending in 1982.

The subjects were over 12,000 men who were thought to have a high risk of heart disease because of three risk factors that are statistically associated with this disease: smoking, high blood pressure and high cholesterol levels.

Half of the men received no special medical intervention. The other half received medical treatment that consistently reduced all three risk factors, compared with the first group.

It was assumed that the group with lower risk factors would, over time, suffer significantly fewer deaths from heart disease than the higher risk factor group.

But that is not the way it turned out.

After 10 years, there was no statistically significant difference between the two groups in the number of heart disease deaths.

The theory persists

We at R.J. Reynolds do not claim this study proves that smoking doesn't cause heart disease. But we do wish to make a point.

Despite the results of MR FIT and other experiments like it, many scientists have not abandoned or modified their original theory, or re-examined its assumptions.

They continue to believe these factors cause heart disease. But it is important to label their belief accurately. It is an opinion. A judgment. But *not* scientific fact.

We believe in science. That is why we continue to provide funding for independent research into smoking and health.

But we do not believe there should be one set of scientific principles for the whole world, and a different set for experiments involving cigarettes. Science is science. Proof is proof. That is why the controversy over smoking and health remains an open one.

R.J. Reynolds Tobacco Company

Figure 7.1. Reproduced with the permission of R.J. Reynolds Tobacco Co.

and *The Pleasures of Cocaine.* A sign in the store referred to the "head" supplies used by frequent drug users. A design on cigarette papers showed a person smoking drugs.

The *Hoffman Estates* decision did not say that commercial speech may be prohibited for all products that might be used for an illegal purpose. Such reasoning could lead to prohibitions on almost all commercial expression. "Peanut butter advertising cannot be banned," a federal judge once observed, "just because someone might throw a jar at the presidential motorcade."[30] But the commercial symbols in *Hoffman Estates* clearly promoted the purchase of commercial products for illegal use.

False, Misleading, and Deceptive Advertising   Commercial speech, to merit constitutional consideration, must not only promote a legal product or service, but must also be true and accurate. The Supreme Court ruled that ads offering prescription drugs, simple legal services, and houses for sale were eligible for constitutional protection because the ads were not false, misleading, or deceptive. The promotion of electricity by Central Hudson Gas & Electric was also eligible for constitutional protection because it did not mislead consumers.

Ads mislead if they make important false statements or leave the wrong impression. The Supreme Court has said commercial speech is misleading if it advertises the price of a complex service that cannot be accurately priced before delivery. In *Bates v. State Bar of Arizona,*[31] the Court said price advertisements for complex legal services, such as complicated divorces and estate settlements, would be misleading because attorneys cannot accurately fix a price on such open-ended, time-consuming tasks before work begins. Only routine legal services that take a fixed amount of time can be accurately priced in advertising that does not mislead, the Court said. Routine services that might be advertised include uncontested divorces and simple adoptions.

The Court has also ruled that attorneys' use of "in-person" sales talks can be prohibited because of the potential for deception. In-person solicitations can be prohibited because, unlike lawyers' advertisements in the media, they present dangers of coercing, intimidating, misleading, and invading the privacy of potential clients. The Court said an in-person appeal for business by an attorney—often to a vulnerable potential client who is distraught by a divorce, an accident, or a death—is deceptive because it "may exert pressure and often demands an immediate response, without providing an opportunity for comparison or reflection."[32] Ads in the media, however, do not present the same potential for misleading clients because media ads do not apply such immediate pressure for a response, the Court said.

Legitimate Government Regulatory Interest   Once it is determined that an advertisement is eligible for constitutional consideration because it accurately promotes a legal product or service, a court's analysis focuses on the constitutionality of the pro-

---

[30]Dunagin v. City of Oxford, 718 F.2d 738, 10 Media L. Rep. 1001 (5th Cir. 1983), *cert. denied,* 104 S. Ct. 3553 (1984).
[31]433 U.S. 350, 2 Media L. Rep. 2097 (1977).
[32]Ohralik v. Ohio State Bar Ass'n, 436 U.S. 447, 457 (1978).

posed government regulation. The second criterion under the *Central Hudson* test is whether the regulation serves a legitimate or substantial government interest. If the speech in question were political rather than commercial, government suppression would require proof of a *compelling* state interest. The lesser value of commercial speech is reflected in the requirement that the government demonstrate only a *legitimate* or *substantial* interest to justify regulation.

The government often can meet the second part of the *Central Hudson* test by demonstrating an interest in protecting consumers from being misled by inaccurate information and in preserving the health, safety, morals, and aesthetic quality of the community. The Supreme Court noted the government's interest in ensuring the accuracy of commercial speech in *Virginia Pharmacy*. The Court ultimately struck down the Virginia statute prohibiting drug price advertising, but not before recognizing Virginia's legitimate interest in ensuring the accuracy of consumer information about prescription drugs. The state has a legitimate interest, the Court said, in ensuring that the "stream of commercial information flows cleanly as well as freely."

In *Central Hudson,* the Supreme Court recognized the legitimacy of the New York Public Service Commission's desire to conserve energy. The Public Service Commission curbed Central Hudson's promotional advertising for electricity as part of a national policy of energy conservation. The Court declared the commission's complete ban on the utility's electricity promotions to be unconstitutionally broad, but not before recognizing the legitimacy of the Public Service Commission's goal to save energy. The Supreme Court has also said that traffic safety and the physical appearance of a city are sufficient state interests to justify banning commercial billboards.[33]

In *Posadas de Puerto Rico Associates v. Tourism Company of Puerto Rico,* the Supreme Court ruled that preserving the health and welfare of the Puerto Rican people was sufficient grounds to ban truthful casino advertising on the island.[34] The Court held that the Puerto Rican government could bar truthful ads on the island for legal gambling casinos while, at the same time, advertising the casinos in the continental United States. The Supreme Court, in an opinion written by Justice Rehnquist, said the Puerto Rican government could bar accurate casino ads on the island because the power to regulate a service such as gambling includes the power to regulate or prohibit advertising.

The Puerto Rican government wanted to ban the ads in Puerto Rico so as not to encourage gambling by Puerto Ricans. The gambling promoted by the ads, Justice Rehnquist said for the Court majority, could result in "disruption of moral and cultural patterns, the increase in local crime, the fostering of prostitution, the development of corruption, and the infiltration of organized crime."

Justices Brennan, Marshall, and Blackmun, who dissented in *Posadas de Puerto Rico,* argued that the First Amendment does not permit suppression of accurate information about lawful products and services. If the government wishes to discour-

---

[33]Metromedia, Inc. v. City of San Diego, 453 U.S. 490 (1981).

[34]Posadas de Puerto Rico Assocs. v. Tourism Co. of Puerto Rico, 478 U.S. 328, 13 Media L. Rep. 1033 (1986). *See also* Princess Sea Indus. v. Nevada, 635 P.2d 281, 7 Media L. Rep. 2474 (Nev. 1981), *cert. denied,* 456 U.S. 926 (1982) (ads for legal prostitution may be barred in counties where prostitution is not legal).

age gambling, Brennan said, it should encourage people to avoid the casinos, rather than deny accurate information about them. Suppression of truthful commercial information should not be used, Brennan said, as a means to discourage consumers from buying legal products and services. To Brennan and the other dissenters, the First Amendment does not permit suppression of truthful commercial speech as a means to control economic behavior.

Direct Advancement of the Government's Regulatory Interest

The third part of the *Central Hudson* test is whether a regulation on commercial speech directly advances the government's legitimate interest. It is one thing to conclude that the government has a legitimate interest in establishing a regulation; it is something else to determine that the regulation would directly advance the state's interest.

To suggest that a regulation on commercial speech will advance a governmental goal assumes that advertising is effective. If advertising does not affect consumers, there is no reason to regulate it. While empirical evidence is sketchy, the Supreme Court has usually assumed that advertising works and that a ban on advertising would therefore help the government to curb fraud, conserve electricity, protect community morals, preserve the environment, or serve other state interests.

In *Central Hudson,* the Court said there is an "immediate connection between advertising and demand for electricity."[35] Therefore, a ban on the electricity promotions would presumably advance the state's interest in conserving electricity. The ban on electricity promotions was declared unconstitutional in *Central Hudson,* not because it would not work, but because the ban was overbroad and therefore violated the fourth part of the *Central Hudson* test.

In the casino advertising case, the Court had no evidence that advertising would encourage Puerto Ricans to gamble, but, writing for the majority, Justice Rehnquist said it was "reasonable" for the Puerto Rican legislature to believe that advertising gambling on the island would increase the number of gamblers. Therefore, Rehnquist concluded that banning casino advertising would directly advance the state interest in curbing prostitution, crime, and other demoralizing activities the legislature said gambling spawned. However, three of the four dissenters in *Posadas*—Justices Brennan, Marshall, and Blackmun—spiritedly disputed Rehnquist's assumption that banning advertising would discourage gambling. In addition, the dissenters were not persuaded that gambling hurt society or that banning ads would benefit it.

The Court's ban on truthful advertising to discourage gambling by Puerto Ricans would seem to encourage advocates of banning ads for alcoholic beverages and cigarettes. Although the sale of alcoholic beverages is legal in Mississippi, a federal appeals court upheld a Mississippi law banning advertising for alcoholic beverages to discourage drinking. The Supreme Court refused to review the decision.[36] The American Medical Association has recommended a ban on all cigarette advertising even though cigarettes are legally sold in the United States.

A federal district court in Oklahoma, however, convinced that a state prohibi-

---

[35]447 U.S. at 569, 6 Media L. Rep. at 1502.

[36]Dunagin v. City of Oxford, 718 F.2d 738, 10 Media L. Rep. 1001 (5th Cir. 1983), *cert. denied,* 104 S. Ct. 3553 (1984).

tion on alcohol advertising would not discourage drinking, enjoined the state from enforcing an ad ban. Although the court said the ban on advertising did not violate the First Amendment, it held that the ban violated advertisers' rights to equal protection of the laws guaranteed by the Fourteenth Amendment. The court said the state statute barring the ads denied advertisers equal protection because the statute only prohibited in-state advertisements. Liquor companies were allowed under the law to bombard Oklahomans with alcohol advertisements through national publications, broadcast stations in neighboring states, and cable programs. The law also permitted beer advertisements within the state. Furthermore, the court noted there was no evidence that banning advertising lowers the demand for alcoholic beverages.[37]

Narrowly Drawn Ban   A regulation on truthful commercial speech must be narrowly drawn to be constitutional, even if the regulation advances a legitimate state interest. Although restrictions on commercial speech are not subject to the *strict scrutiny* that restrictions on political speech are, the Supreme Court said in *Central Hudson* that a regulation on commercial speech cannot be any broader than is necessary to carry out the regulation. The Supreme Court had sometimes interpreted the fourth *Central Hudson* requirement to mean that a regulation on commercial speech had to be the "least restrictive" possible. However, the Supreme Court ruled in *Board of Trustees v. Fox* that restrictions on commercial speech may be constitutional even if they are not the least restrictive.[38]

In *Fox,* the State University of New York at Buffalo had barred Tupperware sales in university dorms under a regulation prohibiting all private commercial enterprises in university facilities. The Supreme Court remanded the case for determination whether the regulation barring all private commercial enterprises was too broad. Writing for a six-judge majority, Justice Scalia said that regulations on commercial speech must be "narrowly tailored" to meet legislative purposes, but not the narrowest possible. Scalia said there should be a reasonable "fit" between legislative interests and the regulations employed to achieve them.

In *Central Hudson,* the Court found the ban on electricity promotions to be unconstitutionally broad because it was more extensive than necessary to further the government interest in energy conservation. The Court recognized that the New York Public Service Commission had a legitimate interest in regulating advertising to conserve energy. But the ban was unconstitutional, the Court said, because it barred promotional information about efficient as well as inefficient uses of electricity.

The Court said the Public Service Commission failed to demonstrate that its interest in energy conservation could not be advanced adequately by more limited regulation. Rather than ban all promotions, the Court said the Public Service Commission might further its conservation policy by ensuring that the utility's advertisements include information about the relative efficiency and expense of different uses of electricity.

Contrary to its ruling in *Central Hudson,* the Court in *Posadas de Puerto Rico*

---

[37]Oklahoma Broadcasters v. Crisp, 636 F. Supp. 978, 12 Media L. Rep. 2379 (W.D. Okla. 1986).
[38]109 S. Ct. 3028 (1989).

ruled that even though the government banned all casino ads in Puerto Rico, the ban was no more extensive than necessary to serve government interests. Justice Rehnquist said the government's policy, which permitted casino ads in the continental United States, was tailored to discourage gambling by local residents while attracting tourists to Puerto Rico's casinos.

Justice Brennan, joined by Justices Marshall and Blackmun, argued in his dissent in *Posadas de Puerto Rico* that the government could serve its legitimate purpose of discouraging gambling with more limited regulations. Rather than suppress truthful commercial expression, Brennan suggested that Puerto Rico increase its law enforcement efforts to curb the undesirable social effects it feared from casino gambling on the island. Brennan said that rather than stop advertising, the island government could guard against the development of corruption and the infiltration of organized crime into casinos. The Puerto Rican government could also enforce laws against prostitution and put limits on betting, Brennan said.

SUMMARY

The First Amendment protects commercial speech, but to a lesser degree than it protects other kinds of expression. The Supreme Court has said that the hardiness and verifiability of commercial speech justify lesser constitutional protections on advertising than on political and social commentary.

Commercial speech has been defined as expression promoting a commercial transaction. Under a four-part test developed by the Supreme Court, restrictions on commercial speech are constitutional if the expression is truthful and promotes a legal product or service. However, in *Posadas de Puerto Rico,* the Supreme Court ruled that even truthful, accurate advertising might be banned. Under the four-part test, truthful commercial speech may be restricted if the government asserts a substantial interest that will be advanced by a regulation. The regulation must also be narrowly tailored to serve government objectives.

UNFAIR AND DECEPTIVE ADVERTISING

Because false, deceptive, and unfair commercial advertisements are outside constitutional protection, they may be banned or altered under a number of federal and state laws. Regulatory agencies may halt or alter deceptive and misleading advertising and require advertisers to substantiate their claims. Advertising is regulated at the state and federal levels.

State Regulations

All 50 states prohibit unfair competition and unfair acts or practices. Under many state laws, consumers as well as competitors can sue to stop deceptive advertising and to recover damages and attorneys' fees.[39] During the Reagan years of deregulation, federal monitoring of deceptive advertising waned, spurring greater regulatory efforts in the states. Consequently, state attorneys general became more aggressive, suing airlines and car rental companies for deceptive advertising.

While states can only regulate advertising within their borders, regulations in important commercial states, such as Texas or Florida, have a national impact. During the Reagan years, state legislatures introduced and occasionally passed bills to regulate the sale of cigarettes, ban tobacco and alcohol advertisements, and require warnings on tobacco packages, including the Sugeon General's finding that nicotine is addictive. Bills to tax advertising were also introduced.

Federal Trade Commission

Despite the increased vigor among state regulators, the most important regulation of advertising occurs at the federal level. Several federal agencies, the most important of which is the Federal Trade Commission, regulate advertising. The FTC's rulings and reports not only define the scope of federal regulation, but also determine standards for state and industry regulatory bodies. In some states, compliance with the Federal Trade Commission Act is a defense in prosecutions under state antideception laws.

The FTC, which operates under the Federal Trade Commission Act of 1914, is a five-member commission whose members are appointed by the president to staggered seven-year terms. No more than three members can belong to the same political party. The commission has a large staff of attorneys, economists, and accountants who originate inquiries, issue reports, and conduct investigations.

The Federal Trade Commission originally had jurisdiction only over unfair and deceptive acts or practices that hurt competing companies. In 1938, however, the scope of the Federal Trade Commission Act was broadened to provide protection for consumers as well as competitors.[40] Although halting false and deceptive advertising is one of the FTC's assignments, the 1600-member agency spends much more of its time on other regulatory activities, including administering the antitrust laws. Indeed, the FTC has rather modest resources to monitor the messages on which advertisers spend $130 billion per year. The agency spends only about $3 million of its $70-million budget to combat false and deceptive advertising. At the heart of FTC advertising regulation is its power to require that advertisers substantiate the accuracy of advertising claims.[41]

During the Reagan presidency, the FTC's regulatory initiatives were curtailed by reduced budgets and the president's ideology of deregulation. Reagan's FTC chairman, James Miller, an economist, shared the president's view that government regulation of business should be reduced. Miller tried to draw the FTC back from regulation, particularly of less significant cases. In the 1980s, the FTC narrowed the definition of deception and demanded more empirical evidence than before on which to base a finding that an advertisement was deceptive or misleading.

---

[39]K. Plevan and M. Siroky, *Advertising Compliance Handbook* 343–45 (1988).
[40]15 U.S.C.A. sec. 53 (1973).
[41]K. Plevan and M. Siroky, *Advertising Compliance Handbook* 73 (1988).

Unfairness

The FTC may stop both unfair and deceptive advertising. Section 5 of the Federal Trade Commission Act declares unlawful unfair competition and unfair or deceptive acts or practices in commerce.[42] The Federal Trade Commission Act defines neither unfairness nor deception. However, unfair advertising is not of great concern to the commission. While a company's failure to substantiate advertising claims may be unfair, a subject discussed in a later section, unfairness issues are more likely to arise in a company's treatment of customers than in advertising.

The commission will find a commercial trading practice to be unfair when it causes substantial harm that a consumer or competitor may not reasonably avoid. The commission is not concerned with trivial or merely speculative harms. In most cases of unfairness, substantial injury involves monetary harm, as when sellers coerce consumers into purchasing unwanted goods or services. In one case, a company acted unfairly by refusing to allow its servicemen to reassemble furnaces they had dismantled until consumers agreed to buy services or replacement parts.[43]

Unwarranted health and safety risks may also support a finding of unfairness. A razor blade manufacturer was found to have acted unfairly when it distributed free samples of blades in newspapers, thus creating the possibility that small children might hurt themselves.[44] A tractor manufacturer was found to have acted unfairly when it failed to tell customers that opening the gas cap after the engine was hot might result in dangerous "geysering" of gasoline.[45]

In a few cases, advertisements have also been found to be unfair. The FTC said a cereal advertisement that focused on naturalist Euell Gibbons picking wild berries for nourishment was unfair because it might encourage children to eat wild berries that could be poisonous.

Deception

The FTC is more concerned with deception than unfairness. *Deception,* like *unfairness,* is not defined in the Federal Trade Commission Act. The FTC, however, has defined a deceptive ad as a material representation or omission that is likely to mislead consumers acting reasonably.[46] Thus, there are three elements for determining whether an advertisement is deceptive: (1) the probability of deception, (2) characteristics of consumers, and (3) materiality.

Probability of Deception Deceptive advertisements are those that either contain express falsehoods or create false impressions that tend to mislead. Courts and the FTC have long held that ads do not have to deceive someone to be deceptive; rather, ads must possess a "tendency," or "capacity," or be "likely" to mislead a reasonable

---

[42] 15 U.S.C.A. sec. 45(a) (1) (Supp. 1989).
[43] Holland Furnace Co. v. FTC, 295 F.2d 302 (1961).
[44] Philip Morris Inc., 82 F.T.C. 16 (1973).
[45] International Harvester Co., 104 F.T.C. 949 (1984).
[46] FTC, "Policy Statement on Deception," *appended to,* Cliffdale Assocs. Inc., 103 F.T.C. 110, 165 (1984).

consumer.[47] It does not matter whether the advertiser intends to mislead; an advertisement may have a tendency to deceive regardless of the advertiser's intent.

Deceptiveness is determined by the overall impression of an advertisement, not by isolated statements within it. Statements that might be susceptible to both a misleading and a nonmisleading interpretation will be considered deceptive.

Audience Whether an advertisement is deceptive depends not only upon its containing material misstatements or omissions, but upon the likelihood the ad will deceive those to whom it is addressed. The FTC has said an ad is deceptive only if it might mislead a consumer "acting reasonably in the circumstances."[48] An advertisement is not deceptive if it would mislead only a few particularly gullible consumers. After all, the FTC has said, a company "cannot be liable for every possible reading of its claims no matter how far-fetched."[49] Thus, for example, the law does not help the consumer who thinks Danish pastry comes from Denmark.[50]

The FTC may determine that an advertisement is deceptive simply by reading or viewing it. But often the FTC will rely on the testimony of experts and the results of consumer surveys. An ad is deceptive if it is likely to deceive a "substantial number" of consumers in the group to which it is directed.[51] An ad that tends to deceive 20 percent to 25 percent of the consumers in a survey is said to deceive a "substantial number."

While many ads are aimed at the general public, others are targeted at subgroups, such as children, the aged, or the sick. An ad is deceptive if it misleads a substantial number of consumers in the subgroup to which it is directed. An ad exaggerating the medicinal powers of a product might not deceive average, healthy adults but could be deceptive if directed to terminally ill consumers desperately seeking a cure.[52] Misleading promises of easy weight loss might deceive the obese but not necessarily the average consumer.[53]

For many years, the FTC has been especially attentive to ads aimed at children because children are "unqualified by age or experience to anticipate or appreciate the possibility that representations may be exaggerated or untrue."[54] For example, children might be deceived by the apparently miraculous performance of toys in an advertisement.

Advertisers are not liable if accurate ads aimed at doctors, lawyers, and other specialists are misunderstood by a typical consumer. Laymen read at their own risk the technical language in ads directed to experts.[55]

---

[47]Cliffdale Associates, Inc., 103 F.T.C. 110, 184 (1984).

[48]"Policy Statement on Deception," *appended to,* Cliffdale Assocs., Inc., 103 F.T.C. 110, 175 (1984).

[49]International Harvester Co., 104 F.T.C. 949, 1057 (1984).

[50]*See* Heinz W. Kirchner, 63 F.T.C. 1282, 1290 (1963).

[51]Bailey and Pertschuk, "Deception Policy Statement Prepared by Commissioners Bailey and Pertschuk and Transmitted on Feb. 29 to the House Energy and Commerce Committee," 46 Antitrust & Trade Reg. Rep. (BNA) 372, 393 (1984).

[52]Travel King Inc., 86 F.T.C. 715, 719 (1975).

[53]Porter & Dietsch Inc., 90 F.T.C. 770, 864–65 (1977), *aff'd,* Porter & Dietsch Inc. v. FTC, 605 F.2d 294 (7th Cir. 1979), *cert. denied,* 445 U.S. 950 (1980).

[54]Ideal Toy Corp., 64 F.T.C. 297, 310 (1964).

[55]Koch v. FTC, 206 F.2d 311 (6th Cir. 1953).

Materiality To be deceptive, advertising that has a tendency to deceive the average consumer must be material. A material statement in advertising, like a material statement in corporate securities transactions, is one that is likely to affect a purchasing decision. A material advertising claim need not actually affect a consumer's decision to buy a product, nor must the consumer lose money for the ad to be considered deceptive. An ad is deceptive if it is likely to, or has the capacity to, affect consumer choices.

The FTC will not undertake costly litigation against false advertising that has no capacity to affect consumer choices. The FTC is not concerned with false advertising claims that are harmless or easily ignored.

Material statements include express claims and deliberately implied claims about a product or service. An omission in an advertisement may also be material if the seller knows or should know that consumers need the omitted information to form an accurate impression. The FTC has found advertising claims or omissions about health, safety, efficacy, durability, performance, warranties, quality, and cost to be material. Indeed, the FTC considers most factual advertising claims about a product to be material. After all, the commission has observed, advertisers would not make factual claims if the advertisers did not intend to affect consumers' choices.[56]

Consumer decisions would be affected, for example, by a material claim that only one brand of air conditioner assures cooling on extra hot, humid days.[57] Likewise, a claim that aspirin relieves pain better than other pain relievers is material,[58] as is a claim that a skin cream contains aspirin. However, it would not be material to say in an advertisement that a tire company's main office is red when it is white. The color of the building would not be material to a consumer's decision to buy tires.

Material statements that are likely to deceive may consist of express falsehoods as well as true statements that imply falsehood.

Express Falsehoods Expressly false statements about product attributes are almost always deceptive. The FTC has defined express claims as ones that make a direct representation. The meaning of express falsehoods, like the meaning of libel *per se,* can be determined from the plain meaning of the words.[59] The message is stated unequivocally. Express falsehoods include a claim that merchandise is "antique" when it is not old enough to qualify as antique,[60] that coffee is "caffeine free" when the brew contains caffeine, or that goods are "fireproof" when they are only fire resistant.[61] Explicit falsity has also been found where merchandise was called "genuine" when it was a simulation or imitation.[62]

It is also deceptive to reprint a newspaper story in an advertisement if the story contains material falsehoods. The U.S. Court of Appeals for the Second Circuit up-

---

[56]*See* "Policy Statement on Deception," *appended to,* Cliffdale Assoc., Inc., 103 F.T.C. 110, 182 (1984).

[57]Fedders Corp. v. FTC, 529 F.2d 1398 (2d Cir.), *cert. denied,* 429 U.S. 818 (1976).

[58]American Home Products, 98 F.T.C. 136, 368 (1981), *aff'd,* American Home Products Corp. v. FTC, 695 F.2d 681 (3rd Cir. 1982).

[59]Thompson Medical Co., 104 F.T.C. 648, 788 (1984).

[60]State v. Cohn, 188 A.2d 878 (Conn. Cir. Ct. 1962).

[61]Perfect Mfg. Co., 43 F.T.C. 238 (1946).

[62]Masland Duraleather Co. v. FTC. 34 F.2d 733 (3d Cir. 1929). *See also* Omega Importing Corp. v. Petri-Kine Camera Co., 451 F.2d 1190 (2d Cir. 1971) (deceptive to confuse place of origin).

held an order prohibiting the Murray Space Shoe Corporation from reprinting newspaper articles that suggested the shoes helped cure foot disorders. In one reprinted article a man said he thought the space shoes helped relieve his high blood pressure. The real purpose of the shoes was to relieve discomfort caused by poorly fitting shoes.[63]

An ad is also deceptive if it contains an expressly false demonstration of a product. In the famous sandpaper shave case, Rapid Shave was made to appear in a television commercial to have the moistening power to soak sandpaper for an effortless shave. The voice in the television commercial told viewers they were seeing proof that Rapid Shave could shave "tough dry sandpaper." However, viewers were not shown sandpaper being shaved. Instead, viewers saw a piece of Plexiglas on which sand had been spread. After Rapid Shave was applied, a razor whisked the sand away.[64]

The ability of Rapid Shave to soften sandpaper was not disputed, at least if considerable time was allowed. However, Colgate-Palmolive, the makers of Rapid Shave, said it substituted Plexiglas for sandpaper only to compensate for the technical distortions of television. Colgate-Palmolive said sandpaper on television looked like unattractive, plain, brown paper.

The FTC and the Supreme Court ruled the Plexiglas mock-up was materially deceptive because it was used as "actual proof of an advertising claim." Even though Rapid Shave could shave sandpaper if enough soaking time was allowed, the Supreme Court said the demonstration was deceptive because it falsely told viewers they were seeing objective proof of a product's performance. The Court said the false demonstration was similar to false testimony by a celebrity or expert. If simulations cannot be shown on television in a truthful manner, the Court said, "this indicates that television is not a medium that lends itself to this type of commercial, not that the commercial must survive at all costs."

The Court's ruling does not foreclose the use of mock-ups to overcome the technical distortions of television. Mock-ups may be used if they are not employed falsely to prove a product claim. For example, an advertiser could use mashed potatoes to represent ice cream in an ad for table linen if ice cream would melt too quickly under hot television lights. However, mashed potatoes should not be used in an ice cream advertisement to demonstrate the velvety texture and succulent colors of ice cream. Props are only deceptive if they are used falsely as proof of a product claim.

Implied Falsehoods More common and more difficult to identify than express falsehoods are statements or omissions in advertisements that create a false impression by implication. The FTC defines implied claims circularly as claims that are not express.[65] An implication can be thought of as a false meaning added to a truthful advertisement by the reader or viewer because of an impression created by an advertisement. For example, a consumer might infer that a tire manufacturer's claims are backed by scientific tests if "technicians" in white jackets attest to the superior stopping power of the tires. If no scientific tests support the tire manufacturer's claims,

---

[63]Murray Space Shoe Corp. v. FTC, 304 F.2d 270 (2d Cir. 1962).
[64]FTC v. Colgate-Palmolive Co., 380 U.S. 374 (1965).
[65]Thompson Medical Co., 104 F.T.C. 648, 788 (1984).

the advertiser establishes a false implication. Ivan Preston, Professor of Advertising at the University of Wisconsin, has identified fifteen categories of implications that may be deceptive.[66] Following are several:

Reasonable Basis Implication   The Federal Trade Commission assumes that advertisers have a *reasonable basis* for the objective claims in their advertisements if they can substantiate their material claims with results from scientific tests or other appropriate evidence. Thus, an advertiser who says its tires stop faster than others should have scientific evidence to back the claim.

An advertiser's ability to support substantive claims is a material element, the absence of which is deceptive. Consumers, the FTC says, are less likely to rely on claims for products and services if they know the advertisers have no reasonable basis for making them.[67] The FTC may find an advertisement deceptive, even if the claim is true, if the advertiser has no reasonable basis for making the claim.

The FTC originated the substantiation requirement in 1972 when it ruled an advertising claim by the Pfizer pharmaceutical company lacked a reasonable basis.[68] Although *Pfizer* was technically an unfairness case, many ad-substantiation cases since *Pfizer* have been pursued with similar results on the basis of deception.[69] In *Pfizer,* the FTC was not satisfied that the pharmaceutical company had adequate substantiation for its claims that Unburn suntan lotion "actually anesthetizes nerves" to relieve pain. The company could offer no scientific data to support the claim. The FTC said that "failure to possess substantiation amounts to a lack of reasonable basis, which in turn is an unfair act or practice under section 5" of the Federal Trade Commission Act.

The FTC said in *Pfizer* that substantiation might be provided through scientific studies, existing medical literature, tests conducted by makers of similar competing products, or, in some cases, the successful wide use of a product. But Pfizer had virtually no evidence for its claims for Unburn tanning lotion.

Advertisers should possess substantiation before they make claims about safety, performance, efficiency, quality, and price. If an advertisement asserts a certain level of scientific support by saying "tests prove" or "studies show," the advertiser must be able to provide results supporting the claim from two scientifically valid tests. If an ad does not claim a certain level of supporting data, the FTC determines a reasonable basis for claims by considering the type of claim, the product, and the consequences for consumers of a false claim. The FTC also considers the benefits of a truthful claim, the cost to the company of developing substantiation, and the amount of substantiation experts in the field believe is reasonable.[70]

The Firestone Tire & Rubber Company issued deceptive and unfair advertisements by failing to substantiate a claim that the company's Super Sport Wide Oval

---

[66]Preston, "The Federal Trade Commission's Identification of Implications as Constituting Deceptive Advertising," 57 *University of Cincinnati Law Review* 1243 (1989).

[67]"FTC Policy Statement Regarding Advertising Substantiation," *in,* Thompson Medical Co., 104 F.T.C. 648, 839–40 (1984).

[68]Pfizer, Inc., 81 F.T.C. 23 (1972).

[69]Ford and Calfee, "Recent Developments in FTC Policy on Deception," 50 *J. of Marketing* 98 (1986).

[70]"Policy Statement Regarding Advertising Substantiation Program," *in,* Thompson Medical Co., 104 F.T.C. 648, 839–40 (1984).

tires "stop 25 percent quicker." The tires did stop a car quicker than other tires on wet concrete, but the company lacked "substantial scientific test data" to prove that the tires performed significantly better in the many different road conditions American motorists encounter.[71] Similarly, a company marketing Acne Satin, a skin medication promoted by singer Pat Boone, lacked substantiation for its claims that Acne Satin "cures acne, eliminates or reduces the bacteria and fatty acids responsible for acne blemishes."[72]

The FTC may reconsider a substantiation ruling if scientific opinion changes. In 1974, the commission prohibited the Sterling Drug Company from claiming that Lysol Disinfectant Spray prevents colds. The FTC's ruling was based on the best scientific evidence of the time, which concluded that colds were transmitted by airborne viruses that would not be affected by Lysol, which was used to clean counters, tables, and other surfaces. However, the commission lifted its ban when new scientific evidence indicated that colds may be transmitted through contact with surfaces that can be cleaned with Lysol. As new research began to appear, the FTC said Sterling could advertise that Lysol can prevent colds as long as successive claims were supported by "competent and reliable scientific evidence."[73]

Proof Implication   Besides the substantiation implication, Professor Preston also identifies the proof implication. A false implication of proof is created if an advertiser misrepresents the evidence presented to substantiate an advertising claim. Ads are deceptive if they misuse test data, create a phony aura of scientific support, or otherwise imply proof that does not exist. In the Firestone advertisement just mentioned, the company created a false implication of proof by saying that the company's "racing research" established that Firestone tires stop 25 percent quicker. The implication was deceptive because, while the company had conducted tests, the company had no tests comparing the ability of Firestone and other tires to stop a car under normal driving conditions.[74]

The U.S. Court of Appeals for the Second Circuit ruled that an advertisement citing a hint of superiority for Bayer aspirin was an accurate presentation of scientific proof. The ad pointed out that a study found no significant difference in the speed with which the tested pain relievers worked. Nonetheless, the ad said, "it is interesting to note that within fifteen minutes, Bayer Aspirin had a somewhat higher pain relief score than any of the other products." While the significance of the higher pain relief score was not known, the court ruled that the ad was not deceptive because it accurately presented the conclusions of the study.[75]

Demonstration Implication   Product demonstrations may also create deceptive implications in advertising. In the Rapid Shave case discussed earlier, a mock-up was misleading because it falsely demonstrated the moistening power of a shaving cream.

---

[71]Firestone Tire & Rubber Co. v. FTC, 481 F.2d 246 (6th Cir. 1973), *cert. denied,* 414 U.S. 1112 (1973).

[72]National Media Group, Inc., 94 F.T.C. 1096 (1979).

[73]Sterling Drug Co., Order Reopening and Modifying 1974 Cease and Desist Order, 48 Fed. Reg. 14891, 14892 (1983).

[74]Firestone Tire & Rubber Co. v. FTC, 481 F.2d 246 (6th Cir. 1973), *cert. denied,* 414 U.S. 1112 (1973).

[75]FTC v. Sterling Drug, Inc., 317 F.2d 669 (1963).

More often, however, a demonstration is true, but nevertheless creates a false impression about how the product will perform in normal circumstances. The FTC found misleading an advertisement in which a sandwich was kept dry under water in a Baggies lunch bag while the sandwich in a competitor's bag was soaked. The demonstration was accurate, but it falsely implied that Baggies were superior to other sandwich bags for keeping food fresh in a refrigerator or lunchbox. "Dunking the sealed bags in a sink of water and swishing them vigorously . . . is not proof of the comparative abilities of the two bags to prevent food spoilage," the FTC said.[76]

The Standard Oil Company of California falsely implied through a demonstration of clean air and a pollution meter that Chevron gasoline with F-310 removed all or most pollutants from engine exhaust. In one ad, a car burning Chevron with F-310 emitted clear exhaust into a large see-through balloon tied to the exhaust pipe of the car. In another ad, the exhaust was contained in a transparent bag encircling the car. In a third, a meter dial labeled "exhaust emissions" pointed to "100" at the "dirty" end of the scale before Chevron with F-310 was used. After "just six tankfuls," the meter pointed to "20," four-fifths of the way toward "0" at the "clean" end of the scale. Meanwhile, another car in the ads, a car whose gasoline did not contain F-310, continued to emit dirty exhaust that clouded the balloon and bag.

The balloon ads were deceptive, the FTC said, because the clear Chevron exhaust appeared to contain no pollutants, when in fact it contained invisible but significant amounts of carbon monoxide and hydrocarbons. Indepedent scientific tests revealed that the F-310 additive did reduce pollutants, but not as much as the balloon and bag demonstrations indicated. The ads were deceptive, the FTC said, "because of the substantial disparity between the visual impact of the demonstrations and the evidence which showed the actual average reductions."[77] The meter, too, was misleading because the drop of 80 units from the dirty end to the clean end did not correspond to the percentage reduction in pollutants a typical motorist would experience from using Chevron with F-310.

The U.S. Court of Appeals for the Ninth Circuit ruled that BBD&O, the advertising agency in the Chevron case, bore responsibility for the deceptive demonstrations. It is not enough that an advertising agency know that products will perform as the manufacturer claims, the court said. The agency also has a responsibility to represent that performance accurately. BBD&O argued that it should not be liable because it based the ads on information that had been validated by independent tests and approved by several departments at Chevron, including engineering, research, and law.

However, the Ninth Circuit said it was not sufficient for BBD&O to satisfy itself only that F-310 did in fact reduce pollution. The agency also had a responsibility to ensure the accuracy of the implicit representations the ads conveyed. Said the court:

> No specialized engineer was needed to put BBD&O on notice that a gauge which drops from a reading of 100 ("dirty") to 20 ("clean") implies a sweeping representation with reference to the change in level of pollution discharge. In light of the advertising agency's active participation in developing this advertising, it was

---

[76]Colgate-Palmolive Co., 77 F.T.C. 150 (1970).
[77]Standard Oil Co. of Calif., 84 F.T.C. 1401, 1470 (1974).

BBD&O's responsibility to assure itself not only that the gauge was not rigged, but also that use of the gauge did not convey a distorted impression.[78]

No Qualification Implication   Advertisements are misleading if they omit a necessary qualification. The FTC ruled, for instance, that a Firestone tire advertisement was misleading because it claimed without qualification that Firestone was "The Safe Tire." The company's claim was supported by the statement that Firestone tires pass all of the company's inspections.[79]

However, while Firestone marketed no tires that failed company inspections, the FTC ruled that the unqualified claim that Firestone tires were "safe" was deceptive because it falsely implied that the tires were free of all defects. Indeed, 15 percent of the respondents in a consumer survey thought the company was claiming its tires were free of defects. But tests available at the time were insufficiently accurate to detect all defects in a tire.

Ineffective Qualification Implication   Consumers are always warned to read the small type in an advertisement for qualifications, but the FTC says ads may be deceptive even if they contain accurate, but ineffective, qualifications. "A qualification presented weakly has the same impact as a qualification completely absent," Professor Preston observes.[80]

The FTC ruled that the advertisements for Chevron gasoline with F-310 were deceptive not only because the clear bags belied scientific tests for pollution, but also because the visual impact of the clear bags overwhelmed the verbal and written qualifications in the broadcast and print versions of the ads. The verbal and written parts of both balloon ads did not claim that the Chevron exhaust was completely "clean," only that it was "cleaner" than the other exhaust. Nor did the ads claim that Chevron eliminated pollution, only that it reduced it. Despite this qualifying language, the Federal Trade Commission ruled that the ads were misleading because the "strong, predominant visual message" of the clear balloons and bags implied a complete reduction in pollutants. "The net impression," the FTC said, "is overwhelmingly influenced by the striking visual portions of the advertisements."[81]

Significance Implication   Insignificant facts stated so that they appear to be significant also create a false implication in advertising. In one case, advertisements for Old Gold cigarettes were deceptive even though they truthfully claimed that Old Golds were found "lowest in throat-irritating tars and resins." Though true, the ads created the false implication that smokers would benefit from choosing Old Golds over other brands.[82]

---

[78]Standard Oil Company of Calif. v. FTC, 577 F.2d 653, 660 (1978).

[79]Firestone Tire & Rubber Co., 81 F.T.C. 398, 457 (1972), *aff'd,* 481 F.2d 246 (6th Cir.), *cert. denied,* 414 U.S. 1112 (1973).

[80]"The Federal Trade Commission's Identification of Implications as Constituting Deceptive Advertising," 57 *U. Cincinnati L. Rev.* 1243, 1281 (1989).

[81]Standard Oil Co. of Cal., 84 F.T.C. 1401, 1471 (1974), *modified,* 577 F.2d 653 (9th Cir. 1978), *modified order,* 95 F.T.C. 866 (1980).

[82]P. Lorillard Co. v. FTC, 186 F.2d 52 (4th Cir. 1950).

The study on which the cigarette ad claims were based was reported in *Reader's Digest*. In its report of the study, *Reader's Digest* concluded that the difference in tar and nicotine among cigarette brands was too insignificant to be important to smokers. One cigarette is "just about as good as another" to "nail down" a smoker's coffin, the *Digest* said.

The FTC ruled, in a decision upheld by a federal appeals court, that the Old Gold ads were deceptive because they falsely implied a significant difference among cigarettes. The advertisements, the court said, used the truth in a perverted way "to cause the reader to believe the exact opposite of what was intended" in the *Reader's Digest* article. Similarly, advertisements for Carnation Instant Breakfast were ruled to be misleading when they claimed the product provided "as much mineral nourishment as two strips of bacon." Bacon, it turns out, is not a good source of the most commonly recommended minerals.[83] Likewise, Gainesburgers' claims to provide all the milk protein a dog needs were of misleading significance because dogs do not need milk protein.[84]

Puffery Implication   While advertising claims are supposed to be factual and represent the experience of the people making them, the law of advertising, like the law of libel, leaves room for subjective statements of opinion. Advertisers may exaggerate or "puff" their products on such subjective matters as taste, feel, appearance and smell. The commission assumes that ordinary consumers do not take puffery seriously.

It is acceptable puffery for an advertiser to say that a foreign sports car is "the sexiest European,"[85] that "Bayer works wonders"[86] or that a motor oil is the "perfect" lubrication, allowing a car to travel an "amazing distance" without an oil change.[87] "So far as we know," a federal appeals court said, "there is nothing perfect' in this world, which undoubtedly means nothing more than that the product is good or of high quality." Such exaggeration is recognized as puffery and creates no false implication.

Puffery becomes deception when exaggerated claims falsely imply material assertions of superiority. The FTC ruled that Jay Norris Company went beyond acceptable puffery when it advertised that a television antenna was an "electronic miracle." The FTC said the statement was one of several exaggerated claims that could lead consumers to believe falsely that the antenna was generally superior.[88]

Expertise and Endorsement Implications   The FTC defines an expert as someone who has acquired superior knowledge of a subject as a result of experience, study, or training. Endorsements by experts and celebrities, unlike statements by company

---

[83]Carnation Co., 77 F.T.C. 1547, 1549 (1970).
[84]General Foods Corp., 84 F.T.C. 1572, 1573 (1974).
[85]Bristol-Myers Co., 102 F.T.C. 21, 321 (1983), *aff'd,* 738 F.2d 554 (2nd Cir. 1984).
[86]Sterling Drug, Inc., 102 F.T.C. at 752, *aff'd,* 741 F.2d 1146, 1150 (1984).
[87]Kidder Oil Co. v. FTC, 117 F.2d 892, 901 *reh'g denied,* (7th Cir. 1941).
[88]Jay Norris, Inc., 91 F.T.C. 751 (1978), *aff'd,* Jay Norris Inc. v. FTC, 598 F.2d 1244 (2d Cir.), *cert. denied,* 444 U.S. 980 (1979).

spokespersons, are regulated because testimonials by experts and celebrities are thought to carry special weight with consumers.[89] If experts claim in an advertisement that a product is superior, FTC guidelines require that the experts have expertise relevant to their product endorsements. Astronaut Gordon Cooper's endorsement of a fuel-saving automobile engine attachment was ruled to be deceptive because the astronaut's expertise was not in the field of automobile engines.[90] Experts are also supposed to have compared a product they endorse with others.

Similarly, a product endorsement by an organization should be based on objective evaluation of the product by the professional standards of the organization.[91] Thus, mattresses endorsed by a chiropractic association should perform to standards set by the profession. The FTC ruled that racing drivers' endorsement of toy cars was misleading because the drivers lacked competence to judge the worth of the cars.[92] A police department or sports team should base its selection of a product for official use on comparative tests with other products.[93]

Neither ordinary citizens nor celebrities need possess special expertise to endorse a product. However, endorsements by celebrities and average citizens imply that consumers generally will experience the same personal satisfaction as the endorsers. If atypical experience is to be demonstrated, such as removal of a particularly stubborn stain from the wash, a disclaimer should be included telling the customer that his or her experience may be different.[94]

According to FTC guidelines, celebrities and common citizens who endorse a product should actually use it; if they discontinue use, they should also stop their testimonials.[95] Singer Pat Boone's endorsement of Acne-Satin, a skin medication, was ruled to be deceptive because, contrary to his testimonials, not all his daughters used the product. Boone was ordered to contribute his share of profits from Acne-Satin sales as restitution for people who bought the product. The advertising agency also paid.[96]

At one time it was necessary to tell consumers if celebrities were paid for their endorsements. Such disclosure is no longer necessary becaust the FTC reasons that consumers will assume celebrities are paid for their testimonials. But an advertisement is supposed to reveal if a typical consumer is paid to endorse a product in an ad. However, it may not be necessary to reveal payment to average citizens if the endorsements are made for consumer "research" or other nonpromotional purposes and are only later used in advertisements.[97]

---

[89]See Comment, "FTC Regulation of Endorsements in Advertising: In the Consumer's Behalf?," 8 *Pepperdine L. Rev.* 97, 701 (1981).

[90]Cooper, 94 F.T.C. 674 (1979).

[91]16 C.F.R. sec. 255.4 (1990).

[92]Mattel, Inc., 79 F.T.C. 667, 669 (1971), *modified,* 104 F.T.C. 555 (1984).

[93]16 C.F.R. sec. 255.3 (1990).

[94]16 C.F.R. sec. 255.2 (1990).

[95]FTC Guides Concerning Use of Endorsements and Testimonials in Advertising, 16 C.F.R. sec. 255 (1990).

[96]Cooga Mooga, 92 F.T.C. 310 (1978).

[97]"Real People Star in Many Ads, But Are They Really Credible?," *Wall Street Journal,* May 23, 1985, at 33.

SUMMARY

A number of federal and state agencies prohibit harmful trade practices. However, the Federal Trade Commission is the main enforcer of truth in advertising. Deceptive advertisements contain material statements or omissions that are likely to mislead reasonable consumers. Ads are deceptive if they contain expressly false statements or demonstrations. Ads are also deceptive if they contain true statements that convey a misleading implication. Deceptive implications may be found in advertisements that lack substantiation, contain misleading proofs or demonstrations, lack sufficient qualification, imply false singificance, puff excessively, and rely misleadingly on expertise and endorsements.

FTC POWERS AND REMEDIES

The FTC has a number of powers to keep advertising accurate. Some powers are future-looking, providing guidance to advertisers so that they can avoid deceptive advertising. Some powers focus on the present, permitting the agency to halt or correct a misleading or deceptive ad. One of its most important powers is the authority to require advertisers to be able to substantiate ads before they are disseminated. Other FTC powers include staff opinion letters, industry guidelines, trade regulation rules, consent decrees, cease-and-desist orders, affirmative disclosure, and corrective advertising. In addition, the FTC as well as advertisers can seek court injunctions against deceptive ads.

Prospective Remedies

The FTC's opinion letters, advisory opinions, industry guides, policy statements, and trade regulation rules are broad statements that tell advertisers before they disseminate advertisements the kinds of statements and practices that may be deceptive. These are *prospective,* or future-looking, guidelines that help advertisers avoid deceptive practices.

Staff Opinion Letters   Staff opinion letters are not specifically mentioned in the FTC's rules. They are a form of quick, free advice that does not bind the commission. If an advertiser wants an informal opinion on whether an ad might violate the law, the advertiser can ask for an opinion letter.

Advisory Opinions   If advertisers want to know more than they can learn in a staff opinion letter about whether a contemplated activity would be legal, they can write to the FTC for an advisory opinion. An advisory opinion, which is more formal than a staff opinion letter, is placed on the public record and protects the requesting party who follows the advice from litigation until such time as the commission might shift its position.[98] However, while the advertiser who follows an advisory opinion is protected from a suit, an advertiser may find the commission's advice burdensome because the commission tends to be stricter in its advisory opinions than in its litigation.

Industry Guides   Under section 18 of the Federal Trade Commission Act, the commission may prescribe "interpretive rules and general statements of policy with respect to unfair or deceptive acts or practices." One form of general statement is an industry guide. Unlike an advisory opinion, an industry guide is written for a whole industry. An industry guide is the FTC's interpretation of federal law. If an advertiser fails to comply with a guide, the FTC may begin adjudicative proceedings.[99]

FTC industry guides prescribe legal practices, often in minute detail, for advertising and labeling of products as diverse as adhesives, dog food, toupees, and textiles.[100] FTC regulations on product endorsements and testimonials are issued in the form of industry guidelines, as are regulations on bait-and-switch advertising and cigarette labeling.[101] Sometimes industry guides are required by Congress. For example, a section of the Fur Products Labeling Act required the FTC to establish a fur products name guide so that animals used in furs would be uniformly identified. One FTC industry guide specifies that the word *free* may be used in an advertisement even if a consumer is charged a small fee for postage and handling.[102] Another industry guide tells broadcast rating companies that broadcast audience rating claims must be based on scientifically respectable surveys of viewers.[103]

Policy Statements   More general than industry guides are statements of policy issued by the FTC. Policy statements tell in general terms the FTC's enforcement attitude. While policy statements do not have the force of law, they do tell advertisers what practices the FTC might challenge.

The commission has issued policy statements encouraging comparative advertising, thus telling advertisers that previous opposition to comparative advertising is no longer FTC policy. In another policy statement, the FTC reaffirmed its commitment to prior substantiation of ad claims.[104] The FTC has also stated a policy to determine on a case-by-case basis whether corrective advertising is appropriate.[105]

Trade Regulation Rules   A more sweeping and legally potent FTC power is the Trade Regulation Rule, or TRR. Under section 6(g) of the Federal Trade Commission Act, the commission may "make rules and regulations for the purpose of carrying out the provisions of the Act." The commission also has authority to issue rules under the Wool Products Labeling Act and other statutes the FTC administers.

Under the rule-making authority, the commission has issued a number of trade

---

[98]16 C.F.R. secs. 1.1 to 1.4 (1989).

[99]16 C.F.R. sec. 1.5. *See, generally,* G. Rosden and P. Rosden, 3 *Law of Advertising* sec. 32.04[2] (1989).

[100]*See* Deceptive Labeling and Advertising of Adhesive Compositions, 16 C.F.R. sec. 235 (1989); Dog and Cat Food Industry, 16 C.F.R. sec. 241; Labeling, Advertising, and Sale of Wigs and Other Hairpieces, 16 C.F.R. sec. 252.

[101]16 C.F.R. sec. 255 (endorsements and testimonials); 16 C.F.R. sec. 238 (bait and switch advertising).

[102]16 C.F.R. sec. 251.

[103]Guidelines for Audience Rating Claims, 4 *Trade Reg. Rep.* (CCH) para. 39,026 (eff. Aug. 27, 1969).

[104]16 C.F.R. sec. 14.15 (1989) (comparative advertising); 49 Fed. Reg. 30999 (1984) (substantiation).

[105]Corrective Advertising: Position Regarding Rule or Policy Statement, 4 *Trade Reg. Rep.* (CCH) para. 39,046 (1979).

regulation rules that, like industry guides, are favored by the commission because they allow for a more uniform and efficient policy than individual commission decisions. Trade regulation rules, like industry guides, affect whole industries, not just an individual company or advertiser.

Trade regulation rules are more potent than industry guides, however. An advertiser who violates an industry guide does not violate the law but may be taken to court on charges of unfair or deceptive practices under section 5 of the Federal Trade Commission Act. But violation of a trade regulation rule is itself a violation of law. An advertiser who violates a TRR can be asked to refund money, return property, pay damages, and pay civil penalties of up to $10,000 a day.

When the FTC wishes to issue a trade regulation rule, it must publish the text of the rule and reasons why the rule is proposed. Advertisers, manufacturers, and the public can then present written comments and testify at hearings. A final rule can be challenged in a federal appeals court within 60 days of its promulgation.

The commission first asserted the power to issue trade rules in the early 1960s, when it issued the rule requiring a health warning on cigarette packages.[106] In the years following, the commission issued a number of rules, often specifying rather mundane requirements such as what information must be included in advertising about the power output of home amplifiers and how the size of TV screens is to be measured (diagonally). One trade regulation rule requires manufacturers to print warnings against breathing the quick-freezing aerosol sprays used for frosting cocktail glasses.[107]

In the 1970s, the FTC issued several trade regulation rules that the commission said were necessary to prevent unfairness. The FTC's power expanded in 1972 when the Supreme Court recognized the FTC's authority to regulate advertising for unfairness.[108] The FTC gained wide authority to issue broad trade regulation rules to prohibit unfair or deceptive practices when President Ford signed the Magnuson-Moss Warranty Federal Trade Commission Improvement Act in 1975.[109] With expanded power under Magnuson-Moss, an activist, liberal FTC issued several proposed rules to correct unfairness. The commission adopted rules regulating eyeglass advertising, requiring publicity for vocational schools to include enrollment and job placement statistics, and requiring funeral directors, credit agencies, used-car and mobile-home dealers to reveal more information to consumers.[110]

Businesses and advertisers opposed these rules because they considered *unfairness* to be too vague a term. The proposed rule that drew the most fire and that illustrated the expansive dimension of *unfairness,* was a plan to ban all television advertising directed at children. The ban was justified, the FTC argued, because the

---

[106]FTC Trade Regulation Rule for the Prevention of Unfair or Deceptive Acts or Practices in the Sale of Cigarettes, 29 Fed. Reg. 8324, 8355 (1964).

[107]16 C.F.R. sec. 432 (1989) (amplifiers); 16 C.F.R. sec. 410 (measurement of television screens); 16 C.F.R. sec. 417 (aerosol sprays).

[108]FTC v. Sperry & Hutchinson Co., 405 U.S. 233, 244–45 n.5 (1972).

[109]Pub. L. 93-637, 88 Stat. 2183, 15 U.S.C. sec. 45 *et seq.* (1975).

[110]*See, e.g.,* Advertising of Ophthalmic Goods and Services, 43 Fed. Reg. 23,992 (1978); Proprietary Vocational and Home Study Schools 43 Fed. Reg. 60796, 60800 (1978); FTC Trade Regulation Rule for the Prevention of Unfair or Deceptive Acts or Practices in the Sale of Cigarettes, 29 Fed. Reg. 8325, 8355 (1964). *See, generally,* E. Rockefeller, *Desk Book of FTC Practice and Procedure* 139–41 (3d. ed. 1979).

relationship between powerful, sophisticated corporate advertisers and susceptible children was inherently unfair.[111] The networks, advertisers, and toy manufacturers, with $661 million in advertising revenues at stake, disagreed. If corporate advertising to children is inherently unfair, they asked, why isn't all advertising unfair? Is even the average adult a match for the refined marketing and psychological skills of Madison Avenue professionals with millions to spend on an ad campaign?

Responding to the criticism of the FTC's aggressive campaign against unfairness, Congress passed the Federal Trade Commission Improvements Act of 1980, which ordered the FTC to abandon its children's advertising rule proposal.[112] The act also barred the FTC from issuing more trade regulation rules in the name of fairness. The prohibition, which has been extended, allows the FTC to ban individual ads as unfair but does not permit the agency to issue trade regulation rules on the basis of unfairness.

Halting Advertisements

If the warnings in advisory opinions, industry guides, and trade regulation rules fail to prevent deceptive advertising, the FTC can halt illegal ads through the use of consent decrees and cease-and-desist orders. In addition, a competing advertiser who might be hurt by a deceptive advertisement can seek an injunction in court.

Consent Decrees   More than 90 percent of FTC cases are settled by consent decrees in which a party agrees to discontinue an advertising practice.[113] Most consent decrees originate when a citizen or—more frequently—a competitor, sends a letter of complaint to the FTC. Commission staff members, either in Washington or at one of the several regional FTC bureaus, may also originate an inquiry. If it appears that ads are deceptive, the staff conducts an investigation. If the investigation reveals that corrective action may be necessary, a proposed complaint may be submitted to the commission. The commission notifies the party of the proposed complaint and asks whether the party would sign a consent order agreeing to discontinue the deceptive practice.[114] In one consent case, the Ford Motor Company and its advertising agency, J. Walter Thompson Company, agreed to stop claiming that the Ford LTD ran quieter than a glider in flight. The FTC said the ad was misleading because a glider makes a lot of noise.[115]

Advertisers have a strong incentive to sign consent decrees. If they do not, the FTC may file a formal complaint against them. The formal complaint is often accompanied by considerable bad publicity, much more than accompanies a consent decree. In addition, an advertiser who signs a consent decree is not required to admit to false or deceptive advertising. Furthermore, a consent decree saves the costs and time of litigation. A signed consent order is published for public comment and becomes final

---

[111]FTC Staff Report on Television Advertising to Children (1978).

[112]5 U.S.C.A. sec. 45 *et seq.* (1980).

[113]G. Rosden & P. Rosden , 3 *Law of Advertising* sec. 33.01 (1989).

[114]Id. sec. 33.02[2]; E. Rockefeller, *Desk Book of FTC Practice and Procedure,* 105–109 (3d ed. 1979).

[115]Ford Motor Co., *Trade Reg. Rep.* (CCH) [1973–1976 Transfer Binder] para. 20,621 (1974).

after 60 days. Failure to abide by a consent order subjects a company to fines up to $10,000 a day for as long as the advertising campaign continues.

Cease-and-Desist Orders If consent cannot be reached, the FTC issues a formal complaint leading to a cease-and-desist order. Before the commission can begin cease-and-desist proceedings, it must determine that the action would be "to the interest of the public" as required by section 5 of the Federal Trade Commission Act. If deception is trivial, it may not be in the public interest to pursue a cease-and-desist order. The FTC has wide discretion in deciding whether the public interest would be served by legal action against an advertisement, but, as Justice Brandeis said, that interest must be "specific and substantial."[116] In deciding whether to take action, the FTC will answer such questions as the number of consumers who may have been deceived, how much money they lost, whether market forces would fix the problem without government intervention, and whether government intervention would be an effective deterrent.[117]

When the FTC issues a complaint against an advertiser, an investigation proceeds to adjudication. The FTC announces the complaint in a press release mailed to more than 1,000 publications and to 20,000 persons on the FTC's mailing list.[118] When the complaint is issued, the case is assigned to an FTC administrative law judge who conducts a hearing much like a trial. The agency has the burden to establish substantial evidence that an advertiser has violated the law. The administrative law judge either dismisses the case or issues a cease-and-desist order that can be appealed to the full commission and then to a federal appeals court.

A cease-and-desist order becomes final after an appeal or after time runs out to make an appeal. Failure to abide by a cease-and-desist order, as with failure to abide by a consent decree, can lead to fines of up to $10,000 a day, but the fines are usually much less. In fact, a company may decide it makes better business sense to continue the ads and sustain the fines than to stop a successful ad campaign.

In one of the most famous and long-running cases, the FTC won a judgment against the makers of Geritol 14 years after a complaint was filed to halt misleading advertisements. The FTC filed a complaint in 1962 charging that the J. B. Williams Company's television advertisements for Geritol were misleading. The FTC said the ads for the vitamin-and-iron tonic misleadingly said the product was an effective remedy for tiredness, loss of strength, and that "run-down" feeling. The FTC found the ad deceptive because Geritol is effective only in a minority of cases where tiredness is caused by a lack of the iron and vitamins in Geritol. In most cases, fatigue is caused by factors not affected by Geritol.

In 1964, the FTC issued a cease-and-desist order telling J. B. Williams to include statements in its ads that the vast majority of people who are run-down do not suffer from iron or vitamin deficiencies that Geritol might correct. Two years later the case was given to the Justice Department when J. B. Williams did not comply with the cease-and-desist order. The company was fined $800,000 in 1973 for violating the

---

[116]F.T.C. v. Klesner, 280 U.S. 19, 28 (1929).

[117]Deceptive and Unsubstantiated Claims Policy Protocol, 4 _Trade Reg. Rep._ (CCH) para. 39,059 (1975).

[118]16 C.F.R. secs. 2.31–2.34 (1989). _See_ Gellhorn, "Adverse Publicity by Administrative Agencies," 86 _Harv. L. Rev._ 1380 (1973). G. Rosden and P. Rosden, 3 _Law of Advertising_ sec. 34.03 (1989).

FTC's order, but a court of appeals ordered a new trial.[119] In 1976, 14 years after the complaint was filed, the FTC won a $280,000 judgment against the makers of Geritol.

At the beginning of another lengthy case in 1971, the FTC told the *Reader's Digest* to cease and desist from promoting magazine subscriptions with simulated checks and money that were deceptively offered as being redeemable for cash or a new car. In 1975, the FTC charged violation of the cease-and-desist order because the *Reader's Digest* was issuing simulated travelers checks and bonds, which, like the checks and money, were deceptively offered as convertible to cash. In 1981, the U.S. Court of Appeals for the Third Circuit upheld a district court assessment of a $1,750,000 penalty for more than 17 million violations of the earlier cease-and-desist order. The courts counted each advertisement mailed as a separate deceptive act. The district court concluded the *Reader's Digest* raised more then $5 million in gross subscription revenues from the deceptive promotions.[120]

Injunctions In some cases of deceptive advertising, particularly where public health might be at risk, the most important FTC goal is to stop the offending advertisement quickly. This can be accomplished with an injunction. Under section 13 of the Federal Trade Commission Act, the commission can ask a federal district judge for an injunction to stop deceptive advertising for food, drugs, or cosmetics.[121] For example, in *FTC v. National Commission on Egg Nutrition,* the FTC obtained a temporary injunction stopping statements asserting there is no scientific edvidence linking egg consumption and heart disease.[122] Usually, however, the commission does not seek a permanent injunction, but prefers to act through the administrative process seeking consent decrees or cease-and-desist orders.[123] But this process is much too slow for companies being hurt commercially by a competitor's deceptive advertisements. Advertisers damaged by competitors' ads often seek injunctions in federal court under the Lanham Act, a subject addressed shortly.

Required Statements

Not only can the FTC halt deceptive advertising and punish the advertiser, it can also alter advertisements to make them accurate. Besides requiring substantiation, the FTC can tell advertisers that they must include certain words or phrases in their ads and occasionally must correct false impressions created by deceptive ad campaigns. The FTC's power to alter the content of advertisements is a power not enjoyed by the government generally. Critics charge that such a power violates the First Amendment as well as the purpose of the Federal Trade Commission Act. The FTC, critics say, is supposed to prevent deception, not require the dissemination of information. But

---

[119]United States v. J. B. Williams Co., 498 F.2d 414 (2d cir. 1974).
[120]United States v. Reader's Digest Ass'n, Inc., 662 F.2d 955, 7 Media L. Rep. 1921 (3d Cir. 1981), *cert. denied,* 455 U.S. 908 (1982).
[121]*See* FTC v. Sterling Drug, Inc., 317 F.2d 669, 671 (2d Cir. 1963).
[122]517 F.2d 485 (7th Cir. 1975).
[123]E. Rockefeller, *Desk Book of FTC Practice and Procedure* 112 (3d ed. 1979).

defenders of affirmative disclosure requirements say that the FTC cannot meaningfully prohibit deception unless it can sometimes require that statements be included in an advertisement. In any case, the FTC can require affirmative disclosure and corrective advertising.

Affirmative Disclosure   The Federal Trade Commission Act does not contain an explicit grant of power for the FTC to order disclosure, but courts have recognized, as a congressional committee did earlier, an advertiser's responsibility to reveal facts necessary to keep an ad from being deceptive.[124] Silence by an advertiser is not necessarily deceptive, but silence is deceptive if it means a consumer might be hurt.[125]

Often a consent decree contains an affirmative disclosure requirement. In one case, the Morton Salt Company agreed to stop advertising Lite Salt in such a way that consumers would think it was more healthful than ordinary salt. In signing the consent order, the company agreed that future advertising of Lite Salt would contain the statement: "Not to be used by persons on sodium- or potassium-restricted diets unless approved by a physician."[126] In another case of affirmative disclosure, the FTC ordered the J. B. Williams Company to tell customers in Geritol ads that a vitamin and iron supplement will probably not correct a run-down feeling. Health warnings on cigarette packages are also a form of affirmative disclosure.

Corrective Advertising   In rare cases, the FTC requires *corrective advertising* to correct the misrepresentation created by a long-term, misleading advertising campaign. A Washington public interest group once proposed that the FTC require corrective advertising whenever the FTC found a deceptive health, safety, or nutrition ad that was part of a campaign of at least a year's duration. But the FTC chose a more flexible, case-by-case approach, requiring corrective advertising only when a long deceptive ad campaign—one perhaps lasting several years—misleads consumers. To determine whether corrective ads are necessary, the FTC will consider consumer surveys, the amount of exposure to the ads, the persuasiveness of the claims, and the naiveté of the audience.[127]

The FTC first required corrective advertising in 1971. In a consent order, the FTC told the ITT Continental Baking Company to correct a false impression created by a long-term series of advertisements for the company's Profile bread.[128] The ads suggested that consumers could lose weight by eating Profile bread because it contained fewer calories than other breads. Actually, Profile bread contained the same number of calories per ounce as other breads. Therefore, if a person kept a better figure while eating ITT Continental's bread, it was because Profile bread was sliced thinner.

---

[124]Committee on Interstate and Foreign Commerce, H.R. Rep. 1613, 75th Cong., 1st Sess. 5 (1937).

[125]Alberty v. FTC, 182 F.2d 36 (1949), *cert. denied,* 340 U.S. 818 (1950); Anderson and Winer, "Corrective Advertising: The FTC's New Formula for Effective Relief," 50 *Texas L. Rev.* 312, 320 (1972).

[126]Morton-Norwich Products, Inc., *Trade Reg. Rep.* (CCH) [1973–1976 Transfer Binder] para. 20,891 (1975).

[127]Corrective Advertising: Position Regarding Rule or Policy Statement, 4 *Trade Reg. Rep.* (CCH) para. 39,046 (1979).

[128]ITT Continental Baking Co., 79 F.T.C. 248 (1971).

In televised corrective ads featuring Julia Meade, ITT Continental showed how a company could fulfill an FTC requirement to correct a long-running, misleading ad campaign without unnecessarily damaging a company's credibility. Meade began the ad with:

> I'm Julia Meade for Profile Bread. And like all mothers I'm concerned about nutrition and balanced meals. So I'd like to clear up any misunderstanding you may have about Profile Bread from its advertising or even its name. Does Profile have fewer calories than other breads? No, Profile has about the same per ounce as other breads. To be exact Profile has seven fewer calories per slice. But that's because it's sliced thinner. But eating Profile Bread will not cause you to lose weight. A reduction of seven calories is insignificant. It's total calories and balanced nutrition that count. And Profile can help you achieve a balanced meal, because it provides protein and B vitamins as well as other nutrients.

In a famous Listerine case, the FTC required the Warner-Lambert Company to make statements in its advertising to correct a long-running campaign claiming that use of Listerine mouthwash would help prevent colds. The company was ordered to include in $10 million of its advertising the statement that Listerine "will not help prevent colds or sore throats." Ten million dollars was the average annual sum spent to advertise Listerine between 1962, when the complaint against Warner-Lambert was issued, and 1974, when the company was ordered to run corrections.[129] Typically, the FTC requires an advertiser to include corrective statements in 25 percent of its advertising for a year following an agreement.

The FTC ordered Warner-Lambert not only to tell consumers that Listerine would not prevent colds, but also to alert readers to the company's earlier misleading advertising by beginning its corrective message with the phrase, "Contrary to prior advertising." Judge Skelly Wright of the U.S. Court of Appeals for the District of Columbia ruled that the FTC's order violated the First Amendment because it required more speech than was necessary to correct the false impression. Judge Wright said the First Amendment imposes a requirement that FTC corrective orders be no broader than necessary to set the record straight. Judge Wright said that requiring Warner-Lambert to confess to its previous misleading ads was not necessary and would amount to an unwarranted humiliation for the company.[130]

Another federal appeals court ruled that the FTC violated the First Amendment when it told a tax preparing company it could not advertise loans as "instant tax refunds." The loans were offered to taxpayers who were scheduled to receive refunds from the IRS. The FTC argued that treating a loan as a refund misled potential borrowers into believing they did not have to meet the usual creditworthiness standards of the finance company to qualify for the loans. However, the court ruled the prohibition on the phrase *instant tax refunds* was an unconstitutional prior restraint on commercial speech "not reasonably necessary" to prevent consumers from being

---

[129]Warner-Lambert Co., 86 F.T.C. 1938 (1975).

[130]Warner-Lambert Co. v. FTC, 562 F.2d 749 (D.C.Cir. 1977), 2 Media L. Rep. 2503, *cert. denied,* 435 U.S. 950 (1978).

misled.[131] The court said the tax preparation company might offer instant tax refunds in its advertising provided the ads made it clear that the "refund" was really a loan.

Competitor Remedies

Consumers, of course, are not the only people hurt by deceptive advertisements. Advertisers, too, may be hurt by the false and deceptive claims of competing companies. However, the FTC offers little immediate relief for a competitor whose major concern is to quickly stop a deceptive ad that may hurt business. Even if the FTC agrees to seek an injunction, the process may be too slow to be of much help to the damaged competitor. Therefore, companies often seek court injunctions themselves to stop the deceptive ads of competing companies.

Companies seek injunctions under section 43(a) of the Lanham Trademark Act of 1946, the same act discussed earlier in the intellectual property chapter. Besides protecting trademarks, the Lanham Act, as amended in 1988, prohibits any person's "false or misleading representation of fact" in "commercial advertising or promotion" that "misrepresents the nature, characteristics, qualities, or geographic origin of his or her or another person's goods, services, or commercial activities."[132] Anyone who believes he or she "is or is likely to be damaged" by deceptive advertising may seek an injunction; it is not necessary to prove actual loss. A plaintiff usually seeks a halt to the offending ad, but he or she may also be entitled to significant monetary damages.

Before the 1988 amendments, competitors could sue under section 43(a) only if the defendant's advertisement contained false statements about his or her own products. After the 1988 amendments, plaintiffs may sue to stop advertisements in which defendants make false claims either about their own products or about the plaintiff's.

Employing the law before 1988, the makers of Minute Maid orange juice halted Tropicana orange juice ads that contained falsehoods about Tropicana. In the ads, Olympic champion Bruce Jenner squeezed fresh oranges and poured the juice into a Tropicana carton as a voice proclaimed, "It's pure, pasteurized juice as it comes from the orange."[133]

The Coca-Cola Company, which sells Minute Maid, claimed the Tropicana ads were misleading because Tropicana orange juice, like most ready-to-serve orange juices, is not packaged as it "comes from the orange." It is pasteurized and sometimes frozen before packaging. Even though the Tropicana ad said the juice was pasteurized, the U.S. Court of Appeals for the Second Circuit granted a preliminary injunction to stop the ads because they were likely to harm Minute Maid. A "not insubstantial" number of consumers surveyed mistakenly believed Tropicana juice came directly from the orange.

Often competitors stop deceptive comparative advertisements under section 43(a). All ads invite comparison, but so-called comparative ads point out the similar-

---

[131]Beneficial Corp. v. FTC, 542 F.2d 611, 619 (3d Cir. 1976), *cert. denied,* 430 U.S. 983 (1977).

[132]15 U.S.C.A. 1125(a) (Supp. 1989).

[133]Coca-Cola Co. v. Tropicana Products Inc., 690 F.2d 312 (2d Cir. 1982).

ities and differences between an advertiser's product and its competitors. The FTC has defined comparative advertising as ads that compare a named or identified competing brand on objectively measurable attributes or price.[134] Although advertisers, the networks, and the FTC once frowned on comparative advertisements, the FTC has said in a policy statement that it encourages companies to name and compare competitors' products in advertisements.[135] Comparative ads are thought to help consumers make better choices. Today, comparative ads are popular.

In a well-known comparative ad case, Johnson & Johnson, the manufacturer of Tylenol, obtained an injuction against ads for Anacin that falsely claimed Anacin was a superior pain reliever.[136] The televised ads claimed Anacin could reduce inflammation from muscle strain, backache, and tendonitis faster than other pain relievers. "Your body knows the difference between these pain relievers . . . and Adult Strength Anacin," the ad said. Unlike Tropicana ad, which did not mention Minute Maid by name, the Anacin ad showed the competing products—Datril, Tylenol, and Extra Strength Tylenol—on the screen. A federal court enjoined the Anacin ads because they left the impression on consumers surveyed that Anacin was a better pain reliever overall. The real superiority of Anacin, if any, was its ability to reduce inflamation.

Several suggestions for avoiding litigation over comparative advertisements have been offered by George and Peter Rosden, authors of a treatise on advertising. Among their recommendations:[137]

- Make comparative ads truthful.
- Avoid subjective claims. Use objective claims that can be substantiated.
- Use reliable independent testing services or public surveying firms to substantiate claims.
- Keep the results of the substantiation.
- Present the comparison fairly.
- Avoid knocking the competitor's business practices.

SUMMARY

The Federal Trade Commission has several powers and remedies to keep the flow of commercial information clean. The forward-looking powers include staff opinion letters, advisory opinions, industry guides, policy statements, and trade regulation rules. In addition, the FTC can halt deceptive advertising through consent decrees, cease-and-desist orders, and injunctions. The FTC can also require that advertisements contain statements necessary to leave an accurate impression or to correct misrepresentation. In addition, companies may seek injunctions under the Lanham Act to halt false or misleading advertisements and promotions by competitors.

---

[134]16 C.F.R. 14.15(b) n.1 (1989).
[135]16 C.F.R. sec. 14.15(b) (1989).
[136]American Home Products Corp. v. Johnson & Johnson, 577 F.2d 160 (2d Cir. 1978).
[137]G. Rosden & P. Rosden, 3 *Law of Advertising* sec. 31.05 (1989).

OTHER FEDERAL REGULATION

Although deception is the major concern of federal regulators of advertising, federal regulations on games of chance and the reproductions of money also affect the media.

Lotteries and Contests

The FTC may regulate lotteries and games of chance as unfair or deceptive under the Federal Trade Commission Act,[138] but the FTC is generally not involved in regulating the advertising or news coverage of lotteries. Until recently, federal mail and broadcast law banned advertising and promoting of lotteries and games of chance. But the country is apparently losing the fear, expressed by a federal judge in 1892, that anti-gambling laws are needed to "protect the citizen from the demoralizing or corrupting influence" of solicitations to gamble.[139]

As of May 1990, the media may advertise all official state lotteries in any state that operates a lottery.[140] The media may also print or broadcast advertising and prize lists of lotteries conducted by nonprofit organizations and by commercial companies, if the lotteries are legal under state law. The commercial lotteries, however, must only be conducted occasionally and not be related to the company's usual business. The media may also broadcast and print information about legal gaming activities on Indian reservations.[141]

A lottery has three elements: (1) prize, (2) chance, and (3) consideration. The prize is the reward, money, trip, merchandise, or other remuneration given the winner. Chance means that luck, not skill, will determine the winner. Consideration, which is often more difficult to recognize than chance or prize, is the effort or expense required of the participant. Consideration is the time one spends to play a game or the money paid to enter a contest.

While publishers and broadcasters may not conduct lotteries themselves, they can conduct promotional contests and advertise the contests of others as long as the promotions are not false or deceptive. To be legal, contests may not consist of all three elements of a lottery—prize, chance, and consideration. Contests may include two elements of a lottery, such as a prize and chance, as long as they do not require the third element, consideration. Many contests avoid the prohibitions on lotteries by basing winning on knowledge or skill rather than chance. Common contests conducted by publishers, broadcasters, and retailers include treasure hunts, drawings, word games, picture coloring, name-that-tune competitions, and cash call-in jackpots.

Section 509 of the Communications Act of 1934 makes it unlawful for a broad-

---

[138]FTC v. R. F. Keppel & Bros., 291 U.S. 304 (1934); Games of Chance in the Food Retailing and Gasoline Industries, Trade Regulation Rule, 16 C.F.R. 419 (1986).

[139]United States v. Horner, 44 F. 677, 679 (S.D.N.Y. 1891), *aff'd,* 143 U.S. 207 (1892).

[140]Charity Games Advertising Clarification Act of 1988, Pub. L. 100-625, 102 Stat. 3205 (Nov. 7, 1988), *codified,* 18 U.S.C.A. sec. 1302–1306 (Supp. 1989).

[141]Indian Gaming Regulatory Act, Pub. L. 100-497, 102 Stat. 2467 (1988). *See* J. Albert, *The Broadcaster's Legal Guide for Conducting Contests and Promotions* (1985).

caster to deceive the public by providing any "special and secret assistance" to a contestant in a contest or to fix or rig a contest through "any artifice or scheme."[142] In addition, FCC rules require broadcasters who conduct or advertise contests to

> fully and accurately disclose the material terms of the contest, and . . . conduct the contest substantially as announced or advertised. No contest description shall be false, misleading or deceptive with respect to any material term.[143]

FCC rules require that stations reveal who is eligible to win, the nature and value of prizes, how to enter, how winners will be determined, and dates of the contest. A disc jockey, TV host, or broadcast promotion director could be subject to a fine of $10,000 and a year in jail for participating in a false or misleading contest. Furthermore, a state could lose its license for willful or repeated violation. Contests may also be prohibited under state law.

The FCC revoked the license of WMJX-FM in Miami, Florida, in 1975 because of deception in two contests. In one, the station announced that contestants could win a $1,000 prize in an Easter egg hunt. The station's program director allowed the promotional announcements to be broadcast even though the station had no prize money to award. In the other, the station announced a $500 reward for the listener who found disc jockey Greg Austin, reported to be wandering around the Miami area in a daze, "his mind boggled," after a trip to the Bermuda Triangle. However, station announcers knew that Austin was in the studio, safely returned from a brief charter boat excursion.[144]

Money

The U.S. Supreme Court ruled in 1986 that it is constitutionally permissible for the government to regulate the manner in which money can be pictured in advertisements and news stories. In *Regan v. Time, Inc.,* the Court upheld a federal statute requiring that money be pictured only in black and white and only either larger or smaller than actual size.[145] The Treasury Department fears that color photos of money in actual size would aid counterfeiters. Therefore, the law prohibits picturing money unless the reproduction is black and white and either less than three-fourths or more than one-and-a-half times the actual size of money.

The *Regan* case arose over a cover picture in *Sports Illustrated* showing a basketball hoop stuffed with $100 bills. The color picture illustrated a story about a basketball point-shaving scandal at Boston University. The Treasury Department tried to seize the plates and other materials used to produce the *Sports Illustrated* cover.

Justice White, in a plurality opinion for the Court, said the government's color and size requirements are not an impermissible content regulation. The Court likened the size and color limitations to limits on the decibel levels imposed on sound trucks

---

[142]47 U.S.C.A. sec. 509 (1962).
[143]47 C.F.R. sec. 73.1216 (1988).
[144]WMJX, Inc., 85 F.C.C.2d 251 (1981).
[145]468 U.S. 641 (1984).

or size and height limits on outdoor signs. All of these regulations constitutionally restrict the manner in which a message is presented, not the content of the message.

The Court also recognized in *Regan* the government's substantial interest in preventing counterfeiting. Barring color pictures of money makes it harder for counterfeiters to gain access to color negatives that can be altered and used for illegal purposes. Size limitations ensure that the illustrations of money themselves are not used as counterfeit money.

The Court did strike down as unconstitutional a content restriction in the law that prohibited the reproduction of money except for "educational, historical or newsworthy purposes in articles, books, journals, newspapers, or albums." The Court said it was unconstitutional to limit speech because of its purpose or subject matter.

SUMMARY

The media may advertise all official state lotteries in any state that operates a lottery. The media may also print or broadcast advertising and prize lists of lotteries conducted by nonprofit organizations and, occasionally, by commercial companies, if the lotteries are legal under state law and if the commercial lotteries are not related to the company's usual business. A lottery must have three elements: chance, prize, and consideration.

The media may reproduce U.S. money in an advertisement or illustration but only if the money is pictured in black and white and is either larger or smaller than real money.

MEDIA'S RIGHT TO REFUSE ADVERTISING

It is well established that the media choose what to broadcast or publish. As Chief Justice Warren Burger said in *CBS, Inc. v. Democratic National Committee,* "For better or worse, editing is what editors are for; and editing is selection and choice of material." In *Democratic National Committee,* a case discussed in chapter 12, the Court ruled that a Washington, D.C., television station had a First Amendment right to refuse to sell airtime for a business group's editorial advertisements.

Earlier the Court had ruled unconstitutional a Florida law requiring newspapers to print replies from political candidates attacked editorially. In *Miami Herald Publishing Company v. Tornillo,* a political candidate argued that newspapers, which are often monopolies in their cities, should be required to accept responses from candidates criticized in their pages. But Chief Justice Burger, writing for the Court, said, "A newspaper is more than a passive receptacle or conduit for news, comment, and advertising." What a newspaper publishes is a matter of editorial judgment that the First Amendment places beyond government control, Burger said.

Before the Supreme Court established the media's First Amendment right to refuse advertising, lower courts had ruled in common law that the media are private businesses free to accept or reject advertising, providing publishers do not violate advertising contracts, the antitrust statutes, or antidiscrimination laws. In *Chicago Joint Board, Amalgamated Clothing Workers of America, AFL-CIO v. Chicago Tribune Company,* the U.S. Court of Appeals for the Seventh Circuit ruled that newspapers are private enterprises that can refuse editorial advertisements.[146]

In *Chicago Joint Board,* the clothing workers union sought a court order to require the *Tribune* and several other Chicago papers to publish the union's editorial ad. The ad opposed the sale of foreign-made goods at Marshall Field & Company, a large department store that advertised in the papers. The union contended the newspapers received so many benefits from the city of Chicago and the state of Illinois that the papers' refusal of the union's ads was not just the refusal of a private business, but the refusal of a business infused with "state action." So entwined were the newspapers and the government that the newspapers' refusal was, in effect, a government refusal to publish the ads, a refusal in violation of the First Amendment, the union argued.

To support its argument, the union cited, among other benefits, the revenues newspapers gained from publishing legal notices, the publishers' privilege to sell newspapers on public sidewalks, and the space provided for reporters at City Hall and other public buildings. These economic benefits amounted to government involvement in the newspaper business, the union said.

But the Seventh Circuit denied that the newspaper's refusal to publish the union's advertisement amounted to a government decision. The government has no stake in the profits a paper might make from publishing legal notices, the court said. Furthermore, the government permits sales of newspapers on public streets and sidewalks, not to benefit publishers, but as a convenience to the public, the court said. Any benefit to media owners is incidental to the public purpose of the benefit. Likewise, reporters are provided space in public buildings, not to benefit the press, the court said, but to allow the public to receive quick reports about government affairs. In sum, the court said there was no direct tie between the newspapers and the government.

The court also rejected the union's contention that First Amendment protections afforded the press impose an obligation on the media to serve as a public forum, publishing all editorial advertisements once one is published. A publisher's presses belong to the publisher, the court said. "The Union's right to free speech does not give it the right to make use of the defendants' printing presses and distribution systems without defendants' consent."

The First Amendment and the common law do not free the media entirely from required publishing and broadcasting. The Federal Communications Act imposes obligations on broadcasters to provide airtime for candidates during elections. The media are also required to provide access to advertisers with whom contracts have been signed. Furthermore, publications considered to be public forums may have to accept all lawful advertising if they accept any. In addition, media may violate antitrust laws if they refuse advertisements because of an agreement among themselves to exclude ads or because of pressure from important advertisers.

---

[146]435 F.2d 470 (7th Cir. 1970), *cert. denied,* 402 U.S. 973 (1971).

SUMMARY

The media may refuse to publish or broadcast advertisements because of both First Amendment and common law precedents. The media's refusal to disseminate an advertisement is not deemed a government refusal in violation of the First Amendment just because the media receive government benefits. However, the media, like other business, must honor their advertising contracts, the antitrust laws, and other legal obligations.

SELF-REGULATION

Despite the elaborate legal apparatus for regulating advertising, self-regulation by the advertising industry has been called the most efficient tool for curbing excesses and illegalities.[147] In the recent era of government deregulation, the FTC also emphasized the importance of regulation from within the advertising industry. With FTC budget cuts and the closure of a number of regional FTC offices, consumers depended on advertisers themselves, more than before, to ensure that advertising is fair and accurate.

While the zeal for deregulation has abated, regulation of advertising by a number of bureaus and agencies outside of government are still important. These regulatory bodies include associations, such as the American Association of Advertising Agencies; the networks, all of which have advertising acceptance guidelines, and individual radio and TV stations, newspapers, and magazines. In addition, some advertisers promote self-regulation to stave off a resurgence of government regulation. In the late 1980s, the Direct Mail Board of Review, Inc., a trade association formed to help regulate direct mail advertising, issued a new Code of Business Ethics. During the same period, the American Telemarketing Association adopted "Telemarketing Standards and Ethics Guidelines."

A leading regulator of the advertising industry is the National Advertising Division of the National Advertising Review Board (NARB). The NARB was set up by a number of trade associations during the most vigorous period of the consumer movement in the early 1970s.

National Advertising Division

The National Advertising Division and the National Advertising Review Board were established in 1971 to promote truth and accuracy in national advertising. These regulatory bodies were created through the cooperation of the American Advertising Federation, the American Association of Advertising Agencies, the Association of National Advertisers, and the Council of Better Business Bureaus. The National Advertising Division, or the NAD as it is called, is "responsible for receiving or initiat-

---

[147]G. Rosden & P. Rosden, *Law of Advertising* sec. 31.02 (1989).

ing, evaluating, investigating, analyzing, and holding initial negotiations with an advertiser on complaints or questions from any source involving the truth or accuracy of national advertising.''[148]

Like the FTC, the NAD investigates advertising claims to see if they are substantiated. The NAD says it "maintains the principle unreservedly" that prior substantiation "is essential for truthful and accurate advertising."[149] Almost all of the 140 cases NAD handled during one year in the 1980s involved substantiation of advertising claims.

The NAD deals only with misleading or deceptive national advertisements. It does not get involved in private disputes between competitors and does not take complaints dealing with local advertising or business practices. Furthermore, the NAD does not entertain questions about the basic performance of products, questions of taste, political and issue advertising, or advertising addressed to lawyers, engineers, or other audiences with special expertise. A related organization, the Children's Advertising Review Unit, tries to prevent exploitation of children through misleading ads, messages that children cannot understand, and ads that disregard the risk that children may imitate dangerous product demonstrations.

The NAD's cases come from the organization's own systematic monitoring of national television, radio, and print advertising, complaints from competing advertisers, and complaints from consumer groups, individuals, and the independent Better Business Bureaus. If the NAD is not satisfied that an advertising claim is substantiated, it will negotiate with the advertiser to modify or discontinue the ad. If an agreement cannot be reached, an advertiser can appeal the NAD decision that an ad is deceptive to an impartial five-member panel appointed by the chairman of the NARB. The review board has 50 members representing national advertisers, advertising agencies, and the public. Members of the board serve a two-year term. In 1987, the NAD resolved 90 advertising complaints.[150]

The NAD has no definitive standards defining untrue or inaccurate ads. It decides each case individually. But NAD brings into the regulatory process the standards of many other agencies and associations, including FTC rules and consent orders, postal regulations, state consumer protection programs, and court decisions, particularly the increasing number of comparative advertising cases. The NAD also relies on the guidelines of the Advertising Research Foundation, network broadcast guides, and professional and trade association guides.

In a typical case, the NAD found there was inadequate substantiation for newspaper ads proclaiming the superiority of Bama Peanut Butter over three other brands compared in taste tests with children in the South. The ad said:

> Peanut Butter lovers say "You Can't Beat Bama!" Jif Can't! Peter Pan Can't! Skippy Can't! In recent taste tests in the South, boys and girls who love peanut butter found Bama Peanut Butter unbeatable! None of the leading brands beat the delicious taste of Bama.

---

[148]Statement of Organization and Procedures of the National Advertising Review Board, sec. 2.1 (June 19, 1985).

[149]National Advertising Division, Council of Better Business Bureaus, Inc., "Self-Regulation of National Advertising: Twelfth Year-End Report," in *NAD Case Rep.,* July 15, 1983.

[150]*See* K. Plevan & M. Siroky, *Advertising Compliance Handbook* 247–51 (1988).

The company's taste tests did show children thought Bama was as good as or better than the other three brands overall, but the kids liked the consistency and the strength of the peanut butter flavor better in one of the competing brands. Because Bama's taste was not preferred in all respects, the NAD found insufficient substantiation for Bama's claim to be preferred by children. The company agreed that claims of Bama's superiority to all three other brands would not be used in future campaigns without more test data to support the claims, but as typically happens, the advertising had already been discontinued.[151]

The NAD has no coercive powers or punitive role, but advertisers cooperate with the NAD. In its first 12 years of operation, no advertiser who participated in the complete process of a NAD investigation and NARB appeal declined to abide by the final decision. In those rare cases where an advertiser refuses to participate in a NAD review, the case may be referred to the FTC or another government agency. Publicity about NAD cases is circulated to the media, businesses, colleges and government agencies in monthly *Case Reports*.

Media Regulation

In addition to the NARB, advertising is regulated by the networks, newspapers, and other media that sell advertising time and space. The media, like the FTC and the NAD, screen advertisements submitted to them for accuracy and fairness and demand that objective claims be substantiated. So valued are network guidelines that advertising associations have urged television networks in recent years to scuttle plans to reduce scrutiny of broadcast commercials. In letters to the networks, the president of the American Association of Advertising Agencies said network attempts to save money by cutting the staff of commercial acceptance departments would invite unwanted government regulation "to fill the void."[152]

For many years, the National Association of Broadcasters' Television Code imposed several limits on advertising by members. These guidelines were more sensitive to the taste and morals of the audience than the law was. To meet the standards of the Television Code, ads not only had to be accurate but also had to be presented "with courtesy and good taste." According to the broadcast code, ads were not supposed to be objectionable "to a substantial and responsible segment of the community."[153] The guides were especially sensitive to the sensibilities of children. The code prohibited the advertising of hard liquor, of firearms except for sport, and of fortune-telling. Personal hygiene products were to be advertised "in a restrained and obviously inoffensive manner."

The NAB Code was abandoned after the Justice Department won an antitrust suit challenging the code's provisions barring advertising "clutter." The clutter provisions prohibited the advertising on member stations of two or more products in a single advertisement lasting less than 60 seconds. In other words, 30-second spots could only contain ads for a single product or two closely related products such as

---

[151]Borden, Inc., *NAD Case Report* (No. 1931).

[152]"Networks Hit for Ad Clearance Cuts," *Advertising Age,* Sept. 12, 1988, at 6.

[153]National Association of Broadcasters, "The Television Code," 21st ed., 1980, sec. IX, in Practising Law Institute, *Legal and Business Aspects of the Advertising Industry 1982,* at 88.

different models of the same vacuum cleaner. The NAB claimed the clutter provisions saved viewers from the confusion of having to watch several short advertisements at one time. The NAB also contended that the clutter provisions did not violate the antitrust law because the NAB code in which the provisions were contained was a voluntary code adhered to only by members of the National Associations of Broadcasters.

The Federal District Court for the District of Columbia agreed with the Justice Department that the NAB clutter provisions violated the Sherman Antitrust Act.[154] While the code was not legally binding on its members, the court said the NAB, in effect, had a monopoly on the industry because the most important broadcasting outlets in the country belonged. The court said adherence to the code was not really voluntary because stations that did not abide by the code could be dropped from membership in the association. The court also said that prohibiting an advertiser from advertising more than one product in a 30-second spot was a restraint of trade that particularly hurt smaller companies that could not afford longer television ads.

After the Justice Department won an antitrust suit against some of the NAB code provisions, the NAB abandoned the broadcast code. However, after the NAB Code had been dismantled, the networks adopted substantially the same advertising standards. All networks have detailed advertising acceptance guidelines. Network advertising acceptance departments will not permit an advertisement to be broadcast if the ad fails to meet standards for substantiation and taste.[155] All three networks require substantiation based on appropriate scientific testing for advertising claims.

A number of the network regulations are rather detailed. For example, the networks have prohibited the use of live models for underwear, as well as testimonials for over-the-counter drugs, ads for hard liquor, and ''ashcanning.'' *Ashcanning* is throwing a competitor's product on the floor or in the wastebasket. Furthermore, one network prohibited ads for toilet bowl cleaners if the camera looked directly into the bowl. Recently the networks, following the lead of local stations, began experimenting with previously rejected advertisements for contraceptives, douches, and other personal products.

SUMMARY

Government regulation is not the only check on the accuracy of advertising. Advertisers themselves and the media monitor advertisements to ensure that the government and public will not find them deceptive. The leading self-regulatory body is the National Advertising Division of the National Advertising Review Board. Many other agencies, as well as the networks and newspapers, monitor advertising. Like the FTC, the National Advertising Division and the media expect advertising claims to be substantiated.

---

[154]United States v. National Association of Broadcasters, 536 F.Supp. 149, 8 Media L. Rep. 2572 (D.C.D.C. 1982).
[155]*See, e.g.,* ''CBS Television Network Advertising Guidelines''; ''NBC Broadcast Standards for Television.''

8

PORNOGRAPHY

"Sex," Justice Brennan once observed, "has indisputably been a subject of absorbing interest to mankind through the ages." This "great and mysterious motive force in human life," he said, is "one of the vital problems of human interest and public concern."[1] Indeed, sex was among the earliest subjects of art. Before the Roman Empire, every acceptable and unacceptable sexual practice known today had been sketched, painted, carved, or sculpted.[2]

Today, sexually explicit materials are a significant part of the mass media. As one commentator concludes, "Society's appetite for sexually oriented works, from *Sports Illustrated*'s swimsuit issue to the burgeoning market in pornographic home videos, continues unabated."[3] By the mid-1980s, records, videos, cable, books, magazines, and films with sexual messages were an $8-billion-a-year business in the United States.[4] In 1990, a record store owner was convicted under the obscenity law for selling 2 Live Crew's rap album *As Nasty as They Wanna Be*, which contains graphic language about sex, genitals, and sodomy.[5]

Most Americans, particularly those older than 40, believe that pornography is potentially dangerous and should be restricted.[6] People fear that exposure to pornography, particularly the violent pornography that has become more popular, makes viewers more tolerant of sexual crimes and may lead to antisocial behavior. Many opponents of pornography were not surprised that just before his execution serial killer Ted Bundy blamed his violence on graphic pornography.[7] Some argue that even if pornography does not lead to antisocial behavior, it is a blight on the community that should be curbed.

Concern over pornography is especially acute today because of the increase in violence associated with sex, not only in graphic pornography but also in the popular media. Films depict women enjoying being raped; soft-core violent pornographic images, sometimes called *brutality chic,* appear in high-fashion magazines, on record covers, and in department store windows.[8] In an example not associated with sex, a popular song by the rap group N.W.A. calls a policeman "a sucker in a uniform waitin' to get shot."[9]

In response, citizens groups have intensified efforts to curb the explicit sex and violence in books, films, cable television, and rock music. In 1986, a pornography commission appointed by Attorney General Edwin Meese urged broader enforcement of laws dealing with sexually explicit materials.[10] In 1988, Congress passed a law to protect minors from being used in sexual materials.[11]

---

[1]Roth v. United States, 354 U.S. 476, 487, 1 Media L. Rep. 1375, 1379 (1957).

[2]Byrne & Kelley, "Introduction: Pornography and Sex Research," in N. Malamuth and E. Donnerstein, eds., *Pornography and Sexual Aggression* 2 (1984).

[3]Note, "Obscenity and the Reasonable Person: Will He 'Know It When He Sees It'?" 30 *B.C.L. Rev.* 823 (1989).

[4]"Porn Wars: Do's and Don'ts," 100 *U.S. News & World Report*, March 10, 1986, at 8.

[5]"Store Owner Convicted of Obscenity in Album Sale," *New York Times,* Oct. 4, 1990, at 10.

[6]Byrne & Kelley, "Introduction: Pornography and Sex Research," in N. Malamuth and E. Donnerstein, eds., *Pornography and Sexual Aggression* 3 (1984).

[7]Gest, "The Drive to Make America Porn-free," 106 *U.S. News & World Rep.*, Feb. 6, 1989, at 26.

[8]Penrod & Linz, "Using Psychological Research on Violent Pornography to Inform Legal Change," in N. Malamuth and E. Donnerstein, *Pornography and Sexual Aggression* 3 (1984).

[9]"Outlaw Rock: More Skirmishes on the Censorship Front," *New York Times*, Dec. 10, 1989, at H32.

[10]"Pornography in U.S. Linked to Violence, Meese Panel Asserts," *New York Times*, May 14, 1986, at 1.

[11]Child Protection and Obscenity Enforcement Act, Pub. L. 100-690, 102 Stat. 4485 (1988).

Yet pornography has its defenders. Even people who find pornography offensive may defend it, as Justice William O. Douglas did, on First Amendment grounds. Douglas argued that even obscenity, which is the most graphic, offensive pornography, is a matter of taste that cannot be prohibited without violating freedom of expression. Matters of taste, like matters of belief, Douglas said, "turn on the idiosyncrasies of individuals. They are too personal to define and too emotional and vague to apply."[12]

Justice Douglas's liberalism did not prevail in the law of obscenity any more than it did in many other areas of communication law. Today obscenity, like false advertising and fighting words, is outside of First Amendment consideration.[13] All fifty states and the federal government have statutes prohibiting obscenity. While obscenity is banned, nonobscene sexual and violent materials are protected by the First Amendment. However, the government may also regulate the sale and distribution of nonobscene pornography.

DEFINING OBSCENITY

Obscenity has not always been a subject of great social concern. Obscenity prosecutions were rare in England through the eighteenth century. John Cleland's *Memoirs of a Woman of Pleasure* was published in England in 1748 without incident. Sexual materials in the American colonies generally were not questioned unless they were antireligious. The law in the eighteenth century was more concerned with preventing blasphemy and heresy than with barring sexual titillation.[14]

Vermont passed one of the earliest American obscenity statutes in 1821, providing for a fine of up to $200 for people who printed, published, or sold any lewd or obscene book, picture, or print. Several other states followed. The first federal law prohibiting obscenity was a customs act enacted in 1842. The law was supposed to keep indecent French postcards outside American borders.[15]

The first major obscenity law and the foundation for today's federal obscenity law was the Comstock Act of 1873, "An Act for the Suppression of Trade in, and Circulation of, Obscene Literature and Articles of Immoral Use."[16] The movement for an obscenity law was led by Anthony Comstock, a strict New England Congregationalist, who had created a committee for the suppression of vice at the YMCA in New York. Similar societies were formed elsewhere. After passage of the Comstock Act, Anthony Comstock was appointed a special agent of the post office to enforce the law. He and the New York Society for the Suppression of Vice received a portion of the fines he collected. Comstock said he destroyed 160 tons of obscene literature and convicted enough people to fill more than 60 railway passenger coaches holding 60 persons each.[17]

---

[12]Paris Adult Theatre I v. Slaton, 413 U.S. 49, 70 (1973) (dissenting opinion).
[13]Roth v. United States, 354 U.S. 476, 1 Media L. Rep. 1375 (1957).
[14]F. Schauer, *The Law of Obscenity* 6–8 (1976).
[15]5 Stat. 566 (1842).
[16]17 Stat. 598 (1873).
[17]J. Kilpatrick, *The Smut Peddlers* 35 (1960), *quoted in* F. Schauer, *The Law of Obscenity* at 13.

In 1957, the Supreme Court ruled in *Roth v. United States* that obscenity deserves no constitutional protection because it is "utterly without redeeming social importance."[18] Roth was convicted under a federal obscenity statute for mailing an obscene book, circulars, and advertising. None of the materials deserved constitutional protection, the Court said, because they made no contribution to the exposition of ideas or truth.

In *Roth* and later cases, the Court of Chief Justice Earl Warren evolved a three-part test for determining whether sexual materials are obscene. The more conservative court under Chief Justice Burger broadened the three-part test slightly to encompass more sexual materials and make obscenity prosecutions easier. The Burger Court's test for obscenity was set forth in *Miller v. California* in 1973.[19]

Miller was a Californian convicted under state law for conducting a mass-mailing campaign to advertise four books—*Intercourse, Man–Woman, Sex Orgies Illustrated,* and *An Illustrated History of Pornography*—and a film titled *Marital Intercourse.* The advertising brochures contained pictures and drawings of men and women, their genitals prominently displayed, engaged in a variety of sexual activities. The Supreme Court, applying its three-part test, found the materials to be obscene.

To determine if a work is obscene, the Court said, it is first necessary to establish that "the average person, applying contemporary community standards" would find that the work, taken as a whole, appeals to the prurient interest. Second, the materials must depict or describe in a "patently offensive" way sexual conduct specifically defined by applicable state law. Third, the work, taken as a whole, must lack serious literary, artistic, political, or scientific value. The test is "conjunctive"; all three parts must be met if a work is to be ruled obscene and therefore outside of constitutional protection.

Patent Offensiveness

The most distinguishing feature of materials that are legally obscene is their patent offensiveness. Many popular sexual materials, including *Playboy* magazine, may be pornographic because they present sexually provocative materials. But sexually oriented films and publications may be pornographic without being obscene. To be obscene, sexually stimulating materials must be patently offensive.

In *Miller v. California*, the Supreme Court said obscene materials might include: (a) patently offensive representations or descriptions of ultimate sex acts, normal or perverted, actual or simulated, or (b) patently offensive representations or descriptions of masturbation, excretory functions, and lewd exhibition of the genitals.[20]

What makes materials patently offensive is their excess of sexual detail, the repetitive nature of the activity, often in a very commercial context. The Supreme Court wants to curb "hard core" pornography. Most obscenity will include scenes of erection, penetration, or ejaculation. Hard-core pornography also emphasizes homosexuality, bestiality, flagellation, sadomasochism, fellatio, and cunnilingus. Photo-

---

[18]354 U.S. 476, 484, 1 Media L. Rep. 1375, 1378 (1957).
[19]413 U.S. 15, 1 Media L. Rep. 1441 (1973).
[20]413 U.S. at 25, 1 Media L. Rep. at 1445.

graphs and motion pictures may have the greatest impact, but textual material and cartoons may also be ''patently offensive.''[21]

In *Hamling v. United States*, the Supreme Court held that advertising brochures that included explicit photographs of heterosexual and homosexual intercourse, fellatio, cunnilingus, masturbation, and group sex were patently offensive.[22] In another case, a federal district court in Florida ruled that a rap album by the musical group 2 Live Crew was also patently offensive. The court said that the graphic rhythmic references to female and male genitalia, human sexual excretion, oral-anal contact and other sexual activities ''makes the audio message analogous to a camera with a zoom lens, focusing on the signs and sounds of various ultimate sex acts.'' Adding to the patent offensiveness, the court said, was the fact that music might be ''more intrusive to the unwilling listener than other forms of communication.''[23]

Mere nudity is not obscene. When the Georgia Supreme Court ruled that the nudity in the film *Carnal Knowledge* was obscene, the U.S. Supreme Court reversed. In an opinion written by Justice Rehnquist, the Court said the film did not show details of sexually intimate encounters that might be obscene. There was no exhibition ''of the actors' genitals, lewd or otherwise.''[24] Therefore the film was not patently offensive.

Similarly, four-letter words are not obscene. Four-letter words may be offensive or indecent, but they are neither sexually arousing nor patently offensive. Four-letter words may be part of graphic and lewd sexual portrayals that are patently offensive, but four-letter words by themselves are not obscene.[25]

Because obscenity law focuses on so-called hard-core pornography, it poses few restraints on most journalists, advertisers, and public relations practitioners. The danger for journalists is using the term *obscenity* too loosely. It is libelous for a journalist to refer to materials as *obscene* if a jury should determine that the materials are not obscene. When no one has been convicted of distributing obscenity, it is safer for the media to refer to *sexual materials* or *erotic magazines*, terms that a jury could say are matters of opinion and not defamatory fact.

Prurient Interest

To be obscene, materials must be more than patently offensive. They must also, taken as a whole, appeal to the prurient interest as determined by the ''the average person, applying contemporary community standards.'' It is not enough that the materials elicit normal, healthy, or lustful thoughts. To be obscene, materials must appeal to a lascivious, shameful, or morbid interest in sex. Materials that are obscene in an everyday sense because some people find them filthy, disgusting, revolting, or repugnant are not obscene legally if they are not patently offensive and do not appeal to the prurient interest of the average person. The prurient appeal may be présented in advertising, books, magazines, and other works.

---

[21]F. Schauer, *Law of Obscenity* 112–113.
[22]418 U.S. 87 (1974).
[23]Skyywalker Records, Inc. v. Navarro, 17 Media L. Rep. 2073 (S.D. Fla. 1990).
[24]Jenkins v. Georgia, 418 U.S. 153, 1 Media L. Rep. 1504 (1974).
[25]Cohen v. California, 403 U.S. 15 (1971).

The Average Person The Supreme Court required in *Roth v. United States* that obscenity be determined by the average person.[26] This ruling liberalized obscenity law. Before *Roth*, many lower courts had used an average-person standard, but the Supreme Court had never formally rejected the influential *Hicklin* test, which barred sexual materials to everyone if they were offensive to children. The *Hicklin* test was the result of a nineteenth-century English case, *Regina v. Hicklin*, in which Lord Cockburn ruled that offensive materials should be judged by the likely effect of the most offensive passages on the most vulnerable members of society, not by the effect of the whole work on the average person.[27]

Lord Cockburn said the intent of the writer of sexual materials, whether to educate or enlighten, was irrelevant if the tendency of the words was to corrupt impressionable minds. Under the *Hicklin* test, a book could be declared obscene if only part of it was found to be obscene to children, the mentally weak, the immature, or other susceptible members of society. Under the *Hicklin* rule, adults who might suffer no ill effects from exposure to pornography could be denied access to sexual materials deemed harmful to children.

In *Miller v. California*, the Supreme Court reiterated its holding in *Roth* that patent offensiveness and prurient interest should be determined by what would be obscene to the average person, not to the youngest and most vulnerable. The average person is the normal adult, not the "highly sensitive or the callous, the educated or the uneducated."[28] Nor is the average person a "puritanical prude"[29] or a person of strange or perverted tastes.

Minors Although the average adult applying contemporary community standards determines what is patently offensive and what appeals to prurient interests, there is a different or *variable* standard for minors. Protecting the health and welfare of children has always been of special concern to courts and legislatures. The states, the Supreme Court has said, have a compelling interest in "safeguarding the physical and psychological well-being of a minor."[30] For this reason, the Court has ruled that sexual materials that would not be obscene to adults can be prohibited for children.

The principle of variable obscenity for adults and children was established in 1968 in *Ginsberg v. New York*.[31] The Supreme Court upheld the conviction of Sam Ginsberg for selling to minors "girlie" magazines that had been found not to be obscene for adults. The magazines showed female buttocks and breasts without full opaque covering as required by a New York statute prohibiting distribution of materials harmful to minors under age 17.

Instead of applying the average-person standard in *Ginsberg*, the Court, in a opinion written by Justice Brennan, held that a state might bar materials as obscene if they appeal to the prurient interests of minors, provided the materials also meet the

---

[26]354 U.S. 476, 1 Media L. Rep. 1375 (1957).
[27]3 Q.B. 360 (1868).
[28]State v. Miller, 112 S.E.2d 472 (W.Va.1960).
[29]State v. Shapiro, 300 A.2d 595 (N.J. Super. Ct. Law Div. 1973).
[30]New York v. Ferber, 458 U.S. 747, 8 Media L. Rep. 1809 (1982), *quoting* Glove Newspaper Co. v. Superior Court, 457 U.S. 596, 3 Media L. Rep. 1689 (1982).
[31]390 U.S. 629, 1 Media L. Rep. 1409 (1968).

other criteria of obscenity—patent offensiveness to minors and lack of serious social value to minors. Serious literature and objects of art that contain nudity or sexual information are not obscene to children any more than they are to adults.

The court in *Ginsberg* did not demand scientific proof that pornography leads to antisocial conduct among children. Instead the Court deferred to the determination of the New York legislature that materials not obscene to adults might be obscene to minors. The Court only required that the law defining what is obscene to minors have a "rational relation to the objective of safeguarding . . . minors from harm."

To protect young minds and bodies, the Supreme Court has also ruled that a state may prohibit the distribution of pictures and films in which children under 16 perform sexual acts. Such materials, the Court said in *New York v. Ferber,* illegally promote the use of minors in pornography, an exploitation of children the state has an interest in halting.[32] Ferber was convicted for selling to an undercover police officer two films of young boys masturbating. The Court noted that in recent years, "the exploitative use of children in the production of pornography has become a serious national problem."

In *Ferber* as in *Ginsberg*, the Court required no proof that participation in pornographic films and pictures damaged a child's psyche. But, the Court noted, "The legislative judgment, as well as the judgment found in the relevant literature, is that the use of children as subjects of pornographic materials is harmful to the physiological, emotional, and mental health of the child."

The Court said the distributors of children's pornography could be punished even though they had nothing to do with the production of the materials employing children. The distribution of children's pornography, the Court said, "is intrinsically related to the sexual abuse of children." Closing the distribution network, the Court said, would cut off the financial incentives essential to pornographic filmmakers.

The Supreme Court has also upheld the constitutionality of a state statute prohibiting the possession of child pornography. In *Osborne v. Ohio*, the Court upheld an Ohio statute that prohibited the possession or viewing of materials showing nude minors.[33] The U.S. Supreme Court said the statute was constitutional, as interpreted by the Ohio Supreme Court, because the Ohio Court did not prohibit possession of all nude depictions of children, but only those in which the nudity constituted "a lewd exhibition" or a "graphic focus on the genitals."

The Ohio statute prohibiting the possession of child pornography, like the statute upheld in *Ferber* prohibiting the distribution of child pornography, attempted to remove the economic incentives to exploit children in sexually explicit films and pictures. Citing *Ferber*, the Court said in *Osborne* that it was reasonable for the state of Ohio to conclude "that it will decrease the production of child pornography if it penalizes those who possess and view the product, thereby decreasing demand." While the Court said the Ohio statute was constitutional, the Court overturned the conviction of Clyde Osborne for possession of four sexually explicit photos of adolescent boys because of faulty instructions to the jury.

In 1988, Congress passed the Child Protection and Obscenity Enforcement Act,

---

[32]458 U.S. 747, 8 Media L. Rep. 1809 (1982).
[33]Osborne v. Ohio, 110 S. Ct. 1691 (1990).

which prohibits selling minors for sexually explicit conduct. The law also requires publishers, printers, photographers, and filmmakers to be able to prove that persons depicted in sexual activity are at least 18 years old.[34]

The law does not protect children only from exposure to, and use in, graphic sexual materials that appeal to the prurient interest. The law also protects children from exposure to *lewd* and *indecent* materials that may have no appeal to the prurient interest. In *FCC v. Pacifica Foundation*, a case to be discussed in the chapter on electronic media, the Supreme Court upheld the Federal Communications Commission's criticism of a radio station for broadcasting indecent four-letter words during the afternoon when children might be listening.[35] Offensive four-letter words, though not necessarily obscene, may be punished, the Court said, when they intrude into the home over the broadcast band when children are listening. Indecent words offend for the same reasons that obscenity offends, the Court said.

Deviants Sexual materials may be obscene not only if they appeal to average adults and minors, but also if they appeal to people with atypical sexual tastes. In *Mishkin v. New York*, the Supreme Court ruled that deviants' pornography is obscene if it is patently offensive and appeals to the prurient interests of the deviant group to which it is addressed.[36] In *Mishkin*, the Court upheld the conviction of a man who had helped to produce and sell 50 books, several of which dealt with sadomasochism, fetishism, and homosexuality.

People stimulated by atypical sexual practices argue there should be no restrictions on the pornography they prefer because it does not appeal to the ''average'' person. Indeed, the average person may find pornography containing deviant sexual practices to be sickening or disgusting. But, the Court said in *Mishkin:*

> Where the material is designed primarily for and primarily disseminated to a clearly defined deviant sexual group, rather than the public at large, the prurient appeal requirement of the *Roth* test is satisfied if the dominant theme of the material taken as a whole appeals to the prurient interest of the members of that group.[37]

Pandering In determining whether sexual materials are obscene, the Supreme Court will consider the commercial methods by which they are marketed. If the materials are aggressively marketed for their prurient appeal, they are more likely to be termed obscene.[38] The assertive marketing of sexual materials for their prurient interest is called *pandering*. So offensive is pandering to the Supreme Court that the justices have upheld obscenity convictions for the commercial promotion of sexual materials that were not themselves obscene.

The Supreme Court upheld the obscenity conviction of publisher Ralph Ginzburg in part because of his aggressive marketing of sexual materials with advertising that was not obscene. In *Ginzburg v. United States*, one of the most controversial

---

[34]Pub. L. 100–690, 102 Stat. 4485 (1988).

[35]438 U.S. 726, 3 Media L. Rep. 2553 (1978).

[36]Mishkin v. New York, 383 U.S. 502 (1966).

[37]*Id.* at 508–509.

[38]Pinkus v. United States, 436 U.S. 293 (1978); F. Schauer, *Law of Obscenity* 83–84.

cases in obscenity law, the Supreme Court upheld Ginzburg's conviction for pandering because of his "commercial exploitation of erotica solely for the sake of their prurient appeal."[39] Ginzburg mailed *Eros*, a hardbound magazine dealing with sex, along with *The Housewife's Handbook of Selective Promiscuity* and another periodical. Four of 15 articles in *Eros* were found to be obscene, but leading literary figures testified at the trial that even these had serious literary value. Some pictures in *Eros* were described by Professor H. W. Janson, a New York University art historian, as "outstandingly beautiful and artistic."[40]

The Court examined the commercial setting of Ginzburg's promotion as an aid in determining obscenity. The ads announcing Ginzburg's publications contained no erotic or explicit pictures or foul language, but Justice Brennan, writing for the Court, found pandering because Ginzburg's enterprise was permeated with the "leer of the sensualist." Brennan said that Ginzburg's advertising emphasized the eroticism of his publications, not their literary value. Even the postmark from Middlesex, N.J., was suggestive. Furthermore, the Court noted that Ginzburg had first tried to get mailing privileges at Blue Ball and Intercourse, Pa.

Justice Douglas, who dissented, later remarked that Ralph Ginzburg went to jail "not for what he printed, but for the sexy manner in which he advertised his creations."[41] Justice Stewart, who also dissented, said Ginzburg had been convicted of "commercial exploitation," something he was not charged with.[42]

Community Standard

The Burger and Rehnquist Courts, reflecting the decentralization of power favored by Republican administrations, tend to leave substantial decision-making powers to the states. Each state, for example, can determine the degree of fault that a private person must prove in a libel suit against the media.

In the law of obscenity, too, the Burger Court augmented the power of localities by ruling in *Miller v. California* that the average person determining whether sexual materials are obscene is supposed to apply a "contemporary community standard." Jurors can draw on their own understanding of the views of the average person in the community to decide what is patently offensive and prurient.[43] The "community" that reflects the average person's values may be the juror's city, county, or state. Often, the community standard may be interpreted by a public opinion poll. Not surprisingly, urban populations are more tolerant of pornography than people in smaller communities.[44]

The Warren Court, like the Burger Court, had used a community standard. But the Warren Court's standard was the same for the whole nation. Chief Justice Burger opposed the national community standard of the Warren years because he thought a

---

[39]383 U.S. 463, 1 Media L. Rep. 1424 (1966). *See also* Splawn v. California, 431 U.S. 595, 2 Media L. Rep. 1881 (1977); Hamling v. United States, 418 U.S. 87, 1 Media L. Rep. 1479 (1974).

[40]P. Magrath, "The Obscenity Cases: Grapes of Roth," 1966 *S. Ct. Rev.* 7, 27.

[41]Paris Adult Theatre I v. Slaton, 413 U.S. 49, 70, 1 Media L. Rep. 1454, 1462 (1973) (dissenting opinion).

[42]383 U.S. at 500, 1 Media L. Rep. at 1423.

[43]Hamling v. United States, 418 U.S. 87, 1 Media L. Rep. 1479 (1974).

[44]Glassman, "Community Standards of Patent Offensiveness: Public Opinion Data and Obscenity Law," 42 *Pub. Opinion Q.* 161 (1978).

single standard for the whole nation was too abstract. It is neither "realistic nor constitutionally sound," Burger said in his opinion in *Miller v. California*, "to read the First Amendment as requiring that the people of Maine or Mississippi accept public depiction of conduct found tolerable in Las Vegas, or New York City."[45]

The Burger Court admitted that using different state and local standards might cause some distributors to censor their sexual materials to conform to the tastes of the most conservative markets rather than risk prosecution in different communities under different standards. But the national obscenity standard of the Warren years did not necessarily encourage more daring sexual materials than the community standard of the Burger years. Even operating under a national standard, a distributor of pornography will not necessarily gear materials to the most tolerant and liberal communities.[46]

Because some communities have more conservative obscenity standards than others, federal officials prosecuting pornographers sometimes practice *venue shopping*, picking a jurisdiction—or venue—in which prosecutors think they have the best chance of finding a conservative jury that will convict for obscenity. People connected to the film *Deep Throat*, for example, were prosecuted and convicted under federal obscenity laws in Memphis.[47]

A case in Alabama illustrates how a local obscenity prosecution may curb national distribution of sexual materials. An Alabama county's obscenity indictment forced a New York City distributor of sex films into bankruptcy when satellite companies ceased beaming the New York firm's movies. Home Dish Satellite Corp. of New York was forced out of business when it was indicted under an Alabama obscenity statute modeled after *Miller v. California*. Home Dish provided X-rated films that were possibly obscene to 30,000 subscribers nationwide and nonobscene R-rated films to another 1.2 million customers. The indictments were brought in Montgomery County, Alabama, where about 50 households subscribed to Home Dish Satellite's sexual films.[48]

Also indicted were GTE Corp., GTE Spacenet Corp., and United States Satellite, all of which provided the satellite transmission for Home Dish. Although satellite companies are normally not liable for the programs they carry, all three satellite transmission firms discontinued their contracts with Home Dish after the charges were brought. Home Dish was then forced out of business before any determination of obscenity was made.

Social Value of the Whole Work

Finally, for a work to be obscene, it must not only be patently offensive and appeal to prurient interests, it must also lack social value when viewed as a whole.

The Whole Work   By requiring that the work be looked at as a whole, the Court in *Miller v. California* reaffirmed its 1957 decision in *Roth* holding that a determination

---

[45]413 U.S. at 32, 1 Media L. Rep. at 1448.

[46]F. Schauer, *Law of Obscenity* at 32 n.13.

[47]United States v. Battista, 646 F.2d 237 (6th Cir. 1981), *cert. denied*, 454 U.S. 1046 (1981).

[48]"Obscenity Law Used in Alabama Breaks New York Company," *New York Times*, May 2, 1990, at 1, 11.

of obscenity should not be made on the basis of only a few isolated passages or pictures. The *Roth* decision rejected the holding in the nineteenth-century English case, *Regina v. Hicklin*, in which an English court ruled that works could be declared obscene if only a few passages endangered children and other sensitive people.[49] Under the *Hicklin* rule, many literary classics were ruled to be obscene because they contained a few offensive passages. Among the books banned in this country were James Joyce's *Ulysses*, D. H. Lawrence's *Lady Chatterley's Lover*, and Theodore Dreiser's *An American Tragedy*.

The *Hicklin* rule was challenged in an American court in a case involving Joyce's *Ulysses*. In a decision upheld on appeal, Judge Woolsey, a federal judge in New York, ruled that *Ulysses* could be imported into the United States because it was not obscene. Taking the book as a whole, Judge Woolsey found it to be a sincere, serious literary effort of which explicit descriptions of sexual acts were a necessary part.[50] The Supreme Court reiterated Judge Woolsey's view when it ruled in *Roth* and in *Miller* that a work should be judged as a whole.

Social Value   Generally in First Amendment analysis, courts avoid judging the value of expression. In the political arena, for example, the courts make no effort to determine whether a politician's promises are practical, far-fetched, or naive. Listeners decide the value of what they hear. But in obscenity cases, the Supreme Court has always used a social-value test to determine if materials are constitutionally protected. In the *Miller* decision, the Supreme Court said that sexual content, to be obscene, must, taken as a whole, lack "serious literary, artistic, political, or scientific value."

The Burger Court's standard of social value broadened the definition of obscenity slightly from what it had been during the years of the Warren Court. The Warren Court had required a plaintiff to prove that sexual materials were, taken as a whole, "utterly without redeeming social value."[51] Liberals on the Warren Court argued that no work should be denied constitutional protection unless it is utterly without value. But Chief Justice Burger said the "utterly without" standard made it too hard for prosecutors to prove that a work was obscene.[52] Indeed, until the Burger Court's decision in *Miller v. California*, it was almost impossible for a prosecutor to prove that materials were utterly without redeeming social value.

Since *Miller*, works may be declared obscene even if they are not utterly without redeeming social value. Because of *Miller*, a work with a fragment of social value may still be declared obscene if the work, taken as a whole, lacks serious literary, artistic, political, or scientific value.

Although *Miller* made prosecuting obscenity a bit easier, *Miller* did not place significantly greater restrictions on pornographic materials than the "utterly without" standard did. Under the *Miller* standard, courts rule that works dealing with political and historical subjects have serious value even if the works are crude and offensive. The movie *Caligula*, for example, was ruled to have artistic value even

---

[49] 3 Q.B. 360 (1868).
[50] United States v. One Book Called "Ulysses," 5 F. Supp. 182 (S.D.N.Y 1933), *aff'd*, 72 F.2d 705 (2d Cir. 1934).
[51] Memoirs v. Massachusetts, 383 U.S. 413, 1 Media L. Rep. 1390 (1966).
[52] Miller v. California, 413 U.S. 15, 22, 1 Media L. Rep. 1441 (1973).

though it contained endless scenes of tasteless sex and violence. Although a federal court found the film to be patently offensive, the film was not obscene because the violence and sex did not appeal to the prurient interest and because, taken as a whole, the film contained artistic effort and creativity. *"Caligula,"* the court said, "clearly contains political, historical, and social themes and subthemes, including the use and abuse of power, dynastic and institutional struggle, the violence and corruption that attends a society bankrupt in moral values, and the fragility of civilization."[53]

A federal court in a case involving 2 Live Crew rejected expert testimony about the political, scientific, and literary value of the rap album *As Nasty As They Wanna Be*. The court said brief phrases in such songs as "Dirty Nursery Rhymes" about Abraham Lincoln were not sufficient in number or significance to give the recording, as a whole, any serious political value. Likewise, the court found insignificant scientific value in such cultural devices as "boasting" which is overstating one's sexual prowess and other virtues. To the court, the rhythm and explicit sexual lyrics were utterly without redeeming social value.[54]

The value of sexual expression—unlike its offensiveness and its appeal to prurient interests—is not determined by the average person applying contemporary community standards. In 1987, in *Pope v. Illinois*, the Supreme Court ruled that the value question of the three-part *Miller* test should be determined by a "reasonable person" rather than by the "average person."[55] The Court's decision in *Pope* may increase First Amendment protection for sexual materials because the so-called reasonable person may find literary, artistic, political, or scientific value in a work where the majority, represented by the average person, would not. In practice, critics, scholars, and other experts frequently help determine the value of a disputed work.

SUMMARY

For a work to be obscene, it must, taken as a whole, be patently offensive and appeal to the prurient interest of the average person applying contemporary community standards. Works are patently offensive if they are "hard-core" pornography containing graphic, lewd displays of the genitals or sexual acts. A work appeals to the prurient interest if it is sexually arousing to the average person. Materials that appeal to the prurient interest of minors or deviants may also be obscene to those audiences even though the materials might not be obscene to the average adult. Materials that are not obscene, but which "pander" in an intense commercial promotion of their sexual appeal, may also be prohibited as obscene. To be obscene, materials must also lack serious literary, artistic, political, or scientific value, as determined by a reasonable person.

---

[53] Penthouse v. McCauliffe, 7 Media L. Rep. 1798, 1804 (N.D.Ga. 1981), *aff'd by an evenly divided court*, 717 F.2d 517 (11th Cir. 1983).

[54] Skyywalker Records, Inc. v. Navarro, 17 Media L. Rep. 2073 (S.D. Fla. 1990).

[55] 481 U.S. 497 (1987)

PRIVACY AND POSSESSION

Prohibitions on obscenity include bans on the sale, importation, and interstate transport of obscene materials.[56] The government may also ban possession of child pornography, the Supreme Court said in *Osborne v. Ohio*.[57] However, in 1969, a divided Supreme Court ruled in *Stanley v. Georgia* that citizens might possess adult obscenity in the privacy of their home.[58]

Stanley was convicted for possession of obscene films found while police were searching his residence for evidence of illegal bookmaking. The Supreme Court reversed an obscenity conviction on the grounds that Stanley had a First Amendment right to receive pornographic information. In ringing language, Justice Marshall, who wrote the Court's opinion, said Stanley's right to receive sexual material had an "added dimension" because he possessed the materials in the privacy of his home. "If the First Amendment means anything," Justice Marshall wrote, "it means that a State has no business telling a man, sitting alone in his own house, what books he may read and what films he may watch." The government, Marshall continued, has no right to "control the moral content of a person's thoughts."

Although the *Stanley* decision upheld a citizen's right to receive obscenity in the privacy of the home, *Stanley* is an aging precedent that establishes no meaningful right to possess obscenity. The constitutional prohibitions on the purchase, import, and interstate commerce in obscene materials seriously erodes whatever right the Court may have established in *Stanley* for citizens to receive obscene materials. The right recognized in *Stanley* to receive and possess obscenity is further limited by the Court's ruling in *Osborne* that prohibitions on the possession of child pornography are also constitutional.

Whatever tenuous right Stanley had to possess obscenity in his home, the Supreme Court has ruled the right does not extend to public theaters. In *Paris Adult Theatre I v. Slaton*, the Court ruled that a downtown Atlanta theater could be barred from showing two obscene films, *Magic Mirror* and *It All Comes Out in the End*, to willing adults. Signs outside the theater announced that the movies were "mature feature films" for adults 21 and older.[59] "If viewing the nude body offends you," one sign said, "Please Do Not Enter." There was no evidence that minors had entered the theater.

The Supreme Court rejected the theater management's argument that adults should have as much right to attend an explicit movie in a theater as Stanley had to possess obscene materials in his home. A public theater, unlike a home, is not a private place, the Court said. The state can regulate a theater as it can regulate any other business. In a public theater, the Court said, it was immaterial that the theater management limited the audience to consenting adults. There are many activities, including prostitution, self-mutilation, and bare-fist prizefighting, which the state prohibits even though adults are willing to participate. The state has an interest, the Court said,

---

[56]*See* United States v. Reidel, 402 U.S. 351 (1971): United States v. Thirty-Seven (37) Photographs, 402 U.S. 363 (1971); 18 U.S.C.A. 1461–1465 (1984).

[57] 110 S. Ct. 1691 (1990).

[58] 394 U.S. 557 (1969).

[59] 413 U.S. 49, 1 Media L. Rep. 1454 (1973).

in protecting "the quality of life and the total community environment, the tone of commerce in the great city centers, and, possibly, the public safety itself."

In a long, detailed dissent to *Paris Adult Theatre,* Justice Brennan argued that obscenity laws should do no more than protect unconsenting adults and children, a conclusion arrived at a few years earlier by the Commission on Obscenity and Pornography appointed by President Lyndon Johnson. Justice Brennan, after wrestling with the question of obscenity for more than 15 years, decided that all definitions of obscenity are too vague to pass constitutional muster.

Brennan also opposed the court's willingness to permit the government to regulate the moral tone of the community. If the state can create a particular moral tone by proscribing what citizens can read or see, Brennan said, then why cannot the state decree what citizens must read?

SUMMARY

The Supreme Court has ruled that adults may receive obscene materials in the privacy of their homes. However, the right to receive and possess obscenity is severely curtailed by constitutional prohibitions on the import, distribution, and sale of obscenity. The right to possess obscenity is further limited by the Court's ruling that possession of child pornography may be barred. The Supreme Court has also held that obscene films may be prohibited in theaters even if admission is limited to adults.

DUE PROCESS AND PRIOR RESTRAINTS

Because obscenity is outside of First Amendment protection, it can be enjoined before distribution as well as punished after. Communities can stop the showing of an obscene film or play or the distribution of an obscene book or magazine. Enjoining obscenity is quicker and cheaper than prosecuting the distributor or theater operator after an obscene film or play has been presented.[60]

Nevertheless, because obscenity is speech, the First Amendment requires that procedures for prior review be followed carefully so that sexual expression is not unduly limited before it is determined to be obscene. In fact, the procedural requirements of First Amendment due process are more clearly spelled out in obscenity law than in other areas of communications law.

Government Burden

First Amendment due process requires that the government shoulder the burden of proving that a film or play is obscene. In *Freedman v. Maryland*, the Supreme Court said theater owners and film distributors do not have the responsibility to prove their

---

[60] Note, "Enjoining Obscenity as a Public Nuisance and the Prior Restraint Doctrine," 84 *Colum. L. Rev.* 1616 (1984).

productions are not obscene. The government agency that would stop the expression must prove that the materials are obscene.[61]

In *Fort Wayne Books, Inc. v. Indiana*, the Supreme Court ruled that government agents may not seize sexual materials before a judge has determined at a hearing that they are obscene.[62] The Supreme Court overturned a decision of the Supreme Court of Indiana holding that all sexual materials might be removed from an adult bookstore before trial on racketeering charges if officials had reason to believe that obscenity was being circulated. The U.S. Supreme Court said the risk of prior restraint on constitutionally protected expression is too high if sexual materials may be seized before they are found to be obscene. The Court said officials may seize a single copy of a book or film as evidence, but they may not take all materials from an adult bookstore before an obscenity determination is made.

Due process also requires that the administrative decision be made rapidly and that the administrator not have the final word on what is obscene. Administrative boards cannot be trusted with the final determination of what is obscene because they are often composed of political appointees. One commentator points out that political appointees do not have the independence and long-term view necessary for determining sensitive First Amendment cases.[63] Only the courts, the Supreme Court has said, have the necessary sensitivity to freedom of expression to determine when prior restraints might be imposed.[64]

Informal Restraints

Injunctions are not the only potentially unconstitutional government restraints on sexual materials. Informal government pressures may also unconstitutionally suppress sexual materials. In 1986, a federal court ruled that a warning letter sent to stores selling *Playboy* and other sexually oriented magazines was an unconstitutional prior restraint. The U.S. District Court for the District of Columbia ruled unconstitutional a letter written for Attorney General Edwin Meese's Commission on Pornography warning drugstore and convenience store chains that they might be listed in the commission's report as sellers of pornography. The letter was sent after one minister testified before the commission that several corporations were selling pornography. To the minister, pornography included *Playboy* and *Penthouse* magazines, publications that have not been found to be obscene. Several thousand convenience stores, including the 7-Eleven Stores, stopped selling nonobscene adult publications such as *Playboy* and *Penthouse* after receiving the letter.[65]

The federal district court said the Meese commission letter was similar to a blacklist that the U.S. Supreme Court ruled to be an unconstitutional prior restraint in *Bantam Books, Inc. v. Sullivan* in 1963.[66] In *Bantam Books*, the Supreme Court ruled

---

[61] Freedman v. Maryland, 380 U.S. 51, 1 Media L. Rep. 1126 (1965). *See also* Vance v. Universal Amusement Co., 445 U.S. 308 (1980) and Southeastern Promotions, Ltd. v. Conrad, 420 U.S. 546, 1 Media L. Rep. 1130 (1975).

[62] 109 S. Ct. 916, 16 Media L. Rep. 1337 (1989).

[63] Monaghan, "First Amendment 'Due Process,'" 83 *Harv. L. Rev.* 518, 522–23 (1970).

[64] Freedman v. Maryland, 380 U.S. at 58, 1 Media L. Rep. at 1129.

[65] Playboy Enterprises v. Meese, 639 F. Supp. 581, 13 Media L. Rep. 1101 (D.C.D.C. 1986). *See* "'Adult' Magazines Lose Sales as 8,000 Stores Forbid Them," *New York Times*, June 16, 1986 at 1.

[66] 372 U.S. 58, 1 Media L. Rep. 1116 (1963).

it was unconstitutional for the Rhode Island Commission to Encourage Morality in Youth to notify magazine and book distributors that some of their publications were objectionable for sale or display to youths under 18. The notices thanked distributors on the list in advance for their cooperation and reminded them that the Rhode Island commission had the duty to recommend prosecution for purveyors of obscenity. Officials were then sent to see what action distributors planned to take.

The Rhode Island commission said it wrote letters and visited distributors simply to advise them of their legal rights. But the Supreme Court said the commission engaged in an informal censorship in violation of the First Amendment. The Court said the Rhode Island commission's blacklists, informal threats, and coercion unconstitutionally suppressed publications. The Court also said the term *objectionable* in the commission's warning notice was vague and left distributors to speculate whether the commission considered a particular publication to be obscene.

Relying on the Rhode Island case, the federal district court in Washington found the Meese commission's letters to convenience stores also to be unconstitutional. The court said the letters suppressed nonobscene publications by threatening to list the store owners as sellers of pornography in the commission's final report. The only purpose of the letters, which did not define *pornography*, was "to discourage distributors from selling the publications; a form of pressure amounting to an administrative restraint of the plaintiffs' First Amendment rights," the court said. The court enjoined the commission from publishing company names in the final report and told the Justice Department to withdraw the letters from those to whom they were sent.

Cutting Funds

Another way for the government to curb obscenity is to bar funding. In 1989, Congress passed a law prohibiting the National Endowment for the Arts and the National Endowment for the Humanities from awarding grants for the creation of obscene art. This was the first time Congress limited arts grants because of content.[67]

The bill's sponsor, Senator Jesse Helms, hoped for a broader ban on the use of government funds to support art with sexual or violent themes. But Congress limited the ban on funds to works that are obscene as defined in *Miller v. California*. The legislation requires the endowment chairpersons and advisory councils to review all art financed through the hundreds of subgrants made each year.[68]

The legislation emerged from controversy over a grant supporting an exhibition of photographs by the late Robert Mapplethorpe. Some of the photos had homosexual themes. Members of Congress were also agitated by a grant to a museum in Winston-Salem, North Carolina, where an exhibit included a photograph of a crucifix suspended in urine. Under the new law, federal funds may not be used to support works that depict sadomasochism, homoeroticism, sexual exploitation of children or individuals engaged in sex acts, if, taken as a whole, the works lack serious literary, artistic, political, or scientific value.

Government curbs on funding of the arts are not a prior restraint. The government, like any patron, may support the art it finds most pleasing. There is a risk,

---

[67] Pub. L. 101–121, 103 Stat. 701 (1989).
[68] "Advisers to Arts Endowment Discuss New Financing Law," *New York Times*, Nov. 5, 1989, at 14.

however, that laws excluding some artistic subjects will cause the national endowments to avoid funding controversial and challenging artists, a result that would be inconsistent with the robust debate encouraged by the First Amendment.

SUMMARY

When the decision is made about what is obscene, the First Amendment requires that due process be followed. This includes placing the burden of proof on the government and providing for rapid judicial review. Threatening letters and other informal regulation of sexual materials by the government may be an unconstitutional prior restraint. Another curb on obscenity, though not a prior restraint, is a government curb on funding of obscene art.

VIOLENCE

A number of attempts have been made to expand the definition of obscenity to include indecency, immorality, sacrilege, and violence. Of special concern in recent years has been the increase in violent pornography, an increase that has led to attempts to prohibit it as Scandinavian countries often do.[69] Another area of concern has been violent themes and lyrics in popular music.

However, violence in American media is generally not restricted unless it is obscene. Violence is not obscene unless it is patently offensive and appeals to the prurient interest. Violence, however, usually does not appeal to prurient interests. Courts are more likely to find violent portrayals revolting than obscene.

The film *Caligula* was ruled not to be obscene despite its endless scenes of disembowlment, castration, decapitation, rape, murder, and other acts of cruelty and sexual violence. While the numerous acts of violence in *Caligula* were offensive to some and boring to others, a federal court said the film was not obscene because the violence did not appeal to the prurient interest. A federal court said the film's "overwhelming depictions of violence, cruelty, and sexual explicitness" were in extremely bad taste and would likely be revolting to the average person. However, the film was not obscene because the violence would not arouse an erotic interest. In fact, the court said the natural rhythm of sex was "obstructed by the fast-paced explicitly sexual depictions.[70]

Women and Violence

Unable to bar violence as obscene, feminists attempted unsuccessfully in Minneapolis and Indianapolis to bar the "graphic sexually explicit subordination of women" as a violation of women's civil rights. In an ordinance adopted by the city council in Indi-

---

[69] R. Randall, *Freedom and Taboo* 62 (1989).
[70] Penthouse v. McCauliffe, 702 F.2d 925, 7 Media L. Rep. 1798 (N.D.Ga. 1981), *aff'd by an evenly divided court*, 717 F.2d 517 (11th Cir. 1983).

anapolis, the feminists said sale and distribution of pornography is "a systematic practice of exploitation and subordination based on sex." This subordination of women in pornography promotes bigotry and contempt and thereby denies women opportunities for equality of rights in employment, education, and access to public accommodations, the ordinance said.

The ordinance also said that pornography denies women their civil rights by encouraging rape and abuse.[71] The ordinance defined pornography as "the graphic sexually explicit subordination of women," whether in pictures or in words. For pornography to be a violation, it was necessary that it represent women in one or more of six "subordinate" ways, including as sexual objects enjoying pain, humiliation, or rape. Women were also depicted in subordinate ways in violation of the ordinance if they were shown as sexual objects being cut up or mutilated, as "sexual objects for domination," or in "scenarios of degradation."

The mayor of Minneapolis vetoed the ordinance on constitutional grounds after the City Council adopted it. The U.S. Court of Appeals for Seventh Circuit also declared the Indianapolis ordinance unconstitutional. The Seventh Circuit accepted the premise of the ordinance that "depictions of subordination tend to perpetuate subordination." The subordinate status of women, the court said, "leads to affront and lower pay at work, insult and injury at home, battery and rape on the streets." However, the court found the definition of pornography in the Indianapolis ordinance to be unconstitutional because it did not include the elements of patent offensiveness, appeal to the prurient interest, and lack of social value as required by the Supreme Court's obscenity ruling in *Miller v. California*.

The court viewed pornography as other courts have viewed racial bigotry, anti-Semitism, televised violence, and biased newspaper stories. Although expression containing bigotry and violence may be repugnant, it is protected by the First Amendment because it is a powerful expression of citizens' political and social views. The discrimination against women that pornography encourages, the court said, "demonstrates the power of pornography as speech." However insidious protected expression may be, the First Amendment does not permit the government to decide what is acceptable and unacceptable speech, the court said.

The Seventh Circuit said a law permitting the portrayal of women only in positions of equality no matter how graphic the sexual content is "thought control." The Indianapolis statute established "an 'approved' view of women, of how they may react to sexual encounters, of how the sexes may relate to each other. Those who espouse the approved view may use sexual images; those who do not, may not."[72] Such limitations on expression are unconstitutional.

Effects of Violence

Since the late 1960s there has been a dramatic increase in the amount of social-psychological research on the effects of pornography. This research was sparked in

---

[71] American Booksellers Association, Inc. v. Hudnut, 598 F. Supp. 1316 (S.D.Ind. 1984), *aff'd*,771 F.2d 324, 328, *aff'd without opinion*, 475 U.S. 1132, 11 Media L. Rep. 2465 (1986).
[72] 771 F.2d at 328, 1 Media L. Rep. at 1107.

part by President Johnson's appointment of the Commission on Obscenity and Pornography in 1968. That commission's task was to study the effect of obscenity and pornography on the public, particularly on minors, and to investigate the relationship of pornography to crime and other antisocial behavior.[73] The Commission on Obscenity and Pornography did not study violent pornography because it was not prevalent at the time.

The commission could find no significant causal relationship between pornography and antisocial conduct. Although the commission recognized public concern about sexually explicit materials, the presidential panel recommended repeal of all regulations limiting adults' access to pornography. Only children and unconsenting adults should be protected from pornography, the commission said. The commission also urged that sex education programs be expanded and that society treat sexuality more openly. Three commissioners issued a dissenting minority report. President Nixon, who succeeded President Johnson before the report was issued, rejected the document as "morally bankrupt."

In 1986, Attorney General Edwin Meese's Commission on Pornography issued a report that registered much more concern than the earlier presidential report about the social effects of pornography, particularly violent pornography.[74] The Meese commission agreed with the earlier presidential commission that mere nudity does no damage to society. The Meese commission also agreed generally with the legal definition of prosecutable obscenity as fashioned by the U.S. Supreme Court in *Miller v. California* and later cases.

However, the Meese commission found a detrimental effect on society from nonviolent pornography that depicts degradation, domination, subordination, or humiliation. Degrading nonviolent pornography as well as violent pornography helps foster erroneous attitudes that women enjoy being raped and that sexual coercion is appropriate, the commission said. The commission also concluded that a broad population holding these beliefs "will commit more acts of sexual violence or sexual coercion than would a population holding these beliefs to a lesser extent." Furthermore, the Meese commission concluded that violent pornography has "a causal relationship to antisocial acts of sexual violence."

The Meese commission's conclusion that violent pornography causes antisocial acts appears to overreach scientific evidence. Professor Neil Malamuth, who testified before the commission, concluded from his studies that exposure to aggressive pornography depicting rape, bondage, and domination can contribute "to a cultural climate that is more accepting of aggression against women."[75] Professor Edward Donnerstein, who also testified before the commission, concluded that exposure to violent pornography stimulates aggressive attitudes in some men.[76] But, while some research links pornography to aggressive attitudes, the Meese commission's conclusion that pornography causes violence in society bears further study.

---

[73] *Report of the Commission on Obscenity and Pornography* 1 (1970).

[74] Attorney General's Commission on Pornography, *Final Report* (1986).

[75] Malamuth, "Aggression Against Women: Cultural and Individual Causes," in N. Malamuth and E. Donnerstein, *Pornography and Sexual Aggression* at 40.

[76] Donnerstein, "Pornography: Its Effect on Violence Against Women," in N. Malamuth and E. Donnerstein, *Pornography and Sexual Aggression* at 79.

SUMMARY

Violence is not unconstitutional in American media unless it is obscene. Sexual violence, however, may not appeal to the prurient interest as sexual materials must if they are obscene. So far, violent pornography does not violate women's civil rights. The Meese commission on Pornography said it found a causal link between violent pornography and violence in society, but social scientists generally do not go so far. Social scientific evidence suggests that exposure to violent pornography may increase one's tolerance for sexual crimes, but evidence linking violent crime to pornography is not clear.

NONOBSCENE SEXUAL EXPRESSION

While obscenity can be banned, nonobscene sexual expression generally cannot be. However, nonobscene sexual expression may be restricted to certain places or times to preserve the community's quality of life. The constitutionality of time, place, and manner restrictions on nonobscene sexual expression depends on the circumstances in each case.[77] The Supreme Court looks at the content, the medium, and the time of day in which materials are presented to determine if they may be prohibited or curtailed. Government restrictions on nonobscene sexual expression should be as narrow as possible and should allow alternative avenues by which the restricted expression may find its audience.

Generally, the government's power to regulate or prohibit sexual expression increases as the expression merges with conduct. Some conduct, such as nude sunbathing, topless waitressing, and massaging, contains no expression and therefore can be regulated without First Amendment consideration.[78] Other nonobscene conduct, such as nude dancing and nude musicals, is mixed with communication and therefore may be channeled to certain times and places.[79] Three acceptable governmental regulations on the distribution of nonobscene sexual materials are zoning, postal, and display laws. The media themselves also regulate the sexual content of their offerings.

Zoning

In 1976, the Supreme Court upheld the constitutionality of Detroit's Anti–Skid Row Ordinance, which required that adult theaters be more than 1,000 feet from adult bookstores, cabarets, and bars. The ordinance regulates constitutionally protected materials that are not obscene but are "characterized by an emphasis" on sex.[80] Detroit passed the zoning provision to prevent a concentration of adult theaters that

---

[77] FCC v. Pacifica Foundation, 438 U.S. 726, 3 Media L. Rep. 2553 (1978).

[78] *E.g.*, South Florida Free Beaches v. City of Miami, 734 F.2d 608 (11th Cir. 1984).

[79] Schad v. Borough of Mount Ephraim, 452 U.S. 61 (1981); Southeastern Promotions, Ltd. v. Conrad, 420 U.S. 546, 1 Media L. Rep. 1140 (1975).

[80] Young v. American Mini Theatres, Inc., 427 U.S. 50, 61, 1 Media L. Rep. 1151, 1155 (1976).

might lower property values, attract transients, and encourage flight of legitimate businesses.

In upholding the constitutionality of the ordinance, the Supreme Court noted that the city had a legitimate interest in "planning and regulating the use of property for commercial purposes." The limitation on adult movie theaters was simply a time, place, and manner regulation on a specific kind of theater, the Court said. The city was not limiting the market for theaters overall; there were still abundant opportunities to open adult theaters in the city.[81]

While the Supreme Court has approved zoning laws to restrict the location of pornographic theaters and bookstores, the Court does not permit zoning laws to ban nonobscene sexual expression. The Court struck down a New Jersey zoning law that barred all commercial live entertainment, including nude dancing, in the Borough of Mount Ephraim. The zoning ordinance was declared unconstitutional because it provided no place where constitutionally protected nonobscene dancing might be performed. The Court said that the borough had not demonstrated that permitting nude dancing would create the difficulties with parking, trash collection, and police protection that prompted the ban on commercial live entertainment.[82]

Ordinances restricting the showing of nonobscene materials must not be too broad. In a Florida case, the Supreme Court struck down an ordinance that prohibited drive-in movie theaters from exhibiting films showing bare breasts, buttocks, or pubic areas if the screen was visible from streets and sidewalks. The Supreme Court ruled that the ordinance was too broad as it applied to adults because it barred adults from seeing nonobscene anatomy on the screen. The Court also said the ordinance was too broad as it applied to children. By preventing the showing of all nudity, the ordinance would have protected children not only from lewd pornography but also from pictures of a baby's buttocks, the nude body of a war victim, scenes from a culture where nudity was common, the opening of some art exhibitions, and pictures of nude bathers.[83] Such a broad content prohibition in a nuisance statute or zoning law is unconstitutional.

Postal Regulations

While zoning has limited power to channel nonobscene messages, another legal method is the postal law. Postal regulations limit but do not prohibit nonobscene pandering advertisements. Reflecting the special concern of legislators and courts for protecting children and privacy, the Supreme Court permits homeowners to stop sexually oriented advertisements from being delivered to their mailboxes.[84] Under postal law, people who receive a pandering advertisement can contact the post office and have their names removed from the mailer's list. The law also says that the sender can be required to mark on the outside that the advertisements are sexually oriented. Ads do not have to be obscene to be halted.

The Supreme Court upheld the constitutionality of the statute in *Rowan v.*

---

[81] *See also* City of Renton v. Playtime Theatres, Inc., 475 U.S. 41, 12 Media L. Rep. 1721 (1986).
[82] Schad v. Borough of Mount Ephraim, 452 U.S. 61, 7 Media L. Rep. 1426 (1981).
[83] Erznoznik v. City of Jacksonville, 422 U.S. 205, 213, 1 Media L. Rep. 1508, 1511 (1975).
[84] 39 U.S.C.A. sec. 3008 (1980).

United States Post Office Department.[85] The Supreme Court unanimously agreed that no one has a right to press even good ideas on an unwilling recipient. The mailer's right to communicate stops at the mailbox of the unreceptive addressee.

Display Laws

Statutes and ordinances may also restrict the display of sexually explicit materials that are not obscene for adults but may be for minors. In a case remanded by the U.S. Supreme Court, the Virginia Supreme Court ruled that 16 books by James Joyce, John Updike, Judy Blume, and other authors would not be banned under a state statute protecting minors from "harmful" material.[86] Some booksellers feared that the books, several of which have considerable literary merit, could be barred under the statute protecting minors from sexually explicit books and films. In an interpretive decision requested by the U.S. Supreme Court,[87] the Virginia court ruled that none of the 16 books would be banned under the statute that bars display of harmful materials in such a way that juveniles might "examine and peruse" them.

The Virginia court also ruled that store owners do not have to hide harmful materials to keep juveniles from examining them. It is sufficient, the Virginia court said, for booksellers to keep sexually explicit materials in their sight so that juveniles may be halted if they attempt to peruse them.

In another case protecting minors, a federal court upheld the use of "blinder racks" that hide the lower two-thirds of the cover of sexual publications. The U.S. Court of Appeals for the Tenth Circuit upheld the constitutionality of a Wichita, Kansas, ordinance barring display of sexual materials to minors but permitting use of the so-called blinder racks. Blinder racks effectively shield minors from sexual materials without unconstitutionally depriving adults of access to legal sexual publications.[88]

A Minneapolis ordinance requiring bookstores to keep materials harmful to minors in a sealed wrapper or behind an opaque cover was also ruled to be constitutional.[89] Adults still have access to the materials by asking a clerk to remove the wrapper, by viewing an inspection copy kept behind the store counter, or by viewing the material in an adults-only bookstore that excludes minors.

Industry and Citizen Regulation

The media go through cycles during which they limit violent and sexual content either to quiet public criticism, to fend off legislative controls, or because they consider it the right thing to do. Self-regulation over a broad range of content poses no First Amendment challenges if the government does not coerce the regulations.[90] In the

---

[85] 397 U.S. 728 (1970).

[86] Virginia v. American Booksellers Ass'n, 372 S.E.2d 618, 15 Media L. Rep. 2078 (Va. 1988).

[87] Virginia v. American Booksellers Ass'n, 484 U.S. 383, 14 Media L. Rep. 2145 (1988).

[88] M.S. News Co. v. Casado, 721 F.2d 1281 (10th Cir. 1983).

[89] Upper Midwest Booksellers Ass'n v. City of Minneapolis, 780 F.2d 1389, 12 Media L. Rep. 1913 (8th Cir. 1985).

[90] *See* Friedan, "The Motion Picture Rating System of 1968: A Constitutional Analysis of Self-Regulation by the Film Industry," 73 *Columbia L. Rev.* 185 (1973).

1930s, the film industry adopted a code aimed primarily at reducing portrayals of crime and violence. Violence waned for 15 years before returning. Broadcasting went through a cycle of lessened violence in the early 1970s in response to concern about the Vietnam War and urban violence.[91]

One of the major media regulators is the Motion Picture Association of America, formed in 1930. The MPAA is a voluntary film-rating board concerned with nudity, profanity, violence, the exploitation of sex, and other antisocial activities. The MPAA classifies films as G for general audiences; PG for parental guidance suggested, but all ages admitted; R for restricted to those 17 or older unless accompanied by a parent or guardian; and NC-17 for which those under 17 are not admitted. A PG film contains more than minimal violence, brief nudity, or nonexplicit sexual scenes. An R-rated film is devoted in some way to themes of sex or violence. An R-rated film may contain harsh language, sexual activity, and nudity, but not explicit sexual activity. An NC-17-rated film contains explicit sexual activity or considerable quantities and varieties of violence.

The MPAA also rates films PG-13, a rating between PG and R. The PG-13 rating was added in 1984 in response to complaints that movies such as *Indiana Jones and the Temple of Doom* are too violent to be rated PG. The PG-13 rating warns parents to exercise special caution in allowing children under the age of 13 to attend a movie. The criteria used to judge the appropriateness of the movie include the presence of violence, sensuality, drugs, and suicide.[92]

An number of citizens' groups pressure the media with varying success to reduce sex and violence. Among these groups are the National Coalition on Television Violence, Women Against Violence Against Women, The Parents' Musical Resource Center, and national PTA groups. The Parents' Musical Resource Center pressured the recording industry to attach warning stickers on albums containing explicit lyrics about sexuality, violence, drug abuse, and suicide.[93] Manufacturers of albums, cassettes, and CD packages agreed to a label that reads: "Explicit Lyrics—Parental Advisory." Terry Rakolta, a Michigan mother, convinced Coca-Cola USA, Procter & Gamble, McDonald's, and other major corporations to cancel commercials on Fox Broadcasting Company's series "Married . .. With Children." Rakolta persuaded the companies that the series was "helping to feed our kids a steady diet of gratuitous sex and violence."[94]

Women Against Violence Against Women pickets pornographic films, including soft-core films the organization considers antisocial. A WAVAW threat to organize a national boycott induced Warner Communications to remove a billboard on Los Angeles' Sunset Strip showing a woman bound and bruised with the caption "I'm Black and Blue from the Rolling Stones—and I Love It."[95]

Courts have ruled that citizens have a First Amendment right to picket pornographic establishments and to try to intimidate patrons and employees of the stores by

[91] *See* Krattenmaker and Powe, "Televised Violence: First Amendment Principles and Social Science Theory," 64 *Va. L. Rev.* 1123, 1128–29 (1978).

[92] "New Film-Rating Category Readied," *New York Times*, June 28, 1984, at 24.

[93] "Companies to Label Explicit Records," *New York Times*, March 29, 1990, at B1.

[94] "A Mother Is Heard as Sponsors Abandon a TV Hit," *New York Times*, March 2, 1989, at 1, D20.

[95] Penrod & Linz, "Using Psychological Research on Violent Pornography to Inform Legal Change," in N. Malamuth and E. Donnerstein, *Pornography and Sexual Aggression* 271–72.

threatening to publish their pictures. Such conduct is constitutional as long as the pickets do not trespass or block entrances.[96]

SUMMARY

Sexual communications that are not obscene may be regulated by time, place, and manner restrictions such as zoning ordinances, postal regulations, and restrictions on the display of materials that would be harmful to minors. In addition, citizens may pressure media to curb sex and violence.

---

[96] Eagle Books, Inc. v. Jones 474 N.E.2d 444 (I11. App. 1985), *cert. denied*, 474 U.S. 920 (1985).

9

THE MEDIA AND THE JUDICIARY

Thus far the book has concentrated on law that punishes injurious publication—broadcasts that hurt individual reputations, ads that mislead consumers, and magazine articles that infringe on copyright. This chapter on the media and the courts is the first of three chapters to focus on news gathering.

News coverage of the courts pits two constitutional rights against each other. The Bill of Rights, in addition to prohibiting the government from abridging free speech and a free press, guarantees the integrity of the criminal justice system. The Sixth Amendment provides that anyone accused of a crime shall have the right to a trial "by an impartial jury," a jury composed of persons who can decide guilt or innocence based only on the evidence presented in a courtroom.

In court, judges can control what jurors see and hear. However, outside the courtroom, jurors often see and hear news stories and gossip protected by the First Amendment that are never allowed into evidence in court. Extensive news coverage about criminal defendants can make it difficult, if not impossible, for them to receive a fair trial, some legal experts contend.

In 1966, the U.S. Supreme Court said that massive sensational media coverage prevented Dr. Sam Sheppard, an osteopath who lived near Cleveland, Ohio, from receiving a fair trial. Sheppard's ordeal began on July 4, 1954, when neighbors he had called discovered Marilyn Sheppard's body in the upstairs bedroom of the family home. Sheppard said he woke up in the middle of the night to find a "form" standing by his dead wife. He claimed he struggled with the intruder but was knocked unconscious. Sheppard immediately became the object of sensational pretrial publicity. The media also helped turn his trial into what has been called a "Roman holiday."[1]

Sheppard became a suspect soon after his wife's death, but he was not arrested for about a month. Meanwhile, local newspapers published a barrage of information and opinions that were never admitted into evidence during his trial. Cleveland newspapers accused Sheppard of impeding the police investigation, emphasized his refusal to take a lie detector test, and quoted a police detective who said Sheppard's explanation of the death was suspect. The newspapers said Sheppard was "getting away with murder" and one ran a front-page editorial asking "Why Isn't Sam Sheppard in Jail?" Within 24 hours of the editorial the authorities arrested Sheppard.

Sheppard's trial began two weeks before the 1954 November election. Both the judge and the chief prosecutor were seeking hotly contested judgeships. In the court-

---

[1]Sheppard v. Maxwell, 384 U.S. 333, 1 Media L. Rep. 1220 (1966).

room, the judge seated newspaper reporters so close to Sheppard and his attorney that the pair had to leave the courtroom to talk without being overheard. Often the movement of reporters in and out of the courtroom made it difficult for the lawyers and witnesses to be heard. Photographers jammed the corridors, taking pictures of jurors, witnesses, lawyers, and Sheppard.

The jury convicted Sheppard of murder. His unsuccessful appeals to three appellate courts were discussed in Chapter 1. Sheppard spent 12 years in jail before the U.S. Supreme Court, in *Sheppard v. Maxwell,* reversed the original verdict on the ground that he did not receive a fair trial. Sheppard was acquitted in a new trial but died a few years later.

While the Supreme Court said that Sam Sheppard did not receive a fair trial because of prejudicial publicity and a carnival-like atmosphere in the courtroom, the Court also stressed the media's role in protecting public oversight of the judicial system. In *Sheppard,* the Court emphasized that judges must ensure that defendants receive trials by impartial juries at the same time they restrict the press as little as possible. The Court's *Sheppard* opinion establishes the framework for much of the rest of the chapter. Although the chapter will focus on the rights of criminal defendants, parties to civil litigation face many of the same issues.

DEFINING JURY BIAS

The U.S. Supreme Court has said that jurors are biased as a matter of law if they are so affected by prejudicial publicity that they cannot set aside preconceived ideas and decide a case solely on evidence presented during a trial. Judges and lawyers often argue that an impartial jury may be impossible to find if a community has been saturated by news reporting of a sensational crime and the arrest of a suspect. However, social scientists have been unable to prove that prejudicial publicity leads to biased jurors.

The Supreme Court and Jury Prejudice

Since 1807, the Supreme Court has said impartial jurors arrive at a verdict of guilt or innocence only on the evidence permitted under the rules of the court. An impartial juror is one free from "strong and deep impressions" based on knowledge acquired outside the courtroom that closes the mind to the unbiased consideration of evidence presented in court. Justice Oliver Wendell Holmes said

> The theory of our system is that the conclusions to be reached in a case will be induced only by evidence and argument in open court, and not by any outside influence, whether of private talk or public print.[2]

The Supreme Court does not require jurors to be completely unaware of the facts and issues of a case. Chief Justice John Marshall, in the treason trial of Aaron Burr,

---

[2]Patterson v. Colorado, 205 U.S. 454, 462 (1907).

first ruled that impartial jurors might form impressions about a case before a trial as long as those impressions could be changed in light of evidence presented in court.[3] In 1975, the Supreme Court held 8–1 in *Murphy v. Florida* that a defendant can receive a fair trial even if every member of the jury knows the defendant's prior criminal record.[4]

The defendant in the 1975 case, Jack Roland Murphy, had become notorious after he helped steal the Star of India sapphire in 1964. Known as "Murph the Surf," Murphy also attracted attention because of a flamboyant life-style. In 1968, he was arrested for robbery and assault. However, before he could be tried on those charges, he was convicted of murder and pleaded guilty to the interstate transportation of stolen securities. The events attracted extensive press coverage. When Murphy was later convicted of the 1968 charges of robbery and assault, he appealed on the ground that the jury had been prejudiced by knowledge of his previous criminal record.

Justice Thurgood Marshall, writing for the Court, said that jurors need not be "totally ignorant of the facts and issues" of a case. He distinguished between "mere familiarity" with a defendant and a "predisposition against him." Marshall said most of the publicity about Murphy was factual and published at least seven months before the jury was selected, too far in advance to inflame prejudice at the time of the trial. Marshall said that none of the jurors indicated that Murphy's past was relevant to the case. The trial court did not have difficulty finding jurors who claimed to be impartial. Only 20 of 78 persons questioned were excused because they had prejudged Murphy's guilt. Neither the atmosphere in the courtroom nor in the community was inflamed, the Court said.[5]

The Supreme Court has said a conviction will be overturned because of prejudicial publicity only if the Court finds identifiable bias in individual jurors or such an extraordinary amount of prejudicial publicity in the media that the "presumption of prejudice" is raised.[6] In 1984, Jon Yount could not convince the Court that publicity had created a "presumption of prejudice" in his second murder trial. In *Patton v. Yount,* the Court upheld Yount's second conviction even though 5 of the 12 jurors had thought, at least at one time, that Yount was guilty.[7] Yount had pleaded not guilty by reason of temporary insanity at his trial after confessing in 1966 to the brutal killing of a female high school student. The Pennsylvania Supreme Court overturned Yount's first conviction because the police had not given him adequate notice of his right to an attorney prior to his confession. In 1970, Yount was convicted a second time and appealed, contending that he did not receive a fair trial because of prejudicial pretrial publicity. A federal appeals court said that 77 percent of 163 people questioned during the jury selection process at the second trial admitted they thought that Yount was guilty.

Yet the U.S. Supreme Court said the trial judge had not erred in finding that the jury was impartial. The Court, in an opinion written by Justice Lewis Powell, Jr.,

---

[3]United States v. Burr, 24 Fed. Cas. 49 No. 14692g (1807).

[4]421 U.S. 794, 1 Media L. Rep. 1232 (1975).

[5]*Id.* at 800–803, 1 Media L. Rep. at 1234–35.

[6]*E.g.,* Irvin v. Dowd, 366 U.S. 717, 1 Media L. Rep. 1178 (1961); Estes v. Texas, 381 U.S. 532, 1 Media L. Rep. 1187 (1965).

[7]467 U.S. 1025, 1035 (1984).

noted that "the extensive adverse publicity and the community's sense of outrage" were at their height prior to the 1966 trial. The second trial occurred when "prejudicial publicity was greatly diminished and community sentiment had softened." The Court said that the two daily newspapers in the county averaged less than an article a month, primarily in the form of announcements, about the Yount proceedings prior to the second trial. Articles during the jury selection process were "purely factual." Furthermore, Powell said, the time between the two trials "had a profound effect on the community and, more important, on the jury, in softening or effacing opinion." The Court decided, 6–2, that the lapse of time between the first and second trials rebutted "any presumption of partiality or prejudice that existed at the time of the initial trial."

In contrast, in 1961 in *Irvin v. Dowd,* the Court overturned a murder conviction where publicity created a "wave of passion" and "pattern of prejudice."[8] The Court found a "buildup of prejudice" in the case of Leslie Irvin, convicted for a December 1954 murder near Evansville, Indiana. Shortly after his arrest in April 1955, the press announced that "Mad Dog Irvin" had confessed to six murders in four months. Headlines announced that he had been placed at the scene of at least one of the murders and identified in a police lineup. One story said Irvin was "remorseless and without conscience." Another discussed the promise of a sheriff "to devote his life" to ensuring that Irvin was executed. In many stories, Irvin was referred to as the "confessed slayer of six." Radio, television, and newspaper stories revealed Irvin's criminal history. The local radio station broadcast curbside opinions of Irvin's guilt by members of the public.

U.S. Supreme Court Justice Tom Clark, who wrote for a unanimous Court, said that the continued adverse publicity fostered a strong prejudice among the people of the county. Of 430 prospective jurors questioned, 90 percent at least suspected Irvin was guilty. A number admitted that if they were in Irvin's place they would not want themselves on the jury. Of the jurors finally seated, 8 of 12 were familiar with the case, including the fact that Irvin was accused of other murders. All eight said they thought he was guilty. Some jurors said they had to be convinced that Irvin was not guilty, contrary to the principle that a person is innocent until proven guilty. One juror said he "could not . . . give the defendant the benefit of the doubt that he is innocent." Another said he had a " 'somewhat' certain fixed opinion" of guilt. Yet all 12 jurors told the judge they could be impartial.

Justice Clark said the statements of impartiality could be given little weight where "so many" jurors "so many times, admitted of prejudice." The jurors' statements reflected a " 'pattern of deep and bitter prejudice' shown to be present throughout the community."[9] The Court overturned Irvin's conviction. He was later convicted in a second trial but sentenced to life imprisonment instead of death as he was after the first trial.[10]

Although the evidence of prejudice was discussed in *Irvin v. Dowd,* none was presented in *Sheppard v. Maxwell,* discussed at the beginning of the chapter. In

---

[8] 366 U.S. at 725, 1 Media L. Rep. at 1180.
[9] Id. at 728, 1 Media L. Rep. at 1181.
[10] D. Gillmor, *Free Press and Fair Trial* 11–12 (1966).

Sheppard v. Maxwell, the Court did not require evidence that jurors were unable to base their verdict on what they saw and heard in the courtroom. The Court said only that there could be no doubt that the deluge of extremely inflammatory publicity referred to early in the chapter reached at least some of the jurors.[11] Relying on its own impression of the potential impact of publicity, the Court criticized the prejudicial publicity, community pressure, and lack of judicial control over activity in the courtroom that led to Sheppard's conviction.

Prejudicial Publicity, Community Pressure, and Decorum in Court

One of the Supreme Court justices most concerned about prejudicial publicity, the late Felix Frankfurter, once asked how "fallible men and women" can reach a verdict based only on what they hear in court when their minds are "saturated" by media coverage for months "by matter designed to establish the guilt of the accused."[12] Frankfurter particularly feared pretrial coverage of criminal proceedings that occurs before jurors are selected. In the Sheppard case, all but one of the jury members who decided that Sam Sheppard was guilty said during the jury selection process that they had read about the case in the newspapers or heard about it on radio or television.

Although legal experts and scholars do not agree on the impact of pretrial publicity, most agree on the kinds of statements and information that may be prejudicial.[13] The U.S. Justice Department, the American Bar Association, and several state bench-bar-press committees have issued similar guidelines designed to limit reporting of crime and court news. Most mention the reporting of:

- Confessions. The Fifth Amendment protects against persons being required to testify against themselves. A confession may be ruled inadmissible evidence at trial if it is made under duress or if a defendant is not properly advised of his or her right to an attorney. However, jurors may have a hard time ignoring a confession that is printed or broadcast. In *Rideau v. Louisiana,* the Supreme Court overturned the murder conviction of Wilbert Rideau after he confessed to a sheriff in the absence of a lawyer to advise him of his rights. Rideau's filmed confession was seen by an estimated 100,000 television viewers living near Lake Charles, Louisiana. The Supreme Court said the televised confession in a very real sense *was* Rideau's trial—at which he pleaded guilty to murder. The Court added that any subsequent court proceedings would be pointless.[14]
- Prior criminal records. A prior criminal record is ordinarily inadmissible because a defendant cannot be convicted on the basis of past criminal history. The prosecution must prove that a defendant committed the crime for which he

---

[11]384 U.S. at 357, 1 Media L. Rep. at 1229. *See also* Rideau v. Louisiana, 373 U.S. 723, 1 Media L. Rep. 1183 (1963).

[12]Irvin v. Dowd, 366 U.S. at 729–30, 1 Media L. Rep. at 1182 (Frankfurter, J., concurring).

[13]*E.g.,* C. Bush, ed., *Free Press and Fair Trial* 16–18 (1970).

[14]373 U.S. at 726, 1 Media L. Rep. at 1184.

or she is currently being tried. Yet jurors may have a difficult time deciding that a person on trial for burglary or murder is innocent if he or she has been convicted of the same crime before. In *Irvin v. Dowd,* the media revealed Leslie Irvin's earlier convictions for arson and burglary after he was arrested for murder near Evansville, Indiana. News stories also disclosed Irvin's juvenile record and a court-martial on AWOL charges. The Supreme Court said the stories were part of "a build-up of prejudice" in the community that led the Court to overturn Irvin's 1955 conviction.[15]

- The results of lie detector tests, blood tests, ballistics tests, and other investigatory procedures. The results of some tests administered by police investigators may not be admitted into evidence in court because the tests were improperly administered. Some tests used to evaluate evidence produce unreliable results. In addition, the fact that a defendant chooses not to take a test may have no bearing on his or her guilt or innocence. Yet, in *Sheppard v. Maxwell,* the Cleveland newspapers headlined Sam Sheppard's refusal to take a lie detector test as if it was evidence he must be hiding his role in his wife's murder. The newspapers also reported the results of blood tests that were never admitted into evidence at trial.[16]

- Character flaws or life-style. Comments from neighbors or other acquaintances, often seen in newspapers, about the life-style of a suspect will seldom be admitted into evidence in court. Frequently the comments reflect rumors or hearsay rather than behavior witnessed firsthand. In the Sheppard case, the Cleveland newspapers emphasized that Sheppard had extramarital affairs that were not documented in court. During the trial, the jurors had access to a newspaper story claiming that Marilyn Sheppard had said her husband had a "Dr. Jekyll and Mr. Hyde" personality.[17] No evidence of the accusation was presented during the trial.

- Potential witnesses, testimony, or evidence. Pretrial statements of potential witnesses may or may not be accurate and may or may not be heard by jurors in court. In the Sheppard case, the newspapers quoted a detective who said blood had been washed from the floor of the Sheppard home before investigators arrived but never testified about the blood in court. In addition, opinions about the credibility of prospective witnesses or the reliability of possible evidence also can mislead potential jurors.

- Speculation by officials. Sometimes law enforcement officers and judges are purveyors of prejudicial publicity. They may make statements about the character, innocence, or guilt of defendants that probably will not be admitted into evidence. In the Sheppard case, a newspaper headline reported that a police captain called Sheppard a "bare-faced liar." The police officer was never called to the witness stand to explain the comment. In the Irvin case, the media reported that at least two officials were determined to make certain that Leslie Irvin was executed.

---

[15]366 U.S. 717, 1 Media L. Rep. 1178 (1961).
[16]384 U.S. at 340, 1 Media L. Rep. at 1221–22.
[17]*Id.* at 348, 1 Media L. Rep. at 1225.

- Other sensational and inflammatory statements. Judges fear press coverage so inflammatory and pervasive that it contributes to a "deep and bitter pattern" of community prejudice. While an accumulation of publicity can contribute to a public perception that the suspect is guilty, particular kinds of media coverage can foster community fears and prejudices. The reporting of man-in-the-street opinion polls, like the one conducted by a radio station in the Irvin case, can be highly inflammatory and may have little relation to the facts of the case. Media use of nicknames such as "Mad Dog Irvin" can suggest guilt. Headlines that demand the arrest of a suspect, as occurred in the Sheppard case, can inflame a community. Strong community bias not only makes selecting impartial jurors difficult, but can also pressure jurors into convicting the defendant. When the Cleveland papers published the names of potential jurors, all received calls and letters from "cranks and friends" with opinions about the upcoming trial.

Finally, legal experts contend that a defendant not only needs to be tried by jurors unaffected by prejudicial publicity, but also needs to be tried in solemn and ordered proceedings free of a carnival-like atmosphere. The Supreme Court once said that the preservation of an atmosphere in court necessary for a fair trial "must be maintained at all costs."[18] In the Sheppard case, the judge did not adequately preserve the decorum of the courtroom when he seated reporters inside the rail that separates the public from the trial participants. Reporters could overhear conversations between Sheppard and his lawyers, and the lawyers and the judge. Reporters also handled exhibits lying on the attorneys' tables. In *Sheppard v. Maxwell,* the Court said the arrangements made for the press inside the courtroom caused Sheppard "to be deprived of that judicial serenity and calm to which [he] was entitled.' "[19]

Measuring Prejudice

No one knows for certain whether extensive exposure to media coverage of the criminal justice process has an impact on jury decisions. In contrast to the result of the Sheppard trial, for example, Watergate defendants John Mitchell and Maurice Stans, cabinet officers in the Nixon administration, were found not guilty in spite of massive nationwide pretrial publicity.

Many observers argue that the values of a fair trial and a free press are often compatible. The Supreme Court acknowledges that the press helps ensure fair trials by allowing public scrutiny of the judicial system.[20] Some scholars point to the fact that extensive pretrial publicity is relatively rare—the majority of crimes receive little or no press coverage.[21] Others contend that there is very little evidence linking pretrial

---

[18]Estes v. Texas, 381 U.S. at 540, 1 Media L. Rep. at 1190.

[19]Sheppard v. Maxwell, 384 U.S. at 355, 1 Media L. Rep. at 1228, *quoting* Estes v. Texas, 381 U.S. at 536, 1 Media L. Rep. at 1188.

[20]*E.g.,* Sheppard v. Maxwell, 384 U.S. at 349–50, 1 Media L. Rep. at 1226; Cox Broadcasting Corp. v. Cohn, 420 U.S. 469, 491–92, 1 Media L. Rep. 1819, 1827 (1975).

[21]*E.g., see* M. Conners, *Prejudicial Publicity: An Assessment* 9 (Journ. Monographs No. 41, 1975).

publicity to jury bias and that the impact of the press on potential jurors is exaggerated.[22]

In fact, the only time researchers listened to actual jury deliberations they said they found that jurors did not make capricious decisions because of bias.[23] The secretly taped jury discussions were but one aspect of a massive study of jury performance completed in 1954. The director of the study, Harry Kalven, said that the jury was "a pretty stubborn, healthy institution not likely to be overwhelmed by a remark . . . in the press."[24]

Soon after the 1954 study, the courts prohibited studies of real juries, fearing the research would influence deliberations. Hence, most research on the impact of crime reporting on jurors comes from studies of public reaction to news stories and research involving mock juries. Not only is research about human attitudes imprecise, but the research is also conducted in circumstances that do not effectively duplicate the experiences of jurors. In the studies, subjects usually are asked to react to prejudicial stories immediately. However, in the case of real trials, people sit on juries months after seeing much of the publicity about a case. In addition, researchers often do not take into consideration that judges frequently admonish real juries to ignore what they have previously read or heard about a case. Further, no one knows whether research results would be different if the persons studied in hypothetical situations were making life-and-death decisions about real human beings.

The most one can conclude from such research is that publication of a defendant's confession or criminal record could convince some jurors that a defendant is guilty. However, some studies suggest that carefully weeding out jurors during the jury selection process can reduce the effects of publicity.[25] In addition, a factor often forgotten by commentators concerned about the impact of prejudicial publicity is the inability of people to absorb everything published and broadcast. Some people pay little attention to news. Even regular news consumers watch and read selectively and forget much of what they have heard or read as time passes. One federal appeals court judge said that he conducted a study in which 94 percent of jurors could not remember stories published about highly publicized cases. The other 6 percent only remembered they had read "something." Less than 1 percent of the total could remember what they had read. Less than half of the 1 percent had determined guilt or innocence based upon what they had read.[26]

Regardless of the lack of research evidence establishing that media coverage of criminal cases influences jurors, courts try to protect defendants against prejudicial publicity.

[22]*E.g.,* Pember, "Does Pretrial Publicity Really Hurt?" *Colum. Journ. Rev.* 16–20 (Sept.–Oct. 1984).

[23]H. Kalven & H. Zeisel, *The American Jury* 492–99 (1966). *See also* Simon, "Does the Court's Decision in *Nebraska Press Association* Fit the Research Evidence on the Impact on Jurors of News Coverage?" 29 *Stan. L. Rev.* 515, 518–20 (1977).

[24]Gillmor, "Free Press v. Fair Trial: A Continuing Dialogue—'Trial by Newspaper' and the Social Sciences," 41 *N.D.L. Rev.* 156, 167 (1965).

[25]*See* Buddenbaum, Weaver, Holsinger & Brown, "Pretrial Publicity and Juries: A Review of Research," Research Report No. 11, School of Journalism, Indiana University (1981); Simon, "Does the Court's Decision in *Nebraska Press Association* Fit the Research Evidence on the Impact on Jurors of News Coverage?" 29 *Stan. L. Rev.* 515, 520–26 (1977).

[26]Remarks by Judge William J. Bauer in "Newspapers Under Fire," in American Society of Newspaper Editors, *Problems in Journalism* 226–27 (1976). *See also* Simon, "Does the Court's Decision in *Nebraska Press Association* Fit the Research Evidence on the Impact on Jurors of News Coverage?" 29 *Stan. L. Rev.* 515, 526–28 (1977).

SUMMARY

The Sixth Amendment guarantees criminal defendants the right to a trial by an impartial jury. The Supreme Court has said that an impartial juror is one free from strong impressions that close the mind to evidence presented in court. Jurors can know something about a defendant as long as they can decide a case on evidence they hear in court. However, the Court has overturned criminal convictions on evidence of massive publicity that has created a "presumption of prejudice" among jurors.

Many judges and lawyers contend that information published before a trial but not introduced into evidence can lead to a biased jury. Prejudicial publicity can include news about confessions, criminal records, results of police tests, and reports of character flaws. It also can include derogatory nicknames, curbside opinion polls, and comments by neighbors and investigating officers. Judges and lawyers also are concerned about the impact of community pressure on jurors. In addition, maintaining order in the courtroom itself is considered essential to guarantee the rights of a defendant.

However, there is no reliable evidence indicating that extensive pretrial news coverage of arrests and pretrial proceedings will endanger the rights of a defendant to an impartial jury. Experiments in laboratory conditions indicate that news of confessions or criminal records might lead to bias in jurors. However, such studies are at best an imprecise mirror of prejudice among real jurors.

REMEDIES FOR PREJUDICIAL PUBLICITY

The Supreme Court's decision in *Sheppard v. Maxwell* marked the fifth time in seven years that the Court had reversed a criminal conviction because of prejudicial publicity or press behavior in the courtroom.[27] In *Sheppard,* the Court responded to the issues raised by prejudicial publicity not by lecturing the press, but by delivering a stinging rebuke to the trial judge for failing to protect Sheppard's right to a fair trial.

Justice Clark, backed by seven of eight other justices, said the trial court judge had not adequately protected Sheppard's right to a trial by an impartial jury. Clark said that, given "the pervasiveness of modern communications and the difficulty of effacing prejudicial publicity from the minds of jurors," trial courts must ensure that the accused can still receive a trial by an impartial jury, free from outside influences.[28]

Clark said the Supreme Court did not want to impose direct limitations on the reporting of public trials because of both the First Amendment and the role of the press in guarding against abuses in the criminal justice system. Clark said justice cannot survive secret trials. He also said that the press guards against the miscarriage of justice by subjecting the police, prosecutors, and the entire judicial process to public scrutiny. But, he continued, no one ought to be punished for a crime without being

---

[27]*See also* Marshall v. United States, 360 U.S. 310 (1959); Irvin v. Dowd, 366 U.S. 717, 1 Media L. Rep. 1178 (1961); Rideau v. Louisiana, 373 U.S. 723, 1 Media L. Rep. 1183 (1963); Estes v. Texas, 381 U.S. 532, 1 Media L. Rep. 1187 (1965).

[28]Sheppard v. Maxwell, 384 U.S. at 362, 1 Media L. Rep. at 1231.

"fairly tried in a public tribunal free of prejudice, passion, excitement, and tyrannical powers."[29]

The Supreme Court said the trial court judge in the *Sheppard* case had failed to protect the defendant in three ways, including two involving the judge's lack of control over the trial itself. The Court said the trial judge (1) did not control the atmosphere of the courtroom and (2) did not control information released to the press during the trial. Both will be discussed later in the chapter.

The third judicial error, said the Court in *Sheppard,* was the judge's failure to protect jurors from the impact of prejudicial pretrial publicity. The Court recommended remedies for prejudicial publicity that generally do not directly interfere with reporting court news. The remedies available include changing the location of the trial, importing a jury, delaying the trial, and conducting different trials for defendants charged with the same crime. Other judicial tools for preventing prejudicial publicity from influencing jurors are excusing potential jurors who demonstrate bias, admonishing jurors, **sequestering** the jury, and scheduling a new trial. These remedies do not prevent extensive coverage of criminal proceedings but may limit the impact of the media on jurors.

Change of Venue

One of Justice Clark's suggestions for protecting a trial against the impact of news stories about a case is a *change of venue.* Change of venue means a shift in the location of the trial. Judges have the authority, within limits specified by state law, to move a trial from the jurisdiction of the crime to one nearby. Moving a trial can be expensive for the county responsible. However, changing the location of a trial is supposed to move the trial away from the scene of the most damaging publicity.

In *Rideau v. Louisiana,* the Supreme Court held that the trial court's denial of a change of venue for Wilbert Rideau violated his constitutional right to a "fair and impartial trial." Rideau had asked that the trial be removed from the Calcasieu Parish trial court after his confession was televised three times in the county. Justice Potter Stewart, writing for the Supreme Court, said the televised confession became Rideau's trial to "tens of thousands of people." Stewart said further court proceedings "in a community so pervasively exposed to such a spectacle could be but a hollow formality."[30]

The success of changing venue depends on the extent and nature of the news coverage about a case. Frequently, if a crime is notorious enough to trigger extensive publicity, it is difficult to move the trial far enough away to find unaffected jurors. For example, could the trial of Lee Harvey Oswald, who was accused of assassinating President Kennedy, have been moved to a place not saturated by massive news coverage? In the Irvin case mentioned earlier, the trial was moved to a county adjacent to the one where the murder was committed, but the move did not substantially improve the defendant's chances of receiving a fair trial.[31] Although a transfer might move the trial from the community with the most at stake, the publicity sometimes follows.

---

[29]*Id.* at 350–51, 1 Media L. Rep. at 1226, *quoting* Chambers v. Florida, 309 U.S. 227, 236–37 (1940).
[30]373 U.S. at 726, 1 Media L. Rep. at 1184.
[31]366 U.S. 717, 1 Media L. Rep. 1178 (1961).

Change of Venire

A *change of venire* changes the jury pool rather than the location of a trial. Occasionally, a judge will request that potential jurors be brought in from a nearby community. In the sensational murder trial of John Wayne Gacy, accused of the sex-related murders of 33 boys and young men in 1979, jurors were bused from Rockford, Illinois, to Chicago. Theoretically, jurors who have been imported have had less exposure to potentially damaging publicity. However, regional newspapers and national television news ensure that information about major crimes achieves widespread circulation. Importing a jury also can be expensive for the county responsible for the trial.

Continuance

A judge who believes that publicity might damage the chances for a fair trial can postpone the trial until publicity subsides. *Continuance,* the legal term for such a postponement, was mentioned by Justice Clark in *Sheppard v. Maxwell* as an alternative when a trial judge is faced with "a reasonable likelihood that prejudicial news prior to trial will prevent a fair trial."[32] The Court noted in *Irvin v. Dowd* that when Leslie Irvin was on trial for six murders the trial court had denied eight motions for a continuance.

Postponement can effectively remove the trial from the publicity surrounding the arrest. Of course, there is likely to be renewed publicity when the trial finally takes place. There are other practical problems. Defendants asking for a postponement may have to waive their constitutional right to a speedy trial. In addition, defendants unable to raise bail wait in jail during the continuance. Furthermore, the longer a trial is postponed, the more likely witnesses or evidence may disappear.

Severance

Severance is a remedy available only when more than one person has been charged with the same crime or related crimes. Two or more defendants are tried separately in an attempt to prevent the publicity related to one from affecting the other.

Voir Dire

Voir dire is the term used for the process of questioning potential jurors prior to selecting a jury for a trial. Potential jurors are asked questions designed to detect bias. The prospective jurors may be asked whether they know the defendant or any of the witnesses. They also may be asked about their occupation, reading habits, or religious beliefs. They may be asked if they have racial prejudices or believe in the death penalty. In theory, the purpose of voir dire is to find persons able to judge a defendant only on the basis of information presented in the courtroom. In practice, each lawyer looks for jurors who might lean toward his or her client or who might be sus-

---

[32]384 U.S. at 363, 1 Media L. Rep. at 1231.

picious of the opposing lawyer. In federal courts, the judge asks the questions. In state courts, the opposing attorneys usually control the voir dire.

The lawyers on each side of a case can challenge any number of jurors "for cause." Prospective jurors will be excused if the judge is convinced they are unfit to serve. For example, a juror may be dismissed for an obvious prejudice or because he or she is a relative of the crime victim. The Supreme Court noted in *Rideau v. Louisiana* that the trial judge had wrongly refused to excuse two deputy sheriffs from the jury in spite of the fact that Rideau had confessed to the sheriff.

In addition to the challenges for cause, each side in a case also can dismiss a limited number of jurors through *peremptory challenges* without giving a reason. The number of peremptory challenges varies with the state and the nature of the case. Lawyers use peremptory challenges to excuse prospective jurors when they cannot persuade the judge to excuse them for cause. An attorney simply may have a "gut feeling" that a given juror has hidden biases. The gut feeling could be based on answers to questions, facial expressions, clothes, or even rumor. Peremptory challenges are also used to excuse jurors who have socioeconomic characteristics that suggest a probable bias, though one that may be hard to detect. For example, the attorney of a man accused of sexually abusing children will often want to excuse mothers from the jury. The judge has no control over a lawyer's peremptory challenges.

In *Irvin v. Dowd,* 430 prospective jurors were examined in a lengthy voir dire that is unusual except in sensational cases receiving widespread publicity.[33] In a voir dire lasting four weeks, 268 prospective jurors were excused for cause because of their belief that Irvin was guilty of murder. More than 100 potential jurors were excused because they opposed the death penalty. Dowd's counsel excused 20 through peremptory challenges, the prosecution 10. Both used all of the peremptory challenges allowed by Indiana law. Other prospective jurors were excused on personal grounds such as health.

Voir dire gives attorneys some control over the nature of the jury that will hear a case. However, some critics assert that voir dire is not very effective. Many judges and lawyers contend that potential jurors say what they believe the attorneys want to hear. The critics say potential jurors can hide bias.

In some trials, behavioral scientists have been used to help lawyers choose jurors. The behavioral scientists conduct extensive research in an attempt to determine what kind of jurors might be sympathetic to the defendant. Then the lawyer tries to seat jurors who fit the profile.

Sequestration

Sequestration is the "locking up" of the jury during a trial. A judge can order that the jurors be isolated under guard. They usually are housed together at a hotel at government expense. They are not allowed to see friends or family or to see news stories about the case in court. Guards screen and monitor phone calls.

Sequestration prevents jurors from hearing others evaluate the evidence or predict the outcome of the trial. Although sequestration cannot be used until a jury is

---

[33]366 U.S. at 727, 1 Media L. Rep. at 1181.

chosen, it effectively keeps jurors from obtaining information from outside the courtroom during the trial. The Supreme Court implied that the judge in the Sheppard trial should have sequestered the jury. Because the judge did not sequester jurors, they were exposed to rumors and opinions during the trial as well as before. Two jurors heard a woman tell Walter Winchell on the radio that Sheppard had fathered her illegitimate child.

However, sequestration is very expensive and it seriously disrupts the lives of jurors, particularly during long trials. Defense attorneys often worry that a sequestered jury will resent the defendant for keeping them from family and friends.

Judicial Admonition

Once a jury is chosen, a judge can instruct jurors to render their verdict on the basis of evidence presented in the courtroom. A judge may tell jurors to avoid reading, watching, or listening to anything about the trial.

The Supreme Court criticized as inadequate the admonitions to the jury issued by the Sheppard trial court judge. He "suggested" and "requested" jurors to avoid reading newspapers, listening to the radio, or watching television. He said that "we shall all feel very much better" if the jurors paid no attention to the media.[34] But, the Court said, the judge failed to "instruct" or "admonish" jurors to avoid the media.

Judges who admonish jurors want to keep them from seeing or hearing information and commentary that may affect their decisions while, at the same time, avoiding the cost and inconvenience of sequestration. The judicial admonition may be the most frequently used, but least binding, of the remedies discussed. However, many judges believe, and one important study found, that jurors take such admonitions very seriously.[35]

New Trial

As a last resort, a criminal conviction can be overturned, as occurred in *Irvin, Sheppard,* and *Rideau.* A retrial involves all the expense and personal trauma of the first trial. Defendants may have to remain in jail if they cannot post bond.

In his *Sheppard* opinion, Justice Clark noted that

> reversals are but palliatives; the cure lies in those remedial measures that will prevent the prejudice at its inception. The courts must take such steps by rule and regulation that will protect their processes from prejudicial outside interferences.[36]

SUMMARY

The majority opinion in *Sheppard v. Maxwell* criticized the trial court judge for failing to protect against prejudicial pretrial publicity, failing to control the courtroom, and failing to restrict the release of prejudicial information during the trial.

---

[34]384 U.S. at 353, 1 Media L. Rep. at 1227.
[35]H. Kalven and H. Zeisel, *The American Jury* (1966).
[36]384 U.S. at 363, 1 Media L. Rep. at 1231.

The opinion suggested that the judge in the Sheppard trial should have used some of the tools available to judges to protect against prejudicial pretrial publicity. The devices available include change of venue, change of venire, continuance (postponement) of the trial, severance of related trials, voir dire, sequestration, admonitions to the jury, and a judicial order for a new trial.

CONTROLLING CONDUCT IN COURT

The Supreme Court stressed in *Sheppard v. Maxwell* that judges must ensure a dignified atmosphere in the court, including control over the behavior of journalists. Justice Tom Clark's majority opinion said the judge in the Sheppard trial should have better controlled the courtroom conduct of reporters. He also should have kept reporters from areas of the courtroom where they could disrupt the trial participants, including the defendant, lawyers, and jurors. The reporters should not have been allowed to sit near the defendant or jurors and should not have been allowed to handle court exhibits. The number of reporters in the courtroom should have been reduced when it became evident they were disrupting the trial.[37]

Judges can also control the use of cameras in court. However, while judicial control over reporters in the courtroom is a matter of settled law, the regulation of cameras in court has changed dramatically in the last two decades.

Both television and still cameras have long been perceived by some judges and lawyers as a threat to the dignity of courtrooms. In fact, photographers have not been allowed in court during trials for most of the twentieth century, a restriction that was held to be constitutional by the U.S. Supreme Court. But in the last 20 years many states have adopted rules allowing camera coverage of trials. The Supreme Court has said that states can develop their own rules as long as the presence of cameras does not violate a defendant's right to a fair trial. Cameras were still prohibited in federal courts in 1990, although an experiment had been authorized.

The Early Ban on Cameras

The hostility to cameras in court is often traced to the sensational trial of Bruno Hauptmann in 1935. Hauptmann was accused of kidnapping and killing the 18-month-old son of Charles and Anne Morrow Lindbergh. Because of the tremendous popularity of Lindbergh, the first person to fly nonstop across the Atlantic, the trial became a media circus. About 700 writers and broadcasters, plus more than 130 still and newsreel cameramen, from around the world moved into Flemington, New Jersey, the site of the trial. The journalism trade publication, *Editor & Publisher,* reported newspaper circulation figures during the trial. On one day, a New York newspaper, the *Evening Journal,* filled 24 columns with news, photographs, and sketches from the trial. The *Evening Journal* also agreed to pay Hauptmann's defense costs in exchange for exclusive stories. The press hired messengers who disrupted the

---

[37]384 U.S. at 358, 1 Media L. Rep. at 1229.

trial by running in and out of the courtroom with copy. Reporters and photographers who could not get into the courtroom jammed the halls. However, news photographers in court created comparatively few problems. Only a few cameras were allowed inside the courtroom, and photographers largely obeyed a judicial order barring pictures while court was in session.[38]

Yet, in 1937, a few years after Hauptmann's conviction, the American Bar Association (ABA) recommended banning cameras in courtrooms as one of several efforts to curb trial publicity. Canon 35 of the ABA's Canons of Professional and Judicial Ethics said cameras, and broadcasts of trials, should be banned because they "detract from the essential dignity of the proceedings, degrade the court and create misconceptions . . . in the mind of the public." Although ABA recommendations are not law, they are significant because states often adopt them as rules governing court proceedings. State bar associations also adopt ABA rules when writing enforceable codes of ethics. In addition, the ABA's rules are considered by judges writing court opinions.

The ABA's opposition to cameras continued for more than 40 years. For the first 35 of the 40 years, photographers were generally kept out of courtrooms. In the mid-1950s, only one state—Colorado—allowed cameras in court. In the early 1960s, Texas also permitted television and still photography. In 1962, televising live events was still relatively new and spectacular, and television coverage of the trial of Billie Sol Estes created a major controversy.

Estes, a Texas grain dealer, became the focus of national media attention when he was charged with fraudulently inducing farmers to buy nonexistent fertilizer tanks and property. A two-day pretrial hearing in Tyler, Texas, was broadcast live by both radio and television. At least 12 television cameramen and still photographers contributed to a courtroom so full that 30 people stood in the aisles. The courtroom, according to one observer, was a "forest of equipment."[39] Microphones stood at the judge's bench, counsel table, and jury box. Cables and wires snaked across the courtroom. Two television cameras were installed inside the bar separating the defendant and jurors from the spectators.

When the trial began, the judge had moved television cameras to a booth constructed in the back of the courtroom. Live coverage was permitted only occasionally during the trial, and reports of the trial were primarily confined to news programs. However, in spite of the more limited camera coverage, Estes appealed his conviction on the ground that broadcast coverage denied him a fair trial. The Supreme Court agreed, 5–4, and ordered a retrial. Estes was later convicted again.

The Supreme Court's majority in *Estes v. Texas* said the press must be allowed as much freedom to report court proceedings as possible, but the preservation of the atmosphere necessary to guarantee a fair trial "must be maintained at all costs." Four of the five justices in the majority believed that the mere presence of television cameras in court violated the Sixth Amendment guarantee of a fair trial to criminal

---

[38] *See generally* State v. Hauptmann, 180 A. 809, 827, *cert. denied,* 296 U.S. 649 (1935); Kielbowicz, "The Story Behind the Adoption of the Ban on Courtroom Cameras," 63 *Judicature* 14 (June–July 1979); and Costa, "Cameras in Court: A Position Paper," Communications Reports, Journalism/Public Relations Research Center, Department of Journalism, Ball State University (April 1980).

[39] Estes v. Texas, 381 U.S. at 604–605 n.2, 1 Media L. Rep. at 1215 n.2.

defendants. The fifth justice, John M. Harlan, said television coverage must be banned at that time in criminal trials of "widespread public interest" and "great notoriety."

Justice Clark, who wrote the court's majority opinion, listed the concerns still voiced by those opposing cameras in court. Cameras and their "telltale red lights" would distract jurors and inevitably lead to the pressure "of knowing their friends and neighbors have their eyes upon them." Cameras were a form of mental harassment for the defendant, Clark said. The "inevitable close-ups of his gestures and expressions," he explained, might overwhelm the defendant's "personal sensibilities, his dignity, and his ability to concentrate on the proceedings before him—sometimes the difference between life and death."[40] Clark also said the presence of cameras impaired the quality of testimony because it could frighten some witnesses and encourage others to exaggerate.

In addition, Clark said, cameras added to the concerns of judges in ensuring that defendants received a fair trial. Judges had to supervise the use of cameras in court and were subject to the "ever-present distraction" of the presence of cameras. Clark also said that elected judges would want to use televised trials as a political weapon. He said the "heightened public clamor resulting from radio and television coverage will inevitably result in prejudice."

While four of the justices in the majority suggested television cameras inherently endangered the constitutional rights of any criminal defendant, Justice Harlan said in a concurring opinion that he was limiting his judgment to only "heavily publicized and highly sensational" trials. Harlan, whose vote was necessary to overturn the first Estes conviction, suggested he might permit cameras in "run-of-the-mill" criminal trials and for educational purposes. Harlan did not want to prohibit the states from experimenting with cameras in the courtroom. He said that television may eventually become "so commonplace an affair in the daily life of the average person" that it would not likely damage the judicial process.[41]

Harlan agreed with the rest of the majority that the First Amendment did not guarantee the right of broadcasters to take television cameras into courtrooms. The majority rejected the argument that courts treated the print media more favorably than the broadcast media. Both print and broadcast reporters were permitted access to courtrooms, Clark said.[42]

Cameras Move into Courtrooms

After the *Estes* decision, every state but Colorado barred cameras from court for nearly a decade. Meanwhile, cameras became smaller and quieter and therefore less intrusive. Film became less dependent on special lighting. The media kept pushing for the acceptance of cameras in court. By the mid-1970s a number of states had experimented with cameras in courtrooms. Among the first were Alabama, Washington,

---

[40]*Id.* at 549, 1 Media L. Rep. at 1193.
[41]*Id.* at 590, 595, 1 Media L. Rep. at 1209, 1211 (Harlan, J., concurring).
[42]*Id.* at 541–42, 1 Media L. Rep. at 1190.

New Hampshire, Texas, and Georgia. By the end of 1980, 22 states had experimented with cameras and another dozen were studying the issue.[43]

A pilot program in Florida led to the Supreme Court test of whether states could allow cameras in court. Florida had first tried to experiment with cameras in 1976. However, the 1976 rules required the consent of all participants, and defendants consistently refused to permit cameras in court. Then, in July 1977, the Florida Supreme Court initiated a one-year test that did not require the consent of everyone photographed during a court proceeding but only the consent of the judge. The other rules of the pilot program were similar to procedures adopted in many other states both before and since. For example, Florida allowed only one television camera and two still cameras in fixed positions in court. If several publications and broadcast stations wanted trial coverage, a pooling agreement had to be arranged. Film and lenses could not be changed while court was in session. No artificial lighting was allowed. The media had to use existing courtroom audio recording equipment and could not record bench conferences between judges and attorneys.

After the year-long Florida experiment, a study found that cameras did not affect the behavior of those in court. Many of the trial participants surveyed believed that jurors and witnesses were slightly self-conscious in front of cameras, but also slightly more attentive. Although a few witnesses refused to testify in front of cameras, the Florida Supreme Court said that physical disturbance by the cameras "was so minimal as not to be an arguable factor" during trials.[44]

Florida's rules were challenged by two defendants who had objected to the presence of cameras at their trial. During the first month of Florida's experiment, two Miami Beach policemen were charged with burglarizing a well-known restaurant. An amateur radio operator overheard the two officers talking on their walkie-talkies during the burglary and taped the conversation. At the policemen's trial, the judge allowed cameras in the courtroom over the objection of the defense. The jury was not sequestered, but jury members were told not to read about the case or watch the local television news. Actually, only 2 minutes and 55 seconds of the trial were broadcast—depicting only the prosecution's side of the case. The policemen were convicted and appealed on the ground that they had not received a fair trial because cameras were in the courtroom. The Florida District Court affirmed the convictions and the Florida Supreme Court declined to review the case.[45]

The U.S. Supreme Court granted *certiorari* and voted 8–0, in *Chandler v. Florida,* to allow the states to continue experimenting with cameras in state courts. Former Chief Justice Burger, a strong critic of cameras in court,[46] wrote the opinion. First, Burger noted that Florida had not suggested that there was a state or federal constitutional right to have cameras in the courtroom. The only question to be resolved was whether the Florida Supreme Court's rules violated the defendants' Sixth Amendment right to a fair trial.

In *Chandler,* Burger noted that only four justices in *Estes* had declared that cameras in the courtroom automatically denied a defendant a fair trial. The Court in

[43]Chandler v. Florida, 449 U.S. 560, 565 nn. 5–6, 7 Media L. Rep. 1041, 1043 nn.5–6 (1981).

[44]*In re* Petition of Post-Newsweek Stations, Inc., 370 So.2d 764, 5 Media L. Rep. 1039 (Fla. 1979).

[45]Chandler v. Florida, 449 U.S. at 568–69, 7 Media L. Rep. at 1044–45.

[46]*See, e.g.,* "No Cameras in Burger's Court," *Broadcasting,* Nov. 19, 1984, at 71.

Estes therefore fell one vote short of ruling that the presence of cameras in court violated the Sixth Amendment. Burger, in asking again whether cameras in court violated the rights of criminal defendants, noted technological changes since *Estes* and the procedural protections in Florida designed to protect the rights of defendants. He acknowledged that there was still a heated controversy over whether the mere presence of cameras in court "invariably and uniformly affected the conduct of participants so as to impair fundamental fairness." Yet, said the chief justice, whatever potential cameras had for interfering with the judicial process, no one had presented data that established that the "mere presence" of broadcast media "inherently has an adverse effect on that process."[47]

The Supreme Court said a complete constitutional ban of cameras could not be justified simply because of a danger to a fair trial in some cases. A defendant must demonstrate that the cameras impaired a jury's ability to decide his or her case fairly, the Court said. Or, a defendant must establish that the presence of cameras, or the possibility of televised coverage, adversely affected any participants, including witnesses. In the *Chandler* case, the majority opinion noted, the police officers had not provided any evidence that their trial was tainted by broadcast coverage.

Chief Justice Burger, in the majority opinion, said the U.S. Supreme Court is empowered to intervene in state procedures only when fundamental constitutional guarantees are being violated. Therefore, Florida and the other states were free to allow cameras in state courts even though "dangers lurk in this, as in most, experiments."[48]

Burger's opinion should not be considered a ringing endorsement of cameras in the courtroom. He said that the Court neither endorsed nor invalidated the Florida experiment. He did not contradict the holding in *Estes* that cameras in the courtroom can, under certain circumstances, endanger the right of defendants to a fair trial. Indeed, he suggested, the Court may take action in a " Roman circus' or Yankee Stadium' atmosphere, as in *Estes,*" or if an unsequestered jury was exposed to "sensational" coverage, as in *Estes* and *Sheppard v. Maxwell. Chandler* was decided only on the grounds that the federal government could not interfere with the rules and procedures of state courts absent a violation of the Sixth Amendment.

Shortly after the *Chandler* decision, the ABA modified its ban on cameras in Canon 35, which had become Rule 3A(7) of the ABA Code of Judicial Conduct. The new rule still prohibits broadcasting, televising, recording, and photography in, or adjacent to, a courtroom unless an appellate court "or appropriate authority" approves. Then a judge can allow camera coverage only under supervision that ensures it is "unobtrusive, will not distract trial participants, and will not otherwise interfere with the administration of justice."[49]

By 1990, 44 states allowed television coverage on either a permanent or experimental basis, as illustrated by Table 9.1 on the next page. Of the 44 states, about three dozen allowed cameras into courtrooms during trials. The rest limited cameras to appellate courts, where there are no juries or witnesses. About a dozen states required

---

[47]Chandler v. Florida, 449 U.S. at 578–79, 7 Media L. Rep. at 1049.
[48]*Id.* at 582, 7 Media L. Rep. at 1050.
[49]American Bar Association, Code of Judicial Conduct, Canon 3A(7) (ABA/BNA Lawyers' Manual on Professional Conduct 1984).

TABLE 9.1. CAMERA COVERAGE OF STATE COURTS

States with Permanent Rules

		Courts	
	Effective Date	Level	Division
Alabama‡	02/01/76	Trial & Appellate	Civil & Criminal*
Arizona	07/01/83	Trial & Appellate	Civil & Criminal
Arkansas†	03/08/82	Trial & Appellate	Civil & Criminal
California	07/01/84	Trial & Appellate	Civil & Criminal
Colorado	02/27/56	Trial & Appellate	Civil & Criminal*
Connecticut	10/01/84	Trial & Appellate	Civil & Criminal
Florida	05/01/79	Trial & Appellate	Civil & Criminal
Georgia	05/12/77	Trial & Appellate	Civil & Criminal*
Hawaii	12/07/87	Trial & Appellate	Civil & Criminal
Idaho	08/27/79	Supreme Court in Boise	
Idaho	10/01/80	Supreme Court on Circuit	
Illinois	01/22/85	Appellate	
Iowa	01/01/82	Trial & Appellate	Civil & Criminal
Kansas	09/01/88	Trial & Appellate	
Kentucky	07/01/81	Trial & Appellate	Civil & Criminal
Louisiana§	04/30/85	Appellate	
Maine	03/13/84	Supreme Court	
Maryland	07/01/82	Appellate	
Maryland†	07/01/84	Trial	Civil
Massachusetts	01/01/83	Appellate	
Massachusetts	01/01/83	Trial	Civil & Criminal
Michigan	01/13/89	Trial & Appellate	Civil & Criminal
Minnesota	04/20/83	Appellate	
Montana	04/18/80	Trial & Appellate	Civil & Criminal
Nebraska	10/01/83	Supreme Court	
New Hampshire	01/01/78	Trial & Appellate	Civil & Criminal
New Jersey	10/08/80	Appellate	
New Jersey	06/09/81	Trial	Civil & Criminal
New Mexico	01/01/83	Dist. & Appellate	Civil & Criminal
New York	01/01/81	Appellate	
North Dakota	07/01/80	Supreme Court	
Ohio‡	01/01/82	Trial & Appellate	Civil & Criminal
Oklahoma‡	02/22/82	Trial & Appellate	Civil & Criminal*
Tennessee‡	02/27/79	Trial & Appellate	Civil & Criminal*
Vermont	09/01/88	Supreme Court	
Washington‡	09/20/76	Trial & Appellate	Civil & Criminal
West Virginia	05/28/81	Trial & Appellate	Civil & Criminal
Wisconsin	07/01/79	Trial & Appellate	Civil & Criminal

(continued)

TABLE 9.1. continued

	Period	Level	Division
	States with Experimental Rules		
Alaska	To 1/15/90, then permanent	Trial & Appellate	Civil & Criminal
Delaware	Extended indefinitely	Supreme Court	Civil
Idaho	Extended indefinitely	Court of Appeals	
Minnesota†	Unofficially extended	Trial	Civil & Criminal
Nevada	Unofficially extended	Trial & Appellate	Civil & Criminal
New Jersey	Indefinite	Municipal Courts	Civil & Criminal
New York	Extended to 5/31/91	Selected Trial Courts	Civil & Criminal
North Carolina	Extended to 6/30/90	Trial & Appellate	Civil & Criminal
Oregon	Indefinite	Appellate	Civil & Criminal
Pennsylvania†	Extended indefinitely	Trial, nonjury	Civil, Superior Court
Rhode Island	Extended indefinitely	Trial & Appellate	Civil & Criminal
Utah#	Completed, awaiting decision	Supreme Court	Civil & Criminal
Virginia	Extended to 6/30/90	Trial & Appellate	Civil & Criminal
Wyoming	Extended indefinitely	Supreme Court	

*Consent of accused required in criminal trials.
†Consent of parties and witness required.
‡No coverage of individuals who object.
§Subject to approval of the individual court.
#Still photography only in trial courts.
Used with permission of National Center for State Courts, 300 Newport Avenue, Williamsburg, Virginia 23187 (November, 1989).

consent of the parties to the proceeding before cameras are admitted. The only states banning cameras from court were Indiana, Mississippi, Missouri, South Carolina, South Dakota, and Texas. Cameras were also still banned in the District of Columbia courts.[50]

The Supreme Court, in *Estes* and *Chandler,* did not provide any guidelines to help determine when cameras violate the right to a fair trial. A few of the states, including Florida, are developing their own rules. In Florida, a judge can exclude electronic media coverage only if it will have "a substantial effect" that would be "qualitatively different" from that of other media coverage. Trial participants ordinarily have to show that they would be injured by the presence of cameras. Relying on the "qualitatively different" test, the Florida Supreme Court upheld the exclusion of cameras from the grand larceny trial of a woman with a history of mental illness. Psychiatrists said that television cameras would increase the woman's anxiety and depression and would interfere with her ability to defend herself and communicate with her attorney.[51] The same court said the "clicking" of cameras in another trial was sufficiently distracting to justify their exclusion from the courtroom.[52]

---

[50]National Center for State Courts, "Summary of TV Cameras in the State Courts" (Nov. 1989).
[51]Florida v. Green, 395 So.2d 532, 7 Media L. Rep. 1025 (1981). *See also* Ariz. Code of Judicial Conduct Canon 3A(7)(b) (1983); B. Beilfuss, Standards on Conduct Governing Use of Audio or Visual Equipment in Courtrooms (April 21, 1978) (memo from Chief Justice of Wisconsin Supreme Court to all Wisconsin judges), *quoted in* Hoyt, "Prohibiting Courtroom Photography: It's Up to the Judge in Florida and Wisconsin," 63 *Judicature* 290 (1980).
[52]Jent v. State, 408 So.2d 1024 (Fla. 1981).

As of mid-1990, the developments in the states had not affected the federal courts. In the spring of 1989, the Supreme Court rejected a request that the Court permit camera coverage of its proceedings.[53] The operating rules for federal courts still ban cameras,[54] and those rules have withstood First Amendment challenges in at least three federal appeals courts. In one decision, the U.S. Court of Appeals for the Second Circuit upheld the decision to keep cameras out of court during the General William C. Westmoreland–CBS libel trial. The court turned down a petition by Cable News Network that had the support of both General Westmoreland and CBS. The court said there was a "long leap" between an acknowledged First Amendment right to attend trials[55] and the yet-to-be-discovered First Amendment right to see a trial televised. Until that leap is made, "television coverage of federal trials is a right created by consent of the judiciary, which has always had control over the courtrooms, a consent which the federal courts . . . have not given."[56]

In 1990, cameras were still not permitted in other federal courts. However, in September 1990, the Judicial Conference of the United States, the policy-making body for the federal courts, authorized a limited three-year experiment in about a half-dozen courts. The conference voted to allow still photography and radio and television coverage of only civil trials and appeals beginning June 1, 1991. Under the rules, judges retained substantial discretion for deciding whether cameras would be allowed for specific cases.[57] Before 1991, the judicial conference prohibited cameras in federal courts because of the burden on judges to monitor camera activity; the psychological pressures on jurors, witnesses, judges, and lawyers; and the risk to "the required sense of solemnity, dignity and the search for truth."[58]

In 1988, the Judicial Conference of the United States agreed to an experiment using video cameras to create official records in federal courts.[59] In addition, in 1989, cameras were allowed into military courts on an experimental basis.[60]

SUMMARY

Judges have the authority to control the behavior of the press within the courtroom. Whether cameras are allowed in state courtrooms depends upon the rules of individual states (see Table 9.1). Many states allow restricted use of cameras in court, a practice permitted by the U.S. Supreme Court as long as the right of a defendant to

---

[53]"High Court Says No to TV, Radio," *Broadcasting,* Nov. 6, 1989, at 78.

[54]*See* Fed. R. Crim. P. 53 and Canon 3A(7) of the Code of Judicial Conduct for United States Judges.

[55]*See* section on "Access to Courtrooms" in this chapter.

[56]Westmoreland v. CBS, 752 F.2d 16, 24, 11 Media L. Rep. 1013, 1019 (2d Cir. 1984). *See also* United States v. Hastings, 695 F.2d 1278, 8 Media L. Rep. 2617, *reh'g en banc denied,* 704 F.2d 559, 9 Media L. Rep. 1582 (11th Cir. 1983).

[57]"Federal Courts Moving to Permit Trial Coverage by Radio and TV," *New York Times*, Sept. 13, 1990, at A10.

[58]Report of the Judicial Conference Ad Hoc Committee on Cameras in the Courtroom 3, 7 (Sept. 6, 1984), *cited in* Westmoreland v. CBS, 752 F.2d at 23 n.10, 11 Media L. Rep. at 1018–19 n.10.

[59]"In Brief . . .," *Access Reports,* Oct. 19, 1988, at 14.

[60]"First Cameras in Military Courts," *News Media Update,* April 15, 1989, at 4.

a fair trial is not violated. Cameras were still not permitted in federal courtrooms in 1990, but an experiment had been authorized.

CONTROLLING PREJUDICIAL PUBLICITY

In *Sheppard v. Maxwell,* Justice Clark's majority opinion stressed that judges, in addition to protecting the jury from prejudicial publicity and controlling courtroom conduct, must control publicity about the trial. Clark emphasized the need to control the disclosure of information by trial participants. At the same time, however, he asserted that the press cannot be prevented from reporting the trial itself. The tolerance for "gagging" trial participants and intolerance for restricting press reports of trials continues to be the Court's policy after 25 years of litigation. In addition, the Supreme Court has held since *Sheppard v. Maxwell* that the press cannot ordinarily be punished for reporting information about the judicial process that is lawfully obtained.

Restraints on News Sources

In the *Sheppard* opinion, Justice Clark said the trial judge in the case should have tried to control the release of information to the press by lawyers, police, and witnesses. Clark said no one who was a part of the trial process, and therefore under the direct jurisdiction of the court,

> should be permitted to frustrate its function. Collaboration between counsel and the press as to information affecting the fairness of a criminal trial is not only subject to regulation, but is highly censurable and worthy of disciplinary measures.[61]

Clark applauded the judge's threat to bar from the courtroom one defense witness, Sheppard's brother, who was accused of trying the case in the newspapers. Clark said the judge would have been within his authority to forbid any lawyer, party, or witness from discussing the case with the press. He said the judge could have barred any participant in the case from revealing Sheppard's refusal to take a lie detector test, the identity of prospective witnesses, the contents of probable testimony, comments about Sheppard's guilt or innocence, or any statements related to the merits of the case. The court also could have requested local government officials to instruct their employees not to disseminate information about the case, Clark said in *Sheppard.*

Even before *Sheppard,* the U.S. Department of Justice had issued a 1965 policy statement governing the release of information by its personnel. Commonly known as the Katzenbach Rules, after then Attorney General Nicholas Katzenbach, the state-

---

[61]Sheppard v. Maxwell, 384 U.S. at 363, 1 Media L. Rep. at 1231. *See also id.* at 357–63, 1 Media L. Rep. at 1229–31.

ment condemned the release of information designed to influence the outcome of a trial. Justice Department personnel were told not to make statements about investigative procedures, evidence, prospective witnesses, confessions, a defendant's character, or arguments to be used in the case. Neither were members of the Justice Department to volunteer information about a defendant's prior criminal record or encourage the news media to obtain photographs of defendants in custody. Authorized personnel could release a defendant's identity, age, and residence; the criminal charge; the identity of the investigating and arresting agencies; the length of the investigation; and the circumstances surrounding the arrest.[62]

Within a few years of *Sheppard,* two additional sets of recommendations designed to control publicity about criminal justice proceedings were released. In 1968, the American Bar Association adopted recommendations intended to prevent publication of the same kinds of information discouraged by the Katzenbach Rules. The report leading to the recommendations became known as the Reardon Report, for Paul C. Reardon, a justice on the Massachusetts Supreme Judicial Court and the chair of the ABA fair trial and free press advisory committee. The Reardon Report standards were primarily intended to control the release of prejudicial information by persons directly involved in court proceedings—lawyers, defendants, witnesses, court personnel, and law enforcement officers. The report recommended contempt citations for anyone who disseminated extrajudicial statements designed to affect the outcome of a trial or who violated a court order not to reveal information disclosed in a closed courtroom.[63] At about the same time the Reardon Report was adopted, similar guidelines for control of the release of prejudicial information were adopted by the Judicial Conference of the United States, the agency responsible for developing policy for the federal courts.[64]

Following the publication of the various guidelines, judges began to issue more orders restraining trial participants and officers of the court, such as lawyers and court personnel, from releasing information to the press. Since the 1960s, the U.S. Supreme Court has refused several opportunities to declare such restraining orders unconstitutional. Therefore, in the 1990s, more than two decades after the Reardon Report, judicial orders prohibiting trial participants from talking to the press are still considered by judges to be an acceptable technique for preventing prejudicial publicity. Both the ABA and the judicial conference still recommend restraining orders on trial participants although both have otherwise adjusted their guidelines since the 1960s.[65]

Judicial restraining orders take a variety of forms, but they usually ban some or all of the persons involved in a trial from discussing the case with reporters. An order may prohibit giving the media specific kinds of information or any information at all.

---

[62] *See* 28 C.F.R. 50.2 (1988).

[63] American Bar Association Legal Advisory Committee on Fair Trial and Free Press, *The Rights of Fair Trial and Free Press* (1969).

[64] *See* Report of the Committee on the Operation of the Jury System on the "Free Press-Fair Trial" Issue, 45 F.R.D. 391 (1968).

[65] *See* Standing Committee on Association Communications of the American Bar Association, *The Rights of Fair Trial and Free Press: The American Bar Association Standards* (1981); Revised Report of the Judicial Conference Committee on the Operation of the Jury System on the "Free Press-Fair Trial" Issue, 87 F.R.D. 519 (1980).

In one notorious double murder trial in Arizona, one with "overtones of organized crime and contract killing," the trial court judge ordered all participants in the case to keep away from news personnel during the proceeding. He said massive publicity since the two murders, including allegations of professional killings and brutality for the purpose of "sending a message," made it necessary to control discussion of the case outside the courtroom. The judge said the restraint order was the least restrictive means to protect the defendants' Sixth Amendment rights to a fair trial.[66]

In the North Carolina trial of Ku Klux Klan and Nazi party members accused of five shooting deaths in Greensboro in 1979, Judge Thomas Flannery, in an order printed in part as Figure 9.1, prohibited potential witnesses from making statements to the press about their testimony. Flannery said the order was necessary to restrain what were expected to be "highly prejudicial" statements affecting the outcome of the trial.[67]

Both the North Carolina and Arizona orders were upheld by appellate courts, as are most orders aimed at restraining trial participants.[68] A restraining order, or "gag" order, is especially likely to be upheld if a judge had considered several alternatives to protect a defendant's right to a fair trial and decided that, without the restraining order, there was at least a reasonable likelihood the defendant would be denied a fair trial. In the North Carolina case, the U.S. Court of Appeals for the Fourth Circuit said the restraining order on witnesses was necessary because of the "tremendous publicity attending this trial" and the "potentially inflammatory" statements that could be expected from the witnesses, many of whom were relatives of the victims. The Fourth Circuit also accepted Judge Flannery's judgment that alternatives, such as changing the location of the trial or admonishing or sequestering the jury, would either be impractical or ineffective.

A restraining order is more likely to be overturned if an appellate court decides that alternatives to the order were not considered and the order was broader than necessary to protect the rights of a defendant. For example, a federal district court in Connecticut overturned a state trial court order prohibiting attorneys from making "any public statement" to the press during a sensational chainsaw murder trial. The federal court acknowledged that, based on the extensive media coverage the case had already received, trial judge Howard Moraghan "could reasonably conclude" that further publicity might endanger the defendant's right to a fair trial. However, the federal court declared the restraining order unconstitutionally overbroad because it prohibited "any" statements by lawyers about the case rather than only those statements that might "reasonably" be prejudicial. In addition, the federal court said, gag orders must be accompanied by evidence that a judge had considered alternatives to closure. The federal court said Moraghan provided no evidence that he considered options to the restraining order.[69]

Appellate courts have not only affirmed restraining orders on trial participants challenged by the press, but also on those challenged by the persons being restricted—the

---

[66]KPNX Broadcasting Co. v. Maricopa County Superior Court, 678 P.2d 431, 434, 10 Media L. Rep. 1289, 1295 (Ariz. 1984).

[67]*In re* Russell, 726 F.2d 1007, 10 Media L. Rep. 1359 (4th Cir. 1984).

[68]*E.g.,* Radio and Television News Ass'n v. U.S. Dist. Court, 781 F.2d 1443, 12 Media L. Rep. 1739 (9th Cir. 1986).

[69]Connecticut Magazine v. Moraghan, 676 F. Supp. 38, 14 Media L. Rep. 2127 (D.C. Conn. 1987).

UNITED STATES DISTRICT COURT FOR THE
MIDDLE DISTRICT OF NORTH CAROLINA

Greensboro Division

MEMORANDUM

During the course of pre-trial proceedings in this case, issues concerning the proper procedures for controlling prejudicial pre-trial publicity have come to the court's attention on several occasions. In addition to numerous other measures outlined herein aimed at ensuring that the defendants in this case are tried based on admissible evidence only and that potential jurors are not prejudiced by pre-trial publicity, the court in May 1983 issued a ban on extrajudicial statements by counsel and witnesses, and modified that Order on October 13, 1983. . . . the October 13 order shall be modified as set forth in an accompanying order.

    2.   The potential witnesses covered by the Order are those who have been notified by the government or defendants that they may be called to testify in this case, and those who are actually called to testify.

    3.   The Order prohibits such potential witnesses from making or authorizing any extrajudicial statement relating to the testimony in this case that such potential witnesses may give, or relating to any of the parties or issues such potential witnesses expect or should reasonably expect to be involved in this case, or relating to the events leading up to and culminating in the shooting incident at Everitt and Carver Streets in Greensboro, North Carolina, on November 3, 1979, if such statements are intended for dissemination by means of public communication.

    4.   Potential witnesses shall <u>not</u> conduct any interviews with the print or electronic media in which the issues described in paragraph 3 are discussed.

    5.   Potential witnesses shall <u>not</u> make any proscribed statements, either orally or in written or demonstrative form, which are intended by such potential witnesses to be disseminated by means of public communication. This includes statements by potential witnesses to any third party whom such potential witnesses authorize, intend, or expect to disseminate such statements by means of public communication.

    6.   Nothing in this Order shall be deemed to prevent or interfere with the right of potential witnesses to discuss this case or any related case fully with counsel.

7. Nothing in this Order shall be deemed to prevent or interfere with the right of any potential witness to testify in court or by way of court authorized depositions or interrogatories in connection with any other case about all events, issues, and persons relevant to such case.

8. Nothing in this Order shall be deemed to prevent potential witnesses from privately soliciting funds to aid in the prosecution or defense of any related case, and such potential witnesses may discuss the events leading up to and following the Greensboro shootings in private, provided such discussions are not intended by such witnesses to result in dissemination of proscribed statements by means of public communication. Potential witnesses are permitted, in aid of their efforts to solicit funds, to send private letters to potential contributors, provided such potential contributors are in no way involved with this case.

Finally, it should be clear that, unlike in the Nebraska Press case heavily relied upon by witnesses' counsel, Nebraska Press Association v. Stuart, 427 U.S. 539, 96 S.Ct. 2791 (1976), this court has at no time banned the press from reporting this case. Although, as authorized by Sheppard, supra, the press will be tightly controlled in its access to jurors and witnesses during trial, and will be confined to certain areas of the courtroom once the trial begins, the press is free to report this case based on its observation of court proceedings. The court hopes, and hereby requests, that the press will cover this case in a responsible and ethical fashion and will avoid publicizing information that is prejudicial and has not been deemed admissible evidence during the trial.

An appropriate Order accompanies this Memorandum, and counsel for the government, defendants, and potential witnesses have been directed to make copies of this Order available to potential witnesses.

Thomas A. Flannery
_____

UNITED STATES DISTRICT JUDGE
Jan. 4, 1984

Figure 9.1. Restraining order—excerpts.

lawyers, witnesses, and defendants themselves. Trial participants sometimes contend that restrictions on their speech are prior restraints in violation of the First Amendment. Appellate courts often reject arguments that a judge cannot limit speech during a criminal proceeding. But the appellate courts do ordinarily require that judges document that the lack of a restraining order would threaten either a defendant's right to a fair trial or the integrity of the judicial system. In *Levine v. U.S. District Court,* for example, a federal appeals court affirmed that a restraining order was necessary to preclude "a serious and imminent threat to the administration of justice" but found the order as issued to be unconstitutionally overbroad. In *Levine,* which arose from the espionage trial of former FBI agent Richard Miller, the trial judge had forbidden attorneys from making any statements to the media about issues "to be resolved by the jury." The judge cited widespread publicity, including a newspaper report that defense lawyers had charged the FBI with exaggerating its case and badgering Miller for five days until he confessed. The Ninth Circuit of the U.S. Court of Appeals said the importance of controlling "the circus-like environment that surrounds highly publicized trials" outweighs the First Amendment rights of attorneys to argue "a client's case in detail in the press on the eve of the trial." However, the Ninth Circuit also said the trial judge's order should have specified statements to be restricted, such as comments about pretrial confessions and the strengths or weaknesses of each party's case.[70]

Appellate courts may be more likely to overturn court restrictions on speech challenged by participants in civil trials and after any trial is concluded. In 1990, the U.S. Supreme Court found unconstitutional a Florida law that punished grand jury witnesses who disclosed their own grand jury testimony. In *Butterworth v. Smith,* Michael Smith, a reporter for the *Charlotte Herald-News,* wanted to include in a news story or book his own testimony before a special grand jury investigating the Charlotte County State Attorney's Office and Sheriff's Department.[71] Smith was called to testify after writing news stories about alleged misconduct relevant to the grand jury's investigation. The prosecutor conducting the grand jury investigation warned Smith that he could be prosecuted under Florida law if he revealed any of his testimony. When the grand jury concluded its investigation, Smith claimed a First Amendment right to publish his own testimony. The state of Florida argued, in part, that grand jury testimony should remain secret so that persons exonerated by grand juries would not be held up to ridicule, witnesses would not fear retribution, and persons about to be indicted would not flee.

The U.S. Supreme Court held unanimously that the First Amendment protects the right of grand jury witnesses to publish their own testimony once the term of a grand jury ends. The majority opinion, written by Chief Justice Rehnquist, said the Florida statute was unconstitutional because it provided for the punishment of speech central to First Amendment values. Rehnquist noted that, under the Florida ban on discussion of grand jury testimony, critics of government could be silenced by calling them before grand juries. In contrast, Rehnquist said, some of Florida's reasons for

---

[70]Levine v. U.S. Dist. Court, 764 F.2d 590, 11 Media L. Rep. 2289 (9th Cir. 1985). *But see, e.g., In re* New York Times Co., 533 N.Y.S.2d 73, 15 Media L. Rep. 2158 (N.Y. App. Div. 1988).

[71]17 Media L. Rep. 1569 (1990). *See also, e.g.,* Hirschkop v. Snead, 594 F.2d 356, 4 Media L. Rep. 2599 (4th Cir. 1979).

grand jury secrecy did not apply to the release of a witness's own testimony after a grand jury had been discharged. Any remaining reasons, Rehnquist said, were insufficient to justify the permanent ban on testimony. The Court did not decide whether grand jury witnesses could publish their own testimony while a grand jury is still sitting or discuss what they had learned about the grand jury proceedings from being a witness, such as the scope and details of the investigation.

SUMMARY

Judicial orders restraining officers of the court and others involved in a case from talking to the press were widely encouraged in the late 1960s. Court orders restraining witnesses, law enforcement officers, lawyers, and litigants are usually upheld by appellate courts if the trial judge decides there is a reasonable likelihood that the jury may otherwise be biased and has considered alternatives.

Restraints Imposed on the Media

While Justice Tom Clark, in *Sheppard v. Maxwell,* authorized restraints on trial participants' contacts with the news media, he did not say that reporters could be restricted from publishing information they obtained about the criminal proceedings. In fact, consistent with the Supreme Court's general intolerance of prior restraints on publication, Clark said the Supreme Court had not authorized restraining press reports of proceedings in open court.[72]

The Supreme Court's prohibition of prior restraints directed at the news media in criminal proceedings may seem curious considering the Court's tolerance of restraining orders on news sources such as lawyers, witnesses, and law enforcement officers. A gag on either a reporter or a reporter's source has essentially the same impact—less information reaching the public. But the Court frequently draws a line between restricting press access to information and prior restraint, saying that while the First Amendment does not give reporters an absolute right to gather news, it does create an almost insurmountable bar to prior restraints on publication.[73]

Protection of the media's right to publish information about criminal proceedings was reinforced in 1976 when five Supreme Court justices said they were not likely to tolerate prior restraints on the news media to stop prejudicial pretrial publicity. In *Nebraska Press Association v. Stuart,* the Court held that a Nebraska court's restrictions on the reporting of a murder investigation and subsequent legal proceedings violated the First Amendment. The case started with a mass murder in the tiny prairie town of Sutherland, Nebraska. Fear ran rampant in the community on the night of October 18, 1975, after residents learned that six members of the Henry Kellie family had been killed. The 850 town residents were alerted to stay off the streets and to be

[72]384 U.S. at 350, 362–63, 1 Media L. Rep. at 1226, 1231.
[73]*E.g.,* Pell v. Procunier, 417 U.S. 817, 1 Media L. Rep. 2379 (1974).

careful whom they admitted to their homes. The next day a neighbor of the murdered family, 30-year-old Erwin Charles Simants, confessed to law enforcement officers. Simants, charged with six counts of premeditated murder, immediately became the focus of nationwide news coverage.

After four days of publicity, County Judge Ronald Ruff issued an order prohibiting the publication of news obtained during public pretrial proceedings. Members of the press also were ordered to observe supposedly voluntary Nebraska Bar-Press Guidelines. The guidelines, agreed to by representatives of the state bar and news media, discouraged the reporting of confessions, opinions about guilt or innocence, statements that would influence the outcome of a trial, the results of laboratory tests, comments on the credibility of witnesses, and evidence presented during the trial outside the presence of a jury. Ruff's order, upheld by District Judge Hugh Stuart, was intended to suppress publication of Simants's confession, statements he had made to relatives, and the results of medical tests related to a sexual assault. When the Nebraska Press Association appealed, the Nebraska Supreme Court upheld the key elements of the Stuart order. Simants was convicted of first-degree murder in January 1976.

Five months later, a unanimous U.S. Supreme Court said the Nebraska court order barring publication of Simants's confession and other information about the case was unconstitutional. Chief Justice Warren Burger, who wrote for five of the nine justices, did not say that prior restraints could never be imposed to protect the rights of a defendant. However, he said, anyone wishing to restrain the media would have the "heavy burden" of demonstrating that a fair trial would not be possible without prior restraint. Burger refused to consider the First Amendment to be more important than the Sixth, or vice versa. Yet, he said prior restraint on publication was "one of the most extraordinary remedies known to our jurisprudence" and should be difficult to obtain. He said that prior restraint did more than "chill" speech—it "froze" it, at least for a time.[74]

To determine whether a prior restraint was warranted in the Simants case, Burger applied a form of the clear-and-present-danger test once used in sedition cases. He said the question was whether the "gravity of the evil" of pretrial publicity, "discounted by the improbability" of its occurrence, merited a prior restraint. Burger looked at three factors:

1. the nature and extent of pretrial news coverage,
2. whether other measures would likely mitigate the effects of unrestrained pretrial publicity, and
3. the effectiveness of a restraining order in diminishing the effect of prejudicial publicity.

Considering the first factor, Burger affirmed trial judge Ronald Ruff's judgment that there would be "intense and pervasive" pretrial publicity that might impair the defendant's right to a fair trial. However, Burger did not believe there was enough evidence that unchecked publicity would have impaired jurors' abilities to judge

---

[74]Nebraska Press Ass'n v. Stuart, 427 U.S. 539, 559, 1 Media L. Rep. 1064, 1072 (1976).

Simants fairly. Burger noted that Ruff found only that the publicity could *possibly* have constituted a clear and present danger to a fair trial. Burger said Ruff's conclusion was necessarily speculative because the judge was dealing with factors "unknown and unknowable." Burger seemed to suggest that it might be impossible to prove that pretrial publicity would lead to a prejudiced jury, and thus impossible to meet the burden of proof necessary to justify a prior restraint.

Second, Burger said, Ruff had not indicated whether alternatives to prior restraint would have protected Simants. Ruff had not said that remedies such as a change of venue or the questioning of jurors during voir dire would not have ensured a fair trial. Ruff had not closed the courtroom, an alternative that Burger implicitly approved in his opinion.

Finally, Burger said, it was not clear that a prior restraint on publication would have halted pretrial publicity in Sutherland. In a town of 850, word of mouth could be more damaging than news media accounts, Burger said. In addition, by law, Judge Ruff could legally try to limit the publicity only within the county. As a county judge, he did not have jurisdiction over network television news and the national wire services.

Although Burger imposed a form of the clear-and-present-danger test on defendants wanting to restrain the press, at least three of the Court's justices would have provided even greater protection for the press. Justice Brennan, who had concurred only in the judgment in the case, said in a separate opinion that prior restraint could never be permitted to ensure a fair trial. Justices Stewart and Marshall joined in Brennan's concurring opinion. In addition, Justices White and Stevens indicated in separate concurring opinions that they might eventually agree to Brennan's absolutist approach.

Meanwhile, Simants's first murder conviction was overturned on the ground that a sheriff supervising the sequestered jury members had tried to influence them. When Simants was retried, he was found not guilty by reason of insanity.

A year after the Supreme Court's decision in *Nebraska Press Association,* the Court affirmed its reluctance to allow prior restraints on court coverage. In *Oklahoma Publishing Co. v. District Court,* a trial judge had allowed the press to attend the detention hearing of an 11-year-old boy arrested for the murder of a railroad switchman.[75] A few days later the judge prohibited the media from publishing the boy's name obtained during the open hearing, and a picture taken immediately afterward without any objections. The Supreme Court noted that, by statute, juvenile proceedings in Oklahoma were private unless explicitly ordered open. However, the Court said in a *per curiam* opinion that, since the press was permitted to attend the hearing, an order to prohibit the publication of information and pictures obtained there was unconstitutional.

Even after *Nebraska Press Association* and *Oklahoma Publishing,* lower courts occasionally issue prior restraint orders on the press, only to have them overturned by appellate courts. Journalists have the choice of obeying prior restraint orders issued by the trial courts, even if they appear to be unconstitutional, or facing a possible contempt citation. Relying on what is known as the Dickinson Rule, appellate courts

---

[75]430 U.S. 308, 2 Media L. Rep. 1456 (1977).

have been reluctant to lift contempt of court citations after journalists have violated a court order. The Dickinson Rule will be discussed in the contempt section of this chapter.

In 1984, the Supreme Court approved an exception to its virtual ban of prior restraints imposed on the news media for trial coverage. In *Seattle Times Co. v. Rhinehart,* the Court said that two Washington state newspapers could be restrained from publishing information they acquired only because they were defendants in a libel suit. The two papers, the *Seattle Times* and the *Walla Walla Union-Bulletin,* had been sued for $14 million by Keith Rhinehart, the leader of the Aquarian Foundation, a religious group believing in communication with the dead. Articles in the two papers said that Rhinehart treated inmates at the Walla Walla State Penitentiary to a 6-hour extravaganza that included "a chorus line of girls [who] shed their gowns and bikinis and sang."[76] During the pretrial fact-finding, the newspapers questioned whether the foundation had been damaged by the stories. They asked the judge to order the foundation to reveal the names of its members and donors for the previous 10 years in order to determine whether donations declined after the stories. The foundation countered that such an order would violate the First Amendment rights of members and donors to privacy, freedom of association, and freedom of religion. The foundation argued that its members would be harassed and donations would drop.

The trial court judge, relying on rules of procedure for the Washington state courts, ordered the Aquarian Foundation to provide the names of members and donors. However, the judge prohibited the newspapers from publishing the information. The newspapers appealed the restriction on publication, but the order was upheld by a unanimous U.S. Supreme Court.[77] Justice Powell, writing the Court's opinion, said the restraint on publication inherent in the trial court's order was not the "classic prior restraint that requires exacting First Amendment scrutiny." Although the order prohibited publication of information obtained through discovery, the same information could be published if acquired in another way, Powell said.

However, Powell continued, even if *Rhinehart* was not a classic prior restraint case, the newspaper's First Amendment rights could be restricted only if an important government interest was at stake. The Court decided that the state of Washington had demonstrated a "substantial" government interest: to protect against the abuse of the court rules that require parties in civil suits to provide information to the opposing party during pretrial discovery. The rules could lead to abuse, the Court said, because they require a party to litigation to reveal any information relevant to the dispute, including materials that may damage an individual's privacy or reputation. The only purpose of the rules, said the Court, was to ensure that litigants such as the newspapers could acquire information important to their defense. Therefore, the Court concluded, the government had an interest in preventing information acquired during discovery from being used for other purposes.

The Supreme Court accepted the word of the Washington courts that the publication of the names of foundation members and donors could lead to their being

---

[76]467 U.S. 20, 10 Media L. Rep. 1705 (1984).
[77]*Id. See also* KUTV v. Wilkinson, 686 P.2d 456, 10 Media L. Rep. 1749 (Utah 1984).

annoyed, embarrassed, or even oppressed.[78] The Supreme Court said the Washington courts did not abuse their discretion by deciding that an order requiring the foundation to reveal private financial records could also prohibit publication of that information. The courts could limit the use of the information because it was only made available by court order so that the newspapers could defend themselves in a libel suit. The information was otherwise not available to the public or the press.

SUMMARY

The Supreme Court, in *Nebraska Press Association v. Stuart,* said that prior restraints on publication to protect the right to a fair trial are ordinarily unconstitutional. The Court said that before trial judges issue prior restraint orders, they must consider the nature and extent of pretrial news coverage, alternative measures to protect Sixth Amendment rights, and whether a prior restraint order would be effective. However, the Court has approved a prior restraint order in a case where newspapers obtained information only because they were parties in a lawsuit.

Punishment after Publication

The Supreme Court, in addition to holding that it is ordinarily unconstitutional to prevent the publication of news about court proceedings, has also ruled unconstitutional after-publication punishment of the media for news about the judicial system. In two cases, one in 1978 and another a year later, the U.S. Supreme Court ruled unanimously that government could not punish the media for truthful news stories absent a compelling government need. The Court held that states could not punish the media even for printing information declared confidential by state law.

In *Landmark Communications v. Virginia,* the Court said the state could not justify the punishment of a newspaper for printing information about a confidential judicial inquiry. The case arose in 1975 when the *Virginian Pilot,* owned by Landmark Communications, identified a judge being investigated by the Virginia Judicial Inquiry and Review Commission, which reviews complaints about the disability or misconduct of judges. An article in the *Pilot* accurately reported that the commission had not filed a formal complaint against the judge. A month after the article, a grand jury indicted Landmark for divulging the judge's name contrary to state law. A Virginia statute provided that dissemination of the confidential information was a misdemeanor. Landmark was found guilty and fined $500.

The Supreme Court of Virginia affirmed the conviction, but the decision was reversed by the U.S. Supreme Court. Chief Justice Burger, writing the Court's opinion, did not discount the need for confidentiality by the judicial review commission. He noted that 47 states had procedures similar to Virginia's for confidential investigations of judicial conduct. Burger said confidentiality encouraged citizens to partic-

---

[78]*See* Seattle Times Co. v. Rhinehart, 467 U.S. at 37, 10 Media L. Rep. at 1712–13, *quoting* Rhinehart v. Seattle Times Co., 654 P.2d 673, 690, 8 Media L. Rep. 2537, 2550 (Wash. 1982).

ipate in investigations. It also protected the credibility of individual judges and the reputation of the judicial system from public disclosure of unsubstantiated complaints.

Burger said the issue was whether confidentiality could be enforced constitutionally by a fine levied for a truthful publication. Burger said that accurate reporting of the conduct of public officials "lies near the core of the First Amendment." He said the article published by the *Virginian Pilot* "clearly served those interests in public scrutiny and discussion of governmental affairs which the First Amendment was adopted to protect."[79]

In contrast, Burger said, Virginia's interest in encouraging participation in the investigation of judges and protecting both the reputation of individual judges and respect for the judicial system did not justify the encroachment on the freedom of the press. Virginia argued that the state's effort to protect confidentiality encourages complainants, witnesses, and judges to take part in the investigations. But Burger noted that more than 40 of the 47 states with review boards did not punish breaches of confidentiality by criminal sanction. In addition, Burger said, the Court had established in libel cases that it would not repress speech that damaged public officials' reputations. Burger also quoted justices who said respect for the court system could not be protected by punishing speech.

Further, Burger criticized Virginia's contention that the article in the *Pilot* constituted a clear and present danger to the administration of justice, a test used in contempt of court cases to be discussed later in the chapter. Burger said the risk of the article's publication injuring individual judges or the operation of the judicial review board fell "far short" of a clear and present danger. Burger said the danger "must be extremely serious and the degree of imminence extremely high before utterances can be punished."[80]

A year later the Supreme Court told the state of West Virginia it could not punish the *Charleston Daily Mail* and the *Charleston Daily Gazette* for printing the name of a juvenile defendant. The two papers identified a 14-year-old who shot and killed a classmate at a junior high school in St. Albans, a small community outside Charleston. Reporters obtained the name by asking witnesses, the police, and an assistant prosecuting attorney at the scene of the incident.

A grand jury indicted the two newspapers for violating a West Virginia law prohibiting newspapers from publishing the names of youths charged as juvenile offenders. Under the law, newspapers, but not broadcast stations, could be fined $100 and editors and reporters jailed for up to six months. The West Virginia Supreme Court prohibited county officials from acting on the indictment and the U.S. Supreme Court, in *Smith v. Daily Mail Publishing Co.*, upheld that judgment.

The U.S. Supreme Court said that a state could punish "truthful information about a matter of public significance" only "to further a need of the highest order." The Court's majority opinion acknowledged the validity of West Virginia's interest in facilitating the rehabilitation of youthful offenders by protecting their anonymity.

---

[79]Landmark Communications, Inc. v. Virginia, 435 U.S. 829, 839, 3 Media L. Rep. 2153, 2157 (1978).

[80]*Id.* at 845, 3 Media L. Rep. at 2159, *quoting* Bridges v. California, 314 U.S. 252, 263, 1 Media L. Rep. 1275, 1277 (1941).

The publicity from one crime could create a stigma that would block employment opportunities, the state argued.

However, the Court said, the state's interest in anonymity was not sufficient to overcome First Amendment rights threatened by imposing criminal penalties for the publication of the names of juveniles. The Court noted that every state protects the anonymity of juveniles, but 45 of the 50 accomplished that objective without criminal penalties. Moreover, the Court said, the statute was unconstitutional because it could not accomplish its goal, protecting the identity of juveniles, since it restricted only newspapers and not the electronic media. Three radio stations had revealed the name of the 14-year-old St. Albans youth who killed his classmate, but none of the stations could be prosecuted under the West Virginia law.[81]

SUMMARY

The Supreme Court has indicated that the First Amendment ordinarily prohibits punishment of the press for the publication of news stories about judicial proceedings. The Court has declared that, absent a compelling governmental interest, states cannot even punish the media for publishing stories based on information that is otherwise protected by law.

Access to Courtrooms

After the Supreme Court demonstrated in 1976 and 1977 its intolerance for prior restraints on publication, at least some trial court judges noted Justice Burger's suggestion in *Nebraska Press Association* that judges might close courtrooms to ensure a fair trial. In the late 1970s, several trial court judges tried to close courtrooms to prevent reporters from acquiring information that could prejudice the outcome of a trial. Indeed, the Supreme Court seemed to sanction court closures in 1979 when it ruled that the press and the public did not have a constitutional right to attend pretrial hearings. However, in the 1980s, the Supreme Court reversed direction and held that the public and the press do have a qualified First Amendment right of access to trials and the jury selection process as well as to pretrial hearings.

The Supreme Court and Access to Trials   The Supreme Court first ruled that the press and the public have a constitutional right of access to courtrooms in 1980. In *Richmond Newspapers v. Virginia,* seven justices agreed that the public has a limited First Amendment right to attend criminal trials. *Richmond Newspapers* marked the first time that the Supreme Court has held that the public has a First Amendment right to observe government proceedings and records.

Richmond Newspapers arose from a series of circumstances that understandably could frustrate a judge. In July 1976, John Stevenson was convicted of the murder of a hotel manager. A few months later the Virginia Supreme Court overturned the con-

---

[81]Smith v. Daily Mail Publishing Co., 443 U.S. 97, 5 Media L. Rep. 1305 (1979).

viction, holding that a bloodstained shirt had been improperly admitted into evidence. A second trial ended in a mistrial in May 1978, when a juror asked to be excused and no alternate juror was available. Stevenson's third trial, in June 1978, also ended in a mistrial when one prospective juror told others about the history of the case.

Before the beginning of the fourth trial, still in 1978, Judge Richard H. C. Taylor closed the trial at the request of the defense. He said he would agree with defense requests if he believed the rights of the defendant were infringed "in any way" and the rights of "everyone else" were not "completely" overridden.[82] Richmond Newspapers, the corporate parent of the *Richmond Times-Dispatch* and the *Richmond News-Leader,* unsuccessfully protested the closure. Stevenson was found not guilty after a closed trial. Richmond Newspapers' posttrial appeal of the closure was denied by the Virginia Supreme Court, but the U.S. Supreme Court granted *certiorari.*

Although a majority of the Court agreed that the Virginia closure order violated the public's right to an open trial, the Court was otherwise divided. The eight justices participating in the case wrote seven opinions. No more than three justices agreed to join any one opinion. Chief Justice Burger, writing the opinion for the Court, said that trials ought to be open to the public because of a tradition of openness in the Anglo-American judicial system, a tradition based on the indispensable role public trials play in the criminal justice system. Burger, supported only by Justices White and Stevens, said that criminal trials have been open "to all who cared to observe" since before the Norman Conquest of England. Burger said that trials have long been presumptively open because public trials discourage perjury and official misconduct during the proceedings. Open trials also inspire public confidence in the criminal justice process. Burger said citizens know they can observe the system at work to see whether it is fair. In addition, public trials allow the public to see "justice done," helping to defuse community outrage after major crimes.

Burger said that not only is "a presumption of openness" inherent "in the very nature of a criminal trial," openness is also guaranteed by the First Amendment. Although the First Amendment does not explicitly mention a public right to attend criminal trials, such a right is implied, he said. The rights specifically guaranteed in the First Amendment, such as freedom of speech and press, the right to assemble peaceably, and the right to petition the government for a redress of grievances, ensure free communication about government, Burger said. "Plainly it would be difficult to single out any aspect of government of higher concern and importance to the people than the manner in which criminal trials are conducted," he added.[83]

For Burger, it followed that the First Amendment right of the press to report court news would lose its meaning if access to that information could be denied. He acknowledged that freedom of the press "could be eviscerated" without some protection for gathering news.[84] Although Burger, in *Richmond Newspapers,* emphasized that the First Amendment right to attend trials belongs to the public as a whole, he also said the press often acted as a surrogate for the public, informing people about

---

[82]Richmond Newspapers, Inc. v. Virginia, 448 U.S. 555, 561, 6 Media L. Rep. 1833, 1836 (1980).

[83]*Id.* at 575, 6 Media L. Rep. at 1841–42.

[84]*Id.* at 580, 6 Media L. Rep. at 1844, *quoting* Branzburg v. Hayes, 408 U.S. 665, 681, 1 Media L. Rep. 2617, 2623 (1972).

Court proceedings

If a motion is made to close a court proceeding, you should raise your hand, stand and say:

"Your honor, I am (your name), a reporter for the (your newspaper). I respectfully request the opportunity to register on the record an objection to the motion to close this proceeding to the public, including the press. Our legal counsel has advised us that standards set forth in recent state and federal court decisions give us the opportunity for a hearing before the courtroom is closed. Accordingly, I respectfully request such a hearing and a brief continuance so our counsel can be present to make the appropriate arguments. Thank you."

Figure 9.2. Above is a sample of a statement journalists should try to read to a judge if a motion is made to close a court proceeding. Every reporter covering courts should carry a similar statement. Many lawyers say that a courtroom confrontation with a judge over the issue of closure can often be avoided if journalists mention to the judge before any court proceeding that their media organizations would appreciate the opportunity to challenge any motion for closure. Most lawyers recommend calling an editor as soon as possible after the issue of closure is raised, so that the editor has the option of calling an attorney. This sample statement is provided by the First Amendment Foundation, Tallahassee, Florida.

court activity. He noted that while attendance in court by members of the public had once been common, people now rely on the media for their information about trials. Therefore, even though journalists have no greater right of access to courts under the First Amendment, "they often are provided special seating and priority of entry so that they may report what people in attendance have seen and heard."[85]

Burger not only based the right of access to courts on the First Amendment right of the press, but also on an expansive interpretation of the First Amendment right to assemble. Burger said that trial courtrooms—like public streets, sidewalks, and parks—are public places where the public and representatives of the media have a right to exercise their First Amendment rights. People assemble in public places, Burger said, "not only to speak or to take action, but also to listen, observe, and learn." He added that people exercising their First Amendment right to be present in a courtroom historically have been thought to enhance "the integrity and quality of what takes place."

Because the press and the public have a right to attend court, Burger said, the trial in a criminal case can be closed only if the state interest in a fair trial overrides the rights of the press and public to attend. Burger criticized Judge Taylor in the Ste-

---

[85]*Id.* at 573, 6 Media L. Rep. at 1841.

venson case for failing to explain the need for closure. Burger said, "No inquiry was made as to whether alternative solutions would have met the need to ensure fairness; there was no recognition of any right under the Constitution for the public or press to attend the trial."

Burger did not explain what circumstances and evidence would demonstrate the "overriding interest" that would justify closing the court. However, in a separate opinion, Justice Stewart suggested that courts might be closed to protect trade secrets or youthful rape victims. Justice Brennan, in a separate opinion joined by Justice Marshall, said that national security might warrant closure.

Brennan's opinion, concurring in the Court's judgment, said a First Amendment right of access secures and fosters self-government. Brennan said arguments for access are strong when based on "an enduring and vital tradition of public entree" and when access assists the governing process. Justice Rehnquist, the lone dissenter, said the Court inappropriately applied the Constitution to a decision that should have been left to the state court system.

Just two years after the Court decided *Richmond Newspapers,* a 6–3 majority affirmed the Court's commitment to public trials. In 1982, in *Globe Newspaper Co. v. Superior Court,* five justices said states could not require that courts be closed routinely during the testimony of minors in sex offense cases. The Court's opinion said closure could be based only on a "compelling" need in individual cases and could last no longer than necessary.

In *Globe Newspaper Co.,* a Massachusetts statute provided that a judge "shall exclude the general public from the courtroom" during a criminal trial "for rape, incest, carnal abuse," or other sex-related crimes when the victim was less than 18 years old. Relying on the statute, a trial court judge in Norfolk County ordered a rape trial closed in 1979. The defendant had been charged with the rape of two 16-year-olds and a 17-year-old. When an appeal by the *Boston Globe* was dismissed by the Supreme Judicial Court of Massachusetts, the U.S. Supreme Court granted *certiorari.*[86]

Justice Brennan, who wrote the Court's majority opinion, agreed that the first of two reasons the state offered for the statute was compelling. The state said it wanted to close courtrooms to protect young victims of sex crimes from further trauma and embarrassment. However, Brennan said, as compelling as that interest was, it did not justify the mandatory closure required by the state statute. Rather, he said, the need for closure must be made on a case-by-case basis. Brennan said the need for closure would depend on the minor's age and psychological maturity, the nature of the crime, the need for the testimony, and the interests of close relatives. He said the court should not be closed if the names of the minors were already in the public record or if the minors indicated they were willing to testify in the presence of the press.

Brennan also said the state had not sufficiently proven its second justification for the statute, that automatic closure encourages minor sex-crime victims to cooperate with law enforcement officials. Brennan said that officials may be able to prove in individual cases that sex offense victims would testify only if they could do so in

[86]Globe Newspaper Co. v. Superior Court, 457 U.S. 596, 8 Media L. Rep. 1689 (1982).

closed court. However, the Massachusetts law requiring closed courts did not guarantee that the testimony would be kept secret. Massachusetts still provided the press with access to court transcripts containing testimony.

Justice Burger, joined by Justice Rehnquist, dissented vigorously to Brennan's opinion. Burger said the decision undercut the state's authority and duty to protect minor victims of crimes. Justice Stevens dissented on procedural grounds.

In general, the decision in *Globe Newspaper Co.* has not affected state efforts to keep juvenile proceedings closed. *Globe* involved an adult defendant in a criminal trial. Only the witnesses were juveniles. Juvenile proceedings are presumptively closed to the public in about half of the states, according to the Reporters Committee for the Freedom of the Press. They are presumptively open in 11 states. Most of the others allow the judge to decide whether the proceedings should be open or closed.[87] States often avoid prosecuting youths in open court as part of an effort to avoid stigmatizing them for life as criminals. States try to avoid treating juveniles as adult criminals so that efforts to rehabilitate them might be more effective.[88] The Supreme Court has not suggested that closing courts during juvenile proceedings violates the First Amendment rights of the public and press.

Opponents to closing juvenile justice proceedings say that public access is as important in the juvenile justice system to ensure against abuse as it is in adult court. Indeed, many observers question whether youths arrested for violent crimes and repeat offenders should not be treated as adults. Several state appellate courts have recently affirmed trial court decisions to open juvenile proceedings to the public. In 1988 and 1989, the supreme courts of Arizona, Ohio, Vermont, and Virginia were among the courts to hold that the public could attend juvenile proceedings. In Ohio, the Supreme Court said state law allows trial judges to decide that the public can be admitted. The Ohio Supreme Court said that a juvenile court judge in Coshocton did not abuse his discretion when he opened a hearing held to consider whether juveniles Daniel Fyffe and Bret McVay ought to be tried as adults. Fyffe and McVay, arrested on charges of murder, argued that their Sixth Amendment rights to a fair trial would be jeopardized if evidence presented in an open hearing was ruled inadmissible during their trial. However, Juvenile Court Judge Fenning Pierce said the public's First Amendment right to attend trials includes juvenile proceedings. He said Fyffe and McVay had not demonstrated that closing the hearing was necessary to protect their Sixth Amendment rights.[89]

If the Supreme Court has not declared that juvenile proceedings must be open to the public, neither has it said that civil trials must be open to the public. The closest the Court has come was a footnote in Chief Justice Burger's plurality opinion in *Richmond Newspapers,* a criminal case. In the footnote, Burger said that both civil and criminal trials have historically been presumed to be open.[90]

---

[87]"Media Gain Juvenile Court Access," *News Media & Law,* Spring 1989, at 21, 23.

[88]*E.g., In re* J.S., 438 A.2d 1125 (Vt. 1981). *See* Day, "Media Access to Juvenile Courts," 61 *Journ. Q.* 751 (Winter 1984).

[89]Ohio *ex rel.* Fyffe v. Pierce, 531 N.E.2d 673, 15 Media L. Rep. 2431 (1988); "Media Gain Juvenile Court Access," *News Media & Law,* Spring 1989, at 21.

[90]448 U.S. at 580 n.17, 6 Media L. Rep. at 1844 n.17. *See also id.* at 599, 6 Media L. Rep. at 1852 (Stewart, J., concurring). *But see* Globe Newspaper Co. v. Superior Court, 457 U.S. at 611, 8 Media L. Rep. at 1696 (O'Connor, J., concurring).

Civil court cases can often be more important to the public than the prosecution of individual criminals. Civil trials often involve such issues as discrimination, voting rights, antitrust, government regulation, and bankruptcy. They also often involve the dangers of cigarettes, drugs, automobiles, and chemical processing plants. News reports of civil litigation may provide the public with information about corporate products and processing techniques normally kept secret.

Recent appeals court opinions have recognized the public's First Amendment right of access in civil as well as criminal cases. Appeals courts are requiring judges to demonstrate a compelling need before closing civil hearings or trials. Judges must also show a potential for harm to litigants or persons not party to a case and severely limit the closure. In 1988, a Maryland appellate court said that a trial court unconstitutionally closed court proceedings arising out of a state investigation into fraudulent automobile repairs. The Maryland Attorney General sued Cottman Transmission Systems, which franchises 150 auto transmission repair centers, for defrauding consumers. The state accused Cottman franchises of falsely telling customers that transmissions in their cars had to be torn apart—at the customer's expense—before problems could be identified. Cottman employees allegedly induced customers to authorize and pay for unnecessary repairs. When the state issued a press release announcing its accusations, Cottman sales dropped 35 percent and a circuit court judge ordered that all proceedings be closed. On appeal, the Maryland Court of Special Appeals noted that federal courts had ruled the public had First Amendment rights to attend civil proceedings as well as criminal proceedings. The Maryland court said the same policy considerations for keeping criminal courts open, such as allowing the public to check for government abuse and fostering public respect for the judicial process, apply to civil courts. The Maryland appeals court said Cottman Transmission had not demonstrated an interest sufficiently compelling to close the court proceedings. Cottman, said the court, only wanted to minimize the damage to its reputation and business, a desire of every business and professional sued. The court recognized the "natural interest" in keeping information damaging to a business's image away from the public, but said that "possible harm to a corporate reputation does not serve to surmount the strong presumption in favor of public access to court proceedings and records." The court said that every business is "entitled to a fair trial, not a private one."[91]

The Supreme Court and Access to Jury Selection

Two years after *Globe Newspaper,* in 1984, a unanimous Supreme Court declared that the jury selection process, as well as the trial itself, must ordinarily be open to the public. In fact, in the first of two closed-courtroom cases named *Press-Enterprise Co. v. Riverside County Superior Court,* the Court treated jury selection as part of the trial. The Court said, in effect, that the public confidence in the criminal justice system, derived in part from public access to the questioning of potential jurors, should generally be given priority over undocumented concerns about the right to a fair trial for the defendant or violations of the privacy of citizens asked to be jurors.

---

[91]State v. Cottman Transmission Sys. Inc., 542 A.2d 859, 15 Media L. Rep. 1644 (1988). *See also, e.g.,* Publicker Industries v. Cohen, 733 F.2d 1059, 10 Media L. Rep. 1777 (3d Cir. 1984); Newman v. Graddick, 686 F.2d 796, 9 Media L. Rep. 1104 (11th Cir. 1983).

In what is known as *Press-Enterprise I,* the Press-Enterprise Company of Riverside, California, successfully appealed the closing of jury selection before the trial of Albert Greenwood Brown, Jr. Brown, a black, had been charged with the rape and murder of a white teenage girl in California. He had been convicted previously of raping a white adolescent girl. The judge refused to allow the voir dire examination of jurors to be open to the public and the press for two reasons. He wanted to protect Brown's right to a fair trial and the privacy rights of jurors who "had some special experiences in sensitive areas that do not appear to be appropriate for public discussion." After a voir dire lasting six weeks, all but three days closed to the press, the judge also refused to release the transcripts of the questioning. California appellate courts refused to review the case, but the U.S. Supreme Court vacated the judge's order and remanded the case for further consideration.

Chief Justice Burger, writing for eight of the nine justices, said the process of jury selection has been presumptively open to the public since the development of trial by jury. Burger contended that the selection of jurors has always been an integral part of the public trial. At times, the courts even selected jurors from members of the public attending the trial. Although Burger said that "no right ranks higher than the right of the accused to a fair trial," he contended the right of the accused and the right of the public to attend the voir dire were closely connected. Burger said:

> The value of openness lies in the fact that people not actually attending trials can have confidence that standards of fairness are being observed; the sure knowledge that *anyone* is free to attend gives assurance that established procedures are being followed and that deviations will become known.[92]

To overcome the presumption that jury selection must be open, Burger said, a judge must first specify an overriding interest, such as the defendant's right to a fair trial or jurors' rights to privacy. Second, the judge must establish that the overriding interest cannot effectively be protected except through closure. For example, Burger said, a judge may decide that closure is the only way to protect the privacy of a prospective juror who, during the voir dire, is asked whether he or she has ever been sexually assaulted. Third, the judge must document in writing why closure is essential to protect a "higher value," Burger said. That is, the judge will need to explain why the answer of the prospective juror is entitled to privacy. Fourth, the closure can last only as long as necessary to meet the needs of the single juror. Burger said the California trial judge in *Press-Enterprise I* had not supported his closure order by findings that either Brown's right to a fair trial or the privacy of the jurors was threatened by questioning the jurors in public.

Justice Thurgood Marshall did not join Burger's opinion although he concurred in the judgment of the Court. Marshall stressed that the constitutional rights of access to all aspects of criminal trials are not diminished when "deeply personal matters" may be discussed. Marshall said a trial court should be required to use the least restrictive means possible to protect a compelling state interest. If closure is necessary, Marshall said, names of jurors could be removed from transcripts so the public could know the substance of their responses to questions. "Only in the most extraordinary circumstances," said Marshall, "can the substance of a juror's response to question-

---

[92]464 U.S. 501, 508, 10 Media L. Rep. 1161, 1164 (1984) (emphasis in original).

ing at voir dire be permanently excluded from the salutary scrutiny of the public and the press.''[93]

The Supreme Court and Access to Pretrial Hearings Since 1984, the Supreme Court has applied a First Amendment right of access to hearings held before the trial begins. Although pretrial hearings are not technically part of trials, they often take on the significance of trials. Legal authorities contend that 90 percent of criminal cases never reach the trial stage, often because they are resolved as a result of pretrial hearings. Consequently, a pretrial hearing often presents the only opportunity for a public proceeding in a criminal case.

Pretrial hearings are often held to determine whether there is enough evidence for a judge to find ''probable cause'' that a defendant committed a crime. Judges may also hold pretrial hearings to consider whether potential evidence, such as a confession or a weapon, may be revealed to a jury during a trial. Judges also hold hearings to consider whether bail should be denied or the courtroom closed.

If a pretrial hearing is reported in the media, people who might be called as jurors can read about and perhaps be influenced by information such as a confession that might not be admissible as evidence during a trial. Since jurors are not selected until a case comes to trial, judges cannot sequester them or order them not to read or listen to reports about pretrial hearings.

In the early 1980s, trial courts were reluctant to open pretrial hearings to the public, in part because of a 1979 U.S. Supreme Court decision. In 1979, before recognizing a First Amendment access to courtrooms, the Court said in *Gannett Co. v. DePasquale* that the press and public do not have a constitutional right to attend pretrial hearings. A divided Court affirmed the ruling of a New York judge to exclude a Gannett newspaper reporter from a pretrial hearing in a second-degree murder case. The Court created a furor when it upheld 5–4 the closure of a hearing to consider whether the confessions of two men should be admitted into evidence at their trial.[94] Not only had the Court upheld the closure of a pretrial hearing, but, at that time, observers did not know whether the decision would exclude the press and public from trials as well. In fact, the ambiguous opinion led to a rash of closures of trials as well as pretrial hearings.[95]

A year after *Gannett*, the Supreme Court ruled in *Richmond Newspapers* that trials are presumptively open to the public under the First Amendment. But the Court did not overrule *Gannett* in *Richmond Newspapers, Globe Newspaper Co.,* or *Press-Enterprise I.* However, in 1986, the Court ruled in *Press-Enterprise II* that the public and the press have a First Amendment right to pretrial hearings held to determine whether there is probable cause to believe a suspect has committed a crime. Although the Supreme Court did not directly overrule *Gannett* in *Press-Enterprise II,* the Court's reliance on the First Amendment right of access cast considerable doubt on *Gannett's* continued validity.[96]

---

[93]464 U.S. at 520, 10 Media L. Rep. at 1170 (Marshall, J., concurring).
[94]443 U.S. 368, 5 Media L. Rep. 1337 (1979).
[95]''Court Watch Summary,'' *News Media & Law,* Aug.–Sept. 1980, at 4.
[96]*See also* Waller v. Georgia, 467 U.S. 39, 10 Media L. Rep. 1714 (1984) (Sixth Amendment right of defendants to public trial extends to pretrial hearings).

In *Press-Enterprise II,* a magistrate in Riverside, California, excluded the press from a preliminary hearing scheduled to determine whether there was probable cause that Robert Diaz, a nurse, had murdered a dozen hospital patients with massive doses of the heart drug lidocaine. The magistrate said closure was necessary because Diaz's case had attracted national publicity and "only one side may get reported in the media." After a 41-day hearing, the magistrate ordered a trial after he determined there was probable cause to believe that Diaz committed the murders. The magistrate refused to release transcripts of the hearing.

The California Supreme Court, upholding the magistrate's order to close the courtroom, said that defendants must only demonstrate a "reasonable likelihood" that a public hearing would prejudice their right to a fair trial. However, the U.S. Supreme Court, by a 7–2 margin, said the First Amendment requires that defendants seeking to close pretrial hearings must demonstrate a greater danger to their rights than a "reasonable likelihood." Instead, the Court said, defendants must provide specific evidence that an open courtroom would have a "substantial probability" of endangering their rights to a fair trial. In addition, echoing *Press-Enterprise I,* the Court said that judges must consider whether alternatives to closure could protect the rights of the defendant. Further, closure must be for as short a time as necessary to ensure a fair trial.

Chief Justice Burger, again writing for the Court, said the same reasons that led the Court to apply the First Amendment right of access to criminal trials and the jury selection process also apply in pretrial hearings. Most preliminary hearings, including those in California, are traditionally open, Burger said. In addition, preliminary hearings are enough like trials that the Court could conclude that public access is as essential to their success as it is to the success of trials. As in trials, Burger said, preliminary hearings in California afford the accused the right to appear before a magistrate, to be represented by an attorney, to cross-examine hostile witnesses, to present evidence on behalf of the defense, and to challenge illegally obtained evidence.

Burger said the preliminary hearing in California "is often the final and most important in the criminal proceeding"[97] and sometimes the only chance for the public to observe the criminal justice system at work in a given case. The attendance of the public and the press at open hearings is also important because, unlike a trial, there is no jury to guard against the "corrupt or overzealous prosecutor" and "the compliant, biased, or eccentric judge."[98]

However, *Press-Enterprise II* and the other recent Supreme Court decisions will not necessarily stop court closures. First, the Supreme Court has said that the right of access is not absolute. Trial judges can constitutionally close courts if they can document an overriding interest that cannot be protected by alternative means and if they can narrowly restrict the closure as required in the *Press-Enterprise* cases. In addition, state courts are still apt to be influenced by state constitutions, statutes, and common law traditions that may have more relaxed standards for public access than the relatively new First Amendment guarantees. While state law cannot contradict the

---

[97]Press-Enterprise Co. v. Riverside County Superior Court (P-E II), 478 U.S. 1, 12, 13 Media L. Rep. 1001, 1006 (1986).

[98]*Id., quoting* Duncan v. Louisiana, 391 U.S. 145, 156 (1968).

First Amendment, substantial leeway for interpretation in individual cases remains after the recent Supreme Court opinions.

In addition, the Supreme Court's recent emphasis on the presumption of openness for trials and pretrial hearings should not affect the historic secrecy of grand juries. Since grand juries prepare indictments, rather than determine guilt or innocence, they play a unique role in the legal system. Reports about grand jury proceedings could disseminate unsubstantiated charges and hearsay that may not lead to an indictment. No judge is present in a grand jury hearing to ensure that the evidence sought is relevant to the investigation. Further, those who testify generally do not have the right to counsel or the right to cross-examine others who testify, as they would during pretrial proceedings and trials.[99] In *Press-Enterprise II,* all nine justices supported opinions emphasizing the importance of secrecy for grand jury proceedings.[100]

SUMMARY

The U.S. Supreme Court emphasized the First Amendment right of the public and press to attend judicial proceedings in four rulings over six years in the late 1970s and early 1980s. In 1980, in *Richmond Newspapers v. Virginia,* the Court said that criminal trials are presumptively open. The public and the press have a First Amendment right to attend trials unless the state can document an overriding interest in closure, the Court said. In *Globe Newspaper Co.,* the Court said that statutes providing for automatic closures are unconstitutional. In *Press-Enterprise I,* the Court said that the First Amendment protects against the closure of the jury selection process. In *Press-Enterprise II,* the Court extended the presumption of openness to pretrial hearings.

In the series of courtroom-closure cases, the Court has established that judicial proceedings can ordinarily be closed only for compelling reasons that are carefully substantiated. A judge must consider alternatives to closure and must limit closure to only as long as necessary. Thus far, most courts considering closure have not distinguished between criminal and civil cases. Grand jury proceedings remain closed, however. Juvenile court proceedings, traditionally closed, are sometimes open to the public.

Access to Court Records

Official court records have long been open for inspection and copying by the public and the press under common law. Recently, many appellate courts have said access to records is also guaranteed by the First Amendment. The Supreme Court has not directly established a First Amendment right of access to judicial records, but the *Press-Enterprise* cases that established a right of access to jury selection and pretrial

---

[99]*E.g., In re* Grand Jury Investigation, 508 F. Supp. 397 (D. Va. 1980).
[100]478 U.S. at 7–9, 20–22, and 24–29, 13 Media L. Rep. at 1004–1005, 1010, and 1011–14.

hearings also included access to sealed transcripts. Chief Justice Burger's majority opinions in both cases seemed to assume that the public has the same right of access to the transcripts of the pretrial hearings as it has to the hearings themselves.[101]

Both state and federal appellate courts usually support a right of access to official court documents, particularly to those used as evidence in court, unless a compelling need for nondisclosure is demonstrated. In a government attempt to prosecute automaker John DeLorean on charges of conspiring to import cocaine, the U.S. Court of Appeals for the Ninth Circuit said in 1983 that court records could be sealed only if "strictly and inescapably necessary" to ensure a fair trial. The Ninth Circuit said a district court judge had improperly closed records pertaining to whether De-Lorean should be confined before his trial and documents containing allegations of government misconduct during the DeLorean investigation. The Ninth Circuit said such pretrial documents are often important to a public understanding of the judicial process. The Ninth Circuit said the public's right of access could only be overcome by a showing that the sealing of the documents "is strictly and inescapably necessary in order to protect the fair-trial guarantee."[102] The appeals court said the district court failed to satisfy all three of the tests that must be applied before documents could be sealed. First, the judge had not demonstrated that there was a substantial probability DeLorean would not receive a fair trial if the documents were released. Second, the judge had not established that alternatives to closure would inadequately protect DeLorean's rights. Finally, the judge did not demonstrate a substantial probability that closure would be effective in protecting Delorean's rights.

Several federal courts have found that the presumption of openness extends to the right of broadcasters to copy tapes used as evidence in court. For example, the U.S. Court of Appeals for the Third Circuit said that broadcasters could not be prohibited from copying tapes made during a controversial FBI "sting" operation known as Abscam. The three major television networks and Westinghouse Broadcasting, Inc., sought video and audio tapes played in open court during the bribery trial of two Philadelphia city council members. The Third Circuit said the broader dissemination of information already made public increased the chance that the Abscam trial could both provide a catharsis for community hostility and ensure that the defendants were treated fairly by judges and lawyers, goals emphasized in the Supreme Court's decision in *Richmond Newspapers*. The Third Circuit said broadcasts of the tapes would give persons other than those who attended the trial a chance to observe a significant public event. The court said defense arguments that additional publicity could prejudice a new trial were only speculative. Even if a new trial was necessary, the court said, the voir dire examination of potential jurors could be employed to avoid seating biased jurors. The Third Circuit also said that tapes could be edited to protect nondefendants whose reputations might otherwise be damaged.[103]

---

[101]*E.g.,* Press-Enterprise v. Riverside County Superior Court (P-E I), 464 U.S. at 510–11, 10 Media L. Rep. at 1166.

[102]Associated Press v. U.S. Dist. Court, 705 F.2d 1143, 1145, 9 Media L. Rep. 1617, 1618 (9th Cir. 1983), *quoting* Gannett v. DePasquale, 443 U.S. at 440, 5 Media L. Rep. at 1367 (Blackmun, J., concurring).

[103]*In re* Application of NBC, 648 F.2d 814, 7 Media L. Rep. 1153 (3d Cir. 1981). *See also In re* Application of NBC [United States v. Myers], 635 F.2d 945, 6 Media L. Rep. 1961 (2d Cir. 1980); United States v. Jenrette, 653 F.2d 609 (D.C. Cir. 1981). *Cf.* United States v. Edwards, 672 F.2d 1289, 8 Media L. Rep. 1145 (7th Cir. 1982).

In contrast, both the Fifth and Sixth circuits of the U.S. Courts of Appeals turned down requests to copy tapes because of perceived risks to the defendants' Sixth Amendment rights.[104] Both courts said that a right of access was only one of many issues to be considered. Both courts relied on *Nixon v. Warner Communications, Inc.,* a 1978 Supreme Court decision that prevented the copying of White House tapes of former President Richard Nixon. In *Nixon,* the Supreme Court held that broadcasters and record companies did not have the right to copy the Nixon tapes for broadcasting and sale to the public. The tapes had been used as evidence at the trials of presidential aides charged with obstructing justice during the Watergate investigation. The Supreme Court acknowledged "a general right to inspect and copy public records and documents" at the discretion of the judge.[105] However, the Court held that the public's common law right of access had been superseded by congressional action creating a procedure for processing and releasing the tapes to the public.[106] The First Amendment had not been violated because the press had been allowed to listen to the tapes and had been given transcripts during the trial.

Federal appeals courts have been divided not only on the right of broadcasters to copy tapes, but also on the media's right of access to records that have not been introduced into evidence in court. Many of the conflicts over access to records involve materials used by lawyers during the discovery process in cases that never come to trial. Chapter 1 of this book discussed the discovery process, which allows both parties in a legal dispute to investigate documents and question witnesses that may be material to a case. A court can compel one party to disclose discovery information to the other, sometimes accompanying the order with a *protective order* guaranteeing that the information will not be made public. A Supreme Court case involving both compelled discovery and a protective order, *Seattle Times v. Rhinehart,* has strongly influenced lower courts since it was decided in 1984. In *Seattle Times v. Rhinehart,* discussed earlier in this chapter, the Supreme Court said a trial court did not abuse the First Amendment when it prohibited newspapers from publishing information obtained through a protective order. The *Seattle Times* and the *Walla Walla Union-Bulletin* had been prevented from printing information about the Aquarian Foundation that the newspapers had obtained during a libel suit. The Court said that prohibiting the publication of information obtained only through a court order was not a classic prior restraint, almost always a violation of the First Amendment. Even so, the Court said, the First Amendment right to publish could only be restricted if a substantial governmental interest was at stake. In *Rhinehart,* the Court said the need to prevent the abuse of the rules requiring compelled discovery overrode First Amendment values. The Seattle and Walla Walla newspapers could not claim a First Amendment right to publish information that might invade privacy and damage reputations if those materials were obtained only because the newspapers were litigants in a civil suit.

Both before and after *Rhinehart,* some courts have ruled that the need to protect

---

[104]United States v. Beckham, 789 F.2d 401, 12 Media L. Rep. 2073 (6th Cir. 1986); Belo Broadcasting Corp. v. Clark, 654 F.2d 423, 7 Media L. Rep. 1841 (5th Cir. 1981). *See also* Oregon *ex rel.* KOIN-TV v. Olsen, 711 P.2d 966, 12 Media L. Rep. 1625 (Or. 1985); United States v. Edwards, 672 F.2d 1289, 8 Media L. Rep. 1145 (7th Cir. 1982).
[105]435 U.S. 589, 597, 3 Media L. Rep. 2074, 2077 (1978).
[106]Presidential Recordings and Materials Preservation Act, Pub. L. 93-526, 88 Stat. 1695 (1974).

such social and economic values as privacy and trade secrets might overcome the right of access to certain court documents. In 1983, the year before *Rhinehart* was decided, the U.S. Court of Appeals for the Sixth Circuit upheld an order protecting information about 423 questionable loans made by the United American Bank. The documents included the names of borrowers, the amounts of each loan, and "extensive discussion of each borrower's financial condition, prospects and personal life." The documents had been sealed under a protective order by a district court judge when they were filed in a suit trying to stop the Federal Deposit Insurance Corporation from closing the bank.

However, before the suit went to trial, the Tennessee Commissioner of Banking ordered the bank closed because of extensive loan losses. The district judge dismissed the bank's lawsuit but permitted the bank to withdraw the personal loan information from the court file. When the *Knoxville News-Sentinel* and the *Knoxville Journal* appealed the district judge's protective order, the Sixth Circuit ruled "the long-established" presumption of public access had to yield to statutory restrictions on the disclosure of bank records. The court cited several federal statutes to support the argument that Congress intended that "the banking records of individuals be kept in strict confidence." The court said the borrowers were not responsible for the litigation and their interest in privacy was "sufficiently compelling to justify non-disclosure." The borrowers had a "justifiable expectation" that their names and financial records would not be revealed to the public.[107]

However, many courts hold that documents in both criminal and civil courts cannot be automatically sealed, even when the information contained in them may not be offered in evidence at trial. For example, the U.S. Court of Appeals for the First Circuit said in 1988 that the federal rules governing civil suits create a presumption that pretrial discovery should take place in public. Therefore, in *Public Citizen v. Liggett Group,* the First Circuit said that documents surrendered in pretrial discovery by the Liggett & Meyers Tobacco Company to the relatives of a lung cancer victim could be made public. The court upheld a lower court decision to release to health associations 18 boxes of research documents prepared by a consultant for Liggett & Meyers. The trial court, in order to protect the company's right to a fair trial, had originally ordered that the documents be made available only to the relatives of the lung cancer victim who were suing Liggett & Meyers. However, the suit was dismissed before a trial could be held, and the documents were never made public. Subsequently, a group of health organizations, including the American Cancer Society and the American Heart Association, sued for access to the research.

Liggett & Meyers claimed a general right of privacy in the documents and argued that allowing public access to pretrial discovery materials would excessively disrupt future litigation. The Public Citizen Litigation Group, representing the health organizations, said the public should know as much as possible about the hazards of smoking.

The First Circuit said federal rules permit the courts to seal pretrial documents in civil suits for "good cause" to protect persons "from annoyance, embarrassment, oppression or undue burden or expense." However, the court said the rules also re-

---

[107]*In re* Knoxville News-Sentinel, 723 F.2d 470, 477, 10 Media L. Rep. 1081, 1087 (6th Cir. 1983).

quire that pretrial discovery be public unless compelling reasons justify denying public access.[108] The court noted that Liggett & Meyers had not argued that documents sought by the health organizations contained trade secrets or other "specifically confidential material" that would have prevented them from being made public.

The Liggett & Meyers case represents a significant development in access litigation in the last several years. Although the law affecting access to pretrial and trial documents has not yet changed substantially, the fight for the disclosure of sensitive court documents has intensified. A few states have recently adopted new laws or court rules that limit the power of courts to seal records connected to litigation.[109] Both public interest groups and the media have become increasingly aware that enormous amounts of information about public issues, such as the health hazards of smoking, are collected by attorneys in civil suits. In addition, the press in particular has been aggressive in seeking documents during the criminal trials of such well-known persons at Lt. Col. Oliver North, the White House aide who helped engineer the exchange of arms to Iran for money to assist the Contra rebels in Nicaragua.

SUMMARY

Most court records are presumed by appellate courts to be open. However, lower court judges may seal records, particularly if the records have not been introduced into evidence in court. Courts have disagreed when asked to decide whether broadcasters can copy videotapes introduced into evidence in court.

VOLUNTARY COOPERATION

An informal remedy for prejudicial publicity is voluntary cooperation among the courts, law enforcement agencies, and the press.

In several states, lawyers, judges, law enforcement officers, and journalists have agreed to voluntary guidelines for the handling of criminal pretrial publicity. In the early 1970s, at least two dozen states adopted guidelines that both encouraged the release of basic information about arrests and discouraged the publication of information prejudicial to the rights of criminal defendants. The guidelines varied widely, but most substantially paralleled the ABA recommendations and the Katzenbach Rules mentioned earlier in the chapter. The guidelines recognized the right of the public to be informed about activities in the criminal justice system and the right of editors to decide what to print. But they also recognized that an accused person is presumed innocent until proven guilty and has the right to a trial by an impartial jury under the Sixth Amendment.

Most of the guidelines, such as those still used in New York, said that law en-

---

[108]Public Citizen v. Liggett Group, Inc., 858 F.2d 775, 789 (1988), *cert. denied,* 109 S. Ct. 838 (1989), *quoting* American Telephone & Telegraph v. Grady, 594 F.2d 594 (7th Cir. 1978).

[109]*E.g.,* "Governor Signs Sunshine-in-Litigation into Law," *Brechner Report,* July 1990, at 1; Tex. Civ. Proc. Rules Ann. R. 76a, 166b.5.c (1990); Lewin, "Press Curbs Increasing in Courts," *New York Times,* Feb. 8, 1989, at 1.

forcement officers should release to the press a suspect's name and address, the identity of the investigating agency, the text of the charge, and circumstances directly related to the arrest. The New York guidelines, like most others, warn against the publication of confessions, the possibility of a guilty plea, opinions about the character or reputation of a defendant, opinions about evidence and potential witnesses, and the results of such investigative techniques as ballistics tests and lie detector tests. The New York guidelines warn that the latter information "may tend to create dangers of prejudice without serving a significant law enforcement function."[110] However, most guidelines, like those in New York, include statements emphasizing that only the media has the right to decide what to publish. The guidelines do not provide for sanctions for violations of the guidelines other than adverse publicity and peer disapproval.

Most of the guidelines were adopted in the wake of the 1966 Supreme Court opinion *Sheppard v. Maxwell.* Press–court relations deteriorated rapidly after the Supreme Court ordered a retrial for Cleveland osteopath Dr. Sam Sheppard. In *Sheppard,* the Court had admonished a trial court judge for not adequately protecting the defendant against sensational news coverage. The *Sheppard* decision marked the fifth time in seven years that the Supreme Court had said that extensive media coverage violated a defendant's right to a fair trial.[111] Soon after *Sheppard,* recommendations leading to restrictions on press coverage were adopted by the American Bar Association, the U.S. Department of Justice, and the Judicial Conference of the United States.

The Supreme Court's *Sheppard* decision also reinforced the findings of a 1964 presidential commission headed by Supreme Court Chief Justice Earl Warren. The Warren Commission had strongly criticized the media for their lack of self-discipline in the news coverage of the assassination of President John F. Kennedy and the subsequent shooting of Lee Harvey Oswald by Jack Ruby. The commission had called for a professional code of conduct that demonstrated the press was sensitive to the rights of defendants to receive fair trials.[112]

Both the Warren Commission and the ABA's Reardon Report recommended that representatives of the bar and the media develop standards for the reporting of criminal investigations and court proceedings.[113] Much of the press feared that formal standards of acceptable and unacceptable criminal reporting might lead to reduced press freedom. However, some media representatives preferred cooperation with law enforcement officers and court officials to officially imposed restrictions on information about trials. As a result, unofficial groups of lawyers, judges, law enforcement officers, and news media personnel in some states developed informal guidelines, such as those in New York. The guidelines generally recognized the problems that specified reporting practices created for the criminal justice system without mandat-

---

[110]The New York Fair Trial Free Press Conference, *Fair Trial Free Press Principles and Guidelines for the State of New York* 2.

[111]*See* Marshall v. United States, 360 U.S. 310 (1959); Irvin v. Dowd, 366 U.S. 717, 1 Media L. Rep. 1178 (1963); Rideau v. Louisiana, 373 U.S. 723, 1 Media L. Rep. 1183 (1963); Estes v. Texas, 381 U.S. 532, 1 Media L. Rep. 1187 (1965).

[112]Report of the President's Commission on the Assassination of President John F. Kennedy 241 (1964).

[113]American Bar Association Legal Advisory Committee on Fair Trial and Free Press, *The Rights of Fair Trial and Free Press* (1969).

ing what the media should print or broadcast. In some states, what became known as bench-bar-press discussions not only produced guidelines but also helped reduce animosity and develop a spirit of cooperation. Some of the bench-bar-press groups established in the 1960s still operate.

However, in the early 1990s, journalists, judges, and lawyers no longer sense the urgent need for cooperation of 20 years ago. In some cases, the bench-bar-press guidelines have been forgotten by the press. More often, guidelines are ignored in sensational cases.[114] Press interest in guidelines waned when judges turned voluntary guidelines into court-imposed orders. *Nebraska Press Association v. Stuart,* discussed earlier in this chapter, arose out of Judge Stuart's order that the press observe the Nebraska Bar-Press Guidelines.[115] In Washington state, a judge turned guidelines into requirements for access to his courtroom.

The Washington case was especially significant because the state had long been a leader in press-bar cooperation. Washington's Bench-Bar-Press Committee adopted guidelines in 1966. The committee, with the support of the Washington State Supreme Court, was more active than many. It sponsored daylong seminars to explain the guidelines and developed subcommittees that could advise judges and the media in cases of conflict.[116] However, in 1981, Superior Court Judge Byron Swedburg told reporters they would not be admitted to a pretrial hearing unless they signed an agreement to abide by Washington's bench-bar-press guidelines. Swedburg wanted to limit pretrial news coverage after the arrest for attempted murder of the girlfriend of the "Hillside Strangler," a man notorious for multiple murders in Washington and California. However, Swedburg said members of the public who were not journalists could attend the hearing without signing an agreement.

Many reporters refused to agree to Swedburg's conditions, believing that his order was a prior restraint. However, in *Federated Publications v. Swedburg,* the state supreme court said Swedburg's order was not a prior restraint, particularly since the judge had set no penalty for violating the agreement. The court said the order was a reasonable means of avoiding a closed hearing.[117] The U.S. Supreme Court refused to review the case.

The implications of *Swedburg* became a major concern for the press. A state supreme court that had encouraged cooperation for 15 years had upheld the mandatory application of a voluntary agreement. Even though the same court seemed willing to ignore *Swedburg* just a few months later,[118] the state's media associations withdrew their support for the guidelines. In addition, the Washington state case troubled the news media in other parts of the country. For example, the Arizona Newspaper Association withdrew its approval of the Arizona guidelines following *Swedburg.* In North Carolina, guidelines were revised to stress the voluntary nature of the bench-bar-press agreements. Even more important, many media representa-

---

[114]Tankard, Middleton, and Rimmer, "Compliance with the American Bar Association Voluntary Free Press-Fair Trial Guidelines," 56 *Journ. Q.* 464 (1979).

[115]*See* State v. Simants, 236 N.W.2d 794 (Neb. 1975).

[116]*See* Standing Committee on Association Communications of the American Bar Association, *The Rights of Fair Trial and Free Press: The American Bar Association Standards* 31–32 (1981).

[117]633 P.2d 74, 7 Media L. Rep. 1865 (1981), *cert. denied,* 456 U.S. 984 (1982).

[118]Seattle Times Co. v. Ishikawa, 640 P.2d 716, 8 Media L. Rep. 1041 (1982). New guidelines for the state were later adopted.

tives to bench-bar-press groups across the county believed the spirit of cooperation had been undermined.

The media reaction to *Swedburg,* however, overlooks the fact that journalists frequently obtain access to information or to court proceedings by agreeing to conditions. In North Carolina, for example, judges sometimes permit reporters to attend juvenile proceedings only on the condition that names not be revealed. Judges, by statute, can exclude the public from a juvenile hearing unless the juvenile requests that the proceeding be open.[119]

Besides bench-bar-press agreements, a second kind of cooperative effort that can affect criminal reporting is a press council. The only surviving press council, in Minnesota, is a private organization with membership divided between journalists and nonjournalists. The council responds to grievances brought by members of the public against the media. It has no authority to punish the media for any errors, but relies on persuasion, peer pressure, and leverage inherent in the publicity of their opinions.

SUMMARY

In the late 1960s, lawyers, judges, and news media representatives met in many states to try to reduce tensions that had arisen over prejudicial pretrial publicity. More than 20 of these groups developed guidelines for the release, and reporting, of information related to criminal justice activity. Once the tension of the 1960s subsided, many of the guidelines fell into disuse. Media cooperation was, in part, threatened when judges required adherence to the guidelines in exchange for access to courtrooms.

CONTEMPT POWER

Judicial Authority

Members of the news media agreed to guidelines for the reporting of criminal proceedings in part because of the power of judges to control the courts. Judges can exercise the kind of control over a trial that was recommended in the 1966 Supreme Court decision *Sheppard v. Maxwell* because judges have the power to punish anyone who disobeys a judicial order.

American judges inherited from the English courts the power to cite for contempt of court any acts of disobedience or disrespect and any acts that interfere with the judicial process.[120] A single judge can decide what kind of conduct constitutes contempt of court, accuse a person of being in contempt, determine that person's guilt, and assess the punishment—sometimes even the same judge who was the object of the contempt. In a matter of minutes, a person can be fined or sentenced to jail.

---

[119]N.C. Gen. Stat. sec. 7A-629 (1986). *See also* Sacramento Bee v. U.S. Dist. Court, 656 F.2d 477, 7 Media L. Rep. 1929 (9th Cir. 1981).

[120]*See* R. Goldfarb, *The Contempt Power* 1 (1963).

The judicial power to summarily cite for contempt of court is an unusual concentration of authority in our system of government. A holdover from authoritarian rule in England, the contempt power ensures judicial authority and order in the court. It gives judges the enforcement power necessary to protect the constitutional rights of persons under the jurisdiction of the courts. Anyone who disobeys a judge, including a journalist, may be faced with a contempt citation. Even if an appeals court later decides that a contempt order was unconstitutional, it may well uphold the fine or jail term imposed by the trial judge. The appellate courts do not want to encourage doubts about judicial authority in the courtroom.

However, there are a few legal limits on the contempt power that curb its abuse. Most of those limits apply to both civil contempt and criminal contempt.

Civil Contempt versus Criminal Contempt

The differences in the two kinds of contempt, civil and criminal, do not parallel the distinctions between civil and criminal law. Rather, civil and criminal contempt can be distinguished by the purpose of a contempt order and a difference in the assessment of penalties.[121]

A civil contempt citation is coercive; it is applied to get someone to do something. The penalty stays in force until the court's directives are obeyed or become moot.

Civil contempt is usually imposed on a person who refuses to obey an order intended to protect one of the parties in a court case. In mass media law, judges most often use civil contempt when a reporter refuses to reveal confidential news sources. Journalists are cited for contempt because they refuse to give possible evidence to one of the parties in a legal dispute. Myron Farber of the *New York Times* was sentenced to jail and fined $1,000 a day for civil contempt after the defense sought his notes in a murder trial. Farber spent 40 days in jail after refusing to let the judge review the notes. William Farr of the *Los Angeles Times* spent 46 days in jail when he refused to reveal a source. Farber was released when the murder trial was over; Farr was released on the order of a Supreme Court justice.[122]

In civil contempt, a judge can order the person charged with contempt to be locked up until he or she agrees to obey the court. In a sense, people charged with civil contempt hold the keys to their own cells. They can free themselves by complying with the court order. Many states have limited the amount of time a person can serve in jail.

In contrast, a criminal contempt citation punishes disrespect for the court, such as obstruction of court proceedings or verbal abuse of the judge. The penalty could be a fine or a specific amount of time in jail, or both. In Colorado, a court held two reporters and their newspaper, the *Boulder Daily Camera,* in contempt after the reporters questioned jurors in a murder trial. As a result of the reporters' actions, the

---

[121]*See* Kutner, ''Contempt Power:—The Black Robe; A Proposal for Due Process,'' 39 *Tenn. L. Rev.* 1, 8 (Fall 1971).

[122]Comment, ''The Fallacy of *Farber:* Failure to Acknowledge the Constitutional Newsman's Privilege in Criminal Cases,'' 70 *J. Crim. L. & Criminology* 299, 303 n.45 (1979).

jurors were dismissed and the jury selection process had to be repeated. In lieu of a fine, the reporters and the newspaper were ordered to reimburse the parties in the case and the state judicial department for the costs of four additional days of trial. The reporters and the newspapers also had to pay the costs incurred by the state for prosecuting them for contempt.[123]

A journalist refusing to reveal confidential sources could be cited for both civil and criminal contempt. A judge can cite a reporter for civil contempt in an effort to coerce a reporter to reveal sources and for criminal contempt for disobeying an order of the court. This happened in the case of Myron Farber, the *New York Times* reporter mentioned above. In addition to his fine and jail sentence for civil contempt, Farber was fined $1,000 and ordered to spend six months in jail—a sentence later suspended—for disobeying the court.

The Supreme Court has ruled that those sentenced to jail for criminal contempt for more than six months have a right to a jury trial.[124] The Court has not yet granted the same procedural right to persons cited for civil contempt.

Limits on Judicial Power

Both the U.S. Constitution and federal law limit the power of judges to cite for contempt of court, particularly for behavior outside of the judge's presence. The limits are important to journalists because they protect the publication of information and comment about the courts.

First Amendment   Three Supreme Court decisions in the 1940s virtually eliminated the use of contempt citations to punish publications or broadcasts about court proceedings, especially for the criticism of judicial behavior.

In 1941, in two cases treated as one, the Supreme Court ruled that contempt citations issued in response to published criticism of judges violated the First Amendment. The Court, by a 5–4 margin, said that judges could not hold journalists in contempt absent a clear and present danger of a miscarriage of justice. In one of the cases, *Bridges v. California,* an official of the International Longshoremen-Warehousemen's Union was held in contempt after he said that a judge's decision in a union dispute was "outrageous." Harry Bridges, in a telegram to the U.S. Secretary of Labor, threatened to "tie up" the docks at the port of Los Angeles and the entire Pacific Coast if the court ruling was enforced. Bridges's comments were published in Los Angeles and San Francisco newspapers.

At about the same time, the *Los Angeles Times* published three editorials commenting about cases pending before judges. The headline of one editorial asked "Probation for Gorillas?" The editorial said that Judge A. A. Scott would be making "a serious mistake" to grant probation to two labor union members who had been found guilty of assaulting nonunion truck drivers. The editorial wanted the "sluggers for pay" and "men who commit mayhem for wages" sent to San Quentin. In *Times-*

[123]*In re* Stone, 11 Media L. Rep. 2209 (Colo. Ct. App. 1985).
[124]Bloom v. Illinois, 391 U.S. 194 (1968). For discussion, *see* Kutner, "Contempt Power:—The Black Robe; A Proposal for Due Process," 39 *Tenn. L. Rev.* 1, 57–66 (Fall 1971).

Mirror Co. v. Superior Court, a trial court had said the editorials were aimed at influencing the disposition of the cases.

Both the *Times-Mirror* and Longshoremen official Bridges were found guilty of contempt of court and fined. The convictions were upheld by the California Supreme Court but overturned by the U.S. Supreme Court. Justice Hugo Black, writing the Court's majority opinion, said "the only conclusion supported by history" is that those who adopted the Constitution "intended to give to liberty of the press . . . the broadest scope that could be countenanced in an orderly society."[125] Black said the contempt citations punished speech about important controversial topics "at the precise time" when the public interest in those issues would be at its peak. Drawing upon language used by the Supreme Court in sedition cases, Black said the criticism of pending court cases could only be punished if there was an "extremely high" degree of imminence of an "extremely serious" evil. Black said the judge in the Bridges case should not be any more intimidated by Bridges's statement than by the enormous implications of the pending decision. In the case of the *Times-Mirror,* Black said the editorials did no more than threaten criticism, which could have been expected anyway.

Five years later, in *Pennekamp v. Florida,* the Supreme Court said inaccurate editorials about a rape case before a Florida court did not present a clear and present danger to the administration of justice. In the editorials, the *Miami Herald* accused judges of protecting criminals more than the law-abiding public. Justice Stanley Reed, writing for a unanimous Court, said

> Free discussion of the problems of society is a cardinal principle of Americanism—a principle which all are zealous to preserve.[126]

Reed said that discussing a case only after its conclusion may not adequately alert the public to the danger of "supposedly wrongful judicial conduct."

Bridges, Times-Mirror, and *Pennekamp* made it clear that the Supreme Court expects judges to have thick skins and that the criticism of judges should not lead to contempt of court charges.[127] However, courts might uphold contempt citations for other kinds of publications. For example, courts might be less tolerant of publications that seek to influence jury decisions. Courts might decide that jurors could be more easily intimidated than judges. In addition, *Bridges, Times-Mirror*, and *Pennekamp* involved only commentary as opposed to prejudicial pretrial publicity or the violation of a judicial order.

Judicial Reach and Due Process   The Supreme Court has not been alone in limiting the use of the judicial contempt power. Congress and many state legislatures have passed laws that limit the ability of judges to hold journalists in contempt for the publication of unfavorable stories or commentary. For example, in 1831 Congress enacted a statute that said that federal judges could hold persons in contempt only for

---

[125]Bridges v. California, 314 U.S. 252, 265, 1 Media L. Rep. 1275, 1278 (1941).
[126]Pennekamp v. Florida, 328 U.S. 331, 346, 1 Media L. Rep. 1294, 1300 (1946).
[127]*See also* Craig v. Harney, 331 U.S. 367 (1947).

the refusal to obey a judicial order or for misbehavior in or near the courtroom that can "obstruct the administration of justice."[128] The word *near* probably refers to the hallway outside the courtroom and maybe the sidewalks or grounds just outside the courthouse.[129]

In addition, persons cited by federal judges for contempt for activity taking place outside a courtroom ordinarily have a right to a notice of the nature of the charge and a hearing. In federal courts, persons who are cited for contempt have the right to an attorney, the right to cross-examine witnesses, the right to offer testimony, and, frequently, the right to a jury trial. If the contempt involves criticism or disrespect of a judge, that judge is disqualified from the proceeding.[130]

Limits on Appeals

The power of judges to cite for contempt of court with only limited opportunities for appeal presents particular problems for journalists when a judge has issued a prior restraint order—that is, a judge orders reporters not to print or publish. After the Supreme Court's decision in *Nebraska Press Association,* a prior restraint order probably would be considered unconstitutional by an appellate court. However, if reporters do not print the news until they can appeal a judge's order, a story may lose its news value. If journalists do print the story in violation of a judge's order, they may be cited for contempt of court.

To add to a journalist's dilemma, a citation for contempt of court traditionally would stand even if an appellate court declared the original prior restraint order unconstitutional. In other words, a journalist could be jailed or fined for violating an order that infringes on the First Amendment. The reason is that appellate courts want to protect the authority of the trial courts even when the trial courts are wrong.

The traditional rule upholding contempt citations—known as the Dickinson Rule—resulted from a decision of the U.S. Court of Appeals for the Fifth Circuit in 1972. In *Dickinson v. United States,* two reporters in Baton Rouge, Louisiana, tried to cover the hearing of a government-sponsored civil rights volunteer accused of conspiring to murder the mayor. A federal district judge ordered the news media not to report testimony given in the public proceedings. Nevertheless, Larry Dickinson and Gibb Adams reported on the hearing in the *Morning Advocate* and the *State Times.* The judge found the reporters in contempt of court and fined them $300 each. The reporters appealed.

The U.S. Court of Appeals for the Fifth Circuit agreed with the reporters that the judge's order was a prior restraint that violated the First Amendment. The Fifth Circuit said that a blanket ban on publication "cannot withstand the mildest breeze emanating from the Constitution."[131] However, the appeals court refused to overturn the contempt order.

Chief Judge John R. Brown said the principle that an injunction must be obeyed,

---

[128]18 U.S.C.A. sec. 401 (1966).

[129]Nye v. United States, 313 U.S. 33 (1940).

[130]Fed. R. Crim. P. 42 (b). *See* R. Goldfarb, *The Contempt Power* at 75.

[131]United States v. Dickinson, 465 F.2d 496, 500, 1 Media L. Rep. 1338, 1339 (5th Cir. 1972), *quoting* Southeastern Promotions Ltd. v. City of West Palm Beach, 457 F.2d 1016, 1017 (5th Cir. 1972).

regardless of the ultimate validity of the court order, was "well-established." Brown said that for the judicial system to work,

> people simply cannot have the luxury of knowing that they have a right to contest the correctness of the judge's order in deciding whether to wilfully disobey it.[132]

Brown suggested that the reporters should have appealed the order rather than violated it. He acknowledged that an appeal created "thorny problems" given the timely nature of news. Brown concluded, however, that a judicial order must be obeyed absent a showing that it was transparently invalid or patently frivolous. He said that the First Amendment does not give reporters the right to violate a judicial order with impunity without "strong indications that the appellate process was being deliberately stalled."

The case against the two reporters was returned to the district court judge. The trial judge upheld his previous contempt order and the fines. The Fifth Circuit affirmed the lower court for the second time.[133]

In 1986, however, the U.S. Court of Appeals for the First Circuit overturned a contempt conviction of a newspaper that disregarded a judge's prior restraint order. In 1986 and in a related opinion in 1987, the court ruled that it was permissible to violate a "transparently unconstitutional" court order if a quick appeal to the order was not available.[134] The First Circuit reversed a contempt citation issued by the U.S. District Court for Rhode Island against the *Providence Journal* for printing, contrary to a judicial order, information about Raymond L. S. Patriarca, a reputed crime boss in New England. After Patriarca died in 1985, the paper obtained from the FBI the results of an illegal wiretap on Patriarca's phone in the 1960s. However, Patriarca's son obtained a court order barring publication in the *Journal* on the grounds that his own right of privacy would be violated. The *Journal* was cited for contempt of court in November 1986 when it printed a story based on the FBI file in violation of the court order.

A three-judge panel of the First Circuit reversed the contempt order in December 1986. The panel said the order was a "transparently invalid" infringement of the First Amendment because the federal district judge had failed to meet the heavy burden of proof required by the U.S. Supreme Court before imposing a prior restraint. The court acknowledged the "bedrock principle" that court orders—even those later found to be unconstitutional—must be obeyed. However, the panel of judges said, "Of all the constitutional imperatives protecting a free press under the First Amendment, the most significant is the restriction against prior restraint on publication." The judges said that when a court order "transparently" violates the First Amendment the court "is acting so far in excess of its authority that it has no right to expect compliance" and the interest in preserving the integrity of the judicial system is not served by requiring it.

---

    [132]*Id.* at 509, 1 Media L. Rep. 1346, *quoting* Southern Railway Co. v. Lanham, 408 F.2d 348, 350 (5th Cir. 1969) (Brown, C. J., dissenting from denial of rehearing *en banc*.)

    [133]Dickinson v. United States, 476 F.2d 373, *cert. denied,* 414 U.S. 979 (1973).

    [134]*In re* Providence Journal, 820 F.2d 1342, 13 Media L. Rep. 1945 (1st Cir. 1986), *modified,* 820 F.2d 1354, 14 Media L. Rep. 1029 (1st Cir. 1987), *cert. dismissed,* 485 U.S. 693, 15 Media L. Rep. 1241 (1988).

In May 1987, the First Circuit, after rehearing the case *en banc,* affirmed the panel's opinion but attached a modification. The full court said that editors in the future who are ordered not to print a story must make a "good faith effort" to appeal a prior restraint before they publish in violation of the order. When editors are ordered not to print a story, the court said, they may publish and still challenge the constitutionality of an order only "if timely access to the appellate court is not available or if [a] timely decision is not forthcoming."[135] The First Circuit said it would have been "unfair" to apply its new requirement to the *Providence Journal* after the fact. Further, the court said, it was not sure whether "timely emergency relief" was available to the *Journal.*

The U.S. Supreme Court dismissed *United States v. Providence Journal* on procedural grounds, leaving intact the First Circuit's ruling in favor of the newspaper.[136] However, the rule in *Providence Journal* holds only for the First Circuit, and does not overturn *Dickinson* in the Fifth Circuit. Neither does the First Circuit's decision change the strong judicial bias generally toward upholding a contempt of court order in spite of the unconstitutionality of the order. Only appellate courts in Illinois[137] and Washington[138] have joined the First Circuit in allowing publishers who defied injunctions to challenge the validity of their contempt citations.

SUMMARY

Judges have substantial authority to cite individuals for contempt of court. Criminal contempt citations are used to punish disruptive behavior. Judges issue civil contempt citations to coerce people into following a court order, such as revealing confidential news sources. Congress, state legislatures, and the courts have provided substantial protection against contempt citations for persons writing about the courts. However, persons ordered not to publish information about court activity may be punished for contempt even if the order itself is ultimately declared invalid.

---

[135]*In re* Providence Journal, 820 F.2d 1354, 14 Media L. Rep. 1029 (1st Cir. 1987).
[136]485 U.S. 693, 15 Media L. Rep. 1241 (1988).
[137]Cooper v. Rockford Newspapers, Inc., 365 N.E.2d 746 (Ill. App. Ct. 1977).
[138]State *ex rel.* Superior Court of Snohomish County v. Sperry, 483 P.2d 608 (Wash.), *cert. denied,* 404 U.S. 939 (1971).

10

PROTECTION OF NEWS SOURCES, NOTES, AND FILM

While many of the conflicts between the courts and the press since *Sheppard v. Maxwell* have been settled or eased, the dispute over protecting journalists' notes, film, and confidential news sources continues to fester. On one side, many judges and lawyers believe that reporters should be required to testify in court like everyone else. On the other side, journalists tend to argue that their ability to report the news often depends on protecting the confidentiality of news sources.

In fact, reporters are frequently willing to go to jail, pay fines, or perform court-ordered community service rather than obey court orders requiring them to reveal the names of sources who provided information in confidence. In one of the most famous cases, *New York Times* reporter Myron Farber spent 48 days in jail and the *Times* paid $286,000 in fines when Farber refused to produce notes of his investigation into suspicious deaths in a New Jersey hospital. Farber's stories in the mid-1970s led to the murder indictment of Dr. Mario E. Jascalevich, who wanted to see Farber's notes for the preparation of his defense.

Farber said he refused to give up his notes because they would have revealed confidential sources he used to prepare his stories. Farber and other journalists argue that many potential news sources would not talk to the media if they suspected their identities would be made public. People who know about official corruption and criminal activity, reporters say, will keep the information to themselves because they fear for their jobs or their safety if they "blow the whistle" publicly. If reporters cannot promise confidentiality to sources, Farber said, there would be less information for the public "on a variety of important and sensitive issues, all to the detriment of the public interest."[1]

But judges order journalists to turn over notes or the names of sources to protect significant social interests such as the Sixth Amendment right of criminal defendants to obtain evidence in their favor and confront witnesses against them. In the case of the *New York Times*'s Myron Farber, Dr. Jascalevich wanted to know what the reporter was told by people expected to be called as witnesses during his trial for murder. Accused of poisoning hospital patients, Jascalevich wanted to know, for example, what Farber was told by Dr. Stanley Harris, the physician for several of the patients who died and who Jascalevich believed to be his "principal accuser."

In addition, law enforcement officials contend that journalists have a civic duty to help convict criminals through their testimony. Officials are frustrated when journalists write stories about drug possession and trafficking, but will not contribute information to related criminal investigations or testify in court. Reporter Robin Traywick was fined $1,400 when she refused to tell a grand jury the sources for stories about cocaine use she published in the *Richmond Times-Dispatch*. The grand jury was convened to investigate allegations in Traywick's stories that lawyers, judges, and other public officials were using cocaine and that some defendants arrested on drug-related charges were inexplicably receiving lenient treatment. Traywick's articles quoted sources who had been promised confidentiality.[2]

Finally, plaintiffs and defendants in civil suits sometimes contend that journalists have information that could determine who wins and who loses their litigation. In

---

[1] *In re* Farber, 394 A.2d 330, 4 Media L. Rep. 1360 (N.J. 1978).
[2] "Journalist Fined $1,400 for Refusing to Testify," *News Media & Law,* March–April 1983, at 46.

particular, plaintiffs suing the media for libel want access to story sources in order to prepare their cases. Richard Hargraves, an editorial writer for the *Belleville* (Illinois) *News-Democrat,* spent 54 hours in jail for refusing to reveal the names of sources for an editorial accusing a country official of lying to the public. The official, Jerry Costello, sued for libel and tried to find out the names of Hargraves's sources in order to prove that the editorial was false. Hargraves was released only when his sources revealed themselves.[3]

For three decades, judges and legislatures have been trying to reconcile the need for evidence in court with the desire of communicators to preserve the anonymity of their sources of information. The result so far is an uneasy compromise. In most states, reporters will not be found in contempt of court for refusing to disclose sources or other information until the importance of the journalists' testimony is demonstrated in court. However, much of the protection for reporters is provided on a case-by-case basis only after a court battle.

This chapter will discuss the statutes and judicial opinions that shield journalists who refuse to testify in court from contempt of court citations. The chapter also will discuss congressional subpoenas, government access to journalists' telephone records, and police searches of newsrooms.

PROTECTION UNDER THE COMMON LAW

Before the 1970s, courts usually held that journalists deserved no special protection when ordered to reveal the names of confidential sources. The courts did not extend to journalists the same common law privilege that protects the confidential relationships between lawyers and clients, doctors and patients, and priests and penitents.

Lawyers and doctors, for example, are usually not required to testify in court because society recognizes they render essential services that depend on confidentiality. Lawyers and doctors cannot effectively provide legal advice or practice medicine if clients and patients cannot be candid. Lawyers need to know all information pertinent to a criminal charge in order to provide the best defense. Doctors need to know intimate details about patient behavior to provide a correct diagnosis. Clients and patients will not be open and honest, and may not seek help in the first place, if they believe that embarrassing or incriminating information will be made public.[4]

However, judges and legal scholars argue that exemptions from the responsibility to testify in court should be kept to a minimum. As more people are excused from telling what they know, fewer remain to contribute evidence in the search for truth in court. Courts generally have refused to excuse reporters from testifying because news sources do not depend on journalists for their personal welfare in the same way that patients depend on their doctors or clients depend on their lawyers. The privilege for journalists, when recognized, is not based as much on a source's need to talk to a reporter as on the need for the public to receive information about crime and corruption that may otherwise not be published. Judges and lawyers argue that what journalists know about crime and corruption should be made public in the courts.

---

[3]"Column Leads to Jail," *News Media & Law,* Nov.–Dec. 1984, at 36.
[4]*See, e.g.,* J. Wigmore, 8 *Evidence in Trials at Common Law,* secs. 2291, 2380a (McNaughton rev. ed. 1961).

In addition, critics of a journalistic privilege contend that reporters do not have the same professional relationship with their sources that lawyers and doctors have with their clients and patients. Most journalists do not have three years of professional education in addition to a bachelor's degree. Journalists do not have to meet educational requirements or pass tests before they can write and publish stories. Journalists are not certified by state governments or subject to review by their peers, as doctors and lawyers are.

Despite the courts' reluctance to protect the confidentiality of the journalist-news source relationship, a limited common law privilege has emerged in a few state[5] and federal courts.[6] Still, most journalists have learned to seek protection from the U.S. Constitution and state statutes when receiving a subpoena, a judicial order to testify in court (*subpoena ad testificandum*) or to produce notes, tapes, or documents in court (*subpoena duces tecum*).

PROTECTION UNDER THE CONSTITUTION: THE FIRST AMENDMENT

Most courts provide a limited First Amendment privilege for reporters refusing to reveal confidential sources. The source of these rulings is *Branzburg v. Hayes,* a Supreme Court decision that appeared to say that journalists do not have constitutional protection when they refuse to reveal their news sources. However, lower courts have relied upon the concurring and dissenting opinions in *Branzburg* to create a limited First Amendment privilege for journalists.

The Supreme Court

In *Branzburg v. Hayes*, a 5–4 majority of the Supreme Court rejected a privilege under the First Amendment for three reporters who had refused to testify before three different grand juries.[7] The Supreme Court decided the cases from California, Kentucky, and Massachusetts with one opinion.

One of the reporters, Paul Branzburg of the *Louisville Courier-Journal,* was appealing two court orders to testify before two grand juries investigating drug use and sales. In 1969, Branzburg had written about two young men he watched making hashish near Louisville. Branzburg promised not to reveal the men's identities. In a second article, in 1971, Branzburg described the two weeks he spent watching and interviewing several dozen unnamed drug users in Frankfort, Kentucky. After each story, Branzburg was ordered to reveal to a grand jury the criminal activity he witnessed. He refused both times. Although a Kentucky law protects reporters from being forced to reveal sources, a state appellate court said the statute did not protect journalists who personally observed criminal acts.

The second reporter in *Branzburg,* Earl Caldwell of the *New York Times,* was

---

[5]*E.g.,* Senear v. Daily Journal-American, 641 P.2d 1180, 8 Media L. Rep. 1151 (Wash. 1982).
[6]See the section on federal statutes and regulations in this chapter.
[7]408 U.S. 665, 1 Media L. Rep. 2617 (1972).

subpoenaed to appear before a federal grand jury in Oakland, California, in 1970. The grand jury ordered Caldwell, who covered the militant black organization known as the Black Panther party, to bring notes and audiotapes of interviews with Panther officers and spokesmen. The grand jury was investigating allegations of Panther threats against the president, Panther involvement in assassination plots, and Panther participation in riots. Caldwell refused to appear and was found in contempt of the grand jury. The U.S. Court of Appeals for the Ninth Circuit reversed the contempt order, and the U.S. government petitioned for *certiorari.*

The third case before the Supreme Court in *Branzburg* also involved a journalist who had refused to answer grand jury questions about the Black Panthers. Paul Pappas, a television newsman-photographer, covered civil disorders in New Bedford, Massachusetts, in 1970. He had been allowed into a barricaded store serving as the headquarters for the Black Panthers while they waited for a police raid. Two months later Pappas told a grand jury what he had witnessed outside the Black Panthers' headquarters; but he would not answer questions about what took place inside the headquarters.

The three reporters told the grand juries that the First Amendment protected them from being forced to disclose confidential information. The reporters argued that journalists often have to promise confidentiality to a source in order to obtain information of value for the public. Each of the three reporters contended that if they were forced to reveal their confidences, people with information important to the public would become reluctant to speak to reporters, "all to the detriment of the free flow of information protected by the First Amendment." Caldwell, for one, argued that simply his appearance before the grand jury, regardless of what he might say, would destroy his working relationship with the Black Panthers. Since grand jury proceedings are secret, Caldwell said, the Black Panthers could never be sure what he had said or refused to say behind closed doors. Caldwell said the uncertainty of his sources about his grand jury appearance would drive "a wedge of distrust and silence between the news media and the militants," resulting in less public knowledge about Panther activities.[8]

Justice Byron White, writing the Court's majority opinion in *Branzburg,* weighed the First Amendment rights of the press against the obligation of every citizen to answer questions relevant to a criminal investigation. He said he could not see why the public interest in law enforcement should be overridden by "the consequential, but uncertain, burden on news gathering" that might result from insisting that reporters testify before grand juries.[9]

White emphasized the importance of the "long-standing principle that the public . . . has a right to every man's evidence,' " particularly during grand jury proceedings.[10] He said that stopping drug trafficking, assassination plots, and violent disorders was a "fundamental function" of government. Grand juries, which determine whether there is reason to believe a crime has been committed and whether there is sufficient evidence to bring charges, play "an important role in fair and efficient law

---

[8]*Id.* at 676, 1 Media L. Rep. at 2621.
[9]*Id.* at 690–91, 1 Media L. Rep. at 2627.
[10]*Id.* at 688, 1 Media L. Rep. at 2626.

enforcement.'' White did not think that reporters should be protected from testifying about someone who had committed a crime or someone who had evidence of criminal conduct. He said the Court could not adopt the theory ''that it is better to write about crime than to do something about it.''[11]

The Court in *Branzburg* put the burden on the press to establish that the flow of news would be constricted if journalists could not withhold the names of sources. White said the journalists had not demonstrated that substantial numbers of sources would remain silent if journalists were forced to testify before grand juries. He said the press had not been hampered in the past by being required to reveal sources, and he doubted sources would be inhibited by the possibility that a reporter might be required to disclose their names in court. White said that sources such as representatives of minority political groups would continue to speak to reporters because they needed the media to disseminate their views. White asserted that sources who were afraid of losing their jobs or who feared for their safety could trust their stories to officials as much as they could to the press.

Branzburg, Caldwell, and Pappas argued for a qualified, rather than an absolute, privilege for reporters to withhold the names of sources. The three did not claim that a reporter should never have to answer officials' questions. Rather, the reporters said they should not have to testify unless the government could establish (1) that a reporter had information relevant to a crime being investigated, (2) that the information was not available from other sources, and (3) that the need for the information was sufficiently compelling to override First Amendment concerns. But White said although the privilege recommended by Branzburg, Caldwell, and Pappas would presumably reduce the number of times that reporters would have to testify, the conditional privilege would not satisfy the needs of the press. Since the privilege was conditional, White said, predicting when and under what circumstances journalists would be compelled to testify would be difficult. He suggested the press could never guarantee a source that confidentiality would be protected by a court.

In addition, White said, establishing the qualified privilege recommended by the three reporters would mean a substantial burden for judges. White said the privilege would force judges to resolve several legal issues each time a reporter was subpoenaed to testify. The courts would have to answer such questions as whether the reporter possesses useful confidential information or whether the law enforcement interest in the information outweighs First Amendment values.

Judges would also have to determine, White said, which citizens would qualify for a constitutional press privilege. Implying that a privilege would have to be limited in order to protect the courts' interest in obtaining testimony, White said that judges would have to determine who was a journalist deserving of the privilege. Defining who was a journalist, he said, was ''a questionable procedure in light of the traditional doctrine that liberty of the press is the right of the lonely pamphleteer who uses carbon paper or a mimeograph.'' He said that lecturers, political pollsters, scholars, and novelists, as well as newspaper publishers, published information gathered from confidential sources. He added

---

[11]*Id.* at 692, 1 Media L. Rep. at 2628.

Almost any author may quite accurately assert that he is contributing to the flow of information to the public, that he relies on confidential sources of information, and that these sources will be silenced if he is forced to make disclosures before a grand jury.[12]

White said news gathering, including the protection of confidential sources, was "not without its First Amendment protections." He said that harassment of the press by officials in order to disrupt a reporter's relationship with news sources "would have no justification." However, White said that it is the job of legislators, rather than the courts, to weigh the need to protect confidential sources against the need for testimony. Congress and the state legislatures have the power to develop a statutory privilege. The task of judges is to uphold the law rather than make it, White said.

Justice Lewis F. Powell, Jr., who concurred with White's majority opinion, wrote separately to emphasize "the limited nature" of the Court's ruling. Powell suggested that newsmen have more First Amendment protection than White had conceded. Unlike White, Powell said the needs of law enforcement and of newsmen should be balanced on a case-by-case basis. He said news personnel might be protected if the information being sought is not directly relevant to an investigation or if the revelation would endanger confidential relationships with sources without "a legitimate need of law enforcement." Powell's opinion suggested that, in some circumstances, he would be willing to vote with the four-man minority to protect journalists who did not want to reveal confidential sources.

Justice Potter Stewart, writing a dissenting opinion, would have granted the three reporters in *Branzburg* the qualified privilege they sought. Stewart, in an opinion supported by Justices William Brennan and Thurgood Marshall, rebuked the "Court's crabbed view of the First Amendment." He said that the "delicate and vulnerable" nature of First Amendment freedoms requires special safeguards. Stewart said reporters have a limited First Amendment right to refuse to reveal sources, a right that stems from society's interest "in a full and free flow of information to the public." Stewart, in contrast to White, said the right to publish information would be severely curtailed without protection to obtain it in the first place.

Stewart, unlike White, believed confidentiality is sometimes necessary to the news-gathering process. Stewart said confidential sources are particularly important for "sensitive" stories involving government officials, political figures, dissidents, and minority groups. He said that government employees and dissidents with information valuable to the public may fear reprisals or censure if they are revealed as the sources behind news stories. They may only be willing to talk in confidence to a trusted reporter. Stewart said the Court's *Branzburg* decision would mean that "a public-spirited citizen, who is not implicated in any crime, will now be fearful of revealing corruption or other governmental wrongdoing." Since journalists could be forced to identify sources under court order, such persons may have to choose "between risking exposure by giving information or avoiding the risk by remaining silent."[13]

Stewart said the Court's decision in *Branzburg* forces journalists into a choice

---

[12]*Id.* at 705–707, 1 Media L. Rep. at 2632–33.
[13]*Id.* at 731, 1 Media L. Rep. at 2643 (Stewart, J., dissenting).

between two bad alternatives. Journalists can risk a contempt of court citation for failing to reveal news sources, or they can violate professional ethics by disclosing the name of a confidential source. Journalists who disclose confidential sources would have difficulty establishing future confidential relationships, Stewart suggested.

Stewart acknowledged the importance of "every man's relevant evidence" in the grand jury process. But he noted exceptions to the requirement to testify, such as the common law privilege protecting confidentiality between doctors and patients and the right against self-incrimination. Stewart said those exceptions to the obligations of citizens to testify protect private interests. He argued that a privilege shielding confidential relationships between reporters and their sources protects a public interest. A reporter's privilege would "insure nothing less than democratic decision-making through the free flow of information to the public."[14]

Stewart said that, until *Branzburg,* the Supreme Court had not made its protection of First Amendment values contingent on proof provided by journalists that the news-gathering process was inhibited. Stewart wanted the burden of proof shifted to the government. He said that officials should have to satisfy "a heavy burden of justification" before forcing a reporter to testify before a grand jury. Stewart said he would require the government to demonstrate there is

1. a probable cause to believe that a reporter has information "clearly relevant" to a specific violation of law,
2. evidence that the information sought cannot be obtained by alternative means less destructive of First Amendment values, and
3. "a compelling and overriding interest in the information."[15]

Two of Stewart's points parallel those in Powell's concurring opinion. Both Stewart and Powell would require that a request for confidential sources be relevant to an investigation. Stewart said the relevance requirement prevents the government from conducting a fishing expedition at the expense of the media. The relevance requirement also could prevent harassment of reporters and sources. Stewart said that, in the case of *New York Times* reporter Earl Caldwell, the government had not shown the probable commission of any new crimes.

Stewart also agreed with Powell that the government must demonstrate a need for a journalist's confidential information. However, Stewart would impose a heavier burden of proof on the government than Powell. Powell only required that a request for information serve a "legitimate need" of law enforcement rather than the "compelling and overriding" interest specified by Stewart.

Stewart agreed with the Ninth Circuit that the government had not established a compelling interest in Caldwell's testimony. Stewart said that Earl Caldwell had argued, without being refuted, that he had nothing to say in testimony that had not already been printed. Stewart said there was no evidence in the court record that Caldwell had information about illegal activities of the Black Panthers that he could give to the grand jury. On the other hand, Stewart believed that Caldwell had demon-

---

[14]*Id.* at 738, 1 Media L. Rep at 2646.
[15]*Id.* at 743, 1 Media L. Rep at 2648.

strated that his ability to report on the Black Panthers would be impaired if he were required to appear before a grand jury.[16]

Finally, Stewart said officials should have to prove they could not obtain the necessary information without forcing a journalist to testify, a point that Powell had not mentioned. Stewart said that if journalists were required to testify when the information was available elsewhere, the flow of information to the public would be disrupted without a resulting benefit to the courts. Stewart said that in the case of Earl Caldwell, the government had not shown that it had tried an alternative means to acquire the information it was seeking. Stewart wanted the government to show that the information it was seeking could not be obtained through police informants, other law enforcement agencies, or other witnesses.

Justice William O. Douglas, the fourth dissenter in *Branzburg,* argued that the First Amendment prohibited the government from requiring journalists to testify.[17] His views, coupled with those of Stewart, Marshall, Brennan, and Powell, added up to five justices who believed in limited First Amendment protection for journalists refusing to reveal their sources. Soon, lower courts began to rely on that arithmetic to create a qualified First Amendment privilege for journalists who refused to disclose confidential information. The Supreme Court has passed up several opportunities to overturn lower court application of the constitutional privilege.

Application of the Three-Part Test

Since *Branzburg v. Hayes,* most appellate courts deciding whether a reporter should be forced to testify have granted the journalist a limited First Amendment privilege. The privilege is usually based on the three-part test advocated by Justice Stewart in his *Branzburg* dissent.

The practical application of a qualified privilege for reporters varies greatly by jurisdiction. Many courts apply the privilege not only when reporters want to protect the anonymity of confidential sources but also when they refuse to produce documents, notes, and video that have not been published or broadcast. Some courts require reporters to establish that their news sources were promised confidentiality before the courts excuse the journalists from testifying.

Not all states base the qualified privilege on the U.S. Constitution. A few state courts have recognized a privilege in their state constitutions[18] or in the common law.[19] On the other hand, courts in some states, including Hawaii and Massachusetts, have rejected a qualified privilege.[20]

The application of a reporter's privilege depends not only on jurisdiction but also on the nature of the court proceeding and on who is seeking the information. Courts regularly rely on the three-part constitutional test when the testimony of journalists is sought for trials, but seldom when reporters are subpoenaed to appear before grand juries.

[16]*Id.* at 746–52, 1 Media L. Rep. at 2650–52.
[17]*Id.* at 712, 1 Media L. Rep. at 2636.
[18]*E.g.,* Zelenka v. State, 266 N.W.2d 279, 4 Media L. Rep. 1055 (Wis. 1978).
[19]*E.g.,* Senear v. Daily Journal-American, 641 P.2d 1180, 8 Media L. Rep. 1151 (Wash. 1982).
[20]Goodale and Moodhe, "Reporter's Privilege Cases," in J. Goodale, ed., 2 *Communications Law 1989,* at 321–76.

Courts ordinarily require reporters to testify before grand juries, particularly if the journalists witnessed criminal activity. The courts consistently follow the lead of the Supreme Court in *Branzburg v. Hayes,* where the Court emphasized the importance of grand juries to effective law enforcement and the need for "every man's evidence." Courts contend journalists deserve First Amendment protection against testifying only if they can establish that grand jury requests for testimony are conducted in bad faith or constitute harassment.[21] Reporters unable to meet this burden of proof are uniformly required to testify before a grand jury when they have witnessed the selling of drugs,[22] the possession of weapons,[23] or assaults.[24]

During trials, journalists are most likely to be required to testify when subpoenaed by the prosecution in criminal cases and by libel plaintiffs in civil cases. They are least likely to be ordered to reveal sources, notes, or tapes in criminal proceedings when a defendant is seeking information and in civil trials when a media organization is not a defendant.

Criminal Proceedings Courts use a three-part constitutional test in most criminal trials to determine whether reporters are required to reveal confidential sources or information in their possession. Usually, the deciding factor is whether the person seeking the information can demonstrate a compelling need.

During criminal trials, prosecutors seek information from the media less frequently than defendants but with relatively more success. Courts tend to take seriously the *Branzburg* admonition that reporters ought to "do something about crime" rather than write about it. Judges say that journalists should help prosecute criminals by testifying during trials as well as before grand juries.

However, criminal defendants trying to subpoena reporters seldom succeed, in spite of the Sixth Amendment right to compel testimony in their favor. Criminal defendants seldom obtain the information they seek because they can rarely meet all three parts of Stewart's test in *Branzburg*. In 1982, a federal appeals court affirmed the quashing of a subpoena served on *Sports Illustrated* because a defendant in a college basketball point-shaving scandal could not demonstrate that the information he sought was necessary to his defense. The U.S. Court of Appeals for the Second Circuit said that James Burke, who had been convicted, also had not shown that he tried to obtain the information from sources other than *Sports Illustrated*.[25]

The Second Circuit blocked Burke's attempt to obtain nearly all of the documents and tapes related to a 1981 *Sports Illustrated* article, "How I Put the Fix In," coauthored by Douglas Looney, a staff writer, and Henry Hill, a career criminal. In the article, Hill told his version of a scheme to fix Boston College basketball games during the 1978–79 season. According to Hill, brothers Rocco and Tony Perla had purchased the cooperation of two key Boston College basketball players, Richard

---

[21]*E.g., In re* Lewis, 377 F. Supp. 297 (C.D. Cal. 1974), *aff'd,* 501 F.2d 418 (9th Cir. 1974), *cert. denied,* 420 U.S. 913 (1975).

[22]Lightman v. State, 294 A.2d 149 (Md. Ct. Spec. App. 1972), *aff'd,* 295 A.2d 212, *cert. denied,* 410 U.S. 991 (1973).

[23]Bursey v. United States, 466 F.2d 1059, 1 Media L. Rep. 2652 (9th Cir.), *reh'g denied,* 466 F.2d 1092 (1972).

[24]*In re* Ziegler, 550 F. Supp. 530 (W.D.N.Y. 1982).

[25]United States v. Burke, 700 F.2d 70, 9 Media L. Rep. 1211 (2d Cir. 1983) *cert. denied,* 464 U.S. 816 (1983).

Kuhn and Ernie Cobb. The two players were paid if Boston College fell short of the point spread set by the bookmakers. Henry Hill and James Burke, a reputed mob boss, were to provide protection if the bookmakers discovered they were being swindled.

The scheme to fix Boston College games collapsed when the team came closer than planned to beating Holy Cross and the conspirators lost substantial sums of money. Soon afterward, Hill testified against his partners in exchange for immunity from prosecution. Burke was sentenced to 20 years in prison. Burke appealed, contending that the trial judge made several errors. One error, Burke argued, was the judge's failure to require that *Sports Illustrated* turn over the documents and tapes related to the Hill-Looney article.

When the Second Circuit applied Stewart's three-part test in *United States v. Burke,* the court said Burke satisfied only one prong of the test. The court said the documents and tapes being sought could have been relevant to his defense, the first part of Stewart's test. They might have contradicted the trial testimony of Henry Hill, who said that he and Burke were to provide protection for the operation from the bookmakers. However, the court said, Burke could not show that the materials were "necessary or critical" to his defense, an adaptation of Stewart's second requirement—that there was a "compelling and overriding interest" in the information. The *Sports Illustrated* documents and tapes were not critical to Burke's case because he only wanted to use them to attack Hill's credibility. The court said that there was already ample evidence to destroy Hill's credibility as a witness. The court said Hill had been convicted for loansharking, extortion, and trafficking in heroin, cocaine, and other drugs. He also had admitted to armed robbery, arson, and hijacking.

The Second Circuit said that Burke could not fulfill the third requirement of the Stewart test either. Burke had not sought the information from other available sources. For example, he had not subpoenaed a witness to the interviews of Hill by the *Sports Illustrated* writer Looney.

Sometimes the application of the three-point test results in a journalist being required to testify, as occurred in *United States v. Criden.*[26] In 1980, the U.S. Court of Appeals for the Third Circuit upheld an order holding reporter Jan Schaffer of the *Philadelphia Inquirer* in contempt of court after she refused to testify during a trial arising from the FBI's Abscam operation. The defendants in the trial, a lawyer and three Philadelphia city councilmen, were charged with receiving bribes from FBI agents posing as Arab sheiks. The defendants argued the bribery charges should be dismissed because the prosecutors purposely released "sensational and prejudicial information," making a fair trial impossible.

After one of the prosecutors, U.S. Attorney Peter F. Vaira, admitted giving Schaffer information, the defendants wanted to ask the reporter what she thought about Vaira's motivation and credibility. Schaffer refused to say whether she had talked with Vaira, arguing that any answers might lead to a disclosure of sources. Schaffer claimed she could refuse to testify under a First Amendment privilege.

However, the Third Circuit said that Schaffer's First Amendment privilege had to be considered in light of the defendants' Sixth Amendment right to compel testi-

---

[26]633 F. 2d 346, 6 Media L. Rep. 1993 (3d Cir. 1980), *cert. denied sub nom.* Schaffer v. United States, 449 U.S. 1113 (1981).

mony in their favor and their Fifth Amendment protection against the deprivation of life, liberty, and property without due process of law. The court, deciding that it had to balance the constitutional rights of Schaffer against those of the defendants, turned to a version of the three-part test.

The Third Circuit said the information sought from Schaffer was both relevant and important. Information about Vaira's motivations and credibility was central to the question of misconduct by the prosecution. In addition, the defendants had demonstrated that they had tried to get the pertinent information from other sources. They had called Vaira to testify, and they had unsuccessfully tried to obtain a report of an investigation of Abscam leaks undertaken by the U.S. Justice Department. They had convinced the court that "only Schaffer" could testify to Vaira's credibility during telephone conversations between the two of them.

Courts have applied the reporters' constitutional privilege not only to the mass media but also to specialized publications. For example, the same court that decided the *Burke* case applied a three-point test when several states subpoenaed documents from an oil industry news service. The states wanted information about prices for petroleum products to use in antitrust litigation. The states argued that oil companies conspiring to fix gasoline prices may have communicated price information through reporters working for *Platt's Oilgram Price Report*. *Platt's* refused to provide documents containing confidential news sources. The U.S. Court of Appeals for the Second Circuit said the states provided no evidence that the names of confidential sources were relevant to the antitrust claims. Further, the states failed to establish that the information could not be obtained elsewhere.[27] Courts have also applied the privilege in cases involving a medical newsletter[28] and publications of the Photo Marketing Association International.[29]

However, unlike the Second and Third circuits of the U.S. Courts of Appeals, some courts refuse to recognize a First Amendment privilege for reporters. The New Jersey Supreme Court upheld fines and a jail sentence for *New York Times* reporter Myron Farber in a case mentioned at the beginning of the chapter. Farber's reporting helped reopen an investigation into 13 deaths in a New Jersey hospital in 1965 and 1966. The investigation led to the indictment of Dr. Mario E. Jascalevich for poisoning five patients in an alleged attempt to discredit their physicians. Prosecutors argued that Jascalevich had killed patients by injecting them with a powerful muscle-relaxing drug, curare, after relatively safe operations.

When Farber refused to provide materials requested by the defense, he was found in contempt of court. The trial judge fined Farber $1,000 and sentenced him to six months in jail. The judge fined the *New York Times* $100,000. In addition, in an effort to obtain Farber's testimony, the judge fined Farber $1,000 a day and sentenced him to jail until he produced the materials. The judge also fined the *New York Times* $5,000 for every day Farber refused to comply with the court's order. In all, the *New York Times* paid $286,000 and Farber spent 40 days in jail.[30] Although Far-

[27]McGraw-Hill, Inc. v. Arizona, 680 F.2d 5, 8 Media L. Rep. 1525 (2d Cir. 1982).

[28]Apicella v. McNeil Laboratories, Inc., 66 F.R.D. 78 (1975).

[29]*In re* Photo Marketing, 327 N.W.2d 515, 9 Media L. Rep. 1087 (Mich. Ct. App. 1982).

[30]Eventually New Jersey Governor Brendan Byrne pardoned Farber and returned part of the fine. Friendly, "Times and Reporter Granted Byrne Pardon in 'Dr. X' Case," *New York Times,* Jan. 19, 1982, at 1.

ber never provided the information sought, a jury found Jascalevich not guilty. Farber was released when Jascalevich was acquitted.

The New Jersey Supreme Court, hearing Farber's appeal of the contempt ruling, said the U.S. Supreme Court in *Branzburg v. Hayes* refused to recognize a First Amendment privilege for journalists. The New Jersey court said the five-man *Branzburg* majority required no consideration of the interests of journalists as Stewart had proposed in his dissent. The court said that a journalist's obligation to appear at a criminal trial on behalf of a defendant ''is at least as compelling as the duty to appear before a grand jury,'' a duty that the U.S. Supreme Court said in *Branzburg* should override any burden on news gathering.[31]

The Farber case illustrates that a court may decide that an individual journalist has no First Amendment right to refuse to reveal news sources in spite of general judicial trends to the contrary. Indeed, Farber was punished in spite of a strong New Jersey law designed to protect journalists from forced disclosure.

Civil Trials   Whether a court demands reporters' sources or notes in civil suits depends in large part on whether a news organization is a party to the suit. If the newspaper or broadcast station fighting a subpoena is not the defendant in a civil suit, the courts will almost always recognize the constitutional privilege and decide in favor of the news medium. When newspapers and broadcast stations are defendants in libel suits, judges are more reluctant to apply a qualified privilege.

Civil Suits: Journalist as Third Party   The courts seldom require writers or editors to disclose information to either party in a civil suit when the journalists themselves are not directly involved in the case. The courts regularly decide that the civil litigants seeking notes or the names of sources in such cases cannot meet the requirements of the three-part test.

Civil suits present different issues than criminal prosecutions. Most important, the Constitution does not give to civil litigants the same power to require testimony on their behalf as it does for criminal defendants. In addition, defendants in civil suits, because they do not face the possibility of jail or death, may have less at stake in the disclosure of information protected by journalists. Furthermore, many civil suits do not have a direct and substantial impact on public health and safety such as criminal cases involving rapes and murders.

A federal appeals court decided the most significant civil case involving confidential news sources in 1972, less than six months after the Supreme Court decided *Branzburg*. In *Baker v. F & F Investment,* the U.S. Court of Appeals for the Second Circuit upheld the right of a prominent magazine journalist to refuse to reveal his source after using a variation of the three-point test. The journalist, Alfred Balk, had written ''Confessions of a Block-buster'' for the *Saturday Evening Post.* The 1962 story, which documented discriminatory real estate practices in Chicago, was based on information supplied by an anonymous source given the pseudonym of ''Norris Vitcheck.'' The source told Balk how he scared whites living near black neighborhoods into selling their houses to him at low prices. ''Vitcheck'' then sold those

---

[31]*In re* Farber, 394 A.2d 330, 334, 4 Media L. Rep. 1360, 1363 (1978).

houses to blacks for substantial profits. Several years after the article appeared, a group of blacks sued about 60 landlords, real estate companies, and real estate investors, contending that they sold homes to blacks for excessive prices. The blacks wanted Balk to identify ''Vitcheck.''

The Second Circuit said the blacks had not demonstrated a sufficiently compelling need for the information to override the First Amendment values at stake. The court distinguished *Branzburg* because, it said, *Branzburg* protected the integrity of the criminal justice system. The court, noting the ''preferred position'' of the First Amendment, said that at least in civil cases the public interest in protecting a journalist's confidential news sources ''will often be weightier than the private interest in compelled disclosure.''[32] In the case at hand, the Second Circuit did not mention the Stewart three-part test but relied on similar criteria. The court said the identity of the source ''did not go to the heart'' of the case, a phrase often used when confidential sources are either not relevant or not necessary to a case. The Second Circuit also noted that according to the trial court judge no alternatives to identifying Balk's source had been tried. The failure of litigants to establish that they have sought other sources is often cited by judges who refuse to require journalists to divulge notes or sources in civil cases.

In addition, courts in civil cases frequently require persons seeking information from journalists to demonstrate that their suits are not frivolous, that is, that the cases have legal merit. Judges appear to be trying to protect the media from divulging information when a suit has no chance of succeeding and may, indeed, have been filed only to discover information held by the media.

Libel Suits   Courts are more reluctant to protect journalists' confidential news sources in civil suits involving media defendants than in suits in which the media are not parties to cases. Courts frequently order journalists to reveal sources and notes when they are subpoenaed by libel plaintiffs. A few judges have strictly limited news media defenses in libel suits when reporters refuse to reveal the names of anonymous sources used for defamatory stories.

Judges generally insist that libel plaintiffs must have the opportunity to prove that newspapers or broadcast stations acted negligently or recklessly when preparing defamatory stories. Federal courts are more likely than state courts to use a variation of the three-part constitutional privilege and more likely to allow a journalist to withhold information in a libel suit. However, even federal courts sometimes order media defendants in libel cases to respond to subpoenas in order for plaintiffs to obtain evidence for their suits.

For example, in *Miller v. TransAmerican Press,* a federal appeals court said the only way the plaintiff could meet his burden of proof in a libel case was to know who accused him of corruption. In *Miller,* the U.S. Court of Appeals for the Fifth Circuit ordered a trucking magazine to disclose a confidential informant even though the court recognized a constitutional privilege for reporters.[33] The court decided that the

---

[32]Baker v. F & F Investment, 470 F.2d 778, 785, 1 Media L. Rep. 2551, 2556 (1972), *cert. denied,* 411 U.S. 966 (1973).

[33]621 F.2d 721, 6 Media L. Rep. 1598 (5th Cir. 1980), *modified,* 628 F.2d 932, 6 Media L. Rep. 2252, *cert. denied,* 450 U.S. 1041 (1981).

editor of *Overdrive* magazine must disclose the only source for the assertion that Teamsters union official Dusty Miller swindled the union's pension fund out of $1.6 million to buy a business. The court said the only way that Miller, as a public figure, could demonstrate that the magazine acted with *New York Times* actual malice was to know the name of the only source of the accusation.

Relying on the three-part test Justice Stewart suggested in *Branzburg,* the Fifth Circuit said that the identity of the person who told *Overdrive* that Miller swindled the union was relevant to Miller's libel suit. The court noted that Miller had tried unsuccessfully to prove that *Overdrive* was reckless through means other than the magazine's confidential source. Miller had searched through notes and documents provided by the magazine and had questioned a union source the magazine had suggested. The court determined that Miller had a compelling interest in *Overdrive's* confidential source because the union official had to prove the magazine knew the story was false or that the magazine had recklessly relied on the source. In order to do that, the court argued, Miller had to know the source of the allegation.

In a modification of the Fifth Circuit's first opinion, the court added that libel plaintiffs must demonstrate that the libel suit was not frivolous before the court would order confidential sources disclosed. The plaintiff would be required to prove essential ingredients of a successful libel suit, that defamation had been published and the defamation was false, requirements that Miller had already met, the court said. The safeguards provided by requiring plaintiffs to meet the Stewart test and basic elements of their burden of proof in a libel suit, the court implied, were essential to protect First Amendment interests. A court order to disclose confidential sources not only risked deterring sources from talking to journalists, but risked retaliation of the plaintiff against the informant, the court said.

However, the Fifth Circuit suggested, the First Amendment interest in confidential sources must yield when plaintiffs need the names of persons relied upon in defamatory stories to defend their reputations. The court noted that the U.S. Supreme Court had ruled, in *Herbert v. Lando,* that journalists have no First Amendment right to refuse to testify when a libel plaintiff is seeking evidence of *New York Times* actual malice. In *Herbert v. Lando,* discussed in Chapter 3, the Supreme Court ruled that journalists do not have a First Amendment privilege to refuse to provide information about how a story is investigated and written. In *Herbert,* which did not involve confidential sources, "60 Minutes" producer Barry Lando was required to tell Lieutenant Colonel Anthony Herbert how he decided what to include in a broadcast critical of the army officer. The Supreme Court said such an exploration into the journalistic process was justified because public-figure libel plaintiffs must prove actual malice.[34] The Court said that plaintiffs could not show knowing falsehood or reckless disregard for the truth if they did not know what writers and editors were thinking when they put a story together.

After the Supreme Court's decision in *Herbert v. Lando,* some courts cited the opinion when requiring journalists to respond to subpoenas for sources and information obtained without promises of confidentiality. Courts required reporters to testify and to produce materials, such as notes and newsroom memos, related to the editorial process.[35]

[34]441 U.S. 153, 3 Media L. Rep. 2575 (1979).

[35]*E.g.,* Cape Publications v. Bridges, 387 So.2d 436, 6 Media L. Rep. 1884 (Fla. Dist. Ct. App. 1980).

In addition, courts have relied upon *Herbert* not only to require media defendants to disclose sources as in *Miller,* but also to justify punitive measures if the sources are not revealed. Several courts after *Herbert* ruled that news organizations refusing to reveal confidential news sources have to defend themselves in libel suits as if the sources did not exist. Some courts even decided that newspapers or broadcast stations refusing to divulge sources have no defense.[36] In New Hampshire, for example, the state supreme court relied heavily on *Herbert v. Lando* when it said that there is "no absolute privilege" that allows the press to refuse to reveal sources of information "essential" to a libel plaintiff's case.[37] In *Downing v. Monitor Publishing,* former police chief Clayton Downing of Boscawen sought the names of sources who had told the *Concord Monitor* that he had failed a lie detector test. The New Hampshire Supreme Court not only affirmed the lower court ruling to compel disclosure of the newspaper's sources but also said a stronger enforcement mechanism than contempt of court might be needed to protect the rights of libel plaintiffs.

The New Hampshire Supreme Court noted that reporters held in contempt for refusing to reveal sources often choose to go to jail rather than to obey court orders to provide information. Putting journalists in jail "in no way" helps a libel plaintiff obtain sufficient information to prove his case, the court said. Therefore, the court decided, if a journalist refuses to reveal a source, the court would assume no source was used. Thus a newspaper or broadcast station may have to prove the lack of recklessness or negligence without using the information gained from the confidential source and even without saying in court that a source existed.

The more uncompromising approaches, like that of *Downing*, have been limited to a minority of cases that became less frequent in the late 1980s. However, the treatment of subpoenas by plaintiffs in libel suits varies widely among the state court systems. Many courts do not rely on the three-part constitutional test, and journalists are usually ordered to disclose their confidential sources in cases before those courts.

Therefore, in libel suits, journalists not only have to weigh the possibility of fines or jail sentences when deciding whether to make promises protecting the confidentiality of sources, but they also have to consider the possibility of having to defend a libel suit. Before publishing a defamatory story, journalists should be confident they can prove to a jury they are accurate and have exercised sufficient care in the preparation of the article without reliance on confidential sources. On occasion, newspapers and broadcast stations may face the dilemma of having to decide whether to break a promise of confidentiality or risk losing a libel case.

PROTECTION UNDER THE CONSTITUTION: THE FIFTH AMENDMENT

Under the rare circumstances that journalists are criminal defendants, they may be able to withhold the names of confidential news sources by relying on the Fifth Amendment to the U.S. Constitution. Anyone charged with a crime can claim the

---

[36]*E.g., see* Mehra, "Sanctions for Reporters Who Refuse to Disclose Sources in Libel Cases," 60 *Journ. Q.* 437 (Autumn 1983).

[37]Downing v. Monitor Publishing, 415 A.2d 683, 686, 6 Media L. Rep. 1193, 1194 (1980).

Fifth Amendment protection against being "compelled in any criminal case to be a witness against himself."

Jerry Seper of the *Arizona Republic,* at risk of being charged with a crime, relied on the Fifth Amendment in 1983. Seper, using confidential sources from within the Internal Revenue Service, had written two stories about an IRS investigation of the United Liquor Company. Following the publication of the articles, United Liquor sued an IRS agent and an unnamed defendant for illegally disclosing confidential information from the company's tax returns. In preparing for the trial, United asked Seper to name the sources for his stories. Seper refused on the grounds that identifying his sources would incriminate him since it was unlawful to publish information obtained from tax returns. The U.S. Court of Appeals for the Ninth Circuit upheld Seper's claim of a Fifth Amendment privilege. The court acknowledged that when Seper said in a deposition that his first story was based on information obtained from two IRS agents, he already had revealed enough that he could be charged with "willfully" publishing tax return information that he had not been authorized to see. But, the court said, in order to successfully prosecute Seper, the government would have to prove that the disclosure to Seper had been "unauthorized," that Seper "willfully" published the information, and probably that Seper knew that the information was given to him illegally. The court said the government would probably have a stronger case if it knew Seper's sources.[38]

The Fifth and First amendments to the Constitution are not, of course, the only sources of protection for journalists who want to refuse to reveal confidential news sources. There are also state and federal statutes and executive guidelines.

SUMMARY

The Supreme Court decided 5-4, in *Branzburg v. Hayes,* that reporters do not have First Amendment protection to refuse to testify before grand juries. Justice White, writing the majority opinion, said that journalists had not demonstrated that they should be accorded a privilege under the First Amendment that allowed them to refuse to reveal confidential sources. However, Justice Powell, casting the deciding vote, said in a concurring opinion that the First Amendment rights of journalists should be measured case by case against the needs of law enforcement. Powell said that journalists should be able to quash subpoenas if they could prove they were being asked for information irrelevant to an investigation or unnecessary to a legitimate need of law enforcement. Justice Stewart, in dissent, said that in order to compel testimony from journalists the First Amendment should be interpreted to require government officials to prove that there was probable cause to believe the information was relevant to a specific investigation, that the need for the information was sufficient to overcome First Amendment interests, and that no alternative way of acquiring the information was available.

Since *Branzburg,* a First Amendment privilege is seldom granted in grand jury

---

[38]United Liquor Co. v. Gard, 705 F.2d 1499, 9 Media L. Rep. 1697 (9th Cir. 1983). *See* Burdick v. United States, 236 U.S. 79 (1915); Blanchard, "The Fifth Amendment Privilege of Newsman George Burdick," 55 *Journ. Q.* 29-36 (Spring 1978).

contexts, and journalists are therefore almost always required to testify when subpoenaed in grand jury investigations. However, in cases not involving grand juries, most appellate courts have added Justice Powell's vote to that of the four dissenters in *Branzburg* and have recognized a qualified First Amendment privilege for reporters refusing to disclose confidential sources. Most appellate courts require persons who want to subpoena a journalist to meet a three-part test based on Stewart's *Branzburg* dissent. Through the protection afforded in the three-part test, appellate courts more often than not decide that journalists do not have to testify in criminal cases. Prosecutors in criminal cases try to subpoena journalists less often than the defense, but generally have a little more success in convincing the courts to uphold a forced disclosure of information. Reporters are seldom required to testify when information is being sought by parties to civil suits that do not directly involve the media. The courts are more reluctant to grant the privilege and to rule in favor of journalists when a newspaper or broadcast station is being sued for libel.

On the rare occasions when journalists are criminal defendants they may be protected from revealing confidential news sources by pleading the Fifth Amendment.

PROTECTION UNDER STATE STATUTES

Although the Supreme Court in *Branzburg* said the First Amendment did not protect reporters from being compelled to testify before grand juries, the Court did not say the Constitution prohibited state legislative protection for confidential sources. Indeed, the Court found "merit" in leaving Congress and the state legislatures free to fashion statutory privileges for journalists.[39]

While Congress has not passed legislation providing protection for journalists,[40] 28 state legislatures have. States that have adopted statutes protecting journalists, known as "shield laws," are Alabama, Alaska, Arizona, Arkansas, California, Colorado, Delaware, Georgia, Illinois, Indiana, Kentucky, Louisiana, Maryland, Michigan, Minnesota, Montana, Nebraska, Nevada, New Jersey, New Mexico, New York, North Dakota, Ohio, Oklahoma, Oregon, Pennsylvania, Rhode Island, and Tennessee. California is the only state to provide for a privilege within its state constitution.[41]

Although the shield laws vary widely, about a dozen state statutes are similar to Alabama's:

> No person engaged in, connected with or employed on any newspaper, radio broadcasting station or television station, while engaged in a news-gathering capacity, shall be compelled to disclose in any legal proceeding or trial, before any court or

[39]408 U.S. at 706, 1 Media L. Rep. at 2633.

[40]*E.g., see* Comment, "The Fallacy of *Farber:* Failure to Acknowledge the Constitutional Newsman's Privilege in Criminal Cases," 70 *J. Crim. L. & Criminology* 299, 310 (1979).

[41]*E.g., see* "Confidential Sources & Information; A Practical Guide for Reporters in the 50 States," *News Media & Law,* Fall 1989 (pullout). *See also* "States Adopt Shield Laws, Amendments," *News Media & Law,* Spring 1990, at 39.

before a grand jury of any court, or before the presiding officers of any tribunal or his agent or agents, or before any committee of the legislature or elsewhere the sources of any information procured or obtained by him and published in the newspaper, broadcast by any broadcasting station, or televised by any television station on which he is engaged, connected with or employed.[42]

The Alabama statute and others like it are considered to be "absolute" in the sense that nothing is said to qualify or give exceptions to the privilege that excuses journalists from having to reveal confidential sources. However, the Alabama law does not shield all journalists. For example, it does not protect the authors of articles written for magazines or business newsletters. In addition, the statute appears to require publication before any protection is provided. Unpublished notes and tapes may be subpoenaed. Further, the statute on its face would appear to protect only a journalist who refuses to reveal the name of a source and not a journalist who refuses to reveal information from notes.[43] The limitations the Alabama legislature has imposed on the statutory privilege are typical of the laws of many states.

Seven of the more important points to consider when evaluating a shield law are: who is protected, whether confidentiality is required for protection, what kind of information is protected, whether publication is required, in what legal forums the privilege can be asserted, whether the privilege can be waived, and whether exceptions to the privilege are specified.[44]

People Protected

Justice White's majority opinion in *Branzburg* questioned how judges could decide who is a journalist for the purposes of a constitutional privilege. White implied that determining who should be protected by a privilege and who should not would be difficult since practically all writers could argue they contribute to the public knowledge. Legislators adopting shield laws have the difficult task of specifying who ought to be shielded from disclosing sources or information in court. The list must be limited in some way or it could prove to be a haven for anyone who does not want to testify in court.

Most of the 28 states with shield laws allow protection for those connected to "newspapers, radio, and television" or the "news media." About a dozen states appear to protect anyone employed by the news media. Another dozen protect only persons involved in the news process, including editors and photographers. One state statute, Alaska's, applies only to "reporters."[45]

Virtually all laws exclude book authors, free-lance writers, academic researchers, and others not working directly in news organizations. Many states, such as Alabama, exclude magazine writers. Michigan amended its shield law in 1986 to protect

---

[42]Ala. Code sec. 12-21-142 (Michie 1986).

[43]*But see* Brothers v. Brothers, 16 Media L. Rep. 1031 (Ala. Cir. Ct. Marshall Co. 1989) (statute protects reporter's documents as well as information about the location of an interview).

[44]For an outline of state shield laws, *see* "Confidential Sources & Information: A Practical Guide for Reporters in the 50 States," *News Media & Law,* Fall 1989 (pullout).

[45]Alaska Stat. sec. 09.25.150 (Michie 1983).

broadcast journalists for the first time.[46] However, a few states, including Alaska, Illinois, and Louisiana—but not California—shield persons engaged in reporting or editorial activities for "motion pictures."[47]

Minnesota and Nebraska have adopted among the broadest descriptions of persons covered by shield laws. The statement of principle in the Minnesota shield law asserts the statute was written to provide a privilege against the disclosure of new sources and other information for the "news media." The law protects any person "directly engaged in the gathering, procuring, compiling, editing or publishing of information for the purpose of transmission, dissemination or publication to the public."[48] Nebraska's law may be even broader than Minnesota's. It protects persons engaged in "procuring, gathering, writing, editing, or disseminating" not only news, but also "other information." In addition, the Nebraska statute applies to "any medium of communication," which includes, but is not limited to, "any newspaper, magazine, other periodical, book, pamphlet, news service, wire service, news or feature syndicate, broadcast station or network, or cable television system." The Nebraska statute appears broad enough to apply to work of communicators such as public relations professionals.[49]

The courts generally interpret shield laws strictly when asked to apply a privilege to a category of persons not specifically mentioned in a state law. For example, a California court ruled in 1982 that a free-lance writer investigating the death of actor John Belushi was not protected under the California shield law when he did not have an agreement with a news organization to publish his work. The California law prohibited contempt of court citations for persons "connected with or employed by" the media. A California Superior Court said the fact that Christopher Van Ness was a published free-lance writer or that he had decided to write about the death of Belushi did not qualify him for protection under the California statute when he was subpoenaed to appear before a grand jury. "Intentions, hopes or expectations to later market a piece of writing" were not sufficient, said the court. Neither did Van Ness qualify for shield law protection because he had tried unsuccessfully to sell his work to at least one magazine and one newspaper. The court said Van Ness had no relationship that he could claim made him "connected with or employed by" either publication. Van Ness only qualified for the California shield law protection once he entered into a "contractual understanding" with NBC. Otherwise, said the court, "any intrusive and self-anointed busybody' " could use the privilege to avoid testifying in legal proceedings.[50]

Sometimes a strict interpretation of a shield statute produces results that seem to nullify the law. In Montana, for example, the shield law specifically protects a person employed by a wire service to gather news from being required to disclose information obtained in the course of his or her employment. However, in 1978, a Montana

---

[46]"Outtakes Not Protected from Grand Jury," *News Media & Law,* Spring 1987, at 30. *See* Michigan v. Storer Communications, 13 Media L. Rep. 1901 (Mich. Ct. App. 1986).

[47]Alaska Stat. sec. 09.25.220 (1) (A) (ii) (Michie 1983); La. Rev. Stat. sec. 45: 1451(f) (West 1982); Cal. Evid. Code sec. 1070 (1966 & West Supp. 1990).

[48]Minn. Stat. Ann. sec. 595.023 (West 1988).

[49]Neb. Rev. Stat. secs. 20-145(2), 146 (1987).

[50]*In re* Van Ness, 8 Media L. Rep. 2563 (Cal. Super. Ct. 1982).

state trial court said the statute protected only reporters and not their employers. Therefore, the Associated Press was ordered to produce an audiotape of a telephone conversation between an AP reporter and a man who admitted shooting a highway patrolman.[51]

Confidentiality Requirement

A few state shield laws specify that a reporter must have promised confidentiality to a source to be protected by the statute. However, most of the state statutes, like that of Alabama, do not explicitly say whether a promise of confidentiality is required for a journalist to be protected under the law.

The Tennessee Supreme Court, among others, has ruled that the state's statute, protecting "any information or the source of any information" from disclosure, protects journalists whether or not they promise confidentiality. The Tennessee court's opinion said the statutory protection for "any" information means "all" information is protected.[52] The court noted that the legislature had not qualified its protection of "any information" in the statute by requiring that a promise of confidentiality be made. The court reversed a lower court decision that would have required the disclosure of "any and all correspondence, studies, reports, memoranda, or any other source material" used by Memphis newspapers for stories about a bridge collapse.

However, some courts have interpreted a shield law to require a promise of confidentiality if the state statute does not explicitly protect journalists from subpoenas when a promise of confidentiality has not been made. For many years, New York state courts said that reporters who had not promised confidentiality fell outside a state law protecting journalists who refused to reveal "any news or the source of any news coming into his possession."[53] Although the New York shield law did not require that a reporter promise confidentiality to a source to qualify for protection, New York state courts ruled that reporters could claim a privilege under the statute only if a promise of confidentiality was made. Therefore, a court in 1984 refused to quash a subpoena for the tape of an interview Mike Wallace conducted for "60 Minutes." During the 7-hour interview in Beirut, Lebanon, George Gregory Korkala freely discussed in front of a camera the selling of weapons to terrorists, a violation of U.S. law. When Korkala was returned to the United States to stand trial, a district attorney subpoenaed the portions of the taped interview that had not been broadcast. Instead of quashing the subpoena, a New York appellate court ordered that the tape be given to a trial court judge to determine, *in camera,* whether the tape was necessary for the prosecution of Korkala.[54] However, six years later, in 1990, the New York

[51]*In re* Investigative File, 4 Media L. Rep. 1865 (Mont. D.C. 1978).
[52]Austin v. Memphis Publishing Co., 655 S.W.2d 146, 149, 9 Media L. Rep. 2070, 2072 (1983). *See also, e.g.,* Hammarley v. Superior Court, 89 Cal. App.3d 388, 4 Media L. Rep. 2055 (Cal. Ct. App. 1979); Aerial Burials Inc. v. Minneapolis Star & Tribune Co., 8 Media L. Rep. 1653 (Minn. Dist. Ct. Hennepin Co. 1982); Brothers v. Brothers, 16 Media L. Rep. 1031 (Ala. Cir. Ct. Marshall Co. 1989).
[53]N.Y. Civ. Rights Law sec. 79-h(b) (Law. Co-op. 1982 & 1989 Supp.).
[54]New York v. Korkala, 471 N.Y.S.2d 310, 10 Media L. Rep. 1355 (Sup. Ct. A.D. 1984). *But see* O'Neill v. Oakgrove Construction Inc., 523 N.E.2d 277, 15 Media L. Rep. 1219 (N.Y. 1988) (a qualified privilege under both the U.S. and state constitutions may protect journalists refusing to divulge nonconfidential materials).

legislature revised its shield law to protect reporters from disclosing information regardless of whether a promise of confidentiality was made.[55]

Information Protected

States are divided over whether to shield reporters from revealing notes and other information as well as sources. Some states protect reporters from testifying only when the journalists want to withhold the name of a source. Other states offer protection against disclosure of any information in the possession of a reporter or other media employee. Only a few state statutes specifically say that outtakes, film, and photographs are protected from forced disclosure.

The Alabama shield law, quoted above, if strictly interpreted, would protect only "the sources" of information obtained by news personnel.[56] However, the Tennessee statute applies to "any information" as well as "the source of any information" obtained for publication or broadcast.[57] Nebraska protects sources, information, and "all notes, outtakes, photographs, film, tapes, or other data."[58]

Although the text of the Pennsylvania state law provides protection only against the disclosure of "the source of information," the state's supreme court has interpreted the language broadly. The Pennsylvania Supreme Court said the "source of information" includes *all* sources of information, including tape recordings, memoranda, notes, and reports.[59]

Most statutes do not protect reporters who have been called to testify about something they have seen rather than to reveal a source or information given to them by a source. More than one court has held that a statute shielding confidential news sources from disclosure does not protect a reporter who witnessed a crime from testifying. Paul Branzburg, the *Louisville Courier-Journal* reporter of *Branzburg v. Hayes,* tried to avoid appearing before two grand juries by arguing he was protected by the Kentucky shield law. Although the Kentucky statute provided without qualification that reporters do not have to reveal their sources, the Kentucky Court of Appeals said the law did not apply to Branzburg's case because Branzburg's own observation was the source of the story. Branzburg was subpoenaed to testify about criminal acts, the making and using of drugs, that he had witnessed.[60] He could not protect the identity of the young men who had made the drugs even though he would have had no story without his promise to maintain their anonymity. Branzburg could have been jailed or fined had he remained in Kentucky. However, he had moved to

---

[55]"New York State Votes Stricter Law Protecting Reporters' Notes," *New York Times,* March 22, 1990, at A16.

[56]Ala. Code sec. 12-21-142 (Michie 1986). *But see* Brothers v. Brothers, 16 Media L. Rep. 1031 (Ala. Cir. Ct. Marshall Co. 1989).

[57]Tenn. Code Ann. sec. 24-1-208(a) (Michie 1980 & Supp. 1989).

[58]Neb. Rev. Stat. sec. 20-145(5) (1987).

[59]*In re* Taylor, 193 A.2d 181, 1 Media L. Rep. 2675 (Pa. 1963).

[60]Branzburg v. Pound, 461 S.W.2d 345 (Ky. 1970), *aff'd sub nom.* Branzburg v. Hayes, 408 U.S. 665, 1 Media L. Rep. 2617 (1972). *See also* Branzburg v. Meigs, 503 S.W.2d 748 (Ky. 1971), *aff'd sub nom.* Branzburg v. Hayes, 408 U.S. 665, 1 Media L. Rep. 2617 (1972). *But see* Brothers v. Brothers, 16 Media L. Rep. 1031 (Ala. Cir. Ct. Marshall Co. 1989) (Alabama shield law interpreted to protect against revealing the location of a reporter's interview with a woman to her ex-husband).

Michigan by the time his case was considered by the U.S. Supreme Court, and Michigan refused to extradite him.[61]

Publication Requirement

Slightly more than half of the 28 state shield laws appear to provide protection whether or not the subpoenaed information is published. About a half-dozen statutes, including Alabama's, require publication in order for the statutory protection to be triggered. State statutes that require publication will not ordinarily protect information or pictures that reporters and editors decide to leave out of newspapers and news broadcasts.

In contrast, Minnesota's shield law protects against the disclosure of "any unpublished information," and therefore a state court quashed a subpoena for half a page of notes a reporter said she did not use or rely on for a story. Minneapolis freelance journalist Joanna Conners turned over to a plaintiff in a libel case her handwritten notes and a transcription of a tape-recorded interview that contained published information. She deleted from the notes and transcripts information she said she did not use.[62]

Where Privilege Can Be Asserted

Most shield laws appear to protect journalists from a subpoena initiated by any legal authority. Others prevent subpoenas only in a narrow range of circumstances.

Most shield laws protect newspersons asked to testify before any administrative, judicial, or legislative body. Some, like the one in Alabama, are more detailed. Alabama protects reporters before "any legal proceeding or trial, before any court or before a grand jury of any court, or before the presiding officers of any tribunal or his agent or agents, or before any committee of the legislature, or elsewhere." A few state statutes cover only civil proceedings or only criminal proceedings. Some indicate that they do not apply in the case of a newsperson asked to testify in a libel suit.

Waiver

Most state shield laws do not address whether a journalist's privilege is lost, or *waived,* when the source becomes known or the journalist discloses part of a confidential conversation. A few statutes indicate that limited disclosure, publication, or testimony by a journalist does not waive the privilege protecting against the forced disclosure of additional information. However, a few shield laws provide that informants can destroy the privilege of a newsperson by revealing their own identity.

Although the New Jersey shield statute does not contain a waiver provision, the state's rules of evidence do. The state's rules declare that a person claiming a privilege

[61]Goodale, "*Branzburg v. Hayes* and the Developing Qualified Privilege for Newsmen," 26 *Hastings L.J.* 709, 719 (1975).

[62]Aerial Burials Inc. v. Minneapolis Star & Tribune Co., 8 Media L. Rep. 1653 (Minn. Dist. Ct. Hennepin Co. 1982).

cannot refuse to testify if any part of the confidential information is disclosed. However, the New Jersey shield law provides for a privilege for information "whether or not it is disseminated." In the case *In re Schuman,* the New Jersey Supreme Court ruled the shield law controlled. The court said *New Jersey Herald* reporter Evan Schuman did not have to appear in court to affirm a story he wrote about a murder confession. The court said that Schuman's disclosures in the story were protected because the state shield law explicitly covered information already disseminated. The court also recognized that the "legislature has continuously acted to establish the strongest possible protection from compulsory testimony for the press."[63]

Sometimes reporters, such as Jan Schaffer of the *Philadelphia Inquirer,* refuse to acknowledge a source even though the source is otherwise revealed. In *United States v. Criden,* Schaffer contended that if she confirmed or denied that she had talked to one source, investigators could determine whether she had talked to other confidential sources. However, the U.S. Court of Appeals for the Third Circuit ruled that Schaffer had to testify after criminal defendants satisfied the three-part test.[64]

Exceptions

Most shield laws, like that of Alabama, are "absolute" in the sense that they do not qualify or limit a journalist's privilege or list exceptions to the statutory protection against the disclosure.

In states that list exceptions to their shield laws, the most frequent limitation is a three-part test similar to the one advocated by Justice Stewart in *Branzburg v. Hayes.* In Tennessee, for example, the state shield law protects a journalist from compelled testimony unless the person seeking the information can demonstrate that (1) the information sought relates to a specific, probable violation of law, (2) the information cannot be obtained through alternative means, and (3) there is a compelling and overriding public interest requiring disclosure.[65] Journalists are shielded from testifying if persons seeking the information cannot meet all three criteria.

A few states require disclosure when necessary to prevent "a miscarriage of justice,"[66] a provision that could be used if a judge believed a reporter's testimony was critical to the defense of a criminal defendant. Some states simply indicate that the privilege can be revoked if disclosure is essential to the public interest.[67]

Pros and Cons of Shield Laws

The benefits of shield laws tend to be both too easily dismissed and too often overestimated. Journalists sometimes overlook the protection of shield laws because they would prefer protection under the First Amendment. Journalists argue that shield laws adopted by legislatures can also be rescinded by legislatures. Journalists contend

[63]552 A.2d 602, 16 Media L. Rep. 1092 (1989).
[64]*See* 633 F.2d 346, 6 Media L. Rep. 1993 (3d Cir. 1980).
[65]Tenn. Code Ann. sec. 24-1-208(c) (2) (A)–(C) (1980 & Michie Supp. 1986).
[66]*E.g.,* N.D. Cent. Code Ann. sec. 31-01-06.2 (1976).
[67]*E.g.,* La. Rev. Stat. sec. 45:1453 (West 1982).

that a constitutional privilege would be more respected by the courts than legislated protection. Reporters and editors also argue that the protection against testifying afforded by statutes is necessarily limited because statutes must define who should be protected and under what conditions. Many news personnel would prefer a broadly stated privilege under the First Amendment that can be interpreted on a case-by-case basis in the courts. The courts could determine when a privilege under the First Amendment should apply without predetermined exceptions.

However, First Amendment protection has its limits as well. A constitutional privilege is unlikely to protect journalists subpoenaed to testify before grand juries and journalists who witness criminal activity. It may not be available in libel litigation. In addition, journalists cannot predict when a court will use the three-part test and how it will be applied in an individual case. Although the privilege available through shield laws is not absolute, journalists ordinarily can determine whether a shield law will apply to their situation. In addition, the mere existence of shield laws helps thwart subpoenas. Lawyers are less likely to seek a subpoena for the purpose of "fishing" for information when a state statute clearly grants a reporter a shield against testifying.

Journalists working in states with shield laws should be cautious before relying on the states' statutes. Shield laws are not only limited by a myriad of exclusions and exceptions, but judges have tended to interpret them strictly. Many journalists and sources have counted on shield law protection only to find that a statute did not apply in their case. Many reporters therefore have faced penalties, including jail, they had not anticipated and might not have risked if they had known no protection existed. A reporter must not only know what a state shield law says but also how that law could be interpreted by the courts.

Judges have not only tended to interpret shield laws strictly, but a few courts have declared that shield laws represent illegal interference by a legislature into the affairs of the judiciary. In 1982, for example, New Mexico's Supreme Court ruled the state's shield law violated the state constitution on the grounds that the legislature could not establish rules governing evidence and procedure for the courts.[68] In addition, courts sometimes rule that shield laws unconstitutionally interfere with the Sixth Amendment rights of criminal defendants. The New Jersey Supreme Court ruled that *New York Times* reporter Myron Farber had to produce subpoenaed materials in the murder trial of Dr. Mario E. Jascalevich despite the state's shield law. The New Jersey court agreed that "it is abundantly clear" that Farber fell under the New Jersey law providing news media employees with the privilege of refusing to reveal information collected during their professional activities. However, the court said the state's shield law conflicted with both federal and state constitutional provisions that gave defendants the right "to have compulsory process for obtaining witnesses" in their favor.[69]

---

[68]Ammerman v. Hubbard Broadcasting, 551 P.2d 1354 (N.M. Ct. App. 1976). The same New Mexico Supreme Court later promulgated a rule providing journalists with a limited privilege. *See also* Farr v. Los Angeles County Superior Court, 22 Cal. App.3d 60, 69–70, 1 Media L. Rep. 2545, 2549 (1971).

[69]*In re* Farber, 394 A.2d at 337–38, 4 Media L. Rep. at 1364–65 (1978).

The lack of complete protection for confidential sources means that a journalist should consider carefully any promise not to reveal the identity of sources. A reporter may want to promise only conditional confidentiality. That is, a reporter will promise to protect the identity of a source unless required to reveal it by a court order. Indeed, some lawyers suggest that reporters require sources to sign affidavits as evidence the source exists. Many news organizations require that editors be told when reporters are using confidential news sources. Journalists should keep in mind that their news organizations may not provide lawyers to help fight subpoenas if the reporters do not adhere to company policy.

SUMMARY

Twenty-eight states have adopted statutes protecting journalists from revealing news sources. These statutes vary greatly, but none protects every writer in all circumstances. Most apply only to news media employees. A few specify that they apply only when confidentiality has been promised. About half of the statutes apply only to the disclosure of sources and not to notes and other information. The rest protect information in the possession of reporters as well. Journalists need to be aware of the limitations of their states' shield laws before relying on them for protection against a court order to testify.

PROTECTION UNDER FEDERAL STATUTES AND REGULATIONS

No federal statute explicitly protects reporters from being ordered to testify in court. However, rules governing the federal courts and regulations issued by the Department of Justice restrict the use of subpoenas served on reporters.

Several courts, for example, have protected reporters from subpoenas under rules of evidence Congress adopted for use in the federal courts. Section 403 of the Federal Rules of Evidence allows judges to quash subpoenas if information sought from reporters would duplicate information already available. In addition, section 17(c) of the Federal Rules of Criminal Procedure limits the use of subpoenas to obtaining evidence that can actually be used during a trial rather than only during the pretrial discovery process.[70] Time, Inc., the parent company of *Sports Illustrated,* used Rule 17(c) to quash a subpoena sought by a man convicted in a basketball point-shaving scandal. In a case discussed earlier in the chapter, James Burke tried during the discovery phase of his trial to obtain documents and tapes related to a *Sports Illustrated* article about efforts to fix Boston College basketball games. In *United*

---

[70]*See also* Fed. R. Evid. 501; Fed. R. Civ. Pro. 16(b)(1), 26(b)(1); Riley v. Chester, 612 F.2d 708, 714 n.6, 5 Media L. Rep. 2161, 2165 n.6 (3d Cir. 1979).

States v. Burke, trial judge Henry Bramwell held that under Rule 17(c) the subpoena was premature. Burke wanted to see if he could discredit the key government witness against him, Henry Hill, by locating any statements by Hill in *Sports Illustrated*'s file that were inconsistent with testimony Hill would eventually give at trial. However, Judge Bramwell said that only after Hill testified during the trial could the judge determine whether *Sports Illustrated* would be required to turn over any materials. Only after Hill's testimony at trial, Bramwell said, could he evaluate the issue of whether Hill had made inconsistent statements. During the trial, Hill would have to show he had a compelling need for the material and could not otherwise obtain it.[71]

In addition to the rules governing the federal courts, the U.S. attorney general issued guidelines in 1973 to limit requests for journalists' confidential sources by federal law enforcement officials. The guidelines were written "to strike the proper balance" between the public interest in an unrestricted flow of information and the public interest in fair and effective law enforcement.[72] Since being amended in 1980, the guidelines apply to civil litigation as well as criminal investigations.

The guidelines reflect the protections for journalists recognized in Stewart's three-part test in *Branzburg v. Hayes.* The guidelines require that before subpoenaing journalists Justice Department employees must seek alternative sources and negotiate with the media when possible. The guidelines specify that the government should seek subpoenas only when there are "reasonable grounds" to believe that the information is relevant and essential to an investigation or case. The scope of the subpoena should be as narrow as possible, limiting the amount of material affected. No subpoena is to be issued without the authorization of the U.S. attorney general.

Justice Department guidelines helped lead to the quashing of a subpoena issued to *Miami Herald* medical writer Patrick Malone. In 1982, federal law enforcement officers wanted Malone to verify statements in an article attributed to Dr. Fredrick Blanton, a Ft. Lauderdale eye surgeon charged with illegally dispensing the drug methaqualone. A U.S. district court quashed the subpoena, saying the government did not follow the Justice Department's guidelines and the qualified First Amendment privilege suggested in *Branzburg v. Hayes.* The government had not negotiated with Malone to see if it could obtain the information it needed without a subpoena nor had it tried to get the information it wanted from anyone besides Malone.[73]

When the Justice Department guidelines were amended in 1980, they included for the first time limitations on subpoenas seeking journalists' long-distance telephone records. The new provisions were added after a federal appeals court ruled in 1978 that the news media had no constitutional right to be notified before telephone companies turned over the records of long-distance phone calls to law enforcement officers. In *Reporters Committee for Freedom of the Press v. AT&T,* several reporters, two newspaper companies, and the Reporters Committee for Freedom of the Press tried to block government access to a journalist's long-distance billing information if the journalist was not told beforehand. The journalists sued AT&T after the

---

[71]United States v. Burke, 7 Media L. Rep. 2019 (E.D.N.Y. 1981), *aff'd,* 700 F.2d 70, 9 Media L. Rep. 1211 (2d Cir. 1983), *cert. denied,* 464 U.S. 816 (1983).

[72]28 C.F.R. 50.10, 6 Media L. Rep. 2153 (1980).

[73]United States v. Blanton, 534 F. Supp. 295, 8 Media L. Rep. 1107 (S.D. Fla. 1981).

company released toll-call records to government officials five times between 1971 and 1974. In one case, the FBI used phone records to try to link Daniel Ellsberg to the publication of the Pentagon Papers, discussed in Chapter 2. In another, the Internal Revenue Service sought evidence to confirm that an IRS employee had illegally divulged information to *New York Times* reporter David Rosenbaum.

The media argued before the U.S. Court of Appeals for the D.C. Circuit that release of the long-distance records without warning journalists violated their First and Fourth amendment rights. The journalists said that government access to reporters' phone records, containing numbers called and the time and date of calls, threatened the confidentiality of sources. The media contended that the government could use the records to identify sources, even sources unrelated to a current law enforcement investigation.[74]

The D.C. Circuit, citing the Supreme Court's decision in *Branzburg v. Hayes,* said that the media had no First Amendment right to prevent the government from seeing telephone records that allow the identification of a news source. In *Reporters Committee,* the court said the First Amendment did not guarantee anyone, including journalists, the right to collect information immune from good-faith investigations by the government. No one, said the court, is insulated from the inhibitions that result from knowing the government has the authority to investigate criminal activity. The court added:

> All citizens when they choose to act surreptitiously are put to some inconvenience; they must lower their voices, put little or nothing in writing, speak and meet outside the presence of third parties; these simple precautions are commonly used, whether the ends be lofty or evil. Plaintiffs are no exception simply because they are "journalists."[75]

In addition, the court said that telephone records are not protected by Fourth Amendment restrictions on government searches. Persons using the phone system knowingly expose their actions to third parties, thus surrendering Fourth Amendment rights protecting private affairs from unreasonable government encroachment. The court said the government was free to investigate criminal activity by examining the telephone records of persons who might have been in contact with a suspect.

The Justice Department guidelines amended after *Reporters Committee* limited any subpoena for telephone records to specific and relevant information essential to an investigation. The guidelines also say the government should pursue alternative approaches to obtaining the information being sought before officials seek a subpoena. The government need not notify the media prior to subpoenaing telephone records if prior notice poses "a substantial threat to the integrity" of an investigation.[76] However, if a news organization is not warned about a subpoena for telephone records, it must be notified within 90 days of the time the subpoena is issued. The U.S. attorney general must ordinarily approve a subpoena for telephone records.

---

[74]593 F.2d 1030, 4 Media L. Rep. 1177 (D.C. Cir. 1978), *cert. denied,* 440 U.S. 949, 4 Media L. Rep. 2536 (1979).
[75]*Id.* at 1059, 4 Media L. Rep. at 1197.
[76]28 C.F.R. 50.10, 6 Media L. Rep. at 2154–55 (1980).

SUMMARY

There is no federal shield law. However, several courts have recognized a privilege for reporters under federal rules of procedure adopted by Congress for the federal courts. In addition, the U.S. attorney general has adopted guidelines designed to limit the use of subpoenas served on journalists.

CONGRESSIONAL AUTHORITY

The judicial branch is not the only arm of the federal government with the power to subpoena reporters and cite journalists for contempt for refusing to disclose sources or information. Although no reporter has been found in contempt of Congress in the last 25 years, a few have been threatened with contempt citations for refusing to testify during congressional investigations.[77] One of the last to be threatened was then-CBS correspondent Daniel Schorr, who refused to tell how he obtained a secret House committee report on the operations of the Central Intelligence Agency. Although Schorr did not reveal his source to the House Committee on Standards of Official Conduct, the committee did not recommend, as it could have, that Schorr be cited for contempt.[78] In previous years, the courts have been reluctant to reverse contempt of Congress citations because of the doctrine of separation of powers.

SEARCH WARRANTS

In the 1970s, a few media personnel faced a legal weapon—the search warrant—more threatening to confidential information than a subpoena. Although subpoenas require reporters to testify in court or produce documents for the court, the recipient of a subpoena can challenge it before complying. In contrast, a search warrant allows no opportunity for a journalist to prepare a response and no opportunity for a court challenge. A search warrant authorizes law enforcement officers to make unannounced searches for journalists' notes and photographs.

Many law enforcement officers prefer search warrants to subpoenas because they do not believe journalists will respond to subpoenas. In addition, the officials fear that journalists will destroy or hide evidence while fighting a subpoena. News personnel fear search warrants because confidential information kept in a newsroom can be seized. Journalists are afraid that a proliferation of newsroom searches would drive potential confidential sources underground. Sources could reasonably decide that journalists could not enforce promises to keep confidential information from law enforcement officers.

---

[77] See *Newsman's Privilege: Hearings Before the Subcomm. on Administrative Practice and Procedure of the Senate Comm. on the Judiciary,* 89th Cong., 2nd Sess. 57–61 (1966). For a discussion of legislative use of the contempt power, *see* R. Goldfarb, *The Contempt Power* 25–45 (1963).

[78] See D. Schorr, *Clearing the Air* (1977); "The Daniel Schorr Investigation," *Freedom of Information Center Report,* No. 361 (Oct. 1976).

Thus far, however, there have been only about a dozen publicized searches of newsrooms in just a half-dozen states. In addition, state and federal statutes have largely neutralized a 1978 Supreme Court opinion that permitted police to conduct unannounced searches of newsrooms.

The Supreme Court said, in its 1978 opinion in *Zurcher v. Stanford Daily,* that the U.S. Constitution permitted the police to search without warning the homes and offices of people who are not criminal suspects. The Court said that neither the First nor the Fourth amendments prohibit law enforcement officers with a search warrant from searching for criminal evidence on property used or owned by law-abiding citizens. The 5–3 decision permitted searches of newsrooms, corporate offices, and private homes and cars.

In *Zurcher,* the Stanford University student newspaper challenged a 1971 search of its office. The search occurred after *Stanford Daily* photographers took pictures of a student takeover of Stanford University Hospital's administrative offices. When policemen tried to remove the demonstrators, violence erupted and several officers were hurt. The injured policemen could not identify most of the people involved. Police photographers did not see the violence.

When the Santa Clara County district attorney saw pictures of the incident in the *Stanford Daily,* he obtained a warrant from the municipal court for a search of the paper's offices for film, negatives, and prints showing the events at the hospital. The warrant said officials had probable cause to believe that "material and relevant" evidence helpful to identifying the persons involved in the violence was in the *Stanford Daily* offices. Documents accompanying the search warrant did not contend that anyone connected with the paper had violated the law. Indeed, the search of the student newsroom did not produce anything that had not been published. The *Stanford Daily* and members of the staff complained that the search violated their rights under the First, Fourth, and Fourteenth amendments.

The Fourth Amendment, as discussed in the privacy chapter, protects citizens "against unreasonable searches and seizures" of their person, houses, papers, and effects and declares that no warrants should be issued "but upon probable cause" specifically "describing the place to be searched, and the persons or things to be seized." The students argued that warrants authorizing searches of places occupied by "third parties," persons not directly suspected of crimes, should not ordinarily be allowed.

The Supreme Court said in *Zurcher* that the Fourth Amendment provides no special exemption for searches involving third parties when authorities have probable cause to believe that they can find criminal evidence. In addition, said Justice Byron White, writing for the Court, the First Amendment does not protect the news media from searches. White said the First Amendment only requires the courts to adhere to Fourth Amendment requirements with "particular exactitude." He said the preconditions for a warrant—probable cause, specificity with respect to the place to be searched and the things to be seized, and overall reasonableness—should provide adequate protection for journalists.[79] Justice White also said that the legislative and executive branches could adopt laws and regulations protecting against the abuse of search warrants.

---

[79]436 U.S. 547, 555–60, 3 Media L. Rep. 2377, 2379–85 (1978).

Journalists feared that the Supreme Court's *Zurcher* opinion would encourage law enforcement officers to use search warrants as an alternative to subpoenas, and those fears were fueled by a few searches conducted shortly after *Zurcher* was announced. In Flint, Michigan, police searched the printing plant of the *Flint Voice,* a monthly newspaper that had been critical of the mayor. In addition, a prosecutor in Boise, Idaho, armed with a search warrant, rummaged through the desks and files of television station KBCI-TV until he found film of a prison riot. The news media launched a major lobbying campaign to encourage state legislatures and the U.S. Congress to adopt statutes that would blunt the impetus for searches triggered by the Supreme Court's opinion in *Zurcher.*

In response to the concerns of the news media, several state legislatures and the U.S. Congress adopted legislation to protect newsrooms from searches. The federal law, the Privacy Protection Act of 1980, severely restricts the use of search warrants to look for or seize information in the possession of public communicators. Only in exceptional circumstances can federal, state, and local law enforcement officers search for criminal evidence in the offices of the news media, book authors, and others who intend to disseminate information to the public.

The Privacy Protection Act puts the most severe restrictions on searches for "work product materials" obtained and prepared for public dissemination. Work product materials are notes, story drafts, film, outtakes, mental impressions, and opinions. The statute prohibits searches for work product materials unless federal and state law enforcement officers can establish beforehand that (1) there is a probable cause to believe a reporter has committed a crime, (2) there is reason to believe that seizure of the materials is necessary to prevent an injury or death, or (3) the materials contain information "relating to the national defense, classified information, or restricted data" as defined under federal espionage laws. The government needs to prove only one of the three in order to meet its obligation under the statute. Under the Privacy Protection Act, the Stanford student newspaper offices could not have been searched. There was no evidence that any student journalist had committed a crime, that the photographs were needed to save a life, or that any student journalist held national security secrets.

The Privacy Protection Act allows officials to search for "documentary materials" under more circumstances than they may search for "work product materials." Documentary materials are pieces of information recorded in tangible form that are obtained during the preparation of a story. Documentary materials do not qualify as work product materials because they are not a journalist's work product or do not contain a journalist's ideas. Government documents or tapes made by hostages are examples of documentary materials. Law enforcement officials may not only search for and seize "documentary materials" when there is reason to believe a journalist has committed a crime, reason to believe a life can be saved, or national security information to protect, but also when a journalist does not produce the materials in response to a subpoena. In addition, law enforcement officers can search for documentary materials if they can demonstrate they have a reason to believe the materials would be altered, destroyed, or hidden if a reporter were served with a subpoena.

The Privacy Protection Act and similar state laws provide public communicators with substantial protection against unannounced searches. Law enforcement officers ordinarily will have to rely upon a subpoena rather than a search warrant to obtain confidential information from the media. However, the provision allowing searches for national security information would have allowed for an unannounced search of the offices of the *New York Times* for the Pentagon Papers.

In addition, despite the statutes, at least a half-dozen news organizations have been subjected to unannounced searches in the last few years. Several searches have taken place in California and Minnesota. In California, both a judge who issued one warrant and officials who conducted a search under a second admitted they had erred. In San Bernardino County in 1988, a judge who issued a warrant for a search of a Riverside television news bureau later admitted the warrant violated California law. The judge had issued a warrant for a search of a bureau of KCBS-TV in spite of a law that prohibited warrants to search for confidential sources or unpublished information. During the search, sheriff's deputies seized tapes never used in a broadcast of a raid on an animal research lab by animal rights activists. The judge ordered the sheriff to return the tapes that were seized. In the second California case, Santa Clara County officials paid the *Viet Nam Nhat Bao* newspaper and the *Tan Van Magazine* $25,000 in compensatory damages after a search for evidence of violations of state welfare laws. Authorities seized not only business records in the 1987 raid, but also editorial matter including unpublished manuscripts, photographs, and letters to the editor unrelated to the allegations of welfare abuse. The publisher of both publications said the seizures forced her to miss deadlines and cancel one issue of the magazine. Santa Clara County officials paid the out-of-court settlement after admitting they should not have taken the material.[80]

SUMMARY

The U.S. Supreme Court decided in *Zurcher v. Stanford Daily* that the First Amendment does not protect communicators from searches for criminal evidence, even when they are not suspected of criminal activity. The impact of the decision has been blunted by state and federal statutes encouraging the use of subpoenas rather than search warrants in most circumstances.

BREACHING CONFIDENTIALITY

This chapter has focused on the efforts of journalists to honor their promises of confidentiality to news sources. Occasionally, however, a reporter or editor decides to reveal the name of a source who wanted to remain anonymous. When two Minnesota newspapers broke the promises of their reporters not to publish the name of a source, the source sued, contending the newspaper violated a binding legal agreement. In 1990, the Minnesota Supreme Court ruled that the *Minneapolis Star & Tribune* and the *St. Paul Pioneer Press Dispatch* had not violated a binding contract when the

---

[80]"FBI, Police Invade Newsrooms," *News Media & Law,* Fall 1988, at 4, 5. *Also see* "Cops Confiscate Student Video of Shoot-out," *News Media & Law,* Spring 1989, at 12.

editors of the papers printed the name of a source who had been promised confidentiality. The court also ruled the broken promise of confidentiality could neither be considered a legal misrepresentation nor enforced through a common law doctrine protecting promises.

The two Minnesota newspapers were sued by Dan Cohen, a public relations consultant and spokesman for the 1982 Independent-Republican gubernatorial candidate in Minnesota. Cohen offered four reporters a confidential tip six days before the election. After being promised that his identity would not be disclosed, Cohen supplied each reporter with documents showing that the Democratic-Farm-Labor party candidate had been convicted 12 years before of shoplifting $6 worth of merchandise. WCCO-TV decided not to use the story. The Associated Press distributed the story but did not identify Cohen as the tipster. However, the editors of the *Star & Tribune* and the *Pioneer Press Dispatch* decided to name Cohen as the source of the story in spite of both the reporters' promises to Cohen and their protests against revealing his name. The editors said that readers needed to know that the shoplifting story came from the opposing candidate's campaign staff in order to gauge the credibility of the information and the motivation behind its release. They said the story of one candidate's campaign "releasing eleventh hour information" about an opponent was more important than a story about a 12-year-old shoplifting charge that had been vacated.

When the stories appeared, Cohen lost his job as a public relations executive with an advertising firm and sued the newspapers. Cohen contended the reporters' agreements with him met the legal requirements for a valid contract: (1) a promise by one person to do something, (2) that is accepted by a second person, (3) in exchange for something of value. Cohen said the reporters' promises not to disclose his identity in return for the campaign information, an agreement that he accepted, was a binding oral contract the editors broke when they published his name. Cohen also argued that the "revocation" by the editors of the reporters' commitment constituted a legal misrepresentation by the newspapers. A jury agreed with Cohen, awarding him $700,000 from the two papers for misrepresentation and breach of an oral contract. The Minnesota Court of Appeals upheld Cohen's contract claim but reversed the jury on the claim of misrepresentation.[81]

The Minnesota Supreme Court affirmed the appellate court decision that the reporters' promises to Cohen did not constitute misrepresentation.[82] The court found no mispresentation, or fraud, because the newspaper reporters did not know that Cohen's name would be printed when they promised to keep his name confidential. Even Cohen agreed, the court said, that the reporters had intended to keep their promises, and were overruled by their editors.

The Minnesota Supreme Court also held that the newspapers' decisions to print Cohen's name in spite of the reporters' promises of confidentiality did not constitute a breach of contract. The court said that although the agreement between the reporters and Cohen involved the elements of a contract—offer, acceptance, and consideration—every exchange of promises is not a binding contract under law. The

---

[81]Cohen v. Cowles Media Co., 445 N.W.2d 248, 16 Media L. Rep. 2209 (1987).
[82]17 Media L. Rep. 2176 (1990).

Minnesota court said that in the news-gathering process, both the reporter and source "understand that the reporter's promise of anonymity is given as a moral commitment" rather than a binding offer and acceptance of an offer. "What we have here," said the court, "is an 'I'll-scratch-your-back-if-you'll-scratch-mine' accommodation."

The court said each party to a confidential source relationship assumes risks in what is more of an ethical agreement than a binding contract. The court noted that the length and conditions of the promise of confidentiality are seldom spelled out. The reporters, said the court, cannot know whether they should have promised confidentiality until they see the information, which is after the promise has been made. The court said that editors make decisions to honor confidential relationships only in the larger context of news developments. Neither the source nor the journalists can predict the consequences of publication, said the court.

The Minnesota Supreme Court also refused to enforce the promises of confidentiality to Cohen through a common law doctrine that requires that a promise be legally enforced if breaking the promise creates an "injustice." The Minnesota court was reluctant to enforce the common law doctrine because the issue of whether Cohen had been treated unjustly required an inquiry into the editorial processes that would inhibit constitutionally protected reporting. The court said it would have to consider such issues as whether Cohen's name was newsworthy, whether Cohen could have been identified only as a "source close to the campaign," and whether publishing Cohen's name was necessary for a balanced story. However, the court said, the controversy over the promise of confidentiality to Cohen arose in "the classic First Amendment context" of a political campaign. The potential for civil damages for decisions made by journalists in the context of political reporting "chills public debate," the court said, "a debate Cohen willingly entered." The court said in Cohen's case an enforcement of the common law would be a violation of the First Amendment.

Two Minnesota Supreme Court justices dissented angrily to the *Cohen* opinion. Justices Kelley and Yetka said that the newspapers broke a contract and should be compelled to keep their promises like anyone else. Justice Yetka said the Cohen decision could lead to less information for the public because some sources may be more reluctant to talk to the press knowing that the press may not be held responsible for breaking promises of confidentiality.

SUMMARY

The supreme court of one state has said that editors' decisions to override reporters' promises of confidentiality did not constitute misrepresentation, breach of contract, or a common law violation of a binding agreement.

11

ACCESS TO INFORMATION

While the First Amendment protects the right to publish information about public issues, it does not guarantee the right to collect information, even information about the government. The U.S. Supreme Court has refused to provide First Amendment protection for the news-gathering process beyond the access to criminal trials discussed in the previous chapter. The First Amendment does not ensure that a reporter can gain entry to a city council meeting, obtain a consultant's report about the quality of drinking water, or visit the site of a nuclear power plant accident.

If the U.S. Constitution does not protect a communicator's access to information, neither does the common law. Traditionally, judges have not required that governmental bodies in the United States meet publicly or allow everyone to inspect their records. However, a right of access to government meetings and records has been legislated in the United States, primarily during the last 30 years.

Access law, like the right to publish, is grounded in American political theory. Since government in the United States is based on the will of the public, citizens need to know what government is doing. Thomas Jefferson said that only an informed electorate could govern effectively.[1] Professor Alexander Meiklejohn wrote that citizens who are denied information will make decisions that are "ill-considered" and "ill-balanced."[2] Professor Thomas Emerson said a democracy without an informed public is a contradiction in terms.[3]

If access to information is important to our system of government, so is the security of government records. National defense depends on secret military tactics and capabilities. Law enforcement officers would have more difficulty catching criminals if suspects could discover what the police knew and planned to do. The government could not obtain tax information, census data, or research results on new drugs if it could not ensure confidentiality. The release to the public of government-held information about the health or finances of individual citizens could infringe on their privacy.

While government officials withhold some records from the public as a matter of public policy, they deny the public access to other information for personal and political reasons. Some officials want to hide embarrassments and improprieties. Other officials believe they can make decisions more efficiently if they do not have to debate every policy option in public. In addition, policy decisions can be justified more easily when officials control what the public knows.

Despite the reasons for withholding information, the American public probably has more access to information about government than people in any other country. In the United States, most legislative bodies meet in public most of the time. Some administrative bodies also meet in public. The public has access to criminal arrest records, property records, and census reports. It also can acquire access to scientific data on the side effects of prescription drugs and to documentation of illegal government surveillance of civilians by the CIA and FBI. The amount of information available to Americans astonished British journalist William Shawcross, who used the federal open records law to research a book that criticized American military incur-

---

[1] *E.g.,* Letter from Thomas Jefferson to Edward Carrington, January 16, 1787, in J. Boyd, ed., XI *The Papers of Thomas Jefferson* 48–49 (1955).

[2] A. Meiklejohn, *Free Speech* 26 (1948).

[3] Emerson, "The Danger of State Secrecy," *The Nation,* March 30, 1974, at 395.

sions into Cambodia during the Vietnam War. After Shawcross obtained much of his information through the Freedom of Information Act, he said, "you could not do this in my country."[4]

This chapter discusses the law of access to the legislative and administrative branches of government and to public places. It begins with a discussion of the Supreme Court's treatment of access as a First Amendment issue. Then it discusses the law of access to public places. Next, the chapter treats federal and state laws controlling access to government records. Finally, the federal and state laws governing access to the meetings of government agencies are discussed.

ACCESS AND THE CONSTITUTION

For many scholars and journalists, the freedom to publish news means little without the ability to gather information. However, the U.S. Supreme Court has ruled in a few cases that the First Amendment does not protect news gathering to the same degree it guarantees the right to print and broadcast the news.

The Supreme Court has said only that the First Amendment guarantees access of the press and public to the courts. The Court has found no First Amendment right of access for the press or public to prisons or prisoners. Lower federal courts have occasionally found a limited First Amendment right to gather news in public places. More frequently, the lower courts have said that public officials cannot selectively exclude journalists from news events and access to sources.

The Supreme Court and Limitations on News Gathering

In the handful of news-gathering cases the Supreme Court has decided, it has set forth three principles. First, the First Amendment does not guarantee a right to obtain information. Second, journalists have no greater rights of access to information than those of any other person. Third, the need for access to information will be balanced against other social needs, such as effective law enforcement and prison security.

The Supreme Court said as early as 1972 that

> it has generally been held that the First Amendment does not guarantee the press a constitutional right of special access to information not available to the public generally . . . . Despite the fact that news gathering may be hampered, the press is regularly excluded from grand jury proceedings, our own conferences, the meetings of other official bodies gathered in executive session, and the meetings of private organizations. Newsmen have no constitutional right of access to the scenes of crime or disaster when the general public is excluded, and they may be prohibited from attending or publishing information about trials if such restrictions are necessary to assure a defendant a fair trial before an impartial tribunal.[5]

---

[4]"All Things Considered," National Public Radio, July 7, 1989.
[5]Branzburg v. Hayes, 408 U.S. 665, 684–85, 1 Media L. Rep. 2617, 2624–25 (1972).

Also in the 1970s, the Supreme Court directly denied journalists a First Amendment right of access to newsworthy information in three prison cases. In the first two, decided on the same day, the Court upheld the constitutionality of prison rules restricting reporter interviews with inmates. The Court said that the First Amendment does not guarantee the press more access to prisons and inmates than is available to the general public. In one of the cases, *Procunier v. Pell*, reporters claimed a First Amendment right to interview specific California prisoners. In California, before 1971, journalists could conduct face-to-face interviews with prisoners on request. However, state prison officials said that the unrestricted interviewing policy was at least partly responsible for five deaths in an escape attempt in August 1971. Officials said the media attention given to the Soledad Brothers, three black inmates accused of killing a white prison guard, led to their notoriety and influence among fellow prisoners. The notoriety and influence led in turn to a breakdown in discipline, officials said. The California state corrections manual was revised to specify that "media interviews with specific individual inmates will not be permitted." In *Procunier v. Pell*, the Supreme Court, by a 5–4 vote, said the prison regulations restricting access did not abridge the constitutional right of a free press.

In the second case, *Saxbe v. Washington Post*, the Court upheld the constitutionality of a federal prison rule that, like the California state manual revision, prohibited interviews with specific prisoners. *Washington Post* reporter Ben Bagdikian had wanted to interview prisoners at Lewisburg, Pennsylvania, and Danbury, Connecticut. The *Post* wanted to find out if inmates participating in strike negotiations had been punished after the prisoners returned to work.

In the first of the two cases, *Procunier v. Pell*, the Court said that although the First and the Fourteenth amendments prevent the government from interfering with a free press, the Constitution does not require the government to give the press access to information not available to the average citizen. Justice Potter Stewart, writing for the Court, said

> It is one thing to say that a journalist is free to seek out sources of information not available to members of the general public. . . . It is quite another thing to suggest that the Constitution imposes upon government the affirmative duty to make available to journalists sources of information not available to members of the public generally.[6]

Stewart said that in the absence of evidence that prison rules were adopted to control specific kinds of expression, the Court deferred to the judgment of corrections officials. Prison officials have to control conduct in the prisons and have the expertise to determine which forms of prisoner communications do not interfere with prison security, Stewart said.

Justice Douglas, writing a dissent backed by Justices Brennan and Marshall, argued that an absolute ban on interviews with inmates selected by the press violates the First Amendment. Not even Douglas, known for his First Amendment absolutism, would grant the press access to prisons without consideration for prison discipline

---

[6]417 U.S. 817, 834, 1 Media L. Rep. 2379, 2386 (1974).

and order. Douglas said he understood the need for "reasonable" regulations on the time, place, and manner of prisoner interviews. However, he said, an absolute ban on press interviews with specifically designated prisoners was "far broader" than necessary to protect legitimate government interests and therefore an unconstitutional limitation on the public's right to know.

Douglas, quoting his own dissent in *Branzburg,* said the press has a preferred position under the Constitution "to bring fulfillment to the public's right to know," which is "crucial to the governing powers of the people."[7] Douglas said the people are responsible for prisons and need to be informed about their condition:

> It is . . . not enough to note that the press . . . is denied no more access to the prisons than is denied the public generally. . . . The average citizen is most unlikely to inform himself about the operation of the prison system by requesting an interview with a particular inmate. . . . He is likely instead, in a society which values a free press, to rely upon the media for information.[8]

Justice Powell, dissenting in both *Pell* and *Saxbe,* said that prison regulations should be no broader than necessary to ensure that individual prisoners do not become media celebrities. Prison officials could, Powell suggested, limit the number of interviews with one inmate during a set time period. Powell said the First Amendment embodies a national commitment to a faith that a free exchange of views is "the surest course for developing sound national policy."[9] The debate has to be informed as well as unfettered, he said.

A few years later, by a 4–3 vote, the Court again upheld restrictions imposed on jail visits, this time regulations adopted by Alameda County, California, Sheriff Thomas Houchins. In *Houchins v. KQED,* the television station sought access to the portion of the Santa Rita jail where an inmate was reported to have committed suicide. A psychiatrist claimed some of his patient-prisoners were physically sick because of the conditions there.

Chief Justice Burger, writing the opinion of the Court, said the Court had "never intimated" a First Amendment right of access to all sources of information under government control. He said a constitutional right to enter the jail could not be based on the public's concern for the condition of jails and the media's role in providing information. The issue in the case was not the right of citizens to receive ideas, Burger continued, but a claim by the press of a special privilege of access that the Court had rejected in *Pell* and *Saxbe.* The media have no right of access "different from or greater than" that afforded the public in general, Burger said. He pointed to a number of ways that reporters can learn of prison conditions, including interviews with prison visitors, public officials, prison personnel, and the lawyers of prisoners. He suggested the public interest in prisons is protected by inspections by the Board of Corrections and health and fire officials.

Burger said the Constitution left the issue of public access to the "political process." It is a legislative matter, he said. Quoting a speech by Justice Stewart, Burger asserted

---

[7]*Id.* at 840, 1 Media L. Rep. at 2388, *quoting* Branzburg v. Hayes, 408 U.S. at 721, 1 Media L. Rep. at 2639.
[8]*Id.* at 841, 1 Media L. Rep. at 2389.
[9]Saxbe v. Washington Post Co., 417 U.S. 843, 862–63, 1 Media L. Rep. 2314, 2322 (1974).

"The Constitution itself is neither a Freedom of Information Act nor an Official Secrets Act.

The Constitution . . . establishes the contest [for information], not its resolution. Congress may provide a resolution, at least in some instances. . . . For the rest, we must rely, as so often in our system we must, on the tug and pull of the political forces in American society."[10]

In addition, Burger said, the Constitution provides no standards for determining when access is appropriate. "Hundreds of judges" would have to apply "ad hoc standards, in individual cases, according to their own ideas of what seems 'desirable' or 'expedient.' "[11] Burger did not want the courts deciding who should have access to what governmental information and under what conditions.

In contrast to the prison cases, the Supreme Court decided in *Richmond Newspapers v. Virginia* that both the public and the press have a constitutional right to attend trials. The Court in *Richmond* found the right of access in First Amendment rights to report about courts, to assemble peaceably, and to petition the government for a redress of grievances. In *Richmond,* the Court relied strongly on the tradition of open courts and the argument that information about the criminal justice system was important to self-government. Chief Justice Burger, writing the Court opinion in *Richmond,* said that prisons, unlike courts, are not traditionally open to the public. In addition, legislatures could oversee the operations of prisons to protect against abuse.[12]

The court has yet to confront directly the constitutional right of access to legislative proceedings, official government records, and news events on public property. Conceivably, the Court's arguments in *Richmond* could apply. Legislative bodies, many government records, and the public streets have long been open to the public, a justification in *Richmond* for protecting access to courts. Access to legislative bodies and government records is important to self-government in a way similar to the way the Court said that access to the courts is essential to the judicial system. Arguably, the First Amendment rights relied upon in *Richmond Newspapers* to guarantee access to trials—the rights to report on government, assemble peaceably, and petition the government—apply to most legislative meetings, public records, and government property. However, until the Supreme Court rules otherwise, the First Amendment has not been held to guarantee a right to gather news outside courtrooms. Only a few exceptions have been noted by lower federal courts.

Federal Lower Courts and Selective Exclusion of Journalists

On a few occasions, lower federal courts have found a First Amendment right of access to news events and news sources. More frequently, however, courts have only said the First Amendment bars public officials from arbitrarily discriminating among journalists trying to gain access to news.

---

[10]438 U.S. 1, 14–15, 3 Media L. Rep. 2521, 2526 [inaccurate text], quoting a printed version of a speech, found in Stewart, "Or of the Press," 26 *Hast. L.J.* 631, 636 (1975).

[11]*Id.* at 14, 3 Media L. Rep. at 2526.

[12]448 U.S. 555, 6 Media L. Rep. 1833 (1980). See discussion in Chapter 9.

While a small number of court opinions have said the First Amendment provides some protection for the right to gather news in public places, special circumstances in the cases make them unreliable as broad precedents. One court said a restriction on press access to one hour per day to the site of a plane crash on public property violated the First Amendment. The court said there was no "reasonable basis" to limit access to such a short period. The court also said the federal agency involved, the National Transportation Safety Board, violated its own regulations when it restricted access so narrowly.[13]

In addition, courts have struck down restrictions on the access of journalists and pollsters to voting locations in at least seven states. The restrictions were adopted by several states during the 1980s to limit "exit interviews" of voters as they left the polls on election day. The statutes were designed to impede the television networks' projections of winners in presidential elections before the polls close in all states. Officials in western states especially argue that projections based on "exit polls" of voters reduce voter turnout for state and local elections held the same day. Officials contend that citizens won't vote if they already know the winner of the presidential race.

However, a federal appeals court ruled unconstitutional a Washington state statute prohibiting interviews of voters within 300 feet of a polling place. In *Daily Herald v. Munro,* the U.S. Court of Appeals for the Ninth Circuit said the First Amendment protected the discussion of governmental affairs and the gathering of news that took place in exit interviews. Therefore, the court said any law regulating exit polling must be narrowly tailored to accomplish a compelling governmental interest. Washington state argued that it must maintain peace and order at polling places, but the Ninth Circuit said the state's statute prohibiting exit interviews of voters within 300 feet of a polling place—the length of a football field—was too broad for that purpose. The statute prohibited all exit polling, the court said, and not simply disruptive exit polling. The Ninth Circuit added that any state intent to prevent network projections of election results through restrictions on election polling is unconstitutional. The court said that official concerns that network projections "might indirectly affect the voters' choice" could not justify the regulation of protected speech.[14]

Laws similar to the one in Washington state have also been overturned by federal district courts in Georgia, Kentucky, Minnesota, Montana, and Wyoming.[15] State appeals courts have struck down similar statutes in South Carolina and Florida. In 1990, Congress considered legislation that would establish a uniform closing time for polls during presidential elections, a bill seen by many officials as a way to settle the election projection controversy.

While the lower courts rarely have found a specific First Amendment right to gather news, they have said the First Amendment bars the arbitrary or capricious exclusion of journalists from sources of news. One federal appeals court ruled that a reporter could only be excluded from covering the White House with other reporters for compelling reasons explained to the journalist.

---

[13]Westinghouse Broadcasting Co. v. National Transp. Safety Bd., 670 F.2d 4, 8, Media L. Rep. 1177 (D. Mass. 1982). *See also* Channel 10, Inc. v. Gunnarson, 337 F. Supp. 634 (1972).

[14]Daily Herald Co. v. Munro, 838 F.2d 380, 14 Media L. Rep. 2332 (9th Cir. 1988).

[15]NBC v. Cleland, 697 F. Supp. 1204, 15 Media L. Rep. 2265 (N.D. Ga. 1988); CBS v. Growe, 15 Media L. Rep. 2275 (D. Minn. 1988); NBC v. Colburg, 699 F. Supp. 241, 16 Media L. Rep. 1267 (D. Mont. 1988). *See also* "Media Win Challenges to Exit Poll Restrictions," *News Media & Law,* Winter 1989, at 22–23.

Robert Sherrill, a reporter for *The Nation* magazine, was denied a press pass by the Secret Service in 1965 without an explanation. The Secret Service did not explain to Sherrill that he was being denied access to the White House because he was considered "a security risk." Sherrill had been convicted previously for assaulting a governor's press secretary. A second assault charge was pending.

The U.S. Court of Appeals for the District of Columbia rejected Sherrill's argument that he had a First Amendment right of access to the White House. Rather, the court said, since the White House voluntarily provided press access, the First Amendment protection for news gathering required that the access not be denied to an individual reporter without a compelling reason. Although protection of the president is clearly "compelling," the court said, the First Amendment requires that restrictions on news gathering be no more rigorous than necessary and that individual journalists not be arbitrarily excluded from sources of information. Therefore, the court said the Secret Service must publish the standards it uses to determine whether a journalist can obtain a White House press pass. The court also required the Secret Service to explain in writing why Sherrill was denied a press pass and provide him an opportunity for rebuttal.[16]

Similarly, in Iowa, a federal court said that a police department could not show its records to one newspaper and refuse to show them to another without a compelling reason. The court said that city officials discriminated by according access to "legitimate" or "established" media and denying access to an "underground newspaper" called *Challenge*.[17] In addition, a female reporter could not be denied access to a locker room in a city-owned baseball stadium while male reporters were allowed in the locker room. The exclusion from the New York Yankees's locker room violated the right of *Sports Illustrated* reporter Melissa Ludtke to pursue her profession. Alternatives to the exclusion of Ludtke from the locker room had to be found to protect the privacy of the baseball players.[18]

Courts have ruled that the First Amendment prohibits officials from denying reporters access to press conferences or sessions of state legislatures as a means of punishment. A federal district court in Hawaii said Honolulu Mayor Frank Fasi could not deny access to his press conferences to a reporter because the mayor did not like the reporter's coverage of his administration. Fasi said stories by Richard Borreca of the *Honolulu Star-Bulletin* were "irresponsible, inaccurate, biased, and malicious." Fasi also had been told that Borreca said the mayor was a crook. The courts said that officials could criticize the work of reporters, but the use of "intimidation" or "discipline," absent compelling reasons, violated the First Amendment.[19]

Some courts have said that access might be denied to specific journalists without violating the First Amendment if officials have a "reasonable basis" for a restriction. In California, a federal district court said the police and sheriff's departments could withhold press passes from a newspaper that did not regularly cover crime news. The court said the police had a reasonable basis for denying press passes to the *Los An-*

---

[16]Sherrill v. Knight, 569 F.2d 124, 3 Media L. Rep. 1514 (D.C. Cir. 1978).

[17]Quad-City Community News Serv., Inc. v. Jebens, 334 F. Supp. 8 (S.D. Iowa 1971). *See also* Legi-Tech v. Keiper, 766 F.2d 728, 11 Media L. Rep. 2482 (2d Cir. 1985).

[18]Ludtke v. Kuhn, 461 F. Supp. 86, 4 Media L. Rep. 1625 (S.D.N.Y. 1978).

[19]Borreca v. Fasi, 369 F. Supp 906, 1 Media L. Rep. 2410 (D. Hawaii 1974). *Also see* Kovach v. Maddux, 238 F. Supp. 835, 1 Media L. Rep. 2367 (D. Tenn. 1965).

geles Free Press, which primarily ran feature stories and news essays rather than spot news. The court said that, considering that the demand for press cards exceeded 1,500 a year, the departments had not acted arbitrarily in limiting press access to the scenes of crimes, fires, and natural disasters "to protect the public safety, health and welfare" and to contribute to the efficiency of law enforcement. The court noted that a primary criterion for a press pass is the need to regularly cover police and fire news. Passes were consistently denied to free-lance reporters, trade papers, college newspapers, and financial publications, the court observed.[20]

In addition to restricting reporters, officials can bar reporting equipment, including cameras and tape recorders, from news events. The U.S. Court of Appeals for the Fifth Circuit, relying on *Pell* and *Saxbe,* upheld Texas regulations prohibiting camera coverage of executions. The court said the limited First Amendment right to gather news does not include filming executions in a state prison. The court refused to interfere with state policy restricting the number of witnesses to executions, whether in person or by television.[21]

The limited constitutional protection for news gathering means that officials are generally not required by law to grant reporters access to news events on public and quasi-public property.

SUMMARY

The Supreme Court, in cases involving access to prisons and the protection of confidential news sources, has said that the First Amendment does not guarantee a right to gather news parallel to the right to publish. The Court has also said that journalists have no right of access to government facilities beyond that of the public. The Court has recognized a First Amendment right for both the public and the press to attend criminal trials.

Other federal courts have said that the First Amendment prohibits officials from denying access to news arbitrarily or discriminating against one reporter or news medium.

ACCESS TO PUBLIC AND QUASI-PUBLIC PROPERTY

Everyone, including members of the press, generally has access to public streets, sidewalks, parks, and public buildings. Several courts have recognized a common law right for everyone to observe, photograph, and record what can easily be seen or overheard in a public place.[22] However, public officials have the authority to deny access to public property when it becomes the scene of a public disorder or disaster

---

[20]Los Angeles Free Press, Inc. v. City of Los Angeles, 88 Cal. Rptr. 605 (1970), *cert. denied,* 401 U.S. 982 (1971).
[21]Garrett v. Estelle, 556 F.2d 1974, 2 Media L. Rep. 2265 (5th Cir. 1977), *cert. denied,* 438 U.S. 914 (1978).
[22]*E.g.,* Harrison v. Washington Post Co., 391 A.2d 781, 4 Media L. Rep. 1493 (D.C. Ct. App. 1978); Jacova v. Southern Radio & Television Co., 83 So.2d 34 (Fla. 1955).

such as an automobile accident or fire. Public safety officers often exclude journalists from the scene. Courts avoid second-guessing police and fire officials who have to make snap judgments while trying to save lives and property.

Anyone who disobeys an official order to move away from the scene of a calamity may be charged with criminal trespass, obstruction, or resisting arrest.[23] The First Amendment provides little or no protection in such a situation. Although police and fire officials are not supposed to act arbitrarily or capriciously, the courts tend to provide them with wide discretion during emergencies. California may be the only state that has adopted legislation permitting journalists access to the scenes of disasters.[24]

Journalists finding themselves in confrontation with authorities at the scene of accidents and disasters on public property have few options. If they refuse to move when ordered to, they may be arrested for interference with officials, disorderly conduct, assault, failure to move on, or other violations even if their presence poses no hindrance to officials. Sometimes police and fire officials do not fully appreciate that journalists are on hand only to gather information for the public.

The New Jersey Supreme Court upheld the conviction for disorderly conduct of a newspaper photographer who refused to obey a state trooper at the scene of an automobile accident. Harvey Lashinsky, a photographer for the *Newark Star-Ledger*, had stopped at the scene of an accident in the median of the Garden State Parkway. Inside a car, a girl was pinned against the corpse of her decapitated mother. Lashinsky took pictures until he was told to back away by a New Jersey state trooper who feared that spilled fuel might ignite or that the gathering crowd might steal property or destroy evidence. When Lashinsky was told to move, he argued with the trooper and was arrested. Lashinsky said he did not intend to interfere with the officer, but was convicted under a New Jersey statute for refusing to move, for arguing with the officer, and for attracting a crowd to the scene.[25]

The media's right of access to quasi-public property is even less secure than its right of access to public property. Quasi-public property is land that serves a public purpose but is not available for use by the general public. Army bases are quasi-public property. They belong to the public, but, unlike public parks, they are not open for regular public use. The site of a nuclear power plant also might be considered quasi-public. The land and buildings may be owned by either the state or a private company, but the facility is dedicated to a public use and is usually regulated and financed by a public agency. Nevertheless, the site of a nuclear power plant is not public land in the sense that it is dedicated to public use for recreation, communication, or other public purpose.

The administrator of quasi-public property, such as a utility, can restrict use to the purposes for which the property is dedicated. In 1984, the U.S. Supreme Court refused to consider the criminal trespass convictions of nine reporters covering a demonstration at the Black Fox nuclear power plant in Oklahoma. The journalists had accompanied antinuclear demonstrators through a hole in a fence at the plant instead

---

[23]*See generally* Middleton, ''Journalists' Interference with Police: The First Amendment, Access to News and Official Discretion,'' 5 *COMM/ENT* 443 (Spring 1983).

[24]Cal. Penal Code sec. 409.5 (d) (West Supp. 1986).

[25]State v. Lashinsky, 404 A.2d 1121, 5 Media L. Rep. 1418 (N.J. 1979).

of staying at a company-approved viewing site on the property. The journalists complained that they would have missed much of the story if restricted to the observation site provided by the Public Service Company of Oklahoma (PSO), which ran the nuclear power plant. Indeed, the PSO, which had been stung by bad publicity from an earlier antinuclear protest, said it wanted to minimize coverage of the demonstration by restricting press access.

The Oklahoma Court of Criminal Appeals said the press had no special right of access. The Public Service Company, the court said, has the power to regulate the quasi-public property to conform to designated uses. Since the Black Fox facility was not dedicated to use by demonstrators, nine reporters were fined $25 each for trespassing with the demonstrators.

The majority of the Oklahoma court rejected Judge Tom Brett's dissenting argument that journalists who are peacefully gathering news on quasi-public property should not be held to strict liability for trespass. Judge Brett argued that journalists' interests in news gathering should be balanced against the threat to property and order. Brett did not see that the press posed a threat to public order or property at the Black Fox plant.[26]

SUMMARY

In the case of access to public and quasi-public property, courts are often inclined to accept the discretion of officials. State statutes specify punishment for those obstructing authority rather than mandating access to journalists.

ACCESS TO RECORDS

While the law determining access to public places is very limited and relatively undefined, the opposite is true for law affecting access to public records and to public meetings. All states and the federal government have adopted statutes mandating access to many government records and meetings.

Most records laws deal with the same issues. Most begin with a statement of purpose declaring that the policy of the state is to maximize the availability of records for the public. Scholars suggest that strong policy statements establish a presumption of openness that allows the courts to interpret access laws broadly. Then most laws address the same concerns: What government agencies are covered by the law? What is a public record? Who has access to the records? How can a person obtain a public record? What penalties exist for punishing officials who withhold public records? What items are exempt from disclosure? Most states and the federal government exempt information related to law enforcement investigations, privacy, and business.

The discussion of records laws will begin with an analysis of the federal Freedom

---

[26]Stahl v. Oklahoma, 665 P.2d 839, 9 Media L. Rep. 1945, 1951 (Okla. Crim. App. 1983), *cert. denied,* 464 U.S. 1069 (1984).

of Information Act, the law controlling documents held by federal agencies. Many of the issues raised by the federal law are also pertinent to the state laws.

Federal Freedom of Information Act

History and Purpose Congress adopted the Freedom of Information Act (FOIA) in 1966 as a bipartisan effort to increase public access to federal documents. The FOIA replaced a 1946 act that recognized the public nature of government records but was treated by federal agencies as an authorization to withhold records instead of a mandate to release them. Beginning in 1955, First Amendment scholar Harold Cross and California Congressman John Moss organized a collection of allies with different motives to push for a new law. For example, the press wanted public access to documents produced by the government. Legal and administrative reform groups wanted regular publication of federal agency rules and opinions.

The FOIA does not include a statement of purpose, but Congress left a clear legislative record of its intent. The Senate report on the bill said the act was supposed

"to establish a general philosophy of full agency disclosure," and "to close the loopholes which allow agencies to deny legitimate information to the public."[27]

The spirit of the law was captured by President Lyndon Johnson, who said as he signed it that

a democracy works best when the people have all the information that the security of the nation permits. No one should be able to pull the curtain of secrecy around decisions which can be revealed without injury to the public interest.[28]

The overriding policy of the FOIA is to disclose whenever possible and to withhold only when necessary. Congress included nine exemptions in the law to balance the public's right to be informed with the government's need to maintain some records in confidence. The U.S. Supreme Court has said that the exemptions do not obscure that "disclosure, not secrecy" is the "dominant objective" of the act.[29]

Since its passage, the act has allowed writers to uncover a wide range of information important to the public welfare. Journalists used the FOIA in 1989 to document how Reagan administration officials at the Department of Housing and Urban Development used department funds to finance projects for prominent Republicans, former colleagues, and friends. Documents obtained through the FOIA also have revealed FBI harassment of Dr. Martin Luther King, Jr., illegal CIA surveillance of domestic political groups, CIA mind-control experiments on federal prisoners, and the experimental use of drugs in a nursing home. The act also has been used to disclose unsanitary conditions in food processing plants, the fat content of hot dogs,

---

[27]S. Rep. No. 813, 89th Cong., 1st Sess. 3 (1965) *as reported in* GTE Sylvania, Inc. v. Consumers Union, 445 U.S. 375, 385 (1979).

[28]Susman, "Introduction to the Issues, Problems and Relevant Law" in "Your Business, Your Trade Secrets, and Your Government," 34 *Admin. L. R.* 117 (1982).

[29]Department of Air Force v. Rose, 425 U.S. 352, 1 Media L. Rep. 2509 (1976).

serious safety problems in nuclear power plants, the increased incidence of cancer among plutonium workers, the presence of poisonous wastes in drinking water, and school district compliance with antidiscrimination laws.

Still, the act is heavily criticized. Journalists charge it is ineffective. They argue that agencies interpret the exemptions broadly and employ a number of procedural ploys to block public access. They say agencies often contend that documents are lost or they simply do not have the staff to process the FOIA requests. Reporters claim that agencies also use delaying tactics until the information sought is no longer newsworthy. On the other hand, law enforcement officers, businesses, and others, contend the act allows too much disclosure, is unfair to businesses submitting information to the government, and is an undue burden on government.

The government estimates that it spent $55 million processing nearly 400,000 requests in 1988.[30] The Department of Health and Human Services reported the largest number of requests that year, about 130,000. The department reported that it cost an average of $70 to fill a request. Some agencies, including the Federal Trade Commission, reported that it cost more than $450 to comply with the average FOIA request. At one time, the FBI employed 400 people to do nothing but handle FOIA requests.[31] Adding to the expense of the FOIA is the fact that it is one of the most litigated federal laws, surpassed only by the civil rights acts, according to one government official.[32] The Justice Department must defend every FOIA suit—which amounted to nearly 575 in one recent year.[33]

Reach of the Act—Defining "Agency"   The FOIA applies to "agency" records. The term *agency* includes

> any executive department, military department, Government corporation, Government controlled corporation or other establishment in the executive branch of the federal government. . ., or any independent regulatory agency.[34]

It applies to cabinet offices such as defense, treasury, and justice, and agencies such as the FBI, that report to them. The independent regulatory agencies subject to the law include the Federal Communications Commission, the Federal Trade Commission, the Securities and Exchange Commission, and the Consumer Product Safety Commission. The act pertains to presidential commissions, the U.S. Postal Service, and AMTRAK. It applies to the Executive Office of the President, including the Office of Management and Budget, but not to the president himself, his staff, or his advisers. Therefore, the act does not apply to the Council of Economic Advisers,

---

[30]"Requests Continue Up, Costs Level Off," *Access Reports,* Oct. 18, 1989, at 3.

[31]J. Rose, in remarks at "The Freedom of Information Act; How Is It Working?", a conference sponsored by the American Enterprise Institute and the Institute for Communications Law Studies, Catholic University of America 20 (Oct. 27, 1983).

[32]R. Rader, in remarks at "The Freedom of Information Act; How Is It Working?", conference transcript, at 24–25.

[33]M. Grunewald, "Administrative Mechanisms for Resolving Freedom of Information Act Disputes," report submitted to Administrative Law Conference of the United States 5 (Dec. 15, 1986).

[34]5 U.S.C. sec. 552 (f) (1988).

established to advise and assist the president.[35] In addition, the act does not apply to records of Congress or the federal courts.

If an agency is covered by the law, the physical location of an office makes no difference. The act applies to local and regional offices of the Internal Revenue Service, the FBI, and other federal agencies.

Reach of the Act—Defining "Record"

The FOIA applies to *records,* which are tangible, and not to *information,* which is intangible. The act requires agencies to provide nonexempt documents in response to a request, but it does not require agencies to answer questions during an interview. The FOIA does not define "record," but two important criteria are whether items function as records and can be copied or reproduced. Paper documents, tape recordings, photographs, and computerized printouts are *records* because they record government activity and can be reproduced. Physical objects such as weapons are not because although they may be a record of government activity, they cannot be reproduced.[36]

The computerization of records has created several issues and problems that are not yet resolved. Congress has said that agencies cannot withhold computerized records from the public if the information would be available under the FOIA as paper documents.[37] However, in many cases, an agency would have to incur an additional expense to develop a software program in order to retrieve the data sought from a computer. Until now, the courts have been hesitant to require agencies "to create" documents to fill FOIA requests. In addition, the development of software by the government raises the question whether computer software itself is a "record" subject to the FOIA. Software does not contain government-held information in the usual sense, but provides the instructions for the storage and manipulation of the information. A further question is whether an agency will be required to provide computerized data in a particular format to the person seeking it. In other words, can a person using the FOIA require that information be provided by a computer disk, a computer tape, or a printout? In 1990, the Justice Department was drafting a federal administrative policy for access to computerized records.[38]

Regardless of physical form or format, an agency must both possess and control a record for it to be subject to disclosure under the FOIA. The statute itself does not explain the conditions necessary before a "record" becomes an "agency record." However, the U.S. Supreme Court has said that an agency must possess a document—that is, it must create or obtain a document—before it can become an "agency record." Not only must an agency have physical possession of a document for it to be an "agency record," according to the Court, but an agency must also exercise "control" over a document.

In a ruling that especially limits public access to studies prepared by private consultants for the government, the Supreme Court said a report about diabetes treatments was not an "agency record" because it was not in the physical possession of a

---

[35]Rushford v. Council of Economic Advisers, 762 F.2d 1038, 11 Media L. Rep. 2075 (1985). *See also* Kissinger v. Reporters Comm. for Freedom of the Press, 445 U.S. 136, 155–58, 6 Media L. Rep. 1001, 1009–1010 (1980).

[36]J.T. O'Reilly, 1 *Federal Information Disclosure* para. 5.03, at 5–9 (June 1984).

[37]Computer Security Act of 1987, Pub. L. 100–235, 101 Stat. 1724 (1988).

[38]*E.g.,* "Agencies Respond to DOJ Computer Survey," *Access Reports,* Nov. 15, 1989, at 1–3.

federal agency. In the case of *Forsham v. Harris,* the diabetes report had been paid for by a government agency, the National Institute of Arthritis, Metabolism and Digestive Diseases. The Federal Food and Drug Administration used the report to develop drug labeling policies. However, the report was prepared and possessed by a team of consultants. The consultants, a private group of physicians and scientists, had studied the effectiveness of various diabetes treatments and kept the data and the patient records. An association of doctors, the Committee on the Care of Diabetics, wanted the results of the study. The Supreme Court, in a 7–2 vote, said the diabetes report was the property of the research group, which was not a government agency. The FOIA applies only to documents that have been created or obtained by a federal agency, the Court said.[39] In dissent, Justice Brennan said a document should be a record subject to the FOIA if it is used by an agency to arrive at a decision and is important to the public's understanding of the decision.

The Supreme Court has also said that an agency cannot be forced to obtain documents that fall under the FOIA if they were not in the agency's possession. In a case decided on the same day as *Forsham,* the Reporters Committee for the Freedom of the Press and the Military Audit Project sought from the State Department the transcripts of Henry Kissinger's telephone conversations when he was Secretary of State and National Security Adviser. Kissinger had donated the records to the Library of Congress, which is not subject to the FOIA, under an agreement that substantially limited public access.

The Supreme Court, in *Kissinger v. Reporters Committee for Freedom of the Press,* said the FOIA only requires agencies to provide access to the records in their possession.[40] The Court said that a federal agency does not improperly withhold a document under the FOIA if the record has been removed from the agency prior to the filing of the FOIA request. In the FOIA, the Court said, Congress only required agencies to disclose information in their possession, and not to create, retain, or retrieve documents they do not possess. In dissent, Justice Stevens said the ruling could encourage outgoing officials to remove embarrassing information from their files.[41]

However, an agency must exercise control over documents, as well as possess them, before they qualify as "agency records" under the FOIA. In another FOIA request considered in the *Kissinger* opinion, *New York Times* columnist William Safire wanted notes of specific Kissinger telephone conversations located at the State Department. The notes were made by Kissinger when he was the National Security Adviser in the White House and therefore were considered to be White House records not subject to the FOIA. The fact that the papers happened to be at the State Department did not give that agency control of the documents, the Supreme Court said. Justice Rehnquist, writing for the Court, said

> We simply decline to hold that the physical location of the notes . . . renders them "agency records." The papers were not in the control of the State Department at any time. They were not generated in the State Department. They never entered the State Department's files, and they were not used by the Department for any purpose.[42]

---

[39]445 U.S. 169, 5 Media L. Rep. 2473 (1980).
[40]445 U.S. 136, 6 Media L. Rep. 1001 (1980).
[41]*Id.* at 161, 6 Media L. Rep. at 1012.
[42]*Id.* at 157, 6 Media L. Rep. at 1010.

If the Court ruled otherwise, Rehnquist said, Kissinger's personal books and memorabilia, which were not government records but were kept in his State Department office, would be subject to disclosure under the FOIA.

If an agency both possesses and controls documents, the Supreme Court said in 1989, the records should be open to the public even if the agency did not create the records or if the records are available elsewhere. In *Tax Analysts v. Department of Justice,* the Court said the Justice Department must provide copies of all federal trial court opinions interpreting tax law to Tax Analysts, a nonprofit organization that publishes a weekly magazine for tax attorneys, accountants, and economists. The Justice Department receives almost all federal court opinions affecting tax law because the department represents the federal government in tax litigation. However, the agency argued it should not have to provide the court opinions to Tax Analysts because the decisions were already available at individual district courts. The Justice Department contended the cost of searching for the opinions in department files would be prohibitive.[43] Tax Analysts asked the Justice Department for the court opinions because it frequently had trouble obtaining them quickly from the "ninety-odd, far flung" federal district courts.

The Supreme Court, in an opinion written by Justice Marshall, said the court tax opinions were "agency records" under the FOIA because the Justice Department first obtained them and then controlled them. The Court rejected a Justice Department argument that documents must be created by an agency in order to be considered "agency records" under the act. The Court said such a ruling "would frustrate Congress' desire to put within public reach the information available to an agency in its decision-making processes." The Court said the Justice Department "controlled" the tax opinions because it acquired them "in the legitimate conduct of its official duties," representing the government in tax cases.[44]

In addition, the Court ruled, an agency cannot withhold files being sought under the FOIA simply because the information is publicly available elsewhere. "If Congress had wished to codify an exemption for all publicly available materials," the Court said, "it knew perfectly well how to do so."[45] The Supreme Court said the Justice Department improperly withheld the district court opinions from Tax Analysts because the opinions did not fit any of the nine exemptions of the FOIA.

Together, *Forsham, Kissinger,* and *Tax Analysts* mean that agencies must both possess and exercise control over documents before the records become subject to disclosure under the FOIA. While an agency cannot be forced to obtain a document because it receives an FOIA request, neither can an agency refuse to honor a request because it did not create a document or because the document is available elsewhere.

Access for Whom?   Under the FOIA, "any person" may submit a request for a federal record.[46] "Any person" includes citizens of foreign countries and persons acting on behalf of organizations such as defense contractors, media companies, and public interest groups.[47]

---

[43]Tax Analysts v. Department of Justice, 845 F.2d 1060 (D.C. Cir.1988).
[44]Department of Justice v. Tax Analysts, 109 S. Ct. 2841, 2848, 16 Media L. Rep. 1849, 1853 (1989).
[45]*Id.* at 2852, 16 Media L. Rep. at 1856.
[46]5 U.S.C. sec. 552 (a) (3) (1988).
[47]J.T. O'Reilly, 1 *Federal Information Disclosure* para. 5.04, at 5–14, 5–15 (June 1984).

With few exceptions, a federal agency cannot consider the purpose of an FOIA request when making a decision to withhold documents. Release of federal records does not depend on the documents serving the "public interest." As one judge put it, the FOIA grants "the scholar and the scoundrel equal rights of access to agency records."[48] If records could be released only for the "public interest," government officials could deny requests for documents for personal or corporate use. If release of records depended on an official's definition of the "public interest," agency personnel could withhold documents because they did not like how the information might be used, an easy end-run around congressional intent to maximize public access to government records. Officials can withhold information only if the records fit into one of the nine exempt categories.

In fact, the FOIA is used extensively for commercial and personal purposes. Businesses, for example, use the act to seek lists of potential customers, marketing information about a competitor's product, and information to sell to the public. Angry consumers have used the act to seek information from the Environmental Protection Agency about a possible administrative action against Volkswagen. The case and the EPA investigation involved the recall of 450,000 Volkswagen Rabbits for the replacement of valve stem seals.[49] In addition, at least one prisoner fighting his criminal conviction filed an FOIA request for arrest records of witnesses against him.[50]

Procedures for Requesting Information

Filing the Request Anyone wanting information from a U.S. government agency may be able to obtain it through informal processes. Persons can ask an agency public information officer and perhaps the agency FOIA officer without making a formal FOIA request, even at a local or regional office. This approach, when it works, saves the time and money involved in a formal FOIA request.

If informal contacts do not succeed, a person can file a formal, written request for the information under the FOIA. Each agency must publish in the *Federal Register* a description of its organization and a list of the people a citizen should contact when making an inquiry under the FOIA. The agency must explain FOIA procedures for that agency and provide indexes identifying the information available.[51] A sample request letter is printed as Figure 11.1. Additional information for preparing a request is available in a booklet, "How to Use the Federal FOI Act," published by the Reporters Committee for Freedom of the Press.[52]

Once a formal FOIA request is made, an agency must release the documents or demonstrate that they fall into one of the exempt categories. Although the law requires the requester to make only a "reasonable" description of the documents sought, the more specific the request, the more likely that it will be filled and the less it will cost. When possible, a document should be described by number, date, title, and author. If an agency decides that some of the information requested falls under

---

[48]Durns v. Bureau of Prisons, 804 F.2d 701, 706 (D.C. Cir. 1986).
[49]*See* Thomas v. EPA, 554 F. Supp. 418 (D.C.N.Y. 1983).
[50]Pollard v. FBI, 705 F.2d 1151 (9th Cir. 1983); A. Adler, ed., *Litigation under the Federal Freedom of Information Act and Privacy Act* 11, 193–94, 203 (10th ed. 1985).
[51]5 U.S.C. sec. 552 (a) (2) (c) (1988).
[52]Available at the FOI Service Center, 800 18th Street, N.W., Washington, D.C. 20006.

```
                                              Your address
                                              Day time phone number
                                              Date

        Freedom of Information Office
        Agency
        Address

            FOIA Request

        Dear FOI Officer:
            Pursuant to the federal Freedom of Information Act, 5 U.S.C.
        § 552, I request access to and copies of (here, clearly describe what
        you want.  Include identifying material, such as names, places, and
        the period of time about which you are inquiring.  If you think they
        will help to explain what you are looking for, attach news clips,
        reports, and other documents describing the subject of your
        research.)
            I agree to pay reasonable duplication fees for the processing of
        this request in an amount not to exceed $___.  However, please notify
        me prior to your incurring any expenses in excess of that amount.[1]
            (Suggested request for fee benefit as a representative of the
        news media:) As a representative of the news media I am only required
        to pay for the direct cost of duplication after the first 100 pages.
        Through this request, I am gathering information on (subject) that is
        of current interest to the public because (give reason).  This
        information is being sought on behalf of (give the name of your news
        organization) for dissemination to the general public.  (If a
        freelancer, provide information such as experience, publication
        contract, etc., that demonstrates that you expect publication.)
            (Optional fee waiver request:) Please waive any applicable fees.
        Release of the information is in the public interest because it will
        contribute significantly to public understanding of government
        operations and activites.[2]
            If my request is denied in whole or part, I ask that you justify
        all deletions by reference to specific exemptions of the act.  I will
        also expect you to release all segregable portions of otherwise
        exempt material.  I, of course, reserve the right to appeal your
        decision to withhold any information or to deny a waiver of fees.
            As I am making this request as a journalist (author, or scholar)
        and this information is of timely value, I would appreciate your
        communicating with me by telephone, rather than by mail, if you have
        questions regarding this request.[3]  I look forward to your reply
        within 10 business days, as the statute requires.
            Thank you for your assistance.

                                              Very truly yours,

                                              Your signature
```

Figure 11.1.   Sample FOI Act request letter.

one of the nine exemptions, only that information can be deleted. The fact that a document includes some classified information is not a sufficient excuse for withholding the entire document.

Response Deadlines   The government agency is required by law to respond to an FOIA request within 10 working days. If access is denied, the agency bears the burden of explaining why. The agency must also advise a person requesting information of the right to appeal to the head of the agency. Answers to an appeal are supposed to be ready within 20 working days.[53]

Agency response time can be extended 10 days if the agency provides a reason for the delay and a date when the information should be available. A delay is only permissible under the law on the "unusual" occasion when a request involves a "voluminous" amount of material, records not available in the immediate vicinity, or the need to consult with another agency.[54]

The Center for National Security Studies has reported that although most of the agencies meet FOIA time limits some do not respond to requests for years. This is particularly true of the CIA, the FBI, and the State Department.[55] The FBI admitted to a backlog of 8,000 requests in 1989. The agency took an average of 326 days to complete the processing of an FOIA request.[56] Many of the delays can be attributed to the large number of requests and the limited number of agency personnel assigned to process them. Agencies are reluctant to commit the resources necessary to handle all requests. Money for FOIA administration comes out of general agency funding. Congress does not specifically fund FOIA administration for fear the agencies would not respond to requests after they exhausted the money allocated.

Critics also accuse agencies of stalling to thwart FOIA requests. NBC correspondent Carl Stern said that when he first asked the U.S. Air Force for the videotape of the 1982 crash of the Thunderbirds, the Air Force precision aerobatics team, he was told no tape existed. Then he was told videotape of the crash was not an agency record. Then he was told it was protected under the privacy exemption. After Stern effectively refuted each argument, he was told by a Pentagon official, "You're never going to get those pictures." Showing the crash on network television, the official said, would defeat the purpose of the Thunderbirds, to generate enthusiasm for the Air Force. Stern said the tactics successfully defeated his original intent, to show the crash in an anniversary segment discussing the costs and benefits of the Thunderbirds.[57]

The courts have tended to tolerate slow agency responses. The courts rely on the FOIA language providing agencies extra time if they are "exercising due diligence" under "exceptional circumstances."[58] However, a federal appeals court said in 1988 that the Air Force Logistics Command could not routinely delay responses to FOIA

---

[53]5 U.S.C. sec. 552 (a) (6) (A) (i), (ii) (1988).

[54]5 U.S.C. sec. 552 (a) (6) (B) (1988).

[55]*See* Adler, ed., *Litigation under the Federal Freedom of Information Act and Privacy Act* 17 (14th ed. 1989); Popkin, "Running the New 'Improved' FOIA Obstacle Course," *Colum. Journ. Rev.*, July–Aug. 1989, at 47; Freedom of Information Act: State Department Request Processing, GAO/GGD-89-23 (Jan. 1989).

[56]"Subcommittee Reviews FBI's FOIA Operations," *Access Reports,* March 7, 1990, at 1.

[57]Remarks at "The Freedom of Information Act: How Is It Working?", conference transcript, at 7.

[58]5 U.S.C. sec. 552 (a) (6) (C) (1988).

requests. Between 1985 and 1987, Logistics Command officers consistently denied requests for summaries of bids on government contracts. Payne Enterprises sells the information to prospective contractors. Logistics Command officers argued that bidders might raise prices if they learned from the summaries that they had no serious competition. The Secretary of the Air Force routinely ordered the Logistics Command to release the information because it did not fit any of the FOIA exemptions. However, the Command took so long to release the documents that they were out of date by the time Payne received them. The U.S. Court of Appeals for the D.C. Circuit ordered the federal district court in Washington to prohibit similar delays, with an injunction if necessary. The D.C. Circuit said the Logistic Command consistently hurt Payne's business by abusing the FOIA.[59]

Fees   As amended in 1986, the FOIA requires that only persons seeking information for commercial uses pay full search and copying costs as well as the costs for officials to review information for possible deletions. All other requesters receive the first two hours of search time and the first 100 pages copied free of charge. Furthermore, requesters using the information for noncommercial purposes cannot be charged for the review for deletions. In addition, representatives of the news media and educational and scientific institutions cannot be charged for searches at all.

The revised FOIA also specifies that all fees will be reduced or waived if the disclosure of the information

> is in the public interest because it is likely to contribute significantly to public understanding of the operations or activities of the government and is not primarily in the commercial interest of the requester.[60]

The 1986 FOI Reform Act directed each agency to establish a fee schedule and standards for determining fee reductions and waivers. The act also instructed the Office of Management and Budget (OMB) to assist the agencies by providing uniform guidelines. Among the hotly debated provisions in the OMB's guidelines were its definition of the groups to be exempt from search charges, including the *news media* and *educational institutions.*[61] Several FOIA users claimed the OMB's definitions excluded too many organizations and allowed the agencies too much discretion to deny waivers. OMB's definitions and their use by federal agencies soon were challenged in court.

The OMB said that the term *news media* was limited to organizations that publish or broadcast information about current events for the general public.[62] The FBI said a Canadian newspaper, the *Southam News,* did not qualify as a *news medium* because it does not disseminate information in the United States. However, federal District Court Judge Harold H. Greene said there is no such restriction in the act. He

---

[59]Payne Enterprises, Inc. v. United States, 837 F.2d 486 (D.C. Cir. 1988).

[60]5 U.S.C. sec. 552 (a) (4) (A) (iii) (1988).

[61]Uniform Fee Schedule and Guidelines, 52 Fed. Reg. 10012 (March 27, 1987). *See* Note, "Developments under the Freedom of Information Act—1987," 1988 *Duke L.J.* 566, 571-73; A. Adler, ed., *Litigation under the Federal Freedom of Information Act and Privacy Act* 179-84 (14th ed. 1989).

[62]*E.g.,* Note, "Developments under the Freedom of Information Act—1987," 1988 *Duke L.J.* 566, 571-72.

directed the agency to waive the search fees for documents that explained why Canadians were denied entry to the United States as subversives.[63]

In 1989, a federal appeals court said that sponsors of the 1986 FOIA Reform Act intended the phrase "representative of the news media" to apply to any persons or organizations regularly providing information to the public. The U.S. Court of Appeals for the District of Columbia ruled that the search fee exemption for the *news media* is available to any FOIA user who "gathers information of potential interest" to the public, uses editorial skills to create a distinct work, and publishes or otherwise distributes the work. The D.C. Circuit, in *National Security Archive v. Department of Defense,* ruled that a nonprofit research institute that disseminates information about foreign, defense, and international economic policy is a *news medium* qualifying for the fee waiver.[64] The court said the National Security Archive obtains information from several sources, exercises editorial judgment, creates indexes and other research tools, and makes its work available to the public. The D.C. Circuit said the archive's intent to sell its work did not constitute commercial use that disqualifies the organization from the fee waiver. The court said the archive's sale of its information is no different, under the FOIA, than the sale of a newspaper.

In addition to the dispute over the meaning of "news media" in the 1986 FOI Reform Act, a controversy has existed over the criteria agencies should use to determine fee waivers or reductions for the disclosure of information "likely to contribute significantly to the public understanding" of government. Although principal sponsors of the reform act said 1986 amendments were intended to counteract elaborate guidelines for fee waivers issued by the Justice Department, the department recommended similar criteria in 1987. The department encourages agency administrators to examine FOI requests to be sure they conform to the statutory language by seeking records, for example, that are likely to *contribute significantly* to the *public understanding* of government. The Justice Department advises agencies they need to analyze the "substantive content" of the records requested and also consider such factors as whether the information is already available to the public and whether the person seeking the documents has any expertise on the subject of the documents. Critics charge that the Justice Department's criteria provide agencies with reasons to refuse fee waivers and encourage government officials to make news judgments that should be left to the media. Since the Justice Department reissued its guidelines in 1987, several agencies have adopted them in spite of the vigorous protests of one of the sponsors of the 1986 amendments, Representative Glenn English. English said that whether the Justice Department liked it or not Congress rewrote the fee waiver provisions "in order to make more people eligible for waivers."[65]

In the *Southam News* case mentioned earlier, the court said the FBI interpreted the amended FOIA fee waiver provisions too strictly when denying a waiver to a Canadian newspaper. When the *Southam News* sought a waiver of copying costs for

[63]Southam News v. Immigration and Naturalization Serv., 674 F. Supp. 881, 892 (D.D.C. 1987), *enforced by* 1987 WL 20241 (D.D.C., Nov. 9, 1987) (No. Civ. A. 85-2721).

[64]National Sec. Archive v. Department of Defense, 880 F.2d 1381 (D.C. Cir.), *cert. denied,* 110 S. Ct. 1478 (March 19, 1990).

[65]"New Fee Waiver Policy Guidance," *FOIA Update,* Winter-Spring 1987, at 3; Note, "Developments under the Freedom of Information Act—1987," 1988 *Duke L.J.* 566, 575–78; A. Adler, ed., *Litigation under the Federal Freedom of Information Act and Privacy Act* 184–92 (14th ed. 1989).

records explaining why Canadians were being denied entry into the United States, the FBI contended no fee waiver was merited because the documents did not "contribute significantly to the public's understanding of government operations and activities." However, District Court Judge Harold Greene, in ordering a waiver of fees, dismissed as "absurd" the contention that publishing information about U.S. immigration policies would not significantly contribute to the public's understanding of government. "Moreover," he said, "it is the very purpose of the FOIA to allow the *public* to decide what will aid its understanding of the government."[66]

Persons charged search fees can expect to pay from $11 to $28 an hour, according to the FOI Service Center, sponsored by the Reporters Committee for Freedom of the Press. The service center said in 1987 that computer charges ran up to $270 an hour. Copying generally costs 15 cents a page.[67] Agencies often charge for unsuccessful searches.

Persons seeking information through the FOIA should request a fee waiver in the initial request if they believe they are eligible. They also ought to put a limit on the money they are willing to spend before the agency conducts the search and does the copying. When no waiver has been granted, the government frequently demands the fee before the documents are released. The fee mounts quickly for several hundred pages. For Carl Stern of NBC News, the fee could have meant a cost of $196 for 1,340 pages. Stern only wanted a few of those pages.[68] Costs also can be cut if persons seeking information are able to look at the documents themselves to determine which pages are necessary, rather than having the agency copy everything it finds. Persons can appeal any charge for an FOIA request. Stern eventually received a fee waiver.

Appeal Procedures and Penalties   If the appeal for access to a record is denied by an agency head, or if the agency does not respond within 20 days, a person requesting information has two options. First, he or she can appeal to the Special Counsel of the Merit Systems Protection Board in the Justice Department. The Special Counsel lacks the power to order the release of any documents, but an inquiry might convince an agency to release information. The facts uncovered in the investigation could be useful in further appeals.[69]

Almost all persons who have exhausted their appeal opportunities within an agency use the second of the two appeal routes outside the agency. They file a complaint in federal district court. The FOIA provides that a suit under the act should be given precedence over most other litigation. A court has the authority to examine the documents at issue, even those that may be related to national security, to decide whether agency records have been improperly withheld.[70] The court can order that the documents be made available if the information sought does not fall under one of the exemptions. The court's decision can be appealed to one of the circuits of the U.S. Courts of Appeals. The judicial examination of documents, known as *in camera* re-

---

[66]674 F. Supp. at 893 (emphasis in original).
[67]FOI Service Center, *How to Use the Federal FOI Act* 5 (6th ed. 1987).
[68]Weinberg, "Trashing the FOIA," *Colum. Journ. Rev.,* Jan.–Feb. 1985, at 21.
[69]5 U.S.C. sec. 1206 (e) (1) (C) (1988).
[70]5 U.S.C. sec. 552 (a) (4) (B) (1988). *See* Kissinger v. Reporters Comm. for Freedom of the Press, 445 U.S. at 150, 6 Media L. Rep. at 1007.

view, was approved by Congress in 1974 over President Ford's veto. Ford believed it was improper for the courts to have the authority to overrule the executive branch on what documents should be classified for the sake of national security. Congress believed a check on executive branch secrecy was necessary.

During the first half of the 1980s, persons seeking federal records won only 11 percent of the appeals before a federal district court. Only 20 percent of FOIA cases reaching a circuit of the U.S. Courts of Appeals were reversed.[71] If a person seeking information wins in court, a judge can assess the government the requester's attorney's fees and other litigation costs.[72]

If an agency refuses to comply with a court order, the court can cite the person responsible for contempt. Persons responsible for improperly withholding information can also be reprimanded, fined, or fired after an investigation by the Civil Service Commission.[73] The FOI Service Center reported in 1987 that no government official had ever been punished.[74]

Persons refused records often are reluctant to appeal agency decisions in court because of the costs. While the court may decide that the government has improperly withheld information and must pay the fees involved, a person losing in court is not reimbursed.

SUMMARY

The thrust of the Freedom of Information Act is to make federal records available to any person. The statute applies to the executive branch with the exception of the White House, but not to Congress or the federal courts. The act applies to records in tangible form, including computer printouts. A document is a record of an agency only if it is both possessed and controlled by the agency. An agency must respond to a written request for a record within 10 working days. In cases of inaction or denial, appeals to an agency head are supposed to be answered within 20 working days. Fees can be charged for searches and for copying but are waived if a request is in the public interest. Most persons who contest agency rejections of record requests in court lose their appeal.

Exemptions An agency must disclose any record that does not fall under one of the nine categories of material that can be exempt from disclosure under the FOIA. However, an agency may choose to disclose a document that fits one of the nine categories as long as another statute does not require the information to be withheld. The U.S. Supreme Court has said that the exemptions only permit, and do not require, a federal agency to withhold documents.[75]

---

[71]M. Grunewald, "Administrative Mechanisms for Resolving Freedom of Information Act Disputes," report submitted to Administrative Law Conference of the United States 11, 13 (Dec. 15, 1986).

[72]5 U.S.C. sec. 552 (a) (4) (E) (1988).

[73]5 U.S.C. sec. 552 (a) (4) (C), (D), (E), (F) and (G) (1988).

[74]FOI Service Center, *How to Use the Federal FOI Act* 8 (6th ed. 1987).

[75]Chrysler Corp. v. Brown, 441 U.S. 281, 293 (1979).

The most important exemptions for journalists are exemption 1, national security; exemption 6, personnel and medical files; and exemption 7, law enforcement investigation records. The most important exemption for business is the fourth, protecting confidential business information. Businesses are also protected by exemption 3, matters required to be withheld by other statutes; 8, banking reports; and 9, information about oil and gas wells. The other FOIA exemptions are 2, internal rules and agency practices; and 5, interagency or intraagency memoranda.

(1) National Security Exemption 1 protects from forced disclosure agency records that could damage the national defense and foreign policy if they were made public. The FOIA grants the executive branch more discretion for withholding national security information than for any other category. Exemption 1 is the only exemption that allows the executive branch, rather than Congress, to spell out the criteria for the release of documents.

In fact, prior to 1974 amendments to the FOIA, Congress had provided no check on executive branch authority to withhold documents in the interest of national security. Before 1974, exemption 1 gave the executive branch unrestricted discretion to withhold materials it had labeled "top secret," "secret," or "confidential." In 1973, in *EPA v. Mink,* the Supreme Court said exemption 1 meant that classification decisions were not subject to court review. In *Mink,* Congresswoman Patsy Mink and 32 colleagues had requested classified documents used by President Nixon to decide whether to conduct a nuclear test at Amchitka Island, Alaska. The Supreme Court said that the language of exemption 1 made it clear that Congress intended to rely on executive branch decision making. The Court said that Congress did not intend that the judiciary question whether agency decisions were justified.[76]

In the year following *Mink,* Congress, over the veto of President Gerald Ford, amended the FOIA to authorize judicial review of materials withheld by the government under exemption 1. Judges were given the authority to decide whether the government has properly classified and withheld information under criteria established by the president. The government must satisfy the court that proper classification procedures are followed and that the records in question "logically fall" into the national security exemption.[77]

The classification scheme being used during the early years of President George Bush's administration was put into effect by his predecessor, Ronald Reagan. Reagan's 1982 executive order used the same three levels of classification as his predecessor, Jimmy Carter: top secret, secret, and confidential. A "top secret" classification is used when officials claim that disclosure of a record could reasonably be expected "to cause exceptionally grave damage to the national security." Records are to be classified "secret" when disclosure could "cause serious damage" and "confidential" when disclosure could cause only "damage." The level of classification controls who has access to documents. All levels of classification protect the records from public disclosure.

The Reagan classification order used by Bush includes language that sounds protective of the public interest in the disclosure of government records. The order "rec-

---

[76]410 U.S. 73, 81–84, 1 Media L. Rep. 2448, 2451–52 (1973).
[77]*E.g.,* Weissman v. CIA, 565 F.2d 692, 2 Media L. Rep. 1276 (D.C. Cir. 1977).

ognizes'' the importance of an informed public and it prohibits government officials from withholding records unless necessary to protect the national security. The Reagan order even specifically bans classification to conceal illegal administrative activities or to prevent the disclosure of embarrassing mistakes.[78]

However, despite the classification order's recognition of the public interest in disclosure, the thrust of most of the document is to encourage classification, thus allowing the government to withhold more information. Reagan's 1982 classification order was the first in three decades to enlarge, rather than decrease, the classification authority.[79] For example, while the classification of a document under the criteria established by President Carter was left up to the officials examining the documents, information meeting the Reagan-Bush criteria must automatically be classified. Officials classifying documents are not currently required to balance the need for security against the public's interest in disclosure, as they were under the Carter administration.[80] Neither are officials required to look for ''identifiable'' harm to national security if the records are released. Rather, the current classification order directs that information shall be classified if disclosure could ''reasonably'' be expected to damage national security. Under the Reagan-Bush classification order, any doubts about classification are to be resolved—at least temporarily—in favor of classification and in favor of classification at a higher rather than a lower level.

Unlike the Carter order, the current classification order provides that unclassified information, possibly information that is publicly available, can still be classified. The current order also provides that information could be classified after the government receives a request for it. Carter's order provided that individual documents could be classified for only 20 years unless a longer term could be specifically justified. Currently, information may remain classified indefinitely without review.

The list of categories of information that can be classified includes military plans, weapons, or operations; intelligence activities, sources, and methods; information about foreign governments; U.S. foreign relations; scientific, technological, or economic matters relating to national security; and programs for safeguarding nuclear materials or facilities.

FOIA suits can challenge the classification of any document. However, the courts have rarely ordered the release of information that the executive branch says should remain classified.[81] Although the amended FOIA authorizes judges to review executive branch classification decisions, judges ordinarily defer to the president, who is given the power by the Constitution to conduct foreign policy and to supervise national security.[82] In addition, most courts seem to share the sentiment of the judge who said that ''few judges have the skill or experience to weigh the repercussions of disclosure of intelligence information.''[83] Judges are seldom willing to second-guess

---

[78]Exec. Order No. 12,356, 3 C.F.R. 166, 8 Media L. Rep. 1306 (1982).

[79]H.R. Rep. No. 97–731, 97th Cong., 2d Sess. 9–12, 43 (1982).

[80]Exec. Order No. 12,065, 3 C.F.R. 190 (1978).

[81]*E.g.,* Note, ''National Security Information Disclosure under the FOIA: The Need for Effective Judicial Enforcement,'' 25 *Boston Col. L. Rev.* 611, 629 (1984).

[82]*E.g.,* Bell v. United States, 563 F.2d 484, 487, 3 Media L. Rep. 1154, 1156 (1st Cir. 1977); Note, ''National Security Information Disclosure under the FOIA: The Need for Effective Judicial Enforcement,'' 25 *Boston Col. L. Rev.* 611, 614–15, 636 (1984).

[83]Weissman v. CIA, 565 F.2d at 697, 2 Media L. Rep. at 1279.

military officers, who classify documents on the grounds that disclosure will reveal confidential sources[84] or jeopardize intelligence sources, methods, or capabilities.[85]

In 1982, a federal appeals court deferred to military judgment when it said that a compilation of combat unit readiness reports had been properly classified as confidential. Although the readiness reports of individual combat units had been unclassified for 20 years, the U.S. Court of Appeals for the District of Columbia held that the Reagan administration had properly classified the compilations under FOIA exemption 1. The court gave "utmost deference" to the contentions of three generals that the disclosure of the records would result in "identifiable" damage to the national security, taking into consideration "the knowledge, experience and positions held by the three . . . regarding military secrets, military planning and national security."[86]

Although Congress has given the courts the authority to examine classified materials in chambers,[87] judges often decline to do so. Typically, courts are willing to accept the government's argument for the need to withhold documents if the government's affidavit is sufficiently specific, not contradicted by other evidence, and apparently made in good faith.[88]

Critics argue that the courts have effectively created a presumption that documents can be withheld under exemption 1 contrary to the presumption of openness that pervades the FOIA generally.[89] However, judges have enforced the procedural requirements of the classification process and insisted on detailed justifications for the classification of individual records. In at least one case, a court decided that the CIA had not demonstrated that disclosing documents about its activities in the Dominican Republic more than 25 years ago would damage national security.[90] In another, the threat of a judicial inspection pressured the CIA into releasing information about two persons with ties to radical political groups.[91]

(2) Agency Rules and Practices   Exemption 2 allows agencies to withhold documents "related solely" to internal personnel rules and practices. The courts have said exemption 2 applies only to management records of little or no concern to the general public. Among the records fitting the exemption are regulations governing filing, parking, cafeteria use, and sick leave.

In the most significant exemption 2 court case, *Department of the Air Force v. Rose,* the Supreme Court said the exemption does not allow the government to withhold documents involving issues of a "genuine and significant public interest." The Court said that exemption 2 could not be used by the U.S. Air Force Academy to withhold summaries of honors and ethics hearings, with the identification of the participants deleted. New York University Law Review editors wanted the summaries for

---

[84]*E.g.,* Lesar v. Department of Justice, 636 F.2d 472 (1980).

[85]*E.g.,* Hayden v. National Sec. Agency, 608 F.2d 1381, 5 Media L. Rep. 1897 (D.C. Cir. 1979), *cert. denied,* 446 U.S. 937 (1980).

[86]Taylor v. Department of the Army, 684 F.2d 99, 109, 8 Media L. Rep. 2214, 2221 (D.C. Cir. 1982).

[87]5 U.S.C. sec. 552 (a) (4) (B) (1988).

[88]Hayden v. National Sec. Agency, 608 F.2d at 1387–88, 5 Media L. Rep. at 1900–1901.

[89]*See generally* Note, "National Security Information Disclosure under the FOIA: The Need for Effective Judicial Enforcement," 25 *Boston Col. L. Rev.* 611 (1984).

[90]Fitzgibbon v. CIA, 578 F. Supp. 704 (D.D.C. 1983).

[91]Turner v. Ray, 587 F.2d 1187, 1212 n.51 (D.C. Cir. 1978); Note, "National Security Information Disclosure under the FOIA: The Need for Effective Judicial Enforcement," 25 *Boston Col. L. Rev.* 611, 637 (1984).

an article about discipline at the military academies. Justice Brennan, writing for a majority of the Court, said the

> general thrust of the exemption is simply to relieve agencies of the burden of assembling and maintaining for public inspection matter in which the public could not reasonably be expected to have an interest. The case summaries plainly do not fit that description. They are not matter with merely internal significance. They do not concern only routine matters. Their disclosure entails no particular administrative burden.[92]

Brennan said the public interest in discipline at the Air Force Academy was obvious given the importance of discipline to military effectiveness.

Under exemption 2, agency staff manuals of interest to the public have created the most controversy. The courts tend to protect the withholding of agency manuals when disclosure might allow individuals to circumvent agency rules, particularly in the case of law enforcement agencies. Two circuits of the U.S. Courts of Appeals have said that exemption 2 allows the Bureau of Alcohol, Tobacco and Firearms to withhold a manual about how to conduct searches and raids.[93] In contrast, the U.S. Court of Appeals for the Sixth Circuit said an IRS auditing manual did not qualify for exemption 2 because the release of the manual contained information of interest to taxpayers as well as to agency employees.[94]

(3) Statutory Exemptions   The third exemption applies to documents that Congress has declared in other statutes to be confidential. The third exemption is often called the "catch-all" exemption because it exempts from disclosure any records Congress has decided to exclude from the general policy of openness under the FOIA.

The exemption applies to Census Bureau records, tax returns, and patent applications. It allows for the withholding of records possessed and controlled by such agencies as the U.S. Postal Service, the Central Intelligence Agency, the Department of Agriculture, the Federal Trade Commission, the Consumer Product Safety Commission, the Veterans Administration, the Equal Employment Opportunity Commission, and the General Accounting Office. The FOI Service Center said that in recent years agencies have cited nearly 100 catch-all statutes to justify withholding information. The validity of most of these claims has not been tested in court.[95]

Under exemption 3, administrators can only withhold documents as authorized by a statute; a federal administrative rule is not sufficient.[96] The exemption specifies that a statute either must (1) mandate that documents be withheld, leaving no discretion for an administrator, or (2) provide precise criteria for determining what should be withheld. In 1984, for example, Congress passed legislation exempting specific operational files of the CIA from the FOIA. The law protects records related to the conduct of foreign intelligence operations, background investigations of informants, intelligence arrangements with foreign governments, and scientific and technical

---

[92]Department of the Air Force v. Rose, 425 U.S. 352, 369–70, 1 Media L. Rep. 2509, 2515 (1976).

[93]Caplan v. Bureau of Alcohol, Tobacco & Firearms, 587 F.2d 544, 4 Media L. Rep. 1851 (2d Cir. 1978); Hardy v. Bureau of Alcohol, Tobacco & Firearms, 631 F.2d 653, 6 Media L. Rep. 2236 (9th Cir. 1980).

[94]Hawkes v. IRS, 467 F.2d 787 (6th Cir. 1972).

[95]FOI Service Center, *How to Use the Federal FOI Act* 11 (6th ed. 1987).

[96]Administrator, FAA v. Robertson, 422 U.S. 255,1 Media L. Rep. 2465 (1975).

methods of obtaining intelligence. Congress passed the law, in part, to help the CIA cope with a huge backlog of FOIA requests. Although most of the records covered by the statute would have been exempted under the national security provision of the FOIA, the legislation was intended to relieve the agency from the time-consuming process of responding to FOIA requests that would eventually be denied. Since Congress has specifically exempted the documents from the FOIA, the CIA no longer must respond to each request for records by searching its files, reviewing documents, and writing a justification for denial.[97]

Congress can, instead of requiring that specific documents be withheld, provide an agency with criteria for withholding records. For example, the National Security Act provides the National Security Agency with criteria when it exempts from disclosure records containing "the names, titles, salaries, or number of persons employed by" the NSA.[98]

Agencies cannot shield documents from disclosure under exemption 3 without specific authorization from Congress or criteria provided by Congress. A federal appeals court said that a statute authorizing the Secretary of State to withhold "foreign affairs expenditures" was too broad to meet the requirements of exemption 3. The statute did not sufficiently specify the records to be withheld.[99]

(4) Confidential Business Information Regulated businesses such as broadcast stations and drug manufacturing companies must submit voluminous amounts of information to regulatory agencies. In addition, businesses seeking government contracts must provide government officials with proprietary information. Exemption 4 protects trade secrets and commercial or financial information businesses send to government agencies on a confidential basis.

The FOIA's impact on businesses was one of the most controversial FOI issues of the 1980s. Businesses themselves file more than half of the Freedom of Information Act requests. Businesses have obtained, through the FOIA, information about government agency procedures, inspection plans, and enforcement policies. For example, businesses can obtain the procedures the Food and Drug Administration uses in its inspections of food processing plants and drug companies to better prepare for FDA visits.

However, most of the business use of the FOIA is for industrial espionage, a term that refers to businesses obtaining information about their competitors.[100] For instance, Suzuki Motor Company has acquired copies of records submitted to the U.S. government by Toyota, information that it cannot obtain from the Japanese government. One scholar reported that a food processing company saved "tens of thousands of dollars" because of an innovation, but any competitive advantage was quickly destroyed when the Environmental Protection Agency mailed the blueprints to a larger competitor for 10 cents a page.[101]

---

[97]Central Intelligence Agency Information Act, Pub. L. No. 98–477, sec. 701, 98 Stat. 2209 (1984).

[98]*See* 50 U.S.C. sec. 402 (1982).

[99]Washington Post Co. v. Department of State, 685 F.2d 698, 8 Media L. Rep. 2206 (D.C. Cir. 1982).

[100]J. Rose, remarks at "The Freedom of Information Act; How Is It Working?", conference transcript, at 20

[101]O'Reilly, "Regaining a Confidence: Protection of Business Confidential Data through Reform of the Freedom of Information Act," 34 *Admin. L. Rev.* 263–64 (1982).

Thus, the Freedom of Information Act has become a window of opportunity for some businesses at the same time it has become a threat to the survival of others. Businesses say they feel trapped by the government. They are required to provide economically sensitive information without being able to control who will see it. The FOIA exemption protects confidential business information only if government agencies choose to use the exemption to deny requests for records. Instead, agencies sometimes choose to release documents that businesses want kept confidential. In addition, agencies sometimes accidentally release sensitive information. For example, in 1982, the EPA gave a secret Monsanto herbicide formula to a competitor because of an agency processing error. The formula for "Roundup" weed killer had been responsible for 40 percent of Monsanto's profits during the previous year.[102] Finally, even if an agency believes that a record may qualify under exemption 4, a court may not. If an agency's decision that sensitive information can be withheld under exemption 4 is appealed, a court may decide to reverse the agency.

Of the two provisions in exemption 4 that may protect businesses, the least used allows agencies to withhold documents that contain trade secrets, commercially valuable information and formulas used and kept secret by a business. One of the most famous examples of a trade secret is the formula for Coca-Cola. Experts disagree on a precise meaning for the term *trade secret*. The FOIA does not define the term and there have been few court opinions.[103] A few courts have said that a trade secret is "any formula, pattern, device, or compilation of information" used in one's business that provides an advantage over competitors. However, a federal appeals court has limited the definition of *trade secret* for the purpose of the FOIA to information directly applicable to the production of goods.[104]

Even if an agency wanted to disregard exemption 4 and disclose a trade secret, it may not be at liberty to do so. Although agencies have discretion over whether to disclose records under FOIA exemptions, the disclosure of trade secrets is prohibited by the Trade Secrets Act.[105] The Trade Secrets Act may *require* agencies to withhold documents they are *permitted* to release under FOIA exemption 4.[106]

Most of the exemption 4 litigation has focused not on the trade secret provision, but rather on the provision protecting confidential "commercial or financial information." This provision covers business sales statistics, overhead and operating costs, information about financial condition, and data about a company's work force. The exemption allows the government to withhold only data submitted by the business seeking the confidentiality and not to information the government collects from other sources. For records to qualify as *confidential* commercial and financial information, according to the courts, the disclosure must be likely to (1) impair the

---

[102]"EPA Lets Trade Secret Loose in Slip-Up, to Firm's Dismay," *Washington Post,* Sept. 18, 1982, at A1. *But see* Stevenson, "Protecting Business Secrets under the Freedom of Information Act: Managing Exemption 4," 34 *Admin. L. Rev.* 220 (1982) (scholar argues that FOIA is not responsible for the release of secret or confidential business information).

[103]*E.g.,* A. Adler, ed., *Litigation under the Federal Freedom of Information Act and Privacy Act* 70–71 (14th ed. 1989); J. Franklin and R. Bouchard, *Guidebook to the Freedom of Information and Privacy Acts,* para. 1.07, at 1–62 (April 1988).

[104]Public Citizen Health Research Group v. Food and Drug Admin., 704 F.2d 1280, 1288 (D.C. Cir. 1983).

[105]18 U.S.C. sec. 1905 (1988).

[106]A. Adler, ed., *Litigation under the Federal Freedom of Information Act and Privacy Act* 83 (14th ed. 1989); J. Franklin and R. Bouchard, *Guidebook to the Freedom of Information and Privacy Acts,* para. 1.08, at 1–74 (April 1988).

government's ability to obtain necessary information in the future or (2) cause "substantial" harm to the competitive position of the company providing the information.[107]

In *Orion Research Inc. v. EPA,* a federal appeals court said the Environmental Protection Agency can withhold details of bids submitted to the agency because disclosure would discourage businesses from submitting novel ideas. In *Orion,* a company that lost a competitive bid wanted to see the winning proposal. The U.S. Court of Appeals for the First Circuit said disclosure "would have a chilling effect" on the willingness of potential bidders to submit proposals. The court said businesses would fear that competitors would learn too much from their submissions.[108]

An agency can also refuse to release records when disclosure would cause substantial competitive harm to the business submitting the data. Federal appeals courts have said that businesses need not show actual competitive harm to justify the government's withholding of documents under exemption 4. Businesses only have to demonstrate that they have competition and that the disclosure of company documents would likely result in a substantial injury to their competitive position. Under this test, a court upheld the Defense Department's refusal to reveal information provided by Norris Industries about one of the weapons the company manufactures. Norris had submitted financial data, including production costs, for the M549 warhead for artillery. The information was sought by Gulf & Western, a competitor that built the first M549 warheads. The U.S. Court of Appeals for the D.C. Circuit, upholding the Army's refusal to disclose Norris's financial data, noted that the Army would soon solicit new bids for the ammunition. The court said that Norris's competitors—including Gulf & Western—could calculate Norris's future bids and pricing structure if the information was disclosed, and could undercut Norris's bids, creating "substantial competitive harm."[109]

Business concerns over the risk of competitive loss through information released under the FOIA increased in 1976 when the U.S. Supreme Court said that businesses do not have the right under the act to block the release of records they have submitted to the government. In *Chrysler Corp. v. Brown,* the auto company tried to block the government's release of detailed employment records of a Delaware assembly plant. Chrysler is one of many corporations under government contract that must report their minority hiring practices to the government. Under Labor Department regulations, much of this information is available to the public.

Chrysler argued that competitors could use the data to raid Chrysler employees and to determine what technology was being used and what equipment was working.[110] Justice Rehnquist, writing for a unanimous Supreme Court, said the FOIA provided no mechanism that would allow a company submitting records to stop an agency from releasing information, even if the documents qualified for exemption 4. The nine FOIA exemptions allow, but do not require, agencies to withhold information. Congress, said Rehnquist, "did not limit an agency's discretion to disclose information."[111]

---

[107]National Parks and Conservation Ass'n v. Morton, 498 F.2d 765 (D.C. Cir. 1974).
[108]615 F.2d 551, 5 Media L. Rep. 2598 (1st Cir. 1980).
[109]Gulf & Western Industries, Inc. v. United States, 615 F.2d 527 (1979).
[110]Chrysler Corp. v. Schlesinger, 412 F. Supp. 171 (1976).
[111]Chrysler Corp. v. Brown, 441 U.S. 281, 293, 4 Media L. Rep. 2441, 2447 (1979).

After *Chrysler,* a business can still bring a "reverse FOIA suit" to block release of business information by arguing that agency release of the records is arbitrary and capricious, an abuse of discretion, or a violation of another law. If the business cannot show a specific statute that requires withholding a record, it will have to prove that release of a record would cause substantial competitive harm.[112]

Businesses wanting to block the release of sensitive information without going to court received help from the Reagan administration in 1987. President Reagan issued an executive order requiring agencies to establish procedures to allow businesses to object before an agency releases "arguably" confidential information. The order directed the agencies to allow businesses submitting information to identify information they believe could be "confidential commercial information" under exemption 4. Under the order, an agency must notify a business when the agency receives an FOI request for information the company has designated "confidential." The agency must allow the business time to object to disclosure, and explain why those objections were overruled if the agency decides to disclose the records anyway.[113]

(5) Interagency or Intraagency Memoranda The widely used exemption 5 protects the deliberative process of executive agencies. Exemption 5 incorporates into the FOIA what is known as "executive privilege." It exempts working documents, circulated within an agency or between agencies, that historically have been considered privileged government communications under common law.

Exemption 5 is designed to encourage open, frank discussion on policy matters, particularly among agency personnel. Officials contend that sensitive issues may be discussed more thoroughly in preliminary stages without the glare of publicity. Many officials argue they are more likely to suggest unconventional ideas if records of their discussions are exempt from disclosure. Officials say they want to be judged by what they decide and not by what is considered while making up their minds. Once an official's position on an issue is made public it is difficult to change, many contend.

Exemption 5 is also intended to protect the public from confusion resulting from premature disclosure of discussions prior to policy adoption.[114] Hence, the courts have said that the exemption protects the deliberative policy-making process, but not purely factual material.[115] Even so, critics claim the exemption can be used to shield documents not related to the decision-making process that would reveal improper or embarrassing behavior by public officials.

Exemption 5 shields policy drafts, staff proposals, studies, and reports. The courts have held the exemption also applies to documents provided by consultants and to witnesses used by the government in policy preparation and self-criticism. In 1984, the Supreme Court decided the exemption protected the U.S. Air Force from disclosing confidential statements made during a "safety investigation" of a 1973 crash. The exemption was necessary, the Court said, to encourage uninhibited fact-

---

[112]A. Adler, ed., *Litigation under the Federal Freedom of Information Act and Privacy Act* 82–83 (14th ed. 1989); J. Franklin and R. Bouchard, *Guidebook to the Freedom of Information and Privacy Acts,* para. 4.04[7][a], at 4–48 (April 1988).

[113]Exec. Order No. 12,600, 52 Fed. Reg. 23,781 (1987).

[114]*E.g.,* Jordan v. Department of Justice, 591 F.2d 753, 772–73, 4 Media L. Rep. 1785, 1800 (D.C. Cir. 1978).

[115]*E.g.,* Coastal States Gas Corp. v. Department of Energy, 617 F.2d 854, 867 (D.C. Cir. 1980).

finding. The Court, in *United States v. Weber Aircraft,* said the confidential testimony was unquestionably intraagency communication protected from disclosure to ensure efficient governmental operation.

The Air Force uses "safety investigations" of accidents, such as the one discussed in Weber Aircraft, to prevent future mishaps. In safety investigations, the Air Force wants as much information as possible, including conjecture, speculation, and opinion. To encourage candid assessments, witnesses are promised confidentiality. Safety investigations are different from formal public investigations undertaken to determine whether anyone should be punished. During the formal investigations, witnesses testify under oath in formal hearings governed by standard rules of evidence.

In the 1973 crash, the pilot, Captain Richard Hoover, was severely injured when he ejected from an F–106B after its engine failed. Hoover and the airman who had prepared his parachute were interviewed during a safety investigation conducted by the Air Force. When Hoover sued the Weber Aircraft Corporation and the Mills Manufacturing Corporation for providing faulty ejection equipment in the F–106B, the two companies wanted access to everything the Air Force knew about the accident.

The Air Force released the entire record of the public investigation and facts gathered during the safety investigation. When it refused to release the confidential portions of the safety investigation, the two companies filed a suit under the FOIA. The Supreme Court, in *Weber Aircraft,* said confidential statements made to crash safety investigators had been privileged in the common law for more than 20 years. The common law recognized a need for "privilege when confidentiality is necessary to ensure frank and open discussion and hence efficient governmental operations."[116]

Exemption 5 does not protect predecision documents that become the basis of final policy declaration. The Supreme Court has said that disclosure after a decision has been made does not endanger the decision-making process. Further, "the public is vitally concerned" with the reasons agencies adopt policies.[117] Hence, materials gathered or prepared during the decision-making process can lose their exemption 5 protection if they become part of a final decision. This is what happened to a memorandum prepared for Watergate Special Prosecutor Leon Jaworski. The memorandum would have been exempt as an intraagency document that outlined the pardoning power of the president of the United States. However, the final report of the Watergate Special Prosecution Force quoted the memorandum in support of an argument that Richard Nixon not be indicted for Watergate crimes. Therefore, the U.S. Court of Appeals for the Seventh Circuit held that the memorandum had become part of a final opinion and could not be exempt under the FOIA.[118]

Courts have also ruled that exemption 5 allows the government to withhold documents protected by the attorney-client privilege. Therefore, exemption 5 protects from forced disclosure an agency's communications with its attorneys, including the U.S. Department of Justice. The exemption also protects documents prepared by an attorney that would reveal case strategy.[119] In addition, the exemption partially pro-

---

[116]465 U.S. 792, 802, 10 Media L. Rep. 1477, 1482–83 (1984).
[117]National Labor Relations Bd. v. Sears, Roebuck & Co., 421 U.S. 132, 152, 1 Media L. Rep. 2471, 2478 (1975).
[118]Niemeier v. Watergate Special Prosecution Force, 565 F.2d 967, 3 Media L. Rep. 1321 (7th Cir. 1977).
[119]*See* FTC v. Grolier, 462 U.S. 19, 9 Media L. Rep. 1737 (1983).

tects confidential commercial information gathered by the government in preparation for awarding contracts.[120]

(6) Personnel or Medical Files   Exemption 6 protects from forced disclosure information in personnel, medical, and "similar" files that "would constitute a clearly unwarranted invasion of personal privacy." Exemption 6 shields more than "highly personal" or "intimate" information. However, agencies have to balance the interest in privacy against the public interest in monitoring the activities of government. The exemption allows the government to withhold personal information if its release would be *clearly unwarranted* when balanced against the legitimate information needs of the public.

Exemption 6 can protect the personnel records of government employees, and documents that reveal any individual's marital status, medical condition, employment, welfare payments, alcohol consumption, and religious affiliation. In addition, exemption 6 has protected the names and addresses of persons affiliated with unions or holding Veterans Administration loans.[121]

The threshold issue in an exemption 6 case is whether a record falls within the definition of "personnel," "medical," and "similar" files. Exemption 6 protects a wide range of personal information because the courts have interpreted the term *similar files* in the exemption broadly. In 1982, the Supreme Court said that *similar* applied to any information about a specific individual held by the federal government. In *Department of State v. Washington Post Co.,* the Court voted 9–0 that citizenship information qualified as a "similar" file and could be withheld. The *Washington Post* had filed an FOIA request asking whether two Iranian officials were U.S. citizens. Justice Rehnquist, writing for eight of the nine justices, said that Congress intended exemption 6 to apply generally to information about individuals held by the government. Rehnquist said a file does not have to contain intimate information to merit withholding. The kinds of files used as a benchmark in the exemption—personnel and medical files—contain significant amounts of information that is not intimate.

Rehnquist said exemption 6 was intended "to protect individuals from the injury and embarrassment that can result from the unnecessary disclosure of personal information."[122] The State Department said that giving the *Washington Post* the information it sought could threaten the safety of the Iranians because of the "intense anti-American sentiment in Iran." The Supreme Court referred the *Post*'s request to the lower courts to determine whether the release of the personal information would constitute a clearly unwarranted invasion of personal privacy.

Before the *Washington Post* case, the Supreme Court said exemption 6 did not create an absolute right to privacy even for personnel, medical, or similar files. In *Department of the Air Force v. Rose,* the Court said that "Congress had made it clear" that information was not to be "insulated from disclosure" simply because it was in a personnel file. Some FOIA requests for personal information fall outside the protection of the exemption. The statute protects privacy interests only against "a clearly unwarranted invasion."

---

[120]Federal Open Market Comm. v. Merrill, 443 U.S. 340, 5 Media L. Rep. 1221 (1975).

[121]A. Adler, ed., *Litigation under the Federal Freedom of Information Act and Privacy Act* 106, 110–12 (14th ed. 1989).

[122]456 U.S. 595, 8 Media L. Rep. 1521 (1982).

In *Rose,* the Court said that Congress intended the term *clearly unwarranted* to be the device to balance the individual right to privacy against the need for the public to know information about government.[123] Personal information was to be exempt from disclosure only if it might harm the individual or expose an individual to unnecessary public scrutiny. The need for privacy in an individual case must be balanced against the FOIA's purpose of opening agency action up to public scrutiny. When New York University Law Review editors sought transcripts of honors and ethics hearings at the Air Force Academy, the Court said discipline in the military academies was a matter of public concern. The Court acknowledged the public's stake in training military officers. The Supreme Court said that a federal district court must examine the transcripts of the hearings to determine whether eliminating direct personal references sufficiently protected the privacy interests of the cadets.

The federal appeals courts have uniformly held that, because exemption 6 provides that an invasion of privacy must be "clearly unwarranted," the scales tilt strongly toward a public interest in disclosure of the information.[124] For example, in *Arieff v. Navy,* a court said that information about prescription drugs ordered by the Office of Attending Physician to the Congress should be released to *Congressional Quarterly.* The Office of Attending Physician serves the medical needs of members of Congress and the U.S. Supreme Court, as well as other officials. The U.S. Court of Appeals for the D.C. Circuit, overturning a lower court decision, said that the name, quantity, and price of the drugs ordered by the Office provided information relevant to monitoring the government's activities, "the 'core purpose' of the FOIA."[125] A federal district court had said that, although *Congressional Quarterly*'s request indicated that information identifying drug recipients could be deleted, release of the records would constitute a "clearly unwarranted invasion of personal privacy." The lower court had said the records, coupled with other publicly available information, "would enable identification of the medical conditions" of specific individuals. However, the D.C. Circuit said that the government had not demonstrated that threats to individual privacy were "more palpable than mere possibility."[126] The D.C. Circuit said the district court could shield portions of the records only if there were more than a "mere possibility" that a specific person could be identified. Otherwise, it said, the records should be disclosed.

The public interest in disclosure is more likely to outweigh privacy concerns when records provide information about the performance of public officials and government agencies. In *Columbia Packing Co. v. Department of Agriculture,* another federal appeals court found a substantial public interest in the personnel records of two former federal meat inspectors. The two inspectors, Joseph F. Mauriello and Domenic L. Germano, had been convicted of taking bribes in a widespread scandal in the meat packing industry. The records were ordered released. The U.S. Court of Appeals for the First Circuit said that ordinarily the individual careers of public servants would be of little general interest. However, public curiosity about the careers

---

[123]425 U.S. at 372, 1 Media L. Rep. at 2516 (1976).
[124]*See* A. Adler, ed., *Litigation under the Federal Freedom of Information Act and Privacy Act* 108 (14th ed. 1989).
[125]712 F.2d 1462, 1468, 9 Media L. Rep. 2302, 2305–2306 (D.C. Cir. 1983).
[126]*Id.* at 1467–68, *quoting* Department of the Air Force v. Rose, 425 U.S. at 380 n.19, 1 Media L. Rep. at 2520 n.19 (1976).

of the meat inspectors was "legitimate." To prevent similar scandals, the court said, the public had an interest in how the inspectors conducted themselves before their discharge and how well they were supervised.[127]

The courts' consideration of the public interest in exemption 6 cases has led to evaluating the purpose of FOIA requests, not ordinarily permitted to be a factor under the FOIA. The FOIA does not require requesters to explain why they are seeking information from the government.[128] However, the reasons for seeking personal information can be factors in the government's handling of exemption 6 requests. In *Wine Hobby USA, Inc. v. IRS,* for example, the U.S. Court of Appeals for the Third Circuit upheld the withholding of the names and addresses of amateur winemakers because the purpose of the request was commercial and "wholly unrelated to the purposes" of the FOIA.[129]

A number of factors besides the purpose of the request can affect a court's balancing of the personal privacy interests and the public interest in disclosure. A frequent consideration, one mentioned earlier in both *Rose* and *Arieff,* is whether references to individuals could be deleted. If so, the records, such as prescription drug information in *Arieff,* can often be released. If not, the courts will order the government to withhold only the part of the information necessary to protect an individual's privacy.[130] Among other factors considered in balancing privacy protection and public interest in disclosure are whether an agency promised confidentiality or whether individuals are thought to have waived their rights to privacy.[131] An agency may decide that a person has waived a right to privacy if he or she provided the government with information in exchange for a benefit, such as a research grant or building contract.[132]

Disclosures of personal information under the Freedom of Information Act are not supposed to be limited by the Privacy Act of 1974, which was intended to give individuals some control over information the government collects and disseminates about them. While the intent of the FOIA is to reveal government operations to the public, the intent of the privacy act is to protect against government misuse of information about identifiable individuals.

Under the privacy act, individuals generally have the right to obtain and amend personal information about themselves. In addition, the privacy act requires government agencies to use a "personally identifiable record" only for the reasons it was collected or for reasons specifically listed in the act itself. Agencies are otherwise prohibited from disclosing personal information without the written consent of the person involved. Agencies must keep track of each disclosure.[133]

The privacy act would appear to mandate that government agencies withhold more information about individuals than could be withheld under the exemptions of

---

[127]563 F.2d 495, 3 Media L. Rep. 1441 (1st Cir. 1977).

[128]A. Adler, ed., *Litigation under the Federal Freedom of Information Act and Privacy Act* 11, 113-17 (14th ed. 1989).

[129]502 F.2d 133, 137 (3d Cir. 1974).

[130]*See* Department of the Air Force v. Rose, 425 U.S. at 378-82, 1 Media L. Rep. at 2518-20 (1976).

[131]*See generally* A. Adler, ed., *Litigation under the Federal Freedom of Information Act and Privacy Act* 118-19 (14th ed. 1989).

[132]*E.g.,* Kurzon v. Department of Health and Human Servs., 649 F.2d 65, 7 Media L. Rep. 1591 (1st Cir. 1981).

[133]5 U.S.C. secs. 552a (b)(3), (a)(7), (e)(1), (b), (c), (d) (1982). *See* J.T. O'Reilly, 2 *Federal Information Disclosure* para. 21.01, at 21-1, 21-2; para. 20.09, at 20-34; para. 22.30, at 22-10 (Dec. 1986).

the FOIA. However, in 1984, Congress passed legislation stating explicitly that the privacy act could not be used by a government agency to deny access to information that should be available under the FOIA.[134] If there is a conflict between the privacy act and the FOIA, the FOIA is supposed to prevail. But even after the congressional action, the privacy act may cause agencies to be cautious about releasing an individual's records under the FOIA. First, the standard of "clearly unwarranted invasion of privacy" in FOIA exemption 6 is so imprecise that agencies are not sure what personal information must be released under the FOIA. Second, if an agency improperly releases records under FOIA, it can be sued for damages under the privacy act.[135]

In addition to the privacy act, another federal statute designed to protect personal privacy is the Family Educational Rights and Privacy Act, often called the Buckley Amendment. The Buckley Amendment permits parents to see their children's school records and prohibits the distribution of personal information without the consent of parents.[136] Schools receiving federal funding may only release what is called "directory information," which includes a student's name, address, telephone, date and place of birth, attendance record, field of study, degrees, and participation in official activities. Grades and health information may not be released. Although the Buckley Amendment may limit the reporting of a few newsworthy disciplinary problems, it should not severely limit the mass media. However, school officials fearing the loss of federal funding could interpret the act to unnecessarily limit access to information about students.

The passage of the FOIA, the privacy act, and the Buckley Amendment were attempts to find a compromise between the interests in personal privacy and disclosure of government-held information. Congress has recognized that

> It is vital to our way of life to reach a workable balance between the right of the public to know and the need of the Government to keep information in confidence. . . . The right of the individual to be able to find out how his Government is operating can be just as important to him as the right of privacy and his right to confide in his Government.[137]

(7) Law Enforcement Investigations Exemption 7 permits the withholding of several records and pieces of information "compiled" for law enforcement purposes. For the documents to be protected under the exemption, an agency can show that disclosure could reasonably be expected to interfere with law enforcement proceedings or investigations, invade personal privacy, or endanger someone's life. Alternatively, an agency seeking to withhold documents could show that disclosure would reveal protected enforcement techniques and procedures or would deprive a defendant of a fair trial.

Exemption 7 is designed to bar the release of documents that would harm a pending government case or disclose investigative methods or sources damaging to future

---

[134]98 Stat. 2211–12 (1984).
[135]J.T. O'Reilly, 2 *Federal Information Disclosure* para. 27.07, at 22–35 (Dec. 1986).
[136]20 U.S.C. sec. 1232 (1988).
[137]H.R. Rep. No. 1497, 89th Cong., 2d Sess. 3–4, in 1966 *U.S. Code Cong. & Admin. News* 2418, 2423.

operations. Prisoners and criminal organizations have tried to use the FOIA to discover evidence and sources used against them, sometimes to destroy the evidence, silence the source, or take revenge.[138] Former FBI Director William H. Webster once said "seemingly innocuous details in FBI records might provide the missing clue" to identify an FBI source to a criminal "or at least narrow down the candidates." Webster added that, "a criminal does not require proof positive before taking action on such information."[139]

The courts, when deciding an exemption 7 case, have employed a two-part test. First, a government agency must demonstrate the documents at issue are information or records compiled specifically for law enforcement purposes. Then it must show that the records fall into one of six categories of documents eligible for withholding.

In the last decade, the Supreme Court has twice been called upon to settle disputes over the meaning of the *compilation* of law enforcement records. In 1989, the Supreme Court said records used for law enforcement purposes are protected by the exemption even if they were originally compiled for other reasons. The court, in *John Doe Agency v. John Doe Corp.*,[140] said the requirement that documents must be "compiled" for law enforcement purposes did not mean that they had to be compiled exclusively for law enforcement purposes. In *Doe v. Doe,* a defense contractor under investigation for fraud sought financial records being used by the government in its investigation. The records originally had been collected by the Department of Defense in its auditing process. The contractor, Grumman Corp., argued that the records could not be withheld under exemption 7 because they had not been originally "compiled" for law enforcement purposes. The Supreme Court said the "plain words" of the exemption contained no qualification suggesting that records had to be "originally compiled" for an investigation. The Court said the dictionary meaning for "compiled" also applied to investigation records originally collected by the government for purposes other than law enforcement and later used in a law enforcement investigation.

In a prior case, the Supreme Court also said that information originally collected for law enforcement does not lose its protection when summarized or reproduced for another reason. In 1982, in *FBI v. Abramson,* an independent journalist wanted information about Nixon administration critics that the White House had received from the FBI in 1969. Howard Abramson's FOIA request asked for a memo from J. Edgar Hoover to White House official John Ehrlichman and information summaries on such people as economist Kenneth Galbraith, antiwar activist Benjamin Spock, and theologian Reinhold Niebuhr. The Court accepted the government's contention that the information had originally been compiled at the FBI for law enforcement purposes. Justice White, writing for a 5–4 majority, said the information would have been exempt from disclosure in its original form under the privacy provision of exemption 7. He said it was still exempt when reproduced or summarized in a new document prepared for a partisan political purpose unrelated to law enforcement.[141]

Exemption 7 applies to most records related to ongoing investigations or proceedings, such as interviews with witnesses, affidavits, and notes taken by investigat-

---

[138]*E.g., see* J.T. O'Reilly, 2 *Federal Information Disclosure* para. 17.01, at 17–4 (Dec. 1982).
[139]Note, "Developments under the Freedom of Information Act—1984," 1985 *Duke L.J.* 742, 751.
[140]110 S. Ct. 1471, 17 Media L. Rep. 1225 (1989).
[141]FBI v. Abramson, 456 U.S. 615, 8 Media L. Rep. 1561 (1982).

ing officers. An investigation qualifying for exemption 7 protection may be related to either civil or criminal proceedings. The proceedings may involve the federal courts or administrative agencies.[142]

In 1986, Congress adopted several amendments that increased the FBI's ability to withhold information, including a provision that authorized the FBI to deny the existence of documents that would reveal that an investigation is under way. The FBI can also refuse to acknowledge the existence of records related to foreign intelligence, counterintelligence, or international terrorism as long as the existence of the records is classified. Before, law enforcement agencies were required to disclose that they possessed the documents being requested and explain why the records had been withheld.[143] Law enforcement agencies had claimed that the admission that records did or did not exist provided the subjects of investigations valuable information that undermined law enforcement efforts.

If an agency establishes that an FOIA request has asked for a record compiled for law enforcement purposes, the next issue considered by the courts is whether the record fits one of the six exempt categories. Exemption 7(a), interference with law enforcement proceedings, is the one most often cited by agencies withholding information. Exemption 7(a) does not apply once enforcement proceedings have ended, such as in a conviction after a trial.[144]

Exemption 7(a) was one of the categories amended in 1986 to increase the FBI's ability to withhold records. Language that permits law enforcement agents to withhold information if access *could reasonably be expected* to cause harm to law enforcement proceedings was added to 7(a) and similar language was added to other categories. Before, records could be withheld only if disclosure *would* damage investigations. The less restrictive language in the 1986 amendments makes it easier for law enforcement officers to withhold information.

Three categories of records that can be withheld under exemption 7 protect the confidentiality of law enforcement sources, methods, and officers. Exemption 7(d) allows agencies to withhold records that could reasonably be expected to disclose the identity of a confidential source, including a state, local, or foreign agency or a private institution. It also protects confidential information furnished by a confidential source during a criminal investigation or a national security intelligence operation. The exemption protects, for example, the identity of persons involved in the Department of Justice witness relocation program.[145] One court said such material should be withheld "not only to protect those citizens who voluntarily provide law enforcement agencies with information, but also to ensure that such persons remain willing to provide such information in the future."[146]

Exemption 7(e) protects from mandatory disclosure documents that would reveal techniques and procedures used by law enforcement investigators and prosecutors. The exemption also protects guidelines for law enforcement investigations or prosecutions if disclosure could reasonably allow people to circumvent the law. The

---

[142]*E.g.*, A. Adler, ed., *Litigation under the Federal Freedom of Information Act and Privacy Act* 123–27 (14th ed. 1989).

[143]Freedom of Information Reform Act of 1986, Pub. L. No. 99–570, 100 Stat. 3207 (1986).

[144]*E.g.*, A. Adler, ed., *Litigation under Federal Freedom of Information Act and Privacy Act* 132 (14th ed. 1989).

[145]Librach v. FBI, 587 F.2d 372 (8th Cir. 1979).

[146]Maroscia v. Levi, 569 F.2d 1000, 1002 (7th Cir. 1977).

exemption is intended to shield information that would allow criminals to anticipate the methods law enforcement officers might use to catch them. Exemption 7(e) can be used by agencies to withhold from disclosure computer programs designed to appre-hend violators.[147] It cannot be used by agencies to withhold routine techniques and procedures such as fingerprinting and ballistics tests.

Exemption 7(f) can protect from disclosure information that would endanger the life or physical safety of any individual, including law enforcement personnel. Hence, a federal appeals court denied Anthony J. Scherer access to the names of law enforce-ment officers who investigated his involvement in the smuggling of guns and ammu-nition to foreign political groups.[148]

Two sections in exemption 7 protect the interests of persons with criminal re-cords rather than the interests of law enforcement officers. One of the least used of the exemptions, 7(b), protects against the disclosure of information that would en-danger a defendant's right to a fair trial or an impartial administrative judgment. A federal appeals court said the government can use 7(b) to withhold documents only if it can show that a trial or administrative proceeding is "pending or truly imminent" and "that it is more probable than not that disclosure of the material sought would seriously interfere with the fairness" of the proceedings.[149] Public disclosure of pre-liminary results in the investigation of an accident, for example, could make it diffi-cult for a defendant to be judged only by what is presented formally before a jury or administrative agency.

The courts have held that exemption 7(c)—permitting the withholding of infor-mation that could reasonably be expected to constitute an unwarranted invasion of personal privacy—requires balancing the privacy right against the public interest in disclosure, much like exemption 6. However, the protection of privacy is given more weight in exemption 7 cases than in exemption 6 cases because of two differences in the wording of the two provisions. First, exemption 7(c) allows the government to withhold records that "could reasonably be expected to constitute" an invasion of privacy while exemption 6 uses a stricter standard requiring a heavier burden of proof. Under exemption 6, agencies can withhold only records that "would consti-tute" an invasion of privacy. Second, exemption 7(c) protects from disclosure re-cords that could be an "unwarranted" invasion of privacy as opposed to records that would be a "clearly unwarranted" invasion of privacy, the language in exemption 6. Courts have interpreted the absence of the word *clearly* in exemption 7 to mean the public interest in disclosure should receive less weight.

In 1989, the U.S. Supreme Court said that under exemption 7(c) FBI "rap sheets" on private individuals are exempt from disclosure even though the informa-tion can be found in state or local public records. In *Department of Justice v. Report-ers Committee for Freedom of the Press,* the Supreme Court held that the disclosure of compilations of citizens' criminal records that do not directly reveal information about government operations is an "unwarranted" invasion of privacy.[150] The Court

---

[147]J.T. O'Reilly, 2 *Federal Information Disclosure* para. 17.11, at 17–72 (Dec. 1987).
[148]Scherer v. Kelley, 584 F.2d 170, 4 Media L. Rep. 1580 (7th Cir. 1978).
[149]Washington Post Co. v. Department of Justice, 863 F.2d 96 (1988).
[150]Department of Justice v. Reporters Comm. for Freedom of the Press, 109 S. Ct. 1468, 16 Media L. Rep. 1545 (1989).

said that federal compilations of personal information, including records stored in centralized computer data bases, can constitute a serious threat to personal privacy.

The FBI's rap sheets, the focus of *Reporters Committee,* contain an individual's history of arrests, indictments, acquittals, and convictions, information that is a matter of public record in local and state law enforcement agencies and courthouses across the country. However, the FBI's rap sheets are a computer compilation of individual criminal records collected nationwide that have traditionally been kept confidential. The FBI operates a nationwide network of local, state, and federal law enforcement agencies that share criminal history information under strict rules. Although most states make conviction data they have compiled available to the public, most limit the release of nonconviction data to criminal complaints, arrests, and dropped charges. Many states withhold information about individuals in the prison system. Investigative data is virtually never available.[151]

In *Reporters Committee,* the Court's decision ended a decade-long search by the Reporters Committee and CBS correspondent Robert Schakne for the criminal records of Charles Medico and his three brothers. The Pennsylvania Crime Commission said that Medico Industries, a family company, was "a legitimate business dominated by organized crime figures." Schakne wanted to know the connection between the company's defense contracts and bribery allegations against former Representative Daniel Flood, a Democrat from Pennsylvania. The FBI released the rap sheet information on three of the Medico brothers after they died. However, the agency refused to release the records of the only living brother, Charles Medico. Schakne and the Reporters Committee argued that the information in the FBI rap sheets was a matter of public record in local government files and therefore ought to be released by the federal government. The Justice Department argued that the release of Medico's rap sheet would constitute "an unwarranted invasion" of his privacy under exemption 7(c).

The U.S. Supreme Court, balancing the importance of individual privacy against the public interest in understanding government operations, unanimously ruled that Medico's records could be withheld. The Court's opinion, backed by seven justices, said that disclosure of a compilation of law enforcement records of a private citizen could reasonably be expected to invade the individual's privacy. Justice Stevens, writing the majority opinion, said that protection of individual privacy meant allowing people to control information about themselves. Stevens relied upon a dictionary to say that "private" meant "intended for or restricted to the use of a particular person or group or class of persons; not freely available to the public."[152] The Court said that although in an "organized" society "there are few facts that are not at one time or another" divulged to someone, individuals have an interest in limiting the wider dissemination of personal information that is publicly available.

Therefore, the Court said, centralized criminal records about individuals are private even though the separate pieces of the information in them are available else-

---

[151]Belair, "State of the Law," *News Media Access to Criminal Justice Information* 17 (1980). *See* D. Pember, "The Burgeoning Scope of 'Access Privacy' and the Portent for a Free Press," 64 *Iowa L. Rev.* 1186–87 (1979) *See also* 28 C.F.R. sec. 20.33 (c) (1989); 28 C.F.R. sec. 20.20 (b) and (c) (1989).

[152]Department of Justice v. Reporters Comm. for Freedom of the Press, 109 S. Ct. at 1476, 16 Media L. Rep. at 1551, *quoting Webster's Third New International Dictionary* 1804 (1976).

where. The Court recognized what it called "the power of compilations to affect personal privacy" in a way that "outstrips the combined power of the bits of information" in them. Justice Stevens said that the information collected in a centralized computer data base threatens privacy more than individual documents scattered in several police departments. He said that

> plainly there is a vast difference between the public records that might be found after a diligent search of courthouse files, county archives and local police stations throughout the country and a computerized summary located in a single clearinghouse of information.[153]

Computers, Stevens said, allow the accumulation and storage of information that "would otherwise have surely been forgotten." Stevens said that, if the information in the rap sheets was "freely available" in other locations, Schakne and the Reporters Committee could have easily acquired it without using the FOIA. In addition, Stevens said, the fact that federal funds were spent to "prepare, index, and maintain" the criminal history files demonstrated that the collection of information was not otherwise freely available.

Stevens also said that Congress had demonstrated it intended to protect the privacy of rap sheets. He said Congress has only authorized a limited use of rap sheets, such as by law enforcement agencies, banks, and the nuclear-power industry. In addition, Stevens said, the FBI's regulations specify that it can stop sharing rap sheet information with any agency that discloses the data to others.

The Supreme Court said that, in addition to the disclosure of the personal information on a rap sheet being an invasion of privacy, such disclosure would be "unwarranted" under exemption 7 if an FOIA request does not seek "official information" about a government agency. The Court acknowledged that citizens have a right to be told "what their government is up to." Therefore, "official information that sheds light on an agency's performance" should be disclosed under the FOIA. However, the Court said, the right of citizens to know about their government is not enhanced by the disclosure of information about private citizens "that reveals little or nothing" about agency conduct. The Court argued that the disclosure of Medico's criminal record would only reveal information about Medico and would say "nothing directly" about Congressman Flood's behavior or the conduct of the Defense Department when it awarded contracts to Medico Industries.[154] If Medico had been arrested or convicted of crimes, the Court said, that "would neither aggravate nor mitigate his allegedly improper relationship" with Flood. The Court acknowledged that there was public interest in Medico's criminal record, but said it was not the kind of public interest Congress intended to serve when it passed the FOIA.

The Supreme Court said that not only was the release of Medico's rap sheet an unwarranted invasion of privacy, but so would be the release of anyone's criminal history record when an FOIA request does not seek information about government. Although exemption 7(c) requires the balancing of the individual interest in privacy and the public interest in disclosure, the Supreme Court ruled the privacy provision

---

[153]*Id.* at 1477, 16 Media L. Rep. at 1552.
[154]*Id.* at 1482, 16 Media L. Rep. at 1556.

of FOIA exemption 7 protects all individual rap sheets and not just Medico's. The Court said it could balance the competing interests in withholding and disclosing records by category of record rather than on a case-by-case basis. "Categorical balancing" was appropriate, the Court asserted, because "the privacy interest in maintaining the practical obscurity of rap-sheet information will always be high." The Court said

> When the subject of such a rap sheet is a private citizen and when the information is in the Government's control as a compilation, rather than as a record of "what the Government is up to," the privacy interest . . . is . . . at its apex while the FOIA-based public interest in disclosure is at its nadir.[155]

When the scale is so tipped, said the Court, decisions can be made for categories of cases rather than examining individual circumstances.

Justice Blackmun concurred in the judgment in *Reporters Committee* but said that rap sheets should not always be exempt from disclosure under the FOIA. In an opinion joined by Justice Brennan, Blackmun suggested that the Court's opinion would, for example, prohibit the disclosure of a rap sheet revealing a congressional candidate's conviction of tax fraud. Blackmun said candidates relinquish the right to keep such information from the public when they choose to run for election. Blackmun said his alternative to the majority's "categorical" exemption would be to "leave the door open for the disclosure of rap-sheet information in some circumstances."

Journalists reacted sharply to the Court's decision. Veteran Supreme Court reporter Lyle Denniston said it was "astonishing" to hear that information about individuals who have had contact with the government "is not the kind" of information the FOIA was designed to provide. Denniston said, referring to the circumstances of Congressman Flood and Medico respectively, that

> the fact that a member of Congress has ties to or does favors for someone who has been in trouble with the police, or the fact that the Pentagon buys goods or services from such a person, says a great deal indeed about the member of Congress or about the Pentagon.[156]

In addition, Denniston questioned whether the public disclosure of accumulated data would interfere with personal privacy any more than the disclosure of scattered pieces of information. In fact, press representatives argue that public access to information compiled in computer data banks is a safeguard against abuse that can occur when only government officials have access to the information. Journalists contend that the biggest threat to individuals from computerized files is not disclosure to the press, but misuse by the government. Citizens are more apt to be damaged by government agencies that rely on inaccurate and dated information stored in data banks than the publication of that information in the media, journalists argue. Media representatives say that public oversight of government records is the best way to protect against abuse.[157]

---

[155]*Id.* at 1485, 16 Media L. Rep. at 1558–59.
[156]"The Press & the Law: Court Bans FOIA Probe of Central Files," *Wash. Journ. Rev.,* May 1989, at 10.
[157]*E.g.,* Kirtley, "Is Big Brother Coming?," 3 *Statewide* (California) *Bench/Bar/Media Newsletter* 6 (June 1988).

(8) Banking Reports   Exemption 8 protects from required disclosure a number of financial reports and audits from banks, trust companies, investment banking firms, and other federally regulated financial institutions. The records are held by such agencies as the Federal Reserve System, the Comptroller of the Currency, and the Federal Home Loan Bank Board. The exemption, though seldom used to deny access to records, has been construed broadly by the courts. The exemption has been interpreted to include information that might reflect on the financial soundness of a bank. It also has been interpreted to protect any information necessary to convince bankers that the information they give the government will be kept confidential.

(9) Information about Oil and Gas Wells   Exemption 9 protects geological and geophysical information and data, including maps, concerning oil and gas wells. Private companies drilling for oil and gas file a considerable amount of information, including maps and seismic reports, with such federal agencies as the Department of Interior, the Federal Energy Regulatory Commission, and the Federal Power Commission. Exemption 9 was designed to prevent speculators from easily acquiring valuable information obtained by others about the location of gas and oil wells. This is the least invoked, least litigated of the exemptions.

SUMMARY

In an effort to balance the government's need for secrecy with the presumption of openness that pervades the Freedom of Information Act, the FOIA provided nine categories of information that can be exempt from disclosure to the public. An agency must disclose any record not falling under one of the exemptions, but has discretion to withhold or disclose information falling into an exempt category.

Exemption 1, the national security exemption, protects from forced disclosure items properly classified according to criteria established by the president. President Bush has been using the relatively restrictive criteria adopted by his immediate predecessor, Ronald Reagan. Even though Congress has given the courts the authority to review records the government wants to withhold, the courts have been reluctant to second-guess the executive branch on matters of national security.

Exemption 2 protects agency management records of little concern to the general public such as parking and sick leave regulations. Exemption 3 allows the withholding of documents Congress has authorized to be confidential in other statutes either by enumeration or by use of criteria.

Exemption 4 protects trade secrets and confidential commercial and financial information. Trade secrets include commercially valuable information and formulas used and kept secret by a business. Commercial and financial information can be withheld only if disclosure would impair an agency's ability to obtain information in the future or cause substantial competitive harm to the business submitting the data. Many businesses are concerned that the FOIA does not adequately protect information they are required to give the government from falling into the hands of competitors.

Exemption 5 allows agencies to withhold information used in the decision-making process of government as long as a document is not publicly revealed to be the basis for a decision.

Exemption 6 protects information in personnel, medical, and similar files that "would constitute a clearly unwarranted invasion of personal privacy." The courts balance the personal interest in nondisclosure against the public interest in the information about government activities. Agencies cannot use the Privacy Act of 1974 to withhold information that must be made public under the FOIA.

Exemption 7 applies to records compiled for law enforcement purposes that, if disclosed, could reasonably be expected to interfere with law enforcement efforts, constitute an unwarranted invasion of privacy, disclose the identity of a confidential source or information provided by a confidential source, or endanger the safety of law enforcement personnel. The exemption also protects from required disclosure many investigative techniques and procedures used by law enforcement officers and information that would deprive a person of the right to a fair trial.

Exemption 8 protects banking reports submitted to the federal government. Exemption 9 applies to maps of oil and gas wells.

State Records Laws

The FOIA attracts so much attention that it may be easy to forget that it applies only to federal records, albeit federal records located all over the country. Many reporters, however, rely daily on state laws giving them access to state, county, and municipal government records. Reporters depend on obtaining county budget documents, city data about the number of housing starts, and reports on the quality of water leaving the local sewage treatment plant.

In most states, the common law requires that government records be open. Access to records through the common law, however, has two major limitations. First, the only persons who can obtain access are those with a legal interest in them—that is, those who would be directly affected by them, often because of a lawsuit. The restriction on access to those with a legal interest in documents does not permit access for the sake of public education through the media. The public and the press have no general right of access in the common law. A second limitation of the common law is that a "public record" is not subject to disclosure unless it is "required to be kept," or is specifically listed as a public record, by state law. This excludes a number of documents.[158]

To augment the access provided by common law, all 50 states have adopted statutes requiring disclosure of public records held by state, county, and municipal governments. The details and effectiveness of these laws vary significantly. In addition, state records laws are frequently adjusted through amendment and court interpretation.

Most open records laws begin with a policy statement expressing the need for accountability of government officials. West Virginia's statute bluntly declares:

> The people, in delegating authority, do not give their public servants the right to decide what is good for the people to know and what is not good for them to know.[159]

---

[158]Braverman & Heppler, "A Practical Review of State Open Records Laws," 49 *Geo. Wash. L. Rev.* 720, 723–24 (1981).

[159]W. Va. Code Ann. sec. 29B-1-1 (Michie 1986).

State records laws routinely apply to executive and administrative agencies of the state, county, and municipal governments. Most states have separate laws for the records of courts and legislatures. New York's FOI law, for example, covers

> any state or municipal department, board, bureau, division, commission, committee, public authority, public corporation, council, office or other governmental entity performing a governmental or proprietary function for the state or any one or more municipalities thereof, except the judiciary or the state legislature.[160]

The factor often determining whether an agency must abide by the public records statute is whether the agency receives public funds.[161] Under Kentucky law, a "body" must conform to the state's open records law if it has been created by a state or local government or receives at least 25 percent of its funds from state or local government.[162]

Most recently adopted laws apply to government records in almost any physical form. For example, South Carolina's FOI law defines public records to include "all books, papers, maps, photographs, cards, tapes, recordings or other documentary materials regardless of physical form or characteristics."[163] Such broad definitions have been held to include computerized records. However, public records laws defining *record* more narrowly may be interpreted by the courts not to apply to computer tapes and microfilm.[164] A few court decisions have said that a state's change to computerized records does not reduce citizens' right of access to records that would have been available in paper form. However, the person seeking the computerized information must be willing to pay for retrieval costs, and officials must be able to isolate the information from confidential data.[165]

So far, only a few state open records statutes have authorized direct public access to government data banks. Florida, often at the forefront of access law, has authorized counties to permit public access to local government data bases at "a reasonable charge."[166] New York has established the Legislative Retrieval Service, a computerized data base providing access to pending legislation and related information.[167]

States define public records not only by their physical form but also in terms of their origin, nature, and purpose. About two-thirds of the states define public records expansively to include anything in the possession of a state agency. Or a public record can be any record made or received in connection with a state law or the transaction of public business. This kind of definition has been interpreted by at least some courts to include the reports submitted to the government by private consultants.[168] A public

---

[160]N.Y. Pub. Off. Law sec. 86(3) (McKinney 1988).

[161]Braverman & Heppler, "A Practical Review of State Open Records Laws," 49 *Geo. Wash. L. Rev.* 720, 730–31 (1981).

[162]Ky. Rev. Stat. Ann. sec. 61.870(1) (Banks-Baldwin Supp. 1989).

[163]S.C. Code Ann. sec. 30-4-20(c) (Law. Co-op. Supp. 1989).

[164]*E.g.,* Minnesota Medical Ass'n v. State, 274 N.W.2d 84, 4 Media L. Rep. 1872 (Minn. 1978); Lorain County Title Co. v. Essex, 373 N.E.2d 1261 (Ohio Ct. App. 1976).

[165]Maher v. Freedom of Information Comm'n, 472 A.2d 321, 10 Media L. Rep. 1509 (Conn. 1984); Kansas *ex rel.* Stephan v. Harder, 641 P.2d 366, 8 Media L. Rep. 1891 (Kan. 1982).

[166]Fla. Stat. Ann. sec. 119.07(1)(b) (1989).

[167]*See* Legi-Tech v. Keiper, 766 F.2d 728, 11 Media L. Rep. 2482 (2d Cir. 1985).

[168]State *ex rel.* Tindel v. Sharp, 300 So.2d 750 (Fla. Dist. Ct. App. 1974).

record also can be defined as any document containing information about public matters. When a state statute is written expansively, state officials and state courts generally interpret it "liberally," that is, with a stress on openness.[169]

However, some states still define records restrictively, limiting public records only to those identified specifically by law. Other states limit public records to what is required by law to be made or kept, the old common law definition. In the past, courts have interpreted the common law language to mean that the statutes must have listed documents that were to qualify as public records, but that reading of the law may be changing. For example, one Ohio court said jail records should be open because "required to be kept" in the state statute did not refer only to records specifically identified by law as those that must be maintained. The phrase "required to be kept" applied to any documents "necessary to an agency's functions and responsibilities."[170]

Both the more expansive and the more restrictive laws tend to allow agencies to withhold the kinds of records exempted by three of the FOIA categories—information declared confidential by other state laws, personal information about individuals, and law enforcement and investigatory information. Ten to 20 states also exempt trade secrets and other business information, a category similar to the fourth exemption of the federal FOIA; department memoranda, much like that of the FOIA's fifth exemption; information related to state litigation; tax return data; and information about land values.

States are about equally divided between those that mandate the withholding of any record exempted from disclosure and those that give an agency discretion whether to disclose exempted material, as the FOIA does. More than a half-dozen states limit the release of records if disclosure would damage the public interest. In Colorado, the custodian of a public record can withhold a record, even if it would ordinarily be available for inspection, if its disclosure "would do substantial injury to the public interest."[171]

A state's records law is not likely to be the sole determinant of whether a document is available to the public. Most states also have a number of laws that restrict the release of government-held documents. Indeed, some of those states with records laws that seem to encourage openness can be more restrictive than they first appear. For example, in North Carolina, about 100 statutes exempt records from disclosure, modifying an otherwise expansive definition of a public record.[172] More than 40 states have privacy statutes that limit the disclosure of agency records. South Dakota protects adoption records, income tax information, and some birth records. More than 20 states have statutes restricting access to "trade secret" or comparable business information.[173]

---

[169]Braverman & Heppler, "A Practical Review of State Open Records Laws," 49 *Geo. Wash. L. Rev.* 720, 734 (1981). *See also* Comment, "Public Inspection of State and Municipal Executive Documents: 'Everybody, Practically Everything, Anytime, Except . . . .'" 45 *Fordham L. Rev.* 1105, 1117–21 (1977).

[170]Dayton Newspapers, Inc. v. City of Dayton, 341 N.E.2d 576 (Ohio 1976).

[171]Colo. Rev. Stat. sec. 24–72–204 (6) (1988).

[172]*See generally* H. Greyard, A Reporter's Guide to the North Carolina Open Records Law (January 1, 1983).

[173]Braverman & Heppler, "A Practical Review of State Open Records Laws," 49 *Geo. Wash. L. Rev.* 720, 724–25 (1981).

State laws either allow "any person" access to state records or limit access to state citizens.[174] A "person" includes corporations, citizens' groups, and associations. Journalists have no greater rights of access than others.[175] In all but a few states, access is not dependent on the reason that a person wants to see a document. For example, a Pennsylvania court said a school district must disclose the names and addresses of incoming pupils to parents opposed to the scheduling of kindergarten classes. The court said the parents had a right to the information even though the parents wanted it in order to enlist opposition to school policy.[176] However, at least Arizona, Rhode Island, and Washington restrict access for "commercial" use.[177] The public records laws of all states except Indiana provide for the right to copy records open to public inspection.[178]

Few state statutes specifically outline procedures to be used for requesting a record. Some states require that a government agency provide an explanation for nondisclosure. All but about a dozen states specifically provide for judicial review of a record custodian's denial of a disclosure request. Many states require, and others permit, an appeal within the agency denying a requested document before the person wanting the record seeks a judicial appeal.[179] The state agency has the burden of proving that withholding the record is justified.

Many state statutes provide for fining or jailing officials who do not comply with state records laws. In 1986, a Detroit official was jailed for one day after the city repeatedly refused to release land records to the *Detroit News* and the *Detroit Free Press*. Even a fine of $250 had not convinced city officials to release the documents. The jailing of the city's director of community and economic development resulted in the release of the records.[180] However, fines and jail sentences are rare, in part because prosecutors do not want to punish their official colleagues. Open records laws in about 15 states provide no penalty for illegally withholding documents.[181]

About 10 states provide for reimbursement of attorney's fees and related expenses to successful plaintiffs. The *Detroit News* received $5,500 for its suit. The *Free Press* did not ask for a reimbursement.

SUMMARY

Every state has an open records law for executive and administrative agencies of state, county, and municipal governments. Most begin with statements establishing a state policy of openness. Most state records laws apply to any documents in the possession of a state agency, with specifically named exemptions. The most common rea-

---

[174]*Id.* at 727.

[175]J.T. O'Reilly, 2 *Federal Information Disclosure* para. 27.03, at 27–9 (June 1985).

[176]Wiles v. Armstrong School Dist., 66 Pa. D. & C.2d 499 (1974).

[177]Ariz. Rev. Stat. Ann. sec. 39–121–.03 (Supp. 1986 & Supp. 1989); R.I. Gen. Laws sec. 38–2–6 (1980 Supp.); Wash. Rev. Code Ann. sec. 42.17.260(5) (Supp. 1990).

[178]Braverman & Heppler, "A Practical Review of State Open Records Laws," 49 *Geo. Wash. L. Rev.* 720, 749 (1981).

[179]*Id.* at 751–53.

[180]"Meetings Laws Improved: Officials Jailed for Secrecy," *News Media & Law,* Winter 1987, at 38.

[181]Braverman & Heppler, "A Practical Review of State Open Records Laws," 49 *Geo. Wash. L. Rev.* 720, 755 (1981).

sons for authorized withholding of documents are privacy, law enforcement records, and items exempted by other state laws. Most recently written laws apply to records in almost any physical form. Most states provide for fines or jail terms for officials who do not comply with the state law, although such stern sanctions are seldom imposed.

ACCESS TO MEETINGS

Neither the First Amendment nor the common law provides the press and the public access to the meetings of federal, state, or local governing bodies. Hence, access can only be obtained through statute.

A strong statute will declare that the purpose of the law is to open deliberations to the public as much as possible and that the law should be interpreted by the courts accordingly. The statute should describe the government agencies that are subject to the law. It will tell how many members must be present for a meeting to be official. It will explain how an agency may close a meeting and under what conditions closure is allowed. It should explain how a citizen can contest a closed meeting and what remedies are available if the law has been violated.

Federal

A federal statute requires several executive agencies to meet in public. Congress has opened up most of its sessions and most of its committee meetings to the public.

Sunshine Act   In 1976, Congress passed legislation requiring about 50 federal agencies, commissions, boards, and councils to meet in public. The Sunshine Act, as it is called, declares that the public "is entitled to the fullest practicable information" about the "decision-making processes" of the federal government.[182] With ten exceptions, any meeting of a sufficient number of members required to take action is presumed to be public.

The Sunshine Act only pertains to agencies subject to the Freedom of Information Act. In addition, the agencies must be headed by boards of more than one member, a majority of whom are appointed by the president.[183] Among the agencies subject to the statute are the Federal Trade Commission, the Federal Communications Commission, the Securities and Exchange Commission, and the National Labor Relations Board.

In 1982, a federal appellate court decided that a board composed of members only indirectly appointed by the president did not qualify as an "agency" under the act. The court rejected the contention of Congress Watch, a public interest group, that the meetings of the Chrysler Corporation Loan Guarantee Board ought to be open to the public. The board, established to lend $1.5 billion in federal funds to the

---

[182]90 Stat. 1241 (1976) (declaration of policy).
[183]5 U.S.C. sec. 522b (a) (1) (1988).

then-failing Chrysler Corporation, was composed of such officials as the secretary of the treasury and the chairman of the Federal Reserve Board. The persons in those positions had been given their jobs by the president, but they had not been appointed to the Chrysler Loan Guarantee Board by the president. Rather, they were on the board because the statute authorizing the loan said the board would include the treasury secretary and the Federal Reserve chairman. The court said that the loan board did not meet the requirements of an agency covered by the Sunshine Act because its members were not appointed to the board by the president, even though they were board members because they were presidential appointees to other positions.[184]

The Sunshine Act, unlike the FOIA, allows public access to discussions prior to official actions. In a suit initiated by the citizen group Common Cause, a federal appellate court said Congress intended that the decision-making process of government be conducted in the open. The U.S. Court of Appeals for the D.C. Circuit rejected arguments of the Nuclear Regulatory Commission that discussions of budget proposals should be closed. The court said that although the FOIA exempted documents prepared as a part of the decision-making process, Congress decided that the discussion of issues prior to decisions must be exposed to public scrutiny.[185]

The Sunshine Act also covers the deliberations of agency subdivisions "authorized to act on behalf of the agency." The U.S. Supreme Court has said that, in order for the law to apply to agency subdivisions, the subdivisions must be considering issues that it can resolve for the agency. Hence, the Telecommunications Committee of the Federal Communications Commission was not "an agency" during informal international conferences referred to as the Consultative Process. The Court said that members of the committee discussed telecommunications issues that did not deal directly with processing common carrier applications, their only official responsibility. The Court said that, in addition, the sessions of the Consultative Process were not meetings within the language of the Sunshine Act. The FCC did not convene the Consultative Process and did not control its procedures unilaterally. The provisions of the Sunshine Act, the Court said, assume that an agency has the power to conduct meetings according to the requirements of the law.[186]

In order to close a meeting, a federal agency must determine that remaining open would lead to a disclosure of information protected by one of the Sunshine Act's 10 exempt categories. The agency also must determine that the public interest does not require that the meeting be open. Seven of the 10 exemptions to the presumption of open meetings parallel exemptions of the FOIA: national security, agency rules, matters exempted by other statutes, business information, matters of personal privacy, investigatory records, and the reports of financial institutions. In addition to the exemption for investigative records, the Sunshine Act exempts accusations of criminal activity or formal reprimands in order to protect the reputations of persons accused but not yet formally charged. Another exemption permits closure for agencies regulating financial matters if a discussion would (1) lead to financial speculation, (2) "significantly endanger" the stability of a bank, or (3) frustrate the implementation of an agency action.

---

[184]Symons v. Chrysler Corp. Loan Guarantee Board, 670 F.2d 238, 7 Media L. Rep. 2363 (D.C. Cir. 1981).
[185]Common Cause v. Nuclear Regulatory Comm'n, 674 F.2d 921, 8 Media L. Rep. 1190 (D.C. Cir. 1982).
[186]FCC v. ITT World Communications, 466 U.S. 463, 10 Media L. Rep. 1685 (1984).

A final exemption to the Sunshine Act allows closed meetings to discuss an agency's issuance of a subpoena or its participation in court action or an administrative proceeding. The exemption is intended to ensure that a premature announcement does not allow people to effectively counter agency plans.[187] The Nuclear Power Commission used the last exemption to block public access to a discussion about the reopening of the nuclear power plant at Three Mile Island in Pennsylvania. The *Philadelphia Inquirer* wanted to attend NRC meetings dealing with the procedural steps to be used in deciding whether the reactor could be reopened. A federal district court ruled the meetings could be closed because they involve preparation for a formal administrative hearing.[188]

The Sunshine Act requires public notice of meetings in the *Federal Register* at least one week in advance. If an agency chooses to close a meeting, it must provide reasons in advance. Anyone objecting to a closure can file a suit in a federal district court. A court can enjoin a closed meeting or require that meetings similar to one just closed be open in the future. The agency must maintain a transcript or recording of any closed meetings. Anyone can sue to obtain a transcript, which can be examined by a judge in chambers.

Even if a suit under the act is successful, no financial penalty can be levied against individual members of an agency and no agency action can be invalidated. The government can be assessed court costs and lawyers' fees. A person suing under the act can be assessed court costs and lawyers' fees if the suit is found to be "dilatory or frivolous."[189]

Federal agencies frequently try to skirt the Sunshine law, observers contend. One news story claimed that one commission stopped meeting, another redefined the word *meeting* to avoid inviting the public, and others vested more power in staffs that can meet informally. It is also suspected that many agencies meet less often to avoid the law.

Congress   The U.S. Constitution provides that each house of Congress should publish "a Journal of its Proceedings . . . excepting such Parts as may in their Judgment require Secrecy."[190] Otherwise, the Constitution specifies that each house may determine its own rules. This includes which sessions should be open to the public and whether cameras ought to be allowed.

Most sessions of the Senate and House are open to the public. Since the 1970s, committee and subcommittee meetings—including bill-drafting sessions—are open to the public unless a majority votes in public to close. The House and Senate also agreed to open conference committee meetings, where representatives of the House and Senate try to reconcile different versions of a bill. A conference committee meeting can be closed only by a public vote of a majority of the Senate conferees or by a vote of the entire House of Representatives.[191]

In 1979, the House of Representatives began television coverage of its proceed-

---

[187]5 U.S.C. 552b (c) (10) (1988).

[188]Philadelphia Newspapers v. Nuclear Regulatory Comm'n, 727 F.2d 1195, 9 Media L. Rep. 1843 (D.C. Cir. 1983).

[189]5 U.S.C sec. 552b (e), (f), (g), (h), (i) (1982).

[190]U.S. Const. art. I, sec. 5.

[191]Congressional Quarterly, *Guide to Congress* 70–72, 110, 114, 455, 470, 928 (3d ed. 1982).

ings. The House controls the cameras and allows broadcasters to use the footage. In 1986, the Senate approved radio and television coverage of its proceedings under similar rules. The committee hearings of both houses are also open to broadcast coverage. However, in 1989, two famous witnesses invoked a House rule that permits persons required to appear before House committees to block broadcast coverage of their testimony. The two were Samuel Pierce, the former Secretary of Housing and Urban Development enmeshed in a scandal of alleged fraud and mismanagement, and Charles R. Keating, the owner of a failed savings and loan institution whose campaign contributions to five U.S. senators were being investigated in 1990.[192]

SUMMARY

The Sunshine Act requires about 60 federal agencies to meet in public. The act applies to agencies subject to the FOIA and headed by a board appointed by the president. Unlike the FOIA, the act allows access to discussions prior to official actions. The act provides for exceptions to openness when the agencies are dealing with 10 topics, most of them mirroring the FOIA exemptions.

Both houses of Congress establish their own rules for access. Most sessions of the Senate and the House of Representatives, and most congressional committee meetings, are now open. The House has permitted television coverage since 1979. The Senate approved broadcast coverage in 1986.

States

All 50 states have adopted open meetings laws—many in the last 15 years. Only Alabama had a modern open meetings law in 1950. In 1962, only 28 states had open meetings laws.[193] The states' open meetings laws are different and many continue to change through legislative amendment and court interpretation. Reporters and public relations personnel need to keep track of legal developments in the state where they work.

Many scholars assert that one of the most important aspects of a strong open meetings statute, as well as a strong records law, is a legislative declaration that the law is intended to open government deliberations and actions to the people.[194] One of the most explicit declarations is from the state of Washington:

> The legislature finds and declares that all . . . public agencies of this state and subdivisions thereof exist to aid in the conduct of the people's business. It is the intent of this chapter that their action be taken openly and that their deliberations be conducted openly.

---

[192]See CNN v. Anderson, 723 F. Supp. 835 (D.D.C. 1989); "Former HUD Head Bars TV Coverage," *New York Times,* Sept. 23, 1989, at 6.

[193]Comment, "Open Meetings Law: An Analysis and a Proposal," 45 *Miss. L.J.* 1151, 1158 (1974).

[194]*E.g., id.* at 1162; Wickham, "LET THE SUNSHINE IN! Open-Meeting Legislation Can Be Our Key to Closed Doors in State and Local Government," 68 *Nw.U.L. Rev.* 480, 488 (1973).

The people of this state do not yield their sovereignty to the agencies which serve them. The people, in delegating authority, do not give their public servants the right to decide what is good for the people to know and what is not good for them to know. The people insist on remaining informed so that they may retain control over the instruments they have created.[195]

Some states indicate that the meetings of all agencies supported by public funds or performing governing functions are open except for explicitly named exceptions. The other states list or enumerate the kinds of agencies that must hold open meetings. The New York open meetings law, like its records law, applies to

any state or municipal department, board, bureau, division, commission, committee, public authority, public corporation, council, office or other governmental entity performing a governmental or proprietary function for the state or any one or more municipalities thereof, except the judiciary or the state legislature.[196]

Laws such as the one in New York leave the status of any unlisted agencies unclear. For example, if a law pertains to "boards and commissions," it is not obvious that it applies to city councils. Many state laws exempt state legislatures, parole and pardon boards, and jury proceedings.[197]

A comprehensive definition of the word *meeting* in a state law can help the public and officials alike know what kind of gathering triggers the statute. For example, the Texas statute defines "meeting" as

any deliberation between a quorum of members of a governmental body at which any public business or public policy over which the governmental body has supervision or control is discussed or considered, or at which any formal action is taken.[198]

In 1990, the Texas Supreme Court said that two of the three members of the Texas Water Commission were in a "meeting" when they discussed a case in the restroom.[199]

States usually require either a quorum or a majority to be present for the meeting to qualify under the law. A majority may or may not be a quorum, which is the number of members required to attend before an agency can conduct official business. In some states, any two members talking to each other is sufficient for a *meeting* under the law, regardless of the size of the government body.

Unlike Texas, some state laws require a meeting to be open only if action is taken. Such an approach, of course, means that meetings can be closed during deliberations. This permits public agencies to reach decisions in private as long as the official vote is public.

But what if members of a public body discuss public business at lunch, during a round of golf, or at a retreat? Social gatherings can be an excuse to do the public's

---

[195]Wash. Rev. Code Ann. sec. 42.30.010 (1972).

[196]N.Y. Pub. Off. Law sec. 86(3) (McKinney 1988).

[197]For a survey of open meetings laws treatment of legislatures, *see* "State Legislatures' Openness Surveyed," *News Media & Law,* Spring 1987, at 33–35.

[198]Tex. Rev. Civ. Stat. Ann. art. 6252–17 (Vernon 1990).

[199]Acker v. Texas Water Comm'n, 1990 WL 55932 (Tex. 1990).

business without public debate. On the other hand, even many advocates of open meetings believe that a law should not prevent officials from socializing together. The Texas open meetings law specifically excludes from its requirements any "social functions unrelated to the public business" and attendance at conventions and workshops as long as there is no public business discussed or conducted. Some other states provide no exclusion for social affairs.

In most states, if a meeting is open to the public, cameras and audio equipment are usually allowed.[200]

All states allow *executive,* or closed, sessions. Executive sessions are most commonly allowed for discussions of the hiring, firing, and disciplining of personnel; real estate transactions; official investigations; security or safety; labor negotiations; and legal suits. Some states also allow executive sessions for discussions that would tend to damage individual reputations.[201]

Journalists frequently believe that public officials at least stretch the meaning of a "personnel" exemption when they close the doors at a meeting. In 1989, the Mississippi Supreme Court said a majority of the Hinds County Board of Supervisors repeatedly violated the state's open meetings law when they went into executive session to discuss "personnel." The court said that under the Mississippi statute, the exemption for "personnel matters" was restricted to "dealing with employees hired and supervised by the board." The board had illegally entered executive session to discuss the hiring of an architect, an independent professional who was not an employee of the board, the court said. Neither was another item discussed in executive session, an appointment to fill a vacancy on the board itself, a "personnel matter," the court said.[202]

Advocates of open government want the decision to close meetings made by a public vote, with the reasons for closure on the record, so that officials favoring closure can be identified. Although the Mississippi open meetings law requires that votes for closure be public, the Mississippi Supreme Court said the Hinds County Board of Supervisors did not always comply. In addition, the court said, the board's announced reasons for closing meetings frequently did not meet the requirements of the state law. First, the court said, the board at least once discussed business in executive session that was not covered by its announcement prior to closure. Second, the board did not adequately describe why it was going into executive session. The court said that for the board "to simply say, 'personnel matters,' or 'litigation' tells nothing" about the reason for closing a meeting. In an expansive reading of the Mississippi law, the supreme court said the requirement that the reason for closure be announced means that a reason must be "of sufficient specificity to inform those present that there is in reality a specific, discrete matter" that needs to be discussed in executive session.

Advocates of open government not only want votes to close meetings to take place in public, but also all final votes on public policy to be on the record. The Mississippi Supreme Court said the Hinds County Board of Supervisors illegally voted to hire an architectural firm in an executive session.

Open meetings laws, to be effective, must include a requirement that the public

---

[200]"Photos Allowed at Meetings," *News Media & Law,* Jan.–Feb. 1984, 49–51.
[201]*E.g.,* N.H. Rev. Stat. Ann. sec. 91–A:3(II)(c) (1977).
[202]Hinds County Bd. of Supervisors v. Common Cause of Miss., 551 So.2d 107 (1989).

be notified of meetings. Requirements that meetings be open are meaningless if no one knows when and where the meetings are taking place. Many statutes require that the times of regularly scheduled meetings be posted and sent to the media. States often mandate that the media, or persons requesting notification, be advised of special or emergency meetings in enough time to attend.[203]

Virtually every state provides a mechanism to enforce the open meetings law, but the enforcement mechanisms are often ineffective because they are rarely used.[204] Prosecutors are reluctant to take action against fellow officials and citizens seldom make the effort or spend the money to challenge closed meetings. Observers believe the number of Florida officials convicted for open meetings law violations—28 since 1977—is unusually high.[205]

Several state statutes provide for short jail sentences or fines for officials responsible for closing meetings illegally. In 1989, three Longwood, Florida, officials were fined $500 each for discussing outside of an official meeting a proposal for the city to purchase a utility.[206] Florida's state law, as well as laws in other states, also provides for civil penalties, eliminating the stigma attached to a criminal conviction.

Some states allow a court to enjoin officials from closing a meeting when the intent to do so is known in advance. Other states provide for the nullification of any law or ordinance passed in an illegally closed meeting.[207] An innovative enforcement tool used only in a few states is the removal from office of officials involved in illegally closing meetings. One of the Longwood, Florida, officials, mentioned above, City Commissioner Rick Bullington, was removed from office by the governor under a provision in Florida's general statutes after he participated in policy discussions outside of an open meeting.[208]

SUMMARY

Every state has an open meetings law. The laws that best protect the public's interest in openness specify that meetings be open during consideration of issues as well as when formal action is taken. State open meetings laws also need to provide for public notice of meetings if the public is to have an opportunity to attend. At least a few state laws prohibit public officials from conducting business at social occasions when members of the public cannot be present. Many states permit closed sessions for discussing personnel matters, real estate transactions, official investigations, security, and labor negotiations. Enforcement of the open meetings statutes is a problem in many states although most have statutory mechanisms, such as fines or short jail sentences, for illegal closure.

---

[203]*E.g.,* Ark. Stat. Ann. sec. 25–19–106(B) (2) (1987).

[204]*E.g.,* Wickham, "LET THE SUN SHINE IN! Open-Meeting Legislation Can Be Our Key to Closed Doors in State and Local Government," 68 *Nw. U.L. Rev.* 400, 496 (1973).

[205]"Successful Sunshine Prosecutions on Rise," *Brechner Report,* Feb. 1990, at 1, 5.

[206]"Two Convicted of Sunshine Violations; One Ousted," *Brechner Report,* Nov. 1989, at 1.

[207]*See* Comment, "Open Meetings Law: An Analysis and a Proposal," 45 *Miss. L.J.* 1151, 1181 (1974).

[208]"Two Convicted of Sunshine Violations; One Ousted," *Brechner Report,* Nov. 1989, at 1. *See* Fla. Stat. sec. 112.52 (1989).

OBTAINING ACCESS: A FINAL WORD

Laws requiring access help journalists. Because of open meetings and open records laws, reporters do not have to rely totally on their own devices to gain access to government meetings and records. However, laws themselves do not guarantee access to records or meetings. Many officials will not be aware of the law. Others may try to ignore it.

Successful reporters learn that access depends on effectively cultivating sources. Officials are more likely to help reporters they know and trust. Reporters should discuss with public officials the interest of the public in obtaining information and make an effort to understand the concerns of their sources. Journalists should consider working with local officials to develop guidelines for coverage of news events.

Many reporters also have learned that persuasion, either friendly or stern, is more likely to open a meeting or a record than the enforcement provision of the state law. Persuasion is more immediate, less expensive, and sometimes more effective. Sometimes, a reluctant official only needs to be convinced that access is required by law. But journalists can use persuasion only if they know and understand access laws themselves. In many states, press associations distribute wallet-sized copies of open meetings and records laws for reporters to carry to meetings. If such information is not provided, a reporter may need to visit a nearby law library.

Reporters also should consult with lawyers to find out how best to achieve access in their state. The best route in some states may be speaking up when asked to leave a meeting. But, in North Carolina, speaking up too vociferously can result in a fine for disturbing the peace.[209] Journalists usually need to record the official reasons given for closure in order for lawyers to challenge it.

If it appears that access has been denied illegally, a reporter should consult first with an editor and then with a lawyer. Only they can decide if a publication wants to pursue legal action. Sometimes a paper or broadcast station will write stories about closure, leave blank spaces where a story would have been published, or use a picture of a closed door to pressure officials to keep meetings open. Few public officials want those who elected them to believe decisions are made in closed ''smoke-filled'' rooms.

---

[209]N.C. Gen. Stat. sec. 143–318.17 (1987).

12

THE ELECTRONIC MEDIA

Most of the law discussed thus far applies to all media. But the Supreme Court has said that the special characteristics of some media may justify special legal controls.[1] The Court has, for example, approved content regulation for the electronic media that is unacceptable for the print media.

The Supreme Court has said that the First Amendment prohibits the government from telling the publishers of newspapers and magazines what to print and what not to print. The government cannot compel newspapers to provide equal space to political opponents or require magazines to limit their publication of pictures and stories that are indecent but not obscene. However, broadcasters must treat political candidates equally and must restrict the airing of "indecent" programs despite deregulation of program content in the last 15 years.

The Supreme Court has said that the regulation of radio and television is justified because physical limitations in the broadcast spectrum make it necessary for government to decide who can obtain a broadcast license. Government therefore can require broadcasters to serve the public interest in return, courts have said.

But the development of new media technologies in the last 30 years has raised questions about the traditional regulation of electronic media. Should broadcast signals sent to homes through a cable that can carry several dozen channels be regulated in the same way as over-the-air broadcasting? Should programming sent paying subscribers be regulated the same as "free" radio and television? Indeed, given the number of media outlets in the 1990s, should broadcast programming itself be regulated any longer?

Because communication through electronic media is constantly improving, regulation is in a state of flux. So far only some of the traditional broadcast regulations are being imposed on programming delivered by some of the "new" media technologies such as cable television, microwave signals, and satellite transponders.

All electronic media—broadcast stations, cable systems, telephone companies, and various new technologies—are governed by the Federal Communications Commission under the authority of the 1934 Communications Act. The purpose of the act is to provide rapid and efficient wire and broadcast communications nationwide.[2] The act controls industry structure and the nature of communications on each medium. This chapter will focus on the issue that most concerns public communicators: the content regulation of the various electronic media, particularly broadcasting and cable.

REGULATION OF BROADCASTING

Broadcasting was first regulated by the Federal Radio Commission under the 1927 Radio Act. Since 1934, the Federal Communications Commission has regulated broadcast programming by licensing and by responding to complaints from listeners and viewers. Programming regulations such as the restriction on indecency and a re-

---

[1] *See* Joseph Burstyn, Inc. v. Wilson, 343 U.S. 495, 503, 1 Media L. Rep. 1357, 1359-60 (1952).
[2] 47 U.S.C. sec. 151 (1982).

quirement that broadcasters provide airtime for federal candidates to public office have been held constitutional by the U.S. Supreme Court.

Framework for Content Regulations

The 1927 Radio Act authorized an independent regulatory commission to decide who should receive broadcast licenses. Although the act prohibited the government from censoring radio, it authorized programming regulation. The Radio Act was upheld by the courts and provided the regulatory framework for the 1934 Communications Act. Thirty-five years later the U.S. Supreme Court upheld the constitutionality of broadcast programming regulation, tolerating government supervision of broadcasting that is not acceptable in the case of the print media.

The First Content Regulation   The first radio stations began broadcasting about 1920. By 1926, nearly 800 broadcasters were using the airwaves any time they chose, at whatever power they chose, and at any frequency they chose. The public grew tired of being unable to listen to one station without interference from others, and radio set sales—once skyrocketing—dropped. Both the public and the radio industry urged Congress to adopt a system for regulating radio.

In the Radio Act of 1927, Congress codified many of the practices that had developed in the absence of legislation.[3] The Radio Act ensured that broadcast stations in this country would continue to be predominantly owned and operated by private citizens rather than the government. However, the act established that no person or business could claim ownership of the airwaves or the right to use them permanently. Because the airwaves were considered a public resource and there were not enough frequencies to accommodate everyone who wanted to broadcast, the newly established Federal Radio Commission (FRC) was authorized to grant licenses, renew licenses, and otherwise regulate broadcasters according to the public interest, convenience, or necessity.[4]

The Radio Act contained a few specific programming regulations at the same time that it declared that the FRC had no "power of censorship over the radio" and that no regulation "shall interfere with the right of free speech by means of radio." In the same paragraph in which the act prohibited censorship, it banned obscene, indecent, or profane language on the radio. The statute also directed that a licensee who allowed a political candidate to use broadcast facilities provide "equal opportunities" to any opponents. In addition, the act required stations to reveal the sponsors of any programming or advertising.[5]

Key legislators believed that, in spite of the no-censorship provision, a station's programming ought to be a factor in determining whether a licensee was acting in the public interest.[6] A federal appeals court soon agreed, ruling in 1931 that the Federal

---

[3]*See generally* E. Barnouw, *A History of Broadcasting in the United States, Vol. I: Tower of Babel* 195–201 (1966).
[4]Radio Act of 1927, 44 Stat. 1162–66, 1168 (1927).
[5]*Id.* at 1170, 1172–73.
[6]*See, e.g.,* 68 Cong. Rec. 4, 111 (1927); *To Amend the Communications Act of 1934: Hearings on S. 1333 Before a Subcomm. of the Senate Comm. on Interstate and Foreign Commerce,* 80th Cong., 1st Sess. 409 (1947) (statement of Sen. Wallace H. White, Jr.).

Radio Commission could refuse to renew a broadcast station's license because its programming did not serve the public interest.[7] The commission had decided not to renew the license of popular Kansas broadcaster Dr. John Romulus Brinkley. Brinkley, who had purchased his medical diplomas, diagnosed the illnesses his listeners described in letters and then prescribed his own medical preparations on the air.[8] The U.S. Court of Appeals for the District of Columbia, in affirming the FRC's decision, said "the character and the quality" of a broadcaster's service was necessarily part of a license review. Judge Charles Robb said the review of a station's programming did not violate the prohibition against censorship in the Radio Act. The commission had the right to "take note of" Brinkley's conduct in considering whether a license renewal would be in the public interest. The prohibition on censorship only barred prior restraints, the court said. Robb said the commission had not subjected Brinkley's programming to scrutiny prior to its broadcast.

A year later, in 1932, the same federal court said the FRC's refusal to renew a license because of defamatory and racist programming did not violate the First Amendment.[9] The court said the government could not interfere with an individual's right to speak, but it could constitutionally regulate the use of the airwaves by those who obtained a permit from the commission to broadcast.

The Supreme Court did not uphold the constitutionality of broadcast program regulation until 1969, 35 years after Congress incorporated the programming provisions of the Radio Act into the 1934 Communications Act.

Broadcast Regulation and the First Amendment

The U.S. Supreme Court said in 1969 that broadcasters can be required to carry programming for the benefit of the listening and viewing public. However, the Court said a few years later that no single individual or group has a First Amendment right of access to the broadcast media. In contrast, the Court has held unconstitutional any government-imposed requirement that the print media publish a particular story.

A First Amendment Right for the Broadcast Audience

In 1969, the Supreme Court upheld the constitutionality of a requirement that broadcasters provide a right of reply to persons whose character has been attacked during discussions of controversial public issues. In *Red Lion Broadcasting Co. v. FCC,* the Court said that giving a person an opportunity to rebut a personal attack enhanced rather than abridged the freedoms of speech and press protected by the First Amendment.

In *Red Lion,* a small radio station and a major broadcast news organization challenged the FCC's personal attack policy, one of a few remnants in 1990 of an otherwise defunct fairness doctrine. The fairness doctrine itself, created in 1949 and eliminated in 1987, required broadcasters to provide diverse viewpoints on controversial public issues. Although the FCC has dropped the fairness doctrine, several court decisions based on the policy remain important to media law and are discussed in this

---

[7]KFKB Broadcasting Ass'n, Inc. v. FRC, 47 F.2d 670 (1931).
[8]*See generally* E. Barnouw, *Tower of Babel* 168–72 (1966).
[9]Trinity Methodist Church, South v. FRC, 62 F.2d 850 (D.C. Cir. 1932).

chapter. In addition, a few policies that grew out of the fairness doctrine, including the personal attack rule, remained intact as of mid-1990.[10]

The FCC first suggested that licensees may have a responsibility to provide time for replies to personal attacks made on the air when the commission announced the birth of the fairness doctrine in 1949. A little more than a decade later, in 1960, the commission said a station that broadcast an attack on someone's character during the discussion of a controversial public issue was required to offer time for a reply regardless of whether the person attacked was willing to pay for it. The FCC said the station must send a tape, transcript, or broadcast summary to the person attacked.[11]

In one of two cases decided by the Supreme Court in *Red Lion,* radio station WGCB of Red Lion, Pennsylvania, challenged an FCC order that it provide free air-time to a writer attacked in a broadcast. In November 1964, WGCB aired a 15-minute program featuring an evangelist, the Reverend Billy James Hargis. Hargis sharply criticized Fred Cook, the author of a book about presidential candidate Senator Barry Goldwater. Hargis said Cook had once been fired from a newspaper for making false charges about a city official. Hargis also said Cook had written for *The Nation,* "one of the most scurrilous publications of the left." In addition, Hargis denounced Cook for attacking the FBI, FBI Director J. Edgar Hoover, and the CIA.[12]

Cook asked radio stations that had aired the Hargis broadcast for free time to reply. WGCB refused and Cook complained to the FCC. When the FCC insisted that the station provide free airtime, WGCB's owner, the Reverend John Norris, appealed to the U.S. Court of Appeals for the District of Columbia. Although Norris argued that the fairness doctrine violated his constitutional rights of free expression, the District of Columbia Circuit upheld the commission.[13]

A year later, a different federal appeals court declared the FCC's personal attack requirements unconstitutional. The U.S. Court of Appeals for the Seventh Circuit struck down the FCC's personal attack rules after they were challenged by a major broadcast news organization, the Radio and Television News Directors Association (RTNDA).[14] The RTNDA contested the rules in a court believed to be more sympathetic to the broadcasters' interests than the court in the District of Columbia. Indeed, as the RTNDA hoped, the Seventh Circuit said the requirement that broadcasters send persons attacked on the air a copy of the attack and offer them a time to reply placed unreasonable burdens on the dissemination of opinion and public issues.

The holding of the Seventh Circuit, coupled with the ruling of the D.C. Circuit, presented the U.S. Supreme Court with conflicting decisions in two federal appeals courts. In response, the Supreme Court unanimously upheld the D.C. Circuit and the

---

[10]The FCC's elimination of the fairness doctrine and preservation of the personal attack rule are discussed later in the chapter.

[11]*See* Times-Mirror Broadcasting Co., 24 P & F Rad. Reg. 404 (1962); Red Lion Broadcasting Co. v. FCC, 395 U.S. 367, 373–75, 1 Media L. Rep. 2053, 2056 (1969).

[12]Red Lion Broadcasting Co. v. FCC, 395 U.S. at 371–73, 1 Media. L. Rep. at 2055; F. Friendly, *The Good Guys, the Bad Guys and the First Amendment; Free Speech vs. Fairness in Broadcasting* chaps. 1, 3, 4 (1976).

[13]Red Lion Broadcasting Co. v. FCC, 381 F.2d 908 (D.C. Cir. 1967); F. Friendly, *The Good Guys, the Bad Guys and the First Amendment; Free Speech vs. Fairness in Broadcasting* 43–50 (1976).

[14]Radio-Television News Directors Ass'n v. United States, 400 F.2d 1002, 1010–12 (7th Cir. 1968).

FCC, holding that the personal attack rules were consistent with both the 1934 Communications Act and the U.S. Constitution.

Justice Byron White, writing for the Court, first said that the FCC had acted within its statutory authority when it required WGCB to give Cook reply time. The Court's opinion said personal attack rules implemented the congressional policy that broadcast licensees must serve the public interest.

The Court also held that the personal attack rules do not abridge freedom of the press. The Court affirmed that the First Amendment can be applied differently to different media. Justice White, in the majority opinion, said the inherent limits in the number of frequencies available on the broadcast spectrum meant that not everyone can operate a broadcast station. Although the broadcast spectrum was being used more efficiently than in the past, White said, the government must still deny some applications for broadcast licenses.

Justice White said that as long as the demand for spectrum space exceeds the frequencies available, no person has a constitutional right to use the broadcast spectrum. He said no one can claim a First Amendment right to broadcast in the same way he or she has a right to speak, write, or print. Therefore, to deny someone a broadcast license so that the airwaves can be more effectively used in the public interest is not a denial of free speech.

At the same time, White said, those who obtain broadcast licenses have no greater First Amendment rights than those who are refused. White said those who receive licenses do not have an unfettered right to broadcast only their own views on public issues or the views of persons who agree with them. The First Amendment does not prevent the government

> from requiring a licensee to share his frequency with others and . . . to present those views and voices which are representative of his community and which would otherwise . . . be barred from the airwaves.[15]

White said the First Amendment protects the public's right to receive information as well as the right of broadcasters to speak. "The people as a whole" retain First Amendment rights in broadcasting. Indeed, "it is the right of the viewers and listeners, not the right of the broadcasters, which is paramount." White said the purpose of the First Amendment is to preserve "an uninhibited market-place of ideas" rather than to allow control of that market by a few:

> It is the right of the public to receive suitable access to social, political, esthetic, moral, and other ideas and experiences which is crucial here.[16]

Because of the limits of the broadcast spectrum, White said, the government could adopt regulations consistent with the First Amendment goal of informing the public so that the people could govern themselves.

White discounted broadcaster arguments that requirements to provide reply time to those attacked on the air would result in self-censorship. He said that arguments

---

[15]395 U.S. at 389, 1 Media L. Rep. at 2062.
[16]*Id.* at 390, 1 Media L. Rep. at 2063.

that the fairness doctrine would force broadcasters to shy away from coverage of controversial public issues were "at best speculative." The fairness doctrine had not yet inhibited broadcasters, he said. Besides, he contended, the FCC had the power to insist that stations give "adequate and fair attention to public issues."[17]

White said the Court was not ratifying every FCC programming decision of the past and future. He said that any attempt by the FCC to prohibit a broadcaster from carrying a particular program would raise "more serious First Amendment issues."

No Individual Right to Discuss Public Issues   Although the Supreme Court declared in *Red Lion* that broadcasters could be required to give persons attacked on the air the right to reply, the Court said a few years later that the First Amendment does not require broadcast licensees to provide airtime to specific individuals or groups who want to present a point of view on public issues.

The 1973 Supreme Court decision *CBS v. Democratic National Committee* combined two cases, as occurred in *Red Lion*. In one, radio station WTOP in Washington, D.C., refused to sell time to an organization of businessmen opposed to United States military involvement in Vietnam. The Business Executives' Move for Vietnam Peace (BEM) wanted to buy a series of one-minute spot announcements expressing its opposition to the war.

In the second case, the Democratic National Committee (DNC) petitioned the FCC to declare that no broadcaster could refuse to run paid editorial advertisements. The DNC wanted the FCC to declare that the committee could buy time from broadcast stations and the networks to present party views and solicit funds. The DNC claimed that many broadcasters had adopted a policy of refusing to sell time for spot announcements advocating positions on controversial public issues.

The FCC ruled that broadcasters could refuse to sell time for comment on public issues, but the U.S. Court of Appeals for the D.C. Circuit reversed the commission. The court said a flat ban on paid public-issue announcements was a violation of the First Amendment right of the public to receive information.[18] However, seven of the nine Supreme Court justices voted to reverse the appeals court and support the FCC. Five justices agreed with Chief Justice Burger when he said that the First Amendment does not require broadcast stations to sell time to anyone wishing to speak out on public issues.

Burger said the Supreme Court should defer, when possible, to the "delicate and difficult" balance of the First Amendment rights of the broadcast media and public established by Congress and the FCC. Burger noted that Congress did not require in the Communications Act that broadcasters provide airtime to specific persons wanting to speak out on public issues. Rather, he said, Congress intended to leave licensees with broad discretion in broadcasting discussions of public issues.

Burger said that the FCC adopted the fairness doctrine, in existence at the time of the Court's decision, to ensure that the public would receive information and views involving public controversies. He said the FCC feared that if access to the broadcast

---

[17]*Id.* at 393–94, 1 Media L. Rep. at 2064.

[18]Democratic National Committee, 25 F.C.C.2d 216, 19 P & F Rad. Reg.2d 977 (1970) and Business Executives' Move for Vietnam Peace, 25 F.C.C.2d 242, 19 P & F Rad. Reg.2d 1053 (1970), both *rev'd* in Business Executives' Move for Vietnam Peace v. FCC, 450 F.2d 642 (D.C. Cir. 1971).

media could be purchased on demand, the discussion of public issues would be dominated by the rich. In addition, Burger said there was a danger that the time allotted for editorializing might be monopolized by one political persuasion.

Burger said the First Amendment does not require that someone other than journalists have the opportunity to decide what issues should be aired. He said the Court did not accept the view

> that every potential speaker is "the best judge" of what the listening public ought to hear or indeed the best judge of the merits of his or her views. . . . For better or for worse, editing is what editors are for; and editing is selection and choice of material.[19]

The fact that both newspaper and broadcast editors "can and do abuse" their power did not justify, in the eyes of the Court, a denial of the journalistic discretion for broadcasters intended by Congress. The potential for abuse was a calculated risk taken "in order to preserve higher values." The Court wanted to avoid substituting the judgment of those who might buy time on the air for the judgment of journalists.

The Court also wanted to avoid the possibility of increased government supervision over the discussion of public issues. Burger said a system of access would require the FCC to "oversee far more of the day-to-day operations of broadcasters' conduct." The commission would have to determine whether specific individuals were given adequate time to present their views and whether particular viewpoints already had been sufficiently aired. Burger was not prepared to "sacrifice" the First Amendment for the questionable advantages of access.

No Right of Reply to the Print Media   Even though the Supreme Court did not require broadcasters to sell time for the discussion of public issues in *CBS v. Democratic National Committee,* the Court's understanding of the rights of broadcasters contrasts sharply with its understanding of the rights of the print media. The Supreme Court's decision in *Red Lion* to uphold the constitutionality of the FCC's personal attack rules provides a stark contrast to a decision five years later involving a right to reply to attacks in newspapers. The same Supreme Court that said a right of reply requirement was constitutional for broadcasters said it was unconstitutional for the print media.

In *Miami Herald v. Tornillo,* the *Miami Herald* challenged a Florida statute, adopted in 1913, that required newspapers to print free replies by political candidates the paper had attacked.[20] The statute made it a misdemeanor for a newspaper to refuse to print the candidate's reply in as conspicuous a place and in the same kind of type as the original charges. In 1972, Pat Tornillo, a candidate for the Florida House of Representatives, demanded to reply to a *Miami Herald* editorial. The *Herald* had charged that Tornillo, the executive director of the Classroom Teachers Association in Miami, had led an illegal teachers' strike a few years earlier. A Florida trial court held that the state law requiring a reply was unconstitutional, but the Florida Supreme Court reversed the decision. The U.S. Supreme Court granted *certiorari.*

---

[19]CBS v. Democratic National Committee, 412 U.S. 94, 124, 1 Media L. Rep. 1855, 1866 (1973).
[20]418 U.S. 241, 1 Media L. Rep. 1898 (1974).

Tornillo argued that an enforceable right of reply to newspaper attacks should be constitutional because the government has an obligation to ensure that a wide variety of views is available to the public. He cited the Supreme Court's declaration in *Red Lion* that requiring broadcasters to provide a right of reply did not violate, but enhanced, the First Amendment.[21] Tornillo argued that the First Amendment rights of the public were in danger because the marketplace of ideas was controlled by a few media owners. He said that national newspapers, national newspaper chains, national wire and news services, and one-newspaper cities limited the ability of members of the public to contribute to debate on public issues.[22]

Chief Justice Warren Burger, writing for a unanimous Court, did not address Tornillo's arguments. However, the Court ruled that a government-enforced right of reply for the print media violated the First Amendment. Burger said that past Supreme Court decisions made it unconstitutional to require a newspaper to print what it otherwise would not. He said press responsibility was undoubtedly a desirable goal, but it was not mandated by the Constitution and, "like many other virtues," could not be legislated.

Burger said that a government-enforced right of access for the print media inescapably "dampens the vigor and limits the variety of public debate."[23] He said the Florida statute was an unconstitutional government restraint on publishing in the same sense as a statute forbidding publication. The required access would increase the cost of printing, require additional composing time and materials, and take up space that could be devoted to something else. Burger said that editors, realizing that they faced a reply requirement, "might well conclude that the safe course is to avoid controversy." As a result, he said, political and electoral coverage in Florida would be "blunted or reduced."

Burger also said that the Florida reply statute was unconstitutional because it intruded into the function of editors:

> The choice of material to go into a newspaper, and the decisions made as to limitations on the size and content of the paper, and treatment of public issues and public officials—whether fair or unfair—constitute the exercise of editorial control and judgment. It has yet to be demonstrated how governmental regulation of this crucial process can be exercised consistent with First Amendment guarantees of a free press.[24]

In *Tornillo,* therefore, the Supreme Court emphasized the rights of the editors and owners of newspapers. In contrast, the Court's opinion in *Red Lion* emphasized the First Amendment rights of the public. In *Tornillo,* Burger did not explain why a right of reply would stifle a newspaper and interfere with the editorial rights of an editor but not do the same to a broadcaster. In fact, in *Tornillo,* Burger did not mention the Court's decision in *Red Lion.*

Many commentators cannot reconcile *Red Lion* with *Tornillo* because, they con-

---

[21]Brief for Appellee, Miami Herald Publishing Co. v. Tornillo, 418 U.S. 241, 1 Media L. Rep. 1898 (1974).
[22]418 U.S. at 249, 1 Media L. Rep. at 1901 (1974).
[23]*Id.* at 257, 1 Media L. Rep. at 1904, *quoting* New York Times Co. v. Sullivan, 376 U.S. at 279.
[24]*Id.*

tend, the economic limitations on the number of newspapers are more severe than the spectrum limitations on the number of broadcasters.[25] In fact, there are about 10,500 broadcast stations compared to 10,000 newspapers.[26] In most major cities, there are more television stations than daily newspapers. Communities wired for cable often receive more than 30 channels of programming.

However, the Court's decisions in *Red Lion* and *Tornillo* had little to do with the number of newspapers and broadcast stations. The Court's decision in *Red Lion* was based on the presumption that limitations of the broadcast spectrum forced the government to decide who could use the finite number of frequencies available. The Court said the chosen few had to serve all. Therefore, the FCC could require that broadcasters provide certain information to the public without damaging their own First Amendment rights. On the other hand, government officials could not determine who could and who could not start a newspaper. Neither could a government official interfere in newspaper content.

The Supreme Court affirmed *Red Lion*'s application to broadcasting as recently as 1984. In *FCC v. League of Women Voters,* the Court reiterated that, because of spectrum scarcity, those who are awarded a broadcast license can be required to provide programming that serves the public interest. The Court commented in a footnote that many critics contend that spectrum scarcity should no longer be the basis of regulation because of the variety of programming available through cable and satellite technologies. In addition, many commentators argue, members of the public now have access to so many media outlets that regulation based on limits of the broadcast spectrum is no longer justifiable.[27] The Court, in *League of Women Voters,* said, however, that it was "not prepared" to reconsider its application of the First Amendment to broadcasting "without some signal from Congress or the FCC that technological developments have advanced so far" that a revision "may be required."[28] Until that happens, Court tolerance of broadcast program regulation allows the FCC substantial freedom to regulate broadcasting within the parameters established by Congress.

SUMMARY

Congress adopted the 1927 Radio Act in order to curb the chaos on the airwaves. The limited number of frequencies available on the broadcast spectrum dictated that not everyone who wanted to could broadcast. The Radio Act established a licensing system for private broadcasters based on the principle of service in the public interest. The act also provided for government supervision of programming but prohibited

---

[25]*E.g.,* B. Schmidt, Jr., *Freedom of the Press vs. Public Access* (1976); Bazelon, "FCC Regulation of the Telecommunications Press," 1975 *Duke L.J.* 213.

[26]Bureau of Census, Department of Commerce, *Statistical Abstracts of the United States 1989,* at 544–49 (109th ed.).

[27]*E.g.,* Fowler & Brenner, "A Marketplace Approach to Broadcast Regulation," 60 *Tex. L. Rev.* 207, 221–26 (1982).

[28]*See* FCC v. League of Women Voters of California, 468 U.S. 364, 376 n.11, 10 Media L. Rep. 1937, 1942 n.11 (1984).

censorship. Early court cases upheld the Federal Radio Commission's regulation of programming. Congress incorporated the radio law into the 1934 Communications Act.

The Supreme Court, in *Red Lion Broadcasting,* said that at least one aspect of program regulation enhanced rather than abridged First Amendment values. The Court said that because of the limitations of the broadcast spectrum the government must choose some persons rather than others to use the airwaves. The public interest requires that those granted licenses must ensure that views other than their own are presented, the Court said. The First Amendment right of the public to receive ideas is paramount.

However, in *CBS v. Democratic National Committee,* the Court said that no one person or group could demand access to the airwaves to discuss their points of view on public issues. The Court said there was no First Amendment right to purchase time on the broadcast media.

In contrast to the Court's decision in *Red Lion Broadcasting v. FCC* that broadcasters could be required to accord a right of reply to persons attacked, the Court said in *Miami Herald v. Tornillo* that newspaper editors could not be required to print something they did not want to publish. A requirement that newspapers print a reply to a personal attack would violate the First Amendment.

Federal Communications Commission

The 1934 Communications Act established the Federal Communications Commission to regulate telecommunications. The five members of the commission are appointed by the president and confirmed by the Senate for staggered five-year terms. There can be no more than three members from one political party.

Although the FCC was established at a time when the only telecommunications media were radio, telegraph, and telephone, the commission has since assumed control over television, cable television, subscription television, teletext, direct satellite broadcasting, and other new telecommunications technologies.

The FCC controls the allocation of the electromagnetic spectrum, the range of electromagnetic energy that includes radio waves, infrared rays, visible light, X-rays, and cosmic rays. The commission allocates the bands of electromagnetic frequencies that can be used to transmit sound and pictures to particular services, such as AM and FM radio, VHF and UHF television, and microwave communications.[29]

The commission also places each electronic media service into a classification such as broadcast, cable, or common carrier, the latter required to transmit the message of anyone who can pay. The classification given to a service determines which FCC rules apply. However, some of the new technologies do not fit neatly into any of the three standard categories, and the FCC has developed specialized regulatory packages for individual media technologies.

Although the FCC's program regulation tends to be one of the most visible parts

---

[29]For a fuller discussion of the electromagnetic spectrum, *see, e.g.,* F. L. Smith, *Perspectives on Radio and Television; Telecommunication in the United States* 234–37 (3d ed. 1990).

of its work, more commission staff time is devoted to such matters as ownership questions, technical issues, and routine paperwork. For example, the commission assigns frequencies, approves the transfer of licenses and the heights of radio towers, and monitors station power. However, because programming regulation is the only commission responsibility directly affecting public communicators, it is the only one discussed in detail in this chapter.

The FCC is responsible for enforcing the programming requirements specified in the 1934 Communications Act. It can also adopt enforceable program policies not specified in the act in order to serve the public interest. The commission's licensing power is its most powerful enforcement tool. It can also fine stations.

Broadcast Policy Making   Both Congress and the FCC participate in the making of broadcast policy, the adoption and enforcement of the government's regulation of over-the-air radio and television. Congress adopts legislation that the FCC executes through administrative proceedings.

In the 1934 Communications Act, Congress both specified a few programming requirements by statute and more generally authorized the FCC to regulate broadcasters according to the "public interest, convenience, or necessity." This vague regulatory guideline permits commissioners to determine, within statutory restrictions, what kinds of broadcast programming should be encouraged and discouraged. Over the years, the commission has at times emphasized the importance of improving broadcast programming and at other times promoted broadcaster independence. During most of the commission's history, it has encouraged locally originated programming. The dominant policy of the FCC during the 1980s was deregulation—doing away with rules rather than adding any or enforcing those rules already in place. The FCC under President George Bush appears ready to protect most broadcast decision making from direct government oversight. At the same time, the commission does not appear to be as tied to the ideology of deregulation as it was during the last decade. The commission can establish programming policies through rule making, opinions settling disputes, and ad hoc announcements.

Rule Making   Official FCC regulations must be promulgated through a formal process of rule making. To adopt a rule, the commission must announce a proposal in the *Federal Register,* allow for public comment, and then print the final rule, also in the *Federal Register.* The personal attack rules contested in the *Red Lion* case were adopted after rule making. A violation of a rule can result in a fine. A violation also may be considered during the license renewal process, to be discussed in the next few pages.

Policy Making through Dispute Settlement   At times, the FCC announces a new policy or a new policy application while settling controversies. One of the most famous examples of policy making through individual case decisions occurred in 1941 in a challenge to the renewal of a radio license in Boston. The FCC discovered that WAAB, under the incumbent licensee, had supported political candidates in editorials and taken sides on public issues. In *Mayflower Broadcasting,* the FCC said for the first time that editorializing by broadcast licensees was not considered to be in the public interest.[30] The FCC, while deciding who should broadcast in Boston, had announced a new interpretation of the statutory language "public interest, convenience, or necessity." In more recent years, the FCC has frequently used individual case opinions to reveal new interpretations of programming policies, such as the enforcement of indecency restrictions and the elimination of the fairness doctrine.

The commission, by making general policy as it decides individual cases, can deal with issues as they arise without going through the time-consuming and burdensome rule-making process. However, policy developed case by case is sometimes adopted without carefully considering all the implications. The results of such policy are harder for the commission to anticipate than if the policy had been more carefully researched, and then scrutinized by the public, in the rule-making process. In the case of the ban on broadcast editorials announced in *Mayflower,* pressure from the broadcast industry encouraged the FCC to reverse its position in less than a decade. In 1949, the commission announced that broadcast licensees could editorialize after all.

Ad Hoc Policy Creation   Sometimes the FCC, in ad hoc decision making, announces a new policy without having a specific case in front of it and without following the rule-making procedure. The FCC engaged in ad hoc decision making in 1949 when it decided that broadcasters could editorialize. In the same document, *In the Matter of Editorializing by Broadcast Licensees,* the commission announced its fairness doctrine, the policy that until 1987 required broadcasters to provide diverse views on controversial public issues. The FCC revealed the fairness doctrine after staff study and several days of hearings focused on the question of editorializing. The commission did not give the public a chance to react to the proposed fairness policy by publishing a draft prior to its adoption. Such policy statements are not enforceable by fines. However, the commission can consider a broadcaster's compliance when deciding whether to renew a license.

Policy Enforcement   The FCC can fine stations for each violation of a programming regulation or statutory requirement. The commission can also take away a broadcaster's license for failing to provide programming that is, as a whole, in the public interest. In practice, the commission rarely punishes broadcasters for the programming they air. In fact, the FCC's reluctance to punish broadcasters has led to an informal mechanism for FCC enforcement, called regulation by the *raised eyebrow,* to be discussed shortly.

Evaluation of Individual Complaints   The commission can enforce violations of the 1934 Communications Act or FCC regulations on a case-by-case basis. The commission has seldom monitored broadcast programming on its own initiative, but has ordinarily relied upon complaints received from viewers and listeners.

When the commission staff receives a complaint that appears to have merit, it asks a broadcaster to respond. After the FCC has examined the broadcast station's reply, it usually decides that a station operated within the discretion allowed broadcasters to make their own good-faith judgments. However, the FCC sometimes or-

---

[30]8 F.C.C. 333 (1941).

ders a broadcaster to provide programming that would rectify a problem indicated in a complaint. Or sometimes the commission writes a letter of reprimand, which is the equivalent of a slap on the hand.

Only rarely will the commission issue an official legal sanction against a licensee for a programming violation. The commission can force a licensee to stop a specific practice with a cease-and-desist order. It can also levy a fine called a *forfeiture*. A licensee can be fined as much as $25,000 a day, but the total for one violation cannot exceed $250,000.[31] Many of the fines for programming have been assessed for failure to identify the sponsor of advertising or for broadcasting information about lotteries. Radio station KWAC of Bakersfield, California, was fined $2,500 in 1973 for broadcasting lottery information and for not informing listeners that announcers were receiving money for broadcasting specifically requested musical selections.[32] Broadcasters have more freedom under federal law to broadcast lottery information than they used to since Congress passed the Charity Games Advertising Clarification Act of 1988, discussed in Chapter 7.

One reason the FCC seldom punishes a station for individual programming violations is that it prefers to consider a complaint in context. That is, the commission prefers to evaluate a complaint only in light of a broadcast licensee's total programming performance for a period of several years, something it can do only during the license renewal process.

Regulating by Licensing   The licensing process is the major enforcement vehicle for the FCC. The commission must approve applications for new licenses, transfers of ownership, and improved broadcast facilities. It also must approve license renewals, including those renewals contested by another applicant or by a petition submitted by listeners or viewers.

The commission licenses only individual stations and not broadcast networks. However, the FCC exercises control over the national networks because each of them owns licensed broadcast stations that must periodically submit renewal applications. In addition, the commission can control the networks through its authority under the 1934 Communications Act to issue "special regulations" to network-owned stations.[33] One of those special regulations is the Prime Time Access Rule, discussed later in the chapter.

The license renewal process provides the FCC with a natural mechanism to enforce programming policies. Each television station must apply for a license renewal every five years. Radio broadcasters must renew their licenses every seven years.[34] The FCC can require broadcasters to submit information about their programming so the commission can evaluate their performance. Licensees failing to comply with programming policies can be refused renewal or granted a renewal for less than the standard term. Licenses can also be revoked at any time. However, in practice, the commission has rarely used the license renewal process to punish broadcasters for violations of programming policies.

---

[31] 47 U.S.C.S. sec. 503 (b) (2) (A) (Supp. 1990).
[32] Liability of KMAP, Inc., Licensee of Radio Station KWAC, 43 F.C.C.2d 158, 22 P & F Rad. Reg.2d 699 (1973).
[33] 47 U.S.C. 301 (i) (1982).
[34] 47 U.S.C. 307 (c) (1982).

The FCC's responsibility during the license renewal process is to determine whether a broadcaster has served the public interest. The FCC claims to review violations of programming regulations and consider whether broadcasters have provided programming to meet the needs and interests of their communities.[35] Broadcast licensees can meet community needs through news and public affairs programming such as documentaries. Educational, religious, and children's programming can also help meet community needs. So can agricultural information, service to minority groups, broadcasts by political candidates, and weather and market reports. The FCC also accepts public service announcements, editorials, and community bulletin boards.[36] The FCC does not currently recommend that a station devote a specific number of hours or percentage of its airtime to programming that meets community needs.

However, during the 1960s and early 1970s, the FCC aggressively encouraged broadcasters to provide programming related to community issues. The commission required broadcasters to ascertain community need through formal procedures. It established guidelines for the amount of informational programming that ought to be aired in the public interest. It also required licensees to submit extensive programming information to the commission.[37] About a half-dozen stations lost their licenses or received short-term renewals, at least in part for failing to provide programming about community issues. The owner of WSWG-AM of Greenwood, Mississippi, for example, lost his license for intentionally failing to broadcast the public issues programming he had promised on his previous renewal application. The station also mislabeled entertainment programs such as the "Miss Hospitality Pageant" as public affairs.[38] WQAL-FM of Cleveland, Ohio, received only a one-year renewal after it devoted less than one percent of its broadcast time to public affairs programming.[39]

In all, the FCC revoked or refused to renew the licenses of about a dozen of the 10,000 broadcasters periodically filing for renewal during the 1970s. Broadcasters were penalized not only for failing to provide programming related to community needs, but also for frequent violations of the fairness doctrine, broadcasting lottery information, distortion of the news, broadcasting too much advertising, and excluding minorities from programming. In many of the cases, station management also lied to the commission.[40]

In contrast, the FCC did not deny the license renewal of a single station between 1940 and 1970 because of a broadcast station's overall programming. Neither did the FCC punish broadcasters for their failure overall to meet community needs and interests in the 1980s. In fact, during the Reagan administration, the commission rescinded most of the regulations adopted in the 1960s and 1970s.

---

[35]Report and Statement of Policy Res.: Commission Programming Inquiry, 44 F.C.C. 2303 (1960).

[36]See Revision of Programming and Commercialization Policies, Ascertainment Requirements, and Program Log Requirements for Commercial TV Stations (Television Deregulation), 98 F.C.C.2d 1076, 1086-88, 1091-94, 56 P & F Rad. Reg.2d 1005, 1014-15, 1018-20 (1984); Deregulation of Radio, 84 F.C.C.2d 968, 978-79, 982-83, 49 P & F Rad. Reg.2d 1, 10-11, 13-14, reconsideration, 87 F.C.C.2d 797, 50 P & F Rad. Reg.2d 93 (1981).

[37]See Chamberlin, "Lessons in Regulating Information Flow: The FCC's Weak Track Record in Interpreting the Public Interest Standard," 60 N.C.L. Rev. 1058, 1067-1103 (1982).

[38]LeFlore Broadcasting Co., 46 F.C.C.2d 980 (1974), license denied, 65 F.C.C.2d 556, 41 P & F Rad. Reg.2d 379 (1977), aff'd, 636 F.2d 454 (D.C. Cir. 1980).

[39]SJR Communications, Inc., 67 F.C.C.2d 1103, 42 P & F Rad.Reg.2d 920 (1978).

[40]Weiss, Ostroff & Clift, "Station License Revocations and Denials of Renewal, 1970-78," 24 J. Broadcasting 69 (1980).

The FCC still insists that broadcasters carry community-oriented programming. However, the commission did not show an inclination during the early years of the Bush administration to initiate enforcement proceedings against any broadcasters who fail to air programs about community issues. In fact, the FCC does not ordinarily know what programming a station broadcasts because the commission no longer requires that station programming records be sent to Washington, D.C.[41] Broadcasters are only required to keep a public file of the station's "most significant" programs about community issues.[42]

Beginning in 1983, the commission evaluated the programming of KTTL-FM of Dodge City, Kansas, only after its license was challenged by a local citizen group and the National Black Media Coalition. Then the FCC decided that the station, operated by Charles and Nellie Babbs, may not have provided programming that met the needs of its audience. The commission ordered an investigation when the station's list of programs did not appear to match the list of community needs. In addition, said one commissioner, "KTTL subjected Dodge City residents to a regular dose of . . . racist, anti-Semitic and socially destructive messages, with no apparent regard for the differing views held by most of its listeners."[43] Eventually, the FCC approved a settlement that awarded the license to the citizen group and paid Charles Babbs, by that time divorced, $10,000 to withdraw his renewal application.

The FCC's move to deregulation during the 1980s did not satisfy Mark Fowler, FCC chairman during most of the Reagan administration. Fowler wanted to eliminate programming regulation altogether. Fowler argued that a broadcaster's service to the public ought to depend only on what the public wants. According to Fowler, "the public's interest, then, defines the public interest."[44] The Fowler commission said stations are inclined to provide public issues programming more because of market incentives than because of regulation. Programming regulation costs too much and infringes on the editorial judgment of broadcasters, Fowler said.[45]

Renewal Challenges   Although the FCC is not closely examining broadcast station programming, a license may be contested by a listener or viewer or by someone who wants to broadcast on the same frequency.

Members of the public have been able to participate in FCC renewal proceedings since the late 1960s. In 1966, a federal appeals court ruled that Mississippi residents could challenge the license renewal of television station WLBT in Jackson, Mississippi, for presenting programming unfair to blacks. The station was accused, for example, of using language offensive to black viewers and presenting only one side of the racial integration controversy. The FCC said the viewers had no legal right to

---

[41]Revision of Applications for Renewals of License of Commercial and Noncommercial AM, FM, and Television Licensees, 87 F.C.C.2d 1127, 50 P & F Rad. Reg.2d 704 (1981); Television Deregulation, 98 F.C.C.2d at 1077–80, 1086–96, 56 P & F Rad. Reg.2d at 1006–1020; Radio Deregulation, 84 F.C.C.2d at 971–72, 1011, 49 P & F Rad. Reg.2d at 5, 32.

[42]Radio Deregulation, 104 F.C.C.2d 505, 60 P & F Rad. Reg.2d 789 (1986); Television Deregulation, 104 F.C.C.2d 357, 60 P & F Rad. Reg.2d 526 (1986).

[43]Cattle Country Broadcasting, 58 P & F Rad. Reg.2d 1109, 1125 (1985) (Rivera, separate statement).

[44]Fowler & Brenner, "A Marketplace Approach to Broadcast Regulation," 60 *Texas L. Rev.* 207, 210 (1982).

[45]Television Deregulation, 98 F.C.C.2d at 1076–91, 56 P & F Rad. Reg.2d at 1005–1017.

challenge the license because viewers—unlike someone competing for the same frequency—had no economic stake in the proceeding. However, the U.S. Court of Appeals for the District of Columbia ruled that viewers had a genuine interest in the license renewal process. The court said that viewers who have no intention of owning a station should still be allowed to challenge the license renewal of a broadcaster who they believe is not operating in the public interest.[46]

During the 1970s, citizen groups filed more than 500 petitions to deny the licenses of radio and television stations.[47] Although few licenses were denied, citizen groups had a major impact on commission procedures and policies. In addition, citizen groups often used the threat of a complaint or license challenge to bargain with broadcast station management for programming changes.

The FCC's deregulation of broadcasting has hurt citizen groups' efforts to challenge broadcasters. The commission has eliminated many of the regulations and guidelines that were once the bases of challenges. In addition, since the commission has severely reduced station record-keeping requirements, groups that want to challenge licenses have to provide more of the documentation of licensee programming themselves.

While deregulation has undermined effective citizen challenges of broadcast licenses, it has not substantially affected challenges by persons who want to replace a licensee. The FCC must choose between the applications of the challenger and the incumbent in a comparative renewal proceeding.

Since 1981, licensees who provide "meritorious" programming have been given a comparative preference during competitive renewal proceedings. Incumbents rendering substantial community service through their programming are accorded a "renewal expectancy," one of several factors evaluated by the commission when two applicants are competing for use of the same spectrum space. The other criteria include:

- Diversification of media ownership. Owners of a newspaper or another broadcast station in the same community, or of significant media holdings elsewhere, are at a competitive disadvantage in a comparative renewal proceeding.
- Owner participation in station management. The FCC favors owners who participate in the day-to-day decisions of station operations rather than absentee owners.
- Owner participation in community activities.
- Minority ownership. The increased participation of blacks and women in the broadcast industry became a commission policy in the 1970s.[48]
- Previous experience as broadcast station owner.
- Personal character of ownership. A criminal record or lack of candor can be significant factors weighed against an applicant.

[46]Office of Communication of the United Church of Christ v. FCC, 359 F.2d 994 (D.C. Cir. 1966). *Accord,* Office of Communication of the United Church of Christ v. FCC, 425 F.2d 543 (D.C. Cir. 1969).

[47]Chamberlin, "Lessons in Regulating Information Flow: The FCC's Weak Track Record in Interpreting the Public Interest Standard," 60 *N.L.C. Rev.* 1067, 1087 n.175 (1982).

[48]Upheld by U.S. Supreme Court in Metro Broadcasting, Inc. v. FCC, 1990 WL 85319.

- Efficient use of broadcast spectrum. One applicant may propose an operation that would be technically superior.
- Proposed program service. The promise of more public affairs and informational programming is a factor only if there is a major difference between competing plans.[49]

The addition in 1981 of a consideration for meritorious programming was added after the U.S. Court of Appeals for the D.C. Circuit reversed one of the FCC's comparative renewal decisions in a continuing dispute between the court and the commission over comparative renewal proceedings. While the FCC had long contended it awarded licenses to the best applicants in comparative renewal proceedings, the court and critics frequently criticized the commission for regularly favoring incumbents. In 1978, in the first of two decisions in *Central Florida Enterprises v. FCC,* the D.C. Circuit said the FCC "arbitrarily" renewed the license of the incumbent, WESH-TV, in a fight for a television frequency in Orlando, Florida. When the court told the commission to reconsider its decision, the FCC again chose the incumbent licensee, Cowles Florida Broadcasting, Inc., over the challenger, Central Florida Enterprises, Inc. However, in the FCC's second decision, it provided an explanation the court said was missing the first time.

In the FCC's second decision in the *Central Florida* dispute, the commission said that Cowles's "substantial" service to the community outweighed both its previous misconduct and Central Florida's superiority in two comparative categories. The FCC said the programming of WESH-TV under Cowles was "sound, favorable and substantially above a level of mediocre." The station's programming had been responsive to community needs, the FCC said, and was praised by several community leaders. The FCC said the favorable programming record overcame the fact that Cowles had violated an FCC rule by moving a studio without permission and that five Cowles subsidiaries had been fined $50,000 for mail fraud. The FCC said WESH-TV's programming record under Cowles also outweighed the fact that Central Florida owned fewer communications properties and offered more owner participation in station management.

The commission also said that Cowles's license should be renewed because the public might receive poorer service if "an untested and undistinguished proposal" replaced a known acceptable service.[50] The FCC said that incumbent broadcasters providing even stronger service than the "sound" and "favorable" evaluation given Cowles should receive a strong preference in comparative proceedings. An incumbent broadcaster providing minimal program service would receive no preference.[51]

The D.C. Circuit accepted the FCC's argument that a licensee's meritorious ser-

---

[49]1965 Policy Statement on Comparative Broadcast Hearings, 1 F.C.C.2d 393, 5 P & F Rad. Reg.2d 1901 (1965); Television Deregulation, 98 F.C.C.2d at 1091–96, 56 P & F Rad. Reg.2d at 1017–20 (1984).

[50]*In re* Cowles Broadcasting, Inc., 60 F.C.C.2d 372, 37 P & F Rad. Reg.2d 1487 (1976), *reconsideration denied and clarified,* 62 F.C.C.2d 953, 39 P & F Rad. Reg.2d 541, *reconsideration denied,* 40 P & F Rad. Reg.2d 1627 (1977), *vacated and remanded sub. nom.* Central Florida Enterprises, Inc. v. FCC, 598 F.2d 37 (D.C. Cir. 1978), *cert. denied,* 441 U.S. 957 (1979), on remand, *reconsideration denied,* 86 F.C.C.2d 993, 49 P & F Rad. Reg.2d 1138 (1981), *aff'd,* Central Florida Enterprises, Inc. v. FCC, 683 F.2d 503 (D.C. Cir. 1982), *cert. denied,* 460 U.S. 1084 (1983).

[51]Cowles Broadcasting, Inc., 86 F.C.C.2d at 1012–16, 49 P & F Rad. Reg. 2d at 1156–60.

vice should receive favorable consideration during a comparative license renewal proceeding, but warned that the new comparative criterion could "degenerate" into an "irrebuttable presumption in favor of renewal." The court noted that the commission had up to that point never denied the renewal of an incumbent television licensee during a competitive challenge.[52] It continued,

> American television viewers will be reassured, although a trifle baffled, to learn that even the worst television stations—those which are, presumably, the ones picked out as vulnerable to a challenge—are so good that they never need replacing.[53]

In 1990, nine years after the 1981 change in the comparative renewal proceedings criteria, the commission was considering specific criteria for evaluating "meritorious" service of broadcast licensees.[54] In addition, the commission was evaluating other proposals to reform the comparative hearing process as well.[55] In the same proceeding in 1989, the FCC adopted rules to reduce the possibility that challengers to licenses could use the comparative renewal process for what has been called *greenmail,* agreeing to forgo what could be a lengthy license challenge in exchange for money.

Under the new rules, the FCC will only approve negotiated settlements between a licensee and a competing applicant if payment to a challenger willing to withdraw is limited to "legitimate and prudent" expenses. In addition, the FCC said it would approve payments only when settlements are made after the completion of a comparative hearing. The FCC said the two limitations on settlements should significantly reduce the number of competing applications filed in order to make quick profits through negotiations with a broadcast licensee. In addition, the commission is asking for more information about a challenger's financial qualifications and ownership plans to determine whether a competing applicant is a legitimate candidate for a license.[56]

Raised Eyebrow   While not an official part of the FCC's enforcement arsenal, the *raised eyebrow* is nevertheless an important ingredient in broadcast programming regulation. The FCC uses the raised eyebrow when it tells broadcasters what kind of programming is expected of them without any intent to use fines or the license renewal process to directly enforce its policy. The commission counts on broadcasters' fears of losing their licenses rather than active enforcement to obtain compliance.[57]

---

[52]*But see* Simon Geller, 91 F.C.C.2d 1253, 52 P & F Rad. Reg.2d 709 (1982), *remanded,* Geller v. FCC, 737 F.2d 74 (D.C. Cir. 1984), *rev'd,* 102 F.C.C.2d 1443, 59 P & F Rad. Reg.2d 579 (1985).

[53]Central Florida Enterprises, Inc. v. FCC, 683 F.2d at 510.

[54]Formulation of Policies and Rules Relating to Broadcast Renewal Applicants, Competing Applicants, and Other Participants to the Comparative Renewal Process and to the Prevention of Abuses of the Renewal Process (Renewal Expectancy), 4 FCC Rcd. 6363 (1989).

[55]Proposals to Reform the Commission's Comparative Hearing Process to Expedite the Resolution of Cases, FCC 90-194 (May 10, 1990) (FCOM-FCC).

[56]Formulation of Policies and Rules Relating to Broadcast Renewal Applicants, Competing Applicants, and Other Participants to the Comparative Renewal Process and to the Prevention of Abuses of the Renewal Process, 4 FCC Rcd. 4780 (1989).

[57]Miami Broadcasting Co., 14 P & F Rad. Reg. 125, 126-29 (1956) (Doerfer, dissenting).

During the 1980s, the raised eyebrow was the only enforcement tool used to encourage licensees to provide children's programming and programming to meet the needs of the communities served.

The effectiveness of the raised eyebrow is made possible by the threat of non-renewal of a license—a life-and-death issue for every broadcaster. The 1934 Communications Act created an ideal environment for regulation by suggestion. The FCC alone decides whether a broadcast station can retain its license, and the statutory standard for renewal—public interest—is vague. Neither the 1934 act nor the FCC explicitly provides a comprehensive list of expectations for licensees. Therefore, when the commission indicates that a specific kind of programming is not in the public interest, some licensees behave as if the suggestion was a mandate.

An example of regulation by raised eyebrow occurred when the FCC became concerned about drug lyrics in many popular songs in 1971. The commission announced that licensees would be held accountable for songs with lyrics containing "glorification" of drug use.[58] The FCC even provided broadcasters a list of 22 songs that became, in effect, a "do-not-play" list.[59] Stations banned such records as "With a Little Help from My Friends" and "Lucy in the Sky with Diamonds" by the Beatles, "Mr. Tambourine Man" by Bob Dylan and the Byrds, and "One Toke Over the Line" by Brewer and Shipley. Some stations even banned records with antidrug lyrics, records with lyrics they could not understand, and records they did not have time to screen for fear that the stations would be subject to FCC scrutiny.[60]

Within two months, the FCC repudiated the list. The commission said that decisions about which records to play are "solely for the licensee" and that the commission "cannot make or review such an individual licensee judgment." But, the commission kept its eyebrow raised by adding that a broadcaster "could jeopardize his license by failing to exercise licensee responsibility in this area."[61]

Some broadcasters still argued that the commission had violated the First Amendment by suggesting they could be punished for playing specific records. Broadcasters also argued the FCC had imposed a requirement on broadcasters that could be adopted only in a rule-making proceeding. The U.S. Court of Appeals for the D.C. Circuit said, however, that it was appropriate for the FCC to tell broadcasters that specific kinds of programming might not be in the public interest. The commission was only reminding licensees of their statutory responsibilities, the court said. The FCC's drug lyrics announcement, the court ruled, did not constitute a threat to the licensee's freedom of speech.[62]

During the 1980s, the commission did not rely on the raised eyebrow as much as it had in the past, at least in part because of its commitment to deregulating broadcasting. Even so, the commission relied on the raised eyebrow in the case of children's programming, to be discussed later in the chapter.

---

[58]Licensee Responsibility to Review Records before Their Broadcast, 28 F.C.C.2d 409, 21 P & F Rad. Reg.2d 1576 (1971).

[59]Yale Broadcasting Co. v. FCC, 478 F.2d 594 (D.C. Cir.), cert. denied, 414 U.S. 914 (1973).

[60]Comment, "Drug Lyrics, the FCC and the First Amendment," 5 Loy. L.A.L. Rev. 329, 348–49 (1972).

[61]Review of Records on Drugs, 31 F.C.C.2d 377, 378, 21 P & F Rad. Reg.2d 1698, 1701 (1971).

[62]Yale Broadcasting Co. v. FCC, 478 F.2d at 599–601.

SUMMARY

The Federal Communications Commission consists of five members appointed by the president. The FCC is responsible for regulating the use of the electromagnetic spectrum; the supervision of telecommunications content is but one of its many functions.

The FCC establishes telecommunications policy through rule making and ad hoc policy announcements. The FCC can control the behavior of broadcasters largely through the licensing process, particularly through the requirement of periodic license renewal. The licensing process has often been used by the commission to encourage broadcasts of programming that meets the needs of listeners and viewers. However, because of deregulation, licensees no longer send programming reports to the commission. The FCC does not ordinarily evaluate licensee programming during the license renewal process unless it receives a complaint from a viewer or listener or a challenge to a license by someone else wanting to use the frequency. The commission seldom punishes licensee programming practices through license nonrenewal, short-term renewal, revocation, or fines, but often tries to encourage compliance with FCC pronouncements through the use of the raised eyebrow.

Regulation of Political Candidate Programming

The FCC not only enforces a general statutory requirement that broadcasters serve the public interest, convenience, or necessity, but also enforces specific programming regulations mandated by statute or by the commission itself. For example, the 1934 Communications Act sets forth two requirements affecting broadcast programming about political candidates. One, the equal opportunities rule, requires that a broadcast station provide time for a political candidate if it has provided time for an opponent. The other, the candidate access law, requires broadcasters to provide reasonable amounts of time for candidates running for federal office.

Equal Opportunities for Political Candidates   The equal opportunities rule (see Appendix B) is one of two kinds of programming required by the first statute regulating broadcasting. The 1927 Radio Act said that if a broadcaster allowed a legally qualified political candidate to use airtime, it had to "afford equal opportunities to all other such candidates for that office."[63] That language, which became section 315 of the 1934 Communications Act, remains an essential ingredient of broadcast regulation in spite of the move to deregulation.

The "equal opportunities" doctrine, sometimes inaccurately called the "equal time" rule, requires that candidates for the same office have the same opportunity to purchase broadcast time during a period of the day when they are likely to attract the same size audience. If a station provides free time to one candidate, free time must be offered to any qualified opponents for the same office.

Critics of the equal opportunities rule say the law does not guarantee equal treat-

---

[63] 1927 Radio Act, 44 Stat. sec. 18 (1927).

ment of candidates. Section 315 does not stop a rich candidate from buying far more time than an opponent can afford. Nor does it stop the broadcast of a newsworthy debate between the candidates of the major parties that excludes independents and so-called "minor party candidates," as will be explained later in this section. In addition, critics say, the equal opportunities requirements may well discourage broadcasters from providing time for political candidates. First, stations may be reluctant to sell time or otherwise provide airtime to the major political candidates, knowing they will also have to provide time to candidates they do not consider newsworthy or to candidates who use the time for racist or vulgar messages. Second, broadcasters often make less money when selling time to political candidates than they could selling the same time to other advertisers. Section 315 requires broadcasters to sell political advertising at their lowest rate for a particular time of day, regardless of the amount of time being purchased.

However, in spite of the problems with the equal opportunities law, Congress is unlikely to rescind section 315. Incumbent politicians believe the law protects them from being denied airtime in the face of an advertising blitz by an opponent. The law also protects incumbents because news coverage of public officials is exempt from the equal opportunities requirements.

Qualified Candidates Section 315 applies only to legally qualified political candidates. The FCC has said a person must meet three requirements to qualify as an official political candidate.

First, a candidate must have publicly announced an intention to run for office. The commission considers filing for office or fulfilling state requirements to appear on the ballot the equivalent of a public announcement. A person is not a qualified candidate simply because supporters are raising funds or because political observers expect him or her to run for office. The FCC said that then-President Lyndon Johnson was not a candidate for the 1968 Democratic presidential nomination when the television networks broadcast an interview with him in December 1967.[64] The commission said that Johnson had not publicly announced his bid for reelection. Senator Eugene McCarthy, who had announced his candidacy, complained that he and Johnson were the opposing candidates for the nomination of their party.

The FCC's decision in the Johnson-McCarthy dispute can create problems for a political candidate challenging an incumbent. The decision encourages an incumbent with substantial public exposure to delay an official announcement that would subject his activities to the equal opportunities rule. However, the commission said that deciding which unannounced candidates were nevertheless candidates would be "unworkable."

The second requirement to be met in order for section 315 to apply is that a candidate be legally qualified for the office. For example, any candidate for president of the United States must have been born in the United States and be at least 35 years old. Former Secretary of State Henry Kissinger, a naturalized citizen, is not eligible to be president and therefore cannot be a legally qualified candidate.

---

[64]Sen. Eugene J. McCarthy, 11 F.C.C.2d 511, *aff'd sub nom.* McCarthy v. FCC, 390 F.2d 471, 1 Media L. Rep. 2205 (D.C. Cir. 1968).

The third requirement for a legally qualified political candidate under section 315 is the most complicated. A candidate seeking an elective office must qualify for a place on the ballot or publicly commit to seeking election as a write-in candidate. For example, in Illinois, candidates for any statewide office must represent parties that received 5 percent of the vote in the preceding election or submit a nominating petition meeting statutory standards.[65]

Under section 315, a person seeking election as a write-in candidate must meet any legal requirements for write-in candidates. A write-in candidate also must make a "substantial showing" as a candidate—that is, engage in such campaign activities as making speeches, distributing literature, maintaining a campaign committee, and establishing a headquarters. Other candidates required to make a substantial showing in order to be considered official candidates are those seeking nomination to public office by a convention or caucus.

Candidates for president or vice president of the United States will be considered official candidates in all states if they qualify in 10 or more.[66] A broadcast station cannot deny equal opportunities to any candidate simply because the person appears to have little chance of winning.[67]

Legally qualified candidates oppose each other only if they are competing for the same votes in a specific election. So, in a general election in November or at another time, anyone running for the same office, regardless of party affiliation, is an "opposing candidate." But in primary elections, only candidates facing opposition within their own party qualify for time under section 315. Hence, Richard Kay, an unopposed candidate of the American Independent Party for the U.S. Senate from Ohio, could not obtain broadcast time to match that given candidates in the contested Democratic and Republican primaries. The candidates offered time included Democratic candidates Howard M. Metzenbaum and John Glenn, both of whom eventually served in the U.S. Senate. The Republican candidates were Governor James Rhodes and Representative Robert A. Taft, Jr.[68]

Time Requirements   The FCC has said emphatically that section 315 requires equal *opportunities* rather than only equal *time*. When a station provides time for purchase by one candidate, it must provide an opponent the same amount of time at a time of day when a comparable audience can be expected. An hour of broadcast time at 9 A.M. Sunday is not equivalent to one during prime-time Sunday evening because the morning program is likely to be seen by substantially fewer people. However, the commission said that giving a candidate 60 one-minute spots throughout the day to respond to an hour-long program during prime time would be more response than the law required.[69]

In addition, candidates must be charged the same rate for political broadcasts. A

[65]Ill. Ann. Stat. ch. 46, para. 10-2 (Smith-Hurd Supp. 1989). *See* Flory v. FCC, 528 F.2d 124 (7th Cir. 1975).
[66]47 C.F.R. sec. 73.1940 (1989).
[67]The Law of Political Broadcasting and Cablecasting: A Political Primer (1984 Political Primer), 100 F.C.C.2d 1476, 1486 (1984).
[68]Kay v. FCC, 443 F.2d 638 (D.C. Cir. 1970).
[69]*See* Bella S. Abzug, 25 F.C.C.2d 117, 19 P & F Rad. Reg.2d 1047 (1970).

broadcast licensee cannot charge one candidate $8,000 for 30 minutes of prime time and the second $9,500.[70]

The FCC relies on a broadcaster's reasonable judgment when it is impossible to provide opportunities that are exactly equal because of mechanical difficulties or other circumstances. The FCC upheld a broadcast station's use of a still picture of former Indiana Senator Birch Bayh when the video failed during the senator's closing remarks in a 30-minute debate. The sound was not affected during the three-minute video interruption.[71]

Under section 315, political candidates cannot demand that broadcast stations allow them to go on the air at any time the candidates choose. A candidate for mayor in Chicago could not demand time in blocks of an hour or more instead of the five-minute segments and spot announcements he was offered.[72] Neither are stations required to provide any individual candidate free time unless free time was first given to an opponent.

In fact, under section 315, a broadcaster need not offer any time at all to political candidates. However, broadcasters cannot avoid election coverage completely. The FCC has said broadcast licensees must provide "substantial" amounts of time for political candidates as part of their requirement to serve the public interest. In addition, the candidate access law, discussed next, requires broadcasters to provide "reasonable" amounts of time for federal candidates for office.[73]

In spite of section 315's mandate of equal opportunity, broadcast stations do not have to limit the time provided for one candidate because an opponent cannot afford to buy the same amount of time. The FCC has recognized that section 315 does not "equalize disparities in the financial resources of candidates."[74]

In addition, a broadcast station is not required to notify a legally qualified political candidate when an opponent has been granted airtime. It is up to the candidate to request the time, and to make the request within a week of the broadcast triggering the statute.[75]

"Use" of Broadcast Time   Section 315 provides that any "use" of a broadcast station by a political candidate entitles opponents to an equal opportunity. The law applies only when the candidate's voice or picture is part of the program or spot. However, not all programming about a candidate constitutes a "use."

Almost any presence of a candidate in a political spot triggers section 315. If the candidate only announces the sponsorship of the ad and the voice can be recognized, that is considered a "use."[76] Therefore, candidate appearances in a paid 60-second political advertisement and a paid 30-minute movie both trigger section 315.

Any broadcast programming involving a candidate that is related to politics or a

---

[70]1984 Political Primer, 100 F.C.C.2d at 1503–1504; 47 C.F.R. 73.1940 (b) (1988).

[71]Sen. Birch Bayh, 15 F.C.C.2d 47 (1968).

[72]Martin-Trigona, 64 F.C.C.2d 1087, 40 P & F Rad. Reg.2d 1189 (1977). However, federal candidates may have some control over the kind of time they can demand. See the next section of this chapter.

[73]1984 Political Primer, 100 F.C.C.2d at 1522–24.

[74]*See* Hon. Thomas Eagleton, 81 F.C.C.2d 423, 426, 48 P & F Rad. Reg.2d 541, 544 (1980), *quoting* Carter/Mondale Reelection Committee, 81 F.C.C.2d 409, 419–20, 48 P & F Rad. Reg.2d 414, 421 (1980).

[75]47 C.F.R. sec. 73.1940 (e) (1989).

[76]*E.g.,* Charles F. Dykas, 35 F.C.C.2d 937, 24 P & F Rad. Reg.2d 920 (1972).

political campaign will constitute a "use" under section 315, even if the airtime is not paid for. An incumbent congressman "uses" a station for a weekly broadcast to his constituents.[77] The equal opportunities requirement also applies to a half-hour special featuring local candidates for mayor.

However, an appearance need not be directly related to politics or a political campaign to become a "use" for the purpose of section 315. The FCC has said that a broadcaster is not expected to determine whether the appearance of a candidate is helpful to a campaign. The FCC has said that distinguishing between political and nonpolitical uses of broadcast time would require highly subjective judgments about content and could lead to increased governmental interference in programming content. Therefore, public officials' on-air appearances on behalf of charities such as the United Fund and Community Chest campaigns are considered candidate "uses" of the airwaves.[78] So are the appearances of television evangelists during worship services, crusades, or their own talk shows if the evangelists are candidates for office.[79]

In 1987, a federal appeals court affirmed the FCC's policy that an appearance on a news show by a journalist who is running for office constitutes a "use" of a broadcast station by a political candidate. In *Branch v. FCC,* the U.S. Court of Appeals for the District of Columbia said a candidate's reporting of the news does not fit the exemption in section 315 for news about candidates,[80] discussed later in this section. The D.C. Circuit affirmed the FCC's ruling that appearances by reporter William Branch required Sacramento television station KOVR to provide equal opportunities to Branch's opponents. Branch wanted to keep his job while he ran for a town council position in Loomis, California. KOVR said it would not provide the airtime necessary to meet the equal opportunities requirements of Branch's opponents during the election campaign. The station said Branch would have to take an unpaid leave of absence during his political campaign.

Section 315 also applies to entertainment programming. Therefore, the broadcast of Ronald Reagan's movies when Reagan was an official political candidate provided anyone opposing him a claim to equal opportunity for airtime.[81] Indeed, the FCC has ruled that an opponent can be granted time for the duration of a movie, or radio or television program, and not just for the limited time a candidate appears on the screen. Section 315 applies to an entire program if the candidate's appearance is "substantial" and the candidate is "integral" to the plot. However, the candidate must have some control over the appearance for it to qualify as a "use."[82]

A candidate's control over a broadcast is a key criterion in determining whether an appearance requires offering opponents equal opportunity for the time of an entire program or only for the amount of time a candidate appears. A candidate's presence in a political spot, however brief, obligates a broadcaster to provide the

---

[77]KNGS, 7 P & F Rad. Reg. 1130 (1952).

[78]*See* United Way of America, 35 P & F Rad. Reg.2d 137 (1975).

[79]Rev. Billy Robinson, 23 F.C.C.2d 117 (1970).

[80]824 F.2d 37 (1987), *cert. denied,* 485 U.S. 959 (1988).

[81]*In re* Adrian Weiss, 58 F.C.C.2d 342, 36 P & F Rad. Reg.2d 292 (1976), *review denied,* 58 F.C.C.2d 1389 (1976); Walt Disney Productions, Inc., 33 F.C.C.2d 297, *aff'd sub nom.* Review of the Pat Paulsen Ruling, 33 F.C.C.2d 835, 23 P & F Rad. Reg.2d 861 (1972), *aff'd,* Paulsen v. FCC, 491 F.2d 887 (9th Cir. 1974).

[82]Gray Communications System, Inc., 19 F.C.C.2d 532, 17 P & F Rad. Reg.2d 305 (1969).

opponent time equivalent to the entire ad. If a candidate is present in only 10 seconds of a 60-second ad, the opponent has the right to 60 seconds. However, if a candidate appears as part of a talk show or variety show controlled by an emcee, an opponent is entitled only to the amount of time the candidate is "on camera or on mike." When Congressman Sidney Yates appeared on a talk program called "Kup's Show" in Chicago, his opponent for the Democratic nomination wanted equal time. The commission said the station was obligated for only the 10 minutes and 9 seconds of Yates's appearance rather than the 40 minutes of the entire program.[83]

Campaign advertising that does not use a candidate's image or voice does not trigger the equal opportunities doctrine.[84] Hence, a series of ads sponsored by a political action committee criticizing the voting record of Missouri Senator Thomas Eagleton was not a "use" of broadcast time because it did not include the image or voice of Eagleton's opponent.[85] Such ads, however, could trigger an aspect of the fairness doctrine called the Zapple Rule, discussed later in the chapter.

Exempt Programming: Newscasts, News Interviews, and Documentaries   Some programming is exempt from the equal opportunities requirement. In a 1959 amendment to the 1934 Communications Act, Congress specifically exempted newscasts, news interviews, news documentaries where a candidate's appearance is incidental to the subject, and live coverage of news events, including political conventions and many political debates.[86]

Congress exempted candidate appearances on bona fide newscasts from the equal opportunities requirements after the FCC ruled that candidate appearances in newscasts triggered equal opportunities requirements. The commission had decided that a third-party mayoral candidate in Chicago should be granted airtime comparable to the news coverage accorded incumbent Mayor Richard Daley and his Republican opponent. The third-party candidate, Lar Daly, no relation to the incumbent, said he was entitled to time when the mayor appeared in news film accepting his nomination and meeting the president of Argentina at the Chicago airport. The FCC agreed.[87] The decision created such a furor that Congress amended the Communications Act the same year. Congress feared the FCC's interpretation of section 315 would "dry up" broadcast coverage of political campaigns. A Senate report said broadcasters would be reluctant to show a political candidate on a news program if the broadcast created equal opportunities obligations. Broadcasters would fear the "parade of aspirants" who would seek free airtime, the report said.[88]

In order for a news program to qualify for the exemption under the 1959 amendment, it must be regularly scheduled and emphasize news. The content must be determined by network or station personnel rather than by any candidate. The FCC has ruled that both the "Today" show and "Sixty Minutes" qualify as news shows. Both

---

[83]*E.g.,* Robert R. Benjamin, 51 P & F Rad. Reg.2d 91 (1982).

[84]Felix v. Westinghouse Radio Stations, 186 F.2d 1 (3d Cir. 1950), *cert. denied,* 341 U.S. 909 (1951); 1984 Political Primer, 100 F.C.C.2d at 1489.

[85]Hon. Thomas F. Eagleton, 81 F.C.C.2d 423, 48 P & F Rad. Reg.2d 541 (1980).

[86]47 U.S.C. sec. 315 (a) (1982).

[87]CBS, 26 F.C.C. 715, 18 P & F Rad. Reg. 238, *reconsideration denied,* 18 P & F Rad. Reg. 701 (1959).

[88]S. Rep. No. 562, 86th Cong., 1st Sess. 9, 10 (1959).

are regularly scheduled and consistently use the news-interview format. The persons interviewed are selected because of their importance and interest to viewers.[89] Interviews with candidates on news shows also are exempt unless a candidate's appearance is based on factors other than news value.[90] The FCC also has ruled that "Entertainment Tonight" and "Entertainment This Week," which provide spot news coverage and news interviews about entertainment, are bona fide news programs exempt from section 315. The commission said the news exemption to section 315 is not based "on the subject matter reported" in a show but on "whether the program reports news of some area of current events." The commission said that any effort on its part to determine "whether particular kinds of news are more or less bona fide would involve an unwarranted intrusion into program content and would be, thus, at least suspect under the First Amendment."[91]

News interviews are exempt from the equal opportunities requirement if they take place on a bona fide news-interview program. Not all interview programs or talk shows qualify. Shows such as "Meet the Press" and "Face the Nation" are considered bona fide news-interview programs. An NBC show called "Tomorrow," featuring Tom Snyder, was not a bona fide news-interview program.[92]

The FCC, when deciding if a news-interview program should be exempt, considers how long the program has been on the air, and whether

1. the program is regularly scheduled,
2. the broadcaster controls the format,
3. the decisions about format and content are based on reasonable journalistic judgments rather than an intention to advance a candidate's political career, and
4. the selection of persons to appear is based on their newsworthiness.

In the case of the "Tomorrow" show, the commission said that the interviews in nearly half of the programs examined were not associated with recent news events. Discussions focused on movie monsters, sexual fantasies, psychic healing, and soap operas.

The requirement that a journalist control the discussion in a bona fide news-interview program was a major issue when the "Donahue" show sought to be exempt from section 315 requirements. In 1984, reversing an earlier decision, the FCC ruled that the "Donahue" show is a bona fide news-interview program. In 1980, the commission had said the audience participation in the show did not leave host Phil Donahue with enough control over the contents of the program to qualify it as an exempt news-interview program. In 1984, the show's producers convinced the commission that Donahue used his skills as a journalist to effectively control the discussion. Donahue could frustrate anyone who tried to use the show to promote a specific political candidate. The commission also decided that although many "Donahue" shows did not focus on current events enough would feature politicians that the show

---

[89] 1984 Political Primer, 100 F.C.C.2d at 1494–97.
[90] See Letter to Citizens for Reagan, 58 F.C.C.2d 925, 36 P & F Rad. Reg.2d 885 (1976).
[91] Request for Declaratory Ruling by Paramount Pictures Corp., 3 FCC Rcd. 245, 64 P & F Rad. Reg.2d 600 (1988).
[92] KRON-TV, 47 F.C.C.2d 1204 (1974).

could contribute to the political debate. The commission said it did not want to stifle what it called innovative approaches to the coverage of politics.[93]

The fact that the "Donahue" show had been regularly scheduled for 15 years was also a factor in the commission's 1984 decision. One-time news interviews or special candidate's programs begun only weeks before an election do not qualify for the news-interview exemption.[94]

While any news interview on a bona fide news-interview program is exempt from equal opportunities requirements, an appearance by a candidate in a news documentary is exempt only if the appearance is incidental to the discussion of an issue of genuine news value. The FCC rejected a request for equal time by Richard Kay, who was competing against Robert A. Taft, Jr., and Howard M. Metzenbaum in 1970 for a seat in the U.S. Senate. Taft and Metzenbaum appeared for 93 seconds in a CBS news documentary, "Television and Politics." The commission ruled that the program focused on the use of television by candidates rather than on either of Kay's opponents.[95]

Exempt Programming: Spot Coverage of News Events The 1959 exemption for on-the-spot coverage of bona fide news events includes live broadcasts of presidential speeches such as the State of the Union message and reports to the nation during international crises. The exemption also applies to political conventions, press conferences held by political candidates, and many forms of debates featuring candidates. On-the-spot coverage also includes the appearances of political candidates at parades, court proceedings, and baseball games.[96]

The spot news exemption was expanded in 1975 to include candidate press conferences and the broadcast of debates between candidates. Before then, the FCC said that Congress intended the spot news exemption to apply only when a candidate's appearance was "incidental" to a broadcast. This interpretation automatically ruled out debates and press conferences, where public officials or politicians were the focal point. In 1975, the FCC revised its interpretation of section 315 in response to a petition by the Aspen Institute for Humanistic Studies.[97]

In ruling on the Aspen petition, the FCC said that live television coverage of press conferences was exempt under the 1959 amendments if

1. a broadcaster made a good-faith judgment that the press conference was a bona fide news event and
2. the licensee did not intend by the broadcast to provide one candidate with an advantage over another.

Applying those guidelines a few years later, the FCC said that the broadcast of a press conference held by President Jimmy Carter was a bona fide news event. Senator Ed-

---

[93]Multimedia Entertainment, Inc., 56 P & F Rad. Reg.2d 143 (1984).

[94]1984 Political Primer, 100 F.C.C.2d at 1498.

[95]*See* Richard B. Kay, 26 F.C.C.2d 235 (1970).

[96]1984 Political Primer, 100 F.C.C.2d at 1500–1502.

[97]Petitions of Aspen Institute and CBS, 55 F.C.C.2d 697, 35 P & F Rad. Reg.2d 49 (1975), *aff'd,* Chisholm v. FCC, 538 F.2d 349, 1 Media L. Rep. 2207 (D.C. Cir.), *cert. denied,* 429 U.S. 890 (1976).

ward Kennedy, who was challenging the renomination of President Carter, complained that the president had used more than five minutes of a press conference to attack him. The networks refused to provide Kennedy time under the equal opportunities rule, and the FCC affirmed the broadcasters' decision. The commission said the press conference was carried live and the networks had covered Kennedy press conferences previously. In addition, the commission said it would not overrule the news judgments of broadcasters absent evidence they intended to promote one candidacy over another. The FCC acknowledged its decision could work in favor of incumbents because they might attract more media coverage than their opponents. On appeal, the U.S. Court of Appeals for the D.C. Circuit agreed that Congress had intended to place "considerable reliance" on the discretion of journalists.[98]

The FCC's 1975 Aspen decision not only allowed live press conferences to be exempt under section 315, but also reversed the commission's long-time policy subjecting debates to equal opportunities requirements. Prior to 1975, presidential debates had not been televised since the 1960 broadcasts featuring Richard M. Nixon and John F. Kennedy. Congress had suspended the equal opportunities rule to allow the Nixon–Kennedy debates.

In 1975, in what is called the Aspen Rule, the commission said that presidential debates are bona fide news events if they are sponsored by nonbroadcast organizations, staged outside broadcast studios, and aired live in their entirety. The commission said the reversal of its earlier policy served the public interest by allowing broadcasters to contribute more fully and effectively to an informed electorate. The FCC said that Congress had chosen to encourage broadcasters "to cover the news to the fullest degree" and to risk that candidates might not receive equal news coverage.[99] The Aspen Rule, upheld by the U.S. Court of Appeals for the D.C. Circuit, meant that broadcasters could air televised debates between major political candidates without owing equal opportunities to so-called minor party candidates. The Aspen Rule led to a series of televised debates sponsored by the League of Women Voters: Carter–Ford in 1976, Reagan–Carter in 1980, and the presidential and vice presidential debates of 1984. The candidates were questioned by panelists selected by the league.

In 1983, in response to a petition by former FCC official Henry Geller and two broadcast organizations, the FCC said that candidate debates sponsored by broadcasters are also exempt from the equal opportunities requirements. The commission said that Congress, when it exempted spot coverage of news events from equal opportunities requirements, intended "to enhance the exercise of broadcasters' good faith news judgments to enable more extensive coverage of political issues."[100] The commission said the risks of partiality to candidates were no greater in broadcaster-sponsored presidential debates than in the news-interview format specifically exempted by the 1959 amendment.

---

[98]Kennedy for President Comm., 77 F.C.C.2d 971, 47 P & F Rad. Reg.2d 810 (Broadcast Bureau), *review denied,* 77 F.C.C.2d 971, 47 P & F Rad. Reg.2d 1537, *aff'd,* Kennedy for President Comm. v. FCC, 636 F.2d 432, 6 Media L. Rep. 1705 (D.C. Cir. 1980).

[99]Petitions of Aspen Institute and CBS, 55 F.C.C.2d 697, 35 P & F Rad. Reg.2d 49 (1975).

[100]Petitions of Henry Geller, 95 F.C.C.2d 1236, 1241, 54 P & F Rad. Reg.2d 1246, 1251 (1983), aff'd mem. sub nom., p. 1392 League of Women Voters Educ. Fund v. FCC, 731 F.2d 995 (D.C. Cir. 1984).

The commission also said that licensees could delay the broadcast of a newsworthy debate more than a day without forfeiting the news exemption. The commission's decision was upheld by the U.S. Court of Appeals for the D.C. Circuit. The first national network-sponsored debate between presidential candidates since 1960 featured contenders for the 1984 Democratic presidential nomination. Walter Mondale, Gary Hart, and Jesse Jackson participated in the debate sponsored by CBS.[101]

In 1987, the U.S. Court of Appeals for the D.C. Circuit said minor-party candidates for president and vice president do not have a right to participate in televised debates. The court affirmed the FCC's decision to reject the complaint of the 1984 nominee for the Citizens Party, Sonia Johnson, who was excluded from the presidential debates between the Republican and Democratic candidates sponsored by the League of Women Voters. Johnson finished fifth in the election with less than 1 percent of the vote. The D.C. Circuit said the FCC had not gone beyond its statutory authority in determining that debates between qualified political candidates are news events exempt from the equal opportunities requirements. The court, relying heavily on the U.S. Supreme Court opinion in *CBS v. Democratic National Committee*, discussed earlier in the chapter, said that no individual has a First Amendment right of access to the broadcast media. The court said the reasonable access and equal opportunities requirements in the Communications Act "ensure that political debate will not be monopolized by one or a very few candidates." The act ensures "that all candidates from all points of the political spectrum will be able to utilize the media."[102]

In 1988 and 1989, the FCC extended the spot news exemption for political coverage to two more forms of debate. The FCC said that coverage of debates sponsored by political parties and political candidates, as well as debates sponsored by broadcasters and independent organizations, can be exempt from the equal opportunities requirement. The commission said that the factor determining whether a debate is exempt under section 315 is its *bona fide* news value and not its sponsor. In 1989, the commission ruled that debates between presidential candidates George Bush and Michael Dukakis were exempt from the equal opportunities requirement even though they were sponsored by the two major political parties. The commission rejected a complaint by minor party presidential candidate Lenora Fulani. The FCC said debates can be exempt as long as broadcasters make good-faith journalistic decisions that the debates are newsworthy. Televised debates, the commission said, do not give the candidates "unbridled power" to advance their candidacies. "Indeed, the adversarial nature of the debate format reduces greatly the chance of any broadcast favoritism."[103] In 1988, the commission exempted the televising of a debate sponsored by Dukakis and Richard Gephardt, two candidates for the Democratic party presidential nomination.[104]

Limits on Broadcaster Censorship of Political Content   A broadcast station has no control over the content of programming aired by political candidates. Section 315

[101]"Political TV Debate Rages," *News Media & Law,* Nov.–Dec. 1984, at 32.

[102]Johnson v. FCC, 829 F.2d 157, 14 Media L. Rep. 1711 (1987).

[103]*In re* Fulani, 65 P & F Rad. Reg.2d 644, 645 (1988), *quoting* Henry Geller, 95 F.C.C.2d 1236, 54 P & F Rad. Reg.2d 1246 (1983), *aff'd sub nom.* League of Women Voters v. FCC, 731 F.2d 995 (1984).

[104]Request for a Declaratory Ruling by WCVB-TV, 63 P & F Rad. Reg.2d 665 (1987).

prohibits broadcasters from censoring the remarks of candidates, even if the statements are racist, vulgar, or defamatory.[105] Hence, the FCC refused to tell stations that they could reject, without being in violation of section 315, the spot announcements of Georgia Senate candidate J. B. Stoner, who proclaimed himself to be a "white racist" candidate. Stoner's ad campaigned against a law he said "takes jobs from us whites and gives those jobs to the niggers." Stoner, chairman of the neo-Nazi National States Rights party, said he was for "law and order with the knowledge you cannot have law and order and niggers too." The commission said the no-censorship portion of section 315 could not be overridden without evidence of a "clear and present danger of imminent violence."[106] The prohibition against censoring candidate programming applies only when the candidate is a part of the broadcast.

Since the remarks of candidates under section 315 cannot be edited for libel, the U.S. Supreme Court decided licensees could not be held responsible for what candidates said in broadcasts subject to the equal opportunities rule. If the licensees were liable for the remarks of a candidate they could not censor, the Court said, they would be penalized for doing what the law required them to do—providing broadcast time for political candidates.[107] Of course, the candidates themselves are legally responsible for remarks they make over the air.

Rates and Sponsor Identification   The equal opportunities provision requires that broadcasters charge political candidates no more than the station's lowest advertising rates 45 days before a primary election and 60 days before a general election. Broadcasters can charge only what they charge their largest-volume advertisers for the same amount of time and same time of the broadcast day. If a radio station charges $200 for a single one-minute commercial, but $125 for each of a package of 15 one-minute commercials, a candidate can buy a single one-minute commercial for $125. The lowest unit rate applies only to programming directly involving political candidates themselves. Before the 45- and 60-day time periods, broadcasters can charge candidates what they normally charge advertisers buying the same amounts of time.[108]

Broadcast stations must reveal who pays for political broadcasts. In addition, the Federal Election Campaign Act requires that an announcement specify who authorized the ad.[109]

Complaint Process   Frequently broadcasters query the FCC if they have a question about the application of the equal opportunities rule. By following the recommendations of the commission, licensees can avoid the expense and hassle of fighting a complaint. If a complaint is filed, and the FCC agrees with the candidate, it usually asks the station to provide the candidate with airtime. A licensee violating section 315 can also be fined.

Access for Political Candidates   While section 315 of the Communications Act requires broadcasters to provide equal opportunities to political candidates, it does not

---

[105]47 U.S.C. sec. 315 (a) (1982).
[106]Letter to Lonnie King, 36 F.C.C.2d 635, 25 P & F Rad. Reg.2d 54 (1972).
[107]Farmers Educ. & Coop. Union of America v. WDAY, Inc., 360 U.S. 525 (1959).
[108]47 U.S.C. sec. 315 (b) (1982).
[109]1984 Political Primer, 100 F.C.C.2d at 1535–36, 1537.

require broadcast licensees to provide time to political candidates in the first place. However, section 312 (a) (7) does require broadcasters to provide time to each legally qualified candidate running for federal office. Under section 312 (a) (7), a broadcast station could lose its license for willfully or repeatedly refusing to provide "reasonable access" or to permit the "purchase of reasonable amounts of time" by federal candidates. The Supreme Court has upheld the constitutionality of the candidate access requirement. Section 312 (a) (7) does not require broadcast stations to provide airtime to candidates for state office.

Congress adopted section 312 (a) (7) in 1971 to ensure that broadcasters would provide time to candidates for the presidency, the U.S. Senate, and the U.S. House of Representatives. Section 312 (a) (7) was adopted, in part, to offset the fact that Congress was amending section 315 to require broadcasters to charge political candidates the station's lowest advertising rates. Congress feared that imposing the low advertising rates would discourage broadcasters from selling time to political candidates when the time could be sold to others at higher prices. Even before the amendment, broadcasters were often reluctant to offer time to one candidate because of the requirement that they provide time to opponents.

The FCC has said that the best way to balance the desires of the candidates for airtime and the interests of the broadcasters under section 312 (a) (7) is "to rely on the reasonable, good faith discretion" of broadcast licensees. Therefore, the commission did not establish a set of rules interpreting "reasonable access" in section 312 (a) (7). However, the commission has said *reasonable access* means that broadcasters should try to accommodate the requests for airtime of individual candidates as much as possible and avoid "blanket bans" on the time available to candidates.

For example, the commission has said *reasonable access* means that broadcasters must ordinarily provide some time for candidates during prime listening and viewing hours. Stations cannot, as a matter of policy, reject all candidate advertising during the most popular listening and viewing hours in order to accommodate commercial advertisers. However, neither are broadcasters obligated to allow candidates to choose the time they wish to air political programming.[110] Such a requirement could significantly interfere with broadcasters' long-term contracts with commercial sponsors of regularly scheduled programming, the commission said.

Similarly, the FCC says, a blanket refusal to run political candidate advertising once a political campaign begins is a denial of "reasonable access" under section 312 (a) (7). The commission requires that broadcasters decide "reasonably" when campaigning has begun on an election-by-election basis. In a decision upheld by the U.S. Supreme Court, the commission ruled that the three national television networks violated section 312 (a) (7) when they turned down requests by the Carter-Mondale Presidential Committee to buy time in December 1979.

The case, *CBS v. FCC,* began with requests from the Carter-Mondale campaign to broadcast a 30-minute campaign film 11 months before the 1980 general election. Campaign officials wanted the broadcast to coincide with President Carter's announcement that he would seek reelection. CBS offered the committee only five minutes of prime time. NBC and ABC said they were not yet prepared to sell any time for

---

[110]1984 Political Primer, 100 F.C.C.2d at 1524–25.

the 1980 campaign. The networks said that demands for equal opportunity to the Carter-Mondale presentation by other presidential candidates so long before the election would disrupt their programming schedule.

Both the U.S. Court of Appeals for the District of Columbia and the U.S. Supreme Court affirmed the FCC's decision that the networks had unreasonably turned down the Carter-Mondale request. The Supreme Court first rejected a contention by the networks that section 312 (a) (7) did not create a new right of access for federal candidates but only codified a broadcaster's public interest responsibility to air programming and advertisements provided by political candidates. The Court said that Congress intended section 312 (a) (7) to mandate a right of access for individual candidates rather than prescribe only a general duty to provide political programming. The Congress, said the Court, intended to increase access to the media for federal candidates.

The networks argued that the FCC's decision that the Carter-Mondale campaign had not been granted "reasonable access" under section 312 (a) (7) interfered with the editorial prerogatives of broadcasters. The networks said the commission had "improperly substituted its judgment for that of the broadcasters."[111] However, the Supreme Court said the FCC had not been arbitrary and capricious when it interpreted section 312 (a) (7) to mean that broadcasters could not adopt a blanket policy of refusing to provide time to all candidates. The commission's requirement that broadcasters consider individual candidates' needs is consistent with the statutory guarantee of access for individual candidates, the Court said. Chief Justice Warren Burger, writing for the six-justice majority, said that a uniform policy might be more convenient for broadcasters, but it would allow them to ignore "personal campaign strategies and the exigencies of the political process."[112]

Burger said the FCC reasonably decided that once a campaign has begun, broadcasters must consider each request for time from a federal candidate on its own merits. Burger said the FCC requires each broadcaster to tailor the response to a request, "as much as reasonably possible," to meet a candidate's purpose in seeking the airtime. Each broadcaster can consider such factors as the amount of time previously sold to the candidate, the disruption of regular programming, and the likelihood of requests for time by rival candidates under the equal opportunities provision of section 315. However, to justify a refusal of a candidate's request, a broadcaster must make a counteroffer or be able to explain to the commission why access would pose "a realistic danger of substantial program disruption."

The Supreme Court rejected the argument that the FCC becomes improperly involved in the election process when it decides when a political campaign has begun. The networks contended that it is their decision, not the FCC's, to determine when a political campaign begins and, consequently, when the access requirements of section 312 (a) (7) apply. The FCC, in its interpretation of section 312 (a) (7), had said that broadcasters may be required to afford access to political candidates before "traditional campaign periods." The commission said the congressional mandate that can-

---

[111]Carter-Mondale Presidential Comm., Inc., 74 F.C.C.2d 631, *reconsideration denied,* 74 F.C.C.2d 657, *aff'd sub nom.* CBS v. FCC, 629 F.2d 1, 5 Media L. Rep. 2649 (1980), *aff'd,* 453 U.S. 367, 7 Media L. Rep. 1563 (1981).
[112]CBS v. FCC, 453 U.S. 367, 389, 7 Media L. Rep. 1563, 1573 (1981).

didates for federal office be given "reasonable access" to broadcast time certainly means that broadcast licensees must provide time to political candidates within 45 days of a primary election and within 60 days of a general election, the time specified for the "lowest unit charge" for candidate advertising in section 315. However, the commission said, the determination of the beginning of an individual political campaign must be based on the "facts and circumstances" of each case.[113]

Burger said the commission does not decide the beginning of political campaigns by selecting arbitrary dates. Rather, Burger said, the commission determines whether a campaign has begun by examining "objective evidence" once it receives a complaint from a candidate that "reasonable access" has been denied. In the Carter-Mondale case, Burger said, the FCC's decision that the 1980 presidential campaign had begun by late 1979 was reasonable. He noted that 12 candidates had formally announced their intention to run. They were collecting endorsements and otherwise campaigning. National campaign organizations were functioning, states had started to select delegates, and the national print media had been covering the candidates for months.

Burger also rejected the contention that section 312 (a) (7) violated the First Amendment by unduly restricting the networks' editorial decision making. He said the access requirement "makes a significant contribution to freedom of expression by enhancing the ability of candidates to present, and the public to receive, information necessary for the effective operation of the democratic process."[114] Burger, following the Supreme Court's reasoning in *Red Lion,* said the First Amendment rights of the candidates and the public therefore outweigh those of the broadcasters.

Burger said the Supreme Court was not approving a general right of access to the broadcast media. Rather, it was approving only a limited right of access for legally qualified federal candidates during a political campaign. He argued that section 312 (a) (7) did not "impair the discretion of broadcasters to present their views on any issue or to carry any particular type of programming."

Justice Byron White, however, writing for the three dissenting justices, argued that the Court had eviscerated licensee discretion. White, the author of the Court's *Red Lion* opinion, contended that the commission overstepped its statutory authority by imposing its own interpretation of when the political campaign began. He argued that the FCC overemphasized the interests of individual candidates at the expense of the discretion of individual broadcasters.

However, one federal appeals court has said that even after the Carter-Mondale decision, broadcasters could refuse to provide free time to federal candidates under section 312 (a) (7). The U.S. Court of Appeals for the D.C. Circuit said the prohibition on a blanket refusal to run a candidate's advertising does not mean broadcasters must provide free time to candidates under section 312 (a) (7). The court rejected a plea by Senator Edward Kennedy that he be granted free time to offset network coverage of President Carter, whom Kennedy was opposing in the 1980 Democratic primaries. The networks had broadcast a half-hour Carter speech and a half-hour

---

[113]Comm'n Policy in Enforcing Section 312 (a) (7), 68 F.C.C.2d 1079, 1091, 43 P & F Rad. Reg.2d 1029, 1045 (1978).

[114]CBS v. FCC, 453 U.S. at 396, 7 Media L. Rep. at 1576.

presidential news conference four days before the Illinois primary. The networks said they would be willing to sell Kennedy time, but would not grant him free time. Kennedy contended that the FCC's decision in the Carter-Mondale case meant that there could be no across-the-board rejection of his request. However, the FCC and the D.C. Circuit said section 312 did not mandate that candidates be given free time. Broadcasters can either provide reasonable access free or sell reasonable amounts of time.[115]

Although section 312 (a) (7) applies only to federal candidates, the FCC has ruled that the public interest standard requires broadcasters to devote substantial time to state and local political campaigns. However, there is no law or regulation specifying that broadcast licensees must provide access to state and local candidates.[116]

SUMMARY

Section 315 of the 1934 Communications Act requires broadcast licensees to provide equal opportunities to legally qualified political candidates. To be considered legally qualified, candidates must satisfy the requirements for office, must publicly announce an intention to run for office, and must qualify for a ballot position or publicly seek election as a write-in candidate. Candidates running for the same office must have access to the same amount of airtime and the chance to appear before about the same size audience.

The equal opportunities rule does not apply to spokespersons for political candidates. Neither does it apply to newscasts, news-interview programs such as "Face the Nation," news documentaries, or live coverage of news events, including political debates. Entertainment programs are not exempt from section 315.

Broadcast licensees must charge political candidates the lowest advertising rates within 45 days of primary elections and within 60 days of general elections. A broadcaster cannot censor the remarks of legally qualified candidates during political broadcasts.

Section 312 (a) (7) of the Communications Act requires broadcast licensees to provide "reasonable access" or permit the "purchase of reasonable amounts of time" by legally qualified candidates for federal office. Stations are not required to provide free time to federal candidates; nor must they give candidates the time of the broadcast day that is requested. However, in the Carter-Mondale case, the Supreme Court affirmed an FCC determination that broadcasters cannot adopt a blanket policy of refusing to provide airtime to all candidates once a political campaign has begun. Broadcasters must consider the individual circumstances of each request for broadcast time by federal political candidates.

---

[115]Kennedy for President Comm. v. FCC, 636 F.2d 432, 436, 6 Media L. Rep. 1705, 1706 (D.C. Cir. 1980).
[116]*E.g.*, 1984 Political Primer, 100 F.C.C.2d at 1525–26.

Regulation of Public Issues Programming: The Fairness Doctrine

Without a doubt, the most controversial broadcast programming regulation in the last 40 years has been the fairness doctrine. However, the FCC repealed the core of its fairness policy in 1987 in a decision upheld by a federal appeals court. The U.S. Supreme Court decided not to review the case.[117]

As of mid-1990, only a few programming policies related to the fairness doctrine remained. Yet several congressional leaders still wanted to reinstate the fairness doctrine.

Fairness: 1949–1987 Broadcasters' obligation to air diverse views on public issues was first declared a policy of the Federal Radio Commission in 1929.[118] In 1949, the Federal Communications Commission announced the twofold duty of broadcasters that became known as the *fairness doctrine.*[119] The FCC required broadcasters (1) to devote a reasonable percentage of airtime to the discussion of public issues and (2) to present contrasting views in the case of controversial issues of public importance.[120] The commission established specific applications of the fairness doctrine for personal attacks, editorial endorsements of political candidates, noncandidate advertising in political campaigns, and issue-oriented advertising.

The fairness doctrine, unlike the equal opportunities rule, applied to discussions of controversial issues and not to broadcasts by political candidates. In addition, the fairness doctrine did not require the equal treatment imposed by section 315. Rather, the fairness doctrine imposed a more general obligation to ensure that diverse ideas were presented.

When deciding fairness doctrine cases, the FCC relied heavily ''on the reasonable, good faith judgments'' of broadcast licensees. Licensees were afforded wide discretion to determine what constituted both a ''controversial issue'' and a ''reasonable opportunity'' for contrasting viewpoints. A broadcast station did not have to air all points of view. No particular person or group had a right to be heard. Broadcasters were given the discretion to determine which views were to be presented and by whom as well as the time and format provided for contrasting viewpoints.

The FCC seldom punished a station for failing to provide a diversity of views. The commission only fined stations for violations of the personal attack rules. Only two stations have ever lost their licenses for fairness violations. The license of WLBT-TV of Jackson, Mississippi, was taken away by a federal appeals court in 1969 for racist programming.[121] WXUR of Media, Pennsylvania, which regularly broadcast only one side of controversial public issues, often ridiculing those who dared to differ, also lost its license.[122]

---

[117]Syracuse Peace Council v. FCC, 110 S. Ct. 717 (1990).

[118]Great Lakes Broadcasting, 3 F.R.C. Ann. Rep. 34 (1929).

[119]*In re* Editorializing by Broadcast Licensees, 13 F.C.C. 1246, 1249–50, 25 P & F Rad. Reg. 1901, 1905 (1949).

[120]Fairness Doctrine and Public Interest Standards; Handling of Public Issues (The Fairness Report), 48 F.C.C.2d 1, 7, 10–11, 30 P & F Rad. Reg.2d 1261, 1273, 1276–78 (1974).

[121]Office of Communication of the United Church of Christ v. FCC, 425 F.2d 543 (D.C. Cir. 1969).

[122]Brandywine-Main Line Radio, Inc., 24 F.C.C.2d 18, 19 P & F Rad. Reg.2d 433 (1970), *reconsideration denied,* 27 F.C.C.2d 565, 21 P & F Rad. Reg.2d 22 (1971), *aff'd on other grounds,* 473 F.2d 16, 1 Media L. Rep. 2067 (D.C. Cir. 1972), *cert. denied,* 412 U.S. 922 (1973).

In 1969, the U.S. Supreme Court declared at least one form of the fairness doctrine, the personal attack rules, to be constitutional. The case, *Red Lion Broadcasting Co. v. FCC,* was discussed earlier in the chapter.[123] After the FCC repealed the fairness doctrine in 1987, all three branches of government debated whether the fairness doctrine was a policy of the FCC that the commission could reverse or part of the 1934 Communications Act that only Congress could repeal.

Eliminating the Fairness Doctrine   The events leading to the FCC's 1987 elimination of the fairness doctrine began with a 1984 commission decision to enforce the fairness doctrine against a Syracuse, New York, television station. When the FCC said a year later that it believed the fairness doctrine violated the First Amendment, a federal appeals court said the commission could not enforce a policy it believed to be unconstitutional. When the FCC announced it would no longer enforce the fairness doctrine, the same court affirmed the commission's decision. Congress subsequently passed legislation codifying the fairness doctrine only to have it vetoed by President Reagan.

In mid-1990, only vestiges of the fairness doctrine—such as rules governing personal attacks and political editorials—were in force. Several members of Congress wanted to send a bill specifically incorporating the fairness doctrine into the 1934 Communications Act to President Bush.

Syracuse Peace Council   The FCC's decision to abandon the fairness doctrine resulted from a dispute over whether WTVH(TV) of Syracuse, New York, had broadcast both sides of a controversy over the construction of a nuclear power plant. The FCC had ruled in 1984 that WTVH(TV) had broadcast advertisements promoting the construction of a nuclear power plant in upstate New York without providing an opportunity for opposing views. The Syracuse Peace Council argued that the economic viability of the nuclear plant was a controversial issue of public importance. The FCC told WTVH that it would have to offer time for contrasting views. Although the station had by the time of the FCC's decision aired views opposing the nuclear facility, it appealed the commission's ruling on the grounds that the fairness doctrine was unconstitutional.[124]

In fact, in 1985, the commission itself issued a comprehensive report declaring the fairness doctrine to be unconstitutional and contrary to the public interest.[125] However, the commission did not eliminate the fairness doctrine in 1985. Rather, it "gave" Congress "an opportunity to review the fairness doctrine in the light of the evidence." The commission said that whether the fairness doctrine violated the First Amendment was a question for the courts.

In 1987, the U.S. Court of Appeals for the District of Columbia denounced the FCC's "two-faced" approach to the fairness doctrine.[126] The court said the FCC acted arbitrarily and capriciously when it held that WTVH violated a policy the com-

---

[123]Red Lion Broadcasting Co. v. FCC, 395 U.S. 367, 1 Media L. Rep. 2053 (1969).

[124]Syracuse Peace Council v. FCC, 867 F.2d 654, 16 Media L. Rep. 1225 (D.C. Cir. 1989), *cert. denied,* 110 S. Ct. 717 (1990).

[125]General Fairness Doctrine Obligations of Broadcast Licensees (1985 Fairness Report), 102 F.C.C.2d 142, 58 P & F Rad. Reg.2d 1137 (1985).

[126]Meredith Corp. v. FCC, 809 F.2d 863, 13 Media L. Rep. 1994 (1987). The D.C. Circuit said the same day it would consider a challenge to the FCC's *1985 Fairness Report.* That challenge was vacated after the FCC ruled the fairness doctrine unconstitutional. *See* Radio-Television News Directors Ass'n v. FCC, 831 F.2d 1149 (1987).

mission itself believed was unconstitutional. The court said the commission could avoid the constitutional question raised by WTVH only by declaring the fairness doctrine did not serve the public interest.

The FCC responded to the D.C. Circuit's 1987 opinion by saying later the same year that the fairness doctrine would no longer be enforced because it conflicted with both the public interest and the First Amendment. In the FCC's second consideration of *Syracuse Peace Council,* it refused to separate its discussion of the public interest and the constitutional issues, arguing that they were "inextricably intertwined."

The FCC said the fairness doctrine thwarted, rather than enhanced, the discussion of controversial public issues. The commission said broadcasters censored themselves because they feared someone would complain their programming was unfair. Broadcasters feared both an FCC ruling that they had been unfair and the expense and damage to their reputation caused by a fairness inquiry. In addition, the FCC suggested, the fairness doctrine "may have penalized or impeded the expression of unorthodox or unpopular opinions."[127] The commission said that several of the broadcasters who had been the focus of fairness doctrine inquiries aired particularly provocative opinions.

The commission also found that the fairness doctrine imposed substantial burdens on the editorial process of broadcast licensees. The commission said it concluded, in its *1985 Fairness Report,* that the enforcement of the fairness doctrine

> requires the "minute and subjective scrutiny of program content" which perilously treads upon the editorial prerogatives of broadcast journalists.[128]

The commission argued that the FCC's intrusion into the editorial judgments of broadcasters was not necessary to ensure the airing of diverse views on important public issues. The commission cited findings in its *1985 Fairness Report* that "revealed an explosive growth" in the number and variety of information outlets since 1969. The commission "repudiated the notion" that a government agency should intervene in the marketplace of ideas.

The FCC also argued that the broadcast media ought to have the same constitutional protection as the print media. It said the application of the First Amendment should not focus on the difference between the printed page and the broadcast spectrum, but on the similar ways the media are used. In addition, the commission said the Supreme Court's 1969 decision in *Red Lion Broadcasting Co. v. FCC* departed from traditional First Amendment reasoning. The commission said the *Red Lion* assertion that rights of listeners were superior to rights of broadcasters violated a fundamental First Amendment tenet—that governmental intervention in the marketplace of ideas should not be tolerated. The commission said,

> The First Amendment was adopted to protect the people *not from the journalists, but from government.* It gives people the right to receive ideas that are unfettered by governmental interference.[129]

---

[127]Syracuse Peace Council, 2 FCC Rcd. 5043, 5049, 63 P & F Rad. Reg.2d 541, 566 (1987), *reconsideration denied,* 3 FCC Rcd. 2035, 64 P & F Rad. Reg.2d 1073 (1988).

[128]2 FCC Rcd. at 5051, 63 P & F Rad. Reg.2d at 569, *quoting* 1985 Fairness Report, 102 F.C.C.2d at 191, 58 P & F Rad. Reg.2d at 1175.

[129]*Id.* at 5057, 63 P & F Rad. Reg.2d at 589 (emphasis in the original).

In *Peace Council,* the FCC not only eliminated the fairness doctrine requirement that stations provide contrasting views on controversial public issues, but it also abolished the ''first half'' of the fairness doctrine, the requirement that broadcasters cover controversial issues of public importance in the first place. The FCC said the two portions of the fairness doctrine were too interrelated to be separated. In addition, the commission said, the first half of the fairness doctrine duplicated another commission policy, the requirement that licensees cover issues important to their communities. Hence, there was no need to retain the first half, the commission said.[130]

The FCC's *Peace Council* decision left intact the personal attack and political editorializing rules and perhaps a fairness rule applying to the supporters of opposing political candidates.[131] Each of the rules will be discussed shortly.

In 1989, in *Syracuse Peace Council v. FCC,* a divided three-judge panel of the U.S. Court of Appeals for the D.C. Circuit said the FCC was not arbitrary and capricious when it eliminated the fairness doctrine.[132] The court said the FCC had adequately demonstrated that the fairness doctrine did not serve the public interest. The court said that, given the ambiguity of the issues, the FCC could rely on its assessment of the ''net effect'' of the fairness doctrine. The court accepted the commission's conclusions that the fairness doctrine substantially deterred the discussion of public issues and that government should not interfere in broadcast programming judgments.

The majority of the D.C. Circuit panel refused to consider whether the fairness doctrine was unconstitutional. Relying on the legal principle that courts should decide cases on constitutional grounds only when necessary, two of the three judges said the commission's determination that the fairness doctrine was contrary to the public interest was a sufficient and independent reason for eliminating it. However, Judge Kenneth Starr said the commission's decision was necessarily tied to First Amendment considerations. Starr said that throughout the FCC's opinion the commission wrestled with the U.S. Supreme Court's constitutional interpretation of broadcast regulation in *Red Lion Broadcasting Co. v. FCC.*

The FCC's Confrontation with Congress   The FCC's *Peace Council* decision may have satisfied a federal appeals court, but it did not satisfy Congress. Although the FCC contends that the fairness doctrine is a commission-initiated policy that the commission can drop, many members of Congress believe that only Congress can repeal the fairness doctrine. Several members of Congress believe that the fairness doctrine was incorporated into the 1934 Communications Act in a 1959 amendment.

The 1959 amendment to section 315 exempted news programs from the requirement that broadcasters provide equal opportunities for political candidates. Congress qualified the exemption by adding that it should not be construed to relieve broadcasters during news programming

> from the obligation imposed on them under this Act to operate in the public interest and to afford reasonable opportunity for the presentation of conflicting views on issues of public importance.[133]

---

[130]*Id.* at 5048, 63 P & F Rad. Reg.2d at 561–62.
[131]*See id.* at 5063 n.75, 63 P & F Rad. Reg.2d at 555–56 n.75.
[132]Syracuse Peace Council v. FCC, 867 F.2d 654, 10 Media L. Rep. 1225 (D.C. Cir. 1989).
[133]47 U.S.C. sec. 315 (a) (1982).

Although the 1959 amendment did not specifically mention the fairness doctrine, the FCC itself argued for the next twenty years that Congress added the fairness doctrine to the statute through the 1959 amendment to section 315. The U.S. Supreme Court seemed to agree when it upheld the authority of the FCC to develop the fairness doctrine in its 1969 *Red Lion* opinion. In *Red Lion,* the Court said Congress "made it very plain" in the 1959 amendment that a broadcaster's requirement to operate in the "public interest" imposed a duty "to discuss both sides of controversial public issues."[134]

However, the FCC, in a deregulatory mood during the Reagan administration, argued in the 1980s that the 1959 amendment did not codify the fairness doctrine. In both a report to Congress and the *Syracuse Peace Council* decision, the commission pointed to a 1986 decision of the D.C. Circuit, *Telecommunications Research and Action Center (TRAC) v. FCC.*[135] The D.C. Circuit said, in *TRAC,* that the congressional adoption of section 315 in 1959 only "ratified" the commission's argument that the fairness doctrine was *authorized* by the public interest standard in the Communications Act.[136] The court said the 1959 amendment demonstrated that Congress considered the fairness doctrine to be an obligation *created by the FCC* and not a statutory requirement, as the Supreme Court had implied in *Red Lion.* Because the fairness doctrine was created by the commission, the commission had the authority to eliminate it, the D.C. Circuit said. The Supreme Court denied *certiorari* in *TRAC,* leaving the appeals court explanation of the 1959 amendment intact.

However, if congressional intent in 1959 was in dispute, Congress has left no doubts about its intent in the last few years. Congress responded to the FCC's *1985 Fairness Report* by prohibiting the commission from changing or eliminating the fairness doctrine before the FCC reported fairness doctrine alternatives to Congress. When the FCC sent its report to Congress on the same day the commission eliminated the fairness doctrine, it knew Congress would object. Just two months earlier Congress had passed a bill explicitly inserting the fairness doctrine into the 1934 Communications Act, legislation vetoed by President Reagan. Later in the same year, Congress attached a rider to a continuing budget resolution that would have incorporated the fairness doctrine into the Communications Act. Congress withdrew the rider when Reagan said he would not sign the bill with the fairness doctrine language included.

In 1990, many members of Congress were committed to ensuring that the fairness doctrine was required by statute. Revival of the policy by Congress was possible because the courts had not ruled the policy unconstitutional. The courts had only said the FCC's decision to abandon the fairness doctrine was within the commission's administrative authority. However, a codification of the fairness doctrine into law might be just as susceptible to a veto in 1990 as it was in 1987. President Bush has said that he, like Reagan, was prepared to veto legislation codifying the fairness doctrine.[137]

---

[134]Red Lion Broadcasting Co. v. FCC, 395 U.S. at 380–81, 1 Media L. Rep. at 2059.

[135]Syracuse Peace Council, 2 FCC Rcd. at 5060 n.46, 63 P & F Rad. Reg.2d at 548 n.46; Inquiry into Section 73.1910 of the Commission's Rules and Regulations Concerning Alternatives to the General Fairness Doctrine Obligations of Broadcast Licensees (Fairness Report to Congress), 2 FCC Rcd. 5272, 5297 n.32, 63 P & F Rad. Reg.2d 488, 496 n.32 (1987). *See* Telecommunications Research & Action Center v. FCC, 801 F.2d 501, 13 Media L. Rep. 1881 (D.C. Cir. 1986), *cert. denied,* 482 U.S. 919 (1987).

[136]801 F.2d at 517–18, 13 Media L. Rep. at 1894.

[137]"Bush Seen as Sending Signal on Fairness Doctrine," *Broadcasting,* April 17, 1989, at 31.

Personal Attacks and Political Editorials The most important, and perhaps the only, fairness-doctrine-related policies in 1990 were rules that required broadcast licensees to provide time for replies to personal attacks and political editorials that had been aired. The FCC said in *Syracuse Peace Council,* and again in its reconsideration of that decision, that it was not at the time eliminating the personal attack and political editorializing rules. The commission said the two rules were being considered in another proceeding.[138]

The FCC first suggested that broadcasters may have to provide time for replies to personal attacks in the 1949 document announcing the fairness doctrine. The commission said that "elementary considerations of fairness may dictate that time be allocated to a person or group attacked" during the discussion of a controversial public issue.[139] The "suggestion" became a formal regulation in 1967. At the same time, the commission adopted a rule that if a station broadcasts an editorial opposing a political candidate or supporting the candidate's opponent, the station must provide an opportunity for a response.

The FCC does not prohibit personal attacks and political editorials; it just requires licensees to provide response time if personal attacks and political editorials are broadcast. The personal attack and political editorial rules are intended to keep the public informed and prevent broadcasters from using their licenses to unduly influence the public.

Personal Attacks The FCC's personal attack rules specify that broadcasters must offer reply time if the honesty, character, or integrity of an identified person or group is attacked during the discussion of a controversial issue of public importance. A person attacked must be notified within a week of the date, time, and identification of the broadcast. A broadcaster must provide a script, tape, or accurate summary of the attack. It must offer a reasonable opportunity to respond over the licensee's facilities without charge.[140]

In *Red Lion Broadcasting Co. v. FCC,* discussed early in the chapter, radio station WGCB of Red Lion, Pennsylvania, had not notified author Fred Cook when it carried an attack implying that his writing was subversive. When Cook asked for free time to reply, he was turned down. The FCC insisted that WGCB provide the free time, but the station appealed first to a federal appeals court and eventually to the Supreme Court. In *Red Lion,* the Supreme Court upheld the FCC's personal attack and political editorializing rules, saying they did not violate the First Amendment.[141]

Even before *Red Lion,* the FCC said a person attacked has the right to respond personally to the attack or to designate a spokesperson. The station broadcasting a personal attack cannot decide who should respond to the attack.[142] The person attacked must be given a chance to reply directly to the attack without being subjected to questions or cross-examination.[143] The commission has not said how closely the amount of time given to a reply must come to matching the length of attack.[144]

---

[138]Syracuse Peace Council, 2 FCC Rcd. at 5063 n.75, 63 P & F Rad. Reg.2d at 555–56 n.75.

[139]*In re* Editorializing by Broadcast Licensees, 13 F.C.C. at 1252, 25 P & F Rad. Reg. at 1907.

[140]47 C.F.R. 73.1920 (1989).

[141]395 U.S. 367, 1 Media L. Rep. 2053 (1969).

[142]*See* Radio Albany, Inc., 40 F.C.C. 632, 4 P & F Rad. Reg.2d 277 (1965).

[143]John Birch Soc'y, 11 F.C.C.2d 790 (1968).

[144]*See* S. Simmons, *The Fairness Doctrine and the Media* 86 (1978).

The FCC has never disclosed any criteria it uses to determine which broadcasts constitute a personal attack. There is little, if any, apparent logic in what kinds of broadcasts have been and have not been labeled personal attacks. The commission has said that personal attacks include allegations of criminal activity, moral turpitude, Communist activity, and the promotion of violence. On the other hand, disagreements over political issues and charges of bad judgment or incompetence tend not to be considered personal attacks.[145] The FCC said an accusation by Dr. Antonio Luque that another doctor engaged in "unethical conduct" that led to the death of two small children was a personal attack. The remark attacked Dr. John Gabler's "honesty, integrity, and character."[146] However, an earlier assertion aired by Dr. Luque that doctors and nurses in a Rome hospital were "incompetent" was not an attack. The FCC said the issue of incompetence related to "ability and knowledge" rather than "honesty, integrity, and character."[147] At least two commentators have warned against relying too heavily on the categories outlined by the FCC. The commentators argue that the distinctions the FCC makes do not always stand up to close scrutiny.[148]

Similarly, the commission's criteria are unclear for determining the *controversy* of a discussion said to carry a personal attack. The FCC has not consistently used the amount of media coverage or the attention paid to the issue by community leaders, information the commission used in other fairness doctrine cases, to determine whether a *controversy* exists in a personal attack complaint. Sometimes the commission provides no rationale for why one issue is a *controversy* and another is not. For example, the commission said without explanation that the dismissal of Dr. Antonio Luque from the City Hospital medical staff in Rome, New York, was a controversial issue of public importance.[149] In contrast, a union election involving federal employees at Fort Bragg, North Carolina, was not a controversial issue of public importance even though it involved 1,230 people directly and affected another 5,000 households indirectly. The FCC said the election was a "narrow" controversy between two unions and not a matter of general importance to the listening audience. The commission said a *controversy* requires evidence of a general public debate.[150]

The personal attack rules apply to attacks made both by station employees and others using the broadcast facilities. Individual stations are even responsible for attacks broadcast by the networks. The rules, however, exempt newscasts, news interviews, and on-the-spot news coverage, including any commentary or analysis, but not news documentaries.

The personal attack rules do not apply to attacks on foreign groups or public figures. Neither do they apply to attacks made by legally qualified candidates or their campaign staffs during political campaigns.

Comments made by the campaign staffs of political candidates are subject to the

---

[145]*Id.* at 79–82.

[146]Dr. John Gabler, 40 F.C.C.2d 579, 27 P & F Rad. Reg.2d 1249 (1973).

[147]Rome Hosp., 40 F.C.C.2d 452, 27 P & F Rad. Reg.2d 1142 (1973).

[148]S. Simmons, *The Fairness Doctrine and the Media* at 82; B. Schmidt, Jr., *Freedom of the Press vs. Public Access* 171 (1976).

[149]Dr. John Gabler, 40 F.C.C.2d 579, 27 P & F Rad. Reg.2d 1249 (1973).

[150]National Ass'n of Gov't Employees, 41 F.C.C.2d 965, 27 P & F Rad. Reg.2d 1309 (1973).

Zapple Rule, which has not yet been specifically eliminated by the FCC.[151] The Zapple Rule holds that supporters of opposing candidates be given about the same amount of airtime during election campaigns. The Zapple Rule complements section 315 of the Communications Act, which requires that broadcasters provide equal opportunities to legally qualified political candidates. Although section 315 does not apply to the supporters of candidates, the Zapple Rule does. Under the Zapple Rule, a broadcaster can invite representatives of the candidates, rather than the candidates themselves, to respond to personal attacks by someone other than political candidates or their supporters. The Zapple Rule allows the licensee to avoid triggering the equal opportunities doctrine, requiring a response from the candidate's opponent.[152]

Under the Zapple Rule, if the supporters of one candidate pay for their time, so must the supporters of the other candidate. If the first group is given free time, the second group must receive free time as well.[153]

The Zapple Rule was created in response to a letter by a former congressional staff member, Nicholas Zapple.

Political Editorials   The FCC requires that broadcasters provide notification, script or tape, and time to reply not only for personal attacks, but also for editorials that oppose a legally qualified candidate or endorse an opponent. The political editorial rule applies only when the editorial represents the views of the broadcast station owner or manager. It has not been applied to political commentators who are not speaking on behalf of the station. Political commentary independent of management views used to be subject to the general fairness doctrine.

A licensee must offer time on the air to the candidate opposed, or legally qualified opponents of the candidate supported, within 24 hours of a political editorial. When stations broadcast editorials within 72 hours of election day or on election day itself, they must notify opposing candidates "sufficiently far in advance of the broadcast" to enable a "reasonable opportunity to respond."[154]

Since editorials do not ordinarily feature pictures or voices of political candidates, the FCC allows the response to them to be given by representatives of the candidates rather than the candidates themselves. Appearances by the candidates themselves would trigger the equal opportunities rule of section 315 and provide additional time to those who benefited from an editorial in the first place.

As in the case of replies to personal attacks, the FCC has not said whether the time for replies to editorial endorsements must exactly equal the length of the original editorial. However, the commission has said that stations giving candidates only a third or a fourth of the original editorial time had not provided "a reasonable opportunity to respond." The same held true when candidates were awarded airtime for only one reply to four editorials.[155]

---

[151]Syracuse Peace Council, 2 FCC Rcd. at 5063 n.75, 63 P & F Rad. Reg.2d at 555–56 n.75.

[152]47 C.F.R. sec. 73.1920 (1989).

[153]Letter to Nicholas Zapple, 23 F.C.C.2d 707, 19 P & F Rad. Reg.2d 421 (1970); 1984 Political Primer, 100 F.C.C.2d at 1534–35.

[154]47 C.F.R. sec. 73.1930 (1989).

[155]*See* Bill Bishop, 30 F.C.C.2d 829 (1971).

SUMMARY

Before 1987, the fairness doctrine required that broadcasters provide airtime for the discussion of important and controversial public issues and, in doing so, that they present a reasonable opportunity for the presentation of contrasting viewpoints. The FCC eliminated the fairness doctrine in 1987, a decision upheld by the courts. Meanwhile, many members of Congress have said they want to ensure that the fairness doctrine is a part of the 1934 Communications Act and therefore beyond the reach of the FCC. Whether the fairness doctrine was codified in 1959 amendments to section 315 of the act is disputed.

A few aspects of the commission's general fairness policy were not abandoned in 1987. Broadcast licensees are still required to provide reply time for personal attacks aired during the discussion of controversial public issues. Broadcasters also must provide political candidates opportunities to respond to editorials attacking them or supporting their opponents. Stations must notify either the person attacked or the candidate, provide them with a script or tape of the attack or endorsement, and allow for a "reasonable opportunity" to respond without charge. The FCC also requires that licensees provide comparable time to supporters of opposing political candidates.

Other Programming Regulation

In addition to regulating personal attacks and candidates' access to the airwaves, the FCC administers a statute restricting the broadcast of obscene, indecent, and profane programming. It also limits the amount of commercial television network programming during prime evening hours. In addition, the commission has warned broadcast stations that they must broadcast children's programming and that they must not distort the news. However, the commission has declined to regulate the amount of advertising on the broadcast media or control broadcast formats.

Obscene, Indecent, and Profane Programming   Both the print and broadcast media can be prosecuted for disseminating obscenity. In addition, broadcasters can be punished for airing indecent and profane programming.

Obscenity in broadcasting, like obscenity in the print media, is governed by the U.S. Supreme Court's decision in *Miller v. California,* discussed in Chapter 8. In an obscenity proceeding, broadcasters, like publishers, can be punished only for material that depicts or describes sexual conduct in a patently offensive way as defined by state law. In addition, a publication or program is obscene only if, as a whole, it appeals to the prurient interest of the average person applying contemporary community standards. To be considered obscene, a program also must lack serious literary, artistic, political, or scientific value.

The FCC says it regulates indecency to protect children in the broadcast audience. Congress imposed a ban on indecency in 1988. However, the U.S. Supreme Court has said in the past that indecency could only be regulated and not banned, and the congressional ban was being appealed in 1990.

Indecency, much like obscenity, depicts or describes sexual or excretory activities or organs in a patently offensive manner. However, indecency, in contrast to obscenity, need not arouse a prurient interest in sex as defined by the average person applying community standards. Rather, indecency, as defined by the FCC, is offensive to the community standards for broadcasting. In indecency, the FCC determines what is patently offensive.

In addition, indecent programming, unlike obscenity, can have social value. The FCC has said that it would consider the "serious merit" of programming as one factor in determining whether a broadcast is patently offensive.[156]

The FCC only takes action against indecent programming if it is broadcast at a time when children could reasonably be expected to be listening or watching.[157]

Defining and Regulating Indecency   Indecency is protected by the First Amendment because the Supreme Court has said that only those materials meeting the *Miller v. California* tests for obscenity fall outside of First Amendment protection. However, in 1978, in *FCC v. Pacifica Foundation,* the Supreme Court ruled that the FCC could regulate indecent broadcasts without violating the First Amendment.[158]

The dispute in *Pacifica* began with an afternoon broadcast of a George Carlin monologue, "Filthy Words," on New York City radio station WBAI(FM). A New York father heard the Carlin satire on the use of language while driving with his son and complained to the FCC. The owner of WBAI, the Pacifica Foundation, said the broadcast was introduced with a warning that the program contained "sensitive language which might be regarded as offensive to some."[159] Carlin begins his 12-minute monologue by saying he will talk about "the words you couldn't say on the public, ah, airwaves, um, the ones you definitely wouldn't say, ever." Then he says the words, repeating them frequently.[160]

The FCC said that words such as *shit, piss, tits,* and *fuck* were indecent because they depicted sexual and excretory activities and organs in a patently offensive manner. The commission said the words were "obnoxious, gutter language" that were indecent because they "debased" and "brutalized" human beings "by reducing them to their bodily functions." The commission said Carlin repeated the offensive words "over and over" during the early afternoon when children were "undoubtedly" in the audience. Although the FCC did not penalize WBAI for the Carlin broadcast, the commission said additional complaints about indecent programming from listeners could lead to sanctions.[161]

The 1934 Communications Act authorizes the commission to fine a station for each day it illegally broadcasts obscenity or indecency.[162] The commission can also revoke a station's license, deny a license renewal, or grant only a short-term renewal

---

[156]*In re* Infinity Broadcasting Corp. (Reconsideration Order), 3 FCC Rcd. 930, 931, 64 P & F Rad. Reg.2d 211, 216 (1987).

[157]*Id.* at 936 n.6, 64 P & F Rad. Reg.2d at 213 n.6.

[158]438 U.S. 726, 730, 3 Media L. Rep. 2553, 2554 (1978).

[159]Pacifica Foundation Station WBAI(FM), 56 F.C.C.2d 94, 98, 32 P & F Rad. Reg.2d 1331, 1336–37 (1975).

[160]The words are *shit, piss, fuck, cunt, cocksucker, motherfucker,* and *tits.*

[161]Pacifica Foundation Station WBAI(FM), 56 F.C.C.2d at 99, 32 P & F Rad. Reg.2d at 1337.

[162]47 U.S.C. sec. 312 (a) (6) (1982).

if a station broadcasts obscene or indecent programming.[163] In addition, the U.S. Department of Justice can fine broadcasters up to $10,000 and jail them for up to two years for violating the federal criminal code.[164]

The FCC's decision to warn Pacifica for the broadcast of the Carlin monologue was reversed by the U.S. Court of Appeals for the District of Columbia, but reinstated by a divided U.S. Supreme Court. Justice John Paul Stevens, in an opinion supported in part by four other justices, said the FCC's warning to WBAI did not violate the 1934 Communications Act or the First Amendment.

Stevens said the FCC did not censor WBAI's broadcast of the Carlin monologue, as Pacifica contended. Stevens said the language in the 1934 Communications Act prohibiting censorship had never been interpreted to forbid the FCC from evaluating broadcasts after they were aired. Neither did the statute prohibit the FCC from imposing sanctions on broadcasters who aired indecent programming, Stevens said. The commission had not edited the "Filthy Words" monologue in advance. Rather, the FCC had reviewed the program after the broadcast as part of the commission's responsibility to regulate licensees in the public interest. Stevens said review of program content after a broadcast is not censorship.

Stevens rejected Pacifica's argument that Carlin's monologue could not be regulated because it was not obscene. Pacifica had argued that the words *indecent* and *obscene* in the federal laws meant the same thing. Pacifica contended that indecent language, like obscene language, must appeal to the prurient interest before it can be punished. However, Stevens argued that the words *obscene, indecent,* and *profane* have different meanings when applied to broadcasting. The term *indecent* refers "to nonconformance with accepted standards of morality," the justice said. Hence, the Court accepted the FCC's conclusion that Carlin's monologue was indecent but not obscene.

The Court also refused to hold that the FCC's ruling that the Carlin monologue was indecent had violated the First Amendment. Stevens said indecent programming can be limited on broadcasting because radio is intrusive and because children could be exposed. First, Stevens said, broadcasting is a "uniquely pervasive presence in the lives of all Americans." Stevens said,

> Patently offensive, indecent material presented over the airwaves confronts the citizen, not only in public, but also in the privacy of the home, where the individual's right to be let alone plainly outweighs the First Amendment rights of an intruder.[165]

Second, said Stevens, "broadcasting is uniquely accessible to children, even those too young to read." He said special treatment of broadcasting was justified because of the societal interests in protecting children and in the interest of supporting parental authority.

Justice Stevens said, in a part of the opinion supported by only three other justices, that the First Amendment might have protected the Carlin monologue if it had been offensive political or social commentary. However, Carlin's use of the "seven

---

[163]47 U.S.C. sec. 307, 308 (1982).

[164]18 U.S.C. sec. 1464 (1988).

[165]438 U.S. at 748, 3 Media L. Rep. at 2562.

dirty words" did not deserve absolute First Amendment protection because the words were not essential to the "exposition of ideas" and were of such little use in the search for truth that any benefit "is clearly outweighed by the social interest in order and morality."[166] Since the words Carlin used were patently offensive and ordinarily lacked literary, political, or scientific value, they could be regulated in some contexts.

In a part of the opinion where he again spoke for the Court's majority, Stevens said important considerations in indecency cases include the time of day of the broadcast, the nature of the program containing the offensive language, the composition of the audience, and perhaps the differences among radio, television, and closed-circuit transmissions. The Court said the Carlin monologue could be regulated because of the repetitive use of the offensive words at a time when children could reasonably be expected to be a part of the audience.

Justice Powell, joined by Justice Blackmun, concurred with most of Stevens's opinion, including the need to protect children from offensive speech on the broadcast media. However, Powell disagreed with Stevens's attempt to regulate speech on the basis of social value. He said the justices should not be deciding which speech is protected by the First Amendment by assessing the social and political value of its content. The social value of speech "is a judgment for each person to make," said Powell, "not one for the judges to impose on him."[167]

Justice Brennan, however, in a dissenting opinion, said that the FCC's regulation of the Carlin speech was unconstitutional. In an opinion joined by Justice Marshall, Brennan said the Court's majority was for the first time prohibiting minors from hearing speech that was not obscene, and therefore was protected by the First Amendment. Brennan said that "surely" preserving speech entitled to First Amendment protection was important enough that listeners could be required to suffer the "minimal discomfort" of briefly listening to offensive speech before they turned off the radio. Brennan chastised Powell as well as the rest of the majority for "censoring" speech like the Carlin monologue solely because the justices found the words offensive. Brennan accused the Court of attempting "to impose *its* notions of propriety on the whole of the American people."[168]

All four dissenting justices, in an opinion written by Justice Stewart, said the FCC could not regulate the "seven dirty words" since the Court agreed that the Carlin monologue was not obscene. The monologue was not obscene because it did not appeal to a prurient interest in sex, the Court said. Stewart said that when Congress passed the law banning "any obscene, indecent, or profane language" from the airwaves, no legislator said that the word *indecent* meant anything different than the word *obscene.*

After the *Pacifica* decision, the FCC at first emphasized the limits of its supervision of indecent programming. For more than a decade the FCC confined its enforcement of indecency to the frequent repetition of sexual or excretory expletives such as *fuck* and *shit.* No broadcasters were punished for airing indecent programming during that time.

---

[166]*Id.* at 746, 3 Media L. Rep. at 2561, *quoting* Chaplinsky v. New Hampshire, 315 U.S. 568, 572 (1942).
[167]*Id.*at 761, 3 Media L. Rep. at 2567 (Powell, J., concurring).
[168]*Id.* at 762, 3 Media L. Rep. at 2567 (Brennan, J., dissenting) (emphasis in original).

However, in April 1987, an FCC that had otherwise deregulated broadcast programming warned broadcasters that the term *indecency* would in the future be applied to more than the repetitive use of George Carlin's "seven dirty words." The commission said that, unlike the recent past, *any* broadcast would be *indecent* if it included a description or depiction of sexual or excretory activities or organs in a manner patently offensive by contemporary community standards for the broadcast medium. The commission said that the context of a broadcast would be an important factor in determining whether the words or depictions are "vulgar" or "shocking" and therefore indecent. Context, the commission said, includes the manner in which the words or depictions are portrayed, whether the portrayal is isolated or fleeting, "the merit" of a program, and whether children might be listening or viewing.[169] The FCC said it would take action against any program that met its definition of *indecency* at times when "there is a reasonable risk that children are in the audience."[170] The FCC emphasized that broadcasters must precede indecent material with a warning even if children could not reasonably be expected to be in the audience.[171]

Between 1987 and 1989, no broadcast licensee was fined for indecent programming. However, in August 1989, U.S. senators told three nominees to the commission during their confirmation hearings that regulating indecency should be a top priority. One of the three, Alfred Sykes, would soon be the new FCC chairman.

Within months of the confirmation hearings, the FCC fined at least a dozen stations for broadcasting "patently offensive" bawdy humor and double entendre containing descriptions of sexual activities that were clearly capable of specific sexual meaning. The commission fined WLUP(AM) of Chicago $2,000 for each of three drive-time broadcasts of the "Steve and Gary Show." In one of the three, co-host Steve Dahl described a *Penthouse* picture of dethroned Miss America Vanessa Williams "licking that other woman's vagina."[172] In another, a caller sang portions of a song called "Kiddie Porn" that referred in graphic language to the male genitals. The FCC also fined WIOD(AM) of Miami $10,000 for playing songs such as "Walk with an Erection" and "Penis Envy" between 10 A.M. and 2 P.M.[173]

However, the FCC also has said it will not take action against rock songs containing explicit sexual language, serious discussions of sex, scantily clad dancing women, or humor without explicit sexual language. The commission refused, for example, to penalize radio station WTMA of Charleston, South Carolina, for broadcasting the word "clocksucker" in a political advertisement opposing the purchase of a clock for city hall. The commission said the ad did not involve a "patently offensive depiction of sexual or excretory activities or organs."[174]

The FCC also ruled that a television broadcast about high school sex education in Seattle was not patently offensive even though it included frank discussions of sexual topics, the use of sex organ models, and the simulated demonstration of birth

---

[169]*In re* Infinity Broadcasting Corp. (Reconsideration Order), 3 FCC Rcd. at 932, 64 P & F Rad. Reg.2d at 216.
[170]*In re* Pacifica Foundation, Inc., 2 FCC Rcd. 2698, 62 P & F Rad. Reg.2d 1195 (1987).
[171]*Id.* at 2701, 62 P & F Rad. Reg.2d at 1197.
[172]*See* Evergreen Media Corp. of Chicago AM, 66 P & F Rad. Reg.2d 1555 (1989).
[173]Letter from Roy J. Stewart, Chief of Mass Media Bureau, FCC, to Michael J. Faherty, Executive Vice President-Radio, Cox Broadcasting Division, Cox Enterprises, Inc. (Oct. 26, 1989).
[174]"FCC Rejects Five Indecency Complaints," *Broadcasting,* April 11, 1988, at 37.

control devices. The FCC said the program, broadcast by KING-TV, was not indecent because the references to sexual and excretory organs and activities were not "vulgar," "lewd," or "shocking." Nor did the sexual references pander or titillate, the commission said.

In 1988, the FCC's policy of expanded enforcement of indecency was upheld by the U.S. Court of Appeals for the D.C. Circuit. In *Action for Children's Television v. FCC,* the court agreed that the FCC's past policy of limiting indecency actions to programs containing the seven dirty words was an "unduly narrow" interpretation.[175] The court affirmed the FCC's assessment that it made "no legal or policy sense" to regulate Carlin's monologue but not other offensive descriptions or depictions of sexual or excretory activity simply because they avoided particular words. The D.C. Circuit said the commission rationally decided that a broader definition of *indecency* was needed.

Channeling Indecency   At the same time the D.C. Circuit held the FCC could expand its enforcement of indecency, the court said the commission had inadequately justified a 1987 warning to broadcasters that indecency between 10 P.M. and midnight might be punished. The court said the commission unconstitutionally infringed on broadcasters' right to speak and adults' right to receive by failing to consider sufficiently why late evening broadcasts of indecency need to be banned to protect children.

Until April 1987, the FCC did not punish indecency broadcast after 10 P.M. because the commission assumed that few children 12 years old and younger would be in the audience. However, in 1987, citing new evidence of children's listening and viewing habits, the FCC told broadcasters they could "safely" air indecent programming only between midnight and 6 A.M.[176]

However, the D.C. Circuit rescinded the FCC's new time limitation, saying that the commission had not demonstrated that children would be listening to the radio or watching television between 10 P.M. and midnight.[177] The court explained that, while the FCC had been restricting indecency to protect children 12 years old and younger, the commission was justifying its new policy with data on the viewing habits of children 12 and older. The court said that if the commission had decided to protect children older than 12 from indecency, it needed to explain why. In addition, the D.C. Circuit said, the FCC needed to provide data on the number of children listening to indecent programs rather than what the commission provided, the number of children listening to all radio stations in a market.

Banning Indecency   In the wake of the D.C. Circuit's opinion, the FCC decided to be cautious by taking action against indecency broadcast only before 8 P.M.[178] However, in September 1988, Congress banned indecency at all times.[179] Congress

---

[175]852 F.2d 1332, 15 Media L. Rep. 1907 (1988).

[176]*In re* Pacifica Foundation, Inc., 2 FCC Rcd. at 2699, 62 P & F Rad. Reg.2d at 1195; *In re* Infinity Broadcasting Corp., 3 FCC Rcd. at 937 n.47, 64 P & F Rad. Reg.2d at 219 n.47.

[177]852 F.2d 1332, 15 Media L. Rep. 1907 (1988).

[178]*See In re* Kansas City Television, Ltd., FCC 89-261 (Aug. 4, 1989) (Westlaw, FCOM-FCC).

[179]Making Appropriations for the Departments of Commerce, Justice, and State, the Judiciary, and Related Agencies for the Fiscal Year Ending September 30, 1988, Pub. L. No. 100-459, sec. 608, 102 Stat. 2216, 2228 (1988).

ordered the FCC to prohibit indecent programming 24 hours a day despite warnings from some of its own members, as well as from legal experts, that a ban of indecency would violate the First Amendment.

Doubts about the constitutionality of a total ban on broadcast indecency were reinforced by a 1989 U.S. Supreme Court decision prohibiting a ban on indecent telephone messages. In *Sable Communications v. FCC,* discussed later in the chapter, the Supreme Court said that nonobscene sexual expression sent by telephone wires is protected by the First Amendment. Therefore, indecent telephone communication could be regulated to protect children but not in a way that would deny access to adults.[180]

Also in 1989, the U.S. Court of Appeals for the District of Columbia Circuit enjoined the FCC from enforcing the congressional ban on indecency.[181] Later in the year, the court remanded to the FCC the constitutional challenge to the ban after the commission asked for the opportunity to establish a case for a 24-hour-a-day restriction on indecency.[182] In the summer of 1990, the commission said in a report prepared for the D.C. Circuit that a 24-hour ban of indecency was a "narrowly tailored" regulation designed to protect children. The commission said the 24-hour ban was "narrowly tailored" because stations would be allowed to broadcast indecent material if they could demonstrate that children were not in the audience at the time of the broadcast. The commission said that a 24-hour ban could be justified because other "narrowly tailored" options to protect children, such as providing a limited time when indecency could be broadcast without punitive action, were inadequate since children watch or listen to broadcasts around the clock. The commission adopted 17 years old and under as the definition of *children.*[183]

In contrast to indecency, the regulation of profane language in the broadcast media is rarely an issue. The legal definition of *profane* language is "irreverence towards sacred things" and particularly "an irreverent or blasphemous use of the name of God." *Blasphemy* is the malicious reproach of God or religion.[184] The FCC is unlikely to punish a station for the isolated use of *God* or *damn* as swear words.[185]

Children's Programming In contrast to the FCC's recent aggressive oversight of indecency has been its disinterest in regulating children's programming. In the 1980s, the commission told broadcasters that they had a responsibility to meet the needs of children but showed no sign of developing or enforcing any children's program requirements.

As a result, in 1990, Congress passed legislation requiring the FCC to consider during the licensee renewal process whether broadcasters served the "educational and information needs" of children. In addition, the new law limits commercials during children's programming to 10½ minutes an hour on weekends and 12 minutes on

---

[180]Sable Communications, Inc. v. FCC, 109 S. Ct. 2829, 16 Media L. Rep. 1961 (1989).
[181]"Chances Slim for 24-Hour FCC Ban on Indecency," *Broadcasting,* Jan. 30, 1989, at 58.
[182]Action for Children's Television v. FCC, No. 88-1916 (D.C. Cir. Sept. 13, 1989).
[183]*In re* Enforcement of Prohibitions Against Broadcast Indecency, in 18 U.S.C. sec. 1464, 1990 FCC Lexis 4213.
[184]*Black's Law Dictionary* 155–56, 1089 (5th ed. 1979).
[185]CBS, 21 P & F Rad. Reg.2d 497 (1972).

week days.[186] President Reagan had pocket-vetoed similar legislation because, he said, it was "counterproductive" and violated the First Amendment.[187]

Children's Educational Programming   Congressional efforts to increase educational television for children are supported by parents and other observers who argue that broadcasters have failed to meet their public interest obligations by providing sufficient "quality" programming for children. Instead, parents argue, children's programs are too violent and foster stereotypes, prejudices, and questionable social values.

The FCC responded to parental concerns and citizen groups nearly 20 years ago in a 1974 children's programming policy statement. In 1974, the commission declared for the first time that children's programming aired by a broadcast station would be evaluated during the license renewal process.[188] The FCC asked commercial television stations to increase the amount of programming for children, to increase educational programming on weekdays, and to air a reasonable amount of educational and informational programming targeted to specific age groups.

Checking broadcaster performance in 1979, the FCC found no increase in the amount of children's programming offered by network affiliates and no significant increase in educational or informational programs. The commission proposed five options for dealing with the "non-compliance" with the 1974 programming policy statement, ranging from rescinding the 1974 document to instituting mandatory programming requirements.[189]

Soon after, however, the FCC lost interest in regulating any kind of programming. FCC Chairman Mark Fowler led a commission committed to letting the marketplace determine broadcast programming. Fowler did not believe the FCC should impose program regulations through its interpretations of the public interest standard of the 1934 Communications Act, and, therefore, the FCC did not address its 1979 proposals until after being ordered to do so by the U.S. Court of Appeals for the D.C. Circuit.[190] Finally, in 1984, the commission did not directly rescind the 1974 policy statement but neither did it mandate children's programming. Instead, the commission said that the "video market" as a whole, including public television and cable television, met the needs of children. The FCC said there were more noncommercial programs, more broadcast stations, and more viewing options because of cable. "In short," the commission asserted, "there is no national failure of access to children's programming that requires an across-the-board, national quota for each and every licensee to meet."[191] The commission said that program selection should be

---

[186]"President's Pocket Unveto Allows Children's Bill to Become Law," *Broadcasting,* Oct. 25, 1990, at 35.

[187]"Reagan Vetoes Bill Putting Limits on TV Programming for Children," *New York Times,* Nov. 7, 1988, at 1. *See also* "Commerce Committee Moves Kidvid Bill over Broadcaster Objection," *Broadcasting,* Oct. 9, 1989, at 40.

[188]Children's Television Report and Policy Statement, 50 F.C.C.2d 1, 31 P & F Rad. Reg.2d 1228 (1974), *reconsideration denied,* 55 F.C.C.2d 691, 34 P & F Rad. Reg.2d 1703 (1975).

[189]Children's Television Programming and Advertising Practices, 75 F.C.C.2d 138 (1980).

[190]Washington Ass'n for Television and Children v. FCC, 712 F.2d 677 (D.C. Cir. 1983); "Court Orders FCC to End Children's Rulemaking before End of Year," *Broadcasting,* Nov. 28, 1983, at 38.

[191]Children's Television Programming and Advertising Practices, 96 F.C.C.2d 634, 651, 55 P & F Rad. Reg.2d 199, 211 (1984), *aff'd sub nom.* Action for Children's Television v. FCC, 756 F.2d 899, 11 Media L. Rep. 2080 (D.C. Cir. 1985).

determined by broadcast licensees and the viewing choices of the audience "with only the rarest of exceptions."

Although the FCC said that each licensee must meet the needs of children as part of its responsibility to serve the public interest, the commission did not suggest the kinds or amounts of programming it expected and it set up no mechanism to monitor the children's programs being broadcast. Commissioner Henry Rivera, in dissent, said that "while a broadcaster has a 'special' duty to children . . . nothing special is required to fill it!" Rivera said the "recitation" of a licensee's duties was "nothing more than a fig leaf to clothe the nakedness of the new policy."[192]

Advertising in Children's Programming   Besides objecting to the lack of educational programming on children's television, parents and citizen groups have also contended that children's programs contain too many ads. They also protest the so-called "program-length commercials," half-hour- or hour-long programs based on a sponsor's product.

In 1974, in its children's programming policy statement, the commission suggested that advertising during children's programs should be limited to $9\frac{1}{2}$ minutes per hour on weekends and 12 minutes on weekdays. However, in 1986, the commission said the 1974 guidelines on advertising during children's programming were no longer in force. The commission said only that eliminating restrictions on commercials during children's programming was consistent with its general policy of deregulation, an explanation unacceptable to the U.S. Court of Appeals for the D.C. Circuit. In the first of two 1987 rulings questioning the FCC's children's advertising policies, the D.C. Circuit said the FCC did not adequately explain why the 1974 guidelines suggesting limitations on advertising time during children's programs were no longer needed. The court remanded the case to the commission, asking for a better justification.[193]

In the second D.C. Circuit opinion in 1987, the court overturned an FCC decision ruling that the producers of program-length commercials need not be identified. In *National Association for Better Broadcasting v. FCC*, the D.C. Circuit said that allowing program-length commercials without adequate labeling betrayed the congressional intent of the 1934 Communications Act.[194] Section 317 of the statute, known as the sponsorship identification requirement, requires that broadcasters identify anyone who pays for a commercial or a program with money, services, or something else of value. Although broadcasters are not required to identify programs or services given to a station for free, gifts cannot be "rewarded" with unexplained airtime for a service, product, or brand name.

In *NABB v. FCC*, citizen groups claimed that KCOP-TV did not tell viewers that "He-Man and Masters of the Universe" was, in effect, a sponsored program by the producers of the toy of the same name. "He-Man," based on an invincible animated hero, is created and produced by Mattel and Group W Productions. Through a common practice known as barter syndication, the companies provided the show to

---

[192]Children's Television Programming and Advertising Practices, 96 F.C.C.2d at 661, 55 P & F Rad. Reg.2d at 245 (Rivera dissenting).

[193]Action for Children's Television v. FCC, 821 F.2d 741 (1987).

[194]National Ass'n for Better Broadcasting v. FCC, 830 F.2d 270 (1987).

KCOP in exchange for two minutes of advertising time during the station's children's programming. The National Association for Better Broadcasting argued that Mattel and Group W should be identified under section 317 because the companies gave "something of value," the "He-Man" program, in order that the cartoon based on their product would be aired. The NABB said "He-Man" was, in effect, given to the station because the advertising time was worth only a small proportion of the program's value. Mattel and Group W spent $14 million on the first 65 episodes of "He-Man" and received in return only $400,000 worth of advertising time.

The FCC ruled that a station did not have to announce that the manufacturer of "He-Man and Masters of the Universe" had provided the station a children's cartoon with the same name. The FCC said the sponsorship identification requirement in the 1934 Communications Act restricted deceptive commercial practices by permitting viewers to determine easily when commercial messages were being broadcast. The commission said that its 1974 children's program policy statement adequately protected children from commercial deception by requiring distinctions between programming content and commercial material. The commission, quoting the 1974 statement, said the arrangement with KCOP-TV would have violated the sponsorship identification rule only if the show "He-Man" was so closely connected to "He-Man" advertising "that the entire program constitutes a single commercial promotion." The commission said that it recognized the commercial goals of the producers of "He-Man," but did not know how to effectively distinguish the motives and program-product ties of Mattel and Group W from the producers and distribution methods of critically acclaimed programs such as "Sesame Street" and "Peanuts." The commission said it had no evidence that programming based on products harms children. The benefit of the programs to product manufacturers was irrelevant, the FCC said, as long as broadcasters believed the cartoons were entertaining or informative and properly distinguished from commercials.

However, the D.C. Circuit said the commission could not avoid Communications Act requirements by hiding behind the 1974 children's programming policy. The sponsorship identification rules apply to all programs, regardless of whether they entertain, the court said. The court noted that members of Congress who drafted the current version of section 317 appeared to believe identification would be required when a company provided to broadcasters without charge a program featuring that company's product or service. The court said that, given the prevalence of barter arrangements for children's programming, the FCC must devise a standard to determine when the exchange of a program for advertising time does not constitute sponsorship of the program and therefore ought to be identified.

Shortly after the two D.C. Circuit opinions, in October 1987, the FCC initiated a rule-making proceeding into children's advertising. The FCC said it would examine commercial time limits for children's programming and the so-called program-length commercials.[195]

Commercials   Neither the FCC nor Congress has shown an inclination to reverse the deregulation of commercials in programming that is not directed to children. However, several federal statutes still regulate commercials.

---

[195]Revision of Programming and Commercialization Policies, Ascertainment Requirements, and Program Log Requirements for Commercial Television Stations, 2 FCC Rcd. 6822 (1987).

In recent years, the FCC has stopped limiting the amount of airtime broadcasters may devote to commercials. In 1984, the commission eliminated its guideline that licensees broadcast no more than 16 minutes of commercials an hour, and it announced it would no longer consider the amount of time devoted to commercials when processing license applications. The commission rescinded a ban on program-length commercials.[196] It also withdrew a policy declaration that the advertising of alcoholic beverages is not in the public interest in communities or states where the sale of alcohol is prohibited.[197] In addition, the commission stopped regulating issue-oriented advertising through the fairness doctrine in the case of WTVH(TV) of Syracuse, New York, discussed earlier in the chapter.

The deregulation of broadcast advertising has been based on the premise that marketplace forces can better determine the number and length of commercials than can FCC rules. The commission said that if stations air more commercials than the public will tolerate "the market will regulate itself"—viewers will not watch and advertisers will not buy time.[198]

However, section 317 of the 1934 Communications Act requires that broadcasters announce the identity of anyone who has purchased broadcast time, a provision mentioned in the previous section.[199] In commercials, use of an advertiser's name or product constitutes sufficient identification of the sponsor. The FCC can waive the sponsorship identification requirement, which it has done for "classified ad" programs and movies produced initially for theaters. Absent the waiver, stations could not broadcast without editing many feature films containing paid-for displays of commercial products.[200]

In addition to section 317, two federal statutes ban the advertising of cigarettes, little cigars, and chewing tobacco on all the electronic media.[201] Violators can be punished by fines up to $10,000.

Prime-Time Access One programming regulation that has survived deregulation is the prime-time access rule. The prime-time access rule limits the amount of commercial television network programming during the early evening hours in the largest 50 markets. Since the top 50 markets reach two-thirds of the viewers, the rule applies, in effect, to all network stations.

The prime-time access rule was adopted in 1971 to limit the dominance of network programming. The rule was intended to (1) encourage local programming and (2) provide a market for independent producers and distributors offering individual broadcast stations programming outside the network structure.

The rule, as it now stands, generally limits the networks to three hours of evening programming other than feature films during the prime-time period from 7 P.M. to

---

[196]Television Deregulation, 98 F.C.C.2d at 1101–1102, 56 P & F Rad. Reg.2d at 1025–26 and 84 F.C.C.2d at 1007–1008, 49 P & F Rad. Reg.2d at 30–31.

[197]*In re* Unnecessary Broadcast Regulation and Inquiry into Subscription Agreements Between Radio Broadcast Stations and Music Format Service Companies, 54 P & F Rad. Reg.2d 1043, 1049 (1983).

[198]Television Deregulation, 98 F.C.C.2d at 1105, 56 P & F Rad. Reg.2d at 1028.

[199]47 U.S.C. sec. 317 (1982).

[200]47 C.F.R. sec 73.1212 (g), (h) (1990).

[201]15 U.S.C. secs. 1335, 4401–4408 (1988). The ban on cigarette advertising was upheld in Capital Broadcasting Co. v. Mitchell, 333 F. Supp. 583 (D.C. 1971), *aff'd sub nom.* Capital Broadcasting Co. v. Kleindienst, 405 U.S. 1000 (1972).

11 P.M. (6 P.M. to 10 P.M. in the Central and Mountain time zones). Exceptions are allowed for children's programs, public affairs programs, documentaries, fast-breaking news, a half-hour of national news if adjacent to an hour of local news, political broadcasts for legally qualified candidates, certain sports activities, and special occasions when a network devotes all of its evening programming time to one program.[202] The FCC also has granted exceptions to Home Shopping Network and a Spanish-language network.[203]

Because of the prime-time access rule, the first hour of prime-time television on network affiliates each evening is dominated by network news and syndicated programs including quiz shows such as "Wheel of Fortune," so-called "tabloid television" such as "Inside Edition," and situation comedies. Although the prime-time access rule has been a factor in the creation of a large number of original programs for syndication, the FCC once conceded that it was disappointed that the regulation did not foster more local programming in the early evening viewing hours.[204]

Formats The FCC has steadfastly refused to regulate broadcast station format. The FCC refuses to tell radio licensees, for example, whether they should broadcast all news, classical music, or rock. The FCC's hands-off policy was upheld in 1981 by the U.S. Supreme Court.

The Court's decision was the climax to a decade-long struggle between the FCC on one side and several citizen groups and a federal appeals court on the other. The citizen groups wanted the FCC to consider proposed station format changes before approving the transfer of broadcast licenses from one owner to another. Frequently the citizen groups were fighting the conversion of the last classical music station in the community into one of many rock stations. In Chicago, the Citizens Committee to Save WEFM-FM wanted the FCC to hold a hearing to determine if the sale of one of the two classical music stations in the area was in the public interest. The owner of WEFM, the Zenith Radio Corporation, wanted to sell the station to GCC Communications of Chicago, a company that planned to change the format to rock music.[205] When the FCC refused to consider whether format changes were in the public interest, the U.S. Court of Appeals for the D.C. Circuit sided with the Citizens Committee. The court said that the commission must hold a hearing when a format unique to a market is being abandoned and a significant number of persons object.

The FCC responded to the court decision with a policy statement insisting that the public interest would best be served if the government did not intervene in format disputes. The commission said the determination of formats should be left to market forces rather than be subject to commission fiat. The FCC said that consumers can decide which formats they want to listen to and what kind of diversity of programming they want.[206] On appeal, the D.C. Circuit overturned the policy statement, ar-

---

[202]47 C.F.R. sec. 73.658(k) (1989).

[203]*In re* The Applicability of 47 C.F.R. sec. 73.658 (g) and 47 C.F.R. sec. 73.658 (k) to Home Shopping Inc., 4 FCC Rcd. 2422 (1989); Univision, Inc., 4 FCC Rcd. 2417, 66 P & F Rad. Reg.2d 170 (1989).

[204]*See* National Ass'n of Indep. Television Producers & Distributors v. FCC, 516 F.2d 526 (2d Cir. 1975).

[205]*E.g.*, Citizens Committee to Save WEFM v. FCC, 506 F.2d 246 (D.C. Cir. 1974) (*en banc*).

[206]Development of Policy re: Changes in the Entertainment Formats of Broadcast Stations, 60 F.C.C.2d 858, 33 P & F Rad. Reg.2d 1679 (1976), *reconsideration denied*, 66 F.C.C.2d 78, 41 P & F Rad. Reg.2d 543 (1977).

guing that some listener interests might not be served if all broadcasters adopted formats that would maximize profits.[207] However, the U.S. Supreme Court reversed the D.C. Circuit. The Supreme Court said that neither the First Amendment nor the Communications Act requires the FCC to review entertainment programming to determine whether a licensee is operating in the public interest. The Court refused to overturn the FCC's preference of relying on market forces rather than "its own attempt to oversee format changes at the behest of disaffected listeners."[208]

Distorted or Staged News

The FCC has also refused to regulate broadcast news closely. The commission has seldom punished broadcasters for distortions in the news, contending that the FCC cannot be "the national arbiter of the 'truth' of a news event."[209] The commission has said that investigations into the accuracy of news stories would discourage broadcasters from examining public issues and would violate the First Amendment.

However, the commission has warned it will intervene if it finds evidence that a broadcaster misled viewers or listeners by intentionally slanting or staging the news. The commission once said "there is no act more harmful to the public's ability to handle its affairs" than purposefully distorting news reports.[210] The commission has expressed concern about the deliberate "acting out" of a "significant event" that did not actually occur.[211] For example, the FCC rebuked WBBM-TV of Chicago for arranging a pot party that the commission said was held for the sole purpose of filming it.[212]

The commission has also said that stations should not intentionally misrepresent events and interviews through editing. The commission has said the normal editing of news film to fit a news broadcast is not intentional distortion. Neither is planning the questions or the lighting and camera direction before a television interview. To find a purposeful misrepresentation of news, the FCC has said, it must see evidence that a station's management instructed reporters and editors to slant the news or it must see a comparison of the film used and not used that demonstrates an intentional distortion of events.

The FCC distinguishes between a deliberate distortion and a "mere" inaccuracy or difference of opinion between a viewer and a station's news staff. The FCC has said it will not enter into disputes over a broadcaster's news judgment. It will not "enter the quagmire" of investigating the credibility of a reporter when a news source claims to have been misquoted. Neither will the FCC punish stations for mistakes that do not go "to the substance of the news." Hence, the FCC excused an inexperienced news staff at WPIX in New York City when it used film a day or more old to illustrate news stories about the Vietnam war, the 1968 presidential campaign, floods, and student demonstrations. The station also used inaccurately written titles to identify pic-

---

[207]WNCN Listeners Guild v. FCC, 610 F.2d 838 (1979).

[208]FCC v. WNCN Listeners Guild, 450 U.S. 582 (1981).

[209]*E.g.*, Hunger in America, 20 F.C.C.2d 143, 151, 17 P & F Rad. Reg.2d 674, 683 (1969); WBBM-TV, 18 F.C.C.2d 124, 131, 16 P & F Rad. Reg.2d 207, 216–17 (1969).

[210]Hunger in America, 20 F.C.C.2d at 151, 17 P & F Rad. Reg.2d at 684.

[211]*See* Hon. Harley O. Staggers, 25 P & F Rad. Reg.2d 413, 414 (1972).

[212]WBBM-TV, 18 F.C.C.2d 124, 16 P & F Rad. Reg.2d 207 (1969).

tures. The FCC said the "inaccurate embellishments" of news stories did not deceive the public about a matter of significance or affect the essentially accurate verbal accounts of the news. The commission renewed the license of WPIX.[213]

The FCC did refuse to renew the licenses of three broadcast stations owned by Star Stations of Indiana, at least in part for news distortion. The FCC said that licensee Don Burden told news personnel at WIFE and WIFE-FM in Indianapolis to give Indiana Senator Vance Hartke "frequent, favorable mention" on the air. Burden also told the news staff at KISN in Vancouver, Washington, to favor Oregon Governor Mark Hatfield over his opponent, Representative Robert Duncan, for a U.S. Senate seat. Burden said he wanted only positive news about Governor Hatfield and only negative stories about Representative Duncan, according to FCC reports. The FCC said that in both campaigns newscasts were used to deceive the public and further Don Burden's private interests rather than to inform the public with honest news judgment. "Such attempts to use broadcast facilities to subvert the political process," the commission said, "cannot be ignored or condoned."[214]

Fright, Violence, Fraud, and Payola   The FCC has eliminated many of its minor programming rules, but the 1934 Communications Act still contains a few miscellaneous provisions that are important to the broadcaster.

One exception to the commission's recent "hands off" approach is occasional pronouncements that broadcasters must warn the public about programming that may frighten listeners. The commission told a Rhode Island radio station in 1975 that it should have advised listeners periodically that a broadcast of H. G. Wells's *War of the Worlds* was not a news report of an invasion by creatures from space. Although the station alerted public officials and broadcast occasional warnings, several listeners were frightened and angry. The FCC told the licensee that the only way to sufficiently ensure that the public would not be alarmed "would be an introductory statement repeated at frequent intervals throughout the program."[215]

The FCC has been reluctant to rule in favor of complaints about violence in broadcast programming.[216] However, in 1989, both houses of Congress passed bills designed to reduce depictions of violence on television. The bills would exempt representatives of the broadcast, cable, and film industries from antitrust action when they meet to discuss reductions in violent programming.[217]

In the 1980's the commission deleted several minor programming policies it no longer believed to be necessary. These included a policy requiring licensees to report the scientific sampling techniques for public opinion polls. The commission also withdrew an expression of "concern" regarding the broadcast of astrological material.[218]

A few other program-related requirements are still mandated by the 1934 Communications Act. By statute, everyone is prohibited from using broadcasting or any

---

[213]WPIX, Inc., 68 F.C.C.2d 381, 43 P & F Rad. Reg.2d 278 (1978).

[214]Star Stations of Indiana, 51 F.C.C.2d 95, 32 P & F Rad. Reg.2d 1151 (1975).

[215]Capital Cities Communications, Inc., 54 F.C.C.2d 1035, 1037, 34 P & F Rad. Reg.2d 1016, 1019 (1975).

[216]Report on the Broadcast of Violent, Indecent, and Obscene Material, 51 F.C.C.2d 418, 32 P & F Rad. Reg.2d 1367 (1975).

[217]*E.g.,* "Congress Returns to Full Fifth Estate Plate," *Broadcasting,* Aug. 14, 1989, at 31.

[218]Unnecessary Broadcast Regulation, 54 P & F Rad. Reg.2d 1043, 1051–52, 1058 (1983).

other form of electronic communication for fraud, the obtaining of money through false pretenses. Violators can be punished by a $1,000 fine and up to five years imprisonment.[219]

In May 1988, the FCC warned broadcasters to adhere to the provisions of the Communications Act banning payola, under-the-table payment to disc jockeys to play particular records.[220] Also illegal is plugola, a secret payment for the promotion of a product or service during broadcast programming; for example, money paid to ensure that viewers see a particular brand of soft-drink when the stars of a show stop at a drink machine. The Communications Act prohibits anyone from offering or accepting money to air programming without the knowledge of a station manager or owner. The statute requires stations to disclose any payments they receive to broadcast specific program content. Violators can be jailed up to a year and fined up to $10,000.[221]

Anyone caught deceiving the public in a quiz show can also be jailed up to a year and fined up to $10,000. The 1934 Communications Act prohibits the rigging of contests based on knowledge or skill through secret help.[222]

SUMMARY

Federal law regulates the broadcast of obscene, indecent, and profane programming. Broadcasters can only be prosecuted for obscenity if programming meets the standards set by the U.S. Supreme Court in *Miller v. California*. The regulation of indecent and profane programming is unique to broadcasting. Broadcasters are seldom punished for airing *profane* language. *Indecency* depicts or describes sexual or excretory activities or organs in a manner patently offensive to the community standards for broadcasting. The FCC only takes action against indecent programming if it is broadcast at a time when children could reasonably be expected to be in the audience.

The U.S. Supreme Court, in *FCC v. Pacifica Foundation*, said the regulation of indecency was constitutional. Although the FCC did not punish a broadcaster for indecency for more than a decade after *Pacifica*, it began to enforce its indecency prohibition in 1987, targeting bawdy humor, sexually explicit double entendre, and detailed descriptions of sexual activity. While the FCC had permitted indecent programming at night, when children were least likely to be listening, Congress passed a bill banning indecency completely. Enforcement of the law has been enjoined until a federal appeals court rules on its constitutionality.

The FCC is reluctant to regulate children's programming and penalize stations for news distortion and news staging. The commission has eliminated most of its advertising regulations. It has also refused to regulate radio station formats and violent programming.

An exception to the FCC's recent deregulation is the prime-time access rule, which limits the amount of commercial television network programming during the early evening hours in major markets.

---

[219]18 U.S.C. sec. 1343 (1988).
[220]Commission Warns Licensees about Payola and Undisclosed Promotion, 64 P & F Rad. Reg.2d 1338 (1988).
[221]47 U.S.C. secs. 317, 507 (1982).
[222]47 U.S.C. sec. 318 (1982).

Noncommercial Broadcasting

So far, the discussion of broadcast regulation has focused on commercial radio and television. Noncommercial broadcast stations also must comply with content regulations such as the equal opportunities rule, the access requirement for federal political candidates, the personal attack rule, and the statute banning indecent and obscene programming. The fact that most noncommercial broadcast stations receive federal funding raises additional issues. Federally funded programming must, by law, be "objective." In addition, noncommercial stations are forbidden to accept advertising. Further, courts have had to protect noncommercial licensees from government attempts to limit their programming discretion.

The federal government first set aside spectrum space for educational broadcasting in 1939. However, it was 1962 before the federal government subsidized noncommercial, educational broadcasting. In 1967, a nonprofit corporation, the Corporation for Public Broadcasting (CPB), was established to dispense federal funds to noncommercial television and radio stations. In the Public Broadcasting Act of 1967, Congress instructed the CPB to help develop quality and diversity in educational broadcasting with "strict adherence to objectivity and balance in all programs . . . of a controversial nature."[223]

In 1976, a federal appeals court said, however, that no government agency, including the FCC, could tell the CPB that its programming was not objective.[224] The U.S. Court of Appeals for the D.C. Circuit upheld an FCC decision that the commission had no authority to enforce the statutory requirement that programming funded by the CPB be objective. Therefore, the FCC refused to act on the petition of a politically conservative citizen group, Accuracy in Media, Inc. (AIM), when AIM complained that two programs funded by the CPB violated the "objectivity and balance" standard. AIM said a program called "Justice?," which examined the American judicial system from a black perspective, was a one-sided and false presentation of controversial black prisoners Angela Davis and the Soledad Brothers. AIM also objected to a second program, "the three r's . . . and sex education," because of its portrayal of opponents to sex education.[225] The D.C. Circuit, upholding the FCC's understanding of the Public Broadcasting Act, denied AIM's petition to the court for review.

The D.C. Circuit said that in order to avoid politicizing public broadcasting the Public Broadcasting Act prohibited any U.S. official or agency from exercising control over the CPB. However, the court noted, Congress could use its funding and oversight functions to protest CPB actions. The court said the combination of public accountability through Congress and protection from programming interference by other governmental agencies struck an appropriate balance between the First Amendment rights of the broadcast journalist and the concerns of the viewing public.

Editorializing The same Public Broadcasting Act that prohibits officials from interfering in CPB programming decisions also bans noncommercial public broadcasting

---

[223]47 U.S.C. sec. 396 (g) (1) (A) (1982).
[224]Accuracy in Media, Inc. v. FCC, 521 F.2d 288, 296 (D.C. Cir. 1975), *cert. denied*, 425 U.S. 934 (1976).
[225]Accuracy in Media, Inc., 39 F.C.C.2d 416, 26 P & F Rad. Reg.2d 687, *reconsideration denied*, 43 F.C.C.2d 851, 28 P & F Rad. Reg.2d 1239 (1973).

stations from supporting or opposing individual political candidates.[226] In addition, the act originally banned editorializing on noncommercial stations receiving government funding. However, in 1984, the Supreme Court, in a 5–4 vote, agreed that the ban on editorializing violated the First Amendment.

The constitutionality of the ban on editorializing had been challenged by the League of Women Voters, California Representative Henry Waxman, and the Pacifica Foundation, the same organization that defended the radio broadcast of George Carlin's ''Filthy Words.'' Justice Brennan, writing the opinion of the Court, said program regulations such as the fairness doctrine were constitutional because they were designed to promote the discussion of public issues. In contrast, Brennan said, the ban on editorializing restricted the very kind of political and social commentary the First Amendment was designed to encourage.[227]

Brennan rejected the argument that the government might control, or be perceived to control, the content of editorials on public broadcast stations through its funding and oversight of public broadcasting. Brennan said that although public broadcasters receive federal funds, they are insulated from government influence. The CPB is governed by a bipartisan structure and required to be balanced and objective when dispersing funds, Brennan noted. In addition, he said, the CPB itself is insulated because the Public Broadcasting Act prohibits official coercion.

However, Brennan said, even if improper government influence on editorials is a real threat, the total ban on editorializing was broader than necessary. Brennan said, for example, that those who want a complete ban have never explained how an editorial ''urging improvements in a town's parks or museums will so infuriate Congress or other federal officials that the future of public broadcasting will be imperiled unless such editorials are suppressed.''[228]

Program Choices   Not only have the courts protected the right of public television licensees to editorialize, but they also have protected the discretion of public broadcasters to choose which programs should be aired. Several stations were challenged by viewers when they refused in 1980 to broadcast ''Death of a Princess,'' a controversial dramatization of the execution of a Saudi Arabian princess for adultery. Saudi Arabia objected to the show, and many U.S. citizens argued that the program could increase tension in the Middle East and endanger the lives of Americans working there. However, some viewers argued that government-operated television stations were public forums that could not deny access to scheduled ''speakers'' such as the producers of ''Death of a Princess.'' Viewers who wanted the program broadcast contended that the First Amendment prohibited public television stations from canceling a program because of its political content.

A federal appeals court said that publicly funded television stations did not violate the First Amendment right of viewers by refusing to carry ''Death of a Princess.''[229] In reviewing conflicting decisions from federal district courts, the U.S. Court of Appeals for the Fifth Circuit said that noncommercial broadcast stations

---

[226]47 U.S.C.A. sec. 399 (Supp. 1990).

[227]FCC v. League of Women Voters of Cal, 468 U.S. 364, 399, 10 Media L. Rep. 1937, 1953 (1984).

[228]*Id*. at 393, 10 Media L. Rep. at 1950.

[229]Muir v. Alabama Educ. Television Comm'n, 688 F.2d 1033, 8 Media L. Rep. 2305 (5th Cir. 1981) (*en banc*).

operated by the University of Houston and the Alabama Educational Television Commission had the editorial freedom to determine which shows to air.

First, the court said, Congress attempted to reconcile the First Amendment interests of the public and government broadcast licensees in the 1934 Communications Act. The Fifth Circuit said Congress tried to protect the right of the public to receive ideas by requiring that broadcast licensees serve the public interest. Congress protected the First Amendment interests of broadcasters, the court said, by giving them substantial journalistic discretion rather than requiring that they give airtime to anyone who wanted to talk about public issues. Under the 1934 Communications Act, noncommercial broadcasters are as free to decide what programming to carry as commercial broadcasters, the court said.

If public broadcast stations are not required by statute to provide access time to viewers, the Fifth Circuit said, neither are broadcasters required by the First Amendment to give up some of their journalistic discretion. The court said that public broadcast stations are not, like sidewalks, public forums under the First Amendment where government cannot control speech. Public broadcast stations are not public forums since, by congressional design and traditional use, station programming is controlled by station management rather than by viewers, the court explained. Public television stations were established for viewers to watch, the Fifth Circuit added, and not for viewers to schedule programming. Therefore, since public broadcast stations are not public forums, viewers have no First Amendment right to compel the broadcast of any particular program, the court said.

Neither did the Fifth Circuit believe that state employees operating public television stations engaged in unconstitutional governmental censorship when they canceled scheduled programs. The First Amendment, the court said, does not prohibit government from exercising editorial decision making over a medium of expression that it controls. The court said that broadcasters inevitably have to make subjective decisions about which programming is in the public interest. Canceling a scheduled program, like scheduling one in the first place, involves the same kind of editorial process. Deciding which programs to broadcast is a job for broadcasters rather than the courts, the court said.

Advertising Although noncommercial public stations control their programming content, they are prohibited from accepting advertising. Public broadcasting is both nonprofit and noncommercial. Public broadcasters cannot be paid for airing promotional announcements for profit-making organizations. However, they can air acknowledgments of contributions as long as the announcements do not interrupt programming. The announcements can include a company's logo and address and a nonpromotional description of the services or products the company offers.[230]

During the 1980s the federal government substantially reduced its spending for public broadcasting. In order to compensate, Congress and the FCC tried to locate nongovernmental funding that would retain the noncommercial status of public broadcast stations.[231] The commission therefore authorized public broadcast licensees to charge for broadcasting the announcements of nonprofit organizations. It

[230]47 C.F.R. secs. 73.503 (d), 73.621 (e) (1989).

[231]_See generally_ Commission Policy Concerning Noncommercial Nature of Educ. Broadcast Stations, 90 F.C.C.2d 895, 51 P & F Rad. Reg.2d 1567 (1982).

also said that public broadcasting stations could carry **teletext**, explained later in the chapter, on a for-profit basis.[232]

Low-Power Television (LPTV)

Low-power television, one of the new communications media most likely to survive in the 1990s, is regulated much like broadcasting but has been exempted from some of the programming requirements.

The name *low-power television* effectively describes the technology. Low-power television employs a standard, but weak, over-the-air broadcast transmitter. A low-power transmitter can broadcast from 10 to 15 miles, depending on its power and the terrain. Typical full-power television transmitters reach 50 to 70 miles.

The FCC has licensed low-power broadcast transmitters since 1956 but did not allow the licensees to originate programming. LPTV transmitters were used primarily to retransmit television signals to rural areas that would otherwise receive poor reception. In 1982, the FCC eliminated the ban on programming origination and invited applications for additional licenses. The FCC hoped low-power television would provide service to both small communities and special-interest groups in large communities not served by stations appealing to large audiences.[233]

In 1990, more than 750 LPTV stations were on the air, and construction permits had been granted for another 1,700.[234] LPTV operators may provide locally originated programming or offer programs provided by educational institutions, syndicators, satellites, PBS, or the national networks. They can provide specialized programming for minorities, offer subscription television in areas not wired for cable, or experiment with various forms of advertising .

To encourage a variety of programming on low-power stations, the FCC has minimized regulation. The commission does not require LPTV operators to offer programming to meet community needs as full-power broadcast licensees are required to do. The rules governing equal opportunities, personal attack, and political editorials apply only to programming originated by the LPTV licensee, and not to programming provided from other sources. LPTV must abide by the restrictions imposed on indecent, obscene, and profane programming.

SUMMARY

Noncommercial broadcast licensees must comply with the same broadcasting regulations imposed on commercial broadcasters. However, the Public Broadcasting Act of 1967 prohibits any government agency, including the FCC, from exercising control over the program decisions of the Corporation for Public Broadcasting. Public broadcasters cannot support or oppose political candidates, but they can editorialize. At least one federal appellate court has said that noncommercial broadcast

---

[232]47 C.F.R. sec. 73.621(f) (1989).
[233]Low Power Television, 51 P & F Rad. Reg.2d 476 (1982).
[234]"For the Record: Summary of Broadcasting and Cable," *Broadcasting*, July 2, 1990, at 61.

licensees have the same freedom to make programming decisions as commercial licensees. Public broadcasters cannot receive funds for promoting commercial products.

The FCC has authorized low-power television licensees to originate programming. The commission has imposed limited programming regulations, hoping that LPTV can increase local programming and serve areas not receiving standard commercial broadcast signals.

CABLE

In 1984, Congress passed the Cable Communications Policy Act, providing for the first time a cohesive and comprehensive regulatory structure for cable television. Under a plan that may be adjusted in the early 1990s, the Cable Act allows local governments to agree to contracts with cable systems within restrictions established by Congress and the FCC.

Before the passage of the 1984 Cable Act, the 20 years of cable television regulation was marked by uncertainty and inconsistency. The FCC, local governments, and the courts fought over the authority to regulate cable, the kinds of programming required on cable, public and governmental access to cable channels, and copyright issues. Government policy hindered rather than aided the development of cable.

As might be expected, the 1984 act did not settle all the controversies surrounding regulation of cable systems. While the act fostered a fiscally healthy industry, boasting more than 50 million subscribers in 1989, the statute also permitted increased cable rates and growing cable control over programming that has angered city officials, media competitors, and consumers. Organizations including the National League of Cities, the Consumer Federation of America, and the National Association of Broadcasters have asked Congress for significant increases in regulation of cable. However, in 1990, the FCC issued a report to Congress encouraging relatively modest changes in the 1984 act that would increase competition for cable systems both from other cable operators and other communications media.[235]

So far, courts are divided over the constitutionality of the 1984 Cable Act and other current regulatory practices. The courts have not determined the extent of government regulation of cable programming that can be tolerated under the First Amendment.

The relationship between cable and broadcasting has been at the center of the 30-year-old battle over how cable ought to be regulated.

Early Regulation

Cable television began in the late 1940s as a way to extend early television service to households out of range of a broadcast signal. One of the first cable systems was

---

[235] *In re* Competition, Rate Deregulation and the Commission's Policies Relating to the Provision of Cable Service, 1990 FCC Lexis 4103.

built by an entrepreneur trying to sell television sets in the mountains of Pennsylvania.[236] Where television reception was poor, few people bought sets until businesses erected antennas on mountain ridges and strung cable into private homes. Such community antenna television systems (CATV) pleased both viewers who received improved reception and broadcasters who reached a larger audience.

By 1961, there were 700 community antenna TV systems.[237] CATV, in addition to serving areas without television, began to be built in communities being served directly by broadcast stations. CATV systems imported signals from distant television stations and, it was charged, refused to transmit the signals from local stations. Regulation began in a piecemeal fashion. At first, some local governments granted permits but the FCC chose not to regulate CATV. Eventually, as a result of broadcast industry pressure, the FCC began regulating cable.

Cable television raised new regulatory issues. Cable signals are sent to homes primarily through a coaxial cable containing wire capable of transmitting several communications services. The cable is installed underground or strung on telephone poles. Because cable television signals are not sent "over the air" through the electromagnetic spectrum, cable operators are not required to obtain broadcast licenses. But cable television affects the livelihood of over-the-air television licensees because cable carries video programming. Cable television can extend the reach of broadcast station signals, but it also can compete with local broadcasters by offering the programming of distant stations and syndicated program suppliers. The programming competition can be particularly harmful to an over-the-air station if the local cable company refuses to carry its signal, forcing viewers to switch off the cable system in order to watch the local broadcaster.

In 1966, the FCC ruled that cable systems must carry all local broadcast signals. The commission also restricted the importation of signals from distant broadcast stations.[238] The Supreme Court upheld the FCC's actions on grounds that the regulation was necessary to ensure "fair, efficient, and equitable" broadcasting service. The Court agreed with the FCC that cable had the potential of damaging the development of local broadcasting by reducing audience and revenues of local stations. The Court ruled that, under the 1934 Communications Act, the FCC had the authority to take action "reasonably ancillary" to its responsibility to regulate broadcasting.

The FCC, having received the Court's approval to regulate, soon adopted additional programming policies for cable. In 1969, the commission required cable operators to originate their own programming as well as carry the signals of local broadcasters. The FCC imposed equal opportunities rules and the fairness doctrine on the newly required cable-originated programming.[239] The Supreme Court, in *United States v. Midwest Video Corp.*, upheld the program origination rules. The Court said that cable systems must serve local communities as much as broadcasters since cable operators had become enmeshed in broadcast service.[240]

---

[236]*E.g.*, T. Baldwin & D. McVoy, *Cable Communication* 5 (1988).
[237]Sloan Commission on Cable Communication, *On the Cable* 31 (1971).
[238]Second Report and Order in Docket Nos. 14895, 15233, and 15972, 2 F.C.C.2d 725, 6 P & F Rad. Reg.2d 1717 (1966), *aff'd sub nom.* Black Hills Video Corp. v. FCC, 359 F.2d 65 (8th Cir. 1968).
[239]*In re* CATV, 20 F.C.C.2d 201, 17 P & F Rad. Reg.2d (1969).
[240]United States v. Midwest Video Corp., 406 U.S. 649 (1972).

In 1976, the FCC required cable operators in the top 100 markets to offer at least 20 channels of programming, to set aside access channels for use by members of the public, and to provide equipment and facilities for the access channels.[241] But this time the Supreme Court, in a second *Midwest Video Corp.* decision, said that the commission had gone beyond its statutory authority. Previous regulations had fostered the goals of broadcasting as determined by Congress, said Justice Byron White, writing for the Court's majority. The access rules, however, deprived cable operators of the ability to determine what kind of programming to provide. White said the Court could not ignore that Congress had strongly disapproved of infringements on the editorial discretion "enjoyed by broadcasters and cable operators alike."[242] The Court did not decide whether the access rules violated the First Amendment.

By the time the Supreme Court had decided *Midwest Video II*, the FCC had already dropped some of its cable program requirements, including the local origination and access rules. The programming had not attracted viewers and had been a major financial burden on a struggling cable industry.

However, while the federal government was deregulating cable, local governments were increasing their control over cable systems through a complex franchising process. A local government usually selected a single cable company to serve the community, frequently after competitive bidding. The government awarded the operator a contract called a franchise, which authorized the construction and operation of a cable system. The community agreed to allow the cable company to dig up city streets and to use other government rights of way to lay cable. In exchange, cable operators promised a variety of programming and high technical quality and set aside channels for use by the public, educational institutions, or the government. Cable operators also paid a percentage of their receipts to cities as a franchise fee.

Cable operators could provide diversified programming because of the development of new satellite program services. In 1975, Home Box Office became the first programming service to use a commercial communications satellite to develop a cable programming network. HBO beamed first-run movies to cable system operators willing to set up a receiving dish and pay a fee. Soon, satellites allowed cable viewers across the country to view a large variety of programming by paying a monthly fee to a local cable company. Much of the nation could choose between the three networks, an all-day Cable News Network, several pay movie channels including HBO and Showtime, an all-sports channel, C-Span's coverage of Congress, religious channels including the one sponsored by Jim and Tammy Fay Bakker's PTL, and "superstations" including TBS of Atlanta and WGN of Chicago that provided old movies and sports.

The number of cable subscribers doubled between 1975 and 1981 and increased by another 50 percent between 1981 and 1985. New cable franchises sprang up nationwide, often after wild bidding by national cable companies. Local governments demanded and received promises for 60 channels of innovative programming, local program origination, local television studios, and two-way cable services.

---

[241]Cable Television Report and Order, 36 F.C.C.2d 143, 24 P & F Rad. Reg.2d 1501 (1972), *clarified,* 59 F.C.C.2d 984, 37 P & F Rad. Reg.2d 643 (1976).

[242]FCC v. Midwest Video Corp., 440 U.S. 689, 4 Media L. Rep. 2345 (1979).

However, the promises were based on naive perceptions of public demand and overly optimistic expectations of the still developing technology. Soon, a short-lived industry boom was at least temporarily over. Cable operators could not afford to deliver on their promises. Many of the new specialized programming networks did not make enough money to survive. Very little use was made of the channels set aside for education and government.

Shortly after the cable business began to sour, the U.S. Supreme Court and the FCC clarified the limits on the power of local governments to regulate cable content. The Court, in *Capital Cities Cable, Inc. v. Crisp*, overturned an Oklahoma statute that conflicted with federal laws.[243] The Oklahoma law prohibited cable systems from carrying advertising for wine, thus forcing cable operators to edit wine commercials out of television network programming being imported into the state. However, cable system operators are prohibited from altering or modifying imported signals by FCC regulations and the federal copyright statute. In 1984, the Supreme Court said in *Crisp* that the federal laws preempted, or overrode, conflicting state and local laws. The cable operators could not delete the commercials from network programming because federal laws forbid it.

The FCC, during the same year, reminded local governments they could only regulate basic cable service, often called the first tier of service. This service, provided to all subscribers at the lowest price charged by the cable system, usually includes the signals of local network affiliates and locally required access channels. The commission said, referring to earlier decisions, that local governments could not dictate what special services, such as movie channels or additional tiers of programming, must be offered by cable operators, or what rates must be charged for those services.[244]

In the rapidly changing regulatory environment of cable in the early 1980s, both the local governments and the cable operators sought more stability and a clearer delineation of authority. At first, neither side was willing to compromise enough to allow legislation acceptable to the other. Finally, in 1984, Congress passed a bill fashioned by the cities and the cable industry.

Cable Communications Policy Act of 1984

The Cable Communications Policy Act of 1984 became the first cable statute adopted by Congress. The law provides for community regulation of cable limited by federal oversight. Communities cannot regulate programming content except in the case of obscenity. However, they can require cable operators to provide access channels. The constitutionality of the act had not been settled by the courts by mid-1990.

Regulatory Framework The 1984 Cable Act incorporates cable regulation into the 1934 Communications Act and gives the FCC restricted authority over the technology.[245] The law authorizes cities to regulate cable through the franchise process.

The Cable Act defines cable to mean one-way video programming and other ser-

---

[243]467 U.S. 691, 10 Media L. Rep. 1873 (1984).

[244]*E.g.*, *In re* Community Cable TV, Inc., 95 F.C.C.2d 1204, 54 P & F Rad. Reg.2d 1351 (1983), *reconsideration denied*, 98 F.C.C.2d 1180, 56 P & F Rad. Reg.2d 735 (1984).

[245]47 U.S.C. sec. 521 (Supp. V 1988).

vices selected by a subscriber. The definition includes pay-per-view television, the one-way transmission of video games, teletext, and **videotex** informational services.[246] Teletext and videotex, which provide data on television or computer screens, are discussed later in the chapter. Cable television does not include two-way communications services such as computerized shopping or banking.

The 1984 cable law allows local governments to determine the number of cable systems they will license. Although the First Amendment prohibits cities from deciding one person can publish a newspaper and another cannot, the 1984 Cable Act permits a city to grant a cable franchise to only one company and to reject other applicants. The 1984 act assumes that the Constitution permits greater regulation of cable television than of the print media because, in part, cable systems must use public rights of way to lay the cable. In addition, it is contended, cable may be regulated because it is a natural monopoly—that is, no more than one cable system can survive in one service area. Continued competition is not economically feasible, it is said, because of the high cost of cable installation and the limited number of potential subscribers.

The 1984 Cable Act specifies that local television stations and telephone companies cannot own cable systems within their service areas, but that local newspapers can.[247] States or cities may operate cable systems, but they cannot control the editorial content.[248]

Constitutionality of the Franchising Process
In mid-1990, the U.S. Supreme Court had not yet ruled on the constitutionality of cable franchising. However, in 1986, the Supreme Court said that cable operators "plainly" had First Amendment interests that might limit the franchise requirements imposed by cities on cable systems.

In *Los Angeles v. Preferred Communications, Inc.*, the Supreme Court said that a suit filed by Preferred Communications against the city of Los Angeles should not be dismissed by the courts.[249] Preferred claimed Los Angeles violated the First Amendment when the city denied the company a cable franchise. Los Angeles said it did not violate the Constitution when it selected only one company to operate a cable system in one area of the city. The Supreme Court, in the 1986 *Preferred* decision, refused to resolve the constitutional argument because it said it needed more information about cable operations before determining whether cities were justified in approving only one cable system. The Court sent the case back to a federal district court in California for a trial, where facts about cable systems could be offered as evidence in the case.

Los Angeles had refused to award Preferred a cable license because the company had not participated in an auction for the single cable franchise in the south central area of the city. The city said that the number of cable franchises had to be limited in order to minimize the demands on public property. The city said that cable wires

---

[246] 47 U.S.C. sec. 522 (5) (Supp. V 1988).
[247] 47 U.S.C. sec. 533 (a), (b) (2), (d) (Supp. V 1988).
[248] 47 U.S.C. sec. 533 (e) (Supp. V 1988).
[249] 476 U.S. 488, 12 Media L. Rep. 2244 (1986).

constituted "a permanent visual blight" and the installation and repair of cable subjected the city to "traffic delays and hazards and esthetic unsightliness."

Preferred argued, on the other hand, that the city violated the company's First Amendment rights by prohibiting it from having a voice in south central Los Angeles. Preferred contended that the public demand for cable service and the space on the utility poles could accommodate more than one cable company. The U.S. District Court for the Middle District of California dismissed Preferred's claims. However, the U.S. Court of Appeals for the Ninth Circuit said the case should be tried. The Ninth Circuit said the city had violated the First Amendment by refusing to issue more than one cable franchise if there was adequate physical and economic capacity.[250]

When the case was appealed to the Supreme Court, the justices said they would not decide the First Amendment question in *Preferred* until they knew, for example, more about the city's use of the utility poles and Preferred's plans for installing and maintaining cable. Justice William Rehnquist, writing for a unanimous Supreme Court, said the values of speech must be balanced against other social interests. He said cable "partakes of some of the aspects of speech and the communication of ideas as do the traditional enterprises of newspaper and book publishers, public speakers and pamphleteers." He said that Preferred wanted "to communicate messages on a wide variety of topics and in a wide variety of formats." However, Rehnquist said, not all speech was "equally permissible in all places and at all times."[251]

After the Supreme Court's decision, the trial court reconsidered *Preferred* and held in two separate opinions in 1990 that the decision by Los Angeles to license only one cable company violated the First Amendment. The city had conceded to the trial judge that the utility poles could accommodate a second cable. Although the city continued to argue that the disruption of city streets and the creation of traffic hazards justified a limitation on the number of cable companies in one area, Judge Consuelo Marshall disagreed. Judge Marshall said the city of Los Angeles had not convinced her the transportation problems were sufficient to outweigh the risks to the free speech right of potential cable operators. Marshall said that if city officials were allowed to choose only one of several applicants for a franchise, officials may unconstitutionally base their decision on program proposals. In addition, Marshall said, although some of the specific provisions of the Los Angeles cable franchising ordinance—such as a franchise fee—were constitutionally permissible, others—including mandated access channels—violated the First Amendment.[252] Los Angeles said it would appeal the decision.

Preferred challenged the constitutionality of the Los Angeles franchise requirements rather than the 1984 Cable Act. However, if appellate courts upheld Judge Marshall's decision, the constitutionality of at least part of the Cable Act itself would be at serious risk. In the meantime, however, the 1984 Cable Act has eliminated control by most local governments over the rates cable operators charge subscribers. It

---

[250]754 F.2d 1396 (1985).

[251]476 U.S. at 495, 12 Media L. Rep. at 2247, *quoting* Cornelius v. NAACP Legal Defense and Educ. Fund, Inc., 473 U.S. 788, 799 (1985).

[252]Preferred Communications, Inc. v. Los Angeles, 67 P & F Rad. Reg.2d 366 (1990); "L.A. Cable Fees OK'd," *Broadcasting*, Sept. 3, 1990, at 24.

also limits the size of franchise fees cities can negotiate with cable companies. It further establishes procedures to protect cable operators from arbitrary refusals by local governments to renew a franchise. Cable operators, on the other hand, are required to provide service to an entire franchise area rather than only to the most profitable neighborhoods.

Constitutionality of Cable Programming Regulation   Although the Supreme Court has not ruled on the constitutionality of the Cable Act, it has affirmed a lower court decision declaring that the regulation of indecency on cable is unconstitutional.

The Supreme Court's affirmation of a ruling that indecency cannot be barred on cable came without comment. The Court upheld decisions by both a trial court and an appellate court that the prohibition of indecency in the Utah Cable Television Programming Decency Act violated the First Amendment.[253] The Utah statute authorized fines of up to $10,000 for cable operators who provided programming that described or depicted human buttocks and genitals and female breasts. The Supreme Court, as well as the U.S. Court of Appeals for the Tenth Circuit, agreed with a district court decision that the Utah statute did not meet the constitutional requirements specified in *Miller v. California* for the regulation of obscenity. For example, the Utah act did not require that restricted material depict or describe offensive sexual conduct or that the material appeal to a "prurient interest" in sex.

Both the Tenth Circuit and the Supreme Court also upheld the district court's decision that *FCC v. Pacifica Foundation*, limiting indecent programming on over-the-air television, does not apply to cable. The district court said government cannot regulate cable as it does broadcasting because the number of cable channels is not restricted by the limits of the electromagnetic spectrum.

In addition, the district court said, cable television is not an "uninvited intruder" in the home in the same way that broadcasting is. A cable subscriber must voluntarily request and pay for the cable service. Cable viewers must pay additional fees for entertainment programming such as HBO or Showtime and can obtain lock boxes to limit the viewing of children. Program guides are generally available, suggested the court. Therefore, the court found "no uninvited intrusion" into family privacy such as when the radio listener complained about the Carlin monologue in *Pacifica*. The parent who filed the complaint in *Pacifica* did not subscribe to radio and did not pay a fee for the Carlin broadcast. No lock box existed and no program guide warned of the content of the monologue, the court said.

Further, the district court added, Utah's effort to protect children through the decency act was unconstitutionally overbroad. The state statute prohibited materials that were indecent but not obscene rather than restricting them to certain times of day, as in the case of *Pacifica*. The statute therefore prevented even consenting adults from viewing nonobscene materials.

In 1988, the Supreme Court let stand an appellate court ruling that said it was unconstitutional for the FCC to require cable operators to carry local television sta-

---

[253]Wilkinson v. Jones, 480 U.S. 926 (1987). *See also* Community Television of Utah v. Wilkinson, 611 F. Supp. 1099, 11 Media L. Rep. 2217 (D.C. Utah 1985), *aff'd sub nom.* Jones v. Wilkinson, 800 F.2d 989, 13 Media L. Rep. 1913 (10th Cir. 1986). *See also* Cruz v. Ferre, 755 F.2d 1415 (11th Cir.1985).

tions on their cable system.[254] The FCC had said that "must-carry" rules were needed to ensure that local television signals can be seen in their communities, especially where most viewers subscribe to a cable system. Cable subscribers, the commission argued, would not tune in to local over-the-air television stations unless the signals were carried on their cable system. Without must-carry, the commission said, cable operators could drop local broadcast stations. Therefore, local broadcasters would have difficulty competing in the marketplace and local broadcast service, long a priority of the commission, would be severely damaged, the FCC said.

However, the U.S. Court of Appeals for the D.C. Circuit said that the must-carry rules violated the First Amendment because the commission had not sufficiently justified the need to protect local broadcasters from cable companies. The commission had not demonstrated that cable operators would drop local stations if there were no must-carry regulations, the court said. In addition, the court added, the commission assumed, rather than proved, that television viewers subscribing to cable believe they can only watch over-the-air television through their cable system. Further, the court said, the must-carry rules were too broad, protecting local broadcasters more than necessary to ensure local broadcast service.

In contrast to the indecency and must-carry decisions, one federal appeals court has said that a city could mandate that cable systems carry locally originated programming. The U.S. Court of Appeals for the Seventh Circuit upheld a fine of $60,750 levied against three affiliated cable companies that failed to provide locally originated programming as required by their franchise with the city of Chicago. The Seventh Circuit said the city demonstrated that the local programming requirement met a substantial government interest and that the requirement was no greater than necessary to serve that interest.

The city of Chicago required cable franchise holders to provide $4\frac{1}{2}$ hours a week of cable programming produced in Chicago specifically for Chicago audiences. The three cable companies fined, known jointly as Chicago Cable TV or CCTV, instead provided programming produced by suburban affiliates that "would be interesting to" Chicago customers.

In *Chicago Cable Communications v. Chicago Cable Commission*, the Seventh Circuit said that although First Amendment interests were "plainly" at stake, cable television can be regulated more than the print media. One reason, the court said, is that cable television systems must use the public streets and rights of way. In addition, the court suggested, the expense of cable facilities creates economic constraints that limit competition much as the physical constraints of the electromagnetic spectrum limit the number of broadcasters. The Seventh Circuit said that cable,

> like other forms of the electronic media, is an economically scarce medium. Unlike the traditional forms of print media, a cable programmer enjoys a virtual monopoly over its area, without the threat of an alternative producer.[255]

---

[254]Quincy Cable TV, Inc. v. FCC, 768 F.2d 1434, 12 Media L. Rep. 1001 (D.C. Cir. 1985), *cert. denied sub nom.* National Ass'n of Broadcasters v. Quincy Cable TV, Inc., 476 U.S. 1169 (1986); Century Communications Corp. v. FCC, 835 F.2d 292, 14 Media L. Rep. 2049 (D.C. Cir. 1987), *cert. denied sub nom.* Office of Communication of the United Church of Christ v. FCC, 486 U.S. 1032 (1988).

[255]Chicago Cable Communications v. Chicago Cable Comm'n, 879 F.2d 1540 (1989), *cert. denied*, 110 S. Ct. 839 (1990).

Therefore, the court continued, local governments, representing cable customers, are "duty-bound" to ensure that the few cable operators use their franchise optimally.

The Seventh Circuit accepted arguments by the city of Chicago that the local cable programming requirement met substantial government interests because it improved communications between Chicago citizens and their government and provided jobs for Chicago citizens, particularly minorities. Furthermore, the court said that Chicago's local programming requirements are "no greater" than necessary to further the governmental interests because the city only requires "a few hours a week" of local cable programming. In addition, the court said, the cable companies are not required to provide "any specific program, kind of show, or editorial viewpoint." The cable companies have "full discretion" over what they provide as long as the programs are geared to Chicago, the court said.

Program Regulation in the Cable Act   The 1984 Cable Act protects programming requirements of cable franchise agreements in effect when the statute was passed.[256] However, the law states that local governments cannot in the future regulate programming services except to require access channels and prohibit obscenity.[257]

Access   Congress wrote two access provisions into the Cable Communications Policy Act, making cable television the only mass medium required to provide access to its facilities by any member of the public.

First, the Cable Act allows local governments to require cable systems to set aside channels for "public, educational or governmental use." During the franchising process, communities can establish the rules and procedures for the use of the so-called PEG access channels. Congress intended that local governments control the content of governmental access channels that might air city council meetings or court sessions but not the public access channels used by private individuals and community groups.[258]

In addition to access channels for public, educational, or governmental use, the cable law requires that larger cable systems make channels available to others on a commercial or "leased" basis. Under the Cable Act, cable systems of more than 35 channels are required to designate for leased access up to 15 percent of their channel capacity. Smaller cable systems have no leased access requirements.[259] Cable operators are allowed to use the channels dedicated for PEG or leased access until someone wants to use them for the designated purpose.

While channels set aside for PEG access are frequently used, channels reserved for leased access are used less often. The leased access channels were supposed to increase program diversity. Leased channels were to operate like telephone lines by allowing anyone who can afford to pay to deliver a message over a cable channel. Many politicians and consumer advocates argued that cable system owners should not have control over every channel on their system. However, many observers have

[256]47 U.S.C. sec. 544 (c) (Supp. V 1988). *See also* Cox Cable, Inc. v. City of New Orleans, 594 F. Supp. 1452 (E.D. La. 1984).
[257]47 U.S.C. 544 (a), (b), (d) (1) (Supp. V 1988).
[258]47 U.S.C. 531 (e) (Supp. V 1988).
[259]47 U.S.C. 532 (b) (1) (D) (Supp. V 1988).

said, the leased access section of the Cable Act allowed cable operators to frustrate access by establishing unreasonable conditions for channel use. In addition, many said, the provisions designed to enforce the access requirements were too cumbersome to be helpful to those who wanted airtime.

The Cable Act allows state and local governments to prohibit the use of leased channels for obscene, lewd, lascivious, filthy, or indecent programming. Fighting words and expression presenting clear and present danger to public order can probably be prohibited as well.[260]

The Cable Act protects cable operators from liability for obscenity, incitement to violence, defamation, invasion of privacy, false or misleading advertising, and the violation of "other similar laws" during programming on any of the access channels.[261] When channels are being used to meet any access requirements, cable operators cannot exercise editorial control except to censor obscene programming.[262] In 1989, a federal judge in Missouri refused to dismiss a complaint that the Ku Klux Klan had been unconstitutionally prevented from using the Kansas City access channel.[263] The Klan accused the city of violating both the First Amendment and the 1984 Cable Act. The Klan contended the city and the local cable company, in order to exclude Klan programming, illegally eliminated the access channel and substituted a channel with programming controlled by the cable operator. City officials and the cable company agreed to restore the access channel when the judge refused to dismiss the Klan's case.[264]

Obscenity and Indecency The control of obscene and indecent programming on cable was a serious concern for the authors of the 1984 Cable Act. The law makes it a crime to transmit obscenity over cable. Anyone found guilty can be fined up to $10,000 and jailed for up to two years.[265] In addition, obscene programming can be prohibited by state law or local franchise agreements.[266] Further, cable operators are required to sell or lease "lock boxes" that subscribers can use to bar the viewing of a channel. Legislators said the lock-box provision would allow parents to restrict the viewing of programming they considered inappropriate for their children. As discussed earlier, the federal courts have said that the banning of indecent programming on cable television violated the First Amendment.

Privacy Protection The 1984 Cable Act was intended to protect not only the sensibilities of cable viewers but also their privacy. The statute protects the privacy of cable subscribers by limiting the collection and dissemination of information about their viewing habits. Cable operators can only collect information about individual

---

[260]C. Ferris, F. Lloyd & T. Casey, 1 *Cable Television Law; Special Supplement—Cable Communications Policy Act of 1984* para. 1.02[1][6], at 5–6; para. 10.02, at 59–60 (1989).

[261]47 U.S.C. sec. 558 (Supp. V 1988).

[262]47 U.S.C. secs. 531 (e), (c) (2), 544 (d) (Supp. V 1988).

[263]Missouri Knights of the Ku Klux Klan v. Kansas City, 723 F. Supp. 1343 (W.D. Mo. 1989).

[264]"K.C. Access Channel Restored after Klan's First Amendment Victory," *Cable T.V. & New Media*, Aug. 1989, at 3.

[265]47 U.S.C. sec. 559 (Supp. V 1988).

[266]47 U.S.C. sec. 544 (d) (1), (d) (2) (A) (Supp. V 1988).

subscribers necessary to provide video services, to bill for the services, or to detect unauthorized reception. The law does not restrict collecting or disclosing aggregate data about customer viewing habits that do not identify individual subscribers.

The law not only limits the information cable companies may collect about subscribers but also requires cable companies to tell individual subscribers what information about them the company collects. Cable operators must disclose the kind of information collected, the intended use of the data, the length of time the information will be kept, and the nature of any disclosure. Subscribers must be advised of their rights to see information about themselves.

Cable operators can only disclose information about a subscriber to a law enforcement officer or other government official if ordered to by a court. Officials seeking information about an individual's viewing habits must first demonstrate to a court that the subscriber is suspected of a crime. The subscriber must then be given an opportunity to object to the disclosure. Subscribers can sue for damages for violations of their privacy under the Cable Act.

One of the few known threats to subscriber privacy occurred before the Cable Act was passed. A movie theater proprietor being prosecuted for showing a movie alleged to be obscene tried unsuccessfully to subpoena a list of cable subscribers who watched the movie via cable. The theater owner contended the list of Columbus, Ohio, cable viewers would allow him to demonstrate the kinds of sexual material acceptable to the average person in the community. The supervising judge issued a subpoena for an aggregate listing of the number of cable subscribers who had watched the movie.[267]

The Cable Act also allows states and cities to enact and enforce privacy protection for subscribers.[268] States that have done so include California, Connecticut, Illinois, Minnesota, New York, Rhode Island, and Wisconsin.[269] Several cities have as well. Individual cable companies and industry organizations also have adopted privacy codes. In addition, many companies have programmed computers to safeguard individualized information.

Other Cable Programming Regulation   Cable operators have not been held responsible for ensuring that programming supplied by others meets broadcast regulations such as those affecting political candidates and indecency. The FCC does not hold cable operators responsible for programming originally provided by over-the-air broadcasters, who are licensed by the commission. Local over-the-air stations and the networks, through the stations they own, are held accountable for the programming they originate. The FCC has not said whether cable operators are responsible for programming provided by the movie channels or the cable networks, which are not licensed by the commission.

The 1984 Cable Act prohibits the FCC from adopting new "requirements regarding the provision or content of cable services."[270] However, programming originated by a cable system must comply with indecency regulation, the equal opportu-

[267] J. Goodale, *All About Cable* (L.J. Seminars-Press) para. 6.07[1], at 6–72 (1986).
[268] 47 U.S.C. sec. 551 (Supp. V 1988).
[269] *E.g.,* C. Ferris, F. Lloyd & T. Casey, 2 *Cable Television Law* para. 17A.07[2], at 17A–20.1 (Oct. 1989).
[270] 47 U.S.C. sec. 544 (f) (Supp. V 1990).

nities rule for political candidates, and the personal attack and political editorializing rules.[271] Legal authorities question whether cable operators must adhere to the requirement that broadcasters provide a reasonable amount of time to political candidates for federal office.[272]

Although cable operators can decide which network shows they want to carry, they cannot delete selected unwanted material, including advertising, from the programs they run.[273] Programs that are locally originated on cable systems must include identification of the sponsors of advertisements.[274] Cable operators must obey federal lottery statutes, as discussed in the advertising chapter. Cable systems are prohibited from carrying cigarette advertising.[275]

Network Nonduplication Rules A few FCC programming rules are intended to protect local over-the-air broadcast stations from the competition of cable systems. One set of regulations, the complicated network "nonduplication" rules, bars cable operators from duplicating a local station's programs by carrying the same programs broadcast by a television station in a distant city. Under the nonduplication rules, a cable system may not import a program such as "LA Law" from a distant city if the local network affiliate carries the program. The nonduplication rules, also called "network exclusivity" rules, protect local broadcasters from split audiences that would lower ratings and thus lower advertising income.

Since the 1970s, the nonduplication rules, which contain several exceptions,[276] have applied only when the "distant signals" on cable duplicated programs broadcast at the same time on local stations. Beginning in 1990, however, the FCC extended the network nonduplication rules to apply not only to a "distant signal" duplicating local station programming at the same time, but also to "distant signals" that duplicate a program offered by local affiliates at any time.[277] The FCC has said that cable systems can "black out" the imported signal duplicating the local signal, carry a substitute, or carry the local station's signal on both its channel and that of the "distant signal."

Syndicated Exclusivity In addition to strengthening the network nonduplication rules in 1990, the FCC reinstated rules that can require cable systems to block out, or substitute for, syndicated programming that duplicates the programming of local over-the-air broadcasters.[278] Since January 1990, over-the-air broadcasters can purchase exclusive local rights to syndicated television programs such as "M.A.S.H." and "Wheel of Fortune." Syndicated exclusivity prohibits cable systems as well as other local broadcast stations from carrying the same program. Cable systems with fewer than 1,000 subscribers, about half of the total number of systems, are exempt from the new rules.

---

[271]47 U.S.C. sec. 315 (c) (1982); 47 C.F.R. sec. 76.205, 76.209 (1990).

[272]*E.g.,* C. Ferris, F. Lloyd & T. Casey, 1 *Cable Television Law* para. 8.07[2], at 8–15–16 (1989).

[273]47 C.F.R. sec 76.55 (b) (1990).

[274]47 C.F.R. sec. 76.221 (1989).

[275]15 U.S.C. sec. 1335 (1982).

[276]47 C.F.R. sec. 76.92 (1990).

[277]Amendment of Parts 73 and 76 of the Commission's Rules Relating to Program Exclusivity in the Cable and Broadcast Industries, Report and Order, 3 FCC Rcd. 5299, 64 P & F Rad. Reg.2d 1818 (1988), *clarified,* Memorandum Opinion and Order, 4 FCC Rcd. 2711, 66 P & F Rad. Reg.2d (1989).

[278]*Id.*

The so-called syndicated exclusivity rules allow a local television station to buy rights to popular programs and block the local cable system from carrying the program on other channels. Before the new rule, the reruns of many popular syndicated programs were often available on several channels at different times of the day in many markets, thus dividing the viewership and the advertising revenue.

The commission, by adopting the program exclusivity rules for broadcasters, reinstated a policy eliminated in 1980. At the time, the commission did not consider the cable industry a threat to traditional broadcasting. However, since 1980, the number of persons watching traditional television programming from local stations and the networks has decreased as viewers of cable services have increased. Cable advertising revenues have soared during the same time. The commission said the new rules encourage a larger variety of programming on cable and give local over-the-air broadcasters the chance to compete equally with networks and cable operators.

The syndicated exclusivity rules were upheld by the U.S. Court of Appeals for the D.C. Circuit in spite of the Cable Act's prohibition against new regulations affecting "the provision or content of cable services." The court said the ban did not prohibit what the court called "content-neutral" rules like syndicated exclusivity.[279]

Cable operators also may be required to black out the broadcast of live local sporting events if all of the tickets are not sold. The FCC has been afraid that teams might refuse to allow the broadcast of sporting events if fans stay home to watch the contests on television.[280]

SUMMARY

Cable television began as a vehicle to extend over-the-air television service into areas beyond the range of broadcast signals. The FCC soon began to regulate cable to protect local broadcasters who feared that cable's ability to bring distant signals into communities would reduce their own viewership. Some of the regulations were lifted in the 1970s after they created major financial burdens for cable operators. Other cable regulations were declared unconstitutional.

But as the FCC deregulated cable, local governments increased their regulation through franchise agreements. Local governments bargained for technical quality and programming in exchange for the right to put cable under public roads. When cable began to provide satellite programming services, competition for community franchises became fierce. However, immediate expectations for the technology were overly optimistic and new cable franchises and programming services struggled. Federal, state, and local governments continued to battle for the right to regulate cable until a compromise between cable operators and city governments resulted in the 1984 Cable Communications Policy Act.

The 1984 Cable Act authorizes local government regulation of cable within the framework of statutory limitations and FCC supervision. The act protects cable operators from arbitrary city decisions but requires them to provide comprehensive

---

[279]United Video, Inc. v. FCC, 890 F.2d 1173, 17 Media L. Rep. 1129 (1989).
[280]47 C.F.R. sec. 76.67 (1990).

community cable service. Cable systems can be required by local governments to provide access channels for public, educational, and governmental use. Larger cable operators are required to set aside channels to lease programming time to anyone who wants to pay for it. The use of cable to transmit obscenity is banned. Cable operators can only collect limited information about subscribers and must tell subscribers what is being kept.

The Cable Act authorized programming regulation imposed by the 1934 Communications Act and the FCC. The FCC requires that cable operators protect local broadcast stations from competitive network programming. The FCC also allows local broadcasters to buy exclusive rights to syndicated programming, preventing cable operators from airing the same program.

The courts have still not settled on a constitutional standard to be applied to cable television. The U.S. Supreme Court has not said how much cable regulation, particularly programming regulation, will be tolerated under the First Amendment. A few federal courts have indicated that the First Amendment rights of cable operators should be more like those of the print media rather than the broadcast media since cable is not constrained by the limits of the electromagnetic spectrum. The federal courts have invalidated both a state's attempt to ban indecent cable programming and the FCC's "must carry" rules. One federal appeals court upheld a Chicago programming requirement.

COMMON CARRIER REGULATION

Unlike broadcasters and cable operators, common carriers have no control over the messages sent through their systems. Common carriers, such as telephone and telegraph systems, are required by law to provide their facilities as a neutral conduit for information sent by others.[281] Common carriers must provide their services to anyone who can pay, without altering the content of the message sent. Traditionally, common carriers have not been allowed to transmit on their own systems messages they generated.

The telephone is the most frequently used common carrier service, and its value to public communicators is increasing. Technological improvements are expanding the potential for automated message services, teleconferencing, and enhanced mobility through cellular radio. Cellular radio is a mobile telephone service made possible by sophisticated computerized switching networks.

Restrictions on Telephone Companies

The laws prohibiting common carriers from transmitting messages they originate have been significantly relaxed in recent years. Long-distance carriers may now deliver their own messages as well as those of others. So can many local telephone companies not considered dominant in their own service areas. Only the seven major

---

[281]47 U.S.C. sec. 201 (1982).

regional Bell operating companies, commonly known as the BOCs, have been banned from providing their own information services to customers.

The BOCs, primarily responsible for local telephone service since they were split off from AT&T in 1982, want to offer revenue producing information services such as electronic yellow pages, news reports, cable television, and home banking services. They argue that if they are allowed to generate information services they will be given the incentive to develop new communications services for consumers. The mass media generally oppose allowing the BOCs to provide information services. Representatives of newspaper, broadcasting, and cable industries argue that the regional companies can abuse their monopoly power as the only companies providing local phone service. The media contend that the BOCs would subsidize their information services with the money they receive as regulated common carriers, allowing them to charge less. The BOCs would then have an unfair advantage in the marketplace, the other media argue. Newspapers also fear that services such as electronic yellow pages will substantially undercut their own classified advertising, one of their chief sources of revenue.

The BOCs, like all telephone companies, are generally prohibited by the 1984 Cable Act from owning cable companies in their service areas. In addition, the BOCs have been prohibited by the 1982 consent decree breaking up AT&T from generating information services to be delivered over phone lines. In 1987 and 1988, U.S. District Court Judge Harold H. Greene, who oversees the consent decree, refused to grant the BOCs waivers that would allow them to provide electronic publishing services. Greene argued that if the regional Bell companies were allowed to compete with other information providers, the BOCs could unfairly favor their own services. The BOCs so effectively control local telephone service, Greene said, they could use their power to give competitors unfavorable access and transmission quality.[282] However, in 1990, the U.S. Court of Appeals for the D.C. Circuit said that Greene had not used the right criteria when deciding to continue the ban on the BOC's provision of information services. The D.C. Circuit reversed Greene and told him to reconsider his opinion, using criteria different than he had used before.[283]

Even before the D.C. Circuit's opinion, Judge Greene permitted the BOCs to transmit on phone lines information services provided by other companies. In fact, in 1988, Judge Greene allowed the BOCs to provide equipment and services necessary as the link, or "gateway," between information providers and information users. The BOCs can provide electronic mail, billing, and other services as long as they do not themselves provide information or do not have a financial interest in the information.

Restrictions on Telephone Users

While the government has not allowed common carriers to edit or censor the messages they deliver, neither has the government itself generally regulated the content of messages sent by common carriers. One of the few exceptions is a ban on fraudulent communication sent by common carriers. In addition, the advertising of cigarettes,

---

[282]United States v. Western Elec. Co., 673 F. Supp. 525 (D.D.C. 1987); United States v. Western Elec. Co., 714 F. Supp. 1 (D.D.C. 1988).

[283]United States v. Western Elec. Co., 900 F.2d 283 (1990).

little cigars, and smokeless tobacco is banned on common carriers, as it is on all electronic media. However, the most controversial ban of telephone content is that of obscene "dial-a-porn."

Congress and the FCC tried several times during the 1980s to restrict the use of telephones by services providing prerecorded sexually explicit messages. Callers pay a fee that is divided between the message service and the telephone company. Parents have complained that the services are readily available to children, who may try to imitate the sexual activities described and who sometimes incur charges of thousands of dollars while listening to dial-a-porn.

In 1989, the U.S. Supreme Court said that Congress could constitutionally ban sexually explicit messages sent by telephone if the content is obscene . But, at the same time, the Court said a ban on the use of interstate telephone lines for indecent dial-a-porn violated the First Amendment.

Congress had attempted, in 1988, to eliminate the business of offering both indecent and obscene sexual messages to callers for a charge. Congress said that persons responsible for providing obscene messages could be fined up to $500,000 and spend up to two years in jail. Under the federal statute, the providers of indecent messages could be fined as much as $50,000 and jailed up to six months.[284] The statute was challenged by Sable Communications, which provides recorded dial-a-porn messages.

In *Sable Communications v. FCC,* the Supreme Court voted 6–3 to uphold the congressional ban on obscene dial-a-porn.[285] Justice Byron White, who wrote the Court's opinion, said the justices had repeatedly ruled that obscenity is not protected by the First Amendment. The Court rejected Sable's argument that Congress had created an unconstitutional national standard of obscenity by passing a federal dial-a-porn ban. Sable said the federal ban on obscene dial-a-porn violated the Court's own standard, discussed in *Miller v. California*, that materials could be judged obscene only in the context of community standards. However, Justice White said the *Miller* requirement that obscenity be determined according to community standards applies to the enforcement of all federal statutes banning obscenity. White said the Constitution allows the barring of dial-a-porn services in any community when the calls are obscene by local community standards.

Justice William J. Brennan, Jr., dissenting, argued that banning even obscene dial-a-porn is unconstitutional. Brennan, in an opinion joined by Justices Marshall and Stevens, said that *obscenity* cannot be defined so that people who create and distribute sexually oriented materials know when they are dealing with constitutionally protected speech and when they are dealing with obscene speech, which is unprotected by the First Amendment.

In contrast to the Court's ruling on obscenity, a unanimous Court in *Sable* ruled that sexually explicit phone messages that are only indecent cannot be banned but can only be constitutionally regulated. All nine justices ruled that since indecency, unlike obscenity, is constitutionally protected, Congress invalidly banned indecent dial-a-

---

[284]Child Protection and Obscenity Enforcement Act of 1988, 102 Stat. 4502, sec. 7524, enacted as Title VII, Subtitle N, Anti-Drug Abuse Act of 1988, Pub. L. 100–690 (Nov. 1988), *amending* Telephone Decency Act, Pub. L. 100–297, 102 Stat. 424 (April 1988).

[285]109 S. Ct. 2829, 16 Media L. Rep. 1961 (1989).

porn instead of only restricting access by children. Justice Byron White, in the opinion of the Court, said it was "another case of burning the house to roast the pig."

The Court rejected an argument that the Court's own opinion in *FCC v. Pacifica Foundation* provided a precedent for a ban of indecent dial-a-porn. The Court said *Pacifica* allowed the seven dirty words to be channeled but not prohibited. In addition, the Court said in *Sable*, *Pacifica* applied to over-the-air broadcasting, where persons turning on the radio or television could be "surprised" by an indecent message they might not have a "meaningful opportunity to avoid." In contrast, the court said, dial-a-porn could not be imposed on a "captive audience." Dial-a-porn, unlike over-the-air broadcasts, the Court said, requires the listener to take "affirmative steps to receive the communication," including dialing the telephone number.

The Court acknowledged that Congress has a legitimate interest in preventing children from being exposed to dial-a-porn. However, the Court said that since indecent speech is constitutionally protected, the regulation of indecent dial-a-porn must be limited so that access by children is restricted without barring access by adults.

The Court suggested that it might find constitutional a narrowly tailored restriction on indecent dial-a-porn such as one the FCC adopted in 1987. The commission, in interpreting a previous statute, had said that dial-a-porn companies would have to restrict access by children by requiring callers to use either a credit card or an access code, or by scrambling calls so that they could be heard only through a descrambling device. Although a federal appeals court in 1988 had upheld the commission's rules as constitutional, the rules could not be adequately tested because of the 1988 congressional ban on dial-a-porn, the Supreme Court said.[286]

The Court rejected the argument that it should defer to Congress, which had implied by its dial-a-porn ban that the FCC's rules would not sufficiently protect children from telephone indecency. The majority said the Court must protect the First Amendment against statutes that restricted speech more broadly than necessary.

Within six months of *Sable*, Congress enacted new legislation prohibiting dial-a-porn services from providing access to indecent messages to persons less than 18 years old or to nonconsenting adults. The new law requires adults who want to hear indecent messages to subscribe to dial-a-porn services in writing. The statute also allows dial-a-porn services to insulate themselves from prosecution by adhering to FCC procedures limiting children's access to explicit sexual messages. The FCC, under the authority of the new law, readopted the restrictions the Supreme Court had referred to in *Sable*. The commission requires dial-a-porn providers to restrict access to their services by requiring credit cards or access codes, or by scrambling their calls so that decoders are necessary.[287]

Even before the 1988 congressional ban on dial-a-porn, the FCC had the statutory authority to prosecute dial-a-porn providers allowing persons under 18 years old to use their services.[288] In 1988, the FCC fined a dial-a-porn provider for the first

---

[286]Carlin Communications, Inc. v. FCC, 837 F.2d 546 (1988).

[287]FCC, "Commission Adopts Final Rules to Regulate Indecent Communications by Telephone," News Report No. DC–1660, June 14, 1990; Regulations Concerning Indecent Communications by Telephone, 79 P & F Rad Reg.2d 3 (1990) (Notice of Proposed Rule Making). *But see* "Telephone Service," 59 U.S.L.W. 2131 (1990) and "Latest Dial-a-Porn Restrictions Too Broad to Satisfy First Amendment,". 59 U.S.L.W. 1034 (1990) (federal district courts enjoin enforcement of new dial-a-porn rules).

[288]Federal Communications Commission Authorization Act of 1983, Pub. L. No 98–214, 97 Stat. 1467 (1983).

time. Audio Enterprises, Inc., of San Jose, California, was not only fined $50,000, but the company also agreed to stop its service until it could effectively deny access by minors.[289] One woman complained to the FCC that six children, ranging from 10 to 13 years old, had made one call of 211 minutes to Audio's dial-a-porn service. Following the call, the woman's 10-year-old daughter was sexually molested by two brothers. The woman said her daughter had encouraged the boys with language the girl had heard during the call.[290]

The telephone companies are also trying to restrict dial-a-porn providers, even though the law requires phone companies to provide their facilities to any paying customer. In January 1988, AT&T stopped paying fees to sponsors of commercial pornographic messages. Some phone companies, such as Illinois Bell, refuse to bill customers for dial-it services they consider objectionable. Others, like Pacific Bell, Mountain Bell, and New York Telephone Company, allow customers to block access to dial-it services from their telephones.[291] An Arizona telephone company's ban on sexually explicit message services has been upheld in court.[292]

SUMMARY

Common carriers are licensed to provide a neutral conduit for information sent by others. Common carriers cannot discriminate in deciding whose content to disseminate. Some common carriers cannot provide their own content. The government provides little regulation of the content of messages sent by common carriers. However, it is illegal to use the telephone for obscene phone calls.

NEW COMMUNICATIONS MEDIA

Several relatively new electronic media do not fit readily into the regulatory models for broadcasting, common carrier, cable, or print. Some of the new communications media grew from recent technological developments in satellites and computer communications. Others are new uses of older technologies such as broadcasting and cable.

In the 1980s, the Federal Communications Commission minimized the regulation of the new media in order to encourage experimentation. The commission wanted the new media to succeed or fail in the marketplace on their own merits.

In the early 1990s, a few of the new communications media have begun to find a

---

[289]Audio Enterprises, Inc., 65 P & F Rad. Reg.2d 1035 (1988).

[290]Audio Enterprises, Inc., 64 P & F Rad. Reg.2d 1681 (1988).

[291]*E.g.*," 'Dial-a-Porn' Industry: Lucrative and Besieged," *New York Times*, June 24, 1989, at 7; "Moves Taken to Restrict Dial-a-Porn," *New York Times*, Jan. 19, 1988, at 11.

[292]Carlin Communications, Inc. v. Mountain States Tel. & Tel. Co., 829 F.2d 1291 (9th Cir. 1987), *cert. denied*, 485 U.S. 1029 (1988).

niche. A few are still searching, and some may not survive. Ironically, the lack of regulation probably slowed the development of some new technologies. Businesses were sometimes reluctant to invest in expensive research and equipment that could quickly be dated because the FCC had refused to set technological standards. In addition, the growth of cable occurred at about the same time many of the new media were trying to get off the ground. Cable could offer a larger variety of programming for less cost to the same viewers sought by most of the new media.

New media that provide services similar to cable television include satellite master antenna television, subscription television, satellite communications, and MDS service. New media that provide electronic publishing include teletext and videotex.

Cable Competitors

Satellite Master Antenna Television (SMATV)   Satellite Master Antenna Television (SMATV) is essentially a small cable system on private property. A cable hooked up to a satellite dish can provide both good television reception and satellite-delivered programming services for the tenants of individual apartment complexes, condominiums, and mobile-home parks.

SMATVs are among the most viable of the new communications systems. About 800,000 to one million subscribers and about 3,000 hotels use SMATV in the United States.[293] Although the $2,500–$4,000 price of large satellite dishes effectively limits SMATV to multi-unit complexes, the cost of linking all television sets in a high-rise is low compared to wiring a neighborhood or town. In addition, SMATV systems have captive customers, need very little marketing, and do not need studios.

Further, SMATV systems are substantially exempt from regulation as long as they do not lay cable across a public right of way such as a road and only serve the tenants of one building or a single-owner complex. The 1984 Cable Act exempted SMATV operators from federal cable regulation, including programming requirements.[294] The Cable Act left unaffected a 1983 FCC ruling that prohibited state and local governments from regulating SMATV.[295] SMATV systems do not have to be licensed as broadcasters since they do not use the air waves.

Subscription Television (STV)   Although subscription television is technologically possible, few over-the-air television stations provided programming on a subscription basis in the early 1990s. A discussion of STV is important primarily because of what the FCC has said about STV regulation.

Subscription television sends scrambled programs over the air to subscribers who have decoding devices attached to their television sets. STV operators must be com-

---

[293]*Channels* Field Guide 1989, at 188, *quoted in* J. Goodale, *All About Cable; Legal and Business Aspects of Cable and Pay Television* para. 5.08, at 5–15 (1989).

[294]47 U.S.C. 522 (6) (1988).

[295]C. Ferris, F. Lloyd & T. Casey, 2 *Cable Television Law* para. 21.11[1] n.6, at 21–26 (Oct.1986). *See* Earth Satellite Communications, Inc., 95 F.C.C.2d 1223, 55 P & F Rad. Reg.2d 1427 (1983), *aff'd sub nom.* New York State Comm'n on Cable Television v. FCC, 749 F.2d 804 (D.C. Cir. 1984).

mercial broadcast licensees or be leasing airtime from commercial broadcast licensees. In the 1980s, STV services charged about $20 a month for one channel of programming—often sports or movies—in the evening hours. STV operators found it difficult to compete with cable, which could offer several channels of programming at about the same cost as a subscription to one STV channel.

The FCC established subscription television as a heavily regulated experimental broadcast service in 1968. In late 1986, however, the FCC reclassified STV as a nonbroadcast technology that would not be subject to broadcast programming regulations. The commission said that although STV uses over-the-air broadcast signals, STV operators do not target their signals for a general audience.

In a decision that affects other subscription-based technologies, the FCC based its deregulation of STV on the nature of the intended audience rather than on the nature of the technology. The FCC said STV operators were not broadcasters because the term *broadcasting* in the 1934 Communications Act refers to communication to a general audience rather than to specific points of reception. STV operators, the commission said, only provide programming to subscribers in a private, contractual relationship and encrypt their programming to prevent its unauthorized use.

Because STV is not broadcasting, it is not subject to broadcast regulations such as the equal opportunities rule for political candidates. Neither, said the commission, are direct broadcast satellites (DBS), which provide direct satellite-to-home communications.[296] The commission suggested STV and DBS would be treated the same as other subscription-based media, such as SMATV and MDS service, each discussed elsewhere in the chapter. The commission's decision was upheld in June 1988 by the U.S. Court of Appeals for the District of Columbia.[297]

Satellite Communications   Satellites are positioned more than 22,000 miles above earth, rotating around earth at the same speed that the planet itself rotates. Satellites therefore keep the same position relative to earth's surface, allowing them to receive signals sent by transmitting stations on the ground and relaying the signals back to "dish" antennas.

Satellites functioning as common carriers—carrying the messages of anyone willing to pay—have been an important part of communications for several years. Satellites can be neutral conduits beaming programming and information for cable systems, broadcast networks, wire services, and newspapers. News video from around the world is seen on the evening news because of satellite delivery. The *Wall Street Journal* and *USA Today* send their newspapers' pages each day by satellite to regional printing plants across the country.

In 1982, the FCC expanded the potential use of satellites by allowing satellite owners to provide more than common carrier services.[298] Since 1982, satellite owners could provide programming themselves and could sell or lease satellite use to whomever they choose. In 1986, HBO began using satellites to deliver movies on scrambled

---

[296]Subscription Video, 62 P & F Rad. Reg.2d 389 (1987).
[297]National Ass'n of Better Broadcasting v. FCC, 849 F.2d 665 (1988).
[298]Direct Broadcast Satellites, 90 F.C.C.2d 676, 51 P & F Rad. Reg.2d 1341 (1982).

signals to individual subscribers owning the receiving dishes costing $2,500 and up. Several other cable programmers have since begun competing for home satellite subscriptions.

The FCC has said that programming sent by encrypted signals to individual subscribers by satellite, like programming delivered by STV, is not *broadcasting* as defined by the 1934 Communications Act. Satellite-delivered programming would only be classified as *broadcasting* if it sent signals to the general public on a nonsubscription basis. Therefore, programming sent by satellite to subscribers only is not subject to broadcast regulation.[299]

The FCC's current regulation for satellites would govern new high-powered satellites that could relay encrypted signals to small private satellite signal-receiving dishes. Entrepreneurs have dreamed since the early 1980s of direct broadcast satellites that would beam multichannel television services directly into homes. During the 1980s, companies believed that the cost of more than $100 million to get such a system operational could not be justified by expected revenues. However, high-powered DBS has been introduced into Japan and Europe, where mountains interfere with over-the-air broadcast signals and cable systems have not been developed. In 1990, one business consortium in the United States was promoting a 108-channel system beamed to plate-sized satellite receiving dishes costing about $300. Another company said it would launch an 80-channel service using a medium-powered satellite.

MDS Service   MDS service, more commonly known as "wireless cable," delivers the same kinds of programming as cable television but via microwave signals instead of coaxial cable. MDS service, as it is called by FCC, is generally cheaper than cable because microwave equipment is cheaper than laying cable. However, MDS service operators cannot ordinarily match the number of channels available on cable systems. In addition, MDS service operators claim that major cable program suppliers will not sell their products to wireless cable.

MDS service is most successful in major urban markets that have not been wired for cable. The Wireless Cable Association estimated in 1990 that between 20 and 30 systems were serving 300,000 subscribers. About the same time, one company served 92,000 customers in Detroit, Washington, and New York with 11-, 14-, and 16-channel systems respectively.[300] MDS operators provide programming that includes MTV, ESPN, Nickelodeon, and superstation TBS.

Wireless cable has evolved in the last decade through the combination of four separate microwave services. The FCC's name for the combination of the four, MDS service, comes from one of them, multipoint distribution service (MDS). Other than MDS, the other media that make up the MDS service are multichannel, multipoint distribution service (MMDS); instructional television fixed service (ITFS); and operational-fixed microwave service (OFS). All four use microwave signals that can be sent in all directions to special receiving antennas on the rooftops of homes, businesses, and apartment buildings. The normal transmitting range is only 15 to 25 miles and reception is only possible when an antenna is in a direct line of sight from the

---

[299]Subscription Video, 2 FCC Rcd. 1001, 62 P & F Rad. Reg.2d 389 (1987), *aff'd*, National Ass'n of Better Broadcasting v. FCC, 849 F.2d 665 (1988).

[300]"Wireless: Going Head to Headend with Conventional Cable," *Broadcasting,* Sept. 18, 1989, at 62.

transmitter. The signal can be blocked by any physical object, including a building, a hill, or even a tree.

Until recently, ITFS channels could be used only by educational institutions for instructional use. OFS has provided video programming for hotels and other businesses and local governments.

Multipoint distribution service offers two channels of programming that have been used to deliver pay movies to condominiums and apartment buildings. However, the two-channel MDS had trouble competing with multichannel cable systems for access to private homes. In an effort to provide a microwave service competitive with cable, the FCC created MMDS and gave MDS and MMDS operators the authority to use OFS and ITFS frequencies. As a result, an MDS microwave system could provide as many as 33 channels by using a combination of MDS (2 channels), MMDS (8), ITFS (20), and OFS (3).

MDS service providers can decide whether each channel will serve as a common carrier, distributing programming prepared by others, or as a vehicle for their own programming. The FCC said in 1987 that MDS service operators would be regulated as subscription services such as STV and DBS rather than as broadcasters, and therefore would not be subject to broadcast regulation such as the equal opportunities rule.[301]

Electronic Publishing

Teletext   Teletext displays information such as news, pages of catalogs, entertainment schedules, and advertising sent to a viewer through a television or a television-like delivery system such as cable, DBS, or MDS service. Teletext is sent through the vertical blanking interval (VBI), the black line that can be seen between the pictures on a television set when the picture is out of adjustment.

A broadcaster can effectively send a set of 100 to 200 pages of text at a time through the VBI portion of the broadcast signal. The pages are on a cycle that repeats every few minutes. They can be displayed on a separate channel or at the bottom of the screen. A teletext subscriber, using a special keypad and decoder attached to a television set, chooses the page desired, and it appears on the screen. Teletext is a one-way information system—that is, signals can be received, but not sent, by the consumer.

Several television stations and networks have experimented with teletext. The experiments usually include news, weather, sports, and such features as movie reviews and quizzes. Teletext is inexpensive for the originator. However, consumer use has been limited by the cost of the decoder, the failure of the FCC to set technical standards for decoders, and such technological limitations as the time it takes for the chosen page to appear.

Although teletext is sent through a broadcast signal, it does not have to comply with the federal candidate access requirement or the personal attack or political edi-

---

[301]Revisions to Part 21 of the Commission's Rules regarding the Multipoint Distribution Service, 2 FCC Rcd. 4251, 63 P & F Rad. Reg.2d 398 (1987).

torial rules. However, teletext operators must meet the requirements of the equal opportunities rule for political candidates.

The FCC had first said in 1983 that teletext would not be subject to any major broadcast programming regulation, including the equal opportunities requirements. The commission said that although teletext is sent by a broadcast signal, it does not by itself take up space on the broadcast spectrum. Broadcasters providing teletext are already required to serve the public interest through their television facilities, the commission argued. Besides, the commission said, teletext provides the kind of information and services seen in the print media rather than in the broadcast media.[302]

However, the U.S. Court of Appeals for the D.C. Circuit did not agree with the FCC's rationale. The court said that the content of teletext could be regulated because it is transmitted over broadcast frequencies that are regulated. The court said the FCC's decision that the obligation to provide equal opportunities for political candidates did not apply to teletext was "plainly at odds" with section 315 of the 1934 Communications Act. The court said reference to a candidate through words or a graphic illustration on teletext would constitute "use" of a broadcast medium under the statute.[303] However, the court upheld the FCC's decision that teletext would not be subject to the federal candidate access requirement. The court agreed that licensees could satisfy their statutory obligation to provide airtime to federal candidates on their regular television signal. The court also agreed that the FCC need not apply fairness doctrine regulations such as the political broadcast rules to teletext. The court accepted arguments that the burdens of the fairness doctrine could impede the development of the technology.

The FCC has chosen to regulate teletext as a common carrier when it provides nonbroadcast data services to businesses.

Videotex   Videotex is the least regulated of the new technologies. Videotex consists of text and graphics transmitted onto a television or computer screen over either telephone lines or a two-way cable system. Videotex systems provide a two-way link between a home terminal and the information held by a master computer. Users can call up pages of information through a keypad.

Videotex as an information system merging text and graphics has not found its niche in the marketplace, even after major experiments by two large newspaper companies, Knight-Ridder, Inc. of Miami and the Times Mirror Co. of Los Angeles. However, several major corporations are developing two-way communications systems for consumer use. Banks, telephone companies, travel agencies, financial service companies, newspapers, and retail stores are actively trying to offer so-called interactive consumer services by combining computer and electronic communications technologies. Limited consumer videotex is in use at information stations in hotels and shopping malls.

Information retrieval systems, so far the most successful linkage of computers and electronic communications, generally provide data without significant graphic

---

[302]Amendment to the Commission's Rules to Authorize the Transmission of Teletext by TV Stations, 53 P & F Rad. Reg.2d 1309 (1983), *aff'd on reconsideration*, 101 F.C.C.2d 827, 57 P & F Rad. Reg.2d 842 (1985).
[303]Telecommunications Research and Action Center v. FCC, 801 F.2d 501 (1986), *cert. denied,* 482 U.S. 919 (1987).

display. Businesses and individuals who own computers, and are willing to pay from $10 to more than $100 an hour, can access one of the more than 2,800 public data bases.[304] Several national data bases such as CompuServe and Dialog provide computerized information services on a wide variety of topics. Specialized data bases are available for such professions as law and medicine. One of the more successful services has been the Dow Jones Information Retrieval Service, providing news and financial information to more than 300,000 subscribers.

Since most videotex is transmitted over telephone lines, regulation is limited to what ordinarily applies to the uses of the telephone. Hence, by federal statute, videotex cannot carry lewd or indecent language or cigarette advertising or be used for fraudulent purposes. Otherwise, the FCC has preempted state regulation of videotex without trying to impose any content regulations of its own.[305]

The 1984 Cable Act controls videotex on cable as long as subscribers are simply seeking information. The Cable Act does not apply to such interactive services as banking and shopping. Theoretically, videotex on cable could be required to abide by political broadcast rules and existing fairness doctrine rules. However, experts argue that the FCC limitation on those regulations for teletext would also apply to videotex.[306] Statutory bans on obscenity, cigarette advertising, fraud, and information about lotteries also apply to cable videotex.

Subscribers using informational videotex are protected by the 1984 Cable Act provisions limiting the collection and dissemination of information about individual users. In addition, many state laws have privacy provisions for two-way cable. Further, key figures in the new industry have considered videotex vulnerable to privacy legislation and have therefore developed a voluntary privacy code similar to the privacy provisions in the cable law. They also have protected subscriber privacy with various encrypting mechanisms.

SUMMARY

While many of the new communications systems have not been overnight successes, several still have a chance to find their place in the market. Many of the new systems are providing services similar to cable television. Satellite master antenna television (SMATV) is a minicable system used to deliver television to apartment complexes and condominiums. Congress and the FCC have chosen not to regulate SMATV and the FCC has prohibited state and local governments from interfering in SMATV operations. Subscription television, because of its relatively low channel capacity, has had trouble competing against cable even after extensive deregulation. The FCC had said that subscription television is not a broadcast service because it

---

[304]*See generally* L. Singleton, *Telecommunications in the Information Age* (2d ed. 1986); J. Aumente, *New Electronic Pathways* (1987).

[305]Amendment of Section 64.702 of the Commission's Rules and Regulation (Final Decision), 77 F.C.C.2d 384, 47 P & F Rad. Reg.2d 669 (1980), *on reconsideration*, 84 F.C.C.2d 50, 48 P & F Rad. Reg.2d 1107 (1980) (often cited as Second Computer Inquiry), *aff'd sub nom.* Computer and Communications Indus. Ass'n v. FCC, 693 F.2d 198, 8 Media L. Rep. 2457 (D.C. Cir. 1982).

[306]Abrams & Ringel, "Content Regulation," in "Symposium; Legal Issues in Electronic Publishing," 36 *Fed. Com. L.J.* 154 (1984); C. Ferris, F. Lloyd & T. Casey, 2 *Cable Television Law* para. 22.04[3][a], at 22–12 (Sept. 1984).

targets its programming through an encrypted signal to subscribers only and not to the general public. The commission also has labeled satellite signals providing television programming as a subscription service. Satellites also act as common carriers.

MDS systems, also called wireless cable, use microwave signals to send entertainment programming to homes and businesses with special receiving antennas on rooftops. Major components of MDS service, MDS and MMDS, have been regulated as common carriers. However, the FCC has said that MDS and MMDS can also provide their own programming without being subject to broadcast programming regulations.

Teletext uses the vertical blanking interval (VBI) on a television set to transmit text into a home or business. It is being regulated as broadcast technology with major exceptions. Videotex uses telephone wires or cable to put text into homes. Depending on the technology used, it is regulated as cable or as a user of a common carrier.

APPENDIX A

THE FIRST FOURTEEN AMENDMENTS TO THE CONSTITUTION

Amendment I

Congress shall make no law respecting an establishment of religion, or prohibiting the free exercise thereof; or abridging the freedom of speech, or of the press; or the right of the people peaceably to assemble, and to petition the Government for a redress of grievances.

Amendment II

A well regulated Militia being necessary to the security of a free State, the right of the people to keep and bear Arms, shall not be infringed.

Amendment III

No Soldier shall, in time of peace be quartered in any house, without the consent of the Owner, nor in time of war, but in a manner to be prescribed by law.

Amendment IV

The right of the people to be secure in their persons, houses, papers, and effects, against unreasonable searches and seizures, shall not be violated, and no Warrants shall issue, but upon probable cause, supported by Oath or affirmation, and particularly describing the place to be searched, and the persons or things to be seized.

Amendment V

No person shall be held to answer for a capital, or otherwise infamous crime, unless on a presentment or indictment of a Grand Jury, except in cases arising in the land or naval forces, or in the Militia, when in actual service in time of War or public danger; nor shall any person be subject for the same offence to be twice put in jeopardy of life or limb; nor shall be compelled in any criminal case to be a witness against himself, nor be deprived of life, liberty, or property, without due process of law; nor shall private property be taken for public use, without just compensation.

Amendment VI

In all criminal prosecutions, the accused shall enjoy the right to a speedy and public trial, by an impartial jury of the State and district wherein the crime shall have been committed, which district shall have been previously ascertained by law, and to be informed of the nature and cause of the accusation; to be confronted with the witnesses against him; to have compulsory process for obtaining witnesses in his favor, and to have the Assistance of Counsel for his defence.

Amendment VII

In Suits at common law, where the value in controversy shall exceed twenty dollars, the right of trial by jury shall be preserved, and no fact tried by jury, shall be otherwise reexamined in any Court of the United States, than according to the rules of the common law.

Amendment VIII

Excessive bail shall not be required, nor excessive fines imposed, nor cruel and unusual punishments inflicted.

Amendment IX

The enumeration in the Constitution, of certain rights, shall not be construed to deny or disparage others retained by the people.

Amendment X

The powers not delegated to the United States by the Constitution, nor prohibited by it to the States, are reserved to the States respectively, or to the people.

Amendment XI

The Judicial power of the United States shall not be construed to extend to any suit in law or equity, commenced or prosecuted against one of the United States by Citizens of another State, or by Citizens or Subjects of any Foreign State.

Amendment XII

The Electors shall meet in their respective states and vote by ballot for President and Vice-President, one of whom, at least, shall not be an inhabitant of the same state with themselves; they shall name in their ballots the person voted for as President, and in distinct ballots the person voted for as Vice-President, and they shall make distinct lists of all persons voted for as President, and of all persons voted for as Vice-President, and of the number of votes for each, which lists they shall sign and certify, and transmit sealed to the seat of the government of the United States, directed to the President of the Senate;—The President of the Senate shall, in the presence of the Senate and House of Representatives, open all the certificates and the votes shall then be counted;—The person having the greatest number of votes for President, shall be the President, if such number be a majority of the whole number of Electors appointed; and if no person have such majority, then from the persons having the highest numbers not exceeding three on the list of those voted for as President, the House of Representatives shall choose immediately, by ballot, the President. But in choosing the President, the votes shall be taken by states, the representation from each state having one vote; a quorum for this purpose shall consist of a member or members from two-thirds of the states, and a majority of all states shall be necessary to a choice. And if the House of Representatives shall not choose a President whenever the right of choice shall devolve upon them before the fourth day of March next following, then the Vice-President shall act as President, as in the case of the death or other constitutional disability of the President.—The person having the greatest number of votes as Vice-President, shall be the Vice-President, if such number be a majority of the whole number Electors appointed, and if no person have a majority, then from the two highest numbers on the list, the Senate shall choose the Vice-President; a quorum for the purpose shall consist of two-thirds of the whole number of Senators, and a majority of the whole number shall be necessary to a choice. But no person constitutionally ineligible to the office of President shall be eligible to that of Vice-President of the United States.

Amendment XIII

Section 1.   Neither slavery nor involuntary servitude, except as a punishment for crime whereof the party shall have been duly convicted, shall exist within the United States, or any place subject to their jurisdiction.

Section 2.   Congress shall have power to enforce this article by appropriate legislation.

Amendment XIV

Section 1.   All persons born or naturalized in the United States, and subject to the jurisdiction thereof, are citizens of the United States and of the State wherein they reside. No State shall make or enforce any law which shall abridge the privileges or immunities of citizens of the United States; nor shall any State deprive any person of life, liberty, or property, without due process of law; nor deny to any person within its jurisdiction the equal protection of the laws.

Section 2.   Representatives shall be apportioned among the several States according to their respective numbers, counting the whole number of persons in each State, excluding Indians not taxed. But when the right to vote at any election for the choice of electors for President and Vice President of the United States, Representatives in Congress, the Executive and Judicial officers of a State, or the members of the Legislature thereof, is denied to any of the male inhabitants of such State, being twenty-one years of age, and citizens of the United States, or in any way abridged, except for participation in rebellion, or other crime, the basis of representation therein shall be reduced in the proportion which the number of such male citizens shall bear to the whole number of male citizens twenty-one years of age in such State.

Section 3.   No person shall be a Senator or Representative in Congress, or elector of President and Vice President, or hold any office, civil or military, under the United States, or under any State, who having previously taken an oath, as a member of Congress, or as an officer of the United States, or as a member of any State legislature, or as an executive or judicial officer of any State, to support the constitution of the United States, shall have engaged in insurrection or rebellion against the same, or given aid or comfort to the enemies thereof. But Congress may by a vote of two-thirds of each House, remove such disability.

Section 4. The validity of the public debt of the United States, authorized by law, including debts incurred for payment of pensions and bounties for services in suppressing insurrection or rebellion, shall not be questioned. But neither the United States nor any State shall assume or pay any debt or obligation incurred in aid of insurrection or rebellion against the United States, or any claim for the loss or emancipation of any slave; but all such debts, obligations, and claims shall be held illegal and void.

Section 5. The Congress shall have the power to enforce, by appropriate legislation, the provisions of this article.

APPENDIX B

FEDERAL COMMUNICATIONS ACT

Section 315. Candidates for public office; facilities; rules

(a) If any licensee shall permit any person who is a legally qualified candidate for any public office to use a broadcasting station, he shall afford equal opportunities to all other such candidates for that office in the use of such broadcasting station: Provided, That such licensee shall have no power of censorship over the material broadcast under the provisions of this section. No obligation is imposed upon any licensee to allow the use of its station by any such candidate. Appearance by a legally qualified candidate on any—

(1) bona fide newscast,
(2) bona fide news interview,
(3) bona fide news documentary (if the appearance of the candidate is incidental to the presentation of the subject or subjects covered by the news documentary), or
(4) on-the-spot coverage of bona fide news events (including but not limited to political conventions and activities incidental thereto),

shall not be deemed to be use of a broadcasting station within the meaning of this subsection. Nothing in the foregoing sentence shall be construed as relieving broadcasters, in connection with the presentation of newscasts, news interviews, news documentaries, and on-the-spot coverage of news events, from the obligation imposed upon them under this chapter to operate in the public interest and to afford reasonable opportunity for the discussion of conflicting views on issues of public importance.

(b) Broadcast media rates. The charges made for the use of any broadcasting station by any person who is a legally qualified candidate for any public office in connection with his campaign for nomination for election, or election to such office shall not exceed—

(1) during the forty-five days preceding the date of a primary or primary runoff election and during the sixty days preceding the date of a general or special election in which such person is a candidate, the lowest unit charge of the station for the same class and amount of time for the same period; and
(2) at any other time, the charges made for comparable use of such station by other users thereof.

(c) Definitions. For purposes of this section—

    (1) the term "broadcasting station" includes a community antenna television system; and

    (2) the terms "licensee" and "station licensee" when used with respect to a community antenna television system mean the operator of such system.

(d) Rules and regulations. The Commission shall prescribe appropriate rules and regulations to carry out the provisions of this section.

GLOSSARY

Absolutism   A theory of freedom of expression holding that the First Amendment prevents all government interference with speaking or publishing. The absolutist position is associated with Justice Black. *See also* Ad hoc balancing; Bad-tendency test; Clear-and-present-danger test; and Definitional-balancing test.

Actual damages   Money awarded to a plaintiff in a libel suit who can demonstrate evidence of harm to reputation. Actual damages can include evidence of emotional distress as well as proof of out-of-pocket money loss.

Actual malice (*New York Times*)   In libel, publication with the knowledge of the falsity of a story or with reckless disregard for the truth. The U.S. Supreme Court has said that both public officials and public figures must prove *New York Times* actual malice in order to win libel suits. *See* Common law malice.

Ad hoc balancing   A judicial weighing, case by case, of reasons for and against publishing to determine whether expression may be halted or punished. Ad hoc balancing is flexible but unpredictable because it relies little on previous cases or set standards. *See also* Absolutism; Bad-tendency test; Clear-and-present-danger test; and Definitional-balancing test.

Adjudicate   To settle a matter.

Appellant   A party in a court case who, having lost in one court, appeals the decision to a higher court.

Appellate courts   Courts that review the actions of lower courts after an appeal by one of the parties in a case. Appellate courts consider only errors of law or legal procedure and do not reevaluate the facts of a case.

Appellee   A successful litigant in a lower court proceeding who opposes an appeal to a higher court.

Bad-tendency test   Discredited judicial test halting or punishing speech that presents only a remote danger to a substantial individual or social interest. *See also* Absolutism; Ad hoc balancing; Clear-and-present-danger test; and Definitional-balancing test.

Burden of proof   The responsibility imposed on one side in a legal conflict to prove its version of the facts.

Certiorari   The name of a petition, or writ, asking the U.S. Supreme Court to review a case. If the writ is granted, the Court will order from the lower court the record of the case for review.

633

Cf.   In a legal citation, an abbreviation that indicates the source cited lends support to the statement in the text although it does not directly document the statement in the text. Literally, *cf.* means ''compare.''

Clear-and-present-danger test   A judicial test that, if applied literally, halts or punishes expression only when there is objective evidence of an imminent, substantial danger to individual or social interests. Sometimes the test has been used to halt speech that presents no clear, imminent danger. *See also* Absolutism; Ad hoc balancing; Bad-tendency test; and Definitional-balancing test.

Common law   The body of law developed from custom and tradition as recognized by judicial decisions. Common law is largely based on the precedent of previous court decisions.

Common law malice   In libel, publishing with improper motive such as hatred, spite, vengeance, or ill will. Proof of common law malice has traditionally defeated common law defenses such as the reporter's privilege to report official proceedings. Proof of common law malice also is often required by persons suing for trade libel or libel *per quod*. *See* Actual malice (*New York Times*).

Content regulation   Regulation of expression because of what is said as opposed to where or when it is said. First Amendment doctrine predisposes courts to consider content regulation unconstitutional. *See also* Time, place, and manner regulation.

Damages   Money awarded to a winning plaintiff in a civil lawsuit. *See also* Actual damages; Punitive damages; and Special damages.

De novo review   A new or fresh review by an appeals court of both law and facts of a lower court decision. Appellate review of facts, in addition to law, is quite rare. But in First Amendment cases, de novo review permits wider protection of freedom of expression. A trial de novo is a new trial.

Defendant   In civil law, the party against whom a lawsuit is brought. In criminal law, the party accused of a crime by the state.

Definitional-balancing test   Judicial balancing of interests after freedom of expression is broadly defined to give it extra weight. Definitional balancing provides more predictable protection to freedom of expression than ad hoc balancing. *See also* Absolutism; Ad hoc balancing; Bad-tendency test; and Clear-and-present-danger test.

Dictum   A remark in a court opinion that does not resolve the legal point in question in the case. The remark may be pertinent to issues in the case, but cannot be part of the court's holding. Dictum does not have the same precedential value as a court's holding.

Discovery   The process before a trial of gathering information that can be used as evidence in a court case. Discovery includes the exchange of information by the two parties to a case.

En banc   A French term used when all the judges of an appellate court decide a case. More typically, a small number of judges, called a panel, decides a case.

Equity   A source of law that allows courts to fashion remedies appropriate to the case at hand. The law of equity enables courts to provide legal remedies other than money damages.

F.R.D. (*Federal Rules Decisions*)   The case reporter for U.S. District Court opinions dealing with rules of procedure.

Fault   Frequently used to mean the media error that must be proven by a plaintiff in order to win a libel suit. Plaintiffs determined to be public officials or public figures must prove *New York Times* actual malice. Individual states can determine the level of fault that must be proven by other plaintiffs, but most states have chosen negligence.

First Amendment due process First Amendment procedural requirements that the government justify prior restraints and other restrictions and that hearings be held at which restrictions may be contested. *See also* Prior restraint.

Fourteenth Amendment Amendment to the Constitution making states—in addition to the federal government—liable for violation of rights protected by the Bill of Rights. A state government that violates the Bill of Rights usually also violates a citizen's right of "due process" guaranteed by the Fourteenth Amendment. *See also* Incorporation.

In camera In private in the judge's chambers, excluding the public.

Incorporation In a series of cases the Supreme Court made state governments liable for violating the Bill of Rights. The Court incorporated the Bill of Rights into the Fourteenth Amendment by holding that state infringements of free speech and other rights violate a citizen's right to due process, guaranteed by the Fourteenth Amendment. *See also* Fourteenth Amendment.

Indictment An accusation issued by a grand jury that charges an individual with a crime and requires the person to stand trial.

Injunction Order from a court telling a person or company to perform or refrain from some act, such as publishing. An injunction is an equitable remedy. *See also* Equity; Prior restraint.

Jurisdiction The authority of a court. A court has jurisdiction over a person when that person must obey the orders of the court. A court has jurisdiction over subject matter when constitutions or statutes give the court the prerogative to decide cases relating to the subject.

Liability Being legally responsible for an act.

Litigant A party in a lawsuit; a participant in litigation.

Malice *See* Actual malice (*New York Times*); Common law malice.

Original jurisdiction A court of original jurisdiction is the first court to decide a case, rather than a court hearing a case on appeal.

Overbreadth First Amendment doctrine by which courts determine that legislation is unconstitutional because it restricts more expression than necessary. *See also* Strict scrutiny; Vagueness.

Party A participant in a legal action.

Per curiam An opinion issued by and for the entire court rather than by one judge writing for the court.

Petitioner A person who petitions a court to take an action, including the initiation of a civil suit or the initiation of an appeal, then as a respondent. *See also* Respondent.

Plaintiff The party bringing the lawsuit; the person complaining.

Political action committee (PAC) Organization established by a corporation, union, or others to solicit and spend money on behalf of political candidates and issues.

Precedent An established rule of law set by a previous court opinion. A precedent for an individual case is the authority relied on for the disposition of the case. The precedent usually comes from a case involving similar facts and raising similar issues as the case at hand.

Preemption The doctrine that allows the federal government to preclude local or state governments from regulating a specific activity.

Prior restraint Restriction on expression before publication or broadcast by injunction, agreement, or discriminatory taxation. First Amendment doctrine favors punishment after publication instead of prior restraint. *See also* Injunction.

Probable cause   A legal standard used by judges, police officers, and grand juries to determine whether there are reasonable grounds for believing a person committed a crime.

Public figure   The U.S. Supreme Court has said that people become public figures for the purpose of libel suits only if they (1) possess widespread fame or notoriety or (2) have injected themselves into the debate of a controversial public issue for the purpose of affecting the outcome of that controversy. In contrast, people can become public figures in privacy law when they involuntarily become part of a news event.

Punitive damages   Money awarded to punish a defendant, rather than to compensate a plaintiff for loss of money or reputation.

Remanded   When an appellate court sends a case back to a lower court, directing the lower court to decide the case consistent with the higher court's opinion.

Respondent   A term used to refer to an appellee, a party opposing the grant of a petition before a court.

Restatement of Torts   A publication of the American Law Institute that attempts to provide a comprehensive statement of the law of torts.

Rule making   A formal process of making administrative law used by such agencies as the Federal Communications Commission and the Federal Trade Commission. An agency must publish a proposed rule in the *Federal Register* and review comments. The rule as finally adopted must also be published.

Sequestration   Physically isolating jurors during a trial; housing jurors, separated from their families, under guard so that they will not be exposed to information or opinions about a case outside of the courtroom.

Special damages   Monetary damages as compensation for loss of reputation that are awarded only on proof of out-of-pocket monetary loss.

Stare decisis   The foundation of common law, the doctrine that judges should rely on precedent when deciding cases in similar factual situations.

Statutory law   Law made by statutes passed by legislative bodies.

Strict liability   A legal doctrine holding that a defendant is liable for an act even if the action was unintentional and without negligence, recklessness, or ill will. In communication law, the concept that a person or business is liable for disseminating a damaging statement even if the comment was made without negligence and not intended to cause harm. Strict liability means that communicators cannot defend themselves by arguing that they performed responsibly and without error on their part. The doctrine of strict liability formerly governed libel law.

Strict scrutiny   Requirement in First Amendment cases that courts abandon the usual presumption that legislation and lower court decisions are constitutional. In First Amendment cases, courts scrutinize restrictions on expression for unconstitutional overbreadth and vagueness. *See also* Overbreadth; Vagueness.

Sub nom.   The abbreviation means that although a second case name in a single citation is different than the first, they both involve the same legal action. The appeal of the case was decided under a different name than was used in the previous decision.

Subpoena   A court document requiring a person to appear in court and testify at a given time and place.

Subscription television (STV)   Television services offered only to subscribers who pay a fee. Subscribers are given a decoder so they can recieve signals that are otherwise scrambled.

Summary judgment   A ruling by a judge that there is no dispute of material fact between the two parties in a case, and that one party should win the case as a matter of law. A summary judgment precludes the need for a trial.

Teletext The transmission of text to viewers through the vertical blanking interval of television sets. Subscribers need a decoder.

Temporary restraining order (TRO) A court order to temporarily prevent action. A TRO is an emergency remedy possible only while the court considers a more permanent solution to a legal problem. A TRO can only be issued for a brief time in exceptional circumstances.

Third party A participant in a legal action only at the behest of one of the two parties directly involved. Third party refers to a person who is neither a plaintiff nor a defendant.

Time, place, and manner regulation Regulation of where and when expression is made, as opposed to what is said. First Amendment doctrine is more tolerant of time, place, and manner restrictions than of content regulations. *See also* Content regulation.

Tort A legal wrong other than a crime or a violation of a contract that is committed by one person against another. Torts include libel, invasion of privacy, and trespass. Relief for a tort is usually sought through monetary damages.

U.S.L.W. (*U.S. Law Week*) A looseleaf legal service that prints the full text of recent Supreme Court opinions.

Vacate To set aside the opinion of a lower court; to rescind, annul, or render a decision void.

Vagueness Doctrine by which courts determine that laws are unconstitutional because average persons would not know ahead of time whether their expression would violate the law. Vague laws affecting expression violate the First Amendment because the uncertainty they create leads to self-censorship. *See also* Overbreadth; Strict scrutiny.

Videotex Two-way home video service linking a television set or video terminal to a computer through telephone lines or cable.

Voir dire The examination of prospective jurors to determine whether they are qualified to sit on a jury.

CASE INDEX

Note: Page numbers in italics refer to the text discussion that includes both facts of the case and points of law. A page number followed by *n* indicates that the case is referred to in a footnote on that page.

SUBJECT INDEX

Direct Mail Board of Review, 365
Disaster scenes, press access, 493
Discipline at Air Force Academy, 510
Disc jockeys, payola, 597
Disclaimers, in advertisements, 330
Disclosures
    campaign finances, 296–97
    corporate finances, 306, 311–23
Discovery process, 17–19, 438, 439
Discriminatory exclusion of journalists, 490–91
Discriminatory real estate practices, 462–63
Discriminatory taxes, 73–75, 77
Disease, and privacy, 182–83
Disobedience of court, 444
Display rights, 251
Dispute settlement, FCC, 551–52
Disrespect for court, 444–45
Dissemination, 109–10, 159, 182, 208
Dissenting opinions, Supreme Court, 13
Distinctive trademarks, 272
Distortion of news, 583, 595–96
Distribution, copyright and, 250–51
District courts, U.S., 8, 9
    See also individual districts
District of Columbia Circuit Court of Appeals decisions, 10
    broadcast format, 594–95
    business information, 513
    cable television, 609
    candidate access to broadcast time, 572, 573–74
    children's programming, 590–92
    classified information, 509
    copyrights, 249
    corporate publicity, 315
    corrective advertising, 358
    fairness doctrine, 576–79
    FCC regulations, 544, 546, 556–59, 564, 568
    Freedom of Information Act, 503
    indecent broadcasts, 585, 588, 589
    noncommercial broadcast, 598, 600
    press access to White House, 491
    public figures, 123
    radio programming regulation, 543
    reporter's privilege, 153, 156
    subscription television, 621
    Sunshine Act, 532
    telephone information services, 616
    telephone records, 477
    teletext, 624
    televised debates, 566–69
    unfair labor practices, 304
District of Columbia courts, 8, 413
    and Freedom of Information Act, 504
    and invasion of privacy, 183
    and NAB Code, 368
    and negligent errors, 239
    and obscenity, 383
Divisibility of copyrights, 250
Divorce, reports of, 102, 155
Doctors, 93, 183, 452
Docudramas, 210, 214

Documentary films, 567, 581, 594
Documents, 6, 181, 480, 497, 506
Dodd, Thomas, 205
Dolan, James, 130
Dolls, based on fiction, 244
Donahue, Phil, 566–67
Donaldson, Michael, 92
Donnerstein, Edward, 387
Dorfman, Dan, 317
Douglas, William O., 12, 65, 69, 88
    and advertising decision, 328
    and confidentiality of sources, 458
    and lobbying, 299
    and pornography, 371, 377
    and press prison access, 487–88
    and third-party monitoring, 199
Dowd, Nancy, 256
Dow Jones Information Retrieval Service, 625
Dow Jones stock lists, 244
Downing, Clayton, 465
Draft card destruction, 77, 82
Dramatic works, 242
Dreiser, Theodore, An American Tragedy, 379
Drew, Elizabeth, 296
Drotzmann's Inc., 104
Drug lyrics, FCC and, 559
Drug paraphernalia, 333–35
Drug price advertising, 327, 328–30, 332, 335, 336
Drug-related cases, confidentiality of sources, 451, 453, 454, 459
Drugs, experimental use by CIA, 495
Dual citizenship, 55–56
Due process, 59–60, 382–83, 385, 447
Dukakis, Michael, debate, 569
Duncan, Carol, 263–64
Duncan, Linda K., 209–10
Duncan, Robert, 596
Dunn, J. Willcox, 158–59
DuPont Good Government Fund, 294
DuPont News, 279–80
Duration of copyright, 245
Duty of care, 232–33, 235–39
Duty to correct material misstatements, 316–17

Eagleton, Thomas, 565
Earnings projections, false, 316
Easton (Pennsylvania) Express, 188
Eavesdropping, 198
Echo Motor Hotel, 252
Economic harm, 238–39
Economic information, classified, 508
Economic report errors, 239–40
Editor & Publisher, 407
Editorial advertising, 34, 114–15, 279–80, 327, 364, 546–47
Editorial discretion, broadcast, 546–47
Editorial function, 27–28, 135–36, 243, 363, 548, 577
    of broadcast news, 595
    of films, 255
Editorializing, 168, 551–52, 598–99
    cable television and, 613
Editorials, 163–65, 304, 445–46, 580, 582

Educational institutions, FOIA costs, 503
Educational programming, 554, 590–91
    federal government and, 598
Educational purposes, fair-use, 258
Effectiveness of advertising, 337
Efficiency claims, 345
Eggs, deceptive advertising, 356
Ehrlichman, John, 520
Eighth Circuit Court of Appeals, 46, 158, 272–73
Elected judges, 409
Elections, 50, 286–98, 300
Electric Autolite Company, 313
Electricity advertising, 331, 337, 338
Electronic mail, 198
Electronic media, 539–26. See also Broadcasts; Cable television; Television
Electronic Specialty Company, 317
Electronic surveillance, 181, 194, 195, 198, 201–2
Electronic yellow pages, 616
Eleventh Circuit Court of Appeals, and copyright, 263–64
Ellsberg, Daniel, 69, 477
Elysium Company, 273–74
Emerson, Thomas I., 32, 34, 36, 485
Emerson (complainant), 154–55
Emotional distress, 228–33
Employees, 160, 167, 247, 302
Employment records, confidential, 513
En banc hearings, 9–10
Enclosures in monthly bills, 284–85
Encrypted broadcast signals, 622, 625
Endorsements in advertising, 349–50
Energy conservation, 338
Enforcement of laws, 14
England, copyrights, 241–42
English, Glenn, 504
English common law, 6, 111
Entertainers, 127, 167, 221, 223
    reproduction of whole act, 225–26
Entertainment programming, 564
"Entertainment This Week," 566
"Entertainment Tonight," 566
Environmental Protection Agency (EPA), 500, 511–12, 513
Epithets, 163–64
Equal opportunities for candidates, 65, 149–50, 560–70, 598, 624
    cable television and, 603, 612–13
Equity law, 7, 8
Eros, 377
Errors, and economic harm, 238
Espionage Act (1917), 62, 76
Estes, Billy Sol, 408
Estes, Murray, 155
Eszterhas, Joseph, 210–11, 213
Ethics, 29
Ethnic groups, libel, 87–88
Evangelists, and politics, 564
Evans, Rowland, 10
Evidence, to prove truth, 145
Exaggerated advertising claims, 349
Exaggerated speech, 161–64